PASSING TIME IN THE Loo

London · New York

Stevens W. Anderson, Editor

Cover design by Satpaul Bhamra

Published by Scarab

ISBN 978 0-9537357-9-2

Gilfillan 24/11

> *Of course everything has been said*
> *that needs to be said—*
> *but since no one was listening*
> *it has to be said again.*
>
> *–Anonymous*

CONTENTS

DREAMSCAPES
exploring the worlds within

continued ...

Futurescapes—science fiction classics

REALITYSCAPES
confronting the waking world

continued ...

Ambitious Pursuits—intrigue and adventure

Wastelands—reaching for relevance

Transcendence and Realities—dealings in self doubt

WALKING BACK IN TIME
the drama of history

PLAYERS OF THE PRESENT
"one man in his time"

Prejudice and Politics—select snapshots

Personal Perspectives—courage and conquest

continued ...

THE STAGES OF MANKIND
colorful theatres of history

Situational Perspectives—through their own eyes

Drama Across Continents—a sampler of cultural histories

CHANGING BACKDROPS
the best and worst of times

Turning Points—anthologies of historical highlights

Cradles of Civilization—setting the stages of today

continued ...

IMMORTAL VOICES

words that live on

THEY MADE A DIFFERENCE
shapers of our world

continued ...

Sports Greats—legends in their own time

Visionaries and Warriors—taking up a cause

Political Profiles—courage and power

POETS AND POETRY
epic verses and versemakers

Paradigm Poetry

Mid- and Late-19th-century Lyricists

Twentieth-century Verse

continued …

Popular Poetry Today

THOUGHTS WORTH PONDERING

musings for the moment

FANTASTIC FACTS
oddities, inquiries and curiosities

DREAMSCAPES

exploring the worlds within

He was so impressed with himself
that he named his sword "Sting,"
after its ability to kill spiders.

Bilbo Baggins – The Hobbit

Achilles advanced
"like the implacable
god of war."

The Iliad

"...the whole idea scares me stiff....
It can't be done by fighting or fair words,
no. So it will have to be done by means
of a trick."

Hazel – Watership Down

"Oh, children, children, why are
you following me?"

Aslan – The Lion, the Witch, and the Wardrobe

Get ready for a headlong plunge into the endless oceans of the human mind and spirit.

Our *"Dreamscapes"* library will carry you through realms of myth, mystery and allegory; of nightmare and visionary hope. And there you will dream, dare, despair and triumph with such richly diverse characters as Sleepy Hollow's love-smitten yet ill-fated schoolmaster Ichabod Crane; the heroically poignant Charlie of Daniel Keyes's *Flowers for Algernon,* who retains his purity of soul throughout a devastating roundtrip journey between imbecility and genius; Middle Earth's Bilbo Baggins, Tolkien's brave and quick-witted hobbit; and Odysseus, honored King of Ithaca, who sets out on an epic homeward journey home reunite with his beloved and faithful Penelope.

So, immerse yourself in these Dreamscapes, and connect with the sourcewaters of all that is best and worst—and all that is truly creative— in the soul of humankind.

Contents

Futurescapes—science fiction classics

... In a matter of some generations
the stupid ones will die out and those with
your discipline will inherit the earth.

Jubal Harshaw – Stranger in a Strange Land

His panic peaked when he
realized that the dark
horseman was carrying his
own head in his lap!

The Legend of Sleepy Hollow

I hate the tests and I hate the amazeds and I hate Alegernon. I never new before that I was dummer than a mouse.

Flowers for Algernon

"You see, Watson," Holmes later explained, "it was perfectly obvious"

The Adventures of Sherlock Holmes

All the pills did was remove every bit of pleasure from the act.

Welcome to the Monkey House

ANIMAL FARM
by George Orwell (1903–1950)

Type of work
Allegorical political satire

Setting
The Manor Farm (represents Russia during and after the Communist Revolution)

Principal characters
Old Major (i.e. Karl Marx), an ancient and venerated boar
Snowball (i.e. Trotsky), a young porcine intellectual
Napoleon (i.e. Stalin), an unscrupulous, aggressively fierce young pig
Boxer (i.e. the Russian worker), a huge, hardworking male horse
Mollie (i.e. the Russian bourgeois capitalist), a frivolous mare
Moses (i.e. organized religion), a tame raven
Squealer (i.e. Russia's propaganda machine), a young pig and fluent orator
Various dogs (i.e. Stalin's secret police), *men* (Capitalist enemies) *sheep, hens and other animals* (those who follow)
Farmer Jones (i.e. Czar Nicholas)
Farmer Frederick (i.e. Germany)
Farmer Pilkington (i.e. England)

George Orwell, a dedicated British Socialist, wrote this classic 1945 fable in embittered protest against what he saw as the perversion of socialism by post--Revolutionary communism in the U.S.S.R. Rather than highlighting factual incidents from the grim cauldron of horrors that had boiled to a climax under the Stalinist regime, Orwell chose to focus an allegorical mirror on the brutal dynamics that blazed beneath the action. And within this mirror, the pigs and sheep and horses of *Animal Farm* move as vivid and grisly reflections of the historical figures and factions they represent.

But Orwell's book mirrors more than the evils of Soviet Communism. Read closely, it is also an impassioned indictment of Capitalism. And read more closely still, the novel reflects the haunted and ironic image of the dark gulf which the author sees opening—perhaps inevitably—between the two eternal poles of idealism and expediency; between all noble ends and their self-betraying necessary means. This little "fairy story," as Orwell calls it, is in the end an angry, eloquent and almost despairing protest against the tragic potential for tyranny in all social institutions—including even language itself—over those very ideals and hopes for human transcendence that they are supposed to nurture and to serve.

Story overview

One day on the Manor Farm, the Old Major, a venerable 11-year-old boar, gathered the animals together. "Now comrades," he said. "What is the nature of this life of ours? Let us face it: our lives are miserable, laborious and short." He went on to detail Farmer Jones's cruel exploitation as he butchered the animals and plundered the products of their labor. "Is it not crystal clear then, comrades," concluded Old Major, "that all the evils of this life spring from the tyranny of human beings? Only get rid of Man and the produce of labor would be our own. All men are enemies. All animals are friends." At this passionate invocation of a world ruled by those whose lives and labor made it fruitful—the animals themselves—everyone broke into a rousing anthem until the disturbance was silenced—for the time being—by a round of shot fired above them by Farmer Jones.

Three days later, Old Major died, and the other pigs—generally recognized as the cleverest of the animals on the farm—began to expound his teachings on "Animalism." Napoleon and Snowball, pre-eminent among the younger pigs, led the discussions, which centered on open rebellion. At first the other animals objected: some were swayed by thoughts of food or loyalty; others, like Mollie, the carthorse—who loved the ribbons that Farmer Jones tied in her hair—actually enjoyed the frills that man provided. The pigs were angered by the apathy that greeted their call to battle. They were equally exasperated by the raven, Moses, who squawked of forbearance, and of a better life "in heaven" after death. Napoleon "had to argue very hard to persuade [the animals] there was no such place." Finally, however, he convinced the group to accept the Animalism credo.

Meanwhile, Farmer Jones, "fallen on evil days," began to neglect the animals. One day he failed to feed them altogether, and they broke into the stalls to get at the food. When Jones and his farmhands burst into the barn, whips at the ready, the enraged animals attacked the men and drove them completely off the farm. The animals were left victorious—and alone.

In their initial elation, the animals burned all the farm implements, along with any other items that smacked of man— including Mollie's ribbons. Then they warily entered the farmhouse—where, to their utter disgust, they found Mollie, trying on a fine ribbon. Seeing how weak and capricious even an animal could be, they agreed that in their new order no animal would inhabit the house, put on clothes, or in any other way imitate humans.

As the first order of business, Snowball removed the Manor Farm sign from the front gate and replaced it with a sign reading "Animal Farm." Then, in great white letters, on the barn wall the pigs painted the Seven Commandments of Animalism:

1. Whatever goes on two legs is an enemy.
2. Whatever goes on four legs, or has wings, is a friend.
3. No animal shall wear clothes.
4. No animal shall sleep in a bed.
5. No animal shall drink alcohol.
6. No animal shall kill another animal.
7. All animals are equal.

Just then, the unmilked cows "set up a loud lowing" of complaint. The pigs, whose forehooves made "good milkers," soon filled many buckets from the cows' swollen udders; but they left the apportionment of the milk until later, after "more important work" in the fields. "When the animals came back in the evening, it was noticed that the milk had disappeared."

Later, when the pigs also appropriated the windfallen apples, they explained that "day and night we are watching over your welfare. It is for your sake that we drink that milk and eat those apples." Napoleon and Snowball now organized committees to put the others to work—though, as managers, they themselves participated in none of the actual labor. But the animals were given all the hay they could eat, and gradually they accepted the pigs' dominance.

For the meantime, Farmer Jones had spread the news of the uprising to his neighbors, Pilkington and Frederick. Frightened by the thought that their own animals might revolt, they agreed to form a contingent of men to launch a counterattack on Jones's farm.

A fierce battle ensued. The animals, led by Snowball, once again drove the humans from the farm. Snowball was wounded in the engagement, and several animals were killed, but the survivors were elated by their inspired resistance. Afterward, Mollie, discouraged by the dearth of ribbons in her life, left the farm, never to return.

Now Snowball and Napoleon began to vie for leadership. Their struggle culminated at a meeting where the animals were to vote on Snowball's plan for a windmill he had designed to supply electricity to the farm, thus easing the animals' burdens. Napoleon appeared at the meeting with a contingent of sheep which he had trained to interrupt Snowball's speech, repeatedly bleating out the Animal Farm slogan "Four legs good, two legs bad"—until no animal could remember what was being said. Then, just before the vote was called, Napoleon summoned a pack of ferocious dogs, who chased Snowball from the farm. After this display, the animals dared not question Napoleon's will; nor did they fail to note that the dogs he always kept around "wagged their tails to him as other dogs did to Mr. Jones."

Even after Napoleon's brainwashing sessions, when some of the animals came forward, fervently confessing their allegiances to Snowball, they were immediately torn apart by Napoleon's dogs—who then set them to building the windmill, which he had once opposed. But it was the workhorse Boxer, in his simpleminded faithfulness, who truly inspired the animals. When Boxer promised that "I will work harder," and agreed that "Napoleon is always right," any objections to the project were silenced.

In constructing of the windmill, the pigs, as usual, did no actual work. While they supervised, Boxer wore himself out hauling huge stones from the quarry. Napoleon then determined that certain "materials" would be needed to finish the mill and decreed that he must bend the "two legs bad" rule—the First Commandment of Animalism—and deal with a man who could make their purchases. The animals were also placed on rations in order that their "surplus" food could be sold to purchase the needed materials. When the hens were told they had to give up their eggs, they put up a brief and futile resistance in which nine hens were killed. The shocked animals consulted the list of commandments; they concluded that they must have had remembered the sixth incorrectly, for it now read "No animal shall kill another animal *without cause.*"

Soon "Comrade Napoleon" had persuaded Pilkington and Frederick to buy wood from Animal Farm. "Napoleon

had forced Frederick to raise his price by twelve pounds"; but Frederick, in turn, swindled Napoleon by paying for the wood with false notes. Enraged and humiliated, Napoleon now prepared for a follow-up attack from Frederick. It came the next morning. Frederick's men managed to destroy the newly finished windmill, but once again were ultimately driven off by the angry animals. The pigs watched the battle from the safety of the farmhouse—and, later, got uproariously drunk on Farmer Jones' whiskey.

Before long, Napoleon had moved into Farmer Jones's house, sleeping in his bed and drinking all his liquor. And when the animals again went to look at the Seven Commandments, they found written, "No animal shall sleep in a bed *without sheets*" and "No animal shall drink alcohol *to excess.*"

Through the never-ending exhortations of Squealer, the animals began to reconstruct the windmill and to accept even smaller rations. Squealer even convinced them—almost—that they had never been happier or better fed. And their "readjustment" hardships were forgotten under endless processions and marches celebrating their victory over Frederick—and honoring their benefactor and greatest hero of all, Napoleon.

As the windmill neared completion, old Boxer was approaching his retirement. One day, as he hauled a great load of stone, the faithful old workhorse collapsed, and Napoleon arranged for a cart to take him "to the hospital." But when the already uneasy animals gathered to wave goodbye to their friend, they were told what was written on the "hospital" van's side: "Alfred Simmons, Horse Slaughterer and Glue Boiler." As they called out to warn Boxer, he tried to escape, but he was too feeble to kick his way out. The next day Squealer assured everyone that he himself had been there at the hospital when Boxer died; the doctor, he said, had just bought the cart from the horse slaughterer. Relieved and chastened, the animals returned to their duties.

At long last, the windmill was rebuilt. But rather than supplying power to the farm, it was used to grind corn—which was then sold for a profit. The suffering animals worked by now out of habit, still under the dim illusion that it was they who ran the farm. "None of the old dreams had been abandoned."

Then one day their illusions were shattered. Napoleon and his charges appeared in the yard, dressed in Jones's clothes and striding on two legs instead of four. In his hoof Napoleon clasped a whip, while the sheep bleated, "Four legs good, two legs better." Indeed, the last Commandment of Animalism had been altered to read, "All animals are equal *but some animals are more equal than others.*"

Later that day Jones's neighbors arrived in their carts to be entertained. The animals gathered around while Pilkington toasted Napoleon for his successful management tactics, tidy profits and his "discipline" of the animals. "If you have your lower animals to contend with," pronounced the human farmer, emptying his mug, "we have our lower classes." In pride, Napoleon announced that the name of "Animal Farm" would revert to "Manor Farm"—and, in the end, the animals could not distinguish which of the guests were men and which were pigs.

WATERSHIP DOWN
by Richard Adams, Avon Books, 1972

Type of work
Dramatic fantasy

Setting
A countryside

Principal characters
A hutch of rabbits, including...
Hazel, the rabbit warren's natural leader
Fiver, Hazel's tiny brother who is a "seer"
Bigwig, a strong, courageous rabbit
Blackberry, a clever and insightful young buck

Story overview

Two rabbits, Hazel and his small brother Fiver, came upon a sign that had recently been erected by humans. Scanning the bold white letters against the bright red background, Fiver began to shake with fear. "Look!" he cried, his eyes widening. "The field! It's covered with blood!"

Although Hazel wasn't alarmed, he knew that his brother had always been quite prescient. Thus they went to see the Chief Rabbit. However, when Fiver predicted an apocalypse and suggested that all the rabbits flee for their lives, the Chief politely dismissed them.

Still, the brothers were determined to save everyone they could. Scampering out of the underground warren, they bumped into a brawny rabbit named Bigwig. Because he had just withdrawn from the Owsla—the military group comprised of the warren's strongest males—Bigwig decided to join the brothers. That night the three rabbits would alert the warren to the danger, then flee for their lives.

As the rabbits gathered to make their final plans, Captain Holly suddenly approached with two guards. "You are under arrest [for] spreading dissension and inciting to mutiny," he barked, pointing to Bigwig. Bigwig, however, resisted. Soon other rabbits joined in the fray. In the end, there were ten rebellious rabbits who escaped the warren after repelling the guards.

The fugitives, fording rivers and scurrying past forests and fields, continued their journey into the following day, when they came across an unusually large and robust rabbit named Cowslip, who invited all of them to come join his warren. Although Cowslip's warren was quite impressive and its inhabitants looked healthy and well-fed, for some reason they seemed uneasy and downhearted. Little Fiver sensed "something unnatural and evil twisted all round this place"; he would have nothing to do with Cowslip's rabbits. Bigwig, though, was now fed up with Fiver's portents of doom. After reprimanding the small rabbit, he went off into the underbrush—only to be caught in a snare!

It was only thanks to fellow fugitive Blackberry's superior intellect that Bigwig was freed from the trap. Indeed, Fiver had been right. Apparently the farmer had been using this warren as a natural larder: the plump rabbits all eventually disappeared, only to reappear on the farmer's plate.

With this revelation, the band of refugees once again set off. After two wet and miserable days of travel, at last they reached the undulating hillside known as Watership Down. The three abandoned rabbit holes there could serve at least as temporary dwellings.

Soon the Watership Down rabbits were joined by two more refugees—a badly wounded Captain Holly, and Bluebell—who brought with them devastating news: Fiver's prophecy had proved true; men had come to the warren home to flood it with poison gas. Only Holly and Bluebell had survived the attack and the long journey to Watership Down.

One day not long after the arrival of the two survivors, Hazel rescued a mouse from a predator. Gratefully, the mouse vowed, "You 'elp a mouse. One time a mouse 'elp a you." Later, Hazel declared, "I think we ought to do all we can to make these creatures friendly. It might turn out to be well worth the trouble."

Then, just a few days later, the rabbits found a wounded black-headed gull, which they cared for until its wing healed. Intent upon finding doe rabbits for mates, they asked the gull, Keehar, to fly over the countryside in search of a neighboring warren. Keehar returned a few days later to report that he had seen four rabbits at a nearby farm, and also a "town of rabbits" to the south. Holly led the Watership Down rabbits to visit the warren at the farm, and met a few adventurous does there who agreed to return with them to the Down.

Shortly afterward, Hazel—now the leader of the Watership warren—went south with young Pipkin, a friend of Fiver's, to recruit still more mates. The "town of rabbits" they found there, however, was actually a dozen or so wire hutches. The penned rabbits eagerly agreed to go home with their visitors, assuming that Hazel could free them. But just then a cat approached, its ears laid ominously back. "Why, you pop-eyed, back-door saucer scraper," Hazel sneered, whereupon the cat pounced. The two rabbits easily outran the enemy, however, and hurried back to Watership Down.

The next night a squadron of rescuers, led by Hazel, returned stealthily to the farm. Unfortunately, as they began freeing the penned rabbits the commotion aroused the guard dog into a volley of barks, and two men came running straight for the hutches. Acting as a decoy, Hazel scurried toward the field. Suddenly a bullet tore into his leg. In agony, he dragged himself into a drain, where he soon "passed into a dreaming inert stupor."

Meanwhile, Hazel's little brother Fiver had managed to escape with a few others into a burrow. Grief-stricken over Hazel's fate, Fiver eventually managed to fall asleep, only to reawaken with a start: His brother was alive—he knew it! Fiver grabbed Blackberry, and the two rabbits raced to Hazel's rescue.

In the meantime, the Watership rabbits came straggling home—without the does they had so gallantly freed. Regrettably, the does had been apprehended by another rabbit group, the Efafra warren. Commanded by a tyrannical rabbit called General Woundwort, this warren had forced the does into the most oppressive labor.

Before long, Hazel came hobbling triumphantly home, between Blackberry and Fiver. Now, however, the warren was faced with another, more complicated problem: now that Watership had recently acquired two does, everyone wanted a doe. They simply must invade Efafra and rescue the captive does. "I'm afraid," Holly said, "I can't have given you a very clear description of Efafra." "Oh, yes," replied Hazel, "you have—the whole idea scares me stiff.... It can't be done by fighting or fair words, no. So it will have to be done by means of a trick." And so the assignment to design a ruse fell upon the clever Blackberry.

At this point, Fiver revealed that he had no dire premonitions about Efafra. It was then determined that Bigwig would play the most dangerous role, while the gull Keehar would serve as scout, guide and messenger. Then all but six of the Watership rabbits set off for Efafra.

The trek took only a few days. Keehar performed his job well, correcting the rabbits' course when necessary and keeping them apprised of Efafran patrols. When a camp was established near a river south of Efafra, Blackberry's plan was presented: after freeing the does, the Watership rabbits would flee, evading the Efafrans to vanish in makeshift boats.

According to plan, Bigwig set off leading the way—only to be captured almost immediately by an Efafran patrol. Thinking quickly, he told his captors that he was fleeing to join their warren. Although suspicious, Woundwort, the Efafran general, viewed the large and self-assured Bigwig as a "distinctly useful rabbit," and he made him an officer.

Efafra, Bigwig soon discovered, had "a depressingly efficient system" abundantly staffed by police, spies and sentries. He would be forced to use all his cunning in order to bring off the escape. Clearly the plan required careful timing: Bigwig would lead the slave-does out of their work areas and Keehar would attack the sentries, while Hazel and the other rabbits waited for them at the woodline.

Soon Bigwig received news that one of the does had been arrested and was being interrogated. They would have to set their plan in motion immediately. Attracting the guards' attention, Bigwig sent the does creeping out of the warren. But where was Keehar? Where was Hazel? Then, glancing behind him, Bigwig saw General Woundwort himself approaching, leading countless troops of grimly determined Efafrans.

Just as the Efafrans closed in on Bigwig, Keehar screeched out his battle cry and descended on the frightened soldiers, who quickly dispersed. When Bigwig and his allies along with Hazel and the does finally reached the woodline, they leapt into their boat. And Woundwort's rabbits—who had by then regrouped—also piled from the bank and into the boat to join them. While the Efafran leader stared in amazement, the boat, filled to overflowing with refugees, launched off into the water.

As the rabbits sailed back to Watership Down, Hazel summed up the adventure by quoting a rabbit proverb: "Our children's children will hear a good story."

For weeks afterwards, everything at Watership Down went smoothly. Then one day Hazel's loyal mouse friend brought news that a new group of rabbits had arrived on the Down. Cautiously investigating, Hazel found Woundwort and 26 other Efafrans encamped not far off. At once, he ordered all the warren's rabbit-holes closed, then he prepared for the siege.

Though Woundwort could no longer count on a surprise attack, he was still determined to have his revenge. The Efafrans thus began digging straight down into the warren. But when the Watership rabbits heard the digging, they concocted a delaying tactic: They would abandon the central chamber, crowd into a large side burrow, and seal up the connecting passages.

As the Efafrans closed in on them, Hazel suddenly remembered the dog at the farm, and in a desperate burst of inspiration burrowed back to the surface and scurried off with Blackberry and Dandelion to the south.

Before dawn the rabbits had reached the farm. While the others waited in the field as decoys, Hazel climbed atop the kennel, bit through the sleeping dog's rope, and stamped his foot to awaken the creature. When the hound opened his eyes to see Dandelion, he lunged, jerking the whole kennel as the rope went taut, then broke, bringing Hazel tumbling to the ground. The dog raced after Dandelion. Then, as Hazel arose, dazed, he felt the raking claws of the pouncing cat.

Back at Watership Down, meanwhile, Woundwort's soldiers had broken into the main chamber, only to find it empty. Now the general stormed the wall and was soon face to face with Bigwig in the tight tunnel. Immediately bloodied, Woundwort backed out of the passage. None of his followers dared to pursue the hulking, grim Bigwig either, so they followed their General out into the open air—and almost into the teeth of the looming dog. "Dogs aren't dangerous!" shouted Woundwort to his scattering troops. "Come back and fight!" They were the last words he was ever to utter.

The racket outside had awakened the little girl who lived in the farmhouse. She immediately ran out the door—just in time to save the poor little bunny from the brutish cat. Later, the doctor came to check on the girl's convalescent mother, and she showed him the injured rabbit. The wound wasn't serious, and the doctor advised her to let the rabbit go. It was a wild creature, he told her, happier in the fields. Then he took the animal to his car. And, taking the girl along for the ride, they drove out to a beautiful meadow and freed the frightened animal.

That was how Hazel returned to a victorious Watership Down, where everyone wanted to know just what had happened to him. "A man brought me in a [car]," said Hazel, "nearly all the way." And they believed him.

Commentary

Although *Watership Down*'s characters are animals, the novel is definitely not a fairy tale. Indeed, reading the book is somewhat like viewing a nature program in which the camera crew has somehow induced the creatures to enact their own, less time-honored version of the Trojan War.

THE LION, THE WITCH, AND THE WARDROBE
FIRST OF THE CHRONICLES OF NARNIA SERIES – by C.S. Lewis (1898–1963)

Type of work
Fantasy and spiritual allegory
Setting
During World War II; a country-house outside London
Principal characters
Lucy, "a very truthful girl"
Edmund and *Susan,* her brother and sister
Peter, another brother, the eldest and bravest of the four
Aslan, Narnia's majestic ruler
The White Witch, an evil enchantress who has cast a spell
on Narnia

Story overview

One rainy day, in a large house in the heart of the English countryside, Lucy Pevensie entered the enchanted world of Narnia through a magical wardrobe. The four Pevensie children had been visiting the Professor in his old house to escape the bombs of World War II that were devastating London. Like all children, they were curious, and had decided to explore the many rooms of the house. Lucy, the youngest, had come across the wardrobe at the end of a long, bare room. Oddly enough, she couldn't feel the back of the wardrobe with her hands. Somewhere in the distance a dim light glowed. As she followed the light, the fur coats in the wardrobe slowly turned to trees.

The light turned out to be an ordinary lamppost. However, Lucy discovered the land of Narnia was anything but ordinary when she spied a faun, half-man and half-goat, hurry past carrying books and parcels. He invited Lucy to tea, and she accepted. They had such a pleasant time—until the faun reluctantly explained that he was under orders to turn any children appearing in Narnia over to the White Witch. Sensing Lucy was a good person, though, he helped her return.

At last Lucy found herself safe in the spare room. Though it seemed as if she had been gone for a dreadfully long time, no one had even missed her. Furthermore, they didn't believe her story.

During a game of hide and seek on yet another rainy day, Lucy and Edmund both hid inside the wardrobe, and suddenly they both found themselves in Narnia. Lucy started off to visit her friend, Mr. Tumnus, leaving Edmund behind. As he surveyed the area, Edmund came face to face with the White Witch. Knowing a child's weakness, she fed him the sweetest and best candy in the world, Turkish Delight. Edmund ate and ate. The more he devoured, however, the more he wanted to eat; in this manner, she persuaded him to reveal much about his brother and sisters. She seemed particularly interested in knowing that there were *four* children in all. When the Turkish Delight was finally gone, Edmund greedily asked for more. But all the Witch gave him was a sweet smile—and the command that he must bring his brother and sisters to her castle between the two hills on the Western horizon. Only then could he have more; in fact, he could have as much as he wanted.

Later, as was bound to happen, all the children found themselves in Narnia via the wardrobe in the spare room. At once, Peter lashed out at Edmund for his nastiness to Lucy. After this unpleasant scene, Lucy suggested they all go and see her friend, Mr. Tumnus. But as they reached the mouth of the faun's cave, they came upon a horrible display of destruction. Mr. Tumnus's door had been ripped off its hinges and the contents of the cave were strewn about and broken. There was no sight of the dear faun, but there was a note left behind stating that Mr. Tumnus, guilty of high treason against the Queen of Narnia, had been arrested, taken before the Queen, and turned to stone. The note was signed by Fenris Ulf, a huge and terrifying wolf, and Captain of the Secret Police.

Lucy could not bear to think of her good friend standing as a cold, lifeless statue in the palace of the White Witch. There was only one thing to do: the faun had saved her life, now she must save his. Susan and Peter were ready to join her, but Edmund had no intention of doing any such thing; his thoughts were only of Turkish Delight. Still, he decided to tag along; it would be difficult finding the White Witch all by himself.

The children encountered a beaver who had been expecting them. He told them how they might find the faun, and about a legend of four children who would sit on the Four Thrones, ending the reign of the White Witch.

"And another thing," he added, "Aslan is on the move." Never had the children felt so much power and dignity at the sound of a name, and they eagerly listened to Mr. Beaver recite another old prophecy about the great lion Aslan: "Wrong will be right, when Aslan comes in sight, at the sound of his roar, sorrows will be no more, when he bares his teeth, winter meets its death and when he shakes his mane, we shall have spring again."

"Ooh!" said Susan, "Is he safe? I feel quite nervous about meeting a lion." "Safe?" replied Mr. Beaver. "Who said anything about safe? 'Course he isn't safe. But he's good. He's the King, I tell you. Word has been sent that you are to meet him, tomorrow if you can, at the Stone Table."

For hours the children and Mr. Beaver discussed Aslan, and their plans to rescue the faun. Suddenly, they noticed that there was one less person at the table. Edmund was gone! Mr. Beaver claimed to have seen treachery in Edmund's eyes from the start; surely he had eaten of the White Witch's Turkish Delight, and was under her spell. "We've not a moment to lose," the beaver cried. "The White Witch will be here as soon as she gets word from Edmund and will try to cut us off from the Stone Table."

Meanwhile, Edmund had indeed located the Witch and had told her everything he knew about his siblings, Mr. and Mrs. Beaver, and Aslan. At once she dispatched Fenris Ulf, along with his best deputy, to storm the party at the home of the beavers. In the meantime, she planned to hinder them from reaching the Stone Table. Taking Edmund along for the ride, she and her dwarves headed out in her sled, pulled by reindeer with bells attached to their harness.

Peter, Susan, Lucy and the beavers had already snatched up a few belongings and were traveling along the frozen river bed that led to the Stone Table. They pressed forward through the intricate patterns of shadow, snow and ice shining in the moonlight, hoping the falling snow would cover their tracks and mask their scent from the Witch's ferocious wolves. When Lucy finally could go no farther, they sought shelter in a secluded cave. There, safe and warm, they slept, but were soon suddenly roused by the sound of bells rending the stillness of the night. They all held their breath in fear, thinking the Witch had detected them. What joy, what relief, to find that it was only Father Christmas! This meant that the Witch's spell was breaking! Calling the children "Sons of Adam and Daughters of Eve," Father Christmas presented each of them with a special present: Peter was given a sword and shield; Susan, a quiver and bow, along with a horn that would always summon help; and then he placed in Lucy's hand a shining diamond vial containing an elixir that would miraculously heal any wounds.

Alas, the snow began to melt, which slowed the witch's sled, enabling the children to reach Aslan and the Stone Table in safety. Beholding the mighty lion in all his glory, the children were at first afraid to approach Aslan. After some nervous discussion, the duty of addressing him fell to the eldest, Peter. He drew his sword, raised it to a salute and said, "We have come—Aslan." Aslan's regal yet gentle voice boomed in reply. "Welcome, Peter, Son of Adam." Surrounded by a half-circle of centaurs and leopards, and a host of other good creatures nearby, he had prepared a festival of music and delicious food.

Aslan then sent forth his swiftest centaurs to recapture Edmund, which they succeeded in doing. But the White Witch was by no means content to lose the kingdom of Narnia without a fight. That night she visited Aslan under the white flag of truce to play her final, most sinister hand. First, she demanded the death of Edmund, according to the laws of the "Deep Magic Since the Dawn of Time." This Deep Magic declared that every traitor belonged to her as lawful prey; for every treachery committed, she had a right to kill, to exact her justice.

Some of Aslan's followers gasped in disbelief; others challenged the Witch to try taking Edmund from them. Susan, utterly horrified, turned to Aslan for guidance: "Isn't there something you can do to work against the Deep Magic?" "Work against the Emperor's magic?" he replied, with something of a frown on his face. Then Aslan gave out a stern warning: "Fall back, all of you, and I will talk to the Witch alone." Minutes later, he returned to announce that the Witch had consented to renounce her claim on Edmund's life. This news brought great relief and cheer.

Lucy and Susan found themselves unable to sleep that night, worrying and wondering. In the morning, they decided to go to Aslan. At first they couldn't find him; then Susan pointed toward the trees at the edge of their camp. A lion with his head bowed low was trudging, slowly, heavily, toward the Hill of the Stone Table. When he spied them, the great lion turned and said, "Oh, children, children, why are you following me?" Lucy responded in earnest: "We couldn't sleep. Please, may we come with you—wherever you are going?" Seeing the love in the children's eyes, Aslan could not rebuke them: "I should be glad of company tonight. Yes, you may come, but you must promise to stop when I tell you, and after that leave me to go on alone." The girls promised. They walked on through the darkness, stroking the glorious fur of Aslan's golden mane to comfort him. Then it was time for him to proceed unaccompanied.

But Lucy and Susan just couldn't return to camp; something awful was about to happen. Hiding in the bushes, they witnessed the saddest, most horrible scene of their entire lives. Aslan made his way to the Stone Table where the Witch and all her evil army were waiting. Revelling, mocking voices filled the air as she tied Aslan to the table and plunged her razor-sharp knife into his side. Lucy and Susan buried their faces in their hands, unable to watch. When it was over, the Witch and her host of evil demons scuttled off to find the four children, and to kill those who had been faithful to Aslan.

Lucy and Susan went to the great lion, whose massive body lay silent on the table. They put their arms around him and wept at his side all that night—until a faint light began to appear on the eastern edge of the sky, and they turned to leave. Then they heard a great cracking sound coming from behind them. They turned to see the table, split into two huge pieces, and Aslan's body, gone. "Who's done it?" cried Susan. "What does it mean? Is it more magic?"

"Yes!" announced a great voice. "It is more magic." Aslan, in all his majesty, then appeared, alive again, his mane glistening in the dawning sun. There was "Deeper Magic from Before the Dawn of Time," he explained, of which the White Witch had no knowledge. "When a willing victim who had committed no treachery was killed in a traitor's stead, the table would crack and Death itself would start working backward."

The children rode swiftly on Aslan's back to the Witch's castle to set the stone captives free. What a joy it was for Lucy and Mr. Tumnus to be together again! They lost not a moment in celebrating as they all ran to battle against the White Witch and her foul army. They arrived just in time to relieve Peter's weary forces and save Narnia. Edmund, sorry for the trouble he had caused, had fought most bravely and had managed to destroy the Witch's powerful wand; but he had been wounded severely. Lucy administered the elixir from the diamond vial and healed him, while Aslan exterminated the wicked White Witch once and for all.

The children ruled Narnia for many years until the day they came across a rusted lamppost in the forest. In the next moment, they appeared in the professor's bedroom, the very moment they had first stepped into the wardrobe.

THE HOBBIT
by J.R.R. Tolkien (1892–1973)

Type of work
Fantasy adventure

Setting
Middle Earth; whenever

Principal characters
Bilbo Baggins, a hobbit
Gandalf, a wizard
Thorin Oakenshield, leader of the dwarf party
Elrond, leader of the elves
Gollum, a small lake dweller
Bard, Lake Town's mayor
Smaug, a terrible dragon

Story overview

Bilbo Baggins, a diminutive, hairy-footed hobbit, was perfectly content to live in his comfortable little hole in the hillside in the quiet village of Hobbiton, had not Gandalf the Wizard come into his life. Gandalf wanted Bilbo to join him and a party of 13 dwarves on a great adventure. Bilbo's hesitance was noticed by Gandalf, but not by the dwarf band, led by Thorin Oakenshield.

Thorin explained that he was the dwarf grandson of Thror, King under the Mountain. A fierce dragon named Smaug had driven the dwarves from their homeland. Now the dwarves aimed to travel to Lonely Mountain, kill Smaug, and reclaim the mountain's treasures. Bilbo would serve as the mission's burglar—even though, as he contended, he knew nothing about burgling.

The party set off in grand style, traveling as best they could the paths dictated by the ancient dwarf maps. One evening, they noticed a campfire in the distance. Bilbo was sent to investigate—and was immediately captured by trolls. One by one, the dwarves followed after him, until they had all fallen into the trolls' trap. The trolls argued about whether to eat their captives now, or wait until later. Gandalf, aware of the troll's slow wit and love of arguing, cleverly prolonged the discussion until daylight, at which time the trolls turned to stone. Rescued, the party searched for the treasure the trolls were sure to keep, and found in the lair some food, coins and swords. The weapons would be particularly useful, as they had no other means of defense. Even tiny Bilbo found a knife, although to him it seemed to be the size of a sword.

The adventurers next made their way to the valley city of Rivendell, where Elrond ruled the land of the elves. A hardy meal and lively conversation ensued. During the chat, Bilbo brought up the topic of runes and maps, and asked Elrond to interpret the writings on the dwarf maps. Elrond, examining the maps, explained that they gave a clue to a secret entrance to Lonely Mountain. The object of the clue would become apparent later.

The treacherous Misty Mountains lay in the path of the party. Scaling these could take days. After a long day's excursion up the trails, the band sought shelter in a snug, dry cave. During the night, however, goblins entered through secret entrances and made off with the party's horses. The dwarves—and a reluctant Bilbo—managed to capture the small band of goblins and bring them before their goblin king. The thieves had nothing personal against the dwarves, they explained in their defense; they only wanted the horses. But then the goblin king spied the writing on the troll-sword which Thorin carried: "Orchrist, the Goblin-cleaver," it read in ancient goblin language. At once the displeased king ordered the whole lot of dwarves killed. But Gandalf come to their rescue—at the last possible moment, as was the habit of wizards. He conjured up a strong wind to blow out the goblins' torches; he then used his sword to kill the goblin king.

Bilbo and the dwarves fled for their lives down the dimly-lighted passageways. During the escape, the unfortunate Bilbo was knocked unconscious and became separated from the rest of the party. When he came to he wandered for hours in the dark mountain corridors. Cold, tired and hungry, he needed to find the way out. As he traveled, Bilbo came across a small ring. It must be a goblin ring, he decided, and dropped the trinket into his pocket.

He soon happened upon a cold, underground lake. Gollum, a small, slimy lake-dweller who feasted on fish and ill-fated goblins who lost their way in the tunnels (not unlike Bilbo), suddenly appeared. Gollum hungrily eyed Bilbo; surely the hobbit would make a tasty treat. But Bilbo was not about to let this happen. Following a brief exchange, they came up with a compromise: Bilbo would submit himself to a game of riddles that would give the winner his wish—either freedom from the tunnels, or a nice dinner. Each took his turn posing a riddle that the other subsequently guessed correctly. Bilbo finally got the best of Gollum with the modest riddle, "What have I got in my pocket?" Gollum, stumped, attempted to stall by mentioning a "birthday present" he had for Bilbo, which he immediately went to find. Returning, Gollum soon deduced that the object in Bilbo's pocket was a ring, for it was none other than the thing for which Gollum had been hunting.

Having guessed correctly, Gollum at once began chasing Bilbo. But Bilbo was already well out in front, running through the tunnels. Unexplainably, Bilbo put on the ring—and was astonished to see Gollum run right past him. Following his assailant, hoping to find an exit, Gollum's own mutterings revealed the secret of the ring: it made its wearer invisible. Bilbo merely had to follow Gollum through the tunnels that led to the surface.

Bilbo presently rejoined the party of dwarves, but kept the ring a secret as he told what had happened. The travelers moved on through the forest toward Lonely Mountain. By and by they were surrounded by vicious wolves. The only place of escape was up into the trees, a place that seemed safe enough—until the trees began to burn. Fearing for their lives, the adventurers again looked to Gandalf to rescue them, but even he could not come up with a solution. This time, their deliverance would come from a different source: eagles. Long ago, Gandalf had rescued and nursed to health the king of the eagles. Now this king had decided to return the favor by having his forces carry the party to safety.

Another near-fatal adventure ensued as the company made its way through the gloomy forest of Mirkwood. They traveled without Gandalf these days, as he was attending to other matters. Day after day they walked, never seeing the direct sunlight. Then they awoke one morning to find themselves covered with spider webs. Bilbo, by donning his magic ring, escaped from the webs and freed the others. As they ran to safety, he used his ring again, along with his sword, to slay many of the hungry beasts. He was so impressed with himself that he named his sword "Sting," after its ability to kill spiders.

When Bilbo returned to the others, he found that they had been captured by wood-elves. Bilbo, still unseen, followed silently and watched as his friends were put in jail. It took weeks to devise a strategy to free the dwarves. It seems that after finishing a barrel of wine, the wood-elves floated the empty barrel back down the river to the humans who produced it. Bilbo freed his dwarf friends, smuggled them to the dock, and secreted them in the empty barrels. One by one he sent them all down the river, hopping on the last barrel himself.

The humans of Lake Town were surprised to find dwarves in the barrels, but when the dwarves explained the situation, all was well. Lake Town lay in the shadow of Lonely Mountain, and the dwarves were pleased that their journey was nearing its end. They traveled the rest of the way to the mountain and began looking for the secret passageway. Bilbo remembered the clues given by Elrond the elf king, and found the camouflaged door that led to the passage opening.

Now came Bilbo's opportunity to be a burglar. The dwarves sent him to steal a piece of treasure. This he did, though awed by the sight of the magnificent and deadly Smaug, still in the castle after all of these years. Smaug could smell Bilbo, but of course could not see him. The hobbit noticed a spot on Smaug where the armor protecting him had fallen away. This spot was near a vital organ, and Bilbo saw this as perhaps the dragon's only weakness in battle. A small bird had followed Bilbo into the cavern, and he made sure he pointed out the weakness to the bird.

As Bilbo left with his small piece of stolen treasure, Smaug became enraged, and vowed revenge against the people of Lake Town. He immediately took to the air, breathing fire on the town and reducing several buildings to ashes. Meanwhile, the bird carried his valuable information to Bard, mayor of the town. Bard, an expert marksman, drew his surest arrow and, taking aim, brought down the evil Smaug, dead.

After many days of uncertainty as to Smaug's demise, the dwarves entered the mountain. Ecstatic at roaming the halls of their ancestors' castle, carved into the mountainside, they assumed their mission was complete and reveled in their good fortune. A bit later, however, Bard appeared at the castle gates asking for a share of the treasure to rebuild the town; it was he who had exterminated the dragon, and certainly Lake Town had sustained much damage. The stubborn dwarf king refused to share the hoard, claiming birthright inheritance to the whole of it. But Bard, equally as stubborn, vowed to fight for what he felt was his fair share. The matter became more complicated with the arrival of an army of wood-elves, who also demanded a portion of the riches.

On the morning of the great battle between the three armies, Gandalf suddenly appeared to announce that an even greater danger approached: the goblins, teamed up with a vicious pack of wolves, were now bent on revenge against the dwarves who had murdered their king. Threatened by a common enemy, the three armies quickly settled their differences and joined forces to fight the goblin swarm. The pitched battle proved to be long-lasting, the goblin forces appearing to gain ground on the battlefield. Then yet another army appeared, that of the eagles. Together with their new allies, the dwarf, human and wood-elf troops emerged victorious.

Victory, however, was not secured without sacrifice. Thorin Oakenshield, the new King under the Mountain, lay mortally wounded. Before dying a noble death, he patched up whatever differences he had with his former enemies, and bid Bilbo a fond farewell.

In time, the dwarves set up a new kingdom in the mountain, summoning all their scattered relatives to join them. The men of Lake Town, who had fought valiantly, gained more than enough treasure to rebuild their city, and the elves shared in the prize as well.

As for Bilbo, he took but two small bags of treasure, enough to last him a lifetime in his humble mien. But he carried with him a wealth of memories of this, his greatest adventure.

Commentary

The Hobbit, published in 1937, was only the beginning of the adventures in Middle Earth. J.R.R. Tolkien followed up this story with his *The Lord of the Rings* trilogy (1954-55) and *The Simarillion* (1977). In the subsequent stories, Bilbo passes the ring down to his nephew, Frodo, who strikes out on many adventures, and also running into Gollum, as had his Uncle Bilbo.

Part of what Tolkien wished to depict in *The Hobbit* were the class divisions so prevalent in his time, symbolized by the new, hostile, warring races of creatures that he imagined. In addition to its being a fanciful adventure novel, the book can also be read as a coming-of-age tale. Bilbo, although mature in years, still needs to learn more about his true self, the one that savors adventure. Here, he tests himself, discovers his gift for helping others, and gradually becomes a better, more caring person as a result of his enlarged understanding.

In this anthology of supernatural tales, the master of suspense and one of history's great film directors selects his "favorite stories about strange and fantastic occurrences."

THE STRANGE VALLEY
by T.V. Olsen

Young Elk, Blue Goose and the shaman's son rode to the hilltop and stared down at the prairie—just another Dakota Valley about a mile across with only a few small oaks and a sparse lacing of buffalo grass enhancing its sandy monotony.

"Is this what you wished us to see, Blue Goose?" Young Elk asked, his voice pricked by annoyance. "Yes," Blue Goose replied. The shaman's son then intervened. "Now that we're here, tell us what you saw the other night." Intently, Blue Goose related how, after hunting, he'd fallen asleep in the valley: "I came awake all at once, and I don't know why. I heard a strange sound, a kind of growl that was very low and steady, and it was a long way off. But it was running very fast in my direction, and I sat in my blanket and waited.... Then I saw it ... a huge beast, as big as a small hill, black in the night and running very close to the ground, and its two eyes were yellow and glaring.... It was bellowing as loud as a hundred bull buffaloes if they all bellowed at once. Suddenly it was gone."

"You should be more careful about what you eat," Young Elk mocked his friend; nevertheless, he "felt a crawl of gooseflesh on his bare shoulders."

Everything had started, he reflected, "early this same summer, on the river of the Greasy Grass that the white men called Little Big Horn, [when] the long haired General Custer had gone down to defeat and death with his troops." In the weeks after the battle, there were those who claimed to have seen dead men "walking the prairie with bloody arrows protruding from them" and to have heard dead voices moaning in the night wind.

"This valley is a strange place," the shaman's son now intoned. "Many strange things happened here in the old days. Men known to be long dead would be seen walking—not as spirits, but in the flesh." Young Elk could not contain his laughter.

"Young Elk does not believe in such things," said the shaman's son. "Why then did he come with us tonight?" Young Elk's reply split the air like a well-flung arrow: "Because, otherwise, for the next moon I would hear nothing from you and Blue Goose but mad stories about what you saw tonight. I'd prefer to see it for myself." And with that, he "kneed his pony forward, down the long grassy dip of hill," his companions following cautiously. But when their ponies "turned skittish" they hesitated. This was a bad omen, the shaman's son warned. "We've come this far," Young Elk countered angrily, "and now we'll see what there is to see, if anything."

Finally the young braves came to a moonlit stretch of sand. "Here is the place," Blue Goose announced—and at that moment the ponies again began shuffling uneasily beneath their riders. Young Elk drew his throwing ax from his belt and toyed nervously with it. Was that low, swelling growl anything more than a figment of his own fear? Then, all at once, as if the young skeptic had suddenly entered into a dream or a delirium, "the two yellow eyes of which Blue Goose had spoken came boring out of night" towards him. Transfixed, Young Elk "flung the ax with all his strength ..."

"I tell you I saw him," the man named Johnny Antelope said, after braking his truck to a tire-screeching stop. "A real old-time Sioux buck on a spotted pony" had attacked the truck. Joe, his trucking buddy, who had been abruptly awakened from his nap, only grunted, "You been on the road too long, kid."

"You white men don't know it all, Joe," Johnny shot back. "This has been our country for a long, long time, and I could tell you some things ... " Indeed, as Blue Goose's grandson, Johnny had heard many stories about the days when the Sioux dominated the landscape.

Stepping out of the truck, the men directed their flashlights onto an object resting on the sand at the highway's shoulder. Johnny ambled over and picked it up: "A Sioux throwing ax," he said. Then suddenly, as the men looked on, spellbound, the wooden ax handle began dissolving and the leather fastenings crumbled into brittle fragments. *Only the stone blade remained in Johnny's hand, as old and flinty and weathered as if it had lain there by the road for an untold number of years ...*

MISS PINKERTON'S APOCALYPSE
by Muriel Spark

As usual, Miss Laura Pinkerton had spent the evening in heated disagreement with her dear friend, Mr. George Lake. But when "something flew in at the window," she screeched, "George! Come here! Come quickly!" Still irritated, George trudged in to gaze upon a small, roundish flying object. "It's a saucer," said Miss Pinkerton, "an antique piece. You can tell by the shape"—an opinion George immediately countered. "It can't be an antique, that's absolutely certain," he stated flatly.

"I should hope I know my facts," rejoined Miss Pinkerton. "I've been in antique china for twenty-three years ... " Even as she spoke, the "little saucer was cavorting around the lamp." Then it took a dive at George's head. "The thing might be radioactive," he howled, ducking. "It might be dangerous."

"It is not radioactive," Miss Pinkerton rebutted, "it is Spode ware." George dodged the saucer again. "Don't be so damn silly," he spat back. But Miss Pinkerton would not be outdone: "I was only judging by the pattern," she explained with professional aplomb.

Later, when a reporter arrived, he took out a notepad and glanced around the room. "Did the apparition make this mess?" he inquired. "Well, indirectly," replied George. "It struck me that there was some sort of Mind behind it, operating from outer space. It tried to attack me, in fact."

"Mr. Lake was not attacked," Miss Pinkerton corrected. "There was no danger at all. I saw the expression on the pilot's face. He was having a game with Mr. Lake, grinning all over his face … " And the quarrel began anew.

Finally, the reporter offered another possible explanation for the sighting: "The lady may have been subject to some sort of hallucination … " At this, Miss Pinkerton's voice was stilled. Then suddenly she looked around. "Oh what a mess!" she giggled uncomfortably. "What an evening! We aren't accustomed to drink, you see…. We really oughtn't have done this…. I can't keep it up, George."

Although George sputtered and protested that they had indeed witnessed an "extraordinary phenomenon" that night, the reporter promptly left. Although George would not disown his story, Miss Pinkerton simply "smiled tolerably" when anyone asked about it. "Flying saucer? George is very artistic," she would invariably respond.

Yet at least one of the neighbors professed absolute faith in Miss Pinkerton's original report. "I have reason to believe this version," the neighbor explained, "because, not long afterwards, I too received a flying visitation from a saucer. The little pilot, in my case, was shy and inquisitive. He pedaled with all his might. My saucer was Royal Worcester, fake or not I can't say."

THE PRAM
by A.W. Bennett

Chorn the undertaker "was a man full of meanness." As such, he had always avoided Old Sam when he saw him tramping through the streets in "his ragged clothes, tattered trilby, beard, [and] oversized shoes." Even the hard-spirited undertaker, however, regarded the old man's oversized baby carriage with a certain amount of respect: "That pram had seen life—and death. It had carried lively, lovely kiddies, scrap metal, a gramophone, fruit, manure, firewood, and a corpse— Barmey Betty. In fact, Barmey Betty had her last and probably only ride in that pram. To Chorn's funeral parlor, Old Sam pushing her."

Simpleminded Old Sam and his beloved Betty "were already full of years when they joined forces," and so they never married, though they lived together in a dilapidated brewhouse, each taking on odd jobs—and constantly dragging the old pram after them. Betty was always chatting about how much she loved the pram, how it served so well for fetching coal and such—and in taking the kiddies for rides. So when she died, Old Sam had fetched Chorn and offered to pay him 21 pounds to perform the burial. And Chorn "agreed to tuck her under for that, provided Sam delivered the cadaver to his parlor." But after loading her remains into the precious pram and wheeling them over to Chorn's, Sam paused to reflect on something: "She told me to look after [this] old pram…. Said I should burn it when I died. She wants the ashes on our grave. Worries me that:

burn it when I die. Not before I die, but when. Takes some thinking about, dunnit?"

"Take your heartbreakings somewhere else," Chorn replied when he heard the old man's request. In fact, the only reason he agreed to tend to Old Sam at all was because he "wanted one thing—the fifty-pound fee … "

After standing next to Betty's coffin during the brief service and whispering a few tearful words down to the stilled body, Sam went away to prepare in earnest for his own burial. "Got to save fifty at least for when I die," he'd say. "Got to have enough for me and the old pram … "

Sam departed this life unexpectedly. Trying to save a drowning toddler, he "walked into a flooded river, although he couldn't swim a stroke." Both victims were rescued, but afterwards Sam contracted pneumonia and died.

After a few words were uttered over the burial plot, Sam "was lowered into the same grave as Betty." Yet, in spite of Old Sam's wishes, the unscrupulous Chorn declined to "burn the old pram on his grave then and there." Rather, he declared, "he'd keep it in his warehouse and burn it later."

One night not long thereafter, as a policeman looked on, mesmerized, "Chorn's warehouse doors slowly slid open [and] out came the old pram and set off—uphill. Nobody pushing it, nobody with it."

The policeman followed the pram as it "rocked on, straight to [Sam's and Betty's] grave." At the site, the pram stopped and the policeman "saw a heap of rags in the pram: a moment later they burst into flame. Evidently the heavy body of the pram was made of wood, dry, for soon it was a mass of flames." As the blaze grew more intense, fiery sparks streaked past the policeman, igniting Chorn's warehouse. And the undertaker, rushing forward in an attempt to save his property, was quickly engulfed in the inferno.

Commentary

With the same inimitable style that he displayed in the selection and production of his screenplays, Alfred Hitchcock (1899–1980) compiled this anthology of ghost stories tinged with both pathos and macabre humor. In fact, the authors here, working in the hallmark tradition of Hitchcock's own movies, have managed to commingle these two strikingly disparate elements in the creation of utterly surreal and unbelievable situations—and yet, somehow, to make us utterly believe in them.

The secret lies to a great extent in the characters they give us. Vividly painted yet wonderfully commonplace, endearingly and very humanly heroic, a rebellious Sioux teenager rides out to confront a ghost truck from the future, a feisty old couple spar with each other for dignity and dominance over the issue of a literal flying saucer, and a chivalrous vagrant exacts the fulfillment of a promise to his beloved—along with an incidental but terrible revenge—from the grave. They provide the reader with a voyage through the many virtual realities of Hitchcock's entertaining, anything-can-happen universe.

Perhaps no other fictional character in the history of literature has enjoyed the phenomenal celebrity of Conan Doyle's Sherlock Holmes. Whether readers refer to the sleuth as the embodiment of Victorian eccentricity, hyperrationalism, or brooding romanticism, they do more than merely confer on him the status of a cultural icon: they imbue him with reality. Through his combined passions of forensics and deductive logic, Holmes—along with his assistant, John H. Watson, M.D., the chronicler of the cases of Sherlock Holmes—is still considered, after over century of sleuthing fame, the greatest private detective in the world.

THE RED-HEADED LEAGUE

When Watson arrived at the Baker Street apartment of Sherlock Holmes one fine October morning, he found his friend already engrossed in conversation with a Mr. Jabez Wilson, an elderly pawnbroker with fiery red hair. "You could not have possibly come at a better time, my dear Watson," Holmes enthused. Then, because he knew that Watson "shared his love of all that is bizarre," Holmes asked Mr. Jabez Wilson to restate his narrative; it was, Holmes promised, "one of the most singular" he had ever heard.

Wilson explained that the whole affair had begun months earlier when a clever assistant, Mr. Vincent Spaulding, had drawn his attention to a newspaper ad which bore the curious headline TO THE RED-HEADED LEAGUE. The ad, Wilson said, announced a "vacancy" in the League for a red-headed man over the age of 21. Moreover, the position would pay a handsome salary of £4 a week "for purely nominal services."

Acting, then, on Spaulding's advice, and on the reflection that his own pawnbroker's business was mostly conducted in the evenings, Wilson had applied and gained admittance to the League. The "conditions" of employment were as simple as they were peculiar: each weekday from 10:00 a.m. to 2:00 p.m. he was to come to the League's office and copy by hand the *Encyclopedia Britannica.* There was one caveat, however: he could not "budge from the office during that time"; if he did, he would forfeit his position forever.

"Eight weeks passed away like this," said Wilson. He had nearly copied the *A*'s and was anticipating moving on to the *B*'s, when "suddenly the whole business came to an end." This morning, he said, when he arrived at work, he had found the office locked and a note tacked to the door: *THE RED-HEADED LEAGUE IS DISSOLVED.* He had come to Holmes because he wanted to find out why the League had played this exotic "prank" on him.

At once Holmes and Watson "burst out into a roar of laughter." As Holmes noted, apart from having been the object of a prank, Wilson had no real grievance. Indeed, he was "richer by some £30," to say nothing of his newly acquired mastery over "every subject which comes under the letter *A.*" Nonetheless, because the tale was so "refreshingly unusual," Holmes agreed to take the case. Before Wilson left, he obtained additional information about Spaulding, who, Holmes reasoned, undoubtedly counted "for a good deal in this mystery of the Red-headed League." Most notably, Holmes learned that Spaulding had come to work at "half wages" and that he spent his idle time in the pawnshop's cellar, ostensibly developing photographs.

The pair took the underground railway to Saxe-Coburg Square, the location of Wilson's pawnshop. Holmes tapped the pavement in front of the shop with his cane two or three times and then knocked at the door. Instantly, he pronounced his deduction that Spaulding was, in reality, the notorious criminal John Clay. Holmes then surveyed the surrounding streets, noting that the Coburg Bank abutted the square. "A considerable crime is in contemplation," he informed Watson. "But today being Saturday rather complicates matters. I shall want your help tonight."

At ten o'clock that evening, Holmes and Watson returned to the bank to meet Mr. Merryweather, its director, and Mr. Jones of Scotland Yard. Merryweather escorted the party into the bank vault and explained that, according to rumor, an attempt might soon be made on the bank's reserve of gold bullion. Holmes nodded presciently. "Matters," he said, would soon "come to a head."

They waited, and after an hour a "gash" of light appeared in the floor; then, through a gaping hole, John Clay lifted himself into the vault, where Holmes immediately seized him by the collar. His accomplice was caught soon afterward.

"You see, Watson," Holmes later explained, "it was perfectly obvious" that it was Clay who had placed the newspaper ad in order to lure Wilson from the pawnshop in the mornings. Then, while Wilson toiled for the bogus "League of Red-headed Men," Clay had tunneled from the pawnshop's cellar to the bank's vault. The note announcing the dissolution of the League, Holmes reasoned, confirmed not only that the tunnel had been completed, but that Clay would immediately put it to use.

"You reasoned it out beautifully," Watson exclaimed. "It saved me from ennui," Holmes yawned, adding as an afterthought that solving these "little problems" helped him in his lifelong "effort to escape the commonplaces of existence."

THE ADVENTURE OF THE SPECKLED BAND

The case "associated with the well-known Surrey family of the Roylotts of Stoke Moran" began, as Watson remembered it, "early in April in the year '83." Holmes had awakened Watson that morning with news that a client, a "young lady ... in a state of excitement," was waiting downstairs.

Watson quickly dressed and together they descended to the sitting-room where the young woman, "dressed in black and heavily veiled," sat shivering in fear. Her name, she began, was Helen Stoner. She lived at Stoke Moran with her stepfather Dr. Grimesby Roylott, "the last survivor of one of the oldest Saxon families in England." The Roylott family had long since fallen into ruin when, thirty years earlier in India, Roylott had met and married Miss Stoner's widowed mother. Her mother, she continued, possessed "a considerable sum of money" which she had bequeathed to Roylott with one provision: that an "annual sum" be given to Miss Stoner and her twin sister Julia if either girl should marry.

Eight years later Miss Stoner's mother had died, and Roylott moved the family to his ancestral estate at Stoke Moran. It was then that "a terrible change" came over him. He became reclusive, quarrelsome and violent; he installed "gypsies" on his estate; and he began to collect "Indian animals," which he let roam "freely over his grounds." Their lives, Miss Stoner reported, quickly degenerated: no servant would stay with them and Julia's hair had already begun to whiten when she died at thirty, two years ago—only a fortnight before she was to marry.

Miss Stoner then described how, on the night of her sister's death, Julia had come to her room and asked if she had "ever heard anyone whistle in the dead of the night." Miss Stoner replied that she hadn't, but later that night, after a storm began "beating and splashing against the windows," she had heard a "low whistle" and a metallic "clang," followed by Julia's scream. When she arrived at her sister's room, she found Julia writhing in terrible pain on the floor. "Oh … Helen!" she shrieked. "It was the band! The speckled band!"

The reason for her visit now, Miss Stoner apprised Holmes, was that she herself was about to marry, and for the past few nights at about three in the morning, she had heard a low, clear whistle. "You have done wisely," Holmes told her, then promising that he and Watson would meet her at Stoke Moran later that day.

Some minutes later the two men were treated to an abrupt visit from Dr. Roylott. He had traced his stepdaughter there, Roylott said. Then snatching up a poker from the fireplace, he bent it in half and warned Holmes not to "meddle" in his affairs.

Holmes and Watson were met at Stoke Moran by Miss Stoner, who allowed them to examine her room. It was a typical "homely" bedroom, except for two details: first, the bell-rope hanging beside the bed was a "dummy"; and second, the rope had been fastened to a ventilator on the ceiling. Holmes then asked to see Roylott's bedroom and, before leaving, instructed Helen precisely on what to do: that night, professing to have a headache, she would retire early; then when she heard Roylott enter his room, she would signal Holmes and Watson with a lamp.

That evening, after Helen's signal, the sleuths slipped into her room and began their "dreadful vigil." The parish clock had struck twelve when, inside the ventilator, they saw a "momentary gleam of light." A half hour later they heard "a very gentle, soothing sound, like that of a small jet stream escaping continually from a kettle." Instantly, Holmes sprang to his feet. "You see it, Watson?" he shouted, striking a light and lashing at the rope with his cane. Then Holmes stopped and looked up at the ventilator. Momentarily, they heard a "horrible cry" in Roylott's room. Entering, they found him dead, staring at a corner of the ceiling. "The band! the speckled band!" Holmes pointed as the "strange headgear began to move" on Roylott's head. It was, Holmes explained, a swamp adder, "the deadliest snake in India."

Initially, Holmes told Watson, he had been distracted by the presence of gypsies and the "use of the word band." It wasn't until he saw the dummy bell-rope, which he surmised was a "bridge" to allow something to pass from the ventilator to the bed, that the "idea of a snake" occurred to him. That knowledge, in addition to the whistle and Roylott's ready "supply of creatures from India," had led him to conclude that he "was probably on the right track." Thus, when the snake descended the bell-rope and Holmes attacked it with his cane, he knew that he had "roused its snakish temper" and that, as it returned through the ventilator, it would attack "the first person it saw"—its master. "In this way," Holmes concluded, "I am no doubt indirectly responsible for Dr. Grimesby Roylott's death, and I cannot say that it is likely to weigh very heavily upon my conscience."

Commentary

We may find it hard to bear in mind as we read Sir Arthur Conan Doyle's elegantly crafted stories that most were composed hastily for magazine sale and were initially targeted at passengers and commuters traveling by train. Perhaps the peculiar constraints of writing for this audience, however, help explain two important features of the prose. First, because he wanted each "adventure" to provide his audience with a complete narrative experience, Conan Doyle (1859–1930) decided against using a serial format. Rather, he fashioned his plots so that they could be read independently of each other. Second, to allow for some complexity of plot without sacrificing clarity, he devised a narrative form wherein each story could be told, as it were, as a variation on a theme.

Thus, apart from the fact all the adventures are narrated by Watson, each of the plots unfolds in essentially the same way. That is, Holmes receives a communication—usually a letter or telegram—followed by a visit from the client. The client in turn recounts a story that requires some action of Holmes, and, prior to that action, an exercise of his brilliant deductive skills in order to solve the case. Once these elements are established, the action ensues. Then as the adventure concludes, Holmes explains the process by which he arrived at the solution.

In all, Conan Doyle wrote 56 adventures and four detective novels featuring Holmes and Watson, an oeuvre which, by the standards of any other reading public, might be considered rather large. Yet for Holmes aficionados, the number is regrettably small.

Throughout his career, William Faulkner populated his fictional Mississippian microcosm, Yoknapatawpha county, with a rich assortment of characters, some morose, some bewildered, some unmerciful, and others living in illusion.

The myriad voices of these characters—and especially of Faulkner's varied first-person narrators—present simultaneously one of the great pleasures and one of the great challenges to Faulknerian prose: the use of unrefined dialects. Usage can convey the most subtle of nuances (as with the uncouth omission of the apostrophe in the donts, cants and aints of the dialogue in "Dry September") or the broad narrative sweep of an unfamiliar colloquial jargon, as found in "Race at Morning" (not summarized here): "Then the lot, home; and up yonder in the dark, not no piece akchully, close enough to hear us unsaddling and shucking corn prob'ly ... that old buck in his brake in the bayou." On a par with Mark Twain, Faulkner stands as an American master in the literary use of vernacular.

A ROSE FOR EMILY

Miss Emily Grierson had posed a delicate problem for the town authorities since the day in 1894 when, upon the death of her father, then-mayor Colonel Sartoris absolved her of paying taxes. When the succeeding mayor and aldermen attempted to undo this arrangement, Miss Emily genteely ignored their tax notices. And thus the years went by, until at last a deputation was duly assembled to call on the elderly maiden.

As the first visitors to enter the Grierson house since Miss Emily had "ceased giving china-painting lessons eight or ten years earlier," the officials noticed a scent of "dust and disuse—a close, dank smell." Aside from the fetid odor and the closed-in aspect of the house, Miss Emily herself "looked bloated, like a body long submerged in motionless water, and of that [same] pallid hue." She dismissed them curtly with instructions to take up the matter with Colonel Sartoris, who had by this time been dead for over ten years.

"So she vanquished them, horse and foot, just as she had vanquished their fathers thirty years before about the smell." This episode had occurred some time after her father's death and Miss Emily's abandonment by her suitor, a Northerner named Homer Barron. Ever since then, neighbors had reported a powerful stench emanating from the Grierson residence. To one disgruntled neighbor Judge Stevens snapped, "Dammit, sir, will you accuse a lady to her face of smelling bad?"

It was around this time that people began to feel genuinely sorry for Miss Emily. While alive, her father had deemed none of Jefferson's young men equal to his Emily and put off each and every one of those displaying an interest. With his passing no one any longer deigned to avail himself of the opportunity—except for the brash Yankee, Barron.

A gregarious, cigar-chomping merchant, Homer Barron took Miss Emily for rides on Sundays. This was enough to thoroughly upset the town citizenry, who found riding out on the Sabbath a poor example to set for their sons and daughters. However, their indignation was suddenly arrested one day by the abrupt departure of Homer Barron, his business in town having concluded. Afterward, Miss Emily herself was rarely seen.

And then the smell came, followed by the sympathy of the townsfolk for miserable Miss Emily, suspected now of dementia as well as lax sanitary practices. For even after the odor had dispersed, Miss Emily continued in the habits of a recluse, employing but one house servant and seeing nobody, save the girls who came to her china-painting classes. Then, when china-painting passed out of vogue and the students stopped coming, she had simply "passed from generation to generation—dear, inescapable, impervious, tranquil, and perverse."

Following Miss Emily's death, the aged manservant showed the ladies who had come to arrange for burial into the parlor, then "walked right through the house and out the back and was not seen again." Not until after her internment was Miss Emily's locked bedroom broken into; and there on the bed, bearing a "profound and fleshless grin," lay Homer Barron. "What was left of him, rotted beneath what was left of the nightshirt, had become inextricable" from the bedclothes which enmeshed him. "Then [it was] noticed that in the second pillow was the indentation of a head."

DRY SEPTEMBER

Sixty-two days without rain—and now this. Talk in the barber shop that evening turned on nothing else. "I dont believe Will Mayes did it," the barber announced. "I know Will Mayes." But the barber's innocent remark struck deeply into a seated youth, who leapt from his chair. "Do you accuse a white woman of lying?" he chided. "You—"

Another speaker tried to quiet the young man: "Shut up, Butch. We got plenty of time." At this chastisement, Butch appeared utterly astounded. "Well, by God!" he exclaimed. Damn if I'm going to let a white woman—"

All at once someone else spoke up, siding with Butch—to be followed in the next instant by the vigorous entrance of one John McClendon. McClendon had fought with distinction in France, and now his "hot, bold glance swept the group." And the weight of his views was more than enough to tip the scales. "Well," McClendon snapped, "are you going to sit there and let a black son rape a white woman on the streets of Jefferson?"

"Did it really happen?" another man asked.

"Happen?" McClendon growled. "What the hell difference does it make? Are you going to let the black sons get away with it until one really does it?" Then he made a savage, encompassing gesture with his arms. "All that're with me get up from there," he challenged. "The ones that aint ..."

The men—some eagerly, others in painful reluctance—made to leave with McClendon. "Boys, dont do that," the barber repeated. "Will Mayes never done it. I know." But paying him no heed, one by one the mob filed out into the street. After a moment's reflection, the barber grabbed his hat and left the shop on a dead run, catching up with the mob just as McClendon and three others were climbing into a car. He got in and they raced away, bound for the ice plant where Will Mayes worked as night watchman.

"Listen here, boys," the barber spoke up, still hoping to head off trouble. "If he's here, dont that prove he never done it? Dont it? If it was him, he would run." But his pleas fell on deaf ears.

"Cut the lights off!" McClendon ordered. They had arrived. McClendon and Butch exited the car and disappeared into the dark, McClendon calling, "Will!... Will!" When three figures returned to the cars, someone muttered, "Kill him, kill the son."

"Not here," said McClendon. "Get him into the car."

"What is it, captains?" asked Will Mayes, a perplexed look on his face as he was pushed into the back seat. "I aint done nothing, 'Fore God, Mr. John.'" With Butch on the running board and Will Mayes sitting between his two captors, McClendon steered the car away from the ice plant—away from town.

"Let me out, John," said the barber. McClendon replied immediately: "Jump out ... " It was then that Will Mayes spoke the barber's name; repeated it in fact. In a burst of motion, the barber threw open the door, perched on the running board, and vaulted into the swathe of black alongside the country road. "Dust puffed about him, and in a thin, vicious crackling of sapless stems he lay choking and retching."

McClendon arrived home around midnight. Removing his shirt, he wiped the sweat from his torso and leaned against the screen door, beyond which "the dark world seemed to lie stricken beneath the cold moon and the lidless stars."

BEYOND

"... The hard round ear of the stethoscope was cold and unpleasant against his naked chest." But what bothered the Judge even more was to have his bedroom jammed with people—neighbors, distant business acquaintances. When the doctor removed the offending instrument, the Judge relaxed for a moment—but only for a moment; just then his housekeeper let go with a tremendous, sustained shrieking.

"Chlory!" he bellowed. "Stop that!" Yet she seemed not to hear. The Judge appealed to others around him to remove the woman, yet none so much as turned in her direction. "Then he flung the covers back and rose from the bed and hurried furiously from the room and from the house."

Still in his pajamas, the Judge buttoned his overcoat, noted with relief the shoes on his feet, and entered the throng of passersby. Then he was through the mass of humanity, standing apart, his face reflecting "quizzical bemusement."

A young man stood nearby, observantly scanning the crowd. When he spied the pajama-clad elderly man, the youth confronted the Judge, asking if he had seen his wife. "I came here to escape someone; not to find anyone," the Judge admitted. "If I were looking for anybody, it would probably be my son."

"Oh. A son. I see," said the other. "Look for him here." At this the Judge laughed rudely. "You mean you don't believe?" the young man said. "Look for him here," he repeated.

The Judge thanked the young man and turned away, only to receive a shock that, for an instant, paralyzed him. He was looking into the irascible features of Mothershed, his grating, cursing utterances filling his ears. "I thought that you were dead ... " the Judge said stupidly, staring at his former business partner. "I remember raising the pistol ... " Mothershed glared with contempt at the Judge. Then he intoned, " ... I know why you are here. You came here looking for that boy."

"No," said the Judge softly. "We never thought, sitting in my office on those afternoons, discussing Voltaire and Ingersoll, that we should ever be brought to this, did we?" Mothershed cursed once more; then he suggested that the Judge meet these very historical characters. The Judge could not control the gasp that emanated from his throat. Were they here, too?

"Sure," Mothershed assured him. "Ingersoll. Paine. Every bastard one of them that I use to waste my time reading when I had been better sitting on the sunny side of a log."

Now heeding Mothershed's directions, the Judge located a "shapeless, gray, sedentary, almost nondescript" figure sitting upon a park bench. This was Ingersoll, the sage lawyer and convincing orator—the man he had worshiped in life.

The Judge took out a picture of his boy and explained how his only son—his only family, his wife having died by then—had a pony that he rode everywhere. "One day they telephoned me at my office," he told the seated form. "He had been found dragging from the stirrups." Should he, the Judge continued, have hope or not in this afterlife? "Give me your word. I will believe."

"Go seek your son," Ingersoll grunted in reply. "Go seek him."

"No," protested the Judge. "I do not require that. To lie beside him will be sufficient for me. There will be a wall of dust between us: that is true, and he is already dust these twenty years. But some day I shall be dust too. And who is he who will affirm that there must be a web of flesh and bone to hold the shape of love?" These final words the Judge spoke "firmly, quietly, with a kind of triumph." Then he hastened home.

Passing the many motor cars lined in front of his estate, the Judge entered the house directly, made his way to the bedroom, and, with great satisfaction, settled himself upon the soft mattress. "Then he heard or felt the decorous scuffing of feet about him, and he lay in the close dark, his hands folded upon his breast as he slept."

These three fantasy pieces, taken from Irving's *The Sketch Book* (first published in 1819), are considered by many to be the best Gothic horror he ever wrote, and are commonly regarded as early-American classics. They demonstrate Irving's innate ability to fascinate readers by combining a witty insight into human nature with remarkable control of the English language.

THE LEGEND OF SLEEPY HOLLOW

East of the Hudson River in New York lay a rustic little village of Dutch settlers named Sleepy Hollow, whose local school board employed as schoolmaster an exceedingly lank fellow by the name of Ichabod Crane. Ichabod was also well-known as a man totally absorbed in the study of local folklore, especially ghost tales, and no tale was too gruesome for him. "His appetite for the marvelous, and his powers of digesting it, were equally extraordinary; and both had been increased by his residence in this spell bound region." He had even come to regard the tales as actual events, and when he heard the moan of the whippoorwill or saw the sparks of fire flies, he would work himself into such a genuine frenzy that he himself "was ready to give up the ghost."

There was one thing, however, that could take Ichabod away from his studies—and that was young Katrina Van Tassel. The local beauty had a number of other admirers, the most formidable of whom was Brom Van Brunt, the leader of the local gang of delinquents.

One evening Ichabod put on his best suit of clothes and borrowed a horse from a neighbor to attend a harvest party at the Van Tassel estate. There he joined a group of fellows who were engaged in telling their best ghost stories. Soon the tales focused on a famous local specter, the headless horseman, who kept nightly vigil in the woods and cemetery near town. First Old Brouwer told of how he had met the horseman on the road one night, and had even raced him—until the devilish rider had come alongside and butted him into the river. Brom Bones then interrupted to tell of an occasion when the specter, unable to catch him, had disappeared in a flash of light.

After the party's end, the schoolmaster began his lonely ride home through the dark woods. The ebony trees creaked in the winds as he neared the crossing where the apparition had first appeared to Old Brouwer and Brom Bones. Then, suddenly, Ichabod became aware of a presence. "Who are you?" Ichabod demanded, his voice trembling and hoarse—but there was no answer. Then he saw it: a headless horseman "of large dimensions ... mounted on a black horse of powerful frame." Ichabod urged his steed to quicken its gate, but his horrifying companion kept time with him. His panic peaked when he realized that the dark horseman was carrying his own head in his lap!

Ichabod desperately kicked at his horse, hoping to outrun the demon and cross the bridge before it could reach him. But when he cast a backward glance, he "saw the goblin rising in his stirrups, and in the very act of hurling his head at him."

Ichabod Crane never returned home, although his borrowed steed arrived without him the following day. His disappearance started quite a stir of gossip in Sleepy Hollow. Some said that Ichabod had been spirited away; others rumored that he had changed residence because of the ghost. And in time Brom Bones was able to win the hand of Katrina. Strangely, though, whenever anyone brought up the bizarre disappearance of Ichabod Crane, Brom would grin with a certain sense of knowing. Some believe the ghost of Ichabod still haunts the "tranquil solitudes of Sleepy Hollow."

THE SPECTER BRIDEGROOM

Long after most of the German nobility had abandoned their drafty castles for more convenient housing, the Baron Von Landshort proudly and peacefully remained in his beloved Katzenellenbogen castle. There was one thing, however, that the Baron cherished nearly as much as his "little fortress": feuding with his neighbors. One particularly deep-seated quarrel yet lingered between the Baron and the nearby Von Starkenfaust family.

The nobleman also had one daughter, who had been nurtured by two maiden aunts into "a miracle of accomplishments." The manners and education of the Heiress were equaled only by her extraordinary beauty.

The rhythm of daily life at Katzenellenbogen castle quickened with the news of the imminent arrival of Count Von Altenburg of Bavaria, to whom the Heiress had been betrothed many years earlier, sight unseen. All the Baron's relatives arrived to celebrate the occasion; *the fatted calf had been killed; the forests had rung with the clamor of the huntsmen; the kitchen was crowded with good cheer—indeed, all things were prepared in the true spirit of German hospitality.*

Meanwhile, the young Count was making his way through the forest accompanied by an old companion of arms, Herman Von Starkenfaust, who was returning home from the army—the very same Von Starkenfaust who was the Baron's traditional rival. When the two comrades were attacked by robbers, they defended themselves valiantly, but the Count received a mortal wound. With his dying breath he pleaded with Von Starkenfaust to "repair instantly to the Castle of Landshort, and explain the fatal cause of his not keeping his appointment with his bride." Despite the family feud, Von Starkenfaust vowed to honor his friend's last wish.

Upon his arrival at the castle, Von Starkenfaust was instantly mistaken for the Count. He was so overwhelmed by the abundant hospitality offered him and by the beauty and grace of the bride that he was scarcely able to speak. Heiress Landshort was likewise captivated by the man whom she supposed to be her bridegroom, and despaired when he suddenly excused himself, claiming that he had an appointment at the cathedral. " … My engagement is with no bride," he stammered, but with "the worms! The worms expect me! I am a dead man—I have been slain by robbers—my body lies at Wurtzburg—at midnight I am to be buried—the grave is waiting for me—I must keep my appointment!" After making this astounding announcement, the cavalier departed.

When the Landshorts learned that the true Count had in fact died, a melancholy dread swept over the castle. The Baron's daughter, horrified and heartbroken, retired to her chamber, accompanied by one of her doting aunts. The old woman fell asleep, but her niece stole to the window and gazed into the night. To her surprise, "a tall figure stood among the shadows of the trees. As it raised its head, a beam of moonlight fell upon the countenance … the Specter Bridegroom!" A scream shook the castle as the aunt awoke and saw the apparition. But for some vague reason the Heiress found something endearing in him, and made her aunt promise not to reveal her infatuation.

When the Heiress was found missing the next morning, the aunt realized that she had to break her promise and relate the terrifying story of the Specter Bridegroom's return. Baron Von Landshort was shocked by the thought of his daughter being carried off by some goblin; the very suggestion of goblin grandchildren was too much to bear! But the mysterious disappearance was soon solved when his daughter and Herman Von Starkenfaust—a real man of flesh and blood—arrived to announce that they had eloped. The Baron forgave his old enemy and their feud was readily forgotten.

Rip Van Winkle

At the foot of the Catskill Mountains, smoke from a little village could be seen curling upwards. In one of its antique houses lived a man by the name of Rip Van Winkle, the descendant of a gallant line of Van Winkles. "He was a simple good natured man; he was, moreover, a kind neighbor, and an obedient, henpecked husband." His temperament made him a favorite among the townsfolk, but his mildness left him under the rule of his wife's sharp-tongued temper. Unfortunately, "a tart temper never mellows with age; and a sharp tongue is the only edged tool that grows keener with constant use." On occasion Dame Van Winkle even drove Rip and his dog Wolf from home into the mountains.

On one such day the pair hiked to a very high spot and engaged in some squirrel shooting. As Rip and his dog were hurrying for home, he heard a voice calling his name. At first he thought he had only imagined it, but then, very faintly, he heard it again: "Rip Van Winkle! Rip Van Winkle"—and there near the path he spied a "short, square-built old fellow, with bushy hair and a grizzled beard." The strange man was trying to carry a heavy keg and obviously needed assistance.

At the stranger's request, Rip helped him haul the keg down a rugged path which led through a ravine into a small amphitheater-shaped clearing, where he discovered many other small people. After sitting down to rest, Rip helped serve the beverage in the keg to them. When he tasted it himself, he found it much to his liking, and drank more and more, until "his eyes swam in his head—his head gradually declined and he fell into a deep sleep."

When Rip awoke, it was morning, and there was no sign of his dog, the clearing, or the little people. A rusted old rifle lay where his gun had rested when he had begun his slumber. He fingered his chin and found, to his surprise, that his beard had grown long. Shrugging his shoulders, he started once more down the mountain, dreading with each step his impending encounter with his shrewish wife.

When he reached his house, it was in shambles. There on the porch sat Wolf, growling at him. "My very dog has forgotten me," Rip lamented. Finding no one at home, he went into the village—which he found very unlike the place he had left the day before! What was more, among the passersby he could not recognize a single face. "Where's Nicholas Vedder?" he asked one old man. Vedder died years ago, was the reply. Rip seemed alone in a world of strangers!

Next he heard a woman speaking to her child: "Hush, Rip," she was saying. Rip Van Winkle asked her name: "Judith Gardenier," was the answer. "And your father's name?" he queried next. "Ah, poor man, Rip Van Winkle was his name, but it's twenty years now since he went away from home with his gun and has never been heard of since." Soon afterward, the woman said, her mother had died.

Rip was comforted to know that the Dame Van Winkle was dead. He revealed his identity to his daughter, and to the whole town. The story of his twenty-year sleep spread quickly. But finally the clamor died down and Rip, "his neck out of the yoke of matrimony," resumed a leisurely life with his children and grandchildren.

Commentary

In the 18th and early 19th centuries, all "great" literature was thought to originate in Europe. Finally, American writer Washington Irving came out with his *Sketch Book* collection—impressing his readership and greatly advancing the short story as an original and accepted literary genre. Indeed, many writers since have discovered America to be a country uniquely suited to the Gothic form, having spawned a host of regional superstitions and being abundantly endowed with a rich Native American folklore. Irving's short fiction and that of other early writers of American Gothic, allowed the United States to gain recognition as a country with a culture and history all its own.

TEN LITTLE INDIANS
(also published as *And Then There Were None*) by Agatha Christie (1891–1975)

Type of work
Murder mystery

Setting
Indian Island, a remote island off the English coast; c. 1930

Story overview

A mixed lot, the island's guests included medical doctor George Armstrong; spinster Emily Brent; African colonel William Blore; Captain Philip Lombard; former governess Vera Claythorne; World War I veteran General John Macarthur; handsome young Anthony Marston; and Judge Lawrence Wargrave. Given Indian Island's mysterious name and their anonymous wealthy host, the guests had envisioned opulence, a private pleasure resort "crowned with a beautiful white house." Instead, they found a barren and vaguely sinister-looking rock jutting up out of the water like a "giant Indian head" rising up from the sea.

That evening after dinner, a shrill, disembodied voice suddenly pierced the room: "Ladies and gentlemen! Silence, please!" Then, one by one, the guests and house servants Thomas and Ethel Rogers alike were charged with sundry acts of "deliberate murder." At first mute with terror, the guests finally began discussing the accusations, and in each case found them to be true; at various points in their lives, all of them had been responsible for the death of others.

Later, the manservant Rogers—whom their absent host, U.N. Owen, had hired sight unseen—admitted that it was he who had played the gramophone record of the voice. "I was just obeying orders," he explained to his overwrought guests, adding that he had assumed the record was "just a piece of music," because it bore the title *Swan Song*.

Unnerved by Rogers' "disgraceful and heartless" joke, their mysterious host, and the news that a storm would prevent the next day's supply boat from coming, Wargrave suggested that they escape the island immediately. Tony Marston, a young, bronzed, god-like fellow, disagreed. "Ought to ferret out the mystery before we go," he urged. Then, raising his glass "to crime!" he "drank it off at a gulp." Suddenly he began to choke and, with contorted face, fell to the ground. Dr. Armstrong rushed to his side. "My God! he's dead," he gasped. Finally, after investigating all possible causes of the tragedy, the group said goodnight and each drifted off to a fitful sleep.

Upon awakening the next morning, they discovered that Mrs. Rogers had apparently died in her sleep—poisoned. Because everyone had trouble absorbing this latest shock, Captain Lombard finally suggested that they needed to find a proper theory to explain the two successive deaths. He then revealed that on the previous night there had been ten "china Indian figures" placed like a centerpiece on the table; now, he counted only eight. Vera Claythorne suddenly recalled that each bedroom contained a framed copy of the old nursery rhyme *Ten Little Indians*, which, as if on cue, Armstrong began to recite:

Ten little Indian boys going out to dine;
One went and choked himself and then there were nine.
Nine little Indian boys sat up late;
One overslept and then there were eight.

Their host, U. N. Owen, Armstrong concluded, "must be a raving maniac!"

As the stormy—and deadly—week progressed, the survivors added new pieces to the puzzle. After General Macarthur was found bludgeoned to death on the beach, Wargrave deduced that their host must be in the house, posing as one of the guests. Indeed, "U.N. Owen"—simply a pun on "Unknown"—was using the nursery rhyme both to forecast how each murder would be accomplished and, in the process, to frighten and divide them:

Eight little Indian boys traveling in Devon;
One said he'd stay and then there were seven.
Seven little Indian boys chopping up sticks;
One chopped himself in halves and then there were six.
Six little Indian boys playing with a hive;
A bumblebee stung one and then there were five.
Five little Indian boys going in for law;
One got in Chancery and then there were four.
Four little Indian boys going out to sea;
A red herring swallowed one and then there were three.
Three little Indian boys walking in the Zoo;
A big bear hugged one and then there were two.
Two little Indian boys sitting in the sun;
One got frizzled up and then there was one.
One little Indian boy left all alone;
He went and hanged himself and then there were none.

Like clockwork, the deaths were carried out. At each, an Indian figure on the dining room table would disappear: Rogers, earlier seen chopping kindling for the fire, was found with a "deep wound" in his head; Emily Brent, poisoned, had a syringe mark on her neck resembling a bee sting; Wargrave, discovered in the dining room, was shot in the back and seated in a highback chair "robed in scarlet with a judge's wig upon his head"; Armstrong simply vanished "clean off the island"; and Blore, "crushed and mangled by a great block of white marble" falling from the terrace, was found with a bear-shaped mantle clock beside his body.

To the two survivors Philip Lombard and Vera Claythorne, Blore's death solved the mystery: Armstrong, the only victim whose body had not been found, was the heinous U.N. Owen. Just as they had begun to trust each other, however, they discovered Armstrong's body on the beach, "flung there by the tide earlier in the day."

In what seemed an odd gesture of pity, Vera suggested they move the body to the house to "get him out of the reach of the sea." Lombard agreed, and while they tugged at the man's bulk, Vera managed to lift Captain Lombard's gun from his pocket and point it at him. "Now look here, dear girl," Lombard puffed, "you just listen—" Then he sprang at her—and Vera, in a flash, shot him "through the heart."

Vera, at once flooded by a sense of panic and "enormous, exquisite relief," returned to the house and started up the stairs. The house, though, "didn't seem like an empty house." She was trying to remember the last line of the rhyme—something about "One little Indian boy left all alone"—when she forced open her bedroom door. There, in the center of the room above a chair, was a hook with a noose tied around it. "Of course," she thought to herself: "He went and hanged himself and then there were none … " Obeying the bizarre command, she walked slowly over to the chair and climbed upon it. Then, with her "eyes staring in front of her like a sleepwalker's," she placed the noose around her neck and "kicked away the chair…"

When Chief Inspector Maine of Scotland Yard filed his report with Assistant Commissioner Legge, his theory regarding the murders remained incomplete. Ten people on an island and not a living soul left. Maine's suspects consisted of everyone who had stepped foot on the windswept speck of land:

• Dr. Armstrong, a drinker and a convenient dispenser of sedatives—and, perhaps, poison, as he had once been accused and convicted.

• The spinster Emily Brent, who, implicated in the death of one of her servants, had written in her rambling diary of "troubled dreams."

• Ex-C.I.D. man Mr. Blore, who amused himself by suspecting everyone else's motives—and who, by committing perjury while testifying in a murder trial, had been responsible for the death of another man.

• Vera Claythorne, an ex-governess with a Coroner's Inquest in her past, had been completely absolved of all guilt; why, even the boy's mother hadn't blamed her for the drowning!

• The life of Captain Philip Lombard didn't bear serious examination, though he was the only one who thought it necessary to carry along a gun.

• General Macarthur, a retired WWI veteran once convicted for the death of his wife's lover, had gruffly admitted to anyone who would listen, "I'll never leave Indian Island alive."

• Anthony "Tony" Marston, as handsome as a Norse god, had hit and killed two college students with his car.

• Justice Wargrave, a reptilian old man once known in the press and in the courts as the "hanging judge," and a man with the blood of countless prisoners—including innocents, perhaps—on his hands.

• And the servants Mr. and Mrs. Rogers, the stammering butler and bloodless cook—said to have induced a heart attack in their former employer—may have needed to fend for themselves when circumstances turned grim.

From the crime scene, Inspector Maine had been able to reconstruct the sequence of the murders, the means by which they were committed, and the apparent motives for each. What he could not explain, however, was the fact that Vera Claythorne's chair "wasn't found kicked over. It was," he told Legge, "like all the other chairs, neatly put back against the wall. That was done after Vera Claythorne's death—by someone else."

Scotland Yard's solution to this seemingly insoluble puzzle would only come later—and then quite by chance—after a trawler fished a bottle from the sea containing a detailed confession, written by the deranged Justice Wargrave, as to how—and why—the murders had taken place:

… For some years past I have been aware of a change within myself, a lessening of control—a desire to act instead of to judge … to commit a murder myself … no ordinary murder … but murder on a grand scale. A childish rhyme of my infancy came back into my mind—the rhyme of the ten little Indian boys. It had fascinated me as a child of two … the sense of inevitability …

I slipped some potassium cyanide into Marston's drink, and … chloral hydrate into the brandy that Mr. Rogers later gave Mrs. Rogers. I killed General Macarthur the next day. About this time suspicion started to grow, and my plan called for an ally. I selected Dr. Armstrong for the part. I killed Rogers [and] in the confusion … I slipped into Lombard's room and [stole] his revolver. Then at breakfast I slipped my last dose of chloral into Miss Brent's coffee …

It was then that I intimated to Armstrong that we must carry our plan into effect. Miss Claythorne screamed the house down when she found the seaweed that I had thoughtfully arranged in her room. They all rushed up, and I took the pose of a murdered man. [Later] I took [Armstrong] behind the house on the edge of the cliff. A quick vigorous push sent him off his balance and … into the heaving sea below. I returned the revolver to Lombard's room. And now came the moment I had anticipated—three people who were so frightened of each other that anything might happen—and one of them had a revolver.

I watched them from the windows of the house. When Blore came up alone I had the big marble block poised ready. Exit Blore. From my window I saw Vera Claythorne shoot Lombard. As soon as that happened I set the stage in her bedroom. Vera Claythorne hanged herself before my eyes where I stood in the shadow of the wardrobe. After entrusting my bottle to the sea I shall go to my room and lay myself down on the bed. I shall be found, laid neatly on my bed, shot through the forehead in accordance with the record kept by my fellow victims. When the sea goes down, there will come from the mainland boats and men. And they will find ten dead bodies and an unsolved problem on Indian Island.

(Signed) Lawrence Wargrave

Commentary

Many critics believe Ten Little Indians (1939) to be Agatha Christie's greatest, most clever mystery; the baffling, impossible, and bizarre intrigue it offers remain unsurpassed. The book's enthusiastic reception may be largely due to the fact that the mystery's solution depends upon the reader's interpretation of actual facts, and not upon unexpected turns of plot.

Many readers simply take pleasure in the novel's artifice and style. But regardless of one's interests, Ten Little Indians will likely capture a most deep-seated, spine tingling curiosity.

24

A STRANGER IS WATCHING
by Mary Higgins Clark, Dell Publishing, 1988

Type of work
Suspense novel

Setting
Contemporary Manhattan and Carley, Connecticut

Principal characters
Arty "Foxy" Taggart, a deranged auto mechanic
Steve Peterson, a widower, editor of *Events* magazine
Neil Peterson, Steve's first-grade son
Sharon Martin, a journalist and social activist
Hugh Taylor, an FBI agent

Story overview

Arty Taggart sat watching the "Today" show in his Biltmore Hotel suite, intensity etched on his face. Sharon Martin, author of the bestselling book *The Crime of Capital Punishment*, was debating the case of 19-year-old Ronald Thompson with Steve Peterson, the editor of *Events* magazine. Thompson was scheduled to die the following Wednesday at 11:30 a.m. for the murder of Peterson's wife Nina two and a half years earlier. Sharon was on the program vehemently arguing that capital punishment was "brutalizing," while Steve maintained, just as vehemently, that the death penalty was imposed only "after exhaustive consideration of extenuating circumstances," and was a just and necessary sentence.

Arty was not paying much attention to what either party said; he was far more interested in simply observing Sharon. The expression in her beautiful eyes made him think "that when she looked directly into the camera she had been looking at him." Incredibly, the deranged man became convinced that this woman, whom he had never met, loved him; that "she wanted him to come for her"—which he intended to do. Arty's plan was to kidnap Sharon and then—precisely at the moment of Ronald Thompson's electrocution—kill her.

Steve and Sharon finished their television appearance. "Can I count on you for tonight?" Steve asked when they found a minute alone. Ironically, he and Sharon had been carrying on a six-month-long romance, even as she fought tirelessly to prevent the execution of his wife's killer. And now, as she nodded to confirm their date, Steve smiled inwardly. At his house that night he intended to discuss marriage with her. He knew that he loved Sharon, and he was not the least bit angry at her passionate opposition to capital punishment. In fact, he felt that Sharon's crusade was a testament to her vitality and her commitment to her own ethics—two attributes that Steve deeply respected.

That evening, however, when Steve returned home, he was surprised to find neither Sharon nor his young son Neil. On a table he noticed "an untouched cup of cocoa and a glass of sherry"; nearby lay Sharon's suitcase, purse and cape. But the house was silent.

Then, stepping into the kitchen, he abruptly froze: on the memo board, written in chalk with uneven lettering, a message stared out at him: *If you want your kid and girlfriend alive, wait for instructions ... Don't call police.* Scrawled beneath this warning was the name "Foxy."

Later that evening, "Foxy" made contact again, this time through a phone call to Steve's neighbor: Steve was to go to a phone booth at a certain Exxon gas station to receive instructions about a ransom. Despite the kidnapper's warning, Steve made an urgent stop on his way to the gas station to talk with Hugh Taylor, an FBI agent who had worked on his wife's murder case. Then he drove on to wait in the phone booth; the kidnapper's call soon came through. "I want eighty-two thousand dollars," demanded a male voice. Steve was directed to appear with the money at a street corner in Manhattan—alone. In turn, Steve insisted on proof that Sharon and Neil were still alive. The voice on the phone agreed to produce an audio tape, then hung up.

Within hours, Arty had taped his hostages' voices, wrapped the cassette in brown paper, and left it, just as he had promised, on the altar of a Catholic church. Shortly afterward Steve and Taylor heard Sharon's voice repeating the ransom terms, followed by Neil's young chirp of assurance: "Dad, I'm all right. Sharon is taking care of me." But Steve's new relief was almost instantly shattered. "Why how nice of you," sang out another voice from the tape. "Do come in."

Steve moaned and let out an expletive. "That's my wife, that's Nina!" The voices of the hostages had been taped over an earlier recording. The kidnapper must have known Nina and spoken with her before her death!

Taylor, skeptical, was at first more inclined to believe that Sharon herself had masterminded the kidnapping as a desperate hoax to postpone Thompson's execution. He believed that she was trying to imitate the voice of Steve's wife on tape as "a cheap clumsy way to link the abduction to Nina Peterson's death." But an expert examination soon confirmed that the voice was indeed Nina's. Now it became only too obvious to both Steve and Taylor that Ronald Thompson was not Nina's killer; the man who now held Neil and Sharon at his mercy was the same man who had murdered Steve's wife.

It was now over 24 hours since Arty, toting a gun, had forced his way into Steve's house, bound the terrified occupants, stuffed little Neil into a duffel bag, and taken both of them away in a stolen car. After driving along the icy streets into Manhattan, the kidnapper had pulled into a parking lot and reached into the back seat to untie Sharon's feet and removed her gag. "If one scream comes out of you, the boy dies," he threatened as he led her down the stairs of Grand Central Station's lower terminal and into an isolated room. Then, pushing Sharon to the floor, he re-tied her bindings, set down the duffel bag, unzipped it, then turned and left the room, closing the door behind him.

Sharon recognized at once that Neil, who suffered from asthma, was having an attack. "Breathe slowly, Neil," she said, trying to comfort him. "You're brave." Soon the boy drifted off to sleep. But before long he awoke with a start. "Sharon, that man, the bad man who tied us up," his voice quavered, "that's the man who killed my Mommy."

Early on the morning of Thompson's scheduled execution, Steve made the lonely trip to deliver the ransom. "Did you have anything to do with my wife's death?" he asked the kidnapper point-blank. But the disguised abductor gave no reply; he simply removed the $82,000 from Steve's suitcase—correctly guessing that the luggage was equipped with an FBI "tracer"—and left, with one terse declaration: "If I'm not followed and the money is all here, you'll be told where to pick up your son and Sharon at eleven-thirty this morning."

After Arty had ascertained that he wasn't being shadowed, he returned to the grimy little room in Grand Central Station to pay Sharon and Neil a final visit. "I'm going to set the clock now," he told them quietly, referring to the timer on his lovingly assembled bomb. Then, re-checking the pair's bindings and putting gags in their mouths, he jeered, "You won't feel anything, Sharon. You'll just be gone and Neil will be gone and Ronald Thompson will be gone." Then, leaning over his beautiful hostage, Arty offered a parting line: "I could have loved you very much, Sharon, as I think you could have loved me." As the door closed behind her kidnapper, Sharon looked "at the glowing face of the clock. It was 8:36." The timer had been set for 11:30. In less than three hours she and Neil would be dead.

While Arty was bending to set the timer for his bomb in Grand Central Station, Steve and Taylor were finally piecing together his identity. One of Neil's after-school babysitters, it turned out, remembered a bar-buddy, an auto mechanic, who had been casually questioning him about the Peterson household. The name of the mechanic was Arty Taggert. But once again Steve's hopes were quickly dampened, when another message came through from "Foxy": At 11:30 that morning, "during an explosion in New York State"—an allusion to the Thompson execution—Neil and Sharon would also be "executed" at an unnamed major transportation center somewhere in New York City.

With less than two hours to act, Steve and Taylor almost succumbed to despair. Then, miraculously, more information came in: another bar customer had recalled hearing Taggert talk about "going to Arizona." More important, they learned that Taggert had stolen the car he was driving from a parking place in front of the Biltmore Hotel, a place where he was soon confirmed as a "recent guest." After making a frantic call to notify the Governor of Connecticut that her state was about to execute an innocent man, Taylor and Steve boarded a police helicopter and headed for the "largest New York City transportation center" located near the Biltmore: Grand Central Station.

Meanwhile, Taggert was already waiting at La Guardia Airport to board a plane for Arizona. Just as his flight was announced, he saw the police closing in. With the cunning of a trapped animal, he managed to elude them—but the suitcase full of ransom money was lost. Enraged, Arty decided that Sharon must be punished for his defeat. "A bomb was too good for her" at this point; she would have to die—"look up at him [and] feel his hands on her throat," just as Nina and his other victims had died.

The killer arrived at Grand Central—now evacuated and echoing with silence—at exactly 11:26. Downstairs waited Sharon, alone and terrified, behind the secret door. In a spasm of orgiastic frenzy, his hands gripped her throat—and began to twist and squeeze. At that moment, Steve and Taylor burst into the room. With Sharon's help, Neil had somehow managed to make his way upstairs to alert his frantic father.

After one frozen moment, Taggert bolted into a restroom, locking the door behind him. Steve snatched Sharon's motionless body up in his arms and dashed up the stairs behind Taylor. Together they cleared the station—just as Taggart glimpsed the "blinding flash" of the explosion that "hurtled him into eternity."

At 11:42 a.m., Ronald Thompson's mother looked up from her prayers to find her son's lawyer standing at the back of the church. "Is it over?" she asked. Yes, explained the lawyer, but not in the way she had expected. Instead, at the last minute it had been absolutely proven that her son was not the murderer of Nina Peterson. Ronald would be coming home.

Sharon, who was just regaining consciousness in a nearby hospital, would be delighted to hear all about Thompson's release later on. But for now all she wanted was to feel "Steve's lips on her cheeks, her forehead, her lips."

Commentary

An immensely popular novelist, Mary Higgins Clark deftly modulates plot with pacing in her suspense tales. In A Stranger Is Watching the early narrative unfolds slowly, alternating its focus from the viewpoints of various characters, then picks up momentum as it moves toward the dramatic final pages.

Born in 1931, Clark began writing professionally to support herself and her children after the death of her husband. She started out by composing short stories for magazines and soon followed with a biography of George Washington, Aspire to the Heavens, published in 1969. But it was not until the release of her third book, A Stranger Is Watching, in 1977, that Clark became widely read. After the work's publication, she emerged as one of the most popular authors in the United States.

"I write for the mainstream," Clark once said in an interview for the Washington Post. "I write about nice people not looking for trouble. They find evil in their own car, home, everyday life." Within this civilized, familiar context, of course, terror, when it comes, seems all the more nightmarish and stark.

'Round the Fire Stories is a collection of chilling English tales intended, as Arthur Conan Doyle's title implies, "to be read 'round the fire." In the grand tradition of his better-known Sherlock Holmes mysteries, Doyle (1859–1930) interweaves cryptic events, plot twists, surprise endings, and characters as diverse as a disgraced banker, an expatriate gourmet and a ship's captain all into intriguing arabesques of adventure, suspense and lush Victorian horror.

THE POT OF CAVIAR

When the Boxer insurrection incited pandemonium throughout northern China, resident Europeans gathered in any safe place they could find. One unfortunate group was huddled together under siege in a little garrison 50 miles from the coast. A nurse, a professor, a priest, a few railworkers, a mother with her teenage daughter, and a German colonel anxiously watched their food supply dwindle as they awaited the arrival of British reinforcements.

On Thursday, the faint echo of gunshots raised the party's spirits; the distant booms, fired by their own troops, marked the almost certain rout of the rebels. This called for a celebration. "The pot of caviar!" exhorted Ainslie, one of the railworkers; and the others joined in: "The pot!" But Professor Mercer, who had produced the delicacy from his own luggage, demurred. "Better wait," he cautioned. "They still have far to come."

Finally the group agreed to save the luxurious fare for dinner, and the conversation turned to bracing anecdotes of past dangers surmounted. When the professor was asked to recount the tale of his own spectacular encounter with death during a battle in another Asian uprising, he seemed strangely disturbed; nevertheless, his eyes burning with the horror of old memories, he reached into the recesses of his mind to retrieve the past.

Years earlier, Mercer had been trapped in another garrison at Sung-Tong, with another group of civilians, including a number of women. The little fort eventually fell to the enemy, but because Mercer was a doctor, his life was spared. "But what about the others?" pressed the colonel. "It is wiser not to ask," the professor warned. "It is better not to speak about such things at all."

At this point the professor's story was interrupted. The gunshots were suddenly getting closer. The company ran outside to judge how long it would be before relief arrived. Only the professor remained behind, as if rooted to his chair, still haunted by vapors from the past. Soon the colonel returned to report the news to him: all was well. Ainslie had gone to the church to await the relief forces and would send a signal of three gunshots as reinforcements approached. Then, still riveted by the story of the Sung-Tong garrison, the German asked, "Could it have been saved?"

"No, everything possible was done—save only one thing," Mercer replied. "No one—above all, no woman—should have been allowed to fall alive into the hands of the Chinese."

The colonel agreed readily on that point, but what, asked the colonel, was the "one thing" that could have been done? Glancing up, the professor slowly replied: "I have seen the death of the hot eggs. I have seen the death of the boiling kettle; I was strapped to a stake with thorns in my eyelids to keep them open, and my grief at their torture was … less than my self-reproach when I thought that I could with one tube of tasteless tablets have snatched them at the last instant from the hands of their tormentors."

Suddenly, all was quiet around the garrison; the guns had fallen silent. The colonel again went outside to see why Ainslie had not fired his signal, only to return moments later with a ghastly look on his face. A wounded man outside the gate had informed him that reinforcements could not get through; the garrison, he said, was sure to fall.

The colonel and the professor kept this grim news from the others. At supper the company celebrated their imminent deliverance by opening and eating the caviar. Only one young girl refused the exotic treat.

Soon, one of the group, a railworker, was slumbering peacefully on the table. He was followed in short order by the nurse, and then by the priest. One by one each of the hideaways drifted into sweet oblivion—until only the girl who had not partaken of the caviar remained awake. Not until then did the professor turn to her with a terrible revelation: This time the "one thing" necessary to save them all from a fate worse than death had been done; the professor had mixed cyanide into the caviar. Now he begged the terrified girl also to partake of the poisonous delicacy, but by then she had collapsed in helpless shock. And it was just at that moment, as the professor felt himself falling into his own death-sleep, that the shouts of British soldiers sounded outside the walls. "What have I done?" cried the professor as the gallant reinforcements burst through the door to their hideaway. *"What have I done?"*

THE SEALED ROOM

The Stanniford house was long since denuded of all furnishings;. Its only ornaments were layers of cobwebs and dust. At the end of the hallway a large door stood closed and sealed, as it had remained for nearly a decade. Felix's father, Stanislaus, had been one of the most successful bankers in all England. However, after a few hapless ventures, he was left owing so much money to his investors that he had simply decided to vanish, leaving his wife and son to fend for themselves.

In the first months after Stanniford's disappearance, Felix and his mother had received two letters from him, the first directing that a seal be immediately placed on the door to the darkroom which Stanislaus had used for his photography, to be removed only by his son Felix upon Felix's twenty-first birthday; until then, the house must remain unrented and unsold. The second letter pronounced that Mrs. Stanniford would see her husband soon, though she had long been an invalid and was now considered on the threshold of death. No further communications were received from the fugitive.

Shortly thereafter, Mrs. Stanniford did, in fact, die, leaving young Felix alone in the blighted house. As years went by, he was forced to sell the furnishings to stay alive. Still, Felix never opened the sealed door.

Finally, on his twenty-first birthday, Felix, as directed, summoned his father's aged clerk Perceval and asked him to turn over the key. "Mr. Stanniford, I hope you will prepare yourself in case any shock should be awaiting you," cautioned Perceval. With many forebodings, the clerk stood by as Felix manipulated the lock—his heart still filled with memories of his master's final confidences. Stanislaus had admitted that his first resolve was to escape disgrace by taking his own life; in the end, he had only hesitated because of the anguish this might cause to his wife. At last, he had entrusted Perceval with two letters to be mailed soon thereafter. Then, voicing his yearning to somehow remain close to them, he had secreted himself to prepare for his disappearance.

The door to the darkroom at last creaked open and a cry of horror escaped Felix Stanniford's throat: seated at the dust-covered desk before him was a shriveled, lemon-colored corpse.

Thus, Stanniford's last promise to his wife—that she would meet him soon—had been fulfilled after all, on the day when the two were rejoined forever in death. And now, as Felix, utterly stricken, sank to the floor, the old clerk reached forward to extract a final letter from the dead man's hand. Scanning its contents, he read aloud:

I have taken the poison, and I feel it working in my veins.... When these words are read I shall, if my wishes have been faithfully carried out, have been dead many years. Surely no one who had lost money through me will still bear me animosity. And you, Felix, you will forgive me this family scandal. May God find rest for a sorely wearied spirit!

THE FIEND OF THE COOPERAGE

The *Gamecock* touched shore. Captain Meldrum, the owner of the small yacht, stepped onto a small tropical island and was greeted by Doctor Severall and Mr. Walker, two business associates who had invited the captain to visit them.

After touring a few points of interest, the three men sat down to dine in a large building with white wooden walls, an iron roof and an earthen floor. This was the cooperage, a place which the island natives

were now avoiding in terror. The specific object of their dread was a harmless-looking bed standing against the far wall of the room. Six days earlier, the watchman who slept in that bed had mysteriously vanished. Since no canoe had been seen and the river surrounding the cooperage was infested by crocodiles, there was no explanation for his disappearance. Then, just three days after that, the new watchman had also come up missing, again leaving behind no clues—no bloodstains and no signs of any violent struggle. The natives were convinced that voodoo was responsible; but this had only left Doctor Severall more determined to solve the mystery. In fact, he had resolved to spend a night in the cooperage himself.

As they discussed these bizarre events, Mr. Walker was suddenly struck by an attack of a fever common to the islands, and began to sink into delirium. The doctor steered the poor man up to the house, gave him a sedative, and put him to bed. Meanwhile, Meldrum decided to stay the night in the cooperage to keep watch with Severall. The men would take turns sleeping.

After dark, a storm hit the island. Outside the cooperage the rain and the flooding river roared together turbulently, but inside all remained calm. Once, during a lull in the storm, Severall did rouse to a faint, satiny, slithering noise outside the window,. But when he got up to investigate, there was nothing to be seen.

When daylight finally came, the mystery was still unresolved. Severall was happy enough, however, because they had both obviously survived. Then, eager for breakfast, the two men went to check on Walker. Upon reaching the house, they were met by a ghastly scene: Walker, still in his pajamas, lay dead on the floor. And it soon became obvious that he had not died of the fever. "The breast bone is gone," said Severall in bewilderment. He looked at Meldrum, shaken; what could have caused such harm?

As the two men raced outside toward the waterfront, they were greeted by another eerie sight: a massive tree trunk, uprooted by the flood, floated by them, and on it lay a human body. The head was flattened, the terrified face stared hideously out at them. And wound around the neck and torso were thick yellow and black coils. "What is it?" cried the captain. "It is our fiend of the cooperage," Severall answered. "The great python of the Gaboon."

Indeed, it must have been the python that Severall had heard slithering past the cooperage during the night. Then, frightened by Severall's movements, the snake had changed course and crawled to the house. There, the sedated Walker was no doubt crushed almost instantly, but before the snake could carry him away, the renewed fury of the storm had frightened it off—to search for yet another victim. And after the serpent had fastened onto its prey, the flood had swept the assassin, along with its final victim, to its own watery death.

THE HOUSE OF THE SEVEN GABLES
by Nathaniel Hawthorne (1804–1864)

Type of work
Gothic mystery

Setting
New England; the mid-1800s

Principal characters
Hepzibah Pyncheon, a sour-faced but tenderhearted old maid

Clifford Pyncheon, Hepzibah's brother

Phoebe Pyncheon, her delightful young cousin

Jaffery Pyncheon, another of Hepzibah's cousins, heir to the Pyncheon fortune

Mr. Holgrave, Hepzibah's tenant, a daguerreotypist (i.e., a primitive photographer)

Nathaniel Hawthorne describes this novel as a "romance." Not to be outdone by other writers of his day, however, who placed great import on framing their work around definite moral lessons, Hawthorne also provided a moral for his story: "That the wrong-doing of one generation lives into the successive ones, and, divesting itself of every temporary advantage, becomes a pure and uncontrollable mischief."

Hawthorne's work is often preoccupied with the themes of witches' curses, family influences, the decay of ancient lineages—and *The House of Seven Gables* is vintage Hawthorne, capturing each of these elements somewhere within the novel's two-century time span.

Story overview

The house stood halfway down Pyncheon Street. It bore unmistakable "traces not merely of outward storm and sunshine," but also of "the long lapse of mortal life, and accompanying vicissitudes that [had] passed within."

But the house was not the first habitation erected on that spot of ground. The carpenter Matthew Maule had originally built a hut for his family on the site, near a pleasant natural spring. But as the town grew the land had come to the attention of Colonel Pyncheon, "a prominent and powerful personage, who asserted plausible claims to [its] proprietorship ... on the strength of a grant from the legislature." Matthew Maule, however, though an obscure man, stubbornly defended what he considered his property.

The dispute was settled only by the death of Matthew Maule. In fact, Maule was executed for witchcraft—and Colonel Pyncheon's had been among the loudest of those voices who had joined in the cry to expedite his sentence.

But who on this earth can be assured of ultimate victory? At the moment of his execution, Maule had pointed his finger toward Pyncheon and proclaimed a curse upon him and his entire posterity. Pyncheon, his energy of purpose undeterred, had torn down Maule's shack and erected in its stead the House of the Seven Gables—though the townspeople had expressed amazement that he would choose the site of an unquiet grave to build a house where "future bridegrooms were to lead their brides, and where children of the Pyncheon blood

were to be born." And perhaps they were correct in their forebodings, for on the day of the great public opening of his new structure, Colonel Pyncheon was found within, sitting dead at his desk beneath his own imposing portrait. The clutter of letters, parchments and blank sheets of paper before him bore mute testimony to the coroner's verdict of "sudden death."

Upon the demise of the Colonel his only son acquired a rich estate, including claim to a vast tract of Eastern lands in the state of Maine. But, unfortunately, Colonel Pyncheon had died without leaving a clue as to where the deeds to those lands might be found. Thus, over the generations, the Pyncheon family wealth slowly deteriorated.

For the better part of two centuries the Pyncheons, though a family filled with eccentrics, lived much like any other New Englanders. In recent years, however, a particularly onerous calamity had befallen their descendants: one member of the clan, Clifford Pyncheon, was adjudged to have murdered his uncle in a fit of rage. When this shamed and ruined family member was finally released from prison as a broken old man, he took up residence with his sister, Hepzibah, who had been willed a life estate in the House of the Seven Gables. These two, along with the current heir, Judge Jaffery Pyncheon, and the youngest of the family, Phoebe, were all that remained of the Pyncheon lineage. The Maule family, it was supposed, had by now become extinct.

Hepzibah, an old maid, tall, with a "long and shrunken waist" and a perpetual scowl upon her face, was mistress of a now dark and chilly house, its once beautifully sculpted grounds withered and overgrown with weeds. She was thankful, therefore, when her young relative, Phoebe, came to live with her. A slender young girl full of sunshine and song, Phoebe brought a smile and a cheery glow with her, quite a contrast to Clifford's "wasted, gray, and melancholy figure." This unfortunate man still loved beautiful things, however, and was especially drawn to Phoebe. For her part, Phoebe also dearly loved her uncle and delighted in cheering him with flowers from her garden.

Still, living with the two reclusive old people was a lonesome task. "The only youthful mind with which Phoebe had an opportunity of frequent intercourse was that of the daguerreotypist" who boarded at Seven Gables, Mr. Holgrave. It is doubtful either would have taken a liking to the other, so different were they, except they both loved working in the gardens and were regularly drawn together there in conversation. During one of these chats Mr. Holgrave spoke up. "Now, this old Pyncheon House!" he began. "Is it a wholesome place to live in, with its black shingles, and green moss that shows how damp they are?... its grime and sordidness, which are the crystallization on its walls of the human breath that has been drawn and exhaled here in discontent and anguish? The house ought to be purified with fire—purified till only its ashes remain!" Holgrave regretted most that he was forced to board there in order to pursue his studies: "I dwell in it for a while, that I may know the better how to hate it," he declared. In fact, Holgrave continued, he had written down a Pyncheon legend which he meant to have published in a magazine:

Matthew Maule, a grandson of the original Maule, had apparently inherited from his ancestor some traits of witchcraft. These powers were enlisted by Gervayse Pyncheon, a descendent of the Colonel, to help him locate the missing document that would secure the family's Eastern properties: Under a hypnotic spell cast by Matthew, Gervayse's daughter Alice reported that, as part of the Pyncheon curse, the document was destined to remain hidden until it was too late to stake a claim.

After securing this knowledge, however, Maule chose not to release Alice from his control. For the rest of her life, whenever he raised his hand, she would do as he bade. He thus induced her to laugh during solemn occasions and to commit all sorts of other undignified acts over the years. Finally, when he forced her go out on a cold night to wait upon his wife, Alice caught pneumonia and died. Maule followed the funeral procession, "the darkest and woefullest man that ever walked behind a corpse! He meant to humble Alice, not to kill her; but he had taken a woman's delicate soul in to his rude grip, to play with—and she was dead!"

Rolling up his manuscript as he finished relating this story, Holgrave found that Phoebe's eyelids were drooping. "A veil was beginning to be muffled about her.... It was evident that, with but one wave of his hand ... he could establish an influence over this good, pure, and simple child, as dangerous ... as that which the carpenter of his legend had acquired and exercised over the ill-fated Alice."

Not long thereafter Phoebe withdrew to the country for a few days to visit her family. Mr. Holgrave remarked that he would not be surprised if the shattered Clifford now crumbled away and the impoverished old maid Hepzibah lost what "little flexibility" she had; both seemed to exist—indeed, breathe and live—because of Phoebe. He now expressed the portent that some new, unforeseen trouble was hovering over Phoebe's relatives, and that the dilapidated house had become a sort of theater stage on which the last of the Pyncheons would meet their doom.

Holgrave's forebodings were ultimately fulfilled the day Judge Jaffery Pyncheon came to visit and presumptuously announced his certainty that Clifford knew the secret of the Pyncheon land grant, lost now for centuries. But when Hepzibah hurried to summon her brother to the Judge's imperious presence, Clifford was not in his room. Panic-stricken, she returned to the parlor to inform Jaffery of his disappearance—only to find Clifford himself at the parlor's threshold. "His face was preternaturally pale" and his finger pointed towards the Judge, who slumped dead and silent in his seat before him. The brother and sister fled the house in fear, leaving Judge Jaffery alone in the home of his forefathers.

On the following day, when Phoebe returned to the House of the Seven Gables, she was met by Mr. Holgrave, looking extraordinarily pale. "His smile, however, was full of genuine warmth, and had in it a joy, by far the most vivid expression that Phoebe had ever witnessed, shining out of the New England reserve with which Holgrave habitually masked whatever lay in his heart." The Judge was dead, he announced, and both Clifford and Hepzibah had mysteriously vanished. Phoebe could not understand the calmness of Holgrave's demeanor. "He appeared ... to feel the whole awfulness of the Judge's death, yet had received the fact ... without any mixture of surprise, but as an event preordained, happening inevitably, and so fitting itself into past occurrences that it could almost have been prophesied." Phoebe longed to throw open the doors and call for the police, but Holgrave convinced her that with Hepzibah and Clifford gone, suspicion would naturally fall upon them. This, he asserted, would be a grave injustice, "because if the matter can be fairly considered ... it must be evident that Judge Pyncheon could not have come unfairly to his end.... This mode of death has been an idiosyncrasy with his family for generations past ... usually attacking individuals about the Judge's time of life, and generally in the tension of some mental crisis.... Old Maule's prophecy was probably founded on a knowledge of this physical predisposition in the Pyncheon race"—a hereditary condition that brought early death to its bearers.

Phoebe still could not fathom what "mental crisis" could have led to such an end—until Holgrave continued with his narrative. The man sitting dead in the parlor, he contended, had 30 years earlier made a desperate search for a will which would cut off his inheritance. In truth, concluded Holgrave, the elder Jaffery Pyncheon had recently drawn up a new will bequeathing his estate to Clifford. Under the shock of discovering his nephew rifling through his papers, however, the uncle had suffered a fatal seizure, to become another victim of the Pyncheon curse. Jaffery had then destroyed the will—and framed Clifford as his uncle's murderer.

When Hepzibah and Clifford returned to the House of the Seven Gables, the truth of Holgrave's account was at last made known to the world. Clifford, released from the decades of anguish heaped upon him by Jaffery, at last remembered the secret sought after by long generations of Pyncheons: As a child, he had discovered an opening concealed behind the portrait of the original Colonel Pyncheon—a compartment containing the long-lost land grant. The document was now worthless—but no matter; the last of the three Pyncheons would inherit Jaffery's wealth.

Holgrave and Phoebe, drawn together through companionship and crisis, now found themselves in love. Still, there was one more secret still to be revealed. "My dearest Phoebe," said Holgrave, "how will it please you to assume the name of Maule? As for the secret, it is the only inheritance that has come down to me from my ancestors. You should have known sooner (only that I was afraid of frightening you away) that, in this long drama of wrong and retribution, I represent the old wizard, and am probably as much a wizard as ever he was. The son of the executed Matthew Maule, while building this house, took the opportunity to construct that recess, and hide away the ... deed, on which depended the immense land-claim of the Pyncheons. Thus they bartered their Eastern territory for Maule's garden-ground."

IVANHOE
by Sir Walter Scott (1771–1832)

Type of work
Historical Romance

Setting
Late 12th-century England

Principal characters
Sir Brian De Bois-Gilbert, a Norman aristocrat and knight
Sir Cedric, a Saxon aristocrat
Sir Ivanhoe, Cedric's son and a brave Saxon knight
Lady Rowena, Cedric's charge, a Saxon beauty of exalted lineage
Isaac of York, a wealthy Jewish merchant
Rebecca, Isaac's enchanting daughter
Richard I, King of England

Story overview

Two Normans, Sir Brian De Bois-Gilbert, a Knight Templar, and Prior Aymer de Jorvaulx, a monk, had been searching in vain for Rotherwood, the manor of the Saxon noble, Sir Cedric. It was with great relief, then, that they happened upon a cloaked and hooded pilgrim who guided them to their destination.

Observing the approach of visitors, Sir Cedric announced to his warder that whether the strangers be "Norman or Saxon the hospitality of Rotherwood must not be impeached..."

That night at dinner, Cedric and his beguiling young ward Rowena were thus joined by the two Norman travelers and the anonymous pilgrim who had guided them to Rotherwood, as well as by one other remarkable guest: Isaac of York, a wealthy Jewish merchant. Despite his wealth, Isaac was marked by his Hebrew lineage as an outcast—fated to be "detested" by commoners and "persecuted by the greedy and rapacious nobility"; only one of Cedric's guests, the kind pilgrim—whose facial features remained obscured by a swarthy cloak—engaged the Jew in conversation.

Sir Brian, meanwhile, regaled the others in attendance with accolades for the great "renown in arms" of Cedric's son, the noble knight Ivanhoe. Actually, Cedric had banished his son to the crusades because of Ivanhoe's devotion to Rowena, whom Cedric wished to ally in marriage with the illustrious Saxon noble Athelstane. Thus when Sir Brian expressed a desire to joust with Sir Ivanhoe, Cedric bristled at Rowena's response: "My voice shall be heard, if no other in this hall is raised, in behalf of the absent Ivanhoe. I would pledge name and fame that Ivanhoe gives this proud Knight the meeting he desires."

Rowena's words elated the cloaked pilgrim—for, in reality, he was none other than Ivanhoe himself in disguise. To his further delight, Rowena later invited him to converse secretly in her chamber. " ... You this night mentioned a name," faltered the lady. "—I mean ... the name of Ivanhoe in the halls where by nature and kindred it should have sounded most acceptably

... I only dare ask you where, and in what condition ... you left him of whom you spoke?"

"He hath, I believe, surmounted the persecution of his enemies in Palestine," Ivanhoe lied, "and is on the eve of returning to England..."

"Would to God," Rowena exclaimed, "he were here safely arrived, and able to bear arms in the approaching tourney ... " She then retired to her bed, and Ivanhoe paid a visit to Isaac's guest chamber—with the warning that he had overheard Sir Brian earlier discuss a plan "to abduct him and steal his money." Isaac despaired at the news. But Ivanhoe reassured him: "I will guide you by the secret paths of the forest, known as well to me as to any forester that ranges in it, and I will not leave you till you are under safe conduct of some chief or baron going to the tournament..."

As promised, Ivanhoe safely conducted the fugitive through the forest. When Isaac later appeared with his daughter Rebecca in the spectators' gallery at the tournament, Prince John—who was acting as regent while his brother and "mortal enemy" King Richard fought in the Crusades—was immediately smitten with the enchanting girl. "Yonder Jewess must be the very model of that perfection whose charms drove frantic the wisest king that ever lived!" he marveled. Indeed, the Prince even considered naming Rebecca as the tournament's Queen of Beauty and Love.

Ivanhoe, however, under the anonymous title of a "Disinherited Knight," fought superbly in the tournament's first matches, defeating six knights, including Sir Brian; and as a reward, he was given the honor of naming the tournament Queen. Of course the Lady Rowena was selected. On the second day of the tournament, according to custom, "the Prince marshalled Rowena to the seat of honour opposite his own." And as the day's events unfolded, it appeared that the Disinherited Knight would again defeat all his challengers. Suddenly, the horseman was set upon by three knights at once—led by the Norman Sir Brian: *The masterly horsemanship of the Disinherited Knight and the activity of the noble animal which he mounted, enabled him for a few minutes to keep at sword's point his three antagonists, turning and wheeling with the agility of a hawk ... and rushing now against the one, now against the other....* Before long, however, "it was evident that he must at last be overpowered."

Then, just at the crucial moment, "the course of the day [was changed]." A knight dubbed the Black Sluggard, who "hitherto had evinced little interest in the event of the fight," suddenly rushed into battle. With the assistance of this enigmatic ally, the Disinherited Knight again proved victorious. He "waved his fatal sword over the head of his adversary," Sir Brian, who had fallen from his wounded horse.

Proclaiming the Disinherited Knight the tournament champion, Prince John instructed him to receive the "chaplet of honour" from Rowena. Then, over the knight's protests, as he knelt before his lady his "helmet was removed." And though "his countenance was as pale as death, and marked in one or two places with streaks of blood," Rowena recognized Ivanhoe. With a "faint shriek," she placed the chaplet on his head. Ivanhoe then kissed his lady's hand—and fainted.

When "Cedric the Saxon saw his son drop down senseless in the lists of Ashby, his first impulse was to order him into the custody and care of his own attendants." His pride, though, prevented him. And he was further vexed when Rowena subsequently refused to "share a throne with Athelstane"; nevertheless, the three set off together for Rotherwood.

En route, they were shocked to find Isaac and Rebecca shrieking by the roadside in distress. They, having set out for Rotherwood along with their wounded friend Ivanhoe—who lay huddled and concealed in the litter—had been stopped by the news "that there was a strong band of outlaws lying in wait in the woods before them"; meanwhile, their frightened servants had fled with all the horses.

Isaac now begged the Saxons to accompany them on their journey. Athelstane at first refused; touched by Rebecca's pleas, however, Rowena persuaded Cedric to help. The travelers thus journeyed together until twilight, "when they were assailed in front, flank, and rear" by three Normans: Sir Brian, Maurice de Bracy, and Reginald Front de Boeuf.

The Normans immediately led their Saxon prisoners to Front de Boeuf's castle. Here, the Saxons were confined together, and the enshrouded and sickly Isaac was tended to by a Saxon "hag" named Ulrica. The others were led to separate chambers.

In his chamber, Isaac learned that Front de Boeuf sought a ransom of "a thousand silver pounds" for his release. If Isaac refused to pay, de Boeuf would torture him to death. Although unaware of her father's plight, Rebecca, in her chamber, was horrified to hear Sir Brian demand her hand in marriage. To silence him, she threatened "to jump from her turret-chamber."

Not long thereafter the Norman castle was attacked by Saxons—including not only the renowned Robin Hood, along with his outlaw band, but King Richard himself, still riding under the dark trappings of the Black Sluggard Knight. During the ensuing battle, the captives managed to make their way outside. There they saw that a "fire was spreading rapidly through all parts of the castle." And as the blaze roiled upward, "Ulrica, who had first kindled it, appeared on a turret, in the guise of one of the ancient furies, yelling forth a war song," until at last she was engulfed by the hungry flames.

Robin Hood then directed de Bracy and the erstwhile captives to "the trysting-tree near Hartwalk Walk." Here, everyone was apprised of the events that had transpired during the battle: Athelstane and de Boeuf had both met their deaths; Rebecca had been abducted by the proud Sir Brian. "Oh," Isaac lamented, "Better the tomb of her fathers than the dishonourable couch of the licentious and savage Templar."

When Isaac visited the Grand Master of the Templars to arrange a ransom for his daughter's return, the Grand Master was outraged. "Spurn this Jew from the gate," he commanded his men. "Shoot him dead if he oppose or turn again." He then sent a messenger to find Sir Brian, who was stunned to hear that "Rebecca . . . is a sorceress and must suffer as such."

"She shall not, by heaven," Sir Brian exclaimed. But Rebecca's fate was now out of his hands. The Jewish maiden was "brought before the tribunal of the Grand Master" on charges of sorcery.

After various witnesses had related incidents purporting to demonstrate her bewitching of Sir Brian, at last Rebecca spoke. "To invoke your pity," she began, "would . . . be as useless as I should hold it mean." She then continued: " . . . I maintain my innocence, and I declare the falsehood of this accusation. I challenge the privilege of trial by combat . . . "

Thus, on the day scheduled for her execution, Rebecca was led to a "black chair arranged near a stake surrounded by faggots, where she awaited a champion to fight for her life." None appeared. At last the Grand Master announced, "Let her prepare for death."

Suddenly "a knight, urging his horse to speed, appeared on the plain." Ivanhoe had come to defend Rebecca. The combat began; and soon the Saxon's opponent, Sir Brian, lay unhorsed on the ground, unable to arise. "Slay him not," the Grand Master commanded. Sir Brian, however, had already died—not by "the lance of his enemy," but by "the violence of his own contending passions."

Then a "clattering of horses' feet" could be heard. King Richard—who was in the process of wresting control of his throne from the treacherous Prince John—had come with Robin Hood to arrest the Norman Knights.

Shortly thereafter, the victorious King invited Sir Cedric to be "a guest at court for seven days." The Saxon now reconsidered his long quarrel with his son—and relented. With the blessing of Athelstane, who had miraculously come back to life at his own funeral, Ivanhoe and Rowena were soon wed, an event celebrated by Norman and Saxon alike.

Following the marriage, Rebecca and her father left England for a safe and prosperous life in Spain. At Rotherwood, meanwhile, Rowena and Ivanhoe "lived long and happily [together], for they were attached to each other by the bonds of earthly affection, and they loved each other the more from the recollection of the obstacles which had impeded their union."

Commentary

Sir Walter Scott noted that he had set *Ivanhoe* in the reign of Richard I because the period lent his narrative a "striking contrast betwixt the Saxons, by whom the soil was cultivated, and the Normans, who still reigned in it as conquerors . . . " In reality, hostilities between Saxons and their Norman conquerors had largely abated by the late 12th century—a fact that has long irritated critics of the novel. Despite this historical inaccuracy, Scott's gripping tale has remained immensely popular largely because of his skillful dramatization of the daily life in Plantagenet England.

Type of work
Epic Greek poem

Setting
Troy; c. 1250–1240 B.C.E.

Principal characters
The Achaeans (Greeks)
Menelaos, King of the Greek city-state Argos, whose wife Helen has been abducted by Paris, a prince of Troy
Agamemnon, Menelaos's brother and also a King of Argos
Achilles, mightiest and most feared of the Achaean warriors
Patroclus, brave Achaean soldier and close friend of Achilles
The Trojans
Paris, a Trojan prince, abductor of the beautiful Helen
Hector, Paris's brother, a powerful Trojan warrior
Priam, King of Troy and father of Paris and Hector
Krypeis and *Briseis*, two women
Various gods and goddesses, each alternately favoring one side or the other

Since the age of Classical Greece, Homer's *The Iliad* and *The Odyssey* have been revered by the West almost as sacred texts. Throughout the ages, his epics have inspired a multitude of other great works in painting, sculpture, music, dance and other literature.

Homer himself remains a baffling figure. According to legend, he was blind and lived on the island of Chios. All that can be said with certainty about the West's most celebrated poet is that he crafted his works in the Ionian dialect of ancient Greece.

It is not difficult to see why *The Iliad* and *The Odyssey* are considered two of the greatest prototypes of world literature. They possess what the critic Harold Bloom has called an "uncanny sublimity." That is, they have about them an imaginative and spiritual grandeur that competes not only "for the consciousness of Western nations," as Bloom says, but also as that consciousness—in its most powerful and instinctual form.

Prologue

The Iliad focuses on events late in the Trojan War, a ten-year conflict between the Greeks and the Trojans which started when Prince Paris of Troy abducted Queen Helen, an Achaean woman famous for her beauty. King Menelaos, Helen's enraged husband, amassed Achaean troops and laid siege to Troy. The story line begins during the war's tenth year of conflict.

In response to the snatching of Queen Helen, the Achaeans have just kidnapped two comely maidens, Briseis and Kryseis, from towns near Troy; Kryseis was taken by King Agamemnon and Briseis was taken by the warrior Achilles.

As the fighting proceeds, the mythological gods also become important characters in the story, and influence the outcome of events at every turn.

Story overview

Hundreds of Achaean warriors lay dying in "transfixing pain" from a plague brought on by the archer god Apollo in response to a plea from Kryseis's grieving father. Soon an Achaean diviner came to prophesy that the plague would not abate unless the woman was returned. When he heard this news, King Agamemnon flew into a frenzy. "You visionary of hell," he thundered at the diviner, "never have I had fair play in your forecasts." Still, Agamemnon finally agreed to return Kryseis, but only under the condition that he be given Achilles' prize, the charming Briseis. Now it was Achilles' turn to be outraged. "You thick-skinned, shameless greedy fool!" the proud warrior confronted his king. Then he swore to fight in the Achaean cause no more, and even beseeched Zeus, the supreme god, to intervene instead on behalf of the Trojans.

True to his word, when fighting broke out again Achilles remained in camp. The Trojan who first came out to battle was Prince Paris, who, as Helen's abductor, was responsible for starting the war. He sported "a cowl of leopard skin ... a longsword at his hip [and] two spears capped in pointed bronze." When Menelaos caught sight of him, he vowed, "I'll cut him to bits, adulterous dog!" Before he could do so, however, Paris changed his mind and retreated behind Trojan lines. His brother, the famed warrior Hector, regarded him contemptuously. "Paris, the great lover, a gallant sight!" he sneered. Thus humiliated, the cowering Paris announced that he would engage Menelaos in a personal duel for Helen and that the outcome would decide the war.

Menelaos agreed to his rival's challenge. Paris came out aggressively, but Menelaos quickly gained the advantage, pouncing on the prince in such a way that he lay "choked by the chin strap" of his own helmet. Alas, at that very moment the goddess Aphrodite intervened. She "hid [Paris] in mist / and put him down in his own fragrant chamber."

"Beyond question, Menelaos is victorious," Agamemnon proclaimed. But the Trojans renewed the conflict, with mortal foes "going for one another like wolves ... / whirling upon each other, man to man," until countless combatants, "prone in the dust, were strewn beside each other." The brave Achaean warrior Diomedes was struck by an arrow in the shoulder; but, although "spirits of blood ... stained his knitted shirt," he did not collapse. "Courage, Diomedes. Press the fight," the goddess Athena urged. Buoyed by her words, Diomedes strode furiously back into battle. After slaughtering many of his foes, he was assailed by the warrior Pandaros. "Guided by Athena," Diomedes managed to strike Pandaros's "nose beside the eye / and shatter his white teeth: his tongue / the brazen spearhead severed, tip from root, / then plowing on came out beneath his chin." Zeus had long since forbidden the gods and goddesses to aspire to sway men's fate. Still, many of them did choose to intervene at one time or another. On this occasion, when the balance of power tipped in favor of the Achaeans, Hector returned from the battlefield to the city to entreat his mother, Queen Hekabe, to make a sacrificial offering to "Athena, Hope of Soldiers." Then he kissed his child and bade an emotional farewell to his wife Andromache. "Unquiet soul," he said to her,

> *do not be too distresse by thoughts of me.*
> *You know no man dispatches me*
> *into the undergloom against my fate;*
> *no mortal, either, can escape his fate*
> *coward or brave man, once he comes to be.*

Andromache tearfully drew away from her husband's embrace; she was certain that he would not "be delivered from Achaean fury." But Hector, a soldier before a husband, met Paris by the gateway of Troy and rejoined the battle.

Meanwhile, Achilles, still angry with his king, pleaded to Zeus to give success to the enemy. As a result, Zeus sent thunder and "burning flashes of lightning against the Achaean army." All of the Achaeans despaired to see this fearful omen at the hand of Zeus. "Board ship for our own fatherland!" ordered Agamemnon, with tears trickling from his eyes. "Retreat! / We cannot hope any longer to take Troy." The king's advisors were shocked by this order of withdrawal and suggested a final maneuver before giving up: that Agamemnon make peace with Achilles and make use of his services. Agamemnon consented to the gambit and dispatched an embassy to speak with Achilles. The great warrior, however, shunned the embassy and ignored their request, announcing that he still planned to "sail homeward" the following day.

That night "Agamemnon lay beyond sweet sleep, and cast about in tumult of the mind," still looking for some way to avoid defeat. He thus decided to confer with a wise old man named Nestor "and see / what plan if any could be formed with him … " Sure enough, the old man devised a ruse to aid his king: Patroclus, Achilles' good friend, would go to battle wearing the great warrior's armor in an effort to demoralize the Trojans. Weary of war and anxious to break his enemy's spirit, Patroclus readily agreed to Nestor's scheme.

The next day, when the great champion "Achilles" appeared on the field of battle, the Trojans were stunned and terrified. But Apollo descended to allay Trojan fears and to address the imposter: "Back, Patroclus, lordly man! Destiny will not let this fortress town / of Trojans fall to you!" Obedient to the god, Patroclus "retired, a long way off," but not beyond the range of Hector, whose spear struck Patroclus "low in the shank" and killed him. The Trojans then removed Patroclus's battle gear and began desecrating his body.

When news of Patroclus's death reached Achilles, he "tore his hair with both hands [and] gave a dreadful cry":

> *I must reject this life, my heart tells me,*
> *reject the world of men,*
> *if Hector does not feel my battering spear*
> *tear the life out of him, making him pay*
> *in his own blood for the slaughter of Patroclus!*

The "lame god" Hephaistos, a designer of superior armor, undertook to outfit Achilles for the task at hand, creating for the warrior a magnificently crafted set of shield and armor. Girding the armor and taking up his shield, Achilles himself appeared on the field and "all the Achaeans gave a roar of joy." By now they had managed to reclaim Patroclus's body and fierce warfare had continued unabated. Agamemnon made amends with Achilles by returning Briseis to him, and before charging into battle, the two men sacrificed a boar to Zeus. With the aid of the gods, Achilles would not taste defeat.

After killing many brave Trojans, Achilles reached the gateway of the city, where Hector awaited him. When King Priam saw his son about to engage the mighty Achilles in battle, he begged Hector to withdraw: "Cut off as you are, alone, dear son, / don't try to hold your ground against this man, / or soon you'll meet the shock of doom … "

Achilles advanced "like the implacable god of war." At first Hector fled from him; three times did the men circle the walls of Troy. Finally, Hector turned and faced his enemy: "Now my soul would have me stand and fight, / whether I kill you or am killed." Achilles, the superior combatant, aimed his spear and "drove his point straight through the tender neck" of Hector, who was dressed in the armor Achilles had given Patroclus. "I beg you by your soul and by your parents," Hector whispered to Achilles before he died, "do not let the dogs feed on me."

The Achaeans gathered around the slain prince, "and no one came who did not stab the body." Priam wept at the defilement of his son's corpse. "Why could he not have died where I might hold him?" he lamented. Unmoved by the father's grief, Achilles persisted in heaping vengeance upon his fallen foe:

> *Behind both feet he pierced*
> *the tendons, heel to ankle. Rawhide cords*
> *he drew through both and lashed them to his chariot,*
> *letting the man's head trail. Stepping aboard,*
> *bearing the great trophy of the arms,*
> *he shook the reins, and whipped the team ahead*
> *into a willing run. A dustcloud rose*
> *above the furrowing body; the dark tresses*
> *flowed behind, and the head so princely once*
> *lay back in dust …*

Returning to the Achaean camp, Achilles left "Hector's body / to lie full-length in dust … " Thus it lay for eleven nights. As the twelfth day dawned, Zeus lost patience with Achilles' mad vengeance and sent his messengers to "beg [Achilles'] mercy" in accepting "ransom for the body." Afterward, Priam visited the Greek champion, who finally took pity on the anguished old man. His rage exhausted, Achilles ordered Hector's body bathed and rubbed with oil before it was returned to Troy:

> *Then in a grave dug deep they placed it*
> *and heaped it with great stones …*
> *So they performed*
> *the funeral rites of Hector, tamer of horses.*

THE ODYSSEY
by Homer (c. 8th century B.C.E.)

Type of work
Epic poem

Setting
Greek islands; c. 1240-30 B.C.E., 10 years after the fall of Troy

Principal characters

Odysseus, King of Ithaca and hero of the Trojan War
Penelope, Queen of Ithaca and wife of Odysseus
Athena, goddess of war
Zeus, supreme god of Olympus
Hermes, messenger of Zeus
Calypso, a beautiful sea nymph
Polyphemus, a Cyclops and the son of Poseidon
Circe, a beautiful goddess and enchantress

Story overview

Ten years after the Trojan War had ended, Odysseus, one of the great Greek heroes, languished on Ogygia, island of the sea nymph Calypso. Calypso, who was in love with Odysseus, had for seven years held him captive, refusing all appeals for release.

Pitying the plight of Odysseus, the goddess Athena called an Olympian council in hopes of persuading her father Zeus to allow Odysseus to return home to Penelope, his wife, in Ithaca. Zeus agreed, and dispatched his messenger Hermes to Ogygia, ordering Calypso to release Odysseus. Reluctantly, Calypso relented and outfitted Odysseus with provisions and a small boat. And finally the homesick warrior set sail for Ithaca. Poseidon, however, enraged that the Olympian council had met in his absence only to rule in favor of Odysseus's release, sent a storm that shipwrecked the hapless sailor on the Phaeacian coast.

Meanwhile in Ithaca, Penelope was besieged by a group of marauding suitors. Led by Antinous, the suitors had encamped in the palace, and as they ate and drank their way through Odysseus's stores of food and wine, they informed Penelope that they would not leave until she selected a new husband from among them.

Odysseus, having been washed ashore naked and unconscious, awakened to find the beguiling Princess Nausica and her maids drying the palace laundry. By this stroke of good fortune, Odysseus was not only clothed but made welcome by Queen Arete and King Alcinous, who promised to give the stranger safe passage home.

The next night at a palace banquet, the Phaeacian court poet Demodocus unwittingly sang of heroic feats achieved during the Trojan War. Deeply moved, Odysseus wept into his cloak. Seeing this, Alcinous asked his guest why the song had made him so distraught, and, for the first time, Odysseus revealed to his hosts his true identity. At Alcinous's request, then, Odysseus agreed to tell the story of his ten years of wandering.

After the Trojan War, Odysseus began, he and his fellow Ithacans—like all the other Greek heroes of the War—had set sail for home. They first laid anchor at Ismarus, which he and his men then sacked and plun-dered. With their ships loaded with Ismarian wine, they then sailed on. Before reaching their next port of call, however, they were blown off course to the land of the Lotus-eaters. There, some of his crew ate the lotus and fell under its lethargic spell, wanting nothing more than "to stay forever, browsing on that native bloom forgetful of their homeland." Forcing the crew members back to their ships, Odysseus again set sail.

They next laid anchor in the land of the Cyclops, a race of one-eyed giants who lived in isolated mountain caves. Odysseus, taking his twelve best men, decided to explore the regions inland. During the expedition, they came upon the cave of the Cyclops Polyphemus, which, they discovered, contained a large cache of cheese. Against the wishes of his crew, Odysseus decided to await Polyphemus's return and to trade his Ismarian wine for the Cyclops' cheese. But when Polyphemus finally appeared with his flock of sheep, it was only to seal off the cave entrance with a huge stone, whereupon he snatched up two Greek crewmen "in his hands like squirming puppies to beat their brains out, spattering the floor. Then he dismembered them and made his meal, gaping and crunching like a mountain lion—everything: innards, flesh, and marrow bones."

Odysseus, known for his cunning, soon devised an escape plan. He offered Polyphemus several casks of wine—gifts, he reminded his captor—that came from Nobody. "Nobody," Odysseus repeated. "Mother, father, and friends, everyone calls me Nobody." After the Cyclops had passed out, drunk, Odysseus sharpened a large pole, laid its point in the fire, and assisted his men in driving the smoldering stake into the Cyclops's eye. "Nobody, Nobody's tricked me," Polyphemus cried out. "Nobody's ruined me!"

Blinded, Polyphemus swore he'd avenge himself—but after he had pastured his sheep. Then, unsealing the cave, he let his sheep pass beneath his hands one by one, so as to ensure that none of his Greek meals were escaping. Again outwitting the sightless beast, Odysseus and his crew tied themselves to the bellies of the animals and delivered themselves, undetected, out of the cave.

After returning to their ships, Odysseus called out to Polyphemus as he shepherded his sheep, taunting him and acknowledging that it was he who had blinded the giant. "Cyclops," he shouted, "if ever mortal man inquire how you were put to shame and blinded tell him Odysseus, raider of cities, took your eye: Laertes' son, whose home's on Ithaca!" In frustration, Polyphemus called on his father Poseidon to curse Odysseus: "Let him lose all companions, and return under strange sail to bitter days at home." Alas, Poseidon heard his son's pitiful request, and thereafter Odysseus and his crew were to be plagued by one catastrophe after another, including contrary winds, the slaughter of many of his crewmen and the wreckage of a number of his ships.

On one occasion, having sailed to Aeaea, the land of the goddess and enchantress Circe, several of the crew were given a drug by their hostess that transformed them into swine. Odysseus, after much pleading, managed to persuade Circe to release his men from the spell—while himself falling prey to her charm and beauty and deciding to remain as her lover.

A year later, prompted by the complaints of his crew, Odysseus once more made ready to sail for Ithaca. These plans were interrupted when Circe informed Odysseus that he first had to make a trip into the underworld for a consultation with the blind prophet Teresias. Thus Odysseus, following Circe's instructions, steered his ship to the edge of the world, where Hades lay in perpetual darkness. After offering up suitable sacrifices, Teresias appeared. The prophet, reading Odysseus's future, alerted him of those suitors who, even at that time, were pursuing his dear Penelope, predicted his ultimate victory over them, and prophesied that Odysseus would die a peaceful death in old age.

When Odysseus and his crew sailed back to Aeaea, Circe warned them of the many perils presented by the return voyage, the most serious of which concerned her father, the sun god Hyperion. In passing his island, she said, the crew was under no circumstances to eat the sacred cattle of the sun. Forewarned, Odysseus departed Aeaea for good.

As Circe had predicted, they passed the Sirens, whose captivating songs had been the undoing of so many sailors; then they sailed on through the narrow straits inhabited by the monsters Scylla and Charybdis; and, finally, having lost all but one ship, they reached the island of the sun god Hyperion, where the exhausted party laid anchor. Weak from hunger, Odysseus's crew killed and ate several of Hyperion's cattle. Although they managed to leave the island intact, Hyperion soon discovered the slaughter. Enraged, he sent a storm that claimed every soul except Odysseus, who was washed ashore on Ogygia. There, he spent the next seven years as Calypso's captive.

At this point, Odysseus ended his story. For his efforts Alcinous and Arete rewarded him with bounteous treasure from the palace coffers. And that night, just as they had promised, the generous king and queen put him on a Phaeacian ship bound for Ithaca.

On board, Odysseus fell into a deep sleep, only to wake the next morning on a beach with his treasure beside him. Momentarily, he believed that the Phaeacians had tricked him and left him marooned on yet another foreign shore. Athena, however, appeared and convinced Odysseus that he was in fact on the island of Ithaca. She then revealed to the intrepid voyager her plan to take revenge on Penelope's obstinate suitors.

Thus it was that Odysseus, disguised in beggar's clothes, went to the farmhouse of Eumaeus, one of his old family retainers, where he was offered food and a bed. Then, three days later Odysseus, still disguised as an old beggar, paid a visit to his palace. The suitors, in the midst of a feast, mocked and derided him. Biding his time, Odysseus covertly set aside the weapons he would soon be needing and secured the rest; lastly, he instructed the women servants to lock themselves in their rooms.

Later that night, Penelope, thinking once more of ways to discourage her rapacious suitors, devised and announced what she considered an impossible feat of strength: she would consent to marry whoever among them could string Odysseus' bow and shoot an arrow through twelve axes. Then she returned to her room. Each suitor attempted and failed even to string the bow. Finally, Odysseus asked if he could try. To roars of laughter, the cloaked figure picked up the bow, applied its string, and sent an arrow whistling through the air. The arrow's flight was checked only after piercing the twelve axes.

Throwing off his disguise, Odysseus sent his next arrow into Antinous's throat, initiating a slaughter that did not cease until every suitor lay limp on the ground.

Upstairs in her room, Penelope was informed that Odysseus and the old beggar were one and the same, and that he had killed every last one of the greedy suitors. Finally the pair were reunited:

Now from his breast into his eyes the ache
of longing mounted, and he wept at last,
his dear wife, clear and faithful, in his arms,
longed for
as the sunwarmed earth is longed for by a
swimmer
spent in rough water where his ship went down
under Poseidon's blows, gale winds and tons of
sea.
Few men can keep alive through a big surf
to crawl, clotted with brine, on kindly beaches
in joy, in joy, knowing the abyss behind:
and so she too rejoiced, her gaze upon her
husband,
her white arms round him pressed as though
forever.

As Teresias had foretold, the couple lived happily into old age.

Commentary

"Where shall a man find sweetness to surpass his own home and his parents?" Odysseus asks in Book IX. This is the question that inaugurates the tale of Odysseus's wanderings and, in a larger sense, the quest that forms the narrative structure of *The Odyssey*. Odysseus's answer is a pained one, made all the more so because the way back to his island home is vexed by the sea god Poseidon. "In far lands," Odysseus answers, the wanderer "shall not [find the sweetness of home], though he find a house of gold." In this respect, writes the critic Harold Bloom, Odysseus the wanderer is confronted with two choices: "heroic endurance or death."

This powerful theme begins with *The Odyssey* and recurs in some of the great masterpieces of Western literature. Virgil's *The Aeneid*, for instance, borrows this theme of nostalgia—of an exile's longing for a *nostos*, or home. Similarly, in our own times, Joyce's *Ulysses* (the Latin name for Odysseus) takes up Homer's theme with the character of Leopold Bloom, the archetypal wandering Jew.

THE AENEID
by Virgil (70 B.C.E.–19 B.C.E.)

Type of work
Epic poem

Setting
Carthage, Sicily and Italy; c. 1250 B.C.E., after the Trojan War and the destruction of Troy

Principal characters

Aeneas, son of the Trojan prince Anchises and the love goddess Venus; leader of the Trojan exiles after the fall of Troy

Juno, the sister and wife of the supreme god Jupiter, and Aeneas's principal divine nemesis

Dido, the queen and founder of Carthage and, for a year, Aeneas's lover

Latinus, the king of Latium and the father of Lavinia, who is fated to marry Aeneas

Turnus, an Italian king who wages war against the Trojans

Deiphobe, the Prophetess of Cumae who guides Aeneas through the underworld

Written in the twilight years of Augustus Caesar's reign, the *Aeneid* recounts in epic form Aeneas's wanderings from the ruins of Troy to his settlement in Italy. The story was left unfinished at Virgil's death. Still, despite its lack of closure, it has remained a central work in our literary canon for over 2,000 years. And with Robert Fitzgerald's superb English translation, the *Aeneid* continues to exert a vital influence on literature today.

The seeds of Virgil's plot are borrowed from Book XX of the *Iliad*. There, just as the Greek champion Achilles is about to kill Aeneas in combat, the sea god Poseidon (or Neptune, as he was called by the Romans) intercedes and spirits Aeneas out of harm's way, for, as Poseidon knows, Aeneas and his descendants are fated to be "lords over the Trojans born hereafter."

Story overview

The goddess Juno loved Carthage above all cities. She knew, however, that Fate had decreed that Rome, which had not yet been founded, would rise up and destroy Carthage in the Punic Wars. Moreover, she knew that the great Trojan warrior-leader Aeneas, whose Italian descendants were destined to build Rome, had just set sail with his fleet from Sicily.

Embittered by Fate, Juno conspired with the wind god Aeolus to send a storm that would make Aeneas's "long ships founder!" But before Aeolus could complete his task, the sea god Neptune intervened and calmed the waters. "Gale-worn," Aeneas laid anchor off the coast of Libya. Although several of his ships had been separated by the storm, Aeneas ordered the remaining Trojans ashore to make a feast of venison and wine.

The next day Aeneas and his friend Achates set off to explore "the strange new places" along the coast. Midway through a forest, they encountered Aeneas's own mother Venus, disguised as a Libyan huntress. Venus related to them a brief history of Carthage and its founding queen, Dido. Then, before leaving them,

she pointed out the road to Carthage and cloaked them "in grey mist" so that no one would "see or accost them" along the way.

Thus enshrouded, Aeneas and Achates entered Carthage and toured the city. Among its marvels, they were particularly struck by Dido's majestic temple, which was decorated with panels depicting "the Trojan battles in the old war, now known throughout the world." Their wonder, though, soon faded when Dido herself appeared, followed by the captains of the missing Trojan ships.

Dido welcomed the shipwrecked Trojans, also expressing her disappointment that Aeneas was not also present. And even as she said this, the mist around Aeneas and Achates vanished. "Before your eyes I stand," he addressed the queen, "the same one you look for." Pleased, Dido arranged a banquet that night to honor the Trojans.

Aeneas, meanwhile, sent word back to his ships that his son Ascanius should attend the banquet. Venus, seizing on Ascanius's imminent arrival as an opportunity to protect Aeneas, plotted with Cupid: disguised as Ascanius, Cupid would attend the banquet and cast a spell on Dido so she would fall in love with Aeneas. The trick worked, and that evening after feasting, an impassioned Dido asked Aeneas to tell his story of the "ruin" of Troy and his years of "wandering all the lands and all the seas."

Reluctantly, Aeneas agreed. When he had finished his tale of the Trojan Horse and the ruin it had brought him—the murder of his wife Creusa on their final night in Troy, the leveling of his country to ashes and, in Sicily, the death of his father Anchises—Dido "ached [with] longing" for Aeneas and felt as if an "inward fire [was] eating her away." Aeneas, for his part, was equally beguiled by Dido's beauty and charms. Looking on, Juno and Venus decided that a union between the unrequited lovers would be mutually advantageous. Thus Juno caused a thunderstorm, which drove the pair into a secluded cave—there, to consummate their love.

Jupiter, incensed that Aeneas was now living with Dido in Carthage, dispatched his messenger Mercury with a warning. "If future histories and glories do not affect you," he told Aeneas, "think of the expectations of your heir ... to whom the Italian realm, the land of Rome, are due." Sobered by Jupiter's reprimand, Aeneas made secret preparations to make "the fleet ready for the sea."

Dido, having uncovered Aeneas's deceit, built a funeral pyre and threatened to take her own life if he left her. Jupiter, meanwhile, dispatched Mercury with a second warning, and, with this reproach fresh in his ears, Aeneas set sail late that night. At dawn, when Dido awakened and learned that Aeneas was gone, she cursed him and his descendants, climbed her pyre, and killed herself. And at sea, Aeneas looked "far astern" at Carthage, where, flaring on the horizon, he could see the blaze of Dido's pyre.

Back in Sicily, Aeneas sponsored Olympic games to observe the anniversary of his father's death. That night Anchises appeared to Aeneas in a dream and informed him that he should sail for Italy. Once there, Anchises continued, Aeneas should seek out the Prophetess at Cumae, who would escort him to the underworld, where Anchises would reveal to Aeneas his fate.

Following his father's instructions, Aeneas sailed to Cumae and met with this esteemed prophetess, Deiphobe. There was a tree, she told Aeneas, sacred to Juno, whose "deep shade" concealed "the golden bough." This bough, which he would need to leave as an offering in the underworld, would be broken off "willingly" if he was "called by fate."

That evening, Aeneas returned to the Sibyl with the golden bough, and, together, they descended into the underworld. She first led him to the river Acheron, where they presented the golden bough to Charon, the ferryman who transported dead souls across the river. Crossing to the other shore, they continued their journey and, as night drew near, arrived finally at Elysium, where Anchises awaited them.

"Have you come at last?" Anchises wept with joy. "Your sad ghost impelled me," answered Aeneas, at which he tried three times to embrace his father—but each time Anchises "slipped through his hands, weightless as wind and fugitive as dream." The father and son made their way to a secluded grove, where Anchises pointed to a mass of souls gathered by the river Lethe. "Souls," intoned Anchises, "for whom a second body is in store."

As together they traversed among these disembodied spirits, Anchises identified some of the "famous children" Aeneas's line would produce: Romulus, the fabled founder of Rome, and Julius and Augustus Caesar, who would "bring once again an Age of Gold." When the pair had "viewed it all," Anchises spoke briefly of the glory and wars that awaited Aeneas, and how he "might avoid or bear each toil to come." Then, after bidding his father farewell, Aeneas and Deiphobe made their way back "to the upper world."

Transformed and revitalized by the revelations of his fate, Aeneas returned to his ships at Cumae and sailed for Latium, the land where, as his father had foretold, he and his descendants would fulfill their destinies. Shortly after they made landfall, Aeneas and the Trojans were greeted by Latinus, the king of Latium. Immediately, Latinus recognized that Aeneas was the foreign prince the oracles had decreed would conquer Latium and marry his daughter Lavinia. "Children of that stock," he knew, "will see all earth turned Latin at their feet, governed by them, as far as on his rounds the sun looks down on Ocean, East or West." Thus, to propitiate the Fates, Latinus offered his daughter Lavinia in marriage to Aeneas.

Meanwhile, Juno, rancorous because Aeneas now stood at the threshold of his destiny, unleashed the Fury Allecto to stir up enmity between the Latins and the Trojans. Juno accomplished her end by inspiring the Italian prince Turnus, Lavinia's principal suitor, to raise an army against Aeneas.

Rumors of impending war quickly spread throughout Latium. Turnus soon commanded a large army anxious to expel the Trojans. While Aeneas enlisted the aid of the city-states Pallanteum and Etruria, Juno convinced Turnus to "raise the flag of war" over Laurenteum, Latium's capital city. "Now," Juno said, "is the time to sound the call for cavalry and war-cars, now!"

Apprised of the war, Jupiter convened a council of the gods on Mount Olympus and made it clear to both Juno and Venus that he would not tolerate further interference. "The effort each man makes," Jupiter proclaimed, "will bring luck or trouble"; the Latins and Trojans would settle their dispute according to "the Fates."

In the meantime, Aeneas returned to the Trojan camps with new allies. In one of the ensuing battles, Pallas, the son of the Pallenteum king Evander, was killed by Turnus and stripped of his armor. Aeneas, lamenting the loss, swore revenge and sought Turnus out on the battlefield.

As the war dragged on, Turnus fell into disfavor among the Italians, and members of his council suggested that he fight Aeneas himself. "Come, sir," one prince taunted him, "if any fighting blood is in you, any native legacy from Mars, go face the man who calls you out to combat!" After the Italian cavalry suffered another major defeat, Turnus reluctantly agreed to confront Aeneas: Lavinia, he declared, would marry the victor.

With their respective armies watching from either side, Aeneas and Turnus met in the field. A battle, however, soon erupted between the armies. As the conflagration spread, Aeneas was struck by an arrow. While he retired behind battle lines to dress his wound, Turnus slaughtered a large number of Trojans in one of the bloodiest battles of the war.

Aeneas, now recovered, saw—and took—the opportunity to seize the undefended capital Laurenteum. When Turnus learned that Aeneas occupied the city, he again challenged him, offering the same terms as before: that the victor would marry Lavinia.

As the two champions met on the battleground one last time, Jupiter reminded the gods that only Fate should determine the outcome of their combat. After dodging a stone, Aeneas threw his spear and hit Turnus, who fell to the ground. Seeing he was now defeated, Turnus asked Aeneas to "return me, or my body ... to my own kin."

For a moment, Aeneas pitied his toppled foe and considered sparing his life. Nevertheless, when he caught sight of the "swordbelt" at Turnus's side, the same weapon that had been stripped from his friend Pallas's body, the sight of this "trophy" brought on rage. "This wound," he cried at Turnus, "will come from Pallas: Pallas makes this offering, and from your criminal blood exacts his due." With that, Aeneas "sank his blade in fury in Turnus's chest. Then all the body slackened in death's chill, and with a groan for that indignity, his spirit fled into the gloom below."

FLOWERS FOR ALGERNON
by Daniel Keyes, Bantam Books, 1967

Type of work
Reflective science fiction
Setting
A big city; contemporary times
Principal characters
Charlie Gordon, a mentally-challenged man
Miss Alice Kinnian, Charlie's adult-school teacher
Dr. Strauss and Professor Nemur, researchers in
　brain function
Algernon, a brain-enhanced white mouse

Like the best of science fiction, Daniel Keyes's *Flowers for Algernon* asks, "How different might a person act if just one thing was changed about him?" In this story, Charlie finds out.

Charlie is a not-quite-happy retarded adult who agrees to participate in an experiment in brain enhancement. For a time the treatments are effective, and as his intellect expands he begins to see a more truthful view of the world around him—but also a more painful view. In spite of the pain, Charlie likes being smart. When he begins to lose all he has gained, though, he is shattered.

The story's vitality stems from the fact that, through reading Charlie's diary, we identify with and care about him. Indeed, in a sense, our superior viewpoint makes Charlie's eventual deterioration more painful to us than it is to him. This amplified sensitivity for those less fortunate in our society is undoubtedly what Keyes wanted to evoke in us.

Story overview

progris riport 1-March 3—*Dr Strauss says I should rite down what I think and remembir and evrey thing that happins to me from now on. I told dr Strauss and perfesser Nemur I cant rite good, but he says it dont matter.* Miss Kinnian at the beekman college center for retarted adults says they might make me smarter. I hope so, but I cant rite what i remember cause I dont remember anything.

progris riport 2-March 4—They told me I dont have to rite progris riport evrey time. Burt gav me a test today. *I think I faled it and I think mabye now they won't use me.*

Martch 6—Burt showd me a paper with a bunch of lines on it. One side said start and the other said finish. I couldnt get what he wanted me to do. Finally he took me in a labertory and showed me a white mouse. He put him in a box with lots of sides like the lines on my paper. Burt said it was *amazed.* He showed me how Algernon, the mouse ran through the amazed. Burt said Algernon was a very smart mouse because he had the operation that I wanted to have. Burt had me try to do my amazed faster

than the mouse, but Algernon beat me every time. Boy is that a smart mouse. *After the operation Im goona try to be smart.* Prof Nemur says Ill be doing something for science and Ill be famus. *I dont care so much about being famus. I just want to be smart like othr pepul so I can have lots of friends who like me.*

March 11—*The operashun dint hert. Dr. Strauss did it while I was sleeping.* The skinny nerse took off the bandages today so I could write. She told me how to spell March. She said it was not rite what they done to me, they was tampiring with things they had no rite to. If god wanted me smart he would have made me that way.

March 13—I got a new nurse today. She showed me how to spell her name. Miss Kinnian came to see me and I told her I dont feel smart yet. She told me it would be a lot of werk and I would have to learn slowly to be smart. I told her after I got smart I was going to find my mom and dad. Maybe they wouldnt send me away no more if they see how smart I am. Miss Kinnian patted my hand and said I have faith in you Charlie.

March 15—I got out of the hospital but I get tested every day on the amazes. I hope I get smart soon. My head herts from trying to remember.

Mar 17—*Mabye the experimint dint werk. Mabye I wont get smart and Ill have to go live in the Warren home. I hate the tests and I hate the amazeds and I hate Alegernon. I never new before that I was dummer than a mouse.*

Mar 21—I went back to work at the bakery. I didnt tell anyone what the surgery was for because I wasnt supposed to. Joe Carp said maybe they opened me up to put some brains in. Frank said I opened a door the hard way. *That made me laff.* Sometimes when somebody does something wrong, they say, dont pull a Charlie Gordon. I dont know what they mean.

Mar 28—Prof Nemur and Dr Strauss put a thing in my room like a TV that whispers to me all night. I dont sleep well with that talking. I heard it say remember, remember, remember. And I did remember how I met Miss Kinnian at the school the first time.

Mar 29—I beet Algernon today. Burt told me that Algernon had the same operation so he was three times smarter than an average mouse. They sent Miss Kinnian to help teach me. She looks younger. I have started to read harder books like Robinson Crusoe. She showed me how to use a dictionary and think about how words sounded.

April 3—Im remembering lots more. I remember when my Mom brought a new baby sister home from the hospital. One day Mom found me holding the baby and started screaming and yelling and everything. I wouldn't have hurt the baby.

April 8—What a dope I am! I learned about punctuation. I want to go back and fix all my writing, but Miss Kinnian said they wanted it just like I wrote it to see my progress. I feel sick inside because I can see that Frank and Joe have been laughing at me. *Now I know what they mean when they say, "to pull a Charlie Gordon." I am ashamed.*

April 21—I remembered Frank and Joe and Gimpy trying to teach me how to make rolls at the bakery, but I couldn't do it on my own. "It's no use," they said, "It doesn't stick." Well, I'm reading lots of books now and its sticking. I would like to go to college and learn more.

May 1—I invited Miss Kinnian to the movie to celebrate the raise I got after I showed Mr. Donner a way to double the productivity of the bakery. I had never realized how attractive Alice Kinnian is. I didn't quite dare put my arm around her. After, we talked about movies and reality and logic. She said, "You're coming along so fast."

May 17—I am now studying at the University library. I am learning several languages and can read a page at a glimpse. I am having troubles in establishing a relationship with Alice. Whenever I try to as much as touch her I get dizzy and very ill. I remember that as a child, whenever I became aroused, mom would beat me with a belt and tell me to never, never go near a girl.

May 20—Today Mr. Donner fired me from the bakery. He said that the other employees had all signed a protest against me working there. *It had been all right as long as they could laugh at me and appear clever at my expense, but now they were feeling inferior to a moron. I began to see that by my astonishing growth I had made them shrink and emphasized their inadequacies. I had betrayed them and they hated me for it.*

June 6—I remember many things from my childhood now, all painful. Dr. Strauss is trying to help me deal with it through therapy. He says that my emotions have not grown as fast as my intelligence. I had a quarrel with Alice. She says I have changed since I became smarter, that I have no patience for anyone. *I am just as far from Alice with an I.Q. of 185 as I was when I had an I.Q. of 70. And this time we both know it.*

June 13—We went to Chicago so that Professor Nemur and Dr. Strauss could present a paper on Algernon and me. There I got into an argument with them because I realized they hadn't read some recent papers in Indian and Japanese that invalidated their theory. I also objected to being treated as an object, either in the past as a retarded child or now as an experimental subject.

July 9—I have been living on my own without contacting the others. I have a woman friend.... I am finishing my concerto and the technical papers for publication. One thing bothers me, though: Algernon is getting very erratic in his behavior ...

July 12—The foundation agreed to my demands for separate research facilities. Nemur and Strauss act like I am trying to steal some of their credit. *I've learned that intelligence alone doesn't mean a damned thing.... Intelligence and education that hasn't been tempered by human affection isn't worth a damn. 4:30 a.m.—I think I see the flaw in the experiment. I've got to get back to the lab and test it on the computer.*

August 26—I have discovered that artificially-induced intelligence deteriorates in direct proportion to its increase. I have sent the pertinent equations and proofs to Professor Nemur. Algernon can no longer do the mazes. Soon I will be like him.

Sept 27—Nemur says that others have confirmed my results. I went to visit my mother and Norma while I still could. I found my mother largely senile, but was surprised by Norma. She was delighted to see me. As we were talking mom suddenly came at me with the butcher knife in her hand. "Get away from her! I told you what I would do if you ever looked at your sister that way!" Norma took the knife from her. I realized that I could finally forgive her for trying to protect Norma. I wept on the way to my car.

October 3—Forgetting things. Going downhill fast. Have thought of suicide to end it all before I lose it all, but keep putting it off. *I'm trying to hold onto some of the things I've learned. Please, God, don't take it all away.*

October 10—Alice was in my apartment when I returned. She said that she wanted to spend what time she could with me, now that I am on her level. I kissed her and waited for the panic, but none came. I have finally experienced what sex can be with love involved!

October 21—Alice is gone. I have lost all languages and can't read the papers I wrote. About all I do is watch TV and sleep. Worse, I have spells of irritation when I hate everyone. Before she left Alice told me that I was worse off than I was before because I had lost Charlie's smile. I don't have anything to smile about.

November 21—*I did a dumb thing today I forgot I wasnt in Miss Kinnians class at the center any more like I use to be. She lookt at me funny when I came in and started to cry and run out. If you ever reed this Miss Kinnian dont be sorry for me. Im glad I got a second chance to be smart because I lernd alot of things that I never even new were in this werld and Im grateful I saw it all even for a littel bit. Im gone to keep trying to get smart so I can have that feeling agen.*

P.S. please if you get a chanse put some flowrs on Algernons grave in the bak yard.

CHILDHOOD'S END
by Arthur C. Clarke, Harcourt, Brace & World, Inc., 1953

Type of work
Prophetic science fiction

Setting
Earth, in the late 20th through the 21st Centuries

Principal characters
Overlord Karellen, Earth's alien master/ supervisor
Richard Stormgren, Secretary-General of the U.N.,
    Karellen's human liaison
Alexander Wainwright, leader of Earth's "Freedom
    League," an organization fighting against Overlord
    rule
Rashaverak, enigmatic Overlord researcher in the area of
    human psychology
Jan Rodricks, a restless graduate student

Story overview

When the Overlords came to Earth in their enormous, gleaming ships, stationing themselves above every major Terran city, humanity was at once alarmed and relieved. For while the conquest of their planet eliminated international conflict, the very soul of humanity—in part defined by that struggle—was also now diminished.

Supervisor Karellen, the apparently beneficent Overlord who administered Terran affairs through the agency of envoy Richard Stormgren, Secretary-General of the U.N., was strangely evasive about his plans for the human race. Regardless, the Overlords had ushered in a Golden Age among the Terrans: with their technologically advanced rule had come true peace, plenty and freedom for the first time in history. Individuals at last were empowered to pursue any field they chose, albeit with limitations on the exploration of space and certain forms of scientific and artistic experimentation. And with pressure for supporting the arms race tidily removed, the world's wealth nearly doubled.

Apart from the question of their ultimate plans for mankind, one other major mystery remained concerning the conquerors: their physical appearance. For whatever reason, the Overlords refused to show themselves in the presence of humans. Even Stormgren, the one earthling authorized to deal directly with Karellen, communicated with the Supervisor only through an opaque grille. Alexander Wainwright, the vocal and devoutly religious leader of the planet's Freedom League, had used this argument to stir up a measure of protest against the Overlord rule—despite the futility of resistance. "We've lost freedom to control our own lives," Wainwright warned.

Finally the Overlords issued an announcement: "In fifty years—two generations from now—we will come down from our ships and humanity will at last see us as we are."

" … In fifty years," scowled Wainwright, "the damage will have been done. Those who remembered our independence will be dead; humanity will have forgotten its heritage."

"Karellen is working for a united world," Stormgren countered, "and I'll do nothing to help his enemies. What his ultimate plans may be, I don't know, but I believe that they are good."

Stormgren's faith may have been justified. Fifty years later, humanity's new Golden Age was in full swing. The Overlords' laws of "Benevolence" were in force, religious faith had become a relic of the past, and the "mad tempo that had so characterized the 20th Century" was now a distant memory. "Humanity had lost its ancient gods. Now it was old enough to have no need for new ones." And now, at long last, Karellen fulfilled his promise. In the presence of worldwide media, the Overlord stepped from his ship. A great collective gasp arose from the onlookers—for before them stood the Devil himself, horned, black-scaled, barb-tailed, and standing over two meters tall. "The most terrible of all legends had come to life out of the unknown past."

But after the Terrans' first collective shudders of shock, the Overlords' planetary administration continued without a hitch. Meanwhile, bathed in the golden after-glow of "a past that could never return," human civilization drifted on. "And no one worried except a few philosophers."

By this time, freed by technology from the need to congregate in cities, humans had begun to migrate to the far reaches of the globe. It was at one of these remote sites, a house owned by jungle caretaker Rupert Boyce on the southern tip of Africa, that a group of party-goers gathered some years later to commemorate Boyce's latest wedding. Among the celebrants were George Greggson, a noted theater designer, and his attractive and vibrant fiancée Jean Morrel, a researcher into the occult. The couple were surprised to find an actual Overlord also in attendance—a scholarly young devil named Rashaverak who had come to inspect Boyce's extensive library on paranormal psychology. Also present was the bride's brother Jan Rodricks, a graduate student in astronomy.

As the party finally wound down, Boyce prevailed upon his remaining guests, including Jan, George Greggson and Jean Morrel, to join him in a séance. Rashaverak, however, elected merely to observe. As the séance unfolded, the Ouija board revealed several baffling messages, including: *BELIEVE IN MAN NATURE IS WITH YOU.*

As the game proceeded, Jan was invited to ask the board a question. Stealing a single glance at the impassive bulk of Rashaverak, the young scientist called out, "Which star is the Overlord's sun?" At once the plate began to move, spelling out the galactic coordinates: *NGS 549672.* At this point the occult game was interrupted; Jean Morrel, who had stood transfixed throughout the proceedings, suddenly toppled over into a faint.

But Jan Rodricks did not forget that configuration. After correlating the figures from the board with the direction in which the Overlord ships had been seen to exit the Solar System, he contacted a well-known oceanographer, a Dr. Sullivan. At that moment, Sullivan was busy readying a large ocean diorama—specifically, a display of a sperm whale fighting a giant squid—for the Overlords to take back to their planet for exhibition. Now Jan presented the doctor with a startling proposition: he himself would stow away, Jonah-style, aboard the whale and visit the Overlords' home.

Several years passed. George and Jean Greggson were now living with their two young children in a colony on a remote South Pacific island. At first the colonizers of New Athens had feared that their isolated community of artists and intellectuals would invite the wrath of Karellen. However, the Overlords appeared to take little notice of the colony.

But the Greggsons were uneasy. Their oldest child Jefferey had begun to experience vividly haunting dreams of exotic, far-off worlds. At last even the skeptical George began to suspect his son's sleeping mind might be connecting with the aura of some remote universe.

Then one night Jean awoke to a faint, incessant hissing sound. Moments later, she stood transfixed in the nursery doorway. There before her, suspended in the air, was her infant daughter Jennifer's favorite rattle, beating rhythmically above the child, who lay unmoving, her eyes closed placidly over a smile of bliss.

Just a few days later, Karellen delivered his final oration to humanity. George and Jean listened in silence; they had already learned the worst—and the best—from Rashaverak: The Overlords, it was revealed, had come to earth, ultimately, not as masters, but as midwives. From time immemorial their race had lived in the service of a vast, disembodied directive network of power which they called the *Overmind*. Of its origins and purposes they knew little, only that it pervaded the universe and yet remained somehow unfinished—seeking endlessly to expand the depth of its wholeness and awareness by merging with ripening sources of consciousness and creativity. And just such a source, teetering at the evolutionary crosspoint between self-annihilation and exaltation, was Karellen's collective mass of humanity. Now humankind was at last about to be liberated from its earthly prison of animal individuality; now at last the human race would rise into cosmic consciousness—*except*, of course, for those over the age of ten. With the onset of adolescence, Terrans were unredeemable, hopelessly sealed off from breakthrough under the armor of individuality. Only the children of earth would inherit the heavens.

The Greggson children had been the first chosen. Jean, during that long-ago African séance, had connected with the Overmind. And she could only have done so, Rashaverak surmised, through the medium of a child—her then-unconceived son-to-be, Jefferey. And now the chain reaction was accelerating. Very soon, children the world over would be conveyed to the remote interior of Australia, there to join together in an endless chain, dancing in wordless rhythm for months and years, while their minds expanded and blended, until they were ready to rise to their waiting destiny.

"My work here is nearly ended," Karellen concluded in his oration. But he did not speak with the ringing tones of triumph. For in fact the Overlords had come to Earth with a dual mission: First, and obviously, to incubate humanity within the safe, nurturing climate that would ensure a productive breakthrough for the Overmind. But they had also come just as they had come before to other worlds on the verge of breakthrough—to search for their *own* salvation. And in this search they had once again failed.

Intellectually, the Overlords were far superior to the Terrans. "Yet," confessed Karellen, "there is something in your minds that has always eluded us…. Our minds have reached the end of their development. So, in their present form, have yours. Yet you can make the jump to the next stage, and therein lies the difference between us."

So the Overlords, with all their superb analytical and technological powers, would return again to their homeworld as barren midwives—still lacking the essential spirit or circuitry that might have made them into priests, poets, artists and prophets who, one day, might have lifted them into the Overmind.

Decades passed away. But due to the time displacement of faster-than-light travel, the stowaway Jan Rodricks, now returning to Earth after his 80-odd-year odyssey among the Overlords, had aged only six months. He found himself back home on a doomed and deserted planet. Of his race, only the one-time children remained—silently awaiting their liberation. Now, very soon, "like a growing plant that consumes the seed which originated and nourished it," the children would swell, merge, and vanish into the Overmind, absorbing the earth itself in their cosmic journey.

"When our ships entered your skies a century and a half ago … " Karellen reminded the desolate Jan, "you feared and recognized us…. We became identified with your race's death … even while it was ten thousand years in the future!"

It was time for the Overlords to leave. Jan, however, chose to stay behind. The last of a noble race, he awaited the ultimate exaltation—and annihilation—of his kind. And it was not long in coming. The Earth trembled slightly, then shimmered as its children, in a violent, outward-spinning wind, finally burst the bonds of their own flesh, devouring the fragile chrysalis that had nurtured them.

In his last radio transmissions to the Overlords, Jan described the tumultuous escape of the Earth's atmosphere and his own ghostly weightlessness as the planetary mass whirled into a pinwheel of disintegration. The transmissions ended in a blur of static.

And looking down *from the lonely height of the stratosphere, Karellen silently saluted the men and women he had known on the vanished planet. "Remember this," he had told them in his last message. "We will always envy you."*

Commentary

In *Childhood's End* Arthur C. Clarke celebrates humankind's spirituality, the force that drives us to transcend, to create, to connect, to prophesy in a realm beyond words. In fact, from his seat in the 1950s when this book was written, Clarke himself proved to be a remarkable prophet.

Perhaps this prescience stands as testimony enough to the validity of the mysterious Ouija board message: "Believe in man. Nature is with you." And the world—*our* world—may end not in a holocaust after all, but in a triumphant metamorphosis.

THE DAY OF THE TRIFFIDS
by John Wyndham (John B. Harris), Michael Joseph Ltd., 1951

Type of work
Science fiction narrative
Setting
London, England; mid–1950s
Principal characters
William Masen, a biologist (and the story's narrator)
Josella Playton, a writer
Coker, a professional speaker and intellectual

Story overview

"W ednesday, May 8th was the day I was scheduled
to have the bandages removed from my eyes,"
said William Masen as he began his story …

But when I awoke in my hospital bed to hear the
distant clock strike eight, I knew that something was
very wrong: by this time I should have already been
washed, dressed and fed. I rang the service bell to
summon a nurse. When there was no response I felt
my way to the door and shouted into the hall, only to
hear hundreds of babbling voices sound an unintelli-
gible response.

I tried to collect my thoughts. I had spent the
evening before listening to the nurses' raving accounts
of a spectacular meteor shower. What a pity it was that
I had to miss it, they kept telling me. But nothing in
what they said seemed to tie in with the chaos I now
sensed around me.

Finally I reached up and tore the bandages from
my eyes. Squinting against the sunlight, I saw a few
people wandering aimlessly on the street below. I
made my way out into the hall—and almost stumbled
into a doctor who was reeling blindly toward me. I
helped him, ranting and shuddering in pain, to his
fifth-floor office, where he grabbed for the telephone.
When he found the line dead, he turned before I could
stop him and flung himself from the window.

Back in the corridors, I dodged between blinded,
babbling fugitives and a litter of dead bodies. In the
downstairs lobby, a sightless mob groped unsuccessfully for the main doors. I immediately fled.

Actually, let me start at the beginning. I had
landed in the hospital in the first place due to a triffid
sting. You see, I was a biologist involved in triffid
research. Years earlier, when laboratories in
Communist-ruled Russia attempted to smuggle some
triffid seeds out of the country, the jet carrying the
seeds had been destroyed as it flew high in the stratosphere. The seeds, dispersed by air currents all across
the globe, spawned a deadly menace. At maturity, the
triffids stood some seven feet tall. They grew roots, so
I guess you could call them plants; but they were like
no plants anyone had ever seen before. At will they
could pluck themselves from the ground and lurch
about on three leg-like appendages. Even more
alarming, the whorl topping every triffid stem "could
lash out as a slender stinging weapon ten feet long,
capable of discharging enough poison to kill a man,"
whereupon it would feed upon its victim's flesh.

Scientists immediately launched into the all but
impossible task of corralling the triffids, which by
now had popped up everywhere. Since they could not
be easily destroyed, the captured plants were
commonly "docked"—a safety precaution involving
removal of the whorl stinger—or else herded behind
enclosures of safety netting. However, because of the
valuable oil they produced, triffids by the thousands
were soon under cultivation in scores of privately
owned nurseries.

On one occasion while I was examining some
rather unusual triffid specimens, a stinger had
reached out and struck my mask. Poison splashed
right through the mesh and blinded me; in fact, only
quick medical attention had saved my life.

Ironically, I seemed to be the only human creature
in the city who could still see. I wandered through the
streets, watching as people felt their way down the
sidewalks, occasionally colliding with one another.
From time to time they broke into store fronts,
searching for food.

Then, suddenly I heard a scream. I turned to see a
woman, her hands tied behind her back, being beaten
in an alley. Since her assailant was completely blind, I
easily rescued her—and was delighted to discover that
she, too, could see! Like me, this young woman had
missed the fateful meteor shower.

Her name was Josella Playton; she was a writer.
Together we commandeered an auto and set out
toward her family home. Alas, when we arrived we
found only decaying corpses strewn upon the floor
and several triffids silently roaming the house. With a
chill I recalled the words of one of my coworkers: "I
tell you," he had said some days before his death, "a
triffid's in a damn sight better position to survive than
a blind man."

Josella and I drove on to Clerkenwell and supplied
ourselves with "the best triffid-guns and masks in the
world." The next morning we hooked up with a small
group of people at the university who, for various
reasons, had also missed the meteor shower. Working
as a unit, we broke into warehouses and scavenged
supplies, loaded up a lorry and headed out of the city.
When night came, we gathered in a small lecture
theater and discussed our long-term plans. Eventually
it was decided that we must abandon the blinded
masses and work for our own survival.

Early the next morning I woke to shouted warnings. "Fire! Fire!" Hurrying down a smoke-filled staircase, I tripped and hit my head on the landing. When I
regained consciousness I found myself a captive. As it
turned out, another group, led by a sighted intellectual named Coker, had hatched a plan different from
ours. Coker's squads were collecting sighted prisoners
to serve as the "eyes" for a company of blind people,
scrounging up food and other necessities for them
"until help arrived." When—and from whom—the
help would come, however, Coker could not say.

My assigned scavenge district was Hampstead, a London suburb; Josella, who had also been captured, was assigned Westminster. Chained between two rough-looking blind "attendant-guards," my 53-member team went to work. At first, my sightless captors could do virtually nothing without me. But soon we began working as a team, rounding up the often infirm, sightless nomads.

On day five of my servitude we came upon another work party, whose sighted guide straightway shot and killed one of my guards. Fearing for my life, when the other guard refused to release me I instantly beat him to the ground, rifled through his pockets for the key, unchained myself, and ran.

Returning to base, I discovered that roving triffids and bands of human marauders had decimated our group; of the survivors, most were desperately ill with plague-like symptoms. Over the next several hours most of them died or deserted the base. I knew the end for all of us was not far distant.

By the next morning, only the dead and the dying—and I—remained. Hoping to find Josella, I struck out for Westminster. Arriving there, I spotted only an occasional triffid and a random blind scavenger weakly stumbling about. No Josella. Even the university had been abandoned.

It was then that I again ran into Coker. Despondent, he admitted that he had been wrong—it's just that he couldn't believe that some kind of help wouldn't come.

At length Coker and I scouted out another band of sighted survivors at Tynsham, led by a Miss Durrant. She reported that my original group, having rejected her ultra-religious, "brotherly" philosophies, had all gone on to Beaminster some weeks earlier.

Trudging to Beaminster, Coker and I merged with a trio of sighted men, a remnant of one of his squads of "hopefuls," and together we scoured the countryside. Finding isolated pockets of survivors huddled together for protection, still there was no sign of my dear Josella. Coker's plan was to return to Tynsham. But suddenly I remembered that Josella had said something about going to Sussex Downs. So, while the rest of our group proceeded toward Tynsham, I, in a crush of loneliness, made for Sussex.

Miraculously, Josella was there. My arms went around her in a relief that was too vast for words. After we stopped hugging and kissing long enough to speak, we shared our hair-raising stories. When Coker's group was overwhelmed by a combination of triffids and plague, Josella had made a terrified beeline for Sussex, the home of her friends Dennis and Mary Brent, who were now with her—and expecting a baby any time.

Several weeks later, I returned to Tynsham to see Coker, only to find that both his and Durrant's groups had been obliterated; apparently, the typhoid-like plague had taken its horrible toll.

By the time I returned to Sussex, Mary's baby had been born. And only a few months later Josella bore our own son, David. We spent the next several years at Sussex, frequently making runs into the nearby towns and cities to forage for the essentials that couldn't be grown on the land. Our only danger now came from the ever-present triffids pushing at our fenced perimeter. Over the years we came up with some ingenious schemes to kill or trap them, but none became a viable solution: the plants seemed uncannily capable of learning from their mistakes.

Then, in our fourth year at Sussex, a man by the name of Ivan, a friend of Coker's, appeared, piloting a helicopter. Ivan reported that Coker, who in fact had survived the plague, had abandoned Tynsham when the epidemic struck. After eventually locating my original university group, which had established itself on the Isle of Wight, Coker had sent Ivan to find us and bring us to join them on the island. We decided to set out in the fall, after spending one last summer at Sussex.

But as it turned out, we were never to see Coker again. Droves of soldiers, who had spotted the smoke given off by the burning logs we'd used to signal the helicopter, arrived in their half-tracks the following day. Their intentions were both simple and terrible: seventeen blind superintendents were to join us at Sussex. The soldiers spoke proudly of being "the first country to get on its feet." Indeed, they offered me an administrative post if I would aid their efforts.

I pretended to warm to this sinister plan; that night we even threw a party for our guests. Then at the height of the celebration, I slipped out and filled all but one of the vehicles' fuel tanks with honey. Finally, as the soldiers slept, we made our break in the one working half-track. As we smashed through the fences of our enclosed compound, the triffids suddenly became our rescuers. Through the breach they filed, heading for the soldiers—who sat wide-eyed in their stalled vehicles.

"And there my personal story joins up with the rest," William Masen ends his narrative. "You will find it in Elspeth Cary's excellent history of the colony."

Commentary

Written in 1951 at the dawn of the Cold War era, John Wyndham's *The Day of the Triffids* painted a dark portrait of humanity's future, a future filled with bizarre adversaries and horrific diseases. The blinding meteor shower and resultant mysterious plague, Wyndham implies, might actually have been the result of malfunctioning military missiles or satellites armed with deadly bacteria colonies. And the triffids themselves were probably developed by the Soviets for use as secret weapons.

Some of Wyndham's doomsday pessimism can be attributed to the general aura of McCarthy-era paranoia that hovered over the early fifties. However, his assertion that a militant five percent of the world's population keeps the other 95% living in fear is as true today as it was then. And despite the powerful developed countries' claims that their "defensive" weapons are safely stored and in competent hands, we can never really know for sure.

ON THE BEACH
by Nevil Shute, William Morrow & Company, 1957

Type of work
Apocalyptic novel

Setting
Australia; the late 1950s in the aftermath of nuclear war

Principal characters
Commander Dwight Towers, heroic captain of the U.S.S. *Scorpion*
Moira Davidson, Towers' heavy-drinking female companion
Lieutenant Peter Holmes, Australian liaison to the *Scorpion*
Mary Holmes, Peter Holmes's wife
John Osborne, a civilian radiation scientist assigned to the *Scorpion*

Written during the 1950s at the height of the Cold War, Nevil Shute's *On the Beach* depicts the aftermath of a nuclear holocaust. As survivors in Australia await imminent death from fallout, some meet their fates with dignity and others with dread. *On the Beach* thus delves compassionately but forcefully into the human psyche. And while many of Shute's characters ultimately fail to attain a state of grace, their anger and sorrow are nevertheless profound. Perhaps, then, Shute's purpose in portraying his characters so vividly is to paint nuclear war as a possibility so repellent as to be unthinkable.

Story overview

Presumably all life in the northern hemisphere had been destroyed a few years earlier by nuclear detonations and radioactive fallout. Survivors in Australia now awaited the inevitable arrival of the billowing mists of fallout that would eventually kill them.

Peter Holmes, a lieutenant in the Australian Navy, had been reassigned as a liaison officer on the U.S.S. *Scorpion*, a former American submarine that had come under Australian command after America's annihilation. Holmes's new commanding officer, Commander Dwight Towers, was a soft-spoken man who, like most displaced Americans in Australia, kept to himself. Thus, in a gesture of goodwill, Holmes invited the Commander to stay the weekend at his oceanside home south of Melbourne. At first, Dwight was disinclined to undertake even the most casual of friendships, as he was about to embark on a long and dangerous research mission up north. Finally, however, he decided to accept the invitation.

When Dwight arrived at Holmes's house, Peter introduced him to his wife Mary and to family friend Moira Davidson, a boisterous, single young woman who drank to excess in order to escape from the war's painful effects. Dwight nevertheless soon developed a very close relationship with Moira. In truth, grief-stricken over the loss of his family in Connecticut, Dwight's pain was every bit as intense as Moira's: ...

His wife and family were very real to him, more real by far than the half-life in a far corner of the world that had been forced upon him since the war. The devastation of the Northern Hemisphere was not real to him, as it was not real to her. He had seen nothing of the destruction of the war, as she had not; in thinking of his wife and of his home it was impossible for him to visualize them in any other circumstances than those in which he had left them. He had little imagination, and that formed a solid core for his contentment in Australia. In Dwight's eyes, then, his wife and children were still alive. "I suppose you think I'm nuts," he once remarked to Moira. "But that's the way I see it, and I can't seem to think about it any other way." Moira, of course, understood.

As it happened, Moira's cousin John Osborne had also been assigned to the *Scorpion* as a civilian radiation specialist. The Australian government intended to send the submarine to the Northern Hemisphere to measure radiation levels and to investigate the source of some recently received radio signals: transmitted from the Seattle area, the infrequent signals indicated that someone might have survived the nuclear devastation. Although John felt flattered that the Navy had recruited him for such important work, he wanted to stay in Australia for a reason that once might have seemed petty: to work on the Ferrari he had purchased from an elderly widow. For John, the race car—which ran on a methanol derivative rather than ever-scarcer petrol—diverted his thoughts from the radiation which was gradually moving southward. Moreover, a lively amateur racing club had sprung up in Melbourne, and the prospect of speeding around curves with other equally reckless drivers invigorated him. Even dying in a fiery collision was preferable to succumbing to painful radiation poisoning.

Finally, however, John, Dwight and Peter were ordered to board the submarine for its northern mission; both Mary and Moira were left with the fear that they would never again see the men they loved. In fact, before Peter left he also became quite worried, and advised his wife what to do in the event of his death if she and their baby became caught in radiation's grasp. In effect she was to give the baby a lethal injection and then take one of the lethal red pills. "I think you're crazy," Mary shot back at him in disgust. "If you say one more word, I'll murder you!" Now it was John's turn to lash out in anger. Staring fiercely at his wife, he murmured, "This is a time when you've just got to show some guts and face up to things!" Later, Mary told him, sobbing, "Oh, Peter, I'm sorry I've been such a fool." Still, she could not really accept the fact that they were all going to die by summer's end. Instead, she would simply tend to her garden and try to savor life until her husband's return.

In contrast, Moira had come to grips with the inevitable, but longed to have more time with Dwight before their lives ended. But now, upon his departure, she sensed that she would not see him again. Keeping her feelings to herself, Moira, in saying goodbye, tried to ease Dwight's mind about the submarine's dangerous mission.

As the weeks passed, Moira, feeling forsaken, stayed with Mary, then went to her parent's farm, where she thought the chores would provide a distraction. Since beginning her relationship with Dwight, she had taken control of her life, curtailing her drinking and even enrolling in a secretarial class at the local university.

Meanwhile, the farther north the submarine went the more restless became its crew. Even after staying submerged for two weeks, the men did not dare to step onto the bridge when they surfaced because of the high radiation levels. When the submarine finally approached the American coast near Seattle, the crew hoisted the periscope to survey what remained of the small suburb of Edmonds, 15 miles north of the city. Suddenly a sailor, an Edmonds' native named Lieutenant Swain, disappeared through a rear escape hatch and began swimming towards his home town. Stunned, the crew looked on as Swain emerged from the water, climbed the rocks, and disappeared amid a cluster of houses. Dwight, in fact, knew that he likely would react similarly if the sub had been sent to Mystic, Connecticut, where he had last seen his own family.

Later, as the submarine entered the region of Puget Sound near where the radio transmissions had originated, John Osborne was fitted into a radiation suit equipped with two hours of air and sent ashore to inspect the radio station. He found no survivors; someone had apparently left a transmitter on, and an open window pane—slapped by occasional gusts of wind—had activated the switch panel.

After this disappointing discovery, the crew set course to test radiation levels further north. Near the Alaskan shoreline they found the levels to be consistently lethal, disproving a popular theory that the fallout gradually was being filtered out of the atmosphere as it blew toward the polar ice caps. Now there was no hope for survival, either on land or at sea.

The submarine pointed south for its long journey back to Australia. At last Dwight and Moira were reunited. Their relationship, however, quickly began to deteriorate. As Dwight continued to grieve for his dead family, Moira slowly came to grasp the fact that she would never marry and have children. For her, the end had already come.

Peter and Mary, on the other hand, coped with their impending fate by retreating into themselves—focusing only on their home, their garden, their baby and the deep love they felt for one another. They planted seeds in the sterile earth, even though they knew they would never germinate. In essence, the Australians, in single-minded reverence, savored each day, brushing aside the knowledge that eventually the ever-advancing death-tide would overtake them. John Osborne, for one, persisted in fixing up his Ferrari—the glimmering sports car that would carry him to death in the upcoming *Grand Prix*.

Now radio broadcasts reported that the southward

seepage of radiation had quickened; the end of life on earth, once calculated for September, would actually come sometime around the end of August. And as predicted, one by one the cities of the Southern Hemisphere—Rio, Cape Town, Sydney—blacked out, as their remaining inhabitants perished. Now there was only Melbourne.

The lone Australian station still sending out newscasts saw a certain bitter irony in the continent's plight: the pesky rabbits that had long plagued Australia's countryside—and escaped all attempts at eradication—would outlive human beings by at least a year.

As radiation sickness beset Melbourne's remaining inhabitants, the red suicide pills began to appear, free of charge, in all the local pharmacies. In fact, when Moira's parents became gravely ill, the older couple ended their lives with the pills.

As the days passed, Dwight, who had finally come to terms with his wife and children's deaths and had taken many pleasant outings with Moira, decided to release the *Scorpion* from its moorings and sink it out beyond the end of the bay. Under skies that were already turning an unnatural color of gray, he bid Moira a tearful goodbye. And as the sub made its way out of port, Dwight emerged from the below deck and walked out onto the bridge. Moira, standing on the gangway, looked on as if in a trance. So, this was the end. *[She] watched as the lower end of the gangway was released, as the lines were singled up ... watched the water swirl beneath her stern as the propellers ran slow ahead and the stern swung out.... Only Dwight with one other was left on the bridge. [He] lifted his hand in salutation to her, and she lifted hers to him, her eyes blurred with tears, and the low hull of the vessel swung away around Point Gellibrand and vanished in the murk.*

Moira drove her car carelessly around the tip of the Point and parked in a spot overlooking a cliff, where she continued watching the submarine as it glided out of the bay and finally plunged out of view. *[She] looked at her little wrist watch; it showed one minute past ten. Her childhood religion came back to her in those last minutes; one ought to do something about that, she thought. A little alcoholically, she murmured the Lord's Prayer.* Then, closing her eyes, she took the pill in her palm, put it to her mouth, and swallowed for the last time.

John Osborne later triumphed in his *Grand Prix* race, but to his disappointment did not suffer the heroic death he had planned. He retired to his shop to do a final tune-up on his Ferrari. Afterwards, he donned his racing suit and goggles, and then he, too, popped a red pill into his mouth.

Waiting for death together at home, Mary and Peter Holmes had made peace with reality. When they finally became too weak to go on, they enjoyed one last cup of tea. Then Peter prepared the syringe, gave the baby her shot, and extracted two pills. "I've had a lovely time since we got married," Mary said gently, touching his arm. "I've had a grand time, too," he replied, kissing her. "Let's end on that."

STRANGER IN A STRANGE LAND
by Robert Heinlein, Putnam, 1961

Type of work
Science fiction

Setting
The United States; post-20th century

Principal characters
Valentine Michael Smith, a human earthling raised by Martians
Gillian "Jill" Boardman, a nurse who helps teach Michael
Jubal Harshaw, a learned doctor, lawyer and writer who befriends Michael

Story overview

Earth's second mission to Mars produced a surprising discovery: a human child born during the first Mars mission had survived his parents' death, whereupon the Martians had nurtured him to adulthood.

When the young man, Valentine "Michael" Smith, was brought back to Earth—or "Terra," as the planet was officially known—the Terran government was understandably anxious to study him, and he was promptly sequestered in a hospital. But, as it turned out, not for long. Fearing that this stranger in a strange land would be an easy prey to bureaucratic exploitation, Jill Boardman, a nurse in the hospital, surreptitiously removed Michael to the home of her friend Jubal Harshaw, a respected author-journalist-doctor-lawyer, and a veteran cynic. Under the tutelage of Jill and Harshaw, the "Man from Mars" began learning about Terran society. In the process, Michael also instructed them and their assistants about Martian ways.

The central goal and fixture of Martian culture was known as *grokking.* "To grok," Michael explained, meant to achieve complete understanding of an object or individual—in rational, emotional, as well as existential terms; to empathize so thoroughly that the observer actually became part of what he observed. Martians placed an especially high value on "Growing Closer" to their companions, and grokking was the doorway to this intimacy. One could never grok properly with his associates, however, without first calling on the "Old Ones," "the "ghosts" of Martians who had voluntarily "discorporated"—who had allowed their bodies to die while their spirits lived on without material substance.

"Sharing water"—the act of offering water to someone—was one of the chief symbolic signs of Growing Closer. In fact, if one shared water with you, he became your "water brother," a loving companion. Everyone in Harshaw's household, including Jill and Harshaw himself, quickly became a water brother to their transplanted visitor.

Along with a disarming otherworldly naiveté, Michael also possessed totally *unearthly* powers. Not only did he show extraordinary intelligence, but he could read with the speed of an electronic scanner

and remember even minute details with photographic precision. Then there were his "magic tricks": he could make people and objects disappear—"twisting them into neverness"—read minds, levitate, and induce telekinesis and teleportation. When his body needed rest, he could put himself into a cataleptic trance, at the same time allowing his spirit, or "essence," to roam about and do as it wished.

In the meantime, after Michael's removal from the hospital, Jill had immediately been charged with kidnapping. Realizing that their protégé could not be hidden forever, she and Harshaw attempted to contact J. Edward Douglas, Secretary General of the Federation, the planetary government of Terra, to open negotiations which they hoped would save Michael's life and grant him his freedom—and, incidentally, ensure their own immunity from prosecution.

At first they were refused contact with Douglas; instead, a State Security patrol was sent to storm Harshaw's estate. But Michael, grokking threats of "wrongness" to his new water brothers, twisted the entire patrol—guns, ships, soldiers and all—into neverness. Afterward, Harshaw was quickly granted access to Douglas. After ascertaining that Michael Smith was well and that he was not being held against his will, the Secretary agreed to meet with a hastily organized Martian Diplomatic Delegation.

As the Terran delegation's spokesman, Harshaw negotiated masterfully. In return for recognizing Michael's status as Mars's earthly ambassador and heir to a vast fortune (since he, the first human to be born on Mars, was legally entitled to a portion of the planet's resources), Douglas was appointed the young man's business manager. Regarding Michael's alleged ownership of Mars, Harshaw rejected the notion that anyone could be said to "own" a planet, particularly an inhabited one; rather, Michael would serve as an ambassador representing Martian interests. This settlement caused grumbling among those members of the Federation council who had sought to gain rich trading concessions on Mars. But at the moment, with the Secretary General's public recognition of Michael's ambassadorial status, their voices were powerless.

At this point, Michael grew curious about Terran religion, which he perceived as a special human means of Growing Closer. (What humans distinguished separately as religion, philosophy, scienc and medicine, to a Martian, through "grokking," were fused as one.) After reading much about human religions, he was especially interested in conversing with Earth's "Old Ones" as he had with the Old Ones on Mars.

Of course, each of Terra's various religious sects was eager to claim the Man from Mars as a convert. The most prominent of these was the Church of the New Revelation, whose adherents, known as the

"Fosterites," made no bones about their calling to be the "salespeople for God." Since Michael concurred with the Fosterites' prime doctrine—that humans were created to "be Happy"—he went to meet with their leader, Supreme Bishop Digby. But upon seeing the man, Michael immediately grokked "wrongness" and twisted the Bishop into neverness.

For a long time Michael told no one of what he had done, fearing that Harshaw and the others would be angry with him. For their part, the Fosterites simply announced that Supreme Bishop Digby had been translated to heaven, a miracle which further strengthened the prestige of the sect.

Another part of Michael's education was learning about sex, which was both unknown and unnecessary for reproduction on Mars. Until he had come to earth, he had never seen a woman—Martians were not gendered beings—and was totally ignorant of reproduction as practiced by humans. Now he saw sex, like religion, as a wonderful way to Grow Closer and obtain happiness, and went on to encourage its practice without regard to marriage. Jealousy and rivalry, he concluded, had caused humans to institute marriage as a form of "property rights" to prevent love from being cultivated between two unmarried individuals.

Reflecting on his "education" and the generally unhappy state of the human race, Michael finally founded his own "religion," which, in truth, was a facade to attract recruits who could be trained in what Michael called "the discipline." The discipline's purpose was to hone in on a select but slowly-widening group of humans, teaching them the advanced, innate skills of Martians. Its highest level was called the "Inner Nest," and those non-territorial humans found worthy of gaining this status engaged in what outsiders denigrated as a sort of free love. The Inner Nest, of course, referred to it as "Water Sharing," a symbolic expression of closeness, brotherhood, togetherness, and unity of mind, heart and purpose.

Michael's soon-thriving "church" directly challenged the Fosterites, who vigorously fought the "decadent" movement—even while secretly engaging in similar practices themselves. As their power and membership began to erode, the hypocritical Fosterites, using their political connections, were able to focus public outrage on the teachings of the Man from Mars. Local governments soon began cracking down on Michael's organization, burning down its main temple and, finally, putting its leader in jail.

Of course, with his superhuman powers, Michael readily escaped from prison and rendezvoused with his followers at a hotel. Wondering if he had failed his disciples, he discussed their predicament with Harshaw. He had tried to teach love; what could be wrong with that? "It's not a message of cheer and hope … " he told Harshaw. "It's a defiance—and an unafraid, unabashed assumption of personal responsibility. But I rarely put it over…. No matter what I said, they insisted on thinking of God as something outside themselves. Something that yearns to take every indolent moron to His breast and comfort him. The notion that the effort has to be their own … is one that they can't or won't entertain."

The seed had been planted, Harshaw countered: " … In a matter of some generations the stupid ones will die out and those with your discipline will inherit the earth. Don't get faint-hearted because only a handful have turned into angels overnight." With this, the Man from Mars grokked in pleasure; truly he had accomplished something of great worth.

Meanwhile, a menacing crowd, whipped into a frenzy by the local Fosterites, had gathered outside the hotel to "do in" the malevolent Martian. Michael stepped outside to speak to them, but the mob was in no mood for listening. Some of its elements threw bricks; others fired guns. In the end, the swarm closed in with fists and clubs. Valentine Michael Smith's final words before he discorporated were unmistakable: "Thou art God."

After burning what was left of Michael's earthly body, the mob at last dispersed. His loyal followers serenely exited the hotel and returned to Harshaw's estate, from there to continue spreading the discipline. They would succeed. It was just a matter of time.

Commentary

Written in 1961, *Stranger in a Strange Land* was especially popular with younger readers, who enjoyed it for precisely the reason their elders abhorred it: Heinlein's irreverent treatment of traditional religious and ethical values. Similarly provocative was Heinlein's interpretation of marriage as a legal fiction allowing one person to establish "property rights" over another.

The Church of the New Revelation represents a composite of many Protestant religions, while the Fosterites' proselytizing tactics savagely caricature the methods used by some contemporary radio and television evangelists. In spite of Heinlein's cavalier treatment of religion in general, Valentine Michael Smith is a strongly messiah-like figure. In the book's final pages, Michael perceives that his work on Earth is complete and goes willingly to his death at the hands of a mob. And his followers continue to teach and apply his discipline, looking forward to the time when, not "the stupid ones," but *they* shall inherit the earth.

Stranger in a Strange Land can disappoint today's reader, for Heinlein displays none of the technical gadgetry modern science-fiction enthusiasts have come to expect. Instead, he creates and directs his theme on the social and cultural aspects of a futuristic society similar to today's. Although Heinlein's Terrans have avoided global thermonuclear war by kindling a form of world government, in the end, petty power-seekers continue to plague the human race. All in all, Heinlein is more interested in defining and examining the constants of the human condition than in exploring what to him were the trifles of technological wizardry.

THE SHORT STORIES OF KURT VONNEGUT
A Collection of Short Stories by Kurt Vonnegut, Bantam Doubleday Dell Publishing, 1950

Kurt Vonnegut established himself in the 1960s as an enormously popular yet enigmatic tragi-comic writer. Indeed, his novels all are notably avant garde, filled with irreverent descriptions and an unorthodox, off-center, underground view of life. Vonnegut's characters are particularly interesting: while they seem to have the world at their feet, fatal flaws always prevent them from gaining true happiness.

These characters in *Welcome to the Monkey House* explore a highly unusual scientific reality, one that may—or may not—determine the future world. Nevertheless, although Vonnegut maintains a guarded optimism about the future of mankind, he is skeptical that technology can make our lives any more safe or "real" than they already are.

HARRISON BERGERON

In the year 2081 all American citizens finally became equal. No one was more attractive than anyone else, no one was smarter, and no one could exhibit any form of inequity without risking immediate punitive action by agents of the United States Handicapper General's office.

George Bergeron was a case in point. Clearly he would have been distinguished by his above-average intelligence, had it not been for the device implanted in his ear that spat a loud noise into his head every 20 seconds to disrupt intelligent thoughts. In contrast, George's wife Hazel wore no such device; she was naturally stupid.

Their son Harrison, taking after his father, was not precisely like everyone else. As 14 years old and seven feet tall, Harrison had been jailed for repeatedly bypassing the handicaps prescribed for him by law.

One day while watching some ballerinas on TV, George realized that they weren't really very good—anyway, no better than anybody else. They were burdened with sashweights and bags of birdshot, and their faces were masked, so that no one, seeing a free and graceful gesture or a pretty face, would feel like something the cat drug in. As these thoughts passed through George's mind, a news bulletin suddenly flashed on the screen: Harrison Bergeron, said to be extremely dangerous, had just escaped from jail.

As George listened in amazement, crashes were heard backstage at the TV studio, and then Harrison appeared onscreen, laden with the Handicapper General's gadgets: "a tremendous pair of earphones … a red rubber ball for a nose," and black caps covering his teeth in order to offset his naturally good looks. Harrison, though, systematically stripping the artificial handicaps from his body, loudly proclaimed himself "The Emperor." Then he turned to one of the ballerinas and invited her to join him as his "Empress." After she, too, had removed her mask and untied the weights from her arms and legs, Harrison directed the musicians to likewise cast off their handicaps and play for them, while he and the woman danced across the stage.

All at once Diana Moon Glampers, Handicapper General of the United States, burst into the studio and fired a shotgun at the pair. Then as she turned the weapon in the direction of the musicians, she ordered them to again don their handicaps or face imprisonment.

At that point the Bergeron's television set burned out. George turned to say something to his wife, but the noise in his head drowned out his thoughts. And Hazel? She knew she had been crying, but could not remember why.

WELCOME TO THE MONKEY HOUSE

Billy the Poet was on a rampage. An infamous nothinghead, Billy refused to take his government-mandated birth-control supplements, even though he faced a $10,000 fine and ten years in prison. The World Government had legislated use of the pills when Earth's human population approached 17 billion. *The pills were ethical because they didn't interfere with a person's ability to reproduce, which would have been unnatural and immoral.* All the pills did was remove every bit of pleasure from the act. The government further tried to manage population growth by encouraging citizens to submit to suicide at "Ethical Suicide" parlors, where, upon request, they could be given a lethal injection.

As it happened, Billy the Poet "specialized" in deflowering the virgins who served as hostesses at the suicide parlors, and the Hyannis Ethical Suicide Parlor was rumored to be Billy's next target. The local sheriff, in fact, arrived to warn hostesses Nancy McLuhan and Mary Kraft that if Billy were to show up, he should be kicked in the groin: nothingheads—unlike those who were numb from taking their ethical birth control pills—were especially vulnerable from the waist down.

Shortly after the sheriff had left, a light suddenly went on in one of the suicide booths that Nancy attended. An elderly man had entered, requesting that his life be taken. Before she could assist him, however, she was handed an envelope with a poem inside. *We were walking through the park, A-goosing statues in the dark*, it read. *If Sherman's horse can take it, so can you.* Obviously, this was the work of Billy the Poet.

Enraged, Nancy nevertheless stormed into the booth to help the old man, who, she learned, did not want to die right away; instead, he began to reminisce about the good old days, those times before J. Edgar Nation had formulated his ethical birth control pills. One day, the old man muttered, Mr. Nation had apparently gone to the zoo, where he saw monkeys playing with their private parts. Shocked, he vowed to develop a pill to prevent monkeys from engaging in what he considered a disgusting habit—without realizing that later the pills would be used on humans as well.

While the old man droned on, Nancy was called away to answer a phone call—from Billy the Poet. After staying on the line so that the sheriff could trace the call, she returned to the booth. What a shock she received when she discovered that the "old man" was really Billy, wearing a mask and packing a revolver. He quickly forced Nancy out the window, down a hidden manhole, and into the sewers of Hyannis. Finally, after a subterranean journey that seemed to last for hours, the pair emerged into the Kennedy Compound, a museum featuring the Kennedy family yachts. Billy then waited for several more hours, until the effect of Nancy's ethical birth control pills could wear off. Finally, he and his "gang" of psychopath women dragged Nancy, fighting and screaming all the way, into Joseph Kennedy's former yacht, where they had their way with her ...

When it was all over, Billy appeared terribly depressed. "Believe me," he told Nancy, "if there'd been any other way—"

"I suppose all the other women just loved it—couldn't get enough of it," she snapped back.

"Nope," Billy spat. "They've all been like you."

"What?" Nancy howled. "What about the women in your gang? You did the same thing to them?"

"Yes," Billy replied forlornly. "They are grateful. You will be too, in time." Then he explained his philosophy: "The world can afford sex, it just can't afford reproduction. The laws today were written by people that forgave themselves and their friends for such activity but were terrified by the natural sexuality of men and women .... But this world is much poorer in the happiness that can be felt between two people now than in those days. That is why I did to you what I did tonight."

Billy placed a bottle of pills on the counter. "I am leaving you these," he said. "If you take one a month, you will never have children. And still you'll be a nothinghead." Then he left.

Nancy picked up the bottle. Its label read: *WELCOME TO THE MONKEY HOUSE.*

REPORT ON THE BARNHOUSE EFFECT

Professor Arthur Barnhouse is missing—and the world is looking for him. At the time the Professor went into hiding, I estimate he was probably 55 times more powerful as the atomic bomb dropped on Nagasaki. Who is he? He is the man who has disarmed the world. The phenomenon he discovered he named *Dynamopsychism*, or *force of the mind*; the press labeled it the "Barnhouse effect."

In a nutshell, Professor Barnhouse found a way to make luck a measurable and controllable force, something gamblers have sought to do for centuries. While shooting craps in the Army, he threw sevens ten times in a row. After bankrupting his roommates, he borrowed some dice and practiced again—with the same results. In both instances, he noticed that the thoughts that immediately preceded the dice roll were identical.

As time went by the Professor's powers grew stronger. He learned to align his brain cells to create physical force. When discharged in 1945, he could remove bricks from a chimney more than three miles away.

I was a graduate student at Wyandotte the first time I met the Professor. Though he was looked upon by the faculty as a harmless eccentric, he and I became friends. I was fascinated by him; what he saw in me, nobody knows.

One day he came to me to ask my help in determining his sanity. "What you must do is simple," he said, speaking softly. "Watch the inkwell on my desk. If you see nothing happen to it, say so, and I'll go quietly—relieved I might add—to the nearest sanitarium." Dutifully I watched as *a high-pitched humming seemed to come from the inkwell; then it began to vibrate alarmingly, and finally to bound about the top of the desk, making two noisy circuits. It stopped, hummed again, glowed red, then popped in splinters with a blue-green flash.*

The Professor went on to tell me how he had cracked boulders, knocked down great oaks and demolished abandoned farm buildings, using only the power of his mind. He confided that he had written a letter to the Secretary of State, asking his advice on how to best apply his remarkable gift in the interests of peace. For months thereafter he suffered the daily ordeal of having to demonstrate his unique power to the military. Although at first he had agreed to reveal the secret to developing these remarkable mental abilities, after constant pressure from the military brass he changed his mind.

The generals, meanwhile, captivated by the far-reaching possibilities of the Professor's gift, had initiated Operation Brainstorm, designed to prove the extent to which his powers could be used to destroy enemy weapons. Retired Navy ships, some 120 of them, were sent to a remote location in the Pacific, while ten V-2 rockets were readied for simultaneous launch and 50 radio-controlled bombers were prepared for a mock attack on the Aleutian Islands. At precisely 11:00 A.M. on a given date, the Professor was told to *concentrate* on all of the material at once, and to destroy as much of it as possible.

The operation was a resounding success; everything was utterly decimated. But even as we sat there, shocked at the totality of the destruction, the Professor escaped, leaving behind a signed message: *Gentlemen, as the first superweapon with a conscience, I am removing myself from your national defense stockpile.*

Since that day, the Professor has systematically annihilated the lion's share of the world's armaments. He has become a willing participant in a rather amusing "war of the tattletales," a war in which each nation's spy network devotes itself to exposing the existence and location of the weapons of other nations.

Of course, the Professor cannot live forever. Until recently I believed that war would be imminent upon his death. However, not long ago I received an encoded note from the Professor. After deciphering the message, I have decided that I will soon be vanishing from society. In short, Professor Barnhouse may die, but the Barnhouse effect will survive him.

THE SHORT STORIES OF CLARK ASHTON SMITH
by Clark Ashton Smith, Ballantine Books, 1971

Clark Ashton Smith (1893–1961) frequently contributed to such early science fiction and horror pulps as *Weird Tales*. His stories rival those of J.R.R. Tolkien in their depth and character development, and rank among the best of early 20th-century fiction, notwithstanding their focus on horror and the supernatural.

This interwoven collection of short stories describes the land and inhabitants of Hyperborea, the mythical country "beyond the North" that was celebrated by ancient Greek poets and historians. The stories often are intended to provide an important "lesson" for the reader—not unlike the morals of *Aesop's Fables*. Smith's protagonists accept challenges to carry out certain tasks. While some characters are driven by noble purposes, some by greed or arrogance, others by force, their fates commonly depend on the merits of their intentions. Such resolutions are consistent with the stories' rather biblical tone.

THE SEVEN GEASES

The intrepid Lord Ralibar Vooz, high magistrate of Commoriom, had led an expedition of twenty-odd soldiers to hunt the elusive and menacing Voormis amid the towering peaks of Mount Voormithadreth. The Voormis, according to legend, were the half-caste offspring of human women and horrible monsters who lived deep within the mountain. Among these monsters was the god Tsathoggua, who purportedly had come to Earth from the planet Saturn.

On the second day of their journey, Lord Vooz and his party reached the highest peak of Voormithadreth. After gazing down and detecting a peculiar wisp of smoke wafting up from among the crags, Vooz left his companions to investigate. He then climbed ridge after ridge, dodging rockfalls and balancing on steep precipices, until he finally came upon an old man chanting incantations by a fire.

The old wizard, Ezdagor, cursed Vooz for his intrusion. Claiming that Vooz had prevented his spell from being effective, Ezdagor dispensed upon the stunned stranger a geas—both a curse and a heroic challenge that would lead its champion onto many deadly paths, but would ultimately set him on the road to glory and honor. Vooz thus could not avoid carrying out Ezdagor's command to follow a large raven-like bird named Raphtontis into the depths of Vormithadreth, and there offer himself up as a sacrifice to the god Tsathoggua.

After barely surviving a battle with the Voormis in their outer caverns, Vooz found the god—in the form of a crouching mass—deep within the mountain: ... *The mass stirred a little at his approach, and put forth with infinite slothfulness a huge and toad-shaped head.* Its eyes seemed to open slightly, "visible as two slits of oozing phosphor in the black, browless face," as if the god had been disturbed from sleep. Because Tsathoggua had recently feasted upon a blood sacrifice, he had no interest in another. Instead, he sent Vooz to report to the spider-god Atlach-Nacha, who resided in the depths of Vormithadreth. Aided by directions from the sorcerer Haen-Dor, Vooz followed Raphtontis into the very heart of the mountain. After traversing the strange genetic-regulating laboratory of the serpent-people, they passed through the Cavern of the Archetypes, immortal beings who controlled the original templates from which all earthly creatures were created. And finally, after many ordeals, Vooz arrived at the loathsome gulf of Abhoth, the father and mother of all cosmic uncleanness: *Here, it seemed, was the ultimate source of all miscreation and abomination ... for the gray mass quobbed and quivered, and swelled perpetually; and from it, in manifold fission, were spawned the anatomies that crept away on every side of the grotto ... like bodiless legs or arms that flailed in the slime, or heads that rolled ...*

The wrathful Abhoth, angered that this trifling mortal should dare to appear before him, imposed upon Lord Vooz one final geas: after finishing his service to Atlach-Nacha, he must find some way to escape Voormithadreth and return to the Outer World, passing back through all the realms in which he had previously sojourned.

After a day's rest, Vooz resumed his journey, with the ugly progeny of Abhoth in pursuit. At long last he reached the web of the spider-god Atlach-Nacha and was quickly forced onto its precarious filaments by his stalkers. Unfortunately, the web had been weakened by the crossing of an earlier creature, and thus gave way beneath Lord Vooz, plunging him into a bottomless chasm.

The god Tsathoggua at last had secured a most noble sacrifice.

THE WEIRD OF AVOOSL WUTHOQQUAN

Fat Avoosl Wuthoqquan was Hyperborea's most avaricious—and prosperous—moneylender. Throughout the kingdom of Commoriom, Avoosl supplied money to needy citizens at very high interest.

One day while heading home for dinner, Avoosl chanced upon a beggar who petitioned him for a minor pittance in exchange for a prophesy, known as a *weird*. Avoosl, a selfish man, refused; whereupon the beggar intoned these words: " ... *Harken to your weird: the godless and exceeding love which you bear to all material things ... shall lead you on a strange quest and bring you to a doom whereof the stars and the sun will alike be ignorant. The hidden opulence of earth shall allure you and ensnare you; and the earth itself shall devour you at the last.*"

Indeed, months later, Avoosl Wuthoqquan sat conducting his usual business when a stranger entered his chambers and asked to borrow money, offering as security a pair of unusually large and perfect emeralds. Such fine gems, thought the moneylender, looking at his nondescript visitor, must certainly be stolen; and when the bargaining had ended, Avoosl had negotiated to give the stranger only two hundred djals for the stones.

After the stranger departed, Avoosl carried the emeralds to the room where he kept his treasures, which included many carefully arranged diamonds, rubies and sapphires. After adding the emeralds to this impressive collection, the moneylender stood back to ogle his hoard.

Suddenly the two emeralds jerked themselves brusquely into motion and rolled off the table to the doorway. Then, to Avoosl's astonishment, they rolled out of his palatial house and down the street. Needless to say, Avoosl was determined not to lose his precious new gems. Once he recovered his wits, he sprinted after them, but they were now a good distance ahead.

The jewels led him on and on, out of the city and into the surrounding farmlands. So intent on the chase that he ignored his growing fatigue, Avoosl was finally beginning to gain on the shimmering stones when they suddenly turned from the road and plunged into the woods. Frantically, the moneylender followed. Soon he spotted an immense subterranean cavern in which the whirling jewels had disappeared. Panting heavily now, he entered deep into the cavern as the emeralds continued to roll just out of his reach. All at once, Avoosl noticed a glowing light in front of him and stepped onto a narrow ledge overlooking an expansive inner chamber—filled with a stockpile of jewels that reached to the roof. It seemed as if all the wealth in the world had been poured into one exquisite pit!

Letting out "a single cry of ecstasy, the man leapt forward from the ledge, sinking almost to his knees in the shifting and tinkling and billowing gems." What his own treasure would look like with this roomful added to it! But Avoosl became immediately alarmed when he observed that his enormous body was gradually sinking into the jewels, as if he were being swallowed by quicksand. Panic-stricken, he struggled to regain the ledge from which he had vaulted.

Avoosl's shrieks were met by an evil cackling voice. Then a very large, pale, beastly entity appeared on the ledge, gaping down with contempt at the fat, greedy man below. "I came in search of my emeralds!" whimpered Avoosl, still slowly sinking amid his abundance. There was no reply. "Help me!" gasped the money-lender. Finally the entity responded: "… *The jewels you seek were stolen from this cavern, to which they always return upon hearing my call. I had let the original thief go, partly because he was but mere skin and bones. Now I realize my good fortune in doing so, for a fat, plump money-lender has taken his place.*"

Wielding a powerful tentacle, the entity then gently lifted Avoosl Wuthoqquan from the pile of jewels and devoured him.

UBBO-SATHLA

Paul Tregardis, a student of the occult and a frequent browser at London antique shops, stumbled upon a strange crystal during his scanning of a local curio. The milky stone was nearly the size of his fist, and its secondary colors seemed alternately to shift from light to dark. After haggling with the dealer, Tregardis purchased the crystal. Now as he again studied it, a strange familiarity burned in him—as if he and the crystal had had a previous encounter. But how? According to the dealer, the stone had recently been unearthed in Greenland, and Tregardis certainly had never traveled to that cold northern land.

When he returned home, Tregardis took out an old Hyperborean manuscript, the *Book of Eibon*, which made reference to crystals. Leafing through it, he finally found a brief passage telling of a cloudy crystal owned by one Zon Mezzamalech, a wizard from the Mhu Thulan region of Hyperborea. The wizard had used his crystal to see into the past and to pursue Ubbo-Sathla, the being said to be the ultimate source of all life on Earth. Ultimately, the wizard had disappeared, the crystal having vanished with him.

Once again Tregardis stared into the crystal orb, and now he began to sense an odd detachment with the object. It was as though he suddenly was imbued with two separate existences—one being that still lived in his London apartment and one that resided somewhere else. Plummeting deeper and deeper into the auras of the crystal, Paul Tregardis suddenly became the lost wizard Zon Mezzamalech. As he stood in this other world and stared into the same crystal, he was now on a quest for knowledge of Ubbo-Sathla and the origins of life. The clouds of the crystal revealed that Ubbo-Sathla guarded two stone tablets, inscribed with the wisdom of the ancient gods who had died before the world was made.

At this point, Tregardis became more than troubled. He felt he was being swallowed up by Zon Mezzamalech's overpowering persona. Although he turned away from the spellbinding orb, he could not help but again yield to its powers. From then on, each day he gazed dreamily into the crystal, grappling to unlock its secrets. And each day "his own person and the world about him became more tenuous and confused than before."

Finally came the day when Tregardis could no longer turn away from the crystal; at last his being had been wholly absorbed by Zon Mezzamalech. Ever after, he would be one with the great wizards in an eerie succession of events that ran backwards toward the beginning of Time, retracing all of history, experiencing the savagery of the barbaric tribes who had invaded pre-Hyperborean civilizations, and even returning to the days of the giant saurian predators and their prey. As time returned from whence it came, Tregardis, now Zon Mezzamalech, allowed the backward-running stream of Time to carry him into oblivion, where he degenerated into a diffused and muddled being who blindly pursued the archetypes of earthly life.

When at last he reached the inscribed tablets guarded by the formless mass of Ubbo-Sathla, Tregardis himself was no more than a primeval ooze, without memory of why he had sought the tablets or how to absorb their knowledge and wisdom. Paul Tregardis, like Zon Mezzamalech in the *Book of Eibon* before him, had mysteriously vanished into parts unknown, bearing the crystal with him.

In 19th-century England many writers penned wonderful tales of horror. America, though, with the notable exceptions of Edgar Allan Poe and Nathaniel Hawthorne, produced few such authors. All this changed in the 1920s. With the advent of pulp science fiction/horror magazines, America acquired a new interest in fantasy. Among the many writers of this genre, H.P. Lovecraft, who died in 1937 at the age of 47, became one of the first American masters of the macabre.

Lovecraft clearly understood the power of the imagination to produce horrific visions. In contrast to contemporary writers like Stephen King, Lovecraft subtly but ominously evokes the imaginative places that make us dread the dark.

THE OUTSIDER

The castle was infinitely old and infinitely horrible, full of dark passages and having high ceilings where the eye could only find cobwebs and shadows. The damp stones were always overshadowed by giant trees, and the rooms were so dark that candlelight barely helped. Although during my many years there I must have been cared for by someone, I cannot recall any person other than myself. I never heard a human voice and I never thought to speak aloud. *My aspect was a matter equally unthought of, for there were no mirrors in the castle.* I imagined myself akin to the figures I saw drawn and painted in books.

Finally there came a time when my longing for light grew so frantic that I could not rest. Even though the castle had one ancient tower that rose above the trees, stairs no longer ascended to the upper part. Soon, however, *I resolved to scale that tower, fall though I might; since it were better to glimpse the sky and perish, than to live without ever beholding day.*

I climbed the pitch-black stairs as far as possible, then raised myself perilously on whatever small footholds I could find until I reached a large dark chamber. Finding a door, I forced it open and saw the light of the moon shining through an opening. I ran to the opening and peered out, expecting to see the tops of trees in the moonlight. What I saw instead astonished me: the monuments and stones of a cemetery. How could I be at ground level?

As I walked through the opening, I was driven by some vague memory to move along a road toward another castle. Unlike the castle I had been raised in, this castle was not in ruins. In fact, the moat was filled and the windows were lit. Guided by the light, I approached the castle and heard sounds of revelry. Peering through a window, I beheld a throng of joyous people. I wanted to join them, so I stepped over the low sill. The people began to scream. In their panic, a few swooned and were dragged away by fleeing companions.

I trembled at the thought of what might be lurking near me unseen. As I moved across the room, I made my first sound, a ghastly moan, as it came into view: *I cannot even hint what it was like, for it was a compound of all that is unclean, uncanny, unwelcome, abnormal, and detestable.* As I raised my hand to ward it off, it came closer. *In one cataclysmic second of cosmic nightmarishness and hellish accident my fingers touched the rotting outstretched paw of the monster beneath the golden arch.* And in that second all the horrific memories returned. I finally recognized the abomination that stood leering at me.

Crashing out of the doorway, I ran back to the cemetery, but I could not force myself down into the dark. Instead, I remain here in hiding, even to this day. *I know always that I am an outsider; a stranger in this country among those who are still men.* I have known this since my reaching hand touched a cold and unyielding surface of polished glass.

THE COLOR OUT OF SPACE

As a surveyor, I had been sent to help with a new reservoir under construction in a rural area of New England. The region was virtually uninhabited. And the few who did live there had a positive aversion to the place. In fact, as I worked in the five acres of grey ash that the locals called "the blasted heath," I found the place quite unsettling.

Amid all this, I one day happened upon the cabin of old Ammi Pierce. Not only was Ammi unusually excited about the reservoir, but he also knew the story of the heath. Naturally, I listened with interest.

Apparently, a meteorite had at one time fallen near Nahum Gardener's trim white house. Scientists came from the university to chip samples from the meteorite, but when they dropped the pieces of glowing coals into a bucket, the pieces flared and then shrunk before their eyes—as did the meteorite itself, until, finally, there was nothing left of the mass of metal.

Although the region's fruit seemed to flourish that fall, it in fact was bitter in taste, wholly inedible. When the grains suffered a similar fate, Nahum claimed that the meteorite had poisoned the soil. Before long, the animals became sick and died, and then Nahum's family also became sluggish and dispirited.

Nahum's son Thaddeus now swore that the trees swayed when there was no wind. Nahum's house and barn, as well as the ground they sat on, took on a glowing luminescence. Then, exactly one year after the meteorite's fall, Nahum was forced to confine his lunatic wife to an attic room. Soon afterward, as all the trees and bushes began to crumble to a grey powder, Thaddeus started to see colors dancing in the water well. He later died and turned to dust. Little Zenas, the middle son, just stared into space, while the youngest, Merwin, had taken to screaming. Finally one day the young boy went to the well, and never returned.

As winter approached, Nahum's wife was transformed into a colorful pile of rags disintegrating in a corner of the attic. Nearby there was the sound of *a sort of heavy dragging, and a most detestably sticky noise as of some fiendish and unclean species of suction.*

At last Nahum called Ammi to come to the sickly, glowing house. In the kitchen he found Nahum, slowly turning to ash. "The color … it burns," Nahum whispered. "It lived in the well … it beats down your mind … it comes from some place whar things ain't as they is here …"

Ammi returned later with the medical examiner and policemen. After draining the shallow well, they found the skeletal remains of many animals and of Nahum's three sons. That very night, as the sun began to set, the well started to glow intensely until its bright colors poured out and filled the night sky. Then, from the top of a ridge, the flabbergasted men watched as the hideously glowing farm crackled and shot into the air before dissolving into grey ash. Still, colors danced in the well.

The residue left behind was never analyzed, because scientists rarely listen to rural hearsay. Ammi told me, though, that there were probably two other capsules in the meteor: one that escaped back into space and one that stayed behind in the well. Although I'll be glad when the reservoir is finished, I know I will never drink there.

THE THING ON THE DOORSTEP

Edward Derby and I had been friends for years. Because I was a painter and Edward a poet, we shared an interest in the dark side of life. Like many of his friends, I was concerned when Edward married the much younger Asenath Waite— daughter of a reputed family of witches.

On the rare occasions when I saw Edward after his marriage, he often expressed a hunch that Asenath had captured him in her shadowy, hypnotic spell. Before long, many people commented on the changes that had come over Edward: although he had never before driven, he now went for long rides in the car; he seemed to be getting younger, even as his wife rapidly aged; he alternately dabbled in the occult; and he had eerily begun to resemble Asenath, both in appearance and deportment.

I at length received word from a rural town marshal that he had found Edward, crazed and stumbling out of the woods. When I went to see him, Edward raved, "I'll kill that entity before I let her, him, it, take me again." After awhile, I was able to calm him. Then as I drove him home, he stunned me by saying that his wife wanted to become male, because a *male* witch could do so much more. In fact, Asenath gradually had been taking over his body, while she had ordered his mind to reside in

her body, which she kept locked in a room. Worst of all, she had begun to increase the time that she spent occupying Edward's body.

Edward actually believed that neither he nor Asenath existed any longer. Her father, he speculated, had now inhabited her body so that he could live eternally. "Tell me," Edward said quite lucidly, "what devilish exchange was perpetrated in the house of horror where that blasphemous monster had his trusting weak-willed half-human child at his mercy?" Edward at once fell silent. Then he explained that he was again himself and that all of his recent studying of the occult had made him ramble on. Clearly, however, I knew that Edward was *not* himself.

One night a few months later, Edward paid me a visit. Before long, he began to sob, saying, "My brain, my brain … it's tugging from beyond—that she-devil—even now—I might have known— nothing can stop that force; not distance nor magic, nor death …"

From that point on, Edward's health rapidly failed. After he was institutionalized, I visited him at the sanitarium twice weekly and listened to him rave. Then, in late January, the sanitarium called to inform me that Edward had recovered. I rushed over to see him, but I immediately realized that the person sitting before me, while rational, was not the Edward I had known.

Later, when my phone rang that night, I answered only to hear strange noises coming from the receiver. A few hours later my doorbell rang. I went to the door. There on the porch, crouched in the shadows, was a slight figure, wearing Edward's clothes and emanating the rankest odor I had ever smelled.

The figure lunged forward with a piece of paper. It was a message in Edward's handwriting, explaining that he had killed Asenath to prevent her from inhabiting his body. Even after burying her in the basement, however, he could still feel her struggling to enter his soul. In fact, earlier that day he had suddenly found himself inhabiting *her* dead corpse. After managing to free himself from the grave, he had written the note. I was the only one who knew the truth and could kill it; it wasn't Edward Derby anymore, but rather something—a demon, maybe—that might have plans to inhabit my body. The only recourse was to cremate it.

As I came to the end of this pitiful message, the horrid creature on my doorstep disintegrated into dust.

When the police investigation was launched, Asenath's crushed skull was found protruding from Edward's clothing. So you see, dear reader, I really didn't kill Edward Derby at the sanitarium. I put holes into some terrible *thing.* But please stop delaying the cremation for post mortems. *I [will not] change souls with that bullet-ridden lich in the mad-house!*

SOMETHING WICKED THIS WAY COMES
by Ray Bradbury, Bantam Books, 1990

Type of work
Phantasmagorical coming-of-age novel

Setting
Green Town, Illinois; 1930s

Principal characters
Jim Nightshade, a quiet and intense 13-year-old
Will Halloway, Jim's neighbor and best friend
Charles Halloway, Will's father, a janitor
Miss Foley, a kind spinster and Jim's and Will's teacher
J.C. Cooger, a carnival owner
G.M. Dark, Cooger's business partner

Story overview

When a salesman appeared in Green Town, Illinois, one late October day and meandered up on the Nightshade's lawn to chat with Jim Nightshade and Will Halloway, storm clouds were gathering overhead. Jim and Will, both 13, were inseparable, although their personalities were quite different. Jim was quiet and somber, while Will seemed more spirited. The salesman handed the boys a bizarre-looking lightning rod and warned them that their house would soon be struck by lightning—unless, that is, they attached the rod to its roof. Then he disappeared.

After affixing the finely etched rod to the peak of Jim's house, the boys headed for the local library to see Will's father, who worked there as a janitor. Will loved his father, although his stiff sluggishness, morose countenance and middle-aged anxiety were conspicuous—as they had been for some time now, following Mrs. Halloway's death. Despite his father's dismal manner, it was he who had first inspired Will's interest in books. But today the boys had too much energy to sit and read, and so, after greeting Mr. Halloway, they raced into town.

As they dashed along the sidewalk, they came upon a crumpled piece of paper: COMING, OCTOBER TWENTY-FOURTH!... Cooger and Dark's ... A thousand and one wonders!... Why, the carnival would arrive that very night! But instead of eliciting excitement, the boys were strangely unnerved by the news, and each quietly returned to his own home.

At midnight Jim heard a faraway sound. *A calliope began to play oh so softly, grieving to itself, a million miles away.* The carnival! Jim bolted out of bed and ran to the window; he could see that Will was also gazing out his window. Then the carnival train came into view, *dream-filled cars that followed the firefly-sparked churn, chant, drowsy autumn hearthfire roar.* Now brimming with anticipation, the boys quickly dressed and scurried outside.

As they ran toward the train, the boys saw shadowy figures climbing out—strangely quiet, like actors in some *silent theater haunted by black-and-white ghosts....* Somehow it all seemed unnatural. "I don't like it," Will whispered. "Yeah," Jim replied, and they raced back home.

The next morning everything was back to normal—or so it seemed. Will and Jim gulped down their breakfasts and rushed back to the site, where festive, lemon-colored side-show tents glistened in the bright sun. Scores of people milled about, and among them was Miss Foley, the boys' jovial schoolteacher. Spying them in the crowd, she strode up to them, gushing in childlike glee, "I love carnivals." Then, surveying the crowd, she said, "I'll buy hot dogs and you eat while I look for my fool nephew." Her nephew, Robert, she explained, had come for an extended visit. " ... I think I'll spy through that Mirror Maze and—"

Will sharply cut her off, mid-sentence. "No," he cried. "People get lost in there." But Miss Foley would not be dissuaded; she took a step, and vanished in the maze of mirrors. "Oh!... Help!" they heard her shriek. Will and Jim took off after her and led her back into the sunlight. Trembling, the teacher explained that she had seen the image of a young girl in a mirror who looked just as she had many years ago. The girl had spoken to her, saying, "*I'm real. You're not!*"

Just as the boys were about to head for home, they spotted a sign near the merry-go-round: OUT OF ORDER! KEEP OFF! Jim, unable to suppress his curiosity, climbed up among the painted animals and mounted a plum dusk stallion. All at once a man's voice brayed out, "Ho, boy, git!" Then a red-haired man reached up and plucked Jim off the horse and took hold of Will, who had rushed over to rescue his friend. A second man with yellow eyes then approached the boys. "Curious?" he asked. "The name is Dark," he went on, "and my friend with the red hair there is Mr. Cooger. Of Cooger and Dark's." The boys had found the owners of the carnival. Mr. Dark, whose arm was covered with tattoos—multi-colored eels, worms, and scrolls—also worked as the circus's "Illustrated Man." Dark asked their names. When both lied, he realized they were trying to fool him and spouted, "Show's over.... Everyone out."

The boys pretended to leave the circus grounds. But when the carnival owners turned away, they scrambled up a nearby tree. There they watched as Dark activated the control box on the merry-go-round—sending it spinning backward, not forward. Then Mr. Cooger *leaped on the back-whirling universe of animals [and] flung himself into a seat.* His face began melting like pink wax. With each rotation of the carousel, the man grew younger—until he emerged from his seat as a boy, who quickly jumped off the ride's platform and ran toward town. Scrambling down from the tree, Jim and Will followed after him.

They lost sight of the man-boy—until they turned onto Miss Foley's street and happened to glance in her window. There, gazing out at them, stood little Cooger. With some hesitation, they walked up to the front door and rang the bell. "Miss

Foley," Will ventured. "You okay?" She assured the boys that she was fine; then she invited them in to meet her nephew. Robert's face, however, was not that of an innocent child, but of a demon, its eyes peering menacingly back at them. Jim and Will were desperate to warn Miss Foley, but they couldn't find the words to explain that her nephew was not who she thought he was.

That night, after everyone had gone to bed, Will and Jim slipped out of their houses to make sure Miss Foley was alright. Hiding behind some bushes, they looked on as "Robert" opened the front door and raced off toward the carnival. Will and Jim sped after him. But to their horror, just as they reached the midway, the man-boy climbed onto the now forward-spinning merry-go-round and was transformed once more—this time into a seemingly 130-year-old man with long, spidery-white hair. Terrified, the boys fled the scene and called the police. By the time the officers arrived, Dark had strapped the withered old Cooger into an electric chair. But now Mr. Cooger had assumed yet another role, that of "Mr. Electro." There was Dark, supplying the ancient figure with jolts of electricity. The officers, delighted with the illusion, simply laughed off the boys' fears.

The police took the frightened youngsters home; however, the night's horrors were not over. Later, both boys awoke to find the carnival's enormous balloon hovering over the Nightshades' roof. At the very same moment the temperature abruptly dropped. "My God!" Jim exclaimed. "Now they know where we live!"

The next morning the boys warily made their way outside. They came upon a little girl weeping near a vacant lot. Staring into the child's eyes, Jim and Will were shocked to realize that she was Miss Foley! They rushed to her house, only to find it empty. "That carnival," Will gravely muttered. "They ... change you so no one ever knows you again ..."

When the boys returned to help the little girl, she had disappeared. Terribly frightened, they hid themselves in a space under the sidewalk that was covered with an iron grate. Above them they could hear the carnival parade passing by. And just as they had feared, several carnival freaks approached the iron grate and tried to reach the boys. To their relief, Mr. Halloway, who was on his way to the library, saw what was happening and came to their rescue. They were trying to explain the danger they were in, when Dark materialized out of nowhere and demanded to know the boys' whereabouts. Mr. Halloway sent him on his way, then bent down and whispered, "Oh, Jim, Will, something is going on." He instructed the boys to stay hidden for the rest of the day. Then he went on to the library to find a book that would offer solutions for such a dire situation.

For the janitor, that day was the longest of his life. Although he didn't understand precisely why the boys were at risk, he was now convinced the carnival was a source of evil. While browsing through the shelves of books, he was struck while reading one of Shakespeare's couplets. *By the prickling of my thumbs, / Something wicked this way comes*, it read. The words sent a shiver up Mr. Halloway's spine. With the lines still echoing in his head, he began to research the carnival's early history.

Later that evening, Mr. Halloway told Will and Jim what he had found: Cooger and Dark's carnival had been on the road for nearly a century, always operating during the month of October. The carnival was evil, and those in it survived by *living off the poison of the sins we do to each other, and the ferment of our most terrible regrets.*

Mr. Halloway's ominous explanation was interrupted when the diabolical Dark, accompanied by his sinister and powerful associate, the Dust Witch, suddenly appeared and used their magical powers to transport Will and Jim back to the carnival. Seizing his pistol, Mr. Halloway hurried to the ominous tents, raised the gun, and shot the Dust Witch through the heart, freeing Will from her power. Then turning, Mr. Halloway and his son saw Jim, as if in a trance, stumbling toward the spinning carousel. Will ran after his friend, but couldn't reach him before he climbed aboard . His father, however, managed to find the power switch and shut off the mechanism.

Jim straightway slumped and fell to the earth as if he were dead. Mr. Halloway tried to think of a way to break the carnival's spell of malice and misery. Then an idea struck him: "Shout, Will," he cried. "Sing, but most of all laugh, you got that, laugh!" Then, following his own advice, Will's father began to whoop, sing and giggle like a child. Immediately the carnival's sideshow tents began blowing away *like the petals of a great black rose.* And as the evil faded into the blackness of night, carried off by the winds of joy, Jim revived and joined in their joyous dancing.

All that remained of the vile circus was the carousel. Before starting for home, Mr. Halloway took a hammer and smashed its control box. Then Jim, Will and his dad started running away from the wilderness, toward home.

Commentary

Best known for his science fiction, Ray Bradbury departs from this genre in *Something Wicked This Way Comes*. As a coming-of-age novel, it charts the passage of two boys from childhood to young adulthood. Will's father Mr. Halloway also profoundly "comes of age," as he teaches his son about both the reality and the sadness of death. Will cannot understand his father's preoccupation with death, until he himself must look death in the face.

Mr. Halloway also teaches the boys about the once-alien concept of a concrete evil. As they begin to accept this new and unpleasant reality, Mr. Halloway himself learns how to avoid being overcome by his fears. "Jump around! Whoop and holler!" he calls to his son as Jim lies close to death. Halloway's strategies, of course, prove successful: the evil carnival is vanquished, and Halloway rediscovers the exuberance and adventure of his youth.

THE DREAMING JEWELS
by Theodore Sturgeon, Dell Publishing Co., Inc., 1950

Type of work
Science fiction classic

Setting
Middle America of the 1950s

Principal characters
Horty Bluett, an abused child who joins a carnival
Armand Bluett, his harsh stepfather
Havana and *Bunny*, two midgets who befriend Horty
Zena, another midget friend who captivates Horty
Kay Hallowell, Horty's friend
Pierre "the Maneater" Monetre, a doctor/scientist who
  runs the carnival

Although frustratingly cryptic at times, Theodore Sturgeon's *The Dreaming Jewels* remains a classic because of its imaginative characters and plot. The winding narrative focuses specifically on people labeled as "freaks," how they view others and how other people view them. Thus, while Sturgeon fails to elucidate fully the genesis and extent of his characters' macabre powers, his insights into human nature are compelling.

Story overview

"What in Heaven's name made you do a filthy thing like that?" Judge Armand Bluett thundered at his eight-year-old adopted son Horty. "And do you plan to take up bug-eating for a profession?" "They weren't bugs," replied the boy, "they were ants." Horty's enraged stepfather then sent him to his room.

Alone, Horty pulled his jack-in-the-box Junky off the closet shelf. Faded and worn, Junky's only redeeming features were his eyes: *They seemed to have been cut or molded ... from some leaded glass which gave them a strange, complex glitter ... Time and again Horty had been certain that those eyes had a radiance of their own, though he could never quite be sure.*

Junky had been given to Horty as an infant in the foundling home, and he gave the boy his only sense of security. As Horty began talking to his old confidant, Armand suddenly stormed into the room, struck Horty hard across the face and swept Junky to the floor, stomping the old jack-in-the-box into a heap of plastic and metal. When Horty struggled to prevent Armand from destroying Junky, his stepfather grabbed Horty, threw him into the closet, and slammed the door. The child screamed as the door crushed his hand. "No use in your yelling," the man railed. "Now I suppose I'll have to get a doctor."

As Armand tramped downstairs, Horty crept out of the closet. Looking down at his mangled, bloody hand, he saw that the door had severed three of his fingers.

With his hand wrapped in a dirty napkin and Junky's pieces in a bag, Horty left the house and went to see his young friend Kay Hallowell. He was running away, he told Kay, but someday he would return. Then he scurried out onto the street, where he leaped into the bed of a passing truck.

The truck's driver was a strange alligator-skinned man named Solum, and to Horty's surprise, all his passengers were midgets. Among them was a small, cigar-smoking man named Havana and two women: Bunny, a tiny giggling woman, and Zena, an enchantingly "beautiful little work of art." Gazing at the lovely Zena, Horty immediately decided to join the traveling carnival.

The next day Zena introduced Horty to the carnival's owner Pierre Monetre. Monetre had once been a brilliant young surgeon who was barred from his medical practice when one of his patients died under mysterious circumstances. Rehired by a laboratory, Monetre had since become a devotee of the occult, particularly fascinated by the possibilities of cell regeneration.

Happening upon a jewel one day in the woods, Monetre had made a remarkable discovery: the crystal was alive and had the capacity, when paired with a similar crystal, to duplicate human beings and other life forms. He also discovered that he could communicate with the glistening crystal in "thought frequencies."

As Zena soon discovered, Horty possessed a similar ability. When he spoke to Junky, the toy's eyes responded, glowing radiantly; the power behind the eyes even regenerated Horty's three severed fingers. After witnessing this miracle, Zena insisted that Horty hide the regeneration from Monetre by wearing gloves. Horty gladly complied with her request. Dear Zena had accepted him as he was—*and his starved ego soaked it up.*

One night as he slept near Zena, Horty heard an angry voice inside himself, saying, "Come here, come here. Come! Come!" Shaken, he slipped out of bed, only to see Zena coming toward him. When Horty told her what had happened, she commanded, "You get back into bed." Then she walked outside into the darkness.

Often at night, Zena also heard a voice: the same voice Monetre "the Maneater" used when he practiced his dark mind control to summon her to his side, where, over wine, he'd speak to her about the crystals and their dreams: *" ... Their dreams live in our world— in our kind of reality. Their dreams are not thoughts and shadows, pictures and sounds like ours. They dream in flesh and sap, wood and bone and blood. And sometimes their dreams aren't finished, and so I have a cat with two legs, and a hairless squirrel.... They're not finished ... they all lack formic acid and niacin.... But—they're alive."*

The Maneater's oppressive mind control had devastated Zena; indeed, his carnival *had exacted a bitter payment for giving her a place to belong* ... "You're different," the gawking crowds seemed to say. "Freak!" In fact, only Horty could comfort her. "I love you, Horty," she'd tell him. "I love you."

As the years passed, Horty felt a sense of belonging that he never had before experienced. He made wonderful friends at the carnival and Monetre usually left him alone. One day, however, Monetre insisted on examining Horty's gloved hand. Consequently, Zena announced that it would be better if Horty left the carnival. She urged him to find Kay and to think about "getting even" with the monstrous Armand.

Horty, passing himself off as a touring guitar player, made his way to a bar Armand had been known to frequent. There found his enemy, in the act of propositioning Kay, now a lovely young woman. But the past dozen years had not been kind to her. Her parents had died, and, to pay for her brother's medical school, Kay had left college to begin work at a law firm. And though she was not easily unnerved, she had always detested the way Judge Armand Bluett leered at her while she worked. Stung by Kay's rebuffs, he had hinted that he could arrange for her boss to fire her or that he could tie up the money from her father's estate. Intimidated by these threats, Kay had agreed to meet him for a drink.

Now seeing the two seated together, Horty's heart leapt. When Armand excused himself to go to the rest room, Horty hurried past and slipped three hundred dollars into Kay's hand, suggesting she use it to get out of town. Upon Armand's return, Kay resisted his offer to meet at his out-of-the-way apartment, but instead made a date with him for the following evening.

"Kay" met Armand the next night; instantly he noticed that she now possessed a new radiance and confidence. Wholly unaware that it was not Kay in front of him, but rather Horty in disguise, Armand promptly hustled his date to his hideaway. However, to his dismay, "Kay" was not feeling the least bit amorous, but only wanted to know if he had ever hurt anyone. "Why, of course not," he replied. "You must remember—my business is justice." But "Kay" abruptly challenged this answer: Was it not true that he had brutally inflicted both physical and psychological pain on someone years before? Then, to Armand's horror, Kay calmly extracted a meat cleaver and chopped off three fingers of her left hand. As Armand vomited, his "date" walked out the door.

Still shaken two days later, Armand visited Monetre in hopes that the carnival owner—now a respected expert in both "strange people" and the regeneration of tissue—could tell him something about Horty, who he had begun to link to the apartment incident. Armand piqued Monetre's curiosity almost immediately when he mentioned that Horty had owned a jack-in-the-box with two jeweled eyes. Suddenly it all became clear: Horty had hidden his regenerated fingers beneath the gloves—fingers that had been restored by the two jeweled eyes. "Zena!" Monetre the Maneater now roared. "Come here!"

Furious, Monetre stalked to Zena's trailer and beat her into submission, whereupon the story of Horty's fingers came spilling out. Then he turned his wrath on Havana, breaking his neck, and on Bunny, hypnotizing her so that she might recall where to find the jeweled eyes.

Zena, meanwhile, had grabbed some money and fled to Horty's apartment. As they spoke, Bunny arrived. Still hypnotized, she revealed that Kay, instead of leaving town, had come to the carnival in search of Horty, and that Monetre and Armand, thinking she was Horty in disguise, had kidnapped her. Hearing this, Horty leaped to his feet. "Horty, wait, wait!" Zena screamed, snatching the jeweled eyes from the table. "Junky's eyes, the jewels—they're you, Horty!" But Horty had already darted past her and out the door.

Zena told Bunny about the jewels. "They're alive," she confided, staring at Junky's eyes. "They think and they speak. They mate. They're alive." Then she added, "These two are Horty." The jewels in the eyes had once belonged to the occultist Monetre, she continued. Thinking them "lifeless," he had thrown the jewels away. A craftsman later had found them and used them for the eyes of the jack-in-the-box—which in time was donated to the foundling home where Horty lived.

Over the years, the jewels had worked their magic on their new owner, little by little transforming the boy until he wasn't human. And now if the sinister Monetre gained possession of the jewels, he would be able to exercise control over Horty.

When at last Horty returned home, Zena informed him of his sinister connection to the jewels. "Why didn't you tell me all this years ago?" he sighed. "All I tried to do was to have you accept, without question, that you were a human being," she finally offered, "a part of humanity, and grow up according to that idea." Still, Horty had one more question: "As a boy, why did I eat ants?" Zena answered bluntly: "Your formic acid was out of adjustment."

Equipped with this new awareness of himself, Horty located Kay. Then, concentrating with all his might, he used the gift of his supernatural mental powers to annihilate the old Armand. When he turned his powers on to Monetre the Maneater, however, the task of elimination proved more difficult. The wily occultist managed to slink behind Horty and inject him with a sedative. With Horty sinking into oblivion, the Maneater, in a meandering speech, then disclosed that he had killed Zena—who, he said, like Horty, was also *unhuman*. What's more, she had been trying to destroy Monetre with a reverse form of mind control.

Finally, when the Maneater turned his back to seize the prized jewels, Horty, sensing his "strength seeping back into his exhausted frame," suddenly leaped up to confront his enemy. In his fear, the Maneater managed to crush one of the jewels in his hand before Horty could take hold of him by the head and twist it several times around. *There was a sound like a pound of dry spaghetti being broken in two, and the Maneater slumped.*

In the end, Horty's glorious victory was mixed with bitter grief. Zena still lay, lifeless, upon her bed. Immediately Horty rifled through Monetre's supplies for some life-giving formic acid. And as soon as he removed the cap, he heard a voice say, "That smells so good, could I have some?" There was Zena, sitting up in bed. *She was big, now; a regular human girl, the way she always wanted to be.* Overjoyed, Horty *took her in his arms and sobbed.* At that moment he knew she would become his wife.

REALITYSCAPES

confronting the waking world

You want to make yourself into my cross. But I am not going to pick up a cross. I'll see you dead … before I let you do that to me."

Seize the Day

"You've put on considerable many frills since I been away"

The Adventures of Huckleberry Finn

"please leave your chewing gum and razors at the door."

Experience

"If you have the guts to be yourself, other people'll pay your price."

Rabbit, Run

Prepare for a wake-up call from dreams to daylight. There are many surprises waiting for you in the *"Realityscapes"* library. And the biggest surprise of all may be the recognition that waking life is even more confusing and hazardous than the exotic world of dreams. The outside world assails us at countless levels and from all directions. As a result, we again are left with the question: "What is there to do?" For instance, what would you do if you were Huckleberry Finn, drifting down the Mississippi with a runaway slave and trying to pick your way through life's muddled maze of rights and wrongs in order to help a friend? Furthermore, how would you, as the partially crippled young Philip in *Of Human Bondage*, respond to the exclusionary pity of your associates?

The world awaits to hear your answers.

CONTENTS

Ambitious Pursuits—intrigue and adventure

Wastelands—reaching for relevance

Transcendence and Realities—dealings in self doubt

"an encyclopedia of modern life."

Walton Litz – Ulysses

Today, when I saw you, I realized that what is between us is no more than an illusion.

Love in the Time of Cholera

"I love you, dang it!"

Cold Sassy Tree

Whispering into hibiscus stalks and listening to breathing, he suddenly saw himself pawing around in the dirt for a not just crazy woman who happened to be his mother.

Jazz

The short stories included in this anthology first appeared in the popular "Reader's Choice" section of *Together*, a family magazine, when its editors invited older readers to send in stories they remembered from their youth.

THE RED WAGON
by Leon Ware

Janice Long loved her job working at the Sunset Valley School for children with special needs. She marveled at "their appreciation for all that was done for them [as well as] the almost complete lack on their part of any feeling of being ill-used by fate." Not all facets of Janice's work, however, were as rewarding as her dealings with the children. On the school's governing board were "some of the city's staunchest citizens," stalwarts who often disagreed with her on policy decisions. Fortunately, Janice had one ally on the board, a "housewife who usually backed [her in the] tussles with the board—most of which were about money and the 'sensible' use of it."

At today's meeting, though, Janice was certain that "there wouldn't be any squabble." A local philanthropist had given the school a check to buy a brand new station wagon for field trips. When the children heard about the check, they had "shouted and clapped and laughed in their delight"; and when Janice asked them to select a color for the station wagon, they had called out in unison: "Red!" One of the boys then wondered, "Please, Miss Long—will it have our name on it?"

"In gold," answered Janice.

But when Janice came before the board to obtain their blessing, "the OK was snagged on the objections of Mason Arnold," an auto-agency owner. It was "rather ridiculous under the circumstances," Arnold said, to insist on a red car—especially when they could save money by buying "a brand-new, last-year's model" from his dealership—a car that happened to be green. When Janice protested, Arnold shot back, "What difference does the color make?" Buying a red car, the teacher insisted, was "a matter of keeping faith with the children."

Finally, the housewife stepped into the discussion. "The color is a little thing—to us, perhaps," she explained. "But ... I was never more sure of Miss Long's excellence in this position than I am right now: You have to keep faith with the children, Mr. Arnold." Moved by her words, the board decided that Janice should go immediately to pick up the red station wagon, bring it back to school, and beep the horn to summon the children as she drove into the parking lot.

When Janice returned, according to plan, and honked the horn, the children "came hurrying out of the school, almost before the ... echo had subsided." As they gathered around the bright new car, towheaded Whitney explored the lettering on the front door with his fingers. "Our name's here!" he cried.

Then Miss Long invited a little girl named Peg to step forward. Grasping Peg's soft, tiny fingers, Miss Long ran them along the slightly raised lettering and read the words aloud: "Sunset Valley School for the Blind."

The tiny girl's dark, blank eyes opened wide with delight. "And is it red, Miss Long?" she asked. Before Janice could answer, however, Whitney, his sensitive fingers still moving over the sleek front fender, answered for her: "Of course it's red, Peggy. Isn't that what we ordered?"

"Oh please," Janice whispered, catching her breath and biting her lip, "let everyone keep faith with them always."

THE LAST LEAF
by O'Henry

Among the many artists who scoured the streets for lodging in Greenwich Village's low-rent 18th-century attics were a pair of adventurous young women who went by the names Sue and Johnsy. At last they set up a studio together on the top floor of a squatty three-story brick building.

"That was in May. In November a cold, unseen stranger ... called Pneumonia ... stalked about the colony, touching one here and there with his icy fingers." And Johnsy, a native Californian unaccustomed to the harsh New York weather, was "touched" to the very bone. Gravely ill, "she lay scarcely moving, on her painted iron bedstead, looking through the small Dutch window-panes at the blank side of the next brick house."

"Sudie"—who had grown up in the cold climes of Maine—became distraught when the doctor informed her that Johnsy had only "one chance in—let us say, ten" of surviving through the winter. He was most concerned because Johnsy seemed to have lost her will to live. "If you will get her to ask one question about the new winter styles in cloak sleeves," he continued more optimistically, "I will promise you a one-in-five chance for her ... "

As soon as the doctor left, Sue burst into tears. After composing herself, she swaggered into Johnsy's room and sat down next to the bed. Johnsy lay silent, her face turned towards the window. At first Sue thought her friend must be asleep. But soon she became aware of an intermittent murmur. "Twelve," said Johnsy faintly; then a few minutes later, "eleven." With her eyes wide open, staring out the window, Johnsy was counting backwards.

"What is it, dear?" Sue inquired, unable to see what had caught Johnsy's attention outside the window: indeed, "there was only a bare, dreary yard to be seen, and the blank side of the brick house twenty feet away. An old, old ivy vine, gnarled and decayed at the roots, climbed half way up the brick wall."

Johnsy had counted down to five before she finally answered. "Leaves," she whispered. "On the ivy vine. When the last one falls I must go, too ... "

"Don't be a goosey," Sue chided. "Why, the doctor told me this morning that your chances for getting well real soon—let's see ... he said the chances were ten to one!" Even so, Johnsy seemed not to hear. "I want to see the last one fall before it gets dark," she said dreamily. "I want to turn loose my hold on everything and go sailing down, down, just like one of those poor, tired leaves."

"Try to sleep," soothed Sue softly. "Don't try to move 'til I come back." Then she dashed downstairs to the studio of the girls' self-appointed protector, a fierce-tongued old emigre named Behrman who earned a sparse living as a fill-in model while drowning his own endless plans to paint "a masterpiece" in bottle after bottle of gin.

"Is dere people in de world mit der foolishness to die because leafs dey drop off from a confounded vine?" Behrman grumbled as he clambered upstairs behind Sue. But once in the apartment both Sue and Behrman fell silent. Together they stared despondently at the ivy vine outside the window, where a "cold rain was falling, mingled with snow."

Johnsy slept through the night. When she awoke the next morning, she asked Sue to draw back the green shade. "Pull it up; I want to see," she whispered. Sue obeyed. "But, lo! after the beating rain and fierce gusts of wind ... there yet stood out against the brick wall one ivy leaf.... Its serrated edges tinted with the yellow of dissolution and decay, it hung bravely from a branch some twenty feet from the ground."

"It is the last one ... " sighed Johnsy. "It will fall today, and I shall die at the same time."

But as the day passed into another stormy night, "the lone ivy leaf still [clung] to its stem against the wall." And when dawn again awakened the young women, the leaf was still there. Johnsy gazed at it for a long time. "I've been a bad girl, Sudie," she said finally. "Something has made that last leaf stay there to show me how wicked I was. It is a sin to want to die."

The following afternoon Sue came to Johnsy's bed, put an arm around her friend and imparted the news she had just received from the doctor: "Mr. Behrman died of pneumonia today in the hospital." He had been found unconscious in his studio a day or so earlier. "His shoes and clothing were wet through and icy cold." Near his side lay "a lantern still lighted ... a ladder ... some scattered brushes, and a palette with green and yellow colors mixed on it."

"... Look out the window, dear," said Sue, "at the last ivy leaf on the wall. Didn't you wonder why it never fluttered or moved when the wind blew? Ah darling, it's Behrman's masterpiece—he painted it there the night that the last leaf fell."

THREE DAYS TO SEE!
by Helen Keller

Blind and deaf, Helen Keller (1880–1968) lived out her life in a world devoid of both sight and sound but filled with the riches of inner vision. As a middle-aged woman in 1933, Miss Keller asked a friend what she had observed on her hour-long walk in the woods. "Nothing in particular," the friend replied. Keller was astonished. "How was it possible," she asked herself, "to walk for an hour through the woods and see nothing worthy of note? I who cannot see find hundreds of things to interest me through mere touch ... "

Here, in her own words, are some of the magnificent woman's heartfelt reflections on the gifts of the senses and their supreme, often unawakened powers to connect us with each other and the universe.

... I have imagined, selecting carefully, what I should most like to see if I were given the use of my eyes, say, for just a three-day period.

... On the first day, I should want to see the people whose kindness and companionship have made my life worth living. I do not know what it is to see into the heart of a friend through that "window of the soul," the eye.... I should call to me all my dear friends and look long into their faces, imprinting upon my mind the outward evidences of the beauty that is within them. I should let my eyes rest, too, on the face of a baby...

In the afternoon I should take a long walk in the woods and intoxicate my eyes on the beauties of the world of nature. And I should pray for the glory of a colorful sunset...

The next day I should arise with the dawn and see the thrilling miracle by which night is transformed into day.... This day I should devote to a hasty glimpse of the world, past and present. I should want to see the pageant of man's progress and so I should go to the museums...

The evening of my second day I should spend at the theater or at the movies. How I should like to see the fascinating figure of Hamlet, or the gutsy Falstaff amid colorful Elizabethan trappings!...

The following morning I should again greet the dawn, anxious to discover new delights, new revelations of beauty. Today, this third day, I shall spend in the workaday world, amid the haunts of men going about the business of life.... I stroll down [a busy street]. I throw my eyes out of focus, so that I see no particular object but only a seething kaleidoscope of color.... [I] make a tour of the city—to the slums, to factories, to parks where children pla.... Always my eyes are open wide to all the sights of both happiness and misery...

At midnight permanent night would close in on me again. Naturally in those three short days I should not have seen all I wanted to see. Only when darkness had again descended upon me should I realize how much I had left unseen....

MAMA MAKES UP HER MIND
by Bailey White, Random House, 1993

One of the South's most gifted storytellers, Bailey White mingles tall tales with poignant reminiscences in *Mama Makes Up Her Mind (and Other Dangers of Southern Living)*. White's spirited collection of vignettes features the antics of a decidedly cantankerous old woman: the irrepressible and willful Mama.

Take, for instance, the time Mama's husband ran off with an archaeological expedition. *The leader of the expedition, a famous physical anthropologist, was a kind gentleman, and he took pity on my mother, who was to be left at home for a year and a half with a farm to run and three unruly children, and he gave her, as a parting gift, his telescope ... The year and a half went by, and my mother studied every distant object she could find, from celestial bodies in the night sky to the pond a mile away from our house ... My father came back, sunburned and irritable. He had presents for us: for my brother, a Persian dagger with a jeweled handle; for my mother, a lamp made out of the bladders of two camels ... My brother developed amazing skills with the dagger and terrorized the neighborhood with feats of knife throwing, and my mother, on a creative whim, turned the camel-bladder lamp upside down and hung it by an electrical cord over the dining room table.... Soon my father went off on another adventure, but this time he never came back. The camel bladder chandelier could not seem to adjust to the climate of south Georgia: in the summer it would droop and swag and stretch in the damp heat until it almost touched the tabletop, and in the winter it would shrink and suck itself into a tight snarl up near the ceiling.*

As the years slowly passed, Mama aged and she couldn't get around much anymore. It was then that she rediscovered the telescope. "Bring me my spyglass!" she'd bellow. Then she'd perch by the window and gaze through the lens. Ultimately, however, one of Professor Meade's family members reclaimed the telescope, but, surprisingly, Mama didn't seem to miss it. *As a premium in the thirty-dollar pledge category for the local public radio station she got a pair of tiny plastic binoculars. Looking through those binoculars was the equivalent of taking three steps closer to your subject ... Now, with the binoculars, she ... could recognize family members when they came to call a moment before they opened the screen door, stepped inside, and said to her, "Put those damned binoculars down, Lila!"*

One summer we made a family trek to a wild island off the coast of north Florida ... Every morning a boat from the local marine lab would pull up and anchor just off shore. People would wade around in the marsh grass with nets and spades and bottles. By the end of the first week the screen was bulged out from the pressure of Mama's binoculars. She didn't seem to understand that they did not give her the same dignity of distance she had achieved with the telescope. "They can see you, Mama," we hissed. But she just pressed the binoculars harder against the screen.

Then one evening a man came up to the house. We recognized him from the morning marine lab group ... "Where is that old woman with the little tiny binoculars?" he asked. Someone went and got her from in the house ... "Would you like to see what we're doing down there?" he said, and very carefully he helped her over the sand to the marsh ... The last we saw of Mama that summer, she was heading for the open ocean. We stood on the dock and waved good-bye. But she didn't see us. She was leaning forward in the bow of the boat with her little plastic binoculars pressed to her eyes, peering out to sea.

Apparently, Mama came by her willfulness naturally, as one "tough-looking Scandinavian woman" learned the hard way when she purchased Mama's ancestral home. No one told her until the last papers had been signed that the house was haunted. *The ghosts are not the ordinary kind—no doors creaking in the night or dogs watching the progress of nothing steadily mounting the circular staircase. These were eating ghosts. On nights near the solstices, people in the house would be awakened by the sounds of slurping, smacking, crunching, and the clink of cutlery. In the morning, something would be missing from the kitchen—a box of shortbread, a ham bone, a jar of artichoke pickles. And in my great-grandmother's garden there would be wide, winding, silvery trails in the dew, something like the tracks of giant slugs.*

Unfortunately for Mama's dinner guests, eating ghosts were the least of the perils visitors might encounter: Mama's cuisine was more frightening still. *My mother eats things she finds dead on the road. Her standards are high. She claims she won't eat anything that's not a fresh kill. But I don't trust her. I require documentation. I won't eat it unless she can tell me the model and tag number of the car that struck it.*

Mama is an adventurous and excellent cook, and we have feasted not only on doves, turkeys, and quail, but robins, squirrels, and, only once, a possum. I draw the line at snakes. "But it was still wiggling when I got there," she argues. "Let's try it just this once." ... And she won't even slow down for armadillos, although they are the most common dead animal on the road these days. "They look too stupid to eat," she says.

If guests survived dinner and were invited to spend the night, an even greater danger awaited them: the guest room bed. *An old aunt of mine temporarily took leave of her senses in 1890-something and went out and bought it. Her sanity returned soon afterward, but by then it was too late. Forty-five strong men had delivered the bed and had set it up in the guest room.... And it is not only a bed: by means of a series of hair triggers and precisely balanced weights and counterweights it can be made to swing up and fold itself into its headboard to reveal on the underside, now nearly vertical, an enormous beveled mirror ... However, as you might imagine, in neither position is the thing satisfactory as a piece of furniture. In the mirror position the top leans out slightly, as if it were yearning to unfold itself and become a bed again, so that your image appears as a monster with a huge watermelon-sized head and dwindles down to a pair of tiny, remote feet almost hidden in the shadows. And as a bed it seems always to be on the verge of becoming a mirror, with the weights and counterweights groaning and the two iron legs at the foot lifting themselves ever so slightly off the floor ... But the worst part is the tendency the bed has in the dead of night when all is quiet in the house, to transmogrify itself into a mirror.... The poor guest wakes out of a strange dream to find the covers bunched on his chest, all his blood settling at his head, and his bare, drained, ice-cold feet pointing to the ceiling. It's hard to recover from this position in the dark of night in a strange house, and usually the guest falls into a trancelike swoon that lasts until morning, when Mama discovers his predicament, snatches the foot of the bed down again, briskly clicks the latch into position, and says, "We should have warned you about the bed."*

Mama's sister Belle was every bit as fearless and headstrong as Mama was. *I remember as a little child watching my Aunt Belle's wide rump disappear into the cattails and marsh grass at the edge of a pond as she crawled on her hands and knees to meet a giant alligator face to face. She was taming him, she said. We children would wait ... with our eyes and mouths wide open, hoping that the alligator wouldn't eat her up, but not wanting to miss it if he did.*

Finally Aunt Belle would get as close to him as she wanted, and they would stare at each other for some minutes. Then my aunt would jump up, wave her arms in the air, and shout, "Whoo!" With a tremendous leap and flop, the alligator would throw himself into the water ... and my aunt would come up the bank drenched and exultant. "I have to show him who's boss," she would tell us.

Whenever Mama and her sister got together wacky adventures were sure to ensue. What happened during a vacation in North Carolina is a case in point. *Last summer it had been fossil hunting in Virginia. This year we were ferrying our way through North Carolina. Aunt Belle had a taste for the peculiar and the exotic. WORLD'S SMALLEST HORSES. SEE A LIVE PERFORMING BEAR. GHOST OF BLACK-BEARD HAUNTS OUTER BANKS ... [And during one of these wild adventures] Aunt Belle learned about the Devil's Hoofprints. People had been trying to fill the holes since 1813, when they first appeared, but they always came back, each one six inches deep and the size of a dinner plate.... "Chickens will not eat out of those hoofprints," she mused. "Imagine that!"*

[So, after procuring a live chicken], my aunt sprinkled a handful of chicken feed in each depression and then instructed," Now put that chicken down." She stood back to observe, and I set the old hen on the ground and stepped aside. The hen squatted there for a minute, then she puffed herself up with a little growl, gave us each a beady-eyed glare, and stalked off into the woods. Pretty soon she was out of sight. We stood there for a moment. Then my aunt said optimistically,"Well, she didn't eat out of them."

Like her sister, Mama had her share of encounters with the supernatural. Her experiences must have been real: old woman though she was, she didn't tell lies and she didn't see visions. That's why we didn't doubt her for a minute when she told us she had seen a flying saucer go over the house early one spring morning.

She was lying in her bed on the screen porch when she saw it coming down. She unlatched the door and went out into the yard for a better look. It was round, flat, silent, and surrounded by yellow flames. It hovered over the garden for minute. Then, without a sound, it was gone. Our dog, who is not the excitable type, barked wildly and ran around and around.

... Since that day, Mama has read everything she can get her hands on dealing with UFOs and extraterrestrial life. I, not being as thorough a scholar as she, just skim the best parts: the pointy-headed creatures that creep and creep through your house at night and stare at you with their almond eyes as you sleep, and the dreaded "men in black" who cleverly insinuate themselves into your company ...

Aliens, however, don't daunt Mama. And reptiles faze even less. Once when I returned from a vacation in New England, she told me that "a big white oak snake" had taken up residence in my bedroom. "I started to put him out," she conceded, "but he gave me that look." So she'd left him there as a permanent guest! *Now I don't have an unnatural fear of snakes, as some people do, but I'm not sure I like the idea of a having one living in the same room with me. "What if he crawls up the bedpost in the dark of night and creeps between the sheets with me?" I ask Mama.*

"These hot summer nights," she says reassuringly, "you'll just be grateful for the coolness of him."

LISTENING FOR THE CRACK OF DAWN
by Donald Davis, August House Publishers, Inc., 1990

A Master Storyteller Recalls the Appalachia of the '50s and '60s.

Listening for the Crack of Dawn is a series of lively vignettes invoking the author's growing-up years in the down-home Appalachia of the mid-1900s. Vintage storyteller Donald Davis celebrates life as he remembers it through the innocent eyes of early childhood, the exuberance of boyhood, and the turbulent adventures of adolescence.

Although oral-based narratives like these inevitably risk loss when committed to paper, remarkably Davis's tales come through with all the wry warmth of their home-grown flavor intact. Here are a few of his tangiest concoctions.

AUNT LAURA AND THE CRACK OF DAWN

*V*ery shortly after I was born, Aunt Laura came to live with us. She was, in reality, my great-aunt, Daddy's Aunt Laura Henry. She had lived, unmarried, with her sister-in-law, my Grandmother Henry, until Grandmother died the same year I was born. After Grandmother's death, Aunt Laura became what Daddy called a "floater." She would live in the spare front bedroom at our house for weeks at a time. After her first such visit [continued for over a month], Mother came out of her room one Sunday afternoon and looked harshly at my Daddy. "It's time," she said, "to take her for a ride." ... We loaded Aunt Laura and her small cardboard suitcase into our old blue Dodge. After a long and scenic ride around Nantahala County, we ended up for a visit at Aunt Hester's house. We returned home alone.

And so the Aunts took their turns "hosting" their Great Aunt Laura. *My brother and I ... loved it when she was with us. She was the first adult in my life who kept loving me no matter what I did. In fact, she liked it more the worse I was. She played with us all the time.*

Aunt Laura was renowned for thinking things through with a pure and poignant enthusiasm. One night in the middle of World War Two, when our Uncle William was off fighting someplace called "Oversees," she took Joe-brother and me outside to study the stars. When we asked why we needed to know the constellations, she answered, "Well, boys, sometimes people grow up and have to go places they don't want to go.... Boys, if you ever ... get homesick, just remember this: everybody lives under the same sky! Just wait until it gets dark, then go outside and look up. If you know them, those stars will take you right home."

Aunt Laura never got married. It was my observation that she simply had very little use for men as a group.... But she did have one great love in her life: She was absolutely and totally in love with Dental Scotch Snuff, and if getting married meant that she had to give up dipping snuff ... well, no man on the face of God's earth was worth that.

Aunt Laura was always the first one up in the morning at our house. One day I asked her how she managed to get up so early. "Why law, son ... I guess I just get up at the crack of dawn!" I was probably four or five years old at the time and had never heard anyone say that. "Can you hear the crack of dawn?" I asked. *She threw her old head back and laughed.... "Why sure, son," she answered. "I hear the crack of dawn and it wakes me up. And I'll tell you what: once I've heard it, nobody else can ... and everybody else in the whole countryside just has to get up the best way they can."* I must have looked pretty disappointed at hearing that, because Aunt Laura glanced down at me and said, "Don't you worry about that. When I'm dead and gone and don't need to get up anymore, I'll leave that to you ... and you'll be the one who can hear the crack of dawn."

One mid-winter morning before sunup Dad roused Joe-brother and me from a sound sleep and took us out to the barn. We waited in silence while he milked the cow; then, without warning, he told us, "Aunt Laura died."

As we walked back toward the house, my mind was sinking under a load of questions.... *We had just passed my favorite black walnut tree, a split-trunked tree you could climb up in the summer and bounce on the long lower limbs of, when very suddenly, the heavy load of ice from last night's storm became too heavy.... From right behind us with a deafening* **crack**, *the entire walnut tree split from top to bottom.*

When Daddy and I jumped around at the sound, we could just see the edge of the sun peeking over the hill below the Burgins' house.... It was the crack of dawn! And I had heard it! And that hearing answered all my questions at once.

The first thing I knew was that Aunt Laura was really dead. I had heard the crack of dawn ... she had left it to me the way she promised.... But the most important thing was, and is to this day, that now when I hear the crack of dawn, I shall never, not even for one single day, be really very far away from my dear Aunt Laura.

EXPERIENCE

*M*rs. Amelia Harrison taught English, although she felt just as strongly about teaching us manners. And every third day she would stand contentedly at the door holding a brown paper bag and singing a little song about "please leave your chewing gum and razors at the door."

Long dubbed "Bad Boy" by friend and foe alike, Billy Barker had what the teachers called a "personality problem." He was also "orally dependent," and was constantly in trouble for chewing in school. At first it was tobacco, but after he was suspended from school and subsequently marched back to the building by his mother—who didn't want to be stuck with his personality problem either—Bad Boy switched to Juicy Fruit gum. In fact, by the time class was out, he usually had a whole pack of Juicy Fruit wadded up in his mouth.

Finally came the day of confrontation. It was during a vocabulary drill, and we couldn't find the word "hubris" in the dictionary. *So Mrs. Amelia ... began to describe and define 'hubris' as "fatal pride. The kind of pride which makes you truly believe that you are not like everyone else ... the kind of pride which makes you feel that none of the normal laws of life apply to you ... the kind of pride which brings you to a great fall in the end ..."* As she droned on, Bad Boy—lost in some dreamworld of his own—very slowly began to chew a full five-stick wad of Juicy Fruit. *Suddenly we realized that Mrs. Amelia, still talking, was looking straight at Bad Boy, unblinking, eyes open widely and set in a focused stare as she talked. "Hubris is like," she went on, searching for an example, "it's like ... it's like ... well, it's like thinking"—she was on her feet now, and moving toward Bad Boy's desk—"you can chew gum out in the open in Mrs. Amelia Harrison's room and somehow get away with it."*

Face to face with Bad Boy, she held out her hand, and with unmistakable authority commanded him to spit it out. And then, just as Bad Boy spit out that gum into Mrs. Amelia's open palm, she reached up and plopped it right on top of his head and smashed it onto his hair with the dictionary she'd been holding in the other hand. *"Those who live by hubris," she kept talking as she walked back to her desk, "always get stuck in the end."*

"Mrs. Amelia had experience."

DAFF-KNEE GARLIC ...

"I was born without kneecaps, so my knees will bend one way just as far and just as fast as they bend the other way. Why, I can run BACKWARDS as fast as I can run forwards." At least that's how Clarence "Daff-knee" Garlic explained it to us. *"It is a great advantage," he would say, "to be able to look at what you're running from while you do it."*

Daff-knee Garlic was the owner, operator, and sole proprietor of the premier educational institution for teenagers in all of Nantahala County, the Sulpher Springs Big-Screen Drive In Theatre. He hired local boys to run the drive-in operation so he could "take charge" in the projection booth—and watch the movies, right along with the customers. One summer three of my friends and I popped dozens of boxes of popcorn, manned the ticket booths and concession stands, collared "slip-ins," cleaned up the grounds and, of course,

participated in "getting the light"—the really educational part of the job: ... *Next to every car which had its parking lights turned on—for curb side service from the concession stand—there were cars in which the show was much better than anything going on on the movie screen. Who could possibly help it if ... we happened to pass by and even casually notice the strange happenings in [these] cars.... We would have worked all night free just ... to "get the lights."*

Mowing the grass was another one of our professional duties—a job done with the aid of two Yazoo High Wheel Mowers. *There was no safety guard of any kind around the whirring rotary blade, which often slung rocks at tremendous velocity in totally random directions. There were actually several holes in the big-screen itself which had come from Yazoo-thrown rocks.*

In addition to his trick knees, Daff-knee had trick toes that pointed almost straight upwards. What's more, he left his toenails uncut to protect the skin on his toes. "Those awful toenails.... They're enough to make a dog sick," my mother once observed.

Once when Daff-knee was out helping us mow, he decided we needed a lesson in efficiency. So he grabbed the big lawnmower—and ran it straight into a wasps' nest. *Daff-knee grabbed the ... mower and began to run backwards, letting go to slap at a new sting with every step. Running backwards as he was, he didn't see a speaker pole and ran straight into it. He stopped dead cold, but the big mower kept coming and rolled over his right foot.... We looked up just in time to see [his] big toe, all in one piece, flying through the air over Budweiser Boulevard, across the fence and out of the drive-in theatre field.*

"There goes my toe," Daff-knee hollered, and took off to retrieve it, with the four of us right on his heels. But Rufus Stanley's big German shepherd/boxer cross-breed, Towser, was faster. Beelining for the falling toe, he opened his jaws, caught it in mid-air, and swallowed it in a single gulp.

In total shock, Daff-knee sat down and began to cry. We drove him to Dr. York's, who gave him a tetanus shot and stitched him together again. Then on the way home we passed Rufus Stanley's house. And *there in the yard stood old Towser, gagging for all he was worth. We watched as, with a great retch, Towser vomited the intact toe onto the ground.... "Whooo, look, Daff-knee," I shouted. "Mama always said that your toenails are enough to make a dog sick.... Daff-knee didn't think it was funny. He also did not want the toe anymore. Later with the help of a long stick, the four of us boys reclaimed it from Towser's lot. We respectfully buried it and erected a small wooden cross over the grave-site.We were certain that the cross caused much confusion to those moviegoers who chose to park there afterwards.*

THE SHORT STORIES OF H. H. MUNRO
by Hector H. Munro (1870–1916)

The short stories of Saki, the pseudonym of Hector H. Munro, comprise a series of independent vignettes, organized into sections, most of which center on a single character. To introduce Saki's works, two sets of vignettes are featured: the tedious and tiring Reginald and equally as taxing Clovis.

I: REGINALD
Reginald

Against her better judgment, the young woman persuaded her cousin Reginald to go to the McKillops' garden party. It was not so much that she was afraid he would *say* anything; it was just that Reginald could be, well, so charmingly annoying. "There will be," he predicted, "the exhaustingly up-to-date young women who will ask me if I have seen *San Toy*; and a less progressive grade who will yearn to hear about the Diamond Jubilee—the historic event, not the horse ... " She gave him two hours to dress before lunch. Reginald spent most of it debating about what tie to wear with which waistcoat.

Arriving at the McKillops', she parked Reginald near a dish of seductive looking desserts and drifted off to a safe distance. She heard with painful clarity the eldest Mawkby girl ask him if he had seen *San Toy*. A mere ten minutes later, Reginald wittily eviscerated old Colonel Mendoza. The Colonel was about to repeat for the umpteenth time how he had introduced golf into India—"When I was at Poona in '76—" when Reginald cooed, "My dear Colonel, fancy admitting such a thing. Such a give-away for one's age! I wouldn't admit being on this planet in '76." The Colonel turned the color of a ripe fig as Reginald calmly glided away.

Mrs. McKillop caught up with Reginald's cousin. Apparently Reginald was doing the room—telling everyone about an irreverent and bawdy burlesque show he had seen. "Your cousin is discussing *Zaza* with the Archdeacon's wife," she winced. "At least *he* is discussing, *she* is ordering her carriage." But when his cousin arrived at Reginald's side, the conversation had changed to weather and the war in South Africa. Reclining in a chair and pretending not to notice that the others were leaving, Reginald suddenly blurted out giddily, "What did the Caspian Sea?"

All at once, the room showed symptoms of a stampede. She grabbed her cousin and asked for their own carriage, vowing never to take him to a garden party again. "Never ... you behaved abominably ... 'What did the Caspian see?'" Reginald, regretting a missed opportunity, replied, "After all, I believe an apricot tie would have gone better with the lilac waistcoat."

Reginald at the Theatre

Reginald and the Duchess regarded each other with mutual dislike and scientific interest. She thought him ethically below standard; he thought her inexperienced. Ethical conduct, said the Duchess, had certain well-defined limits. "So, for the matter of that, has the

Russian Empire," Reginald answered dryly. "The trouble is that the limits are not always in the same place." The Duchess disapproved of the idea of evolution. Staring straight at the woman, Reginald replied that the process was far from complete in most of the people he knew.

Among numerous other things, the Duchess disliked Reginald's irreverence towards the Church of England. But she let that pass to skewer him instead on patriotism, Empire, Imperial responsibility, love of country, and Anglo Saxon brotherhood. "When the theatre season is over," Reginald rejoined, "and we have the time, you must explain to me the exact blood-brotherhood and all that sort of thing that exists between a French Canadian and a mild Hindoo and Yorkshireman, for instance." To her retort that, after all, England *was* "spreading the benefits of civilization all over the world" and organizing relief efforts for every case of misery and want, Reginald observed that each time one animal *feeds*, another is being *fed upon*. The Duchess gave up: "Oh, you're simply exasperating. You've lost all sense of moral proportion."

II: THE CHRONICLES OF CLOVIS
The Stampeding of Lady Bastable

Mrs. Sangrail virtually bribed Lady Bastable into watching Clovis while she went away to the MacGregor's by offering to cancel her outstanding bridge account in return for the favor. Clovis arrived at the breakfast table just as the deal was struck. "Just think," Mrs. Sangrail said coyly, "Lady Bastable has very kindly asked you to stay on here while I go to the MacGregor's." Clovis made suitable remarks in a very unsuitable fashion. He had hoped, after all, to teach the MacGregor boys how to play poker-patience, since they could afford to learn. Well, it was one thing to make a deal behind his back, but quite another to make him honor it.

Clovis soon found a way to foul his mother's arrangement. After breakfast, Lady Bastable retired, as usual, to her morning-room to read the paper, where she always expected to find news of the great social upheaval—the horrible "jacquerie" that she predicted would soon roll across the country to kill everyone of quality. ("It will come sooner than we think," the Lady often knowingly remarked.)

Shortly after her withdrawal, Clovis frantically burst into the kitchen, howling, "Poor Lady Bastable! In the morning-room! Oh, quick!" Moments later, a full coterie of servants, with Clovis several steps ahead, dashed into the room. "The jacquerie!" Clovis shrieked before fleeing out the French window. "They're on us!" Lady Bastable, confronted with a roomful of storming domestics—including the gardener, sickle still in hand—without hesitation followed Clovis through the window.

Alas, lost dignity is not quickly—nor inexpensively—restored. Halfway through lunch, Mrs.

Sangrail was presented with an envelope on a silver plate. It contained a check for Lady Bastable's bridge account. And "the MacGregor boys learned how to play poker-patience; after all, they could afford to."

The Background

Clovis complained to his journalist friend of an art critic who talked of certain pictures as "growing on one," as though they were "a sort of fungus." At this, the journalist told him the story of Henri Deplis.

A Luxemburger and commercial traveller, Deplis had come into a small inheritance, most of which he frittered away. Once while on business in Italy, he contracted with Andreas Pincini, a renowned tattoo artist, to cover his back with a representation of the *Fall of Icarus*, in return for 600 francs. It was acclaimed by all who saw it as Pincini's greatest masterpiece, but before Deplis could settle his account, the artist died and Deplis discovered that he had but 405 francs to pay Pincini's widow. The widow, indignant, canceled the sale of Pincini's masterpiece and donated it to the city of Bergamo.

Deplis thereupon discovered that he could not publicly display his back, on which Pincini's masterpiece was etched, without permission from this city's governors, which permission was never granted. Nor was Deplis allowed to leave Italy, since the Italians had a strict law forbidding the removal of artwork from the country. After the initial excitement had died down, a German art expert came forward to testify that the *Fall of Icarus* was not a genuine Pincini, but had been executed by one of his students. Italian experts refuted this claim, and eventually all of Europe was drawn into the controversy. Deplis' testimony on the subject was felt to be invalid, inasmuch as he had been under the influence of pain-deadening narcotics while the design was pricked into his skin.

Despondent, Deplis fell into the throes of anarchy. One day during an angry debate held at the Italian Anarchists Congress, an opponent poured corrosive over Deplis' back, destroying the *Icarus*—and doing no small damage to the masterpiece's background, the blighted Deplis. When Deplis was well enough to leave the hospital, he was dropped off at the French border as an undesirable alien.

Today, the journalist concluded, Deplis can be seen on the streets of Paris. "He nurses the illusion that he is one of the lost arms of the Venus de Milo, and hopes that the French Government may be persuaded to buy him."

A Matter of Sentiment

It was the eve of the great horse race, the Derby, but no member of Lady Susan's house party had yet placed a bet. No clear favorite had emerged, as no horse held a commanding position, as the sporting prophets had made no cogent predictions. Colonel Drake, a professor of military history, was the only guest with a definite choice, but he was completely useless because his choice altered every three hours. Unfortunately, Lady Susan objected entirely to racing. In fact, she disapproved of almost everything, it was said, and were it not for her great kindness and her equally great wealth, she would have been unbearable. Still, the house party found it maddening to drop such an enthralling discussion when Lady Susan approached and to suppress mention of it while in her presence.

Suddenly there was a breakthrough. Mr. Motkin, Lady Susan's butler, had a second cousin who worked in a stable at the track. Escaping the house on a ruse, he returned with a tip on the horse *Better Not*—and the next morning a packet of telegrams left the house with instructions for the bookmakers.

The afternoon telegram, however, brought bad news. Clovis reported to all assembled, including Lady Susan, that *Sadowa* had won the race. Lady Susan's countenance brightened at once: she had put money on *Sadowa*. "Why on this horse?" Mrs. Packletide asked, breaking the amazed silence. Smiling, Lady Susan explanation was that the Franco-German war had always interested her. "And when I saw there was a horse running in the Derby called after one of the battles in the war, I said I must put some money on it." Everyone groaned, but no one more deeply than the professor of military history, for Sadowa had most certainly been fought, not in the Franco-German War, but near the end of the Austro-Prussian conflict.

Commentary

Hector Munro's stories, set in an upper-class English milieu during the late-nineteenth and early twentieth centuries, are invariably amusing and cleverly ironic concoctions. Even when the social context is unfamiliar to contemporary readers, Munro's wit connects and enlightens the scene, as when the hapless Mr. Deplis becomes captive to the work of art on his back, or when finicky Lady Susan, the most unlikely bettor, wagers on a horse and wins brilliantly—because of her own historical error.

Yet, beyond the wry humor, Munro savages the manners and attitudes of the Victorian upper crust. He uses Clovis and Reginald as critics, ridiculing the insularity, arrogance and snobbishness that typified the world Munro knew best. Reginald, acting the lampooning clever rogue at a stuffy party, sends out scores of pointed barbs designed to burst the Imperial English bubble. Munro, who would later die defending Britain in World War I, did indeed have some feeling for "the French Canadian and the mild Hindoo," and opposed all avowals of Anglo-Saxon superiority.

Even the unfortunate Henri Deplis is a vehicle for foresighted political commentary. That "all of Europe" became involved in the squabble over the authenticity of Deplis' tattoo pointed up for Munro's contemporaries the fragility of the European balance of power.

And finally, Munro's deftly drawn portraits of a people who take themselves too seriously, provide timeless targets of humor. Artfully intertwined with the author's political convictions, these portraits make Munro's tales so vivid, so lucid, that perhaps only Voltaire and Moliere could be said to have written superior satire.

THE ADVENTURES OF TOM SAWYER
by Mark Twain (1835–1910)

Type of work
Juvenile adventure novel

Setting
The small town of St. Petersburg in antebellum
Missouri

Principal characters
Tom Sawyer, a ten-year-old boy
Aunt Polly, Tom's guardian
Huckleberry Finn, Tom's best friend
Injun Joe, a half-breed scoundrel
Muff Potter, the town drunk
Becky Thatcher, a girl who captures Tom's interest
The Widow Douglas, an elderly townswoman

Story overview

For Tom Sawyer, St. Petersburg was more than a
friendly frontier town located on the banks of the
Mississippi. It was a place of adventure. A
resourceful and scrappy lad, Tom lived with his Aunt
Polly, and spent his free time fishing, playing, and
trying to avoid school and chores.

One beautiful Saturday afternoon when most boys
were at play, Aunt Polly stuck Tom with the task of
whitewashing her fence. But Tom heard another boy,
Ben Rogers, coming down the lane and had an idea. He
began to paint with great zeal.

"Say, I'm going in a-swimming I am," Ben crowed.
"Don't you wish you could? But of course you'd
druther work—wouldn't you?" Tom answered Ben
nonchalantly: "What do you call work?"

"Why, ain't that work?" Ben asked, referring to the
whitewashing. "Well, maybe it is, and maybe it ain't,"
Tom countered. "All I know is, it suits Tom Sawyer."
Ben guffawed. Surely Tom couldn't *like* the task.
"Like it?" Tom replied. "Well, I don't see why I oughtn't
to like it. Does a boy get a chance to whitewash a fence
every day?"

This line of reasoning "put the thing in a whole
new light. Ben stopped nibbling his apple … 'Say,
Tom,' he offered, 'let me whitewash a little … '" Before
long, other children came by and wanted a turn at
whitewashing. Not only was the fence soon finished,
but Tom also had collected many treasures in exchange
for the privilege of tending to that old fence, including
Ben's apple, a kite, and a dead rat (*and* some string to
swing it on).

A boy as inventive as Tom had no trouble figuring
out how he could attract the attention of sweet Becky
Thatcher later that summer. Tom would woo Becky by
winning a Bible in a Sunday School contest. To ensure
success, he'd trade marbles and toys for the tickets that
the Sunday School superintendent awarded the children each time they memorized a scripture. The superintendent was amazed when Tom, who had recited very
little scripture, proudly presented 28 tickets. To Tom's
surprise, when he stepped up to claim the Bible, he was
asked to give the names of Jesus's first two apostles. The
eyes of the whole congregation were fixed upon him,

and although the question was repeated, the boy
remained silent. Finally Tom breathed deeply and
almost shouted, "David and Goliath!"

In fact, in all of St. Petersburg there was only one
other boy half as high-spirited as Tom: Tom's friend,
Huckleberry Finn. The envy of all the boys in town,
Huck had no family except for a drunken father. With
this advantage, he could do whatever he pleased. Thus,
one night he and Tom stole off to the graveyard to
perform a wart-curing spell. When they arrived, they
happened upon a frightening scene: Muff Potter, young
Doc Robinson, and a local criminal named Injun Joe
were digging at a fresh gravesite. The men hoisted up a
coffin and pried it open.

When the drunken Potter demanded more money
from the doctor for helping him secure a cadaver, a
fight ensued. Snatching up a knife from the ground,
Injun Joe went for Robinson, who had already felled
poor Potter with a board. When the doctor spun
around, Injun Joe thrust the knife blade into his chest.

After doing in Doc Robinson, Injun Joe placed the
knife in Potter's limp hand. Then when the man came
to, Injun Joe convinced the bewildered fellow that it
had been he who had killed the doctor. "Why, you two
was scuffling," he recounted, "[you] snatched the knife
and jammed it into him … " Potter sputtered, "It was
all on account of the whiskey … I never used a weapon
in my life…. " The two men then fled the graveyard.

Terribly shaken, Tom and Huck finally reached
safety—and swore that they would never breathe a
word of what they had seen. Nobody crossed Injun Joe
without paying with his life.

As it happened, the next day the whole town was
abuzz about the murder. After one of the townsmen
recognized the knife left at the scene as Muff Potter's
and Injun Joe had given his statement to the Sheriff,
Muff was put in jail to await trial.

Tom, Huck and a friend named Joe Harper, meanwhile, had decided they wanted to leave town and
become pirates. Late one night the three boys set sail on
a makeshift raft for Jackson Island. As they spent the
next day swimming, fishing and exploring, it struck
them that they had discovered the perfect life—no
school, no washing, no one to tell them what to do.

That afternoon, however, the boys heard the
sounds of a cannon and saw a ferryboat approaching,
clearly in search of the missing boys. "Somebody's
drownded," Tom cried. "It's us!" That night after Joe
and Huck fell asleep, Tom quietly left camp and
returned to his house. Peering inside, he saw his
Aunt Polly, his sister Mary, his brother Sid, and
Mrs. Harper, all mourning the boys' death. This gave
Tom an idea. He paddled back over to the island
and announced to Huck and Joe that they would
attend their own funeral!

Disguised, the three boys sat through the first
part of the service in the church gallery. Then they
rustled down the stairs and walked down the church

aisle. Needless to say, Aunt Polly and Mrs. Harper were ecstatic to see the boys alive.

Doc Robinson's murder, meanwhile, was on everyone's mind—and, finally, the date for Muff Potter's trial arrived. What, with the stack of evidence against him, Muff had to have done the deed. When Injun Joe took the stand and convincingly lied about how Muff had murdered the good doctor, Tom and Huck stood by "expecting every moment that the clear sky would deliver God's lightnings upon his head." But God's judgment never came. Tom couldn't stand by and see Ol' Muff hanged. So on the third day of the trial, he came forward to tell what he had seen that night. In the middle of his testimony, a loud crash rang out. Everyone turned to see that Injun Joe had sprung from his seat and disappeared out the window.

Now that he had established Muff's innocence, Tom went back to pirating—and to courting Becky. Once, she accidentally tore a page in the schoolmaster's book and the schoolmaster began questioning all the children about it. Knowing that Becky would be unable to lie, Tom suddenly leaped up and confessed. He received a whipping, but won Becky's admiration.

Having succeeded with Becky, Tom now set out in earnest with Huck to find hidden treasure. They had just started prying up the floor in an old house when they heard voices. After they crept upstairs, the boys peered down through the floorboards. There below were Injun Joe and another bandit. Tom almost fainted on the spot.

With the boys still gazing on, the men dug until one of their knives hit wood. They then removed a box filled with gold coins. After discussing where they might re-bury the gold, the scoundrels grabbed the box and left the house. Minutes later, the two boys scurried home.

Determined to discover where the treasure was re-hidden, Huck kept an eye on the tavern where Injun Joe was staying. When he noticed Injun Joe and his accomplice leave the tavern toting a large bundle one night, he trailed the criminals, who headed straight for the home of the kind Widow Douglas. "Her husband was rough on me … " Huck heard Joe say. "He made me horsewhipped! … do you understand? He took advantage of me and died. But I'll take it out on her." Huck was horrified. Acting quickly, he enlisted the help of a nearby farmer, and Widow Douglas was rescued from harm. Soon the whole town was chattering about how Huck had saved the widow's life.

That same evening Tom, Becky and some of their friends went on a picnic to McDougal's Cave. After exploring the many splendid caverns, most of the children returned to town. Tom and Becky, however, got lost in the cave. When Aunt Polly and Becky Thatcher's mother discovered that the children were missing, they became hysterical.

Poor Tom and Becky wandered from one narrow chamber to another. Becky soon began to cry. Finally settling down to sleep, they hoped someone would find them. When they awoke some hours later, Becky shared with Tom a piece of cake she had brought. Then their candles burned out; darkness closed in.

Finding a kite-string in his pocket, Tom tied one end to a protruding rock and set out in search of an exit. Just as he reached the end of the string, a candle and a hand suddenly appeared twenty yards ahead of him; then Injun Joe came into view. Tom stood paralyzed by fear—but Injun Joe in his haste had apparently failed to see Tom. Badly shaken, he returned to Becky, and eventually they discovered a small gap in the rock—a whole five miles away from the cave's main opening—and managed to crawl out and hitch a ride back into town.

Tom and Becky spent nearly a week recovering from the ordeal. When Huck finally was able to visit his friend, Tom told him about seeing Injun Joe in the cave and about his suspicion that the gold was hidden there. Judge Thatcher, however, already had had the cave's entrance barricaded with a triple-locked iron door to prevent other children from being lost there. When Tom heard this news, he turned white. "Injun Joe's in the cave!" he cried. A posse was organized to ride to the cave, and when the door was unlocked, Injun Joe lay just behind it, dead.

The morning after Injun Joe's funeral, Huck and Tom made their way back inside the cave. Tom led Huck to a large rock marked with a cross. They hoisted up the rock and found a natural chasm—where the treasure-box lay. Filling two sacks with coins, the boys stashed the rest of the gold in the Widow Douglas's woodshed. But by the time they reached her house, a crowd had gathered to hear the Widow's news. Putting her arms around the mangy Huck, she told him he could come and live with her; why, he'd saved her life, and forever after she'd clothe, educate, and take excellent care of him. "Huck don't need it," Tom broke in. "Huck's rich!" Then he ran outside to fetch the money. The coins amounted to over twelve thousand dollars! Judge Thatcher put the money into safekeeping and promised the boys an allowance of a dollar a day.

Huck moved in with the grateful Widow Douglas; he went to school, he used a knife and a fork, he washed regularly. But he never would have consented to such "civilized" things if Tom, true adventurer that he was, had not promised to assemble a "respectable" band of robbers—with Huck as one of its chief marauders.

Commentary

Samuel L. Clemens was born in Hannibal, Missouri, in 1835 and spent his boyhood on the banks of the Mississippi. He began writing under the pen name "Mark Twain" when he was about twenty-six. He is best known for his characters Tom Sawyer and Huckleberry Finn. Tom, the adventurous, all-American boy, is in reality a rather complex character. On the one hand he does everything possible to avoid school and church; at the same time he is highly principled, always trying to do the right thing—according to his rather romantic ideals. The importance of this novel—and its equally beloved companion volume, *Huckleberry Finn*—is in the rich, colorful portrait Twain paints of an unforgettable American era.

THE ADVENTURES OF HUCKLEBERRY FINN
by Mark Twain (1835–1910)

Type of work
Juvenile adventure novel and satire

Setting
Missouri's mid-19th-century backwoods and
the banks of the Mississippi River

Principal characters
Huckleberry Finn, a lively country boy
Tom Sawyer, Huck's friend
Pap Finn, Huck's reprobate, drunkard father
Jim, a runaway Negro slave
The Widow Douglas, Huck's guardian

According to Ernest Hemingway, modern American literature begins with *Huckleberry Finn*, Twain's sequel to *Tom Sawyer*. Mellowed by the introduction of real pathos, deepened by a new attention to Huck's developing consciousness—and conscience—and broadened by its undercover exploration of social and political ambiguities, the book is obviously a richer and more sophisticated work. But what distinguishes it as proudly and quintessentially American is its unabashed use of the first-person Missouri vernacular narrative voice.

Naturally, Twain's characteristic humor peppers *Huck*'s pages. Indeed, Twain prefaces the story with a warning that "Persons attempting to find a motive in this narrative will be prosecuted; persons attempting to find a moral will be banished; persons attempting to find a plot in it will be shot." Nevertheless, the novel explores significant social issues, including the legitimacy of hierarchal social relationships.

Story overview

This story starts out sometime in the mid-1800s in the placid little Mississippi township of Hannibal, Missouri. Some months earlier, Tom Sawyer and his friend Huck had discovered an honest-to-God chest of gold. The two lucky, lively boys had split the twelve-thousand-dollar treasure, and trustworthy Judge Thatcher was safeguarding their money in trust. Meanwhile, the Widow Douglas and her sister Miss Watson had taken the rough-hewn Huck under her wing—and into their home—to try to "civilize" him. Although he managed to put up with school and even learned some religion, the boy didn't take too well to Miss Watson's determined efforts to squelch his swearing and smoking.

Then one day Huck spied some footprints in the snow, and realized that his no-good, drunken father was back in town, no doubt with an eye on his son's money. Huck, in response, immediately rushed over to Judge Thatcher's to sign away his rights to the treasure. He left feeling unburdened and satisfied; now he owned nothing at all to fret over.

Late one night not long afterward, Huck found his Pap, pale and ragged, crouched in the corner of his room. "You've put on considerable many frills since I been away," Pap spat in contempt. "You drop that school, you hear? I'll learn people to bring up a boy to put on airs over his own father." Then Pap asked outright about the money. Huck gave him the dollar he had, whereupon the old man left. But the next day—declaring himself Huck's legal guardian—Pap showed up on Judge Thatcher's doorstep, demanding more money. Naturally, the judge refused to turn over a single red cent.

Well, Pap got to feeling more and more desperate, until finally one pleasant spring day the elder Finn kidnapped his son and took him to stay in a remote log hut on the Illinois side of the Mississippi. Huck reveled in the fishing and hunting, but he didn't like being kept under lock and key when Pap went into town, nor was he fond of the beatings he received when Pap staggered home drunk. One night after Pap almost killed him, Huck decided it was time to make his escape.

The next night, while Pap was in town, Huck sawed a piece out of one of the logs in the cabin wall, crawled out the hole, and carefully replaced the chunk. Then he smashed in the cabin door with an ax and dribbled pig's blood on the ground. Then, for effect, he stuck a few of his own hairs on the bloody ax blade. He sure hoped Pap would think that he had been killed.

For three days the boy happily camped out on Jackson Island. Then, out on a ramble one night, he saw something that caused his heart to jump "up amongst [his] lungs": a campfire. To his relief, he saw that the blaze was tended to by Jim, Miss Watson's Negro slave. Jim, meanwhile, stared wildly at what he presumed was Huck's ghost. "Doan' hurt me—don't!" he wailed. "I alwauz liked dead people, en done all I could for 'em … "

When Huck finally calmed Jim down enough to explain that his death had been fabricated, Jim confided that he'd run off from home after hearing that Miss Watson was planning to sell him downriver. And so the fugitives made camp together.

Then one night after a heavy storm had swollen the river, Jim and Huck found a dilapidated frame house floating by on the current. Inside they found a dead man lying amongst a scattered deck of cards and empty whiskey bottles. Jim warned Huck not to look at the man's face—it was too "gashly." Together they searched the rooms for useful goods and sent the house on its way.

As time passed, Huck found himself itching for news from town. One day he dressed up in a girl's calico dress and bonnet and stepped daintily into Hannibal to gather some gossip. Lisping out questions in a high-pitched voice, he learned that some townsfolk thought poor dead Huck had been killed by his Pap, who had up and disappeared himself just a few days earlier; others thought Jim must have done the deed, since he and Huck had vanished on the same night. In fact, some men were talking about going to Jackson Island later that night to see if they could roust Jim. Double-fast, Huck hurried back to

Jim's side. "There ain't a minute to lose," he warned. "They're after us!"

Within minutes, the fugitives had loaded up Jim's raft and started down the Mississippi. Their plan was to board a steamship north, where Jim could earn money to buy the freedom of his wife and children. But Huck couldn't help feeling guilty; after all, Jim was a runaway: he was Miss Watson's property. Huck finally decided that he would turn Jim in the next chance he got. But when a boatload of men appeared looking for runaways, Huck told them that he was sharing the raft with his sick father—who was lying inside the tent with a bad case of smallpox. That sent the men paddling away in a hurry. Huck felt a few pangs of guilt about helping a man on the lam, but he knew his conscience would kill him if he betrayed a good friend like Jim. So, the travelers continued downstream, encountering one adventure after another.

Then one night after drifting into a bank of thick fog, they heard the unmistakable sound of a steamboat bearing down on them. Immediately they leaped into the water to avoid being mashed. When Huck at last pulled himself up on shore and called out for Jim, there was no answer.

Soon afterward, further downriver, Huck was taken in by a rich family named Grangerford. The Grangerfords were good, generous people, treating Huck to all the comforts he could want. But they were somehow caught up in a bitter feud with another family named Shepardson—for reasons no one could remember.

One day the Grangerford slave who attended Huck asked him to come into the woods to see "some snakes." Rather than snakes, however, Huck found his old friend Jim there, hidden in the underbrush. But tragically, that very night, while Huck was gone, a battle was touched off between the feuding families in which the entire Grangerford clan was killed. "I wished I hadn't ever come ashore that night to see such things," Huck later grieved. "I ain't ever going to get shut of them."

So once more the raft-mates set off down the Mississippi. A few days later they took two fellows on board with them who professed to be from royal families: one said he was a duke, while the other claimed to be a king. Although Huck knew they were lying, he decided to play along.

The two hucksters stopped periodically at towns along the river to carry out get-rich schemes. At one such village the King learned that a wealthy man named Peter Wilks had just died, leaving three thousand dollars to his three daughters. The King likewise had learned that Wilks's deaf-and-dumb brother would be arriving soon for the funeral. He gathered as much information as he could about the brother and then coached the Duke to impersonate him. Sure enough, the poor daughters entrusted the "uncle" with their entire inheritance.

Disgusted by these shenanigans, Huck slipped into the scoundrels' room that night to reclaim the money, which he then stashed safely in the dead man's coffin

for the daughters to retrieve. The next day the real brother showed up, and the Duke and the King were hauled away to jail. But just as Huck and Jim were untying their raft to move on, the two escape artists came running down the bank to rejoin them. It was all Huck could do to keep from crying.

The next day the foursome stopped off at another town. After running some errands, Huck returned to the raft to find Jim gone. The Duke had sold the runaway, complained the King—"and never divided with me, and the money's gone."

Immediately Huck set off to the rescue. But to his surprise, at the plantation where Jim had been imprisoned he was greeted by a woman who gave him a loving squeeze and called him Tom—Tom Sawyer! She was Tom's own Aunt Sally, who obviously had taken Huck for her nephew, due to arrive for a visit. So, in order to help out Jim, Huck gladly assumed Tom's identity.

When Tom eventually showed up, the boys shared a grand reunion. They decided that Huck would pretend to be Tom's cousin, Sid, whenever they were around Aunt Sally. Then Huck told Tom about Jim's predicament and revealed his plan to steal the key, unlock the door to the hut where the slave was being kept, then head off downriver. Tom, however, had been reading pirate books; he favored digging a tunnel into the hut. That plan sounded infinitely more complicated and dangerous, so naturally they immediately settled on it.

When the tunnel was finally completed, Tom wrote an anonymous letter to Mr. Phelps, the plantation owner: There is a desperate gang of cutthroats going to steal your runaway ... to-night. Then the boys made their way through the tunnel into Jim's hut. Fleeing into the darkness, the three were pursue by Phelps and a posse of gun-toting farmers. Alive and free for the moment, they reached the raft. But Tom had caught a real live bullet in the leg, and the group was soon recaptured.

Back at the Phelps' farm, Jim was again securely locked up. Soon cries could be heard to hang the double runaway. Suddenly Tom sat upright in bed. "They hain't no right to shut Jim up!... He's free as any cretur that walks this earth. Old Miss Watson died two months ago, and she ... set him free in her will."

"Then what on earth did you want to set him free for?" cried Aunt Polly.

"I wanted the adventure of it!" Tom replied.

Jim was immediately released. Phelps then fed him and gave him a suit of clothes, while Tom gave him forty dollars for being such a respectable prisoner. Although Tom was now ready to return home, Huck was reluctant to join him for fear of his Pap. Hearing this, Jim made a sad confession: "He ain't a-comin' back no mo', Huck. Doan' you 'member de house dat was float'n down de river, en dey wuz a man in dah, kivered up, dat wuz him."

And so Huck headed back on the double toward the Widow Douglas's house—before Aunt Sally made good on her threat to adopt him.

THE KITCHEN GOD'S WIFE
by Amy Tan, Ivy Books, 1991

Type of work
Intergenerational novel
Setting
20th century China and California
Principal characters
Pearl Louie Brandt, a 40-year-old Chinese-American woman
"Winnie" (Weili) Louie, Pearl's Chinese mother
Wen Fu, Weili's harsh first husband
"Helen" (Hulan) Kwang, Weili's friend and partner

Story overview

"Pearl, [you] have to go, no choice," Winnie informed her daughter by telephone. Pearl did not particularly want to attend the engagement party for her Aunt Helen's son or the Buddhist funeral for her Auntie Du, but, as usual, she dutifully agreed to go.

The first person to greet her at the engagement party was her cousin Mary. Pearl was extremely hurt and unhappy that Mary had told her mother, Helen, about a very private piece of news: Pearl's newly diagnosed multiple sclerosis. Helen and Winnie were very close friends, so it was only a matter of time, thought Pearl, until her own mother knew.

Pearl had meant to tell her mother herself—eventually. But, remembering the cancer that had killed her father years before, she could predict what Winnie's response would be: She "would search in her mind for the causes, as if she could undo the disaster by finding the reason why it had occurred.... According to my mother *nothing* is an accident. She's like a Chinese version of Freud ... "

Now as Pearl gazed at her mother during the banquet, she reflected, "I feel as lonely as I imagine her to be." Then suddenly she felt a hand on her shoulder and looked up to see her Aunt Helen. In a voice that could not be refused, the older woman invited her into the kitchen. "I have a brain tumor," Helen candidly announced once they were alone. "Everyone wants to keep this news from me, okay. They want to be nice before I die.... [So, Pearl], it makes my heart and shoulders heavy that your mother does not know [about your illness].... You must tell your mother, Pearl."

"Auntie Helen, you know I can't tell my mother that," Pearl protested. "You know how she is." Auntie Helen's response came as a startling revelation: "Maybe [your mother] has secrets too."

The next day was Auntie Du's funeral. Afterwards, Winnie presented her daughter with a family heirloom: Auntie Du's famous good-luck icon, the Chinese Kitchen God. Elaborately stationed on what resembled a miniature stage and surrounded by gold-leafed Chinese characters signifying luck, was the picture of a man with "two long whiskers, shaped like smooth, tapered black whips." According to Winnie, the Kitchen God was not "like Buddha," but one of the lesser gods.

In the beginning, Winnie explained, the Kitchen God had been a rich farmer named Zhang. One day Zhang brought a concubine to live in his household. Eventually the new favorite forced Zhang's wife to leave. Then when the concubine and Zhang had spent all of the family fortune, the woman left too, and Zhang, now too poor to buy bread, eventually fainted from hunger. When he came to, he found himself in the kitchen of his good wife. He was so ashamed that he jumped into the fireplace—and the wife watched "her husband's ashes fly up to heaven in three puffs of smoke."

And so farmer Zhang became the Kitchen God, "watching over everyone's behavior ... And once a year, seven days before the new year, Kitchen God flew back up the fireplace to report whose fate deserved to be changed, better for worse, or worse for better."

Not long after giving her daughter the Kitchen God, Winnie's own life abruptly changed. Helen received a letter from China with astonishing news: Winnie's first husband, a harsh man named Wen Fu, had died on Christmas Day. "Can you imagine?" Winnie fumed. "Even to the end he found a way to make me miserable.... How can I sing 'Silent Night,' 'Joy to the World,' when I want to shout and say, So glad he is dead!"

But this was only the beginning of Winnie's distress. Helen now insisted that she reveal the story of her own early life in China with Wen Fu. Winnie demurred; those secrets were shameful and sordid. But Helen's firmness prevailed. Reluctantly, Winnie called her daughter and asked Pearl to come the next day.

"It is the same pain I have had for many years," the older woman, seated next to Pearl, began. "It comes from keeping everything inside, waiting until it is too late. I think my mother gave me this fault.... She left me before she could tell me why she was leaving ... "

Winnie's mother had been raised between two worlds. She was born in Shanghai to a wealthy, educated family and attended a missionary school that encouraged her independence and enthusiasm for foreign customs. But later she had followed tradition by entering into an arranged marriage with Jiang, a rich merchant with four other wives. When Weili—Winnie's Chinese name—was born, the young mother doted on the child. But one day when Winnie was six years old, her mother argued with Jiang, and then ran away. Winnie never saw her again. Jiang sent Winnie to live on a distant island with her paternal uncle and his family, so that her face and mannerisms would not remind him of his wife. Although the family treated her well, Winnie never really felt as if she "belonged."

After Winnie grew up and married Wen Fu, her husband showed her the meaning of cruelty in every way. He had married her only because of her family's great wealth, and she knew little happiness as a bride. "A woman always [has] to feel pain, suffer and cry, before she [can] feel love," her mother-in-law often told her. And this message was daily reinforced by Wen Fu, who forced the innocent girl to use foul language and to humble herself on her hands and knees to beg him for his love. " … He would complain," Winnie remembered, "telling me I was not a good wife, that I had not passion, not like other women he knew … "

It was in 1937, during the early days of her marriage, that Winnie first met Helen, the wife of Wen Fu's military boss. Although Helen was an unschooled chatterbox with "the manners of a village servant," Winnie could not help but respond to her warmth and wit. Throughout the horrible years of war, the two women remained friends as they moved from one Chinese city to another to escape Japanese attacks.

Meanwhile, Wen Fu had impressed all the other men in the air force with his bravado. Even his boss mistook his swagger for courage. Secretly, Wen Fu disparaged his boss—and despised Helen.

As the war raged on, Winnie's relationship with her husband grew steadily worse. After her first baby, a girl, was born dead, Wen Fu's only comment was, "At least it was not a boy." Winnie gave the baby the name of *Mouchou*, or "Sorrowfree," because she had never known sorrow.

After injuring himself in a jeep accident, Wen Fu's behavior grew even more monstrous. He humiliated and beat his wife mercilessly, and when another girlchild, *Yiku*, was born to them, he beat her as well. Eventually, baby Yiku died as a result of Wen Fu's cruelties. "Good for you," said Winnie as she cradled the little corpse in her arms. "You've escaped. Good for you."

When she again became pregnant, Winnie decided to name her next child *Danru*, or "Nonchalance," in the hope that the baby would never become attached to anything. But when her son was born, little Danru adored his mother as much as she loved him.

Wen Fu did not beat his son as he had Yiku, but he continued to terrorize and humiliate Winnie, even inviting a favorite mistress to live in their house. After his mistress left and the war ended, he moved his family back to Shanghai, where they lived in the mansion that belonged to Winnie's father. Jiang had been enfeebled by a stroke and was so weak that he gladly allowed his son-in-law to take over his finances. As Wen Fu busied himself spending the old man's fortune, Winnie and Danru took the opportunity to escape. They moved into a shelter, where Winnie struck up a romance with an old acquaintance, Jimmy Louie, a Chinese-American who worked as a translator for the U.S. government. Before long, she and Danru moved in with Jimmy, who provided them with the first real taste of family happiness. But, tragically, little Danru died during an epidemic, and soon afterwards Wen Fu had his wife imprisoned for stealing his son and "letting him die," and for "deserting her Chinese husband to run off with an American … "

In great anguish, Jimmy returned to the United States. Thanks to his financial support and to Helen's tireless efforts, Winnie was eventually released from prison. After tricking Wen Fu into divorcing her, she prepared to join Jimmy in America. But when Wen Fu learned that he had been outwitted, he accosted Winnie and put a gun to her head. "Beg me, beg me to let you be my wife," he shouted. Then he raped her. Soon after, Winnie left China forever.

Still, there was one important fact left for Winnie to divulge. "And nine months later," she told Pearl, "maybe a little less, I had a baby. I had you." Stunned at the obvious implications of this confession, Pearl broke into sobs.

Her mother took her hand. "Of course every baby is born with *yin* and *yang*," she comforted. "This *yin* comes from the woman. The *yang* comes from the man. When you were born I tried to see whose *yang* you had. I tried to see your daddy…. You looked like Mouchou. You looked like Yiku. You looked like Danru, Danru especially. All of them together. All the children I could not keep but could never forget."

Out of the blue Pearl felt her shock begin to retreat—melting behind the dawn of a new awareness: Barriers were down; a bridge had been crossed. She and her mother were at last united as women. It was not hard at that moment for Pearl to reveal her own secret, the multiple sclerosis. "It's nobody's fault," she finished. "There's nothing you can do about it."

Winnie was aghast. "How can you think this way? What do you call this disease again? Write it down. Tomorrow I am going to Auntie Du's herb doctor. And after that, I will think of a way."

Minutes later Pearl faced one last surprise. "I don't really have a brain tumor," confessed Helen. "I made it up!… Well, you had a secret, your mother had a secret. I said I was going to die so that you both tell each other your secrets…. And now you are closer, mother and daughter, I already see this."

"I am laughing, confused," thought Pearl, "caught [between Helen and Winnie] in endless circles of lies. Or perhaps they are not lies but their own form of loyalty, beyond anything … that I will ever understand."

Commentary

Like her first novel, *The Joy Luck Club*, Amy Tan's *The Kitchen God's Wife* has won universal acclaim. Through the intergenerational struggles of her characters, Tan evokes a marvelously mythic, complex and exotic world, a world that nevertheless remains startlingly contemporary and accessible. And the fact that Tan's characters rarely forget to laugh, in spite of their desperate circumstances, greatly increases this accessibility. The novel's humor, just as in the Greek epics, becomes a gallant response to fate. If Winnie has been victimized, she is not the victim of Wen Fu—whom she challenges—but rather of fate, of dynamic forces larger than life itself.

Even the Kitchen God himself is not exempt from Winnie's mockery. At the end of the novel Winnie buys her daughter "a lady statue" to replace the Kitchen God. "You should tell her everything," Winnie, smiling, urges Pearl. "She will wash away everything sad with her tears … See her name: Lady Sorrowfree, happiness winning over bitterness, no regrets in this world."

MEMORY OF KIN – STORIES ABOUT FAMILY BY BLACK WRITERS
edited by Mary Helen Washington, Doubleday, 1991

As Mary Ellen Washington compiled her collection of 19 stories and 12 poems, she gradually began to see "family as a living mystery, constantly changing, constantly providing us clues about who we are, and demanding that we recognize the new and challenging shapes it often takes." In fact, Washington's anthology challenges the notion that there is a single form of the "ideal" family.

Memory of Kin's writers explore various sides of the family. For instance, in "Just Like a Tree" (1968), a quilted, staccato tale of pilgrimage, Ernest J. Gaines's ten distinct narrators define "family" as *those who care* rather than those who are related by blood. Likewise, in "Roselily" (1972) teacher and writer Alice Walker re-evaluates the function of marriage by revealing a bride's full range of giddy and troubled thoughts as she stands at the altar. And, finally, in "Adventures of the Dread Sisters" (1989), poet, playwright and political journalist Alexis de Veaux demonstrates that a "functional family" need not fit the traditional father, mother, 2.5 children, one-dog prototype.

Thus, Washington submits, "Like the 24 storytellers in this collection, we too become artists, re-creating our family in an imaginative act, retrieving what is lost by reconstructing our own 'memory of kin.'"

JUST LIKE A TREE
by Ernest J. Gaines

Young Chuckkie struggled to stay warm next to his mother Leola in the wagon. She, her husband Emile, her mother Gran'mon and Chuckkie were on their way to say good-bye to "Aunt Fe," who was heading North to escape the unhealthy climate of the South. Chuckkie looked on in amusement as his father fought to get the family mule, Mr. Bascom, to pull the wagon.

As they lurched to a stop in front of Aunt Fe's house, Chuckkie jumped off the wagon to guide Mr. Bascom through the gate. As the wagon rolled through, however, it scraped the fence, tearing half of it down. At the sound of the ruckus, the whole houseful of family and friends who had come to see Aunt Fe off came bustling out.

Later, Chuckkie's mother found Aunt Fe sitting by the fireplace, trying to look happy. "Aunt Fe," Leola ruminated. " … The name's been 'mongst us just like us own family name. Just like the name o' God." She then recalled all the times she had washed clothes for Aunt Fe. Gloomily, Leola approached Louise and exclaimed, "Louise, moving her from here's like moving a tree you been used to in your front yard all your life." She even offered to take Aunt Fe home to live with her and her family, but Louise replied that it wouldn't be right: they weren't Aunt Fe's kin.

Louise's husband James, meanwhile, decided that he needed to show these country folks a good time.

He pulled out his whiskey bottle and began dumping it in the eggnog pot, though Louise held back his hand. Dumbfounded, he glanced around at all the poor, backward masses who were going to drink eggnog straight. "I mean, there's about ninety-nine of them. Old ones, young ones, little ones, big ones, yellow ones, black ones, brown ones—you name them … they're here. And what for? Brother, I'll tell you what for. Just because me and [Louise] are taking this old chick out of these sticks."

"I want me some eggnog," young Ben O repeated over and over. "Well, you ain't getting none," Gran'mon replied, picking up a potato chip and throwing it toward Ben O but hitting Chuckkie instead. Chuckkie then turned and hit Ben O, setting off a wrestling match. Leola rushed from the kitchen, snatched the two tussling boys from off the floor, shook them gently, and ordered them to kiss and make up. Chuckkie kissed Ben O on the jaw, but Ben O refused to kiss Chuckkie—until his mama whipped him with his daddy's belt. Then he kissed Chuckkie, "feeling like he wanted to spit."

In the meantime, Aunt Clo had been thinking of how heartless it was to take Aunt Fe away from the place where she'd lived for so many years. "Be just like wrapping a chain round a tree and jecking," Aunt Clo believed. "Then you hear the roots crying, and then you keep on jecking, and then it give, and you jeck some mo', and then it falls. And not till then … you see the big hole in the ground and piece of the taproot still way down in it—a piece you won't never get out no matter if you dig till doomsday."

Elsewhere in the room, Uncle Chris listened in delight as Lionel told the wildest lies. Everybody laughed; maybe it would take their minds off Aunt Fe's leaving. Why just the other day when Pa had gone by to tell Uncle Chris about Aunt Fe's decision, Chris had broken down and cried, right there by the front gate.

Several miles away from the bustling house, Anne-Marie's car slithered through the mud toward Aunt Fe's. Despite the storm, she had to pay her respects to her former nanny. After her mother had died, Aunt Fe had cooked for her father—and had nursed her back to health several times.

Finally Anne-Marie pulled into the drive. As she approached the house she heard laughter wafting out onto the porch; but the moment she stepped inside, the revelry stopped. Now everyone gawked silently as Anne-Marie handed a package to Aunt Fe. "Just think of it—a white lady coming through all of this for one old darky," one of the men mumbled. But Aunt Fe wasn't fazed in the least. Opening the package, she removed the 79-cent scarf, kissed it, and thanked Anne-Marie profusely—whereupon Anne-Marie knelt down and buried her face in Aunt Fe's lap, weeping. A few minutes later she got up and walked out of the house.

Then Emmanuel suddenly appeared—and again the house turned deathly silent. Emmanuel was responsible for Aunt Fe's leaving. But Aunt Etienne spoke up to defend him; it wasn't his fault. "It started," she insisted, "when one man envied another man for having a penny mo' 'an he had, and then the man married a woman to help him work the field so he could get much's the other man…. And soon the other man had bought him a slave to work the ox so he could get ahead of the other man." The squabble had been going on for a million years, she continued. Emmanuel was just doing what the slaves had done in earlier times—except that instead of raising his arms he was bowing his head.

Emmanuel now stood before Aunt Fe. His voice barely above a whisper, he asked if she knew he loved her. She nodded. Then he turned and reminded everyone there of what Aunt Fe had told him when he was enraged over his great-grandpa's lynching: "I was so angry I felt like killing. But it was you who told me get killing out of my mind," he said, eyeing Aunt Fe. "It was you who told me I would only bring harm to myself and sadness to the others if I killed."

As the crowd began filing out of the house, tears streaming down their cheeks, Chuckkie's grandmother, Aunt Lou, sidled over to Aunt Fe, still sullenly seated by the fireplace. "Well, Fe?" Aunt Lou said, waiting quietly for Aunt Fe's response.

Finally, Aunt Fe, in her majestic yet quiet voice, said, "I ain't leaving here tomorrow, Lou." Aunt Lou, taking Aunt Fe by the hand, sang her a termination song; then she helped her into her nightgown. Leading her into the bedroom, Lou watched Aunt Fe kneel by her bed, praying for a long time, before she took one long last breath. "Sleep on, Fe," Lou said. "When you get up there, tell 'em all I ain't far behind."

Roselily
by Alice Walker

*D*early *Beloved, we are gathered here …* Roselily's mind drifted into nothingness when the marriage ceremony began. As the preacher's voice droned on, she escaped into a fantasy of playing dress-up in her mother's white robe and veil—and of not already having three children. The man beside her glared at the congregation, whom he considered backward, while the bride thought "of ropes, chains, handcuffs, his … place of worship … where she will be required to sit apart with covered head." But after this ritual her groom would take her away from Mississippi to the South Side of Chicago, where she and her children would have a chance at respectability.

If there's anybody here that knows a reason why these two should not be joined together …

In her mind Roselily heard the preacher, but her thoughts had shifted to her fourth child—now living with his well-to-do father in New England. Then she reflected on her dead mother, "and the long sleep of grandparents mingling in the dirt." Seeing her father and sisters in the yard, she wondered about her new life; her fiance had promised her a home, a place where she could sit down to an occasional rest. She regretted that she hadn't "asked him to explain more…. But she was impatient. Impatient to be done with sewing. With doing everything for three children, alone."

Did she love this man standing next to her? There were, of course, things she loved about him—his pride, his sobriety. And she imagined she would "[love] the effort he will make to redo her into what he truly wants." But what did *she* want? Only "to live for once," something she'd never, ever done.

Let him speak now or forever hold his peace …

"The rest she does not hear … " Suddenly Roselily felt "a kiss, passionate, rousing, within the general pandemonium." And as the townspeople lined up to congratulate them, her new husband stood apart. He knew he was different; he was not a Christian. But he will take his bride to Chicago. "Her husband's hand is like the clasp of an iron gate. People congratulate."

Adventures of the Dread Sisters
by Alexis de Veaux

*W*e *crossing The Brooklyn Bridge. Traffic is slow going.* The Dread Sisters were on their way to Manhattan, trying to be on time for the "Rally Against Government Trucks Hauling Nuclear Waste Through Harlem." They were going to protest, even though for over a week they had been told that there was nothing to worry about. The girl reflected about this: *I might be only 15 but even I know ain't nothing safe. Not on no city street. Anything could happen. So I don't believe nothing the government says.*

Nigeria didn't like being late. Toni, another of the sisters, had refused to come along. She was in high school and boy crazy—and besides, she never could wake up before noon on a Saturday. Now the girl's mind again turned to their mission: *Nigeria and me, we call ourselves The Dread Sisters. We're not real sisters…. But she raised me. So we are definite family.*

Dreadlocks trailed down the backs of both Dread Sisters, like African women shown in text books. Nigeria, in fact—like a carved African sculpture with a red leather Nefertiti-shaped crown—looked as if she stepped right out of one of the photos. She was a painter who used to work on Atlantic City's boardwalk, drawing charcoal portraits. She still had the crisp 20-dollar bill she got for her painting of an old black lady dressed in black. The picture captured the woman's essence. That was in 1967, the year Langston Hughes died.

Now the wind was picking up; the girls shivered. They would never make it on time. Suddenly Nigeria jumped out of the car. "If you can't get to the rally when it starts," she bellowed, "start the rally wherever you are." And the Dread Sisters each took a lane, passing out anti-nuclear waste transport flyers to stranded motorists on Brooklyn Bridge.

Type of work
Coming-of-age novel

Setting
Cold Sassy Tree, Georgia; early 20th century

Principal characters
Will Tweedy, the story's sensitive and perceptive
  adolescent narrator
Will's Grandpa Ruck Blakeslee
Love Simpson, a milliner from Baltimore who marries
Grandpa following the death of his wife

Story overview

According to the tale young Will Tweedy spun for his friends, his flat-chested Aunt Loma, a new mother, didn't have enough milk to feed a jaybird and eventually had to resort to nursing a pig to increase her flow. When Loma heard the story, she decided to help her nephew channel his creativity in a different, more appropriate direction. "I've decided you ought to be a writer," she told Will, presenting him with a "special" notebook. Will then faithfully recorded subsequent events as they happened.

The town of Cold Sassy had gotten its name from the ancestors of Will's grandmother when they migrated from North Carolina to Georgia. While they were building their houses, the family camped on a ridge under some big sassafras trees. Later, visitors referred to the settlement as "thet cold sassafras grove" or "them cold sassy trees." Although in 1906 many townspeople figured they had "out-growed" the tawdry name and wanted to change it, Ruck Blakeslee, Will's grandpa, would not hear of it. Inasmuch as he owned the town grocery store—and thus was an influential man—the official name remained Cold Sassy, Georgia.

Ruck Blakeslee was known for doing the unexpected, but on the day he announced to his two daughters that "I'm aimin' to marry Miss Love Simpson," they were appalled: not only was Miss Love young enough to be their sister, she was also a free-thinking suffragette who was undoubtedly only after their father's money. And worst of all was the fact that their father was planning to remarry only three weeks after their beloved mother had died. "She's dead as she'll ever be ain't she?" he responded to their protests. "Well ain't she?"

Unlike his mother and his Aunt Loma, Ruck's 14-year-old notebook-scribbling grandson could see the advantages to the marriage. After all, Grandpa had explained he could either "hire ... a colored woman or get married.... And tell you the truth, hit's jest cheaper to have a wife." In the few weeks since Granny's death, both Grandpa and his house already had begun to look a mess. Now Love would be there to take care of both—and Will was sure she would never try to take Granny's place.

Grandpa had truly *loved* Granny. Although she was a no-nonsense Southern woman, she had always struck Will as gentle and refined. *She didn't fuss at Grandpa about not having the house wired for electricity, [nor his refusal]* to hook into the new water main and sewer *system.* Instead, she and Grandpa kept on "going to Egypt," which was what everybody in town called going out to the privy. Although some folks gossiped that the hardships of her primitive life with Grandpa had finally brought on the stroke that killed her, Will knew better. Like her garden, where she had cultivated over 60 varieties of roses, Granny had enjoyed a full life. As she lay in bed dying, Grandpa had presented her with one of the scarlet buds from the garden. "I remember you had a red rose like this'n in yore hair the day I decided to marry you," he whispered. And he remembered how Granny had once told him, "Mr. Blakeslee, I wouldn't even mind dyin' if'n I could be buried in a bed of roses." After she died, Grandpa had worked tirelessly making blankets of roses to fill the "deep yawning hole" at her gravesite.

So, at any rate, Grandpa and Miss Love eloped. And afterwards no one but Will went to call on them. When he arrived to help Miss Love get settled in her new house, he found Grandpa hard at work and Miss Love playing the piano and singing "Ta-ra-ra-boom-de-ay," followed by "I'm Only a Bird in a Gilded Cage." At the sight of Grandpa's new wife, Will, seeing Miss Love's pretty face and low-cut dress, felt as if he were on fire.

Miss Love was full of plans for the house; already it looked different from when Granny had lived there. To Will's surprise, when Grandpa came in from work he said very cheerfully, "Miss Love, do you think you could trim my hair some?" Miss Love was delighted. "With a close haircut, a thin mustache and no beard, you'll look—distinguished!" she said. And when she was finished, Grandpa looked years younger. "I do recollect seeing thet feller somewheres before," he mused, gawking at himself in the mirror. "Ain't he a buster though!"

"How come you married my grandpa?" Will asked Miss Love after Grandpa returned to the store. "Partly I married your grandfather so I would have a family," she answered, adding that everyone in her own family had died. Then she went on to explain that she and Grandpa had "a marriage in name only"; they didn't love each other, but Grandpa needed someone to be his housekeeper, and he'd agreed to deed the house and furniture to Miss Love after his death.

Their conversation was interrupted when a stranger barged in on them, a man in a cowboy hat with a fancy saddle draped over his arm. Miss Love stood there like she'd gone numb, her hands on her mouth. Then to Will's complete amazement, the man strolled over to Love and "kissed her right on the mouth ... like he was starved and she was something to eat." And Miss Love—why she was "kissing him back, no doubt about it." To Will's horror, the man proposed to Love on the spot. The saddle was an engagement gift he'd brought all the way from Texas, he explained. Tremulously, Miss Love replied, "You write me I'm not good enough for you, and now two years later—"

"I've come back for just one reason," the man broke in. "I love you." And just about that time, Grandpa walked back in through the door. When he heard about the proposal, he seemed neither angry nor jealous. Instead, he offered the man a drink and was "the friendliest host you ever saw."

"So do you want to marry him or don't you?" Grandpa finally asked Love when the stranger had left. Miss Love sobbed and shook her head: "If I weren't married to you, I still wouldn't marry him." And no more questions were asked.

Grandpa's affection for his bride grew stronger with each passing day. He was a new man, far more adventuresome and warm than he'd ever been. Not only did he buy Love a racehorse to go with her new saddle, he also was planning to take her on a buying trip to New York. Although he normally sent Will's Papa to do the buying for the store, this time Grandpa wanted to enjoy the trip with Miss Love.

The news depressed Mama. For once, *she*'d hoped to accompany Papa on the trip north—and now she had yet another reason to dislike her father's new wife. To cheer her up, Papa bought a big shiny red Cadillac car that made everyone in Cold Sassy proud for Mama. Thrilled, Mama exclaimed, "Oh, won't she be jealous"— and Will knew that the "she" referred to Miss Love.

As it turned out, though, Will himself enjoyed the car more than anyone. Quickly learning how to drive, he savored climbing behind the wheel to run errands for his father. One day, he happened to see his pretty schoolmate Lightfoot McClendon walking along the road, and he pulled over to pick her up. After driving for a while, they stopped to take a leisurely walk on the grounds of a cemetery. "I shore wisht I could get one a-them angels for Pa," Lightfoot said, pointing to a beautiful headstone. Then she began to cry, mumbling to Will about her father's tragic death. Without thinking, Will took the girl in his arms and kissed her. The memory of that kiss stayed with him for a long time.

After Grandpa and Love returned from New York— with presents galore and a new car for themselves—Will developed a new, more compassionate appreciation for his grandfather. One night when the three of them went out for a drive in the Blakeslee's new Pearce, they had an accident and were forced to spend the night in a stranger's house. Time passed, and Will couldn't get to sleep. Finally, around midnight, he heard his grandfather get out of bed and go to his wife. "Don't, Mr. Blakeslee," Miss Love began to cry. "How dare you try to . . . to use me like I'm a . . . Why, I trusted you!"

"I love you, dang it!" Will, wide-eyed, heard Grandpa grouse. "Love, I've been waiting for this minute ever since the day I laid eyes on you!" Although he'd hated himself, he'd "hankered after" Love "like a schoolboy," and, while he'd loved his wife and prayed for her recovery, Grandpa also knew "thet if'n she died" he wanted to marry Love. "You poor, dear man. I'm so very sorry," Miss Love murmured. Then she made a confession of her own: when her old cowboy fiancé learned that many years earlier she had been raped by her father, he had broken their engagement; hurt and

rejection followed. Tenderly, Grandpa told her, "Hit don't make no difference, Miss Love."

Soon Will had his own problems to confront. Learning that Lightfoot was going to marry a boy who worked in Grandpa's store, Will found himself praying that something would happen to his rival that would prevent their marriage. But to Will's horror, the one something happened to was Grandpa. One night robbers broke into the store and hit Grandpa, knocking him out. When he regained consciousness, it wasn't the pain that bothered him so much as it was his sense of humiliation. "You're alive," Love sighed tenderly. "That's all I care about." Then, she confessed, "You dear, dear man. I love you."

But that wasn't the end of it: Grandpa was injured more severely than anyone suspected; soon he developed a bad chill and a cough that turned into pneumonia. Miss Love, heartbroken, nursed him, as the rest of the family gathered at his side. Closing his clouded eyes, Grandpa spoke to Granny—presumably, the last words that would ever leave his lips. Then, as Will duly recorded in his notebook, suddenly his fever broke, and Miss Love delightedly told him that she was expecting their baby. Afterwards, holding hands, Grandpa and Miss Love fell asleep. Hours later, when Love awoke, Grandpa was dead.

As he had requested, Grandpa was buried in a plain pine box next to Granny. A band played parade music, and there was a "funeral party" after the burial. Then Miss Love took the opportunity to speak to Grandpa's family and friends about her love for Grandpa. And now that she was expecting his baby, Cold Sassy seemed like home to her—a place where she should raise their child.

A month after Grandpa died, the town's name was changed. He had always said the only way it would happen was "over his dead body." And, Will wrote, he had been right.

Commentary

When journalist Olive Ann Burns (1924–1990) learned that she was chronically ill, she began her work on *Cold Sassy Tree*. Burns's semi-autobiographical novel grew out of vignettes from her own family's history in Georgia, just as Will Tweedy's story grows out of his journal notations.

At first reluctant to write in the notebook his Aunt Loma gives him, Will quickly discovers that his journal can memorialize all the changes that are taking place around him. He is, of course, preserving recollections of bewildering and exhilarating transformations in both his own adolescent life and the world around him. The arrival of Love Simpson in Cold Sassy, with her low-cut bodices and newfangled enthusiasms seems both to symbolize and to catalyze the reformative rhythms of Cold Sassy. Eventually, the town turns against its own name—both endearingly and embarrassingly quirky in a new age dedicated to rounding off rough edges. And an era ends, along with an old man's life, as a new child is born.

THE ACCIDENTAL TOURIST
by Anne Tyler, Alfred A. Knopf, 1985

Type of work
Realistic character novel
Setting
Contemporary Baltimore and Paris
Principal characters
Macon Leary, a middle-aged author of travel guides
Sarah Leary, his unhappy wife
Muriel Pritchett, an eccentric young dog trainer

Story overview

Macon Leary was startled to learn that his wife wanted a divorce. Sarah calmly informed him that she intended to find a place of her own when they returned home after their vacation, which, like so many other events of the past year, they had been unable to enjoy. Ever since their 12-year-old son Ethan had been murdered during a hold-up at the Burger Bonanza, the once-exuberant Sarah had become withdrawn and the ever-guarded Macon had turned into an insomniac. Although they both knew that losing a child put "a terrible strain" on a couple—even people like the Learys who had been together for almost 20 years—they were now too depressed to envision a means of saving their marriage.

After Sarah moved out, Macon "marveled at how an empty space could be so full of a person" who was absent; he was not, however, entirely opposed to living alone. Unlike his wife, Macon had countless strategies for getting things done efficiently, such as wearing "tomorrow's underwear [to bed] so he wouldn't have to launder any pajamas."

In addition to being spared Sarah's "lack of method," Macon could now become totally immersed in his work. The author of *The Accidental Tourist* travel guides—designed for business travelers who liked to "pretend that they had never left home"—Macon loved "the virtuous delights of organizing a disorganized country" on paper, "classifying all that remained in neat, terse paragraphs [and] dithering over questions of punctuation."

Unfortunately, Macon hated to travel. So it was only with the greatest effort that he could force himself to prepare for a trip to England shortly after Sarah had left him. As always, he followed the advice he gave in his guide books: *One suit is plenty.... The suit should be a medium gray. Gray not only hides the dirt; it's handy for sudden funerals.... Bring only what fits in a carry-on bag.... Add several packets of detergent so you won't fall into the hands of foreign laundries.*

Nevertheless, Macon was now confronting a particular problem that had not found its way into *The Accidental Tourist*: how to find someone to care for a temperamental pet. Edward, the Welsh corgi that his son had adored, had become cranky since Ethan's death. Sometimes he even nipped at people—and who wants to dog-sit a nippy, cranky dog? Finally, in desperation, Macon hit upon a solution: the Meow-Bow Animal Hospital.

The receptionist at Meow-Bow, a thin young woman with "aggressively frizzy black hair," surprised Macon by asking, "Can't you leave him at home with your wife?" When Macon explained rather coolly that he was divorced, the woman ignored the snub. "I'm a divorcee myself," she responded. She then went on to introduce herself as Muriel Pritchett.

Upon Macon's return from England, Muriel told him that she and Edward had "just got on like a house afire." In fact, she continued, "He just fell in love with me." Muriel, it so happened, prided herself on being a dog trainer who specialized in dogs that bite, and she was eager—overly eager, from Macon's point of view—to train Edward. She was not "some amateur," she assured Macon; she had success with "biters, barkers, deaf dogs, timid dogs," even attack dogs.

"You think it over and call me," she prodded him before he managed to get out the door with Edward in tow. "Or just call for no reason! Call and talk." Macon, of course, who abhorred superfluous conversation of any kind, had no intention of phoning a stranger, least of all one who sported "blackish lipstick" and "preposterously high-heeled sandals." A few days later, however, Muriel called him. "I was just wondering how Edward was doing," she said. "I still think he ought to be trained." Macon tried to brush her off, but Muriel jabbered right on. "You and me could have a drink or something," she suggested, or, if he preferred, she would cook Macon dinner. "I think for now I'll try to manage on my own," he mumbled as he hung up.

As it happened, Macon soon found that he could *not* manage. One day, carrying Edward down to the basement—where lately he had begun to feed the dog—he tripped and broke his leg. As a result, he was reluctantly moved back to the house where he had lived as a child so that his younger sister Rose could care for him. Rose already cooked and cleaned for her other two brothers, Porter and Charles, with whom she still shared the house. Perhaps because they had been raised by their grandparents, the Leary children had grown up to be rather stodgy and peculiar. In Rose's case, such eccentric behavior included alphabetized canned goods on the kitchen shelves and painstakingly planned menus. She had certainly never expressed much interest in romance. Consequently, Macon was stunned and embarrassed about the way she fussed over his publisher Julian on the day he dropped by to check up on Macon. He was also shocked by Edward's behavior that day: the dog barked ferociously at Julian; when Macon intervened, the dog snarled and then bit his hand. And so, a few days later, Macon called Muriel.

Naturally, Muriel was delighted that Macon needed her help. "Five or six times a week I'll come out for however long it takes," she told him. And true to her word, she arrived the next day. To Macon's surprise, simply by hissing, clucking her tongue and gently prodding Edward, Muriel induced the dog to obey. Throughout their session, Muriel yammered on enthusiastically about her family—and even about her hair, which she herself referred to as a "fright wig."

Macon had never met anyone like Muriel. Although he tried to deny it, he became increasingly drawn to her each time they met. Predictably, his family considered the woman to be utterly outlandish. "Imagine a flamenco dancer with galloping consumption," Rose said to Charles and Porter one day. "That's Edward's trainer." Still, Macon marvelled at Muriel's honesty and exuberance. She—unlike Sarah—was an optimist, a survivor who had worked hard to rear her young son and to make something of her life after her husband had walked out on them.

But Muriel's son, Alexander, left Macon feeling uneasy. He was a "small, white, sickly boy with a shaved-looking skull," and despite the fact that he bore no resemblance to Ethan, he nonetheless evoked memories of Macon's own son. In fact, when Muriel invited Macon to her house for dinner, he thought, *I just can't.*

"I lost my son," Macon eventually blurted out. "I can't go to dinner with people! I can't talk to their little boys!" Silently, Muriel took Macon in her arms and hugged him; a while later, they made love for the first time. That night Macon felt a sense of well-being he had not experienced since Ethan's death.

Not long afterwards, Macon moved in with Muriel and Alexander. He discovered that despite her endless banter about makeup, cellulite and thrift stores, Muriel had the uncanny ability to "pierce his mind like a blade." He also began to bond to Alexander: he worried about the boy and wanted to please him; he found himself helping him with homework, buying him pizzas and taking him shopping for new clothes. Muriel, though, still shell-shocked from her husband's abandonment, began to fear that Macon too would leave. "Oh for pity's sake," he'd say in response.

Still, on the day his sister married Julian Edge, Macon found himself reconsidering his relationship with Muriel. Moreover, talking again with Sarah, who was Rose's matron-of-honor, seemed "so natural," so pleasantly intimate. He had always been a traditionalist, he remembered. He was still a Leary, uncomfortable with flamboyance and change.

To add to his alarm, Macon now realized that Muriel reminded him of his mother Alicia, a "war widow" who had left her young children in the care of her Leary in-laws so that she could enjoy the company of various men. Observing his mother at the wedding standing beside Muriel, Macon entertained a disturbing thought: *Maybe in his middle age he was starting to choose his mother's style of person, as if concluding that Alicia—silly, vain, annoying woman—might have the right answers after all.*

Soon after the wedding, Macon left Muriel—the woman with whom he had planned a trip to Paris and had even discussed marriage—to return to Sarah.

For a while both Sarah and Macon were delighted by the familiarity of their old routines. They bought furniture and flowers and ate at their favorite restaurant. They became increasingly aware, however, that Ethan's death had created a void in their companionship that they were still unable to fill. Before long, Macon called Muriel. Their strained conversation didn't last long.

Then, embarking on another reluctant European business trip, Macon was astonished to see Muriel suddenly materialize on the plane that was transporting him to Paris. "I called your travel agent," she told the blustering traveler. "You don't own this plane!"

Try as he might, Macon could not avoid Muriel once they landed in Paris. She had booked a room at his hotel and she persisted in inviting him to dinner until he acquiesced. The first night they went to the Burger King on the Champs-Elysees; the next they went to an elegant restaurant. Notwithstanding, when Muriel later asked him to spend the night with her, he declined. Alone in his room, he slept fitfully. Then, when he awoke the next morning, he hurt his back and had to stay in bed all day because of the fierce pain.

Sarah immediately flew to Paris to be with her husband. In addition to bringing him medicine and vowing that she intended to fulfill his business obligations while he was laid up, she announced that they could enjoy a "second honeymoon, sort of." Sarah also told him, rather nonchalantly, that she had run into Muriel. Despite her insistence that she had been unfazed, Sarah could not help asking Macon, "Was the fact that she had a child what attracted you to that woman?" A few moments later Sarah said evenly, "You could have stopped her if you'd really wanted…. You could have taken steps."

That night Macon lay awake, thinking. It was true: he had not taken steps very often in his life and it was time to "learn to do things differently." He was packing his bags when Sarah woke up the next morning. "You're going back to that woman," she said. "You'll be one of those mismatched couples no one invites to parties. No one will know what to make of you."

"I'm sorry, Sarah," he sighed, putting his arm around her. "I didn't want to decide this."

Macon walked out of the room, down the stairs, and out of the hotel. Two blocks away he found a taxi. On his way to the airport, the driver passed the hotel and Macon saw Muriel standing there. *"Arretez!"* he commanded the driver. As the taxi lurched to a halt, he saw a "sudden flash of sunlight" before Muriel opened the door and got in.

Commentary

Anne Tyler, born in 1941, is a prolific Pulitzer-Prize-winning writer. Acclaimed most frequently for her compassionate depictions of offbeat characters, Tyler has also earned accolades for her imaginative renderings of Baltimore, the city where she has spent much of her adult life.

Baltimore has nourished other notable writers, such as Poe and Mencken; Dickens, however, is the author with whom Tyler shares the greatest affinity. As the writer Joseph Mathewson has noted, Tyler's "writing has a lot of Dickens's humanity … as well as a certain lack of fear, which came more easily to his own century than it does, alas, to ours." Truly, fearlessness, as it is so movingly embodied in the character of Muriel, emerges in *The Accidental Tourist* as a necessary prerequisite to happiness and survival.

RABBIT, RUN
by John Updike, Ballantine Books, 1960

Type of work
Psychological novel

Setting
Mt. Judge, Pennsylvania; ca. 1960

Principal characters

Harry "Rabbit" Angstrom, a 26-year-old former high-school basketball star, who now demonstrates kitchen gadgets for the Magipeel Peeler Co.

Janice Angstrom, Rabbit's pregnant wife and mother of their son, Nelson

Marty Tothero, Rabbit's former high-school basketball coach

Ruth Leonard, a prostitute

The Reverend Jack Eccles, a young Episcopal minister who seeks to "heal" Rabbit, but soon finds himself as confused as his protégé

Story overview

It was late March, the month when "love makes the air light" and "things start anew." Harry "Rabbit" Angstrom was walking home along the back alleys of Mt. Judge, a suburb of Brewer, when he happened on a group of kids playing basketball. Although he was still dressed in the cocoa-colored suit he'd worn to work that day as a demonstrator for the Magipeel Peeler Company, Rabbit couldn't resist the impulse to show these kids how a "natural" played the game. Indeed, during his junior and senior years of high school Rabbit had broken the county's B-league scoring records. "Hey," he called out, taking off his coat, "O.K. if I play?"

Reluctantly, the youngsters chose up sides. As he raced with the kids up and down the asphalt court, Rabbit sank "shots one-handed, two-handed, under-handed, and out of the pivot, jump, and set." After a while the kids grew sullen. "O.K.," Rabbit finally said, "the old man's going." And, picking up his coat in one hand, "like a letter," he began to run.

When he reached home he found his seven-months-pregnant wife Janice in front of the TV set watching the *Mouseketeers*. As often happened in the afternoons, Janice had been drinking Old-fashioneds. "You're a mess," her husband told her. Rabbit, who didn't drink, couldn't help baring his disapproval, even if it meant initiating a quarrel—which, as usual, it did.

When their argument subsided, Rabbit agreed to retrieve their car, parked at his mother-in-law's house, and to pick up their son Nelson from a friend's house on the way back. Just as he was about to leave, Janice called out to him from the kitchen to ask if he minded buying her a pack of cigarettes while he was out. Squinting down at his faint yellow shadow on the door, Rabbit suddenly felt certain he was about to be caught in some sort of "trap."

It was already dark by the time Rabbit sprinted up to the curb in front of the Springer home. Rather than confront Janice's parents, he ducked into the car and drove off. Still caged by the same stifling sense of claustrophobia, he was suddenly struck by the thought that

he never again wanted to see downtown Brewer— "that flowerpot city" where he worked. An overpowering impulse hammered against his ribs, and Rabbit aimed the car southwest. He would "drive all night, through the dawn through the morning," he decided. Then he would "park on a beach, take off [his] shoes and fall asleep by the Gulf of Mexico."

But after several hours it seemed that the farther he drove into West Virginia away from Pennsylvania, the more the landscape resembled "the country around Mt. Judge." In fact, if anything, the net of the trap felt "thicker now." Instinctively, Rabbit swung the car around and headed north again, following the radio's "warm-weather reports" back to Brewer.

At dawn as he approached the outskirts of town, Rabbit stopped at the apartment of his old basketball coach, Marty Tothero; perhaps Tothero could give him a place to sleep—and maybe some advice on how to redeem his crumbling marriage.

Tothero was delighted to see "wonderful Harry Angstrom" again and gladly put him up. But when Rabbit awoke later that afternoon, he discovered that his coach was less interested in advising him on his marital problems than in taking him out to dinner. "Have I got a girl for you!" Tothero smiled. The girl turned out to be Ruth Leonard, a prostitute, and Rabbit's prearranged date. "Well," Ruth greeted him when they arrived at the restaurant, "you're a big bunny."

That night Rabbit slept at Ruth's apartment; the next morning he decided to move in with her. "In all the green world," he thought, "nothing feels as good as a woman's good nature." He had, however, two concerns: first, since the car had been a gift from Janice's father, he wanted to leave it for his wife at their apartment; and second, he needed to get his clothes.

Everything went smoothly at first. Rabbit was able to drop off the car and pack his clothes at the apartment without bumping into Janice. But as he was leaving he was spotted by Jack Eccles, the young Episcopal minister whom Janice's parents had called in to mediate their daughter's marital problems. Eccles flagged Rabbit down and asked him bluntly if he intended to return to Janice. No, Rabbit replied, he didn't. Then, almost in the attitude of confession, he described his relationship with his wife. It was as if he had been "glued" to their marriage, he said, until it had suddenly occurred to him "how easy it was just to get out ... " Eccles, realizing it would be unwise to pressure Rabbit further, invited him to play golf the next Tuesday. For some reason, Rabbit accepted.

Tuesday arrived. While the twosome made their way around the golf course, Rabbit explained to Eccles that he felt he was on some sort of "quest." There was "something" out there, he said, gesturing vaguely toward the landscape, "that wants me to find it."

"All vagrants think they're on a quest," the minister replied. Then, since Eccles knew that Rabbit's flight from Brewer had cost him his job with Magipeel, he notified him that Mrs. Smith, a wealthy widow, was looking for a gardener at her estate. Rabbit applied, and easily got the job.

For a time, Rabbit's life seemed idyllic. He delighted in the "simplicity" of planting a garden, a labor he likened to getting "rid of something by giving it to itself." And surprisingly, as his friendship with Reverend Eccles deepened, Rabbit discovered that the man of God had lost his own faith; the center of his existence had been shattered. Although Rabbit had never experienced anything remotely comparable to faith, Eccles was now—like him—a man hungering for new meaning and companionship.

Rabbit's ties to Ruth also grew more rooted. As she blithely pointed out to him one day: "You've got Eccles to play golf with every week and to keep your wife from doing anything to you. You've got your flowers, and you've got Mrs. Smith in love with you. You've got me." Later, Rabbit conceded to her that leaving Janice had taught him an "interesting" lesson: "If you have the guts to be yourself, other people'll pay your price."

But after a few months Rabbit's life once more began to sour. First it seemed to him that Ruth, lately, had been "trying to make him feel guilty about something." And then, early one June morning, there was a call for him. "Harry," Eccles told him in muted tones, as though his buried voice were reaching up for Rabbit from beneath the ground, "your wife has started to have the baby."

It was still dark as Rabbit dressed; repeatedly he assured Ruth that it was his duty to go to the hospital. Ruth did not respond. "Hey," he said finally. "If you don't say anything I'm not coming back." Still, Ruth remained silent.

That morning, when little Rebecca June Angstrom was born, Rabbit decided to give his marriage a second chance. And for a brief period after Janice and the baby came home from the hospital, he felt "lucky, blessed, forgiven"—in a state of grace; he even attended services at Eccles's church "to give thanks" for his daughter. "God, Rebecca, thank you," he said as he kneeled, adrift on "the senseless eddies of gladness."

But once again Rabbit's bliss was short-lived. Later that same Sunday night as they lay in bed, he and Janice argued: he wanted to make love; she, reminding him that she was not yet fully recovered from childbirth, refused. Angry, Rabbit bolted out the door and headed for Ruth's apartment—leaving Janice to drink her misery away.

The next afternoon Janice's mother called. Sensing that something was wrong, she announced over her daughter's protests that she was on her way to the apartment. Janice, by then drunk almost to oblivion, blundered through the house for awhile in a desperate effort to tidy things up. Then she drew a bath for the baby. As she knelt by the tub and placed the child in the water, suddenly little Rebecca slipped from her hands and sank "like a grey stone." By the time Janice was able to wrest her daughter from the water, she knew that "the worst thing that has ever happened to any woman in the world [had] happened to her": she had drowned her own daughter.

When Rabbit returned home that evening after a futile search for Ruth, he walked into the nightmare of his daughter's death. Now he began to think that if he and Janice could endure this tragedy, their marriage might survive. At Rebecca's funeral, though, it struck him that everyone somehow blamed him for what had happened. "Don't look at me," he finally said. "I didn't kill her." Then to clarify his own confusion, he pointed at Janice and blurted, "She's the one." A sea of faces, "blank with shock," turned toward Janice—and Rabbit whirled around and began to run.

He ended up once again at Ruth's. This time he found her home—with the news that she was pregnant. Rabbit tried to convince her to have the baby. "Will you marry me?" she demanded. When Rabbit replied that he'd "love to," she challenged him to divorce Janice. "If you can't work it out," she said, "I'm dead to you; I'm dead to you and this baby of yours is dead too."

"That's fair," Rabbit, blinded by hope, answered.

Rabbit suddenly felt hungry now; he decided to step out to buy some groceries. "I'll be right back," he told Ruth. But once he got outside, an air of apprehension overtook him. Instead of heading to the market, he turned and began walking in the opposite direction. Then, as he groped with the old indefinable, elusive urge to be free, his junket picked up speed. "His heels hitting heavily on the pavement at first but with an effortless gathering out of a kind of sweet panic growing lighter and quicker and quieter, he runs. Ah: runs. Runs."

Commentary

Rabbit, Run (1960), the first in a tetralogy of novels which follows with *Rabbit Redux* (1970), the Pulitzer-Prize-winning *Rabbit Is Rich* (1981), and *Rabbit At Rest* (1990), elicited widely divergent critical views. Alfred Kazin, for instance, praised the book for its rich language and its insightful portrayal of a society characterized by "an increasing disbelief in marriage as the foundation of everything." Norman Mailer, in contrast, found Updike's prose deeply flawed, too often filled with "self-indulgent, tortured sentences," and the narrative "routine" and lacking in real moral vision.

Kazin and Mailer did agree, however, on one point: Rabbit's anxious evasions and escapes gradually erode his moral center of gravity, and leave him unable to act decisively. While the Rev. Eccles agonizes over his own lost moral center, Rabbit, who never had a moral center to begin with, continues to run from his future, hoping to return to the shining past of his carefree, basketball-star high-school self—a past where he was in charge, where he knew how to act and what to do. As a result, his growing need for escape—both from the "trap" of social conventions and institutions (his marriage) and from the price of personal freedom (the assumption of responsibility for his own acts and decisions)—becomes an end in itself. "Running," as the book's title implies, becomes Rabbit's one "moral imperative," the symbolic flight of an escape artist par excellence.

O. Henry—the pseudonym of William Sidney Porter—was born in Greensboro, North Carolina, in 1862. Trained as a pharmacist in his uncle's drug store, at age 20 Porter left home and went to Texas, where, for several years, he supported himself by working a string of itinerant jobs. In 1887 he moved to Austin, where he met and married Athol Estes Roach. It was here that Porter found a job with the First National Bank of Texas, a job which eventually led to his being charged with having embezzled $5000.

Porter, rather than stand trial, fled the country and ended up in Honduras, where, apparently, he hoped to establish himself and then send for his family. In the interim, however, his wife contracted tuberculosis. So, in 1897, he returned to the States and was arrested. His wife died, and shortly thereafter Porter began a five-year sentence in the Ohio State Penitentiary. It was while in prison, one story goes, that he adopted his pseudonym, after the prison's warden, Orrin Henry.

Porter served three years and was released in 1901. In 1903 he moved from Pittsburgh to New York, and it was here—in the "rush and throb of real life"—that he enjoyed his most productive years as a writer. In the tradition of Bret Harte—whose gold camp stories had mythologized the California frontier of the 1850s—Porter's stories of turn-of-the-century New York sought to ennoble the struggle of immigrants to survive, perhaps enrich themselves on the economic margins of urban society. It is in this context, and employing Harte's device of the so-called "trick ending," that these stories come to us.

THE FURNISHED ROOM

The unending stream of residents in the "red brick district of the lower west side" was as ephemeral as time itself. There, among the decaying red mansions of an earlier era, the newly-arrived immigrants and transients of the city could find, for a modest weekly rate, a furnished room in which to live. Thus, as a result of having been host to a thousand dwellers, each of the district's houses had accumulated its own ghosts, its own "tales to tell."

One night a young man set his bag down on the steps of one of these houses—the twelfth he had been to that evening—and, "wiping the dust from his hatband and forehead," rang the bell. "Come in," said the housekeeper when asked if she had a room. "I have the third floor, back, vacant since a week back."

He followed her upstairs and down a long lichen-colored carpeted hallway and pushed open a door. "It's a nice room," she said. "It ain't often vacant." Then she pointed out its amenities, which included a large closet and cooking gas, and recalled that its most recent occupants—a vaudeville team—had been happy there that summer. "Do you have many theatrical people rooming here?" the young man wanted to know. In particular, he was interested in a "Miss Eloise Vashner"—a stage singer who was "medium height and slender, with reddish, gold hair and a dark mole near her left eyebrow." The housekeeper replied that she didn't know the woman, adding with a shake of the head, "Them stage people have names they change as often as their rooms."

The young man, who in fact loved Miss Vashner, remained convinced that she was living somewhere in New York. Ever "since her disappearance from home" five months earlier, he had searched the city—from the most elegant theaters to the meanest dance halls—and always the answer to his "ceaseless interrogation" had been the "inevitable 'no'." Now he was beginning to worry he might never find her in a city that seemed increasingly like a "monstrous quicksand, shifting its particles constantly."

He paid an advance on his room and settled into a chair, listening "while the room, confused in speech as though it were an apartment in Babel, tried to discourse to him of its diverse tenantry." Every mark, it seemed, from the "splattered stain" on the wall to the "chipped and bruised" furniture, was a sign, a signature left by the long procession of tenants who'd preceded him. The young man sat there, "inert," reading these "characters of a cryptograph," when he suddenly detected the "sweet odor of mignonette," the same odor she, Miss Vashner, had "made her own."

"She has been in this room," he breathed, springing to his feet. Suppressing his excitement, he rushed down the hall and knocked on the housekeeper's door, again asking her to recite the names of all those who had occupied the room in the weeks previous. None, however, fit Miss Vashner's description. Dejected, he returned to his room. It seemed "dead" now, and the "perfume of mignonette" had disappeared. Staring at the yellow, singing gaslight, he walked over to the bed and began to tear its sheets into strips, which he then stuffed "into every crevice around windows and door." Then he "turned out the light, turned the gas full on again and laid himself gratefully upon the bed."

The housekeeper sat in her room with a friend. "I rented out the third floor, back, this evening," she said. "And did ye tell him, then?" the friend asked, referring to the girl who had killed herself "wid the gas" there the week before. The housekeeper replied that she hadn't. "Rooms," she said, were "furnished for to rent," and people were likely to "rayjict the rentin' of a room if they be tould a suicide has been after dyin' in the bed of it." Finally, in a casual reference to the suicide, the housekeeper observed that the girl would have been considered "handsome"—if it were not "for that mole she a-growin by her left eyebrow."

BRICKDUST ROW

Alexander Blinker was annoyed. His trip to the North Woods would have to be postponed a day so that he could meet with his lawyer and sign some documents pertaining to his vast holdings. "Oh, property!" shouted an exasperated Blinker. "Let's have it all at one dose tomorrow," he said to his attorney, Mr. Oldham, "signatures and property and snappy rubber bands and that smelly sealing-wax and all." Oldham glanced at his client and sighed, "I'll try to remember to drop in at eleven tomorrow."

At the unfolding of a hot afternoon, Blinker decided that rather than dine at the Club that night he would go to Coney Island. He caught a cab to a North River pier, stood in line to buy a ticket like everyone else, and then, after being "trampled upon and shoved forward," at last "found himself on the upper deck of the boat staring brazenly at a girl who sat alone upon a camp stool." He hadn't meant to stare; it was just that "the girl was so wonderfully good looking" that he had forgotten his manners.

She, however, was also staring back at him, and as a gust of wind blew up, he grabbed his straw hat and sat down next to her. "How dare you raise your hat to me," she said with a mocking smile. "I didn't," he replied, and then corrected himself. "I didn't know how to keep from it after I saw you." They talked pleasantly for a while. In the course of their chat he learned that "she was twenty, and her name was Florence." She trimmed hats, she told him, in a millinery shop, and shared a "furnished room with her best chum Ella."

Soon the boat landed at Coney Island, and before they knew it they were swept ashore on "a great human wave of mad pleasure-seekers." Blinker was disgusted by the "vulgarity" of it all, by the "shrieking" masses of sticky children and insolent youths who, in his view, brutally contradicted "all the tenets of a repression and taste" he'd so carefully cultivated in his life. But when he glanced at Florence, his impression suddenly changed. She returned his look of repugnance with a "quick smile and upturned, happy eyes, as bright and clear as the water in trout pools." He saw in her eyes, for the first time in his life, the "right" to be happy—a look that humbled him. Now, with Florence on his arm, they joined the "hundred thousand true idealists" and took "everything in, one by one."

At 8:00 that evening they caught the "returning boat and sat, filled with pleasant fatigue, against the rail of the bow, listening to the Italians' fiddle and harp." The morning's anxieties about signatures and property had melted away, and in their place was "Florence," this extraordinary girl whose "name was as pretty as she was."

The boat had just "turned its nose towards its slip" at the pier when it was struck on the side by a steamer, up near the stern. Quickly the boat began to take on water. As the passengers began to panic, Blinker turned to Florence and called out how much he loved her. She smiled and said, "That's what they all say." Blinker could only assure her he was serious and that, because he was rich, he could "make things all right" for her.

"That's what they all say," the girl repeated, as if the words were a refrain in some "little, reckless song." And Blinker, at this second censure, found himself quite disturbed—not only because she didn't believe him but also because she grouped him with an anonymous "they." She was not a "wallflower," she insisted, and she met these men she referred to either "on the boat, sometimes in the park, sometimes on the street." Blinker was even more exasperated that she found "it necessary to pick up every Tom, Dick, and Harry" she met in public. "Why don't you entertain your company in the house where you live?" he asked incredulously.

Florence gazed at him calmly. "If you could see the place where I live," she explained, "you wouldn't ask that. I live in Brickdust Row. They call it that because there's red dust from the bricks crumbling over everything…. There's no place to receive company. You can't have anybody come to your room. What else is there to do?" she asked him. "A girl has got to meet the men, hasn't she?"

The boat, though severely damaged, managed to dock safely. Blinker walked Florence to within a block of her home. She thanked him for the pleasant evening, and he, after muttering something in reply, "plunged northward till he found a cab."

The next morning at 11:00 Blinker met with his lawyer. After signing his name at least 30 times, he barked at Oldham that now he wanted to "get to the woods." But the attorney had one piece of business to conclude, having to do with "some buildings, fifteen in number," which, he reminded Blinker, had "new five-year leases to be signed." Blinker's father, Oldham continued, had "contemplated a change in the lease provisions, but never made it. He intended that the parlors of these houses should not be sub-let, but that the tenants should be allowed to use them for reception rooms." Oldham was about to describe the location of the house when "Blinker interrupted him with a loud, discordant laugh."

"Brickdust Row for an even hundred," Blinker guessed. "Do what you want with it," he told Oldham, rising to put on his hat. "Remodel it, burn it, raze it to the ground. But, man, it's too late, I tell you. It's too late."

LOVE IN THE TIME OF CHOLERA
by Gabriel Garcia Marquez (translated by Edith Grossman), Knopf Publishing, 1988

Type of work
Magical realism
Setting
Columbia, South America; late 19th, early 20th
   centuries
Principal characters
Dr. Juvenal Urbino de la Calle, a respected doctor
Fermina Daza, de la Calle's beautiful and headstrong
   wife
Florentino Ariza, a romantic who adores Fermina
America Vicuna, Florentino's beloved young relative

In *Love in the Time of Cholera*, Nobel prize-winning
novelist Gabriel Garcia Marquez displays the same
narrative skills that marked his earlier masterpiece *One
Hundred Years of Solitude*. In a style critics have dubbed
"magical realism," Garcia Marquez constructs a novel in
which the characters and landscapes are more reminiscent of mythology than of contemporary fiction. Yet
despite its disregard for chronicle and description, *Love
in the Time of Cholera* is remarkably accessible: its story
of aging, disease and death is a testament to human
nature and to the powers of love. No matter how eccentric Marquez's characters may be, at heart they are
simple, homespun philosophers who bask in their
ability to dream and to love.

Story overview

D
r. Urbino was thinking of changing his clothes
for the funeral of his chess partner Jeremiah
Saint Amour, who, at the age of seventy, had
committed suicide. Outside, Dr. Urbino could hear his
wife's parrot chattering in the mango tree. "You
scoundrel!" he shouted at the bothersome bird. "You're
even more of a scoundrel, Doctor," the bird replied.
With that, Dr. Urbino marched over to the tree, climbed
the ladder that rested beside it, and ascended to the
fourth rung, where he reached to seize the parrot in a
death grip. Ironically, however, clutching the bird
triumphantly, Dr. Urbino lost his balance and fell to his
own death.

While Dr. Urbino's demise was "memorable," his life
had been even more so. Everyone in town recalled that
the doctor's "drastic new methods" of hygiene and
treatment had put an end to "the last cholera epidemic
suffered by the province." He also had been responsible
for the restoration of the Dramatic Theater, and had
even taken a test ride in the "aerostatic balloon" that
provided the first airmail service to a nearby Colombian
town. Certainly he had always appeared to be an exemplary citizen.

Only Urbino's wife Fermina knew anything of his
shortcomings. And the most grievous of these—at least
from her point of view—was that the doctor had once
had an affair, an affair which he had confessed to his
priest. As incensed by her husband's confession as she
was by the affair itself, Fermina had shrieked, "You
might as well have told the snake charmer in the

market." Then, to avoid the gossip that certainly would
be spread, she left Urbino.

Fermina, however, "thought she would die of joy"
when her forsaken husband had come to bring her
home two years later. After all, she loved him: not only
had they raised two children together, traveled to
Europe, and taken part in the wondrous balloon expedition, but they had also grown accustomed to each
other.

Lately, after so many years of marriage, 72-year-old
Fermina had begun to treat her 80-year-old husband
like "a senile baby" and to realize that "they were not
capable of living for even an instant without each
other." So it was with profound shock and horror that
she watched him fall off the ladder by the mango tree.
Mustering all her courage, she insisted that a "vigil" be
held in the doctor's home, "with mountain coffee and
fritters and everyone free to weep for him in any way
they chose."

It was at this vigil that Fermina learned that
someone had been praying for her husband's death for
more than 50 years. This person was Florentino Ariza,
the man to whom, as a headstrong and beautiful adolescent, Fermina had once scribbled a note on a sheet of
paper from her notebook: *Very well, I will marry you if
you promise not to make me eat eggplant.* Receiving
Fermina's acceptance, the shy Florentino had developed
a new "confidence and strength." But despite his ardor,
he had still acquiesced to his mother's wishes that the
wedding be postponed for two years so that the two
would be "very certain of their affections."

Perhaps, then, it was inevitable that young Fermina,
following her return from an extended vacation, had
suffered a change of heart. She had become—or so she
thought—"more polished and intense, her beauty
purified by the restraint of maturity." Accordingly, after
seeing Florentino again, she had summarily dismissed
him from her life with another note: *Today, when I saw
you, I realized that what is between us is no more than an
illusion.*

Naturally, Florentino had been crushed. And his
despair had mounted when he learned a few months
later that Fermina had decided to marry "the most
desirable of bachelors," Dr. Juvenal Urbino.
Brokenhearted, Florentino embarked on a "curative
journey" aboard one of the boats in his uncle's fleet. The
voyage, while it didn't erase the image of Fermina's
wedding and honeymoon, did offer one consolation: a
mysterious and beautiful female passenger had taken a
fancy to him and brought him under her irresistable
spell. Thus began Florentino's lifelong obsession with
the pleasures of the flesh.

Soon after this shipboard encounter, Florentino
came to the conclusion that his love for Fermina Daza
could be replaced by an "earthly passion"; and all too
happy to oblige him was a certain Widow Nazaret who,
upon first meeting Florentino, threw herself at him
with all the fire and fervor she could muster. From this

experience, Florentino learned that although he was timid and delicate and "dressed like an old man from another time," he possessed the power to make women "yield without conditions, without asking him for anything, without hoping for anything from him except the tranquility of knowing that they had done him a favor."

Shortly after his affair with the widow Nazaret had ended, he moved on to "the abandoned little birds of the night," and then to Ausencia Santender, who was "almost fifty years old and looked it," but loved him with a yearning that was intoxicating.

It was not until he was an old man and had met America Vicuna, that Florentino again fell in love. As a distant relative, he had been appointed guardian of the 14-year-old America, who, owning a passion matching his own, was "ready to learn about life" from the venerable Florentino.

For two years Florentino and America reveled in each other. Then one Sunday their ardor was interrupted by the tolling of the Cathedral bells. When Florentino learned that the bells were ringing because of Dr. Urbino's death, he at once deserted America and dashed to the widow's house. For even the past 50 years of passions had not been able to eradicate the love of his youth. Try as he might, he had never been able to surrender "the throb of longing in his heart" for Fermina Daza.

Now, viewing the remains of his rival stretched out on the bed in the master bedroom of the couple's house, Florentino noted that finally Urbino was "wallowing in the indignity of death." Eagerly he pushed through the throng of mourners to speak to the grief-stricken Fermina.

"Fermina," Florentino cried, "I have waited for this opportunity for more than half a century, to repeat to you once again my vow of eternal fidelity and everlasting love." Caught up both in grief and arrogance, Fermina could barely contain her fury. "Get out of here," she roared. "And don't show your face again for the years of life that are left to you."

Florentino, unfazed, retreated from his beloved. Fermina, for her part, tried to forget the impropriety of this man, who, despite his baldness and his false teeth, looked quite fit for his age. True, she had occasionally thought of him over the years—and sometimes fondly—but she was not a sentimentalist by nature.

Nevertheless, on her first night as a widow, Fermina dreamt not of her dead husband, but of Florentino.

As the days passed, Florentino became more determined than ever to win Fermina's love. Consequently, he began to avoid America and to devote all of his time to agonizing over Dr. Urbino's widow.

To his surprise, three weeks after their confrontation, the love-struck old man received a letter from Fermina. Although her words were inspired by "blind rage," Florentino was delighted, and, in answer, he typed her a letter with a "rational and measured" tone. Fermina then sent a second letter, this time obliquely apologizing for her first note. So it was that Florentino began to write her daily.

Fermina received these letters warmly. When they finally met again, she confessed that he had provided her with "serious and thoughtful" reasons to go on living. They began to see each other frequently, chatting or playing cards, and eventually they decided "to take a pleasure cruise along the river" on one of the boats in the fleet that Florentino now owned.

It was on this journey that Fermina fell in love with Florentino. They did not, however, feel like "belated lovers." Instead—lounging on the river, smoking, sipping anisette, or lying in each other's withered arms—they felt "beyond the pitfalls of passion," as if they had discovered the very "heart of love." During their cruise, Fermina often mourned her husband; and on the same cruise Florentino learned that America had committed suicide. Even in their times of sadness, the grieving lovers held true to one another; such pain only intensified their devotion to one another.

As the voyage neared its end, Florentino and Fermina decided that returning home would "be like dying," and so they resolved to remain afloat on the river. It was their aim to keep "going, going, going"—forever.

Commentary

As *Love in the Time of Cholera* opens, we learn that Jeremiah de Saint Amour has taken his own life. To quell "the torments of memory," the 72-year-old Saint Amour has inhaled "aromatic fumes of gold cyanide" so that he will "never be old." Indeed, that night he had stretched out on his cot and bade his lover, "Remember me with a rose." While they are very minor characters in the novel, Saint Amour and his beloved serve as important points of reference because, clearly, theirs is a love unable to endure the "ravages of time."

In contrast, Dr. Juvenal Urbino and his wife Fermina Daza sustain their love for over 50 years. Theirs never has been a passionate attachment, but rather a relationship based on tolerance and a somewhat grudging respect. In fact, it is only upon her husband's death that Fermina fully realizes how much he loves him.

After the funeral, however, Fermina makes the firm decision to go on with life. Rather than simply endure the ravages of age, she flourishes. It is, of course, Florentino who strengthens her resolve. Through her new companion's patient courtship, she emerges "glorified," "beautified," restored with "the untamed character she had displayed at the age of twenty."

Fermina and Florentino, however, do not attempt to recapture their youthful infatuation; when Florentino regales Fermina on the boat, he is not leading them on a voyage into the past, but instead is propelling them into a more profound, ageless future, "beyond the pitfalls of passion, beyond the brutal mockery of hope and the phantoms of disillusion," and toward a love "more solid the closer it came to death."

This love endures far beyond the attachments of youth—as poor America Vicuna, who dies for love, must finally acknowledge—and revels even in "the sour smell of old age." It is a love engendering a life "that has no limits."

Type of work
Contemporary lyrical novel
Setting
New York City and rural Virginia; mid 1800s to 1926
Principal characters
Violet Trace, a thin and attractive 50-year-old woman
Joe Trace, Violet's handsome husband
Dorcas Manfred, Joe's 18-year-old girlfriend
Alice Manfred, Dorcas's aunt
Felice, Dorcas's best friend

Story overview

There were actually *two* Violets—or so Violet often thought to herself. There was the Violet whom neighbors had begun to call "Violent" after she'd brandished the knife at Dorcas's funeral. Long before the funeral however, *that* Violet, after suffering a series of miscarriages, had tried to steal another woman's baby. Mostly, though, *that* Violet seethed quietly. At night she would tiptoe into the living room to stare at the photograph of Dorcas. It sometimes confused and worried her to think that she might somehow be falling in love with the dead girl, even though she used "brand-new cuss-words" to curse her husband Joe because he loved Dorcas, too.

The *other* Violet slept with a doll, despite the fact that she was 50 years old. Of course, she had once been strong, "a snappy, determined girl and a hardworking young woman, with the snatch-gossip tongue of a beautician"—the trade that she had taught herself. This second Violet, though less dangerous than the first, was also extremely tenacious. Not only had she obtained a spacious uptown apartment near Lenox Avenue "by sitting out the landlord, haunting his doorway," but *this* Violet had also won the love of Joe Trace.

Joe Trace was, in fact, the only thing Violet had ever won. She had met him when she was only 17, back in the days when she was baling hay in Virginia. She remembered how they rode all day in haying time— she and her sisters, and her grandmother True Belle— then "assembled at dawn, ate what was handed out and shared the meadows and the stars with local people who saw no point in going all the way home for five hours sleep."

Despite the hardships, Violet's Grandma True Belle never complained. She had spent her entire life toiling on behalf of other people, first as a slave, then as a laborer, and finally as a surrogate mother to the children of her daughter Rose Dear, who had thrown herself down a well. After Rose Dear's suicide, True Belle had raised her grandchildren, including little Violet, whose mother's death haunted the girl so terribly that it often seemed that "the well sucked [Violet's] sleep."

So it was not surprising that when Joe Trace fell out of a tree one night and landed with a thump on the ground near her sleeping place, Violet "claimed him." The moment she saw him in the moonlight, she determined never to let go of him.

What Violet did not know about Joe Trace was that he, too, was haunted by the ghost of his own lost mother. Raised from infancy by a kindhearted foster family, Joe had grown up without any knowledge of the birth parents who abandoned him. In fact, he had chosen his own last name to commemorate his unknown origins: his father and mother had "disappeared without a trace."

But Joe had finally learned who his mother was when one day on a hunting trip he casually asked one of his companions about the fiercely deranged woman who haunted the woods—"Wild," as she was known among the locals. What would it take "to kill Wild if they happened on her?" Joe wondered coolly. But his companion had lashed out at him, saying, "Now, learn this: she ain't prey…. You know that woman is *somebody's* mother and *somebody* ought to take care." As soon as Joe heard these words he'd realized that Wild was his birth-mother, and from that moment "Wild was always on his mind." The rest of his life was devoted "to hunting her," to killing the dazed mother who lived in the woods, constantly shaming her son: *Whispering into hibiscus stalks and listening to breathing, he suddenly saw himself pawing around in the dirt for a not just crazy woman who happened to be his mother … who orphaned her baby rather than nurse him or coddle him or stay in the house with him. A woman who frightened children, made men sharpen knives, for whom brides left food out (might as well— otherwise she stole it). Leaving traces of her sloven unhousebroken self all over the country.*

Joe became obsessed with Wild. Even after he met Violet, married her, and moved to New York, he could not get his mother out of his mind. Even after he'd peddled Cleopatra beauty products in the city for years, he could still not help wishing "he had never been born."

For a while, after Joe turned 50, it had seemed to him that Dorcas Manfred was a reason to live. At 18, "Dorcas should have been prettier than she was"; but even though she "had all the ingredients … the hair, the color, the shape," there was something about her that "didn't fit." Dorcas seemed as if she wanted men "to do something scary all the time." Joe, however, failed to see that aspect of her; instead, he saw a frightened young girl, a child whom he thought he could take care of. And there was another side to Dorcas that Joe responded to as well: the girl "knew better than people his own age what that inside nothing was like"; Dorcas filled the nothing in him, "just as he filled it for her." So Joe spoiled Dorcas with gifts: phonograph records, silk stockings, Schrafts chocolates and scented water—a liquid "in a blue bottle that smelled like a whore." And Dorcas promptly became Joe's "personal sweet—like candy."

Like Joe, Dorcas had been adopted. Her aunt Alice Manfred had taken Dorcas in after her parents died. But the relationship had been rocky from the start. Alice had always been worried about the little girl who "went to two funerals in five days and never said a word." Her father had been "stomped to death" during a race-riot and her mother had subsequently been "burnt alive." When Dorcas finally broke down and told Joe Trace about her mother's tragic death, she cried in his arms. At such times, Joe would tell Dorcas things he never would have thought of telling his wife, things such as how he longed to find his mother in the woods, how he wanted to see her "give him a sign, her hand thrust through the leaves, [which] would be enough to say that she knew him to be the one, the son she had ... and ran away from, but not too far."

Given his attachment to Dorcas, it stunned everyone—especially Joe himself—when he ended her life. After telling him one day that she'd grown tired of him, that he made her "sick," that if he ever "brought her another bottle of cologne" she would "drink it and die," Dorcas walked out of the room, got on a streetcar and took up with another man—younger, "tireless and a little cruel." Her new boyfriend never gave "her a present or even thought about it," but she was happier with him than she had been any time before.

Joe was staggered. He could not believe that she would leave him—abandon him—as his mother once had. Hearing one evening that Dorcas was attending a party, Joe went there, hoping to find her sitting there sad and all alone. Instead, there she was, smiling and dancing in the arms of her new beau. Overcome by pain, Joe raised his gun, took aim, and squeezed the trigger. Because no one in the crowded room was certain just who had killed the girl, Joe was never arrested.

But Violet knew. For a few days she waited, wondering when her husband would come home again. Then, finally, on the day of the funeral, she recalled the knife she used to clean the parrot's beak and claws. Snatching it up, Violet rushed out of her apartment and down the street to the church, pushed through the mourners at the funeral, and slashed "the girl's haughty secret face," just as they were preparing to close the casket.

Horrified, the boys and men in the gathering tackled the kicking and growling Violet and threw her out onto the street. The frenzied woman then turned and ran home. As soon as she reached her apartment, she opened the doors to all her caged birds "and set them out the windows to freeze or fly, including the parrot that said, 'I love you.'"

Following Dorcas's death, time seemed to almost stand still for Violet. Joe finally returned home, but in their apartment "a poisoned silence floated through the rooms" as, for each, the memory of the deceased girl persisted. Grief-stricken over what he had done, Joe became sluggish, while Violet grew more and more obsessed with discovering everything she could about her dead rival. Persistently, Violet called on Dorcas's Aunt Alice. And gradually softening to the strange, sad

woman who had carved up the face of her niece, Alice finally forgave and befriended her. Eventually Alice even gave Violet a picture of Dorcas.

At night, Joe and Violet frequently tiptoed into the living room to stare at the photograph, which Violet had gently placed on the mantle. "Dorcas? Dorcas," they would take turns saying.

One day Dorcas's friend Felice unexpectedly showed up on their doorstep. The girl had been at the party on the night when Dorcas was murdered. In fact, she had phoned for an ambulance—an ambulance that hadn't arrived until the next morning, Felice explained, "because it was colored people calling it." If the ambulance had arrived that night, Dorcas, who was slowly bleeding to death, would probably have lived.

After Felice's visit, the Traces's lives took a turn for the better. Joe found a new job at a nearby speakeasy called "Paydirt," while Violet cooked for him and tended to the new bird she'd bought. Now they would often crawl into bed after dinner and Joe would take Violet's hand and "put it on his cheek, his stomach." And Violet would rest her hand there contentedly, as though on "the sunlit rim of a well."

Commentary

Toni Morrison, born in 1931, is the first woman and the first African-American writer to have won both the Pulitzer and Nobel Prizes. Since the publication of her first novel *The Bluest Eye* in 1970, she has captivated readers with her lyrical prose and unforgettable characters, characters who often have been violently uprooted from their families and who spend their lives searching for lost mothers, for the nurturing and security they have never known.

In *Jazz*, as in her earlier works, Morrison powerfully evokes a well-honed sense of Black history for her readers. For her, history achieves its greatest impact when viewed through the filter of individual experience—through "the interior life of ... a small group of people" who give voice to the collective sufferings of a race. Within this historical context, her characters live, struggle, and ultimately achieve grace.

Time, in Morrison's novels, is cyclical; it is mythical, sacred, a sort of time that defies contemporary notions of progress and linear development. Indeed, Morrison's characters find the strength to survive only insofar as they can integrate their own experiences with those of the past. *Jazz* shifts back and forth between rural, Antebellum Virginia and New York City, shortly after the Armistice. Furthermore, she allows the events of the novel to unfold from the point of view of various characters—including an enigmatic narrator, a strangely insistent anonymous "I" who leads us into the novel's harmonic idioms and compelling rhythms so reminiscent of musical jazz. It is through this anonymous narrator that we gain profound respect for Joe, Violet, and Dorcas. Whatever their transgressions, the narrator reminds us that there is always a hidden reason that must be explored, a context, a complex "state of mind" that must be understood.

SEIZE THE DAY
by Saul Bellow, Viking Press, 1956

Type of work
Psychological novel

Setting
New York City; 1950s

Principal characters
Wilhelm Adler, an emotionally ravaged young man
Dr. Adler, Wilhelm's perfectionist father
Margaret, Wilhelm's ex-wife
Olive, his girlfriend

Saul Bellow's *Seize the Day* chronicles one day in the life of "Tommy" Wilhelm Adler—a day which captures the whole agony of a man's descent into emotional and financial ruin. Though he is already well into middle age when we meet him, Wilhelm is still not free to accept responsibility for his life; forever frozen into his early role as the family failure, he behaves as a helpless, forsaken child, flailing and howling as he slides down into hell.

"I expect help!" wails Wilhelm. But his cries are left unanswered; help is not forthcoming; no kind, wise parent appears to rescue the doomed spiritual orphan. Release and "help" are at last attained only through his own symbolic "death."

As the book's introduction conveys, Wilhelm's "search to affirm his own humanity not only moves the reader through deep pity, but arouses an identification with that search as expressive of what everyone who would come to terms with himself must undergo." At the same time, Bellow raises some probing questions for each of us: Just how much and what kinds of financial, emotional or spiritual support do parents and children owe to one another? And to what extent does a man's monetary worth determine his inner value?

Story overview

Emotional brutality had marked the 40-odd-year relationship between Wilhelm Adler and his father, "Doctor" Adler, the respected diagnostician. Fastidious in both dress and manners, Doctor Adler had a face marked by "a wholesome reddish and almost translucent color, like a ripe apricot. The wrinkles beside his ears were carved deep because the skin conformed so tightly to his bones. With all his might, he was a healthy and fine small old man." The doctor had little tolerance for his son's slothful ways, and, even long years after Wilhelm had reached adulthood, he treated him as if he were a spoiled, messy child. The fact that Doctor Adler insisted upon calling Wilhelm by his childhood nickname, "Wilky," typified the father's domination over his son. In fact, whenever he found himself trapped in his father's presence, "Wilky" actually reverted to markedly childlike behavior, stammering and fidgeting uncontrollably.

It was characteristic of Dr. Adler to judge a man on the size of his bank account. As a matter of pride, he often lied to friends about Wilhelm's earnings, pretending that his son—who had recently been laid off from his latest job with a toy manufacturer—was a successful businessman.

Wilhelm's pleas to his father for financial relief, however, were met only with formulated homilies from the doctor's well-rehearsed litany: "There's a poor man with a bone condition which is gradually breaking him up.... I've learned to keep my sympathy for the real ailments."

That Wilhelm was also "gradually breaking up," not from any physical disease but from a progressive state of financial and spiritual decay, was a reality which his father refused to apprehend. To him, only money and medicine—the two palpably useful commodities that he knew and respected—were real. Doctor Adler's only recommendation was that his son undertake hydrotherapy or muscle massage.

And now, as Wilhelm confronted his father with a last desperate plea for money, the doctor's disgust erupted into an irrevocable dismissal: "Go away from me now, it's torture for me to look at you, you slob!... You want to make yourself into my cross. But I am not going to pick up a cross. I'll see you dead ... before I let you do that to me."

Wilhelm's estranged wife Margaret also had dismissed him from her conscience. She refused to give him the divorce he asked for, yet still insisted that he "agree to support her and the two children"—despite the fact that he was nearly bankrupt. In addition, she held him solely responsible for everything that had gone wrong with his life: for his unemployment, his impotence, and their family breakup. When he begged for mercy, her reply was immediate and brutal: "How did you imagine it was going to be, big shot? Everything made smooth for you?"

Margaret had even denied Wilhelm the companionship of the family dog. "Four years ago when we broke up I gave her everything—goods, furniture, savings," he remembered bitterly. "I tried to show good will, but I didn't get anywhere. Why when I wanted Scissors ... she absolutely refused. Not that she cared a damn about the animal ... "

Margaret's unyielding, unsympathetic spite had spilled over to contaminate Wilhelm's new attachments, too. After his separation, he had fallen madly in love with a girl named Olive who promised to marry him "once he was divorced"—but Margaret would not let him go. Now his romance with Olive had begun to crumble. "When she would get up late on Sunday morning she would wake him almost in tears at being late for Mass. He would try to help her hitch her garters and smooth out her slip and dress and even put on her hat with shaky hands…. She got out a block from church to avoid gossip… "

Perhaps Wilhelm's pain had really begun as a teen, with the death of his mother. He was, after all, his mother's son; it was from her that he had inherited "sensitive feelings, a soft heart, a brooding nature, a tendency to be confused under pressure." The doctor's mistreatment of both his wife and son had also made them equal partners in sorrow; they shared the iron bonds of the mutually oppressed. "You were set free when Ma died," Wilhelm once accused his father. "You wanted to forget her… "

Though other authority figures in his life had generally ignored him, Wilhelm could recall that his mother had cared enough at least to attempt once to dissuade him from what she considered a "foolish" course of action. On the day he had announced his decision to become an actor, Doctor Adler, ashamed of his son, had literally turned his back on Wilhelm. "Mama was the one who tried to stop me," Wilhelm recalled, pondering the incident, "and we carried on and yelled and pleaded…. Poor Mother! How I disappointed her."

Declining his mother's appeal that he go into medicine with his father, Wilhelm had moved to Hollywood anyway and taken on the name "Tommy Wilhelm"—dropping the searing "Adler." And he had actually been hired a few times, though only as an "extra." (Dr. Adler had often tried to explain his son's new name: "I uphold tradition. He's for the new.")

But "Tommy" had left Hollywood when his alleged "agent" finally shared with him the fact that he was wasting his time trying to be an actor; and since then, his forays into various business ventures had all somehow led into shadowy dead ends. Finally, desperate to earn his father's approval and to meet the support payments demanded by his wife, Wilhelm had invested his last seven hundred dollars in lard futures. His investment partner, Dr. Tamkin, a self-proclaimed psychologist with the mesmerizing gift of persuasion, had promised him huge returns. "I am at my most efficient," Tamkin had boasted with customary exuberance, "when I don't need the fee. When I only love … The spiritual compensation is what I look for. Bringing people into … the real universe. That's the present moment. The past is no good to us. The future is full of anxiety. Only the present is real—the here and now. Seize the day."

But Wilhelm's association with Dr. Tamkin had proved only one in a long line of disastrous attempts to find nurturance—to be loved and watched over by a sympathetic parent. Once again he had placed his trust—not to mention his money and his fragile psyche—in the wrong hands. Tamkin had claimed that the "whole secret to this type of speculation is in the alertness. You

have to act fast—buy it and sell it: sell it and buy it again…. Get to the window and have them wire Chicago at just the right second." Yet when the time came to sell, Tamkin had dawdled—and the golden moment was lost. And then, predictably, the wizard had disappeared, leaving his raving, almost lunatic disciple to search for him in the streets.

"What a creature Tamkin was when he took off his hat!" Wilhelm now marveled in despair. "The indirect light showed the many complexities of his bald skull, his gull's nose, his rather handsome eyebrows, his vain mustache, his deceiver's brown eyes."

In the end, even God the Father had seemed to fail Wilhelm. His petitions to heaven all went unheard or ignored. "Oh, God," he prayed. "Let me out of my trouble. Let me out of my thoughts. For all the time I have wasted I am very sorry. Let me out of this clutch and into a different life. For I am all balled up… " But God did not release Wilhelm from his weighty burden of selfhood. No, "the spirit, the peculiar burden of his existence lay upon him like an accretion, a load, a hump. In any moment of quiet when sheer fatigue prevented him from struggling, he was apt to feel this mysterious weight, this growth or collection of nameless things which it was the business of his life to carry about."

Now jobless and destitute, abandoned by every being whose love he had craved and solicited, Tommy Wilhelm Adler realized that his only hope for relief lay in death. Wandering randomly into the funeral service of a stranger, he gazed enviously down at the figure in the coffin. "The dead man … had two large waves of gray hair at the front. But he was not old. His face was long and he had a bony nose, slightly, delicately twisted. His brows were raised as though he had sunk into the final thought. Now at last he was [at] the end of all distractions…. And by his meditative look Wilhelm was so struck that he could not go away."

Then the funeral music started up, and Wilhelm's moment of epiphany swelled into being. "The flowers and lights fused ecstatically in [his] blind, wet eyes; the heavy sea-like music came to his ears. It poured into him where he had hidden himself in the center of a crowd by the great and happy oblivion of tears. He heard it and sank deeper than sorrow, through torn sobs and cries toward the consummation of his heart's ultimate need." Jolted out of his lonely, vulnerable trajectory into another, more peaceful orbit, he had experienced a catharsis, an annihilation of his faltering former self and an acceptance of himself as a lone, free creature. In a single climactic moment of rebirth, Wilhelm Adler had at last come to terms with his own humanity; at once he found himself resurrected, strengthened, serene, intact, whole.

THE SHORT STORIES OF JOHN CHEEVER
Taken from *The Short Stories of John Cheever*, Alfred A. Knopf, 1978

A writer for most of his 70 years, John Cheever (1912–1982) was insatiably fascinated by the dynamics of human relationships and the unique responses of ordinary individuals to the shifting entanglements of life. The following three stories, originally published in magazines as part of a series, illustrate in part the breadth of his interest and style.

THE BROTHERS

When Tom was 17 and his brother Kenneth was 20, their parents had finally ended their bitter, hate-filled marriage. Now, four years later, the brothers still turned primarily to each other for love and support, and did most of their socializing together. Among their joint acquaintances was a vivacious matron named Amy, who, in a gesture of maternal warmth, extended a standing invitation for the brothers to visit her and her adolescent daughter Jane at their New England farm.

Late one Saturday afternoon the brothers arrived at the farmhouse. Amy greeted them happily and made small talk while they waited for Jane to return from riding her mare. Just in time for dinner, Jane finally came in—and immediately began to flirt with Kenneth. But the older boy seemed to be totally indifferent to her, preferring to converse with Tom instead. Tom, noticing that Jane was stung by the rejection, wondered what, if anything, he should do.

That night after dinner the young people went for a drive. When they returned, Tom dropped Jane and Kenneth at the door while he parked the car in the barn. A minute later when he entered the house, he found the pair chatting on the couch, and silently crept upstairs to bed. Kenneth ignored Jane's gentle urging to stay and get better acquainted, instead, following his brother up the staircase.

Kenneth came into the bedroom, happily chattering on and on about the brothers' upcoming trip to Canada. Sensing the excitement in his brother's voice as he spoke of the skiing and fishing they would do, Tom said nothing, although he felt somewhat concerned. "It was the first time it had occurred to [him] that their devotion to each other might be stronger than their love of any girl, or even than their love of the world."

The next morning Tom awoke early and rowed a dinghy far up the Merrimack River, hoping to force Kenneth to pay some attention to Jane. But it was not to be: he found Kenneth waiting for him at the landing when he returned. Later that afternoon, Kenneth pried himself into a conversation with Tom about cars and barely acknowledged Jane's presence. She was seething with jealousy, but tried one last time to gain the older brother's attention. "Want to go for a walk with me, Kenneth?" she asked. Kenneth merely turned to Tom and asked if he wanted to join them. When Tom said no, Kenneth also declined. Jane, fed up, disappeared into the barn; she did not return until after nightfall,

when the brothers had started back to the city.

Tom now knew he had to go away—not only for Kenneth's sake but for his own. On the night after their return from the farm, he caught a bus to New York City, claiming that he had to find work. Eventually, when Kenneth realized why Tom had left, he decided to return to Amy's farm the next weekend. But now Jane showed no interest in him whatsoever. Kenneth wandered pensively into the cornfields. He and his brother, he mused, "had tried to give their lives some meaning and order, and for love of the same world that had driven them together, they had to separate. He walked through the fields clutching involuntarily at the air, as if something were slipping from his grasp, and searching and looking around him like a stranger at the new, strange, vivid world."

THE BELLA LINGUA

Wilson Streeter, an American expatriate living in Rome, was struggling to learn Italian. His "sense of being an outsider would change, he thought, when he knew the language." His teacher was Kate Dresser, another American expatriate. The death of her husband, an officer with the foreign service, had left her with an adolescent son, Charlie, to support. By teaching Italian, doing translations and dubbing English dialogue into old Italian movies, she was able to eke out a living without help from their relatives in Krasbie, Iowa.

Wilson met with Kate on Tuesdays, Fridays and Sundays, and began to move quickly through the language's nuances. After he finished studying the classic *Pinocchio*, he started on *I Promessi Sposi*, and planned to finish up the course with Dante's *Divine Comedy*.

One day Wilson's teacher asked him to come by on Thursday to do her an unspecified favor. Not until he arrived did Kate explain: "My father's brother—my Uncle George—is coming, to try and take Charlie home. I don't know what to do. I don't know what I can do. But I would appreciate it if there was a man here."

Wilson had known that there was tension between Charlie and his mother; now he understood why. Kate had easily embraced her adopted culture, while Charlie had done everything he could to preserve his identity as an American. He dressed in jeans and a leather jacket, and refused to learn Italian. Uncle George's arrival was sure to change the balance of power between them and give Charlie the upper hand. Kate wanted moral support from another expatriate. Good enough; he would help her out.

Uncle George's trip to Rome via Naples had done nothing to give him a positive impression of Italy. To celebrate his first vacation in 43 years, he had signed up for one of those ill-conceived bus tours favored by blue-haired old women wearing costume jewelry. Lamentably, few of the natives had shown him the courtesy of speaking English. Then in some small nameless town, thieves had overpowered him and stolen his wallet. Not surprisingly, when Uncle George's bus finally pulled into Rome, he found it to be a rather ugly city, filled with "trolley cars and cut-rate furniture stores and torn-up streets and the sort of apartment houses that nobody ever really wants to live in."

When Wilson arrived at Kate's *sala* at seven, Uncle George had not yet appeared. As usual, Charlie showed up in his customary "American uniform"—tight jeans with upturned cuffs, pink shirt and loafers—and went on incessantly about baseball.

When at last Uncle George appeared at the door, he looked at Wilson and asked hopefully, "Speaka da English?" Wilson answered dryly, "I'm an American"—whereupon Uncle George launched into a diatribe on Italian culture: "All I see is statues of men without any clothes on … " Soon turning to his niece, he cut straight to the point: "The boat sails on Saturday, Katie, and I want you and the boy to come home with me." A heated discussion followed, which did nothing but reconfirm that while Charlie wanted to go with him, Kate insisted on staying in Italy. She countermanded each of Uncle George's arguments, replying, "No nice friends, no kitchen, no garden, no shower bath or anything else will keep me from wanting to see the world and the different people who live in it." Softly, she added, "You'll miss Italy, Charlie." The embrace between mother and son was one of goodbye.

At Wilson's next Italian lesson, he noticed that Kate's apartment seemed bigger somehow; he rightly concluded that Charlie and his gear were gone. At the end of the lesson Kate made no mention of her son nor of Uncle George; she simply complimented Wilson on his progress and reminded him to buy a copy of *Divine Comedy* for the next week.

THE WORLD OF APPLES

As a Bascomb, aging American poet laureate, wandered through his villa in Monte Carbone, Italy, swatting flies and ruminating over the fact that he had not yet received the Nobel Prize. The flies notwithstanding, Asa preferred Italy to the States. On Fifth Avenue in New York, strangers were continually stopping him for autographs; in Italy he could lead a quieter, more peaceful existence and write without interruption.

But Asa was perturbed by something else now: his dreams had become blatantly obscene. Earlier in the spring he'd accidentally stumbled upon a couple making romantic overtures in the woods above his home. When he returned to work, the sight of the couple dominated his thoughts—and his mental images of their ecstasy were obstructing his creative energies.

As time passed, he found himself producing work that was increasingly banal and mediocre, such as the ballad of "The Fart That Saved Athens"—which he crumpled up and burned in the stove. The next morning he could come up with nothing better than a lurid tale which he called "The Confessions of a Public School Headmaster." To top things off, that same afternoon 14 students from the University of Rome appeared at his villa and, in a chorus of adulation, began chanting "The Orchards of Heaven," the opening sonnet from his latest book *The World of Apples*. Asa was embarrassed by the praise, especially when he thought of his morning's work on the sala-cious adventures of the schoolmaster.

Inexplicably, the hapless laureate now seemed fixated in the course of a pornographer. In ten days he wrote the most ribald stories: "The Confessions of a Lady's Maid," "The Baseball Player's Honeymoon," "A Night in the Park," and some 60 dirty limericks, all of which he burned. A trip to Rome even failed to clear his head. He returned to his villa only seeking to take comfort in the works of Petronius and Juvenal, so full of bawdy merriment. But then, those poets were classicists; their works did not inspire the guilt that writing his own poems did.

Ultimately, Asa grew desperate. In a penitent mood, he climbed to the church at the top of Monte Giordano to offer such prayers as he knew. "God bless Walt Whitman. God bless Hart Crane," he prayed, hoping this would invoke his muses. "God bless Dylan Thomas. God bless William Faulkner, Scott Fitzgerald, and especially Ernest Hemingway." When daylight faded, he spent the night at a nearby inn.

The next morning Asa walked down from Monte Giordano past a mountain pool. There he discreetly watched as an old man undressed, bathed in the cold mountain water and innocently played in the small waterfall that fed the pool. After his bath, the old man dressed and left, and Asa, too, felt cleansed somehow. He remembered a similar incident involving his own father that had occurred when he was child. Now in a rite of emulation he stepped, naked, into the torrent of water, and bellowed the way his father had. And "when he stepped away from the water he seemed at last to be himself."

Asa returned triumphant to Monte Carbone. *In the morning he began a long poem on the inalienable dignity of light and air that, while it would not get him the Nobel Prize, would grace the last months of his life.*

Commentary

John Cheever is considered a virtuoso of characterization. The people in his stories are a unique blend of individual glory and idiosyncrasy: an old writer purges himself of his vices through a self-styled rite of self-baptism; a woman decides to move on with her life and away from her American roots, even at the price of losing her son; two grown brothers cling to one another at the expense of their individuality—until they must part to grow any further.

Many of Cheever's characters feel a compelling need for rebirth. The innate desire human beings have for some sort of cleansing or baptism is universal. He uses a variety of devices to symbolize his characters' personal awakenings—and perhaps, vicariously, our own.

Type of work
Modern detective fiction

Setting
Present-day Los Angeles, California

Principal characters

Lieutenant Peter Smith, Special Services Division police
detective and liaison with the Los Angeles Japanese
community

John Conner, a Special Services detective on indefinite
leave

Eddie Sakamura, a wealthy Japanese playboy

U.S. Senator John Morton, a powerful player in Japanese
trade

Mr. Ishigura, a respected Japanese businessman

Story overview

Lieutenant Peter Smith received a call informing
him that there had been a murder at the grand
opening of Nakamoto Towers. Now the Japanese
hosts were demanding a Special Services liaison officer
at the crime scene. On his way, Smith picked up Captain
John Conner, who spoke fluent Japanese and was one of
the most knowledgeable men in the division.

Upon their arrival a Mr. Ishigura stepped forward.
After introductions, he said, "The only reason there's a
problem here tonight is that your colleague is unreasonable." Apparently an imprudent agent named Graham
had threatened to interrogate everyone at the reception
regarding the murder—including highly influential U.S.
senators and a number of celebrities. At best, Graham
was "a pain in the ass," and it was generally known he
had no liking for the Japanese.

As they approached the crime scene on the 46th
floor, Smith and Conner noticed that a Japanese was
standing behind the yellow tape, taking photographs.
The man was part of the corporation's security staff, Mr.
Ishigura explained.

They learned that the strangled woman, Cheryl
Lynn Austin, 23, was a known party girl, having been
seen with some of the city's highest rollers. Next, the
detectives met with the building's security guard. They
wanted to view the security video tapes for the 46th
floor. The man told them he had come on duty after the
murder took place, and that the guard he was to relieve
was nowhere in sight. Instead, he found a Japanese man
in his office. It soon became evident that this fellow had
removed one of the security tapes.

The following morning Smith and Conner found
the other security guard sitting in a bar. He told them
that he had left his shift early the night before after his
supervisor had replaced him. His supervisor? "Japanese
... New guy.... Never seen him before." When the
agents stood to leave, the guard said, "I'll write down my
phone number for you," and scribbled something on a
napkin. When they got in the car, Conner handed his
partner the napkin, which bore a message in block
letters: THEY STOLE THE TAPES.

The next day, acting on a hunch, Smith and Conner

visited the TV station that had covered the Nakamoto
opening. They viewed the tapes of the celebration and
saw Cheryl Lynn "laughing with Eddie Sakamura....
But from time to time, her eyes flicked away [as] if she
was waiting ... for someone to arrive ... " When
Sakamura "became aware that he did not have her full
attention," he pulled her roughly to him. Then someone
stepped in front of the camera and they were lost in the
crowd.

Smith and Conner drove to a Beverly Hills club that
Eddie Sakamura often frequented, but were told that he
was attending a party at a house in the hills. As the
detectives approached the house, a large man appeared
at the front door. After showing their badges and asking
to speak with Eddie, they stepped inside and immediately spotted both Eddie and Senator John Morton, a
powerful framer of Japanese trade.

A guard confronted the pair; unless they had a
search warrant, he told them, they would have to leave.
"Mr. Sakamura is a friend of mine," Conner insisted.
Now the guard moved toward him threateningly, but
Conner quickly pinned the man to the floor.

At the disturbance, Eddie Sakamura ambled over
and agreed to answer questions about Cheryl's murder.
He coolly denied that he'd been with Cheryl that night
or that he had taken the tapes, though the guard had
said the man who took the tapes had a burn mark on his
hand, exactly like the one on Eddie's.

After leaving the club, the detectives headed to the
morgue, where the medical examiner described the
peculiarities of the woman's wounds, and concluded, "I
don't think there's any question: we're looking at a case
of sexual asphyxia." Just then Conner received a telephone call: Mr. Ishigura of Nakamoto Corporation had
delivered a box of video tapes to police headquarters. At
last, it seemed, Ishigura was cooperating in the investigation.

When the detectives examined the tapes showing
the murder scene, Conner found a spot where Eddie
Sakamura's face appeared reflected in a mirror. They
gathered up the tapes and left.

Smith dropped Conner off at his home and was
headed to his own apartment when the car phone rang.
It was agent Graham; he was outside Eddie Sakamura's
home with a warrant for Sakamura's arrest, and wanted
Smith's help with the bust. For once, Graham was doing
things by the book.

When Smith joined him, the two detectives went to
the door and kicked it open. Behind two shrieking party
girls, both men suddenly spied a "dark figure running
down the stairs." By the time they had dashed back
outside, Eddie's Ferrari was already speeding away, a
police backup unit in hot pursuit. "I got to the concrete
embankment about thirty seconds after the Ferrari hit it
flat out at a hundred and sixty kilometers an hour,"
Smith later reported. Upon impact the gas tank
exploded and flames shot into the sky, leaving the car
nothing more than a smoldering hulk of metal.

The following morning, dispatch sent Smith two intriguing messages. Eddie had called at 1:42 a.m. with urgent news about the missing tape, followed by a call from the assistant chief of police—which left him very nervous because, unless there was a problem, Jim Olson never called before ten in the morning.

"Looks like we got ourselves a rattlesnake by the tail," Olsen told Smith when he returned the call. " … Last night was a prime screwup … nobody got the names of the girls…. They're cutting Sakamura's body out of the wreck this morning to ship what's left to the morgue." The chief, assuming that the videotapes proved that Sakamura had killed the girl, was closing the investigation.

Smith hurried to the lab to make copies of the tapes—before anything happened to them. Along with a technician there, Theresa Asakuma, Smith scrutinized the tapes and found that some of them depicted the murder quite plainly, though the murderer's face was still obscured. Theresa volunteered to study them for more clues. Smith and Conner then went to see Senator Morton—who had seemed abnormally interested in knowing whether or not the investigation was formally wrapped up.

When the detectives returned to the lab, Theresa informed them that the tapes had been doctored. "The shadows don't match," she reflected. "They're in the wrong place … " Then Smith and Connor remembered the man they had found taking pictures at the murder scene. "Do you remember how he moved?" Conner asked excitedly. Yes, there had been something odd about him. "He never turned around," Smith answered. "He backed up all the way…. He was repeating the walk of the girl and the killer in reverse, so … he would have a good record of where the shadows in the room were."

Conner left, but Theresa and Smith continued to examine the altered tapes. "There," she suddenly exclaimed. "They forgot to erase that one." And, sure enough, peering at the monitor, Smith could make out the indistinct image of a third man—not the man who had been involved with, and murdered, Cheryl, but another. At last, after many more hours of video enhancement, they could clearly make out the face of this other man: Eddie Sakamura.

The tapes had definitely been tampered with. Using clever imaging techniques, there they could see, super-imposed on the tape, a reflected image of what appeared to be Eddie Sakamura. Theresa kept working to generate more detail. Then suddenly they saw the face of the real murderer. They were stunned into silence as they recognized the smiling countenance of Senator John Morton. After snapping a Polaroid photo of the screen, Smith left to find Conner.

The detectives tracked down Morton. They found him preparing to appear in a commercial about how America was losing its economic competitiveness to foreigners. "I have nothing to say to you gentlemen," Morton grunted. But when Conner told him that he had a videotape that revealed the real identity of Cheryl Austin's killer, Morton began pacing the room. He sidled toward the window and looked down on the sound-stage, where he saw a familiar figure. It was Eddie Sakamura—alive! Just at that moment the phone rang. It was Theresa Asakuma; she had uncovered another flaw on one of the last tapes.

During the few minutes Smith was on the phone, the senator disappeared upstairs. Conner raced after him, but caught up with him too late: Morton had already jammed the barrel of a gun in his mouth and pulled the trigger.

The detectives reported the suicide and stayed on the scene until police officials arrived. Then they had something else to worry about. "That damn Eddie," Conner grumbled. " … Didn't you notice how he acted around Ishigura? He was too confident…. He should have been frightened and he wasn't." Racing to Eddie's home, they found his body floating face down in the swimming pool.

The next morning both detectives met with Theresa, who said she had something to show them on the tapes. In one sequence the men saw Cheryl's body lying motionless on the conference table; but although the tape was rolling, nothing was happening. Then Theresa began to describe the next scene as they watched it. "It was a static scene. And then I saw, clearly, the girl's leg twitch … Now the girl's arm … The fingers closed and opened." At that point in time, Cheryl was still alive.

"Now watch the clock," Theresa said, pointing at a spot on the tape. It said 8:36. The tape ran for two more minutes, but the clock, frozen at 8:36, never moved. Smith then produced a tape he had found—one presumably left by Eddie Sakamura—in his apartment the night before. There, "in crisp black and white … they saw Morton leave the girl behind on the table." Then the figure of another man appeared, cautiously entering the room. "It was Ishigura," Smith said aloud; it was he who had actually done the killing in hopes of fingering the senator. Ishigura was seeing to it that Morton would pay for his threats to back down on several important trade agreements. There was Ishigura, cool as can be: "very deliberately, he walked to the edge of the table, placed his hands on the girl's neck and strangled her."

Rushing to Nakamoto Towers, Smith and Conner found Ishigura in a meeting. All at once a young Japanese aide passed into the conference room, approached a distinguished-looking gray-haired man, and whispered something to him. The older gentleman stood and slowly left the room; one by one, the others followed. After some time Smith and Conner entered the room. "Mr. Ishigura," Conner said, "would you please stand?" The man didn't move. "Show them the tape," Conner said. Peter played the tape, which showed Ishigura strangling the girl. "When you are through with your charade, you will find me outside," Ishigura said indignantly. Then he stood, left the room, and walked out onto the terrace.

By the time the tape had ended, the terrace was empty. From the railing, the detectives saw that Ishigura had landed in freshly-poured concrete. In the distance, sirens wailed, echoing through the streets.

THE HUNT FOR RED OCTOBER
by Tom Clancy, Naval Institute Press, 1984

Type of work
Military suspense fiction

Setting
The United States, the Soviet Union, and aboard the Soviet submarine Red October; 1980s

Principal characters
Marko Ramius, Captain First Rank of the
    Red October
Jack Ryan, agent of the Central Intelligence Agency
James Greer, Ryan's superior
"Judge" Moore, Director of the Central Intelligence Agency
Ronald Jones, U.S. Navy sonar technician

STORY OVERVIEW

When *Red October*, the most powerful nuclear submarine ever produced by the Soviet Union, plunged deep into the sea on December 3, only Captain Marko Ramius knew that this would be her final voyage. Rather than keep his scheduled rendezvous with a group of attack subs and battleships of the Soviet fleet, Ramius intended to defect to the Americans, making the *Red October* his personal weapon of vengeance against the motherland.

Before setting out, the captain mailed a letter announcing his defection; the news would reach the high levels of Soviet government only after he had made his move. Of course it would only be a matter of time before the Soviet fleet would be dispatched to sink or expropriate his vessel and to execute him as an enemy of the state. But Ramius had great confidence in his own abilities and felt sure that he could escape detection.

Even as Ramius's scheme was being played out in the Atlantic, Jack Ryan, a mid-level analyst for the Central Intelligence Agency, sensed something unusual afoot. Called back to Washington from his post in London, where he had been given a set of classified documents obtained by the British Secret Service, Ryan began to unravel the mystery of *Red October*.

Arriving in the Washington office of his boss, James Greer, Ryan and his superior examined photos of the submarine and speculated about the reasons for the two large doors in its fore and aft sections. Having obtained proper clearance, Ryan took the photos to a friend, Skip Tyler of the Naval Academy. Tyler advised Ryan that the doors probably indicated a tunnel drive, a propulsion system the U.S. Navy had once tried and then abandoned as unworkable. Tyler noted that the jet-like action of a tunnel drive greatly reduced noise and that if *Red October* boasted such a system, the sub would be able to travel virtually undetected.

As Ryan gathered intelligence, the *USS Dallas*, an American sub in the North Atlantic, was routinely monitoring Soviet submarines. Ronald Jones, a top-notch sonar technician, sat at his station in his usual trance-like pose. All at once there came over his earphones a short rumbling noise, but computer analysis attributed the "funny signal" to mere magma displacement. Jones felt uneasy with that analysis and asked his superior officer to inform the Captain.

"You against the machine again?" the captain complained good-naturedly. Jones was still struck by the easy informality of his commanding officer, even after three years on nuclear subs.

"Skipper," Jones replied, "the computer works pretty well most of the time, but sometimes it's a real kludge.... For one thing, the frequency is all wrong." Jones couldn't really say what the signal meant: "I don't know, Captain. It isn't screw sounds, and it isn't any naturally produced sound that I've heard. Beyond that ... "

"Well, keep at it," the commander advised. "No sense letting all this expensive gear go to waste."

Back in Washington, CIA Director "Judge" Moore summoned Greer and Ryan to his office. Moore, whose nickname "Judge" derived from his years as a federal magistrate, had received a communique from "CARDINAL," a well-placed CIA mole working in the Soviet hierarchy. The message revealed the reason for a recent surge in Soviet naval activity: one of the USSR's most state-of-the-art nuclear subs was missing. All available Soviet ships had been put on alert to retrieve her at any cost, lest she sink—or, worse, fall into American imperialist hands.

The Soviets knew the Americans would immediately detect their massive naval force, steaming for U.S. shores. It seemed to give the impression of an all-out invasion aimed directly at the United States—if it were not for the obvious flaws of such a transparent strategy and the lack of accompanying air power.

Because he had done his homework on Ramius, Jack Ryan was able to guess the true motive for the massive enemy fleet action: the Soviet captain intended to defect—and now the Soviet Union knew it too. Ramius, Ryan had learned, was disillusioned with the Soviet government and sought revenge for two reasons: first, for his wife's death at the hands of an incompetent Red Army physician; second, for years of oppression by the Communist Party that he had come to view as abusive and ridiculous. Ramius wanted Party apparatchiks to pay for their abuses with the loss of *Red October*.

Ryan felt that the facts supported his hypothesis—unless CARDINAL's story was misinformation aimed at duping or misdirecting the CIA. Even though such a possibility was real, Judge Moore instructed Ryan to brief the President and Joint Chiefs of Staff about his theory and to investigate the accuracy of CARDINAL's story through independent sources.

Meantime, aboard the *Red October*, Ramius was maintaining radio silence—supposedly to avoid being detected by the Americans; the ruse worked, as most of his crew became convinced of the secrecy of their mission. In fact, he had first secretly killed the Zampolit, or political officer, who posed a threat to the defection, and convinced the enlisted men that the officer had died in an unfortunate accident. Next he had consulted with his fellow officers, who intended to defect with him. Little did Ramius and the *Red October* officers realize that sonarman Jones had succeeded in tracking their vessel and that the Americans were now entirely aware of their intention to defect.

Ramius and his officers plotted their strategy: when Red October neared American shores, the officers would create a fake radiation leak in order to distract the crew. By creating this feeling of imminent danger, they would then prepare the crew to evacuate the sub, voluntarily putting themselves into American hands.

For Jack Ryan, meanwhile, events were moving very quickly—perhaps too quickly. He was sent to the *HMS Invincible*, a British ship in the North Atlantic, with orders to have the battleship assist in defusing a possible Soviet threat. The battleship was to make contact with *Red October* and ascertain Ramius's intention to defect. If a defection was verified, the British ship was to evacuate the crew from the sub, then transfer them first to the United States then back to the Soviet Union. The *Pigeon*, another British ship in the *Invincible*'s battle group, was to protect the *Red October* until two American attack subs could escort her safely into American waters. Once the *October*'s crew had been removed, Ryan himself, assisted by several others, was to board her and guide her into a hiding place in an American missile submarine bay, shielded from Soviet satellites. The Soviet crewmen would be tricked into believing *Red October* had been destroyed when the Americans detonated an old submarine in the vicinity.

Tensions ran high and many cat-and-mouse confrontations with Soviet aircraft over the Atlantic ensued as both superpowers raced to reach the *Red October*. The American *Dallas* was first on the scene, and convinced Ramius to surface near the *Invincible*. Morse Code messages were quickly transmitted to the Russian captain via his periscope, and his intent to defect was verified. However, when Ramius realized that, despite the silent tunnel drive, he had been discovered by the Americans, he was nothing short of incredulous: "How can this be? They knew where to find us—Exactly! How? What can the Americans have? How long has the ... USS Dallas been trailing us?"

By means of a prearranged signal—a single solar ping—Ramius agreed to rendezvous with the American force at 33N 75W, where the evacuation plan would be set in motion. Ryan was elated that his theory had been vindicated and *Red October* secured.

His delight was short-lived, for a deadly confrontation lay ahead. As the American subs and *Red October* sped northward, an Alfa-class Soviet sub,

the *V.I. Konovalov*, under command of the brilliant Captain Tupolev, a former student of Ramius, waited to intercept them.

Although *Red October* was flanked by three American subs, Tupolev recognized her unique sonar signature: undoubtedly, it was that of a Soviet sub, the very submarine he had been sent to hunt and destroy. Quickly, he moved to attack. "Range seven thousand, six hundred meters. Elevation angle zero," the sonar operator reported. Tupolev donned a headset allowing direct communication with the fire control officer, who was entering data into the on-board computer. It was a simple problem of target geometry. "We have a solution for torpedoes one and two.... Prepare to fire.... Flooding tubes," Tupolev ordered. Impatient, the officer reached past the petty officer and flipped the switches himself. "Outer torpedo tube doors are open.... Recheck firing solution!" Tupolev barked. "Solution confirmed, Comrade Captain," came the reply, bringing Tupolev's command: "Fire one and two!" Two Mark C torpedoes were released in the direction of *Red October* at a slow but certain 41 knots.

Who would win this battle of wits—former student Tupolev, or Ramius, his teacher? Ramius adroitly ordered the *October* to turn into the torpedoes, in order to display a minimum profile—but the move was made too late. One torpedo struck the sub mid-stern, tearing a huge hole in her side. The only thing that saved her were her huge nickel-cadmium battery arrays, which had been designed for just such a blow.

The tense chase continued, with the three American subs alternately lunging toward the *Konovalov* and then withdrawing—until Ramius took a bold step. He rammed the Soviet ship, sending it to the bottom of the sea.

A few days later, *Red October* was brought into the American missile submarine dock to be scrutinized. Ramius and his officers were whisked away by the CIA—first to be debriefed, then to enjoy free lives in the United States. Ryan, bleary-eyed from lack of sleep, was routed home on a flight to London. But his superiors had no intention of letting him rest long; this bright young analyst would be a key member of many future intelligence efforts.

Commentary

The Hunt for Red October presents a fascinating look into the sophisticated war machines of the Cold War era. The CIA and its intelligence operations are shown in a favorable light, while Soviet characters are depicted as serving their country capably and honorably, albeit with thinly veiled disgust for the Party and its trappings.

Perhaps the most significant objective of the book is to educate the reader as to the vast scope of international military activity that goes on from day to day and the mutual respect between soldiers and sailors of all nations.

LORD JIM
by Joseph Conrad (1857–1924)

Type of work
English morality and adventure novel
Setting
Malaysia and the Far East
Principal characters
Lord Jim, an intelligent young man who brands
    himself a coward
Captain Marlow, a seaman who takes an interest in Jim
Dain Waris, a young Patusan warrior, and Jim's friend
Doramin, father of Dain Waris
Cornelius, a skulking Patusan trader
Jewel, Cornelius's daughter, and later, Jim's wife
Rajah Tunku Allang, an evil Patusan chieftain
Brown, a treacherous buccaneer

Joseph Conrad's *Lord Jim* ranks among the best novels ever written. Through the enigmatic Jim, Conrad explores the many faces of human character—courage versus cowardice, honor versus dishonor, as well as the fall and redemption of self esteem and the plight of society's lost souls.

Conrad's writing evolved from his own experience as a seaman. He forsook his native Poland after the Russian oppression of the 1800s, a self-condemned act of cowardice with which he apparently came to terms when he wrote *Lord Jim*.

Story overview

The boy, an outcast known simply as Jim, was raised in obscurity on the English coast and trained to go to sea, where he would experience a series of crises which would bring him face to face with his own human frailties. During his first voyage all hands were summoned to recover passengers from two vessels that had collided during a storm. Caught up in the confusion of the moment, Jim hesitated to risk his life—and so another boy carried out the heroic rescue. Although Jim later felt guilty, he made light of the incident and claimed he was brave enough to confront any peril.

While aboard another ship some time later, Jim was injured and set aground at an eastern port to convalesce. Thirsting for action, when he recuperated he immediately signed onto the *Patna*, an archaic iron-sided ship whose captain disdained the 800 Mecca-bound Muslim pilgrims who were his passengers. Jim, considering himself superior, remained aloof from the *Patna*'s gross skipper and his liquor-soaked crew.

One night in the middle of the Red Sea the ship struck some floating wreckage, sustaining damage to the hull. Sent to check the bulkhead, Jim saw that it was half-full of water and assumed it would soon burst apart and drown everyone. Before long, a storm hit and the panicked skipper gave orders to abandon ship. At first Jim was bent on standing by his post. But at the last minute, certain that any moment the ship's hull would rupture, he flung himself over the side of the ship into the lifeboat: "His confounded imagination

had evoked for him all the horrors of panic, the trampling rush, the pitiful screams, boats swamped." Then came the awful realization that, with that single act of cowardice, he had descended into an "everlasting deep hole" of fear and self-loathing.

Jim later learned that the *Patna* and its passengers had not sunk, but had been towed safely to port by a French vessel. When the skipper and crew learned that there was to be an official inquiry conducted on the incident, they either disappeared or descended into panicked dementia, leaving Jim, alone, to face the inspectors. Though Jim also had a chance to escape, he wanted to salvage what was left of his tattered honor.

Jim insisted on a hearing, infuriating the conducting officer, Brierly. With a flawless record to protect, Brierly was not about to have a young man's lack of mettle ruin it. He asked a Captain Marlow to give Jim two hundred rupees to run away. But Jim refused to defect: "I may have jumped but I won't run away. I'm not good enough."

Drawn to the wholesome-looking lad, Marlow saw in Jim a reflection of his own soul and defended the young man before the tribunal. In the end, however, Jim's seaman's certificate was revoked and news of his humiliation followed him to every harbor.

In time, with his friend Marlow's aid, Jim took on employment as a water clerk, brokering cargo for ships. But still ashamed of his actions and feeling "no better than a vagabond," he fled to yet another port. "Dash it all!" the youth exclaimed to Marlow as they again perused Jim's misadventure with the *Patna*. "I tell you [the bulkhead] bulged. A flake of rust as big as the palm of my hand fell off the plate all of itself."

While guilt over the incident often haunted him, Jim eventually came to believe that he had done his penance. One day he cried, "Jove! I feel as if nothing could ever touch me." But Captain Marlow knew from experience that Jim would not be completely free of guilt until he could redeem himself. Meanwhile, he would have to "face it out and wait for another chance."

Months later Marlow introduced Jim to a wealthy merchant named Stein, who operated a trading post near the Malaysian port of Patusan. Right away Stein was impressed with Jim. In fact, he hired the intelligent young man to replace Cornelius, an inefficient Patusan trader who had been overseeing Stein's trading post. When Stein gave Jim his silver ring so that he could convince the local Malay chief, Doramin, that he was a trusted ally, Jim again felt powerful, as if he might overcome the specter of his own trepidation and self-hatred.

While traveling up the river to Patusan territory, Jim was captured by Rajah Tunku Allang, a ruthless chief who routinely tortured and killed the Patusan people. Jim managed to escape by vaulting over the wall of Allang's stockade and running away before the surprised guards could overtake him. When he reached the next village, he collapsed, but managed to gasp Doramin's name in the hope that the locals would help him. The villagers took him to Doramin's house, where Jim produced the silver ring "and was received … into the heart of the community" as a trusted comrade. Jim befriended Doramin's son, Dain Waris, and the two young men worked together to overthrow Rajah Tunku Allang.

Finally Jim made his way to the trading post, where he found Cornelius to be positively despicable—a man who exhibited "an inexpressible … stealthiness, of dark and secret slinking." Cornelius greatly resented the young man for coming to displace him; even more, he feared Jim would take his daughter, Jewel, away from him. Jim stayed at the trading post for the next six weeks, during which time he and Jewel did indeed fall in love. Infuriated by the youthful sailor's presence, one night Cornelius tried to kill him in his sleep, but Jewel arrived just in time to forewarn her lover.

The couple decided to marry and to remain in the Patusan empire—but far away from Cornelius. Although they were very happy, Jewel could not help but fear that Jim in time would become homesick and leave her.

In Patusan, meanwhile, Doramin's people suffered many abuses at the hand of Tunku Allang and his attaché, Sherif Ali. Jim, like a modern-day Moses, resolved to deliver their victims from bondage. First he commanded Doramin's warriors to drag two seven-pound cannons to the hill overlooking Serif Ali's fort and to open fire. The bombardment quickly reduced the fort's walls to rubble. After leading an assault on the ruined encampment, Jim and Dain Waris routed Ali's men and took Tunku Allang prisoner.

When Jim returned from the battle, the villagers greeted him as a hero, appointing him as the great Lord Jim. They even attributed divine powers to him, insisting that "Jim had carried the guns up the hill on his back, two at a time." And so the legend of Lord Jim expanded throughout the land.

But peace would not last long. Soon a notoriously cruel Australian buccaneer named Gentleman Brown was led to Patusan by Cornelius. Brown and his fellow cutthroat seamen were in search of provisions to plunder. Although Jim was absent at the time, the Malay people drove Brown and his marauders onto a hillock near Sherif Ali's ruined fortress. Brown nevertheless plotted to enslave the Malay and to kill Lord Jim.

When Jim returned Doramin and Dain Waris urged him to attack the wily pirate. But Jim decided first to appeal to Brown's sense of honor; surely he could persuade the mercenary to give up his weapons and leave Patusan in peace. Jim thus arranged a meeting.

Without knowing Jim's history, Brown nevertheless detected the young man's guilty past, hinting that he and Jim were alike—both hiding from society and its harsh indictments. Thrown off guard by Brown's words, Jim failed to convince his adversary to give up his weapons. "You shall have a clear road or else a clear fight," Jim warned. Brown, however, refused to strike a deal. Doramin again prodded Jim to lead a raid against Brown and his men, but Jim persuaded the chief to allow them to leave I peace, pledging to give up his own life in the event any Malay was harmed.

After Jim had sealed the agreement with Brown, his men, led by Cornelius, began their retreat downriver. But Cornelius, still lusting after revenge, coaxed Brown's pirates to open fire on the Malays' riverside camp. Amid the heavy volley of bullets, the chief's son, Dain Waris, along with many of his men, fell. Afterwards, Brown's men escaped, but Cornelius was caught and stabbed to death.

Following the attack, Dain Waris's body was brought to Doramin. On the young man's finger was Jim's silver ring, worn as a symbol of love and trust. Now Lord Jim had broken that trust. As the ring was removed from his son's lifeless hand, Doramin let out a "fierce cry, deep from the chest, a cry of pain and fury."

Meanwhile, Jim's servant tried to convince him either to fight or flee for his life. Jim refused, announcing that, as promised, at dusk he would surrender himself up to Doramin. "Nothing can touch me," he declared. Jewel, however, was hysterical that her beloved Jim would forfeit his own life to pay for a scoundrel's crime. She clung to him so fiercely that Jim had to summon a servant to break her grasp. "You are false," she shrieked as he marched off toward Doramin's village. "Forgive me," he called to her, refusing to look back. Jewel called after him, "Never! Never!"

Jim boldly made his way to Doramin's house, while villagers whispered their disbelief that he would honor his word. As he drew near, Jim saw the shrouded body of Dain Waris. Approaching it, he lifted a corner of the sheet and gazed at his dead friend's sallow face. "He hath taken it upon his own head," said one onlooker. Jim then turned to face the chieftain. Surrounded by torches, he sat, a scowl on his face, with two flintlock pistols resting on his knees. "I am come in sorrow," Jim murmured. "I am come ready and unarmed." Doramin said nothing, but "from his throat came gurgling, choking, inhuman sounds [and] his little eyes stared with an expression of mad pain, of rage, with a ferocious glitter."

Two servant men helped Doramin to his feet, whereupon the ring rolled from his lap, coming to rest at Jim's feet. Jim stood in the light of the torches, his head bowed. Doramin "clung heavily with his left arm round the neck of [the] bowed youth, and lifting deliberately his right, shot his son's friend through the chest."

According to legend, "the white man sent right and left at all those faces a proud and unflinching glance. Then with his hand over his lips he fell forward" at the grieving father's feet. In death, Lord Jim had finally overcome fear. Ironically, even in the minds of Doramin and his people, he was a hero.

THE DEERSLAYER
by James Fenimore Cooper (1789–1851)

Type of work
Realistic North-American colonial adventure novel

Setting
Lake Glimmerglass, New York; 1740

Principal characters

Natty Bumppo, a skilled young woodsman known as
Hawk-eye to the Mingo Indians and as *Deerslayer* to the
Delaware

Henry March (Hurry Harry), a large, reckless
woodsman

Tom Hutter, a settler living on a Glimmerglass-Lake
houseboat

Judith Hutter, Tom's beautiful daughter

Hetty Hutter, Judith's half-wit sister

Chingachgook, Mohican chief and friend of Deerslayer

Hist (Wah-ta-wah), Chingachgook's love

Rivenoak, a Mingo chieftain

The *Deerslayer* (1841) is the first of Cooper's classic
Leatherstocking Tales about early American fron-
tiersman Natty Bumppo, stories that address many
conflicting themes often revisited in the 20th century:
reverence for nature, contrasted with the contention
that civilization must destroy nature; the paradox of
considering Native American "savages" somehow both
inferior and superior to Christian colonists; and the sad
truth that people of integrity often find themselves
isolated from the community in which they live.
Cooper also implies that the Christian settlers were
hypocritical, preaching one thing and doing another
insofar as their treatment of Native Americans was
concerned.

Deerslayer's code of conduct is based on respect for
every living thing, a belief that proves a source of
conflict for many who seek to seize upon "the American
dream." When he engages in a shooting contest with a
Mohican chief and kills several waterfowl, he later
expresses regret, saying, "We've done an unthoughtful
thing in taking life with an object no better than vanity."

Cooper lived both in Europe and America. After
writing some 32 novels, he died in 1851 near Lake
Glimmerglass in Cooperstown, New York.

Story overview

Natty Bumppo, known as the Deerslayer, and
Henry "Hurry" March were traveling through
the woods to Tom Hutter's home at Lake
Glimmerglass. Deerslayer planned to rendezvous in the
area with Chingachgook, a Mohican chieftain, and
Hurry had come to see Hutter's eldest daughter, Judith,
whom he adored. If she were already married, Hurry
vowed, he would kill her husband. When Deerslayer
threatened to inform the other settlers if Hurry went "a
murdering," the enormous woodsman took ahold of
Deerslayer and shook him until his bones rattled. But
Deerslayer remained calm. "You may shake until you
bring down the mountain," he said, " ... but nothing
but the truth will you shake from me."

When the two men reached Hutter's fortified cabin,
they could not find him or his houseboat.
Remembering that Hutter occasionally moved it from
one side of the lake to the other, they boarded a canoe
and went in search of him.

Being in Mingo territory, it was natural to speak of
Indians as they paddled. Hurry regarded Indians as
"half-human"; to him, taking their scalps for money
was totally justifiable. Deerslayer strongly disagreed.
Even though it was a customary practice for "savages" to
take scalps, it was wrong for Christians, who understood that "God made all ... alike."

At last the men came upon Hutter's houseboat and
Hurry introduced Deerslayer to Hutter and his two
daughters. Judith was just as beautiful and refined as
Hurry had boasted, while her younger sister Hetty was
sweet, but dull and slow-witted. There was little time
for talk, however; the Mingos were on the warpath, and
Tom was anxious to maneuver the boat away from
shore. Even as he sank his pole into the lake, six Indians
bolted from the trees and attempted to jump aboard.
Five warriors landed in the water. As the sixth struggled
to gain his balance on deck, Judith pushed him in after
them. Shots rang out from other Indians on the bank.
Deerslayer urgently pulled Judith inside the boat as her
father guided their craft safely out of range.

Deerslayer had come to the area on a mission of
mercy: to help his friend Chingachgook rescue his lover,
Hist, from the Mingos. But now Hutter and Hurry
wanted Deerslayer to help them raid the Mingo camp
for scalps. On moral grounds alone Deerslayer strongly
opposed the idea, but finally did agree to stay behind on
the boat and defend Hutter's two daughters. Hutter and
Hurry paddled off toward the Mingo encampment. But
as Deerslayer made his way back to the houseboat, he
heard the screams of his friends coming from the forest,
and knew the white men had already been captured.

As Deerslayer's canoe approached the shoreline, he
was confronted by a Mingo. The two discharged their
weapons simultaneously. The Mingo's bullet missed;
Deerslayer's did not. The maimed Indian, before crum-
pling to the ground, rushed forward in a frenzy of rage
and threw his tomahawk, which Deerslayer caught in
mid-flight. Before returning to the boat, the woodsman
tended to the needs of his dying enemy. Then, after
informing the girls of their father's and Hurry's
predicament, he paddled to a nearby rendezvous with
Chingachgook to plan the rescue of all three prisoners.
He found that Chingachgook had already scouted the
Mingo camp, where he'd caught a glimpse of Hutter
and Hist, unharmed. But as the two friends talked, they
saw Hetty resolutely rowing by in one of the canoes
toward the enemy camp, on a rescue mission of her
own. Deerslayer did not go after her, and later assured
Judith that her sister was safe; Indians did not harm
those they considered slow-witted.

At the Mingo camp Hetty argued with Chief
Rivenoak, trying to convince him to release her father.

"Love your enemies," she preached, quoting from the Bible. "Do good to them that hate you." Rivenoak replied, "Why does [the white man] forget himself all [the Bible] says?" Confused, the simple girl broke down in tears.

The white prisoners were soon freed in exchange for some ivory chess pieces which Judith and Deerslayer had found in Tom Hutter's weathered old sea chest—whereupon Hurry tried improvidently to shoot his erstwhile captors. Although he was thwarted in his attempt by Deerslayer, the Mingos then threw a bundle of blood-dipped sticks on the white men's boat to show that they were still on the warpath. And by the time Hurry, Tom and Chingachgook returned to the Mingo camp to rescue Hist, the Indians had moved.

When they finally located the new campsite, the men crept forward and found Hist in one of the tepees. But before they could free her, a Mingo squaw detected their presence and ran to alert the rest of the camp. Deerslayer, acting as a decoy, distracted the Mingos so that the others could escape, but was captured in the process.

The jubilant Mingos hauled the woodsman to the center of their camp, where Chief Rivenoak, calling Deerslayer by his Mingo name, tried to persuade him to abandon his friends and join up with the tribe. "Hawkeye should have been born a [Mingo]," he declared. Deerslayer, who had been raised by the Delawares, admitted that, though "white in blood," he was "a little redskin in feelin's and habits…. [Hutter] is not a man to gain my love," he added, but still he could not betray his companions.

After Chingachgook and Hist had arrived at the houseboat, Hutter and Hurry decided to backtrack to Hutter's lakeside cabin. There, however, they found the Mingos awaiting them. As the two entered the cabin, the Indians struck. Within seconds, Hutter lay dying on the ground. Hurry managed to escape out the back door.

Judith and Hetty returned to the cabin, just in time to hear Hutter direct them with his last gasp to "look in the chest—'tis all there." And indeed, following a fitting ceremony and after depositing their father's body into the lake, the young women opened his old sea chest. Inside they found documents showing that Hutter was not, in fact, their father. He had married their mother when they were babies, after their own father had abandoned them. What's more, Hutter had apparently once been a pirate—which explained why he had insisted on living on a boat.

Meanwhile, the Mingos sent Deerslayer back to the cabin with a proposal: all the men, including himself, could depart in peace if Hist and the Hutter girls would agree to surrender themselves in their stead and live among the Mingos. Deerslayer promised to deliver this ultimatum and to return to his captors if the bargain was rejected.

Judith, who had come to care for Deerslayer, was stung that he would even consider these conditions. "And do you bring such a message to me?" she rejoined. "Am I a girl to be an Indian's slave?" Humbled by her words, Deerslayer prepared to return to the Mingos and face certain torture.

He left his mournful friends and returned as pledged to the Mingos, who marveled at his sense of honor. "My people are happy in having captured a man and not a skulking fox," Rivenoak told him. Then he offered Deerslayer his life if he would marry the widow of the Indian he had killed earlier. When Deerslayer declined the offer, the widow's brother, very much insulted, launched a tomahawk at his chest. With cat-like quickness, the woodsman caught the weapon in flight and flung it back, striking the Indian between the eyes. Then, in the resulting pandemonium, Deerslayer fled.

The furious Indians lost no time in recapturing their quarry. This time they bound him and began to use his body for target practice, bringing their bullets closer and closer with each shot. But Deerslayer, wounded and bleeding, did not flinch. Then, completely unexpectedly, Hetty again appeared in camp, pleading once more for the Indians to exercise mercy. "You are tormenting your friend in tormenting this young man," she said. But Rivenoak ignored her. "Let the paleface show how little he cares for [Mingo] bullets." They shot at him again, but Deerslayer only mocked them, saying, "We've squaws among the Delaware that could outdo your greatest endeavors." At these words, the Indians became more inflamed.

Then Judith also appeared, disguised as an old woman, and attempted to barter for Deerslayer's life. Her efforts failed, however, when the confused Hetty exposed her sister's true identity. By now thoroughly enraged by the events, Rivenoak lit a circle of fire around his bound enemy. But at just the last moment, Chingachgook and Hist raced into camp, leapt the flames, and cut Deerslayer loose. As he sprang free, a Mingo lunged at Chingachgook with his knife. Hist deflected the blade, and Chingachgook then launched his own knife at the warrior, killing him. Deerslayer seized a rifle, whereupon he and his friends, though greatly outnumbered, prepared to fight for their lives.

All at once at the height of the fighting, a British army platoon broke through the clearing, with Hurry March at the lead. The soldiers opened fire on the Mingos, sending them scurrying into the brush. But Hetty was fatally wounded in the skirmish. "I wish you would try to be more like Deerslayer," she told Hurry with her dying breath. Then, raising her eyes to the sky, she gasped, "I see Mother and bright beings beyond her in the lake." Like Tom, she was buried in Lake Glimmerglass.

Weeks later, Judith bluntly asked Deerslayer to marry her. Turning to her, he gently explained that he desired freedom more than he desired the lovely Judith.

Fifteen years passed, and Deerslayer again visited Lake Glimmerglass, along with Chingachgook and Chingachgook's son, Uncas. There, by the side of the water, they found Hutter's cabin and boat, both ravaged by time—melancholy monuments to the people who had lived and died there.

THE SHORT STORIES OF GUY DE MAUPASSANT
Taken from *The Complete Short Stories of Guy de Maupassant*, Hanover House, 1955

Guy de Maupassant became one of the predominant short story writers of the 19th century. Rivaled only by Anton Chekov in his mastery of the genre, de Maupassant wrote some three hundred short stories in the span of ten years. These accounts often examine what he saw as the hypocrisy of contemporary French society and the decadence of its citizenry.

A LUCKY BURGLAR

One evening as three young men sprawled drunkenly in an art studio "discussing war and the uniforms of the empire," the host tippler suddenly leapt to his feet and pulled out the military uniforms of a Hussar, a grenadier, and a cuirassier. Arranging themselves in their battle gear, the friends executed an intricate drill. Then, after commanding his men to "drink like troopers," the host brought down weapons from the studio wall: a pistol, an enormous gun with a bayonet attached, a battle ax. Appointing himself general, the host split open a dummy's head with his ax while his second in command lunged into its breast with his bayonet. After thoroughly maiming the dummy, all three reeled about the studio.

Opening a cupboard, the companions were startled to find an old man crouched inside—doubtlessly a burglar. Immediately, they slammed and locked the cupboard door. Consultations ensued. Should they starve the intruder, "blow him up with dynamite," or perhaps just smoke him out? Finally, starvation impressed them as most fitting. This decided, they merrily toasted the health of their victim.

Eventually the general decreed that it was time to take a peek. Barking like lunatics, his fellow "madcap" cronies dashed to the cupboard, hauled their captive out, bound him hand and foot, and stood back to observe this "haggard-looking, white-haired old bandit, with shabby, ragged clothes."

"We will try this wretch," the general determined. Accordingly, the prisoner was officially condemned to die. Moreover, it seemed appropriate to execute him on the spot. "Say, you don't mean it, do you?" the old man groaned. But they demanded that the recreant kneel—"for fear that he had not been baptized"—and then poured a glass of rum on his head while ordering him to confess his sins.

Suddenly the prisoner began to scream. They quickly gagged him and put their guns to his head. But when they pulled the triggers, nothing happened—evidently, the weapons had not been loaded. Then one soldier intervened; in reality, he said, "they had no right to shoot a civilian," so the poor wretch was tied to a board and lugged to the police station. The chief of police saw their effort

as nothing more than a "great lark," and declined to keep the man in custody. The three captors dragged their prisoner back to the house.

"By jingo!" the old fellow cried when they ungagged him. "I have [had] enough of this." Moved by the old man's ordeal, the three still tipsy friends plied him with punch and exchanged toasts as if he were "a long-lost friend." In the end, when dawn broke, the captive stood up, saying, "I am obliged to leave you; I must get home." No matter how hard they begged, the man declined to stay. "Look out for the last step," the host cautioned as the old burglar walked out the door.

THE DEVIL

As the aged peasant woman lay on her deathbed, the physician chided her son: "Honore, you cannot leave your mother in this state; she may die at any moment." But Honore, a thrifty farmer of Norman descent, thought otherwise: he needed to collect his wheat; it was, after all, the season for reaping. His 92-year-old mother—though almost too sick to speak—was also "still possessed by her Norman avariciousness"; she agreed that her son should "get in his wheat and leave her to die alone." The incensed doctor threatened that if Honore did not find someone to attend to the poor woman, he would leave Honore himself to "die like a dog" should he become ill.

Troubled about the cost of hiring an attendant, Honore went to call on La Rapet, the old washerwoman who "watched the dead and dying of the neighborhood." La Rapet was herself greedy and stingy in the extreme; nevertheless, she welcomed Honore cordially and even offered him the special price for her services—"twenty sous by day and forty by night"—that she reserved for clients of modest means. "No, I would rather you ... fix a price until the end," Honore said. "I will take my chance one way or the other." La Rapet, though "tempted by the idea of the possible gain," feared that the miserly farmer might take advantage of her. Hence, she insisted on first seeing the patient.

After examining the dying woman, La Rapet grunted, "You will have to give me six francs, everything included." Honore flew into a rage. Yet, remembering his crops, he agreed to her price. Then he left La Rapet to tend to his mother.

La Rapet went home that night and returned the next morning, bitterly disappointed to find the old woman still alive. How long would she live? After waiting impatiently for a few hours, La Rapet asked her patient, "Have you ever seen the devil?" The poor woman said weakly that, no, she had not. La Rapet went to work: *She took a sheet out of the cupboard and wrapped herself up in it; then she put the iron pot onto her head so that its three short, bent feet rose up like horns.* Next she "took a broom in her right hand and a tin pail in her left," and threw the pail suddenly upward so that it clattered noisily to the ground. La Rapet then climbed on a chair near the bed, shrieking and prodding the old woman with the broom. Although the dying woman "made a superhuman effort to get up and escape," she was too frail. After letting out a deep sigh, she finally expired. La Rapet closed the dead woman's eyes and said the prayers for the dead with dutiful solemnity—and with great contentment, for she had come out 20 sous ahead. This fact did not escape Honore either when he came home that evening and found his mother had died.

THE NECKLACE

Mathilda Loisel lamented "the shabby walls, the worn chairs, and the faded stuffs" of her apartment. Life had disappointed her; she had been born "into a family of clerks" and then had "allowed herself to marry a petty clerk," although her looks and charm had once seemed to promise better things.

One night her husband thought he would surprise Mathilda with an invitation to a ball at the residence of the Minister of Public Instruction. To his amazement, Mathilda flung the invitation angrily onto the table. "What do you suppose I have to wear to such a thing as that?" she challenged him, bursting into tears. "How much would a suitable costume cost?" he asked. Calculating silently, she finally told him that four hundred francs would cover the expense. Against his better judgment, the frugal clerk agreed to give his wife the money.

Soon after buying the dress, Mathilda again became distraught. Now she was "vexed not to have a jewel, not one stone, nothing" to adorn herself with. Perhaps she could borrow jewelry from her modish and well-fixed friend, Madame Forestier, suggested her husband. Mathilda realized this was so.

To Mathilda's delight, Madame Forestier presented her with a stunning array, inviting her to choose whichever piece she liked. Mathilda had to try on much of the jewelry before selecting "a superb necklace of diamonds."

The ball turned out to be a dazzling event, and Mathilda was "a great success." Resplendent in her new dress and sparkling necklace, she felt "intoxicated with pleasure." Basking in "the triumph of her beauty," she did not even think of leaving until four in the morning, whereupon she dashed out of the ballroom—so the other women wouldn't notice that she did not have rich furs—and into the street where her husband was hailing a cab.

When she had closed the door to their apartment, Mathilda could not resist "a final view of herself in her glory." Removing her cloak, she gazed at herself in the mirror, only to shriek in dismay: the necklace was missing! Her husband

hastened to retrace their steps—without success. All he could do was contact the police and put a notice in the newspaper.

Her husband, beside himself with concern, instructed his wife to write a letter to Madame Forestier to the effect that the clasp of the necklace had broken, so they had taken it in for repairs. A week passed, and Mathilda's husband reached despair. "We must take measures to replace this jewel," he resolved.

Spotting a replica of the lost necklace in a shop window, the unhappy couple inquired after it. To their horror, the price was thirty-six thousand francs. What else could they do but resort to Mathilda's husband's inheritance and borrow the rest, about half the total amount.

When Mathilda returned the necklace to Madame Forestier, the Madame did not even bother to open its case; rather, she gently rebuked Mathilda for keeping the necklace for so long.

Subsequently, Mathilda's life changed radically. No longer able to afford a maid, she discovered the "horrible life of necessity": washing, scouring, doing the laundry, going to market. When she and her husband finally paid off their debt—some ten years later—Mathilda had become "the crude woman of a poor household." So when it happened that she spotted Madame Forestier out on a stroll, Mathilda was at first hesitant to approach her old friend. Still, so many years had passed; why not reveal the truth?

"Oh! my poor Mathilda! How you have changed," the gentlewoman exclaimed when Mathilda addressed her. "Yes," Mathilda continued, "I have had some hard days since I saw you, and some miserable ones—and all because of you!" Madame Forestier, of course, was taken aback. And on hearing Mathilda's story, her friend was thoroughly shocked—the diamonds had been "false," a trifling piece of costume jewelry: "Oh my poor Mathilda! They were not worth over five hundred francs!"

Commentary

Born in Normandy, France, Guy de Maupassant (1850–1893) developed an early interest in literature. He was more fortunate than most aspiring writers, in that one of his mother's friends was the great French novelist Gustave Flaubert. Indeed, in a story like "The Necklace," many elements are reminiscent of Flaubert. Clearly, the character of Mathilda owes something of her temperament to Flaubert's Madame Bovary.

De Maupassant, however, did not become a strict adherent of any epochal movement. Instead, he borrowed techniques from various schools to highlight the milieu of his complex and pathetic characters, who, like Mathilda, the dying woman, and the burglar, are often destroyed by greed, materialism, or the cruel whims of others.

Pearl Buck (1892–1973) was a prolific writer. And as in her most famous novel *The Good Earth*—in which cultural differences between East and West are explored—"home" often emerges as an important theme in her short fiction.

There is in the stories profiled below a sense in which the characters, to the extent that they are turned against their homes, become identical in their sufferings. In this respect, the accounts may be seen as versions of the same narrative—a narrative of expulsion and exile.

ENCHANTMENT

Boarding the commuter train, Roger Kentwell fought his way through the crowded cars, looking for a place to situate himself for the hourlong ride home. In the third car he spotted an empty seat and, though he "hesitated ... to sit beside a strange woman," he made his way down the aisle and asked, "Is this seat taken?"

"No, it isn't," the woman replied. But it was only after he had seated himself that he "felt a shock of surprise" at seeing a woman so "absolutely beautiful." As he closed his eyes, he thought immediately of his wife Ruth, who would be waiting for him outside the station. Ruth was more than just a part of his life: she was "the earth in which were his roots." Now, however, it occurred to him that, until now, he had never really thought about how women looked.

"Will you help me?" the woman suddenly whispered to him. "What can I do for you?" he asked, instantly on guard. She smiled weakly and said, "Just let me walk beside you, wherever you get off. As soon as we leave the station I shall not need you."

Roger reluctantly agreed to help her, then settled back in his seat. "Ruth was not beautiful," he thought to himself, and yet it was also true that "beauty was the last essential to happiness between a man and a woman ... a chance possession."

Soon the train pulled into the station and Roger found Ruth standing on the platform. Though he wasn't sure why, the sight of her made him feel uncomfortable: he hadn't wanted Ruth to see him walking beside this beautiful creature. "Well, dearest," he greeted her, ignoring the woman who had now fallen a step behind him. Roger could tell instantly that Ruth had noticed the lady, who thanked him and went on her way.

In the car, Ruth remarked how "terribly pretty" the woman appeared. "I always notice really beautiful women," she told Roger, "because I'm so ugly." He protested that she was "the dearest woman in the world and the only one I have ever thought of." Yet, he knew that something had changed between them; it was as though "the beautiful woman ... had set a standard of beauty between them ... "

At dinner, Ruth startled her husband. "It's ridiculous of me," she said, referring to their years of happiness together, "but I'd trade them all for this moment, just to hear you protest that I am really—quite beautiful." Then she excused herself from the table, saying she would join him shortly in the living room for coffee. "The fire," she added, "is laid ready just to touch with a match."

Upstairs, Ruth undressed in front of the mirror; a sense of "lonely wretchedness" crept over her. She had always known that Roger had fallen in love with her not "passionately, but slowly, half unwillingly. She had courted him with exquisite skill, never pursuing, always gently making herself indispensable to him." Then in the years after their marriage, she "had done nothing but built around him the enchantment of her pleasantness." That night at dinner, however, she felt certain that her "enchantment" had been shattered—her husband had almost seen her as she was.

After removing her pale green dress, Ruth put on one of dull red velvet and returned downstairs to Roger, who was sitting by the fireplace. For a moment she thought she detected in him a sign that, in fact, her enchantment was broken. "You know?" she said of her mood, "I think it was that green dress! I don't think I'll ever wear it again."

Roger examined her, and as he did she could see an expression of relief pass across his face. "Silly," he said to her. "Come and pour my coffee!"

PARABLE OF PLAIN PEOPLE

If only the overlords could be "removed by some stroke of heaven," lamented Wang the Eldest, "he could have managed very well." Wang was the first to admit that his life was uncommonly blessed. He owned a small but productive farm, where, with the exception of luxuries like tea and cloth, he was able to raise everything his family needed.

Wang was also fortunate to have two sons, both of whom were good young men. The oldest had married the daughter of his best friend, and shortly after had borne twin sons. Thus, to Wang's delight, the "affairs of his house were arranged and the generations were proceeding in order." His second son, though frail and sickly, proved no less a delight to him. In an effort to bring "silk-making in the house and take his second son from the fields," Wang had managed to betroth him to a silk weaver's daughter. And only a few months after their marriage, his new daughter-in-law—this "Fairy of Silk-weaving," as he called her—had brought so much money into the house that Wang's family became more prosperous than it had ever been. Surely, if not for his overlords, "he would have had no troubles" at all.

Even when his second son's first child was stillborn, Wang remained stoical, if not sanguine.

There would be other children, he prophesied; and, less than a year later, a daughter was born. When famine struck, Wang assured his family that they would weather it "as they had weathered other famines, generation after generation." Again, they survived. In every way, Wang felt "he could have lived in peace and in plenty if it had not been for these overlords."

In all, there were three overlords in the village: the first, Li, "was a rich and powerful man" whom Wang feared most; the second was a magistrate, who routinely had men beaten and imprisoned when they failed to pay their taxes; and the third overlord was an outlaw, a marauding warlord who plundered from the rural peasants. "I have no troubles except for these men," Wang repeated. "Of what use is any good I have, when these men are my overlords?"

After giving his problem a great deal of thought, Wang lit upon a solution. He cut down his orchards, burned his house, torched his fields and flooded his land. "Now," Wang told his family, "now we are free. We are beggars, but we have beggared ourselves at least."

THE SILVER BUTTERFLY

"I tell you of my mother," the Chinese man began. And so, even though it was already dark, the American man shut his eyes and listened. He had come to Hong Kong "to hear the true stories of men and women" who had escaped mainland China. Now this storyteller began a story about his mother's life in a small village by the Yangtze River.

His mother, he said, had been a concubine, and before he was born she had lived on his father's estate. The first son born to them, this man's oldest brother, had died at the age of five. His mother, he surmised, had loved his brother best, because each time she "saw a little child about [his brother's age], a boy, she coaxed him to come to her and fed him sweets."

When the revolution dawned on China some years later, his "father was accused, as a landlord, by his tenants." It didn't matter that he was well-liked in the community; it was simply the custom that tenants demanded "the execution of their landlords." Consequently, his father was strung up by his thumbs in a tree and, as the family watched, flayed to death.

Afterwards, the man continued, the Party moved his family into a one-room "co-operative" on a commune. He was married by then, and he and his wife would work each day digging in the riverbank to lay the pilings for a great bridge. His mother, however, whose "brain was muddied," was by then too old and confused to work. Since food in the commune was rationed according to one's work, his family was forced to survive on only two rations. When he finally broached this subject with his "commander," he was told that his mother would have to work.

Inasmuch as his family's house had been converted to a nursery for the commune, the Party assigned his mother to work there. One day "a little boy of five years, or thereabouts, was brought to the nursery, crying." The moment his mother saw the boy, she was reminded of her son who had died. And so she began to love the child, which "was her great crime."

His mother's return to her old house had stimulated memories of her life as a concubine. One day, in this "dream of confusion," she remembered that years ago she had hidden three pieces of jewelry behind a brick in the wall of the shed. Of these pieces, the most valuable among them was "a butterfly of filigree silver set with small good pearls."

"The next day, it happened that the boy [whom she had taken for her son] cut his hand." Wanting to comfort him, the mother led the boy to the shed and showed him the silver butterfly. "See how pretty," she told him. "This is your butterfly. I will keep it for you, so that no one can take it from you, but it is yours. We will look at it every night. Here, take it in your hand."

Each night they would return and gaze in secret at the silver butterfly. But the boy told another child about the butterfly and that child, for "a bit of sugar," told the directress. Since luxuries were not allowed in the commune, the boy was severely beaten and the man's mother was "sentenced to be denounced at the next meeting of the commune."

"On the day of the meeting," the man continued, "I hid myself in the crowd." His mother, her hands bound behind her back, was forced to make her way through the vicious mob. When she fell to the ground, the man said, he knew "it was time to kick her. Everybody was watching me and I was afraid. I stepped forward to do what I had to do. In that moment she looked up and saw me…. When I saw that she knew me, I tried to look angry. She was bewildered for a moment, and then she smiled."

"Is that the end?" the American man asked.

"No," said the man, "but there is an end." After his mother was released from the hospital, she went to the little boy, who was still recovering from his own beating, and "coaxed him to come with her to the shed." Once there, she held him and whispered to him that she had now become "a burden" to her son—the son who had been made to strike her. "I cannot help him by living," she told the boy. "I see this…. So come with me, my child, my little one. Let us go to a better place."

The boy responded by asking if he could see the silver butterfly, and she answered, "We will go to the river. There are butterflies there." At the water's edge the woman picked the boy up in her arms and "walked into the water until it covered her head and the child's head and she did not step back." That, the man said, "was the end."

ULYSSES
by James Joyce (1882–1941)

Type of work
Experimental novel
Setting
Dublin Ireland; June, 1904
Principal characters
Leopold Bloom, a canvasser at the local newspaper
Molly Bloom, his wife
Stephen Dedalus, a recent college graduate
A host of characters, including a number of
    journalists, an old mariner, a caretaker, priests,
    and several drunken soldiers

In nearly every imaginable way, James Joyce's novel is like no other—and that's aside from its presenting such anomalies as a 50-page-long running sentence (filled with a wife's ruminations), its stream-of-consciousness flavor, and its innovative, twisting, 750-plus-page pseudo-plot. Massive, mythic—and, due to its earthiness, still frequently placed on the "adult" shelf at the library—*Ulysses*, first published in 1922, is probably the most ambitious and multi-dimensional jigsaw puzzle ever assembled out of the English language. But the novel is also something much more pivotal than a juicy literary crossword: it is the work that ushered the world's English-language readers and writers into the landscapes of 20th-century modernism.

In a sense, modernist and post-modernist narrative begins with Joyce. Like T.S. Eliot's influential poem "The Waste Land," Joyce's *Ulysses* grows out of the early 20th century's drastic redefinition of civilization. While Europeans of the late 19th century had assumed that technological advancements would foster peace, prosperity and unchecked progress, artists and intellectuals of the new century not only started questioning technology's contribution to humanity on moral and ethical grounds, but they also began to allocate "progress" to the realm of myth. Thus, writers like Joyce and Eliot focused on the dissolution of the old order.

In the tragic wake of World War I, writers discovered both a profound pessimism and a new emphasis on the individual. Freud, of course, had recently posited the existence of the *id*—a great psychic repository of unconscious impulses and urges that lay deep within the human soul. Armed with this new knowledge, writers and artists like Joyce courted a far less optimistic view of the individual and his experiences than previous Romantic-era writers had entertained.

In *Ulysses*, for example, Joyce chooses to depict individual experience as far too fragmentary and multi-textured to be subjected to the constraints of traditional plot. Thus, no "story" of any real consequence emerges in the novel. In lieu of a traditional narrative, Joyce focuses on the psychology and perceptions of Leopold Bloom, the "middle-aged Irish Jew" who is Joyce's modern Ulysses. Like Homer's timeless Greek voyager wending his way

home to Ithaca after the Trojan War, Bloom lives a life of exile, wandering from adventure to adventure, before he returns home to his wife.

In contrast to Homer's epic *The Odyssey*, in which heroes and gods are truly heroic and godly, Joyce's Ulysses—Bloom—is left trudging the wasteland streets and pubs of lower-middle class Dublin in search life's meaning—or, at very least, some sort of steppingstone on the pathway leading "home."

Bloom's errant wanderings are depicted in a single, "ordinary" Dublin day. And as the routine of this day unfolds, the reader is offered what critic A. Walton Litz calls "an encyclopedia of modern life." Litz goes on to say that no matter how we view *Ulysses*, the ways in which we can approach it are "almost endless. We can only conclude that the best reading of the work is the one that yields the greatest number of related perspectives."

Story overview

June 16, 1904 began as an ordinary day in the city of Dublin. As the early summer sun began to spread her majesty over that vast borough, Stephen Dedalus awoke. Dawn had come, as usual, much too soon. The life of the young Latin poetry instructor lacked any hint of happy anticipation. Still in mourning for his mother, who had died of pneumonia the year before—vainly pleading with her son to pray for her soul—Stephen brooded once again over his guilty memories and the appallingly aimless condition of his life. He had no faith, no true friends. What's more, he received no sympathy in his grief from his roommate and only close companion, the vulgar, bullying medical student Buck Mulligan. "O, it's only Dedalus whose mother is beastly dead," Mulligan mocked.

Having extracted himself from bed, Stephen made his way to the academy. "Tell me now, what is a pier," he asked a pupil. But he did not get the expected Latin translation. "A pier, sir. A thing out in the waves," offered the boy, helpfully. After spending the entire morning in such tedia, Stephen finally realized what it was that kept him in a sort of paralyzed, hopeless conspiracy with these boys: in them he saw his own awkward, fearful, impoverished childhood.

When at last class was dismissed, the principal of the academy, Mr. Deasy, approached Stephen with a manuscript in his hand. "It's about the foot and mouth disease," Deasy explained. In effect, he wanted Stephen to use his influence with the local newspaper to have the article published as a public service item. And since Stephen did not feel he was in any position to deny the request, he made his way to the newspaper offices.

On the other side of town, meanwhile, a middle-aged Jewish man named Leopold Bloom, who worked as an ad saleman at the newspaper, was just beginning his day with an appetizing breakfast of grilled mutton kidneys, which "gave to his palate a fine tang of faintly scented urine." Bloom carried a dead weight within him: since the death of their infant son Rudy he had found himself unable to make love to his wife Molly. And yet, in the aftermath of Rudy's death, both had often sought comfort in the arms of others.

After breakfast Bloom rode off in the carriage to the funeral of his friend Patrik "Paddy" Dignam. As the service commenced, however, he suddenly decided that he detested funerals. "My kneecap is hurting me," he thought as he knelt in prayer. In truth, the whole affair reminded him of little Rudy, and of his own father, who had died a suicide. At one point, gazing ahead at the coffin, he wondered, "Which end is his head?" Then, as his mind strayed further and further from the here and now, Bloom's brief respite from work was over.

Most of salesman's dismal working day was spent trying to negotiate the terms of advertising space with a tea merchant named Keyes. The editor, Myles Crawford, was aghast when he reviewed the final agreement for approval. Keyes was a bloody cheat, he screamed. "He can kiss my royal Irish arse."

Later in the day, Stephen Dedalus arrived at the newspaper office to talk with the staff about the Deasy article. Crawford, still peeved by the Keyes incident, was not in favor of printing a piece dealing with the loathsome and ridiculous subject of foot and mouth disease. His readers wouldn't stand for it; they'd read anything but an article about a damned disease. "All balls!" howled the editor. "Give them something with a bite in it. Put us all into it, damn its soul ... "

At daylight faded Stephen, still flushed from drink, met up with Mulligan and some other young scholars at a local tavern. In time their talk turned to a rousing analysis of *Hamlet*. Hamlet was a Jew, one of the young men spat out, scowling. Stephen quickly rebutted this with the notion that the Prince of Denmark indeed represented the playwright Shakespeare himself. "He wrote the play in the months that followed his father's death," Stephen contended.

As for Leopold Bloom, after he left the office he made his way from the pubs to the seaside. There he happened upon a flirtatious lass named Gerty, who leaned back against a rock, exposing her bare thighs and knickers: ... *She was trembling in every limb ... and she wasn't ashamed and he wasn't either to look in that immodest way like that because he couldn't resist the sight of the wondrous revealment half offered* ... "O sweet little, you don't know how nice you looked," thought Bloom as the girl left. "I begin to like them at that age ... "

Bloom staggered back toward the taverns, the pictures in his mind coming one right after another: there was his dearly departed Rudy; why did his eleven-day-old man-child have to die? Then came the lurid vision of his wife—in bed with one of his cordial acquaintances. Now his only recourse was to "drown his sorrows." He arrived at the pub just in time to catch the last of Stephen's discourse on *Hamlet*. The conversation then moved on to civic issues. Mulligan frequently would turn to stare in the direction of a certain Jewish patron while he voiced his supercilious views: "For the enlightenment of those who are not so intimately acquainted with the minutiae of the municipal abattoir as the morbid-minded esthere and embryo philosopher who for all his overweening bumptiousness in things scientific can scarcely distinguish an acid from an alkali."

After a few more hours of drinking and enduring such bluster, Bloom made his way to Mabbot Street, a nearby lane of enticing ill-repute. Stumbling onward, he received sad, ethereal visitations from his dead father, then from an anonymous bearded woman, then from his wife, and, finally, from his lover. In this state, he came across Stephen again, who, in a similar state of despondency, was revisited on the spot by the ghost of his dead mother, begging her son once more to pray for her soul.

Strolling on together, Bloom and Stephen stopped to cavort with a group of prostitutes—until two soldiers happened upon the scene and took exception to Stephen's surly demeanor. In concert, they struck the young scholar and knocked him, bleeding, to the ground.

As the soldiers continued on down the lane, Bloom helped Stephen up, brushed him off, and handed him his hat. For refreshment, they then trudged on to a seaside café, there to hear a scruffy old sea veteran recount his grandiose tales. "I seen a crocodile bit the fluke of an anchor," he boasted. " ... I seen icebergs plenty, growlers. I was in Stockholm and the Black Sea ... " Bloom and Stephen listened on in rapturous envy; never had either of them braved such wonderful explorations.

Quite recovered from the beating he had taken, Stephen accompanied Bloom home, where they mulled over the intricacies of music, religion, and life. As the night wore on, Bloom implored his new young friend to stay—to leave his reckless circle and come live with him and his wife. And even though Stephen refused, both men now knew that, despite an age difference of 16 years, their lives were irrevocably intertwined.

After insisting that his wife arise early and prepare his breakfast, Bloom now finally drifted off to sleep—leaving Molly Bloom lying there awake, thinking. Thinking of her most recent lover ... of her girlhood ... of the mysteries of the human body ... of the possibility of Stephen Dedalus—a refined young writer—coming to live with them ... and, at last, of her long-past courtship with Leopold Bloom—of "how he kissed me under the Moorish wall and I thought well as well him as another and then I asked him with my eyes to ask again yes and then he asked me would I yes to say yes ... "

And so the woman's thoughts flowed on, pungent, earthy, homey—while her far-wandering husband snored in the darkness at her side.

THE PRINCE OF TIDES
by Pat Conroy, Houghton Mifflin, 1986

Type of work
Mythological realism

Setting
South Carolina and New York City; the 1940s to the
1980s

Principal characters
Tom Wingo, an unemployed coach/English teacher
Savannah Wingo, Tom's twin sister, a poet
Luke Wingo, Tom and Savannah's older brother
Lila Wingo, their beautiful mother
Henry Wingo, their father, a shrimper
Susan Lowenstein, Savannah's psychiatrist and, later,
     Tom's confidante

Story overview

Although 36-year-old Tom Wingo had a wife and
three daughters whom he dearly loved, he was still
tormented by the "wreckage" of the family that he
had been born into. He had grown up near the town of
Colleton, on a small island that his great-grandfather
had actually won in a horseshoe game. The island's
natural beauty had delighted Tom, his twin sister
Savannah, and their older brother Luke; all three of them
spoke of the place "religiously." Their home life, however,
was nightmarish: Lila, their beautiful mother, was
obsessed with her social standing and refused to
acknowledge the pain her husband Henry inflicted on all
of them when he berated and beat them. She ignored the
cruelty, even as it happened, insisting instead on maintaining "family loyalty."

Inwardly unable to endure this "egregious" charade,
the Wingo children bore wounds, deep and festering. As
an adult, the oldest son Luke became a loner who ultimately "heard voices and began to see the faces of his
family materialize on the branches of trees." Wandering
the marshlands where he had been born, he was to suffer
an early and violent death, a tragedy still contained by an
aura of mystery.

Like her brother Luke, Savannah often hallucinated.
As a young woman she had moved to New York and
become a well-known poet. Though she tried valiantly to
repress her pain, she nevertheless had more than once
been crushed by the bone-deep urge to destroy herself.
Horrified by his twin sister's anguish, Tom desperately
tried to impart the appearance of normalcy by striving to
become the "irreproachable figure [that his] parents
always wanted."

But in the end, the past overwhelmed Tom, too. He
suffered a nervous breakdown and lost his job teaching
English and coaching high school football. He still
longed to please his wife Sallie, a medical internist who
was now the sole support of their family. But Tom's
depression prevented him from satisfying Sallie,
emotionally or any other way. Adding to his despondency was the fact that he had not seen Savannah in
three years. He'd also become increasingly troubled by
Luke's death and by the growing hatred he now felt for
his mother.

Tom arrived in New York that day, a devastated man.
Not only was Savannah in the hospital after yet another
suicide attempt, but he had also just discovered that his
wife was having an affair. "Hold me tight, Tom,"
Savannah had often said to him while they were growing
up, and he had always tried to defend his sister—first
from the blows of their father and from the coldness of
their mother, and later from her "own screams and
wounds, [which] sustained the imperishable beauty of
her art. [Yet] there were no dark poems in Savannah's
work, only beautiful fruit surrounded by flowers that
could put the taster forever to sleep on thorns dusted
with cyanide ... "

It became immediately clear to Tom that Savannah's
poetry fascinated her psychiatrist, Susan Lowenstein.
"Who is The Prince of Tides?" Dr. Lowenstein demanded
the moment Tom walked into her elegant New York
office. Completely unnerved, Tom retorted, "Why don't
you ask Savannah?" He simply could not bring himself to
tell this stranger that the phrase—the title of Savannah's
most recent book—referred to their dead brother Luke.
The doctor's reply to this was cool: "I will when she's able
to speak to me." Until then, though, Susan wanted Tom
to tell her about his sister's background.

Susan Lowenstein grated on Tom. She was "breath-
takingly beautiful, one of those go-to-hell New York
women with the incorruptible carriage of a lioness"—
and as the soft-spoken, smooth-mannered gentleman
who had fulfilled Lila Wingo's best visions for her son,
Tom resented the doctor's brash, polished intensity.

Although Tom had confronted Savannah before in
states of catatonic retreat, he was still deeply saddened
when Susan took him to her room. Protectively, he knelt
by the bed where his mute sister lay "curled like an
embryo" and gently crooned her a melody they had sung
together as children.

Later, when Tom learned that Savannah had been
"covering herself with her own excrement"—after
narrowly escaping death from this latest wrist-slashing—
his antagonism toward Susan Lowenstein eased. Their
dinner-date that night initiated the first in a line of
probing and intimate conversations. Finally Tom
decided to stay in New York to meet with Susan regularly
in hopes of coming to terms with his own torn feelings as
the son of a family whom "fate had tested a thousand
times, and left defenseless, humiliated, and dishonored."

At one of their dinners, Tom told Susan about the
day when life had literally begun for him and Savannah:
The tide was rising and a hurricane was gathering force
off the South Carolina coast. The 85-year-old former
slave who attended the twins' birth, had died protecting
the infants from the storm. Every year afterward, the
Wingo children had visited her grave.

Aside from the isolation of being "raised Catholic in
the deep South" on a remote island, the Wingo children
had also suffered terribly from the violence that permeated their lives. In addition to their father's sadistic and
unpredictable beatings, they had been terrorized by a

stalker, an immense man with murderous eyes. After chasing the children out of the woods one day while their father was away in the Korean War, the giant had walked out to stare lasciviously at their mother. "I want you," he had shouted to Lila. And as he turned away, they heard the giant laughing. "I'll be back."

The following week the stalker reappeared, only this time he was brandishing a knife in his meathook-like hand. Lila and her children fought back by pelting him with open jars full of black widow spiders from their basement—and once again he retreated into the darkness.

As the extraordinary history of the Wingo household slowly unfolded, Susan listened with deep interest. Tom found himself increasingly aware of the vibrant, compassionate and vulnerable woman that lay beneath the assertive, clinical poise. After hearing about Tom's anguish over his wife's affair, Susan confessed that her husband, Herbert, a famous violinist, was also involved with another woman. Now more than ever, Savannah's two protectors seemed of one heart.

Then Susan asked Tom if he would coach her adolescent son Bernard, who longed to play football. When Tom agreed, the developing relationship with Bernard soon incited Herbert Lowenstein's jealousy. Aware that both his son and his wife had become smitten with this enigmatic Southerner, Herbert accosted Tom in Central Park and announced that he was sending Bernard away to music camp.

Shortly after this confrontation, Tom was taken aback by an invitation from Herbert to a dinner party. Not surprisingly, the dinner had been engineered as an occasion for Herbert to embarrass his wife and insult his Southern rival. To his dismay, the plan backfired. When he heard Susan repeatedly belittled and himself publicly branded as anti-Semitic, Tom simply turned and left the party. And to his delight, Susan followed. Soon afterward she moved in with Tom.

While Tom still cared deeply for his wife, in Susan's arms he found both comfort and excitement. With her, Tom could let out all the horrors and wonders of his early life. By now he had told her all about his father Henry Wingo—how on one occasion he had brought home a Bengal tiger to rent out at parties.

And then, at last, Tom disclosed details of the day when the stalker had arrived for yet a third time at the door of the Wingo house, accompanied by two depraved companions. Bursting into the living room, the three men had raped Lila, Savannah and Tom, and threatened to kill them. It was Luke who had saved them—along with the Bengal tiger. Lured from its cage by the eldest son, the tiger came padding into the house to confront his mother's attacker, tearing him into a hundred bloody shreds. In the ensuing chaos, Tom grabbed a marble statue and beat in the head of his own assailant, driving "fragments of his skull deep into his brain," while Savannah "cut her rapist in half" with a shotgun.

"This didn't happen," Lila had gasped afterwards. "This did not happen." Then, at their mother's direction, Tom and Luke had carried the three savaged bodies into the woods for burial, while Lila and Savannah cleaned the blood and viscera from the walls and floor. True to her word, Lila never mentioned the ghastly event to anyone, not even to her husband. Henry Wingo came home from work later that night to a clean house and a fish dinner—and afterwards Savannah made her first attempt at suicide.

Lila's children were not surprised when, years later, she divorced their brutal and bewildered father to marry into a prominent local family. It was this marriage that set the events into motion which would lead to Luke's undoing: In her divorce settlement, Lila was awarded the family's small island, a property which her new husband convinced her to sell to a company that produced materials for nuclear weapons and power plants. Luke, with his passionate attachment to the island, had been outraged. A former Vietnam War hero, he "initiated guerrilla actions," unintentionally causing the death of four men in the derailment of a train. Now a wanted man, Luke then disappeared into the wild coastal marshes which he knew so well. While he had never meant to kill innocent people, he was considered to be extremely dangerous, "a murderer and a crackpot." Having slipped into madness, he was finally spotted and callously shot down while making "a sentimental visit to the island where he grew up." After the funeral Tom and Savannah took the body of their beloved brother out on a boat and dropped it overboard.

As Tom's story came to an end, Susan held him in her arms. Shortly afterwards, Tom realized that, while he might never be able to "measure the cost of loving a family so deeply and with such a cold fury," he now had finally found the strength to put his life in order. With great sadness and gratitude, he bade goodbye to Susan and set off on the journey home.

Long after he and Sallie had reclaimed and forgiven each other, long after he and Savannah had turned to the task of reforging their lives, Tom still often found himself alone in his car late at night, whispering, "Lowenstein, Lowenstein, Lowenstein … " —affirming once more the healing relationship that had led him back home.

Commentary

Like his narrator Tom Wingo, Pat Conroy grew up along the coast of South Carolina. *The Prince of Tides* undoubtedly draws heavily on many of the author's own experiences as the self-professed son of a domineering father and a class-conscious mother, whose rigidity helped precipitate their children's rebelliousness.

The fictional story of Tom, Luke and Savannah, however, takes a decidedly idiosyncratic form. Not only do the adult children of Henry and Lila Wingo find themselves unable to conform to the distorted expectations of their parents, they remain in a denial so deep that it not only recolors but often obliterates memory. Alienated from both themselves and each other by the madness of dissociation, it is only through restored memory and disclosure, which Susan Lowenstein so powerfully invokes in the novel, that the Wingos can begin to heal and to share their "capacity for homage and wonder."

THINGS FALL APART
by Chinua Achebe, McDowell, Obolensky., 1959

Type of work
Ethnographic adolescent novel

Setting
Nigeria's Igbo villages; turn of the 20th century

Principal characters
Okonkwo, a middle-aged Igbo farmer and warrior
Nwoye, Okonkwo's disappointing "womanly" oldest son
Ikemefuna, a virile boy who comes to live with Okonkwo

Story overview

Okonkwo lived with his three wives and their children in the Igbo village of Umuofia, feared by all its neighbors for its power "in war and in magic." Subsisting largely on yams, the villagers were obliged to appease the wrath of many gods each season in order to secure a plentiful harvest. And when they finally reaped their yams, they always held a great harvest feast.

Okonkwo, however, unlike the other villagers, did not find release or joy in this celebrating; he much preferred the daily rounds of tending his fields. Indeed, his dedication had made him a prosperous man. He also distinguished himself as a warrior. In his youth he had routed the notorious "Amalinze the Cat" in a wrestling match and, recently, he had taken his fifth head in combat with Umuofia's enemies. Thus the warrior's fame, resting "on solid personal achievements," had spread through all the adjacent Igbo villages. This particularly gratified Okonkwo because it set him apart from his dead father, Unoka.

Unoka was said to have been cursed by a bad *chi*—the personal god-spirit who accompanied each man through life and swayed his fate. In life, the spiteful little god had caused his crops to fail; even more deplorable, Unoka had acquired a reputation as a man who disdained war. His *chi* also had plagued his death, causing him to suffer a fatal "swelling" that "was an abomination to the earth goddess." Due to the loathsome nature of this disease, Unoka's body had been carried away to be buried in the Evil Forest to prevent polluting Umuofia or its people. The man had been so ill-fated in every respect that Okonkwo's "one passion [was] to hate everything his father had loved."

Then an event occurred in Umuofia that was to profoundly change Okonkwo's life. To compensate for the murder of a woman from Umuofia by a villager in Mbaino, a virgin and a young boy from Mbaino were sent to Umuofia. The boy, Ikemefuna, was placed under Okonkwo's care and sent to live in the house of Okonkwo's first wife, who treated him as kindly as she treated her own sons.

In contrast to his wife's tenderness, Okonkwo dealt harshly with Ikemefuna, standing over him with a "big stick" when he would not eat his yams. To be sure, all of Okonkwo's children and wives "lived in perpetual fear of his fiery temper," an anger which he reserved most passionately for his eldest son, Nwoye—whose disposition reminded Okonkwo of his own bedeviled father. Preferring to stay home and hear the "womanly" stories of his mother rather than joining in the manly labors of his father, Nwoye was as gentle and peace-loving as his grandfather had been. The disappointing boy was even less virile and intrepid than his beautiful younger sister Ezinma, in whom Okonkwo found some consolation.

It was with relief, then, that Okonkwo watched as his new charge, Ikemefuna, ripened into a lively, popular and highly industrious youth. As the seasons passed, Okonkwo grew very fond of the boy; in many respects he thought of him as an ideal son. Moreover, this exemplary new brother gradually "kindled a new fire" in the meek and sluggish Nwoye.

Then one day, three years after Ikemefuna's arrival, Okonkwo received a visit from one of Umuofia's respected patriarchs. The esteemed visitor told Okonkwo that the "Oracle of the Hills and the Cave" demanded Ikemefuna's sacrifice. At the same time, the wizened patriarch cautioned that Okonkwo must "not bear a hand in his death."

Two days later the village elders came for the young man. Told that he was being led back to Mbaino, Ikemefuna nevertheless felt a great foreboding as he trudged through the forest alongside the men of Umuofia. Frequently Ikemefuna's mind turned to his mother and sister in Mbaino: Would they recognize him? What if his mother was dead? To soothe his nerves, Ikemefuna recalled a song from his childhood, and sang to himself.

All at once, one of the men "growled at him": the boy had fallen behind. Glancing around, Ikemefuna realized with a chill of fear that Okonkwo had quietly joined the group. An instant later, he found himself struck down by a blow from an unseen machete. "My father, they have killed me!" he cried out. Afraid of being thought weak, Okonkwo immediately dashed forward and slashed at the fallen boy with his own machete.

When Okonkwo returned from the forest, Nwoye avoided him. Instinctively he knew that Ikemefuna had been killed. Deeply shaken, "something had given way inside" Okonkwo's eldest son. Nwoye would never again be the same.

But Ikemefuna's death had also deeply shaken his great lion of a father: *[Okonkwo] tried not to think about Ikemefuna, but the more he tried the more he thought about him. [In time] he was so weak that his legs could hardly carry him. He felt like a drunken giant walking with the limbs of a mosquito. Now and then a cold shudder descended on his head and spread down his body.*

Subsequent events deepened Okonkwo's despair. First, the ancient patriarch who had brought word of Ikemefuna's sacrifice died. Umuofia's warriors, their bodies painted and adorned in "raffia skirts," danced in the great sage's honor. In a frenzy, they then dashed about brandishing machetes and firing guns. Among them, Okonkwo raised his gun for the final salute to the deceased and, by accident, his bullet struck and killed the dead man's son. Okonkwo knew that the only atonement for this deed was seven years banishment, for it "was a crime against the earth goddess to kill a clansman."

Early the next morning Okonkwo set off with his three wives and their children to begin their new life in exile, withdrawing to the village where his mother had been born. Okonkwo straightaway set to work building huts for his family and planting yams so that he might prosper in the new village. But still he was troubled: Okonkwo's deepest desire had always been to "become one of the lords of the clan" in his home village of Umuofia. Now it occurred to him that his own *chi* might be as malevolent as his father's had been.

Seeing Okonkwo's distress, his maternal uncle offered solace: "A man belongs to his fatherland when things are good and life is sweet. But when there is sorrow and bitterness he finds refuge in his motherland. Your mother is there to protect you. She is buried there. And that is why we say that mother is supreme." Okonkwo took these words to heart, rapidly adapting to his new home.

During his second year in his motherland, however, Okonkwo received troubling news: white Christian missionaries had settled in Umuofia, bringing with them their "great evil" and gradually winning many converts. One of these converts was his own son Nwoye, who, upon baptism, had renounced Okonkwo, declaring, "He is not my father."

Okonkwo fumed with hatred; he despised the white intruders and hoped the villagers would wage war on them. How he missed the "bold and warlike" men they once were!

At last the seven years of exile elapsed. After providing a great feast for his maternal kinsmen, Okonkwo and his family set off for home, eager to rebuild their lives. But upon his return Okonkwo found that his fatherland had undergone profound changes. White men had begun to govern the whole region with support of those who had converted to the new faith. Outraged, Okonkwo sought to convince the villagers to "drive away" or slaughter the foreigners, but to no avail. Then one day a white man profaned the earth goddess by removing the mask from one of the village's ritual dancers; for this grave sacrilege the people of Umuofia burned down the new Christian churchhouse.

For a brief moment Okonkwo knew once more a feeling akin to happiness; the men of Umuofia had not lost their courage after all. But his joy evaporated when, a few days later, he and other villagers were arrested and sent to jail to pay for the burning. Starved and beaten, Okonkwo's old fury returned.

After his release from jail, Okonkwo made his way to the village marketplace, where a council was to be held. "All our gods are weeping," said one of the speakers. "We must root out this evil." Suddenly, five court messengers, Okonkwo's former friends who now worked for the new government, appeared in the crowd. "The white men," one of them announced loftily, "whose powers you know all too well, have ordered this meeting to stop."

Okonkwo immediately drew his machete and decapitated the nearest messenger. Then, cleaning his blade on the sand, he turned and disappeared into the crowd. The local District Commissioner and his soldiers set out to re-arrest the Igbo warrior. But upon reaching his compound, they were disappointed: In a nearby bush, Okonkwo had hanged himself.

"It is an offense against the Earth," one of the villagers said, referring to Okonkwo's suicide. Thus, like his father before him, Okonkwo was doomed to be "buried like a dog" in the forest and to suffer forever after the scorn of his people.

Commentary

"Things fall apart," reads William Butler Yeats' classic poem. "The center cannot hold."

Chinua Achebe, born in 1930, grew up in an Igbo tribal village. Like the characters in *Things Fall Apart*, Achebe and his family lived through the trauma of being trapped between radically distinct cultures. "I think that I'm much more a part of a transitional generation than any other," Achebe once stated. "And this is very exciting. Of course it carries its penalties, since you're in no-man's-land." And it is just this anguished journey through no-man's-land that underscores the whole narrative in *Things Fall Apart*.

In the opening pages we find Okonkwo, who has managed to carve himself a "place" in Umuofia, working feverishly to avoid spiritual exile from his "fatherland." His tender firstborn son Nwoye pursues the "womanish" interests that leave him stranded between Umuofia's separate male and female worlds, already an inhabitant of a literal no-man's-land where the torch of Okonkwo's own legacy—one hitherto sired by his outcast father—will obviously be extinguished.

Upon this scene Ikemefuna, a young exile from his own fatherland, seems to descend as a miraculous savior, redeeming and reconciling father and son. But when the hour of the young redeemer is come, and he is led away for sacrifice, Okonkwo makes a rash, unsanctioned leap towards the glory of final self-denial—and falls, cursed, into the abyss of the outcast.

The nourishing womb of the Motherland constitutes yet another no-man's-land. And when Okonkwo re-emerges into the world of manhood, Umuofia, his fatherland, has already been lost to the foreign fathers of white civilization. Okonkwo's suicide completes the tragic cycle, as the evil *chi* that so viciously plagued his father completes its work on him.

"It's possible to write about commonplace things and objects using commonplace but precise language, and to endow those things … with immense, even startling power," Raymond Carver once said of his stories. The message of this statement may, in part, account for the broad appeal of Carver's truly startling tales.

WHAT WE TALK ABOUT WHEN WE TALK ABOUT LOVE

They sat at the table drinking gin, and as the afternoon light poured into the kitchen from the big window behind the sink, they "somehow got on the subject of love." Mel McGinnis, a cardiologist, was telling his friends, Nick and Laura, and his second wife, Terri, that, in his opinion, the only "real love" was "spiritual love." Terri disagreed. She remembered more complex experiences with love; to prove her point, she related how an ex-boyfriend had "loved her so much he tried to kill her." According to Mel, that kind of love belonged to "the kick-me-so-I'll-know-you-love-me school." In the kind of love he was talking about, Mel affirmed, "you don't try to kill people."

"If you call that love," he insisted, "you can have it." Mel took down a second bottle of gin from the cupboard and poured another round of drinks. They raised their glasses in a toast: "To love." Then they "grinned at each other like children who had agreed on something forbidden." Before long, Mel launched into a gently bombastic discourse on what real love wasn't. First, he said, there was "carnal love"; then, "sentimental love." And there had been a time once, he confessed, when he'd loved his first wife "more than life itself." But now he hated her guts, he stated flatly; and this change of heart had led him to conclude that "all this love we're talking about" would, in the end, "just be a memory" anyway. "Am I wrong?" he wanted to know, by now just a little drunk. "Mel, we love you," Laura said. "Love you too, Laura," Mel replied. "And you, Nick, love you too…. You guys are our pals."

But Mel still hadn't said all that he wanted to say about love. The bottle made its way once more around the table, and he commenced a story—a story that would "make us feel ashamed," he said, "when we talk like we know what we're talking about when we talk about love."

He told of a case in which an older couple had suffered "the works" after a youthful drunk driver had plowed his dad's pickup into their camper. Following two weeks in intensive care, the injured twosome was transferred to a private room, where they lay covered in bandages from head to foot. Their only exposed parts were the little "eye-holes and nose-holes and mouth-holes."

Mel shook his head in disbelief, then resumed. Every day, he said, when he treated the husband for his wounds, he would press his ear against the husband's mouth-hole, and the husband would tell him how his "heart was breaking" because he couldn't turn his head to see his wife. "Can you imagine?" Mel asked.

By then everyone was more than a little drunk; daylight was fading. Mel suggested they polish off the gin and go out to dinner, but no one moved from the table. Nick thought he could hear his heart pounding—in fact, he could hear everyone's heart, beating in rhythm. Still, he didn't move. He was overcome by "the human noise [they] sat there making, not one of [them] moving not even when the room went dark."

FEATHERS

Jack and Bud were coworkers. One day in the lunchroom—about eight months after Bud and his wife Olla had had their first baby—Bud invited Jack and his wife, Fran, out to their house for supper. It would be just the four of them, he said. "You and your missus, and me and Olla. Nothing fancy. Come around seven."

When Jack got home that night and told Fran about the invitation, she "wasn't too thrilled." She felt that the two of them didn't really "need other people." In fact, it was this very attitude that explained why Jack and Fran were not planning on having children of their own.

Nonetheless, as Jack and Fran pulled up the long, graveled driveway to Bud and Olla's house, they heard a strange wailing cry—"May-awe, may-awe!" Then they saw "something as big as a vulture [flap] heavily down from one of the trees" and land right in front of the car. Fran had never seen a live peacock before and she said so. Jack could only repeat "Goddamn" over and over again.

After supper, the peacock again took up wailing, and Olla told Bud to let the bird in. Bud boasted that he had paid "a hundred bucks for that bird of paradise," then grinned, saying, "I got me a woman with expensive taste."

Just then the baby awoke and began to cry, so Olla brought him to the table. Jack "drew a breath" and stared: to call the baby ugly, he thought, would be to do it credit. The child had "no neck to speak of" and it was so "pop-eyed" that it looked as if "it was plugged into something." Bud allowed that "he's no Clark Gable," then quickly added, "But give him time."

Fran had just begun to play patty-cake with the child when the peacock once again appeared. As the enormous bird "ran its long neck across the baby's legs" and "pushed its beak in under the baby's pajama top and shook its stiff head back and forth," it was all too obvious the two creatures were involved in a game they had played before.

There was a moment during that evening when Jack realized he "felt good about almost everything."

He could barely "wait to be alone with Fran," to tell her what he was feeling—how he'd closed his eyes at the table and wished to "never forget or otherwise let go of that evening."

Jack's wish came very tangibly true. When they got home that night, Fran turned to her husband and said, "Honey, fill me up with your seed!" For her, that evening had immediately changed everything. "Goddamn those people and their ugly baby," she would later say. "And that smelly bird."

For Jack, though, the change had come about more gradually. He was still adjusting to having his own family, he explained—not to mention the fact that he and Fran almost never talked anymore. Still, he remembered how that night at Bud's they'd hugged each other goodnight and Olla had given Fran some peacock feathers to take home. He remembered how Fran had sat close to him in the car and had "kept her hand" on his leg all the way home.

A SMALL, GOOD THING

It was Saturday afternoon, and Ann Weiss was ordering a birthday cake for her son Scotty. The baker, an older, sullen man, took down her phone number. Then, looking up at her just once, he said, "Monday morning."

But on Monday morning Scotty was hit by a car on his way to school. After the accident he was able to walk home, but as he started telling his mother what had happened he suddenly "closed his eyes, and went limp."

Of course, the birthday party was canceled. Day passed into night at the hospital, and the boy had not regained consciousness. Even so, Ann and Howard were reassured by Dr. Francis's diagnosis that Scotty was "in a very deep sleep—but no coma."

Late that evening Howard decided to go home to wash up and change clothes. The phone was ringing as he entered the house. When he picked up the receiver, a voice on the other end said, "There's a cake here that wasn't picked up." Distraught and tired, Howard shouted, "I don't know anything about a cake," and hung up.

The next morning Scotty was taken to Radiology for a brain scan. Howard and Ann had sat up all night, hugging each other and praying; "they were together in it, this trouble." When Scotty was finally brought back to the room, Dr. Francis spoke for the first time about the possibility of a coma. Still, he insisted, there was "no good reason" why Scotty "shouldn't come around. Very soon."

At last Howard persuaded his wife to go home for an hour or so to freshen up. She had just arrived when the phone rang. "Mrs. Weiss," said a male voice. "It has to do with Scotty, that problem. Have you forgotten about Scotty?" Then the speaker hung up, leaving Ann half-crazed with anxiety.

When Ann returned to the hospital, her husband broke the news: the doctors had decided to operate. But just then, Scotty opened his eyes. They tried talking to him, but after awhile "his eyes scrunched closed, and he howled until he had no more air in his lungs." It was all over in less than a minute.

The doctors explained that the cause of death was "a hidden occlusion … a one-in-a-million circumstance." When Howard and Ann, grief-stricken, returned home, once again the phone began to ring. "Your Scotty," the man's voice said, "I got him ready for you…. Did you forget him?"

By now thoroughly overwrought, Ann screamed and hung up; she would "like to shoot" the man and "watch him kick," she told her husband. Then it dawned on her that it was the baker's voice. "Drive me down to the shopping center," she stammered, turning to Howard.

Warily, the baker let the distraught couple in. At once Ann took out after the man, shouting that they were Scotty's parents and that Scotty was dead. At this, the man cleared a table and asked them to sit down. "Let me say how sorry I am," he began. He was "just a baker"; years ago, perhaps, he had been "a different kind of human being." The truth now, he explained, was that he didn't "know how to act anymore."

"Please," he begged, "let me ask you if you can find it in your hearts to forgive me?" Seeing the sincerity mirrored in the old man's eyes, the distraught couple took off their coats as the baker set coffee and hot cinnamon rolls on the table. "I hope you'll eat," he urged them. "Eating is a small, good thing in a time like this."

For the first time since Scotty's accident, Howard and Ann were hungry. As they ate, the baker spoke of his own isolated existence, of what a dismal loneliness it was to be "childless all these years." Then he brought out a loaf of dark bread. Breaking it open, he asked them to smell it. "It's a heavy bread," he told them, "but rich." They ate as much as they could. And as they continued to talk into the night, "they did not think of leaving."

Commentary

Raymond Carver (1938–1988) writes in a friendly, familiar style that puts most readers instantly at home. At the same time, there is within his conventional working-class characters a profound sense of estrangement. Perhaps it is this paradox that gives the stories their edge and resonance.

In "A Small, Good Thing," for instance, the baker is so isolated by his work that he barely remembers what it once felt like to be a "human being." In "Feathers," Jack and Fran's marriage is so fragile that a simple dinner with casual acquaintances forever alters the course of their lives.

Yet the things-really-are-as-bad-as-they-seem pathos and bleakness evident in Carver's sketches are what make his hard-luck stories at once memorable, meditative and funny. We see in them a series of American grotesques—similar in nature to the urban paintings of Edward Hopper or the frontier tales of Bret Harte; a chain of events, of human beings at once disfigured by progress and cut off from their pasts.

Isaac Babel (1894–1941) published his first story in 1916, the year before the onset of the Russian Revolution. Subsequently he participated in both the Revolution and the Civil War that followed. Stark, realistic, violent, intensely personal, many of his tales are based on his experiences and observations during these periods, and on his service with Russian forces in Poland during the 1920s.

The following stories focus on characters caught up in personal predicaments: the devastation of personal identity amid one's high hopes and the harsh and very private realities of pre-holocaust conditions.

GEDALI

Sabbath evenings made the young man melancholy. Since the Revolution, the Jewish quarter of Zhitomir was a shadow of its former vibrant self. He walked to the market, but beheld there only its death; gone were the days of fat and plenty. Later on, he found half-blind Gedali, who had continued to hold onto his shop even after all the other shopkeepers had fled or been killed. Gedali and his young, dispirited visitor sat on empty beer barrels and talked of the Sabbath—and of the Revolution.

Gedali blessed those high-spirited days in Poland when the revolution had interrupted a pogrom that had cost him his sight. Though Gedali loved music, he had handed over his phonograph to the State when threatened with a firing squad. The young soldier who had come to collect had told him, "She cannot do without shooting, because she is the Revolution." Gedali, puzzled, had replied, "The Revolution is the good deed of good men. But good men do not kill…. Then how is Gedali to tell which is Revolution and which is Counter-Revolution?"

Now the two men, one jaded with age, the other still touched with youthful hope, became quiet as they watched the first star pierce the sunset sky, marking the beginning of the Sabbath. "Jews should be going to the synagogue," Gedali stated solemnly—but the young man could only think that there was a scarcity of good people, of good Jews in Zhitomir. He asked of Gedali if Jewish biscuits and a glass of tea could be made available for the Sabbath. "Not to be had," Gedali answered over his shoulder as he limped away. The Sabbath was coming, and Gedali, founder of Zhitomir's revolutionary front, made his way to the synagogue to pray.

THE STORY OF MY DOVECOT

Young Babel yearned to own a dovecot, a coop or home for pigeons. His father promised the wherewithal to build and populate it, but only if Babel passed the entrance exams to the preparatory class of the secondary school of Nikolayev. After much angst and many long nights of rote memorization, Babel at last did pass the exams, and in the autumn of 1905, as promised, his father gave him the money he sought.

Grandfather Shoyl helped build the dovecot with materials secured by Babel. Then, on the morning of October 10, 1905, the very day Emperor Nicholas bestowed on the Russian people a constitution, Babel set out toward the bird market to purchase his six doves. He would not be deterred, even though gunshots could be heard off in the distance. As he left the bird dealer's stall, a neighbor walked by and reported that "Grandfather Babel has been constitutioned to death." Grandson Babel commenced the walk back to his home, only to be accosted by Makarenko the Cripple and his wife, Kate. "What's that you've got in your sack?" Makarenko asked, snatching the bag from Babel's hands. Opening it to find Babel's long-coveted pigeons, the crippled man took one out and examined it for a moment, then dealt young Babel a crushing blow with the hand holding the bird, knocking him to the ground. "Their spawn must be wiped out," growled Makarenko's wife. "I can't a-bear their spawn, nor their stinking menfolk." Babel, stunned, felt the bird's blood and guts trickle down his temple. Weeping bitterly, he staggered to his feet and furtively made his way home down secluded alleys and backstreets. When he arrived, he found Grandfather Babel lying dead in the dusty yard.

AWAKENING

All the people among Babel's family acquaintances—merchants, fishermen, carpenters, clerks and brokers alike—had insisted that their children study music. Naturally, Babel's parents wanted the same for him. After all, many master musicians had grown up in Odessa: Mischa Elman, Zimbalist, Gabrilowitsch, even Jascha Heifetz. The boy's father could endure poverty, perhaps, but fame he must have. Thus, thrice weekly young Babel went to Zagursky's house for violin lessons. Much to his father's displeasure, however, no amount of practice could make Babel a master violinist. " … The sounds dripped from my fiddle like iron filings," he later recounted, "causing even me excruciating agony, but my father wouldn't give in."

What Babel really wanted was to be a writer. Even as he scraped his way through violin exercises, he devoured the pages of Turgenev or Dumas secreted under the pages on his music stand. During the day he told his friends improbable tales; at night he committed them to paper.

The bookish lad finally managed to escape from Zagursky's den of horrors. As a fugitive schoolboy loitering near Odessa's harbor, he met up with Mr. Trottyburn, a retired sailor who befathered the multitude of young truants spending their days in the port, far away from work, school—and violin lessons. Trottyburn encouraged his young charge to write. "One must suppose there's a spark of the divine fire in you," he remarked after a brief scrutiny of a story Babel had composed. Yet Trottyburn was scandalized that Babel cared nothing for the natural world; the boy could not name a single bird, tree, shrub or flower. "A man who doesn't live in nature, as a stone does or an animal," the old man scolded kindly, "will never in all his life write two worthwhile lines." Babel pondered these words as he returned home. Where could he acquire a feeling for nature?

The aspiring writer's answer did not come that afternoon, for Mr. Zagursky finally arrived to check on the reason for Babel's three-month absence. Catching a glimpse of his former instructor coming up the walk, Babel hurriedly locked himself in the bathroom to escape his father's almost certain wrath. After everyone had gone to sleep, he emerged and stole outside. In the depths of night he headed towards the port, only to be corralled by his Aunt Babka and taken to his grandmother's house. "The moonlight congealed on bushes unknown to me, on trees that had no name. Aunt Bobka held me firmly by the hand so that I shouldn't run away. She was right to. I was thinking of running away." Still the thought ran through his head: How would he attain a feeling for nature?

HOW THINGS WERE DONE IN ODESSA

Babel asked Arye Lieb how it happened that Benya Krik had ascended the ranks to become "King" of Odessa's gangsters; why not Froim Grach, Kolka Pakovsky, or Chaim Drong? So Lieb recounted to his assemblage of boys the story of Benya Krik, bidding them to "forget for a while that you have glasses on your nose and autumn in your heart," to forget their studies and let their imaginations roam.

Krik was the son of a wagon driver, but he dreamed of being something bigger. He went to Froim Grach and confided that he wanted to be *somebody*—and to be somebody, he was willing to rob anybody. A council of gangsters was held and a decision rendered: unleash Krik on Tartakovsky the storeowner—also known as "Nine Holdups," because he had already been robbed nine times, and as "Kike-and-a-half ... because no one Jew could hold all of the sheer nerve and all the money that Tartakovsky had." And so it was arranged.

The tenth robbery of Tartakovsky's store was progressing quite smoothly, until Savka, a member of Krik's gang, staggered drunkenly onto the scene and improvidently shot and killed the store's clerk, who had been meekly handing over the money and jewels.

Later, Tartakovsky offered one hundred rubles to the aunt of the dead clerk, Pesya, as a token compensation for the loss of her nephew. Krik became enraged when he heard of this perfidy. He raced over to the aunt's home, barged into the negotiation with Tartakovsky, and won for the bereaving Pesya a much better settlement: a five-thousand-ruble lump sum and fifty rubles each month. Krik, himself mourning the clerk's untimely death, arranged for the unfortunate young man to have the grandest funeral Odessa had ever seen. And after the funeral, Krik entreated the mourners to attend a similar ceremony for Savka, the group's reckless—and unfortunate—gunman, who had been interred in the Jewish cemetery next to the grave of the hapless clerk.

Following the funerals, everyone but Krik and his three associates had fled the graveyard as if they were running from a fire. "I wasn't there personally," Lieb concluded his account, "but the fact that the cantor, the choir, the Burial Society didn't ask any payment—that I did see with the eyes of Arye Lieb."

And Arye Lieb ended with this declaration: "Now you know everything.... You know who was the first to utter the word 'King.' That was Moses [the Lisper]. And you know why he didn't give this name to Grach the One-Eyed or to Kolka the Crazy. You know everything. But what's the use, if you still have glasses on your nose and autumn in your hearts?"

Commentary

Babel brings to vibrant life the experience of growing up as a Jew in his hometown of Odessa, mixing objectivity and tenderness with humor, cruelty, and elements of wild fantasy. These surrealist components are especially evident in "How Things Were done in Odessa." We enter the action through the eyes of young boys being told a story—itself a soft, sentimental scene. The tale of Benya Krik which unfolds, however, is at once cruel and fantastic. Early on the story seems credible enough (and, sadly, in our modern age, all too familiar). But as the events progress, the picture of a gangster negotiating with one of his victims to secure a pension for the aunt of another victim begins to stretch the bounds of credibility. Yet, only after we finish the story do we wonder how we were able to suspend disbelief.

The more realistic "Awakening," on the other hand, involves a familiar dilemma: the struggle of a growing child to choose between parental expectation and the assertive demands of his own soul.

Though Babel's stories were ostensibly political, presented as portraits of life among the peasant and Jewish populations of pre-World-War-II Russia, apparently many Soviet officials were not at all pleased by the works. Isaac Babel disappeared forever during the Stalinist purges and pogroms of the late 1930s. It is unclear whether he was executed by Stalinists or if he died later in a Nazi concentration camp after Germany invaded Russia in 1941. Whichever is the case, Russian and Jewish literature were made the poorer by Babel's untimely death.

ROLL OF THUNDER, HEAR MY CRY
by Mildred Taylor, Dial Books, 1976

Type of work
Young adult fiction
Setting
Mississippi; 1933
Principal characters
Cassie Logan, a fourth-grade girl
Stacey Logan, her twelve-year-old older brother
"Mama," Mary Logan, their mother
"Papa," David Logan, their father
"Big Ma," their grandmother Caroline
T.J. Avery, Stacey's bothersome friend

Story overview

Even though their mother was a teacher, the Logan children didn't like going to school. Their days were filled with rote lessons, drab textbooks and whippings. Nevertheless, every morning from October to March—when they were not needed to pick or plant cotton—Cassie Logan, her big brother Stacey, and their two younger brothers set off on the hour-long trek to the dismal old schoolhouse.

The children "could have more easily endured the journey" had it not been for the Jefferson Davis school bus that always zipped up behind them and doused them in mud. Stumbling to avoid the mud-shower, the children knew they were simply "comical objects" for the white driver and students on the bus, who yelled racial epithets at them as they passed.

"Big Ma, it ain't fair," the children complained. Though Big Ma knew far better than her grandchildren how difficult it was to be scorned by "ignorant white folks," she "was not one for coddling." She simply replied, "You jus' keep on studying and get a good education and you'll be all right."

Big Ma untiringly maintained the land that her husband had bought for the family way back in 1918. Born a slave, Paul Edward Logan had worked long hours as a carpenter so that he could purchase 400 acres of good farmland from the Grangers, who had once owned the largest plantation in the area. But now Paul Edward was dead, and Harlan Granger, who still held onto a ten-square-mile tract abutting the Logan's acreage, was out to reclaim the property that his family had sold. Of course, Big Ma would never consider giving up her family's land. She made sure that the taxes and mortgage were paid, even if everyone had to do without. And from spring to fall, Papa worked in Louisiana laying railroad track to reduce the debt. "You ain't never had to live on nobody's place but your own," he'd once told Cassie, "and long as I live and the family survives, you'll never have to ... "

In the meantime, Cassie had concerns of her own, not the least of which was the horrid school bus. Stacey, though, devised a plan to stop that bus from splashing them. One day he, Cassie and their little brothers dug dirt from the road's center, forming a pothole. Then they hid in the bushes and watched as the bus "careened drunkenly" in the drooping earth and "died." While the white students piled out into the mud and "moved spiritlessly toward home" on foot, Cassie thought gleefully, "A well-maneuvered revenge!"

However, that night Cassie's glee turned to terror when Joe Avery, the father of Stacey's talkative, pesky friend T.J., arrived at the Logan home. "They's ridin' t'night," he told Mama. "It don't take but a little of nothin' to set them devilish night men off."

The children were hurriedly sent to bed. But Stacey and Cassie already knew all about the night riders. Just a few days earlier T.J. had related how the night men had gone over to the Berrys' house and put "a match to 'em." Mr. Berry and his nephews had been "burnt near to death." Tonight, thought Cassie, they must be out to avenge the school bus. "Stacey," she whispered, "they're coming after us!"

It was a long time before Cassie finally succumbed to sleep. When she woke, it was "still nightly dark" outside and she could see "a caravan of headlights" moving toward the house. One of the cars pulled into the driveway and a man got out. He "stared at the house for several long moments" before he got back in and drove away, followed by the others. "Waves of terror swept over" Cassie as she lay trembling into the dawn.

It was not until a week later that Cassie found out from T.J. that the night riders had at first mistaken the Logans' house for Sam Tatum's. It seems Tatum had called a white merchant named Wallace a liar; in retaliation the night men had hunted Tatum out and tarred and feathered him.

Even though everyone knew that the Wallaces were among the night men who had "poured kerosene over Mr. Berry and his nephews and lit them afire," the black sharecroppers had no choice but to shop at their store: despite the high interest rates they charged and the drinking and gambling that went on at the store, the town's black citizens relied on credit with the Wallaces to buy their wares. Although Mama had gone from house to house in the black community, trying to convince them to do their buying in Vicksburg, even she knew her plan would be difficult to carry out. Who in Vicksburg would extend credit to the sharecroppers?

Then over the Christmas holidays Mr. Wade Jamison, Big Ma's white estate lawyer, offered to back the credit himself. "I'm a Southerner born and bred," he explained in his soft-spoken way, "but that does not mean that I approve of all that goes on here."

In the days following Mr. Jamison's offer, Mama took shopping orders from various black families. Then one morning Papa and his friend Mr. Morrison climbed into the wagon and set off to Vicksburg.

The shopping trip was a success. But shortly after Papa's return, he received a visit from Mr. Harlan Granger, who was piqued because Papa's brother

Hammer had recently bought a silver Packard almost identical to his own. But what really disturbed him was the Logans' "traveling store." "Seems to me," Granger frowned, "you folks are just stirring up something." Then he threatened to foreclose on their mortgage if they missed a payment. "You plan on getting this land," Papa said, "you're planning on the wrong thing." Harlan Granger only grinned.

One day after Mama caught T.J. cheating on an exam, the boy stormed out of her class to report her to Kaleb Wallace, a member of the School Board. Wallace immediately appeared at Mama's classroom—accompanied by fellow board member Harlan Granger. Granger interrupted Mama's history lesson on slavery in the South. "I don't see all those things you're teaching them in here," he said, holding up a textbook. "All that's in that book isn't true," explained Mama evenly. "You so smart," Granger hissed, "I expect you'd best forget about teaching altogether … thataway you'll have plenty of time to write your own book." Mama had lost the job that helped pay the mortgage.

Papa insisted on taking Stacey along on his next shopping trip to Vicksburg. "I want [Stacey] strong … not a fool like T.J.," he said, although Mama worried because she had heard that Wallace might make trouble for them.

On the night that Papa, Stacey and Mr. Morrison were due to return, the family waited nervously. "Something's happened to them! I can feel it!" Mama finally blurted out. And her fears were soon confirmed. When the wagon appeared, Papa lay cradled in Mr. Morrison's arms. Men in a truck had driven by and shot him, the bullet just grazing his head. Then, as he had fallen to the ground, the wagon had rolled over Papa's leg. Mr. Morrison had struck one of the Wallace boys as the truck sped away, and it was rumored that the boy's back was broken.

Mr. Morrison brought Papa into the house and laid him on the bed. He was barely conscious, and his broken left leg jutted out awkwardly. "But who'd shoot Papa?" Cassie cried out in disbelief. "Can't nobody just shoot Papa!" But the concern for now was Mr. Morrison's safety; the Wallaces surely would retaliate.

Sure enough, just days later while Mr. Morrison was out on an errand, Kaleb Wallace found him. Spewing venom, he railed, "I oughta cut your heart out. I'm gonna come get you for what you done!"

Before long the bank—at Granger's and Wallace's urging—demanded that the Logans pay off their mortgage in full. "Said our credit's no good anymore," Papa told his family. Then he promised, "We ain't gonna lose the land …. Trust me."

In fact, his brother's Packard provided unexpected help: Hammer sold it to pay off the loan. "What good's a car?" he smiled. "It can't grow cotton. You can't build a home on it."

Still, the Logans could not forget Wallace's threat. One night Cassie lay listening to Mr. Morrison's mournful singing on the front porch: *Roll of thunder, hear my cry; Over the water, bye and bye. Ole man's comin' down the line; Whip in hand to beat me down.*

But I ain't gonna let him, Turn me round. Suddenly the girl heard a strange sound and opened the door to her room. There stood T.J. She stared "in horror at the deep blue-black swelling of his stomach and chest." T.J. explained that after he and some white friends had broken into a gun shop, one of the white boys had smashed the owner's head in with an axe, before turning on T.J., beating him and leaving him behind to take the blame.

Terrified, Cassie and her brothers helped T.J. to the Avery house. As they turned towards home, they saw the headlights of the night riders. Within seconds the white men had broken into the house and wrenched the Averys out by their feet. Pulling T.J. aside, they began kicking at his mutilated stomach.

Just then, Mr. Jamison arrived. "Y'all let the sheriff and me take the boy," he called out. The mob ignored him. Ropes in hand, they began dragging T.J. outside. "Papa'll know what to do," Stacey frantically whispered to his sister as they turned and ran for home.

Hearing what had happened, Papa grabbed his shotgun and "disappeared into the night." And as "the thunder banged menacingly" outside her window, "Big Ma fell upon her knees and prayed a powerful prayer." Then everyone waited silently. All at once Mama "sniffed the air." The cotton was on fire. Big Ma and Mama instantly began filling buckets and dipping burlap in water. "You set one foot from this house," Mama told her children as she dashed out the door, "and I'll skin you alive."

Early the next day the youngsters learned what had happened. Seeing the flames, everyone in the community—both black and white—had rushed to the cotton fields to put out the fire. They all thought that lightning had caused the blaze. But the Logan children knew better: Papa "had started the fire [to] stop the hanging."

T.J. was arrested; the law would now determine his fate. The long night was finally over. Yet, before she slept, Cassie cried for T.J.—and she cried for the land.

Commentary

Mildred Taylor, one of the country's foremost writers of children's literature, received the coveted Newbery Medal in 1977 for *Roll of Thunder, Hear My Cry*. Like most of Taylor's fiction, this novel reflects the author's fascination with the vivid oral narratives that she heard as a child during summer visits with her Mississippi relatives. She credits the South for the sense of family, community and history that reinforces her writing.

The impact of history is everywhere apparent in *Roll of Thunder*; it fills the Logans' lives and shapes their thinking. Mama, especially, sees an honest confrontation with history, no matter how painful, as essential. Even when her job is on the line, she will not teach the sanitized version of Southern slavery found in the school's textbooks. This portrayal of a "docile, subservient people, happy with their fate" is contrary to her heritage. For Mary Logan, truth and freedom are synonymous.

CATCH–22
by Joseph Heller, Simon & Schuster, 1961

Type of work
Satirical black humor

Setting
Pianosa, an island off the coast of Italy; the last months of World War II

Principal characters
Captain John Yossarian, an unwilling American Air Force bombardier
Orr, Yossarian's tentmate
Doc Daneeka, the squadron's flight surgeon
Captain R.O. Shipman, the chaplain
Colonels Cathcart and *Korn,* two vain and scheming group commanders

Story overview

During the closing months of World War II, Colonel Cathcart resolved to get his picture in the *Saturday Evening Post* and be promoted to the rank of general. In a characteristic act of false valor, he volunteered his 256th Squadron for a bombing mission to destroy the bridge at Ferrara, boasting that the squadron could execute the mission within 24 hours. But now for seven days straight they'd missed their target.

In a bid for redemption—and possible early discharge—Lieutenant John Yossarian offered to take his unit of six bombers over the bridge a second time. Their first run over the target had been a dismal failure when Yossarian's navigator had become disoriented and was unable even to find the Ferrara bridge. But this time out, he vowed, he would prove himself.

That Sunday, as the American planes again approached the target, every German anti-aircraft cannon in the area was aimed directly at them. Yossarian concentrated on his sights while releasing his bombs. When he finally looked up, he noticed the plane above him was engulfed in flames. He watched in horror as it crashed unceremoniously into the sea, its pilot killed.

The loss of the plane and its crew disturbed Colonel Cathcart. "It's just that it looks so lousy on the report," he told Yossarian. "How am I going to cover up something like this in the report?" Yossarian suggested that the colonel award him, as squadron leader, a medal. The colonel agreed, and Yossarian received both the Distinguished Flying Cross and a promotion to the rank of captain.

Yossarian believed that virtually everyone around him was crazy, especially Colonel Cathcart, who had successively raised the number of flying missions from 25 to 30, and then to 35. Moreover, Yossarian found it incredible that even "strangers he didn't know shot at him with cannons every time he flew up into the air to drop bombs on them." Others, of course, thought it was Yossarian who was crazy. His symptoms, as recorded by the squadron's physician, included "a homicidal impulse to machine-gun strangers, retrospective falsification, and an unfounded suspicion that people hated him and were conspiring to kill him."

The 256th Squadron was next assigned to fly a mission over Bologna. But Yossarian did all in his power to ensure that nobody even got near the target. He knew that his fellow bombardiers shared his feelings. Luckily, rainy weather delayed them at first. When the skies cleared, Yossarian added laundry soap to the sweet potatoes in the mess hall, inducing an epidemic of diarrhea. Yet another whole day was lost to allow the rain-soaked runway to harden enough for the planes to take off. Then later that night he stole into the compound and redrew the bomb line so that it extended above their target city. When Cathcart saw the map in the morning, he was overjoyed to see that Bologna had already been miraculously bombed and this week's reports would be spared the smirches of Yossarian's blunderings.

Eventually, the commanding officers realized that in truth the city had not yet been bombed, and ordered their fighters to shell it. Yossarian again deliberated on how he might scuttle the mission. Approaching the target, he tore out the cords of his intercom, thus breaking communication with the pilot and forcing his plane to turn back. The other men, however, flew on to complete the mission successfully.

The next day Colonel Cathcart received orders to bomb the city again, and this time Yossarian was assigned to fly lead. As his plane flew in over the target and the enemy's anti-aircraft gun let loose with a furious barrage, Yossarian lost his nerve. Dropping his bombs prematurely, he left the formation. Then, from a safe distance, he watched his own and another squadron of planes get blasted out of the sky. Among them was the plane belonging to Orr—Yossarian's stocky, buck-toothed tentmate—which was forced to crash-land. In fact, almost every time Orr went up he had to ditch his craft.

Several days later Orr invited Yossarian to go up in a plane with him so that he could teach him how to crash-land—in case it ever came in handy. Yossarian refused, thinking Orr, like all the rest, was crazy.

Later, during a mission over Avignon, Yossarian realized that his buddy Snowden, the plane's radio gunner, had been shot. "I'm cold, I'm cold," Snowden whimpered, ashen-faced, as he reached toward a stain near his armpit. Yossarian "ripped open the snaps of Snowden's flak suit and heard himself scream wildly as Snowden's insides slithered down to the floor in a soggy pile and just kept dripping out."

After that debacle Yossarian vowed never again to put on a uniform; he'd "lost his nerve ... because Snowden lost his guts." This time when the heroic bombardier lined up to receive his medal, he stood in formation stark naked; he had made up his mind to spend the rest of the war in the hospital, easily confusing the doctors with symptoms from a blessed liver condition that fell just short of being jaundice.

Yossarian had always felt comfortable and safe in the hospital. For one thing, he could distract himself by opening and censoring the enlisted men's letters, closing each with an amazingly different and inventive signature. For another, he knew that there, if he started screaming, someone would come running to help. Besides, fewer people died there. "They couldn't dominate Death inside the hospital, but they certainly made her behave."

It was in the hospital that Yossarian was visited by company chaplain R.O. Shipman, a quiet, introverted Anabaptist who doubted his own usefulness. During one visit Yossarian's comrades asked the chaplain to speak to Colonel Cathcart to convince him not to raise their bombing quota again. Summoning his nerve, the chaplain suggested that Cathcart bring in troops stationed in Africa to replace his men. The colonel brushed off the chaplain's advice, but Shipman persisted. In particular, he mentioned Yossarian: "He's in a very bad way, sir. I'm afraid he won't be able to suffer much longer without doing something desperate." Cathcart was unconvinced.

Still, after the chaplain had departed Cathcart began to second-guess himself: "Maybe sixty missions were too many for the men to fly.... But he then remembered that forcing his men to fly more missions than everyone else was the most tangible achievement he had going for him."

Yossarian, meanwhile, busily tried a different tack: he would feign insanity and force the doctors to send him home. "You're wasting your time," Doc Daneeka told him flatly. "Sure, I can ground you by filling out a slip saying you're unfit to fly. But there's a catch"—*Catch-22*. The contradictory essence of Catch-22, the doctor explained, was that he could send home anyone whom he thought was crazy. If, however, Yossarian *asked* to be sent home, then the doctor could not consider him crazy, because feeling threatened by a dangerous situation was a purely rational response. Besides, Daneeka added, if he started grounding men or sending them home, Headquarters might up and reassign him to the Pacific: " ... All they've got in the Pacific is jungles and monsoons. I'd rot there." Yossarian pled for Doc's understanding. "I'm asking you to save my life." But Daneeka only smiled sullenly: "It's not my business to save lives."

After completing a total of 71 missions, Yossarian made a last-ditch effort to stay alive: he refused to fly again. Even as fat-cat officers and supply clerks were profiting from the war by selling government goods on the black market, the absurdities of Catch-22—which by now had cost the life of his friend Orr—were sending countless men to their graves. When word of Yossarian's defiance spread, other fliers' attitudes deteriorated, too. Before long, the commanding officers realized they had a problem on their hands: "The men with seventy missions were starting to grumble because they had to fly eighty.... Morale was deteriorating and it was all Yossarian's fault."

While they pondered what to do, Yossarian took an unauthorized leave to Rome. He knew that going AWOL could lead to a court-martial, but the pressure he felt was even less bearable than the thought of losing his freedom. Walking through the dark, rain-swept streets of the city, he witnessed horrible scenes of poverty and brutality. A youngster without shoes or a coat plodded along in the freezing drizzle. Further on, a man cudgeled a small boy, while an uncaring crowd looked on. "The night was filled with horrors." He felt like a psychiatrist walking through "a ward full of nuts, like a victim through a prison full of thieves." When the bombardier returned to his bed, two military policemen arrested him for having left without a pass.

By now the officers had decided what to do with their resident nonconformist. Colonel Korn greeted Yossarian with a smile and told him they were sending him home—with a promotion and another medal. But only on one condition: he had to play along with the big boys and give a good report. The alternative, they told him, was a court-martial. They still did not acknowledge that they were assigning the men too many missions. But the other fly-boys would be easier to discipline after Yossarian was gone, especially if he consented to endorse their authority.

Yossarian reluctantly agreed to the deal. But guilt soon overwhelmed him; he would be betraying his men. When he asked Shipman for advice, the chaplain replied only that "you must do whatever you think is right ... " It was then that Yossarian knew he could not double-cross his men; yet he also knew he could not fly another bombing mission.

Within minutes after Yossarian had made the decision to desert, Chaplain Shipman rushed in with news that Orr, whom they all had thought dead, was still alive and had made it to Sweden. Yossarian was elated; Sweden was neutral territory, and American soldiers could stay there under comfortable conditions for the duration of the war. Now he understood why Orr had gotten shot down on practically every mission he'd flown: he was practicing crash-landings in the ocean so he could escape to Sweden. "It's a miracle of human perseverance, I tell you," the chaplain added. "And that's just what I'm going to do from now on! I'm going to persevere ... "

Following Shipman's lead, Yossarian laced up his boots and headed north. He had survived war's insanity.

Commentary

Joseph Heller's imaginative, irreverent use of comedy in *Catch-22* forces the reader to re-examine what at first may seem insanely funny. Combat scenes often begin on a humorous course, only to be replaced by overwhelmingly horrible scenes. A similar form of "black comedy" is apparent in the different motives of the commanding officers, resulting in a heightened perception of the frightening effects of misused power.

Yossarian's moral progression is an important theme in the novel. After deserting and being brought back to the squadron, he confronts three choices: save his own life and thereby leave his buddies to deal with the irrational Colonel Cathcart; go to prison for crimes he did not commit; or desert, knowing he has already served his country beyond the so-called "line of duty." By choosing to run away instead of submitting to Korn's "odious deal," Yossarian is not escaping from his problems. Rather, he is finally accepting the responsibility to act on his moral beliefs.

Vladimir Nabokov (1899–1977) once remarked, "While I keep everything on the very brink of parody, there must be, on the other hand, an abyss of seriousness." The interplay of solemnity and humor in his work underscores the double-edged nature of life, which contains elements of both comedy and pathos. In addition, Nabokov's vagueness about time and place hurls his readers into a fractured and unreal world.

"THAT IN ALEPPO ONCE ..."

Although I can produce documentary proofs of matrimony, V.'s friend wrote him in a letter, *I am positive now that my wife never existed.* They had married, the letter continued, not long before the "gentle Germans" thundered into France. The groom was a journalist, and his criticisms of the Nazi regime were sure to breed trouble. So the couple was intent on fleeing to New York, where the bride's uncle lived. Unable to obtain proper emigration papers, however, they were forced to settle for a move to Nice. His wife greatly mourned the loss of their dog, which they were obliged to leave behind. *The honesty of her grief shocked me,* he wrote, *as we had never had any dog.*

The newlyweds traveled by train, stopping along the way at the city of Faugeres. Unfortunately, while he was in the station buying food, the train left without him. He sent frantic messages to all the stops between Faugeres and Nice, to no avail. After several months, he finally found his wife in Marseilles. They were enormously relieved to be together again, and promptly began the long, torturous process of applying for visas to America.

In the meantime, he tried to get his wife to tell him what had transpired during the time they were separated. She told him several tales; each differed wildly. According to one story, she had taken up with a group of refugees and found shelter at a Russian church. Later, she claimed that she had met a traveling salesman who abducted her and took advantage of her. In yet another version she told how she had run off with the salesman of her own accord.

On the day their visas were issued, he arrived at their apartment to discover that she had disappeared with all of her belongings. He made a few inquiries, all without success. He did run into an elderly acquaintance, who berated him for having done away with the dog back in Paris.

Despondent, he took a boat to America. On board, he encountered a doctor who claimed to have known his wife in Marseilles. The doctor said she had told him about her husband, who was planning to meet her shortly with their bags and visas. *It was at that moment,* read the letter's final paragraph, *that I suddenly knew for certain that she had never existed at all.* Her uncle's address in New York, he later ascertained, was no more than an alley between two buildings.

Still, sometimes he felt the desire to go look for her. At the same time, he feared to make the attempt. *It may end in Aleppo if I am not careful,* he closed. The war was raging on, and Aleppo was a dangerous place to be.

SCENES FROM THE LIFE OF A DOUBLE MONSTER

Floyd was trying to resolve a question that he and his brother had been asked years ago. Could they recollect, a doctor had once inquired, the very first time either of them realized the peculiarity of their condition and destiny? Floyd and Lloyd had been born conjoined twins, wed forever at their navels. They had shared the same umbilical cord in the womb. Their mother had died immediately after their birth—shocked beyond measure by their condition, Floyd conjectured—and were left to be raised by their Grandfather Ibrahim.

After thinking it over, Floyd remembered that by age three or four he had started wondering about his strange relationship with his brother. By age nine, he decided, "I knew quite clearly that Lloyd and I presented the rarest of freaks."

Soon Grandfather Ibrahim began exhibiting them for money. Floyd had never felt shame or revulsion at his condition. However, the first time he ever saw another child—a "normal" child, a child other than Lloyd, that is—he concluded that he must be a person with two shadows. He reflected on the strangeness of it all: he and the other child both cast shadows in the sun, but Floyd "possessed yet another shadow, a palpable reflection of my corporal self." And looking on at the awestruck boy, who stood gazing at the conjoined twins, Floyd merely wondered if he "had somehow managed to lose his [shadow], or had unhooked it and left it at home. Indeed, Lloyd and Floyd were complete and normal; he was neither."

The twins, though unashamed, lived in fear of one person: their Uncle Novus. They knew that he was determined to steal them from their grandfather and sell them to a showman or a carnival. So, one day, thinking they had little time left to enjoy themselves, they decided to visit the Black Sea. They had lived near its shores their entire lives, but had never seen it. This was their only chance to "do what we were absolutely forbidden to do: go beyond a certain picket fence, open a certain gate."

But as they emerged from a stand of cypress trees onto the beach, they saw Uncle Novus waiting for them with his carriage. They tried to flee, but he easily snatched them up and pitched them into a large box. They would never again see their home.

Now, 20 years later, Floyd thought back on the moment of their abduction. Had some adventurous mariner stepped out on the shore just then, would he have experienced the thrilling trace of some ancient enchantment as he confronted a gentle, two-headed mythological monster framed by cypress and white stone? "But, alas," Floyd reminisced, "there was nobody to greet us there save ... our nervous kidnapper, a small doll-faced man wearing cheap spectacles..."

CONVERSATION PIECE, 1945

I have a disreputable namesake, the writer began, *complete from nickname to surname, a man whom I have never seen in the flesh but whose vulgar personality I have been able to deduce from his chance intrusions into the castle of my life.* The writer's double did indeed seem to be both real and disreputable. For example, one time in Nice a young woman called on the writer at his hotel, took one look at him, apologized, and left. The writer also learned that his double had once borrowed (and never returned) a copy of the "Protocols of the Wise Men of Zion," a fraudulent document whose only use was to incite anti-Semitic pogroms. And while lecturing in Zurich, the writer had been arrested in a restaurant for the other man's crime of violence: smashing three mirrors.

After emigrating to the United States, the writer thought he had escaped his evil twin. Then one month he had received a phone call. A woman's voice on the other end invited him to attend a lecture about the war. The caller had assured him that he "would be very, very much interested in the discussion."

Yes, when he attended the lecture he found that he was interested—but also deeply disgusted. The lecturer, a Doctor Shoe, made apology after apology for German atrocities committed against the Jews, but then turned around and equated those atrocities to the Allied bombing of Leipzig, Munich, and Dresden. When the writer could stand no more, he retrieved his coat and galoshes, and stormed out. But not before he had announced to his hostess, "You are either murderers or fools, or both, and that man is a filthy German agent."

A week later, he received a letter:

Esteemed Sir,
You have been pursuing me all my life. Good friends of mine, after reading your books, have turned away from me thinking that I was the author of those depraved, decadent writings. In 1941, and again in 1943, I was arrested in France by the Germans for things I never had said or thought. Now in America, not content with having caused me all sorts of troubles in other countries, you have the arrogance to impersonate me and to appear in a drunken condition at the house of a highly respected person. This I will not tolerate. I could have you jailed and branded as an impostor, but I suppose you would not like that, and so I suggest that by way of indemnity...

The amount demanded was actually quite modest.

TIME AND EBB

A 90-year-old scientist had survived a disease that he and everyone else thought would kill him, and now he was resolved to write his memoirs. He discov-

ered, however, that while his early memories were remarkably clear, his recent recall was frustratingly confused. *I cannot,* he scrawled, *remember the name of the eminent scientist who attacked my latest paper, [just] as I have also forgotten those other names which my equally eminent defenders called him.* Stymied by this phenomenon, he decided to content himself with contrasting the world of his childhood with the world of his old age.

He was born a Jew in Paris, but his family had fled to the United States to avoid the tortures another nation had inflicted upon his race. He remembered thinking that the "skyscrapers" of New York were quaintly misnamed. To his childish eyes, they did not grate against the sky at all, but seemed to merge delicately and serenely into the sunset, their pulsating lights merging softly with the twilight.

As a child he had also been fascinated by airplanes, though he doubted anyone born since the 1970s would remember them as fondly as he did. There was such a romance about them in those early days. *A boy would know planes from propeller spinner to rudder trim tab,* he recalled, *and could distinguish the species by the pattern of exhaust flames in the darkness.* One of his most cherished boyhood experiences was imitating the drone of an engine as he watched a plane approach, growing larger as it roared overhead. Then slowly it would shrink into the distance until *nothing but a lone star remained in the sky, like an asterisk leading to an undiscoverable footnote.*

Commentary

Tragicomedy is Nabokov's stage; timelessness is a major component in his fiction. Consider the newlyweds in "That in Aleppo Once ... " At the beginning of the story we chuckle at the thought of a man deducing that his wife never existed. Then as we read on, the tale turns to tragedy when we comprehend that she is a woman who in fact physically exists, and lives in a web of lies and deceit.

A similar development occurs in "Scenes From the Life of a Double Monster." Initially it is amusing when Floyd says that the first child he ever saw was neither complete nor normal. But the mild humor is transformed into pathos when we learn that the conjoined twins have previously been abducted by their uncle, sold to strangers, and made to live out their lives under the gawking eyes of circus goers.

"Conversation Piece, 1945" also stretches the limits of credibility. A writer is haunted by an apparent double throughout his life; in the end he is contacted by this disreputable doppelgager —who has likewise been troubled by the antics of the writer.

"Time and Ebb" is a more tender and melancholy story. An aged scholar writing his memoirs, perhaps in an attempt to liberate himself from the painful thoughts of his own mortality, becomes lost in reverie about the early days of flying machines. Ultimately, he leaves his readers in a state of wistful reminiscence, in much the same way as he was left behind by his vanishing airplanes.

Type of work

Semi-autobiographical account of a young man's
painful progress towards maturity

Setting

England, Germany and France; late 19th, early 20th
centuries

Principal characters

Philip Carey, an awkwardly handicapped but
intelligent and responsive young student

Hayward, Philip's intellectual friend

Sally, Philip's long-awaited bride

W. Somerset Maugham refers to *Of Human Bondage*,
published in 1915, as an "autobiographical novel." In a
sense, perhaps, writing this book helped Maugham to
exorcise the unhappy recollections of his own early life.

The plot is almost void of explicit action; instead, it
transports the reader on a journey through one young
man's developing selfhood as he struggles to find a
center of meaning in the callow world around him. The
intensely personal drama follows Philip Carey through
his many new beginnings, aborted careers and relationships, and finally to his epiphanic proclamation: "
… If one has lived thoroughly, then life has a meaning
and a pattern as rich, though as unsymmetrical, as
those formed by the colors [of] an oriental rug."

Story overview

Torn from the home of his dying mother as a
young boy, Philip Carey was sent to live with his
uncle, the vicar in a small English village. It was
with mixed feelings, however, that the childless clergyman and his wife took on the guardianship of their
sensitive, club-footed nephew.

Soon after Philip's arrival at the vicarage, they
decided to enroll him in a religious boys' school where
the students were encouraged to aspire to Holy
Orders. Though at times bitterly frustrated by his
impairment, nine-year-old Philip relied on his astute
mind to survive and excel among his classmates.

Over the next several years a wave of religious
fervor spread through the school. Always eager for
new experiences, Philip joined the circle of the devout,
and every night before the lights went out he read
earnestly from the Bible.

One night he came across a passage that particularly excited him: *If ye have faith, and doubt not …
whatsoever ye shall ask in prayer, believing, ye shall
receive.* When he heard the same words repeated in a
sermon on the following week, the young boy received
them as an epiphany. Fervently he fell to his knees and
asked God to make his club foot whole; for the rest of
his holiday break he continued in this attitude of
prayer.

When at last school reconvened and Philip saw
that his abnormality was still not repaired, he
consulted his uncle. "Supposing you asked God to do
something, and really believed it was going to happen,

like moving mountains, and you had faith and it didn't
happen, what would it mean?" he asked. The uncle
replied curtly: "It would just mean that you hadn't got
faith." Although he did not see how his faith could
possibly have been any stronger, Philip did not demur.
Perhaps this passage, like many other Biblical verses
his elders had explained to him, somehow meant
something quite different from what it actually said.

But as the next few years passed, Philip found he
could no longer fully embrace the passion of his
former faith; daily religious exercise slipped into mere
formality, his classes became cumbersome, and the
prospect of ordination oppressed him. After much
argument, Philip's aunt and uncle allowed him to
continue his studies in Germany under the guidance
of a local professor. There, Philip experienced for the
first time in his eighteen years a sense of beauty and
freedom.

After three months at school in Heidelberg, Philip
was assigned a new roommate, a scholarly 26-year-old
Englishman named Hayward. Though new acquaintances generally tended to disgust him, Philip rapidly
took a liking to his fellow student, soon finding
himself thirsting for their daily walks and discussions.

When Hayward left Heidelberg to tour Italy, Philip
was at a loss. Back home in England, however, he
struck up a close friendship with the daughter of a
former rector, a Miss Wilkinson. In the meantime, his
guardians took him aside to discuss his future. Philip
flatly refused to attend Oxford University, where his
uncle had hoped he could study on a scholarship for
his degree. But his aunt continued to aver that there
were only three professions worthy of a gentlemen:
Army, Church, and Law. With his club foot and his
unwillingness to accept ordination, the first two
options were ruled out; this left only Law.

Immediately, Philip's uncle contacted the family
solicitor. Though this gentleman said that though he
had no room for Philip as an apprentice in his own
law firm, he knew of a position elsewhere. Philip,
sensing that a move to London would be a great
opportunity, accepted the position and made plans to
leave within the month.

Meanwhile, over time Philip had grown ever
fonder of Miss Wilkinson. One Sunday evening while
he was calling on her family, the object of his interest
complained of a headache and coyly retired to her
room. Not surprisingly, Philip offered to stay and
attend her, if necessary, while the others left for an
engagement. When the house had emptied, he crept
up to the door of Miss Wilkinson's room. After what
seemed like hours, he finally turned the handle—and
there she stood, wearing just her petticoat. In that
instant, a sensation of horror washed over him. Was
this love? But despite his revulsion, he also felt a tinge
of conceit. After all, even with his deformity, another
human being had finally demonstrated an attraction
to him.

Not long after the tepid consummation of his attachment to Miss Wilkinson, Philip set off for London. Unfortunately, the novelty of his new work quickly evaporated. Some nights he would just sit outside a window, watching the people and wondering if he would ever experience any sense of true belonging or joy.

Spring came, and Philip looked forward to Hayward's London homecoming. His hopes were dashed, however, by a letter from his friend that extolled the delights of springtime in Italy; Hayward had decided to stay on and enjoy them. "There are only two things in the world that make life worth living, love and art … " the letter continued. "My feeling is that one should look upon life as an adventure [and] expose oneself to danger. Why do you not go to Paris and study art? I always thought you had talent."

When the end of the year came, Philip decided to act on Hayward's advice. But his uncle would have no part of this plan: "… Going to Paris to be an artist," he sputtered. "What a Bohemian idea." Why, no true gentleman, his uncle added, would participate in such an act. "Well," Philip replied disgustedly, "… I'm beginning to doubt I'm a gentleman."

Since his uncle had refused to provide for him in Paris and it was still three long months before Philip, now twenty, would receive his small inheritance, he ended up scrounging for bed and board at Anitrano's Art school in Paris, where he learned there was very little work to be found in painting unless one did portraits for rich Americans.

With the advent of summer, many Parisian artists retired to the countryside. Philip, finally sustained by his inheritance, joined in the sabbatical. He had but one life to live, he reminded himself earnestly, and it was important to do things right.

But after two years of the artist's life, Philip received some frank advice from his art teacher to the effect that he should get out while he could. Feeling sufficiently liberated, if not successful, he returned to the vicarage, where his aunt had recently died.

It was during this interlude at the vicarage that Philip first read Darwin's *The Origin of Species*. In the "struggle for life" depicted so graphically between its covers, the young man found an intensity and grandeur that he had never before encountered. Raptly turning the pages, he was swept by a flood of new religious elation. On one side of his life lay society's barren and repressive formalities; on the other, like a sun, shone the laws of natural selection. At last he had found the true measure of Good and Evil.

Now 25 and resplendently armored in his new Darwinian vision, Philip once again set out to conquer life in London. The exam he had passed earlier to certify for his accountancy easily qualified him to enter medical school; romance, too, soon crept back into his life in the emaciated form of a consumptive young waitress named Mildred.

But the star of Darwinian optimism soon burned itself out. Every morning Philip awoke with tortured thoughts of Mildred—who snubbed and belittled him at every turn. Desperately the lover persevered—only to find himself recoiling in disgust when Mildred at last relented to his advances. In some perverse way, spurning the love he had finally won from the woman who had once enthralled him brought a new dimension of freedom to Philip's life.

Philip returned to his medical studies with a new—and well-grounded—vigor. When he took the exam for the third time, he passed it with honors and stepped into his new career as an out-patient clerk at the hospital.

Then, when he was in his late twenties, life suddenly passed once again out of Philip's control. It was 1914, and world war had reared its hideous head. Soon nearly all of Philip's old friends and classmates were dead or fighting in the trenches; no one knew where the future of Europe lay.

To distract himself, Philip carelessly played the stocks—and disastrously lost. He could no longer afford medical school, and he was soon put out on the street. Though he had always been poor, until now the possibility of starving had never entered his mind. Poverty of this order was for Philip—as it was for every respectable middle-class Englishman—a disgraceful and dehumanizing disease. The crippled orphan from the vicarage who had fought to form a niche for himself in the world now once again found himself on the outside looking in.

Through the next months Mr. Altheny, a kind-hearted acquaintance from Philip's hospital, often invited the young man to dine with him and his family. And finally, with Altheny's assistance, Philip landed a job as a clerk in a department store.

As the war raged on, Philip avoided the places he had frequented in happier times. His great consolation was a ripening friendship with Mr. Altheny's daughter Sally. That same year his uncle passed away, leaving him enough of an inheritance to finish medical school—and to ask Sally to marry him.

Finally, at the age of thirty, Philip Carey was able to find peace in a world that had both enslaved and rejected him. He now saw the underlying sameness of all the elusive dreams and passions that had once repressed him. From his first childhood ardor for a Biblical God through his worshipful pursuit of Hayward's intellect, of art and Bohemianism, of Darwinian struggles, and of an unobtainable woman, he had been chasing the same chimera: "… All his life he had followed the ideals that other people, by their words or their writings, had instilled in him, and never the desires of his own heart. Always his course had been swayed by what he thought he should do and never by what he wanted with his whole soul to do."

Now, "with a gesture of impatience," Philip put all of this aside. Henceforth, he would follow his own soul. As he pressed his hand in Sally's and walked out onto the street, he saw that the cabs and omnibuses and people were hastening in every direction—and that "the sun was shining."

Ernest Hemingway (1899–1961) served as a volunteer ambulance driver at the Italian front during World War I. In later years he became a big-game hunter, a restless adventurer, and an American expatriate who lived in 1920s Paris. These experiences emerge in much of his fiction, particularly in the following stories, which are among his most popular.

THE SNOWS OF KILIMANJARO

Harry, living with his wife in the wilds of Africa, was dying from the gangrene that had spread down his right leg. Yet he felt no pain and no horror at what he knew was coming. His only regret was that he had so much more to write—all the tales he had saved for the time he could do them justice. Now he was determined not to fail; he would pick up a pen and write those stories.

"I wish we'd never come here," sighed Harry's wife. If only they had remained in Paris, where this sort of thing was unheard of. "What have we done," she murmured, "to have this happen to us?"

Harry, a pragmatist in such matters, only could respond that he'd either forgotten to put iodine on the deep abrasion he'd received, or had acted too late. Then he turned on her; she was to blame. It never would have happened, he mumbled, if she hadn't left her people, the old Westbury, Saratoga, Palm Beach people, for him. That's why it had happened.

"That's not fair," she countered. "I love you. Don't you love me?"

"No," he answered.

Searching his mind for times when all was right with the world, Harry saw himself standing with his pack at a railway station in Karagatch, saw the woodcutter's house with the big porcelain stove at Gauertal, and remembered the time the deserter had come there with bloody feet in the snow to escape the gendarmes who were tracking him. "He had never written a line of that, nor of that cold, bright Christmas day ... [when] ... Barker had flown across the lines to bomb the Austrian officers' leave train, machine-gunning them as they scattered and ran."

Now, in the stark light of the real Africa, here was Harry's wife, crying because of his words. He told her he was sick, that he was crazy, that he did love her as he'd never loved another. Then he turned, contradicted himself, and called her a *bitch*, crying, "I'm full of rot and poetry!"

Harry awoke later that evening and found her gone, out shooting game. He thought back to how he'd become involved with her, of how

the relationship was over for him the moment it had begun. He'd told himself he was going to write about rich people, that he was not really one of them, merely a spy in their country. But now he would never do it; he'd grown soft sharing in his wife's opulent life. And now his abilities had dulled and his desire to work had ebbed to a halt—until he did no work at all.

She returned later with some meat. As they talked and drank together, he realized how cruel he'd been earlier. Only then did it occur to him—with jolting clarity and remorse—that he was really dying. "It came with a rush; not as a rush of water nor of wind; but of a sudden evil-smelling emptiness, and the odd thing of it was that the hyena slipped along the edge of it."

He thought of how he had quarreled with his wife, how he'd argued with all of the women he'd loved. One time before traveling to Constantinople, he and the woman who was then his wife had argued. Afterwards, he'd picked up prostitutes, trying to lessen the hurt. When that didn't work he sent his wife a letter telling about his activities and how he couldn't kill the hurt. He'd witnessed the horrors of battle, but lived to return to Paris to find the lovers' quarrel over and forgotten—until the day his letter had arrived, ending the relationship. " ... He had always thought he would write it finally. There was so much to write ... but now he never would."

Maybe, just maybe, he could write something, he contemplated, before he died. But he had no strength, and his current wife had never learned to take dictation. So he was left to ponder all those things he *should* have written: the log house and the Black Forest after the war, the passionate and gay French quarters, the ranch. His mind turned to the half-wit boy who'd shot a man, and who, afterwards, had allowed himself to be taken to the sheriff under the mistaken certainty that he would be rewarded for having kept the man out of the hay. He thought of his war buddy, Williamson, hit by a stick bomb, caught in the barbed wire, begging for someone to kill him.

Now as Harry's head drowned in such thoughts, he felt a very real weight upon his chest. "It crouched now, heavier, so he could not breathe. And then, while [the servants] lifted the cot, suddenly it was all right and the weight went from his chest."

Morning had dawned, and Harry could hear the droning of old Compton's plane. Compton, a veteran pilot, had earlier loaded him into the craft. Then—just the two of them—they had lifted off, soaring high into the sky through a storm. At last, "all he could see, as wide as all the world, great, high, and unbelievably white in the sun, was the square top of Kilimanjaro."

The woman awoke to the whimpering of a hyena. As she lay in the darkness, she could not hear her husband breathing.

A CLEAN, WELL-LIGHTED PLACE

It was late and everyone had left the cafe except an old man who sat in the shadow the leaves of the tree made against the electric light. Two waiters watched him. One, the more seasoned of the two, remarked to his companion that the old man had tried to hang himself the week before; his niece had found him and cut him down. "Why?" asked the younger one. "Fear for his soul," the older waiter replied.

Mention of the elderly gentleman's attempt on his own life brought a new turn to the conversation. The younger waiter immediately wanted to know if he was a man of wealth. Yes, he had plenty of money. And so the question lingered: Why had he tried to kill himself?

"I wish he would go home," grumbled the young waiter. "I never get to bed before three o'clock. I have a wife waiting in bed for me." At this, his companion revealed that the old man had also once had a wife, and maybe he would be better off if he still had her. Now all he had was his niece to look after him.

Some minutes later, when the old man ordered another drink, the young waiter refused to bring it. Resigned to his fate, the old man sighed, paid his tab, and left. *The waiter watched him go down the street, a very old man walking unsteadily but with dignity.*

As the two waiters closed up for the night, the unhurried one asked why the younger hadn't let the old man stay and drink. His answer was harsh: he was in a hurry to get home to his wife. Upon hearing this the older one responded that he hated to close up so soon. There were those who needed a clean, well-lighted place—those who did not want to go home to bed. He would stay behind and close up later. "Good night," said the younger waiter, disappearing out the door.

Later that night, making his way home after closing down the cafe, the older waiter stopped by a bar and tried to speak with the barman. The barman wasn't at all interested in conversation, and the waiter left after one drink, deciding that "he disliked bars and bodegas. A clean, well-lighted cafe is a very different thing."

Now he would go home and maybe sleep before daylight. He was sure it was only insomnia, and many people must have it.

FATHERS AND SONS

One lazy Sunday morning Nicholas Adams steered his car down the empty streets of a small town, "under the heavy trees ... that are part of your heart if it is your town and you have walked under them, but that are only too heavy, that shut out the sun and dampen the houses for a stranger." He drove straight through into the countryside, through fields forgotten until springtime. In his mind, Nick hunted those fields, sizing up each clearing for signs of quail.

His father had taught him to hunt, his keen-sighted father, who, Nick judged, "saw as a big-horn ram or an eagle sees, literally." He had loved his father very much. But, for Nick, it was not good to call up such a remembrance too often—for his father had killed himself. Someday, Nick resolved, he would write about that—but not yet; he wasn't ready yet for such a painful burden. Perhaps he would write about other things first, like his first love, an Indian girl named Trudy.

Suddenly Nick's thoughts were interrupted by his own son, who, sitting beside him on the seat, asked what it had been like when he was little. Nick hesitated, then told the boy about hunting with Trudy and her brother, and with his father. Yes, the boy's grandfather had been a good shot; in fact, Nick had always gathered that his dad was disappointed with his son's shooting skills. "I don't feel good never to have even visited the tomb of my grandfather," the boy said finally.

"We'll have to go," Nick said. "I can see we'll have to go."

Commentary

Ernest Hemingway is renown for his ability to conjure up powerful characters and storylines using a minimum of narrative. In "A Clean, Well-Lighted Place," for instance, the characters reveal themselves almost entirely through dialogue. The old man is the most defined of the three main characters, yet he says very little. Rather, his character unfolds from the waiters' discourse.

Hemingway's settings are likewise characterized by an economical use of language, a skill perhaps developed during the author's early days as a journalist and war correspondent. Though widely regarded as a man of action, most of Hemingway's shorter works employ very little action, relying on introspective dialogue and description rather than dramatic events to propel the story along. "Fathers and Sons" is aperfect case in point, consisting almost entirely of conversation; "action" occurs only within the protagonist's private thoughts.

The characters who appear in the fifteen stories that comprise *Dubliners*, though widely diverse in age, occupation and ethical constitution, are bound by a common setting—the city of Dublin—and by the quirks of Irish culture, a subject of which Joyce never tired.

COUNTERPARTS

"Mr Alleyne wants you upstairs." Hearing this, Farrington muttered an oath and stood up from his desk. Heavily, for he was a large man, he climbed the stairway and entered his boss's office. There was Alleyne, his head "so pink and hairless that it seemed like a large egg" as he bent over his papers.

"Farrington! What is the meaning of this?" Mr Alleyne began his reprimand. "Why have I always to complain of you?" As Alleyne carried on, Farrington "stared fixedly at the polished skull which directed the affairs of Crosbie & Alleyne, gauging its fragility." Yet he managed to stifle the rage that rose in his own throat. He felt the need for a drink. At length, the red-faced executive officer finished his not uncommon tirade and growled, "Are you going to stand there all day?... Go downstairs and do your work."

Farrington returned to his desk, but he was so angry that he could only "stare stupidly at the last words he had written." Exiting the premises with a practiced deceit, Farrington sought O'Neill's shop, where he could soothe his dry throat with a beer.

Upon Farrington's return to the office, the chief clerk informed him that Mr Alleyne had been asking for him again. He knew that he had no time to complete the transcription his boss was expecting, and hoped his boss would not notice that "the last two letters were missing." Now he found his anger returning. "He felt strong enough to clear out the office single-handed. His body ached to do something, to rush out and revel in violence."

All at once Mr Alleyne was standing in front of him, shouting in a fury. "Do you think me an utter fool?" Caught off guard, Farrington took a moment to respond—and when he did, his answer surprised him as much as it did his coworkers. "I don't think, sir," he stammered, "that that's a fair question to put to me."

Mr Alleyne turned scarlet; he twitched and shook his fist. "You impertinent ruffian!... " he screamed. "You'll apologize to me for your impertinence or you'll quit ...!"

When the workday was over, Farrington "felt savage and thirsty and revengeful, annoyed with himself and with everyone else." He'd apologized to Mr Alleyne, but he knew that his boss would now harass him relentlessly—and things were bad enough already. Once again he craved a drink. As he walked through the crowded streets of Dublin, he began to compose a witty narrative about his momentary triumph over Mr Alleyne, as he would relate it to the boys in the bar. Indeed, Flynn, O'Halloran and Leonard, his drinking chums, considered Farrington's telling of the incident at work highly amusing and found his final rejoinder superb.

A bit later Leonard introduced his friends to another young man named Weathers, a performer of sorts who volunteered to take them to a pub where some "nice girls" of his profession could be met. In mock politeness, O'Halloran offered to excuse Farrington from the adventure—"because he was a married man"—but Farrington declined to be excluded.

At the pub, Weathers greeted two young women. Farrington exchanged a few glances with one of them, but when she left the room she brushed past him without looking back. Instantly Farrington's anger flared again—anger at his lack of money, and anger at Weathers, whom he now saw as a sponge.

Now Weathers sat at their table, displaying his biceps and boasting. Farrington's friends called upon him to upstage the braggart in an arm-wrestling contest. But Weathers bested the hulking Farrington, not once but twice. When another man dared to voice approval of Weathers' technique, Farrington rose up to challenge the meddler. But O'Halloran tactfully called for a final round of drinks.

After a night of arm-wrestling and noise-making, Farrington, discontent, found himself alone, waiting for his tram to appear. Arriving home at last, he let himself in at the kitchen door and bellowed for his wife. A little boy, one of his five children, greeted him and lit the lamp. Farrington roared at the tyke, "What's for my dinner?"

An expression of agony came over the boy's face. "I'm going ... to cook it, pa," he answered. But his father had reached his breaking point. "You let the fire out!" he brayed, seizing a walking stick from behind the door. The child sank to his knees, awaiting the blows. "By God, I'll teach you to do that again. Take that, you little whelp!"

With blood streaming from his thighs, the boy begged, "Don't beat me, pa! And I'll ... and I'll say a Hail Mary for you.... I'll say a Hail Mary for you, pa, if you don't beat me ... I'll say a Hail Mary ... "

THE DEAD

When Miss Julia and Miss Kate staged their annual dance, it was guaranteed to be the success it had always been. But on this occasion the elderly sisters were feeling a certain agitation due to the unexpected tardiness of their favorite nephew, Gabriel Conroy. It was, after all, well past ten o'clock, and the dance was already in progress. The doting aunts were also fretting over the possibility that Freddy Malins might arrive even more drunk than usual.

At last Gabriel and his wife Gretta appeared on the snowy doorstep and were met by the maid. Soon after, Aunt Julia came to announce the arrival of Freddy, hinting that Gabriel must hasten to assess the newcomer's condition. "It's such a relief," said Aunt Kate to Gretta, "that Gabriel is here."

All took to dancing and socializing. When the waltz ended, a young lady sat down to play the piano. Gabriel "liked music, but the piece she was playing had no melody for him." Retreating from the drawing room, he returned only when he perceived the recital's conclusion.

For the next dance Gabriel was paired with a Miss Ivors, a "frank-mannered" young woman who invited her partner to bring his wife on a tour of the Atlantic coast. When Gabriel replied that he was more inclined to take a cycling excursion of Belgium or France, Miss Ivors became indignant. "And haven't you your own land to visit," she sputtered, "that you know nothing of your own people, and your own country?" Suddenly annoyed, Gabriel retorted, "O, to tell you the truth, I'm sick of my country, sick of it!" The dance ended and Gabriel escaped to a "remote corner of the room." Alone at last—that is, until his wife found him. "Gabriel, Aunt Kate wants to know won't you carve the goose as usual?"

After assuming his position at the head of the table, Gabriel commenced carving while Aunt Julia and Aunt Kate circled the table, "getting in each other's way and giving each other unheeded orders." When all were served Gabriel announced, "Kindly forget my existence, ladies and gentlemen, for a few minutes," and with that he commenced eating his meal.

Near the end of the feast "a few gentlemen patted the table … as a signal for silence," whereupon Gabriel rose from his seat to address the assemblage on the merits of Irish hospitality as personified by his aunts. He finished his eloquent discourse by proposing a rousing toast to the hostesses, who were quite overcome with emotion. Indeed, his speech was a great success, as was the event which it capped.

Gabriel and Gretta left the house in the company of a certain conceited tenor who would share their cab until they got out at the hotel. His wife strolling before him, Gabriel walked along, remembering some of their intimate moments together. But the tenor's presence forced Gabriel to restrain his passion.

Despite the tenor's objection, when they arrived home Gabriel tipped the driver hand-somely. When Gretta took his arm, the light pressure she applied filled him with a rush of desire. The aged porter saw them to their room, then departed.

Gretta immediately came to her husband's embrace, but the "serious and weary" expression she wore defied him. "You look tired," Gabriel said, at which she stretched upwards and kissed him, cooing, "You are a very generous person, Gabriel." The words filled his heart with joy. "Just when he was wishing for it she had come to him of her own accord." He stroked her hair—and yet again he sensed a resistance. "Gretta dear, what are you thinking about?"

Breaking free from his arms, she turned and collapsed in tears on the bed. Gently, Gabriel urged her to tell him what was troubling her. "I am thinking about a person long ago," she finally replied. He was a young man, a boy really, she sniffed, named Michael Furey, who had died at the tender age of 17. Then she added: "I think he died for me."

At this confession, a vague terror overcame Gabriel. "While he had been full of … tenderness and joy and desire, she had been comparing him in her mind with another…. He saw himself as a ludicrous figure, acting as a pennyboy for his aunts … orating to vulgarians and idealizing his own clownish lusts." The disillusionment in his voice betrayed him when he next spoke: "I suppose you were in love with this Michael Furey, Gretta." But she broke down in a fit of grief; Gabriel, holding in his sorrow, walked to the window and peered out at the darkness.

Later, as Gabriel imagined Gretta's "first girlish beauty," without which Michael Furey had been unwilling to live, tears welled up in his eyes and his thoughts "approached that region where dwell the vast hosts of the dead."

All across Ireland the snow was falling—even settling upon Michael Furey's cold grave. The soul of Gabriel Conroy "swooned slowly as he heard the snow falling faintly through the universe and faintly falling, like the descent of their last end, upon all the living and the dead."

Commentary

In the preceding two stories, even the apparently dissimilar protagonists, Farrington and Gabriel, share a comparable sense of impotence: Farrington is forced to submit to a man he detests, while Gabriel—caught up in Gretta's memories of a dead youth—feels powerless to seduce his own wife. However, the two men react to their common frustrations in totally opposite ways. The scorned office worker explodes in a flurry of rage and brutality; the bon vivant, on the other hand, manages to move beyond anger to a deeper understanding, a higher spiritual plane.

EAST OF EDEN
by John Steinbeck (1902–1968)

Type of work
Allegorical novel—a study of good and evil
Setting
California's Salinas Valley; early 1900s
Principal characters
Adam Trask, a wealthy idealist
Cathy "Kate" Ames Trask, his wife
Aron and *Caleb Trask*, their twin sons
Lee, the Trask's Chinese houseboy
Samuel Hamilton, Adam's friend, a Salinas rancher

Story overview

"There are monsters born in the world to human parents." And Cathy Ames, "born with the tendencies, or lack of them, which drove her all of her life," was just such a creature. As though nature concealed a trap, Cathy was beautiful and innocent in appearance—a pretty child who grew to become a pretty woman. But "even as a child she had some quality that made people look at her, then look away."

On a farm in Connecticut in the wind-up years of the 19th century, lived two bachelor brothers, Adam and Charles Trask. The sons of a Civil War veteran who'd left them a fortune, the Trask brothers had never gotten along; they simply didn't agree on anything. Recently, Adam had been trying to convince his brother that they should move to California, the land of opportunity. But Charles wasn't interested.

One night as the brothers debated this issue, they heard a scratching at the door. Investigating, they found a woman on the stoop, beaten and left to die. Adam immediately brought her inside.

Despite his brother's opposition, Adam was determined to keep the woman at the house and nurse her back to health. She healed slowly, but "Adam couldn't remember ever having been so happy. It did not matter that he did not know her name. She said to call her Cathy and that was enough for him."

But just as Adam fell utterly in love with Cathy, Charles grew to utterly mistrust her. Even on the day when the couple married, Charles made no attempt to hide his displeasure. Cathy would destroy Adam, he warned. And that very night, while Adam slept, Cathy slipped out of the room and went to Charles's bed. The next day, Adam took his new bride and headed for California.

The newlyweds moved into a ranchhouse situated in the Salinas Valley. When Cathy discovered that she was with child, Adam immediately hired a Chinese servant, Lee, to help her through her pregnancy. He also contacted a neighbor, Samuel Hamilton, about digging some new wells on his property.

Over the course of that first summer Adam and Samuel became friends. Like Charles, however, Samuel too distrusted Cathy. He couldn't put his finger on anything in particular; all he could say was "something's wrong."

Eventually, Cathy gave birth to twin boys. She rested for a week, then announced that she was leaving. When Adam tried to stop her, she picked up his Colt revolver, shot him through the shoulder, then walked out of the house.

Adam withdrew in despair. A year went by, and he remained immobilized. At length, Lee, who'd been single-handedly raising the still-unnamed twins himself while trying to take care of Adam, appealed to Samuel Hamilton for help. Samuel first tried talking to Adam; when talk failed to jolt his friend out of his detached, grey-water world, he raised one of his heavy fists and struck Adam in the face.

It worked, and the two men went to the long-overdue task of naming the twins: the dark-haired boy—curiously resembling his uncle Charles—Adam called "Caleb"; the other, fair-haired child was given the name "Aron."

Time passed, and Adam and Samuel grew older. One day when the twin boys were eleven, Samuel came to visit. Over dinner, the two men, together with Lee, discussed the biblical account in Genesis. Lee remarked how, for many years, the question of Cain's redemption had puzzled him. In one translation, he pointed out, God *promises* Cain that he will conquer sin; in another God *commands* Cain to conquer sin. Yet in the original Hebrew version, according to Lee, God says that Cain MAY conquer sin—an idea expressed by the word "Timshel." Adam favored the latter concept. Cain's fate was *not* set in stone; it offered possibilities of human freedom and choice.

After dinner, Samuel shared with Adam a secret he'd kept hidden for many years: Cathy was in Salinas, the owner of the most vicious and depraved whorehouse in the county. He'd never told Adam for fear of hurting him, but now felt he could no longer hold his silence.

A few weeks later, Samuel died. After attending the funeral in Salinas, Adam, curious, sought out his estranged wife. "She was still pretty … " was his first thought on seeing her, "but her outlines were not sharp anywhere…. The work of the years had been subtle." He saw this woman, who now went by the name "Kate," as she truly was: twisted and filled with anger. Before he left town, Kate told him how much she hated him; Adam answered that it didn't matter anymore. Truly, "Samuel's funeral and the talk with Kate should have made Adam sad and bitter, but they did not. Out of the grey throbbing, an ecstasy arose. He felt young and free."

The twins sprouted quickly. Now virtually grown men, they very much reminded Adam of himself and his brother in their youth. Caleb—or "Cal" as he preferred to be called—was cynical, worldly and cruel—much like Charles; Aron, like his father, was an idealist, loved by everyone. Young Aron refused to hear the occasional rumors about his mother; instead, he scrupulously trusted his father's sentimental stories about her death.

When the Trask family moved into Salinas so that the youths could attend a better school, the same pattern continued. Cal soon took to wandering the streets late at night. Since the restless youth made no trouble, however, the police let him alone.

From fragments of talk overheard in pool halls, Cal slowly came to a knowledge of his mother. Finally one night he located Kate's house and saw what went on there. He reacted strangely to this unveiled truth: instead of hurting for himself, he became concerned for his father. Toward Adam, he grew more and more protective; he wanted to make up somehow for his father's suffering. The old rebellious hatred and jealousy he'd previously held toward his brother seemed to have retreated from his soul.

As his father's new self-appointed guardian, Cal took it upon himself to learn all he could about Kate. He shadowed her for weeks until she finally confronted him. When he introduced himself, distant memories turned to clear recollections; the shadows of years past faded from her eyes. Finally she escorted her son into her grey, windowless "inner sanctum." As they spoke, Cal began seeing the sinister, sinful side of his mother, and vowed never to become like her. She was not part of him.

The nation was plunging headlong towards world war. Adam had recently lost a great deal of money in a disastrous business venture, while Aron yearned to complete college but lacked the funds. As the war fever heightened, Cal came up with a plan to help his father—and maybe Aron, too: he borrowed $5000 from Lee and enlisted Samuel Hamilton's son Will to be his partner. They would grow beans on the old King City ranch—a crop that would skyrocket in price when the fighting broke out. Aron, meanwhile, left for college, still financially strapped, with visions of becoming a minister.

Adam Trask was appointed to the Salinas draft board, a job he performed well and honestly, but also sadly. "He could not get over the feeling that the young men he passed to the army were under sentence of death." What's more, he feared that someday he would be forced to induct his own boys.

Aron returned home for Thanksgiving, disillusioned with the monotony of college life and ready to quit. Conversely, Cal was exuberant; his moneymaking scheme had flourished and he planned to present his father with a gift over dinner.

At last, dinnertime arrived. After picking at the pudding, Cal handed his father a red-ribboned package. Inside was fifteen thousand dollars in cash. The father's face folded into a frown. From whom had his son stolen this money? When Cal answered that he'd earned it by selling beans to the Army, Adam shook his head: "I send boys out ... and sons will die ... not one will come back untorn.... Son, do you think I could take a profit on that?"

Later that evening Cal took his reluctant brother Aron to visit their mother. Early the next morning, Kate was found in her inner sanctum, dead from a drug overdose. When her will was read, it was found that she had left her entire estate to her son, Aron Trask.

Cal sat in his room, pondering what he'd done, of how his brother had sobbed like a child leaving Kate's place, and then disappeared into the night. Hoping beyond hope that some sort of sacrifice might bring his brother back, Cal burned, one at a time, each of the crisp new bills that he'd tried to give his father.

Days later, Adam Trask, now suffering from forgetfulness, deteriorating eyesight and deepening depression, received a letter from Aron. *Dear Father*, it began. *I'm in the Army. I told them I was eighteen.*

On May 28, 1918, American troops carried out their first major offensive of the war. Within the day a telegram arrived at the Trask home: Aron had been killed in action. When he heard the news Adam immediately fell to the floor, the victim of a massive stroke.

At the hospital, after Adam had been stabilized, Cal shuffled up to his father's bedside and confessed everything he had done that pivotal Thanksgiving night. By taking Aron to see Kate, he was indirectly responsible for his brother's death. He was sorry, he explained. But Adam only stared into the blackness. His ever-faithful servant Lee begged on Cal's behalf, imploring Adam to forgive his only remaining son. Adam, trembling with exertion, merely arose and whispered a single word: "Timshel!"

Then he slept.

Commentary

Steinbeck's *East of Eden* can be interpreted as an elaboration of the Book of Genesis: A good and pure man seeks to create a paradise in California but is thwarted by the deeds of his helpmeet; their two sons bear names and traits much like those of Cain and Abel—Aron, the favorite, can do no wrong while, in contrast, Cal's every deed is a vain attempt to win favor from his father. And in the end, like Cain, he figuratively slays his brother after his own "offering" to Adam is rejected.

Though intimations appear throughout the book to the effect that a pattern of good balanced against evil repeats itself in every generation, the real question seems to be what is *good* and what is *evil*. Steinbeck's work also carries the message that no human being is all good or bad.

The notion of "Timshel" is vital to Steinbeck's purposes. Wrapped up in the word's meaning is the possibility of redemption, not through delivering up an offering—a hollow gift of grace—but through personal, proper choice and action. Adam denies evil, and thereby fails to cope with it. Cathy, by contrast, is "born" evil; she *has* no choice. Her rage fills the void left by her inability to love. And Aron symbolizes innocence betrayed—an individual locked out of the chance to become either good or evil. Cal, as the only member of his family to have developed to the point where he really is human, at first refuses to recognize his evil, then eschews it and tries to "protect" the innocence of others, and finally betrays it altogether, taking upon himself the consequences of his own actions.

TESS OF THE D'URBERVILLES
by Thomas Hardy (1840–1928)

Type of work
Impressionist novel

Setting
19th-century England

Principal characters
Tess Durbeyfield, a beautiful farm girl
Alec d'Urberville, her wealthy suitor
Angel Clare, her lover and, later, husband

Story overview

"Don't you really know, Durbeyfield, that you are the lineal representative of the ancient and knightly family of the d'Urbervilles, who derive their descent from Sir Pagan d'Urberville ...?" the parson asked.

"Never heard it before, sir," said John Durbeyfield, a penniless chicken-trader. The parson nodded, "Well, it's true."

Once Durbeyfield had digested this news, it was not long before the entire village had heard about the distinguished heritage of "Sir John." Thereafter, John and his wife began a busy round of pub-hopping to celebrate their newfound nobility and formulate plans for reclaiming the wealth of the d'Urbervilles, leaving their oldest daughter, Tess, with the chores of caring for her six brothers and sisters, making deliveries for her father—and dragging her parents from the pub each night.

Then, after an accident killed the family horse, Mrs. Durbeyfield dispatched Tess to see Mrs. d'Urberville, one of their newly claimed relatives, who lived close by. It was suggested that after informing the woman of their kinship, Tess might appeal for money to purchase a new horse.

At the d'Urberville estate Tess was greeted by Alec d'Urberville, the woman's handsome yet manipulative son. Alec explained to his attractive visitor that his invalid mother was unable to appear. He also revealed that his family were not in fact d'Urbervilles at all, but from a line of Stokes who had simply appropriated an unused title as their own. Though the young man made her vaguely uncomfortable, Tess chatted politely for a time, then took her leave—unaware that she had left her host enamored and intrigued.

Thus the thing began.... She was doomed to be seen and marked and coveted that day by the wrong man, and not by a certain other man, the right and desired one in all respects. Days later Tess received a letter, ostensibly from Mrs. d'Urberville—but actually written by Alec—inviting her to come and manage the d'Urberville's fowl farm. At her parents' urging, she agreed to go.

For weeks Tess labored at the d'Urberville farm, all the while hounded by the infatuated Alec. He tried to force himself upon her at every opportunity. She held off his advances—until one night when she accepted his offer for a ride home. On the way Tess fell asleep; she was still deep in slumber when Alec veered off the main path. When she awakened, they were lost in a dark fog deep in the forest. Out of fright and exhaustion, Tess finally succumbed to Alec's passion.

Soon afterwards, Tess learned that she was pregnant. Ashamed, she returned home and recounted what had happened. Her mother, only mildly shocked, was disappointed when Tess told her she was not going to marry Alec. Tess spent most of that winter indoors to hide her swelling belly. Then, after the child was born, she returned to work in the fields.

Just a few months after its birth, Tess's baby died. The griefstricken mother tried to give it a decent burial, in spite of the fact that it hadn't been baptized.

The sorrows of the past two years had taken their toll. Longing to start a new life away from her heartless parents, Tess took a job as a milkmaid in Talbothay, a village to the south. Once she had left home, she became more and more hopeful that she could put the past behind her.

She settled comfortably into her new position, boarding with a dairyman, his family, and three other milkmaids, Marian, Izzy and Retty. Though the male hands good-naturedly teased Tess, she ignored them all.

Then one day Angel Clare, a fellow farmworker, came to call on Tess. She recognized instantly that Angel was intelligent, educated—and something of a dreamer. He was also unimpressed by religious dogma and saw nothing special in Tess's d'Urberville heritage. He told her that he was apprenticing at the dairy in order to someday establish a farm of his own. Hearing of his high aspirations, "Tess seemed to regard Angel Clare as an intelligence rather than as a man."

The three other dairymaid boarders were likewise enthralled with Angel, and talked about him constantly. Tess, for her part, tried to persuade Angel that any of the three would make a worthier companion than herself. Angel, however, was alone captivated by Tess; despite her protests and lack of formal education, he found her "an exceedingly novel, fresh, and interesting specimen of womankind."

One day when Tess and Angel were alone, he took her by the arms and pulled her close to him. She was at once pleased and distraught; the experience with Alec was still too near the surface, and she was afraid to tell Angel of her past. He sensed her discomfort. After apologizing, he reprimanded himself for allowing his feelings to overcome his judgment, then left.

But Angel soon returned to ask Tess to marry him. At first she hesitated. Though she loved him, she felt she could never be worthy of him. Nevertheless, after much persuasion, Tess agreed to marry Angel on the coming New Year's Eve.

As the marriage date drew nearer, Tess fell into despair. How could she reveal her secret and still keep Angel's love? A few weeks before the wedding, Tess resolved to tell Angel about her past. Since she could not bring herself to confront him in person, she wrote him a letter and slid it under the door of his room. She was puzzled the next day when Angel, cheery as usual, said nothing about the letter.

Finally the day of the wedding arrived. Still guilt-ridden and baffled by Angel's reaction to her confession, Tess went to his room. There she found the letter, unopened—still jammed under the carpet near the door, just as she had left it. Panicking, she tried again to confess her secret to Angel, but he put her off; they could trade confessions after the wedding, he said. So the simple ceremony took place as planned, and the newlyweds departed for their honeymoon at the old d'Urberville family manor.

During dinner that night, Angel announced that it was time to set the record straight: He earlier had had an encounter with a prostitute in London. Relieved beyond measure that his confession was so similar to hers, Tess related the events that had marred her own past. But to her utter dismay, Angel—the Angel whom she had always known as so generous and charitable—would not forgive her. "Forgiveness does not apply to the case!" growled her new husband. "You were one person; now you are another." Beneath his layers of kindness and generosity, Angel was, in fact, a moralizing hypocrite. He could not love someone who had proven to be so different from the pure and innocent young girl he had imagined.

To avoid a scandal, Angel refused to accept a divorce. At last, he gave Tess some money and sent her away with the hope that they might reconcile at a future time.

Angel's family, waiting eagerly to meet his bride, was naturally disappointed when he returned home alone. He explained that his plan was to open a farm in Brazil and gave them the impression that his wife would stay with her family until she could join him there.

Meanwhile, at her home a few miles away, Tess, feigning happiness at her marriage, also claimed that she would soon join her husband in South America. With this, she turned over to her family half the money Angel had given her and left in search of employment. A letter from Marian, one of the Talbothay milkmaids, informed her of a job on the Flintcomb Ash farm—a place as bleak and formidable as its name. The labor there turned out to be brutal; but worse, at Flintcomb Ash, Tess discovered that after rejecting her, Angel had asked Marian's friend Izzy to accompany him to Brazil. This revelation shattered any hope for a reconciliation.

On her way into town one day, Tess passed by a large crowd gathered to hear a preacher. The man's voice was a familiar one: it was Alec d'Urberville! He had apparently repented of his predations and become a barnyard preacher. Tess hurried away, but not before Alec had sighted her.

Not long afterwards, Alec showed up at Flintcomb Ash, explaining that he had come to an understanding of his moral obligation. Now his wish was to wed the woman he had dishonored. Tess begged him to leave; she was already married. But Alec insisted that she forget about her estranged husband and marry him instead. Following months of Alec's vows and visits, Tess wrote a last impassioned letter to Angel, imploring him to come back or send for her before something regret-table happened.

In the meantime, Tess learned that her parents had taken ill, and once again she returned home. Life there became progressively hopeless. First, her father died; then the lease expired and the family was turned out of their home. Resolved in his pursuit of Tess, Alec suggested that the family stay at his estate. She initially rejected his offer, but facing the prospect of homeless-ness, she relented. And once she was installed at the d'Urberville estate, Alec convinced Tess to marry him.

Meanwhile, Angel had made his way home, sick and weak from the hardships suffered in Brazil. Deeply moved by the pleas in Tess's letter, he was now deter-mined to find her and make amends. Upon their reunion, however, Tess greeted him with sobs. "It is too late," she told him. Alec "has won me back to him."

When the confused and painful exchange was over, Alec angrily inquired about Angel's visit. Tess turned and rebuked him bitterly: "You have torn my life all to pieces. My sin will kill him and not me. O God I can bear this no longer." Alec's only response was to mock her, cursing Angel to her face. In a rage, Tess seized a knife, thrust it into his chest, and ran from the house.

" … I have killed him!" Tess confessed when she reached Angel's side. "I have done it—I don't know how. Still I owed it to thee and to myself, Angel." Embracing desperately, they took a vow never to part again.

Fleeing into the woods, the couple came to an aban-doned house, where they remained for five days. At last, in quiet and seclusion, they found the bliss that had so long eluded them. On the sixth day they trekked north-ward to Stonehenge. But feeling that her fate was closing in around her, Tess made Angel take a vow: For her sake, should anything happen, he should marry her younger sister Liza Lu. Angel promised to abide by her wish.

The next morning, Tess was arrested. She was sentenced to hang for the murder of Alec d'Urberville. From atop a hill Angel and Liza Lu watched as a black flag was raised, signaling that Tess's worldly trials were over.

Commentary

Like many of Hardy's works, this literary gem was publicly rejected due to its dark and sensual themes. The writer eventually turned to poetry, forsaking novels entirely.

The plot of Tess is built around an indiscretion. At first it appears the author condemns Tess for her act and sides with Angel Clare, whose very name connotes virtue. Nonetheless, as the story progresses the reader is led to feel that Tess is the one who has been ill-treated by the "monstrously cruel," self-righteous Angel. This growing sympathy for her, along with the portrayal of Alec as a scheming, sadistic predator, leaves Tess somewhat justified in her killing the man who has destroyed her life. Indeed, afterward, she is granted a brief measure of happiness with Angel. But the author never quite condones her crime, and in the end justice prevails as she recieves the ultimate penalty for her actions.

WALKING BACK IN TIME

the drama of history

*I've broken
my leg, that's it.
I'm dead*

Touching the Void

*As soon as we are born the world gets
to work on us and transforms us ...*

E.H. Carr – What is History?

**Behold—the only thing
greater than yourself**

Omoro – Roots –
The Saga of an American Family

"the election was over they could
do almost anything they damned
well pleased."

General John Mitchell – All the President's Men

All the world's a stage, and its people merely players… opened Shakespeare in "As You Like It." And he had a point. History seems to display much of both the Bard's literary and casting skills, and his flair for the dramatic.

The *"Walking Back in Time"* library offers you living, breathing, colorful casts of characters, changes of scenery, and dramatizations that make history real, vital and relevant. This collection of book summaries starts out with the spotlight focused on more recent dramas—with all their heroes, villains and chanting choruses.

A Kaffir Boy from apartheid South Africa tells the story of his struggle, along with a defecting Soviet *MiG* pilot and a British traveler who follows the footsteps of Marco Polo. Then the scene shifts, to highlight crucial and colorful regional subplots. And for the final act we go back in time to recorded history's earliest cradles, until we have experienced at least a sizeable fragment of what has gone before.

Finally led full-circle back to the world we know today, we find ourselves better able to frame more coherent visions for the next act in the ever-unfolding drama of history. The actors are waiting in the wings, the props are in place.

So, part the curtains and let the action begin!

CONTENTS

Heat is to India what fog is to England and smog is to California

India

THE STAGES OF MANKIND
colorful theatres of history

continued …

CHANGING BACKDROPS
the best and worst of times

"You have six minutes of fuel left."

MiG Pilot – The Final Escape
f Lieutenant Belenko

IMMORTAL VOICES
words that live on

"I have offended God and mankind because my work did not reach the quality it should have."

Leonardo da Vinci (1452-1519) – Famous Last Words

"Natives have usually very little feelings for animals"

Isak Dinesen – Out of Africa

I was lying there with dead all round me....
Behind me I could hear the groans of the
wounded. Every now and then one of them
would call out, "Mother, Mother."

Cannon Fodder

WHAT IS HISTORY?
by E.H. Carr, Random House, 1961

Author/historian Edward Hallett Carr was born in London in 1892 and educated at Trinity College, Cambridge. His collection of essays titled *What Is History?* was published in 1961. Now considered a classic, it is a work invaluable to anyone willing to gaze beyond what previous generations regarded as "inherently historical."

French philosopher Voltaire once defined history as "a pack of tricks played upon the dead by the living." Carr is slightly more kind, suggesting instead that history, in fact, is "the perspective of historians," a perspective which is in a constant state of transformation. "When we attempt to answer the question, What is history?" he writes, "our answer, consciously or unconsciously, reflects our own position in time, and … the society in which we live." The just-give-me-the-facts stance of 19th-century historians, for example, often saved them from thinking for themselves. Though this no-nonsense viewpoint at least encourages the historian to get the facts straight before plunging into the realms of interpretation, it also eventually runs straight up against the next big question: "*Which* facts?" In effect, "Not all facts about the past are historical facts, or are treated as such by the historian." So, asks Carr, what facts *will* we select to enshrine as valid "historical" facts? In fact, is there any way to discern the existence of one authentic, solid, irrefutable, "backbone" of historical fact?

No, replies Carr; there is not. By the second half of the 20th century, the factual backbone of 19th-century history had come under close scrutiny—and relegated to the status of a mirage. "History" was found to be, in effect, the creation of the persons writing it and our own notions of truth as shaped by the careful arrangement of selected "facts." Historians must inevitably sift among an infinity of facts to choose those he will pass along. He must interpret and judge from the very beginning. All history, then, is "subjective."

"This element of interpretation enters into every facet of history," notes Carr. "Our picture has been pre-selected and predetermined for us, not so much by accident as by people who were consciously or unconsciously imbued with a particular view and thought the facts which supported that view worth preserving."

"What had gone wrong [in the 19th century]," Carr continues, "was the belief … that facts speak for themselves and that we cannot have too many facts …" As historian Benedetto Croce cogently observes, these "fact-fetish" historians fail to grasp the point that "All history is 'contemporary history'…. Essentially [we look at] the past through the eyes of the present and in the light of its problems…. " Or in the words of another contemporary historian, Michael Oakeshott, "History is the historian's experience. It is 'made' by nobody save the historian …"

Carr finally puts all these arguments into one compact capsule: "The facts of history never come to us 'pure'….: they are always refracted through the mind of the recorder."

And the message here to the reader is equally to the point: "Study the historian before you begin to study the facts. [Remember that] by and large, the historian will get the kind of facts he wants." Of course "the duty of the historian to respect his/her facts is not exhausted by the obligation to see that [the] facts are accurate. He must seek to bring into the picture all known or knowable facts relevant, in one sense or another, to the theme on which he is engaged and to the interpretation proposed."

If this rule is not taken into account, Carr insists, the historian will likely fall into one of two historical heresies: The "scissors-and-paste history," where history is "a child's box of letters with which we can spell any word we please," or the heresy of propaganda, where the historian warps facts to suit a ruling party. "Either you write scissors-and-paste history without meaning or significance; or you write propaganda or historical fiction, and merely use facts of the past to embroider a kind of writing which has nothing to do with history." Hence, what the historian must do, Carr avers, is as follows: *The historian starts with a provisional selection of facts and a provisional interpretation in the light of which that selection has been made—by others as well as by himself. As he works, both the interpretation and the selection and ordering of facts undergo subtle and perhaps partly unconscious changes through the reciprocal action of one or the other. And this reciprocal action also involves reciprocity between present and past, since the historian is part of the present and the facts belong to the past. The historian and the facts of history are necessary to one another. The historian without his facts is rootless and futile; the facts without their historian are dead and meaningless.*

So how does Carr finally answer the question *What is history?* In essence he replies that there is no final answer. He sees "good" or "true" history as a dynamic, evolving relationship; as "a continuous process of interaction between the historian and his facts, an unending dialogue between the present and the past."

Now Carr addresses the roles of society and the individual: *As soon as we are born the world gets to work on us and transforms us … into social units. Every human being at every stage of history or pre-history is born into a society and from his earliest years is molded by that society…. Both language and environment help to determine the character of his thought; his earliest ideas come to him from others, [as] the individual apart from society would be both speechless and mindless. The lasting fascination of the Robinson Crusoe myth is due to its attempt to imagine an individual independent of society. The attempt breaks down. Robinson is not an abstract individual, but an Englishman....; he carries his Bible with him and prays to his tribal God. The myth quickly bestows upon him his Man Friday; and the building of a new society begins.*

"We shall arrive at no real understanding either of the past or of the present if we attempt to operate with the concept of an abstract individual standing outside society," Carr insists. "Civilized man, like primitive man, is molded by society just as effectively as society is molded by him. You can no more have the egg without the hen than you can have the hen without the egg." In a few words, no one can stand completely outside his or her own society.

The effects of *individual* experience are equally as biasing as those of social experience. The common-sense view of history spoken of earlier treats history as "written by individuals about individuals. This view was certainly taken and encouraged by nineteenth-century liberal historians, and is not in substance incorrect. But it now seems over-simplified and inadequate, and we need to probe deeper.... The men whose actions the historian studies were not isolated individuals acting in a vacuum: they acted in the context, and under the impulse of a past society."

[The individual historian is merely] another dim [human] figure trudging along in another part of the procession. And as the procession winds along, swerving now to the right and now to the left, and sometimes doubling back on itself, the relative positions of different parts of the procession are constantly changing, so that it may make perfectly good sense to say, for example, that we are nearer today to the Middle Ages than were our great-grandfathers a century ago or that the age of Caesar is nearer to us than the age of Dante. New vistas, new angles of vision, constantly appear as the procession—and the historian with it—moves along.

In essence, the historian, as a product of history, is an integral *part* of the history he is recording. Taking these views even further, Carr writes: "Great history is written precisely when the historian's vision of the past is illuminated by insights into the problems of the present"; there exists an interactive, ongoing dynamic relationship between the historian's *present* and the *past*. Carr's purpose here is to validate two important truths: "First ... you cannot fully understand or appreciate the work of the historian unless you have first grasped the standpoint from which he/she approached it; second, that standpoint is itself rooted in a social and historical background."

To demonstrate how easily history can be twisted to the individual historian's unique pen and the rapidity by which historians can change their personal points of view—and through their writings change not only one society or social order, but a succession of different orders—Carr cites the example of the great and copious German historian Meinecke, who covered a lengthy series of "revolu-

tionary and catastrophic changes in the fortunes of his country":

Here we have in effect three different Meineckes, each the spokesman of a different historical epoch, and each speaking through one of his three major works. The Meinecke of Weltburgerthum and Nationalstaat, *published in 1907, confidently sees the realization of German national ideals in the Bismarckian Reich and— like many nineteenth century thinkers ... identifies nationalism with the highest form of universals.... The Meinecke of* Die Idee der Straatsrason, *published in 1925, speaks with the divided and bewildered mind of the Weimar Republic: The world of politics has become an arena of unresolved [moral] conflict external to politics.... Finally, the Meinecke of* Die Entstehung des Historismus, *published in 1936, when he had been swept from his academic honors by the Nazi flood, utters a cry of despair, rejecting a historicism which appears to recognize that whatever is, is right, and tossing uneasily between the historical relative and a superrational absolute. Last of all, when Meinecke in his old age had seen his country succumb to a military defeat more crushing than that of 1918, he relapsed helplessly in* Die Deutsche Katastrophe *of 1946 into the belief in a history at the mercy of blind, inexorable change.... What interests the historian is the way in which Meinecke reflects back three—or even four—successive, and sharply contrasted, periods of present time into the historical past.*

The point is that "it is not merely that [history] is in flux. The historian himself is in flux. [So], if the philosopher is right in telling us that we cannot step into the same river twice, it is perhaps equally true, and for the same reason, that two books cannot be written by the same historian." It follows that "the historian who is most conscious of his own situation is also more capable of transcending it ... more capable of appreciating the essential nature of the differences between his own society and outlook and those of other periods and other countries ..."

Hence Carr suggests to any student of history to first study the historian, "study his historical and social environment. The historian, being an individual, is also a product of history and of society; and it is in this twofold light that the student of history must learn to regard him."

And so, Carr's question *What is history?* must be answered not once, but every time a reader's eyes flow over the words and accounts of society's historians, present past or future. "History cannot be written unless the historian can achieve some kind of contact with the mind of those about whom he/she is writing." Once that connection has been established, one can truly begin to understand past societies and individuals. For "the function of the historian," Carr concludes, "is neither to love the past nor to emancipate himself from the past, but to master and understand it as the key to the understanding of the present."

ROOTS – THE SAGA OF AN AMERICAN FAMILY
by Alex Haley, Dell Publishing, 1976

"Alex Haley's taking us back through time to the village of his ancestors is an act of faith and courage," says James Baldwin of Haley's extended family record, "but this book is also an act of love, and it is this which makes it haunting…. It suggests with great power how each of us … can't help but be the vehicle of the history which produced us."

The 200-year saga of *Roots* certainly compels us to listen to the chronicles of modern-day African-American families, to grieve for the brutal mistreatment of the slaves, whose lives we relive through Haley's feeling narrative, and to rejoice in the hard-won triumph of Kunta Kinte's descendants. Ultimately, *Roots* confers upon all non-Native Americans, as the children and grandchildren of immigrants from throughout the world, a renewed appreciation of our own progenitors and a strengthened sense of both our own individual roots and identities and the common links of humanity that unite us.

In a Mandinka village upriver from the coast of Gambia, West Africa, a manchild was born to Omoro and Binta Kinte. The parents named the boy Kunta Kinte to designate him as a member of the Kinte family who would become a proud and honorable hunter, provider and tribesman.

Filled with love for his firstborn, Omoro carried Kunta into the brush, lifted him toward the stars, and uttered the traditional words of blessing and oblation: *Behold—the only thing greater than yourself.*

Raised to take his place as a village leader, Kunta grew quickly. At fifteen he had finished the "manhood training" required of Mandinka boys and emerged from his initiation rites as an accomplished hunter, tireless, dignified, courageous, and well versed in his tribal lore.

Kunta thus began to assume the responsibilities of a young bachelor in the village. After morning prayer, he would inspect various huts to ensure their cleanliness. He also farmed his own rice patch, which contributed to his family's supply.

Fruitful at all of his tasks, Kunta felt most virile when he took his turn as a village sentry, watching to warn the people if *toubob*, or white men, appeared. Tragically, one day as he went to the forest to search for wood to build a drum, Kunta himself was captured by the *toubob*. Beaten senseless, stripped naked, and chained, he was carried away to the beach. Then, with his head shaven, he was loaded along with hundreds of other captives onto what seemed a huge canoe, with a vault where people were crowded in the darkness onto small shelves. As the ship lurched into deeper waters, Kunta knew he would never again see his home.

During the four long months that followed, the captives were taunted, beaten, fed wretched food, and left for days to swelter in the hold. Enduring many sicknesses as well as the ever-present stench of death, Kunta only vowed more deeply to always remember who he was—the son of the Kintes, a "mighty Mandinka man."

When the boat finally touched land, Kunta was appalled to see more throngs of *toubob*. Even worse, were those laboring among them who possessed the skin of Africans yet dressed and talked like his white captors.

Kunta was poked, spat upon, whipped. Finally he was sold to work in the plantation fields, where his only thought was of escape. One day he finally ran away. *His muscles, so long unused, screamed with pain, but the cold, rushing air felt good upon his skin, and he had to stop himself from whooping out loud with pleasure of feeling so wildly free.*

Kunta was soon recaptured. But the exhilaration of this short burst of freedom impelled him to flee the fields again and again and again. After his fourth flight, two men cut off half his foot. Half delirious from shock and blood loss, Kunta promised himself that "he would take revenge—and he would escape again. Or he would die."

Kunta was then relocated to a new plantation, where a fierce and gentle slave woman named Bell nursed him slowly back to health. Although he would never condone the heathen ways of the pork-eating slaves around him, Kunta now knew that, like them, he would have to learn some of the *toubob*'s words in order to survive. And as Kunta began to learn the new language, he gradually came to value his associations with the other slaves. He also found himself drawn closer to middle-aged Bell, though he retained the conviction that "no matter what, he must never become anything like these black people." Eventually they "jumped the broom" together in a slave-sanctioned gesture of marriage. And when their daughter was born, Kunta, with "Africa pumping in his veins," hobbled out under the stars and, baring the "infant's small black face to the heavens … spoke aloud to her in Mandinka: *Behold, the only thing greater than yourself!*" He named her Kizzy, which in Mandinka meant "you stay put"—referring to his wish that she should never be sold away.

But Kizzy did not stay put. Her downfall was ordained when her parents broke the great decree in slave-holding society: they allowed her to learn to read. Thus, at sixteen, when Kizzy was caught trying to forge a traveling pass for the young runaway slave with whom she had fallen in love, she was promptly sold. On her first night at the new plantation, she was visited by her new "massa," and was soon heavy with child.

Even though her baby was not the deep beautiful black of her father and mother, Kizzy adored little George. Proud of her ancestry and determined to never let the memories of her father slip away, she taught her son everything African that she could remember. "Dat river is de *Kamby Bolongo*," she would tell him, just as her father had told her. "An' dat ol' guitar, dat dere's a *ko* in African…. You always 'member dat you grandaddy's name be *Kintey!*" And George did remember. "I gwine tell my chilluns 'bout gran'pappy," he promised his mother.

Years later, as an adult, George was put in charge of raising and matching his "Massa Lea's" gamecocks; ever after he was referred to as "Chicken George." And soon the gifted George himself became his master's prize possession. He ultimately married a slave named Matilda, with whom he had eight children. And after each new birth, the family would gather around to hear their father relate the story of his noble grandaddy: *He were a African dat say he name "Kunta Kinte." He call a guitar a ko, an' a river "Kamby Bolongo," an' lot mo' things wid African names. He say he was choppin' a tree to make his li'l brother a drum when it was fo' mens come up an' grabbed 'im from behin'. Den a ship brung 'im 'crost de big water to a place call 'Naplis. An' he had runned off fo' times when he try to kill dem dat cotched 'im an' dey cut half his foot off!*

The recitation of these stories took on even greater meaning as George's master fell upon hard times and spoke of selling off his slaves. But before any selling could take place, George was lost in a wager over a cockfight and was sent to England to train roosters for a British master. The remaining family—except for Kizzy, who by then was too old to "fetch a decent slavin' price"—was sold to a nearby plantation owner.

Tom, the fourth son of Chicken George and Matilda, was now the head of the family. He learned the blacksmith trade, a skill which allowed him to travel to various plantations where he was paid for his labor. Tom saved every penny that the master allowed him to keep.

It was on one of his "smithin' rounds" that Tom met a half-Indian slave girl named Irene, with whom he promptly fell in love. When they were married, Tom's kind master, Murray, bought Irene and moved her into her husband's cabin.

Meanwhile, after nearly three years in England, Chicken George returned home with the freedom papers his master had promised him. When he arrived, he found his wife and children gone and his mamma, Kizzy, dead. Locating his family's new plantation, though he longed to stay there with them, he found that it was unlawful for a free black man to live in slave quarters. George thus headed north to find work so that he could buy his family's freedom.

Back on the plantation, Irene, who often overheard conversations in the master's house, became enthralled by accounts of someone "up nawth called massa Lincoln," who wanted to set the slaves free. Later, on the day they learned that Lincoln had been elected President, Tom enlisted as a blacksmith for the Southern cavalry. War had begun.

The Southerners were jubilant; there was steady talk of "kickin' those Yankees clear back to England…!" Such talk nearly crushed the slaves' hopes; freedom was a long way off.

Then, on New Years Day, 1863, Matilda dashed from the Master's house to the cabin, shrieking, " … It jes come over de railroad telegraph wire Pres'dent Lincoln done signed 'Mancipation Proclamation' dat set us free!" A wild celebration broke out. Tom's nephew raced to the chicken coop, shouting, "Ol' hens quit layin', you's free!—and so's ME!"

However, the family's jubilation was short lived. Without provisions, they soon realized that they could go nowhere until Chicken George returned. Within a week, they were back sweating in the fields.

At last, one happy afternoon, Chicken George swept in rambling on about a settlement in western Tennessee that needed families to build the town. And before long the family was on their way to Tennessee, "where de land so black an' rich, you plant a pig's tail an' a hog'll grow."

The soil truly was rich, and, at last, they were together. Tom, who took on the last name "Murray," after his former master, quickly established himself as the town's blacksmith. Now unimpeded, he prospered. Tom and Irene's daughter, Cynthia, married a hardworking and highly respected young black man named Will Palmer, and soon the couple were blessed with a young child named Bertha. Once again the family—who by now had built both a church and a general store—assembled to hear the stories of "dat ol' African Kintey…"

Well-versed in her heritage, Bertha grew into a bright young woman who went to college to become a teacher. She fell in love with a young man named Simon Alexander Haley, and after their marriage, she gave birth to a baby boy—a boy whom his parents named Alex.

Young Alex Haley, always hungry for stories about "the old days," spent more time with Grandma Cynthia and Grandpa Will than with anyone else. He listened intently to each tale about "ol' African Kintey."

As an adult, Haley became an accomplished writer. For 30 years he traced his family's past; finally he traveled to Juffure, his ancestral village in Gambia, where he studied the language and spoke with a *griot*, or storyteller. In stunned silence, Haley listened to the old man as he recited the history of a village holy man, Kairaba Kunta Kinte, who, by a second wife, Yaisa, over two centuries earlier, had begotten a son named Omoro. Omoro, at "thirty rains," took to wife a Mandinka maiden named Binta Kebba, and they begat four sons, Kunta, Lamin, Suwadu, and Madi. Then one day their oldest son, Kunta, "went away from his village to chop wood … and he was never seen again …"

This old village *griot*, Haley wrote, "had no way in the world to know that he had just echoed what I had heard all through my boyhood years on my grandma's front porch in Henning, Tennessee…"

Tracing the steps of his abducted forefather, reliving the long voyage from West Africa to Maryland, the author Alex Haley (1921-1992) had unearthed his roots. Even after the passing of seven generations, he was able to introduce to the world the wrenching and wonderful story of his forebears—the family of Kunta Kinte.

THE HIDING PLACE
by Corrie ten Boom, with John and Elizabeth Sherrill, Chosen Books, 1971

The Dutch survivor of a German extermination camp, Corrie ten Boom (1892-1983) inspired countless admirers around the world with her faith- and compassion-promoting "speaking ministry." Her story radiates a faith in God's love and forgiveness that will never die.

In January 1937, the ten Boom family celebrated the 100th anniversary of their watch-making business. That happy day, with the threat of war still distant, 45-year-old Corrie, her brother Willem, her father, her sisters Betsie and Nollie, as well as virtually everyone else in the city of Haarlem joined in the festivities at the *Beje*—as the ten Boom house was called. After the party, Corrie went upstairs to think: *I didn't know it then ... that there was any future to prepare for in a life as humdrum and predictable as mine. I only knew as I lay in my bed at the top of the house that certain moments from long ago stood out in focus against the blur of years.*

Corrie recollected how as a young girl her father had often read aloud to them, and how once she had been particularly baffled by the words of a psalm: *Thy word is a lamp unto my feet, and a light unto my path.... Thou art my hiding place and my shield.* The words made Corrie wonder, "What kind of hiding place? What was there to hide from?"

Although life had been exciting and happy in the *Beje*, Corrie learned over the years to accept the fact that she—like Betsie—would never wed. She had been devastated in her youth when Karel, the man she had loved, married another woman. "God loves Karel, even more than you do," her father had tried to comfort her, "and if you ask Him, He will give you His love for this man, a love nothing can prevent, nothing can destroy. Whenever we cannot love in the old, human way, Corrie, God can give us the perfect way."

Corrie later learned that her father's words had given her "the secret that would open far darker rooms than this—places where there was not, on a human level, anything to love at all."

A few years after the ten Booms' anniversary party, these "darker rooms" became reality when the Germans invaded Holland. The ten Booms had long used the ample rooms of the *Beje* to house many of Haarlem's Jews. As Willem, a minister, became active in the Dutch underground, he helped his father and sisters aid their Jewish friends. The ten Booms were able to meet the many needs of their boarders, including the ration cards that Corrie obtained illegally. The underground even surveyed the *Beje* to find a "hiding place" for Jews in case of a raid and then built an elaborate secret chamber leading to Corrie's bedroom.

When the dreaded raid finally came, Corrie was in bed with the flu. "So you're the ring leader!" growled a Gestapo agent, bursting into her room—where, moments earlier, Corrie had groggily looked on as the Jewish boarders scrambled to safety. "Tell me now, where are you hiding the Jews?" Admitting nothing, Corrie was led downstairs where another Gestapo agent beat her and demanded, "Where is your secret room?"

Corrie cried out; she did not know. The Gestapo agent flew into a rage. "... If you won't talk, that skinny one will." Then he began clubbing Betsie.

Before the day had ended, all the ten Booms were arrested. The next day they were transported to a Gestapo "court" in the Hague, where Corrie and her sisters were separated from their father. "God be with you!" Corrie called to him as she and her sisters were led away by a matron. "And with you, my daughters," he replied.

In the women's prison at Scheveningen, Corrie and her two sisters were assigned to separate cells. As the months wore on she learned that Willem, Nollie and several of the others had been released. But not long after receiving this happy news, a letter from Nollie arrived: *I have news that is very hard to write you. Father survived his arrest by only ten days. He is now with the Lord ...*

That same month in 1944, Corrie finally received a hearing. Led to a hut where she met her interrogator, Corrie was surprised when the man treated her kindly and allowed her to speak about the Bible. The following day, after again calling her to his hut, the man confessed, "I could not sleep last night, thinking about the book where you have read such different ideas. What else does it say in there?" Corrie replied, "It says ... that a Light has come into this world, so that we need no longer walk in the dark. Is there darkness in your life, Lieutenant?" After a long pause, he sighed. "There is great darkness," he told her. "I cannot bear the work I do.... I wear a uniform, I have a certain authority over those under me. But I am in prison, dear lady from Haarlem, a prison stronger than this one."

A few weeks later, the lieutenant arranged for Corrie to see her family under the pretext of a reading of her father's will. She learned that Willem's son Kik had been arrested and deported into Germany. Still, she was relieved to learn that some of their Jewish boarders were safe, and she was grateful to receive a small Bible from Nollie.

This Bible proved to be a source of comfort during the terrible months ahead. Not long after her reunion with her family, Scheveningen was evacuated. In the crowd of women herded into a train car, Corrie was reunited with Betsie—a blessing for which Corrie was immensely grateful. "The four months in Scheveningen had been our first separation in fifty-two years," she later wrote. "It seemed to me that I could bear whatever happened with Betsie beside me."

When the train stopped, the sisters found that they were still in Holland, at Vught, "a concentration camp for political prisoners." Malnourished and exhausted, the women were questioned, finger-printed, and finally "marched along a path between twisted rolls of barbed wire and through a wide gate into a compound of low tin-roofed barracks." Locked in their new quarters, Corrie asked her sister, "How long will it take?" Betsie answered, "Perhaps many years. But what better way could there be to spend our lives?... Corrie, if people can be taught to hate, they can be taught to love! We must find the way, you and I, no matter how long it takes..."

Betsie's capacity for love constantly amazed her sister. Although Corrie frequently raged silently at her German captors, Betsie forgave and sought to understand everyone, even the Dutch informant who had facilitated the raid on the *Beje*. "I ... pray for him whenever his name comes into my mind," Betsie explained one night. "How dreadfully he must be suffering!"

As the months in Vught slowly passed, Corrie learned that "the usual prison term for ration-card offenders—as she and Betsie had been designated by the Germans—was six months," and she began to count the days until their release. But they were not discharged on that date; instead, they were sent on an overcrowded freight train to Ravensbruck—a "women's extermination camp" in Germany.

Ravensbruck, for the few who were not sent to the crematorium, would be far worse than Vught. Not only were the women herded naked into the shower room past jeering S.S. men, but they also had to submit to the "recurrent humiliation of medical inspection," back-breaking labor, and the nightly crowding onto reeking, flea-infested straw-covered platforms.

Although she had been searched upon arrival at the camp, Corrie had managed to retain her Bible. It proved to be the only solace for the ten Boom sisters and their fellow prisoners, who held covert nightly religious services in the barracks. Alas, as Betsie's faith multiplied, her health deteriorated amid daily beatings and inadequate food. Only after she had contracted a blistering fever did the guards permit her to receive medical treatment and to be reassigned to the "knitting brigade," which worked inside the barracks. Nonetheless, the winter chill, which was extreme even indoors, further weakened Betsie, and she was eventually moved to the hospital.

Mercifully, a hospital worker arranged for Corrie to spend one final moment with her beloved sister, who, appearing as "a carving in old yellow ivory," lay naked on a cot. Corrie prayed, in gratitude: *For there lay Betsie, her eyes closed as if in sleep, her face full and young. The care lines, the grief lines, the deep hollows of hunger and disease were simply gone. In front of me was the Betsie of Haarlem, happy and at peace.*

Three days after Betsie's death, Corrie was unexpectedly called into the admission barracks and given a slip of paper that read CERTIFICATE OF DISCHARGE. Stunned, Corrie was presented with new clothing and a railway pass, before being taken into a room for a physical examination. But then came another turn: "Edema," the doctor snapped as he studied her feet. "Hospital!" As a guard led Corrie away, he explained, "They only release you if you're in good condition."

The hospital turned out to be "the most savage place yet." She recalled: *Around me were survivors of a prison train which had been bombed on its way here. The women were horribly mutilated and in terrible pain, but at each moan two of the nurses jeered and mimicked the sounds.* Corrie tended to the wounded—finding bedpans and presenting one particularly sensitive woman with her prized Bible—until the day came when the doctor finally approved Corrie's discharge and she boarded the first of many trains on her long journey home. It was New Year's Day, 1945, and Corrie now recalled with wonder a few of the optimistic words Betsie had murmured the day she died: "By the first of the year, we will be out of prison!" She recalled more of her sister's final remarks: "We must tell people, Corrie. We must tell them what we learned."

Reunited with those who remained of her family, Corrie began to organize meetings; she would see that Betsie's dream of "a home here in Holland where those who had been hurt could learn to live again unafraid" was realized. Following one of these meetings, a wealthy woman offered her estate, Bloemendaal, to serve as just such a home. Later, after Holland was liberated, Corrie donated the *Beje* to widely-hated former Dutch informants for the Gestapo, while Bloemendaal opened its doors to the Gestapo's victims.

In the years following the war, Corrie ten Boom traveled the world, raising contributions for Bloemendaal and speaking about Betsie's life and faith. Of all the countries that Corrie visited, Germany was the nation she perceived to be most in need.

Speaking in Munich once, Corrie recognized the face of one of the S.S. men "who had stood guard at the shower room door in the processing center at Ravensbruck." With no hint of embarrassment, he approached her and said, "How grateful I am for your message, Fraulein! To think that, as you say, He has washed my sins away!"

Face to face with one of her captors, Corrie's blood ran cold. He had found religion, he went on. "I know that God has forgiven me for the cruel things I did there, but I would like to hear it from your lips as well. Fraulein," he said, extending his hand, "will you forgive me?"

Corrie, momentarily stunned by the gesture, wrestled with her feelings until a calm came over her. She took his outstretched hand in hers—and in that instant, she said, *a current seemed to pass from me to him, while into my heart sprang a love for this stranger that almost overwhelmed me.... "I forgive you, brother!" I cried. "With all my heart!"*

ALL THE PRESIDENT'S MEN
by Carl Bernstein and Bob Woodward, Simon and Shuster, 1974

All the President's Men is a compelling record of an American president's fall from power. Moreover, it is a fascinating account of two reporters' dogged pursuit of a story which takes them and the country on an unlikely, behind-the-scenes tour of Washington politics and power. As the characters and their illegal activities are paraded before the American public, they come to represent a sort of contemporary Vanity Fair—Washington Style.

Of all Woodward's and Bernstein's carefully groomed sources, it is the enigmatic "Deep Throat" who most adds a human dimension to the scandal. Described simply as a frail, chain-smoking figure whose fatigue registers in his blood-shot eyes, Deep Throat is the book's moral center of gravity, the wise teacher who despairs for the country. It is he who knows, first hand, that the United States is being governed by a band of "not brilliant guys" who will "stop at nothing" to serve their own ends.

On the calm Saturday afternoon of June 17, 1972, the city editor of the *Washington Post* was startled to learn that five men, wearing "business suits" and "surgical gloves," had been arrested for burglarizing the Democratic National Committee headquarters in Washington's posh Watergate Complex. Policemen had seized more than $2,000 from the prowlers, along with "a walkie-talkie, 40 rolls of unexposed film, two 35-millimeter cameras, lock picks, pen-size tear-gas guns, and bugging devices …"

Post reporter Bob Woodward "snapped awake" the moment the city editor called him to cover the burglary. When he arrived at the newsroom, Woodward learned that he was not the only reporter assigned to the break-in: Carl Bernstein was already on the phone tracking down information on the case. A 28-year-old college drop-out who had the reputation for being able to overpower other reporters, Bernstein had a nose for pushing himself into a good story and getting his byline on it. Neither Bernstein's tactics nor his "counterculture" appearance impressed Woodward, a Yale graduate and a registered Republican.

Woodward had no time to waste worrying about his competitive colleague, and he left for the courthouse to attend the preliminary hearing of the burglary suspects. All of the suspects claimed to be "anti-communists"; three of them were Cuban-American. But the one who most intrigued Woodward the most was James W. McCord, Jr., who told the judge that he was a security officer for the CIA. "Holy shit," Woodward murmured, and rushed back to the Post to write his story. As yet, however, he could not give an "explanation as to why the five suspects would want to bug the Democratic National Committee offices, or whether or not they were working for any other individuals or organizations."

In addition to Woodward's story about the burglary, a piece by Bernstein also appeared in the Sunday *Post*, reporting that four of the suspects "had been involved in anti-Castro activities and were also said to have CIA connections." That same morning the Associated Press reported that McCord had served as the security coordinator of the Committee for the Re-election of the President (CRP).

"What the hell do you think it means?" Woodward asked Bernstein. Bernstein shrugged; he knew nothing about McCord or his involvement in the break-in, but this new facet of the case suggested that it was time their pooled their resources. By the end of the day, the reporters had a profile of McCord, an ex-FBI agent and former CIA officer. He had apparently worked full-time for the CRP, despite a public denial issued that day by former Attorney General John Mitchell.

After assimilating this information, Woodward began typing the day's story. Bernstein studied the crude draft and went back to his desk to rewrite it. Within a short time they had established an efficient work pattern: "Woodward, the faster writer, would do a first draft" and Bernstein would later rework it. Often they worked through the night, all the while maintaining individual master phone-number lists, which they used to unearth leads and document their facts. "The working relationship between Bernstein and Woodward" soon developed into a formidable alliance.

Woodward developed a profound respect for the aggressiveness and tenacity that had once made him resent Bernstein. Similarly, Bernstein came to value Woodward's talent for eliciting information from his sources. Indeed, as the months went by, these sources revealed the identities and activities of various high-level CRP executives. Woodward learned that Maurice Stans, Nixon's chief fund-raiser and CRP finance chairman, had received a check for $25,000 that was later deposited in the bank account of one of the Watergate burglars, suggesting White House involvement in the conspiracy.

Meanwhile, Bernstein pursued his own contacts. A bookkeeper at CRP disclosed that the committee's Finance Counsel, G. Gordon Liddy, had been involved in the conspiracy as well as "Mitchell's principal assistants … the top echelon." Another source, Hugh Sloan, former Treasurer of the CRP and the committee's "sacrificial lamb," provided Bernstein with the most damning information of all. Sloan maintained that John Mitchell, while still the Attorney General of the United States, "had authorized the expenditure of campaign funds for apparently illegal activities against the political opposition."

When Mitchell learned that the *Post* planned to run a story linking him to the break-in, he was furious. Bernstein phoned Mitchell for a reaction. "All that crap, you're putting in the paper?" ranted Mitchell, "It's all been denied." Mitchell then proceeded to threaten the *Post's* publisher Katherine Graham, making it clear that when "the election was over they could do almost anything they damned well pleased."

Shocked by Mitchell's outburst, Bernstein called the newspaper's Executive Editor Benjamin Bradlee, who was equally stunned. Bradlee instructed Bernstein to quote Mitchell verbatim, and, in spite of desperate pleas from the CRP's Deputy Press Director, the *Post* printed the story.

Mitchell's involvement in the conspiracy was soon confirmed by one of Woodward's favorite sources. "Deep Throat"—as the paper's staff had dubbed the anonymous voice—held a "position in the Executive Branch" of government, and clearly deplored the "switchblade mentality" that permeated Nixon's administration. As Woodward secretly met with his anonymous source in a garage early one morning, he was shocked by the picture of the White House and the CRP that Deep Throat painted. "You can safely bet," Deep Throat told the reporter, "that fifty people worked for the White House and CRP to play games and spy and sabotage and gather intelligence. Some of it is beyond belief." Then Woodward asked if the White House had "been willing to subvert … the whole electoral process." Deep Throat just nodded.

During their meeting, Deep Throat warned Woodward that the government wanted "to single out the *Post*. They want to go to court to get your sources." And, sure enough, after the paper ran stories denouncing Republican smear tactics and implicating in the conspiracy attorney Donald H. Segretti and Dwight Chapin, Deputy Assistant to the President, the CRP and the White House retaliated. The CRP's campaign director issued a statement at a press conference on October 18, accusing the *Post* of using "innuendo," "hypocrisy" and "huge scare headlines" to attack the President and promote Democratic rival George McGovern. Then, on October 25, White House Press Secretary Ron Zeigler accused the newspaper of "shabby journalism" and of a "well conceived and coordinated" effort "to discredit [the] Administration and individuals in it."

"This is the hardest hardball that's ever been played in this town," Bradlee told Woodward and Bernstein. Despite Bradlee's and Graham's steadfast support, the two journalists were occasionally unnerved by the magnitude of the situation in which they had involved themselves. In fact, when they began to connect White House Chief of Staff H.R. Haldeman to the conspiracy, there were times when they actually feared for their lives. Deep Throat, for one, had warned Woodward to "Be careful!" By all accounts, Haldeman was a man who would stop at nothing and who took pride in calling himself "the President's son-of-a-bitch."

Bernstein also felt unsettled by Haldeman, though for very different reasons. At times he wondered if he and Woodward were being set up by unscrupulous sources. "What if Haldeman had never asked for authority over the money," he worried, "or had never exercised his authority."

At this point the reporters made a serious mistake: They had misrepresented a statement that Sloan—always an amiable and reliable source—had made and had then "compounded their mistakes" by over-zealously prejudicing a source at the FBI. As Deep Throat would later point out, their hasty deductions had made everyone actually feel *sorry* for Haldeman, initiating for the reporters "the worst possible setback."

It wasn't until after Election Day on November 11 that Bernstein found a long-awaited opportunity to meet with Segretti, who confirmed that Chapin received "his orders from Haldeman…. Everyone is out to crucify me,"

Segretti added, tearfully, " … the White House, the press." Shortly afterward, Bernstein met with a CRP secretary who informed him that John Erlichman, Nixon's Assistant for Domestic Affairs, had met with the conspirators, including Hunt and Liddy, in the Executive Office Building.

In January of the following year, Liddy and McCord were found guilty of several counts of conspiracy. Judge John Sirica, however, noted that he was not satisfied that "all the pertinent facts" had become available and hoped that the upcoming Senate investigation might very well "get to the bottom" of Watergate.

Before the trial began, Woodward and Bernstein collected more incriminating evidence that reached into the highest echelons of the White House. Deep Throat confirmed that, like Mitchell, Charles Colson, Special Counsel to the President, "had direct knowledge" of Watergate. Moreover, the investigators learned "that Hunt and Liddy were being routed information from national-security wiretaps." Infuriated by the *Washington Post* stories, the CRP issued subpoenas for the reporters and their notes.

Although the subpoenas were thrown out of court, the *Post* received another, far more serious threat: "Everyone's life is in danger," Deep Throat told Woodward just before the Senate hearings on Watergate began. Apparently, the CIA had bugged both the *Post* building and the reporters' homes, and Nixon, by now a "secretive, distrustful" man, was suffering "fits of … depression."

Presumably, the President's indignation and depression did not diminish, for there were even more "rampaging" to come. As the Senate hearings progressed, Presidential Counsel John Dean was fired and Haldeman and Erlichman resigned; the White House was in a state of utter confusion. "It's every man for himself," one source told Woodward, "get a lawyer and blame everyone else."

By the spring of 1974, the House Judiciary Committee had begun investigating the possibility of Nixon's impeachment. The President reportedly possessed taped conversations from the Oval Office—conversations which could prove damaging not only because of their content but also because they had apparently been "tampered with." That spring many of Nixon's men, including Magruder, Segretti and Dean, pleaded guilty to various obstruction and conspiracy charges; others—Haldeman, Erlichman, Colson and Mitchell—were indicted. By now, the entire country spoke of little else but the conspiracy Woodward and Bernstein had uncovered.

President Nixon, under threat of impeachment, resigned his office as President of the United States on August 9, 1974. Although his successor Gerald Ford officially pardoned the deposed President the following year, Nixon's documented participation in illegal efforts to ensure re-election and the subsequent cover-up attempt proved not only to shatter his political career but to tarnish the office of President. As a result of having violated the public's trust and tampering with one of the chief features of democracy—free and open elections— Nixon's involvement in Watergate also placed an element of doubt in the minds of Americans about all successors to the office, a doubt that persists to this day.

OUT OF AFRICA
by Isak Dinesen, Random House, 1938

In 1914 Karen Blixen (1885-1962) sailed to the colony of British East Africa (present-day Kenya) to marry her Swedish cousin Baron Bror Blixen. When the couple divorced seven years later, Karen remained as manager of the coffee plantation that she and the Baron had jointly owned outside Nairobi. When the coffee market collapsed in 1931, however, she finally had to leave her beloved Ngong Hills. Returning to her native Denmark that year, she compiled her recollections and impressions, and published them under the pseudonym Isak Dinesen.

The resulting work, *Out of Africa* is neither novel nor autobiography, but rather a collection of personal essays which vividly reveal the author's great admiration for Africa's people, wildlife and landscape. These individual observations and reminiscences can, in most instances, stand on their own, apart from the larger work. But taken together the writings form an elaborate and intricate mural, with each phrase contributing an indispensable pictorial element. Through Dinesen's eyes, we see the interaction between two very different cultures—the cosmos of the African natives and the world of the European colonists. We discover a land of varied geographical features: lush forests, burning deserts, soaring mountains, expansive valleys. And we learn of a woman's immense love for a place and its inhabitants, the affinity of an immigrant who has found her spiritual home.

Baroness Karen Blixen first met Kamante, the son of one of her squatters, while he was herding his family's goats on the grass plains. Observing the gaunt boy whose legs were covered with sores, Madame Blixen reflected, " ... He looked extraordinarily small, so that it struck you as a strange thing that so much suffering could be condensed into a single point." After trying unsuccessfully to cure the boy with home remedies, the baroness carried him to a nearby church hospital.

Three months later, Kamante returned to his goats, healed—and converted to Christianity. "I am like you," he beamed, apprising Madame Blixen of his new religion. From then on he remained at her home as a houseboy. It was "as if he took it for granted that now he belonged there."

Kamante shared a unique relationship with the European woman; without her, as he explained, he "should have been dead a long time ago." He demonstrated his appreciation with a "benevolent, helpful, or perhaps the right word is, forbearing, attitude" towards the baroness. In a particularly touching example of concern for his mistress, he pointed out that the book upon which she was working was not really a book, but rather merely a loose bundle of papers. As evidence, he brought in a copy of *The Odyssey*, announcing, "This is a good book. It hangs together from the one end to the other. Even if you hold it up and shake it strongly, it does not come to pieces.... But what you write ... is some here and some there. When the people forget to close the door it blows about.... It will not be a good book."

Madame Blixen responded to this critique, assuring the boy that "in Europe the people would be able to fix it together." But a few days later she overheard Kamante explaining to the other houseboys that, in Europe, the book Madame Blixen was writing could be "made to stick together, and ... even made as hard as the Odyssey.... He himself, however, did not believe it could be made blue."

Kamante was an unusual character, defying many of the traits Karen Blixen attributed to the natives. "Natives have usually very little feelings for animals," noted Madame Blixen, "but Kamante differed from type here, as in other things." It was Kamante who took charge of Lulu, a young bushbuck antelope who, as a fawn, had become a member of the household. Bottle-fed by Kamante, Lulu grew to be a "slim delicately rounded doe, from her nose to her toes unbelievably beautiful.... On the strength of this great beauty and gracefulness, [she] obtained for herself a commanding position in the house, and was treated with respect by all."

Nevertheless, Lulu was still a wild creature at heart, and one evening she disappeared. A week-long search ended in vain. When Madame Blixen expressed her fear to Kamante that Lulu had fallen prey to the leopards by the river, Kamante reassured her: "Lulu is not dead. But she is married." A few days later the two watched as Lulu returned to the house to eat the maize Kamante had left out for her. Delighted, the baroness wrote:

It also seemed to me that the free union between my house and the antelope was a rare, honorable thing. Lulu came in from the wild world to show that we were on good terms with it, and she made my house one with the African landscape, so that nobody could tell where the one stopped and the other began.

Equally important to the isolated writer were those visitors who brought news from the outside world, news "good or bad, which is bread to the hungry minds in lonely places." Guests at the plantation varied from the Prince of Wales to Kinanjui, Chief of the Kikuyu tribe. Sometimes the farm was the site for tribal dances, known as Ngomas; at other times it served as a sanctuary for fellow Europeans who found themselves down on their luck in Africa.

Probably Karen's favorite guest was Denys Finch-Hatton, a British immigrant to Africa. When not leading a safari, he was frequently to be found at the farm. There the two expatriates would sit "into the small hours of the morning, talking of all the things we could think of, and mastering them and laughing at them."

"When I had no more money, and could not make things pay, I had to sell the farm," explains the author, recounting her last year in Africa. The news saddened everyone: the squatters who worked the farm, the servants in the house, and the large circle of travelers to whom the farm was a second home. And for Karen Blixen herself, who awakened each morning and thought, "Here I am, where I ought to be," a state of denial set in:

It was a curious thing that I myself did not, during this time, ever believe that I would have to give up the farm or to leave Africa. I was told that I must do so by the people round me, all of them reasonable men ... and all the facts of my daily life pointed to it. All the same nothing was farther from my thoughts, and I kept on believing that I should come to lay my bones in Africa.

It had been arranged that she would remain on the farm only until the last crop of coffee was harvested. Still reluctant to accept her destiny, the baroness nevertheless prepared to leave, like "a blind person who is being led, and who places one foot in front of the other, cautiously but unwillingly." Because the new owners intended to sell the land rather than farm it, she began making frequent trips to Nairobi to find new land where the squatters could live. She then proceeded to sell her furniture and many of her possessions. Later, she would reflect:

When in the end, the day came on which I was going away, I learned the strange learning that things can happen which we ourselves cannot possibly imagine, either beforehand, or at the time when they are taking place, or afterwards when we look back on them. Circumstances can have a motive force by which they bring about events without aid of human imagination or apprehension.

Madame Blixen had carefully instructed her houseboys to close the doors of her empty house once she was out of sight. They did not obey, but left the doors wide open to show they wished her to come back again. Undoubtedly a door would always remain open in Karen Blixen's heart, a doorway of hope through which she might someday return to her beloved Africa.

Commentary

The theme of *Out of Africa*, like the continent itself, is an imposing and unwieldy mosaic for any writer to conjoin, but perhaps even more so for one who has lived within the African experience and thus passed beyond simplistic preconceptions and superficial observations. Dinesen superbly presents an Africa of contradictions and extremes. It is a community articulated by natives and immigrants; it is a land inhabited by creatures as common as fireflies and as majestic as lions. For Dinesen, however, each is an essential part of the continent's landscape; singly and combined, they *are* Africa.

Like Africa itself, Karen Blixen, the woman behind Dinesen's narrative voice, is made up of contradictions and extremes. Dinesen is an astute observer of Africa's people and cultures. Yet, paradoxically, she frequently and strangely seems unaware of the destructive impact of her own colonial enterprises. She can assail, for example, a colonial policy that strips the native population of its land, and, at the same time, fail to see her own complicity in the very policy she attacks. Dinesen, in fact, owned six thousand acres of land in a country that prohibited its own native-born "noble savages" from owning even one acre.

Dinesen's whole attitude toward the "noble savage" is yet another of the author's incongruities. At times she seems oblivious to the suffering of the native people; at other times she seems to suffer along with them, accurately recognizing, for instance, both the relationship and the difference between the discovery of the "noble savage" and the subsequent destruction of the cultures and cultural wisdom of Africa's native inhabitants by imperialistic Europeans: " ... It is more than their land that you take away from the people.... It is their past as well, their roots and their identity."

Another area wrought by contradictions and extremes is seen in passages where Dinesen discusses animals, both wild and domestic. She frequently praises the beauty and majesty of the native wild animals, but also finds sport in hunting these same beasts. One moment she extols the virtue of the lion or giraffe, and the next she is taking a bead on the splendid creature down the scope of a rifle. Dinesen's fondness of hunting and her respect of the African wilds are not necessarily irreconcilable; but they do form an intriguing manifestation of the contradictions she embodies.

Perhaps these contradictions escaped her shrewd eye—or possibly her own complicity merely made the paradox an uncomfortable subject for her to confront. Perhaps the ability to live among contradictions, to adapt between one extreme and another, was requisite in a land that was itself in tremendous flux; a land at once being divided asunder and pushed forward by the clash of cultures, yet held together by the tenacious grasp of its inhabitants—wild animals, native dwellers, and immigrants alike. Regardless of Dinesen's intent, the incongruities she presents in her work ultimately serve to challenge the reader to examine his or her own preconceived notions.

KAFFIR BOY
by Mark Mathabane, Macmillan Publishing Co., 1986

Kaffir Boy is the autobiography of Mark Mathabane, a black boy who grew up during the days of apartheid in South Africa—where the word "kaffir" has the same connotation as the derogatory term "nigger" in the United States. He was born in the crowded ghetto of Alexandra, where his parents gave him the name of Johannes. Somehow, through a combination of talent, great discipline, and a series of happy accidents, he found his way past the sealed ghetto to become one of the few black South African tennis stars of the early 1970s.

The Road to Alexandra
Many of Johannes's first gripping childhood memories are of police raids on the shack where he lived with his parents and a growing number of brothers and sisters. Typically, the boy would be sleeping naked on a piece of cardboard, covered with newspaper, when the black "Peri-Urban" policemen came pounding at the door. All blacks had to have a legal pass to live in Alexandra or they could be carried off to jail.

The worst finally happened when Johannes was seven years old: His father Jackson was laid off from work as a laborer and a few weeks later was arrested at a bus stop for "being unemployed." Almost a year later, when the starving family had given him up for dead, Jackson Mathabane returned from jail—gaunt, his proud faith in his manhood irreparably shattered. And as the father retreated sullenly into drink, gambling and hopeless fantasies of revived tribal glory, Johannes's mother became the champion of her son's dream to get ahead.

Other early memories were of coping with hunger. For a time Johannes and his family scavenged for scraps in a garbage dump. On one occasion he accompanied a gang of boys to an address where they had been promised food for easy work, only to learn it was a house of prostitution. Sometimes he suffered dreadful hallucinations brought on by semi-starvation.

Life in the South African ghettos held many lessons to be learned. For instance, when Johannes taunted some laborers, performing what he considered the demeaning work of emptying the ghetto latrines, the men promptly forced him to jump in a bucket of excrement. The boy never made fun of *anyone* again. And at the age of six he grasped another critical reality, when he was introduced through movies to the white world. It didn't take long for Johannes to realize that in South Africa whites had everything and blacks had nothing.

Passport to Knowledge
One day when he was about seven, Johannes's mother woke him early and took him to stand in a long line to be registered for the Bovet Community School, a local outlet for white-ordained "Bantu" (black) education. Students at the black community schools had to provide their own books, uniforms and fees; they were

discouraged from any associations with European (white) culture or literature, and were taught exclusively in African tribal languages. Nevertheless, it was recognized that education "embodied the hope for a meaningful future for black people," and it was hoped that some students would stay in school at least long enough to learn to write their names. The boy's mother knew that without an education, her son would probably wind up on a dead-end road as a *tsotsi*—one of the many murderous ghetto gang members.

Johannes resisted the school's harsh discipline and inflexible code of behavior, but loved learning and became the top pupil in his class. Even the heart of his father was touched; smiling, Jackson gave his son 60 cents to pay for his next year's expenses.

The boy continued to do well in school—although he was often caned for lacking books, not wearing the established uniform, or for failing to pay his fees. Between these canings and a growing sense of isolation at home, the young boy stopped eating and sleeping. At one point he even considered suicide. But his mother, then jobless and six months pregnant, reminded him that his sisters and brother looked up to him. "Stay in school," she said. "As soon as I find a [new] job, I'll buy you books and uniforms."

The family's father opened a beer-selling business, and conditions briefly improved. Johannes even brought in a little extra money by reading and writing letters for migrant workers. Then, when he was ten years old, his life hit a turning point: his Granny took him to meet the Smiths, the white family who employed her as a maid. Impressed with the boy, the Smiths began paying him to do odd jobs. They also provided him with used books and hand-me-down clothes. These were precious items to Johannes, but the Smith's adolescent son, Clyde, still stung the "kaffir boy" with his taunts.

Clyde's insults only made Johannes more aware that learning to express himself effectively in English would be a key tool in lifting himself above the chronic violence of the ghetto.

Meanwhile, Johannes had found a new love: the Smiths had given him a used tennis racket, and he began pounding a tennis ball against the walls of the Alexandra Stadium. He liked the thought of playing tennis because he knew that his success would depend largely on his own efforts—under the direction of a "mulatto" coach named Scaramouch, who soon became Johannes's full-time coach, as well as a surrogate father.

Passport to Freedom
As the youngster's life revolved more and more closely around school, reading and tennis, he resisted both his mother's efforts to win him to Christianity and his father's insistence that he spend three months in "mountain school" and be initiated into tribal manhood. Even as this family tug-of-war intensified,

Johannes's relationship with his father steadily worsened. The boy greatly feared that all this turmoil would hurt his school work; yet when primary exam results came out, he had scored so high that he was awarded a government scholarship for all three years of secondary school. His mother sobbed with joy; even his father's harsh rebukes were softened.

Although classes in the black secondary school were taught in English rather than the familiar tribal Isongas, Johannes's grades remained high—and his interest in tennis jumped to a new level. Toting along a notebook, he visited bookstores to copy pointers from tennis books. Then, to help focus all his energies on schoolwork and tennis, he took up yoga and committed to sexual abstinence.

In 1972 and 1973 Johannes began competing in tennis tournaments. He also obtained work at a white tennis ranch called Barretts, where, in an impulsive rebellion against the oppressive Afrikaner government, he gave his name as the English-sounding "Mark."

For years black South Africans living under apartheid had idolized American black heroes like Martin Luther King, Jr. and Muhammad Ali. Now all black South Africans, including Mark, looked forward to the visit of Arthur Ashe, the distinguished African-American tennis star. Ashe was cheered wildly as he won matches against local white professionals, and Mark wondered if he could ever hope to become like him. As he returned to the dreary reality of life in the ghetto, that hope seemed more impossible every day.

Then in 1974 Mark won his first tournament championship; his trophy was prominently displayed in the bar at Barretts. The following year he became the first player from Alexandra chosen to represent the southern Transvaal black junior tennis squad in the national tournament. But more and more he felt like a stranger in his own country. His wide and voracious interests—which included reading and classical music as well as the desire to match up against the best tennis players in the world—all convinced him that he belonged in another world.

In June of 1976 black riots scarred the country, triggered by a new legal requirement to conduct secondary Bantu school classes in Afrikaans rather than English. Police opened fire on students in Soweto, cutting them down mercilessly. The rebellion soon spread to Alexandra, where Mark angrily joined in the looting. Finally, though, he came to ask himself whether he was willing to kill to obtain black freedom. He found the very question demoralizing.

Meanwhile, Andre Zietsman, one of South Africa's rising white tennis stars, befriended Mark and taught him the finer points of the game. While they played together illegally on white courts, Andre, who had been to America, told an incredulous Mark how blacks in the United States were able to use the same libraries, gymnasiums and taxis as whites. As he listened, Mark felt a great longing to see this "promised land" for himself. Whenever he met an American player, he asked for addresses to universities so that he could write for information about tennis scholarships.

Then the death of imprisoned black activist Steven Biko spawned a new wave of interracial violence. In response, the Afrikaner government cracked down hard. Army vehicles became a common sight in Alexandra. Although some blacks considered him a pacifist traitor, Mark sought his familiar refuge in books and tennis.

During all this unrest, the Black Tennis Foundation tried to force the total integration of tennis by boycotting the prestigious South African Breweries Open tournament. Mark, contending that the boycott only enabled whites to turn their backs on the black cause, played anyway; as a result the Foundation banned him for life from its ranks. But soon afterwards he had the good fortune to meet Stan Smith and Bob Lutz, the number-one doubles team in the world. Eventually Smith became a close friend, and encouraged Mark's efforts to go to the United States. He also sponsored Mark as a player in two white tournaments.

As the first black to be admitted to a white junior tennis squad, Mark was soon invited into the homes of his team members, where he was able to debunk some of their misconceptions about blacks and to revise some of his own biases against whites. But there were still setbacks and discouragements. For example, when a prestigious white club called The Wanderers agreed to admit Mark to membership, they added that, because of apartheid laws, he would have to shower with the servants. Angered, Mark became more intent than ever on getting out of the country.

Then one night the inevitable occurred: Mark was arrested and jailed for "intruding" in a white neighborhood without a pass. Since the only route to get a pass was a job outside the ghetto, Andre Zietsman helped him land a position with a bank at the kingly sum of 290 rands a month—three times the combined earnings of his parents.

Months passed, and Gaffney College in South Carolina offered Mark an all-expense-paid tennis scholarship. But he still had to wait—for the South African government did not favor blacks leaving the country. "Why do you want to study in America? Came the query. "You leave the country and start telling Americans lies about how bad things are . . ." But at last Mark had in hand all the necessary papers—and a plane ticket.

When it was his time to get on the bus to the airport, Mark's family bid him a tearful good-bye. He turned for a last look at them, standing in a row in front of their shack, and was so overcome with emotion that he wanted to turn back. Instead, he followed his destiny.

Though tennis was the vehicle that helped lift Mark Mathabane out of the Alexandra ghetto, he ultimately dedicated himself to a notable career in journalism and public speaking. "Using the pen to fight against injustice and racism" remains his goal and mission.

MiG Pilot – The Final Escape of Lieutenant Belenko
by John Barron, McGraw-Hill Book Co., 1980

Lieutenant Viktor Ivanovich Belenko, deputy commander of the Soviet Air Force's 3rd Squadron, awoke on a September morning in 1976, and peered out the window of his apartment at the blinding sunrise. *Today,* he told himself, *would be the day. Yes, today would definitely be the day ...*

After a distasteful breakfast at the officers' mess, Belenko met with his regimental commander. "Today we fly," the commander barked. "Our mission is a vital mission, for we will fire our rockets."

Belenko knew that he must maintain an air of normalcy. He donned his tattered cotton flight suit and inspected his automatic pistol. That he even carried a gun stemmed from a tragic incident: several months earlier a pilot had successfully ejected from his plane in a wilderness area—only to be found weeks later dead of starvation. Now all Soviet MiG pilots carried a pistol, and the furnishings of their MiG-25s included basic survival gear.

Today Belenko's squadron would practice intercept maneuvers, then return to base. But the day's plans held much more for Belenko. If he was successful, today would mark his first step away from a barren existence; today he would begin fulfilling his dream.

At 12:50 P.M. the pilot lined up with the rest of his squadron, released his brakes and surged down the runway. Then, climbing to 19,000 feet, he suddenly jammed the stick forward and plunged into a power dive. At 100 feet he leveled off, hoping to evade the ever-probing Soviet radar. For him to attempt to take a MiG-25 so low was potentially suicidal; even at 1,000 feet the cumbersome planes were difficult to control.

Flying so close to the water, Belenko twice had to swerve to avoid hitting fishing vessels. Soon he would have to bring the jet back up to the thin air at 20,000 feet so as not to deplete his fuel supply. But for now he had to fly low to avoid long-range Soviet radar, as well as the missile-bearing ships which patrolled offshore.

At 1:11 P.M., when it finally rose from the sea to 20,000 feet, Belenko's MiG appeared as an unidentified blip on Japanese radar. Eleven minutes later he breached Japanese airspace. Immediately several F-4 *Phantom* jets scrambled to intercept him. They would have to find him on their own; the band on his radio was so narrow he could only communicate with other MiGs.

Thirty minutes after takeoff, the fighter pilot throttled back and began gliding downward. Scarcely sustaining airspeed in order to facilitate interception, he hoped that by descending he would also break free of the clouds.

Three times during his descent the MiG pilot sliced through the clouds into thin layers of blue sky—only to be engulfed anew in a blanket of dirty gray clouds. Now, worry crept in: Where were the *Phantoms* that would guide him to a safe landing?

An airstrip at the city of Chitose, which lay toward the middle of Hokkaido behind a range of mountains

on the island's southwestern peninsula, was Belenko's target. But by the time he finally spotted land, he had no more than 18 minutes of fuel left. Hopefully this would carry him to Chitose. He could always eject from the craft, but the preservation of the MiG-25 was his utmost concern. He decided to stay low for visibility, even though it would further compromise his fuel.

At 1:42 a red warning light flashed and a panel lit up with the message "You Have Six Minutes Of Fuel Left." Then suddenly a calm, firm female voice advised him from a hidden recording device: "Caution, Oh-six-eight! Your fuel supply has dropped to an emergency level. You are in an emergency situation." Continuing his flight into the unknown, Belenko replied aloud, "Woman, wherever you are, tell me something I don't know. Tell me where is that aerodrome."

Thus progressed Viktor Belenko's escape from the Soviet Union. But why Belenko, of all people? He had never been in trouble, never associated with dissidents.

The answers began in Belenko's childhood. Having been raised by an aunt in Donbas after his parents' divorce when he was two years old, he had lived out his boyhood in a mud and straw hut. Confined to the hut every winter for lack of suitable footwear, the boy's first shoes were actually a pair of slippers sewn from the sleeves of an old jacket.

In school Viktor became a voracious reader, devouring everything he could put his hands on. Authors were his true parents, his role models and his best teachers. One of these mentors in print, the French aviator and author Antoine de Saint-Exupery, instilled in the life-hungry boy a desire to fly. Later, after suffering a beating by four older boys, Viktor also devoted himself to boxing and physical fitness.

But above all, throughout his life, Viktor had asked himself questions: *Why is our country always unprepared for the harvest? ... How can we have a cholera epidemic when we are told we have the best medicine in the world ... You mean they have a Communist party in the U.S.? They allow it? ... If people in America are starving and out of work, who is driving all those cars I see [on the news and in movies]?...*

Upon graduation from school, Viktor had joined a military auxiliary, where he was selected as one of 40 men to receive pre-flight training. In time he became a pilot, one of the most coveted jobs in the Soviet Union.

But even in flight school questions about America kept vexing the young man's mind. America was filled with decadence and internal strife, he was told. America was the "Main Enemy"; Americans were the "Dark Force." The My Lai massacre in Vietnam was portrayed as the ultimate example of American inhumanity and degeneracy; Lt. William Calley had ordered the slaughtering of hundreds of innocent men, women and children. *But why are the Dark Forces putting him in jail?* Belenko reflected. *If they are pure and true Dark Forces the officer did just what they wanted. Why not give him a medal?*

Then one day, while scanning an intelligence report on the U.S. Navy's F-14, Belenko had learned that its radar could detect aircraft 180 miles away, lock onto multiple targets moving at four times the speed of sound 100 miles away, and fire six missiles simultaneously. He could not believe the report: *Our radar, when it works, has a range of fifty miles. Our missiles, when they work, have a range of eighteen miles. How will we fight the F-14? It will kill us before we ever see it! If our system is so much better than the Americans, why is their technology so much better than ours?*

Belenko's skepticism had gradually grown into a deep-seated rejection of the Soviet system. And now, faced with the loss of his only son, who had been taken by Belenko's estranged wife to a city thousands of miles away, the pilot had no ties to bind him to his country.

Now barely maintaining airspeed, Belenko watched the altimeter drop. Then at 250 feet the world lit up and he could see an airstrip—a commercial airfield at Hakodate. The runway was only two-thirds long enough to land a *MiG*. But with no fuel left for any other choice, he jerked the controls into the tightest turn possible, pulled up to avoid an oncoming *Boeing 727*, dove at the runway, and touched down at 220 knots. Deploying his drag chute and slamming down again and again on his brakes, he grimaced as the craft screeched toward the end of the runway and skidded into a field, finally stopping just short of hitting a huge antenna.

Viktor was quickly ushered into the airport and closeted with officials. But the pilot would say little: his only stated wishes were that his aircraft be put under guard and concealed, and that he be granted political asylum in the United States. These requests, when translated, brought an outburst of cheers and applause. Within minutes the news flashed around the globe: Belenko had delivered the Soviets' most super-secret aircraft into the hands of the Free World.

Not long afterwards a KGB officer, functioning as a Soviet embassy official, was sent to interview Belenko: "All your relatives, your wife, your father ... your mother, your aunt ... have joined in sending a collective letter to you," the agent said. Belenko knew it was a lie: *How could they get them together so quickly from all over Russia?* "I flew to Japan voluntarily and on purpose," he told the agent matter-of-factly. "I on my own initiative have requested political asylum in the United States. Excuse me. Our conversation is over."

Aboard a 747 on his way to Tokyo, Belenko was admitted to the flight deck: *How could only three men manage such an enormous plane?* he wondered. *The rest of the crew must be hidden somewhere ...*

On his arrival in America, the Soviet pilot's doubts persisted. Meeting with CIA officers, Belenko mused on their appearance: *They are too trim, too healthy, dressed too expensively ... too friendly.... They are trying to fool me.* Later, on visiting a supermarket for the first time, he laughed at the expensive shopping carts and the seemingly endless isles of food: *If this were a real store, a woman in less than an hour could buy enough food in this one place to feed a whole family for two weeks. But where*

are the people, the crowds, the lines ... *This is not a real store.... It's a showplace of the Dark Forces.* And upon entering a modest apartment for the first time, it finally struck him as too much: *Who ever heard of a worker's apartment with two bathrooms and carpet all over the floors and machines that wash the dishes ...?*

The CIA were disposed to grant Belenko almost anything he asked. After all, the enormity of what he had supplied them, in the *MiG-25*, defied calculations in both monetary and defense terms. But they were surprised by the still-suspicious pilot's first request: he wanted to work on a farm—absolutely the worst place to live in his homeland. Now, however, he witnessed firsthand the modern equipment and growing and harvesting techniques, the high standard of medical care, the lavish availability of high-tech TVs, radios and calculators—not to mention the fact that they were available to American farm workers and their families.

Above all, Belenko noticed the autonomy of the people. He was astonished: *Why, a common laborer on this farm is better off than a Soviet fighter pilot.... They are free people.... Look at the harvest!*

What! You mean they pay a doctor twice as much as a fighter pilot? You mean you pick your own doctor, and if he makes you wait too long or you don't like the way he treats you, you go to another doctor?... They lied. All these years, they lied, and they knew they were lying.

A color television set in the Soviet Union cost a worker approximately five months' wages.... You can buy a car in this country as easily as a loaf of bread!

... How can they afford to let everybody just get up and go anywhere he pleases whenever he wants? What keeps order in this country?

At the close of his interrogation by CIA agents, Belenko was informed that his great service to the United States was to be repaid via "a generous income for the rest of his life." Not a materialist by nature, Belenko did not rejoice at financial security; he still saw much that he needed to accomplish—with English language proficiency at the top of the list. Accordingly, now cloaked under a new identity, Belenko did two things: he bought a car and enrolled in an intensive English program.

When, after making rapid progress, he hit a patch of resistance in his language studies, Belenko's teachers suggested that he "tramp around the country, practicing English." And this he did. From Appalachia to the Rockies, from Kansas City to San Francisco, Belenko traveled compulsively, still astounded by American "superabundance." Speeding across "the breadth of Texas in fewer than twenty-four hours," Belenko struggled with the impulse to drive straight to the Soviet Embassy. *Great stakes rode with him*; what a boost for Party morale his rejection of American society would mean: all Soviets would be inspired by this "New Communist Man who had seen and judged."

At last, however, the "fever broke." Exhausted, Belenko pulled over to the side of the road. His heart already told him just what a CIA friend would soon be reassuring him: "Viktor ... the United States is more your homeland than the Soviet Union ever could be."

TOUCHING THE VOID
by Joe Simpson, Harper & Row, 1988

After ten days of hard climbing in the Andes, Joe Simpson found himself in a pitch-black icy chasm with no food or water, his leg severely fractured. His climbing partner—his only hope—had, in desperation, cut his safety rope and left him for dead.

Touching the Void is Joe's riveting account of their adventure—their heroic struggle to reach the mountaintop, the terrifying series of incidents that left Joe disabled in an icy abyss, and the superhuman tenacity that brought him home alive

DAY 1-6: At base camp 15,000 feet high in the Peruvian Andes, Joe Simpson and Simon Yates prepared to scale the unclimbed west face of Siula Grande, rising another 6,000 feet above them. They spent two days selecting their route and waiting for a break in the weather, well aware that the towering cumulus clouds moving in to rain on them in the afternoons were bringing fresh snow—and the risk of avalanche—at higher elevations. At one point they started up the fractured, contorted glacier spilling over the mountain's south ridge. But powdery, waist-deep snow soon forced them back in exhaustion.

On day six, after gorging from their supply crates to fortify themselves for the rigorous struggle ahead, the climbers loaded their backpacks with equipment and set out again. That night they bivouacked in a snow hole, hoping for warmth

DAY 7: Peering from their snow hole early the next morning, the climbers were greeted by blue ice fields sparkling under clear, sunny skies—perfect climbing weather. Simon led out, hammering iron pitons into the ice with frost-brittle fingers; Joe, tethered by a 150-foot rope, followed, constantly off balance by the obtruding angle of the sheer wall. Alternating the lead, they continued up another 1,000 feet, then 2,000, wondering when the icefields would ever end.

As night fell, the pair climbed cautiously over the crumbly, honeycombed ice. Finally a tube-shaped wall reared up sharply out of the dark and the good ice gave way to mushy powder. With one last desperate move, the climbers propelled themselves onto the slopes above, where they dug in for the night.

DAY 8: Joe and Simon had bivouacked at 19,000 feet, roughly 2,000 feet from the summit. Just a few hours' climb to go. Despite the thin air, they made good progress ascending up a 55-degree ramp of ice. Then, for the first time, they caught sight of the summit itself—nothing more than a huge overhanging cornice.

From that point on, they encountered every possible deterrent, from bare rock to waist-deep snowfields. After four hours of wrenching work—and a sparse, hard-won 300 feet—they decided to bed down for the night. Two hours and one hundred feet later they gulped down their last freeze-dried meal and settled into their sleeping bags.

DAY 9: Morning dawned with clear skies and no wind. It looked like the climbing would be easier. Before them, rising only another 100 feet, stood the summit. Simon took the lead, leaving Joe behind to take photos. Then Joe also clambered to the top, the euphoria reflecting in his face.

Their joy would be short-lived, as suddenly another storm moved in and the climbers watched the ridge below them disappear into the clouds. Within minutes, they were totally enveloped in a white-out. It was 2:30 P.M.

Together the men weighed their options: Should they stay put or move down? Then for a brief moment the sky brightened and Joe caught a glimpse of the ridge. Encouraged, Simon set out towards it. Within a minute, however, the clouds swirled back in and he was lost from Joe's sight. The rope slowly running through Joe's gloves was the only sign that his partner was still there. Then all at once the rope whipped through his hands, a deep explosion echoed through the clouds, and Joe was jerked chest first into the snow. He called out to Simon; no answer. He waited. A full 15 minutes passed before he heard Simon's relieved, exultant cry: "I've found the ridge!"

"One minute I was climbing, the next I was falling," Simon explained when Joe finally caught up with him. He had broken away a 40-foot cornice and fallen with it; only the rope had saved him from a 4500-foot drop.

DAY 10: As they felt their way along the mountain, often sinking in snow up to their chests, a feeling of helplessness descended on the pair. The going was slow and their fingers were showing signs of deep frostbite. Finally they realized that the ridge they were traversing was one vast horizontal cornice.

At last Joe spied another way off the ridge. Crouching down on his knees, he lowered himself over the edge and kicked the steel-plate crampons attached to his boots into the ice wall below. Without the slightest warning, there was a sharp crack—and he was falling. He hit the slope below with both knees locked. Then, with a second, bone-splintering crack below his left knee, his body exploded in pain. The impact catapulted him over backwards and down the east face.

I've broken my leg, that's it. I'm dead, were Joe's first thoughts. The impact had driven his lower leg bones all the way up through the knee joint. His rope slackened, a sign that Simon was coming his way.

Hour after hour, Simon lowered Joe patiently down the mountain face, slackening the rope until it ran out, then digging himself out of his snow seat and climbing down to where Joe was waiting—to begin the procedure all over again. Nightfall brought a relentless storm, making communication impossible. Each time Joe was lowered, his crampons would snag, wrenching his mangled leg up toward his body. " ... There would be a flare of agony as the knee kinked back, and parts within the joint seemed to shear past each other with a sickening gristly crunch." By the end of the fourth descent, Joe was in so much agony that his leg shook uncontrollably.

Visibility worsened, as did the angle of the slope. At one point Joe screamed for Simon to go slow, but his words were lashed away by the savage wind. Then all at once Joe felt himself hurled outward into space. Clawing at the near-vertical cliff-face, he had triggered an avalanche of loose snow, and now he was dangling in mid-air, suspended over a deep crevasse.

The constant, ever-increasing pull on his line soon told Simon that Joe was in trouble. Then the rope began to cut into his own waist, draining strength from his body; within seconds he would be pulled out of his snow seat. If that happened, both of them would be killed. He weighed the options. Then, with trance-like calm, he reached down and cut the rope.

Moments earlier, Joe's lamp had gone out; above him all he could see were stars. Then all at once the stars went out, too, and he was falling. "I fell silently, endlessly into nothingness, as if dreaming of falling," Joe recalled. And then a blinding thud against his back shattered the stillness of the dream. He bounced, and fell again, deeper into a crevasse. When next he struck something solid, he lay there, stunned. "I couldn't breath. I retched.... Nothing.... I shut my eyes, and gave in to gray fading shadows..."

Joe was overwhelmed by panic and pain as breath and consciousness returned to him. Groping through the dense blackness with his fingers, he discovered that he had landed on some type of ledge or snow bridge. He anchored himself with a piton to the ice. He decided that if he was going to die, he would at least die trying. Pulling his hammer up from below, he beat a piton into the ice to anchor himself. Lastly he drew in the rope—and stared in disbelief at its end: it had been cut. Cut!

In shock, grief and anger, Joe began lowering himself even deeper into the void. When he came to the end of the rope, he resolved, he would simply slip off and die in the plunge. But as he descended, ever so slowly, a surprising shaft of sunlight caught his eye, and a glimmer of hope welled up in him. With renewed strength he began hacking steps in the ice wall; somehow he must reach the light. Planting his axe, he gingerly pulled himself up the jagged steps towards salvation, hopping with his good leg. An ascent that would have taken the average hiker no more than ten minutes exacted from Joe more than half a day of agony. But finally, near total collapse, he poked his head like a gopher out of the abyss to behold the most awesome, gratitude-inspiring sight of his life: he was free again.

DAY 11: Joe was now 200 feet above the glacier and six miles from base camp—a half-day's stroll for a healthy climber, but for him at least a three-day ordeal. In torturous anguish, he began hopping, dropping and sliding downward. From time to time his crampons would catch, wrenching his broken leg up behind him. Finally, in anguish, he reached down, unhooked the spikes with his axe, and rid himself of them entirely.

All the while Joe kept hearing a voice in his mind that prevented him from drifting off into a death sleep: *Go on, keep going ... faster. You've wasted too much time. Go on ...* Darkness fell, and a heavy wind came up. Once again he fell face down in the snow; and for a long while he lay there, defeated. But then the voice intensified: *... Don't sleep, don't sleep, not here. Keep going. Find a slope and dig a snow hole ... don't sleep.*

DAY 12: Joe awoke half-frozen and screaming; then he realized he was no longer in the crevasse. Everything now hinged on his ability to maintain his bearings and find a route that would take him off the glacier. Halfway through the day he found himself in what looked like familiar surroundings. Trying to stand, he peered towards the horizon, fighting the sharp, prickling pains which he recognized as the onset of snow-blindness. At length he caught sight of the rockfields, the pass where they had set up base camp.

When Joe finally reached the rocks, his stamina was spent. Nevertheless, he struggled onward, fighting drowsiness, pain, the urge to quit. Using his foam mat and the straps from his crampons, he fashioned a splint around his knee and again stood. His head reeled in torment as he took a weak step, then another. Each time he collapsed, he lay exhausted in a timeless semi-stupor.

DAY 13: *Must reach camp today,* Joe thought. *Surely Simon had to be there, he'd have been there two days now.* Again and again he clawed his way up to take a hop, and again and again he fell. "I thought how far I had to go and how far I had come. Part of me wanted to give up and sleep.... The voice countered this." At one o'clock he finally stumbled into the narrow, lake-dotted pass that opened onto their base camp, Bomb Alley—home territory at last.

By three o'clock Joe had come to the end of the rock fields. Every now and then he would spot a boot print, and his confidence soared. Then it was four o'clock—close to dark; now he had to hurry. An hour later he inched his way along the divide that led to the campsite. As darkness fell, using his axe as if on ice, he hacked into the mud wall and hauled himself up. "SIIMMMOONNN!" he groaned. Only eerie echoes returned.

Hours of blackness sifted by; all sense of time and place were lost. Staggering dazedly onward, Joe found himself in a dry river bed. Somewhere on the edge of the bed were the tents. "SIIMMMmoonn ... Please be there, you must be there." A crisp snow beat against his face—and the night remained black and silent.

Then, as if out of nowhere, lights appeared. *Something floated and glowed ahead of me. A semicircle of red and green ... a space ship ... then muffled sounds. A spray of yellow light suddenly cut out from the colors in a wide cone ... voices, not my voices ... the tents!! They're still there. Then, [Simon's voice.] "Joe! Is that you? JOE! Joe! God! Oh my God! ... look at you. Lift him, lift him ... God Joe, how? How?"*

O nce while Thor Heyerdahl and his wife were visiting a little island in the Marquesas group called Fatu Hiva, they listened intently as old Tei Tetua—the sole survivor of his tribe—discussed the ancient Polynesian god and chief, offspring of the sun, Tiki. "It was Tiki who brought my ancestors to these islands where we live now," Tei Tetua explained. "Before that we lived in a big country beyond the sea." His words were nearly drowned out by the waves crashing in on the eastern shore—always from the east.

As the old man's words haunted his sleep late into the night, Heyerdahl pondered: "It was as though time no longer existed, and Tiki and his seafarers were just landing … on the beach below." Then a thought struck him, and he said to his wife, "Have you noticed that the huge stone figures of Tiki in the jungle are remarkably like the monoliths left by extinct civilizations in South America?"

Heyerdahl returned to his native Norway with a plan to research the ancient origins of the South Sea islands' native cultures. Although oral tradition held that the earliest Polynesians had been immigrants from Asia (the first groups disembarking around 500 A.D.E. and the second in 1100 A.D.E.), Heyerdahl could not reconcile the technologically advanced civilizations of the orient with the less sophisticated cultures of the Pacific. He supposed that the first Polynesians had come from the opposite direction, from the Americas. Not only did the stone heads and the waves breaking on the eastern shore of Fatu Hiva lead him to this conclusion, but while in Peru he had read the Inca legends of the sun-king: Kon-Tiki had been the Incan leader of the legendary white, bearded men who, after being defeated in battle, had escaped to the Pacific coast, then disappeared to the west. In fact, the first European explorers had been surprised to find entire Polynesian families—said to be direct descendants of Tiki—who looked almost white.

Heyerdahl examined the possible connection between ancient Peru and Polynesia in a manuscript, which he later submitted to various experts. All flatly rejected his theory. One professor of anthropology insisted that no South American culture had the technology in the year 500 to cross the 4,000 miles of Pacific Ocean to reach the first of the Polynesian Islands. When Heyerdahl protested—citing evidence that, far from being a primitive people, these early sailors were expert astronomers and were equipped with well-constructed balsa-wood rafts—the professor smiled. "Well, you can try a trip from Peru to the Pacific islands on a balsa-wood raft." And so the Norwegian resolved to do just that.

Heyerdahl calculated that the minimum time for a raft to make the trip would be 97 days—four months at the outside. He then turned his attention to finding a crew. Herman Watzinger, a Norwegian engineer, was the first to link up with Heyerdahl. After determining that they would need four additional crew members, the would-be sailors enlisted the services of Erik Hesselberg, an experienced seaman, who could use a sextant to plot their course. Two other Norwegian war heroes, Knut Haugland and Torstein Raaby, both skilled in radio transmissions, would receive reports on weather conditions.

Still lacking a sixth crew member, Heyerdahl and Watzinger tended to other aspects of the expedition: first, they obtained financing from private lenders and free food rations from the American War Department, secondly, they attended to legal matters with the government of Peru; and finally, they traveled to South America to a jungle area near the city of Quevedo—a region frequented by headhunters and bandits—in order to obtain the large balsa logs.

After floating the logs down the Rio Palenque to the coast, Heyerdahl and Watzinger began to assemble their raft in the Peruvian naval docks, where they came across their the sixth crew member, Bengt Danielsson, a Swede who had studied Amazonian Indians. Before long, the other crew members also arrived to help build the raft. Supporting a bamboo hut and a large square sail, the vessel was made up of nine huge balsa logs lashed together with long ropes—which experts insisted would fall apart within a few weeks—and long centerboards to keep the 40-foot craft gliding forward, as well as a long steering oar. It was an exact replica of rafts described by the earliest Spanish explorers.

On April 28, 1947, the day after the raft had been christened Kon-Tiki in honor of the legendary voyager, a tug boat towed the raft out to sea. Without an engine, the first few days would prove to be the most difficult and treacherous. Still trying to learn how to steer their raft, the crew worried that cross-currents would smash them back into the rocky coast rather than keeping them afloat on the Humboldt Current that could carry them across 4,000 miles of open water to their destination.

The genius of the raft's design, however, soon presented itself. Unlike a large ship—designed to plow through surging waves—the relatively tiny raft could ride up and down on the surf. If several large waves came in succession, though, whoever was steering had to hold on tight and wait for the water to drain, to avoid being swept overboard.

That first night the waves were so big that two men had to struggle with the steering oar to keep the raft from capsizing. For the next three days they battled the sea, taking turns at the helm. By the fourth day the sea had calmed, and the exhausted crew was relieved to find that their craft's ropes showed no sign of wear. Although the logs seemed to be absorbing water, the voyagers later learned that the balsa sap in the freshly cut logs kept water from saturating—and sinking—them.

Well out on the open seas, the crew became acquainted with their new sea neighbors. Flying fish regularly came thudding onto the deck, which the crew gathered up for breakfast. On one occasion they found on their raft a "snakefish" (*Gempylus*), previously thought to be extinct.

For their own safety, the crew used hooks, harpoons and ropes to discourage sharks from approaching the raft. Harpoons often shattered on the shark's rough skin; several heavy fish hooks hidden in a dolphin fish and lashed onto a strong line proved to be more effective. But later, the seafarers found a more exciting method of clearing the area of sharks: holding a piece of fish over the edge of the raft, a daring "fisherman" would lure the shark to jump up out of the water. In that instant the sailor would seize the shark by the tail and haul it on board.

Sharks were not the only potential menace. The crew had been warned against the giant octopuses found in an area of the Humboldt Current. While they never encountered one of the enormous creatures, they were surprised several times when smaller specimens came flying on board, using a sort of jet propulsion to leap high into the sky in order to avoid their pursuers.

On board the *Kon-Tiki* each man performed daily duties: Bengt worked as steward; Herman took readings with meteorological and hydrographical equipment; Knut and Torstein operated the radio equipment; Erik patched the sail and spliced ropes; and Heyerdahl tended to the logbook, collected fish and plankton specimens, and filmed the expedition. In addition, everyone took turns cooking and steering.

For both solitude and amusement during the long journey, a few of the men would tie a safety line to a rubber dinghy, climb in, and row off alone for a few hours. At first the sight of the tiny, crude *Kon-Tiki* bobbing in the waves made them laugh. But later, as Heyerdahl recalled, "when we saw the silhouette of our craft grow smaller and smaller in the distance ... a sensation of loneliness sometimes crept over us."

Because the current made it impossible for the raft to turn around, the crew knew anything or anyone that fell behind its path would be irredeemably lost. Understandably, then, the crew was momentarily horrified when Herman fell overboard. Quickly, Knut tied a safety line around his waist and swam out to where Herman floundered, and they were drawn safely back to the raft.

Although two storms ended up damaging the steering oar and loosening the ropes and centerboards, they were nonetheless confident that the *Kon-Tiki* was still sound enough to reach their destination.

Heralding land days in advance, boobies and other short-range fowl first appeared, followed by increasing numbers of birds. Then, just after six o'clock on July 30, Herman woke Heyerdahl. "Come out and have a look at your island!" Now, for the first time in over three months, they saw land. The current, however, had already pulled them too far past the island for them to put in ashore. Although they spotted two more islands the next day, the voyagers decided to head for Angatau. Three days later, when they reached the island, the crew deemed the south side the most suitable for a landing—if they could find a break in the treacherous reef that surrounded it. All day they maneuvered in and out of the reef, elated by the prospect of soon setting foot on solid earth after 97 days at sea.

As they circled the island, there appeared two natives, rowing through a passage in the reef to greet them. Astonished to find that the *Kon-Tiki* lacked a motor, the natives helped the crew as they tried to breach the shallow reef. Despite the efforts of natives from four additional seagoing canoes, the unrelenting current swept the raft farther and farther from shore.

Unable to reach Angatau, the crew maneuvered the *Kon-Tiki* through the dangerous reef of Raroia. Though they hoped to sail north of the Raroia shoal, the wind changed and they quickly decided to head for the southern side of the reef. There they became caught in a northern current; surely their craft would strike the reef within a few hours.

During their final hours on the *Kon-Tiki*, the crew scrambled to save what remained of their provisions. Finally the moment came when the raft, with its confident crew, crashed through the breakers and onto the reef. Wave after wave passed over the vessel, battering the hut, before the crew could salvage its provisions and leap onto the reef, away from the murderous breakers.

At last, the six men waded to one of the palm-shaded islets and set up camp. "When I reached the sunny sand beach, I slipped off my shoes and thrust my bare toes down into the warm, bone-dry sand," Heyerdahl recalled. " ... The voyage was over. We were all alive."

A few days later, natives arrived from a neighboring island. They listened spellbound to the story as it was translated by their chief of the *Kon-Tiki*, named after their ancestor, and then helped to pull the wrecked craft over the shoal and into the lagoon. Returning to the natives' village, the crew happily waited for the ship that would transport them and the battered *Kon-Tiki* to the world beyond.

Although *Kon-Tiki*'s voyage had not proven that the Polynesians initially had emigrated from South America, the journey demonstrated conclusively that a balsa-wood raft could sail the 4,000 miles from Peru to Polynesia—a feat perhaps accomplished many millennia earlier in which a similar craft carried a people who would plant coconut palms, create a paradise for themselves, and foster a new civilization.

THESE GOOD MEN
by Michael Norman, Crown Publishers, 1989

On Friday, April 19, 1967 the soldiers of Golf Company, Second Battalion, 9th Marine Division moved out on a routine rescue mission. As they advanced cautiously into North Vietnam, Michael Norman's ten-man Charlie squad paused at Bridge 28, which spanned the Quang Tri River. There they found not only the bodies of those troops they had hoped to save, but also the enemy. For the next three days Norman's company engaged in an intense fire-fight. When the battle was over, only half of the company's 110 men survived to walk away.

Five years later Norman began to feel over-whelmed by rage. As he later recalled: *I was sure that I had walked off the battlefield a more knowing man. Those who survive such a long and lethal assault emerge with at least a small piece of truth, some little lesson, a sliver of light. Maybe, across the years, chasing bylines and a bigger house, I had simply lost it.* Longing to understand the full impact of his war experiences, Norman finally decided in the spring of 1984 to organize a reunion of war buddies. ... *In search of the ineffable, I set out to find the men I once held close, intimates side by side under a flame-white sun and at night belly to back in a fighting hole.... Those men had been a mirror of me; likely they, too, carried home some small verity. Perhaps my comrades had been more provident and not let a thing so dearly won slip so easily away.*

Norman first flew to Mesquite, Texas, to see Craig Belknap, whom he could still remember seeing that day on the bridge, crouched behind the bullet-riddled body of Tommy Gonzales. Although Norman vividly recalled Craig, drenched in blood, being lugged down the road on a stretcher, now, almost 20 years later, he was unprepared for the shock. Craig's right foot and leg, which had been hit by mortar fire, were stunted and twisted so that he limped badly. All that remained of his right hand were two semi-rigid fingers and a fused thumb. Embracing his old friend, Norman wept.

Craig later explained that though he had come home from Vietnam a hero, he also "had come home a drunk." His girlfriend Jean left him soon afterward, and although he had married another woman with whom he had children, he remained an alcoholic who suffered extreme physical and emotional pain. "I wanted to understand it," Craig shook his head. "I wasn't getting any answers."

Finally, after years of anguish, Craig had gone into treatment and had emerged a recovered alco-holic. He subsequently began counseling addicts and alcoholics, and, although he and his wife divorced, Craig found comfort in a resumed rela-tionship with his old girlfriend Jean.

Next, Norman contacted Michael Tom Williamson, a tall, thin Oklahoman who had been nicknamed "Squeaky" because an operation he had undergone as an adolescent had left his voice with a distinct whine. He had been among the first in Norman's rescue squad to set foot on Bridge 28. Although he'd escaped the ambush unscathed, Squeaky remained psychologically tormented by the death of his close buddy Gonzales. Months after the incident, Squeaky, as an eager new lieutenant, had led his men into another ambush and had stepped on a mine. Suffering eye injuries and brain damage from exploding metal fragments, he was sent home.

After "recovering," Squeaky enrolled in college. It was a miracle that he attended his classes at all, not only because he had been partially blinded, but also because he had remained in mental anguish all those years. In any case, one class short of graduation, Squeaky dropped out of college and out of life—as, earlier, he had dropped out of a marriage.

Together with his second wife Georgia, Squeaky launched a cross-country junket, bedding down in a tent and surviving on government disability checks. Because he suffered continual vision loss, he finally contacted a surgeon who performed cornea trans-plants—and who located and removed a remaining "floating" metal fragment from his eye. When he submitted his insurance claim, however, the govern-ment refused to pay for the surgery unless Squeaky could identify the person who had caused the injury. Though he was able to laugh at his misfortune, the terrible absurdity did not escape the veteran's notice.

Soon Norman found himself on a flight to Newark, New Jersey, to see Frank Ciappio, his old platoon commander. Dubbed "Demo Dan"—"because he liked to blow things up"—Frank was a real soldier's soldier, surviving many battles in Vietnam. In fact, because he served as a father figure for many of his men, Frank had signed up for an extra tour of duty.

One day, in the middle of a fire-fight, Frank found one of his buddies lying face down in the mud, dead, and something just snapped inside of him. He suddenly became afraid. Gone was his concern for his men; his only thought now was to get out of the war alive. As it happened, Frank contracted malaria and was soon shipped home—but "he never forgot his kids or recovered from the feeling that he had abandoned them."

Frank later married and became a stock broker. But the war—and his kids—continued to haunt him; he drank heavily and frequently turned violent. Marine psychologists told him that he suffered from "Post Traumatic Stress Disorder," but identifying his "disorder" did little to cure him. All treatments failed. Embittered by his experiences, Frank now claimed that he would send his son to Canada before he let him fight in a war like Vietnam's.

After spending several days with Frank, Norman traveled to Savannah, Georgia, to look up Bob Hagan and Charles Whitfield. Second Lieutenant

Hagan had once bragged that he was going to win the Congressional Medal of Honor. But when the fighting on Bridge 28 broke out, Bob had frozen, paralyzed with fear. Now, as Norman talked to Hagan's parents, he learned that Bob had been awarded the Silver Star for heroism in a later battle, had re-enlisted, and then been reported missing in action. "The more I heard, the more I wanted to know," Norman writes. "Hagan was a conundrum; the man who had wanted to cut and run; the man who had tried to shoulder the standard." What was the difference between a coward and a hero? Norman couldn't say. Bob was probably just a man at war with himself.

Charles Whitfield, it turned out, was still living in Savannah. In a campaign after the "bridge battle," "Whit" had received a sniper bullet in the back of the head—a bullet, incidentally, that had been intended for Norman. Over a period of months as he recuperated in a hospital, Whit had managed to overcome his bitterness about the war and his injuries, and had found peace by acknowledging the abilities he retained. As his wife now told Norman, "I think the war was where Charles derived a lot of his strength, his values, and character."

Norman next located Mike Caron and Dave Buckner. He was pleased to find Mike doing well and working as a manager-in-training for a tire company in West Haven, Connecticut. "Quite simply ... the bravest man I'd ever met," at Bridge 28 Mike had repeatedly risked his own life to drag the dead and wounded from the field of fire. In spite of what he had gone through in Vietnam, the experience had left his psyche fairly intact.

In contrast to Mike, whose wife comforted and supported him, Dave Buckner's spouse had recently left him and filed for divorce. Now living in London, he had remained in the Marines, even though he had once threatened to "do in" a superior officer: Dave had refused to take a hill as ordered, and instead had simply raised his rifle and squinted down its sights at the officer—who backed down. The humiliated officer had subsequently kept Dave from being promoted to Lieutenant Colonel—though he had deserved the promotion many times over. Eventually, Norman learned, Dave won his promotion. Norman grinned widely when he heard this news, because, as Dave so often expressed, "I love the Marines. When they triumph, I just love it."

Dave's enthusiasm for the military was not at all shared by Doc DeWeese, who had been the company's senior medical corpsman. A former divinity student who abhorred war, Doc had always been a gentle, compassionate soul. In fact, the day after Bridge 28, Doc had cared for Norman when he suddenly went into convulsions. After Norman had been stabilized, Doc refused to allow his evacuation after hearing that psychiatrists behind the lines were treating battle fatigue with electro-shock therapy. Instead, he gave Norman tranquilizers and stayed by his side for two weeks until he recovered.

After so many years, Doc had seemed excited when Norman talked with him over the phone. When they met at the airport, though, he acted rather cold and distant. As they drove into Seattle, Doc finally admitted that Norman's visit had upset him. "It's like somebody coming back from the dead," he explained.

In Doc's case, it wasn't just damaging memories that bothered him: the war had literally destroyed his faith in God and he had been unable to return to divinity school. "Every man I zipped in one of those horrible green body bags," he confessed, "a little bit of me died."

After beginning work as a guidance counselor, Doc had finally realized that he was gay, a revelation that troubled him. Nevertheless, the prospect of the reunion seemed agreeable, and he promised to come.

Indeed, when the reunion finally took place in the spacious backyard of the Norman home in Montclair, New York, Doc was there to honor their comrades who had died on Bridge 28. Beth, Norman's wife, had set empty chairs at the flag-adorned tables to mark their ultimate sacrifice.

The weekend passed by too quickly; men wept openly when they bid their goodbyes. It was then that Norman knew why he had gone to so much trouble to arrange the reunion: *I know now why men who have been to war yearn to unite. Not to tell stories or look at old pictures. Not to laugh or weep on one another's knee. Comrades gather because they long to be with men who once acted their best, men who suffered and sacrificed, who were stripped raw, down to their humanity.... I know them in a way I know no other men. I have never given anyone such trust.*

Psychologists studying Vietnam War veterans and the phenomena of post-war stress often contend that the veterans' anger is related to politics. Perhaps to some extent this is true, but what the veterans primarily suffer from is their terrible memories—memories that just won't let them live in peace. In fact, Norman maintains that the Vietnam War experience is unique in that it exposed more dramatically ... the lunatic motives that lead to organized butchery and the awful waste that results from it. In our era, it was easy to see that the sacrifice had been for nothing and that perhaps nothing was worth that sacrifice.

In the end, however, Norman was able to find within his Vietnam experience a deep and abiding consolation. When his second son was born, he and Beth asked Craig Belknap to be the infant's godfather, a rite that reunited them, not merely as comrades in arms, but as best friends. There was Craig, holding the baby. For Norman, it was a pivotal scene: *On that Saturday in September, far from the field of battle ... I knew that the men of Golf Company had done more than just survive the fighting or come through the long aftermath.... We had truly come out ahead ...*

Nick Danziger, a 24-year-old British artist, set out with a backpack and a dream to retrace the Silk Road, the ancient trade route mapped out by Marco Polo that stretches from east China to the gates of Europe. Traveling by foot and local transport, with only $1500 in his pocket, Danziger journeyed from London to Peking in the space of 18 months. En route, he lived with the local people, pitted his wits against government bureaucracies and broke formidable cultural barriers at every new way station.

As he planned his itinerary, Nick applied for travel permits from Middle Eastern and Asian countries. After months of waiting, with only Pakistan having responded, he finally decided to forgo visas and make the journey by hook or by crook. In the end, he felt that the experience would be worth the risk of jail—or perhaps even worse—for it would "promote greater understanding of the people along its route …"

London to Istanbul

Nick traveled by rail from Victoria Station in London to Istanbul, the same city where Marco Polo had begun his journey in the late 13th century. Then, hitchhiking south along the Aegean and Mediterranean coasts, he stopped intermittently to pick tomatoes and converse with the locals. After meandering inland through southern Turkey, he ended up in Cappadocia. The surreal landscape of this Turkish backland is filled with rock cones, capped pinnacles and craggy ravines, forming endless warrens in which thousands of early Christians once took refuge from Arab raiders. Even today entire cities are built right into the soft rock; the homes and furniture, including tables, chairs, beds, windows and disc-shaped doors, are all carved from stone.

Into Syria

With no visa to cross the Turkish border south into Syria, Nick tried to slip past a secondary border post. At the ramshackle hut, two frontier guards apprehended him—and then invited him to join them in tea and backgammon. With a one-week visa in hand, he next hopped a battered bus east to Aleppo, where he found his way into a sleazy night club. Out of the smoke and pulsating music emerged a sultry belly dancer, swishing between the tables as patrons stuffed folded bills into her gold-braided bikini. Later Nick discovered the exotic siren was a Canadian national who taught dance at UCLA. It was, after all, a small world.

Back to Turkey

Crossing back into the eastern part of Turkey, Nick discovered a culture entirely different from that of the west; both the landscape and the people were hard and angry. Bitter Kurds, hailing from enclaves in many Middle-Eastern countries but denied a homeland of their own, made up most of the population. There, camped along the border of Iran, he found tens of thousands of Kurdish refugees, displaced by the recent Iran-

Iraq war. As he continued southward, he doubted that the Iranian border guards, with their hatred of "the Great Satan in the West," would let him pass into their country. But he decided to try anyway, using some forged documents he had obtained. And as luck would have it, the Iranian guard, nursing a machine gun, stamped Nick's passport and put him on the first truck that happened by. Dropped off on the edge of a dusty little town and unable to speak a word of Farsi, he eventually wandered into a bus station and called out, "Tehran," which fortunately sounded the same in both Farsi and English.

Revolutionary Iran

Nick found Tehran to be a city of dualities: Buildings were covered with slogans proclaiming the virtues of the "People's" Revolution, radios blurted out extremist chants, and television channels aired a continuous barrage of military propaganda. However, subtle signs of defiance appeared everywhere: a word whispered against Khomeini, forbidden water sipped during Ramadan, rock music played low late at night.

Near Shiraz, Danziger made a dangerous junket to the ancient city of Persepolis, founded by Darius the Great about 500 B.C.E. Marveling at the immense bas-relief sculptures portraying representatives of vassal peoples to the Persian court, Nick lamented, "It's one of the world's cultural tragedies that such a work of art should now be so inaccessible."

In the northeastern Iranian province of Khorassan Nick lobbied the Afghan *mujahideen*—the Islamic guerrilla at war with Soviet invaders—to smuggle him into their country. At first the soldiers refused; but a few days later a stranger cornered him and surreptitiously whispered, "You will leave here for a place near the border tomorrow afternoon!"

Clandestine Afghanistan Crossing

As it turned out, Danziger didn't leave Iran the next day, but he was taken to a safe house by two Afghani brothers who swapped his British clothing for the garb of the *mujahideen*—turban, baggy pants and a *shalwar camise*, the long-tailed Afghan shirt worn outside the trousers. After several failed and frightening attempts, he finally was spirited across the border into Afghanistan. "We traveled at night, skirting Soviet patrols and trying to make the next village before sunrise."

When he reached the fabled city of Herat, which over its twenty-five hundred years of existence had witnessed the passage of Alexander, Ghengis Khan and Tamerlane, Danziger was shocked to find it a bombed-out ruin under Soviet seige; the Soviet *MiG* attacks were unrelenting; a number of times he barely escaped death.

Eventually a respected *mujahideen* commander Ismail Khan befriended the traveler and allowed him to accompany his band of freedom fighters, who were heading towards Pakistan to secure arms from supporters. The group journeyed on horseback, alternately evading and attacking Soviet forces. Nick came to love these proud and courageous freedom fighters. To show his solidarity with their struggle, he wore the guerrilla "uniform" they had given him throughout the rest of his journey.

At the Pakistani frontier, the *mujahideen* learned that the Soviets were preparing to seal off the border; Nick would be trapped inside war-torn Afghanistan. Miraculously, the night before the Soviet assault began, a smuggler offered to sneak the entire company across the border in a battered army truck. It was a harrowing trip as they crept past Soviet patrols and inched around land mines in narrow desert canyons. Three times the truck broke down, and three times Nick concluded that "it was all over." But just before dawn they saw a glow on the horizon and recognized the frontier town of Chaman. They were in Pakistan.

Across Pakistan

Danziger's objective now was to traverse Pakistan and cross into China through the Himalayan Khunjerab Pass—before this still-prominent trade route was closed by winter snows. Afghan freedom fighters were welcome in Pakistan, so Khan's group of *mujahideen* hired a bus to take them to the mountain city of Quetta, along the way passing some three million tent-dwelling refugees from the recent civil war. In Quetta, Nick bought a first-class ticket to the northern city of Peshawar, near the western border of China, and for the first time in months enjoyed a bed and a shower. Because winter was fast approaching, he hurried on by transit wagon from the Pakistani capital of Islamabad to Gilgit.

The Roof of the World

At 15,000 feet above sea level, the Himalayan highland where China, Russia, Pakistan and Afghanistan converge is one of the most remote areas on earth. After venturing through several high mountain villages, Nick bribed a Pakistani official with a bottle of Scotch to stamp his passport and allow him to cross over into China on a truck convoy.

Xinjiang Province, China

In the city of Tashkorgan near the border of then-Soviet Nadzhikstan, Nick was struck by the beauty of the Tadzhik people—tall and lean with a beautifully exotic combination of Eastern and Western facial features. "The people gazed at our convoy of trucks as though they were spaceships."

After winding through steep mountain passes, the band reached the Uighur town of Kashgar, a major center of commerce during the Middle Ages. The faces of the Uighurs were tanned, wrinkled and hardened by the extremes of temperature in the high mountains. The men were proud and dignified, and wore long black corduroy coats fastened at the waist with scarves.

On the next day, Sunday, the town held a great bazaar. As Danziger roamed through the marketplace, the awe-struck Uighurs all wanted to touch his beard and feel his skin. "Never in all my travels," Nick wrote, "have I enjoyed so much my first day in a new country."

Two weeks later a Chinese official granted him special permission to traverse inland China over the great Takla Makan Desert, an honor that had not been accorded a foreigner since the Communist revolution.

The Great Takla Makan Desert

After beginning the trek, Nick quickly learned that other officials were not pleased to see him wandering so far inside China. They insisted that he be accompanied by a guide. When he managed to slip away for a few days and take a camel caravan to some nearby villages, he was arrested and almost jailed. Finally he resigned himself to completing the long, cold and tedious trip through the heart of China by bus—a vehicle which broke down many times, once for as long as 27 hours.

At his wits' end, Nick left the bus at the town of Dunhuang and, after walking along the main highway for three days, hitched a ride to Lhasa—the forbidden city. The gun-toting drivers of the vehicle must have been bandits; military men would have turned him in. It was a long but spectacular journey, winding past yak herds and glaciers scattered over the plateaus of Tibet.

Forbidden City

In Lhasa, the holy center of Tibetan Buddhism, Nick saw a group of people who were making a ritual walk around a carved deity. In order to earn merit in the next life, occasionally they would stop and bow before the object.

The women of Lhasa were considered so disarmingly attractive that a former Dalai Lama had once ordered them to blacken their faces with soot so he would not be distracted by their beauty. Nick found that he wholeheartedly concurred with the Dalai Lama's assessment.

Leaving Lhasa, Nick spent several more weeks in Tibet. Again he was arrested, but this time there was no room for compromise: he was ordered to leave the country by plane the next day. But that night the dauntless explorer, determined to avoid deportation, slipped past a drowsy sentry, made his way to the road, hitched a ride with a convoy of pilgrims and headed northeast for the Mekong River in central China.

Into the Heart of China

Nick entered into the densely populated Sichuan Province. "In an hour of traveling," he observed, "I passed more people than I'd seen in the whole of Tibet." He was low on money, but it was now late spring and warm enough for him to sleep outdoors. Ranging freely, he took a boat down the Yangtze River to Wuhan, and then an east-bound train to Peking. He writes that it's "worth traveling by train to Peking just to see the station. I felt positively ant-like."

Home

His money now exhausted and his goal of traversing the famed Silk Route achieved, Nick could not even afford a flight back to England—nor, in light of the incredible journey behind him, did he desire such a facile method of travel. Instead he chose to work his way home on a cargo ship, completing a travel adventure that may have been unparalleled since the days of Marco Polo.

In *The Medieval Underworld*, Andrew McCall provides a compelling but disturbing analysis of lawbreakers during the Middle Ages. Contextualizing medieval criminality in terms both of history and religion, McCall explains how society regarded and punished witches, prostitutes, thieves, swindlers, beggars, heretics and homosexuals. Moreover, McCall makes it clear that legal compliance and social conformity were essential survival mechanisms during this period of intolerance, violence and social strife.

In treating the history of the Middle Ages, the points of interest McCall chooses to focus on are fascinatingly unique.

The Middle Ages

The Middle Ages are often thought of as a dark interlude in the progress of Western civilization. Coined by an Italian of the 15th century, the term "Middle Ages" designates the eleven centuries of ignorance and fear that elapsed between the fall of Rome in about A.D.E. 395 and the emergence of the Renaissance in 14th-century Italy.

In essence, the Middle Ages began with the barbarian conquest of the Roman Empire. The ensuing society was developed from an uneasy synthesis of Christianity and paganism. Thus, as Western Europe was steadily raided by Magyars, Saracens, Moors and Vikings, the early Middle Ages were wrought with violence. Ordinary citizens, powerless to defend themselves, consequently turned to territorial warlords for protection. Although these relationships initially were voluntary, they eventually spawned Western European feudalism. In fact, by the end of the 11th century, not only had Christianity become the established religion but feudalism had also determined the established social order. However, over the next few centuries as trade routes gradually extended into far-off regions, more towns emerged, money circulated, the demand for labor increased, and many serfs liberated themselves from their lords. Clustering in towns, the freed serfs began to change the order. As McCall points out, *the Middle Ages had in fact been, for all the talk of an Immutable Order, an age of evolution and flux; an age during which ideas and institutions, secular and ecclesiastical, had been developed, adapted and amended ... an age during which the whole fabric of Western European civilization had, in short, been in a state of continual metamorphosis.*

Crime and Punishment

Medieval society had two conflicting sets of laws: the law of each autonomous region and the law of God (or, Canon law). Secular law combined elements of Roman and Germanic legal systems: Germanic law demanded that the accused prove his innocence, while Roman law put the burden of proof on the accuser (a defendant was presumed "innocent until proven guilty"). In contrast to secular law, religious law maintained that authority

from God was transmitted through God's representatives on earth. Moreover, according to the Church, every "crime" was a "sin" requiring penance, and it was the Church's duty to extract confessions so that the guilty might repent. Besides various means of torture, barbarous rituals were instituted to "draw out" these confessions.

Among these rituals, trial by ordeal was one of the most commonplace. The accused was scalded with boiling water and judged guilty or innocent depending on whether or not welts formed once the bandages were removed. In another popular ritual, trial by battle, the accused was deemed innocent only if he was victorious on the field. Although the Church later tended to rely more heavily on sworn testimony to determine guilt and to put more trust in human evidence, the rack, the pulley, the iron boot and various forms of water torture and other instruments to inflict pain still continued to be used.

If medieval society was not known for its amiable judicial standards, it nevertheless demanded active and observable justice; thus, in order to preserve social order, punishment became an important public event. Not only were stocks and gallows usually set up outside churches, but executions were also carried out in town squares, where corpses of the executed remained for days. Criminals who escaped death often had their flesh branded with hot irons or their limbs crudely amputated. According to McCall: *Conformity at every level ... and in all matters became essential for the salvation of the soul: to achieve the purpose of his earthly life the Christian was obliged not only to submit to the decisions of the Church courts and of royal justice but also to abide by the customary law of the region in which he lived or was staying.*

Richman, Poorman, Beggarman, Thief

Although medieval armies and mercenaries were bellicose, the poor were responsible for much of the period's violence and crime. During the 13th and 14th centuries, for instance, when people were devastated both by unemployment and by the plague, crime became a way of life. Thus as new and larger towns sprang up along travel routes and rivers, beggars and thieves flocked there to prey on the numerous urban dwellers. Certainly, it was much easier to "make a living" scavenging along city streets than in rural yards.

Of all medieval towns, those in France entertained the most organized groups of beggars and thieves: the *Malingreux*, for example, collected charity by making themselves appear as if they were suffering from horrible lesions, while the *Pietres* patronized street corners feigning disability. Similarly, in London men gathered on curbs to collect alms by perpetrating a more novel hoax: they pretended to have had their tongues torn out by an iron hook, displaying the appendage—which actually was a piece of tongue-shaped leather—to sympathetic passersby. "It was seldom difficult," McCall writes, "either for locals who turned to crime, or for fugitives from other areas, to become absorbed into the shifting underworld of thieves, beggars, fences, pickpockets and receivers of stolen goods which no medieval town of any size was without."

Prostitutes

The Church denounced prostitution as an invention of the Devil. However, St. Augustine inferred more than once that if prostitution were suppressed "erratic lusts would overthrow society." Consequently, the enterprise became an "admissible evil" in medieval society—a least-of-two-evils type accord.

As new towns were established, prostitution flourished and eventually took on a more organized demeanor. Official brothel zones proliferated just outside city walls, often contributing sizeable revenues to both church and state. Kings and town councils taxed the brothels, while Popes and bishops leased the "official" property. Indeed, in 1347, Queen Joamma of Naples built a splendid brothel quarter for the prostitutes of Avignon. Other luxurious establishments soon followed at Toulouse, Angers, Strasbourg and elsewhere. However, "prostitution in general remained, throughout the Middle Ages, closely linked with poverty, misery, crime and disease."

Homosexuals

It is difficult to determine how widespread homosexuality may have been in the Middle Ages because there were not many records of cases brought before the authorities. As Christianity took hold of medieval Europe, however, it is clear that the Old Testament story of Sodom became a parable against homosexuality, inasmuch as the crime of the Sodomites was widely presumed to have been such relations. Because St. Augustine had declared that "those sins which are against nature, like those of the men of Sodom, are in all times and places to be detested and punished," people in the Middle Ages viewed death by burning as an appropriate penalty for homosexuality. Interestingly, although female homosexuality was denounced, it was not criminalized as was male homosexuality.

Heretics

In 311, Emperor Constantine found that an alliance with the Church would boost his power. He realized that it was essential for the Church to command obedience and to retain Christian uniformity of belief by stamping out heresies. Therefore, in the year 1230 the Inquisition was enacted by Pope Gregory XI. Though it was intended to stop heresies from spreading, it eventually caused them to multiply. Consequently, in the 12th century many groups such as the *Arius* and the *Montanists* emerged to preach against the corruption of the Church.

In the eyes of the Church, some of the worst heretics belonged to the *Beguines*, a female cult who possessed vernacular translations of the scriptures. Because the Church strongly opposed public use of the texts, maintaining that proper training was required to make correct scriptural interpretation, the ability to read and write and understand Latin was usually confined to the clergy. Many Christians indeed suspected that there were things in the texts that the Church did not want them to learn. Actually, however, there were doctrines that the Church taught that did not appear in scripture. There was no mention of Purgatory, for instance, of indulgences, or of the Pope's all-encompassing influence in the Church. "It was chiefly as a result of the Catholic Church's inability to fulfill the role which the Bible-reading dissenters thought it should play," notes McCall, "rather than because of the spread of Eastern gnosticism or the agitation of fanatical revolutionaries, that medieval Papacy's battle to preserve uniformity of religious belief in a total Christian society was finally lost."

Sorcerers and Witches

As far as the medieval Church was concerned, anyone who practiced magic for any purpose was trying to control the universe, and thus was engaging the Devil. Inasmuch as subjects such as alchemy or astrology were considered evil, anyone who possessed such books was accused of sorcery. Furthermore, the accumulation of knowledge, especially in the natural sciences, was considered a dangerous practice.

Such ideas derived from the earlier Roman and barbarian cultures, which affirmed that certain people possessed the power to work magic. In the Middle Ages these people were labeled "witches." Most "true" witches were women, since females were thought to be more susceptible than males to the persuasions of demons. McCall writes: *Most accusations of sorcery and witchcraft seem to have been made as a result either of personal quarrels or actual attempts to work magic . . . like curing illness or turning metal into gold, which would not today be considered in any way reprehensible.*

Jews

Persecution of Jews inevitably resulted from their cultural practices or religious beliefs. Jews of the classical period became regarded as outcasts; their rights and property were seized. Later during the Middle Ages, anti-Semitism became more virulent, and the Jews had to take their place among those of the medieval underworld.

Inasmuch as medieval Jews had been sentenced by Christians as social subordinates, it was easy to connect any stroke of bad fortune to the "monstrous Jews." Whenever a disaster occurred, it was a Hebrew affliction. Jews were even accused of poisoning wells to spread the Black Death. Although Christians considered Jews to be sub-human, they believed that in the Last Days the Jews would be spared eternal punishment by their conversion to Christianity.

The Middle Ages, then, as McCall's *The Medieval Underworld* points out, was a time of great upheaval. As an amalgam of superstitious beliefs and dog-eat-dog cruelty, century after century of the world's inhabitants endured lives of horrible living conditions and unimaginable fear.

CANNON FODDER
by A. Stuart Dolden, Blandford Press, 1980

Few who fought in World War I are still alive. For most of us, the "war to end all wars" seems a rather quaint and pale precursor to both the high-tech threat and the savage chaos that distinguish our current conflicts around the globe.

But all wars create their own versions of hell. During the years of World War I, the 20th Century was still in its infancy, and aircraft were still daringly experimental. Thus, infantry foot soldiers advanced slowly across Europe, digging trenches every few feet while contending with massive artillery fire and poison gas. Generals used their young fighters to gain ground, apparently unmoved by the loss of life. Because the generals regularly "fed" their front-line soldiers to the enemy cannons, their infantrymen soon became known as "cannon fodder."

One of these young infantrymen, an English Private named A. Stuart Dolden, kept a journal to record his four years as a soldier. Dolden's journal—pages filled with the horror, the day-to-day misery, the occasional boredom, the inevitable bright and dark humor that colored life for him and his war-stressed comrades—was later published as a book, *Cannon Fodder*.

1914–15

In November, 1914, after completing his schooling as a solicitor (attorney), Dolden enlisted in the London Scottish infantry regiment. After several months' training, he was assigned to a battalion commissioned to dig trenches near the front lines. In July the battalion arrived in the small village of Varennes, France, where they set in with pick and shovel under the summer heat. Their first battles were not with the German enemy, but with the ravenous lice that sucked their blood. Then in August they headed out toward the front lines, first by train, then by foot.

Near Vermelles, Dolden and his Company-D colleagues moved into behind-the-lines trenches. Their new homes consisted of dugouts—four- or five-foot deep holes tunneled off to the side of the main trench. Some of the trenches, like "Park Lane," were named nostalgically; others took on more foreboding monikers such as "Rotten Row" and "Death Valley."

Dolden was assigned a box of "bombs" (grenades) which had to be kept at the ready, even as he slept. For four days straight, under nearly constant artillery fire, he dug trenches and dugouts and carried water up the communications trenches towards the front. Finally he was sent to the rear—and allowed to remove his boots. He also had his first hot bath in four months—a great luxury, even though the bathwater was only one inch deep.

One night while he was on guard duty in the rest area, Dolden heard the footfalls of a drunken non-commissioned officer coming up the path, followed by a sudden groan as the officer stumbled into the *midden*

where the farm manure was stacked. The officer emerged in an indescribably unsavory but intact condition—only to discover later that he'd lost his false teeth in the manure pile. Just as well he didn't find them, Dolden supposed.

Using a grenade of 1914 was an unpredictable adventure. Soldiers were instructed to light the detonator, hold the bomb for three or four seconds, then throw it as far as possible. It never worked right, especially when things got wet—as they usually did.

On one assignment to storm a German position, Dolden's company followed a shallow trench up toward the front lines, then, as ordered, they lit and tossed their grenades. As usual, however, it was raining and the devices didn't explode. All at once bullets began hailing down on them from all sides; they were caught in the crossfire between the Germans and their own troops. A bullet splattered through the head of their lead grenadier, and they were forced to crawl in file over his limp body in the struggle back to their regiment—picked off one at a time along the way. One of the soldiers who died that night was Dolden's best friend Johnny Walker. Now Dolden knew first hand—and bone deep—the meaning of the term "cannon fodder."

Soon the regiment was moved to a new area so close to the front that while they spaded the rocky earth they could hear their German counterparts at work just yards away. During the day Dolden's unit cowered in their trenches under continual artillery fire. *No matter which way we turned, we seemed to run into bursting shells. The only thing to do was to crouch down at the bottom of the trench and with palpitating hearts wait and hope for the best.*

One day, after digging a trench far in advance of their lines, the journalist's unit mounted a surprise attack on the enemy. As they rushed forward, German machine-gun fire cut into their ranks. Dolden felt a bullet strike his right thigh. Unable to move in either direction, he huddled in the open along with a few others as the shells rained down around them. The Sergeant-Major handed him a German trenching tool, and Dolden, lying flat, burrowed until he could cover his head and shoulders with earth. Then he turned to hand back the tool to its owner, but the Sergeant-Major did not respond: He had already taken a hit. *I was lying there with dead all round me.... Behind me I could hear the groans of the wounded. Every now and then one of them would call out, "Mother, Mother."*

Out of a brigade of 5,000 men, only 600 survived that day's combat. Of the 20 soldiers in Dolden's platoon, he was one of only three who returned alive to his unit.

1916

His thigh healed quickly, and Dolden soon found himself assigned to serve as cook for a new company. He "had not the faintest idea about cooking," he noted in his journal, and followed with the observation that "ignorance seemed to be the only qualification for a job in the army."

The camp came under bombardment almost every day as they prepared for the Battle of the Somme. Dolden's quartermaster often bragged that he brought his cooks closer to the action than any other company—and he wasn't lying. But after a few months, since two-thirds of the company had been killed and "we didn't need so many cooks" anymore, Dolden was reassigned to combat duty. For seven successive nights he and two other privates were ordered to crawl out in advance of the front lines and, whatever situation they encountered, to hold their position until dawn. After that week-long nightmare of blessed survival, Dolden was gratefully reinstated as a full-time cook.

Back in the world of gourmet cookery, the would-be chef began to wonder about all the engorged bluebottle flies that swarmed through the camp. Then, climbing a ridge one day, he almost stepped on a corpse. French and German bodies lay strewn everywhere, feeding the bloated flies.

In addition to the constant shelling, the flies, the rain and the corpses, Dolden's regiment had to contend with one other formidable challenge: mud. As he wrote: *We had already experienced … all the incidences of warfare on other sectors of the line … but after our trip to the Somme I realized what a truly demoralizing effect mere mud could have.*

In November, Dolden was finally granted leave to go home. After ten days of hot baths and meals with real silverware, however, he returned to the battle lines—to sleep at night on boards floating on the trench waters.

1917

The shelling persisted unabated through New Year's. By then the weather had grown absolutely frigid, and as natural food became scarce, rats became the soldiers' most prolific enemy. Dolden suspected that they were feeding on the dead. Once a rat fell on Dolden's face while he was sleeping, its filthy feet slipping into his mouth before he could reach up and kill it.

When the unit was transferred to Arras in the spring, conditions were no better: the soldiers had to battle the mud again, while their bodies were attacked by vermin of every sort. As they stumbled toward their destination, covered from head to foot in the muck, one horse harnessed to Dolden's cookstove wagon became so swamped in mud that they had to shoot the delirious animal and then drive over it to continue down the road.

But at last, by late June, Dolden could see that the Allies were making progress. Their unit took possession of more and more abandoned German trenches. Some of these huge excavations were 30 feet deep and capable of housing 50 men.

Summer passed and the weather again turned colder. The troops slipped on the icy floorboards of the trenches and battled the chill in their bunkers covered only by a ground cloth. Christmas Day brought only short rations and more cold. But a few days later Dolden and four companions were able to visit an old French lady in the countryside, who cooked ten-egg omelettes for each of them, served with potatoes, chicken, chocolate, cigars and champagne. At that moment, Dolden could believe that perhaps it wasn't such a bad war after all!

1918

Upon returning to France after taking another brief leave, Dolden's unit was sent to stay at a reserve area. One day a shaggy, smelly goat ambled by and started helping himself to their food. When the men tried to drive it away, the outraged goat launched a counterattack, sending them scurrying onto tables for refuge. *The animal stayed just as long as it wished, and then just before dark ambled gently out of the yard, and we were able to come down from our perches.*

Back at the front, the Germans dug in and launched a furious barrage of artillery and bombing. They shelled so far into the rear of the Scottish regiment that the front-line fighters were often safer than the men in the reserve areas.

This was also the point during which gas attacks became a real hazard. All Company A cooks had to visit the hospital for poisoning; one Company B cook was blinded by gas. Once, after a particularly explosive German shelling, Dolden and a companion named Robertson discovered a whitish substance covering the bottom of the trench. They argued a while about whether it could be gas—the enemy had never before been known to lace their shells with chemicals—and finally an expert was called in. He took one whiff and bolted, with Dolden and Robertson not far behind. The gas made them gravely ill. After a painful recuperation, he accompanied his regiment, cooking faithfully away, as they assumed various front-line positions.

Whenever the troops were about to march to the front, and whenever they came trudging back, Dolden boosted their British spirits with—what else?—hot, steaming tea. Ironically, in fact, after four years of fighting the Germans, it was tea that nearly took him permanently out of action. One day as he struggled to pry open a tea canister that had stood near the fire, he was scalded by a blast of steam that might have left his face scarred for life had it not been for the quick action of a comrade who rubbed the Company's entire one-day butter ration over his burns.

Dolden's regiment at length found themselves chasing the Germans back home through France and Belgium. During this "orderly retirement," as the Kaiser's army euphemistically called it, the retreating enemy routinely scorched the earth—burning field, killing farm animals, then poisoning the carcasses in order to deprive the advancing Allies of provisions.

Finally, on November 11, 1918, Dolden received word that a cease-fire was in effect. When the Armistice followed a month later, he went home. After four years of marching over half of Europe—and watching so many others march straight into needless death—he vowed never again to walk any further than he had to. It was a vow he kept religiously throughout the rest of his life.

In the West women experienced an autonomy never before dreamed of, and with this freedom came the necessity to solve their problems in any way they could. Making do became an art shared by both sexes, and "women's work" soon came to mean whatever had to be done...

Concerned that "history seldom tells the stories of the eight hundred thousand women who also came West," Cathy Luchetti offers "not an academic history" of those American women who ventured west between 1830 and 1910, but a "document of human experience." She makes use of letters, diaries, journals and photographs to reconstruct the life stories of eleven female pioneers of the western frontier.

Luchetti's informative introduction offers an overview of both the hardships and the opportunities that confronted the women of the West. Those who migrated on the wagon trains, for example, encountered not only "limited water supplies and scant privacy [but] unsanitary trail conditions [that] contributed to disease and death," and women died at a rate 22 percent higher than their male counterparts. Those who managed to maintain their health were expected to serve as nurses to the less fortunate. As a result, women cultivated a mastery of "herbs, bone-setting, and delivering children," which made their "value to the pioneer community inestimable."

In "Minority Women," the book's second section, Luchetti challenges the stereotype of the "slave-like" position of early Native American women. "While some tribes did hold women in very low esteem," she writes, "other tribes were matrilineal, tracing their ancestry through the mother and bestowing great importance upon women." In fact, while "white women were ... unable to vote, to own their own property or to sign a contract unassisted ... Indian women went into marriage fully endowed with their own property, which remained their own and could not be touched by male relatives."

In this section Luchetti also relates the moving stories of the thousands of Black and Chinese women and girls who occupied the West. Many were sold as slaves and then consigned to a life of prostitution on the West Coast.

The eleven personal histories that round out the remaining chapters of *Women of the West* reflect the author's concern with diversity; the women profiled emerge from varying religious, racial and economic backgrounds. Three of the most illuminating are featured here.

Miriam Davis Colt (1817–)

The twelfth child of 17 coming into the home of a poor New York City tanner, Miriam Davis began working as a housekeeper at the age of 15, using her modest earnings to supplement the family's income and to pay for her own education. After eight years of work and study, Miriam earned her teaching certificate and took a position in Parishville, New York, where she met and married fellow teacher William H. Colt. The two were working and living in Montreal when Colt and his affluent parents decided to join an experimental vegetarian settlement in Kansas. The family immediately purchased 720 acres of land—sight unseen—from the U.S. Government and set out for the rugged frontier.

Despite the privations and perils of the journey west, Miriam faithfully recorded in her personal journal the family's itinerary and the way the West of 1856 appeared through her urban eyes: *May 1st— Take a walk out to the levee—view the city, and see that it takes but a few buildings in this western world to make a city.*

But as the Colts drew near to their new home, Miriam's sense of wonder gave way to uneasiness. On May 12 she mused: *The ladies tell us they are sorry to see us come to this place; which shows us that all is not right. [We] are too weary to question ...* But the very next day, she asks her journal: *Can any one imagine our disappointment this morning, on learning ... that no mills have been built; that the directors, after receiving our money to build mills, have not...* She found herself even more devastated to learn that many families, feeling duped by the directors, had accepted their financial losses and abandoned the project long before the Colts' arrival.

Living in cloth tents, surviving on milk and corn-bread, and occasionally waking to find rattlesnakes in their beds, the Colts and other remaining members of the colony began to see some yield from their labors, when, in mid-June, Miriam's journal reports: *... Pumpkins, squashes, melons, cucumbers, beans, peas, potatoes, and tomatoes are thriving finely.* Miriam, tired of burning the hems of her dresses while cooking over open fires, soon dismissed her Victorian mores and adopted a new mode of dress—shorter "Bloomer dresses," in which she "can bound over the prairie like an antelope."

But the colony's revival was short-lived: malaria struck several members and the water supply was nearly dried up by the first of July. The sickness, threats from local Indians, and the loss of the family oxen convinced Miriam and William to leave Kansas. And when the couple and their two children departed on September 2 after only four short months on the prairie, they were nearly penniless. William's parents and sister—all of whom chose to stay behind with the colony—died shortly thereafter.

Miriam and William's infant son died a few weeks into their journey, and William himself perished in the ensuing weeks, leaving Miriam and her daughter, Mema, stranded in Missouri until local citizens came to the rescue and arranged for their return to New York. In an effort to earn money to support herself and her daughter, Miriam Davis Colt again picked up her pen and wrote about her year on the prairie. The memoir, *Went to Kansas*, was published in 1862.

Sarah Winnemucca (c. 1844–1891)

The granddaughter of a Piute chief, Sarah Winnemucca roamed the northern Nevada deserts. Having spent part of her youth with a trader's family, she became fluent in English and served as a translator between her tribe and the U.S. Army. During her life Sarah traveled and lectured on behalf of her people; one result of this dedication is her book *Life Among the Piutes* (Luchetti's source for Winnemucca's biographical profile).

Sarah Winnemucca writes of her own beginnings: *I was born somewhere near 1844, but am not sure of the precise time. I was a very small child when the first white people came into our country. They came like a lion, yes, like a roaring lion, and have continued so ever since.* Before long rumors began to spread through the Nevada territories that white men were killing and eating Indians. Then came that memorable morning: sensing that whites were approaching Sarah's tribal village, the alarmed Piute women buried Sarah and the other young girls in order to protect them from the fearsome Caucasians: ... *Our mothers buried me and my cousin, planted sage brush over our faces to keep the sun from burning them, and there we were left all day.... Can any one imagine my feelings buried alive, thinking every minute that I was to be unburied and eaten up?...*

The following spring Sarah suffered more heartache when whites fired on her father, grandfather and uncles as they fished in the Humboldt River: *The widow of my uncle who was killed, and my mother and father all had long hair. [After the massacre we] cut off their hair, and also cut long gashes in their arms and legs ... for this is the way we mourn our dead.*

Increasingly aware that her people were called "savages" by the whites, Sarah interpreted the difference between whites and Indians. Piute children are "taught to love everybody," she explained, and "don't need to be taught to love [their] fathers and mothers. Among her people, all were equal: "a tenth cousin is as near ... as [a] ... first cousin." Moreover, Sarah continued, Piute women were honored and respected by their husbands, who, following the birth of a baby, assume all of the wife's household work for the 25 days afterward. And "if [the father] does not do his part in the care of the child, he is considered an outcast."

Throughout her life Sarah attempted to bridge the gap between her people and the white settlers, most notably when she worked for the U.S. Army as an interpreter during the Bannock war. Though she helped save many lives on both sides, the outcome of the war was not favorable to her tribe, whose members, half-starved, were forced to walk in the dead of winter to a prison camp in the Washington Territory. Though half her family perished during the trek, Sarah continued to work for some time as an interpreter. Finally disgusted with the white government's broken promises, she retired from public life around 1884 and founded an Indian school near Lovelock, Nevada, which closed shortly before her death in 1891.

Elinore Pruitt Stewart (1876–1933)

Born in Fort Smith, Arkansas, Elinore Pruitt was one of nine children in a family so poor that she did not own a pair of shoes until she was six years old. When her parents died of a fever, Elinore, just 14, took a job with the railroad and assumed responsibility for her brothers and sisters. She compensated for her lack of a formal education by reading newspapers and asking questions. At the age of 22 she married and began writing articles for the Kansas City Star, but her career as a journalist was cut short by the death of her husband just four years into their marriage. With a young daughter to support, Elinore moved to Denver to work in the home of the genteel Mrs. Coney (to whom all of Elinore's published letters are addressed).

Finally, at age 33, the young mother answered an advertisement for a housekeeper that had been placed by a Wyoming sheep rancher, Clyde Stewart. And, as fate would have it, they married after Elinore had spent only six weeks in his employ. Still, she never allowed the union to interfere with her desire to homestead her own parcel of land.

Shortly after her arrival in Wyoming, Elinore proudly wrote to Mrs. Coney: *Well, I filed on my land and am now a bloated landowner. I waited a long time to even see land in the reserve ...* But not content with merely owning a plot of ground—which was, in itself, quite an accomplishment for a woman in her time— Elinore learned how to work it, and to "do many things which girls more fortunately situated don't even know have to be done." *Among the things I learned to do was ... run a mowing machine.... I got sunburned, and my hands were hard, rough, and stained with machine oil, and I used to wonder how any Prince Charming could overlook all that in any girl he came to. For all I had ever read of Prince Charming had to do with his "reverently kissing her lily-white hand," or doing some other fool thing with a hand as white as a snowflake.... Well, when my Prince showed up ... he was delighted as well as surprised. I was glad because I really like to mow.*

Indeed, Elinore came to believe that involvement in homesteading could raise women from subjugation and lift the poor out of poverty. In one of her later letters she urged women to "get out and file for land." ... *Any woman who can stand her own company ... and is willing to put in as much time at careful labor as she does at the washtub, will certainly succeed; will have independence, plenty to eat all the time, and a home of her own in the end.*

Elinore Pruitt eventually lost her life as a result of her labor of love: in 1926 she was seriously injured when a covey of quail scattered in front of her horses, causing her to fall beneath the hay mower she was driving. Having never fully recovered from those injuries, she died in 1933.

BLACK COWBOYS
by Paul W. Stewart with Wallace Yvonne Ponce, Philips Publishing, Inc, 1986

"Look at that drugstore cowboy," Paul Stewart said to his cousin, pointing to a black man in a cowboy hat. "Who's he trying to fool? Everybody knows there are no Black cowboys." Stewart's cousin assured him, however, that the man was in fact a real cowboy, and since that day in Denver in 1960, Stewart has been on a quest.

What he learned in the intervening years is that after the Civil War more than 8,000 black cowboys—and girls—lived in the Old West. Many worked as cattle ranchers, rodeo stars, farmers and sheriffs. The result of Stewart's long quest is *Black Cowboys*, a history he compiled from taped interviews with these pioneering men and women and their descendants. A blend of true-life stories and photographs, the book makes for fascinating reading.

When the Civil War ended in 1865, Americans resumed their westward expansion. Not surprisingly, the Indian tribes resisted this encroachment on their lands, and to combat this "threat" Congress organized four black regiments—the 9th and 10th Cavalries and the 24th and 25th Infantries. Given a monthly salary of 13 dollars as well as food, clothing and shelter, young blacks eagerly signed up for five-year tours of duty. The Indians called the black troops "Buffalo Soldiers," and held in great esteem their fighting ability, valor, discipline, and loyalty to their superior officers.

For the most part, the contributions of these units have gone unrecognized. For example, the black 10th Cavalry in Cuba rescued Theodore Roosevelt and his "Rough Riders" at the battle of San Juan Hill, but only Roosevelt and the Rough Riders are acknowledged in the history books. "Though their contributions have been downplayed," writes Stewart, "the Buffalo Soldiers truly were the super heroes of the often violent, savage and barbarous West."

Many of these Buffalo Soldiers went on to distinguished careers after their military service. Willie Kennard, for one, applied for the job of marshal in the wild mining town of Yankee Hill, Colorado, in 1874. The mayor promptly sent Kennard to arrest a man, holed up in the saloon, who had just killed the father of a girl he'd raped. Kennard shot the man's guns off his belt before he could grab them, and brought him in for trial. Kennard later served as town sheriff.

Stewart points out that not all the blacks in the Old West were men. Mary Fields, who stood six feet tall and weighed upwards of 200 pounds, was born a slave in 1832. After her escape from slavery, she held a number of jobs in Montana. When her restaurant business folded, Fields got a job as a mail coach driver, regularly "combatting extremely inclement weather, fending off wild wolves, and earning a reputation for delivering the mail."

In her later years Fields managed a laundry. Once, spotting a man who owed her money, she seize him by the coat, threw him to the ground, and put her foot on his chest. "If you don't pay me the $2.00 you owe me for that laundry," she growled, "you won't get up." The man paid up his debt.

The unsavory Ned Huddleston (alias "Isom Dart") and Benjamin J. Hodges were the black versions of Butch Cassidy and the Sundance Kid. Huddleston, also known as "The Black Fox," was an outlaw with a compassionate streak but a lot of bad luck. Born a slave in 1849, he moved down near the Mexican border after emancipation and made a living stealing horses. Later he gave up outlawing for mining, but an unscrupulous partner spent all his money and drove him off the claim.

Huddleston was later jailed when a cook for whom he worked mysteriously disappeared. When the cook returned and the hapless cowboy was released, he turned to breaking wild horses for a living and took an Indian wife named Tickup. Later, he joined a group of horse thieves, moved to Oklahoma, and spent his remaining days ranching—though many alleged he supplemented his own stock with that of his neighbors. In 1900, as Huddleston sat in front of his cabin, a hired killer gunned him down.

Benjamin Hodges—a forger, cattle thief, trail driver and confidence man—lived in Dodge City, Kansas. A rancher once dickered over the price of some cattle Hodges was selling. After the rancher struck what he thought was a good bargain and swaggered into the saloon to boast of it, someone suggested that he check the brands on the cattle: Sure enough, many of the steers he had bought were his own! The embarrassed rancher refused to pressed charges. Although Hodges did go to trial many times, he was never convicted, and lived to a ripe old age, regaling children with his tales of the old West.

A more respectable, law-abiding cowboy was John Ware, who referred to himself as "the first 'Smoked Irishman' to raise cattle in the Southwest." The six-foot-three, 200-pound Ware became known for his great strength while working on the Quorn ranch in 1888. *The Quorn boys were proud of their top rider's strength so they arranged a lifting contest between John and a hefty newcomer.... The first lift with hay hooks on a weigh scale was a draw, so the beam was set up a couple of hundred pounds. John lifted mightily and the hay hooks straightened out in his hands. The contest was over.*

On another occasion a couple of strangers came to the Quorn ranch to dispute the ownership of a horse. Ware convinced them to leave by taking out his .45-caliber Colt revolver and asking, "Shall I kill 'em now, boss, or will I wait 'til they take the horse?"

Some black cowboys distinguished themselves by their innovative horsemanship and rodeo riding. Around 1900, rodeo rider Bill Pickett originated an event called *bull-dogging* (steer-wrestling). Using no hands, Pickett would bite into the animal's tender nose and thus bring it to the ground. Eventually Pickett earned a fortune performing in Wild West Shows. He was later enshrined in the National Rodeo Hall of Fame.

Jessie Stahl, another remarkable entertainer, sometimes rode his broncs backwards. He was also famous for a practice called "Hoolihanding," in which he chased a steer on horseback, leaped onto its neck, grabbed its horns, and drove them into the ground with such force that the steer couldn't pull them out. (The stunt was later outlawed by the Humane Society.)

James Arthur Walker, an all-around cowboy of considerable talents, was born in Texas in 1868. His sister remembered that as a young man he would often perform the trick of spurring his horse to a gallop, jumping off, hitting the ground, and jumping back on—a feat perfected by Walker years before this "Hollywood Hop" was made famous by the cowboy stars of the silver screen.

Some black cowboys achieved great financial success as ranchers and businessmen. Two prominent examples from Colorado were Andrew Jackson Steele and Harvey Groves. Steele, who owned three farms, several rental houses and a number of coal mines, began with only a livery stable and a saloon. He fathered four sons, all of whom went on to attend universities and to hold jobs of considerable responsibility.

In 1890 rodeo cowboy Harvey Groves achieved a measure of fame denied most black cowboys in the West. President Theodore Roosevelt presented Harvey with angora chaps and gold spurs for taking first prize in a bronco-riding contest in Colorado Springs. Groves later became a successful businessman and was often mentioned in the *Colorado Statesman*, one of the first black newspapers.

The Groves family lived in Manitou, Colorado, at a time when the Ku Klux Klan had a strong following. In 1916, when drinking fountains in Manitou began displaying "For Whites Only" signs, one of the Groves brothers took a shotgun and an ax and destroyed all the drinking fountains in town—while the town sheriff looked on. *He told the sheriff, "Don't bother me and I won't bother you." He was later fined $40 for ... destroying public property, but that ended the segregated drinking fountains.*

During his life of 83 years, Matthew "Bones" Hooks engaged in three fruitful careers and made the transition between the era of the Old West and that of modern-day America. He also carried a reputation of returning good for evil.

Born in 1868, young Hooks worked at several different ranches. In Texas, one owner had "Bones" castrated to prevent him from impregnating any of his seven daughters. After working on the range for almost 30 years, in 1909 Hooks became a porter for the Santa Fe railroad. *His love of horses and talent for riding never left him.... While he was on duty as a porter, he overheard a conversation about a horse that*

had a reputation of being impossible to ride.... "Bones" ... rode the horse to a standstill...

In 1930 Hooks left the railroad and became a social and equal rights activist. He started the "Dogie Club," an orphanage for boys, as well as the first Boy Scout troop in Amarillo, Texas. Hooks died in 1951, deeply mourned by the community he'd serve so well.

Other blacks in the West found success as blacksmiths. Dennis Brown, born in 1878, was a blacksmith apprenticed at the age of 12. Those who knew him said "he had the uncanny ability to just look at something and tell its measurements." By the time he mastered his craft, he "could fashion most anything out of iron." People from hundreds of miles away would take their horses to him to shoe.

Racism prevented many great black rodeo cowboys from achieving the fame and fortune they deserved. Marvel Rogers, one of the finest riders of all time, was banned from competing in white rodeos and had to make "hat rides"—passing a hat around to the spectators. He wowed onlookers by riding with a lit cigar in his mouth and emitting puffs of smoke at every leap of the horse or bull. Sadly, this legendary rider suffered much abuse from white riders. "Frequently his boots were used as comfort stations," Stewart notes, "and they'd set fire to the bales of straw where he slept."

Mose Reeder, a rodeo cowboy born in 1885, often rode under the name "Gaucho the Corral Dog." Reeder, says Stewart, best summed up the hardships of the black cowboy on the rodeo circuit: *Your lot as a Black cowboy meant that you drew the roughest horse. If that didn't eliminate you, the next horse you got would be one that wouldn't buck. A non-bucking horse meant no points and that would definitely rule out any hopes of winning. Or, they'd classify you as a professional which would automatically eliminate you or they'd tell you that all the applications for an event were already filled.*

Despite persecution, black cowboys continued to make inroads. Willie (Smokey) Lornes staged the first Black rodeo in Denver in 1947 to give African-Americans the opportunity to compete for prize money. Marvel Rogers later founded the American Black Cowboy Association and worked as the arena manager for the first Black rodeo in New York City. In 1982, three years after Marvel's death, Charles Sampson became the first Black World Champion bullrider.

After having long neglected the history of black cowboys, writers and historians have finally begun to acknowledge their substantial contributions to the development of the Old West. Stewart writes: *Some were hardworking, law-abiding citizens, others were noted because of their lawlessness.... The dangers of the trail were not the only worries of the Black cowboy. Racial prejudice was practiced openly, sometimes at the hands of a trail boss who could inflict indignities of the worst kind.... It is important that these men ... not be forgotten—for they too played a prominent role during that significant period of American history.*

A preeminent chronicler of Native American history and culture, Frank Waters has been nominated for the Nobel Prize in Literature five times. His book *Brave Are My People* gives an account of the tragic lives of 15 noted Native American heroes who lived on the North American continent between 1600 and 1900.

According to Waters, when Columbus arrived the Indian population of North America was about five million. By 1910, the population had been reduced to fewer than 200,000.

Although the Native American population has subsequently increased to nearly two million, indigenous Americans still contend with "prejudice, injustice, [and] the lowest poverty level in the country." But Native Americans, Waters points out, are an extraordinarily resilient people: *They have endured through the centuries because of their loving respect for the earth and their sense of unity with all that exists . . .*

Powhatan

In the late 1500s, the Algonquians—led by Wahunsonacock, who was later named *Powhatan* by his tribe, after the name of his village—were united in a 200-village confederacy that stretched across the whole Eastern seaboard. Not long after the English settled Jamestown in 1608, Captain John Smith led a group of colonists upriver to meet with Powhatan. The chief offered to trade corn for weapons, but Smith refused. Eventually Powhatan did provide the starving colonists with corn, but he expressed his concerns to Smith: "Captain Smith, I know the difference between peace and war better than anyone else in my country. . . . But that you are said to come to destroy my country so much affrights all my people as they dare not visit you. . . . What will it avail you to take that by force which you may quietly obtain with love, or to destroy them that provide you with food?"

Nearly half of the 900 Jamestown colonists died that winter, and more would have perished had the Powhatans not taught them to make wigwams and to plant indigenous crops. In spite of the many deaths, however, new bands of colonists were sent to America with strict orders to "make a profit for the [British] stockholders by any means." *Instead of clearing new forest land [the colonists] drove the Powhatans off t heir own fields, burned their villages, and worked those captured as slaves.* In retaliation, the natives killed a number of colonists and captured John Smith, whose life was spared by Chief Powhatan's daughter, Pocahontas.

When the British settlers decided to grow tobacco, they took possession of additional lands, which the Powhatans defended. In retribution, the colonists took Pocahontas as a hostage.

For months Powhatan received no word of his beloved daughter. Eventually he learned that she had converted to Christianity and had married a planter named John Rolfe. Soon after her marriage, Pocahontas sailed to England, where she was received at court. Three years later she died of smallpox, and within a year of her death, her aged father Powhatan, a disillusioned old peacemaker, also died.

Thayendanegea (Joseph Brant)

Because of his prodigious abilities, the trustworthy young Mohawk Thayendanegea was chosen as a Pine Tree Leader. Clearly, like the stalwart and upright pine tree, Thayendanegea was destined to not only assist the hereditary chieftains in carrying out their decrees, but, in his own right, he would become a leader of his people. Since the whites called his Mohawk father "Brant," he became known as Joseph Brant.

In the early 1760s Brant's sister married the Englishman William Johnson, who encouraged the Indians to join the British in fighting the French. Thirteen-year-old Joseph was among those who eagerly joined the conflict, and in return for his services Johnson helped to educate him.

In due course Brant sailed to England and served as secretary to Colonel Guy Johnson, a post which allowed him to address some of England's most influential government ministers. In one speech before Parliament in 1775, Brant proclaimed: "Indeed, it is very hard, when we have let the king's subjects have so much land for so little, they should want to cheat us in this manner of the small spots we have left for our women and children to live on. We are tired out in making complaints and getting no redress." Bolstered by these words, the British government promised to restore Mohawk lands if the tribe would support the crown against the American revolutionaries.

Brant returned to America, but his alliance with the British divided the Iroquois League, as some tribes chose to ally themselves with the colonists. The Mohawks and British lost the war, of course, but Brant was never captured to stand trial. Still loyal to the British, he escaped to Canada, where he spent the rest of his life translating the Bible into Mohawk.

Interestingly enough, when the Iroquois Confederation of Five Nations was replaced by a new confederation—a realm comprised of 13 colonies—the new American nation followed Mohawk tradition by adopting the eagle and the pine tree as prominent national symbols.

Red Jacket

The Seneca Sagoyewatha became known as *Red Jacket* because of his distinguished service to the British during the Revolutionary War. Later, however, he allied himself with the Americans in the War of 1812. But throughout all of these conflicts he always remained a strong opponent of Anglo encroachment. In a speech to the British Parliament, Red Jacket, a renowned orator, said the following: " . . . Your forefathers crossed the great water and landed on this island.... They found friends and not enemies. They told us they had fled from their own country for fear of wicked men and had come here to enjoy their religion.... We took pity on them.... We gave them corn and meat; they gave us poison in return..."

After growing increasingly dependent on alcohol, Red Jacket was deposed as chief in 1827 and died three years later.

Mangus Coloradas

As a boy Mangus Coloradas was called *Don-ha*, "He-Who-Just-Sits-There," because he always sat up late listening to the discussions of his Apache elders. This habit continued into adulthood, when he is said to have remarked, "Action is useless unless it is the fruit of thought. The heart, the mind, the time must work together."

Toughened by their environment, the Apaches (originally a Canadian people who had migrated southward into Southwestern regions of the United States) disdained farming and herding. Rather, they supported themselves by raiding Mexican settlements across the border—raids often led by the towering Don-ha. It was during one of these raids that Don-ha chose a Mexican girl to be his third wife. The story goes that the brothers of his first two wives became enraged at this, and he was obliged to kill them. When he appeared before his new wife with his arms covered in blood, Don-ha received his adult name: *Mangus Coloradas*, or the quasi-Spanish version of "Red Sleeves."

When the Mexicans put a bounty on Apache scalps, American trappers set an ambush as a means of collecting as many as they could. Their plan was to invite Chief Juan Jose and a large band of Indians to a feast. Then as the women and children came forward to accept a gift of free corn, the Americans fired a cannon upon them, killing many Apaches. The suspicious Mangus Coloradas, who had kept himself apart from the crowd, escaped and returned to his people with news of the massacre.

After suffering other similar atrocities, the Apaches finally turned the full brunt of their rage against the Americans. In 1861 the Arizonian newspaper reported: *We are hemmed in on all sides by unrelenting Apache. Within six months, nine-tenths of the whole male population have been killed off, and every ranch, farm and mine in the country has been abandoned in consequence.*

By the time the territory of Arizona was created in 1863, Mangus was 70 years old and knew he had little time left. He agonized over which of his sub-chiefs [Victorio, Cochise, Cadette or the young renegade Geronimo] to appoint to take his place.

As his final act of bravery, Mangus Coloradas marched into a U.S. Army camp carrying a flag of truce. Wishing to discuss the problems of his people with the commanding officers, they refused to listen. Instead, they tried to provoke him to violence so that they would have an excuse to kill him. At first Mangus, standing erect, ignored their provocations. But when the soldiers began prodding his flesh with red-hot bayonets, he flinched, whereupon the soldiers shot him for "attempting escape."

Sequoyah

The half-breed Sequoyah had obtained some schooling. Therefore he became fascinated by the "talking leaves" that the white men used to communicate with others far away; that black marks on paper could convey meaning seemed to him almost magical.

After joining other Cherokee to help Andrew Jackson fight the Creek Indians, Sequoyah, crippled in the fighting, returned home frustrated by the American government's insatiable hunger for Indian land. He reasoned that if the Cherokee had a written language of their own, they would be better equipped to defend themselves. For four years he labored to develop a Cherokee script, attempting to model it after the ancient Chinese system which used a different character for each word—an overwhelmingly enormous task. Unfortunately, the tribe became impatient with Sequoyah's delay and burned down his cabin—and with it his painstaking work.

Meanwhile, the American government had forced the Cherokee to accept territory in Arkansas in exchange for their land in their Tennessee and the Carolinas. So it was in Arkansas that Sequoyah resumed his work. In three years he devised a new, more efficient written language that employed 86 phonetic characters, one for each sound in the Cherokee tongue. Although he repeatedly demonstrated it to the chiefs, they remained unimpressed.

Sequoyah's fellow Cherokees, however, avidly adopted the script after discovering that it took a Cherokee child only about a month to become proficient in the new writing, whereas mastering the English script took all of four years. As the popularity of the written language spread, Sequoyah purchased a printing press and began publishing a newspaper in Cherokee. Sequoyah became famous and, for a time, his people prospered.

In the meantime, the U.S. Government continued to coerce the Cherokee into accepting more bad land trades. Then, when gold was discovered in Cherokee territory and white settlers tried to uproot them again, the Cherokee fought back in the American courts. Despite having won a Supreme Court decision protecting their property, 13,000 Cherokees were forcibly removed to Indian Territory in an exodus that became known as the "Trail of Tears." During the trek 4,600 Cherokee died.

Sequoyah subsequently disappeared into the Southwestern regions of the U.S. and began a search for the remains of the Cherokee language in the languages of other tribes. Later, when the Indian Territory applied to become a state, Indians voted almost unanimously to name the state "Sequoyah." The U.S. Government, however, insisted that it be called "Oklahoma."

El Inca Garcilaso de la Vega was born seven years after the Spanish conquest. As the son of a Spanish conquistador and his native concubine, a Peruvian princess directly descended from the twelfth Inca, de la Vega grew up hearing the oral histories of the Incas that later provided the foundations for his *Royal Commentaries.*

De la Vega's European heritage, of course, also shaped his points of view. The teachings of the Catholic Church, for example, formed his distaste for Incan gods and icons, which he referred to as "demons." But despite his orthodox religious convictions, his history of the Incas and their subsequent defeat by the Spanish is generally free of the cultural biases so common among the early European chronicles. Indeed, Garcilaso's privileged understanding of both the Spaniards and the pre-Columbian Peruvians makes his *Commentaries* arguably the most illuminating of all the early histories that delineate the New-World conquest.

Written in 1604, the first of the *Commentaries'* two volumes depicts some four-and-a-half centuries of life under the Incas before the Spaniards' arrival; the second, written in 1616, details events of the Conquest and its aftermath.

"Once we were kings, now we are vassals!" the young future historian often heard his grown-up Peruvian relatives exclaim. In response, the curious young lad finally asked his uncle to tell him the history of their ancestors, the Quechua peoples of the Andes who were led by the Great Incas.

" ... At one time, all the land ... was nothing but mountains and desolate cliffs," began the storyteller. "The people lived like wild beasts, with neither order nor religion.... Seeing the condition they were in, our father, Inti, the Sun was ashamed for them, and he decided to send one of his sons and one of his daughters from heaven to earth, in order that they might teach men to adore him and acknowledge him as their god ... "

Thus, to his son Manco Capac and his daughter Coya Mama, the Sun gave a rod made of gold. "At the spot where, with one single thrust, it disappears entirely," the father advised them, "there you must establish your court." Then the Sun-father set his children down on the shores of Lake Titicaca and pointed them north. They began their journey along the Andean plateau-lands, trying the rod as they went; but not until they reached the Cuzco Valley did the rod disappear into the ground when they pushed it.

Finding the radiant Lord "and his sister-bride" in their valley, the Quechua inhabitants joyfully "assembled around the two *Incas* [their word for 'divine leaders'], ready to follow them wherever they might lead."

Manco Capac and Coya Mama spent the rest of their lives establishing "natural and reasonable laws" in their mountain kingdom. Among the most important

rules were those governing royal succession: so that the Sun's blood would "not be mixed with human blood," the great Incas would emulate Manco Capac, marrying only their own sisters, passing their thrones in turn to their eldest sons. The ten legitimate Incas who followed Manco Capac obeyed these royal laws of succession, and, in accordance with the Sun's wishes, continued to expand their territories and to build magnificent temples in honor of their gods.

Then, sometime near the beginning of the European 15th century the eleventh Inca, Huaina Capac, modified the divine rule of succession. Abrogating his throne required him to install his legitimate son, Huascar, as sovereign over all the Inca dominions. Instead, however, he proposed to install his illegitimate son, Huascar's half-brother Atahualpa, as ruler over the Andean kingdom of Quito, while leaving coastal Peru and other conquests to Huascar.

Huascar agreed peaceably to this division; but shortly thereafter, the Inca received unsettling news: "strange people, of a type that was quite unknown" had been spotted sailing along the coast. Unaware, of course, that the ship belonged to the great Spanish explorer Balboa, who "had just discovered the Southern Sea," the Inca regarded the sighting as an omen—the first of many "bad omens," including floods, earthquakes, and comets, that began to appear in his kingdom. Subsequently, he predicted that the "strange people" would eventually conquer his dominions. "I order you to obey and serve them," the Inca said before he died.

A few years after the death of Huaina Capac, the new Peruvian Inca, Huascar, began to worry about his half-brother's growing power. He sent a message to Atahualpa, demanding that he refrain from further territorial expansion and that he acknowledge Quito as a "vassal state" of Peru. Enraged, Atahualpa sent "more than thirty thousand warriors" to capture Huascar in his capital of Cuzco. Then, after imprisoning Huascar and torturing and slaughtering thousands of his friends, relatives and loyal subjects, Atahualpa boldly proclaimed himself sole Inca.

Encamped on the isthmus of modern-day Panama, meanwhile, two Spaniards "of very noble lineage," Diego de Almagro and Francisco Pizarro, had formed an alliance with the purpose of conquering Peru. Pizarro, who had first laid eyes on the Inca kingdom from Balboa's ship, now immediately commandeered another ship and left for the southern coast. He was soon followed by Almagro.

The expedition was plagued by hardships. Whenever the Spaniards attempted to go ashore, they encountered hostile Indians. Almagro was blinded in one eye by Quechua arrows, and many of his crew members were killed. And although they were elated to see natives "decorated with emeralds and turquoises, [and] gold nails driven into their faces," once again they were driven away by arrows. Utterly exhausted,

Almagro and Pizarro finally sighted the beautiful city of Tumbez, "with its fortress, its temples, palaces, and countless houses." Still, only one brave man, Pedro de Candia, dared go ashore. Convinced that the bearded Candia "was the son of the Sun and that he had come from heaven, [the Quechuas] brought him to the temple, which was entirely paneled with gold, in order that he might see how deeply they revered their god, who was also his father."

When Candia returned to the ship and told his story, the Spaniards, fortified by the realization that Peru "promised to be richer than anything ... encountered thus far in the Indies," promptly disembarked for the march inland.

As the conquistadors, led by Pizarro and the noble Hernando de Soto astride their magnificent steeds, approached the capital city of Cajamarca, they were greeted by Atahualpa's soldiers. Bowing down at the feet of their awe-inspiring visitors, the Indians led them to the Inca's sumptuous palace, and Pizarro and de Soto bowed themselves down in turn before the ruler's "solid gold throne." Then, as a sign of love and peace, Atahualpa rose to embrace the Spanish commanders and to offer them food and drink—including "all sorts of fresh and dried fruits, various breads, [and] resin wine." The Spaniards were "dumfounded to see such ... courtesy among people who, until then, they had imagined to be rustics and barbarians." They retained enough presence of mind, however, to advise Atahualpa that "of all the princes in this world," the Pope and King Carlos V of Spain were the most powerful, and that it was their will that the Peruvians give up their idols and worship "the only real God."

Unable fully to comprehend the miserable translation of the Spaniards' inept native interpreter Felipe, Atahualpa nonetheless answered: "I am delighted, divine lords, that you and your companions should have succeeded in reaching such remote regions as these, and that, thus, you should have confirmed the exactness of the events forecast by our ancestors.... I should like to consider this moment as the happiest we have ever experienced ... "

The following morning the Spanish visitors "divided their cavalry ... into three groups of twenty men, [who] went and hid behind a wall," while Pizarro "went to await King Atahualpa at one end of the main square." As soon as the king arrived—on a litter surrounded by thousands of his subjects—Pizarro sent a Dominican priest, Vincente de Valverde, to speak to him.

With "cross in hand," Friar Vincente told the great ruler that if he wished to avoid war, he would have to convert to Christianity and yield up his kingdom to Spain. Atahualpa replied eloquently: "My vassals and I accept death and whatever else you may choose to do with us ... in order that the last wishes of my father, Huaina Capac, may be fulfilled"; Atahualpa added, however, that he was surprised to be asked to pay tribute to King Carlos, rather than to God.... But if you say that I owe nothing to any one of these ... it seems to me that I owe even less to Carlos, who was

never lord of this land, and has never even seen it."

At this point, impatient with the long exchange, the Spaniards suddenly "sprang from their hiding places and attacked the Indians," seizing their jewelry and defacing a gem-encrusted gold icon. Since Atahualpa had forbidden the Peruvians to wound the Spaniards—even if his own person came under attack—the ambush ended in a massacre. "More than five thousand Indians were killed, [even though] there were on hand more than thirty thousand armed Indian fighters, and the Spaniards numbered one hundred and sixty!" Then they seized and shackled Atahualpa, and jailed him within his own temple.

Atahualpa assured his captors that his envoys would ransom him with gifts of unprecedented wealth. And indeed, soon after his imprisonment, immense quantities of "gold and silver began to flow into Cajamarca." But even with this, the Spaniards soon started "to grumble, saying that the Inca was poking fun at them, and that his envoys, instead of collecting gold and silver, were simply levying troops to come and free him."

Two Spanish parties, meanwhile, had left Cajamarca to explore other regions of Peru. While Pizarro traveled to the fabled temple of Pachacamc and marveled at its "unbelievable riches," de Soto and his men visited Sausa, where they met with the imprisoned Inca Huascar. "When your commander-general hears what injustice has been done to me," Huascar told de Soto, "he will surely return my kingdoms to me, and I shall give him much more gold than my brother could ever have promised him." Impressed, de Soto's Spaniards left with Huascar's promise for Cuzco.

Meanwhile, Atahualpa had concluded "that poor Huascar's death would assure him life and liberty"—since the conquistadors would then have all the riches they could possibly desire—and thus had surreptitiously sent orders to guards in Sausa to execute the deposed Inca. But after his half-brother's death, Atahualpa was not set free; instead, he was "tried for the death of Huascar" and for conspiring "to massacre the Spaniards"—a false charge leveled by the unscrupulous interpreter Felipe. Despite the objections of many Spaniards, Atahualpa was sentenced to be burned alive—a common fate for "pagans" of that era. In order to avoid this grisly prospect, Atahualpa agreed to be baptized—after which he was "garroted [fastened, then strangled] on a stake driven into the ground." Although Pizarro had agreed "to have him put to death in order to be freed of the responsibilities that Atahualpa's captivity entailed," the Spaniard "went into mourning for him, and ordered solemn funeral rites in his honor."

Thereafter, "even until this very day," as de la Vega concludes the sweeping narrative that his Quechua uncle began for him when he was a child, "the Spaniards [have] remained supreme masters of [the] Peruvian kingdoms, there being no one left to oppose them or even contradict them, because all the Indians, whether they belonged to Quito or to Cuzco, had remained, after their kings were gone, like sheep without a shepherd."

THE FATAL SHORE – THE EPIC OF AUSTRALIA'S FOUNDING
by Robert Hughes, Alfred A. Knopf, Inc., 1986

Robert Hughes's magnificent history examines the painful colonization of Australia. Between 1788 and 1868, he relates, 160,000 British castoffs of the "criminal class"—men, women and children—were shipped to the newly discovered continent. Although Australia had never before been inhabited by Europeans, and thus seemed strange and hostile to its new arrivals, they gradually established settlements that grew in size and number, until the vast land was transformed into a flourishing nation.

To vividly depict the lives of Australia's early settlers, Hughes studied hundreds of documents, including numerous letters and diaries. Consequently, as he has written, *The Fatal Shore* "is largely about what [the convicts] tell us of their suffering and survival, their aspirations and resistance, their fear of exile and their reconciliation to the once-unimagined land they and their children would claim as their own."

The Harbor and the Exiles

England's 18th-century rulers had so mismanaged the nation's economy that the vast majority of people were impoverished, unable to eat unless they stole food. In hopes both of discouraging theft and of ensuring a cheap labor force in the nation's horrid factories and industrial plants, the government passed extremely harsh laws: theft of property of less than 40 shillings was punishable by seven years in prison, while theft of property worth more than 40 shillings was punishable by hanging.

Despite these severe penalties, thievery continued, and by the 1770s England's prisons were vastly overcrowded. Even though many convicts had previously been sent to America, the Revolution had put an end to that practice. Thus, England—which now had begun "warehousing" prisoners on retired, disease-ridden ships—sought a new solution.

A Horse Foaled by an Acorn

When crime first took its dramatic rise, the Georgian citizenry deduced that England's population largely consisted of criminals who should be eliminated. Public hangings thus became commonplace. Often viewed as social events, hangings were attended by hundreds, even thousands, of people, who frequently referred to the tripod-shaped gallows as the "three-legged mare" and to the condemned as one who was to be "foaled by an acorn."

As time passed, however, the public increasingly viewed the condemned as heroic rather than criminal, and fewer convicts were sentenced to death—which put the government right back in the position of having to deal with increasingly overcrowded prisons. In time Britain's leaders hit upon the idea to ship convicts to the vast Southern Continent discovered by Captain James Cook in 1770.

The Geographical Unconscious

Before Cook's discovery, "the lands south of the equator were thought, even by educated Europeans, to be inhabited by grotesque humans and strange mythical creatures." This notion, however, was somewhat dispelled by Cook, who wrote that the Aborigines "are far happier than we Europeans; being wholly unacquainted not only with the superfluous but the necessary conveniences so much sought after in Europe ... " Concluding that such a primitive and timid people would pose no threat, the British subsequently encountered larger groups of Aborigines on the southern, New South Wales coast; and as a result of this contact, the native population was reduced from 300,000 to 30,000 within one hundred years.

Having deemed Australia the appropriate place to deposit the dregs of England, the British loaded 736 prisoners (including 155 women) on to a fleet of 11 vessels on January 26, 1788. Most of these inmates had been imprisoned for petty crimes: *Thomas Hawell went down for seven years for stealing one live hen.... Elizabeth Powley, twenty-two ... raided a kitchen and took a few shillings worth of bacon, flour and raisins.... Elizabeth Beckford, seventy, got seven years [for having] stolen twelve pounds of cheese.*

However minor their infractions, all of the prisoners—most of whom were seasick and in shock throughout the journey—had to endure abominable conditions. Not only were they deprived of light and fresh air on the ships' lower decks, but they were also chained together, assaulted by vermin and the stench of excrement, vomit, and rotten food. What's more, they had no idea that "they were going on the longest voyage ever attempted by so large a group of people. If they had been told they were off to the moon, the sense of loss and fear could hardly have been worse ... " Finally, on the evening of January 19, 1789, land was sighted, and the surviving 696 feeble passengers disembarked at Botany Bay.

The Starvation Years

As the fleet's captain, Arthur Phillip, and his officers surveyed the landscape—"a flat heath of paperbark scrub and gray-green eucalyptus, stretching featurelessly away under the grinding white light of the Australian summer"—they realized they were ill-prepared to work the land. Worse still, most of the provisions left on the ships had spoiled.

By February 7th, after huts and tents had been erected for the convicts, Phillip sensed that hunger was not their only problem. On that day, as "the judge-advocate read the Royal instructions giving Phillip, as Governor, the power to administer oaths, appoint officers, convene criminal and civil court and emancipate prisoners," the captain surmised that no one else in the First Fleet shared his dream of a colony of free immigrant settlers. Indeed, it soon became evident that the marines and officers hated both the convicts and Aborigines, and despised the impartial way justice was meted out by the governor. Moreover, relations between the Aborigines and the convicts were hostile.

Then in 1790 the colony became desperate for food. Rations were cut to survival level. Soon work-weary convicts began to turn against each other, and what little morale they had was destroyed. To make matters even more fraught, the guards "grew peevish; they could not make up their minds on simple matters; they hallucinated.... They often beat the convicts senseless, sometimes killing them.... Shortages bred stony, grasping men who robbed one another like jackals snarling over a carcass ..."

Bolters and Bushrangers

The convicts quickly realized that "in Australia it was easy to escape. The hard thing was to survive." While some were able to hijack or stowaway on ships, most were caught, only to be shot or hanged. Some runaways became "bushrangers." With their "long ratty hair, thick beards, roughly sewn garments and moccasins of kangaroo hide, a pistol stuck in a rope belt, a stolen musket [and] a polecat's stench," they roamed the bush for over 80 years killing countless kangaroos and Aborigines, or terrorizing newly-arrived settlers. Despite their brutalities and outlaw deeds, the bushrangers—similar to America's Old West outlaws—became Australian folk-heroes.

The Government Stroke

After the turn of the century, convicts were assigned to work for settlers who emigrated with the promise of free land and cheap labor. Gregory Blaxland, one of these newcomers and "the first capitalist-farmer to emigrate," received from the government some "4,000 acres of land in perpetuity ... and forty convicts to work them with."

Critics of "assigned service" considered the practice slavery. Convicts, however, could be paid for a portion of their labor, and they could also sue their masters—who were forbidden to inflict corporeal punishment—for ill-treatment. Moreover, convicts were freed after serving a fixed term of labor, and their children were always born free. While not as brutal as slavery in America, Australia's system of enforced labor soon created a stagnant economy.

Gentlemen of New South Wales

Most of Australia's first settlers suffered either from a rather violent obsession with land acquisition or from a pronounced boredom with their former lives. After relocating, their new rural lives tended to exacerbate their British class-consciousness. Thus, for instance, they believed that Australia's men "could be roughly sorted into three kinds of people. There were opportunists struggling to be gentlemen; convicts and outcasts waiting to be opportunists; and the failures, who could never become anything." Because most colonials had come to New South Wales to make their fortunes quickly and then return to England, few identified with the more prominent residents of the land they called Australia—a term from *austral*, meaning "southern," which was initially synonymous with condescension or abuse. In fact, decades passed before Australians took pride in their sovereign nation and unique culture.

Metastasis

In the early 1820s back in England, an unsuccessful attempt at prison reform was made: a famine, coupled with a deteriorating economy, quickly impoverished rural workers, who turned increasingly to crime. Even as the crime rate surged out of control, liberal opposition to the "transportation" (deportation) system was strident. " ... The English authorities knew—and in fact had come to accept—that their ways of dealing with crime had failed.... The crime rate in England had not dropped; thus one had to conclude that

transportation did not deter." Nevertheless, now addicted to transportation, England had increased the yearly shipment of convicts to almost 3,000 by 1824, but by then Australia's voluntary settlers had begun to outnumber convicts and emancipists. In 1825, responding to the settlers' demands for harsher treatment of prisoners, newly appointed governor Ralph Darling approved the use of "cat-o'-nine tails, whose whistle and crack [became] as much a part of the aural background to Australian life as the kookaburra's laugh."

The Aristocracy Be We

By 1850 the liberals' clamor against transporting convicts had grown louder. The end of the system did not come about because of moral outcries, however, but rather because of two miners, John Lister and Edward Hargraves, who had discovered gold west of Australia's Blue Mountains. Two months after the find in February of 1851, a thousand diggers were tunneling on the banks of Summerhill Creek and the road over the Blue Mountains was choked with columns of men. By mid-1852, 50,000 miners were unearthing hundreds of tons of gold, most of which was shipped back to England. The following year, as over 30,000 more emigrants flooded the Southern Continent, England slowed the shipping of convicts to eastern Australia and Tasmania to a trickle.

The End of the System

Early in 1868 "the last convict ship to Australia landed ... at Fremantle [Western Australia], eighty years to the month ... since Arthur Phillip brought the First Fleet to ... Sydney Cove." Twenty years later, when colonial Australia celebrated its centennial, few convicts were still alive, and the government actually tried to suppress the memory of their "stain." For decades no Australian history book even mentioned the transportation of convicts; records of trials and convictions were burnt so as not to inflict "social pain" on innocent descendants.

In 1901 the six Australian colonies were federated to form an independent Commonwealth—and at this point, ironically, measures were introduced to prevent immigration by non-whites. In 1974, Australia, under Gough Whitlam, abolished the "white Australia" policy in favor of one which was nondiscriminatory.

Although for 80 years England had dumped its refuse on the "fatal shores" of what it deemed a worthless land, Australia struggled to develop a distinctive culture, and, until quite recently, chose to ignore its so-called tarnished origins. Nowadays the thriving nation credits these rejected "criminals" as the cornerstone of its strong, vibrant culture.

Perhaps the history of Australia's "fatal shore" was best captured in 1918 by poet Mary Gilmore, who wrote of the debt Australia owed its unwilling founders:

I was the convict
  Sent to hell,
To make in the desert
  The living well:
I split the rock;
  I felled the tree—
The nation was
  Because of me.

INDIA
by Stanley Wolpert, University of California Press, 1991

*A*ll of us who wear cotton cloth, use the decimal system, enjoy the taste of chicken, play chess or roll dice, and seek peace of mind or tranquility through meditation are indebted to India. Surprisingly few Americans have much more than a superficial understanding of her deep-rooted civilization, or the causes of her complex modern problems and recurring conflicts.

Stanley Wolpert's compelling book *India* not only sheds greater understanding on the societal and religious differences between East and West, but allows readers to vicariously experience that nation's centuries'-long contributions to world culture and the frustrations endured by her people. India is unique for its sheer endurance. The nation has survived "every invasion, every natural disaster, every mortal disease and epidemic, transmitting an unmistakable imprint on three-quarters of a billion modern bearers."

Wolpert further states: *India is the world's most ancient civilization, yet one of its youngest nations. Much of the paradox found there is a product of her antiquity and youth. Everything is there, usually in magnified form. No extreme of lavish wealth or wretched poverty, no joy or misery, no beauty or horror is too wonderful, or too dreadful, for India. Nothing is 'obviously true' of India as a whole.*

One example of the India paradox is that Indians are among the world's most sensual and yet most austere people. Sex is worshiped as religious ritual in the same land that invented monasticism. Alongside the cars of the upper classes and buses of the middle class, roll "bullock carts" loaded with market produce, and people riding bicycles or walking to their daily destinations.

In a similar way, India is a land that is at once startlingly beautiful and menacing: *Heat is to India what fog is to England and smog is to California. She sizzles from March to early November. Crop yields are considerably lower than other nations, but may be attributed to the enervating heat.* Birds and lizards make their nests in the beams of urban dwellings, and snakes, even poisonous ones, are considered good luck. Still, "children are taught early never to reach under a tablecloth or into any dark closet that might have insufficient light to reveal the coiled body of a sleeping cobra."

Even India's famous mountains are marked by paradox. The Himalaya range, which includes both the tallest and the youngest mountains in the world, provides runoff waters to the fertile lower plains and acts as a barrier against outside invasion; yet it also acts as a wall, segregating the national sections from each other and contributing to divisiveness within India—a condition which has left her actually more vulnerable to conquest by outsiders.

India's history, though shrouded in myth, has its roots in historic reality; the epic tales must be sifted for whatever genuine gems that remain. Apparently, more than 4,000 years ago an Aryan people living along the river Indus enjoyed a highly sophisticated, urban, commercial civilization, which was destroyed by severe earthquakes and floods. An oral history was preserved by scattered groups of priests, or Brahmans. Later, around 2,000 B.C.E., their writings were recorded in books called the *Vedas*, early scriptures comprising hymns, prayers, and rituals of war and religious sacrifice.

About 1,000 B.C.E., India discovered iron, ushering in an era of rapid change during which territorial kingdoms evolved. The *Mahabharata* and *Ramayana* epics were recorded during the next 300 years. These literary works, rich in legend, lore, character and custom, tell much of what is known of the period. During this time when many Indians became tired of war and sought ways of achieving peace, *Karma*, the doctrine of reincarnation and teachings of the relationship between the illusory material world and the profound reality of the spiritual world, came into existence. Roughly 500 B.C.E., Buddha's teachings of peace, as opposed to the Brahmans' war-like offerings, gained popularity.

At the end of the 6th century B.C.E. there were a dozen religiously affiliated princely states in India engaging in skirmishs that continue even today. A common strategy of the competing princes was to release a white stallion—followed by cavalry—let him run free for a year, and then claim all the lands that the animal had traversed. Of course, the current landowner would try to kill or capture the stallion to protect his land from being taken and prove his own sovereignty, and thus "ancient India's miniwars began."

Alexander the Great crossed into India in 326 B.C.E. His dreams of world unity inspired Chandragupta Maurya to unite the Ganges and Indus valleys for the first time. Maurya's philosophy of government included such ideas as "spying on the loyalty of wives and closest ministers, also generals and lesser bureaucrats." Maurya's grandson, Ashoka, who reigned from 269 to 232 B.C.E., emulated his grandfather's policies for nine years. Then a particularly bloody war, costing hundreds of thousands of lives, forced him to change strategies. "He decided to follow the paths of war no more, advocating love and nonviolence as the worthiest ideals for empires." These ideals are still remembered today, and many would seek to return to the "golden age" of the Mauryan Empire.

Persians, Scythians and Chinese now poured over the border, each influencing politics. Chandra Gupta II, a Hindu imperial ruler who lived around the year 375, resumed India's era of glory. He also inspired Kalidasa, "the Shakespeare of India," to write "Shakuntala," a drama about human weakness which has since provided historians with great insights into the daily life of that period.

In the year 711 adherents of Islam slashed their way through southern India for the first time; they would "continue their assault on Indian soil for the next thousand years," and during the last 500 years their monarchs—including Mahmud of Ghazni, who annually raided Hindu temples—ruled much of India.

Those jihads ("holy wars") left a bitter legacy of communal hatred in the hearts and minds of India's populace, undermining all attempts to reunify the nation under Muslim rule. The final Islamic wave came about 1526 with Akbar the Great's 50-year reign over the Empire, his Mughal court initiating a "general policy of religious tolerance of Hindus" and wooing royal Hindu families with "beauty, luxury, sensuality, pageantry, and the trappings of power." Soon after, Muslim monarchs returned to Islamic orthodoxy with a vengeance, beheading gurus for refusing to convert to Islam. The Sikhs, another important Indian religion, turned more militant as a result of their persecution.

As the Mughal empire diminished, the forces of the West began to encroach on India. Vasco da Gama began to trade in spices, which allowed Portugal to prevail upon India for almost 100 years. British rule then came to India under the auspices of that country's East India Company—an alliance that would forever change the face of the nation. *Many new ideas, techniques and institutions came to India as a consequence of Western Rule. Private ownership of land, as well as technological inventions, including post and telegraph systems, made enduring changes, whose legacies continue to help modernize Indian life.*

Change brought problems as well as profit. The East India Company, increasingly corrupt, ran roughshod over the Indian people, multiplying abuse that climaxed in the Indian War of 1857. "But [the country] was too divided by unbridgeable gulfs of belief, by doctrines that taught them to hate or mistrust one another." So much brutality would be remembered from the War that Indians would always have difficulty in thinking of themselves as Indians rather than as Brahmans or Afghans or Mughals. Indeed, "even after scar tissue appeared," and "long after the bleeding actually stopped ... young Indians began to awaken to the realization that before they could free India from the shackles of British rule they would have to unite themselves."

Mohandas Gandhi was arguably the greatest leader in Indian history. He returned to his homeland in 1906 after a 13-year stint in South Africa, where racial discrimination changed his life forever. Gandhi was also inspired by Christian concepts of love and self-effacing poverty, the Vedic belief in "the Real" as "the True," and the Buddhist and Hindu ideal of nonviolence, which he defined as "Love." In India, Gandhi argued that he could "move the world" by combining these forces in nonviolent measures. Subsequently, "he adopted the dress (*dhoti*) and preached that modernity was 'Satanic,' crushing human souls and destroying all the good and beautiful things of nature."

After World War I the British imposed martial law upon India. Gandhi, denouncing such "heinous" laws, organized protest marches across the country. When Reginald Dyer, a British brigadier, ordered his troops to open fire on Indians without warning, Gandhi, in an effort to throw off the British yoke, "called upon Indians everywhere to boycott any and everything British until it ground to a halt." Gandhi sought the support of Muslims as well as Hindus and instructed his disciples "to welcome suffering, to court prison, even death, if need be." But when an angry mob burned two dozen Indian police, Gandhi confessed that he had made a "Himalayan blunder" in assuming his followers were ready to carry out a peaceful mass protest. He retired to an isolated village for almost ten years.

Still, Gandhi did not forget his dream of independence for India. In 1930 he led a band of disciples in gathering their own salt at the seashore near Dandi. This act was illegal, since the government had decreed that salt could only be purchased from British stores. Millions if Indians followed Gandhi's example, and soon the jails were full. At the same time, the leader of the Muslim faction, Jinnah, was demanding a separate Moslem state—an independent state that would be called Pakistan.

In 1942, with Japanese troops at India's gates, Britain partially acquiesced by proposing "Dominion Status" for India. In 1947, however, when the British balked at these terms, a year of civil war commenced. Gandhi walked from village to village trying to restore peace, but when he moved on the madness returned, the mayhem and bloodlust continued. He was assassinated on January 30, 1948, never seeing the peaceful India he had so often envisioned.

India's first general election, held late in 1948, took four months to complete, owing to the monumental task of preparing lists of 173 million Indians qualified to vote, 80 percent of whom were illiterate. The Nationalist candidate Jawaharlal Nehru, who had taken over the reins of government at Gandhi's death, was elected. Nehru, himself incorruptible, realized that great power also brought a degree of impotence. Although he was able to articulate the problems of the people, he presented few palpable solutions to India's social and economic troubles.

Nehru's daughter, Indira Gandhi, was elected as India's Prime Minister in 1966. Indira made many needed changes, but her fatal weakness was "her passion for power and her unbridled ambition for herself and her sons." She postponed elections so often that militant Sikhs eventually murdered her.

Indira's son, Rajiv, was elected President in December 1984. In his inaugural address he declared: "We talk of the high principles and lofty ideals needed to build a strong and prosperous India.... But we obey no discipline ... follow no principle of public morality, display no sense of social awareness.... Corruption is not only tolerated but even regarded as the hallmark of our leadership."

In closing, Wolpert remarks: *All of the above is but to say that India's present and future continue to reflect her past. So India keeps changing, but Indian faith in cyclical change makes every return to past norms or traditional values and beliefs seem somehow natural, more proper than what might be viewed as "backsliding" in the West. Indira Gandhi once noted, "India has not ever been an easy country to understand." Perhaps it is too deep, contradictory and diverse, and few people in the contemporary world have the time or inclination to look beyond the obvious.*

CHINA: A MACRO HISTORY
by Ray Huang, M.E. Sharp, Inc., 1988

In *China: A Macro History* Ray Huang traces Chinese history from 1600 B.C.E. to the beginning of the 20th century.

Characterizing China's history as the struggle between the traditional ruling dynasties and the great social and geographical forces that eventually defeated them, Huang writes: *Chinese history differs from the history of other peoples and other parts of the world because of an important factor: its vast multitudes.... Presiding over the land mass of the East Asian continent, the center of gravity of this enormous entity seems always to have been wrapped in some form of mysticism. In the imperial period as well as in the very recent past, practical problems had to be translated into abstract notions in order to be disseminated.... Sometimes form counted more than substance. For the bureaucracy operating under such a system, truth resided with authority; both had to move from the top downward.*

The Shang Dynasty

Although an ancient *Xia* dynasty was purported to have existed around 2000 B.C.E., the first dynasty for which there is archaeological evidence is the *Shang* dynasty, founded around 1600 B.C.E. The Shang, primarily a pastoral people, moved their capital more than six times in their 500-year history. They differed from later Chinese civilizations in that they allowed women relatively more freedom, consumed more alcoholic beverages, and practiced human sacrifice without remorse. More importantly, however, they possessed a sophisticated writing system that even modern Chinese readers can understand.

The Start of the First Empire: The Zhou and Han Dynasties

Around 1000 B.C.E. the warrior King Wu conquered the Shang, inaugurated the *Zhou* period, and inaugurated an age of "culture, peace and virtue."

However, the Duke of Zhou, King Wu's younger brother, soon devised a schematic infrastructure for the new empire, indiscriminately dividing land along preconceived, geometric lines and taking no thought of the people's needs. *If today such a system were to be imposed on the United States, the uneven shore lines of Michigan would be ignored; in organizing the state we would endow it with boundaries as straight and neat as those of Wyoming....* The vast country then consisted of series of small farms laid out on a grid, an agricultural society ruled by a highly ritualistic central government.

In 771 B.C.E. invasions from "barbarian" tribes caused the Zhou to move their capital to the eastern part of the country. Hence, historians designate the Zhou period before 771 as the time of the Western Zhou and the period from 771 B.C.E. until 221 B.C.E. as the Eastern Zhou. The power of the Zhou kings declined during this period and ended between 403 and 221 B.C.E., when land was divided according to a feudal system.

During this period two schools of thought formed. Mencius, a philosopher often referred to as the "Second Sage" (Confucius being the first great Sage), spoke of "charity" and "universal compassion." *Legalism*, on the other hand, was used to justify even the most tyrannical acts of China's first sovereign emperor, Qin Shi-huang-di, who sent huge armies to subjugate weaker states.

Having conquered all rivals by 221 B.C.E., this king of Qin, Shi-huang-di, immediately moved to consolidate and centralize his new dominions, organizing China along the lines of his native Qin state. Although he standardized the writing system and the units of measurement, Qin Shi-huang-di also had "seditious" books burned and Confucianist scholars who opposed his views buried alive. No philosophy but Legalism, which sanctioned his atrocities, could be read or discussed.

Qin Shi-huang-di's dynasty died along with him in 206 B.C.E. Divided into factions, the government then dissolved. Four years passed before a former police officer named Liu Bang founded the *Han* dynasty. Laying claim to the first emperor's dominion, the Han ruled China's sixty million inhabitants.

Emperors who succeeded Liu Bang worked in stages to centralize the government. The fifth emperor, Han Wu-di (141-87 B.C.E.), for example, encouraged a Confucianist code of conduct for the empire's civil servants and proclaimed "the promotion of Confucianism to the disparagement of all other schools." *The teachings of Mencius, which held that the state had a stake in the livelihood of the populace, were similarly endorsed without reservation.*

In practice, however, the Confucianist code of honor proved unrealistic when it came to guiding everyday government operations. The heavy taxes imposed on China's millions of farmers, for instance, were impossible to collect, and the government collapsed under its own weight and corruption. As the Han period ended, Zhang Rang, a palace eunuch who wielded political power, reflected the general cynicism of the time when he said to his opponents: "You said that we inside the palace are corrupt. Please tell me, Sir, from the ministers on down, who is loyal and who is honest?"

The Second Empire: The Sui, the Tang and the Song Dynasties

In the year 220, China experienced a period of disunity, which lasted until 581. The North split into 16 "transient & overlapping" kingdoms, while the South passed through four short dynasties. A warlord named Yang Jian united the North in 581, then conquered the last of the four Southern dynasties in 589, reunifying China and ushering in the Second Empire, under the Sui, Tang, and Song dynasties.

The short-lived *Sui* dynasty was first to offer its people literacy examinations, a practice the later *Tang* dynasty (618-906) also adopted. Whereas the recommendation system of the Han had led to the domination of government offices by clans, the examination system created a highly educated bureaucratic class.

Under Tang rule the empire experienced "the most splendid and satisfying period in the history of China's imperial era." Government efficiency prevailed, and many glorious battles were fought and won.

Then, in 906, the ruling empress Wu Zetian effected a small but real revolution. Empress Wu rejuvenated the bureaucracy in her time, but the Tang fell into decline after her death. Indeed, Huang notes: ... *The ideal state did not endure because, gradually, the central leadership became indolent and irresponsible.... The bureaucracy not only expanded its membership but also multiplied its pay scale. Emperors and ministers degenerated in character [and] there were no common efforts that profitably tied the governing and the governed together ...*

After the collapse of the Tang, the empire again dissolved into separate states. Thus the *Song* dynasty, lasting until 1279, never ruled over the whole empire, yet was marked by prosperity, cultural advancement and artistic excellence. Decentralization also proved beneficial: ... *With the government's center of gravity shifting down to the provincial level, the governance was more responsive to the local situation.*

The Third Empire: The Yuan, the Ming, and the Qing Dynasties

The Mongols under Khublai Khan conquered China in 1279, inaugurating the Third Empire. The Mongols' mobile culture helped make them superior horsemen and irrepressible warriors, but did not prepare them to rule: *The Chinese used to say that the Mongols, after conquering the world on horseback, intended also to rule it on horseback.* The Mongol dynasty, the *Yuan,* lasted until 1368, when the *Ming,* an "introverted and noncompetitive state," came into power.

The founder of the Ming, Zhu Yuanzhang, installed the most centralized government China had yet seen. Moreover, he outlawed sea voyages and forbade participation in warfare outside the empire's boundaries. As the Ming government began its slow decline, its system of taxation failed. And as supply lines broke down and armies were left to scavenge for food, an army of peasant rebels rose up to seize the capital city of Beijing. Emperor Zhu Youjian hung himself before the rebels could overtake him, leaving behind a message that read: *Bandits, I invite you to quarter my body, but I forbid you to do harm to my subjects, any one of them!*

Unable to crush the peasant revolt, the Ming commander invited the Manchus into Beijing to kill the rebels. The Manchus, alien conquerors though they were, quickly adapted themselves to Chinese culture, and initiated the *Qing* dynasty. While at first the Qing did much to reinvigorate the Ming institutions, they made few fundamental changes.

Now as the Renaissance transformed European life, the Celestial Empire remained static, isolated from the world, content to live under the "self-restraint and mutual deference" of the Confucian code: *The calm and orderliness that emanated from this system commanded admiration abroad. It was only in the early nineteenth century when the commercial interests of the West became established in force along the China coast that the Confucian style of statecraft, projecting an ideal perfection, more a fiction than a reality ... quite suddenly*

appeared to be a cheap form of government that was neither solid nor flexible.

Post-Dynasty Governments

Entering the 19th century, the empire suffered crushing defeats at the hands of English and French military expeditions. During the Opium Wars, the Chinese fought to stop Westerners from peddling the drug. But as the Chinese rose up to expel the Westerners, the wars that followed proved to expose the weaknesses of the nation's static system. Western domination of the Chinese was total. To compound matters, the empire also had entered into combat against Taiping rebels—Christian Chinese peasants who actually had lived in China for years—a fight which resulted in 20 million deaths before the rout of the rebels in 1864.

The Chinese soon instituted the massive "Self-Strengthening Movement," a program aimed at modernization. But the movement's purpose was singular: *China wished to take advantage of Western technology to boost its military strength ... nothing else. It was guns and steamships that the reformers wanted....* These attempts to graft Western factories and machines onto the changeless, passive Imperial bureaucracy ultimately failed. But, Huang contends, ... *We can now see that failures though they seemed to be, they were necessary steps toward an immense revolution ...*

With Japan's increasing influence on the region's economy and trade, China's ability to control its own destiny waned. In 1898, for a period of 103 days, the emperor Guangxu issued a series of edicts calling for complete reorganization of government services along Western lines; China must be transformed into a modern nation, Guangxu implored. But the move toward Westernization was proclaimed in a characteristically un-Western manner. The "Hundred Days' Reform," in line with traditional make-believe, invoked an age-old doctrine that truth always emanated from the top downward. A pronouncement from the throne was a deed accomplished, according to the practice. Guangxu's brave attempt at reform failed, and the powerful Empress Dowager Cixi put him under house arrest. Then in 1900, Cixi, resenting increased foreign presence in China, declared war on all related foreign powers. The delegation of Westerners in Beijing was besieged, but eventually Western troops put down the Chinese forces in what was called the "Boxer Rebellion."

Following the deaths of Guangxu and Cixi, and the failure of the Boxer Rebellion, the revolutionaries in China, led by Sun Yat-sen, managed to take over the government in October of 1911, forcing Guangxu's widow to abdicate. After 2,132 years, China's imperial age had ended; the giant hand of revolutionary Communism would rule the giant empire from that time forward.

Summary Note

Although he does foresee an increase in pro-democracy militancy and expresses his hope that China is on the path leading to eventual liberation from Communist rule, Huang admits that it remains to be seen what the giant empire's future will be.

AFRICAN CIVILIZATIONS REVISITED – *FROM ANTIQUITY TO MODERN TIMES*
by Basil Davidson, Africa World Press, 1991

asil Davidson's *African Civilizations Revisited* provides a history of Africa from the vantage point of outsiders who came in contact with its early cultures. Drawing on more than a hundred sources, Davidson's book offers Westerners—who often define "civilization" as only a culture bearing armies and navies, with suit-and-tie-wearing inhabitants, and with a wealth of written chronicles—a uniquely pristine, though often tragic, view of African history.

Anthropology, Davidson argues, seems to indicate that the evolution of humanity's ancestors from apes occurred in Africa. All non-human ancestors disappeared 12,000 years ago; humans were producing food across the vast plain of what is now the Sahara Desert 9,000 years ago. By the first millennium B.C.E.—well before any European contact was made—groups of African *homo sapiens* had developed an iron-based culture and had begun trading with other clans on the African continent.

Though African natives were at one time a single people (or possibly several peoples, according to Davidson), the advent of the iron-pointed spear paved the way for the eventual fracturing of ancestral stocks into a great number of "tribes." Ghana was the earliest of the West African kingdoms, awakening around the year 500. East Africa, a more isolated and developed nation, sprang up in the area of Katanga about 300 years later.

Around the 11th century, during a time when large stone structures were being built in South Africa—and large, sophisticated cities had sprung up in many parts of the continent—the white man arrived, interrupting the advance of African civilization: *European invasion arrived in the mid-stream of a time of major internal adjustment. It struck Africa at a moment of confusion that was itself the product of new pressures and needs. Thereafter, nothing could ever be the same.*

Antiquity

The oldest written records pertaining to Africa come from Egypt and are dated about 2300 B.C.E. The documents' author, Harkhuf, made four journeys south into Africa, bringing back ivory, ebony, incense, grain, panthers and even dancing pygmies: "My lord sent me," Harkhuf writes, "together with my father … in order to explore a road to this country [of the south]. I did it in only seven months and I brought all [kinds of] gifts from it.… I was very greatly praised for it."

About 450 B.C.E. the Greek historian Herodotus traveled to a region now called Aswan and to the capital city of Meroe in northern Africa. Detailing his journey, Herodotus recalls watching the curious way in which the Carthaginians conducted trade with the people of western Libya: first, the Carthaginians laid their wares on the seashore and returned to their boats; next, the natives came to lay a quantity of gold on the beach, then retreated; finally, the Carthaginians returned to look at the gold, and if they were not satisfied with the amount, retreated to the boat until more gold was added. "There is perfect honesty on both sides," writes Herodotus. "The Carthaginians never touch the gold until it equals in value what they have offered for sale, and the natives never touch the goods until the gold has been taken away."

Early East Africa

Many centuries separated Herodotus's visit to East Africa and that of the next reliable recordkeeper. The most successful East African city-state, situated on an island on the southern coast of Tanzania, was Kilwa, a municipality set up sometime in the blur of early antiquity. "Kilwa is one of the most beautiful and well-constructed towns in the world," recounts Ibn Battatua, an Arab adventurer. Kilwani legends tell of the island being settled by ancient sailors from Persia, but the inhabitants were clearly black Muslim, largely Swahili. The city of Kilwa controlled gold exports from southern Africa between the 13th and 16th centuries, before being conquered by marauding pagan Zanj bands and left in ruins.

The Portuguese, who for centuries had sought the source of Africa's legendary silver and spice deposits, also came to explore African coastal regions. Eventually their exploits spelled ruin for the East African traders, but it is through these Portuguese plunderings that we have any record of these early African civilizations. Vasco da Gama wrote about his landing on the East African coast: *They forthwith began to play on four or five flutes, some producing high notes and other low ones, thus making a pretty harmony for Negroes who are not expected to be musicians.* The Portuguese sailors, firing their cannons, then went about the business of subjugating the population and extracting the riches they came for.

Da Gama also recorded his landing on Mozambique Island, where he saw Muslims dressed in clothes of "fine linen or cotton stuff, with variously colored stripes, and of rich and elaborate workmanship," as well as Indian ships laden with great quantities of native treasure for transport back to India.

Chinese records also document trade with East Africa, dating to at least 863. Here was a group of people, Chinese historians wrote, "who eat only meat and drink the blood from cattle mixed with milk." The Chinese expressed disgust to find that Arabs often raided the continent for slaves.

Early West Africa

African culture produced exquisite artistic creations. Anthropologists have found bronze and terra cotta figurines in West Africa that have been dated to the Nok culture, which thrived there between 900 B.C.E. and A.C.E. 200. After the Nok reign, in-migration of

Africans from the east resulted in a government that strictly controlled the indigenous artistic population. In 455 an Arabian merchant, Al Bekri, wrote his observations: *The king of Ghana can put two hundred thousand warriors in the field, more than forty thousand being armed with bow and arrow ...* Following the proscribed regal and formal ceremonies, the king met with his people "to listen to their complaints and set them to rights," ruling fairly in all matters brought before him and delivering verdicts according to sound judgment.

In about 1240 the ruler of Mandingo prevailed in a great battle against a rival king; the result marked the beginning of the empire known as Mali, located in West Africa. Those who eventually migrated into Mali and settled there were of the Muslim faith. In 1324 the esteemed emperor of Mali, Kankan Musa, made a pilgrimage to Mecca. On his way, a historian writes, he passed through Cairo. As Musa made his way through the throng that had gathered to witness the meeting between Egypt's proud Sultan and the high emperor of Mali, it is recorded that Masa generously distributed so much gold to the people as he went that the price of gold in Egypt foundered for more than a decade.

Central Africa

The Portuguese Alcanova reported the sophisticated methods of the African's gold mining and refining: ... *They dig out the earth and make a kind of tunnel, through which they go under the ground a long stone's throw, and keep on taking out from the veins the ground mixed with the gold, and when collected, they put it in a pot, and cook it much in fire; and after cooking they take it out, and put it to cool, and when cold, the earth remains and the gold is all fine gold ...*

Portuguese records describing the inland empire of Monomotapa (Zimbabwe and western Mozambique) show that this area was the source of much of the gold exported from Africa in the early centuries of Western incursion.

By the late 17th century the Portuguese had "fatally intervened in the affairs of Monomotapa," writes a Portuguese sailor, but they were too weak to impose a system of law and order, and so the door to chaos was opened.

West Africa Meets Europe

A new phase of history began when West African gold, spices, jewels and ivory were taken for trade directly to Europe rather than traded through the middlemen of the Sahara: *[The trading] was brusque and bloody to begin with, an affair of squalid raids and running fights, but soon calmed to a more or less regular trading partnership.*

Seeing how wealthy they could become, the Portuguese claimed a monopoly on access to West Africa. In doing so, however, they insulted King Don Fernando of Spain, who authorized a navy to sail to Africa and humble the pride of the Portuguese. A band of Spanish fishermen, hearing of Don Fernando's plan, sent ships to Guinea in advance of the Spanish

monarch's ships. There they offered to trade with the native king and hosted the people to a banquet on their fine vessels. After all had eaten, the fishermen offered to show their guests the holds of the ship, and when the entire assembly was below deck, the Spaniards closed and fastened the hatches and sailed away. In addition to the king himself, they had captured a total of 140 "African nobles of superb physique."

The king protested the captivity of his people, and when they reached Spain, he alone was freed. Alonso de Palencia records the ruler's response to his and his people's incarceration: *That savage [the king] maintained a certain regal authority during his captivity ... dignity in his countenance, gravity in speech, prudence in conduct, and courage in adversity.On reaching his country, he exercised such cunning in order to avenge himself on his treacherous oppressors that, in spite of the distrust with which they traveled, he succeeded in securing some and keeping them as hostages for as many others of his relations.*

As England, France and others entered into trade with Africa, Portugal immersed itself in the slave trade to support its colonies in America. One tribal emperor in the Congo protested this practice to the Portuguese king: ... *The merchants are taking every day our natives, sons of the land and the sons of our noblemen and vassals and our relatives ... and so great, Sir, is the corruption and licentiousness that our country is being completely depopulated.* The Congo emperor recognized that his own people's desire for the Portuguese goods was so great that some would trade others of the tribe to obtain riches, so he begged the Portuguese monarch to end all such trade. His pleas went unanswered.

Richard Eden of England, in depicting the West African communities he visited, characterized himself as thoroughly "dumbfounded" to find advanced civilizations made up of highly skilled craftsmen—not at all the primitive, backward societies he had read about. In 1554, after describing the ingenious methods by which these people created their beautiful artifacts, fishhooks, daggers, and cloth, he wrote: *They are very wary people in their bargaining, and will not lose one sparke of golde of any value. They use weights and measures, and are very circumspect in occupying the same. They that shall have to do with them, must use them gently; for they will not trafique or bring in any wares, if they be evil used.*

Despite their wariness, though, the African civilizations were increasingly exploited by the Western world. All during the 18th century and most of the 19th, the various proud, independent African cultures suffered the expanding impacts of colonialism, bigotry, racism and slave trade. The riches of the continent were heavily exploited, while the interior went largely unexplored. As Davidson concludes: *The "technology gap" between Europe and Africa widened so far in the eighteenth century that Europe's conquest of Africa in the nineteenth was to seem, for most Europeans, right and even necessary.... By 1900 there was hardly any part of Africa which had yet to feel the impact of Europe's drive for material possession.*

LEGENDS, LIES AND CHERISHED MYTHS OF AMERICAN HISTORY
by Richard Shenkman, William Morrow and Company, 1988

*W*e usually admit that Americans are somewhat ignorant of history, but we don't realize how ignorant.... Not only have they forgotten what they should remember, but they have remembered what they should have forgotten.... With time facts fade. But myths seem to go on and on.

Thus Richard Shenkman introduces us to our false memories of American history. Analyzing myths in 17 categories from *Art* to *War*, each section—indeed, each page—shoots down dozens of myths.

Presidents

America's greatest Presidents have long been considered heroes, protagonists beyond reproach. Shenkman unmasks such illusions:

• George Washington was a veritable saint—and no one seems to remember anything that disagrees with that image. He admits to despising his mother—but we remember him only as a devoted son; he was a clever businessman who accumulated a fortune speculating in frontier lands—but we think of him as a simple and trustworthy farmer; his own records show that he was something of a dandy and wore all the latest fashions—but no one speaks of him as being vain. On the other hand, critics have suggested that he fathered several children by his slaves, a claim that is completely at odds with the historical record. In fact, Shenkman suggests, "Washington treated his slaves with respect and compassion and never once is known to have made any advances toward them." And, as near as we can tell, Washington was sterile, unable to have children.

• Likewise, the charge that Thomas Jefferson carried on for years with a beautiful slave name Sally Hemmings isn't easily proved or disproved. One of the most prominent Jefferson authorities discounts the rumor, arguing that Jefferson wouldn't have been willing to seduce a person who didn't have the right to say no. Jefferson's opinions about the press are also varied. Sometimes he asserted that the press was more important than the government itself; but on other occasions he would refuse to even recognize the rights of the press as included among the Constitution's basic freedoms.

• Fortunately, many of the myths told about Abraham Lincoln are true. He *did* carry important papers in his hat; he *did* grow a beard at the suggestion of a child; and he *had* worked as a rail splitter. However, there are also an abundance of fables. He winced when referred to as "Abe," and few called him by that name. The Gettysburg Address was not written on the train on his way to give the speech. In fact, he gave far fewer speeches than is generally believed, and seldom made extemporaneous comments—primarily out of a fear of appearing foolish. Although he did enjoy hearing and telling an occasional joke, he was quite serious and fiercely ambitious. Truly, he deplored slavery, but was not an abolitionist, until necessity forced it on him.

• So entrenched are the myths about the "American Camelot," that John Kennedy is still considered one of the two or three most admired U.S. Presidents. Among the many legendary tales are the ones about his war record and his literary skills. Kennedy, for instance, always maintained that his *PT-109* was split in two during an attack on a destroyer; in truth, it was rammed during a lull in the fighting when he and his crew were caught napping. Kennedy rescued one man, not the three he claimed to have saved. Both his undergraduate thesis and his book *Profiles in Courage*, which won the Pulitzer Prize, were largely drafted by others.

The Family

The fundamental myth of the American family is that it is a fixed and stable institution. Not so, says Shenkman. In colonial times most of the child-rearing was handled by the fathers and not the mothers. Children were treated as little adults, given heavy responsibilities and provided with very few playthings.

Similarly, despite the myth, colonial Americans did not generally live together in extended families. In fact, elderly adults were often ousted from their homes by their children and sent off to fend for themselves. (It was during the Victorian era that epithets such as "old goat" and "geezer" came into use.)

Americans believe that the family today is suffering from new, unprecedented failures. History, however, does not bear this out. For example, divorce is not a recent scourge. In the 1880s America saw more divorces than any other civilized nation. Though the divorce rate is higher today than in previous decades, this may not be a symptom of a problem getting worse, but a sign of a problem getting better. That is, more people are willing to bring unhappy marriages to an end. We also perpetuate the fear that divorce creates a glut of one-parent homes, but America has always had one-parent homes, although from a different cause: the early death of a parent. As a matter of record, in the 19th century Americans had the same proportion of single parent homes as they have today. *Americans idealize the families of the past and fear the worst for present families. The facts show, however, that divorce is not unique to our times, single-parent homes are not solely the creation of modernity, and since colonial times American families have changed repeatedly.*

War

We tend to think of the American Revolution as being distinct from revolutions today, somehow more genteel and less bloody. In reality, America's fight for freedom had much in common with today's revolutions. No matter how unsullied it may appear in our myths, "real revolution is bloody and fearful." One measure of this violence is the way we treated those who stayed loyal to the English king. Loyalists commonly lost all their property, were tarred and feathered, sometimes killed. Eighty thousand fled to Canada, to live out their lives in poverty. In truth, almost as many Americans fought for England as fought against it.

The *minutemen*, far from being middle-class patriots, were often farmers and tradesmen—poor, landless, out of work, and out of hope. What's more, they were not very good shots. We are infused with the image of the British Redcoats marching in line while the wily colonists bombarded them from behind rocks and trees. Actually, such guerrilla warfare was rare. For the most part the war was fought in classic European style, as Americans feared that the use of guerrilla warfare might diminish their society.

There is a myth that the dying Benedict Arnold put on his American uniform. In truth, he languished the last three days of his life in a delirious lethargy. Similarly, Davy Crockett did not die fighting to the end at the Alamo; rather, he and several others were captured and executed by Santa Ana's forces.

No two historians can fully agree about the causes and other details concerning the Civil War. For one, Shenkman asserts that the institution of slavery was no worse in American than in other countries. Likewise, Andersonville prison may have been a vile place to be held captive, but the Confederates didn't plan the deaths of 12,000 Union prisoners: they just couldn't provide any better care; the prisoners were eating as well as their guards.

We often think the sinking of the *Lusitania* precipitated American intervention in World War I, but the fact remains that the United States didn't intervene until two years later. And the Germans, embroiled in the conflict, didn't invent submarine warfare: they just perfected it, as almost a century and a half earlier George Washington had commissioned a primitive one-man submarine to blow up a British warship during the Revolutionary War.

As for the infamous Nazi death camps of World War II and the well-publicized Allied accounts of the horrific sights discovered in them at war's end, these horrors, in fact, were not unexpected. Indeed, Shenkman insists, long before the publicizing of these death camps, the "evidence that Jews were being slaughtered by the millions had been abundant and overwhelming for years." Perhaps the Western world's journalists couldn't quite believe the early accounts themselves; hence the terse reports that were published in the newspapers were often buried on inside pages.

The myth remains that America was forced to drop the atomic bomb on Japan in order to spare millions of lives. According to Shenkman, the reality is that the Japanese emperor was at the time on the verge of surrender. In like manner, claims that the American military misled the government into thinking that they could win an easy victory in Vietnam are wrong, says Shenkman. In actuality, the military warned that victory in Vietnam would require up to a million soldiers and seven years' time. Even the legendary French patriot Charles de Gaulle warned Kennedy against involvement. As we now know, that warning and those that followed went unheeded.

Holidays

Nothing is sacred, writes Shenkman—not even holidays. Americans, for instance, celebrate their Independence on the wrong day. Records clearly show that a break from England was declared in Philadelphia by the Continental Congress on July 2, 1776, and an announcement to that effect published in the papers that very night. True, the Declaration of Independence was adopted on July 4, but most didn't even sign it until a later date. Congress itself celebrated independence on July 8th.

"Until the Civil War, Christmas was but scantly observed," Shenkman notes. In 1659 the Massachusetts Bay Colony actually passed a law prohibiting any forms of Christmas observance, imposing heavy penalties on those who did not comply. Only after the Civil War, when retailers discovered the commercial possibilities of such holiday sales, did Christmas find favor. By 1870, December was a merchant's biggest month.

Folklore

Sometimes what we think of as mythical, is actually real—or at least has solid, historical roots. Casey Jones, John Henry, and Mrs. O'Leary were actual people, though most historians cannot substantiate the myth that O'Leary's cow triggered the great Chicago fire.

• Johnny "Appleseed" Chapman was a real person who tramped the Ohio Valley planting trees—but he wasn't poor and he wasn't a hermit. He was, in fact, a successful nurseryman.

• Sam Wilson, in his day, became America's own "Uncle Sam." Wilson supplied meat to the troops during the War of 1812 and it was stamped "US," for the United States. It was an imaginative dock worker who then claimed that the initials stood for *Uncle Sam*—Sam Wilson's nickname—and, ever since, government property has been "Uncle Sam's."

"Just as there are real people falsely believed to be mythical," writes Shenkman, "so there are mythical figures falsely believed to be real." Mother Goose is one of these. The myth is that Mother Goose was Elizabeth Foster Goose from Boston. True, there really was an Elizabeth Goose, but she had nothing to do with the nursery rhymes, which were written by a Frenchman, Charles Perrault (who, incidentally, also invented the tales of Cinderella and Sleeping Beauty). The wrong connection with Elizabeth Goose resulted from a claim by a descendent many years later.

Everyone knows that Paul Bunyan was merely the product of American folklore. In reality, he was the creation of an advertising man to sell the products of the Red River Lumber Company. Thus he is as authentic a folklore hero as today's Mr. Clean or the Jolly Green Giant.

Shenkman concludes that "many of the best-known stories from history are false." But, he adds, Americans are not to blame for knowing so much that is not worth knowing. Even historians have been taken in. As E.M. Forster wrote, "Nonsense of this type is more difficult to combat than a solid lie. It hides in rubbish heaps and moves when no one is looking."

THE CANADIANS
by Andrew H. Malcom, Time Books, 1985

In 1535 a French sailor named Jacques Cartier sailed up the St. Lawrence River in hopes of finding a passageway to the Pacific. As the river narrowed, Cartier put ashore at a Huron village and asked where he was. "Kanata," the Hurons replied, referring to the name of their village. When Cartier returned to France, he announced that he had discovered a vast new land called "Canada."

"It was," writes Andrew Malcom, "a suitably symbolic beginning for Canada, misnamed, misunderstood, and mistaken for somewhere else." In his book *The Canadians,* Malcom takes his readers on an astonishing tour of Canada's unique history, vast landscape, diverse peoples and burgeoning economy.

As Malcom reminds his readers, neither the French nor the British were the first settlers of Canada. "The first pioneers," he says, "came several thousand years before Cartier." Drawn by migrating animal herds, the Eskimos and other tribes wandered from Asia across the Bering Strait into Alaska. Once there, Malcom contends, they moved "down the coast and inland [to Canada], where they developed the languages and skills and patience and cooperative social structure so suitable for their survival in their harsh environment." Malcom illustrates their unique adaptation to the land by pointing out that while the Eskimos "had 100 words for different kinds of 'snow,' [they had] no words for 'war'; they were too busy fighting the Canadian climate to face off against each other."

Despite the fact that Cartier "discovered" Canada in 1535, Malcom notes that it took the French another 75 years before they were able to establish a permanent settlement near Quebec City; the Canadian winters were simply too severe to endure. The British also had their difficulties colonizing the Canadian wilderness. *In 1610, [the explorer] Henry Hudson pushed west through the ice until a mutinous crew, fearful of continuing farther into the depths of Canada's harsh elements, set him adrift to perish in the vast bay that later carried his name.*

Malcom speculates that Canada's brutal geography and ruthless climate goes a long way in explaining its "mosaic" history and character. In a sense, he says, the isolation imposed by natural elements have created "archipelagos" of language, culture and tradition. Thus, for instance, in the absence of a strong national identity, Canadians did not attain independence from Great Britain until 1867. Then, notes Malcom, it had to be forced on them "by a British government anxious to create some kind of political entity to forestall expansion from the south by the well-armed and newly re-United States."

One of the most remarkable characteristics about Canada is the disparity between its land mass and its population. Although its population barely exceeds 25 million, Canada is second only to Russia as being the largest country in the world. It is, writes Malcom, a sort of "distorted parallelogram of almost 4 million miles of land and water stretching far beyond the average citizen's scale of belief." *East to west, it spans 4,545 miles and one-quarter of the world's time zones. Scattered across this area like a few specks of pepper on a huge freezer-room floor are the people, huddling together along the porous border with the United States.*

While the majority of Canadians live in cities close to the U.S. border, much of Canada's northern tundra remains inhospitable, inaccessible and unexplored. As Malcom remarks: *The North is but one of the many distinct geographical regions that have made Canada what it is today—and kept it from being more.* Indeed, the tundra is so harsh that few animals or plants can survive. Nonetheless, the *Inuits,* as the "Eskimos" prefer to be called, have managed to endure in the frozen north for centuries. Perhaps, Malcom suggests, it has something to do with their rather unique perspective, a perspective that can best be summed up by their word *ionumut,* which means "It can't be helped."

Although most Canadians never confront the hard realities of the Inuits, many have learned to accept a degree of isolation and self-sufficiency that would be unthinkable to most Westerners. As a result, perhaps, Canadians tend to identify themselves *regionally* rather than *nationally,* and, though they love their country, they generally disdain the displays of "patriotism and loud bragging" that might be seen in, say, the United States. Also in stark contrast to its neighbor to the south, Canada does not think of itself so much as a "melting pot" for its myriad immigrants than as "a mosaic of separate pieces with each chunk becoming part of the whole physically but retaining its own separate color and identity."

Thus, while Quebec's separatist impulses may not be applauded, it is tolerated. Toronto, in fact, acquiesces to the demands of its many ethnic groups by sending out tax statements in English, French, Chinese, Italian, Greek and Portuguese. Similarly, Newfoundland, which did not join Canada until 1949, enjoys a unique set of traditions and a "distinctive Irish flavored English" that refuses to give way to any form of "Canadian" identity. As one journalist recently told a foreigner, "Oh, I'm not Canadian either. I'm from Newfoundland."

Of all Canadians, perhaps none is more endangered than the Inuits. Although they have adapted to their unforgiving terrain for millennia, they are losing their traditional means of subsistence and face potentially disastrous consequences. Television, in the minds of many, is to blame. Now living in houses and buying their food from stores, many young Inuits must not only be retrained in "survival skills" to avoid death in the Arctic, but they must also learn to develop a perspective on the images of urban life they see daily on the TV screens: "*They come in for the simple struggle of a nomadic life on the tundra*," one worried high school teacher told me in a cafeteria serving hot dogs, hamburgers, and a strange delicacy called carrots to children reared on seal and caribou, "*and they are exposed without any preparation to jiggling bosoms, talking horses, and colossal spaceship struggles for galactic dominance. If you're brought up with it, you can weed out the garbage. But if everything is a fantasy, how do you discern what is real and what values to embrace? It's a terribly disorienting for these kids.*"

Consequently, some Canadian schools have begun using television to help educate Inuit children. Teachers use sitcoms to analyze and question mainstream culture as well as generate discussion about traditional Inuit values. Of course, educators find they must also adjust to Inuit customs: classes, for instance, must be scheduled around Inuit "hunting patterns," and recess is often cancelled when polar bears encroach on the schoolyard.

In contrast to their Arctic countrymen, urban Canadians enjoy the same comforts and high standard of living as their American counterparts. Not only do they take pleasure in the "delightful and delicious ethnic diversity" of large cities like Toronto and Quebec, they also have a strong tradition in the arts. Some of North America's finest musicians, dancers, actors, writers and journalists are Canadian. Interestingly, however, while native Canadians such as Peter Jennings, Hume Cronyn, Colleen Dewhurst, Margaret Atwood and John Kenneth Galbraith are widely praised in the United States, Canadians often seem close-mouthed or even perturbed by the accomplishments of their countrymen. As Malcom contends: *It has often been true, especially to and for Canadians, that though famous in their own country, they did not really ever attain true fame until they had become widely known in the United States, where their fans or followers ignored their Canadianness. Then, by some perverse twist of the psyche, Canadians back home finally accepted them as worthy of note …*

Such attitudes, over time, seem to be changing. As Canada matures and Canadians become more appreciative of their richly diverse culture, they are rediscovering distinctively Canadian voices and images. Canadian arts are flourishing, while the "relics of the bad old days when being Canadian meant always having to say you were sorry" are rapidly vanishing.

Not surprisingly, then, Canada has strived to differentiate itself from the United States. According to Malcom, an essential aspect of "Canadian identity" is that they are not "Americans." Although Canadians enjoy a similar level of affluence and, at the same time, substantially lower crime rates and infant mortality, they nonetheless tend to feel "overwhelmed" by their southern neighbors. Despite its national sovereignty, Canada cannot help but be influenced by the economy, politics, defense strate-

gies and environmental policies of the United States: *The American influence is so widespread that American bashing is a frequent and often politically profitable phenomenon in Canada, requiring a certain sophistication that has not always been present among American politicians. They need to know when the tweaking of Uncle Sam's nose or the kicking of another anatomical part requires a response and when, being aired solely for domestic Canadian consumption, it had best be met by a dignified and possibly more powerful silence lest it seem to prove the point of American interference to no American advantage whatsoever.*

Given the "misunderstandings, frictions, and misinterpretations," Canada and the United States have enjoyed remarkably peaceful relations. The United States did invade Canada twice—once during the American Revolution and again during the War of 1812—but for the most part the twin giants have shared an "unusual closeness" predicated on respect and convenience. As Malcom notes: *Each country has provided an accommodating and familiar safety valve for the discontented of the other. Thus, many draftees fled to Canada during the Vietnam War, while many Canadians emigrated to the United States during the 1930s when the economy did not begin to improve in Canada as it had in the south.*

Now, Malcom asserts, the movement from north to south tends to take the form of "bilateral trade," which exceeds \$120 billion a year. Moreover, just as Americans have recognized for years that in North America the "natural market forces are north-south," Canadians themselves have recently begun to benefit from this realization.

According to Malcom, Canada's emergence has stimulated internal debate around "two broad areas": *the use of imagination and research and development (R&D), and changing the country's ties with the United States.* In terms of the first issue, Malcom writes that R&D has proved "a vital spark for future jobs and investments" and has helped to "spawn a kind of high-technology Silicon Valley North." As for its ties with the United States, the author observes that there is much dissent among Canadians. On the one hand, he notes, there is a reticence to identify too closely with the United States; as one Canadian professor expresses it, it's "[no] longer true that what is good for the United States is automatically good for Canada." On the other hand, there is a recognition that trade "is the fastest-growing element of the world's economy and that no two lands anywhere trade more than Canada and the United States [do]."

In Malcom's view, the two countries would do well to "face a hard fact": *With the import of trade rising in most domestic economies, magnifying the already intimate relationship of Canada and the United States, scarcely anything is domestic anymore. Virtually everything has an impact somehow on the other country, whether it is a winter frost in Florida that hikes the price of Canadian salads or a government drilling policy that boosts the costs of Canadian natural gas piped into midwestern American homes.*

FAMOUS LAST WORDS
by Barnaby Conrad, Doubleday & Company, Inc., 1961

One of the world's literary necrophilics, or "last-words" hobbyists, Barnaby Conrad offers his collection as a window into the lives and souls of their speakers. He remarks that "after reading thousands of deathbed utterances, one is struck and comforted by how comparatively pleasant dying is reported to be. Especially when compared with other ordeals. Such as living, for example."

This volume contains "byelines" that date from 600 B.C.E. to modern times. Many of the individuals are well known; some entirely unfamiliar. Yet their comments live on, evoking our compassion, our laughter, and our understanding. (For this summary, the book's "passing remarks" have been sorted into various categories.)

Heroic Last Words

Conrad notes that the dying often treat their own deaths or the plights of their loved ones heroically in their final words.

Abigail Adams (1744-1818)

While lying upon her deathbed, President John Adams' wife told her husband: "Do not grieve ... my dearest friend, I am ready to go, and—John, it will not be long."

Robert O'Hara Burke (1820-1861)

One of the first white men to explore the Australian continent, Burke died of starvation on his journey, after writing these words: *I hope we shall be done justice to. We have fulfilled our task, but ... we have not been followed up as we expected, and the depot party abandoned their post. King has behaved nobly. He stayed with me to the last, and placed the pistol in my hand, leaving me lying on the surface as I wished.*

John Calvin (1509-1564)

"Thou bruisest me, O Lord, but it is enough for me that it is Thy hand."

Saint Joan of Arc (1412-1431)

Burned at the stake for heresy, she said in her dying breath: "Ah, Rouen! I have great fear that you are going to suffer by my death ...! Jesus, Jesus!"

Affectionate Last Words

Tender souls, in spite of their suffering, prove their mettle to the very end.

Andrew Jackson (1767-1845)

The 7th President of the United States died surrounded by his family: "Oh, do not cry. Be good children, and we shall all meet in Heaven."

Arria, wife of Caecine Paetus (c. 42)

Commanded by the emperor to kill himself, the Roman hesitated. Instead, Arria snatched up the knife and plunged it into her own breast, saying, "Paetus, it doesn't hurt!"

Augustus Caesar (63 B.C.E.-A.C.E. 14)

"Live mindful of our wedlock, Livia, and farewell."

James, "The Just" (A.C.E. 62)

As the brother of Jesus was being stoned to death, he was said to cry out: "O Lord God, Father, I beseech Thee to forgive them, for they know not what they do."

Dutiful Last Words

At death's door, there are some who leave with their sense of duty and decorum intact.

Dominique Bouhours (1628-1702)

Bouhours was a grammarian to the end: "I am about to—or I am going to—die: either expression is used."

John Jay (1745-1829)

The American statesman died after a long life of public service. "I would have my funeral decent, but not ostentatious. No scarfs—no rings. Instead thereof, I give two hundred dollars to any one poor deserving widow or orphan of this town, whom my children may select."

Anna Pavlova (1885-1931)

The prima ballerina, most famous for the dance from *The Death of the Swan*, saw her own dying in terms of her art: "Get my 'Swan' costume ready!"

Commodore Isaac Hull (1773-1843)

Hearing that he would soon die, Hull summoned the undertaker, his lawyer, and his biographer. He calmly put his affairs in order and then said, "I strike my flag."

Humorous Last Words

Dying is serious business, yet some leave this life chuckling—or leave a smile on the faces of those left behind.

Anne Boleyn (1507-1536)

On the occasion of her execution, she said, "The executioner is, I believe, very expert; and my neck is very slender."

Baron Henry Richard Vassal Fox Holland (1773-1840)

The English Whig statesman said about George Selwyn, who enjoyed executions and corpses: "If Mr. Selwyn calls again, show him up; if I am alive I shall be delighted to see him, and if I am dead, he would like to see me."

Joel Chandler Harris (1848-1908)

Asked if his condition had improved any, the creator of the *Uncle Remus* stories replied, "I am about the extent of a tenth of a gnat's eyebrow better."

Agemore de Gasparin (1810-1871)

Gasparin's wife wished to follow her frail husband up the steps: "No, you know I like to have you go before me."

Ethan Allen (1739-1789)

When told by the parson that the angels were waiting, the former soldier shot back, "Waiting, are they? Waiting are they? Well, Goddamn 'em, let 'em wait!"

Comtesse de Versailles

In his *Confessions*, Rousseau described the Comtesse's aristocratic passing: "In the agonies of death she broke wind loudly. 'Good!' she said, turning around, 'a woman who can fart is not dead!'"

Henry Ward Beecher (1813-1887)

An energetic orator and preacher of exceptional vitality, Beecher, at 74, was a game patient. When the doctor asked him how high he could raise his arm, he replied, "Well, high enough to hit you, doctor."

A.E. Housman (1859-1936)

After receiving sedation, Housman listened to his doctor tell a risqué story and then said, "Yes, that's a good one, and tomorrow I shall be telling it on the Golden Floor."

Poignant Last Words

To the afflicted, death either comes as welcome relief or a time to reflect on lost opportunities.

John Keats (1795-1821)

After a long struggle with consumption, the great poet consoled his devoted friend: " … Lift me up, for I am dying. I shall die easy. Don't be frightened! Thank God it has come."

Queen Elizabeth I (1533-1603)

The queen silenced the Archbishop of Canterbury as he was enumerating her achievements: " … All my possessions for a moment of time."

Sir William Schwench Gilbert (1836-1911)

At the age of 75, Sir Arthur Sullivan's famed collaborator went for a swim in a lake with two young women. When one became frightened, Sir William swam to her saying, "Put your hands on my shoulders and don't struggle. Gilbert died immediately of a heart attack from the exertion, but the girl was saved."

Paul Gauguin (1848-1903)

The French impressionist, dying in the South Seas, appealed to a missionary: "Dear Monsieur Vernier, would it be troubling you too much to ask you to come to see me? My eyesight seems to be going and I cannot walk. I am very ill." Minutes later he was found dead.

Benjamin Franklin (1706-1790)

"Poor Richard" delivered his last aphorism when his daughter urged him to roll over so that he could breathe more easily. He responded, "A dying man can do nothing easy."

Chilling Last Words

Death delivers a deadline for regrets. Some, of course, do not give in to the promptings.

Carl Panzram (died 1930)

Prior to his execution, this murderer of 23 people replied when asked to pronounce his last words, "I wish the whole human race had one neck and I had my hands around it."

Michael Bestuzhev-Ryumin (died 1826)

A convicted Russian revolutionary, the first rope broke at his hanging, after which he said, "Nothing succeeds with me. Even here I meet with disappointment."

Profound Last Words

As in life, many world greats died pondering on the imponderables.

John Luther Jones (1864-1900)

On his gravestone, famous Casey Jones's last words appear: *To the memory of the locomotive engineer, who … as "Casey Jones" became part of folklore and the American language. "For I'm going to run her till she leaves the rail—or make it on time with the southbound mail."*

Charles Hodge (1797-1878)

The Presbyterian clergyman said to one of his children: "Why should you grieve, daughter? To be absent from the body is to be with the Lord, to be with the Lord is to see the Lord, to see the Lord is to be like Him."

Dr. Joseph Green (died 1873)

Looking up at his doctor, the renowned surgeon said, "Congestion." Then, taking his own pulse, he remarked, "Stopped," and died.

Anaxarchus (died c. 350 B.C.E.)

The Greek philosopher was bludgeoned to death, repeating the thought, "Pound, pound the pouch containing Anaxarchus; yet pound not Anaxarchus."

Leonardo da Vinci (1452-1519)

The gifted da Vinci died in the king's arms, saying, "I have offended God and mankind because my work did not reach the quality it should have."

Unspoken Last Words

If actions do speak louder than words, at death's door they become all the louder.

Wolfgang Amadeus Mozart (1756-1791)

Mozart's last act was an attempt to vocally reproduce the sounds of the drum in his great work in progress, *Requiem*.

Inspiring Last Words

The dying often speak sagaciously or enigmatically.

Marquis de Pierre Simon Laplace (1749-1827)

The French astronomer and mathematician's final comment was: "What we know is not much; what we do not know is immense."

Barnaby Conrad states that the best-known of all last words are from Thoreau. " … Asked whether he had made his peace with his God, [Thoreau] answered calmly that he was not really aware that they had ever quarreled."

And a final word from the author expresses his sorrow for the great last words that have never been remembered: "What pains me is to think of … all the touching or inspiring or illuminating last moments of the unfamous that have gone unrecorded."

100 EVENTS THAT SHAPED WORLD HISTORY
by Bill Yenne, Bellwood Books, 1993

When he set out to compile a list of 100 events that have significantly altered world history, Bill Yenne knew some would object to his choices. However, his purpose was not to argue the merits of each event but "to make history accessible—and fun." The result is a collection of readable, single-page "event summaries" that are both entertaining and informative.

The great events in Yenne's list involve fields as diverse as law, religion, science, politics, communications and ideas. Included are discussions of personalities such as Moses, Jesus, Buddha, Gutenberg, Genghis Khan, Newton and Einstein, as well as glimpses into world-altering "events" such as the Dark Ages, the plagues, the Renaissance, the Reformation, the discovery and development of the Americas, major world conflicts, and space travel. You are cordially invited to sample and savor them all in the complete work.

What follows is a scant version of Yenne's book. His self-imposed one-page limit and his chronological scheme force certain historical developments to show up in fragments. In the interest of space and continuity, some of his summaries have been recombined into a single review.

The Dawn of History

There was no particular moment when *prehistory* became *history*. Rather, it was a gradual process. There is evidence, writes Yenne, that humans lived on all continents at least 30,000 years ago. History began independently for each scattered group as they learned to communicate, then to tell stories; eventually the stories became legends, a kind of oral history. Although we have lost most of those early legends, a few remnants have been handed down to our day. "The dawn of history [began when] legends were first passed from one generation to the next."

Humans probably began banding together about 20,000 B.C.E., forming largely nomadic tribes. Then about 8000 B.C.E., people in the Middle East learned to cultivate fields and gardens and to herd sheep and cattle. It was there in ancient Mesopotamia that the first permanent cities were built. As these vestigial social units developed recognized sets of rules and traditions to govern themselves, the "Fertile Crescent" of land that arcs through present-day Iraq, Syria and southern Turkey between the Tigris and Euphrates rivers became the cradle of Western civilization.

The Written Word

Although humans were drawing pictures on rocks as early as 35,000 B.C.E., Yenne claims, it was not until about 3500 B.C.E. that the idea of developing a system of widely understood symbols, or letters, to represent speech and ideas was born. The first such phonetic alphabet was the cuneiform alphabet fostered by the ancient Sumerians. This system actually preceded Egyptian hieroglyphics, which used stylized pictures as symbols. The cuneiform alphabet was the forerunner of the Hebrew and Arabic alphabets, as well as those of the Romans and Greeks. The Roman alphabet forms the basis of most European alphabets of today, while the most profound influence on the Russian and Slavic alphabets was early Greek writing. Somewhat later, the Chinese picto-form alphabet was developed and became the cornerstone of other Asian alphabets.

The Might of Rome

"The *Roman Empire* was perhaps the most significant political entity in the history of the Western world ... " The city of Rome was supposedly named after *Romulus*, the mythical survivor of twins nursed by a wolf after a jealous relative threw them in the Tiber River. Around 750 B.C.E. Romulus or his counterparts founded Rome and began a policy of empire-building and annexing neighbors that lasted for a thousand years.

During the first 500 years, Rome consolidated its control over Italy; then it began looking west. The major power in the western Mediterranean was the city of Carthage on the north coast of Africa, founded in 814 B.C.E. by the Phoenicians. As Rome continued to expand its dominion, the two city-states collided, resulting in the three Punic Wars. The first (264-241 B.C.E.), won by Rome, was primarily a naval battle. During the second war (219-201 B.C.E.), however, the Carthaginian general Hannibal defeated Rome's allies in Spain, then crossed the Alps to win victories in northern Italy. But in his hasty assault, Hannibal was outflanked by the Roman general Scipio, who promptly turned to strike at Carthage itself. Hannibal returned to defend the city, but lost to Scipio on the Plain of Zama in 202 B.C.E.

The third war was comparatively anticlimactic. Rome remained a republic until 44 B.C.E. By that time the city-state had come to see itself as "having a 'manifest destiny' to subjugate and rule as much of the known world as possible." Leading a military campaign that captured what is now France, most of Britain and parts of Germany, General Julius Caesar returned to Rome with his army, deposed the chief consul, Pompey, and proclaimed himself absolute "dictator for life." Fourteen years later, after Julius Caesar's brutal assassination, his nephew Octavian accepted the title of "Emperor"—and became the illustrious Augustus Caesar.

Rome's rise to prominence and Julius Caesar's dreams of expanding the realm in the Mediterranean converged at a historical turning point. By the time of Caesar's death, he had transformed Rome, the first European superpower, into a true "empire."

The Code of Hammurabi and the Magna Carta

As the city-states of Mesopotamia and the great kingdoms of Egypt evolved, their citizens intermingled and old tribal customs gave way to social chaos. The need for some new, unifying order became crucial. Finally, during the reign of King Hammurabi of Babylon (1792-1750 B.C.E.), the first true legal code was written. The *Code of Hammurabi* was engraved on a slab of stone for all to read, and consisted of 282 laws denouncing specific crimes against man and state, and imposing penalties for each. The *Code* also stipulated Babylon's governmental structure and its religion, since the king was also the chief priest. Thus, the *Code of Hammurabi* represented the first time a subject people were allowed to hold a monarch accountable for his actions and demand that he rule by formal, accepted, published edicts rather than by his changing whims—a major milestone in the development of democratic civilization.

Much later, in 13th-century England, King John, described as "greedy, distrustful and incompetent" by all who knew him, held ultimate control over his subjects. John soon alienated the Pope, the commoners, and even his own nobles and land-owners. Finally, in 1215 these latter two groups united and sent John an ultimatum demanding that he agree to relinquish some control of the government to the tax-payers. Reluctantly, he thus signed this *Magna Carta* (literally, "Great Charter").

The *Magna Carta* recognized the rights of all "free" taxpaying citizens. Quickly it became the basis for the modern English legal system—and, eventually, legal systems worldwide—affording individuals rights to trial by jury and to a fair tax structure. Even more importantly, the *Magna Carta* established that kings were not above the law, but must ultimately answer to the people.

The document was further refined in 1679 when the English Parliament forced Charles II to accept the policy of *habeas corpus* ("you must have a *body of evidence*") as specific law. Thereafter, English courts had to possess reasonable evidence of wrongdoing before charging or jailing a person, and monarchs could no longer imprison anyone without demonstrable cause, a principle now embodied in most democratic governments.

The Decades of Discovery

Although Isaac Newton and others made a number of breakthroughs in basic science in the late 1600s, the major advances in applied science took place in the 19th century. In 1824 Joseph Niepce discovered that an image printed by the sun on a coating of silver chloride could be permanently fixed with other chemicals. The pictures produced by this technique he called heliotypes ("sun"-types). Niepce's partner Louis-Jacques-Mande Daguerre perfected the process in 1839 and called his pseudo-photographs *daguerreotypes*.

Then in 1879 inventor George Eastman found a way to mass produce photographic plates in quantity. Ten years later he was able to market strips of celluloid, or "rolls of film," inaugurating today's photographic wonders. Later, Friese-Greene of England and American Thomas Edison cultivated the concept of developing multiple images on a strip of film and then projecting a light through them. If the images were rolled past the light fast enough, the illusion of motion was reproduced on the screen. As early as 1895, the first "motion pictures" were shown in Paris.

In 1876, following the invention and implementation of Samuel Morse's Morse Code and Claude Chappe's high-speed telegraph system, Alexander Graham Bell demonstrated a device which electrically converted the human voice so that, like telegraph pulses, it could be transmitted over metal wires, then converted back to sound at the listener's end. Bell's patent application beat an independent competing application by only two hours, thus securing him credit as the inventor of the telephone system.

Later, in 1895, Guglielmo Marconi, employing Heinrich Hertz's discovery of radio waves eight years earlier, made possible the sending of wireless messages—which spawned the 20th-century's telecommunications boom.

The Fall of Soviet Communism

By 1990, with the dramatic fall of the Berlin Wall and the disbandment of the Polish Communist Party under Lech Walesa's *Solidarity* government, "a wind of change was blowing through Eastern Europe."

Several revolts attempted by Soviet satellites had, years earlier, already been violently crushed, and Stalin, Khrushchev and Brezhnev in turn had come and gone, each having ruled with an iron fist. The Afghan uprising of 1979, however, had added a terrible burden to the USSR's already mounting economic problems. Then in 1985 the new reform-minded Soviet president Mikhail Gorbachev promised the people a new system of government favoring *glasnost* (openness) and *perestroika* (restructuring). He also advocated greater autonomy for Eastern Europe, adding steam to the forces that were already splintering the Soviet Union. Gorbachev still hoped to hold the Union together; "however, Communism had already begun to crumble, and only the iron bands of totalitarianism held the pieces in place." Now as these bonds were loosened, the 15 satellite republics spun out of Soviet control.

Thus ended a 70-year experiment in expansionist centralized totalitarianism; and thus also ended an imposed world order. In the international and regional confusion that has manifested itself since the breakup of the Soviet Union, it remains to be seen what direction the world will take next from this latest historical turning point.

In *The March of Folly*, Barbara Tuchman treats a disturbing pattern in human history: folly in government. She defines her topic as "the pursuit by governments of policies contrary to their own interests, despite the availability of feasible alternatives." Moreover, says Tuchman, a policy must be deemed *folly in its own time*—because "nothing is more unfair than to judge men of the past by the ideas of the present."

To further expand her definition, Tuchman poses the question: *Why does governmental folly so often prevail over common sense?* She subsequently supports this premise through many historical examples of indecision, indiscretion, and recklessness.

The foolhardiness of Israel's King Rehoboam, for instance, divided the nation in two. When his people demanded that he ease the burden of forced labor, Rehoboam instead listened to his counselors' advice to heap additional abuses upon the people. Israel immediately seceded from the House of David, leaving Rehoboam to rule over Judah to the north. In response, the King declared war on his former subjects in hopes of reuniting the tribes of Israel. Instead the Israelites, reduced and divided, were conquered by the Assyrians and driven from their land.

The conquest of Mexico was also based on folly. Because the Aztec ruler Montezuma believed that the Spaniards were supernatural beings who had accompanied the god Quetzalxoatl to Mexico, he inadvertently invited the Spaniards to seize control of his kingdom. Although many Aztecs warned Montezuma that the Spaniards were not gods but altogether human, he ignored his people's counsel—and the invaders moved in to crush the native cultures. Perceived as a coward and a traitor, Montezuma was subsequently assassinated by his subjects. Still, his error in judgment has remained one of the costliest in history.

Another prime example of folly was Japan's World War II bombing of Pearl Harbor. Despite many warnings and the knowledge that a war with United States would probably occasion their defeat, the Japanese decided to attack the U.S. Pacific Fleet. Blinded by dreams of creating a Japanese empire, Emperor Hirohito apparently became incensed by the United States' refusal to make raw materials available to his country. Japanese leaders reasoned that in order to ensure unrestricted transport of such materials, it would be necessary to remove the threat of U.S. naval action in the Pacific. Clearly, Hirohito never stopped to consider that an attack on American territory would instead push the U.S. into full-blown combat.

"The ultimate outcome of a policy is not what determines its qualification as folly," Tuchman emphasizes. "It qualifies as folly when it is a perverse persistence in a policy demonstrably unworkable or counterproductive." To demonstrate that poor decision-making has existed throughout history as a persistent attribute of government, she spotlights four major world events.

The Trojans Take the Wooden Horse Within Their Walls

The legend of the Wooden Horse may or may not be historically accurate; nevertheless, it is one of the most famous stories of the Western world. Because of its significance to Western civilization and its reflection on human judgment, the sacking of Troy is a uniquely important example of folly.

Why would the Trojan commanders opt to bring a suspicious-looking wooden horse into their city while they were at war? Indeed, Trojan King Priam mocked those of his courtiers who advised him to destroy the horse, and instead brought it inside the city gates. Then, while the Trojans slept, Greek troops who had hidden themselves inside the structure crept out and laid siege to the city.

Tuchman attempts to put Troy's lesson into perspective: *Although the gods are its motivators, what [the tale of Troy] tells us about humanity is basic.... It has endured deep in our minds and memories for twenty-eight centuries because it speaks to us of ourselves, not least when least rational.*

The Renaissance Popes Provoke the Protestant Secession

The Popes of the Renaissance era enjoyed great authority throughout most of Europe. Although the six Popes who reigned between 1470 and 1530 were extremely corrupt and perverse, they were nevertheless responsible for some remarkable undertakings, such as uncovering classical treasures, paving roads, assembling the Vatican library, and rebuilding St. Peter's Cathedral. And indeed the Popes were by no means the only decadent Renaissance rogues. Still, if the Popes had not made such a public display of scandal and corruption, the cry for reform would have been far more subdued.

As it was, Popes Alexander VI and Innocent VIII kept mistresses and sired many illegitimate children. But these indiscretions did not bother their followers nearly as much as the Popes' continual military rampages, lootings, tortures, executions, and their obsession with luxurious garments and jewels, the combined effect of which nearly drained the whole of the papal revenues.

Later, by the time Leo X was made Pope, the Church was focusing its attention on making money. "God has given us the Papacy, let us enjoy it," Leo cackled. His favorite way to acquire wealth was by selling indulgences: partial remissions of God's temporal punishments. Although indulgences were not invented by Leo, he popularized the belief that by purchasing indulgences individuals could both atone for future sins and reduce the time their souls spent in Purgatory.

When Leo later authorized the sale of indulgences in Germany, he scoffed at the objections he received. Finally, after Leo had excommunicated many of his German detractors, Martin Luther led the "protestants" to an eventual break from Catholicism.

The Renaissance Popes, says Tuchman, thus displayed a persistent folly in that they were "deaf to disaffection, blind to the alternative ideas it gave rise to, blandly impervious to challenge, unconcerned by the dismay at their misconduct and the rising wrath at their misgovernment, fixed in refusal to change, almost stupidly stubborn in maintaining a corrupt existing system. They could not change it because they were part of it, grew out of it, depended on it."

The British Lose America

Why did King George III insist on trying to force the American colonists into submission, even when cautioned that the harm would outweigh any conceivable gain? Britain sought to maintain its sovereign status in America, and as such, believed it had the right to tax the colonists. The colonies, however, rejected the idea of taxation without representation; since they were denied any seats in Parliament, Britain had no right to tax them.

Taxation, then, was forced on the colonists. Then when the 1765 British Stamp Act was levied, requiring that colonists affix revenue stamps to all official documents, they rebelled. Although King George was fully aware that America yearned for greater independence and less interference, he was not about to bend.

While most colonists had never contemplated rebellion or separation, a decade of provocation from Britain caused them to rethink their position. George responded by immediately calling for a declaration of rebellion to "force those deluded people into submission," disregarding recurrent advice to send a peace commission to America, withdraw troops, recognize independence, and try to maintain rapport. Despite the fact that both Parliament and the British public protested sending a militia to quell the uprising, the King persisted, sensing the loss of America would bring him shame and ruin. As Tuchman points out: *If the British actors before and after 1775 had been other than they were, there might have been statesmanship instead of folly, with a train of altered consequences reaching to the present. The hypothetical has charm, but the actuality of government makes history.*

America Betrays Herself in Vietnam

One of America's own lessons in folly took place in Vietnam shortly after World War II. When President Franklin D. Roosevelt chose to help the French reestablish their colonial rule in Vietnam, he miscalculated the depth of commitment to self-rule of that country's citizens, believing that the Vietnamese would not be ready for self-rule until they were tutored by a democratic nation.

As French involvement increased, various resistance groups arose in Indochina, and the Indochinese Communist Party eventually took control of the scattered independence movement. Now under a consolidated power, the Communists declared that they would take up arms to win their autonomy. Roosevelt was disturbed that an anti-interference party had been formed, but was thoroughly infuriated that it was a *Communist-based* party. Washington thus intensified its efforts to help France retain power in Vietnam.

Later, during the late 1940s, Roosevelt's successor Harry Truman came up with the theory that any Communist movement in Indochina actually reflected a Soviet conspiracy to take over the world. In an attempt to squelch this plot, he gave France $10 million in military aid and urged the French to continue to maintain forces in Vietnam. Backed by Truman's guarantees that he was acting in their best interests, Americans soon became convinced that French victory was "essential to the security of the free world." The United States armed forces, meanwhile, took a passive stance. Even as the Soviets moved in to crush Hungary and assumed political jurisdiction of nearby Cuba, America minimized the danger: a band of Communists in faraway Vietnam did not pose a threat to American security.

Why didn't the American government learn from the French army and Foreign Legion's defeat at the hands of small companies of Asian guerrilla soldiers? Why did the government ignore French general Charles de Gaulle's advice that negotiation was the only path to victory, and that a war in Vietnam could not be won? According to President John Kennedy—who inherited the Vietnam impasse in 1961—the French and American struggles in Vietnam differed in that the French "were fighting for a colony, for an ignoble cause, [whereas] we're fighting for freedom, to free them from the Communists, from China, for their independence."

By 1963, America was fully involved in an undeclared war in Vietnam, and by the time Richard Nixon took office, public support for the conflict had dwindled. Indeed, the war's purpose was unclear to most Americans. In spite of urgings from Nixon's top advisors to find alternative solutions to end the war, Nixon—even as his predecessors had done—challenged conventional wisdom. Why did some of America's best minds underestimate the determination of Vietnam to resist foreign intervention? Ultimately, who or what was to blame? "Not ignorance," answers Tuchman, "but refusal to credit the evidence and ... refusal to grant stature and fixed purpose to a 'fourth-rate' Asiatic country were the determining factors, much as in the case of the British attitude toward the American colonies. The irony of history is inexorable."

Clearly, in the case of Vietnam, possible losses and possible gains were not properly calculated. "Human casualties are bearable when they are believed to have served a purpose," Tuchman writes. "[However], they are bitter when, as in this case, 45,000 killed and 300,000 wounded were sacrificed for nothing." The misfortune for America, she believes, was the absence of a leader who had the courage to end the Vietnam War.

Still, even today, the march of folly persists. It is, though, perhaps only in hindsight that we can realize how truly foolish governments can be. *The March of Folly* thus reveals far more than a few accounts of senseless choices; Tuchman's book leaves us wondering why we do not learn from history—and if we ever will.

*M*en have always liked to believe in their own influence and direction in the course of time. These claims, however, sometimes conceal the truth. This book is about an unexpected source of change, which has hitherto been obscured because man has been looking too closely at his fellow men ...

Scholars have long recognized the impact of crop failures and the rise of new crops on world history, but they have not always appreciated the full scope of that impact. Now, after meticulously studying 80 separate plants, Henry Hobhouse has identified five which have clearly changed the course of world events: quinine, sugar cane, tea, cotton and the potato.

Quinine

Malaria, a disease common to many parts of the world, is caused by a parasite transmitted by the *anopheles* mosquito. After the mosquito bites a victim, the parasite travels to the liver and damages the blood's red corpuscles. Fever, weakness and death often follow.

In ancient times the concentration of people in cities near mosquito habitats led to the infection of whole civilizations. Malaria was also a major player in dictating the outcomes of wars: before World War I, more soldiers died of malaria than died in combat.

There is a story told that in 1638 the wife of the Spanish viceroy in Lima, Peru lay critically ill with malaria. A desperate physician finally tried a native cure containing the bark—or "kina," in the local Quechua language—of the cinchona tree. The wife was miraculously healed, and she and the physician later carried the cure back to Spain, where it was soon hailed as the wonder drug of the age.

Elements of this story may be fictional, but cinchona bark did become a major new trading commodity during the mid 1600s. Because harvesting the bark usually killed the tree, over time the high demand for the new product—by now known in English as *quinine*—threatened to eliminate its source. The British were particularly concerned about this scarcity because of debilitating malarial outbreaks in their Indian colonies. Then in the 1860s British adventurer Clement Markham managed to bring a few cinchona plants from war-torn South America to England. Samples were also transported to India, where a Scottish gardener named McIvor found a way to harvest an annual crop from the trees without destroying them. The Dutch also began cultivating cinchona plantations.

The search for a chemical substitute for quinine began in 1834, with research efforts concentrated in England and Germany. By 1940 an artificial quinine had been developed from coal tar; it soon became one of the underpinnings of German industry.

Without quinine, India would still be an underpopulated country. What's more, the industrial development of much of the world in the 19th and 20th centuries has been based on cheap Oriental labor—a force that would have been vastly weakened without quinine. And finally, without artificial quinine for the Allied troops in Asia, Japan probably would have prevailed in World War II.

The triumphant success of quinine, clearly one of the pivotal plants of world history, leads one to ponder what other potential wonder drugs are being destroyed right now with the rapid destruction of the Amazon rain forest.

Sugar Cane

Sugar cane is a grass native to Polynesia, but apparently roots of the plant washed up and flourished on other tropical shores. It was first refined for its sugar content in India about 700 B.C.E. Over the next 2,000 years the demand for the substance—which many considered to hold magical properties—grew steadily, particularly in cold countries where grapes, with their natural sweetness, were not available. The value of sugar also expanded with the growth of bitter hot drinks—coffee, tea, chocolate—that required a sweetener to make them palatable. But Hobhouse argues that the dominant factor in the growing demand for refined sugar is its addictive power.

Extra energy is produced in a sudden flood when refined sugar is ingested, and demands on the digestive system are lessened. This means that enzymes needed to break down more complex, natural foods are not produced, so the stomach has more difficulty digesting them. As a consequence, fewer nutrients are absorbed and ever greater quantities of sugar are required to boost energy. Since the "sugar addict's" blood-level rises and falls rapidly with the intake of sugar, frequent reinforcement is necessary, spawning a craving "which is chemical, not psychological," claims Hobhouse. After illegal drugs, tobacco and alcohol, sugar "is the most damaging addictive substance ..."

But even worse than the impact of refined sugar on the individual human body has been its impact on society. Soon after Columbus's voyages, sugar cane became the crop of choice in the Caribbean, which by 1800 boasted 80% of the world's sugar production—not to mention 80% of the world's slave trade. As a labor-intensive crop during both planting and harvesting, sugar cane required many workers to supply enough of the commodity to meet demands. Whole tribes of Native Americans in the area resisted slavery—and died for their defiance. Africans were brought in, and soon the black slave trade became big business. "It was ... the first time in history that one race had been uniquely selected for a servile role." An estimated 10 million African slaves were imported to the New World in the 1700s alone; five to ten million more died en route. For the most part, slaves didn't live long in sugar production; about ten percent of the labor force had to be replaced every year.

By the early 1800s there was growing opposition to the slave trade among civilized societies. About the same time, the cultivation of sugar beets in temperate countries aided in the decline of sugar cane production. Yet the tragic effects on the black race had already taken their inestimable toll. "It will take many generations to build the ... sense of community [in the old slave-colony countries] that the humblest African peasant takes for granted," Hobhouse contends.

Tea

In the 1700s, fifty tons of tea were being imported annually to England; by 1800 the amount had increased to 15,000 tons a year. In the decade between 1830 and 1840 alone, tea exports from China averaged over 100,000 tons, worth about $3 billion in today's dollars. Smuggled, non-taxed tea imports may actually have doubled these numbers.

Tea is a product with more bulk than weight. The shippers hauling it needed to put their valuable cargo in the middle of the holds to keep it from water leakage and spray; the light weight of the tea, however, required that something heavier be used for ballast—preferably another marketable commodity. Fine Chinese porcelain, or "China," which was nearly as precious as the tea, soon became the product of choice.

At first the tea and china were paid for mostly with gold, silver and copper. But as European wars created inflationary conditions, the costs of tea traders rose more rapidly than their revenues. In a bid to balance the books, opium was soon seen as a viable, though illegal, trade substitute. Since the profitability of the trade was great, both Chinese and European sovereigns looked the other way.

Thus, "for a pot of tea ... Chinese culture was nearly destroyed." According to Hobhouse, it remains to be seen whether the present Chinese government can restore the lost vitality of a brilliant civilization. (It is interesting to note that Japan separated itself from the opium trade and progressed at a time when China and India declined in influence.)

Cotton

Cotton cloth appears to have originated in what is now Pakistan; it appeared in Europe during the 10th century, but remained a rare though highly coveted fabric. Then at the beginning of the 19th century the American South, putting Eli Whitney's newly invented cotton gin to use, captured the bulk of the market for its vast network of plantations. As a result, cotton became king.

Most cotton weaving was done in the north of England, where the high value of the cloth inspired the invention of machines to speed up the work. The resulting Industrial Revolution, for all its benefits, soon obliterated the old cottage weaving industry and left the new class of British mill and factory workers in an even worse condition than many black American slaves.

But American slaves also suffered from the Industrial Revolution and the expanding cotton market. Before the cotton boom, land owners had worked beside their slaves under reasonably good conditions. With the founding of huge plantations, however, owners left the control of their slaves to often brutal overseers.

After the importing of slaves was banned in 1834, American slave-owners turned to slave breeding to resupply their workforce. Meanwhile, several serious efforts to free the slaves foundered on the problem of

how or whether to compensate the owners for their very valuable "property." It finally took a devastating war, and a million casualties, to free four million Negro slaves.

The Potato

The white potato originated in the highlands of the Andes Mountains and was probably brought to Britain by Sir Francis Drake about 1586. For most Europeans, potatoes soon became just another garden crop.

But not in Ireland; there the potato was seen as a heaven-sent answer to the challenges of the land. Unlike grain crops, potatoes flourished in Ireland's mineral-poor soil. Furthermore, growing a potato crop took only ten to fifteen weeks a year. And the Irish people prospered.

Between 1760 and 1840, Ireland's population grew from 1.5 million to 9 million, a six-fold increase. But this phenomenal expansion only set the stage for disaster. In 1845-46 the great Irish potato blight struck, and for several years after potato crops were utterly ruined. About one million people died of starvation and malnutrition, and there followed great waves of emigration; by the commencement of World War I, a total of five and a half million Irish citizens had fled the island.

The British occupiers of Ireland reacted to this tragedy with massive indifference. "It is not unreasonable to share the Irish peasant's loathing of the English reaction ... " Hobhouse writes. "They wanted food, they got words; they wanted work, they got eviction. Ireland needed investment; the island was told to look after its own poor.... Soon, in some areas, there were not enough living to bury the dead."

When Irish immigrants flooded to America (in some cities making up 30% of the population), they brought their anti-English sentiments with them, eventually swaying much of American policy and profoundly altering much of recent history. Had the United States and England stood united, arm in arm against aggression in other parts of the world, Hobhouse contends, two catastrophic world wars that shaped the 20th century might have been avoided.

In *Seeds of Change* Hobhouse has woven strands of data collected from agriculture, economics, history and other disciplines into a fascinating real-life, worldwide detective saga. But in the end, this book is not only about the influence of a small assortment of crop plants on the fortunes and failures of civilization; it is about the impact of our human choice on human destiny.

Even if readers take the stance that history is ruled by economics, and that nations and individuals must inevitably act to promote their own gain, it is easy to see that both 19th-century slave-breeders in the American South and self-serving Chinese sovereigns who "looked the other way" during the heyday of the opium trade were taking a disastrously shortsighted view.

Those of us in today's world, faced with unprecedented potential for both the enhancement and the annihilation of human life, *Seeds of Change* and books like it can help in the urgent search for answers to the age-old human question, "What shall we do?"

DISEASE AND HISTORY
by Frederick Cartwright, in collaboration with Michael D. Bidiss, Dorset Press, 1972

In *Disease and History*, Frederick Cartwright and Michael Bidiss succeed in making the connection between disease and historical change, arguing that disease may have altered the course of history by influencing significant world events. Theirs is a unique perspective, and within it they raise some interesting questions: Was plague more destructive to the Roman Empire than invading armies? Was the Black Death responsible for ending feudalism? Did syphilis turn Ivan the Terrible into a savage tyrant? Did typhus destroy Napoleon's empire? Was smallpox partially to blame for helping the Spaniards defeat the Aztecs? "The ills that have plagued man," the authors write, "are as much a part of their civilization as are their prevention and cure."

Disease in the Ancient World

One of the most significant events in history was the fall of the Roman Empire, and, insist the authors, one of the major contributors to its downfall was plague. The early Romans had developed a system of public health and sanitation that remained unequaled until the middle of the 19th century. Aqueducts brought pure water into the city, public lavatories were plentiful, daily personal hygiene was an everyday part of life, government regulations saw to the freshness of perishable foodstuffs, and cremation instead of burial was almost exclusively practiced. However, though Romans were clean, they did not know the cause of disease, and therefore had no way of protecting themselves from it.

At its height, "all roads led to Rome." Stretching from the Sahara to Scotland and from the Caspian Sea to Portugal, the Empire's numerous sea routes and roads also ended up serving as the highways for disease, the authors insist. For example, in the first century B.C.E. a severe variety of malaria first appeared in Rome and remained for 500 years, killing hundreds of thousands. In the year125 the plague of Orosius sent so many people to their graves that whole villages and towns had to be abandoned. The plague of Justinian soon followed, daily killing some 10,000 people; so many died that ships were often loaded with bodies and abandoned at sea. "When we consider the frightful sequence of pestilence that smote the empire ... " the Cartwright and Bidiss note, "we need hardly search for a more potent cause of disaster."

While the plagues of the first three centuries almost certainly contributed to the Empire's decline, they also helped Christianity establish itself as a world force. Christianity could not have succeeded at that time had Rome not been ravaged by disease. The new religion, with its belief in a life after death and its claim to healing powers, offered hope to the victims of plague, rapidly swelling the religion's ranks.

The Black Death

The Black Death was a worldwide pandemic, reaching southward into Africa, northward to Scandinavia and Russia, and eastward to China. The tendency today is to assume that an outbreak of such a nature and on such an expansive scale "just cannot have happened." Italian humanist-poet Petrarch, who lived in France while the Death ravaged Europe, prophetically wrote that future generations would "not believe, could not imagine the towns and fields littered with the dead."

The Black Death was a pneumonic type of bubonic plague which could be spread by fleas from rats as well as by breath and saliva. It probably first broke out on the Crimean shore of the Black Sea, then spread east into Russia, India and China. It finally reached Italy through trade and quickly spread throughout Europe, reaching Moscow in 1352. Historians estimate that some 24 million people were exterminated.

The Black Death affected world history in at least two ways. First, it forced peasant laborers in England to become mobile, bringing an end to the already weak feudal system. Second, ships from the ravaged Scandinavian countries carried the plague to Viking settlements in Greenland. There, the inhabitants transported the disease to the coast of Canada, where the plague likely had a deadly impact and completely changed the early history of North America. "The Black Death was not just another incident in the long list of epidemics which have smitten the world. It was probably the greatest European catastrophe in history."

The Mystery of Syphilis

A puzzling question in medical history is how and why syphilis suddenly appeared in Europe at the end of the 15th century. One theory holds that it derived from the African *yaws*, a skin disease indistinguishable from syphilis. Yaws, the theory continues, after it was brought to Spain and Portugal through slave trade, underwent a transformation from the non-venereal variety to the syphilis we know today.

When the disease first emerged in Europe, it was much more virulent than it is now. Indeed, syphilis devastated Europe, and millions suffered, both directly and indirectly. One of the most intriguing, well-documented and far-reaching cases is that of Ivan the Terrible. When at age 17 he first became the Russian czar in 1547, he established a judicious legal code, reformed the all-powerful Church, banished oppressive nobles and instituted freedom of speech. Unfortunately for Ivan—and for Russia—he soon began to suffer from cerebral syphilis, and the savage tyranny began. Brain damage led to fits of insanity during which he routinely had people flogged, tortured, burned, boiled, roasted over slow fires and pushed under lake ice. In one such episode, he even slaughtered his own son. Thousands of Russians died under Ivan's demented direction, and Cartwright and Bidiss argue that, as the disease dragged Ivan slowly down to paralysis and eventual death, millions of Russians were affected. In the end, the authors say, "it is possible that Russian history was radically changed by

Ivan's failure to pursue the comparatively liberal and almost benevolent policy of his opening years."

General Napoleon and General Typhus

Napoleon's armies made up the greatest fighting force since Rome, helping him conquer all of Europe except Britain. Napoleon's power, however, was finally brought to ruin in 1812 with the destruction of his Grand Army. And, Cartwright and Bidiss suggest, Napoleon's primary adversary was not Wellington, but rather typhus.

Typhus, which is transmitted via body lice, became Napoleon's most formidable foe not long after he opted to invade Russia. Everything went as planned for the 600,000 invading troops, until they reached Poland. There, in close, unsanitary quarters, many were quickly infected by the typhus bacteria. Forced into retreat by the combination of cold, hunger, Russian insurgents and typhus, when it was all over, less than 40,000 men were left standing. One can only imagine what would have become of Europe and the rest of the world if Napoleon had fulfilled his dreams. Instead, "his Grand Army was destroyed by his own impatience and by the ill-luck of encountering typhus fever, and his empire never recovered from the destruction of that army."

The Impact of Infectious Diseases

Diseases that have become tamed in civilized communities are generally lethal when introduced to distant peoples by explorers, missionaries or traders. One such disease is smallpox, which had vexed Europe, Asia and Africa since the 10th century. Primarily a childhood disease in Europe, when smallpox was introduced to a new community, it was found to affect individuals of all ages.

In the early 16th century, after Spain had already established colonies in the West Indies, Hernando Cortez and his crew disembarked on the coast of the Yucatan peninsula, bringing with them smallpox, mumps and measles. Within six months almost every village of New Spain was suffering the effects of one or more of the maladies. By the time Cortez defeated the Aztecs in 1519, nearly half of Mexico's indigenous population had been infected. "There is no doubt," the authors insist, "that imported disease played as great a part as the Spanish conquerors in the destruction of the Aztec race, if not a greater one."

Queen Victoria and the Fall of the Russian Monarchy

In a sense, Cartwright and Bidiss argue, Queen Victoria was indirectly responsible for destroying the House of Romanov and bringing Lenin and the Bolsheviks to power in Russia. Victoria carried the gene for hemophilia, a disease that manifests itself in males and is induced by the lack of a clotting-agent protein in the liquid part of the blood. A hemophiliac may bleed to death if inflicted with even the most minor of injuries.

Victoria's daughter, Alice, and her granddaughter, Alix, both inherited the gene for hemophilia. Alix

married Nicholas II, who became Czar of Russia, and they had one son and heir to the throne, Alexis, a victim of hemophilia. In the beginning of his reign, Nicholas was determined to uphold his autonomy, but after the near revolution of 1905, the Russians formed a parliamentary government called the Duma and presented Czar Nicholas, Alexis's father, with a compromise: they agreed to retain the Czardom only if Nicholas abdicated the throne in favor of his son, who would become a constitutional monarch under the tutelage of the Duma. Balking at the prospect of being parted with his all son, Nicholas refused the terms.

At this time, anarchy and disillusionment spread among the Russians. Frequent famine led to a bread riot, which quickly escalated into a revolution led by the Bolshevik party, who rose up and began executing the imperial family. As Cartwright and Bidiss point out, one can only speculate what course Russian history might have taken had Nicholas consented to the Duma's terms. The authors examine the myriad possibilities: *A young, helpless boy might have inspired sympathy, might have formed a rallying point and allowed the shaken Russian people to regain equilibrium. Russia might conceivably have rallied around her young [Czar]; then the history of the world would have been very different.*

Man-made Problems of the Present and Future

"A great part of our civilized life depends upon the addition of amenities (technological advances), [and] very few of these amenities are entirely innocuous," note the authors. To prove their point, they cite the drug thalidomide, a common sedative administered to pregnant women during the early 1960s, which was later found to cause birth defects. In this case, the cure, while temporarily serving humanity's purposes, proved worse than the symptom.

For thousands of years man had no knowledge of the cause of disease, and therefore no means to cure it. He accepted that out of one thousand children, 250 would die within the first year of life; it was common knowledge that an adult could not live beyond the age of 40. By the middle of the 19th century, however, man had gained a better knowledge of bacteria and thus could experiment in preventing and curing some diseases.

With rising life spans, populations shot upward. Between 1300 and 1750, Europe's population went from 80 to 150 million; in the following century, another 115 million were added. Since then, world population has increased at an astronomical rate. The authors thus end with an ominous warning: *Medicine, social, therapeutic, and preventive, has given the human race opportunities for a longer and more healthy life. It has enabled the world population to expand. In doing so, it has brought problems which may be insoluble. Advancing technology has given us comforts and amenities undreamed of two centuries ago. In doing so, it has brought problems which also may be insoluble.... The solution will lie in the hands of one or all of man's age-old enemies, Famine, Pestilence, and War.*

THE RISE AND FALL OF THE GREAT POWERS
by Paul Kennedy, Random House, Inc., 1987

*W*hy is it that throughout history some nations gain power while others lose it? To answer this question, historian Paul Kennedy examines nearly half a millennium of history from 1500 to the early 1980s, tracing what he calls a recurrent "pattern" according to which "victory went to the economically strong side, while states that were militarily top-heavy usually crashed to eventual defeat."

As Kennedy contends: *The triumph of any one Great Power ... or the collapse of another, has usually been the consequence of lengthy fighting by its armed forces; but it has also been the consequence of the more or less efficient utilization of the state's productive economic resources in wartime, and further in the background, in the way in which that state's economy had been rising or falling, relative to the other leading nations in the decades preceding the actual conflict. For that reason, how a Great Power's position steadily alters in peacetime is as important to this study as how it fights in wartime.*

The Rise and Fall In the East

The widely held image of extensive eastern empires possessing fabulous wealth and vast armies was a reasonably accurate one ... and [their populations] seemed far more favorably endowed than the peoples of the states of western Europe. Among all of the great pre-modern civilizations, according to Kennedy, "none appeared more advanced ... felt more superior, than that of China." Its population in the 1500s ranged from 100 million to 130 million in contrast to Europe's 50 to 55 million. Moreover, China boasted a highly refined culture, a "unified hierarchic administration," large cities, huge libraries, sophisticated technologies and agricultural methods. But China remained isolated, preoccupied with preserving and recapturing the past; creating a future based on foreign trade hardly entered their minds.

In contrast, the Ottoman Empire, which ruled over large parts of the Middle East as well as territories in Europe beginning in the 10th century, was intent upon conquering new lands. The Muslims posed a substantial threat to the Christians, who hoped to gain access to regions in India and Africa that ultimately became Islamic. Nevertheless, the Ottoman Empire began to suffer from "strategic overextension, with a large army stationed in central Europe, an expensive navy operating in the Mediterranean, troops engaged in North Africa, the Aegean, Cyprus, and the Red Sea, and reinforcements needed to hold a rising Russian power." The Ottoman Empire consequently began "to falter, to turn inward," as the Chinese had done, and finally "to lose the chance of world domination."

The Mogul Empire likewise deteriorated from within. Although enormously wealthy and strategically astute, the Moguls, starting with the Mongol Genghis Khan in 1526, became notoriously decadent: *The brilliant courts were centers of conspicuous consumption which the Sun King at Versailles might have thought excessive. Thousands of servants and hangers-on, extravagant clothes* and jewels and harems and menageries, vast arrays of bodyguards, could be paid for only by the creation of a systematic plunder machine. Tax collectors, required to provide fixed sums for their masters, preyed mercilessly upon peasant and merchant alike; whatever the state of the harvest or trade, the money had to come in.

As Mogul reign extended throughout India, the Empire, during the late 17th and the 18th centuries, declined in power in the face of opposition from Hindus and of European commercial expansion. Even while the Mogul Empire foundered, both Japan and Russia demonstrated signs of "political consolidation" and economic growth. In Japan, "nationwide peace was good for trade ... and the increasing use of cash payments made merchants and bankers more important." They were not, however, permitted "social and political prominence" and thus had no access to the "new technological and industrial developments that were occurring elsewhere." Like China, Japan "deliberately chose ... to cut itself off from the world."

In its early beginnings, Russia was similar to Japan. Both countries remained aloof from the West, although Western realms consistently challenged both countries' military expansionism. But unlike Japan, Russia was "economically underdeveloped" and encompassed a vast region inhabited by a number of different tribes. Compounding Russia's problems were "severe social defects: the military absolutism of the czars, the monopoly of education in the hands of the Orthodox Church ... and the institution of serfdom, which made agriculture feudal and static." These problems, though, did not keep Russia from acquiring new lands and "imposing upon its new territories the same military force and autocratic rule which was used to command the obedience of the Muscovites."

The Rise and Fall In the West

Kennedy asks: *Why was it among the scattered and relatively unsophisticated peoples inhabiting the western parts of the Eurasian landmass, that there occurred an unstoppable process of economic development and technological innovation which would steadily make it the commercial and military leader in world affairs?* Sixteenth-century Europe's weaknesses were actually more apparent than its strengths. For instance, geopolitically speaking, the continent of Europe was quite "vulnerable." Yet, unencumbered by a "centralized authority and unilateral thinking"—hindrances that checked the economic growth and political diversity of other powers during this time period—"Europe's greatest advantage was that it had fewer disadvantages than the other civilizations." Playing on its economic, technological and military strengths, Europe eventually assumed world leadership.

Consistent with the prevailing patterns of struggle for world dominance, Europe's authority did not go uncontested. With the advent of Martin Luther's "revolt against papal indulgences," Europe became a "continent with large numbers ... drawn into a *transnational* struggle over religious doctrine ... and as a consequence, it became virtually impossible to separate the power-political from the religious strands of the European rivalries which racked the continent during this period." The major threat to peace in the region was the "Habsburg bid for mastery." The Habsburgs, a prominent European royal family/dynasty originating in Switzerland during the 10th century, had gained the imperial title and subsequent power through a series of advantageous "dynastic marriages," inheritances, and papal endowments. However, overextended by military conquests, the wealth of the Habsburg dynasty gradually dissolved—as did their power.

As Habsburg influence crumbled, various European states, step-by-step, evolved into "Great Powers" with distinctive national identities. The period between 1660 and 1815 was thus wrought with tremendous power struggles, which, Kennedy writes, resulted in "the maturing of a genuinely multipolar system of European states," where decisions were made "on the basis of 'national interests,' rather than for transnational, religious causes." During this period, "Spain, the Netherlands, and Sweden, fell into second rank," and five new, more potent nations emerged: France, Britain, Russia, Austria and Prussia.

Despite Napoleon's attempts to bring foreign European nations under French rule, the other Great Powers prevailed. Because the spiraling costs of war led Britain to create an advanced system of banking and credit, the country achieved an economic advantage that helped to frustrate Napoleon's campaign. Moreover, Britain, like Russia, at this time began to expand its sovereignty to other continents.

In the period from 1815 to 1915 a "strategic equilibrium" emerged, supported by all of the leading powers. Governments, particularly in the United States and Russia, now focused on domestic stability and expansion of their borders. During this period of relative stability the British Empire took its place as a global force. England owned a "virtual monopoly [on] steam-driven industrial production, [and] the spread of industrialization to other regions soon began to tilt the international power balances away from the older leading nations and toward those countries with both the resources and organization to exploit the newer means of production and technology."In fact, the Crimean War, the American Civil War and the Franco-Prussian War brought defeat to those nations that had "failed to modernize their military systems."

Soon the pace of technological change and uneven economic growth created a complex and unstable international environment. After the 1880s, the Great Powers competed for strong military alliances and for additional Third World territories to increase economic and strategic capabilities. During this period "indices of economic power were tending more and more to fundamental shifts in global balances.... Despite their best efforts, traditional great powers [except for Germany] were falling out of the race," while the newly formed Soviet Union and the United States were moving to the forefront.

The period between 1900 and 1950 marked the beginning of a bipolarization of power that proved unusually stressful for the *middle* powers. Germany, for example, gained victory over the eastern front during World War I, only to be defeated within a few short months. To the west, Germany's "allies were similarly collapsing in the Italian, Balkan and Near Eastern theaters of the war," primarily as a result of American military and economic aid. *Austria-Hungary was gone, Russia was in revolution, Germany defeated; yet, even in victory, France, Italy and Britain itself had suffered heavy losses. The only exceptions were Japan, which further augmented its position in the Pacific, and the United States, which by 1918 was indisputably the strongest power in the world.*

With the Soviet Union isolated under the Bolshevik regime and America withdrawing from foreign engagements after World War I, the international system was more "out of joint with economic realities than at any time" during the previous four centuries. Between the great world wars, "Britain and France, although weakened, were still at the center of the diplomatic stage, but by the 1930s their position was being challenged by the militarized, revisionists states of Japan, Italy and Germany.... The United States remained by far the most powerful manufacturing nation in the world, and Stalin's Russia was quickly transforming itself into an industrial superpower." The shadow cast by these two giants produced a dilemma for "the status-quo middle powers" during World War II; "in fighting off German and Japanese challenges, they would most likely weaken themselves as well." Indeed, the apprehensions of the middle powers soon were confirmed: *France was eclipsed, and Britain irretrievably weakened.... The bipolar world had arrived ... and military balance had once again caught up with the global distribution of economic resources.*

Following World War II, the Cold War became a fact of life in the bipolar world. Nuclear weapons now guaranteed a completely transformed "strategic" and "diplomatic landscape." From the 1960s to the 1980s, the United States and the Soviet Union remained the dominant powers, their rivalry resulting in an "ever-escalating arms race which no other powers felt capable of matching ... "

And today, "global productive balances have been altering faster than ever before; the Third World's share of total manufacturing output, depressed to an all-time low ... after 1945, has steadily expanded"; Europe has become the world's largest trading unit; China is impressively "leaping forward"; and Japan's postwar economic rate has overtaken Russia in total GNP. Meanwhile, since the 1960s both "superpowers" have shown "sluggish" growth rates, with "their shares of global production and wealth" steadily shrinking. Once again, a "multi-polar" world—including China, Japan, the EEC (European Economic Community), the Soviet Union and the United States—has emerged. Writing in 1987, before the unforeseen breakup of the Soviet Union and its "satellites," Kennedy nevertheless forecasts that those nations which vie to become one of the Great Powers must "grapple with the age-old task of relating national means to national ends. The history of the rise and fall of the Great Powers has in no way come to a full stop."

THE HISTORY OF THE DECLINE AND FALL OF THE ROMAN EMPIRE
by Edward Gibbon (1734–1794)

Since publication of British historian Edward Gibbon's monumental six-volume *Decline and Fall of the Roman Empire* between 1776 and 1788, scholars have debated why Rome fell. Indeed, Gibbon asserts, for more than 12 centuries—from Rome's "golden age" (a two-century period beginning around the year 180) to its final political and physical disintegration in 1461—the city hastened its own ruin.

The massive work itself deserves all the adulation accorded it over the centuries. Manifesting a dramatic, polished style and an unparalleled depth of accuracy, it has been designated the most authoritative study of Rome ever written, though modern historians point to Gibbon's penchant toward taking the Roman perspective as a bias detrimental to his writing.

The lively and extremely complex history begins with a description of the Roman Empire at the height of its glory (A.C.E. 96-180). After the death of Marcus Aurelius, the Empire, under Commodus, began its long, leisurely decline—the causes of which the author briefly explains. Actually, Gibbon was more interested in documenting and recounting historical events than in diagnosing Rome's ills. Thus the work is filled with a menagerie of fascinating anecdotes and milestones, with Rome's great and gradual fall taking a relative back seat.

It is beyond doubt that the Roman Empire was extremely powerful. Military strategists have for centuries studied its war machines, its generals' tactics, its awe-inspiring technological advances. Ironically, says Gibbon, the Romans destroyed themselves—their intricate government, their majestic cities—all while operating under a rich and vast society made up of highly knowledgeable citizens.

Myriad historians have puzzled over the fall of the Great Roman Empire. Some claim that a shortage of manpower played a part in its collapse. Others insist that its populace became debilitated by blood poisoning from the lead used to fashion pipes and pottery, or cite evidence that Rome fell victim to repeated bouts of plague. And still others argue that the intermixing of races—"strong" Aryan blood mixing with that of "weak" barbarian races—played a hand in its decline in power and in its ultimate destruction. Sexual permissiveness has also been widely touted as the cause, especially by Christian and Jewish clergy, who hold in contempt the habitual orgies said to have been common among the ancient Roman aristocracy.

But Gibbon offers documentation suggesting more simple, plausible grounds for Rome's fall, reasons dealing both with politics and simple economics. In fact, he focuses most of his attention on the Empire's physical/structural decline.

Strangled by economic despotism from within, invasion from without, a subsequent intrusion of foreign beliefs and a crumbling superstructure, Gibbon says, the prevailing successive Roman governments failed to uphold even the most basic social policies by which they had operated for almost a thousand years:

"keep the peace, keep the roads open, and do business with everyone."

At the close of his history, Gibbon writes: *After a diligent inquiry, I can discern four principle causes of the ruin of Rome…. I. The injuries of time and nature. II. The hostile attacks of the barbarians and Christians. III. The use and abuse of [building] materials. And IV. The domestic quarrels of the Romans.* Throughout the lengthy narrative—filled with inquiries into emperors' actions both patriotic and tyrannical, accounts of barbarian onslaught, and Rome's gallant efforts to survive amid overwhelming odds—these causes are contested.

I. Physical Decay and Destruction

Certain that Rome's material decay gradually led to its societal, spiritual and intellectual decline, Gibbon writes: *The art of man is able to construct monuments far more permanent than the narrow span of his own existence. Yet these monuments, like himself, are perishable and frail; and in the boundless annals of time his life and his labors must equally be measured as a fleeting moment…. The silent lapse of time is often accelerated by hurricanes and earthquakes, by fires and inundations … and the lofty turrets of Rome have tottered from their foundations.*

During Nero's despotic four-year reign (A.C.E. 64-68), when a fire struck Rome, "innumerable buildings, crowded in close and crooked streets, supplied perpetual fuel for the flames…"

[Then] in the full meridian of empire the metropolis arose with fresh beauty from her ashes; yet … memory … deplored [the] irreparable losses, the arts of Greece, the trophies of victory, the monuments of primitive or fabulous antiquity.

II. Christianity Triumphs; Rome Declines

In clarification of the assertion that "attacks of … Christians" was a principle cause of Rome's decline, Gibbon defended himself: He saw in Christianity an alien influence that ultimately served to dilute the already severely truncated spiritual fabric of Roman society. When the tenets upon which the Roman civilization was built were altered, Gibbon asserts, Roman society began to weaken and wobble. Just as a human being straying from his values—either through omission or commission—morally weakens, a state disregarding the ethics upon which it has rested for centuries becomes impotent. And what is lost cannot easily be regained.

In effect, Christianity's victory sent Rome's true "golden age" into decline; as Romans embraced the lofty new doctrines of the Christians, Rome's might faded, becoming nothing more than a distant mythology.

However harmful Christian presence was to Rome, the complex series of events leading to its downfall were only exacerbated by the Roman government's campaign against the Christians, which continued from the reign of Nero to that of early-4th-century emperor Constantine the Great. While sincerely averring that the emperors were not as harsh in their treatment of Christians as some would claim, Gibbon of course denounces the atrocities perpetrated on Rome's perceived enemies: various "barbarian" tribes, Jews, and Christians.

Gibbon offers evidence supporting his claim that accounts of martyrdom were greatly exaggerated—both in terms of numbers and cruelty—and that, in many cases, Christians brought martyrdom upon themselves by goading the Romans to violence: *The personal guilt which every Christian had contracted, in ... preferring his private sentiment to the national religion, was aggravated [to] a very high degree [by] the religious assemblies of the Christians, who had separated themselves from public worship.... [Their] pious disobedience ... made their conduct, or perhaps their designs, appear in a much more serious and criminal light.*

Five factors attributed to Christianity's rapid growth: *I. The inflexible, and, if we may use the expression, the intolerant zeal of the Christians ... II. The doctrine of a future life ... III. The miraculous powers ascribed to the primitive church ... IV. The pure and austere morals ... V. The union and discipline of the Christian republic, which gradually formed an independent and increasing state in the heart of the Roman empire.* Thus, the Roman myths and creeds failed to hold its adherents, further rending the fabric of Roman society.

"The Edict of Milan"

In the year 313, Gibbon notes, the Emperor Constantine finally became weary of the persecution of Christians and made a radical turnaround. Hoping no doubt to put the devout passions and loyalties of this resilient sect at the services of the Empire, he "adopted Christianity as the official religion of the Roman Empire." Under his Edict of Milan, "Christians were ceded rights to inherit and dispose of property as they wished" and were empowered, under auspices of the Emperor, to elect their own church government. Unfortunately, the universal toleration of Christianity had no sooner been decreed than the Church and Empire were split by the factions rising out of the Donatist and Arian heresies (i.e. dogmas of two rival schismatic Christian sects). The former were confined to Africa, but the latter inflamed the entire domain, which remained in bitter debate until Constantine intervened by convening the Council of Nice, in which he pronounced himself in favor of the Nicene Creed. This was the orthodox dogma of Christianity.

This religion's "insidious germ" served not only to stretch the military forces of the Empire and to fuel heated contests between increasing numbers of religious and social factions, but resulted in higher-ups of the Church coming to have increasingly greater influence on matters of state, a condition which proved to mire the Empire in assorted entanglements for the next 700-odd years.

The Final Straw—Internal Strife Eventually Brings About a Mistreatment of History's Relics

"I have reserved for the last the most potent and forcible cause of destruction," Gibbons writes. That is "the domestic hostilities of the Romans themselves." In 476, Odoacer, a German (barbarian) chieftain, serving under various Roman commanders, rebelled and deposed the last western Roman emperor, Romulus Augustulus. After acknowledging Zeno as overlord of the eastern empire, Odoacer ruled Italy for 27 years. With Odoacer's assassination by Theodoric the Great in 493, Rome entered into a series of alliances with other barbaric kingdoms. However, territorial expansion brought conflict with the Frankish king Clovis, and his death left the Empire leaderless—and ripe for Byzantine annexation.

In this confused and turbulent scene of personal and public bewilderment, the Romans themselves, fearful of further invasion, began disemboweling the city of its greatest treasures in order to supply building materials to construct their fortresses: ... *The statues of the gods and heroes, and the costly ornaments of sculpture ... became the first prey of conquest or fanaticism, of the avarice of the barbarians or the Christians.*

As the centuries wore on, Rome's continued rule by Byzantine and French emperors—who held vastly different beliefs and values than their subjects and were willing to violate the most sacred of Roman laws—triggered frequent periods of internal strife, sedition and civil war in the city. *At such a time ... when every quarrel was decided by a sword and none could trust their lives or properties to the impotence of law ... the cities were filled with [hostility, and] to this mischievous purpose the remains of antiquity [such as temples and arches] were most readily adapted.*

With neither sovereign nor senate to protect it from Arab raids and the increase of papal authority, Rome—both its past might and its future promise—had nearly fallen. *Even the churches were encompassed with arms and bulwarks, and the military engines on the roof of St. Peter's were the terror of the Vatican and the scandal of the Christian world.... "The houses," says a cardinal poet of the times, "were crushed by the weight and velocity of enormous stones; the walls were perforated by the strokes of the battering-ram; the towers were involved in fire and smoke; and the assailants were stimulated by rapine and revenge."*

As the end of the great Empire's power was sealed, no emperor had the power to salvage it. As an ecclesiastical state in schism with its own, long history, Rome's influence was a relic of history: *"Behold,"* says the laureate, *"the relics of Rome, the image of her pristine greatness! Neither time nor barbarian can boast the merit of this stupendous destruction; it was perpetrated by her own citizens.... Your ancestors have done with the battering-ram what the Punic hero could not accomplish with the sword."*

Rome's might had finally been laid to waste; it no longer commanded the respect of its neighbors. And on further reflection, many people would have to agree with Gibbon's concluding thoughts: ... *Instead of inquiring why the Roman Empire was destroyed, we should rather be surprised that it had subsisted so long.*

One of the great flowerings of Western civilization sprang to life at the end of the 4th century B.C.E. with the establishment of the Mediterranean port city of Alexandria. Bearing the name of its illustrious founder, Alexander the Great, and laid out—as many ancient visitors described it—"like an emperor's cloak" sweeping down to the Egyptian seashore, the capital of the Ptolemaic dynasty soon became the cultural center of the Hellenistic world.

At the heart of the city's glory stood the Library and Museum of Alexandria. Within the walls of this great complex, labeled by one Greek poet as "The Cage of the Muses" (hence the edifice's title of "museum"), the Ptolemies and their royal librarians managed to systematically collect, study, translate and classify all the books of the ancient world. The debt we owe to the Library and its creators and curators is immeasurable. Similarly, the magnitude of the loss we have suffered through its mysterious destruction sometime between the first six centuries A.C.E. is incalculable.

In *The Vanished Library*, Luciano Canfora combines the intellectual rigor of a historian with the narrative gifts of a novelist to resurrect the ancient splendors of the Library and Museum. Dividing his fascinating work into two parts—the first a narrative history of the Library and the second an annotated bibliography of his sources—Canfora also lays out a carefully reasoned and provocative scenario to explain the mystery of the fire that destroyed the Library—a conflagration that has haunted Western culture for centuries.

Canfora begins his chronicle with an overview of the historical forerunners of the Library and Museum of Alexandria. There are two, in particular, to which he draws our attention: the *Ramesseum* in Thebes, which was the mausoleum of the Egyptian pharaoh Rameses II; and the *Peripatos* in Athens, which housed the *Lyceum*—the school founded by Aristotle.

Comparing ancient eyewitness accounts of the Library and the mausoleum of Rameses II, Canfora suggests that the Ramesseum served as the architectural model for the Museum complex. Canfora, for that matter, argues that the "two buildings ... were identical." Both contained a "covered walk" which "gave access to numerous rooms or chambers," including a "sacred library" in the Ramesseum. Both opened onto a huge, circular, "sumptuous room with the triclinia or couches." Finally, both buildings were "organized" around the *Soma*, or body, of a dead ruler. "The *Soma* of Alexander [the Great]," says Canfora, "was to be found [within] the Museum ... precincts, just as the *Soma* of Rameses was to be found [within] the hall in the Mausoleum."

But if the Museum owed its architectural legacy to an Egyptian pharaoh, the spiritual breath that created and sustained it was Greek. Specifically, it was the breath of Aristotle, caught and molded into solid reality by the driving hand of Alexander the Great.

As Canfora reminds us, Alexander was born in the mid-4th century B.C.E. into the royal house of Macedonia—at that time still a semi-barbaric, untamed cultural outpost in the minds of the heartland Greeks to the South. His father, King Philip II, anxious to implant the refinements of high Hellenic culture within his borders, dared to invite Aristotle himself—appealing to the illustrious thinker's own origins as a native Macedonian son—to come back home and serve as the young Alexander's personal tutor.

Aristotle accepted; and, not surprisingly, by the time the Macedonian prince turned his hand to the conquest of the Middle East, the Hellenic vision, as embodied by Aristotle, had been burned into his blood. At the core of Alexander's great campaigns blazed the ideal of a great, new, unified world order, enlightened throughout by the culture and language of Greece. "Pray for a new heart among mankind," he told his generals; and the key to achieving that "new heart" lay in the establishment of new Hellenic cities and cultural centers throughout the lands of their conquest.

At Alexander's death in 323 B.C.E., the three generals who divided his empire among them retained this ardent—and shrewdly practical—vision. In fact, Ptolemy, now designated as the new ruler of Egypt, eagerly commissioned another disciple of Aristotle—Demetrius, the ex-governor of Athens—to educate his own son at Alexandria. And this son was to become Ptolemy II, the greatest ruler of the Ptolemaic dynasty, and the founder of the Library and Museum.

Following Alexander's vision and Aristotle's personal example at the Preipatos in Athens, Demetrius and Ptolemy quickly expanded the scope of the Library collection, beginning with a series of "books on kingship and the exercise of power." Canfora writes: ... *They had calculated that they must amass some five hundred thousand scrolls altogether [in order] to collect at Alexandria "the books of all the peoples of the world." [Wherefore] Ptolemy composed a letter "to all the sovereigns and governors on earth" imploring them "not to hesitate to send him" works by authors of every kind: "poets and prose-writers, rhetoricians and sophists, doctors and soothsayers, historians, and all the others too." He gave orders that any books on board ships calling at Alexandria were to be copied: the originals were to be kept, and the copies given to their owners.*

In this way, Canfora observes, Ptolemy I and his successors quickly and purposefully built up a "Universal Library" of several hundred thousand scrolls. Endlessly acquisitive and curious, the Ptolemies and their royal librarians continued throughout several centuries to enlarge the Library's collection. In one project, for instance, the Library not only acquired all "the books of Jewish law," but also conducted a symposium in which "the Sages of Jerusalem" were invited to Alexandria to translate the *Pentateuch* (first five books of scripture) into Greek. All the while, the Museum's librarians made copies of the books and transcribed the rapidly deteriorating scrolls into book form.

As the Museum's collection grew, its curators undertook the operation of cataloguing and classifying all its holdings according to genre. The result—the famous *Catalogues of Callimachus*—gives us a tantalizing glimpse of the Library's extensive collection: *Callimachus devoted six sections to poetry and five to prose: his categories included epics, tragedies, comedies, historical works, works of medicine, rhetoric and law, and miscellaneous works.*

Of these writings, many had been produced at the Library itself. The Greek geographer and historian Strabo, for example, wrote the Egyptian portions of his classic work *Geography* while he was a resident scholar at the Library. Apollonius of Rhodes compiled the classic epic *Jason and the Argonauts* while serving as the royal Librarian. In the field of literary scholarship, the Library and its staff amended and organized the *Iliad* and the *Odyssey* in the forms that we currently read them. The day's most distinguished scholars lectured in its great hall. In short, presided over by the ghost of Aristotle, the Library of Alexandria played a key role in conserving and shaping Western culture as we know it today.

It is easy to see, then, why the building's destruction—and the mystery surrounding it—have plagued the imagination of historians for some two millennia. The most widely accepted historical accounts attribute the catastrophe to Julius Caesar, who, ironically, frequently attended lectures there. According to Roman annals, during the Alexandrian war (48 to 47 B.C.E.) Caesar torched the Ptolemaic fleet which lay anchored in the city's harbor. Ancient sources go on to report that the fire spread to the shipyards and then to the warehouses "in which 'grain and books' were stored." The crucial question that then remains, of course, is whether these "forty thousand scrolls of excellent quality" were part of the Great Library. Canfora thinks not. Returning to his earlier discussion of the architectural resemblances between the Library and the Ramesseum, he notes that our uncertainty about the Library's location derives from the way we have come, over time, to define the word *library*. The Latin-based -*arium* ending which gives us our English "libr-*ary*," *does* in fact denote either a "room" or "receptacle" (solarium, planetarium, etc.). However, the etymological derivation of the word in the original Greek—and, for that matter, in Canfora's own Italian—*bibliotheke* translates instead to mean a "case," an "envelope" or a "shelf" rather than a room or building in which books are placed. Canfora maintains, then, that the Alexandrian *Library*, like the "sacred library" of the Ramesseum, must have been a shelf or a series of shelves which ran part way round the circular walls of the *inside* of the Museum: *Since the treasures of the Museum cannot possibly have been outside the palace walls, let alone stored in the port alongside the grain depots, we need hardly stress that the scrolls which went up in flames were quite unconnected with the royal Library.*

Canfora has another explanation for the forty thousand books that burned in the port warehouses. He recalls that Seneca often attacked "the fashionable taste that led so many rich people [in Rome] to fill their houses with thousands of books, collected [not for study but] for the sake of mere ostentation." So, he argues, the books that were destroyed might much more plausibly have been volumes waiting in storage for export to the personal libraries of wealthy Romans. Moreover, Canfora observes that the resident Library scholar/historian Strabo, writing just 20 years after the port fire, makes no mention of the loss of any books from the Library.

Canfora proposes another theory to account for the Library's ultimate ruin: a demolition of the royal palace and its attached museum that took place some 600 years later. Using a history of the Islamic conquest of Alexandria in the year 641, he suggests that the Library's collection was burned on the orders of the Arab Caliph Omar. Shortly after Omar's general, Emir Amrou Ibn el-Ass, had conquered Alexandria, he apparently wrote to Omar asking him what he should do about the city's extraordinary library. After a delay of several weeks, Amrou received his answer from Omar: *"As for the books you mention, here is my reply. If their content is in accordance with the book of Allah, we may do without them, for in that case the book of Allah more than suffices. If, on the other hand, they contain matter not in accordance with the book of Allah, there can be no need to preserve them. Proceed, then, and destroy them."*

Canfora writes that Amrou, though greatly saddened by the Caliph's orders, then "set about his task of destruction": *The books were distributed to the public baths of Alexandria, where they were used to feed the stoves which kept the baths so comfortably warm. [Islamic historian] Ibn al-Kifti writes that "the number of baths was well known, but I have forgotten it…. They say," continues Ibn al-Kifti, "that it took six months to burn all that mass of material."*

The only volumes spared, notes the Emir in his chronicle, were the works of Aristotle—whom the Arabs already knew and revered as an astronomer and logician from the days when his works were first made known to them by the Greek rulers of the Middle East after the conquests of Alexander the Great.

In the epilogue to his extraordinary history, Canfora attempts to contextualize the significance of the Library of Alexandria, noting that it was "the starting point and the prototype" of all libraries to come. Because of the vast historicity of the Museum's collection and its irreplaceable nature, Canfora considers the wanton destruction of the majestic edifice at Alexandria especially lamentable: *The great concentrations of books, usually found in the centres of power, were the main victims of [the] ruinous attacks, sackings and fires…. In consequence, what has come down to us is derived not from the great centres but from "marginal locations," such as convents, and from scattered private copies.*

THE HISTORIES
(And the History of the Persian Wars) by Herodotus of Halicarnassus (c. 484–425 B.C.E.)

*T*his is the setting-forth of the research of Herodotus of Halicarnassus so that neither will the things done by men be forgotten with the passage of time nor will the great deeds and wonders which have transpired, some among the Greeks, and others among the barbarians, be without fame...

Thus begins Herodotus's massive nine-volume work, titled, appropriately, *The Histories*, considered to be the first true historical treatise. Though Sumerian and Egyptian scribes had earlier set down in print various events, they usually wrote their accounts to flatter their contemporary political authorities.

Herodotus was the first to organize diverse events around a common narrative theme. In fact, his *Histories* stands as the first great work of prose extant in Western literature; all previous works had been written in verse for oral performance. Moreover, it is on the strength of Herodotus's work that the word *history* has come to possess its present meaning.

The Histories largely focuses on the conflict between East and West, Asia and Europe—or the Greeks and the "barbarians"—which culminated in the Persian Wars of 490 and 480 B.C.E. The first half of the work, Books I through V, deals mostly with the rise of the Persian Empire. The remainder details the conflict between the Persians and the Greek city-states.

Herodotus's purposes in writing were not strictly historical. His record primarily was intended to be entertaining, for Herodotus was a great storyteller. He admits: "Digressions are part of the plan," and thus his history contains a large number of fascinating stories, including many of dubious authenticity.

The Story of Croesus

Typical of the writer's quasi-historical narratives is the story of *Croesus of Lydia*. Non-Greeks, the Lydians were most noted for their invention of coinage. Lydia's ruler, Croesus, belonged to a family called the *Mermnadae*. According to Herodotus, their dominion began when Gyges, Croesus's great-great grandfather, usurped the throne of King Candaules.

Now Candaules, or so the story goes, was exceedingly fond of his wife; to him, she was the most beautiful of women and he continually praised her comeliness to his bodyguard Gyges. To prove her beauty to Gyges, Candaules persuaded the reluctant servant to hide in the royal bedroom and observe her as she disrobed. Gyges did spy on the queen, but she spotted him doing so and suspected that her husband was responsible. The next day she summoned Gyges and presented him with an ultimatum: "Gyges, there are two courses open to you, and you may take your choice between them. Kill Candaules and seize the throne, with me as your wife; or die yourself on the spot, so that never again may your blind obedience to the king tempt you to see what you have no right to see." Not surprisingly, Gyges opted for the first alternative.

Although many Lydians objected to the prospect of Gyges as king, they eventually were persuaded to accept him, so long as his authority was confirmed by a pronouncement of the oracle at Delphi. The priestess of Apollo indeed confirmed that Gyges would rule, but announced that Candaules's descendants would be avenged in the fifth generation.

Many years later, Gyges's descendant Croesus extended the Lydian Empire throughout the territory of the Greek city-states. As fifth in the line of Gyges, however, Croesus was destined to be deposed.

As it happened, among the many famous visitors to Croesus's city of Sardis was the Athenian constitutional reformer Solon. Croesus, quite smug about his own prosperity, asked the well-traveled Solon to name the man, among the many he had met, whom he regarded as the most happy. "An Athenian called Tellus," was Solon's reply.

Taken aback, Croesus asked Solon to defend his choice. Solon explained that Tellus had lived to see sons and grandsons born, and had died a glorious death in battle. The Athenians subsequently had provided a public funeral for this honorable, happy man.

Now Croesus demanded to know Solon's second choice, and this time he named Cleobis and Biton, two brothers who had pulled their mother in an oxcart to the festival of the goddess Hera, as the happiest. They died in answer to a maternal prayer that they be granted "the greatest blessing that can fall to mortal man." No man, regardless of his prosperity, added Solon, can be called "happy" until he has *died* happily. Croesus considered this explanation foolish, and sent Solon away.

Some years later, King Cyrus, founder of the Persian Empire, marched on toward Sardis, took the city, and captured Croesus. As predicted by the Oracle, Croesus and his great empire had fallen.

On the orders of Cyrus, Croesus and 14 young Lydian boys were chained to a great pyre to be burned alive. Realizing that he was about to die, Croesus reflected upon his conversation with Solon long ago and thrice uttered the name of the Athenian: "Solon ... Solon ... Solon ... " Cyrus, overhearing the invocation, sent an interpreter to find out what was meant by it. Upon hearing Croesus's explanation, Cyrus wanted to spare his life—but it was too late: the fire had been lit. As a last resort, Croesus called on Apollo to save him, whereupon that diety sent a storm which doused the flames.

Such a tale, at least from a modern perspective, may seem out of place in a historical account. As stated earlier, however, Herodotus's purposes were different than those of a modern historian: *My business is to record what people say, but I am by no means bound to believe it—and that may be taken to apply to this book as a whole.*

Preserving the Ancient Tales

While entertaining, Herodotus's quasi-fictional accounts have also proven to be enlightening. There are at least two instances, for example, when he reports views that he did not find credible but which seem perfectly reasonable to the modern reader. The first deals with why the waters of the Nile rise at the summer solstice. Presenting three commonly held views, Herodotus denounces the third, although it is the one we know to be correct today: " ... The water of the Nile comes from melting snow ... " Since hotter climates were found to be farther south, and the source of the Nile is to the south, this explanation seemed highly implausible. He had no way of knowing, however, that many snow-capped mountains lie in the vicinity of the equator.

The second example of Herodotus's commitment to accurate recording is even more interesting. He relates that a Phoenician crew, commissioned by Pharaoh Neco, circumnavigated the African continent. While Herodotus does not question the fact that the voyage took place, he doubts the report that "as they sailed on a westerly course round the southern end of Libya [by which he means "Africa"], they had the sun on their right—to the northward of them." We know that this is just what one would expect, traveling west in the Southern Hemisphere. But, of course, Herodotus was ignorant to the fact that the earth is roughly spherical. A more "scientific" historian would, no doubt, have neglected to mention such an unlikely detail.

The Culture of Ancient Egypt

One of the most important of Herodotus's digressions is the whole of Book II, which encompasses a detailed description of the cultural idiosyncrasies of ancient Egypt. Egyptian customs included both circumcision—which seemed frightening and distasteful to the Greeks—and mummification. He notes that, from a Greek point of view, the Egyptians often reversed the usual roles of men and women: for instance, Egyptian women went to the marketplace to shop, while the men remained at home, weaving.

Especially engrossing is Herodotus's comparison of Egyptian religious practices with those of the Greeks. He observed substantial underlying similarities between Greek and Egyptian religious beliefs, and did not fail to draw an obvious conclusion: Greek gods were, in many cases, borrowed from the Egyptians. He then goes on to equate Egyptian deities with their Greek counterparts. Thus, the god Amun "is the Egyptian name for Zeus"; Osiris is simply an Egyptian Dionysus.

In some cases, Herodotus's assumptions are probably incorrect. He nevertheless was the first author to suggest that cultures borrow ritual practices and religious beliefs from each other.

The Persian Wars

From the latter part of Book V through Book IX, the historian focuses much more closely on his major theme: the famed Persian Wars. When Aristogoras of Miletus persuaded the Ionian city-states to revolt against the Persian Empire in 499 B.C.E., he enlisted the help of the Athenians, who sent 20 warships. The combined Greek forces launched an attack on Sardis, by then a provincial capital of the Persian Empire, plundering the temples and burning much of the city. Soon afterward the Greeks and Ionians first were defeated at sea by the Persian fleet, and then the Persians struck back, invading Greek and Ionian lands. By 493 B.C.E. the revolt had been completely suppressed.

Meanwhile, a formidable advocate of Athenian naval supremacy named Themistocles initiated two major confrontations between Greeks and Persians. He began by calling upon Persian Emperor Darius to send military aid. Still stung by the role the Athenians had played in Sardis's earlier defeat, Darius dispatched a fleet of ships carrying both infantry and cavalry to challenge Athens. The fleet alighted on the east coast of Attica at the Bay of Marathon, leaving the Athenians, aided only by their allies the Plataeans, to confront a Persian force four times as large as their own. But against all expectations, the Athenians achieved a stunning victory: by what could only be attributed to "the graces of the gods," the Athenians and their allies suffered 192 casualties while the "barbarians" and their allies lost 6400.

The final Persian response was delayed by the death of Darius in 486 B.C.E. Six years later, however, his successor, Xerxes—accompanied by a fleet of unprecedented size—personally led a mighty army to battle the Greeks. Although the Persian army initially met with little resistance, they were eventually confronted by a heroic force of 300 Spartans at the narrow mountain pass of Thermopylae. A Greek named Ephialtes then covertly informed Xerxes of a second mountain pass by which, if followed, would allow the Persians also to attack from the rear. Xerxes and his legion subsequently were able to surround and annihilate the Spartan forces, then press southward to occupy Attica and burn to the ground the evacuated city of Athens.

By use of a clever ploy, the Greeks convinced the Persians to believe that they had "trapped" the entire Athenian fleet in the Bay of Eleusis. But in the ensuing naval battle the mighty Athenians showed their true strength and utterly defeated the Persian fleet.

His ships either sunken or badly crippled, Xerxes had no way to supply his massive land forces. Returning to Persia with some remaining ships, Xerxes left the core of his army on the Greek mainland under the command of Mardonius. During the next summer of 479 B.C.E., though, Mardonius was defeated at the Battle of Plataea and the remnant of the Persian fleet was overwhelmed and sunk at Mycale off the coast of Asia Minor.

Thus ends Herodotus's stirring narrative of the Persian Wars. While not always factual in every detail, his account largely is reliable, and every bit as exciting as the imaginative tales that illuminate today's movie screens.

Played out against the backdrop of the classical Greek "Golden Age," the intermittent conflict between the city states of Athens and Sparta and their allies lasted from Hellenic 431 B.C.E. to 404 B.C.E. For a collective first- and second-hand narrative of the first 20 years of the conflict, we have the remarkable *History of the Peloponnesian War* by the Athenian general Thucydides, who spent two decades in exile after a defeat in the battle for the city of Amphipolis.

Thucydides' work is a rare trove among ancient historical records. Aside from its great literary charm, the general's compilation sets a unique standard for accuracy. As the author himself explains: *And with reference to the narrative of events, far from permitting myself to derive it from the first source that came to hand, I did not even trust my own impressions, but it rests partly on what I saw myself, partly on what others saw for me, the accuracy of the report being always tried by the most severe and detailed tests possible.*

Only in the still-famous speeches he cites does Thucydides favor literary elegance over stringent accuracy: ... *It was in all cases difficult to carry them word for word in one's memory, so my habit was to make the speakers say what was in my opinion demanded of them by the various occasions, of course adhering as close as possible to the general sense of what was really said.* Thus, for instance, Pericles's oration at the funeral of a fellow statesman was probably slightly embellished to help clarify the ideals of Athenian democracy: "Our constitution does not copy the laws of neighbouring states; we are rather a pattern to others than imitators ourselves. Its administration favors the many instead of the few; this is why it is called a democracy. If we look to the laws, they afford equal justice to all in their private differences.... The freedom we enjoy in our government extends to our ordinary life.... We throw open our city to the world, and never by alien acts exclude foreigners from any opportunity of learning or observing.... We cultivate refinement without extravagance and knowledge without effeminacy.... In short ... I doubt if the world can produce a man [who is] graced by so happy a versatility as the Athenian ..."

Even with its self-congratulatory overtones, this 2500-year-old speech remains one of the most eloquent and widely celebrated defenses of an open society.

The Early Years

For years the great city of Sparta—located on the southern Greek peninsula of Peloponnesus —had objected to Athens' expansionist gestures. As friction mounted between the governing Athens and the power-seeking peninsular city-state, relations between the two formerly neighboring—though discordant—cultures turned sour.

The first phase of the war—often known as the Archidamian War in honor of King Archidamus, who commanded Sparta's ground forces—lasted just over a decade, and ended in a virtual stalemate. Though the Athenians and their allies enjoyed an overwhelming naval superiority, the Spartans possessed enough of an advantage on the land to keep their rivals (literally) at bay.

Nearly every spring during this period the Spartans and their allies occupied the promontory of Attica, including the countryside surrounding Athens. Adhering to the policy of their great leader Pericles, the Athenians refused to fight and instead retreated behind the walls of their city. Unfortunately, this tactic brought tragedy: after their first retreat Athens was beset by a plague, which killed a quarter to a third of the population, including Pericles. Overall, however, the occupation of Attica by Sparta and its allies had little political effect, since the Athenians were able to farm most of their own crops within the radius of the city defenses, and import their grain by sea.

With ample food supplies, the Athenians were thus able to conduct brief sorties into enemy territories to block ships from transporting goods. One of these sorties, in 425 B.C.E., led to the turning-point of the Archidamian War. On his way to Corcyra, the Athenian commander Demosthenes landed at Pylos on the west coast of the Peloponnesian peninsula. Finding a suitable and easily fortified harbor, Demosthenes took the radical step of securing it for permanent occupation, forcing the Spartan troops in Attica to sail back to Laconia in order to protect their homeland from Western invaders. Alas, the enormous Spartan fleet was intercepted and destroyed by the vastly superior Athenian navy, led by Eurymedon and Sophocles. After a 72-day battle, a Spartan detachment of 300 infantrymen—trapped by the Athenians in Pylos—finally surrendered.

The defeat at Pylos was a severe blow to Sparta. Overly eager to recoup those who had been taken captive—many of them the sons of Sparta's most prominent families—the Spartans again left themselves vulnerable to attack by Athenian forces in Pylos, who found they could launch raids into Spartan territory virtually unimpeded.

Even after four long years of bitter attack, however, Sparta had some hopes for victory. The advantages of the city's enemies were partially offset by the campaign of the Spartan commander Brasidas, "liberator of Hellas," in Chalcidice, a peninsula where the Athenians held several major colonies. Brasidas set out and, within two years, through conquest and coercion, had conquered several economically crucial Athenian allies. His campaign was almost as damaging to the Athenians as the capture of Pylos was to the Spartans. In 422 B.C., however, both Brasidas and his Athenian counterpart Cleon were killed in battle near Amphipolis.

After the demise of these two outspoken supporters of prolonged warfare, a peace settlement was, in 412 B.C.E., at last arranged by the Athenian general Nicias and the Spartan king Pleistonax. And for the next three years there was no more bloodshed.

The Sicilian Campaign

In 415 B.C.E. Sicilian leaders enticed the Athenians to undertake a campaign in their island, which was at war with neighboring Selinus. Although few Athenians were sufficiently knowledgeable of Sicily to warrant such an undertaking, they anticipated an easy and profitable victory. Encouraged by the popular and ambitious general Alcibiades, the Athenians dispatched a massive armada of 4,000 troops and 300 horsemen, led by Alcibiades, Nicias and Lamachus.

After these three generals had arrived in southern Italy, a messenger arrived from Athens to demand that Alcibiades return: he was to be tried in Athens in connection with what was known as "The Affair of the Hermae," an incident involving a band of drunken young men who had blasphemously defaced many Athenian statues of Hermes. The trusted Alcibiades was allowed to return aboard his own ship. But instead of heading homeward for Athens, he turned sail to Sparta, where he sold his military expertise to his appreciative erstwhile enemies. On Alcibiades' advice, the Spartans soon sent a sizeable force to Syracuse, drawing Nicias and Lamachus to focus their attention on the capture of that city. This proved to be an absurd and highly futile project, inasmuch as Syracuse was almost as large and prosperous as Athens. Lamachus was killed early in the campaign, and Nicias confirmed his reputation as a fumbling and indecisive leader. In short order, the Syracusans, guided by the savvy Gylippus, blocked the Athenian troops by sea and by land.

The stubbornly determined Athenians sent Nicias reinforcements of another 73 ships and 5,000 infantrymen, under the able command of General Demosthenes. Upon seeing what his forces would go up against, Demosthenes confided to his intimates that he favored abandoning the invasion; however, he never dared confront Nicias with this appraisal, and before long the entire Athenian fleet was blockaded in the harbor. In one of the greatest debacles of the war, after waging two unsuccessful sea battles against the Syracusans the Athenians burned most of their own ships and attempted to escape overland. The retreat was suicidal: ... *The dead lay unburied, and each man as he recognized a friend among them shuddered in grief and horror; while the living whom they were leaving behind, wounded or sick, were to the living far ... more to be pitied than those who perished.... They had come to enslave others, and were departing in fear of being enslaved themselves...*

Following this disastrous rout, most of the surviving Athenian forces surrendered. Nicias and Demosthenes were put to death and the captive Athenian soldiers were either sold as slaves or "deposited in the quarries." Thucydides writes: *This was the greatest Hellenic achievement of any in this war.... [The Athenians] were beaten at all points and altogether ... their fleet, their army—everything was destroyed, and few of the many returned home.*

The Final Decline of Athens

Towards the end of the Peloponnesian War, Athens gradually declined in influence. Sparta's allies, which now included the mighty city of Syracuse, built a fleet to rival that of Athens, and, one by one, the city lost almost all the client states which had comprised its empire. Some of the city's wealthiest citizens suspended operations of the Ekklesia, the governing body in Athens, and tried to make peace with Sparta on any terms. Due to military opposition, their attempt failed.

The account of Thucydides ends in 411 B.C.E. For a history of the last years of the war, we are indebted to soldier-essayist Xenophon—unfortunately, neither as accurate nor as elegant as Thucydides. In his work *Hellenica*, Xenophon tells how Sparta and its allies entered into an alliance with the Persian Empire. Alcibiades was allowed to return to Athens and was elected supreme commander of the Athenian fleet, but the Athenians subsequently blamed him for their defeat near Ephesus, whereupon they elected ten new generals, including Pericles, the son and namesake of the celebrated early statesman.

Soon afterward the Athenians enjoyed their last significant victory of the war with the Battle of Arginusae. A fleet of 150 Athenian ships met and defeated Lysander's 120-vessel force, sinking 70 of the Spartan ships, along with the 14,000 men they carried—including Lysander himself. A sudden storm, however, prevented the Athenians from rescuing the sailors from 25 of their own sinking vessels. And when Athens' citizens heard this, they angrily sought to depose the eight generals who had been present at Arginusae, eventually bringing six of them to trial. This was an unconstitutional act, but the members of the presiding committee, the *prytany*, eventually gave in to the public outcry and sentenced the generals to death in a near unanimous vote. The single dissenter was the philosopher Socrates, who "would do nothing at all that was contrary to the law."

As the war dragged disastrously on the Athenian fleet was virtually destroyed after its commanding general Conon ordered it ashore on the European side of the Mediterranean in search of provisions. Under Spartan attack, Conon managed to escape to Cyprus along with eight ships. The *Paralus*, the official state warship of Athens, was subsequently sent to Piraeus, a Greek seaport, with an account of the defeat: *As the news of the disaster was told, one man passed it to another, and a sound of wailing arose.... That night no one slept. They mourned for the lost, but still more for their own fate. They thought that they themselves would now be dealt with as they had dealt with others...*

Besieged by both land and sea, the starving Athenians were compelled to concede defeat in April of 404 B.C.E. There followed the Reign of the Thirty Tyrants—under Spartan dominion—during which Athens's most brutal oligarchs exercised their power to despoil their political enemies. After many executions and confiscations of estates, the Thirty were defeated by Athenian exiles returning from Thebes at the Battle of Munychia. Soon thereafter the Spartan King Pausanias proclaimed a general amnesty and dismantled the Spartan garrison which had controlled Athens. Democracy thus was restored, but never again would Athens attain the status of an imperial power.

WHEN EGYPT RULED THE EAST
by George Steindorff and Keith C. Seele, The University of Chicago Press, 1957

The history of Egypt as an autonomous, sovereign state begins around 2800 B.C.E. and ends with the Persian conquest in 525 B.C.E. Because of the sheer span of its history, then, it is difficult to give an adequate account of the ascent and ultimate decline of Egypt—nor a sufficient feeling for the great influence its culture has had on the world—in a single volume. Steindorff and Seele solve this problem in their masterpiece *When Egypt Ruled the East* by focusing on the period of the New Kingdom (1546 to 1085 B.C.E.), while treating the Old Kingdom, the First Intermediate Period and the Middle Kingdom more as preface, and the Decline (1085 to 322 B.C.E.) as epilogue. Their strategy has merit, since Egypt's most famous and colorful characters date from this period. Moreover, because the period is so rich, the authors can treat several aspects of Egyptian culture—such as religion, art and hieroglyphic writing—topically. On the other hand, the reader should be aware that some very colorful aspects of Egyptian culture belong to earlier periods. In particular, the Great Pyramids of Giza were built for Khufu, Khafre and Menkaure, pharaohs of the Fourth Dynasty of the Old Kingdom (before 2500 B.C.E.); these remarkable edifices were already "ancient" when the New Kingdom began.

Steindorff and Seele begin their history with the Hyksos invasion and the subsequent war of liberation. The Hyksos, foreign invaders who ruled northern Egypt from about 1725 to 1600 B.C.E., set up their capital at Avaris in the Nile Delta. Nobody knows exactly who the Hyksos were. Since they had numerous fortified settlements in Palestine, however, scholars believe they must have been either Semites or Hurrians; the fact that they were skilled in the use of horses and chariots suggests they were a military aristocracy like the Hurrians. In any case, during the first century of Hyksos rule a new line of Egyptian kings, skilled in the progressive arts of warfare, arose in Thebes. At first these Theban kings were vassals of the Hyksos, but by about 1600 B.C.E. the Theban ruler Sekenrere rebelled against his Hyksos overlords. From his mummified remains we know that Sekenrere met a violent end, having sustained blows to his left jaw and forehead, as well as a blow to the head so severe that it fractured his skull, exposing the brain.

Sekenrere's sons, Kamose and Ahmose, carried on a war of liberation against the Hyksos in the city of Avaris and their Nubian allies in the far south. Kamose, who died young, laid siege to Avaris, but failed to capture it. The younger son Ahmose succeeded in capturing the city and, once having driven the Hyksos out of the land, in pursuing them to Sharuhen, their stronghold in southern Palestine. After a three-year siege Sharuhen fell as well, so that the victory over the Hyksos in Egypt was complete. Having defeated the Hyksos in the north, Ahmose attacked their Nubian allies, restoring Egyptian rule in the south as well.

Following a long and relatively peaceful reign, in 1546 B.C.E. Ahmose was succeeded by his son Amenhotep I, the first pharaoh of the 18th Dynasty. Unlike the Egypt of the Old or Middle Kingdom, the Egypt of the New Kingdom was an imperial power with a standing, professional army equipped with chariots, archers and bronze weapons.

Amenhotep was succeeded by his son Thutmose I, who is generally regarded as the founder of the Egyptian Empire and the first pharaoh to fully exploit Egypt's newly-acquired military prowess. Not content to exact tribute from just a few allies in southern Palestine, Thutmose led his armies all the way across Palestine and Syria to the shores of the Euphrates, which the Egyptians described as "that inverted water which flows southward when flowing northward." Although the "conquests" of Thutmose proved ephemeral and Egyptian rule was not established in Syria and Palestine until near the end of the long reign of Thutmose III in 1450 B.C.E., Thutmose I's Syrian campaign may be regarded as Egypt's emergence as an international power.

Thutmose I and his chief consort, the "Great Royal Wife" or crown princess, had two sons—Wadjmose and Amenmose—and two daughters—Hatshepsut and Nefrubity. Of these children, only the Princess Hatshepsut survived her father.

Tradition had for centuries dictated that only men could serve as pharaoh, and also that a pharaoh be succeeded by the husband of his eldest daughter. With this in mind, Thutmose married his daughter Hatshepsut to her younger half-brother Thutmose II, who took power upon his father's death in 1508 B.C.E. Yet when the frail Thutmose II died after a reign of only four years, his son, Thutmose III, was deposed by Hatshepsut, his mother-in-law, the Great Royal Wife herself.

For Hatshepsut, to rule Egypt as a mere regent or "power behind the throne" was not enough. Thus she openly assumed the title of pharaoh and claimed to reign by divine right as the daughter of Amun. In fact, between 1504 and 1482 the Egyptians lived in peace and prosperity under the rule of Hatshepsut and her chancellor, Senenmut. During her administration she rebuilt or restored the temples which had been destroyed or neglected by the Hyksos. She also erected two giant obelisks (one of which still stands in the temple of Amun at Thebes) and saw to the construction of one of the great monuments of Egyptian architecture—her temple at Deir el Bahri.

Hatshepsut designated her daughter, the Princess Nefrure, to succeed her, but her plans were thwarted when Thutmose III returned to Egypt in 1482 B.C.E. to have Hatshepsut killed and her allies banished. Afterwards, Thutmose III did his best to obliterate the memory of "Pharaoh" Hatshepsut and her consort. And, except for a few inscriptions he apparently overlooked, Hatshepsut's name was removed from most of the numerous monuments of her reign.

Having at last achieved undisputed rule, Thutmose

III undertook a series of military campaigns in Syria to the northeast and in Nubia to the south. Over a period of 19 years Thutmose III brought the principalities of Palestine and Syria under firm Egyptian control. He replaced recalcitrant dynasties when necessary, installed princes sympathetic to Egypt, and educated the eldest sons of subject princes in Thebes to prepare them to replace their fathers, if and when necessary.

Following the reign of Thutmose III there was almost a century of peace in the Ancient Near East. The three great powers of Egypt, Mitanni and Babylon engaged in amiable diplomatic relations. This stability lasted until Egypt lost most of its Asiatic empire during the reigns of Amenhoteps III and IV, fanatics of religious reform who initiated a period of cultural and military neglect in Egypt that lasted from 1412 to 1366 B.C.E. Apparently disturbed by the growing wealth and political power of Amun (the personification of wind or breath, represented either as a ram or goose)—which constituted a long-term threat to the economic well-being and political stability of the Egyptian state—Amenhotep IV launched an attempt to systematize the complicated Egyptian pantheon, instituting a form of monotheism in its place, while decreeing that the worship of Aton would be the new and only state religion. (This new theology embodied a radical departure from Egyptian tradition. Aton was depicted not as a person or animal, but as a sun disk from which emanated hands [the rays of the sun] grasping the ankh [a cross with a loop at the top], the hieroglyphic sign for "life.")

In accordance with this proclamation, Amenhotep and his wife Nofretete had all polytheistic references stricken from the histories and chiseled from the temples. Thereafter, all persons bearing names compounded by "-amun" (meaning "Amun is satisfied") were ordered to change their names. Amenhotep himself gladly complied, and from that time forward adopted the name Akhnaton, meaning "He who is beneficial to Aton." Subsequently the government seat was transferred from Thebes to Akhetaton.

Akhnaton, his mind centered on religious reform, "not only made no attempt to reassure or lend material aid to the faltering representatives of Egyptian power in western Asia but rather, through his fanatical devotion to his religious innovations, brought Egypt to the brink of ruin." For this reason, no doubt, Akhnaton's religious reforms (which met with little resistance during his lifetime) were promptly overturned by the nobility shortly after his death. Still, his brief reformation was accompanied by a renaissance in the arts whereby a naturalism took hold in painting (doing away with traditional lateral representations of the face in which the observable eye appears in a frontal perspective), in bas relief, and especially in portraiture. The famous "caryatid statue" of Akhnaton with its long, floppy ears, thick lips and skinny, unmuscled arms carries naturalism to the extreme of caricature. And one of the best-known of Egyptian artifacts, the celebrated bust of Queen Nofretete, accurately portrays her long, thin neck.

Meanwhile, Egypt's Syrian empire crumbled. In the north, its dependencies fell to the Hittites and their allies; and southward "in Palestine the situation was no better." (It is worth noting in passing that this is the earliest Egyptian reference to the people who later came to be known as Hebrews. There is no corroborating Egyptian evidence to support the biblical claim of Hebrew captivity in Egypt proper. The Hebrews first appear as wandering merchants settling down in Syria-Palestine.)

Akhnaton and Nofretete had as yet failed to beget a male heir. With Nofretete having fallen into disgrace, Akhnaton tried to produce an heir through two of his daughters. Finally, approaching death, he gave the hand of a daughter to Tutankhaton (known to us as Tutankhamen), then a nine-year-old nephew-prince. This fair boy-king would succeed the dying Egyptian pharaoh.

Tutankhaton's reign, however, was short-lived. Following his own untimely death in 1357 B.C.E.—and his well-publicized entombment—the aged regent Eye ruled as pharaoh. With Eye's subsequent death, one of Akhnaton's desperate daughters—who had been married to both her father and to Tutankhaton—wrote to the Hittite Emperor Supiluliumas I, requesting that he send one of his sons to be her husband and pharaoh of Egypt. But a group of assassins, disgruntled by this arrangement, murdered the son before the marriage could take place. Harmhab, a former commander-in-chief of the army of Tutankhaton, then marched with his army to Thebes, where he was hailed as new pharaoh. This mighty Harmhab, who ruled from 1353 to 1319 B.C.E., then set out to reclaim the lands lost under Akhnaton's rule.

Before the childless Harmhab's death, he named a favored general, Pramessu, to succeed him. Pramessu became known as Rameses I—the first in a long line of Ramesids, under which Egypt regained most of its previous lands. By 1284 B.C.E. the stability of the region was restored through a treaty with the Hittites. However, at the same time, all the great achievements of Egyptian culture belonged to the past. No subsequent achievement of Egyptian art bears favorable comparison with the best works produced under the reign of the 18th Dynasty; no later literary work bears favorable comparison with the classical literature of the First Intermediate Period.

Indeed, after the death of Rameses III (1198 to 1167)—who had successfully repelled Hittite aggression—the history of Egypt is one of gradual political, economic and cultural decline. Between 663 and 525 B.C.E. Egypt enjoyed a brief renaissance, induced by a vigorous foreign trade and by a nostalgic longing for the glories of the past. Following the conquest of Alexander the Great in 332 B.C.E., Egypt also enjoyed a cultural revival of sorts, since Alexandria became the greatest cultural center in the Eastern Mediterranean during the Hellenistic period. But the great scientific and literary achievements of Alexandria were triumphs of Greek rather than Egyptian culture. The great pharaohs ruled no more.

ELIE WIESEL
"The Perils of Indifference"

As a teenager Elie Wiesel and his family were deported by the Nazis from their native Hungary to the Auschwitz extermination camp in occupied Poland. After months of slave labor, starvation rations, atrocious living standards and brutal treatment, the prisoners were hastily marched out of Auschwitz at the approach of the Russian Army, then transported via cattle car to Buchenwald in Germany, where Wiesel's father, mother and a younger sister eventually died.

Upon being liberated by American troops in April 1945, the young man moved to Paris, taking work as a journalist. He later emigrated to the United States, where, as a professor in the Humanities and author of some 40 books, he has received numerous honors, including the 1986 Nobel Peace Prize and the Presidential Medal of Freedom.

Wiesel accepted President Bill Clinton and First Lady Hillary Clinton's invitation to speak in a series of White House "Millennium Lectures," centering on creating a better, more humane world. On April 12, 1999, in the East Room, Wiesel delivered his impassioned speech.

... Fifty-four years ago to the day, a young Jewish boy from a small town in the Carpathian Mountains woke up ... in a place of eternal infamy called Buchenwald. He was finally free, but there was no joy in his heart. He thought there never would be again.

Liberated a day earlier by American soldiers, he remembers their rage at what they saw. And even if he lives to be a very old man, he will always be grateful to them for that rage, and also for their compassion. Though he did not understand their language, their eyes told him what he needed to know—that they, too, would remember, and bear witness.

And now, I stand before you, Mr. President— Commander-in-Chief of the army that freed me, and tens of thousands of others—and I am filled with a profound and abiding gratitude to the American people.

Gratitude is a word that I cherish. Gratitude is what defines the humanity of the human being ...

We are on the threshold of a new century, a new millennium. What will the legacy of this vanishing century be? How will it be remembered in the new millennium? Surely it will be judged, and judged severely, in both moral and metaphysical terms. These failures have cast a dark shadow over humanity: two World Wars, countless civil wars, the senseless chain of assassinations—Gandhi, the Kennedys, Martin Luther King, Sadat, Rabin—bloodbaths in Cambodia and Nigeria, India and Pakistan, Ireland and Rwanda, Eritrea and Ethiopia, Sarajevo and Kosovo; the

inhumanity in the gulag and the tragedy of Hiroshima. And, on a different level, of course, Auschwitz and Treblinka. So much violence, so much indifference.

What is indifference? Etymologically, the word means "no difference." A strange and unnatural state in which the lines blur between light and darkness, dusk and dawn, crime and punishment, cruelty and compassion, good and evil.

What are its courses and inescapable consequences? Is it a philosophy? Is there a philosophy of indifference conceivable? Can one possibly view indifference as a virtue? Is it necessary at times to practice it simply to keep one's sanity, live normally, enjoy a fine meal and a glass of wine, as the world around us experiences harrowing upheavals?

Of course, indifference can be tempting—more than that, seductive. It is so much easier to look away from victims. It is so much easier to avoid such rude interruptions to our work, our dreams, our hopes. It is, after all, awkward, troublesome, to be involved in another person's pain and despair. Yet, for the person who is indifferent, his or her neighbors are of no consequence. And, therefore, their lives are meaningless. Their hidden or even visible anguish is of no interest. Indifference reduces the other to an abstraction.

Over there, behind the black gates of Auschwitz, the most tragic of all prisoners were the "Muselmanner," as they were called. Wrapped in their torn blankets, they would sit or lie on the ground, staring vacantly into space, unaware of who or where they were, strangers to their surroundings. They no longer felt pain, hunger, thirst. They feared nothing. They felt nothing. They were dead and did not know it.

Rooted in our tradition, some of us felt that to be abandoned by humanity then was not the ultimate. We felt that to be abandoned by God was worse than to be punished by Him. Better an unjust God than an indifferent one. For us to be ignored by God was a harsher punishment than to be a victim of His anger. Man can live far from God—not outside God. God is wherever we are. Even in suffering? Even in suffering.

In a way, to be indifferent to that suffering is what makes the human being inhuman. Indifference, after all, is more dangerous than anger and hatred. Anger can at times be creative. One writes a great poem, a great symphony, one does something special for the sake of humanity because one is angry at the injustice that one witnesses. But indifference is never creative. Even hatred at times may elicit a response. You fight it. You denounce it. You disarm it. Indifference elicits no response ...

Indifference is not a beginning, it is an end. And, therefore, indifference is always the friend of the enemy, for it benefits the aggressor—never its victim, whose pain is magnified when he or she feels forgotten. The political prisoner in his cell, the hungry children, the homeless refugees—not to respond to their plight, not to relieve their solitude by offering them a spark of hope is to exile them from human memory. And in denying their humanity we betray our own.

Indifference, then, is not only a sin, it is a punishment. And this is one of the most important lessons of this outgoing century's wide-ranging experiments in good and evil.

In the place that I come from, society was composed of three simple categories: the killers, the victims, and the bystanders. During the darkest of times, inside the ghettoes and death camps … we felt abandoned, forgotten. All of us did.

And our only miserable consolation was that we believed that Auschwitz and Treblinka were closely guarded secrets; that the leaders of the free world did not know what was going on behind those black gates and barbed wire; that they had no knowledge of the war against the Jews that Hitler's armies and their accomplices waged as part of the war against the Allies.

If they knew, we thought, surely those leaders would have moved heaven and earth to intervene. They would have spoken out with great outrage and conviction. They would have bombed the railways leading to Birkenau, just the railways, just once.

And now we knew, we learned, we discovered that the Pentagon knew, the State Department knew. And the illustrious occupant of the White House then, who was a great leader, knew—and I say it with some anguish and pain, because, today is exactly 54 years marking his death—Franklin Delano Roosevelt died on April the 12th, 1945, so he is very much present to me and to us.

No doubt, he was a great leader. He mobilized the American people and the world, going into battle, bringing hundreds and thousands of valiant and brave soldiers in America to fight fascism, to fight dictatorship, to fight Hitler. And so many of the young people fell in battle. And, nevertheless, his image in Jewish history—I must say it—his image in Jewish history is flawed.

The depressing tale of the St. Louis is a case in point. Sixty years ago, its human cargo—maybe 1,000 Jews—was turned back to Nazi Germany. And that happened after the Kristallnacht, after the first state sponsored pogrom, with hundreds of Jewish shops destroyed, synagogues burned, thousands of people put in concentration camps. And that ship, which was already on the shores of the United States, was sent back.

I don't understand. Roosevelt was a good man, with a heart. He understood those who needed help. Why didn't he allow these refugees to disembark? A thousand people—in America, a great country, the greatest democracy, the most generous of all new nations in modern history. What happened? I don't understand. Why the indifference, on the highest level, to the suffering of the victims?

But then, there were human beings who were sensitive to our tragedy. Those non-Jews, those Christians, that we called the "Righteous Gentiles," whose selfless acts of heroism saved the honor of their faith. Why were they so few? Why was there a greater effort to save SS murderers after the war than to save their victims during the war?

Why did some of America's largest corporations continue to do business with Hitler's Germany until 1942? It has been suggested, and it was documented, that the Wehrmacht could not have conducted its invasion of France without oil obtained from American sources. How is one to explain their indifference?

And yet, my friends, good things have also happened in this traumatic century: the defeat of Nazism, the collapse of communism, the rebirth of Israel on its ancestral soil, the demise of apartheid, Israel's peace treaty with Egypt, the peace accord in Ireland. And let us remember the meeting, filled with drama and emotion, between Rabin and Arafat that you, Mr. President, convened in this very place. I was here and I will never forget it.

And then, of course, the joint decision of the United States and NATO to intervene in Kosovo and save those victims, those refugees, those who were uprooted by a man whom I believe that because of his crimes, should be charged with crimes against humanity. But this time, the world was not silent. This time, we do respond. This time, we intervene.

Does it mean that we have learned from the past? Does it mean that society has changed? Has the human being become less indifferent and more human? Have we really learned from our experiences? Are we less insensitive to the plight of victims of ethnic cleansing and other forms of injustices in places near and far? Is today's justified intervention in Kosovo, led by you, Mr. President, a lasting warning that never again will the deportation, the terrorization of children and their parents be allowed anywhere in the world? Will it discourage other dictators in other lands to do the same?

What about the children? Oh, we see them on television, we read about them in the papers, and we do so with a broken heart. Their fate is always the most tragic, inevitably. When adults wage war, children perish. We see their faces, their eyes. Do we hear their pleas? Do we feel their pain, their agony? Every minute one of them dies of disease, violence, famine. Some of them—so many of them—could be saved.

And so, once again, I think of the young Jewish boy from the Carpathian Mountains. He has accompanied the old man I have become throughout these years of quest and struggle. And together we walk towards the new millennium, carried by profound fear and extraordinary hope.

NELSON MANDELA
"The Rivonia Trial," "Our March to Freedom" and "Glory and Hope"

From prisoner to president, Nelson Mandela sacrificed his personal life for the cause of his fellow South Africans. After he gave up a promising legal career, his public actions quickly carried him to the heights of civil rights leadership and made him a symbol of heroic black resistance to the government's apartheid regime.

As an integral member of the African National Congress (ANC) and the *Umkhonto we Sizwe* ("Spear of the Nation"), Mandela sought the liberation of blacks, who had endured untold hardship and violence. Mandela and other political colleagues were hunted by police and ultimately jailed.

Charged under the Suppression of Communism Act, Mandela defended himself against the death penalty in the Rivonia Trial. Late into the night he wrote his statement—an explanation of the ANC, of Umkhonto, of himself and of his people—then collapsed from exhaustion. Six months after the trial opened, on April 20, 1964, he delivered his four-hour defense. After hearing it, the judge sentenced Mandela and seven other defendants to hard labor and life imprisonment.

"The Rivonia Trial"

Our fight is against real, and not imaginary hardships, or, to use the language of the State Prosecutor, "so-called hardships." ... We fight against two features which are the hallmarks of African life in South Africa.... These features are poverty and lack of human dignity, and we do not need Communists, or so-called "agitators," to teach us about these things.

... The whites enjoy what may well be the highest standard of living in the world, whilst Africans live in poverty and misery. Forty per cent of the Africans live in hopelessly overcrowded and in some cases, drought-stricken reserves.... Thirty percent are labourers, labor tenants, and squatters on White farms and work and live under conditions similar to those of the serfs of the Middle Ages. The other thirty per cent live in towns where they have developed economic and social habits which bring them closer, in many respects, to white standards. Yet ... forty-six per cent of all African families in Johannesburg do not earn enough to keep them going ...

The complaint of Africans, however, is not only that they are poor and Whites are rich, but that the laws which are made by the Whites are designed to preserve this situation. There are two ways to break out of poverty. The first is by formal education, and the second is by the worker acquiring a greater skill at his work and thus higher wages. As far as Africans are concerned, both these avenues of advancement are deliberately curtailed by legislation.

The present Government has always sought to hamper Africans in their search for education.... There is compulsory education for all white children at virtually no cost to their parents.... Similar facilities are

not provided for African children.... The present Prime Minister said during the debate on the Bantu Education Bill in 1953: "When I have control of Native education, I will reform it so that Natives will be taught from childhood to realize that equality with Europeans is not for them.... People who believe in equality are not desirable teachers for Natives. When my Department controls Native education, it will know for what class of higher education a Native is fitted, and whether he will have a chance in life to use his knowledge."

The other main obstacle to the economic advancement of the Africans is the industrial colour bar by which all the better jobs of industry are reserved for Whites only. Moreover, Africans ... are not allowed to form Trade Unions, which have recognition under the Industrial Conciliation Act.... The Government often answers its critics by saying that Africans in South Africa are economically better off than the inhabitants of the other countries in Africa.... Our complaint is not that we are poor by comparison with people in other countries, but that we are poor by comparison with White people in our own country, and that we are prevented by legislation from altering this imbalance ...

The lack of human dignity experienced by Africans is the direct result of the policy of White supremacy. White supremacy implies Black inferiority.... Hundreds and thousands of Africans are thrown into gaol each year under pass laws. Even worse than this is the fact that pass laws keep husband and wife apart and lead to the breakdown family life ...

... Africans want to be part of the general population, and not confined to living in our ghettos. African men want to have their wives and children to live with them, where they work, and not be forced into an unnatural existence in men's hostels. African women want to be left with their menfolk, and not to be left permanently widowed in the Reserves. Africans want to be allowed out after eleven o'clock at night and not to be confined in their rooms like little children. Africans want to be allowed to travel in their own country and to seek work where they want to, and not where the Labor Bureau tells them to. Africans want a just share in the whole of South Africa; they want security and a stake in society.

Above all, we want equal political rights, because without them our disabilities will be permanent. I know this sounds revolutionary to the Whites in this country, because the majority of voters will be Africans. This makes the White man fear democracy.

But this fear cannot be allowed to stand in the way of the only solution which will guarantee racial harmony and freedom for all. It is not true that the enfranchisement of all will result in racial domination. Political division, based on color, is entirely artificial and, when it disappears, so will the domination of one color group by another. The A.N.C. has spent half a century fighting against racialism. When it triumphs it will not change that policy ...

During my lifetime I have dedicated my life to this struggle of the African people. I have fought against White domination, and I have fought against Black domination. I have cherished the ideal of a democratic and free society in which all persons live together in harmony with equal opportunities. It is an ideal which I hope to live for, and to see realized. But my lord, if needs be, it is an ideal for which I am prepared to die.

When released from prison 27 years later, Nelson Mandela was 71 and white-haired. Smiling as he left the jail, he raised his hand in the clenched-fist salute of the ANC and made his first speech since his trial. A crowd of 50,000 and a television audience of millions heard Mandela once again pleading for human rights.

"Our March to Freedom"

Friends, Comrades and fellow South Africans, I greet you all in the name of peace, democracy and freedom for all. I stand here before you not as a prophet but as a humble servant of you, the people. Your tireless and heroic sacrifices have made it possible for me to be here today. I therefore place the remaining years of my life in your hands ...

The apartheid destruction on our subcontinent is incalculable. The fabric of family life of millions of my people has been shattered. Millions are homeless and unemployed. Our economy lies in ruins and our people are embroiled in political strife ...

... We have no option but to continue ...

... Our march to freedom is irreversible. We must not allow fear to stand in our way. Universal suffrage on common voters' roll in a united, democratic and non-racial South Africa is the only way to peace and racial harmony.

... It is an ideal which I hope to live for and to achieve. But if needs be, it is an ideal for which I am prepared to die!

Though Nelson Mandela, his family and his compatriots suffered persecutions and bans for three decades, they unrelentingly struggled to draw attention to the plight of Africans. Finally, as President of South Africa, he addressed the people of Pretoria on May 10, 1994. Displaying an uncommon graciousness toward his former captors and opponents, Mandela expressed his hopes for reconciliation and democracy in his inaugural speech.

"Glory and Hope"

Your majesties, your royal highnesses, distinguished guests, comrades and friends: Today, all of us do, by our presence here, and by our celebrations in other parts of our country and the world, confer glory and hope to newborn liberty.

Out of the experience of an extraordinary human disaster that lasted too long must be born a society of which all humanity will be proud.

Our daily deeds as ordinary South Africans must produce an actual South African reality that will reinforce humanity's belief in justice, strengthen its confidence in the nobility of the human soul and sustain all our hopes for a glorious life for all.

... To my compatriots, I have no hesitation in saying that each one of us is as intimately attached to the soil of this beautiful country as are the famous jacaranda trees of Pretoria and the mimosa trees of the bushveld.

... That spiritual and physical oneness we all share with this common homeland explains the depth of the pain we all carried in our hearts as we saw our country tear itself apart in a terrible conflict, and as we saw it spurned, outlawed and isolated by the peoples of the world, precisely because it has become the universal base of the pernicious ideology and practice of racism and racial oppression ...

We deeply appreciate the role that the masses of our people ... have played to bring about this conclusion. Not least among them is my Second Deputy President, the Honorable F.W. de Klerk.

We would also like to pay tribute to our security forces ... for the distinguished role they have played in securing our first democratic elections and the transition to democracy, from bloodthirsty forces which still refuse to see the light.

The time for the healing of the wounds has come. The moment to bridge the chasms that divide us has come.

The time to build is upon us.

We have, at last, achieved our political emancipation. We pledge ourselves to liberate all our people from the continuing bondage of poverty, deprivation, suffering, gender and other discrimination ...

We dedicate this day to all the heroes and the heroines in this country and the rest of the world who sacrificed in many ways and surrendered their lives so that we could be free ...

We understand it still that there is no easy road to freedom. We know it well that none of us acting alone can achieve success. We must therefore act together as a united people, for national reconciliation, for nation building, for the birth of a new world.

Let there be justice for all.

Let there be peace for all.

Let there be work, bread, and water and salt for all.

Let each know that for each the body, the mind and the soul have been freed to fulfill themselves.

Never, never and never again shall it be that this beautiful land will again experience the oppression of one by another and suffer the indignity of being the skunk of the world.

Let freedom reign. The sun shall never set on so glorious a human achievement!

God bless Africa!

MARTIN LUTHER KING, JR.
"I Have a Dream"

D r. Martin Luther King, Jr., trained as a Christian minister, spoke out on behalf of the poor and the black in America. An intelligent and well-educated orator, Dr. King participated in and led nonviolent protests against segregation and inequity.

The powerful and eloquent speech "I Have A Dream" was delivered August 8, 1963, at the Lincoln Memorial in Washington, D.C. Inspired by the enormity of the task before him, the Reverend had worked, writing out his speech in long-hand, until four o'clock the previous morning. King then delivered his petitions to nearly a quarter of a million protesters who had assembled to urge Congress to pass President Kennedy's civil rights bill ensuring jobs and equal rights. Although large marches previously had been held throughout the South, this was, as Philip Randolph, dean of the black American leaders, later described, a "convocation of national scope and gargantuan size."

King was keenly aware of the volatile nature of the issue and of the gathering itself. His stirring call to action defined the moral basis of the civil rights movement—and became the highlight of the rally. King's eloquence paved the way for The Civil Rights Act of 1964, and earned him the 1964 Nobel Peace Prize.

I am happy to join with you today in what will go down in history as the greatest demonstration for freedom in the history of our nation.

Five score years ago, a great American, in whose symbolic shadow we stand, signed the Emancipation Proclamation. This momentous decree came as a great beacon light of hope to millions of Negro slaves who had been seared in the flames of withering injustice. It came as a joyous daybreak to end the long night of captivity.

But one hundred years later, the Negro is still not free. One hundred years later, the life of the Negro is still sadly crippled by the manacles of segregation and the chains of discrimination. One hundred years later, the Negro lives on a lonely island of poverty in the midst of a vast ocean of material prosperity. One hundred years later, the Negro is still languished in the corners of American society and finds himself in exile in his own land. And so we've come here today to dramatize a shameful condition.

In a sense we have come to our nation's capital to cash a check. When the architects of our republic wrote the magnificent words of the Constitution and the Declaration of Independence, they were signing a promissory note to which every American was to fall heir. This note was a promise that all men, yes, black

men as well as white men, would be guaranteed the "unalienable Rights" of "Life, Liberty, and the pursuit of Happiness."

It is obvious today that America has defaulted on this promissory note insofar as her citizens of color are concerned. Instead of honoring this sacred obligation, America has given the Negro people a bad check, a check which has come back marked "insufficient funds."

But we refuse to believe that the bank of justice is bankrupt. We refuse to believe that there are insufficient funds in the great vaults of opportunity of this nation. And so, we have come to cash this check—a check that will give us upon demand the riches of freedom and the security of justice.

We have also come to this hallowed spot to remind America of the fierce urgency of Now. This is no time to engage in the luxury of cooling off or to take the tranquilizing drug of gradualism. Now is the time to make real the promises of democracy. Now is the time to rise from the dark and desolate valley of segregation to the sunlit path of racial justice. Now is the time to lift our nation from the quicksands of racial injustice to the solid rock of brotherhood. Now is the time to make justice a reality for all of God's children.

It would be fatal for the nation to overlook the urgency of the moment. This sweltering summer of the Negro's legitimate discontent will not pass until there is an invigorating autumn of freedom and equality. Nineteen sixty-three is not an end, but a beginning. Those who hope that the Negro needed to blow off steam and will now be content will have a rude awakening if the nation returns to business as usual. There will be neither rest nor tranquility in America until the Negro is granted his citizenship rights. The whirlwinds of revolt will continue to shake the foundations of our nation until the bright day of justice emerges.

But there is something that I must say to my people, who stand on the warm threshold which leads into the palace of justice: In the process of gaining our rightful place, we must not be guilty of wrongful deeds. Let us not seek to satisfy our thirst for freedom by drinking from the cup of bitterness and hatred. We must forever conduct our struggle on the high plane of dignity and discipline. We must not allow our creative protest to degenerate into physical violence. Again and again, we must rise to the majestic heights of meeting physical force with soul force. The marvelous new militancy which has engulfed the Negro community must not lead us to a distrust of all white people, for many of our white brothers, as evidenced by their presence here today, have come to realize that their destiny is tied up with our destiny. And they have come to realize that their freedom is inextricably bound to our freedom.

We cannot walk alone. And as we walk, we must make the pledge that we shall always march ahead. We cannot turn back.

There are those who are asking the devotees of civil rights, "When will you be satisfied?" We can never be satisfied as long as the Negro is the victim of the unspeakable horrors of police brutality. We can never be satisfied as long as our bodies, heavy with fatigue of travel, cannot gain lodging in the motels of the highways and the hotels of the cities. We cannot be satisfied as long as the Negro's basic mobility is from a smaller ghetto to a larger one. We can never be satisfied as long as our children are stripped of their self-hood and robbed of their dignity by a sign stating: "For Whites Only." We cannot be satisfied as long as a Negro in Mississippi cannot vote and a Negro in New York believes he has nothing for which to vote. No, no, we are not satisfied, and we will not be satisfied until "justice rolls down like waters and righteousness like a mighty stream."

I am not unmindful that some of you have come here out of great trials and tribulations. Some of you have come fresh from narrow jail cells. And some of you have come from areas where your quest for freedom left you battered by the storms of persecution and staggered by the winds of police brutality. You have been the veterans of creative suffering. Continue to work with the faith that unearned suffering is redemptive.

Go back to Mississippi, go back to Alabama, go back to South Carolina, go back to Georgia, go back to Louisiana, go back to the slums and ghettos of the northern cities, knowing that somehow this situation can and will be changed.

Let us not wallow in the valley of despair, I say to you, my friends. And even though we face the difficulties of today and tomorrow, I still have a dream. It is a dream deeply rooted in the American dream.

I have a dream that one day this nation will rise up and live out the true meaning of its creed: "We hold these truths to be self-evident, that all men are created equal."

I have a dream that one day on the red hills of Georgia the sons of former slaves and the sons of former slave owners will be able to sit down together at the table of brotherhood.

I have a dream that one day even the state of Mississippi, a state sweltering with the heat of injustice, sweltering with the heat of oppression, will be transformed into an oasis of freedom and justice.

I have a dream that my four little children will one day live in a nation where they will not be judged by the color of their skin but by the content of their character.

I have a dream today!

I have a dream that one day in the state of Alabama, with its vicious racists, with its governor having his lips dripping with the words of "interposition" and "nullification"—one day right there in Alabama little black boys and black girls will be able to join hands with little white boys and white girls as sisters and brothers.

I have a dream today!

I have a dream that one day every valley shall be exalted, and every hill and mountain shall be made low, the rough places shall be made plain, and the crooked places will be made straight; "and the glory of the Lord shall be revealed and all flesh shall see it together."

This is our hope, and this is the faith that I go back to the South with. With this faith, we will be able to hew out of the mountain of despair a stone of hope. With this faith, we will be able to transform the jangling discords of our nation into a beautiful symphony of brotherhood. With this faith, we will be able to work together, to pray together, to struggle together, to go to jail together, to stand up for freedom together, knowing that we will be free one day.

This will be the day when all of God's children will be able to sing with new meaning:

My country 'tis of thee, sweet land of liberty, of thee I sing.

Land where my fathers died, land of the pilgrim's pride,

From every mountainside, let freedom ring!

And if America is to be a great nation, this must become true. And so let freedom ring from the prodigious hilltops of New Hampshire. Let freedom ring from the mighty mountains of New York. Let freedom ring from the heightening Alleghenies of Pennsylvania! Let freedom ring from the snowcapped Rockies of Colorado! Let freedom ring from the curvaceous slopes of California!

But not only that: let freedom ring from Stone Mountain of Georgia! Let freedom ring from Lookout Mountain of Tennessee! Let freedom ring from every hill and molehill of Mississippi—from every mountainside, let freedom ring!

Wand when this happens, when we let freedom ring, when we let it ring from every village and every hamlet, from every state and every city, we will be able to speed up that day when all of God's children, black men and white men, Jews and Gentiles, Protestants and Catholics, will be able to join hands and sing in the words of the old Negro spiritual: "Free at last! Free at last! Thank God almighty, we are free at last!"

MAHATMA GANDHI
"Nonviolence Is ... My Faith"

Slight of build yet possessing impressive physical and moral strength, Mohandas K. Gandhi led the people of India in a fight for independence. His unique approach to social change required courage, nonviolence and truth. Noncompliance and self-suffering— including fasts and hunger strikes—together with media campaigns and public speaking were his nonviolent methods for social action.

As leader of the Indian National Congress, which adopted his *satyagraha* (passive resistance) principles, his political path included imprisonments, great personal suffering and, ultimately, collaboration with the English when, in 1967, they acceded to Indian self-government.

Trained as a lawyer in London, Gandhi spent 21 years in South Africa working for Indian rights. Constantly shadowed by the police, he was arrested many times by the British, arrests which provided the impetus for the reform Gandhi was seeking. Thus in 1922 he was charged with sedition for articles published in *Young India*. Upon the conclusion of his trial on the 18th day of March, Gandhi was allowed to give the following prepared statement to the packed Indian courtroom prior to his sentencing. In his preliminary remarks, he welcomed full punishment for his activities against the government. However, had he not acted as he did, he would have failed in carrying out his duty to his people. When the judge finally sentenced him to six years in prison, Gandhi thanked him for his courtesy.

●

... I wanted to avoid violence. Non-violence is the first article of my faith. It is also the last article of my creed. But I had to make my choice. I had either to submit to a system which I considered had done an irreparable harm to my country, or incur the risk of the mad fury of my people bursting forth when they understood the truth from my lips. I know that my people have sometimes gone mad. I am deeply sorry for it and I am, therefore, here to submit not to a light penalty but to the highest penalty. I do not ask for mercy. I do not plead any extenuating act. I am here, therefore, to invite and cheerfully submit to the highest penalty that can be inflicted upon me for what in law is a deliberate crime, and what appears to me to be the highest duty of a citizen. The only course open to you, the Judge, is ... either to resign your post, or inflict on me the severest penalty if you believe that the system and law you are assisting to administer are good for the people. I do not expect that kind of conversion. But by the time I have finished with my statement, you will have a glimpse of what is raging within my breast to run this maddest risk which a sane man can run.

I owe it perhaps to the Indian public and to the public in England ... that I should explain why from a staunch loyalist and co-operator, I have become an uncompromising disaffectionist and non-co-operator. To the court too I should say why I plead guilty to the charge of promoting disaffection toward the Government established by law in India.

My public life began in 1893 in South Africa.... My first contact with British authority in that country was not of a happy character. I discovered that as a man and Indian, I had no rights ... as a man because I was an Indian.

But I was not baffled. I thought that this treatment of Indians was an excrescence upon a system that was intrinsically and mainly good. I gave the Government my voluntary and hearty cooperation, criticizing it freely where I felt it was faulty but never wishing its destruction.

Consequently, when the existence of the Empire was threatened in 1899 by the Boer challenge, I offered my services to it.... Similarly in 1906, at the time of the Zulu "revolt," I raised a stretcher bearer party and served till the end of the "rebellion." On both occasions I received medals and was even mentioned in dispatches.... When the war broke out in 1914 between England and Germany, I raised a volunteer ambulance corps in London consisting of the then resident Indians in London, chiefly students. Its work was acknowledged by the authorities to be valuable. Lastly, in India when a special appeal was made at the War Conference in Delhi in 1918 ... I struggled at the cost of my health to raise a corps in Kheda.... In all these efforts at service, I was actuated by the belief that it was possible by such services to gain a status of full equality in the Empire for my countrymen.

The first shock came in the shape of the Rowlatt Act, a law designed to rob the people of all real freedom. I felt called upon to lead an intensive agitation against it. Then followed the Punjab horrors beginning with the massacre at Jallianwala Bagh and culminating in crawling orders, public floggings and other indescribable humiliations.... But in spite of the forebodings and the grave warnings of friends ... I fought for co-operation ... hoping that the Prime Minister would redeem his promise to the Indian Mussulmans, that the Punjab wound would be healed, and that the reforms, inadequate and unsatisfactory though they were, marked a new era of hope in the life of India.

But all that hope was shattered.... The Punjab crime was whitewashed, and most culprits went not only unpunished but remained in service, and some continued to draw pensions from the Indian revenue and in some cases were even rewarded. I saw too that not only did the reforms not mark a change of heart, but they were only a method of further draining India of her wealth and of prolonging her servitude.

I came reluctantly to the conclusion that the British connection had made India more helpless than she ever was before, politically and economically. A disarmed India has no power of resistance against any aggressor if she wanted to engage in an armed conflict with him.... She has become so poor that she has little power of resisting famines. Before the British advent India spun and wove in her millions of cottages just the supplement she needed for adding to her meager agricultural resources. This cottage industry, so vital for India's existence, has been ruined by incredibly heartless and inhuman processes.... Little do town dwellers know how the semi-starved masses of India are slowly sinking to life-lessness. Little do they know that their miserable comfort represents the brokerage they get for the work they do for the foreign exploiter, that the profits and the brokerage are sucked from the masses. Little do they realize that the Government established by law in British India is carried on for this exploitation of the masses. No sophistry, no jugglery in figures can explain away the evidence that the skeletons in many villages present to the naked eye. I have no doubt whatsoever that both England and the town dweller of India will have to answer, if there is a God above, for this crime against humanity, which is perhaps unequaled in history. The law itself in this country has been used to serve the foreign exploiter.... My experience of political cases in India leads me to the conclusion that in nine of every ten, the condemned men were totally innocent. Their crime consisted in the love of their country. In ninety-nine cases out of a hundred, justice has been denied to Indians as against Europeans in the courts of India. This is not an exaggerated picture. It is the experience of almost every Indian who has had anything to do with such cases. In my opinion, the administration of the law is thus prostituted, consciously or unconsciously, for the benefit of the exploiter.

The greater misfortune is that the Englishmen and their Indian associates in the administration of the country do not know that they are engaged in the crime I have attempted to describe. I am satisfied that many Englishmen and Indian officials honestly believe that they are administering one of the best systems devised in the world, and that India is making steady, though slow, progress. They do not know that a subtle but effective system of terrorism and an organized display of force on the one hand, and the deprivation of all powers of retaliation or self-defense on the other, have emasculated the people and induced in them the habit of simulation. This awful habit has added to the ignorance and the self-deception of the administrators.... Affection cannot be manufactured or regulated by law. If one has no affection for a person or system, one should be free to give the fullest expression to his disaffection, so long as he does not contemplate, promote, or incite to violence.... But the section under which mere promotion of disaffection is a crime ... I have studied some of the cases tried under it, and I know that some of the most loved of India's patriots have been convicted under it. I consider it a privilege, therefore, to be charged under that section. I have endeavored to give in their briefest outline the reasons for my disaffection. I have no personal ill-will against any single administrator, much less can I have any disaffection towards the King's person. But I hold it to be a virtue to be disaffected toward a Government which in its totality has done more harm to India than any previous system. India is less manly under the British rule than she ever was before. Holding such a belief, I consider it to be a sin to have affection for the system. And it has been a precious privilege for me to be able to write what I have in the various articles tendered in evidence against me.

In fact, I believe that I have rendered a service to India and England by showing in non-cooperation the way out of the unnatural state in which both are living. In my humble opinion, non-cooperation with evil is as much a duty as is co-operation with good. But in the past, non-cooperation has been deliberately expressed in violence to the evil-doer. I am endeavoring to show to my countrymen that violent non-cooperation only multiplies evil, and that as evil can only be sustained by violence, withdrawal of support of evil requires complete abstention from violence. Non-violence implies voluntary submission to the penalty for non-cooperation with evil. I am here, therefore, to invite and submit cheerfully to the highest penalty that can be inflicted upon me for what in law is a deliberate crime, and what appears to me to be the highest duty of a citizen. The only course open to you, the Judge and the assessors, is either to resign your posts and thus dissociate yourselves from evil, if you feel that the law you are called upon to administer is an evil, and that in reality I am innocent, or to inflict on me the severest penalty, if you believe that the system and the law you are assisting to administer are good for the people of this country, and that my activity is, therefore, injurious to the common weal.

CHIEF JOSEPH
"Let Me Be a Free Man"

Leader of the Nez Perce, Young Chief Joseph worked to fulfill his promise to his "Old Chief" father by becoming a statesman and government advocate for the American Indians. Although his dying father asked that the tribal homeland never be sold, he of course could not foresee that the land in fertile Oregon would be taken from his descendants. "My father was the first to see through the schemes of the white men," Chief Joseph noted, "and he warned his tribe to be careful about trading with them. He had suspicion of men who seemed so anxious to make money. I was a boy then, but I remember my father's caution. He had sharper eyes than the rest of our people."

"Thunder Traveling Over the Mountains," as Young Chief Joseph was known to his tribe, deplored the violent fighting with the U.S. troops that broke out when the Nez Perce were required to surrender their land and move onto a reservation. Rather, the Chief resolved to lead his people to safety in Canada—a rambling march of 1,000 miles through the mountains of the Northwestern United States. Skillfully guiding his clan, the Chief managed to avoid the troops, except during a battle he won in Montana. Finally captured 30 miles from their destination, the Nez Perce were relocated onto reservations. His robes displaying bullet holes, Chief Joseph surrendered in 1877, with these words.

Tell General Howard I know his heart. What he told me before, I have it in my heart. I am tired of fighting. Our chiefs are killed, Looking-Glass is dead, Ta-Hool-Hool-Shute is dead.... It is cold, and we have no blankets; the little children are freezing to death. My people, some of them, have run away to the hills, and have no blankets, no food. No one knows where they are—perhaps freezing to death. I want to have time to look for my children, and see how many of them I can find. Maybe I shall find them among the dead. Hear me, my chiefs! I am tired; my heart is sick and sad. From where the sun now stands I will fight no more forever.

With the aid of an interpreter and from an enforced new "homeland" in Oklahoma, the Indian leader defended his people to the American public. In an attempt to sway public opinion and facilitate justice, Chief Joseph published the following essay in the April, 1879, issue of the *North American Review*. His eloquent plea for human rights is, as T.J. Stiles describes, "as powerful as anything written by the founding fathers."

My friends, I have been asked to show you my heart. I am glad to have a chance to do so. I want the white people to understand my people. Some of you think an Indian is like a wild animal. This is a great mistake.... I will tell you in my way how the Indian sees things. The white man has more words to tell you how they look to him, but it does not require many words to speak the truth. What I have to say will come from my heart, and I will speak with a straight tongue. Ah-cum-kin-i-ma-me-hut (the Great Spirit) is looking at me, and will hear me.

My name is In-mut-too-yah-lat (Thunder Traveling Over the Mountains). I am chief of the Wal-lam-wat-kin band of Chute-pa-lu, or Nez Perces (nose pierced Indians). I was born in eastern Oregon, thirty-eight winters ago. My father was chief before me. When a young man, he was called Joseph by Mr. Spaulding, a missionary. He died a few years ago. There was no stain on his hands of the blood of a white man. He left a good name on the earth ...

Our fathers gave us many laws, which they had learned from their fathers. These laws were good. They told us to treat all men as they treated us; that we should never be the first to break a bargain; that it was a disgrace to tell a lie; that we should speak only the truth; that it was a shame for one man to take from another his wife, or his property without paying for it. We were taught to believe that the Great Spirit sees and hears everything, and that he never forgets; that hereafter he will give every man a spirit-home according to his deserts: if he has been a good man, he will have a good home; if he has been a bad man, he will have a bad home. This I believe, and all my people believe the same.

We did not know there were other people besides the Indian until about one hundred winters ago, when some men with white faces came to our country.... These men were Frenchmen, and they called our people "Nez Perces," because they wore rings in their noses for ornaments. Although very few of our people wear them now, we are still called by the same name.... Our people were divided in opinion about these men. Some thought they taught more bad than good. An Indian respects a brave man, but he despises a coward. He loves a straight tongue. The French trappers told us some truths and some lies.

... All the Nez Perces made friends with Lewis and Clarke, and agreed to let them pass through their country, and never to make war on white men. This promise the Nez Perces have never broken. No white man can accuse them of bad faith, and speak with a straight tongue.... But we soon found that the white men were growing rich very fast, and were greedy to possess everything the Indian had...

... There came a white officer (Governor Stevens), who invited all the Nez Perces to a treaty council. After the council was opened he made known his heart. He said there were a great many white people in the country, and many more would come.... If they were to live in peace it was necessary, he said, that the Indians should have a country set apart for them, and that in that country they must stay. My father, who represented his band, refused to have anything to do with the council, because he wished to be a free man. He claimed that no man owned any part of the earth, and a man could not sell what he did not own.

My father left the council...

Eight years later (1863) was the next treaty council. A chief called Lawyer, because he was a great talker, took the lead in this council and sold nearly all the Nez Perces' country. My father ... said to me: "When you go into council with the white man, always remember your country.... The white man will cheat you out of your home. I have taken no pay from the United States. I have never sold our land." In this treaty Lawyer acted without authority from our band. He had no right to sell the Wallowa (winding water) country . That has always belonged to my father's own people, and the other bands had never disputed our right to it...

... The United States claimed they had bought all the Nez Perces country outside of the Lapway Reservation, from Lawyer and other chiefs, but we continued to live on this land in peace until eight years ago, when white men began to come inside the bounds my father had set. We warned them against this great wrong, but they would not leave our land, and some bad blood was raised. The white men represented that we were going upon the war-path. They reported many things that were false...

... Our young men were quick-tempered, and I have had great trouble in keeping them from doing rash things.... I know that my young men did a great wrong, but I ask, who was first to blame? They had been insulted a thousand times; their fathers and brothers had been killed; their mothers and wives had been disgraced; they had been driven to madness by whisky sold to them by white men; they had been told by General Howard that all their horses and cattle which they had been unable to drive out of Wallowa were to fall into the hands of white men; and, added to all this, they were homeless and desperate.

I would have given my own life if I could have undone the killing of white men by my people. I blame the young men and I blame the white men ...

We retreated as rapidly as we could toward the buffalo country. After six days General Howard came close to us, and we went out and attacked him, and captured nearly all his horses and mules.... We then marched on to the Yellowstone Basin.

On the way we captured one white man and two white women. We released them at the end of three days. They were treated kindly. The women were not insulted. Can the white soldiers tell me of one time when Indian women were taken prisoners, and held three days and then released without being insulted?...

I thought of my wife and children, who were now surrounded by soldiers, and I resolved to go to them or die. With a prayer in my mouth to the Great Spirit Chief who rules above, I dashed unarmed through the line of soldiers ...

... We could have escaped from Bear Paw Mountain if we had left our wounded, old women, and children behind. We were unwilling to do this. We had never heard of a wounded Indian recovering while in the hands of white men ...

... I could not bear to see my wounded men and women suffer any longer; we had lost enough already. General Miles had promised that we might return to our own country with what stock we had left. I thought we could start again. I believed General Miles, or I never would have surrendered ...

... They all say they are my friends, and that I shall have justice, but while their mouths all talk right, I do not understand why nothing is done for my people. I have heard talk and talk but nothing is done. Good words do not last long unless they amount to something ...

... When I think of our condition my heart is heavy. I see men of my race treated as outlaws and driven from country to country, or shot down like animals ...

Let me be a free man—free to travel, free to stop, free to work, free to trade where I choose, free to choose my own teachers, free to follow the religion of my fathers, free to think and talk and act for myself—and I will obey every law, or submit to the penalty.

Whenever the white man treats the Indians as they treat each other, then we will have no more wars. We shall all be alike—brothers of one father and one mother, with one sky above us and one country around us, and one government for all. Then the Great Spirit Chief who rules above will smile upon this land and send rain to wash out the bloody spots made by my brothers' hands from the face of the earth. For this time the Indian race are waiting and praying. I hope that no more groans of wounded men and women will ever go to the ear of the Great Spirit Chief above, and that all people may be one people.

In-mut-too-yah-lat-lat has spoken for his people.

YOUNG JOSEPH

SUSAN B. ANTHONY
"Citizen's Right to Vote"

At the age of 52, and shortly before her trial in June of 1873, Susan B. Anthony delivered a speech to defend women's right to vote in accordance with the Constitution. She had previously been arrested for voting in the 1872 Presidential Election, an event which attracted national attention. In defending her action Anthony wielded the phrase: "… it was we, the people; not we, the white male citizens; nor yet we, the male citizens; but we, the whole people … who formed the Union … to secure … the blessings of liberty."

Well-educated for a woman of her time, Anthony taught school between the ages of 15 and 30, while she and her family worked in support of the American Anti-Slavery Society. Always the crusader, she then organized and led America's first women's temperance league. Writing, lecturing and leading efforts for legislation, the women's rights leader traveled extensively in America and Europe. Together, she and Elizabeth Cady Stanton established the National Woman Suffrage Association.

Although her speeches often met with taunts and ridicule, Anthony's persuasive words and intelligent leadership inspired her followers. In fact, after her death in 1906, her followers picked up the work she had led until women won the right to vote with passage of the 19th amendment in 1920.

Friends and Fellow Citizens: I stand before you under indictment for the alleged crime of having voted at the last presidential election, without having a lawful right to vote. It shall be my work this evening to prove to you that in thus doing, I not only committed no crime, but instead simply exercised my citizen's rights, guaranteed to me and all United States citizens by the National Constitution, beyond the power of any State to deny.

Our democratic-republican government is based on the idea of the natural right of every individual member thereof to a voice and a vote in making and executing the laws. We assert the providence of government to be to secure the people in the enjoyment of their inalienable rights. We throw to the winds the old dogma that government can give rights. No one denies that before governments were organized each individual possessed the right to protect his own life, liberty and property…. The Declaration of Independence, the United States Constitution, the constitutions of the several States and the organic laws of the Territories, all alike propose to protect the people in the exercise of their God-given rights. Not one of them pretends to bestow rights.

"All men are created equal, and endowed by their Creator with certain inalienable rights. Among these are life, liberty and the pursuit of happiness. To secure these, governments are instituted among men, deriving their just powers from the consent of the governed."

Here is no shadow of government authority over rights, or exclusion of any class from their full and equal enjoyment. Here is pronounced the right of all men, and "consequently," as the Quaker preacher said, "of all women," to a voice in the government. And here, in this first paragraph of the Declaration, is the assertion of the natural right of all to the ballot; for how can "the consent of the governed" be given, if the right to vote be denied?... The women, dissatisfied as they are with this form of government, that enforces taxation without representation—that compels them to obey laws to which they never have given their consent—that imprisons and hangs them without a trial by a jury of their peers— that robs them, in marriage, of the custody of their own persons, wages and children—are this half of the people who are left wholly at the mercy of the other half, in direct violation of the spirit and letter of the declarations of the framers of this government, every one of which was based on the immutable principle of equal rights to all. By these declarations, kings, popes, priests, aristocrats, all were alike dethroned and placed on a common level, politically, with the lowliest born subject or serf. By then, too, men, as such, were deprived of their divine right to rule and placed on a political level with women. By the practice of these declarations all class and caste distinctions would be abolished, and slave, serf, plebeian, wife, woman, all alike rise from their subject position to the broader platform of equality.

The preamble of the Federal Constitution says: We, the people of the United States, in order to form a more perfect union, establish justice, insure domestic tranquility, provide for the common defense, promote the general welfare, and secure the blessings of liberty to ourselves and our posterity, do ordain and establish this Constitution for the United States of America.

It was we, the people, not we, the white male citizens, nor yet we, the male citizens; but we, the whole people, who formed the Union. We formed it, not to give the blessings of liberty, but to secure them; not to the half of ourselves and the half of our posterity, but to the whole people—women as well as men. And it is downright mockery to talk to women of their enjoyment of the blessings of liberty while they are denied the use of the only means of securing them provided by this democratic-republican government—the ballot.

The early journals of Congress show that, when the committee reported to that body the original articles of confederation, the very first one which became the subject of discussion was that respecting equality of suffrage …

James Madison said:

"Under every view of the subject, it seems indispensable that the mass of the citizens should not be without a voice in making the laws which they are to obey, and in choosing the magistrates who are to administer them.... Let it be remembered, finally, that it has ever been the pride and the boast of America that the rights for which she contended were the rights of human nature."

These assertions by the framers of the United States Constitution of the equal and natural right of all the people to a voice in the government, have been affirmed and reaffirmed by the leading statesmen of the nation throughout the entire history of our government.

... For any state to make sex a qualification that must ever result in the disfranchisement of one entire half of the people is ... a violation of the supreme law of the land. By it the blessings of liberty are forever withheld from women and their female posterity. To them this government has no just powers derived from the consent of the governed. For them this government is not a democracy; it is not a republic. It is the most odious aristocracy ever established on the face of the globe. An oligarchy of wealth, where the rich govern the poor; an oligarchy of learning, where the educated govern the ignorant; or even an oligarchy of race, where the Saxon rules the African, might be endured; but this oligarchy of sex, which makes father, brothers, husband, sons, the oligarchs over the mother and sisters, the wife and daughters, of every household which ordains all men sovereigns, all women subjects, carries dissension, discord, and rebellion into every home of the nation.

... It is urged that the use of the masculine pronouns he, his and him in all the constitutions and laws, is proof that only men were meant to be included in their provisions. If you insist on this version of the letter of the law, we shall insist that you be consistent and accept the other horn of the dilemma, which would compel you to exempt women from taxation for the support of the government and from penalties for the violation of laws. There is no she or her or hers in the tax laws, and this is equally true of all the criminal laws.

Take for example the civil rights law which I am charged with having violated; not only are all the pronouns in it masculine, but everybody knows that it was intended expressly to hinder the rebel from voting. It reads, "If a person shall knowingly vote without his having a lawful right." ... I insist if government officials may thus manipulate the pronouns to tax, fine, imprison and hang women, it is their duty to thus change them in order to protect us in our right to vote ...

Webster, Worcester, and Bouvier all define a citizen to be a person in the United States, entitled to vote and hold office.

... I submit that in view of the explicit assertions of the equal right of the whole people ... this omission of the adjective "female" should not be construed into a denial; but instead should be considered as of no effect.... No barriers whatever stand today between women and the exercise of their right to vote save those of precedent and prejudice, which refuse to expunge the word "male" from the constitution.

The only question left to be settled now is: Are women persons? And I hardly believe any of our opponents will have the hardihood to say they are not. Being persons, then, women are citizens; and no state has a right to make any law, or to enforce any old law, that shall abridge their privileges or immunities. Hence, every discrimination against women in their constitutions and laws of the several states is today null and void ...

Is the right to vote one of the privileges or immunities of citizens? I think the disfranchised ex-rebels and ex-State prisoners all will agree that it is not only one of them, but the one without which all the others are nothing. Seek first the kingdom of the ballot and all things else shall be added, is the political injunction ...

... It is upon this just interpretation of the United States Constitution that our National Woman Suffrage Association, which celebrates the twenty-fifth anniversary of the woman's rights movement next May in New York City, has based all its arguments and action since the passage of these amendments. We no longer petition legislature or Congress to give us the right to vote but appeal to women everywhere to exercise their too long neglected "citizen's right." We appeal to the inspectors of election to receive the votes of all United States citizens, as it is their duty to do. We appeal to United States commissioners and marshals to arrest, as is their duty, the inspectors who reject the votes of United States citizens, and leave alone those who perform their duties and accept these votes. We ask the juries to return verdicts of "not guilty" in the cases of law-abiding United States citizens who cast their votes, and inspectors of election who receive and count them.

We ask the judges to render unprejudiced opinions of the law, and wherever there is room for doubt to give the benefit to the side of liberty and equal rights for women, remembering that, as Sumner says, "The true rule of interpretation under our National Constitution, especially since its amendments, is that anything for human rights is constitutional, everything against human rights unconstitutional." It is on this line that we propose to fight our battle for the ballot—peaceably but nevertheless persistently—until we achieve complete triumph and all United States citizens, men and women alike, are recognized as equals in the government.

FREDERICK DOUGLASS
"American Slavery"

Born a slave, Frederick Augustus Washington Bailey suffered greatly, and ultimately changed his surname to *Douglass* to avoid capture as a runaway slave. Douglass became a powerful orator whose words moved his sympathizers and enraged his opponents. Because of his background as an ex-slave who tirelessly worked for abolition, he was regarded as an unusually credible speaker.

With the 1845 publication of his autobiography—seven years after escaping as a runaway—Douglass feared his identity would be revealed to his previous owners. He thus traveled to England to ensure his safety and to plead the cause of slaves. Shortly after his arrival in Britain, May 12, 1846, he delivered this classic speech on American slavery.

Returning to America—his freedom now purchased—Douglass continued his work: he founded an anti-slavery newspaper, led attacks against segregated schools, supported the underground railroad for runaway slaves, recruited blacks for the Union Army, and worked in government. Amid loud cheers, Douglass arose and faced his audience:

I feel exceedingly glad of the opportunity now afforded me of presenting the claims of my brethren in bonds in the United States, to so many in London and from various parts of Britain, who have assembled here on the present occasion. I have nothing to commend me to your consideration in the way of learning, nothing in the way of education to entitle me to your attention; and you are aware that slavery is a very bad school for rearing teachers of morality and religion. Twenty-one years of my life have been spent in slavery—personal slavery—surrounded by degrading influences, such as can exist nowhere beyond the pale of slavery; and it will not be strange, if under such circumstances, I should betray, in what I have to say to you, a deficiency of that refinement which is seldom or ever found, except among persons that have experienced superior advantages to those which I have enjoyed. But I will take it for granted that you know something about the degrading influences of slavery, and that you will not expect great things from me this evening, but simply such facts as I may be able to advance immediately in connection with my own experience of slavery.

Now, what is this system of slavery? This is the subject of my lecture this evening—what is the character of the institution?... I have found persons in this country who have identified the term slavery with that which I think it is not, and in some instances, I have feared, in so doing, have rather (unwittingly, I know,) detracted much

from the horror with which the term slavery is contemplated.... I am here to say that I think the term slavery is sometimes abused by identifying it with that which it is not. Slavery in the United States is the granting of that power by which one man exercises and enforces a right of property in the body and soul of another. The condition of the slave is simply that of the brute beast. He is a piece of property—a marketable commodity, in the language of the law, to be bought or sold at the will and caprice of the master who claims him to be his property; he is spoken of, thought of, and treated as property...

... This is American slavery; no marriage—no education—the light of the gospel shut out from the dark mind of the bondman—and he forbidden by law to learn to read. If a mother shall teach her children to read, the law in Louisiana proclaims that she may be hanged by the neck.... Three millions of people shut out from the light of knowledge! It is easy for you to conceive the evil that must result from such a state of things...

... The slaveholder resorts to all kinds of cruelty ... starvation, the bloody whip, the chain, the gag, the thumb-screw, cat-hauling, the cat-o-nine-tails, the dungeon, the bloodhound, are all in requisition to keep the slave in his condition as a slave in the United States.... The bloodhound is regularly trained in the United States, and advertisements are to be found in the southern papers of the Union, from persons advertising themselves as bloodhound trainers, and offering to hunt down slaves at fifteen dollars apiece...

... And all this is necessary: it is necessary to resort to these cruelties, in order to make the slave a slave, and to keep him a slave.... When I was treated exceedingly ill; when my back was being scourged daily; when I was whipped within an inch of my life—life was all I cared for ... I was not thinking of my liberty; it was my life.... But let him [the slave] know that the whip is burned; that the fetters have been turned to some useful and profitable employment; that the chain is no longer for his limb; that the blood-hound is no longer to be put upon his track; that his master's authority over him is no longer to be enforced by taking his life—and immediately he walks out from the house of bondage and asserts his freedom as a man...

... Some of the most awful scenes of cruelty are constantly taking place in the middle states of the Union.... If you would see the cruelties of this system, hear the following narrative. Not long since the following scene occurred. A slave-woman and a slave-man had united themselves as a man and wife in the absence of any law to protect them as a man and wife. They had lived

together by the permission, not by right, of their master, and they had reared a family. The master found it expedient, and for his interest, to sell them. He did not ask them their wishes in regard to the matter at all; they were not consulted. The man and woman were brought to the auctioneer's block, under the sound of the hammer. The cry was raised, "Here goes; who bids cash?" Think of it—a man and wife to be sold! The woman was placed on the auctioneer's block; her limbs, as is customary, were brutally exposed to the purchasers, who examined her with the full freedom with which they would examine a horse. There stood the husband, powerless, no right to his wife.... She was sold. He was next brought to the auctioneer's block. His eyes followed his wife in the distance; and he looked beseechingly, imploringly, to the man that had bought his wife, to buy him also. But he was at length bid off to another person. He was about to be separated forever from her he loved. No word of his, no work of his, could save him from this separation. He asked permission of his new master to go and take the hand of his wife at parting. It was denied him. In the agony of his soul he rushed from the man who had just bought him, that he might take a farewell of his wife; but his way was obstructed, he was struck over the head with a loaded whip, and was held for a moment; but his agony was too great. When he was let go, he fell a corpse at the feet of his master. His heart was broken. Such scenes are the every-day fruits of American slavery...

... But you will ask me, can these things be possible in a land professing Christianity? Yes, they are so.... While America is printing tracts and bibles; sending missionaries abroad to convert the heathen; expending her money in various ways for the promotion of the gospel in foreign lands—the slave not only lies forgotten, uncared for, but it is trampled under foot by the very churches of the land. What have we in America? Why, we have slavery made part of the religion of the land...

... Instead of preaching the gospel against this tyranny, rebuke, and wrong, ministers of religion have sought, by all and every means, to throw in the background whatever in the Bible could be construed into opposition to slavery, and to bring forward that which they could torture into its support. This I conceive to be the darkest feature of slavery, and the most difficult to attack, because it is identified with religion, and exposes them who denounce it to the charge of infidelity ...

... I love the religion that comes from above, in the "wisdom of God," which is first pure, then peaceable, gentle, and easy to be entreated, full of mercy and good fruits, without partiality and without hypocrisy.... I love that religion that makes it the duty of its disciples to visit the father-less and the widow in their affliction. I love that religion that is based upon the glorious principle, of love to God and love to man; which makes its followers do unto others as they themselves would be done by.... It is because I love this religion that I hate the slaveholding, the woman-whip-ping, the mind-darkening, the soul-destroying religion that exists in the southern states of America. It is because I regard the one as good, and pure, and holy, that I cannot but regard the other as bad, corrupt, and wicked. Loving the one, I must hate the other; holding the one I must reject the other ...

... I am here because you [Britain] have an influence on America that no other nation can have.... There is nothing said here against slavery that will not be recorded in the United States. I am here, also, because the slaveholders do not want me to be here; they would rather that I were not here. I have adopted a maxim laid down by Napoleon, never to occupy ground which the enemy would like me to occupy. The slaveholders would much rather have me, if I will denounce slavery, denounce it in the northern states, where their friends and supporters are, who will stand by and mob me for denouncing it ...

... I expose slavery in this country, because to expose it is to kill it. Slavery is one of those monsters of darkness to whom the light of truth is death. Expose slavery, and it dies. Light is to slavery what the heat of the sun is to the root of a tree; it must die under it.... Slavery shrinks from the light; it hateth the light, neither cometh to the light, lest its deeds should be reproved. To tear off the mask from this abominable system, to expose it to the light of heaven, aye, to the heat of the sun, that it may burn and wither it out of existence, is my object in coming to this country.

I want the slaveholder surrounded, as by a wall of anti-slavery fire, so that he may see the condemnation of himself and his system glaring down in letters of light. I want him to feel that he has no sympathy in England, Scotland, or Ireland; that he has none in Canada, none in Mexico, none among the poor wild Indians; that the voice of the civilized, aye, and the savage world, is against him. I would have condemnation blaze down upon him in every direction, till, stunned and overwhelmed with the shame and confusion, he is compelled to let go the grasp he holds upon the persons of his victims, and restore them to their long-lost rights.

Here, then, is work for us to do ...

GEORGE W. BUSH
"After September 11"

On Tuesday, September 11, 2001, four passenger airliners were hijacked, then crashed, killing nearly 3,000 people. The attack was carried out by four Mideast terrorist groups whose would-be martyrs had boarded flights, posing as passengers, then forcibly commandeered the aircraft. Two of the jumbo jets were diverted to New York City, where the hijackers piloted them into the twin towers of the World Trade Center. The impact and subsequent fire collapsed both 110-story towers, killing 2,752 persons, including hundreds of rescue workers.

One of the other four jets was flown into the Pentagon in Washington, D.C., killing all aboard plus 125 military personnel. The other jet had been rerouted also toward Washington, but went down short of the intended target when passengers, knowing the hijackers' aim, attempted to overpower the terrorists. All aboard were killed.

Nine days later, on Thursday, September 20, President George W. Bush addressed the American people in a Joint Session of Congress.

... In the normal course of events, presidents come to this chamber to report on the state of the Union. Tonight, no such report is needed. It has already been delivered by the American people. We have seen it in the courage of passengers who rushed terrorists to save others on the ground.... We have seen the state of our Union in the endurance of rescuers working past exhaustion. We've seen the unfurling of flags, the lighting of candles, the giving of blood, the saying of prayers.... We have seen the decency of a loving and giving people who have made the grief of strangers their own.

My fellow citizens, for the last nine days, the entire world has seen for itself the state of the union, and it is strong. Tonight we are a country awakened to danger and called to defend freedom. Our grief has turned to anger and anger to resolution. Whether we bring our enemies to justice or bring justice to our enemies, justice will be done ...

... I thank the world for its outpouring of support. America will never forget the sounds of our national anthem playing at Buckingham Palace, on the streets of Paris and at Berlin's Brandenburg Gate. We will not forget South Korean children gathering to pray outside our embassy in Seoul, or the prayers of sympathy offered at a mosque in Cairo. We will not forget moments of silence and days of mourning in Australia and Africa and Latin America. Nor will we forget the citizens of 80 other nations who died with our own ...

On September the 11th, enemies of freedom committed an act of war against our country. Americans

have known wars, but for the past 136 years they have been wars on foreign soil, except for one Sunday in 1941. Americans have known the casualties of war, but not at the center of a great city on a peaceful morning. Americans have known surprise attacks, but never before on thousands of civilians. All of this was brought upon us in a single day, and night fell on a different world, a world where freedom itself is under attack.

Americans have many questions tonight. Americans are asking, "Who attacked our country?"

The evidence we have gathered all points to a collection of loosely affiliated terrorist organizations known as al-Qaida.... Al-Qaida is to terror what the Mafia is to crime. But its goal is not making money. Its goal is remaking the world and imposing its radical beliefs on people everywhere.

The terrorists practice a fringe form of Islamic extremism that has been rejected by Muslim scholars and the vast majority of Muslim clerics.... The terrorists' directive commands them to kill Christians and Jews, to kill all Americans and make no distinctions among military and civilians, including women and children.

This group and its leader, a person named Osama bin Laden, are linked to many other organizations in different countries.... They are recruited from their own nations and neighborhoods and brought to camps in places like Afghanistan, where they are trained in the tactics of terror. They are sent back to their homes or sent to hide in countries around the world to plot evil and destruction.

The leadership of al-Qaida has great influence in Afghanistan and supports the Taliban regime in controlling most of that country. In Afghanistan we see al-Qaida's vision for the world. Afghanistan's people have been brutalized, many are starving and many have fled ...

[Those] who commit evil in the name of Allah blaspheme the name of Allah. The terrorists are traitors to their own faith, trying, in effect, to hijack Islam itself. The enemy of America is not our many Muslim friends. It is not our many Arab friends. Our enemy is a radical network of terrorists and every government that supports them. Our war on terror begins with al-Qaida, but it does not end there. It will not end until every terrorist group of global reach has been found, stopped and defeated.

Americans are asking, "Why do they hate us?"

They hate what they see right here in this chamber: a democratically elected government. Their leaders are self-appointed. They hate our freedoms: our freedom of religion, our freedom of speech, our freedom to vote and assemble and disagree with each other.

They want to overthrow existing governments in many Muslim countries such as Egypt, Saudi Arabia and Jordan. They want to drive Israel out of the Middle East. They want to drive Christians and Jews out of vast regions of Asia and Africa …

We have seen their kind before. They're the heirs of all the murderous ideologies of the 20th century. By sacrificing human life to serve their radical visions, by abandoning every value except the will to power, they follow in the path of fascism, Nazism and totalitarianism. And they will follow that path all the way to where it ends in history's unmarked grave of discarded lies.

Americans are asking, "How will we fight and win this war?" We will direct every resource at our command—every means of diplomacy, every tool of intelligence, every instrument of law enforcement, every financial influence and every necessary weapon of war— to the destruction and to the defeat of the global terror network…. Our response involves far more than instant retaliation and isolated strikes. Americans should not expect one battle, but a lengthy campaign unlike any other we have ever seen. It may include dramatic strikes visible on TV and covert operations secret even in success.

We will starve terrorists of funding, turn them one against another, drive them from place to place until there is no refuge or no rest. And we will pursue nations that provide aid or safe haven to terrorism. Every nation in every region now has a decision to make: Either you are with us, or you are with the terrorists. From this day forward, any nation that continues to harbor or support terrorism will be regarded by the United States as a hostile regime. Our nation has been put on notice, we're not immune from attack. We will take defensive measures against terrorism to protect Americans …

These efforts must be coordinated at the highest level. So tonight, I announce the creation of a Cabinet-level position reporting directly to me, the Office of Homeland Security …

This is not, however, just America's fight. And what is at stake is not just America's freedom. This is the world's fight. This is civilization's fight. This is the fight of all who believe in progress and pluralism, tolerance and freedom. We ask every nation to join us …

Americans are asking, "What is expected of us?"

I ask you to live your lives and hug your children. I know many citizens have fears tonight, and I ask you to be calm and resolute, even in the face of a continuing threat…. We're in a fight for our principles, and our first responsibility is to live by them. No one should be singled out for unfair treatment or unkind words because of their ethnic background or religious faith.

I ask you to continue to support the victims of this tragedy with your contributions…. I ask for your patience with the delays and inconveniences that may accompany tighter security and for your patience in what will be a long struggle. I ask your continued participation and confidence in the American economy. Terrorists attacked a symbol of American prosperity; they did not touch its source …

And finally, please continue praying for the victims of terror and their families, for those in uniform and for our great country. Prayer has comforted us in sorrow and will help strengthen us for the journey ahead …

After all that has just passed, all the lives taken and all the possibilities and hopes that died with them, it is natural to wonder if America's future is one of fear. Some speak of an age of terror. I know there are struggles ahead and dangers to face. But this country will define our times, not be defined by them. As long as the United States of America is determined and strong, this will not be an age of terror. This will be an age of liberty here and across the world.

Great harm has been done to us. We have suffered great loss. And in our grief and anger, we have found our mission and our moment. Freedom and fear are at war. The advance of human freedom, the great achievement of our time and the great hope of every time, now depends on us …

It is my hope that in the months and years ahead life will return almost to normal. We'll go back to our lives and routines, and that is good. Even grief recedes with time and grace.

But our resolve must not pass. Each of us will remember what happened that day and to whom it happened. We will remember the moment the news came, where we were and what we were doing. Some will remember an image of a fire or story or rescue. Some will carry memories of a face and a voice gone forever …

I will not forget the wound to our country and those who inflicted it. I will not yield, I will not rest, I will not relent in waging this struggle for freedom and security for the American people.

The course of this conflict is not known, yet its outcome is certain. Freedom and fear, justice and cruelty, have always been at war, and we know that God is not neutral between them.

Fellow citizens, we'll meet violence with patient justice, assured of the rightness of our cause and confident of the victories to come. In all that lies before us, may God grant us wisdom, and may he watch over the United States of America.

Thank you.

Politically active during the breakup of the Soviet Union, Boris Nikolayevich Yeltsin will be remembered as the first popularly elected president of Russia. Thus in 1991, after the old Soviet Union had all but disappeared, Yeltsin suddenly was vitally important to the fate of all Russians.

Trained as a construction engineer, Yeltsin had joined the Communist party as a youth. Although a protégé of Mikhail Gorbachev who came to oppose many items on the President's political agenda, Yeltsin did initially support—in concept, at least—the principles of *glastnost* (free and open discussion) and *perestroika* (economic and political reform). In fact, the up-and-coming statesman backed efforts to crush a coup attempt by Communist hardliners.

Upon being elected, Yeltsin called a constituent assembly and drafted a new Russian constitution. When he later met with other world leaders, the President worked to end the Soviet-era deception in international relations.

The occasion of the following eulogy was the funeral of three young people who had been killed during a Communist uprising in August of 1991. The state used the emotion of the moment to rally public sentiment against old politics. The nationally televised funeral proceedings were conducted by religious leaders, a clear sign to the nation that the Communist regime had at last succumbed to the will of a free people.

"Eulogy"

Dear relatives and loved ones of Dmitri Komar, Vladimir Usov, and Ilya Drichevsky, dear fellow countrymen and Muscovites:

Today many millions of Muscovites, the whole of Russia, are parting with our heroes, with our defenders, and with our saviors. Of course, we are not parting with their names forever, because from now on their names are sacred names for Russia, for all the people of our long-suffering Russia.

When television and radio reported about the coup on Monday, the hearts of millions and millions of mothers and fathers trembled most of all, because they were scared for their children. Because it was young people, it was our children, who more than anyone else rushed to defend Russia's honor, its freedom, its independence, and its democracy, to defend its parliament.

Yes, from now on, this square, on which a battle raged for three days, on which tens of thousands of Muscovites kept vigil, will be called the Square of Free Russia.

The enemy is cruel and, of course, bloodthirsty, especially when he knows that if he loses no one will take him in. All the participants of the putsch are arrested. Criminal proceedings have been started

against them, and I am sure that they will be made to answer for everything.

But even today, how cynical the words of arrested [former head of the KGB, Vladimir A.] Kryuchkov sound, the man who yesterday said that if he could do it over again he would have started a little faster and more energetically, and that the most important thing was to behead Russia.

This entire plot, and we must understand this very clearly, was aimed in the first place against Russia, its parliament, its government, its president. But all of Russia stood up to its defense: Moscow, Leningrad, the Urals, the Far East, the Kuzbass, practically all regions of the republic, although there were some regions which immediately put up banners and slogans expressing loyalty to the Extraordinary Committee. These officials already have been dismissed from their posts. And the prosecutor's office is considering their cases.

But we cannot resurrect those who died at the walls of our White House. We pay tribute to their courage, those who have become Heroes of the Soviet Union in death. I bow down to the mothers and fathers of Dmitri, Volodya, and Ilya, and I express to them my deep condolences, and to all their relatives and loved ones. Forgive me, your president, that I could not defend, could not save your sons.

In this day of Russia's national mourning, we, of course, need to strengthen our unity to energetically act further. We have cleared ourselves a path. Our deceased heroes have helped us to do so. This is a difficult day for us, a hard day. But it could have been even worse, because the enemies are already like cockroaches in a bottle, trying to eat each other. They are pointing fingers at each other, asking who played a more important role in the plot, revealing to each other the lists of people they wanted to kill first, second, third, fourth.

Only the first twelve victims in these lists were designated to be killed at 6 p.m. on August 19 during the storming of the House of Soviets. So it was not in vain the Muscovites were here, defending the honor of Russia.

It was a difficult loss, and the memory of it will be with us forever. For that reason, our heroes, sleep peacefully and let the earth be soft for you.

In early October of 1993, President Yeltsin quashed another Communist coup—one that had joined forces with a Nazi faction. Subsequently, on October 6, 1993, Yeltsin delivered the following speech to the People of the Russian Federation.

"The Cost of Political Indifference"

Esteemed citizens of Russia, on October 3 and 4, Russia experienced a great tragedy. Gangs of murderers broke into state offices, they humiliated people who they took hostages. They captured city buses and trucks. The militants had a great amount of weapons, ammunition and military equipment. The lives of peaceful civilians were in mortal danger.

There was an armed mutiny, planned and prepared by the leaders of the former vice-president, the leaders of some parties and public organizations.

Among them were the National Salvation Front, including its arm "Labour Russia," some Communist parties and groups, the Nazi-style "Russian National Unity" and some others. Nazis and Communists merged in this damnable cause, the swastika joined the sickle and hammer.

Former people's deputies were among the organizers and active participants of the mutiny.... They used their deputy immunity as a shield from behind which to incite violence, stimulate mass unrest, organize mass-scale bloody rioting and unleash civil war.

The aim was to establish in Russia a bloody Communist-Nazi dictatorship. It is now clear that all this had been prepared for many months.

The bloodletting events of that night compelled [us] to bring regular army units into Moscow. The difficult decision was made to storm the Supreme Soviet building, which had turned into the stronghold of terrorism.

The actions of the militants were coordinated from the House of Soviets (parliament building). Illegal armed groups were formed inside it. Calls to storm the Mayor's office building, the Ostankino (television broadcasting centre) and the Kremlin came from the House of Soviets.... All preparations for the mutiny were carried out while sham negotiations were being conducted.

Why did we put up with the organizations in Russia which acted legally not only calling for violence but also preparing it. They were not duly rebuffed by either the prosecutors or by the law-enforcement agencies.... The Supreme Soviet and the Congress became their chief patrons. As a result, every new sortie became more insolent and menacing.

The chief lesson for us is that democracy must be dependably protected. The State must use force wherever there is a threat of violence, a threat to the lives and safety of citizens. There can be no democracy without this.

All those who took part in the rioting with arms in their hands will be punished in accordance with law. All proponents of Nazi and Communist ideas who instigated the mutiny will be made answerable under the law. There can be no all-forgiveness to communistic nazism in Russia ever again.

I think that the constitutional court has to take much of the blame for what had come to pass. This agency has long since abandoned its most important principle—the court's independence from political time-serving.

The court appeared to overlook how endless amendments violated the Russian constitution, overlook the glaring contradictions in the constitution which were deliberately enhanced by the Congress.

I announce with full responsibility: most bodies of Soviet power are directly responsible for the extreme aggravation of the situation in Moscow. The system of Soviets showed full disregard for the security of the state and its citizens and thus put a full stop to its own political life.

Esteemed compatriots, having experienced the fearful days and nights, we can nonetheless be confident—no civil war has been unleashed in Russia. The mutineers in our capital remained strangers. The Muscovites despise and condemn them.

They failed to split the country, to split the Army and the State.

But the problems exposed by the mutiny are extremely serious. We need a normal democratic constitution as we need air to breathe. We need a united Russia. Playing at regional isolation is contrary to the interests and will of the majority of the country's population. We need full reform of the army and security agencies.

We need to consistently carry on economic transformations and support for all efforts the government makes in this direction.

But I would like to warn (people). If you think that the situation is completely back to normal, you are making a big mistake. Passions have not yet abated. Any careless, irresponsible word can enflame them again. I am appealing to the sense of civic responsibility of journalists.

Dear Russians, the most fearful things are now past. But in order to make peace and quiet inviolable in our country, we must pool efforts in strengthening our state, strengthening democracy. Elections to the Federal Assembly—and, I believe, new local bodies of representative power—will take place on December 12.

All politicians, parties and movements who have not smeared themselves with direct involvement in the mutiny are guaranteed equal opportunities.

In the past few days we came to understand the immense cost of political indifference. It is unable to save anyone or secure personal safety. Can one sleep quietly when one's house is being set on fire?

I am calling on you dear compatriots, to take an active part in the elections and vote for the worthiest, competent, clever and intelligent people. Those who are unable to betray.

Dear compatriots, the nightmare of the black days is over. Do not say that someone has won and someone lost. At this moment, these are inappropriate, blasphemous words. We have all been scorched by the deadly breath of fratricide.

People have died, our compatriots. They cannot be brought back. Grief and suffering have entered many families.

No matter how different outlooks may be, all of them are children of Russia, this is our common tragedy, our common grief, great grief.

Let us remember this insanity in order to never let it recur.

RONALD REAGAN
"Tear Down This Wall"

On June 12, 1987, American President Ronald Reagan's address to the people of West Berlin included a line that became etched in the hearts of freedom-loving people everywhere. The Berlin Wall, built by Communists in August 1961 to keep Germans from escaping Communist-ruled East Berlin into Democratic West Berlin, had long served as a stark symbol of division and mistrust. The Cold War was well over three decades old when President Reagan— the "Great Communicator," as he was known—railed against the Soviet regime's continued violation of people's rights. Twelve feet thick and a hundred miles long, it surrounded the city. Scores of East Germans had died in the attempt to breach the barrier, circumvent its electrified fences and skirt its guard posts.

A little over two years later, East Germans demanded that the wall be opened to allow citizens to travel freely between the two Berlins. And by the end of 1990, upon the collapse of Communism in Eastern Europe, the wall was torn down altogether, signaling the imminent end of the Cold War era.

... Twenty-four years ago, President John F. Kennedy visited Berlin, speaking to the people of this city and the world at the City Hall. Well, since then two other presidents have come, each in his turn, to Berlin. And today I, myself, make my second visit to your city.

We come to Berlin, we American presidents, because it's our duty to speak, in this place, of freedom. But I must confess, we're drawn here by other things as well: by the feeling of history in this city, more than 500 years older than our own nation; by the beauty of the Grunewald and the Tiergarten; most of all, by your courage and determination...

Our gathering today is being broadcast throughout Western Europe and North America. I understand that it is being seen and heard as well in the East. To those listening throughout Eastern Europe, a special word: Although I cannot be with you, I address my remarks to you just as surely as to those standing here before me. For I join you, as I join your fellow countrymen in the West, in this firm, this unalterable belief: Es gibt nur ein Berlin. [There is only one Berlin.]

Behind me stands a wall that encircles the free sectors of this city, part of a vast system of barriers that divides the entire continent of Europe. From the Baltic, south, those barriers cut across Germany in a gash of barbed wire, concrete, dog runs, and guard towers. Farther south, there may be no visible, no obvious wall. But there remain armed guards and checkpoints all the same.... Yet it is here in Berlin where the wall emerges most clearly; here, cutting across your city, where the news photo and the television screen have imprinted this brutal division of a continent upon the mind of the world ...

President von Weizsacker has said, "The German question is open as long as the Brandenburg Gate is closed." Today I say: As long as the gate is closed, as long as this scar of a wall is permitted to stand, it is not the German question alone that remains open, but the question of freedom for all mankind. Yet I do not come here to lament. For I find in Berlin a message of hope, even in the shadow of this wall, a message of triumph.

In this season of spring in 1945, the people of Berlin emerged from their air-raid shelters to find devastation. Thousands of miles away, the people of the United States reached out to help. And in 1947 Secretary of State—as you've been told—George Marshall announced the creation of what would become known as the Marshall Plan. Speaking precisely 40 years ago this month, he said: "Our policy is directed not against any country or doctrine, but against hunger, poverty, desperation, and chaos."

... In West Germany and here in Berlin, there took place an economic miracle.... [Your] leaders understood the practical importance of liberty—that just as truth can flourish only when the journalist is given freedom of speech, so prosperity can come about only when the farmer and businessman enjoy economic freedom. The German leaders reduced tariffs, expanded free trade, lowered taxes. From 1950 to 1960 alone, the standard of living in West Germany and Berlin doubled.

Where four decades ago there was rubble, today in West Berlin there is the greatest industrial output of any city in Germany—busy office blocks, fine homes and apartments, proud avenues, and the spreading lawns of parkland. Where a city's culture seemed to have been destroyed, today there are two great universities, orchestras and an opera, countless theaters, and museums. Where there was want, today there's abundance—food, clothing, automobiles.... From devastation, from utter ruin, you Berliners have, in freedom, rebuilt a city that once again ranks as one of the greatest on earth. The Soviets may have had other plans. But my friends, there were a few things the Soviets didn't count on—Berliner Herz, Berliner Humor, ja, und Berliner Schnauze. [Berliner heart, Berliner humor, yes, and a Berliner Schnauze.]

In the 1950s, Khrushchev predicted: "We will bury you." But in the West today, we see a free world that has achieved a level of prosperity and well-being unprecedented in all human history. In the Communist world, we see failure, technological backwardness, declining standards of health, even want of the most basic kind—too little food. Even today the Soviet Union still cannot feed itself. After these four decades, then, there stands before the entire world one great and inescapable conclusion: Freedom leads to prosperity. Freedom replaces the ancient hatreds among the nations with comity and peace. Freedom is the victor.

And now the Soviets themselves may, in a limited way, be coming to understand the importance of freedom. We hear much from Moscow about a new policy of reform and openness. Some political prisoners have been released. Certain foreign news broadcasts are no longer being jammed. Some economic enterprises have been permitted to operate with greater freedom from state control.

Are these the beginnings of profound changes in the Soviet state? Or are they token gestures, intended to raise false hopes in the West, or to strengthen the Soviet system without changing it? We welcome change and openness; for we believe that freedom and security go together, that the advance of human liberty can only strengthen the cause of world peace. There is one sign the Soviets can make that would be unmistakable, that would advance dramatically the cause of freedom and peace.

General Secretary Gorbachev, if you seek peace, if you seek prosperity for the Soviet Union and Eastern Europe, if you seek liberalization: Come here to this gate! Mr. Gorbachev, open this gate! Mr. Gorbachev, tear down this wall!

I understand the fear of war and the pain of division that afflict this continent—and I pledge to you my country's efforts to help overcome these burdens. To be sure, we in the West must resist Soviet expansion. So we must maintain defenses of unassailable strength. Yet we seek peace; so we must strive to reduce arms on both sides ...

As I speak, NATO ministers are meeting in Iceland to review the progress of our proposals for eliminating these weapons. At the talks in Geneva we have also proposed deep cuts in strategic offensive weapons. And the Western allies have likewise made far-reaching proposals to reduce the danger of conventional war and to place a total ban on chemical weapons.

While we pursue these arms reductions, I pledge to you that we will maintain the capacity to deter Soviet aggression at any level at which it might occur.... But we must remember a crucial fact: East and West do not mistrust each other because we are armed; we are armed because we mistrust each other. And our differences are not about weapons but about liberty. When President Kennedy spoke at the City Hall those 24 years ago, freedom was encircled, Berlin was under siege. And today, despite all the pressures upon this city, Berlin stands secure in its liberty. And freedom itself is transforming the globe ...

In Europe, only one nation and those it controls refuse to join the community of freedom. Yet in this age of redoubled economic growth, of information and innovation, the Soviet Union faces a choice: It must make fundamental changes, or it will become obsolete.

Today thus represents a moment of hope. We in the West stand ready to cooperate with the East to promote true openness, to break down barriers that separate people, to create a safe, freer world. And surely there is no better place than Berlin, the meeting place of East and West, to make a start ...

And I invite Mr. Gorbachev: Let us work to bring the Eastern and Western parts of the city closer together, so that all the inhabitants of all Berlin can enjoy the benefits that come with life in one of the great cities of the world ...

With our French and British partners, the United States is prepared to help bring international meetings to Berlin. It would be only fitting for Berlin to serve as the site of United Nations meetings, or world conferences on human rights and arms control or other issues that call for international cooperation.

There is no better way to establish hope for the future than to enlighten young minds, and we would be honored to sponsor summer youth exchanges, cultural events, and other programs for young Berliners from the East. Our French and British friends, I'm certain, will do the same ...

One final proposal, one close to my heart: Sport represents a source of enjoyment and ennoblement, and you may have noted that the Republic of Korea—South Korea—has offered to permit certain events of the 1988 Olympics to take place in the North. International sports competitions of all kinds could take place in both parts of this city. And what better way to demonstrate to the world the openness of this city than to offer in some future year to hold the Olympic games here in Berlin, East and West? In these four decades, as I have said, you Berliners have built a great city. You've done so in spite of threats.... What keeps you here? Certainly there's a great deal to be said for your fortitude, for your defiant courage. But I believe there's something deeper, something that involves Berlin's whole look and feel and way of life—not mere sentiment.... In a word, I would submit that what keeps you in Berlin is love—love both profound and abiding.

Perhaps this gets to the root of the matter, to the most fundamental distinction of all between East and West. The totalitarian world produces backwardness because it does such violence to the spirit, thwarting the human impulse to create, to enjoy, to worship. The totalitarian world finds even symbols of love and of worship an affront ...

As I looked out a moment ago from the Reichstag, that embodiment of German unity, I noticed words crudely spray-painted upon the wall, perhaps by a young Berliner: "This wall will fall. Beliefs become reality." Yes, across Europe, this wall will fall. For it cannot withstand faith; it cannot withstand truth. The wall cannot withstand freedom.

And I would like, before I close, to say one word. I have read, and I have been questioned since I've been here about certain demonstrations against my coming. And I would like to say just one thing, and to those who demonstrate so. I wonder if they have ever asked themselves that if they should have the kind of government they apparently seek, no one would ever be able to do what they're doing again.

Thank you and God bless you all.

Born in a village on the Nile River Delta, Anwar el-Sadat rose through the ranks of military and government leadership. After being trained in the military, Sadat worked to overthrow the government and rid Egypt of British influence. Twenty years before becoming Egypt's vice president in the 1960s, the young activist had served a prison sentence for his revolutionary activities. Sadat, however, ultimately became his country's president and served for 11 years until his assassination at the hands of Islamic extremists in 1981.

One of Sadat's primary goals was to end the longstanding Arab-Israeli conflict. Once an accord was reached, Sadat and Israel's Prime Minister Menachem Begin were awarded the 1978 Nobel Peace prize.

Although Sadat had refused to initiate diplomatic relations with Egypt's longtime foe, he finally, at the peril of his life, accepted an invitation to Jerusalem to plead his case for a peace treaty. In November 1977, Sadat spoke to the Israeli Knesset, charging his words with an emotional appeal for peace.

I come to you today on solid ground to shape a new life and to establish peace. We all love this land, the land of God: we all, Moslems, Christians, and Jews, all worship God.

Under God, God's teachings and commandments are love, sincerity, security, and peace.

I do not blame all those who received my decision when I announced it to the entire world before the Egyptian People's Assembly. I do not blame all those who received my decision with surprise and even with amazement—some gripped even by violent surprise. Still others interpreted it as political, to camouflage my intentions of launching a new war.

I would go so far as to tell you that one of my aides at the presidential office contacted me at a late hour following my return home from the People's Assembly and sounded worried as he asked me, "Mr. President, what would be our reaction if Israel actually extended an invitation to you?"

I replied calmly, "I would accept it immediately. I have declared that I would go to Israel, for I want to put before the people of Israel all the facts."

I can see the faces of all those who were astounded by my decision and had doubts as to the sincerity of the intentions behind the declaration of my decision. No one could ever conceive that the president of the biggest Arab state, which bears the heaviest burden and the main responsibility pertaining to the cause of war and peace in the middle East, should declare his readiness to go to the land of the adversary while we were still in a state of war…

Here I would go back to the big question: How can we achieve a durable peace based on justice? In my opinion, and I declare it to the whole world, from this forum, the answer is neither difficult nor is it impossible despite long years of feuds, blood, faction, strife, hatreds, and deep-rooted animosity.

The answer is not difficult, nor is it impossible, if we sincerely and faithfully follow a straight line…

In all sincerity I tell you we welcome you among us with full security and safety. This in itself is a tremendous turning point, one of the landmarks of a decisive historical change. We used to reject you. We had our reasons and our fears, yes.

We refused to meet with you, anywhere, yes.

We were together in international conferences and organizations, and our representatives did not, and still do not exchange greetings with you. Yes. This has happened and is still happening.

It is also true that we used to set as a precondition for any negotiations with you a mediator who would meet separately with each party.

Yes. Through this procedure, the talks of the first and second disengagement agreements took place.

Our delegates met in the first Geneva conference without exchanging direct word. Yes, this has happened.

Yet today I tell you, and I declare it to the whole world, that we accept to live with you in permanent peace based on justice. We do not want to encircle you or be encircled ourselves by destructive missiles ready for launching, nor by the shells of grudges and hatreds…

I hail the Israeli voices that call for the recognition of the Palestinian people's right to achieve and safeguard peace.

Here I tell you, ladies and gentlemen, that it is no use to refrain from recognizing the Palestinian people and their right to statehood as their right of return. We, the Arabs, have faced this experience before, with you. And with the reality of the Israeli existence, the struggle which took us from war to war, from victims to more victims, until you and we have today reached the edge of a horrible abyss and a terrifying disaster unless, together, we seize this opportunity today of durable peace based on justice.

You have to face reality bravely, as I have done. There can never be a solution to a problem by evading it or turning a deaf ear to it. Peace cannot last if attempts are made to impose fantasy concepts on which the world has turned its back and announced its unanimous call for the respect of rights and facts.

There is no need to enter a vicious circle as to Palestinian rights. It is useless to create obstacles; otherwise, the march of peace will be impeded or peace will be blown up. As I have told you, there is no happiness based on the detriment of others.

Direct confrontation and straightforwardness are the shortcuts and the most successful way to reach a clear objective. Direct confrontation concerning the Palestinian problem and tackling it in one single language with a view to achieving a durable and just peace, lie in the establishment of that peace. With all the guarantees you demand, there should be no fear of a newly born state that needs the assistance of all countries of the world.

When the bells of peace ring, there will be no hands to beat the drums of war. Even if they existed, they would be stilled …

Ladies and gentlemen, peace is not a mere endorsement of written lines. Rather, it is a rewriting of history. Peace is not a game of calling for peace to defend certain whims or hide certain admissions. Peace in its essence is a dire struggle against all and every ambition and whim.

Perhaps the example taken and experienced, taken from ancient and modern history, teaches that missiles, warships, and nuclear weapons cannot establish security. Instead, they destroy what peace and security build.

For the sake of our peoples and for the sake of the civilization made by man, we have to defend man everywhere against rule by the force of arms so that we may endow the full of humanity with all the power of the values and principles that further the sublime position of mankind.

Allow me to address my call from this rostrum to the people of Israel. I tell them, from the Egyptian people, who bless this sacred mission of peace, I convey to you the message of peace of the Egyptian people, who do not harbor fanaticism and whose sons—Moslems, Christians and Jews—live together in a state of cordiality, love and tolerance.

This is Egypt, whose people have entrusted me with their sacred message. A message of security, safety, and peace to every man, woman, and child in Israel. Let all endeavors be channeled toward building a huge stronghold for peace instead of building destructive rockets.

Introduce to the entire world the image of the new man in this area so that he might set an example to the man of our age, the man of peace everywhere. Ring the bells for your sons. Tell them that those wars were the last of wars and the end of sorrows. Tell them that we are entering upon a new beginning, a new life, a life of love, prosperity, freedom, and peace.

You, sorrowing mother, you, widowed wife, you, the son who lost a brother or a father, all the victims of wars, fill the air and space with recitals of peace, fill bosoms and hearts with the aspirations of peace. Make a reality that blossoms and lives. Make hope a code of conduct and endeavor.

The will of peoples is part of the will of God. Ladies and gentlemen, before I came to this place, with every beat of my heart and with every sentiment, I prayed to God Almighty. While performing the prayers … I asked the Almighty to give me strength and to confirm my belief that this visit may achieve the objective I look forward to for a happy present and a happier future.

I have chosen to set aside all precedents and traditions known by warring countries. In spite of the fact that occupation of Arab territories is still there, the declaration of my readiness to proceed to Israel came as a great surprise that stirred many feelings and confounded many minds. Some of them even doubted its intent.

Despite all that, the decision was inspired by all the clarity and purity of belief and with all the true passions of my people's will and intentions, and I have chosen this road considered by many to be the most difficult road.

I have chosen to come to you with an open heart and an open mind. I have chosen to give this great impetus to all international efforts exerted for peace. I have chosen to present to you, in your own home, the realities, devoid of any scheme or whim. Not to maneuver, or win a round, but for us to win together the most dangerous of rounds embattled in modern history, the battle of permanent peace based on justice.

It is not my battle alone. Nor is it the battle of the leadership in Israel alone. It is the battle of all and every citizen in our territories, whose right it is to live in peace. It is the commitment of conscience and responsibility in the hearts of millions.

When I put forward this initiative, many asked what is it that I conceived as possible to achieve during this visit and what my expectations were. And as I answer the questions, I announce before you that I have not thought of carrying out this initiative from the precepts of what could be achieved during this visit. And I have come here to deliver a message. I have delivered the message, and may God be my witness.

I repeat with Zachariah: Love, right, and justice. From the holy Koran I quote the following verses: We believe in God and in what has been revealed to us and what was revealed to Abraham, Ishmael, Isaac, Jacob and the thirteen Jewish tribes. And in the books given to Moses and Jesus and the prophets from their Lord, who made no distinction between them. So we agree.

Salam Aleikum—Peace be upon you.

Dubbed the "Iron Lady," Margaret Thatcher earned the distinction of being the first woman to hold the office of British Prime Minister—and the first prime minister to serve three consecutive terms. Among her primary objectives included reversing Britain's economic decline and reducing the role of government in the lives of its people.

Before entering politics Thatcher received degrees in chemistry from Oxford University. Later, as a research chemist, she studied to become a tax lawyer and, eventually, after joining the conservative party, was elected to the House of Commons. Her goal in government was to reintroduce "Victorian values" and to encourage state thrift and self-reliance.

In her first speech as party leader on October 10, 1975 at Brighton, Thatcher was met with cheers and foot-stamping as she encouraged national pride and financial responsibility.

"Let Me Give You My Vision"

Whenever I visit Communist countries their politicians never hesitate to boast about their achievements. They know them all by heart; they reel off the facts and figures, claiming this is the rich harvest of the Communist system. Yet they are not prosperous as we in the West are prosperous, and they are not free as we in the West are free.

Our capitalist system produces a far higher standard of prosperity and happiness because it believes in incentive and opportunity, and because it is founded on human dignity and freedom. Even the Russians have to go to a capitalist country—America—to buy enough wheat to feed their people—and that after more than fifty years of a State-controlled economy. Yet they boast incessantly, while we, who have so much more to boast about, forever criticize and decry. Is it not time we spoke up for our way of life? After all, no Western nation has to build a wall round itself to keep its people in.

So let us have no truck with those who say the free enterprise system has failed. What we face today is not a crisis of capitalism but of Socialism. No country can flourish if its economic and social life is dominated by nationalization and State control.

The cause of our shortcomings does not, therefore, lie in private enterprise. Our problem is not that we have too little Socialism. It is that we have too much ...

Of course, a halt to further State control will not on its own restore our belief in ourselves, because something else is happening to this country. We are witnessing a deliberate attack on our values, a deliberate attack on our heritage and our great past, and there are those who gnaw away at our national self-respect, rewriting British history as centuries of unrelieved gloom, oppression and failure—as days of hopelessness, not days of hope ...

We must not be bullied or brainwashed out of our beliefs. No wonder so many of our people, some of the best and the brightest, are depressed and talking of emigrating.... They are giving up too soon. Many of the things we hold dear are threatened as never before, but none has yet been lost, so stay here, stay and help us defeat Socialism so that the Britain you have known may be the Britain your children will know.

These are the two great challenges of our time—the moral and political challenge, and the economic challenge. They have to be faced together and we have to master them both.

What are our chances of success? It depends on what kind of people we are. What kind of people are we? We are the people that in the past made Great Britain the workshop of the world ...

We are a people who have received more Nobel Prizes than any other nation except America, and head for head we have done better than America, twice as well in fact.

We are the people who, among other things, invented the computer, the refrigerator, the electric motor, the stethoscope, rayon, the steam turbine, stainless steel, the tank, television, penicillin, radar, the jet engine, hovercraft ... carbon fibers, et cetera—and the best half of Concorde.

We export more of what we produce than either West Germany, France, Japan or the United States, and well over ninety per cent of these exports come from private enterprise. It is a triumph for the private sector and all who work in it, and let us say so loud and clear.

With achievements like that, who can doubt that Britain can have a great future, and what our friends abroad want to know is whether that future is going to happen ...

Let me give you my vision: a man's right to work as he will, to spend what he earns, to own property, to have the State as servant and not as master—these are the British inheritance. They are the essence of a free country and on that freedom all our other freedoms depend.

But we want a free economy, not only because it guarantees our liberties, but also because it is the best way of creating wealth and prosperity for the whole country, and it is this prosperity alone which can give us the resources for better services for the community, better services for those in need ...

Some Socialists seem to believe that people should be numbers in a State computer. We believe they should be individuals. We are all unequal. No one, thank heavens, is quite like anyone else, however much the Socialists may pretend otherwise. We believe that everyone has the right to be unequal. But to us, every human being is equally important. Engineers, miners, manual workers, shop assistants, farmworkers, postmen, housewives—these are the essential foundations of our society, and without them there would be no nation. But there are others with special gifts who should also have their chance, because if the adventurers who strike out in new directions in science, technology, medicine, commerce and industry are hobbled, there can be no advance. The spirit of envy can destroy; it can never build. Everyone must be allowed to develop the abilities he knows he has within him, and she knows she has within her, in the way they choose.

Freedom to choose is something we take for granted until it is in danger of being taken away. Socialist Governments set out perpetually to restrict the area of choice, and Conservative Governments to increase it. We believe that you become a responsible citizen by making decisions for yourself, not by having them made for you. But they are made for you by Labour all right!

Thatcher's strength and resolve during the Falkland Islands crisis—when the British rose up against the occupying Argentine Government—greatly increased her popularity. The strong-willed stateswoman delivered the following speech at a rally of Conservative women in Cheltenham on July 3, 1982.

"The Falklands Factor"

Today we meet in the aftermath of the Falklands Battle. Our country has won a great victory and we are entitled to be proud. This nation had the resolution to do what it knew had to be done—to do what it knew was right.

We fought to show that aggression does not pay.... We fought with the support of so many throughout the world.... Yet we also fought alone—for we fought for our own people and for our own sovereign territory.

Now that it is all over, things cannot be the same again, for we have learned something about ourselves—a lesson which we desperately needed to learn.

When we started out, there were the waverers and the fainthearts: the people who thought that Britain could no longer seize the initiative for herself; the people who thought we could no longer do the great things which we once did; and those who believed that our decline was irreversible.... There were those who would not admit it ... but—in their heart of hearts—they too had their secret fears that it was true: that Britain was no longer the nation that had built an Empire and ruled a quarter of the world.

Well, they were wrong. The lesson of the Falklands is that Britain has not changed and that this nation still has those sterling qualities which shine through our history. This generation can match their fathers and grandfathers in ability, in courage, and in resolution. We have not changed. When the demands of war and the dangers to our own people call us to arms—then we British are as we have always been: competent, courageous and resolute.

When called to arms—ah, that's the problem. It took ... the demands of war for every stop to be pulled out and every man and woman to do their best.

British people had to be threatened by foreign soldiers and British territory invaded and then—why then—the response was incomparable. Yet why does it need a war to bring out our qualities and reassert our pride? Why do we have to be invaded before we throw aside our selfish aims and begin to work together as only we can work, and achieve as only we can achieve?

That ... really is the challenge we as a nation face today. We have to see that the spirit of the South Atlantic—the real spirit of Britain—is kindled not only by war but can now be fired by peace.

We have the first prerequisite. We know we can do it—we haven't lost the ability. That is the Falklands Factor. We have proved ourselves to ourselves. It is a lesson we must not now forget. Indeed, it is a lesson which we must apply to peace just as we have learned it in war. The faltering and the self-doubt has given way to achievement and pride. We have the confidence and we must use it.

Just look at the Task Force as an object lesson. Every man had his own task to do and did it superbly. Officers and men, senior NCO and newest recruit—every one realized that his contribution was essential for the success of the whole. All were equally valuable—each was differently qualified.

By working together, each was able to do more than his best. As a team they raised the average to the level of the best and by each doing his utmost together they achieved the impossible. That's an accurate picture of Britain at war—not yet of Britain at peace. But the spirit has stirred and the nation has begun to assert itself. Things are not going to be the same again ...

And so toady, we can rejoice at our success in the Falklands and take pride in the achievement of the men and women of our Task Force. But we do so, not as some last flickering of a flame which must soon be dead. No—we rejoice that Britain has rekindled that spirit which has fired her for generations past and which today has begun to burn as brightly as before.

Britain has found herself again in the South Atlantic and will not look back from the victory she has won.

The 35th President of the United States, John F. Kennedy was 44 when inaugurated on January 20, 1961. His first address to the country was a clarion call for a new day of government. Delivered outside of the Capitol Building in Washington, D.C., the sermon exuded youth, idealism, and a sense of history. His Lincolnesque use of language was especially poignant, given both presidents were assassinated before their term of office was complete.

•

"Inaugural Address"

We observe today not a victory of a party but a celebration of freedom, symbolizing an end as well as a beginning, signifying renewal as well as change. For I have sworn before you and Almighty God the same solemn oath as our forbears prescribed nearly a century and three-quarters ago.

The world is very different now. For man holds in his mortal hands the power to abolish all forms of human poverty and all forms of human life. And yet the same revolutionary belief for which our forbears fought is still at issue around the globe—the belief that the rights of man come not from the generosity of the state but from the hand of God.

We dare not forget today that we are the heirs of that first revolution. Let the word go forth from this time and place, to friend and foe alike, that the torch has been passed to a new generation of Americans, born in this century, tempered by war, disciplined by a hard and bitter peace, proud of our ancient heritage—and unwilling to witness or permit the slow undoing of those human rights to which this nation has always been committed, and to which we are committed today at home and around the world.

Let every nation know, whether it wishes us well or ill, that we shall pay any price, bear any burden, meet any hardship, support any friend, oppose any foe to assure the survival and success of liberty.

This much we pledge—and more.

To those old allies whose cultural and spiritual origins we share, we pledge the loyalty of faithful friends. United, there is little we cannot do in a host of cooperative ventures. Divided, there is little we can do—for we dare not meet a powerful challenge at odds and split asunder ...

To those peoples in the huts and villages of half the globe struggling to break the bonds of mass misery, we pledge our best efforts to help them help themselves, for whatever period is required—not because the Communists may be doing it, not because we seek their votes, but because it is right. If a free society cannot help the many who are poor, it cannot save the few who are rich.

To our sister republics south of our border, we offer a special pledge—to convert our good words into good deeds—in a new alliance for progress—to assist free men and free governments in casting off the chains of poverty ...

To that world assembly of sovereign states, the United Nations, our last best hope in an age where the instruments of war have far out-paced the instruments of peace, we renew our pledge of support ...

Finally, to those nations who would make themselves our adversary, we offer not a pledge but a request: that both sides begin anew the quest for peace, before the dark powers of destruction unleashed by science engulf all humanity in planned or accidental self-destruction.

We dare not tempt them with weakness. For only when our arms are sufficient beyond doubt can we be certain beyond doubt that they will never be employed.

But neither can two great and powerful groups of nations take comfort from our present course—both sides overburdened by the cost of modern weapons, both rightly alarmed by the steady spread of the deadly atom, yet both racing to alter that uncertain balance of terror that stays the hand of mankind's final war.

So let us begin anew, remembering on both sides that civility is not a sign of weakness, and sincerity is always subject to proof. Let us never negotiate out of fear. But let us never fear to negotiate.

Let both sides explore what problems unite us instead of belaboring those problems which divide us. Let both sides, for the first time, formulate serious and precise proposals for the inspection and control of arms, and bring the absolute power to destroy other nations under the absolute control of all nations.

Let both sides seek to invoke the wonders of science instead of its terrors. Together let us explore the stars, conquer the deserts, eradicate disease, tap the ocean depths and encourage the arts and commerce. Let both sides unite to heed in all corners of the earth the command of Isaiah, to "undo the heavy burdens and to let the oppressed go free."

... All this will not be finished in the first one hundred days. Nor will it be finished in the first one thousand days, nor in the life of this Administration, nor even perhaps in our lifetime on this planet. But let us begin.

In your hands, my fellow citizens, more than mine, will rest the final success or failure of our course. Since this country was founded, each generation of Americans has been summoned to give testimony to its national loyalty. The graves of young Americans who answered the call to service surround the globe.

Now the trumpet summons us again—not as a call to bear arms, though arms we need; not as a call to battle, though embattled we are; but a call to bear the burden of a long twilight struggle, year in and year out, "rejoicing in hope, patient in tribulation," a struggle against the common enemies of man: tyranny, poverty, disease and war itself …

In the long history of the world, only a few generations have been granted the role of defending freedom in its hour of maximum danger. I do not shrink from this responsibility; I welcome it. I do not believe that any of us would exchange places with any other people or any other generation. The energy, the faith, the devotion which we bring to this endeavor will light our country and all who serve it, and the glow from that fire can truly light the world.

And so, my fellow Americans, ask not what your country can do for you, ask what you can do for your country.

My fellow citizens of the world, ask not what America will do for you, but what together we can do for the freedom of man.

Finally, whether you are citizens of America or citizens of the world, ask of us here the same high standards of strength and sacrifice which we ask of you. With a good conscience our only sure reward, with history the final judge of our deeds, let us go forth to lead the land we love, asking His blessings and His help, but knowing that here on earth God's work must truly be our own.

On June 26, 1963, after visiting the Berlin Wall that at that time divided East and West Germany, President Kennedy spoke to an enormous crowd of Germans.

"Ich bin ein Berliner"

… Two thousand years ago the proudest boast was "civis Romanus sum." Today, in the world of freedom, the proudest boast is "Ich bin ein Berliner." (I appreciate my interpreter translating my German!)

There are many people in the world who really don't understand … what is the great issue between the free world and the Communist world. Let them come to Berlin. There are some who say that communism is the wave of the future. Let them come to Berlin. And there are some who say in Europe and elsewhere we can work with the Communists. Let them come to Berlin. And there are even a few who say that it is true that communism is an evil system, but it permits us to make economic progress. Lass' sie nach Berlin kommen. Let them come to Berlin.

Freedom has many difficulties and democracy is not perfect, but we have never had to put a wall up to keep our people in, to prevent them from leaving us. I want to say, on behalf of my countrymen … that they take the greatest pride that they have been able to share with you, even from a distance, the story of the last 18 years. I know of no town, no city, that has been besieged for 18 years that still lives with the vitality and the force, and the hope and the determination of the city of West Berlin. While the wall is the most obvious and vivid demonstration of the failures of the Communist system, for all the world to see, we take no satisfaction in it, for it is, as your Mayor has said, an offense not only against history but an offense against humanity, separating families, dividing husbands and wives and brothers and sisters, and dividing a people who wish to be joined together.

What is true of this city is true of Germany— real, lasting peace in Europe can never be assured as long as one German out of four is denied the elementary right of free men, and that is to make a free choice. In 18 years of peace and good faith, this generation of Germans has earned the right to be free, including the right to unite their families and their nation in lasting peace, with good will to all people. You live in a defended island of freedom, but your life is part of the main. So let me ask you as I close, to lift your eyes beyond the dangers of today, to the hopes of tomorrow, beyond the freedom merely of this city of Berlin, or your country of Germany, to the advance of freedom everywhere, beyond the wall to the day of peace with justice, beyond yourselves and ourselves to all mankind.

Freedom is indivisible, and when one man is enslaved, all are not free. When all are free, then we can look forward to that day when this city will be joined as one and this country and this great Continent of Europe in a peaceful and hopeful globe. When that day finally comes, as it will, the people of West Berlin can take sober satisfaction in the fact that they were in the front lines for almost two decades.

All free men, wherever they may live, are citizens of Berlin, and, therefore, as a free man, I take pride in the words "Ich bin ein Berliner."

WINSTON CHURCHILL
"The Locust Years," "Blood, Toil, Tears and Sweat," "This Was Their Finest Hour" and "The Iron Curtain"

"It was the nation and the race dwelling all round the globe that had the lion's heart. I had the luck to be called upon to give the roar." Not only was Sir Winston Leonard Spencer Churchill one of the world's greatest statesmen, in his lifetime he was a noted speaker, painter, soldier, war reporter, historian and biographer. Writing history, Churchill also made history during his political career in Great Britain.

Having resigned from the position of First Lord of the Admiralty, the post he held for four years and would hold again in three years, Churchill participated in the House of Commons' debate on defense in London on November 12, 1936. Warning that Germany was stronger in the air than France and Britain, in this, one of his greatest speeches, Churchill urged a confrontation with the enemy.

●

"The Locust Years"
... The Government simply cannot make up their minds, or they cannot get the Prime Minister to make up his mind. So they go on in strange paradox, decided only to be undecided, resolved to be irresolute, adamant for drift, solid for fluidity, all-powerful to be impotent. So we go on preparing more months and years—precious, perhaps vital to the greatness of Britain—for the locust to eat. They will say to me, "A Minister of Supply is not necessary, for all is going well." I deny it. "The position is satisfactory." It is not true. "All is proceeding according to plan." We know what that means...

Owing to past neglect, in the face of the plainest warnings, we have now entered upon a period of danger.... The era of procrastination, of half-measures, of soothing and baffling expedients, of delays, is coming to its close. In its place we are entering a period of consequences.... We cannot avoid this period; we are in it now. Surely, if we can abridge it by even a few months, if we can shorten this period when the German Army will begin to be so much larger than the French Army, and before the British Air Force has come to play its complementary part, we may be the architects who build the peace of the world on sure foundations.

Two things, I confess have staggered me.... The first has been the dangers that have so swiftly come upon us in a few years, and have been transforming our position and the whole outlook of the world. Secondly, I have been staggered by the failure of the House of Commons to react effectively against those dangers.... I say that unless the House resolves to find out the truth for itself it will have committed an act of abdication of duty without parallel in its long history.

●

Three days after becoming Prime Minister of Great Britain, Churchill spoke to the House of Commons on May 13, l940. Aired on BBC radio that evening, Churchill's words became famous throughout the world both for their memorable phrases and their refusal to acknowledge the prospect of defeat.

"Blood, Toil, Tears and Sweat"
It must be remembered that we are in the preliminary stage of one of the greatest battles in history, that we are in action at many points in Norway and in Holland, that we have to be prepared in the Mediterranean, that the air battle is continuous and that many preparations have to be made here at home. In this crisis I hope I may be pardoned if I do not address the House at any length today.... I would say to the House, as I said to those who have joined the Government: "I have nothing to offer but blood, toil, tears and sweat."

We have before us an ordeal of the most grievous kind. We have before us many, many long months of struggle and of suffering. You ask, what is our policy? I will say: It is to wage war, by sea, land and air, with all our might and with all the strength that God can give us; to wage war against a monstrous tyranny, never surpassed in the dark, lamentable catalogue of human crime. That is our policy. You ask, What is our aim? I can answer in one word: Victory—victory at all costs, victory in spite of all terror, victory, however long and hard the road may be; for without victory, there is no survival. Let that be realized; no survival for the British Empire, no survival for all that the British Empire has stood for.... But I take up my task with buoyancy and hope. I feel sure that our cause will not be suffered to fail among men. At this time I feel entitled to claim the aid of all, and I say, "Come, then, let us go forward together with our united strength."

●

After the Nazis—with their aggressive, high-speed, highly mechanized "blitzkrieg" war machine— invaded much of Europe, Churchill issued a call to arms. Broadcast to millions four hours after being delivered in the House of Commons, this address became the most famous of all the war's speeches. Noting that French resistance to Hitler had deteriorated, Churchill, in the final bold paragraphs presented below, braced his country to continue the fight alone.

"This Was Their Finest Hour"

... However matters may go in France ... we in this island and in the British Empire will never lose our sense of comradeship with the French people. If we are now called upon to endure what they have been suffering, we shall emulate their courage, and if final victory rewards our toils they shall share the gains, aye, and freedom shall be restored to all. We abate nothing of our just demands: not one jot or tittle do we recede. Czechs, Poles, Norwegians, Dutch, Belgians have joined their causes to our own. All these shall be restored.

What General Weygand called the Battle of France is over. I expect that the Battle of Britain is about to begin. Upon this battle depends the survival of Christian civilization. Upon it depends our own British life, and the long continuity of our institutions and our Empire. The whole fury and might of the enemy must very soon be turned on us.

Hitler knows that he will have to break us in this Island or lose the war. If we can stand up to him, all Europe may be free and the life of the world may move forward into broad, sunlit uplands. But if we fail, then the whole world, including the United States, including all that we have known and cared for, will sink into the abyss of a new Dark Age made more sinister, and perhaps more protracted, by the lights of perverted science.

Let us therefore brace ourselves to our duties and so bear ourselves that if the British Empire and its Commonwealth last for a thousand years, men will still say, "This was their finest hour."

●

Less than a year after war's end Britain's wartime leader came out strongly to warn the world of the spread of Communism. In the course of the speech he coined the term "iron curtain," defining the line between Europe's free Western nations and those Eastern European countries in the shadows of the Soviet empire.

The setting was March 5, 1946, at Westminster College, in Fulton, Missouri, where Churchill first received an honorary degree and then was introduced by Missourian, President Harry Truman.

"Iron Curtain"

The United States stands at this time at the pinnacle of world power. It is a solemn moment for the American democracy. For with this primacy in power is also joined an awe-inspiring accountability to the future ...

I have a strong admiration and regard for the valiant Russian people.... There is deep sympathy and goodwill ... toward the peoples of all the Russias and a resolve to persevere through many differences and rebuffs in establishing lasting friendships.

It is my duty, however, to place before you certain facts about the present position in Europe. From Stettin in the Baltic to Trieste in the Adriatic an iron curtain has descended across the Continent. Behind that line lie all the capitals of the ancient states of Central and Eastern Europe. Warsaw, Berlin, Prague, Vienna, Budapest, Belgrade, Bucharest and Sofia; all these famous cities and the populations around them lie in what I must call the Soviet sphere, and all are subject, in one form or another [to an] increasing measure of control from Moscow ...

I do not believe that Soviet Russia desires war.... But what we have to consider here today while time remains, is the permanent prevention of war and the establishment of conditions of freedom and democracy.... Our difficulties and dangers will not be removed by closing our eyes to them. They will not be removed by mere waiting to see what happens; nor will they be removed by a policy of appeasement ...

Last time I saw it all coming and I cried aloud to my own fellow countrymen and to the world, but no one paid any attention.... [War] could have been prevented, in my belief, without the firing of a single shot, and Germany might be powerful, prosperous and honored today; but no one would listen and one by one we were all sucked into the awful whirlpool.

We must not let it happen again. This can only be achieved by reaching now ... a good understanding on all points with Russia under the general authority of the United Nations Organization and ... by the whole strength of the English-speaking world ... in the air, on the sea, all over the globe, and in science and in industry, and in moral force ...

If we adhere faithfully to the Charter of the United Nations and walk forward in sedate and sober strength, seeking no one's land or treasure, seeking to lay no arbitrary control upon the thoughts of men ... the high roads of the future will be clear, not only for us but for all, not only for our time but for a century to come.

In a few short paragraphs President Abraham Lincoln dedicated the cemetery on the battlefield of Gettysburg, Pennsylvania, in ceremonies honoring the 43,000 casualties of the three-day battle that marked the turning point of the Civil War. The speech would long be remembered and revered, for his words not only dedicated a cemetery but unified a country that had for two years been torn by war.

Interestingly, the President had not been expected to speak at the cemetery's dedication on November 19, 1863—in part because he was not considered to be a particularly eloquent speaker and in part because Edward Everett had been invited to commemorate Gettysburg's dead. Everett, a Harvard professor, was widely regarded as the North's most gifted orator. After Lincoln had finished reading his three-minute "Gettysburg Address" to the crowd, Everett immediately congratulated the President and delivered his own speech, clearly not expecting to have his own words diminished by Lincoln's.

The immediate impact of the President's address was minimal. Perhaps because his high-pitched, Kentucky-accented voice was not ideally suited to oratory, few in the crowd were impressed by Lincoln's beautifully crafted words. The British *Times*, in fact, summarily dismissed his speech by stating, "The ceremony was rendered ludicrous by some of the sallies of that poor President Lincoln." Newspapers in the United States also found the speech "silly" or "embarrassing." And Lincoln himself, after the speech, commented, "That speech won't scour. It is a flat failure and the people are disappointed." (On the farms where Lincoln grew up, when wet soil stuck to the mold board of a plow they said it didn't "scour.")

However, as the days passed and Lincoln's sermon appeared in print, people began to marvel at the personal depth of compassion and presidential debt of gratitude that his words conveyed. Indeed, few speeches can rival "The Gettysburg Address." As scholar Gilbert Highet points out, Lincoln was a "literary artist, [and] 'The Gettysburg Address' [is] a work of art." Not only was Lincoln profoundly influenced by classic literature, the Bible and Shakespeare, but he also fully understood and deftly manipulated rhetorical devices. His powerful diction and profound allusions, Highet contends, have produced a literary masterpiece that "belongs to the same world as the great elegies and the adagios of Beethoven."

The great President's poetic words, spoken in only three minutes' time, are engraven in stone at the Lincoln Memorial—and upon the hearts of freedom-loving people everywhere.

•

"The Gettysburg Address"

Fourscore and seven years ago our fathers brought forth on this continent, a new nation, conceived in liberty and dedicated to the proposition that all men are created equal.

Now we are engaged in a great civil war, testing whether that nation—or any nation so conceived and so dedicated—can long endure. We are met on a great battlefield of that war. We are met to dedicate a portion of it as a final resting place of those who have given their lives that that nation might live. It is altogether fitting and proper that we should do this.

But, in a larger sense, we can not dedicate, we can not consecrate, we can not hallow, this ground. The brave men, living and dead, who struggled here, have consecrated it, far above our poor power to add or detract.

The world will very little note nor long remember what we say here, but it can never forget what they did here.

It is for us, the living, rather, to be dedicated here, to the unfinished work that they have thus far so nobly carried on. It is rather for us to be here dedicated to the great task remaining before us, that from these honored dead we take increased devotion to that cause for which they here gave the last full measure of devotion, that we here highly resolve that these dead shall not have died in vain; that this nation shall, under God, have a new birth of freedom, and that government of the people, by the people, for the people, shall not perish from the earth.

•

Born into poverty, Abraham Lincoln faced defeat throughout his life. He had lost eight elections, had twice failed in business, had suffered a nervous breakdown. After serving in the Illinois state legislature and in Congress, he was not reelected and was subsequently rejected for the job of Illinois's land officer. Nevertheless, he doggedly pursued his political career. While he failed to be elected—twice—and lost his attempt at the Vice-Presidential nomination, Lincoln eventually was voted in as President of the United States of America.

Now taking the oath of the Presidential office for a second time on March 4, 1865, President Lincoln displayed his greatest strengths. He expressed his insights and convictions clearly, and in the process revitalized and healed a nation that had suffered four long years of internal strife. Though only subdued hand clapping and occasional cheers punctuated the address, reporters noted that tears coursed down the faces of those in the audience.

However physically drained the President must have been from presiding over a nation "torn from within," Lincoln continued to see those widows and soldiers who flowed from all parts of the country to visit him at the White House. Referred to as "Father Abraham" by millions of his countrymen, the President implored the nation to mend their differences and work together to rebuild what had been so tragically shattered.

"The Second Inaugural Address"

Fellow countrymen: At this second appearing to take the oath of the presidential office, there is less occasion for an extended address than there was at the first. Then a statement, somewhat in detail, of a course to be pursued, seemed fitting and proper. Now, at the expiration of four years, during which public declarations have been constantly called forth on every point and phase of the great contest which still absorbs the attention, and engrosses the energies of the nation, little that is new could be presented. The progress of our arms, upon which all else chiefly depends, is as well known to the public as to myself; and it is, I trust, reasonably satisfactory and encouraging to all. With high hope for the future, no prediction in regard to it is ventured.

On the occasion corresponding to this four years ago, all thoughts were anxiously directed to an impending civil-war. All dreaded it—all sought to avert it. While the inaugural address was being delivered from this place, devoted altogether to saving the Union without war, insurgent agents were in the city seeking to destroy it without war—seeking to dissolve the Union, and divide effects, by negotiation. Both parties deprecated war; but one of them would make war rather than let the nation survive; and the other would accept war rather than let it perish. And the war came.

One-eighth of the whole population were colored slaves, not distributed generally over the Union, but localized in the Southern part of it. These slaves constituted a peculiar and powerful interest. All knew that this interest was, somehow, the cause of the war. To strengthen, perpetuate, and extend this interest was the object for which the insurgents would rend the Union, even by war; while the government claimed no right to do more than to restrict the territorial enlargement of it. Neither party expected for the war, the magnitude, or the duration, which it has already attained. Neither anticipated that the cause of the conflict might cease with, or even before, the conflict itself should cease. Each looked for an easier triumph, and a result less fundamental and astounding. Both read the same Bible and pray to the same God; and each invokes His aid against the other. It may seem strange that any men should dare to ask a just God's assistance in wringing their bread from the sweat of other men's faces; but let us judge not that we be not judged. The prayers of both could not be answered; that of neither has been answered fully. The Almighty has His own purposes. "Woe unto the world because of offenses! For it must needs be that offenses come; but woe to that man by whom the offense cometh!" If we shall suppose that American Slavery is one of those offenses which, in the providence of God, must needs come, but which, having continued through His appointed time, He now wills to remove, and that He gives to both North and South, this terrible war, as the woe due to those by whom the offense came, shall we discern therein any departure from those divine attributes which the believers in a Living God always ascribe to Him? Fondly do we hope—fervently do we pray—that this mighty scourge of war may speedily pass away. Yet, if God wills that it continue, until all the wealth piled by the bondman's two hundred and fifty years of unrequited toil shall be sunk, and until every drop of blood drawn with the lash shall be paid by another drawn with the sword, as was said three thousand years ago, so still it must be said "the judgements of the Lord are true and righteous altogether."

With malice toward none; with charity for all; with firmness in the right, as God gives us to see the right, let us strive on to finish the work we are in; to bind up the nation's wounds; to care for him who shall have borne the battle, and for his widow, and his orphan-to do all which may achieve and cherish a just and lasting peace, among ourselves, and with all nations.

GEORGE WASHINGTON
"The Temple Speech" and "The Farewell Address"

As the first Commander-in-Chief and first President of the United States, George Washington (1732-1799) profoundly influenced his contemporaries and future Americans with his persistence, discipline and sense of duty.

Born in Virginia, Washington received no formal education as a child, but read widely. He later was trained as a surveyor and subsequently explored his interest in land development. When the French encroached on Virginia territory Washington began both his political and military careers, participating in local government positions and acting as leader of the state militia. After serving as an exemplary general of colonial forces during the Revolutionary War, he retired to his beloved Mount Vernon plantation—until the country would call on him again to lead the fledgling government.

On March 15, 1783, various officers sought grievance for back pay. As the angry and resentful commanders gathered in a hall called the "Temple" in New York, Washington unexpectedly arrived to speak to them. The tide of insurrection gradually turned as the President and Commander-in-Chief reminded his friends of their collective vision and purpose. His address left them in tears and once more willing to put their faith in Congress.

"The Temple Speech"

Gentlemen: By an anonymous summons, an attempt has been made to convene you together; how inconsistent with the rules of propriety, how unmilitary, and how subversive of all order and discipline, let the good sense of the army decide.

… If my conduct heretofore has not evinced to you that I have been a faithful friend to the army, my declaration of it at this time would be equally unavailing and improper. But as I was among the first who embarked in the cause of our common country. As I have never left your side one moment, but when called from you on public duty. As I have been the constant companion and witness of your distresses, and not among the last to feel and acknowledge your merits. As I have ever considered my own military reputation as inseparably connected with that of the army. As my heart has ever expanded with joy when I have heard its praises, and my indignation has arisen when the mouth of detraction has been opened against it, it can scarcely be supposed, at this late stage of the war, that I am indifferent to its interests.

But how are they to be promoted? The way is plain, says the anonymous addresser. If war continues, remove into the unsettled country … and leave an ungrateful country to defend itself. But who are they to defend? Our wives, our children, our farms, and other property which we leave behind us…. If peace takes place, never sheathe your swords, says he, until you have obtained full and ample justice; this dreadful alternative, of either deserting our country in the extremist hour of her distress or turning our arms against it (which is the apparent object, unless Congress can be compelled into instant compliance), has something so shocking in it that humanity revolts at the idea. My God! What can this writer have in view, by recommending such measure? Can he be a friend to the army? Can he be a friend to this country? Rather, is he not an insidious foe? Some emissary, perhaps, from New York, plotting the ruin of both, by sowing the seed of discord and separation between the civil and military powers of the continent? And what a compliment does he pay to our understandings when he recommends measures in either alternative, impracticable in their nature?…

For myself (and I take no merit in giving the assurance, being induced to it from principles of gratitude, veracity, and justice), a grateful sense of the confidence you have ever placed in me, a recollection of the cheerful assistance and prompt obedience I have experienced from you, under every vicissitude of fortune, and the sincere affection I feel for an army I have so long had the honor to command will oblige me to declare, in this public and solemn manner, that, in the gratification of every wish, so far as may be done consistently with the great duty I owe my country and those powers we are bound to respect, you may freely command my services to the utmost of my abilities.

While I give you these assurances, and pledge myself in the most unequivocal manner to exert whatever ability I am possessed of in your favor, let me entreat you, gentlemen, on your part, not to take any measures which, viewed in the calm light of reason, will lessen the dignity and sully the glory you have hitherto maintained; let me request you to rely on the plighted faith of your country, and place a full confidence in the purity of the intentions of Congress…. And let me conjure you, in the name of our common country, as you value your own sacred honor, as you respect the rights of humanity, and as you regard the military and national character of America, to express your utmost horror and detestation of the man who wishes, under any specious pretenses, to overturn the liberties of our country, and who wickedly attempts to open the floodgates of civil discord and deluge our rising empire in blood.

By thus determining and thus acting, you will pursue the plain and direct road to the attainment of your wishes. You will defeat the insidious designs of our enemies, who are compelled to resort from open force to secret artifice. You will give one more distinguished proof of unexampled patriotism and patient virtue, rising superior to the pressure of the most complicated sufferings. And you will, by the dignity of your conduct, afford occasion for posterity to say, when speaking of the glorious example you have exhibited to mankind, "Had this day been wanting, the world had never seen the last stage of perfection to which human nature is capable of attaining."

[Washington then gazed out at his sullen audience and drew a letter from his pocket, to which he wished to refer. Squinting at the writing in the letter, the mighty General could not go on. He then drew from his waistcoat pocket an item very few of his listeners had seen him use—a pair of glasses.]

Gentlemen, you will permit me to put on my spectacles, for I have not only grown gray but almost blind in the service of my country.

After declining to serve a third term as President, in his last words to the young country, September 17, 1796, he issued warnings and beseeched the citizenry to seek harmony in the nation.

"The Farewell Address"

Friends and fellow citizens: The period for a new election of a citizen, to administer the executive government of the United States, being not far distant, and the time actually arrived when your thoughts must be employed in designating the person who is to be clothed with that important trust, it appears to me proper, especially as it may conduce to a more distinct expression of the public voice, that I should now apprise you of the resolution I have formed to decline being considered among the number of those out of whom a choice is to be made ...

Here, perhaps, I ought to stop. But a solicitude for your welfare, which cannot end but with my life, and the apprehension of danger, natural to that solicitude, urge me on an occasion like the present to offer to your solemn contemplation, and to recommend to your frequent review, some sentiments which are the result of much reflection, of no inconsiderable observation, and which appear to me all important to the permanency of your felicity as a people ...

... Citizens by birth or choice, of a common country, that country has a right to concentrate your affections. The name of "American," which belongs to you, in your national capacity, must always exalt the just pride of patriotism.... With slight shades of difference, you have the same religion, manners, habits and political principles. You have in a common cause fought & triumphed together. The independence & liberty you possess are the work of joint councils, and joint efforts; of common dangers, sufferings and successes ...

While then every part of our country thus feels an immediate and particular Interest in union, all the parts combined cannot fail to find in the united mass of means and efforts greater strength, greater resource ... greater security from external danger, a less frequent interruption of their peace by foreign Nations, and ... an exemption from those broils and wars between themselves ...

... Of all the dispositions and habits which lead to political prosperity, religion and morality are indispensable supports. In vain would that man claim the tribute of patriotism who should labor to subvert these great pillars of human happiness—these firmest props of the duties of men and citizens.... And let us with caution indulge the supposition that morality can be maintained without religion. Whatever may be conceded to the influence of refined education on minds of peculiar structure, reason and experience both forbid us to expect that national morality can prevail in exclusion of religious principle.

... Promote, then ... institutions for the general diffusion of knowledge. In proportion as the structure of a government gives force to public opinion, it is essential that public opinion should be enlightened ...

Observe good faith and justice towards all nations. Cultivate peace and harmony with all. Religion and morality enjoin this conduct. And can it be that good policy does not equally enjoin it? It will be worthy of a free, enlightened, and at no distant period a great nation to give to mankind the magnanimous and too novel example of a people always guided by an exalted justice and benevolence.... Can it be that Providence has not connected the permanent felicity of a nation with its virtue? The experiment, at least, is recommended by every sentiment which ennobles human nature. Alas! is it rendered impossible by its vices?...

The great rule of conduct for us in regard to foreign nations is, in extending our commercial relations to have with them as little political connection as possible. So far as we have already formed engagements let them be fulfilled with perfect good faith....

In offering to you, my countrymen, these counsels of an old and affectionate friend, I dare not hope they will make the strong and lasting impression I could wish, that they will control the usual current of the passions, or prevent our nation from running the course which has hitherto marked the destiny of nations ...

Though in reviewing the incidents of my administration, I am unconscious of intentional error. I am nevertheless too sensible of my defects not to think it probable that I may have committed many errors. Whatever they may be, I fervently beseech the Almighty to avert or mitigate the evils to which they may tend. I shall also carry with me the hope that my country will never cease to view them with indulgence, and that after forty-five years of my life dedicated to its service with an upright zeal, the faults of incompetent abilities will be consigned to oblivion, as myself must soon be to the Mansions of rest.

Relying on its kindness in this as in other things, and actuated by that fervent love toward it which is so natural to a man who views in it the native soil of himself and his progenitors for several generations, I anticipate with pleasing expectation that retreat in which I promise myself to realize, without alloy, the sweet enjoyment of partaking in the midst of my fellow-citizens the benign influence of good laws under a free government—the ever-favorite object of my heart, and the happy reward, as I trust, of our mutual cares, labors, and dangers.

PATRICK HENRY
"Give Me Liberty or Give Me Death"

Though mainly remembered for his "Give me liberty or give me death" speech, the radical advocate for separation Patrick Henry (1736-1799) played a prominent part in the American Revolution. Educated in law, his oratorical and debate skills were highly prized in the new, would-be republic. Elected to the House of Burgesses (the Virginia Colony's legislative body), Henry enacted legislation that appeared to any British loyalist to be high treason. In so doing, he was known as a principal catalyst of the Revolution.

Over the years, the significance of and fascination with Henry's address took on a life of its own. In fact, the speech, pronounced on March 23, 1775, was not even written down until much later, its words recorded as best as could be remembered by an eyewitness. Still, they did cause quite a stir at the time, as the crowd leapt to its feet as one and shouted, "To arms! To arms!"

No man thinks more highly than I do of the patriotism, as well as abilities, of the very worthy gentlemen who have just addressed the House. But different men often see the same subject in different lights; and, therefore, I hope it will not be thought disrespectful to those gentlemen if, entertaining as I do opinions of a character very opposite to theirs, I shall speak forth my sentiments freely and without reserve.

This is no time for ceremony. The question before the House is one of awful moment to this country. For my own part, I consider it as nothing less than a question of freedom or slavery; and in proportion to the magnitude of the subject ought to be the freedom of the debate. It is only in this way that we can hope to arrive at truth, and fulfill the great responsibility which we hold to God and our country. Should I keep back my opinions at such a time, through fear of giving offense, I should consider myself as guilty of treason towards my country, and of an act of disloyalty toward the Majesty of Heaven, which I revere above all earthly kings.

Mr. President, it is natural to man to indulge in the illusions of hope. We are apt to shut our eyes against a painful truth, and listen to the song of that siren till she transforms us into beasts. Is this the part of wise men, engaged in a great and arduous struggle for liberty? Are we disposed to be of the number of those who, having eyes, see not, and, having ears, hear not, the things which so nearly concern their temporal salvation? For my

part, whatever anguish of spirit it may cost, I am willing to know the whole truth; to know the worst, and to provide for it.

I have but one lamp by which my feet are guided, and that is the lamp of experience. I know of no way of judging of the future but by the past. And judging by the past, I wish to know what there has been in the conduct of the British ministry for the last ten years to justify those hopes with which gentlemen have been pleased to solace themselves and the House.

Is it that insidious smile with which our petition has been lately received? Trust it not, sir; it will prove a snare to your feet. Suffer not yourselves to be betrayed with a kiss. Ask yourselves how this gracious reception of our petition comports with those warlike preparations which cover our waters and darken our land. Are fleets and armies necessary to a work of love and reconciliation? Have we shown ourselves so unwilling to be reconciled that force must be called in to win back our love?

Let us not deceive ourselves, sir. These are the implements of war and subjugation; the last arguments to which kings resort.

I ask gentlemen, sir, what means this martial array, if its purpose be not to force us to submission? Can gentlemen assign any other possible motive for it? Has Great Britain any enemy, in this quarter of the world, to call for all this accumulation of navies and armies? No, sir, she has none. They are meant for us: they can be meant for no other. They are sent over to bind and rivet upon us those chains which the British ministry have been so long forging.

And what have we to oppose to them? Shall we try argument? Sir, we have been trying that for the last ten years. Have we anything new to offer upon the subject? Nothing. We have held the subject up in every light of which it is capable; but it has been all in vain. Shall we resort to entreaty and humble supplication? What terms shall we find which have not been already exhausted? Let us not, I beseech you, sir, deceive ourselves.

Sir, we have done everything that could be done to avert the storm which is now coming on. We have petitioned; we have remonstrated; we have supplicated; we have prostrated ourselves before the throne, and have implored its interposition to arrest the tyrannical hands of the ministry and Parliament.

Our petitions have been slighted; our remonstrations have produced additional violence and insult; our supplications have been disregarded; and we have been spurned, with contempt, from the foot of the throne! In vain, after these things, may we indulge the fond hope of peace and reconciliation. There is no longer any room for hope. If we wish to be free—if we mean to preserve inviolate those inestimable privileges for which we have been so long contending—if we mean not basely to abandon the noble struggle in which we have been so long engaged, and which we have pledged ourselves never to abandon until the glorious object of our contest shall be obtained—we must fight! I repeat it, sir, we must fight! An appeal to arms and to the God of hosts is all that is left us!

They tell us, sir, that we are weak; unable to cope with so formidable an adversary. But when shall we be stronger? Will it be the next week, or the next year? Will it be when we are totally disarmed, and when a British guard shall be stationed in every house? Shall we gather strength by irresolution and inaction? Shall we acquire the means of effectual resistance by lying supinely on our backs and hugging the delusive phantom of hope, until our enemies shall have bound us hand and foot?

Sir, we are not weak if we make a proper use of those means which the God of nature hath placed in our power. The millions of people, armed in the holy cause of liberty, and in such a country as that which we possess, are invincible by any force which our enemy can send against us.

Besides, sir, we shall not fight our battles alone. There is a just God who presides over the destinies of nations, and who will raise up friends to fight our battles for us. The battle, sir, is not to the strong alone; it is to the vigilant, the active, the brave.

Besides, sir, we have no election. If we were base enough to desire it, it is now too late to retire from the contest. There is no retreat but in submission and slavery! Our chains are forged! Their clanking may be heard on the plains of Boston! The war is inevitable—and let it come! I repeat it, sir, let it come.

It is in vain, sir, to extenuate the matter. Gentlemen may cry, Peace, Peace—but there is no peace. The war is actually begun! The next gale that sweeps from the north will bring to our ears the clash of resounding arms! Our brethren are already in the field! Why stand we here idle? What is it that gentlemen wish? What would they have? Is life so dear, or peace so sweet, as to be purchased at the price of chains and slavery?

Forbid it, Almighty God! I know not what course others may take; but as for me, give me liberty or give me death!

THEY MADE A DIFFERENCE

shapers of our world

Certain individuals—spouses, family members, close friends—touch our lives in daily, direct, and very personal ways. Yet, ironically, many of those who shape our thoughts and actions most profoundly are people we've never actually meet face to face. Think of the movie stars we worship (for better or worse), the sports heroes we try to imitate, the politicians we grumble about … These are the movers and the shakers of the world. And the waves they make reverberate on into the future. Bob Hope, Lucille Ball, Charlie Chaplin and Mark Twain are all dead, yet they still make us laugh. We still swivel to Elvis's early rock rhythms and move to the Gershwins' jazzy melodies; 30 years later, the glamour of Marilyn Monroe still dazzles; again and again we plunge into Spielberg's alternate movie-screen worlds; we still marvel at the skill and determination of Muhammad Ali, the "Babe" and Billie Jean King; the legacy of warriors like George Patton and Margaret Thatcher is still outlined in borders on the map.

And then the occasional Helen Keller, Albert Schweitzer and Geronimo comes along to enlarge our human consciousness and broaden the scope of our compassion and our ideals of justice.

There is a common thread that runs through the lives of all these diverse individuals: steadfast, even stubborn; creative, almost to a fault; confident, focused and courageous ... these are all those who have dared to stand out and to give their personal best in whatever vision of life they aspired to. And whatever their faults, these are those mortal champions who, over the past hundred years or so, have thrown themselves authentically, energetically, wholeheartedly into life, and who, in the process, have shaped and colored the world we live in today. In other words, *"They Made a Difference."*

"Didn't you hear me? I said I was The Greatest"

Muhammed Ali – The Greatest: My Own Story

CONTENTS

As an artist, Spielberg is a mirror, not a lamp

Steven Spielberg – The Man, His Movies,
and their Meaning

Sports Greats—legends in their own time

Visionaries and Warriors—taking up a cause

Political Profiles—courage and power

"But I'm a chemist.
I know it won't work."
The Iron Lady – A Biography of Margaret Thatcher

One prominent cartoonist,
Carey Orr, warned Walt
off with the comment that he
wasn't "cynical" enough for
newspaper cartooning.
Leonard Mosley – Disney's World: A Biography

"Can't I be anything else?"
Marilyn Monroe

*Overnight the children became defenders
of their people against the government.*
Higher Than Hope – The Authorized Biography of Nelson Mandela

DON'T SHOOT, IT'S ONLY ME
by Bob Hope with Melville Shavelson, Putnam, 1990

Bob Hope (1903-2003) was an American comedy legend, dispensing his dosages of on-the-road good will through four wars and countless other military engagements around the world. In giving tribute to his country, Hope's autobiography *Don't Shoot, It's Only Me* reads like "a love song to my girl: America, warts and all."

"The terrible thing about growing older is that it lasts so long," Hope writes. "You start telling jokes to make a living and one morning you wake up and find you've written the history of half a century. Or your writers have. Accidentally."

Bob Hope began entertaining the nation in 1938, first in films with *The Big Broadcast* and then on radio. To achieve his goal of becoming the most popular comedian on radio, he hired the best up-and-coming writers. He also honed an earthy, staccato, fast-paced delivery: *My method ... was to deliver a series of one-liners, joke joke joke.... I would zing a joke and then start on the next line and wait for the audience to catch up. Then I'd ad-lib, "laugh first, figure it out later." If someone laughed a little late, I'd ask, "Which one are you working on?"*

Hope began entertaining U.S. troops in 1941. During World War II everyone seemed to play a part—even President-to-be Ronald Reagan. Here's the story as Hope tells it:

An actor named Captain Ronald Reagan put in a short hitch at Armed Forces Radio Services Headquarters. Captain Reagan's only military experience up to that time had been saluting Colonel Jack Warner whenever Ronnie's option came up. On one careless occasion, someone decided to make Reagan Officer of the Day. One of my writers, now part of the unit, phoned him, disguising his voice.

"Captain Reagan? This is Lieutenant Colonel Whitney of the Fifty-Fourth on secret orders from General McNair. I have a company of one-hundred men en route to Camp Roberts and we're running late. Can you provide bivouac?"

There was a short pause while Ronnie quickly consulted his military dictionary.

"Yes sir!" he replied, and immediately hung up and called Abbey Rents to deliver a hundred army cots. There was no arrangement for sleeping at AFRS. All the sleeping was done at typewriters.

Almost immediately the telephone rang again. "Lieutenant Colonel Whitney here. Very sorry, I miscounted, captain. Our unit on this maneuver actually consists of one hundred and fifty men. Does that present any logistical problem?"

"The impossible we do immediately," Reagan said, believing he had just coined a phrase. He hung up and frantically phoned Abbey Rents for fifty more cots.

Then came the final phone call. "Captain Reagan? You know of course, the Fifty-fourth is a cavalry unit. Be sure you have enough hay."

Ronnie phoned the prop department at Warner Brothers. They tell me there was straw blowing around in the wind at Sunset and Western for weeks after that.

In another story he tells of something that happened right after Reagan's re-election: *Ronnie topped all my jokes that year, making up one of his own. Testing the microphone for his weekly radio broadcast, he said, "My fellow Americans, I'm pleased to tell you today that I've signed legislation that will outlaw Russia forever. We begin bombing in five minutes."*

Somehow, the joke got put on the air. If it had been Orson Welles who had said it, it would have caused a national panic. But since it was Reagan, Hope writes, nobody took it seriously. "They just figured Nancy had forgotten to make out his cue cards."

Hope also shares stories about other American presidents—among whom were both his greatest victims and his greatest friends. During World War II, for example, Franklin D. Roosevelt—who "was either loved or hated," depending on whose side you were on—told a joke about himself that Hope enjoys retelling:

During the fighting on Guadalcanal in the Pacific, an American marine was disappointed because he hadn't had a chance to shoot at the enemy. He hadn't even seen one of them.

"Okay," his commanding officer said, "go up on top of the next hill and yell, 'To hell with Hirohito!' Believe me, that'll bring the Japs out of hiding fast."

So the marine went up on the hill and hollered, "To hell with Hirohito!"

A Jap came out of the jungle and shouted, "To hell with Roosevelt!"

"Just my luck," said the marine. "I can't shoot a fellow Republican."

Hope organized shows for the USO and went on tour, raising the spirits of American troops and their allies. During one show, he remembers, he was telling a joke, when a tank burst through the crowd and came towards the stage. *I didn't think the joke was that bad, but I'd never met a critic with a Sherman tank before, so I got ready to jump off the platform, when suddenly it stopped right in front of me. The turret popped open and a guy got out wearing a tanker's crash helmet. He dragged a folding chair up after him and sat down on it and crossed his legs.*

"Make me laugh," he said.

Hope had them rolling in the aisles ever since.

Hope always made certain to surround himself with beautiful film stars, singers and dancers when on tour. He recalls that one night it got so crowded at a party for servicemen at the Hollywood Canteen that "if a soldier wanted to tune the radio, he had to squeeze past Lana Turner, Hedy Lamarr, Dinah Shore and Betty Grable just to change the station. I must have heard 148 different programs."

Everything was not always rosy for Hope and his band of "Hope Gypsies." A war was on, and enemy snipers and pilots rarely cared who was sleeping in a hotel or riding in a plane or bus. His entertainers often came under fire. As dangerous as touring was, however, sometimes it was just old-fFashioned bad luck that caught up to Hope, as was the case in his first experience handling a plane, the *Catalina*:

I waited until everyone else in our group was asleep before begging our Navy pilot to let me do the driving. He was a little dubious about turning the controls over to a civilian, especially after I asked him which way was reverse, but he wanted an introduction to [my wife] Frances and he figured, how much harm could a stupid civilian do in a couple of minutes?

He put everything on automatic pilot and went back to talk to Frances. I have an idea the Catalina discovered who was flying it and the left engine fainted. The pilot came racing into the cockpit and ordered me out of the seat. He started checking the instruments and the motor kept complaining until finally he feathered the prop. We went into a dive, and he yelled, "Jettison everything we don't need!"

I raced into the back and tripped over Barney [one of the stage people], who was just getting out of his berth. I had kidded him so much about how the planes we were in were going to crash, he didn't believe me when I told him we were in serious trouble.

"How can it be serious?" he asked. "Your option was already picked up."

I dragged him up to the cockpit and showed him the feathered prop.

"That's supposed to be going around," I told him.

He swallowed hard and said, "Spare me the technical crap, how long have we got to live?"

The plane kept losing altitude and by that time everybody was awake and throwing everything overboard, including the scotch. Barney got indignant when we started eyeing him. [Then] he told me to throw my wallet overboard, since it was the heaviest thing on the plane.

When World War II ended, the Hope Gypsies hung up their fatigues and put away the box lunches—but by then their leader was already addicted to the thrills of "playing" for the armed forces. And when the "Korean Conflict" heated up, he was off and "playing" again. But entertaining during the Korean War proved to be a different experience for Hope and his Gypsies. The war was unpopular back home as well as at the front. And the front itself fluctuated wildly; once, in a battle-torn area, they even arrived ahead of the Marines. The war kept Hope, Frances and company cracking jokes and cheering the troops on for three years straight, both in sub-zero weather as well as in the sweltering heat of summer.

After the war's end, Hope went back to his TV and radio shows and film career; the Hope Gypsies were put into mothballs. Then in 1958 he decided to do one of his TV specials from Moscow—a first of its kind. After much wrangling, his travel visa finally

came through and, keeping his writers "chained to a typewriter on the way over," Hope set off. Using Russian talent to back himself, the show went off with few hitches—though the comedian had to convince Soviet officials that Americans made jokes about their leaders all the time before they would release the film for viewing.

In 1964 the Hope Gypsies were called out of retirement to play for thousands of advisers in a nasty little Southeastern Asian skirmish. The country was Vietnam:

There are some cynics who say I never met a war I didn't like. They're the ones who've never smelled it up close, in the hospital wards.... Every time I walked out on stage, I was face-to-face with the kids who were doing the actual fighting.... They were very much alive and preferred to stay that way. I was only interested in doing what I could.... Toward the end in 'Nam, when the G.I.s at Lai Khe started booing the jokes, I knew it was finished.

Hope's tour, a goodwill phenomenon tethered by a long string of entertainment and jokes, had ended; Vietnam had been a long haul. All wars are terrible, but this one, Hope noted, proved to be even nastier than most: "less to laugh at." And the danger was greater than ever. There was even a plot hatched by the Viet Cong to assassinate the comedian. By the slimmest of margins, it didn't succeed.

Between 1974 and 1990, Hope worked on his occasional TV specials and made appearances on various other shows. In the late '80s and early '90s, he returned to the field, entertaining troops in Beirut and the Persian Gulf.

On October 2, 1989, Bob Hope did a vaudeville show. But not just any vaudeville. He was on stage with George Burns. Hope teased that between them they totaled 179 years old.

At the end of that special night, Hope, with the help of a ladies' hat from the audience, played the feminine half of Burns and Allen. *It was a strange feeling, being half of Burns and Allen, even in fun,* Hope recounted. *The two of them had been the real vaudeville, and one of the true love stories of another generation. I wondered what George was thinking, but I couldn't see through the cigar smoke. But after we danced "Tea for Two" together, George said, "Say goodnight Gracie," and I said, "Goodnight Gracie," and he smiled and we walked offstage, arm in arm.*

The team of Burns and Hope had finally made the Big Time.

Lucille Ball, one of the world's best-loved comedians, was a "wild, tempestuous, exciting child with enormous energy, flair, and style," says her cousin. "She saw things in a way nobody else did. She was a reactor—she reacted to everything. Running away from home was reacting. It was always very dramatic when we were caught. And that was the point. What she really wanted was to play a scene."

Lucy was born August 6, 1911 in Celoron, New York. Four years later her father died and the family moved in with her grandfather, whose natural exuberance and love of life clearly influenced Lucy; her flair for acting rapidly emerged. One day she insisted on running next door to entertain some kids who had the measles. So, her mother looped a rope around the little girl's waist and hooked it to a pulley so "Miss Busybody" could run freely back and forth—still harnessed.

Throughout Lucy's school years her mother encouraged her to act, dance and sing. When she turned 15 she dropped out of high school to enroll in a drama academy in New York City. Shortly afterward, however, the academy notified Lucy's mother that she "was wasting her money."

Lucy decided to become a show girl. "I answered an Earl Carroll tryout," she recalled. "I rehearsed for two weeks, then a man told me I was through. I went home and cried. I got picked for a Shubert show. We rehearsed for two weeks and I was fired again. That time I really suffered."

Lucy often returned home to take any odd job she could find: soda jerking, clerking, anything at all to keep her going. She ate only when she could find a "one-doughnut man." This, she explained, "is a guy who sits at the counter and orders coffee and doughnuts. He drinks his coffee, eats one doughnut and puts down a nickel tip. I'd do a fast slide onto his stool, yell for a cup of coffee, pay for it with his nickel, and eat the other doughnut."

At 18 Lucy collapsed from malnutrition and fatigue while doing a modeling job. "It taught me that without your health, you ain't got nothin'," she explained. After recuperating, she signed a contract as a poster girl for a Goldwyn movie in California and appeared in ten films in 1933 and 1934. But by then she was a "last year's girl," so she moved to Columbia Pictures. She sent for her family, and they lived together in a rented house on Ogden Drive.

No sooner had they moved than Columbia dropped Lucy's option. She hurried over to RKO and found a lower-paying job working "halfway between an extra and a bit." It was at RKO's talent school where she finally got her break while studying drama under Lela Rogers, Ginger's mother. "It was real acting experience," Lucy recalled. "We had a stage, scripts to get our teeth into, and an audience."

She soon scored a hit in Stage Door. Busier than ever, she made seven films in 1938 and even more in 1939. One of her friends remembered, "Everything was an adventure, a great burst of joy and it was infectious."

During this joyful period, Desi entered Lucy's life. "I was in the room when Desi and Lucy first met, and it was like love at first sight," fellow dancer and actress Ann Miller recalled. "When he first was introduced to her, her eyes just lit up." Lucy's life changed noticeably when she began to date Desi. "We couldn't have learned more if we'd been in college," Lucy explained. "His department was facts, figures and sports, especially horse racing. Mine was women—I taught Desi a lot about women."

In 1940 the couple eloped. Justice of the Peace John P. O'Brien took them to the Byram River Beagle Club. "Maybe it doesn't sound very romantic," Lucy recalled, "but actually it was. The judge took us there because he said all young people who were going to spend a lifetime together should start off in as romantic a setting as possible."

"Marrying Desi was the boldest thing I ever did," Lucy confessed. "He frightened me." Desi lived dangerously, and danger did not appeal to his new wife.

Soon after her marriage, Lucy made some striking changes. While preparing for her first MGM movie, the chief hair stylist dyed her hair a bright red, which forever after became her trademark. When people remarked that nobody ever had that shade of hair, she firmly said, "I do. When I chose this shade, things began to break for me. It gave me just the right finishing touch before the cameras." Life magazine regarded Lucy's first film at MGM as her "first real opportunity to become a big-time star."

During these years, according to friends, Lucy was "down to earth and refreshingly non-Hollywood." Desi, however, began to travel frequently, and the strain on their relationship increased. Then, as the country went to war, Special Services assigned Desi to a hospital near Van Nuys. He was not far from their Northridge ranch but was still not living at home. By now their marriage was in a shambles. Lucy was an old-fashioned young woman who believed in fidelity and "one man." Desi, on the other hand, liked to "fool around."

Their frequent separations and frenetic schedules soon made the couple long for tranquility. Even Desi grew tired of nightclub life and turned his thoughts to starting a family. Although Lucy became pregnant in 1940, it ended in miscarriage during a strenuous vaudeville tour with Desi.

In September 1944, Lucy filed for divorce. Although she reconciled with Desi the day before, she felt obliged to act according to plan for fear the publicists would make her look foolish. The following morning Lucy and Desi read the newspaper stories proclaiming them "divorced"; their continued cohabitation, though, automatically voided their divorce decree.

When Lucy again became pregnant, the duo conceived their famous television show. Working with a team of writers, they originated their characters: Desi would play a band leader named Ricky Ricardo and Lucy would play his zany wife. The first six scripts were sent to CBS and approved on the condition that the show be filmed live. "I Love Lucy" premiered on CBS-TV on October 15, 1951.

During the show's first season, 39-year-old Lucy gave birth to Little Lucie. Desi was overjoyed. Working hard both to care for their baby and to perfect their show, the stars managed to keep their marriage intact.

Soon "I Love Lucy" was second in popularity only to "The Red Skelton Show." Not only did the series establish a new and energetic comedy team, but it seemed to provide a glimpse into a real-life happy marriage. In fact, when Lucy became pregnant again, they decided to make Lucy's character "expectant"—a very wife-like thing to be in the 1950s. By this time the couple had pooled their talents to achieve stardom and financial security— and, outwardly, at least, they seemed the ideal couple.

Unfortunately, stardom also made them victims of McCarthyism. During the height of Senator Joe McCarthy's 1953 purges of Communist influence, Lucy found herself in the midst of a "witch hunt." Her grandfather had been a Socialist, and, to please him, Lucy had apparently registered as a Socialist in 1936. After newspapers reproduced her registration card without including the word "Canceled," Lucy testified, "I am not a Communist now. I have never been. I never wanted to be. Nothing in the world could ever change my mind."

Despite the McCarthy investigation, "I Love Lucy" remained popular until 1957. When the show ended that year, Lucy told a reporter, "We've loved our work and we've loved being pioneers, but the time has come to let somebody else 'enjoy' it. We're a little brain-weary, you know."

After the show went off the air, Lucy started Desilu workshops so other actors could benefit from her experience just as she had benefited from Lela Rogers' training. "It's the same old vicious circle," she said. "You can't get a job unless you've acted, and you can't act unless you've had a job. We're just trying to give them exposure." Lucy's endeavor was hailed as the only practical workshop to come out of TV production.

The workshop kept Lucy's mind off her personal problems. Although she and Desi had quarreled constantly and had often separated, the public never knew. Following a bitter argument, Desi moved out for the last time and Lucy took the children to New York, where she was to appear in a Broadway musical comedy. The production, however, did not enjoy a long run: Lucy became ill with a severe viral infection and lost the part to another actress.

Her health eventually improved and her spirits lifted. Then she met and married Gary Morton. "He's just a wonderful guy," Lucy explained. "I guess he was a candidate since he made me and my children happy."

For the next two years Lucy turned the management of Desilu Productions over to Desi. During this time she introduced a new series, "Mission: Impossible," which became the biggest hit since "The Untouchables."

In 1967 Charles Bludhorn, president of Gulf and Western Industries, finally persuaded Lucy to sell Desilu, which gave Lucy the freedom to pursue acting. To her surprise, the first "not typically Lucy" story she had ever done— "Yours, Mine and Ours"—became a big hit. Subsequently, she formed Lucille Ball Productions and introduced a popular new show: "Here's Lucy." At first she sought to include her children in the series in an effort to protect them from the dangers of adolescence. Sadly, her plan wasn't successful: Desi Jr. soon began to abuse both alcohol and drugs.

Lucy, as always, was concerned about public opinion. Young Desi once explained: "The basic concern of my mother and stepfather has been protection of the family name. I never felt it was all that important." He eventually turned to them for help. According to Lucy, there was "a difference between being concerned and being nosy, but it took me a while to convince Lucie and Desi of that."

During the mid-70s, Lucie grew tired of being called "little Lucie," a feeling her mother didn't share. As time passed, she went all out to rid herself of the moniker. On one occasion she answered the telephone by saying, "This is young Lucie," for her mother's benefit. Irritated by it all, Mom snapped back, "And this is old Lucy!"

After completing a film version of "Mame," Lucy decided to cut back drastically on her schedule. Desi Jr. was still in and out of drug rehabilitation centers, and she wanted to spend as much time as possible with her family.

Lucy was inducted into the Television Hall of Fame in 1983. Three years later Desi died and Lucy underwent thyroid surgery— giving rise to reports that "she was resentful that she was having to slow down while others her age … still had the health to maintain full-time careers." In 1989, she did a show with Bob Hope. She looked wonderful at the time, but only a few weeks later she was rushed to the hospital after suffering a massive heart attack. Open-heart surgery at first seemed successful and she started to recover. Then her aorta suddenly ruptured. Lucille Ball, the queen of laughter, was dead.

Although Lucy is gone, the public has certainly not forgotten her. International syndication of the Lucy shows reinforces in the public mind that *Lucy will be forever young, forever funny, forever loved— Forever LUCY.*

IF I CAN DREAM: ELVIS' OWN STORY
by Larry Geller and Joel Spector, Simon and Shuster, 1989

In 1964 Larry Geller became Elvis Presley's personal barber. The first time he cut the young singer's hair, he was treated to a philosophical dissertation on life and its meaning. "I've always known that there had to be a purpose for my life," Elvis droned. "I've always felt an unseen hand.... From millions and millions of lives ... why was I picked out to be Elvis?"

Eight years earlier, at 21, Elvis seemed to materialize out of nowhere onto the entertainment scene, and in two short years he had become a "super-star," "larger than life," the "King" of Rock and Roll. According to Geller: ... *Much of the appeal and the love people have for him transcends and probably has little to do with his talent.... When asked about the reason for his success in [the] early days, he told one reporter, "Because God let me come along at this time."*

Elvis Aron (later corrected to Aaron) Presley was born January 8, 1935, to Gladys Love Smith Presley and Vernon Elvis Presley, in East Tupelo, Mississippi ... in the family's two-room shack. Gladys was a devoted mother, and made sure her son attended church and school by taking him herself.

As a member of the First Assembly of God Church, Elvis was introduced to music early. "Man," he once told Geller, "the first thing I could remember in life was sittin' on my mama's lap in church ... all I wanted to do was run down the aisle and go sing with the choir. I knew it then; I had to sing." He made his first major step toward fulfilling that dream in July of 1953, when he made a recording at Sam Phillips' recording studio in Memphis, Tennessee. When asked who he sang like, Elvis is said to have answered, "I don't sound like nobody." This soon became evident; he had a sound all his own.

In July 1954 Elvis recorded "That's All Right," a song that became an overnight hit: *Following quickly came a series of firsts: first interviews, first press, first concerts. From the very start it was clear that Elvis had something—dark, potent, strange and irresistible. One Memphis paper headlined a piece on the new local star "He's Sex!" With a few exceptions, Elvis' early performances were as exciting as and possibly even more suggestive than what the nation finally saw in 1956.*

He went on to release a long line of hits, and his career skyrocketed. His personal appearances, including a landmark performance on the Ed Sullivan Show, were "enough to inspire girls to carve his name into their skin with penknives and demolish cars with their bare hands. [He] changed the way millions of kids viewed themselves and their world.... Elvis was it."

He achieved millionaire status almost immediately, and was soon being featured in movies. In 1957 he returned to Memphis and bought Graceland, a 23-room mansion that had fallen into disrepair. The house sat on 13 acres of wooded land in Whitehaven, a Memphis suburb.

March of 1958 saw the rock idol inducted into the Army. After receiving basic training at Fort Hood, Texas, he rented a house off base where he and his parents could live. But shortly thereafter his mother became ill and the family returned to Memphis. Two days later she died. Elvis was devastated by the loss, and went into seclusion until the Army sent him to West Germany to complete his tour of duty. Returning to civilian life, at age 25 Elvis worried that "his moment of fame" had already passed him by. It was true that many things had changed. While in Germany he had met a girl, 14-year-old Priscilla Beaulieu, with whom he had fallen in love and whom he intended to marry.

During the '60s Elvis committed to making several more movies, which kept him in Hollywood for several months of each year. However, he never did feel comfortable around "Hollywood types"; he was inherently a loner, "part of a crowd that only he belonged to." Still he craved companionship and found it in the "Memphis Mafia," his personal cadre of traveling friends and assistants. Geller, as his barber, joined this close-knit group and became Presley's close friend, confidant and spiritual advisor.

Elvis preferred to drive his motor-home back and forth between Memphis and the west coast. His loathing of Hollywood, however, usually caused him to delay leaving until the last possible moment, which led to non-stop junkets. It was during one such trip that Geller first sensed that Elvis might have a problem with drugs. "Elvis [suddenly] extended his hand towards me," he relates. In it were Dexedrine tablets, a potent amphetamine. "Take these," he said, " ... we'll be driving. We want to be alert."

The singer had also become a voracious reader of religious books. On another occasion a road-weary Elvis confided to Geller, "All I want is to know the truth, to know and experience God.... I believe, only nothing happens, and I want it to." Perhaps, Geller suggested, Elvis was trying to cram too much into his brain at once. "Before God," Geller told him, "you're no different from anybody else.... You're not favored because you're Elvis Presley." Elvis then looked out the window of the bus at a cloud mass that had formed. "Do you see what I see?" he asked. In the shape of the cloud he had imagined the image of Soviet dictator Joseph Stalin. Perhaps God, Presley surmised, "[is] trying to show me what he thinks of me." And then he startled Geller by voicing his wish to die, to infuse God into his life in some way. "Then it happened!" As they continued to watch the wind-driven cloud, "the face of Stalin turned right into the face of Jesus."

This incident had a lasting effect on the young singer. One minute he loved being "the King"; the next he yearned to become a monk so he could worship the King of Kings. "I want to be with God now," he moaned. Geller, for his part, was troubled by the situation: *Elvis was an extremist ... and spiritual studies were no exception.... Rather than using this experience to ... correct and redirect his life, he embraced it as [an] excuse to abandon his life altogether.*

Elvis expressed his spiritual rebirth publicly in the album *How Great Thou Art*, a collection of gospel hymns that earned him a Grammy Award for "Best Sacred Performance." Two more Grammys would follow, one for *He Touched Me* ("Best Inspirational Performance," 1972) and another in 1974 for the song "How Great Thou Art."

Elvis's personality and star status meant "the outside world was a distant place he ventured into but never really lived in.... His life existed on the inside ... " He never even went grocery shopping or on a vacation, but remained isolated in the past and in the company of his money. Money gave Elvis freedom, freedom to buy anything—which he did to excess. Despite his love of money, he was also very generous, giving away cars, condos, mobile homes—and not just to his friends: he lavished total strangers with extravagant gifts. If he heard of someone in need, he would help.

In April 1967 Geller was weighing the possibility of severing his ties with Elvis, when he received a call asking that he come to Graceland. "We're all going to Vegas," trumpeted Elvis's voice. Geller declined. The very next day he was surprised by a newspaper headline: ELVIS PRESLEY IS MARRIED. He had finally wed his Priscilla. The teenage girl had moved to Memphis from Germany in 1962. But over time their marriage became one of appearance only: "Priscilla was like a little sister to me...." explained Elvis. "She grew up, and the person that grew up and I are just apart. We're not in love with each other."

Finally Geller did retire from the Memphis Mafia, informing Elvis by letter that "their time together had been precious ... but I feel that it is time to part ... " For the next five years he had no contact with Elvis. During that time the star regained his title as King of Rock and Roll, principally by means of a "comeback special" on TV. By that time eight years had passed since he had performed for a live audience.

The following year, 1969, he made his Las Vegas debut, which put him back on the record charts as well: "Suspicious Minds" became a number-one hit; in 1970 a documentary on his Vegas show was released; the year after he was named to "America's Ten Outstanding Young Men" by the U.S. Jaycees. America's love affair with Elvis was on once again.

Then in 1972 Priscilla left Elvis. Despite the distance that had grown between them, it was a crushing blow. That same year Geller went to Vegas to see Elvis perform, and their friendship took up right where it had left off five years before. But Geller was still uncomfortable with Elvis's lifestyle: the singer was touring constantly, eating all the wrong foods, and filling his head with drugs. News of the abduction of Patty Hearst had also made him paranoid someone would kidnap his daughter, Lisa Marie.

Further complicating his life was his association with agent/manager Colonel Parker, who had become a compulsive gambler. No casino would turn the Colonel away, and in one night alone Parker gambled away $1.4 million of Elvis's money. He also positioned himself "to take the maximum amount of Elvis' earnings as fast as possible." Among other things, he sold off the recording masters of all of Presley's pre-1973 songs and took nearly half the $5.4 million sale price for himself. To satisfy his own vices, Parker put even greater pressure on Elvis to perform, and Elvis turned even more frequently to prescription drugs; he even experimented once or twice with cocaine and marijuana. Occasionally the singer would attempt to resolve his substance abuse by checking into a hospital. But he had been using drugs for so long, and his tolerance was so high, that his behavior usually seemed normal. Even on those occasions when he would forget his lyrics and he appeared on-stage overweight and under-prepared, the audience still loved him.

In 1976 Elvis found a new love, a woman named Ginger Alden. Their passion for each other, coupled with his love of entertaining, renewed his vitality—at least when he was on stage. Night after night he could pull off a magical performance, somehow, despite his weakening health.

Then one night as Elvis left the stage, he seemed to have lost his vision entirely. In this blinded state, he slipped and twisted his ankle. His staff became increasingly concerned.

On August 15, 1977, Geller returned to Memphis from Los Angeles and phoned his friend: "It's me, E. I just checked into my room." Elvis replied, "I'm in bed, trying to get rested ... for the tour. Would you mind if I called it a night?" Then he asked, "Lawrence, did you bring that book on the Holy Shroud of Jesus?"

"Do angels have wings?" Geller asked in turn. Of course he had; Elvis had been wondering about the authenticity of the shroud of Turin for weeks, and had asked Geller to find him a book that probed the shroud's mysteries.

"Yeah, and don't forget," joked the King, "Angels fly because they take themselves so lightly." This was the last time Geller would ever hear him speak.

The next morning as he drove toward Graceland, Geller saw helicopters hovering overhead. We were driving up to the gates when [Elvis's] Uncle Vester spotted me.... He looked at me blankly ... then said, "Didn't you hear what happened? ... Elvis died."
It didn't register ... "Elvis what?"
"He just died, Larry. Elvis died."

MARILYN: NORMA JEANE – *THE WOMAN WHO WILL NOT DIE*
by Gloria Steinem, H. Holt, 1986

Marilyn Monroe is still very much a part of everyday American life. Her famous smile and celebrated figure live on in posters and magazines; curiously, her persona seems to fit into the modern montage as well as any current actress or model. Other famous people have been remembered, but not like Marilyn Monroe.

"One simple reason for her life story's endurance is the premature end of it …," Gloria Steinem writes in this comprehensive biography. "When the past dies, there is mourning, but when the future dies our imaginations are compelled to carry it on." Indeed, when Monroe took her own life, many imagined that they might have helped her and ultimately saved her. Primarily, then, it is her vulnerability that has made her personal legend survive. As Steinem notes, "Her terrible openness made a connection with strangers."

Norma Jeane, The Girl

Norma Jeane Baker was born near Los Angeles, California on June 1, 1926, to Gladys Baker, a 24-year-old divorcee. Gladys had hoped to marry Norma Jeane's father, C. Stanley Gifford, a "Clark Gable-looking salesman," but on Christmas Eve, when she told him she was pregnant, he abandoned her. Gladys was devastated, and Marilyn, too, ultimately would be hurt: all her life she would yearn for a father. In fact, later in her life, when she tried to contact Gifford, he refused to have anything to do with his daughter.

Although Norma Jeane's mother loved her, she had to board her daughter with a neighbor family so that she could retain her job at a film lab. Eventually Gladys was able to buy a small white bungalow where she and Norma Jeane could live together. Marilyn, a naturally shy girl, recalled feeling a new sense of freedom and happiness when she moved in with her mother.

But the idyll was short-lived. In January of 1934 Gladys, weakened by the strain of working double shifts, withdrew into "her own interior world" and remained in an institution for most of her life.

Gladys's friend, Grace McKee, subsequently helped pay Norma Jeane's board as she moved to a succession of foster homes. When Grace remarried in 1935, however, she felt she had no option but to place the girl in an orphanage. "I saw this sign," Marilyn recalled, "and the emptiness that came over me, I'll never forget. The sign read: LOS ANGELES ORPHANS' HOME. I began to cry…. When a little girl feels lost and lonely and that nobody wants her it's something she never can forget as long as she lives."

When Norma Jeane was 11 she left the orphanage, again to move from family to family, until Ana Lower (Aunt Ana), a loving, gentle woman, accepted her into her home. Unfortunately, Ana was too old to assume legal custody, and when Norma Jeane was 16, an arranged marriage seemed the best alternative.

Many biographers assert that Marilyn exaggerated the emotional neglect—and possible physical abuse—she may have experienced growing up. Notwithstanding, her pain was legitimate, and it did instill in her a remarkable empathy for people from all walks of life.

A Working Career

After marrying, Norma Jeane was singled out by a photographer who was taking action shots of people aiding the war effort. "I'm going to take your picture for the boys in the Army to keep their morale high," he beamed as he snapped picture after picture of the buoyant young woman at the factory where she worked. And upon seeing the photos, the largest modeling agency in California hired Norma Jeane full-time. "When she walked in," one of the agency's other models recalls, "it was like the room stopped, and everyone in the room knew she was going to get the job, and she did." Her career swiftly accelerated. Howard Hughes at RKO studios ordered a screen test, and his interest prompted Twentieth Century-Fox to quickly endorse her contract.

Norma Jeane promptly became "Marilyn Monroe"—and increasingly came to believe that her survival, her need "to prove she was alive, to be noticed, to belong, to be loved and to work, depended on her body." Although the budding actress initially resisted bleaching her hair, she finally relented in order to win a six-hour modeling assignment. She also lowered her "squeaky speaking voice" and mastered a new smile so that there would appear to be more space between her nose and mouth. By the time she had fully developed her "Marilyn" persona, she could turn it on and off like a light switch. "I just felt like being Marilyn for a moment," she would explain.

Although Marilyn appeared in roles as the standard "dumb blonde," she took her work as an actress seriously. Spending her weekly salaries on drama, dancing and singing lessons, she once remarked, "I knew how third-rate I was … but, my God, how I wanted to learn!… I didn't want anything else. Not men, not money, not love, but the ability to act. With the arc lights on me and the camera pointed at me, I suddenly knew myself. How clumsy, empty, uncultured I was! A sullen orphan with a goose egg for a head. But I would change … "

Marilyn thus began studying with one of the foremost acting instructors of the time, Lee Strasberg, who later named her, along with Marlon Brando, as "one of the most talented actors" he had ever met.

But in spite of her efforts to be taken seriously, Hollywood continued to offer her the same vapid roles—and she took them only because she wanted to work. Eventually, of course, she felt used and resentful. Frustrated with those that admired her for her physical attributes, she once said, "Can't I be anything else?"

Marilyn, though, shrewdly appraised Hollywood's attitude toward sex, and tried to use it to her advantage. "If [I] didn't go along, there were twenty-five girls who would," she explained. "You can't sleep your way into being a star ... " she told a British journalist. "But it helps."

Despite owning a strong work ethic, Marilyn displayed some highly unprofessional habits. She was always late, a failing that prompted a reporter to blame her for several weeks of extra shooting on *The Misfits* set—a charge that led Marilyn to attempt suicide.

In addition to tardiness, Marilyn was known for her innate fear. Not only was she afraid to meet new people, she often, in "sheer primal terror," vomited before entering the sound stage.

Addicted to sleeping pills and tranquilizers, Marilyn once blamed her dependence on an inability to sleep—restlessness owing to earlier childhood trauma. In fact, studios of the '50s and '60s used drugs routinely to keep their most valuable performers working. Interestingly, Marilyn's addiction did not seem to interfere with her work; though too fond of pills and champagne, "she was still a beautiful and a good actress to the end."

In addition to acting, Marilyn's great passion was learning. Ashamed that she hadn't finished high school, she read voraciously and was particularly interested in poetry and politics. Even in her last interview she pleaded with the reporter to end the story with something of substance: " ... What the world really needs is a real feeling of kinship. Everybody: stars, laborers, Negroes, Jews, Arabs. We are all brothers. Please don't make me a joke. End the interview with what I believe." The reporter didn't listen.

Fathers and Lovers

Marilyn longed for someone to take the place of the father she'd never known. Although Jim Dougherty was willing to fill this role, he was a merchant marine who was often away from home, leaving Marilyn to turn to her blossoming career and to other men for affirmation. After two years of marriage, she filed for divorce.

Freed from her marriage, Marilyn engaged in several affairs. Finally, though—perhaps "to fulfill the pink-and-white American sex-goddess image that the public expected of her"—she chose baseball star and "handsome stoic" Joe DiMaggio to be her "true" first husband. But DiMaggio soon fell from the pedestal his wife had put him on, splintering the marriage: he resented her career and her immodest way of dressing, and did not share Marilyn's interest in education. On one special occasion she gave him a medal engraved with a quote from *The Little Prince*: "True love is visible not to the eyes, but to the heart, for eyes may be deceived." DiMaggio's mystified response was, "What the hell does that mean?"

Nine months after the wedding, the two separated. Following the split, DiMaggio became both paranoid and violent, once even raiding an apartment where he believed she and a lover were staying. Despite his anger and jealousy, ultimately it was DiMaggio who arranged her funeral, and who spent the night before the services in a vigil over her casket. As a fact of poignancy and irony, Marilyn "was buried with his flowers in her hands."

Upon divorcing DiMaggio, Marilyn promptly married Arthur Miller. She once said that talking with the famed playwright for the first time was "like a cool drink when you've got a fever." For his part, Miller was seriously in love; what's more, he was "touched by her profound connection to children and to nature, and even defended her sexual way of dressing ... " However, problems developed as early as their honeymoon, when Marilyn discovered disparaging notes Miller had written about her, which set her to speculating that she was "only a grist for his writerly mill." After that, Miller took on the role, not of Marilyn's father, but as her caretaker; they never reconciled their differences and soon became, as his maid Lena Pepitone remembers, "two people who were so polarized that Miller rarely emerged from his study or ate meals with his wife."

Marilyn again turned to the comforts of other men, including striking up a serious relationship with Yves Montand and probable relationships with Frank Sinatra and both Jack and Bobby Kennedy. Indeed, as she talked of remarrying and having a baby, "friends were stunned by both her lack of discretion and her lack of realism."

In 1962, following her rumored break-up with Bobby Kennedy, the increasingly erratic Marilyn was fired from the film *Something's Got to Give*. Shortly thereafter, on August 5th, Marilyn, "her image ... so dependent on a sensuous youthfulness that it was bound to self-destruct," was found dead in her bedroom, the phone receiver in her hand. The official cause of death: acute barbiturate overdose.

The speculations as to the cause of Marilyn Monroe's death range from the well-reasoned to the bizarre. Having evaluated them all, Steinem concludes that, in all likelihood, Marilyn's death was by her own hand—though suicide may not have been her aim. Perhaps, writes Steinem, "she meant to die for the evening—but not to die forever."

Who Would Marilyn Be Now?

"We can imagine many futures for Norma Jeane ... " Steinem muses. "If acting had become an expression of [her] real self, not an escape from it, one also can imagine the whole woman who was both Norma Jeane and Marilyn becoming a serious actress and wise comedienne.... But Norma Jeane remained the frightened child of the past. And Marilyn remained the unthreatening half-person that sex goddesses are supposed to be. It is the lost possibilities of Marilyn Monroe that capture our imaginations. It was the lost Norma Jeane, looking out of Marilyn's eyes, who captured our hearts.... If we learn from the life of Marilyn Monroe, she will live on in us."

THE AUTOBIOGRAPHY OF MARK TWAIN
edited and arranged by Charles Neider, Harper & Row Publishers, Inc., 1959

Samuel Langhorne Clemens—best known by the pen name Mark Twain—is one of the most original and gifted American writers. Since his death in 1910, his stories have been adapted countless times for stage and film productions, some fairly effectively; but the full beauty of Twain's works can be encountered only on the page.

A fan of Twain's works considering which of his books to read next could do no better than to pick up his autobiography. In setting down his life story, Twain withdrew from a traditional autobiographical format. Eschewing hard facts and definite chronological order in favor of a tangled series of journal entries, newspaper clippings, remembrances and banterings, he was, as usual, simply out to tell a good story.

Twain intended that his account be published posthumously. He wrote, as he said, "from the grave," offering an honest—sometimes brutally honest—audit of himself and others. As Charles Neider says in the book's introduction: *[Twain] had produced his share of work in the world; he had outlived most of the people he cared for; the world was in a bad way and he was not averse to leaving it. And so he reminisced, and by so doing he amused himself—reminisced on his own terms ... not according to some theory of autobiographical composition.*

And so Twain begins his train of self-musings, appropriately enough, with his birth.

I was born the 30th of November, 1835, in the almost invisible village of Florida, Monroe County, Missouri.... The village contained a hundred people and I increased the population by 1 per cent. It is more than many of the best men in history could have done for a town.

The Clemens family consisted of Twain, his older siblings Orion and Pamela, and his parents, John Marshall and Jane Clemens. Another brother and sister, Benjamin and Margaret, would both die before he was seven. His brother Henry came along some two years later and, according to Twain, "I think that the unbroken monotony of his goodness and truthfulness and obedience would have been a burden to [my mother] but for the relief and variety which I furnished in the other direction." In his book *Tom Sawyer*, Henry served as the inspiration for Sid.

When Twain was still very young, his family moved to Hannibal, Missouri. There he often spent a few months a year on the farm of his uncle John A. Quarles. A lot of the people, places and events in Twain's most notable stories, he claimed, were plagiarized from his childhood. His Uncle John's farm, for example, was relocated to Arkansas in *Tom Sawyer, Detective*, and *Huck Finn*. Similarly, in the middle-aged slave "Uncle Dan'l," Twain said, he found a "faithful and affectionate good friend, ally and adviser," but also a model for "Jim." Thus, between the semi-fictional characters and the real-life people, Twain confessed that he sometimes got confused. *When I was younger I could remember anything, whether it had happened or not; but my faculties are decaying now and soon I shall be so I cannot remember any but the things that never happened.*

One of the boy's earliest memories was of an incident which occurred on his first day of school, when he was four and a half. He committed some small offense and, despite a warning that he had broken one of the rules, he proceeded to break it a second time. The penalty was a whipping, and Mrs. Horr, trusting in the boy's judgment, sent him out to find a suitable switch. The switch Twain presented to her was quite suitable for his purposes—but not for hers. *She said she would try and appoint a boy with a better judgment than mine in the matter of switches, and it saddens me yet to remember how many faces lighted up with the hope of getting that appointment. Jim Dunlap got it, and when he returned with the switch of choice I recognized that he was an expert.*

Twain's father died in 1847, whereupon he was taken from school to serve as an apprentice printer for the Hannibal Courier. Two or three years later, his brother Orion returned from his job as a journeyman printer in St. Louis and purchased the other local newspaper, the *Journal*. Orion had never had much of a head for money, and it wasn't long before he had to move the whole works into the family's house. Finally, in 1853, Orion abandoned the paper altogether and ran off to Keokuk, Iowa, to get married. Soon after that, Twain followed his brother's example and ran off himself to St. Louis. From there he went to see the big world—which, for Twain at the time, consisted of New York and Philadelphia. By the end of the following year he was back working for Orion amid the splendors of Keokuk.

Because Orion could never afford to pay his workers, however, Twain soon set off again. This time he found himself in New Orleans, where, for five hundred dollars borrowed money, he trained as a river pilot. "Within eighteen months," Twain reported, "I [had] become a competent pilot, and I served in that office until the Mississippi River traffic was brought to a standstill by the breaking out of the Civil War." In June of 1861 he served as a second lieutenant in the Confederate Army. But his service would be short-lived: *I resigned after two weeks' service in the field, explaining that I was "incapacitated by fatigue" through persistent retreating.*

A few years later, after signing on to work out

west with the Virginia City *Enterprise*, Twain was sent to Carson City to report on Nevada's legislative session. When several lines of his weekly column proved to be rather unkind to the legislators, they, in turn, became rather unkind towards him. *And so*, Twain writes, *I presently began to sign the letters, using the Mississippi leadsman's call, "Mark Twain" (two fathoms, or twelve feet) for this purpose* ...

From Nevada he headed out to San Francisco to become the sole reporter for the *Morning Call*; later, the Sacramento *Union* sent him to do a story on the sugar interests in the Sandwich Islands (now Hawaii), where he was encouraged to "break into the lecture field"—and did so. After a slow start, he lectured his way throughout California and Nevada. Then he decided to tour Europe, sending letters about his travels to the *Daily Alta California* for 20 dollars each. His book based on this tour, *The Innocents Abroad*, was published in 1869.

Then "in the beginning of February 1870," Twain writes, "I was married to Miss Olivia L. Langdon, and I took up my residence in Buffalo, New York." Once married, he gave up the lecture circuit for a few years. Lamentably, during his absence the circuit became flooded with charlatans and money-grabbers. When he returned to it in 1884, he said, the audiences had to be taught all over again what to appreciate.

The couple's first child, Langdon Clemens, was born the 7th of November, 1870, and lived only 22 months. This loss would have been greater had they not by then also had a daughter, Suzy, who was born a year and a half later. Suzy proved to be a blithe, happy yet contemplative girl with a direct conduit to her father's heart. Another daughter, Clara, was born two years after Suzy, and Jean some seven years after that.

In 1872 Twain wrote *Roughing It*, which, like *The Innocents Abroad*, was published through Elisha Bliss and the American Publishing Company. It was some ten years—and several books later—Twain dryly notes, that he was able to figure out just how badly he had been "swindled by those people." In his early years he knew nothing about royalties nor "above cost of manufacture profits" and such. "From my pen to their pockets" went the proceeds from some of Twain's most popular books—including *Tom Sawyer*. *[Now Bliss] has been dead a quarter of a century.... My bitterness against him has faded* away *and disappeared. I feel only compassion for him, and if I could send him a fan I would.*

Despite the dishonesty of his publishers, Twain was far from impoverished; "my money and I undertook some great adventures." Once, for the cost of $15,000, he took out a patent on a minor invention. After watching his money fly away for a few years, he put the manufacturing and selling details into the hands of another, equally capable

fellow. *At last, when I had lost forty-two thousand dollars on that patent I gave it away to a man whom I had long detested and whose family I desired to ruin. Then I looked around for other adventures—* the second of which cost him only ten thousand dollars; and his third, an attempt that kept him suitably occupied for 16 months at a loss of some $32,000, consisted of an investment in some sort of fantastic coal-burning steam engine thing. After all that, starting up an insurance company seemed like a good idea; and perhaps it was, since he lost just $23,000 on the venture.

By then Twain was finally becoming more careful with his money. And it was then that a Mr. Alexander Graham Bell approached him with an offer to invest in some invention of his called the telephone, but Twain wasn't interested. Bell finally persuaded a dry-goods clerk in Hartford into investing his life's savings of five thousand dollars. *I was sorry for that man when I heard about it. I thought I might have saved him if I had had an opportunity to tell him about my experiences.*

In 1884 Twain set up his own publishing company—and put it in the incapable hands of his nephew-in-law Charles Webster. *Huckleberry Finn* soon appeared, and the author once again took to the lecture circuit.

As impossible as it sounds, my nephew-in-law, who specialized in printing only truly bad books, drove the publishing company into ruin by 1893. And at the age of 58 Twain found himself in debt to no less than 96 creditors. To pay them off, his wife, his daughter Clara and he yet again hit the lecture circuit. By 1899 they were not only free from debt but eighteen thousand dollars in the black—the total sum of which was shortly gone after he trumpeted, "Put it in Federal Steel."

The last quarter of a century of my life has been pretty constantly and faithfully devoted to the study of the human race—that is to say, the study of myself, for in my individual person I am the entire human race compacted together. I have found that there is no ingredient of the race which I do not possess in either a small way or a large way.... As a result, my private and concealed opinion of myself is not of a complimentary sort. It follows that my estimate of the human race is the duplicate of my estimate of myself.

In August of 1896, after a brief illness, Suzy Clemens died at the age of 24. Then in 1902 his wife Olivia's health began to fail—mainly from nervous exhaustion. Jean was also ailing and bedridden at this time but, thanks to Clara, her mother was spared the details.

"Olivia, my beloved wife," Twain wrote, "died on June 5, 1904. She was my life, and she is gone; she was my riches, and I am a pauper." Jean died on Christmas Eve, 1909. "Possibly I know now what the soldier feels when a bullet crashes through his heart."

Twain himself died shortly afterwards, on April 21, 1910.

STEVEN SPIELBERG – THE MAN, HIS MOVIES, AND THEIR MEANING
by Philip M. Taylor, Continuum Publishing, 1992

I think Hollywood will forgive me once I'm 55, I don't know what they'll forgive me for, but they'll forgive me when I'm 55.

Inspired filmmaker Steven Spielberg's success is unmatched in his field. His talent for creating films with universal appeal is certainly unique; however, it was a talent long unrecognized by the Academy of Motion Picture Arts and Sciences—who, as of this biography's 1992 publication date, had not awarded Spielberg even one Oscar. It seems Spielberg had been placed in a creative straightjacket: if he did films his audience loved, the critics hated it; when he broke out of his proven formula to please the critics, the audience hated it. This unfortunate phenomenon may be what he was referring to when he observes that we have probably seen the most successful films he will ever make, "but I don't think you have seen the best of what I can do as a filmmaker." In fact, Spielberg's colleagues often joked that a film could never hope for an Oscar if it suffered from the three S's: success, special effects, and Spielberg.

But Spielberg claims he is not bothered by the critics' view of his work. "I just make the kind of films that I would want to see," he shrugs.

So what is it about this man that makes the public love him, while the very industry in which he works ignores him? Critic Martin Amis astutely sums up the Spielberg phenomenon: *As an artist, Spielberg is a mirror, not a lamp. His line to the common heart is so direct that he unmans you with the frailty of your own defenses, and the transparency of your most intimate fears and hopes.*

Spielberg admits that his best creations spring from a vivid collection of impressions engraved in his first memories. Almost all his films are geared to evoke the pure, primitive images and emotions of early youth—especially *his* youth. And his own preoccupation with childhood, adolescence and nostalgia keeps us predictably spellbound.

Born in Cincinnati, Ohio, in 1947, Spielberg was raised in an era of great political agitation; surprisingly, however, he never really involved himself politically: he was too busy watching TV and the movies. "For children, it is the universe as it is," he reflects. "For adults, who think they know better, it is the universe as it should have been."

The character actors Spielberg uses in leading roles are very much like ourselves. Thus, by placing these people in extraordinary situations, he challenges his viewers with the critical question, "What would you do?" Again and again we are implicitly asked: "Would you board a giant alien spacecraft if one arrived?" "Would you hide a feeble alien in your room and ask the authorities for help if it were dying?"

This identification between audience and character has been a key element in Spielberg's success.

Richard Dreyfuss has been chosen to star in a number of his films for that very reason. As Spielberg explains: " … Most of us are like Richard Dreyfuss. Few of us are like Bob Redford or Steve McQueen."

Spielberg speaks freely about his professional intentions and aspirations; on the other hand, he is not as willing to share the details of his private life. Yet, through his films we can glean a great deal. For example, there is the "yearning-for-home" theme that runs rampant throughout Spielberg movies. In *E.T.* the plot centers around a lost alien's quest to return home; in the 1989 film *Always,* "home" is life itself; and in *Jaws* Robert Shaw's character sings "Show Me the Way to Go Home." Spielberg explains: "I've lived in so many places since I was a child I felt I never really had a home, and that's a feeling many people can respond to."

The movie-maker describes a "semi-unhappy" childhood and parents who constantly bickered. He found a measure of escape by turning to television—though he admits to being frightened by much of what he saw. He specifically recalls a documentary on snakes that left him crying and trembling in fear—a la his future Indiana Jones hero.

As an adult Spielberg was finally able to take out his revenge on TV through the movie *Poltergeist* (1982), a story about a family who is invaded by hostile supernatural entities via the television set.

Movies also left their early mark of inspirational trauma: "The first three movies I ever saw were all Walt Disney films, and they scared the bejeezus out of me … " remembers Spielberg. Ironically, he also credits Disney with influencing him more than any other filmmaker.

Spielberg's mother, Leah, played a leading role in his early life. She not only encouraged but catered to her young son's filmmaking obsession. Once she intentionally overcooked a gallon of cherries jubilee sauce in a pressure cooker until it exploded so her son could film the gooey mess all over the kitchen. "We never said no," she remembers. "We never had a chance to say no. Steven didn't understand that word."

"The weird skinny kid with acne," as Spielberg describes his boyhood self, was rarely accepted by his schoolmates. To make matters worse, just as he would begin to make friends in each new neighborhood, he found his family gearing up for yet another move. Hence, the perennial loner retreated for companionship into the recesses of his TV tube.

The introspective young TV addict began making movies when he was twelve. By age 16 he had mastered his father's 8mm movie camera and produced a two-and-a-half-hour science-fiction epic called *Firelight,* about a team of scientists investigating mysterious lights in the sky. His father, finally resigned to Steven's propensity toward film, rented the local cinema for one night, and the $500 epic made a profit of $100.

Soon after this initial success, the family moved to San Jose, California, where his parents, after years of turmoil, decided to divorce. In the film *Back to the Future* Spielberg focuses on a boy's attempt to recreate his own life, sending his primary character back into the past to try to patch up—in advance— his parents' failing marriage.

Despite the trauma of his mother and father's split, the move to California proved happily fateful for Spielberg. To the detriment of his college studies, all of his efforts were now concentrated on getting his films before Universal Studio executives. And, finally, with a hastily produced 22-minute dialogue-free flick called *Amblin*, his talent was recognized.

Before long the 21-year-old Spielberg had quit college and signed a historic seven-year contract with Universal TV Production—a contract he soon came to resent. Still, driven to create films, he bit the bullet and worked out his professional apprentice-ship by directing various episodes of shows such as "Night Gallery," "Marcus Welby, MD," "The Psychiatrists" and "Columbo."

It wasn't long before the college dropout found himself swapping script ideas with a diverse group of talented young filmmakers, including George Lucas, Francis Ford Coppola, Martin Scorsese and Brian De Palma, who were able to share advice among them-selves when there was none to be had elsewhere.

Spielberg and the American Present

In Spielberg's first cinema releases—*Duel* (1971), *The Sugarland Express* (1974) and *Jaws* (1975), he was able to experiment with techniques that would later become trademarks of his filmmaking style.

Then, because he "couldn't find anybody who would write it the way I wanted it," Spielberg took two years off and wrote *Close Encounters of The Third Kind* himself. He hired J. Allen Hyneck as a consultant for the film, an interesting choice since Hyneck was a former U.S. Government UFO expert who had resigned after seeing evidence that didn't concur with his skepticism. As he recalls: "I really found my faith when I heard that the government was opposed to the film. If NASA took the time to write me a 20-page letter, then I knew there must be something happening."

Close Encounters brought out one of Spielberg's greatest talents: directing children. The movie was first and foremost a celebration of innocence—as well as the first American film ever made suggesting that alien life might be amicable rather than hostile.

Spielberg and the American Past

The highly successful *Indiana Jones* trilogy was the product of a ten-year "gentlemen's agreement" with George Lucas, a joint pact to make a series of films patterned after the cliffhangers they had both enjoyed as kids.

In 1985, between the first and second *Indy* films, Spielberg was prompted to depart from adventure to direct Alice Walker's *The Color Purple*. In this, his first major "people picture," he drew from his own memories to create a realistic portrayal of the pain involved in separation. The motion picture was nominated for 11 Oscars, yet failed to win a single Academy Award.

Spielberg and the American Future

With the release of *E.T.*, his most personal film to date, Spielberg made a significant departure from Hollywood moviemaking. By portraying a race of ugly yet lovable aliens who, despite their superior technology, are just as afraid of us as we are of them, Spielberg made a statement against the Cold War which then still loomed over the world. *E.T.* was undoubtedly Spielberg's most inspired and memo-rable masterpiece—a long-awaited love story born out of his closest and innermost memories and fantasies. The work involves a child lost from its parents, the universal human symbol of naked betrayal of innocence. "Towards the end of *E.T.*," Taylor writes, "barely able to support my own grief and bewilderment, I turned and looked down the aisle at my fellow sufferers: executive, black dude, Japanese businessman, punk, hippie, mother, teenager, child. Each face was a mask of tears."

Nearly a decade after *E.T.*'s release, Spielberg began work on his ultimate autobiographical project: the story of Peter Pan. "I've always been Peter Pan," the filmmaker once admitted. "In a way it's typecasting for me." However, rather than focusing on lost childhood, *Hook*, starring Robin Williams, turned out to be a piece on lost father-hood. "It's an allegory for all of us adults," explains Spielberg.

Today's Spielberg is an even-tempered man who does not smoke, drink or use drugs; he also works 20 hours a day. His only vice seems to be biting his nails. He does, however, occasionally suffer from bouts of depression, but he claims he does his best work when he is "in the pits emotionally." Although he elicits great love and joy from his children—the offspring of several different relationships—he is a man whose adulthood has "never quite proved as satisfying as his childhood."

Taylor points out that Steven Spielberg will soon have lived for half a century. Yet he himself some-times muses that he is simply becoming an older Peter Pan. And whatever he decides to do in the future, it is certain that if he is to be dragged from his childhood, it will have to be kicking and screaming.

Summary Note: In 1993 Spielberg may finally have achieved official Hollywood adulthood with *Schindler's List*, acclaimed by both critics and audi-ences, for which he at last received an Oscar as Best Director. In 1994 he was 'named the highest-paid entertainer in the world, earning 350 million dollars.

DISNEY'S WORLD: A BIOGRAPHY
by Leonard Mosley, Stein & Day, 1985

Walter Elias Disney was born on December 5, 1901, to Elias and Flora Disney, the last of their four sons. Walt's father had grown up in a rowdy, rambunctious family, but he had developed into a stern, religious man who tolerated no improper behavior. Elias's strict, tyrannical rule seemed to drive away all of his children at one point or another.

When Walt was five his family moved to Marceline, Kansas. His father had worked in many trades, but now he wanted to settle permanently into farming. Walt always remembered the Marceline farm years fondly; he got along much better with the farm animals than he did with his harsh father or his two domineering oldest brothers. The ducks, cows and chickens that he tended on the farm became his first real friends. He called them by name, talked to them, and frequently sat down to sketch them.

Life in Marceline was also brightened for Walt by the visits of his Uncle Ed—a small, wizened-faced, elf-like man whom Walt took to calling "Uncle Elf." On every visit zestful Uncle Elf would cavort with his nephew in the fields around the farm. In later years, Uncle Elf became the model for Jiminy Cricket, Pinocchio's loyal, spry and optimistic conscience.

Meanwhile, as Elias Disney's drought-stricken crops withered in the Kansas heat, his farming dreams slowly began to fade away. About this time, his two eldest sons, Herbert and Raymond, ran away from home, unable to tolerate his iron-fisted rule. Their embittered father disowned them, refusing even to acknowledge their existence. Not long afterwards, he became critically ill, and the Disneys finally had to sell their farm.

In Kansas City, their next home, Elias obtained a distribution route for a local newspaper. Though he had to hire and pay some "outside" paper boys, he also worked his two youngest sons, Roy and Walt, without compensation, claiming that he was investing their money. Roy vocally resented this, and finally stormed out of his father's door—just after Herbert had returned to try to make peace. When the family's finances dwindled, the Disneys were again forced to move, this time to Chicago, where Walt found summer work as a news carrier on the Union Pacific Railroad.

The growing young man spent the next school year in Chicago at McKinley High School, where he became enamored of Su Pitowski, the most beautiful and unattainable girl the shy Walt had ever known. Her involvement in the school newspaper, *The Voice*, prompted him to volunteer his services as junior art editor and to originate a section in the paper for his cartoon, "The Tiny Voice."

At the tail-end of World War I in 1917, 16-year-old Walt, too young and too skinny to enlist in the military, became a volunteer for a Red Cross unit. While traveling in Europe, he continued to correspond with Su and earned extra money around camp with his artwork.

Walt's homecoming was not all joy. First of all he discovered that Su Pitowski had already married another man. Then, for months on end there were quarrels with his father over what vocation Walt should now pursue. Elias insisted that his son go to work at a jelly factory; Walt wanted to be a professional illustrator. Walt chose to do it his way—and, true to family tradition, the last Disney son walked defiantly out the door.

Although one prominent cartoonist, Carey Orr, warned Walt off with the comment that he wasn't "cynical" enough for newspaper cartooning, his brother Roy finally secured him a two-month apprenticeship with the Pesmen-Rubin agency. There Walt met Ub Iwerks, another apprentice. When both Walt and Ub were let go at the end of the season, they went into business for themselves as "Iwerks and Disney." And soon they were earning twice their former wages.

But the ever adventurous Walt soon looked away from newspaper comics into the field of animation. He took a brief apprenticeship with a job at Kansas City Film Ad Company and thereafter formed his own company, Laugh-O-Gram Films. When Laugh-O-Gram went bankrupt, Walt was left with a handful of clothes, a camera, fifty dollars and enough loose bills to buy a train ticket to Los Angeles. He headed for Hollywood to try his hand at acting while he tended brother Roy, who was recovering from tuberculosis.

Roy encouraged Walt to return to his cartoons, and finally persuaded him to send a copy of *Alice's Wonderland*, an old Laugh-O-Gram cartoon, to a distributor named Margaret Winkler. She liked it and immediately agreed to finance Walt's work. Taking on Ub Iwerks as a partner, he began producing more Alice comedies.

Within a couple years, however, Walt's new company was also foundering, inundated by mounting production costs. Meanwhile, Margaret Winkler had married and turned her business over to her husband, Charles Mintz, who was not nearly so appreciative of Walt's work.

Searching for a vehicle to recapture the slipping appeal of the *Alice* comedies, Walt worked with Iwerks to create "Oswald the Lucky Rabbit." The new character quickly became a hit, but now trouble arose in earnest between Walt and Charles Mintz. To keep the cartoonist in line, Mintz signed all of Walt's animators, except Ub Iwerks and a few others, to contracts working for him. Then, as co-owner of the Oswald character, along with Universal Pictures, Mintz aspired to produce future Oswald cartoons without Walt. Walt replied by slamming an Oswald button down on Mintz's desk. "Here, you can have the little bastard, he's all yours!" he shouted. Within weeks, Walt had founded Walt Disney Studios and introduced a new character: Mickey Mouse.

At first, Walt's financial problems threatened to derail Mickey's career. The first two Mickey Mouse films met with polite applause at 1928 sneak previews, but no distributor offered to pick them up; and without Mintz, Walt found himself desperately short of capital.

Undeterred, Walt set to work on yet another Mickey Mouse cartoon—*Steamboat Willie*. Demonstrating the scenes for his animators, he would shrilly squeak out Mickey's captioned lines—for a silent cartoon. "If only we had sound," Ub said, "you'd bring the house down …"

In 1929 Walt announced that *Steamboat Willie* would be released with full sound. To achieve this, he agreed to work with sound expert Pat Powers, who demanded that Walt use his studio's equipment exclusively for the next year. By the end of that year, Powers saw what a sensation Mickey was and tried to steal the character by stealing the one man he figured Walt could not do without: Ub Iwerks.

Walt fought on. His staff of young animators rose to the occasion. In the end, he recovered all the rights to his Mickey Mouse films and distributed them through United Artists.

Understandably disillusioned with short cartoons, Walt now resolved to carry out a feature-length project based on the romantic fairy tale *Snow White*. Roy considered the idea ridiculous: no one would pay to see a full-length cartoon feature. But Walt went ahead with the project, and in 1938, thanks to his own obsessive vision and his animators' herculean efforts, *Snow White and the Seven Dwarfs* became a smash success.

The leaves on Walt's laurels for *Snow White* were still green when he came up with the idea for his next project: bringing *The Sorcerer's Apprentice*, a Dukas Symphony inspired by Goethe's classic fable, to film. Because the Dukas work was too lengthy for a short cartoon and too short for a feature, Walt engaged the services of Leopold Stokowski and the Philadelphia Symphony Orchestra to expand the score. Buoyed by the success of this daring experiment, he soon began piecing together another film, the frolicking, semi-abstract musical adventure *Fantasia*—working from an assortment of classical symphonies and ballets. But upon its release, *Fantasia*, undoubtedly a masterpiece, was a box office flop. It took years to recover its costs, and with the onset of World War II, Disney Studios found itself once more deep in the red.

Ironically, many of the Disney films that lost money in the late '30s and early '40s would later become his best-loved classics, including *Fantasia, Dumbo, Sleeping Beauty, Alice in Wonderland, Pinocchio* and *Bambi*. And of course the Disney characters "born" during this era—Mickey and Minnie Mouse, Donald Duck, Goofy, Pluto, the Three Little Pigs, and a dozen others—would become 20th-century legends.

The struggling Disney Studios, with its cadre of loyal employees, had previously been untouched by the union strife that struck every other major studio in Hollywood. However, in 1941 Disney became embroiled in a feud with Herbert Sorrell of the Screen Cartoonists Guild. In the heat of the power struggle, the Guild moved in and forced a strike. Instead of settling through a mediated vote, as proposed by Walt,

the strikers called for a boycott, which forced the studio to concede to their wishes. Finally, Disney Studios became a unionized shop. After this defeat, Walt was a changed man, bitter and more demanding of his employees.

While on vacation in 1947, Walt flew to Alaska. His fascination with the antics of seals soon prompted another new adventure: *Seal Island*, the first non-animated Disney nature documentary. It was followed by a series of 30-minute nature films, the Disney "True-Life Adventures," which helped pay off the company's heavy debt and skyrocketed Disney Studios into the forefront of film-making—just in time for Walt to announce his next project: a recreational park in Anaheim, California.

Walt envisioned Disneyland as a theme park—a pioneer version of simulated reality that the whole family could enjoy. To come up with the needed capital, he created a new company, WED, and began searching for backers—only to find that the banks were not interested either. Amusement parks at that time were little more than carnivals—dirty, rickety, unsavory—and financiers had a hard time catching Walt's vision of "something different."

At last Walt engaged ABC TV network to produce the weekly "Walt Disney Presents" series in return for funds to build his latest dream. Then on land that had once been an orange grove, Disneyland became a reality. Since its opening in 1955, it has expanded through the decades—and made money every year.

After the release of his much-celebrated film *Mary Poppins* in 1964, Walt's enthusiasm for managing Disney Studios and WED began to wear thin. He had always smoked heavily, coughing and hacking his way through the halls of the studio over the years, and now his health was deteriorating.

But Walt Disney was congenitally unable to rest. Already he had begun work on a new secret project: Disney World. Disturbed by the horde of speculative businesses that had clustered around Disneyland, he had secretly bought up huge tracts of land near Orlando, Florida, amassing some 30,000 acres. Decades later, Disney World would arise there, just as Walt had envisioned it: a larger, more varied version of Disneyland, uncontaminated by commercial sleaze and housing a pristine "City of Tomorrow"—the EPCOT Center, a model community where the employees of Disney World could live and play.

But Walt didn't live to see the completion of his City of Tomorrow. In October 1966 a doctor informed him that cancerous nodules had been found in his lungs and immediate surgery was required. In November he left the hospital with one less lung; but even as his health declined precipitously, Walt pushed ahead on EPCOT.

On December 15, 1966, Walt Disney, the tireless, true-life genius-magician loved throughout the world by children young and old, passed away. After a brief, informal funeral, his body was privately cremated—several hours before his adoring public and employees heard the news.

ME: STORIES OF MY LIFE
by Katharine Hepburn, Knopf (Random House), 1991

Katharine Hepburn was born on May 12, 1907, in Hartford, Connecticut, to Thomas Norval Hepburn, a medical doctor, and Katharine Martha Houghton, a strong-willed social activist. Though the grandparents on her mother's side died when Kate was young, they instilled in her the value of education and self-sufficiency. "Knowledge! Education! Don't give in! Make your own trail," she remembers them saying.

The Hepburn household was lively—and *very free*; there were virtually no rules. The children were always climbing trees and swinging on a homemade trapeze, which draped all the way across the property. Hepburn's memories include exploring the nearby woods, organizing afternoon teas on tree stumps, riding on sleds behind Dad's car, and spending summers at their coastal home in Fenwick, Connecticut, where she learned to dive off a pier. Years later, when actress Jane Fonda was struggling to do a somersault dive during the filming of *On Golden Pond*, the 70-year-old Hepburn teased, "If you can't do it, dear, I'll do it for you. It's one of my specialties."

They were also an upbeat household. Even upon the death of Kate's younger brother Tom, her parents refused to let themselves or their family wallow in remorse. "They moved on into life.... They simply did not believe in moaning about anything.... We were a happy family. We are a happy family."

Though she knew it was unavoidable, Kate was not too excited about going off to Bryn Mawr, the prestigious all-girl college which her mother had attended. She had spent most of her youth with her brothers, and the thought of living with wall-to-wall girls repulsed her. Her first year at Bryn Mawr was just as difficult as she had imagined. Her aloofness led a number of her schoolmates to brand her a conceited, "self-conscious beauty." But during the second year she roomed with a girl she had come to know and trust, and college life improved.

Kate had always practiced "acting" as a child, putting on neighborhood shows and clowning around for the family; now, at school, she was given the opportunity to act in significant productions. During her senior year she met Edwin Knopf, who ran a reputable theater company in Baltimore. After graduation, she asked Knopf for work and was ecstatic when he hired her. "My God! I had a job!" she remembers exulting. "He gave me a job!"

Knopf's theater provided the neophyte actress with an ideal learning environment. She recalls the first time she had to be fitted for a costume. She arrived at the stage at 10:00 A.M., expecting to avoid the rush, only to find that she was last in line—and stuck with the worst costume.

"Then something very strange happened," she recalls. "One of the girls came up to me and said, 'I was the first here. I want you to take my costume. It's the prettiest.'" Kate protested—"Oh no, I couldn't"—but the other girl insisted: "I'm not going to be an actor. And I think that you are going to be. I mean, I think you are going to be a big star. I want you to have it." Hepburn later looked back on that milestone: "Can you imagine anyone being so generous? Wasn't I lucky? Lucky."

Of course, the pieces of Hepburn's acting career didn't always fall into place so easily. Her first major stage performance was in a play called *The Big Pond*. During the first rehearsals she worked as an understudy for the lead actress, but she soon became convinced that she could do a far superior job as the lead herself. One day she was asked to stay and play a scene. "Pushed by a sort of frenetic boiling-over, I must have read it very well." Almost immediately the producers fired the lead and hired Hepburn. "This was happening just as I had imagined it would.... I was arriving."

Then, early on during the play's first performance Hepburn feigned a French accent that brought the house down. "Well ... that's that," she thought. "I'm a star." But her overconfidence caused her pitch and tempo to rise, the result being that no one could understand her for the rest of the night. She was swiftly replaced.

Her next big play, *These Days*, closed after only a week, and Hepburn again found herself on the streets, willing to accept any role she was offered. Then one night she got lucky again: a stranger approached and asked if she was in the theater. She would like to be, she said. And through this inauspicious exchange she received an invitation to work with the Theater Guild. The work was not steady, but she did appear in some lesser plays.

Hepburn's voice needed a lot of work. "I think that I was so excited by life and living and my future," she says of those first hectic years, "that I was simply wound up so tight I didn't—couldn't—relax." And this tautness was reflected in her vocal timber. With work and time, however, those same gravelly tones—which had once been considered her least valuable asset—became a Hepburn trademark.

In New York Hepburn also began spending more time with friends—men like Jack Clarke, who had first linked her up with Edwin Knopf, and Clarke's best friend, Ludlow Ogden Smith. Hepburn soon began pairing off with the debonair and sensitive Ludlow, or "Luddy," as she called him. It was with him that she lost her "virtue." "I mean, I guessed that Luddy knew what he was doing—and I didn't object. So we did it," Hepburn recalls. "He was my beau from then on. Listen, let me tell you—yes, he was my beau but—and that's the biggest *but* you've ever heard: He was my friend!"

In time, Kate and Luddy were married. Hepburn had thought she could give up acting and settle down in Pennsylvania, but that lasted only two weeks. She was in love with herself as much as she was with Luddy, and she was compelled to pursue her acting career. Her new husband supported her decision. "I don't know what I would have done without Luddy," Kate still professes affectionately.

Kate continued with her stage career. Then in 1930 she also decided to take on California and the movies. To get the part she coveted, starring alongside John Barrymore in George Cukor's *A Bill of Divorcement*, she knew she would have to beat out Lawrence Olivier's then-wife, Jill Esmond. On the trip by train to California, however, Hepburn caught several flecks of steel rail in her eye. When her agent, Leland Hayward, met her in Hollywood, her eyes were blood-red and sore. " ... We got fifteen hundred dollars for that ... ?" asked another agent when he caught a glimpse of her. "She's an original," replied Hayward. "... Get a load of those eyes," the other responded. "What's she been drinking?"

But Hepburn got the part. For that matter, she made five movies in 18 brief months after her arrival in Hollywood; and, just as important, she made her way into the industry's most prominent social circles, cultivating close friendships with some very influential men:

Motion-picture director **George Cukor**: "George really liked me—and I really liked him.... [He] was my best friend in California. We made many pictures together—always happily.... He loved to entertain and I loved to be his guest.... It was as if George and I had been brought up together.... The same liberal point of view—the same sense of right and wrong. I miss him."

Leland Hayward: After separating from Luddy, Kate spent much time with her agent. "We were like an old married couple.... We just enjoyed—enjoyed—enjoyed.... Leland wanted to marry me, but I really did not want to marry."

Billionaire-aviator-entrepreneur-movie producer **Howard Hughes**: Hughes began following one of Hepburn's plays on tour. In Chicago he stayed at the same hotel as the cast, and he and Kate had dinner together. They "had dinner the next night too—so ... " The pair seemed to fall into a relationship out of loneliness. The newspapers said they were going to marry, "but when it came right down to 'What do we do now?'—I went East and he stayed West.... I always thought it was lucky that we never married—two people who are used to having their own way should stay separate."

Hughes suffered from hearing loss, a handicap that caused him much social discomfort and added heavily to an already deep sense of isolation. Later, after he had injured himself in a plane crash, his doctor gave him an open prescription for morphine—"and Howard found this blank road more comfortable than the endless life struggle. One cannot blame him, but it was very sad. He was a remarkable man."

L.B. Mayer, head of MGM: "He was not stupid, not crude. He was a very sensible fellow, and extremely honest.... I can say that he was the most honest person I ever dealt with in my life."

Mayer and Hepburn were sincere friends, and he came to rely on her judgment in important decisions.

However, Hepburn recalls, " ... His life was his work. When the work ceased, he really sort of died.... [He] would have loved to have been a most witty, charming and fascinating creature. I don't think he was particularly." But in his work "he was wild—He was a romantic. He believed."

And, of course, **Spencer Tracy**. It was with Tracy that this strong and self-willed striver came to learn a new, selfless kind of love. "He was there—I was his. I wanted him to be happy—safe—comfortable. I liked to wait on him—listen to him—feed him—talk to him—work for him. I tried not to disturb him—irritate him—bother him—worry him, nag him. I struggled to change all the qualities which I felt he didn't like. Some of them which I thought were my best I thought he found irksome. I removed them, squelched them, as far as I was able.... We lived a life which he liked. This gave me great pleasure."

The madcap Tracy, "Irish to the fingertips," was a master at making Hepburn laugh. They made nine pictures together and stayed with each other for 27 years. During this time Hepburn finally divorced Luddy, but Spencer remained married to his wife until his death. She had given birth to a deaf child, and it did not sit right with Spencer to leave his family in such circumstances—though he did not actually stay with them, either. In retrospect, Hepburn thinks it would have been better to "straighten things out." Still, the time they spent together, at least for her, was "absolute bliss." She adds: "If he hadn't liked me [a lot too] he wouldn't have hung around."

Tracy died of a sudden coronary in 1967, shortly after he and Hepburn had completed filming *Guess Who's Coming to Dinner?* "I wonder if they found my little painting of flowers I put under his feet," the actress writes of the viewing and funeral. She continued living in the home they had shared for ten more years, making movies and trying to let go of "the thing called LOVE." By the time of her autobiography's publication in 1991, she had starred in 43 films, among them *The Lion in Winter; Rooster Cogburn* (she was extremely fond of John Wayne, whom she likened to a cotton shirt—"It stays clean but it makes you sweat"); *On Golden Pond*; and *The Corn is Green*.

Up until her death in 2003, the actress spent much time at her childhood summer home in Fenwick, which she helped restore after a hurricane. There she was able to garden and relax. To the end, having survived a serious automobile accident, she was grateful for the gift of life: "You suddenly realize what a tremendous opportunity it is just to be alive. The potential. If you can keep a-goin'—you actually can do it.... It's when you stop that you're done." Asked how she was doing, her likely reply was, "Fine, if you don't ask for details. That's about it, isn't it?"

Her book's final chapter is filled with thank-you's, as Katharine Hepburn credits her friends, family, agents and others for helping to make her life memorable. "Memories—all there—Oh thank you.... What would I have done without that backing?... Yes, lucky!"

THE GERSHWIN YEARS
by Edward Jablonski and Lawrence D. Stewart, Doubleday and Company, 1973

. . .   *True music ... must repeat the thought and aspirations of the people and the time. My people are Americans. My time is today.... They ask me what I am trying to do, and I can only say I am trying to express what is in me.... There are thousands who have the same feelings and are mute. Those of us who can must speak for those who cannot—but we must be honest about it.*

– George Gershwin, 1926

The children of Russian Jewish immigrants, George and Ira Gershwin were born within two years of each other—Ira in 1896 and George in 1898. They grew up in a family with a home life that was both intense yet amazingly relaxed: Gershwin birthdays were never observed, the parents often couldn't remember that Ira's real name was actually *Israel*, they moved 28 different times in the New York area, and worked in many different businesses. Their unusual background fostered in both boys a versatile sense of self-sufficiency.

At age six George heard an automatic piano in a penny arcade playing Rubinstein's "Melody in F," somehow instilling within him a life-long habit of keeping a scrapbook for music. "The peculiar jumps in the music held me rooted," he wrote. Thus was born his love for what would later become called "musical jazz."

In 1910 the family bought a piano so that Ira could take lessons. It was the younger George, however, who first pounded out, apparently by ear, a current popular song of the day. So, it was decided that he, not Ira, should continue with the lessons.

George's teachers soon recognized his potential and began instructing him in musical theory. Influenced both by classical composers and by the ragtime music which defined the era, the 15-year-old took on work as a "piano pounder" for a Tin Pan Alley music producer.

Then in 1917, shortly before his 20th birthday, George quit the piano-playing job so as to have more time for his own compositions. To support himself, he worked on producing piano rolls and as an accompanist. His first song was published that same year, and others soon followed.

During this early productive period, George employed several different lyricists and wrote the score for several musicals. His first big success was a lively title song called "Swanee." Although the musical that showcased the tune soon folded, Al Jolson had heard the song and immediately adopted it as his trademark. Sales of Jolson's recorded "Swanee" shot into the millions; George Gershwin was fast gaining the reputation as a songwriter whose tunes would enjoy lasting fame.

While George pursued his path into the world of music, Ira had become fascinated with writing. As a teen he wrote bits for newspapers, but he, too, ultimately found his way into the music business. Working as a librettist coming up with the lyrics for different musicals, he first wrote under the name *Arthur Francis*, to dispel the idea that he was trying to ride on the coat-tails of his brother's success. While Ira eventually supplied lyrics for some of George's most famous songs, his collaborations with other songwriters were more successful.

Then in the early '20s, jazz stormed onto the musical scene. When bandleader Paul Whiteman thought of doing a concert based on the new music—to show the public that it was not a "tool of the devil," as some had suggested—he contacted George. Whiteman asked George to prepare something for an upcoming concert. The songwriter quickly began arranging a piece from scraps of music, combining jazz with classical elements that had been floating around in his head. It was Ira who proposed the title that has been famous ever since: *Rhapsody in Blue.*

Whiteman's concert failed to stir the audience—until Gershwin's piece began. As the last note played, the applause was spontaneous and tumultuous. While a few critics discredited the music, the public loved it.

The first complete all-Gershwin-scored musical, "Lady, Be Good," opened in 1924. Starring a pair of newcomers named Fred and Adele Astaire, it was an immediate hit. A year later "Tell Me More" opened its long run in London. During this time George continued working on classical scores; the climactic triumph of this period was his beautiful and critically acclaimed *Concerto in F* for piano and orchestra. After its release, the critics lauded the "natural gift" of its creator and the "improvisatory ... effortless quality" of the music. Granted, "he did not write by the book although he was thoroughly familiar with its contents."

In 1926, after attending London's premier of *Lady, Be Good*, George spent time in Paris. While there he received the inspiration for the opening theme of what later became *An American in Paris*, a symphonic, rhythmically exciting poem—and American through and through. Two years later he returned to France and completed the work. Due to its unique style, many referred to it as a "tone-poem"; others termed it "jazz ballet." Whatever it was, most listeners considered it fantastic.

Even after *An American in Paris*, some of George's friends begged him to give up serious music and stick to song-writing; others argued that if he gave up commercial composition he could be a great success as a classical composer. George resisted both bits of advice and insisted that he could do both "serious" and popular music—and do them both well.

One night George had trouble sleeping, so he picked up a new best-selling book: DuBose Heyward's *Porgy*. Struck by the work's powerful and dignified characterization of American blacks, he dashed off a letter to Heyward, suggesting a collaboration on a musical version of the story. But because of conflicting schedules, the two men would wait six years to formalize their agreement and to begin work.

During that six-year period, George and Ira together composed a number of well-received

Broadway musicals, as well as one forgettable Hollywood musical. Included among their greatest works from these years were the sparkling musical comedies *Lady Be Good* (1924), *Tip-Toe* (1925), *Oh. Kay* (1926), *Funny Face* (1927), and *Girl Crazy* (1930). The duo then turned to political satire with the comedies *Strike Up the Band* (1930), *Of Thee I Sing* (a 1931 spoof on presidential elections) and *Let Them Eat Cake* (1933). Each of these productions broke new ground in musical theater.

In *Of Thee I Sing*, for instance, rather than tacking verses and choruses onto the usual self-contained story, the Gershwins originated the idea of letting the songs themselves carry part of the story line—rather like an opera. The musical won a 1932 Pulitzer Prize for the story's authors, George Kaufman and Morrie Ryskind, and its lyricist, Ira Gershwin. (Oddly, the composer, George Gershwin, was overlooked.)

In 1933 the Gershwins and Heyward finally reached an agreement on *Porgy and Bess*, and Heyward started to revise the script. But once again previous commitments slowed progress of the work. Heyward ended up doing the lyrics as well as the libretto, with Ira contributing ideas and suggestions.

For a while their commitments were such that they could only collaborate long distance. Then, when George returned to the project—becoming involved in all elements of the opera, including casting and stage design—two years passed before he could finish his score and orchestrations.

When *Porgy and Bess* finally opened in the fall of 1935, it was an initial success with audiences. But, once again, the critics didn't know what to make of something that was neither purely musical nor purely operatic. This lukewarm critical reception took its toll: the "folk opera," as George called it, failed at the box office—but only after 134 performances and a brief tour. Everyone involved lost money, but George was convinced that *Porgy* was some of his best work. Time has proved him correct, as the black folk opera is now considered the most popular piece ever written by an American.

Only a few months after the closing of *Porgy*, George and Ira signed up to work on three movies. The first, "Shall We Dance?" again featured Fred Astaire, now with Ginger Rogers; the second, "Damsel in Distress," was yet another Fred Astaire hit; and the final film was a Goldwyn review. Although George was generally displeased with the movie producers' use of his music, these films contained some of the Gershwins' best songs, including such favorites as "They Can't Take That Away From Me" and "Shall We Dance?"

Meanwhile, George fell in love—apparently for the first time in his life—with film goddess Paulette Goddard. The relationship was not to be, however. Tragically, he soon began to suffer disturbing personality changes, dizzy spells, and lack of coordination. Initial medical examinations failed to reveal a malady, but within a few months he was diagnosed as having a brain tumor. Surgery proved futile: George did not recover. On July 11, 1937, at only 38 years of age, one of America's most gifted, prolific and innovative composers was gone.

After his brother's death Ira worked with a variety of composers to produce several modest Broadway plays. He later achieved his greatest success in Hollywood, where he wrote lyrics for "The Barkleys of Broadway," starring Fred Astaire, "A Star is Born," with Judy Garland, and "The Country Girl," featuring Bing Crosby and Grace Kelly.

In stark contrast to the social dynamism of his brother, Ira was an avowed introvert. "I've always felt that if George [hadn't] pushed me into lyric writing," he divulged toward the end of his life, "I'd have been content to be a bookkeeper."

And true to his bookkeeper nature, Ira had kept photographs and personal accounts of his and George's early years, information which he gladly provided to biographers and musical historians.

The last refrain that the Gershwin brothers completed jointly was the chorus to "Our Love Is Here to Stay." Following George's death, Ira went on to complete the lyrics, which summed up his feelings about his brother and himself:

The more I read the papers,
The less I comprehend
The world and all its capers,
And how it all will end.
Nothing seems to be lasting,
But that isn't our affair;
We've got something permanent
I mean, in the way we care.

A critic once purported that George and Ira Gershwin couldn't possibly write good music because they hadn't suffered enough. Indeed, aside from George's untimely death, the Gershwins' lives certainly always seemed to flow smoothly. But in reality, the brothers had their share of flops to overcome, critics to silence, shattered professional dreams to rebuild. Their courage and determination were hallmarks of their success as clearly as was their talent.

Jablonski and Stewart's work points out the highs and the lows in the careers of the talented pair. It also provides us with peeks at score sheets, handwritten lyrics, and dozens of photographs. The biographers also detail how and why the Gershwin brothers' music has endured the test of time. Now, nearly 60 years after the Gershwins attained the pinnacles of their careers, musicians are still recording and performing their tunes, the many melodies and songs that still touch our heartstrings. After all, who can forget their penetrating musical comedies "Fascinating Rhythm," "I Got Rhythm," "All To Myself," "Lady, Be Good," "Clap Yo Hands," "Someone to Watch Over Me," "'S Wonderful," "Biding My Time," "Embraceable You," "But Not for Me," "Summertime," "I Got Plenty of Nuttin'," "It Ain't Necessarily So," "Shall We Dance," "They Can't Take That Away From Me," "Nice Work If you Can Get It," "Love Walked In," "Love Is Here to Stay," *An American in Paris*, or *Rhapsody in Blue*?

CHARLES CHAPLIN: MY AUTOBIOGRAPHY
by Charles Chaplin, Dutton Publishing, 1992

Charlie Chaplin was many things to many people. A comic genius, a lover, a dreamer, a fighter—and most assuredly, a legend. He rose from the humblest of beginnings in England to great fame across the world, and helped put a little town called Hollywood, California, on the map. He made the world laugh and weep at the same time. Most of all, Chaplin, as the vulnerable and jauntily bedraggled Little Tramp, introduced *humanity* to the screen.

Chaplin penned his 480-page autobiography over a period of six years and endless rewrites. The final product is a neatly written and accurate tour de force. He neither glorifies any particular achievement nor minimizes his failures or the squalid settings of his youth. An inherently modest man, he portrays himself as a life-sized human being confronting life-sized challenges.

The Workhouse Years

Charles Spencer Chaplin was born to a pair of unrenowned vaudeville performers, Charles and Lily Chaplin, in 1889. About one year after the boy's birth, his father and mother separated, and Charlie spent his early years with his mother and older brother, Sydney, bunking in various back rooms of their Kensington Road home. The family led a meager existence, especially after Lily's damaged vocal cords curtailed her performances and her estranged husband refused to pay more for the family's upkeep. When Charlie was just over six years old, the family entered the Lambeth Workhouse.

With no means of support, Charlie and Sydney were sent to the Hanwell School for Orphans and Destitute Children. The school was not a happy place for the two homesick children, but Charlie did learn to read and write.

The Early Acting Years

A few years after she entered the workhouse Charlie's mother was declared insane, and the boys were sent to live briefly with their father and his new wife, both alcoholics. When Lily retrieved the boys after her recovery, the family eked out their meager existence with odd jobs. Sydney signed on as a ship's bugler, and, though he was often at sea, his wages helped the family survive. Then during one of Sydney's absences, Lily suffered another mental breakdown. At age 11, Charlie was left to take care of himself.

At this point Charlie's life finally changed for the better. He registered with Blackmore's Agency, a theatrical company, and was given the part of Billie, a page-boy in the play Sherlock Holmes. After two successful 40-week tours, he went without work for ten months. Sydney, meanwhile, had joined Karno's Comedy Company and pushed Mr. Karno to give Charlie a part. When the manager finally did offer the boy a tryout, Charlie's ad-libbing won him a one-year contract to play in a burlesque slapstick called "The Football Match."

After playing in England and France, Mr. Karno decided it was time to try America. The troupe was fairly well received in the United States, and Charlie at once fell in love with the welcoming towns of the Midwest, accompanying the troupe on a second American tour, which received lavish reviews. But he did not stay with the company. During this second tour, Mack Sennett signed Charlie to star in movies.

As founder and owner of the Keystone Studios, home of the Keystone Cops, Sennett's early films always revolved around a chase. This didn't sit well with Charlie, so when directors tried to push him into the trademark slapstick style, he balked. There was a brief row; but when the box office receipts started rolling in from an earlier film—done more in Charlie's own style—Sennett allowed Charlie to call his own shots.

The Little Tramp is Born

One day, as the story goes, Sennett told Charlie that he needed some gags for a new movie. "Put on a comedy make-up," Sennett directed. "Anything will do." Rummaging through the studio's wardrobe, Charlie chose a too-tight jacket, baggy pants, a cane, a derby hat and over-sized shoes, each item intended to contradict the others. Finally, because Sennett had mentioned that he looked too young, Charlie added a small paste-on mustache to lend an air of maturity.

Charlie began strutting about, swinging his cane in front of Sennett. The character evolved spontaneously from the clothes and make-up. As gags and comedy scenes quickly flowed into a lively stream, Sennett giggled until he began to shake. "You know," he gasped finally, "this fellow is many-sided, a tramp, a gentleman, a poet, a dreamer, a lonely fellow, always hopeful of romance and adventure." With that, "Charlot" the Little Tramp was born.

In the ensuing months Charlie went on to write, direct and star in many more Keystone Studio films.

The Middle Years (1915–1923)

Within a year Charlie Chaplin had become a huge success. But the contract with Sennett expired at the end of 1914. Charlie had been making a film every two weeks and he knew he could not keep up such a furious pace. But in order to slow down, he needed a steady income. Sennett refused his star's request for a $1000-a-week contract, but Essanay Films came up with a better offer: $1250 a week in salary, plus a $10,000 signing bonus—an immense amount of money for 1915. Charlie signed with Essanay.

Meanwhile, he continued to put out a new film every two to three weeks. Burn-out took its toll. He had few friends and socialized little, rarely fixing his gaze on anything but work. After finishing a film, he usually spent the next few days in bed, depressed and exhausted. Then when another idea invaded his mind, he got up and went back to work.

Charlie's films were big box-office attractions. An adoring public eagerly awaited each one. The Little Tramp inspired merchandise, songs and poems. As the income from his films steadily climbed, Charlie negotiated a deal that gave him an additional $10,000 per picture.

By now Sydney was working alongside Charlie and, because he understood legal jargon, took over the negotiations. When the Essanay contract expired, Sydney struck a bargain with The Mutual company, a major agreement which lasted for two years and produced 12 films.

Charlie never worked for one company for more than a couple of years. Always very aware of his triumphs, he was driven to achieve more and more. Subsequently, he *got* more. As his fame grew, however, he didn't care for the attendant publicity. Whenever he traveled his destination was wired ahead by the studios, and all along the route people gathered and waited for him to speak. He had become America's reluctant darling.

After fulfilling the Mutual contract, Charlie entered the happiest time of his career. Twenty-seven years old and free, he was soon to be a millionaire; money flowed in from all his movies. Although he had few close friends, during this period he made several lifelong associations—with a young actor named Douglas Fairbanks; with actress Edna Purviance, who stayed on the payroll at Chaplin Studios until her death; and with screen favorite Mary Pickford. Charlie also enjoyed cordial acquaintances with celebrities and dignitaries from across the globe: William Randolph Hearst, Gandhi, Sir Winston Churchill, Khrushchev, Einstein, and many, many others. He was never a lonely man; he simply preferred solitude to company.

In late 1917 Chaplin met Mildred Harris. After several months of dinners, dances and moonlit walks, he married her. At the time of the wedding, she thought she was pregnant—but this turned out to be untrue.

Meanwhile, Sydney negotiated a new contract with First National for a whopping $1,200,000. When Sydney told his brother the sum of the deal, Charlie's laconic reply was, "Hum-um, I suppose that is wonderful." He would almost certainly have kept making movies even for far less money. He enjoyed the stimulation too much to let go.

First National lacked a studio to go along with its generous contract, so Charlie built a studio in California and started immediately on several films. Married life affected him, though, and he cut back to a couple of full-length movies a year.

Then, during the 1919 cutting of "The Kid," a wildly popular movie featuring Jackie Coogan's four-year-old son Jackie Jr., Charlie and Mildred separated.

After completing his First National contract in 1923, Chaplin began making movies for United Artists, the company he had created together with Fairbanks and Mary Pickford.

The Late Movies (1923–1957)

By now Charlie was making very few films, averaging only one every four years. He was busy with a second wife, whom he would not talk about—then a third wife, Paulette Goddard, with whom he starred in "Modern Times" and "The Great Dictator"—and finally, a fourth, Oona O'Niel, the daughter of playwright Eugene O'Niel. In Oona, Chaplin finally found a woman who loved him not for money or fame, but for himself—and who did not aspire to a movie career of her own.

At this point changing technology posed a problem for Chaplin. Talking pictures had been ushered in; silent films had entered their twilight years. Although he produced two more silent films, "City Lights" and "Modern Times," which proved to be roaring successes, it was obvious that he could not go on as he had.

Yet part of the Little Tramp's loveable, innocent appeal had always been tied to his muteness. Chaplin was faced with a dilemma. In his next film—a talkie called "The Great Dictator"—he found an ingenious way to let the Little Tramp stay on: Chaplin played two roles, appearing both as Hitler and as the dictator's look-alike, an amnesiac Jewish barber, who just happened to be a soft-spoken version of the Little Tramp.

With World War II looming on the horizon, Chaplin was invited by the government to speak on the question of American intervention on the Soviet front. Charlie, who considered himself to be a "citizen of the world," favored sending American and British troops to relieve "our Russian comrades" on the battle lines. Entering the war at all, however, let alone offering aid to Communist Russia, was unthinkable to many Americans. Chaplin political opinions opened a firestorm of criticism. The media degraded him mercilessly, accusing him of being a Communist; eventually he was called before the Committee on Un-American Activities.

After that, Chaplin's stardom waned and his films suffered several forms of censorship. Eventually, facing attempts by the IRS to discredit his name and cries to jail him, Charlie left for a vacation in Europe and was barred from returning to the U.S. Exiled from the land in which he had lived for over 40 years, he moved to Switzerland and produced one final film, "The King in New York." He devoted his remaining years to his wife and daughters, and, later, to his grandchildren.

[In 1973 Chaplin returned to Hollywood to accept a special "Lifetime Achievement" Oscar at the Academy Awards presentations. A standing ovation and the tears that flowed down his own cheeks and those of the audience were testimony to the place that Charlie Chaplin had always retained in the hearts of Americans. In 1976 he was knighted by the British crown; a year later, in Switzerland, Sir Charles Spencer Chaplin passed away.]

ACCIDENTAL MILLIONAIRE – *The Rise and Fall of Steven Jobs at Apple Computer*
by Lee Butcher, Paragon House, 1988

Shortly after his birth in 1956, Steven Jobs, an orphan, was adopted by Paul and Clara Jobs of Mountain View, California. But the real story of Steven Jobs began in the eighth grade, when he formed a friendship with Stephen Wozniak, his future partner and co-founder of Apple Computers. In truth, it was an unlikely collaboration, because Jobs, in fact, had nothing to do with designing the first Apple computer. As Wozniak tells it: *Reporters would ... ask "Well, did he develop the hardware?" I said "No." Then they would ask, "Well did he develop the software?" I had to answer "No ... I created the whole computer."*

Jobs did take an electronics course in high school, but, far from being a computer prodigy, he dropped out of the program after a year. Instead, working nights and weekends at an electrical shop, he became an expert scrounger, reselling cheap finds at a profit.

Jobs, with his abrasive, aggressive style, made a negative first impression almost everywhere he went; but his persuasiveness was ultimately hard to resist.

After being caught up in the hippie movement of the late '60s and early '70s, he enrolled at Reed College in Portland, Oregon. He quit, however, after only one semester, and, seeking enlightenment, turned to the study of Yoga and Zen Buddhism. It was during this period that he moved to a $25-per-month room, where, reportedly for three weeks he lived on Roman Meal and milk from the college cafeteria.

Soon Jobs fast-talked his way into a job at Atari Electronics, where he enjoyed his first business success. Atari had found that in Germany their games interfered with local TV reception, so they sent Jobs to resolve the problem. When he arrived at the German office, the local engineers were so stunned by his bizarre appearance and eccentric, often caustic behavior that they cabled Atari to make certain they had sent the right man. But somehow, to the amazement of everyone, Jobs solved the problem.

The next assignment for Atari's new wunderkind was in India, where he was dismayed by the abject poverty he saw. Rethinking his devotion to yoga, he went home convinced that "Thomas Edison had done more to improve the human condition than all the gurus that had ever lived."

Back at Atari headquarters—which at the time was in tremendous turmoil—Jobs was demoted to the level of consultant. Again, however, fortune prevailed. Atari offered him a bonus to design a game that used a ball to smash a brick wall, and Jobs asked his old friend Wozniak for help, offering to split with him the modest earnings.

Meanwhile, Wozniak had offered a new computer design to Hewlett-Packard, which, at the time, saw no future in personal computers. It was Jobs who caught a glimpse of the possibilities and convinced his friend that they could sell printed circuit boards to computer hobbyists. Within months they had signed a partnership agreement, and Apple Computer was born on April Fools Day, 1976—"Apple" because it was sleek, simple, and possessed a wholesome, educational connotation.

Jobs first approached The Byte Shop, a store that sold computer kits, to market their circuit boards. Instead, The Byte Shop placed an order for 50 *complete* computers—promising to pay "between $489 and $589" per unit. Jobs and Wozniak were flabbergasted; the total return, $25,000 to $30,000, far exceeded their wildest expectations.

Next, a supplier agreed to sell them $20,000 in parts—enough to assemble 100 computers—on credit. With help from family members and friends, the pair put computers together in Jobs's parents' home and garage. Even though these first "completed" computers were actually very incomplete—including no power supply, software, monitor, or keyboard—the Byte Shop accepted them. Wozniak then went on to create a cassette interface and BASIC software to enhance the computers, and finally to design a video interface. Jobs also convinced an Atari engineer to come up with a companion power supply—and, with a keyboard, at last they had a viable working unit.

Aside from securing a few personal loans, Jobs found no investors interested in Apple; amazingly, even as late as 1978, no one could fathom potential in an inexpensive "personal" computer. Bankruptcy threatened. Commodore, Hewlett-Packard and Atari were all approached about buying the company, but each time negotiations fell through.

Finally Jobs decided Apple needed a better image. Using all his persuasive powers, he convinced the prestigious Regis McKenna Advertising Agency to represent them. "It was one of the most important associations the small company could have arranged."

Over time, Jobs also interested "Mike" Markkula, a 33-year-old retired engineer and multi-millionaire, in Apple. Markkula gave the venture his "organizational skills, business experience, and a steadying influence over the mercurial Jobs." On January 3, 1977, Markkula, Wozniak and Jobs incorporated the Apple Computer Company.

Markkula, who "had no desire to run the business," soon convinced his new partners that the company needed to be professionally managed. He hired Michael Scott, an engineer he had worked with, as president of Apple.

With the addition of "professional guidance and a thin cushion of operating capital," Apple grew rapidly, moving from Jobs' garage to a building in Cupertino, California. Markkula created a business plan, Scott ran daily operations, and Wozniak pushed his team to ready the Apple II for the West Coast Computer Faire. Jobs, meanwhile, "who had no real responsibility," was content to "flit from desk to desk, ruffling feathers and ... making himself feared and unpopular."

Jobs's semi-obscure vision now was to see the Apple II "stand out [aesthetically] as a swan against a background of ugly ducklings" and attract those in the hard-core business market. "Steve had a great deal to do with … the computer housing," Wozniak does admit. Indeed, it was Jobs who helped design a stylish plastic case and the Apple logo—a rainbow-colored apple with a bite taken out of one side.

But nothing went smoothly at Apple during those early days. "Steve had no ability to manage people," Wozniak says. "He ruled by intimidation, yelling and screaming…. People were terrified of him." He also gained "a reputation for being rude and overbearing with outside people with whom Apple did business."

By the time the Computer Faire rolled around, Apple had completed three computers. In the next few weeks they received orders for 300—100 more than the total number of Apple I's already sold.

The company had finally achieved a strong sense of community. Its employees came early and stayed late, "partly because they wanted to and partly because Jobs expected it." But despite the company's cohesion, Apple soon acquired a reputation for not fulfilling commitments. Finances stayed tight. What's more, "Jobs' unwillingness to accept his own limitations did not prevent him from getting involved in things he didn't understand. People working on projects started to dread seeing him … "

Meanwhile, Scott, engaged in almost daily shouting matches with Jobs, delighted in highlighting his adversary's sometimes peculiar behavior. With great glee he revealed that Jobs refreshed himself by sitting on the toilet tank, putting his feet in the bowl, and flushing.

In 1978 Apple introduced the first disk drive for a personal computer, beating out Commodore and Tandy. Sales immediately jumped. More investors came on board, while public relations pushed the rags-to-riches tale of two poor teenagers starting a computer company in a garage. Jobs and Wozniak quickly became cult heroes. Erroneously, Jobs got credit for much of the design for the Apple I and II, and accepted it as his due.

Jobs often talked about how much he cared for employees—but his actions seldom showed it. "You couldn't believe anything the guy said," Wozniak recalls, disgustedly. "He would say one thing and do another…. Steve will use anybody to his own advantage."

Yet as one employee observes, Jobs "also had a sweet side, the hippie part of him who had gone to India soul-searching … " When an employee once was hospitalized with cancer, Jobs visited him daily and "paid for … a private room and … all the medical expenses."

In 1979 Jeff Raskins, an Apple engineer, presented his idea for a new, more powerful computer to be targeted at business users—hooked up with something he called a "mouse." But, as Raskins relates, Jobs would not give the idea a chance: "He ran around saying, 'No! No! It'll never work.'"

Jobs fought Raskins's idea for two years. Then in 1982 he abruptly changed his mind and took over the Macintosh division of the company, driving Raskins out of the organization and splitting Apple into two bitter camps. "The Macintosh division had the best of

everything: … biggest parties, highest salaries, and more stroking from Jobs," remembers Wozniak. " … You never heard the Apple II mentioned. We were generating most of the company's revenue and the Apple II was the best-selling computer in the world."

Then mighty IBM finally entered the personal computer market. "Apple looked at IBM with condescension and arrogance, much the way it looked at suppliers, retailers, and the personal computer infrastructure," and by 1983, IBM had managed to "steamroller" its competition and grab a 30% market share.

In 1983 Apple hired John C. Sculley, formerly of PepsiCo, to replace Scott, who had resigned in 1981 as president of the company. Sculley struggled to turn Apple around, restructuring the firm and cutting much of its bloated bureaucracy.

But even as Sculley worked magic on one end of the company, Jobs's design constraints crippled the Mac. One disgruntled Mac owner complained: "It's like having a Maserati with a one-gallon gas tank." By November, 1984, only 200,000 Macintoshes had been sold. Apple had held back from ousting their folk-hero, but they finally brought Jobs to heel early in 1985—a move long overdue.

By this time Jobs's nemesis, the Apple II, had set all-time highs in sales, generating a whopping two-thirds of Apple's 1984 profits. Sculley had promised that the Mac would be made expandable, capable of running IBM programs. But since Jobs refused to make the enhancements, Sculley found himself in a dilemma: Even though Jobs, as the Macintosh division manager, technically worked under Sculley, the company president, "as chairman of the board, Jobs was Sculley's boss."

At last Sculley chose to hire Jean-Louis Gassee, of Apple France, to replace Jobs as manager of Macintosh. In a last desperate maneuver, Jobs called for Sculley's resignation. At an ensuing emergency meeting of the executive committee, Sculley, however, made it clear that it was he who ran Apple—and Jobs was summarily moved to "a remote office … called Siberia."

Jobs still remained as Apple's board chairman, and with undimmed tenacity set out to start a new company. Presenting a list of employees he wanted to take with him—all key people at Apple, "it was clear … that Jobs intended to go into direct competition [with Apple]." Without delay, the board fired Jobs and sued for potential damages.

Jobs settled out of court, agreeing: (1) not to hire Apple employees for three years; (2) not to produce products that competed with Apple's; and (3) to submit any product developed by his new company, "NeXT," for approval by Apple prior to marketing. Then, in a typical act of defiance, he sold all but one of his shares in Apple.

Billionaire H. Ross Perot has since "invested twenty million dollars in NeXT, buying 16 percent of the company." In Perot, Jobs had "found a formidable ally, and, if he succeeds with NeXT, the stigma of his 'accidental' success at Apple may at last vanish."

Dave's Way – A New Approach to Old-Fashioned Success
By R. David Thomas, G.P. Putnam's Sons, 1991

*I*n 1940, at the age of eight, I dreamed that I would one day own the best restaurant in the world. All of the customers would love my food, and all of my employees would do everything they were supposed to do. But, most important, everyone would think I was a good boss, and every day when I walked into the restaurant, people would be glad to see me. The realization of that dream molded Dave Thomas into the man he always dreamed of becoming—a good boss who most of his employees know simply as "Dave," and the founder of one of America's most popular and successful fast-food restaurant chains.

Dave's earliest memories were of his adoptive mother dying: *It seemed like a strange dream to me. I didn't know people were supposed to die and I didn't know who would replace her. My grandmother, Minnie Sinclair, explained that my mother had gone to heaven where she would watch over me.*

After Dave's mother died, his father had a hard time settling into jobs. He and his son were constantly on the move. Dave often spoke fondly of the summers he spent with his grandmother: *She could be tough if she wanted to, but you could see the warmth in her eyes. She was a special motivator. If you did the right thing, she could make you feel ten feet tall, and very, very special.*

One thing Dave especially admired about his grandmother was that she always seemed to have money: "She managed better than anyone I ever saw," he wrote. "She got so much out of so little, and she never acted poor." It was from her that he learned his most valuable lessons, lessons that made him a success: *Make a lot out of a little, but don't cut corners. Work hard and have fun. Be strict but caring, and pray.*

As two "hardy bachelors," the boy and his father constantly ate at restaurants, enabling Dave to become a restaurant connoisseur. His favorite place was a hamburger stand close to their apartment, where he always ordered the thickest milk shake they made. Later it became the model for his Wendy's "Frosty" dessert: *I knew what customers expected and what kind of service and quality was acceptable. I overheard complaints and compliments and soaked them all in.*

Growing up, Dave worked many jobs. As a 12-year-old he lied about his age to get a job at Walgreen's Drug Store. When the manager later became suspicious and confronted Dave, he wasn't fired: he simply refused to schedule Dave for any shifts. "You'll never keep a job!" his dad screamed when he heard of the incident. "I'll be supporting you for the rest of your life!" After that experience, Dave resolved never to lose a job again.

Realizing that "If somebody paid you, it was up to you to perform," Dave went to work at the Regas Restaurant, taking orders and filling out invoices.

Six months later he and his father moved again, forcing him to ride the Trailways bus to work and back. Later, when summer came, Dave decided to rent a room in town so he could work 12-hour days. He summed up his lessons at the Regas this way: *Make a clean, neat impression. Do everything you can to make customers happy. Set tough standards, but back up your employees when necessary. Build your peoples' confidence. Reward motivation and determination. TRY.*

The twosome moved once again, this time to Fort Wayne, Indiana, where the manager of the Hobby House hired Dave "because of his attitude." One day as he waited on tables, he noticed a man in a suit sweeping floors. He later learned that the fellow was the owner of the Hobby House, Phil Clauss. It was a revelation, and Dave determined then that one day he would be the kind of owner Phil Clauss was.

When his father moved yet again, Dave remained in Fort Wayne. He had a "family" at the restaurant, he told his dad. "Someday," he promised, "you'll be proud of me."

Fifteen years old and on his own, Dave attended high school and worked a fulltime job. Finally, the pressure became too severe, and after the tenth grade, he quit school. The lesson he learned was passed on to many youngsters: *Get a job, don't be discouraged, try hard work and get an education. Find people you can learn from.*

Dave joined the Army at 18 and received some culinary training and experience as a mess-hall cook. When he was sent to Germany, "Sergeant Thomas" found that the mess halls were truly "a mess" and badly under-supplied. Trading surplus stock for necessary supplies, he gradually improved the quality of food.

The mess halls themselves were dingy, dismal places in which to eat. Again, through some shrewd trades, Dave obtained a truckload of 500 gallons of paint and ordered that the walls be given a good coat. Morale improved dramatically. This was one time, he chuckled, that "I enjoyed being a big shot."

Before long the manager of the Enlisted Men's Club hired Dave with the orders to turn around the failing operation. By focusing on more and better menu selections, he had the club running in the black within months.

After receiving his Army discharge in October 1953, Dave returned to Hobby House, where Phil was waiting for him, apron in hand. It was at this time that Dave met Lorraine, one of the spunkiest waitresses he'd ever known. After a year of courting, the couple were married.

Dave and Phil made a lot of adjustments to Hobby House's menu, which eventually hurt the business. However, the business partners worked well together, blending Phil's hustle and upbeat attitude with Dave's promotional and organizational talents. With their combined skills they built a loyal core of customers.

On one occasion shortly after Colonel Sanders had come out with his new chicken franchises, Phil wanted to buy into one. In Dave's opinion it was a big mistake. Then one day, out of the blue, Colonel Sanders walked in the door at Hobby House, sat down, and ordered a meal. He and Dave started talking, and by the end of the conversation, Dave was sold.

The advent of Kentucky Fried Marketing was a turning point in the restaurant business for several reasons. Takeout food required proper packaging. In addition, people seemed to enjoy having a real person—the grandfatherly Colonel himself—back up their food. Sanders reinforced what Dave already knew: high standards and cleanliness make customers *feel good*—the real ingredient to business success.

In 1962 Dave and Lorraine moved to Columbus, Ohio, to try to turn around four of Phil's poorly-managed stores. Dave's plan called for a complete overhaul, "firing all the managers (they just weren't cutting it), painting all the stores, daily reports so he could stay on top of things, slimming down the menus, focusing the business, and adding a large dose of promotion." In just five short years he made good on his plan. Not only had he acquired 40% ownership of the stores, but he'd also purchased $10,000 in stock, which, in those five years had grown into a million-dollar investment.

Dave credited Lorraine with keeping his priorities in order: his family and personal life didn't suffer at all. As in most areas, he suggested a few simple rules for couples working together: *Guard your spouse's free time, share authority, think flexibility, keep an eye on the calendar and be careful of timing.*

In 1968 Dave sold his stock in the KFC franchise. About that same time the company offered him a 300-store regional manager's job. Dave's ambition to own a burger place looked like it was still a distant dream.

Then came the turning point that put him on the right path: he lost his job at KFC over a disagreement involving stock purchases, conflicts of interest, and hurt feelings. At 37, Dave was out of work.

National Diversified, a restaurant enterprise in which Thomas owned some stock, offered him a job with the Arthur Treacher's Fish and Chips chain. National's Len Imke, a friend and fellow manager, spent much time listening to Dave's plans and dreams. One day Len announced that he had a building for his new employee to rent, a place where he could try out his ideas. Dave jumped at the opportunity.

The menu would be simple: three kinds of made-to-order burgers, chili, french fries, a Frosty, and assorted beverages. The name for the store came from the nickname of his fourth child, Melinda Lou, dubbed "Wendy" by the older children. At eight, little Wendy was the hit of the party when the first Wendy's opened on November 15, 1969. Within two years three more outlets were opened, each fostering a down-home, family-type atmosphere.

Dave says the market trends that made Wendy's a success were obvious: *People wanted choices. They were tired of poor quality. People were on the move and adjusting to a more complicated way of life. People were ready for an upscale hamburger place.*

What exactly is it that made Wendy's different? Dave believed that his way of doing business, which gave people what they want, was unique. He noticed, for instance, that most hungry customers didn't want to stand in a lines: *Lines really say to the customer: self-service. Serve yourself, buddy, because we sure aren't going to serve you. This is a scramble system. You're either tapping a toe waiting or jumping for the next line that just opened up.* With that in mind, Dave came up with a more efficient, less frustrating system: a zig-zag line with just one, very outgoing, warm person taking orders: "They can make a little quick conversation, so we become a more personable place." If customers get too piled up, Wendy's sends another order-taker down the line: "As long as the line moves, people are happy." Dave employed the same time-and-money-saving techniques at Wendy's drive-through window.

Dave considered customer feedback as crucial to Wendy's supplying better service. On any given day over 500 customer checklists were given out to gauge how customers were feeling, and to assess overall employee satisfaction.

Regarding advertising, Dave was the first to say: "Tell the truth. Have a sense of humor, don't expect it to be cheap and be believable." Sometimes just the mention of a key word or the recreation of the right situation could capture the attention of a nation and give you the edge: Remember Clara Peller of "Where's the Beef" fame?

Dave's management philosophy was most simple: *HARASSMENT.* By this he meant keeping at someone until they either did what you think they should be doing or until they proved that their way was better. But he cautioned to use restraint in this method of motivation: "Only harass people you care about."

Filled with humor and advice, *Dave's Way* is entertaining and valuable for anyone trying to find his way in an increasingly complex and competitive world. His down-to-earth suggestions for coping with everything from shyness to starting your own business epitomize his dream—one he made come true: *There isn't anything in my life that I haven't been able to do. Well, maybe there is one thing. I would like to be able to sing like Perry Como or Nat King Cole…. Maybe someday I'll wake up and decide to take singing lessons…. Imagine the commercials they could cast me in then!*

Branded the richest man in America, Sam Walton once said: "The next thing we knew all these reporters and photographers arrived, I guess to take pictures of me diving into a swimming pool full of money they imagined I had, or to watch me light big fat cigars with hundred-dollar bills while the hootchy-kootchy girls danced by the lake." The picture conjured up by this statement is so patently unlike the real Sam Walton that by the time you come upon it in the book, you just have to laugh. "We're not ashamed of having money," he added at the time, "but I just don't believe a big showy lifestyle is appropriate for anywhere. I'm not sure I ever figured out this celebrity business. I can't believe it was news that I get my hair cut at the barbershop. Where else would I get it cut?"

Walton, born March 29, 1918, grew up in Missouri during the Great Depression. He sold and delivered milk for the family, sold papers and magazine subscriptions, and raised and sold rabbits and pigeons. His mother was a special motivator. She told Sam that "he should always try to be the best he could at whatever he took on." So he always pursued everything he was interested in with a "passion to win." In high school he was voted class officer several years, played every sport (never losing a football game), and earned his Eagle Scout award at age 13—"the youngest Eagle Scout in the history of the state of Missouri at that time."

Throughout college Walton worked at least three jobs at once, carried a full class load and was active in every organization he could join. He also learned a secret of leadership early in his campus years: *Speak to people coming down the sidewalk before they speak to you.* He called everyone by name whenever possible and soon they recognized him and considered him their friend.

When he realized that even with the same hectic pace he still couldn't afford to attend the Wharton School of Finance, he decided to look for a job. After accepting an offer to work for JC Penney as a management trainee, Walton would wander around the other two stores at the intersection on his lunch hour. Canvassing thus became his mode of informal job training.

In 1943, as an ROTC graduate, Walton was ready to ship out, but was sidelined by the Army because of a minor heart irregularity. Still in town, he stopped by a local bowling alley, where he met Helen, his future wife, out on a date with her boyfriend. Not in the least bit shy, Walton stepped up to her and blurted out the old line, "Haven't I met you somewhere before?" Helen could immediately recognize that Walton was someone who knew where he was headed. She told her parents she was "going to marry someone who had that

special energy and drive, that desire to be a success." Later she amended her qualifications: "I certainly found what I was looking for, but now I laugh sometimes and say maybe I overshot a little."

During their first two years of marriage, the new family moved 15 times—until Helen finally insisted that they settle down in a small town, one having no more than ten thousand residents. Sam willingly agreed, so they bought a Ben Franklin store in Newport, Arkansas. The operation, however, turned out to be a real loser; Walton knew little about running a store. Still, looking back, he says, "It was a real blessing for me to be so green and ignorant. I learned a lesson that has stuck all through the years: you can learn from everybody." That included John Dunhams's Sterling Store across the street. "Sam was always over there checking on John," Helen remembers. "Always. Looking at his prices, looking at his displays, looking at what was going on. He was always looking for a way to do a better job."

At first Walton ran his store by the book. Ben Franklin's supervisor sent all the merchandise and told him what to do. Then he started doing things his own way. He wanted to buy direct from the manufacturer and run special promotions, but the manufacturers feared the wrath of Franklin's home office. So Walton would "hitch a homemade trailer to the car, drive it into Tennessee and stuff it with whatever he could get good deals on. Then he'd haul it back, price it low, and just blow that stuff out the store. It drove the Ben Franklin folks crazy …"

As time went on he tried lots of promotional things: a popcorn machine on the sidewalk; a soft ice cream machine in the store. "One of the biggest contributions to the later success of Wal-Mart may have been his constant fiddling and meddling with the status quo."

Before long Walton opened a small department store next to the Ben Franklin and hired his brother Bud as manager. "That Newport store was really the beginning of where Wal-Mart is today," he said. "We did everything. We would wash windows, sweep floors, trim windows. We did all the stockroom work, checked the freight in. Everything it took to run a store. We had to keep expenses to a minimum. That is where it started. Our money was made by controlling expenses."

Of course, Walton's success commanded a price. Knowing he had nowhere else in town to move, his store's landlord decided not to renew the lease at any cost. He did offer to buy it at a fair price, with the idea of turning it over to his son. At that discouraging point, Walton had no other alternative: "It didn't seem fair. I blamed myself for getting suckered into such an awful lease and I was furious at the landlord. I didn't dwell on it. I've always thought of problems as challenges. I don't know if it changed me any. I did read the leases a lot more carefully after that. Helen and I started looking for a new town."

In the spring of 1950 Walton and his family went store hunting. They found a man willing to sell his place in Bentonville, Arkansas, about half the size of Newport. "It was just a sad looking country town," Helen said of the area, "but I knew right after we got here that it was going to work out."

By 1952 Walton had driven to Fayetteville and signed a lease on a site for a second outlet. Now called Walton's Five and Dime, the stores were set up as self-service, pay-at-the-front establishments, a new philosophy to the industry. In a bid to keep the store's name simple yet retain a part of himself, the name Wal-Mart was introduced. And by 1962 several Ben Walton franchises and three Wal-Marts were in operation.

Then the competition started moving in. Gibson's stores—taking a tip from Walton—began copying what Walton was doing, which propelled Walton to "roll out the stores" just as quickly as he could: "Had we been capitalized we would never have tried the small-town America stores. The big lesson that we learned was that there was much, much more out there than we ever dreamed of."

As the stores expanded, new ways of handling distribution, warehousing, management and accounting were needed. Walton continued to explore new management methods, furthering the concept of what it meant to be a "team." Saturday morning management meetings became a place to "share information, lighten everybody's load, and to rally the troops." The most important ingredient of Wal-Mart's success, according to its founder, was that "if you take care of the people in the stores, they will take care of the customers in the same manner. But you have to work at it because that little personal touch means a lot."

Walton hired good people wherever he could find them—most often from other stores. People liked him and were willing to risk coming into what at times may have seemed disastrous circumstances. He loved to buy huge quantities of an item, then advertise extensively. Such tactics set the company apart and were hard to compete with, especially price-wise. "The philosophy is that stores are full of items that can explode into big volume and profits if you are just smart enough to identify them and take the trouble to promote them." He often traipsed all over town to check out the competition, always with an eye to saving himself and his customers money on good merchandise.

Even with his busy schedule, however, he spent time with his family on long camping trips. His son Jim says, "Dad said you've got to stay flexible. We never went on a trip that wasn't changed at least once after the trip was underway. Dad thrived on change."

Despite Walton's success, problems did at times linger. Merchandise often didn't arrive at the stores on time, and there was a constant shortage of trained manpower. He opened 50 stores a year, hired managers with little retail experience, put them on the sales floor for six months and then "put them in line for the next store." Walton's belief in people gave them the confidence to try it "his way" in "their own store"—and they thrived. His motto that "desire and a willingness to work make up for a lack of experience" was not just a collection of idle words. He expected his executives to listen and then turn around and share good, workable ideas with associates. He realized that "folks who stand all day on their feet get exhausted and frustrated too and need someone to share it with who is in a position to find a solution."

In 1974, at age 56, Walton was free of debt, his business was doing well, and he wanted to step back a little. After appointing Ron Mayer as CEO and chairman of Wal-Mart and Ferold Arend as president, Walton demoted himself to chairman of the Executive Committee.

But before long things began to go downhill. "What they had was a semiretired founder who didn't want to go away, on top of an old-line bunch of store managers at war with an ambitious young guy with ideas of his own," conjectured Walton. Numbers were good during that period, but the company continued to line up on two different sides. When Walton finally called Mayer 30 months later and admitted that he wasn't going to retire after all, Mayer left, taking many of the senior managers with him.

The new team Walton succeeded in putting together "was even more talented, more suited for the job at hand than the previous one." As he became more comfortable in his limited hands-on role, he did learn to step back emotionally. As the company grew he continued to pursue the same principles that made it great in the first place: "Put the customer first, communicate, keep your ear to the ground, push responsibility and authority down, force ideas to bubble up, stay lean and fight bureaucracy, and always give something back."

Walton fought the effects of bone cancer during the final two years of his life. "He took his medicine," his son remembers, "but never dwelled on either the illness or its potential cures. He seized the day, flying his plane to visit his beloved associates, and worked on this book."

Just three weeks before his life ended at age 74 on April 5, 1992, he received a Presidential Citation from President Bush, the Medal of Freedom. The down-to-earth atmosphere Walton stubbornly sought to marshal in his stores was not a put-on, but the real thing. Rising from Arkansas store clerk to the heights of a man having captured the American Dream, Sam Walton always gave more than he took.

THE AUTOBIOGRAPHY OF ANDREW CARNEGIE
by Andrew Carnegie, Houghton Mifflin Company, 1920

I intend to tell my story, not as one posturing before the public, but as in the midst of my own people and friends ... to whom I can speak with the utmost freedom, feeling that even trifling incidents may not be wholly destitute of interest for them.

And so begins the story of Andrew Carnegie, the Scottish immigrant who accumulated one of the great fortunes in America—then gave most of it away. Written in the warm, confidential voice one would expect of a friend, Carnegie's autobiography offers its readers a rich tapestry of advice, insight, anecdotes and worldly experience.

Born in 1835, Carnegie grew up in the prominent Scottish town of Dumferline. The deep-seated history and poetic tradition of the hamlet touched him and "set fire to the latent spark within, making him something different and beyond what, less happily born, he would have become."

Carnegie descended from an intellectual and political family. His intensely patriotic forbearers despised the privileged classes, favoring instead American republicanism, specifically its "denunciations of monarchical and aristocratic government" and its belief in "a home for freemen in which every citizen's privilege was every man's right."

In 1848, when Carnegie was 13, his family fell on hard times and subsequently emigrated to America, settling with relatives in Pittsburgh. Andrew's father secured work for his son first as a bobbin boy in a cotton factory and later as a steam engine operator—work much too hard for a youth. "But ... " Carnegie remembered, "my hopes were high, and I looked every day for some change to take place. What it was to be I knew not, but that it would come I felt certain if I kept on."

In 1850 Carnegie left the factory to work as a messenger boy for a telegraph office. "From the dark cellar running a steam-engine ... I was lifted into paradise, yes, heaven, as it seemed to me, with newspapers, pens, pencils, and sunshine about me." In addition to becoming acquainted with "the few leading men of the city," soon he was supervising the delivery office, earning an unprecedented salary of thirteen dollars and fifty cents a month. His parents were elated. "No subsequent success," he wrote, " ... ever thrilled me as this did."

At 17 Carnegie became a telegrapher, earning 25 dollars a month. He and his closest friends also joined a debate society, where he learned the art of public speaking. "Make yourself perfectly at home before your audience," he advised, "and simply talk to them, not at them. Do not try to be somebody else; be your own self and talk, never 'orate' ... "

Young Carnegie quickly rose through the ranks of the firm. His family's situation improved, but in 1855 his father died, "just as we were becoming able to give him a life of leisure and comfort ... "

Around this time Carnegie made his first investment—a hard-earned 500 dollars—and discovered the ease with which money could be generated: "It gave me the first penny of revenue from capital—something I had not worked for with the sweat of my brow." He also bought a one-eighth interest in a firm that manufactured the first sleeping cars for railroads. Then, in 1859, the 24-year-old Carnegie was named superintendent of the railroad's Pittsburgh Division at an annual salary of 1500 dollars.

When the Civil War erupted the young executive was called to Washington to help organize the railroad transport of soldiers and supplies. While there, he worked with both President Lincoln and General Ulysses Grant.

Near the close of the war, Carnegie, back at work for the railroad, went into business forging new rails for the railroads and organizing the prosperous Pittsburgh Locomotive Works. He also helped form the Keystone Bridge Company, which thrived at a time when most other bridge builders were going under. He attributed his success to hard work and the quality production he demanded: *There has been no luck about it. We used only the best material and enough of it, making our own iron and later our own steel. We were our own severest inspectors, and would build a safe structure or none at all.... This policy is the true secret of success.... A high standard of excellence is easily maintained, and men are educated in the effort to reach excellence.... The surest foundation of a manufacturing concern is quality.*

Carnegie and his partners implemented the first cost accounting system for the complicated manufacturing process. Also at this time he invested in the newly drilled Pennsylvania oil wells, and by 1865 his investments commanded so much attention that he retired from railroad service, determined to increase his fortune. "Thenceforth," he recalled, "I never worked for a salary. A man must necessarily occupy a narrow field who is at the beck and call of others."

In 1867 Carnegie moved to New York, where "the whole speculative field was laid out for me in its most seductive guise." He considered buying stocks to be a form of gambling, claiming that "speculation is a parasite feeding upon values, creating none." Hence, he resolved not to "own any stock that was bought and sold upon any stock exchange." Rather he decided that the proper policy was "to put all good eggs in one basket and then watch that basket."

I believe the true road to preeminent success in any line is to make yourself master in that line.... My advice to young men would be not only to concentrate their whole time and attention on the one business in life in which they engage, but to put every dollar of their capital into it.

In 1871 Carnegie and his partners became the first American firm to utilize the "dross" (waste) from coal mines through an English process of washing and cooking. They were also first to hire a chemist to determine the quality of the ore from various mines. Utilizing recent scientific advances, they discovered that many manufacturers were discarding perfectly usable raw materials.

Carnegie founded a company in 1873 that manufactured steel rails using the new "Bessemer" process. For each of his ventures he was able to choose the very best men to run the factories, handle the machinery, and manage the workers. It was this uncanny ability to perceive excellence in men—"the faculty of knowing and choosing others who did know better than myself"—for which he credited his success. Indeed, Carnegie wrote, "I did not understand steam machinery, but I tried to understand that much more complicated piece of mechanism—man."

In 1878 Carnegie embarked on a world tour, taking "several pads suitable for penciling" to make notes, which he later published as *Round the World*, his first book. While traveling, he read the works of Confucius, Buddha, "the sacred books of the Hindoos," and the teachings of Zoroaster: *The result of my journey was to bring a certain mental peace. Where there had been chaos there was now order. My mind was at rest. I had a philosophy at last. The words … "The Kingdom of Heaven is within you" had a new meaning for me. Not in the past or in the future, but now and here is Heaven within us.*

Four years after his return, Carnegie published his second book, *An American Four-in-Hand*, from notes he made while on a coach trip through England and Scotland. Then in 1886 his mother and brother died within a few days of each other, whereupon he wrote, "I was left alone in the world." The next year, in his mid-40s, Carnegie married Louise Whitfield in New York. Soon a daughter was born to them. And in the decade that ensued, Carnegie's business endeavors—and fortune—expanded threefold.

"The one really serious quarrel with our workmen in our whole history," Carnegie disclosed, arose in 1892 while he was away in Scotland. At the height of this Homestead Strike, which pitted disgruntled workmen against their bosses, Carnegie prepared to return to America. But his partners begged him to stay away, complaining that he "was always disposed to yield to the demands of the men, however unreasonable." In truth, he remembered, the bargaining philosophy which he pursued was quite rare: *My idea is that the Company should be known as determined to let the men at any works stop work; that it will confer freely with them and wait patiently until they decide to return to work, never thinking of trying new men—never.*

Because of the ensuing Homestead riots and the massacre of ten picketers by security forces, much of the general public came to believe that Carnegie was unsympathetic to the working man. Ironically, the reverse was true; the industrial mogul had always enjoyed a friendly relationship with his laborers. In fact, once, upon learning that an employee named McLuckie had been forced to flee the country after the Homestead troubles, Carnegie immediately offered to send the destitute man money. McLuckie, upon receipt

of the cash, remarked, "Well, that was damned [good] of Andy, wasn't it?" The comment delighted "Andy." "I would rather risk that verdict of McLuckie's as a passport to Paradise," he quipped, "than all the theological dogmas invented by man." Another worker at the mill told the steel magnate that the Homestead predicament wouldn't have come up in the first place had Carnegie been there. When he confessed that he couldn't have offered a better settlement than his partners, the man replied, "Oh, Mr. Carnegie, it wasn't a question of dollars. The boys would have let you kick 'em, but they wouldn't let that other man stroke their hair."

In 1901 Carnegie elected to follow the advice he himself had given in his most recent book *The Gospel of Wealth*; that is, to cease his "struggle for more wealth." He sold The Carnegie Steel Company to John Pierpont Morgan and began "the infinitely more serious and difficult task of wise distribution." He eventually gave away more than 350 million pre-inflation dollars: four million dollars to a pension fund for his mill workers; a ten-million-dollar grant for the founding of the Carnegie Institution of Washington; and a five-million-dollar donation to create the Hero Fund (a pension for the families of heroes "who perish in the effort to serve or save their fellows"). He also founded libraries in his native Scotland and in America, established a pension fund for university professors, and donated millions of dollars to universities on both sides of the Atlantic.

Denouncing war as "the foulest blot upon our civilization," Carnegie devoted much of his last 20 years to the cause of world peace, providing funds for the building of a Temple of Peace in the Netherlands— "the most holy building in the world because it has the holiest end in view." He also wholeheartedly supported the idea of an International Court to arbitrate disputes between nations.

Carnegie conferred with many of the most famous men of his time: Mark Twain, Matthew Arnold, William Gladstone, Herbert Spencer, and President Benjamin Harrison, with whom Carnegie argued against going to war with Chili. When many speculated that the magnate had been reserved in speaking with the President, Harrison replied, "I didn't see the slightest indication of reserve, I assure you." Carnegie also met the German Kaiser, whom he congratulated in 1912 for ruling for over 25 years without going to war. But Carnegie worried about the Kaiser's "military caste," saying, "Until militarism is subordinated, there can be no World Peace."

The great philanthropist ended his *Autobiography* on a sorrowful note: *As I read this today [1914], what a change! The world convulsed by war as never before! Men slaying each other like wild beasts! I dare not relinquish hope …*

Carnegie died in 1919, having given away the better part of his vast wealth. He spent his life and fortune striving to answer this single, most germane question: "What good am I doing in the world to deserve all my mercies?"

HENRY FORD – *THE WAYWARD CAPITALIST*
by Carol Gelderman, The Dial Press, 1981

*W*hen Henry Ford left his Dearborn, Michigan farm at age sixteen and headed for Detroit, only one out of five Americans lived in cities; when he died in Dearborn at eighty-three, this proportion was exactly reversed. More than any other man, Ford helped bring about this revolution when he introduced industry to the assembly line and put the nation on wheels with his inexpensive Model T. Yet, as Carol Gelderman reveals in *Henry Ford: The Wayward Capitalist*, this pioneer of modern manufacturing despised cities, believing they were a cradle of social disorder.

Born in 1863, the grandson of an Irish immigrant and the son of a farmer, Henry took an early interest in mechanical things. But after he saw a self-propelled steam engine for the first time in 1876, he realized that he "knew only the periphery of the mechanical world which so fascinated him." So, three years later he moved to Detroit to work in a machine shop.

In Detroit, 25-year-old Henry married Clara Bryant, to whom he'd shown sketches of the "horseless carriage" that someday he would build. Clara put her whole heart into Henry's project. Recognizing her faith as an important factor in his success, he referred to her as "the great believer."

In 1893 Ford produced his first working engine from pieces of scrap: *The handwheel of an old lathe acted as flywheel. A piece of discarded pipe became a cylinder…. A piece of fiber with a wire through its center served as a spark plug.* Then on June 4th, 1896, he completed his first vehicle, a "quadricycle," which had no brakes and no reverse gear.

In 1899 Ford lost the financial backing of three Detroit businessmen, who had grown impatient with his insistence on building the "perfect" vehicle. After either antagonizing or frustrating Detroit's wealthiest citizens over the next four years, Ford eventually joined forces with a coal merchant named Alexander Malcomson, who, along with other investors, contributed $100,000 to establish the Ford Motor Company in 1903. In the first year the investors were paid dividends of $98,000 on their initial $100,000 investment.

"I think you are creating a social problem with your car," a young lawyer subsequently told Ford. "No, my friend, you're mistaken," Ford replied. "I'm not creating a social problem at all. I am going to democratize the automobile. When I'm through everybody will be able to afford one … "

True to his word, Ford introduced his Model T as the "motorcar for the great multitude." He then built an enormous assembly plant in Highland Park, near Detroit, where by 1913 he had put together the first moving assembly line, which eventually enabled the plant to turn out a new car every 24 seconds. As demand and production increased, he lowered the price of the Model T from $950 in 1909 to $490 in 1913. "The principle," Ford said, "is to decide on your design, freeze it, and, from then on, spend all your time, effort, and money on making the machinery to produce it, concentrating so completely on production that, as the volume goes up, it is certain to get cheaper per unit produced."

Not only did auto-maker keep lowering prices, but in 1914 he also doubled his employees' pay and shortened their work day from nine to eight hours. His generosity incited an uproar. Although most members of the press praised him and the "new economic era" he had inspired, Ford's fellow industrialists condemned him, protesting that the higher wages and shorter hours would "permanently undermine the peace and contentment of the lower classes [and would] breed revolution." But to Ford, the "mad socialist of Highland Park," the changes made sense: his workers now had more incentive to work diligently and efficiently. Indeed, Ford's profits soon skyrocketed.

While World War I raged, Ford, a staunch pacifist, nevertheless put his factory at the disposal of the U.S. Government to produce cars, boats, tractors and ambulances. After the war Ford went back to making Model T's again, and, at President Woodrow Wilson's behest, tried unsuccessfully to win a seat in the U.S. Senate.

The following year, 1919, Ford bought out his company's minority stockholders for $106 million and gained complete control of the Ford Motor Company: *Never had anyone risen so meteorically; in 1902 Ford had yet to design a car for the market, but seventeen years later he owned a complex of factories worth at least a billion dollars. Henceforth he could act with no restraint upon his massive power.*

That same year Ford sued the *Chicago Tribune* for libel. The newspaper had printed the editorial "Ford Is an Anarchist," attacking his anti-preparedness stance during the early year of World War I. Subjected to a scathing interrogation by the *Tribune*'s lawyer, Ford's ignorance, even in regards to common points of history, was exposed. After the trial the major newspapers again released a bevy of statements belittling the auto-maker. Unfortunately, Ford failed to realize that he had divided America: *It was no coincidence that the urban press damned Ford for his ignorance while provincial papers loved him for his simplicity.*

The mockery and abuse heaped upon him depleted Ford's natural optimism: *… His idealism gave way to cynicism, his faith in others' judgements was undermined, throwing him back on his own instinctive decisions.* Isolating himself from the public, Ford only sought the company of simple men who would not scorn him for his lack of education: *The cruel ridicule of his altruism, he perceived, came always from educated, highly literate city dwellers. Never did any farmer misunderstand Henry Ford…. Ironically, the man who now looked on the city as the source of misanthropy had done more than anyone else to accelerate the rise of congested urban centers.*

Then in 1921, while the country suffered from a recession, Ford had to lay off some 20,000 workers.

Because of his reluctance to deal with administrative duties, his secretary, Ernest G. Liebold, became the second most powerful man in the company. Charles Sorenson, Ford's production chief, also prospered by carrying out "unpleasant assignments," such as overseeing the firings of many employees in 1920 and '21. In addition to Liebold and Sorenson, Harry Bennett—a roughneck with ties to organized crime whom Ford had hired to protect his grandchildren from kidnapping—became increasingly powerful in the company.

The change in Ford's labor policy dismayed Henry's son Edsel, whom the elder Ford had made president of the company in 1918. As time went on, Ford, hiding behind his cadre of eager executives, began to visit the plant less often and became increasingly remote. Although he maintained all along that Edsel was in charge, Ford "refused to relinquish authority." In fact, Edsel "had to run to meet his father as if he were a junior executive." Clearly, Ford—the son of a tough farmer—considered his own son "too soft"; in addition, he resented Edsel's upper class friends.

Harry Bennett, meanwhile, took increasing control of the company: *He bragged that he was closer to Ford than Edsel was, and no one disagreed with him.... When someone wanted something from the boss he went through Bennett, not Edsel.... "Mr. Ford worshiped Edsel," Bennett admitted, "but he insisted that Edsel do everything his way."*

Edsel began urging his father to manufacture a sleeker, more modern automobile. Ford Motors, its outdated "Tin Lizzie" virtually unchanged from 1908 to 1927, had started losing ground on other, up-and-coming car manufacturers, and Ford dealers nationwide had asked for alterations in their product. But Ford's answer was short and sweet: *"Well, gentlemen, so far as I can see the only trouble with the Ford car is that we can't make them fast enough."* What Henry failed to understand was that Americans wanted more than low price.... *They wanted style.*

Finally in 1927, Edsel, with Henry's support, designed a new car called the Model A, which proved wildly popular. To produce the new vehicle, however, the company had to re-tool all its factories, resulting in a tremendous backlog of orders. Ford eventually was able to increase production to a total of 6,400 fully-assembled cars a day, a figure which accounted for one-third of all cars and trucks sold in 1929.

Ford Motors had become "America's first vertically integrated industrial empire." As the company acquired mines, ships and a railroad, Ford controlled every step in the manufacturing process, from extracting the ore from the ground to seeing the finished car roll off the assembly plant. Even while he erected the company's mighty Rouge River, Michigan plant, Ford also collected artifacts of America's rural past, which were later placed in a museum of 18th- and 19th-century rural life. "All the relics have one thing in common," Ford proudly said of his collection, "they are all things used by run-of-the-mill people, not by the elite.... The everyday lives of ordinary folk have been overlooked by historians ..."

Meanwhile, as the country wallowed in the midst of the Great Depression, Ford's mind, will and mouth got him into trouble. Blind to the severity of economic conditions, he optimistically pronounced that now that the people of Detroit had lost their jobs, they could "go back to their farms" where they belonged. A year later, in 1930, he offered this candid observation: "It was a mighty good thing for the nation that the condition which we misnamed prosperity could not last." And later that year he declared that the Depression was a "wholesome thing in general. If we could only realize it, these are the best times we ever had." His off-the-cuff remarks struck his contemporaries as highly insensitive: *Never again would he be the untarnished hero of grass-roots America; his callous statements shocked and bewildered the millions who had always idolized him.*

His assembly-line workers were also quickly disillusioned. Goaded mercilessly by brutal foremen—consisting mostly of Harry Bennett's cronies—hundreds of workers, accused of loafing or of simply talking to other employees, were laid off. Although Edsel complained of Bennett's willingness to use violence and intimidation to break up union-forming activities, Ford continued to let Bennett handle such matters as he thought best.

Ford employees longed for the younger, considerate Henry Ford, the man who hadn't been afraid to address company matters. As Bennett accumulated more and more power, executives loyal to Edsel were summarily dismissed or transferred; Liebold's and Sorenson's teams of executives were also forced out.

Then in 1943, debilitated by the stress of constant feuding, Edsel died. For all intents and purposes, Bennett—under Henry Ford's indifferent eye—now held the keys to the company.

Devastated by his son's death, Ford experienced periods of disorientation and memory loss, and became increasingly dependent on his wife Clara. Bennett quickly began purging the company of Edsel's supporters, replacing them with men who "knew nothing about production or business." Furthermore, many of Bennett's top people were ex-convicts, "ex-pugs and thugs," who terrorized company employees.

Over time, Clara, backed by Edsel's widow, convinced Henry to name Edsel's son, Henry II, president of Ford Motors. Seizing the reigns of the long-neglected firm, Henry II immediately fired Bennett and his henchmen. As the younger Ford reorganized the corporation from top to bottom, employee morale soared. "I guess young Henry knows what he's doing," his proud grandfather said months before his condition entirely deteriorated.

After Ford's death on April 7, 1947, one Detroit newspaper eulogized: *No other man ever so changed the face of the world in his lifetime as did Henry Ford.... Not for the few but for the millions ... he opened new vistas of space ... [placed] in the reach of the greatest number of people a useful product which would lift the whole level of living.... Ford established a new age—it might also be said a new civilization ...*

HANG TIME – *DAYS AND DREAMS WITH JORDAN*
by Bob Greene, Doubleday Publishers, 1992

Bob Greene published his insightful book about Michael Jordan prior to Michael Jordan's retirement from basketball in 1993. Michael allowed Greene to travel with him during two world-championship seasons, and to share in his dreams.

Greene writes: *We had been talking about that word—that word "dream"—and how often people seemed to use it when referring to him.* Interestingly, Greene adds, Michael seldom dreams, and when he does it's rarely about sports. When he does dream about sports, however, it's about baseball—and being a pitcher.

Bob Greene met Michael Jordan quite by accident. At the time Greene was a newspaper journalist who often wrote about child abuse. One case he reported involved an eight-year-old boy named Cornelius McGee who had been systematically abused by his mother—abuse that had been so brutal and unthinkable that Cornelius's little brother Lattie had died at his mother's hands. Cornelius, Greene learned, had a passion for basketball, and when the Chicago Bulls' management heard about the boy they invited him to a game. Greene recalls that when he and Cornelius entered the arena, the boy was too overwhelmed; he just stared in awe. As Greene led him downstairs, "a door opened and a man came out. Cornelius looked up, and his eyes filled with … total disbelief." He tried to speak but no words would come out.

"Hi, Cornelius," the man said. "I'm Michael Jordan." Michael knelt down, spoke quietly … then stood and said, "Are you going to cheer for us?... We're going to need it."

According to Greene, Michael often makes special efforts for children. Once, Greene reports, a little boy in a wheelchair was sitting outside the stadium after a game. As Jordan hurried to his car, he noticed the boy: *[He] had every excuse not to notice; the boy [couldn't even] motion to him. But he did notice. Something about Jordan—maybe it was the peripheral vision that serves him so well on the court, or … compassionate radar … he walked over to the boy and got down on the ground beside him and spoke…. The boy's father had a camera, he tried to snap a picture. The camera didn't work. Jordan noticed … he stayed beside the boy until the father was able to make the shot.*

In the months that followed, Greene was frequently impressed by Jordan's heartfelt acts of generosity and affection. He seemed always to have time for people, especially those with handicaps. Greene learned many other interesting facts about Jordan as well. For instance:

Jordan had once been cut from his high school team. "I went through the day numb," he recalls. "I had to wait until after school to go home…. I hurried to my house and I closed the door of my room and I cried so hard. It was all I wanted—to play on the team." Writes Greene: *There can't be many professional athletes in any sport who were cut from their high school teams.*

Jordan had set himself apart from most professional athletes by arriving early for every game, at a time when only the vendors, ushers and a few police officers are in the stadium. Then, all alone, Greene noted, he would embark on his routine—shot after shot. *Jordan would stand near the out-of-bounds line … his back toward the basket. The ball boy … would fire him the pass. Jordan … would wheel and jump … and shoot.* Then he would repeat the process, over and over.

Jordan never appeared undressed in the locker room. "It's not that I disapprove of women in the locker rooms," he insisted. "My feelings about it are the same for men as for women. Out of respect for myself, and for other people, I could not appear undressed in front of them." In fact, Michael normally would appear for post-game interviews wearing a suit and tie.

Greene took immediate note of the impact Jordan had on the game as well as his team's success: *In the year before Jordan arrived in town, there had not been a single sellout. Some nights there had been scarcely three thousand souls rattling around the cavernous structure.* Upon Jordan's arrival, the Bulls sold out nearly every game, and tickets were nearly impossible to buy for the team's road games.

If any of Michael's family attended a game, he had to know where they were sitting so he could look up and see them to know that they were safe. Otherwise, he couldn't concentrate on the game.

Michael, undisputedly one of the world's greatest athletes, can't swim. When he's at a party where there's a pool, he stands far away from it. "I'll look to see where the deep end is," he grins, a little embarrassed, "Even when I'm … near the shallow end I won't stand very close … "

Jordan once invited four impoverished boys who were standing outside the stadium to see a game. Since, after every home game he made it a practice to stop at a nearby street corner to talk with the boys. A garrulous multi-millionaire lingering in a rough neighborhood late at night to check up on how some boys are doing in school clearly isn't standard procedure.

Michael Jordan is a hero and an inspiration to millions of basketball fans. Who are *his* heroes? "My heroes are and were my parents…. I can't see having anyone else as my heroes…. It wasn't that the rest of the world would … think they were heroic…. But they were the adults that I saw constantly, and I admired what I saw."

Jordan never paid attention during pre-game meetings: "I never follow along. I'm never paying attention…. My whole life, I never did…. I'm not listening." Why? "I know what to do."

Jordan didn't seem to feel pressure the way most people do. Leading his team to championships, defending his NBA scoring title … knowing every fan expected him to play like Michael Jordan every night might seem stressful to some, but Michael claimed it wasn't for him: "The basketball court, during a game, is the most peaceful place I can imagine…. I'm really by myself out there … the rules say that no one can talk to me or walk up to me when I'm playing…. [It's] one of the few times in my life, I feel like I'm untouchable. I'm not untouchable anywhere else."

On June 20, 1984, the NBA held its annual draft of college players. The Houston Rockets chose Akeem Olajuwon with the first pick. The second player selected was Sam Bowie, taken by the Portland Trail Blazers. The team with the third pick … the Chicago Bulls … selected Michael Jordan of the University of North Carolina. The third pick! How would the sports pages have changed if Portland or Houston had picked Michael instead?

In terms of what his physical talent, his work ethic, and his mental preparation have contributed to his unparalleled success, Michael was typically self-deprecating. "So much of it was timing, so much of it was just good luck…." he claimed, adding, "I'm serious. Everyone tries to figure out why all of this has happened to me, and there are all these theories, and no one is willing to consider how much of it was just luck…. I'm telling you luck has played more of a role than anyone understands."

Traveling with Michael, the journalist recalls: *All season long my companions at the press table had been telling me that when the playoffs started, it would feel as if something brand new was beginning. "You'll feel it as soon as you walk into the building."* And, confirms Greene, they were right. Now security was tighter: *no one without a ticket or a playoff credential slipped by…. [The Bulls], for their part, were wearing black basketball shoes rather than their regular white ones—a playoff tradition*, Greene learned. *The most striking difference … was not the excitement of the games, but the fact that for the first time … the faces of the opponents were the same night after night.* The arena itself became frenzied, "almost claustrophobic." Because the opposing team was now a regular fixture, the fans' "hatred" for various players surfaced. Players like Isaiah Thomas, Dennis Rodman, and especially Bill Laimbeer had insults hurled at them constantly.

Laimbeer, as it turned out, could be quite disagreeable. At one of the 1991 playoff games against Detroit, Greene sat next to Consuelo Hill, who had sung the national anthem at one of the regular games against the Pistons and had been invited back for the playoff game. As Greene spoke with her, she seemed rather disheartened. Then she said, "After the game in January, I went up to Bill

Laimbeer to ask for his autograph, [telling him that she had sung the national anthem]. "He just looked at me and said, 'I don't care if you sang a whole concert.'"

Later, as the playoff game neared its end, it became obvious that the Bulls would win and Phil Jackson removed his starters. As they relaxed on the bench, Jordan gazed over in our direction "until he caught Consuelo Hill's eye … [and said], 'I just wanted to tell you that I thought you did a very good job on the anthem.'" The journalist observes: *Whatever would happen in the NBA Finals would happen. The real championships in life are not won on a basketball court.*

The Bulls went on to defeat Detroit and face Los Angeles in the finals—a best-of-seven-game event that brought the celebrities out of the woodwork. Jack Nicholson, Elizabeth Taylor, Arnold Schwarzenegger, even Princess Diana expressed interest in tickets—and a desire to meet Jordan.

In game five, with the Bulls up three games to one, the Lakers had made a strong run in the fourth quarter to take the lead. During a time out, Greene borrowed some binoculars: *I looked through the glasses at the Bulls' bench. "Look at that…. He's not going to let them lose." Later I would learn that Jordan's father had said the same thing … he had looked at the bench during that time out, and he realized that there was no way his son was going to leave the Forum a loser tonight. Jordan … was as intensely focused as any person I could ever imagine seeing…. [And when] the final buzzer sounded: Bulls 108, Lakers 101.*

Whenever Jordan had talked … about a championship, the words seemed uncharacteristically dry and cold; [there was] something missing…. Now on a portable [TV] … there was Jordan … sitting in front of his cubicle, embracing the world championship trophy, weeping uncontrollably…. Of course he had never been able to put into words what [this] would mean. There are only two reasons for us not being able to talk about something: When it means nothing to us. And when it means everything.

As the 1991-92 season arrived, Greene could see an undeniable media "backlash" against Jordan. Later that year Jordan's gambling habits were exposed when a nightclub owner was found shot to death. In his briefcase were photocopies of three checks totaling $108,000, all signed by Michael.

The season, however, went well for Chicago. The Bulls stormed through the playoffs to meet Portland in the finals. In just six games the Bulls defeated the Blazers to repeat as world champions.

Greene writes of Jordan on that memorable night: *The last time I saw him … he was standing on top of the scorer's table … he had done his job, and he was free…. He didn't dream about basketball. That's what he had told me all those months ago. But I do. I didn't used to, but now I do. The dreams are vivid and bright … and they will stay with me forever.*

BILLIE JEAN
by Billie Jean King with Frank Deford, The Viking Press, 1982

I have always disliked the labels that were arbitrarily placed on me, whether in feminist, heroic, or less flattering terms. This book may serve to remove some of those misconceptions. At times I may be tough and at other times extremely sensitive. I'm an individual.

In this candid autobiography Billie Jean King reflects upon her personal life and upon her role as a trailblazer. After growing up in a working-class family, she broke into the world of country-club tennis and eventually became a popular champion to both sexes in a sport previously dominated by men. Though her career spanned two decades and included an amazing 20 "Grand Slam" titles (championships in tennis's "big four" tournaments: Wimbledon, and the U.S., Australian, and French Opens), this book deals more with her personal musings on the game, on her role in changing the game, on her rivalries, and on her personality.

King also offers her own version of her well-publicized lesbian affair with Marilyn Barnett. Once she feared that she would always be labeled by the affair, regardless of her other accomplishments. Now she uses the episode as a forum to attack all labels placed on her and on other people.

Growing Up Supplemental

As a child Billie Jean King's first ambition was to be a missionary. However, she soon discovered that she was athletically inclined, but realized that there was no future for girls in team sports. Golf, to her, was too slow; she might drown in swimming. So she opted to play tennis, even though her working-class family did not have enough money to pay for a racket or a tennis dress.

Even now Billie Jean mourns that there are few underprivileged children who participate in tennis. She wants tennis to become a game that everyone plays. To this end, she visits and sponsors tennis clinics in low-income neighborhoods.

Feeling out of place with the country-club set didn't stop Billie Jean; in fact, she liked being different from everybody else. *I also like being successful. I somehow always knew that I would succeed. I had a great sense of destiny from the time I was very young. I remember one incident so vividly. When I was only about five or six years old, I was standing with my mother in the kitchen.... I told her flat out that when I grew up I was going to be the best at something. She just smiled and kept peeling potatoes or doing whatever it was she was doing. She said, "Yes, dear; yes, of course, dear," as if I had simply said that I* was going to my room or ... whatever. So, I always felt different that way.

Billie Jean suffered from bad knees, bad eyes, and breathing difficulties. But her will to succeed at tennis carried her over all these hurdles, and she was not surprised when she began to excel.

As much as she always loved the game, Billie Jean was prepared to give it up when she married Larry King, to "have babies—lots of them, as far as I was concerned." But Larry wanted her to continue. He also supported her when businessman Bob Mitchell offered to send her to Australia to train with world-renowned coach Mervyn Rose. Later, King was to recall: *I always wanted to be special, to be the best in one thing. I've always thought it would be easier for me just to be comfortable ... but I really had no choice. I was driven.*

Always on the Cusp

That drive also led Billie Jean to accept the challenge to play a match against Bobby Riggs, a self-proclaimed male chauvinist. Their showdown in Houston's Astrodome created a media frenzy, drawing over 30,000 enthusiastic fans and a television audience of 40 million. In retrospect, King is convinced that the only reason she beat Riggs was that she despised what he stood for: not only the myth of male superiority, but also the dominance of men's tennis over women's tennis in terms of money and popularity. She admits that she was shaking until the crossover after the first game, when she glanced at Bobby and saw that he was scared, too. Suddenly all her doubts left her; all she feared was the unknown, and Bobby was now a familiar entity. After that, Billie Jean won the match quite handily. Only one thing bothered her: that everyone else at the match, including Bobby, seemed to have more fun than she did.

But even though King didn't enjoy herself much, she quickly perceived how saliently her victory had enhanced her reputation. Interestingly, it gave her a certain credibility that even her victories at Wimbledon and Forest Hills had not. Even more importantly, she saw how much her victory over Riggs meant to others. Women still tell her that their husbands had to do the dishes for a week because she won that classic "battle of the sexes."

"This Would Make a Great Book"

Billie Jean is often disturbed by the inordinate amount of attention paid to female athletes' personal lives. She laments that, more often than not, they are stereotyped as lesbians. *I have often been asked whether I am a woman or an athlete. The question is absurd. Men are not asked that. I am an athlete, I am a woman.*

This conflict made it all the more painful for King to go public with the fact that, while she was married, she had an affair with a woman. The woman was hairdresser Marilyn Barnett, who King had met in 1972; Billie Jean had never lived as a lesbian before that time. When Marilyn later threatened to sue Billie Jean for part of the fortune she had accumulated, King decided to hold a press conference rather than let Marilyn break the story. She knew that press attention would create a circus-type spectacle, for she was already a controversial celebrity, characterized as tough, loud, brash and insensitive.

What bothered her most about the publicity was that she would be judged on her perceived faults and failures rather than on her achievements and triumphs. The scandal completely ignored Billie Jean as a person and focused on labels. *It is important to keep me in perspective, and to remember the massive changes that I was experiencing at this time. My whole world was in flux.* She also feared that public disclosure of the affair would reflect unfavorably upon women's tennis in general.

Starting with Chris and Jimmy
Billie Jean complains that "players today have no sense of history. They don't feel a part of anything grand or dear or lasting. As a matter of fact, most of them pretty much accept it that tennis began with Chris Evert on the women's side and Jimmy Connors on the men's."

Billie Jean believes that Connors is the one American player who is almost universally admired by female professional tennis players. She contends that although he can be vulgar and even foolish on the court, he gives so much of himself that women can't help but love him.

Evert's participation in the sport was also important, "not only for women's tennis, but for me personally because it gave the press a duel to play up." Although King and Evert were portrayed as opposites by the press, Billie Jean does not feel they are so very different. Unfortunately, the arrival of the mild-mannered Evert on the tennis scene stereotyped King in an even more unfavorable light. When she finally decided to hire Pat Kingsley as her public relations agent, Pat turned down the account at first: she did not want to handle a "tough bitch."

Billie Jean does not identify with the image the media has created for her. In slugging it out with Evert on the tennis court, the press inevitably—and inaccurately, she claims—characterized the matches as contests pitting "monster" against "maiden." In fact, Billie Jean acknowledges nothing but great fondness and admiration for Evert.

Playing for the Love of It
Billie Jean admits that she is jealous of the money that team players make. However, she more deeply regrets the lack of recognition given to tennis players, when compared to that of other athletes. Entire towns unite to give their football and baseball teams parades or "days" in their honor. In contrast, when Billie Jean won Wimbledon three years in a row, few outside of the tennis community even knew about it.

But just as in other sports, the tennis community does spoil its stars. *It's really impossible for athletes to grow up. As long as you're playing, no one will let you. On the one hand, you're a child, still playing a game. And everybody around you acts like a kid, too. But on the other hand, you're a superhuman hero that everyone dreams of being. No wonder we have such a hard time understanding who we are. But either way, you see, the usual response is to spoil the athlete—child or god.*

She also explains that being a star can often be very annoying: *You can't ever win. Surely only a selfish bitch would refuse to donate one of her extra rackets to a worthwhile cause. Only a hundred worthwhile causes a year asking for a racket apiece ... plus autographed photos, clothes, shoes, balls.... "Wouldja, couldja, canya Billie Jean? Just this one time ... " The aggravation never stops.* The most important part of being a champion, she concludes, is playing the game.

In spite of the negative aspects of her fame, King believes that tennis has become the sport for today's woman, and that sports will become a vehicle for upward mobility among girls in the same way as it has always been for boys. *In fact, I would suggest that in tennis (and possibly other sports as well) women are every bit as tough as competitors as the men. If not more so.... Making women's sports acceptable and making women's tennis into a legitimate big-league game was a crusade for me, and I threw my whole self into it in ways that exhausted me emotionally and physically.*

King hasn't allowed the trials of that crusade to discourage her from carrying the banner a few more miles. Despite the trespasses into her personal life, she plans to continue her quest to vanquish labels. *So I'm not going to just wash away. I promise you that. I'm going to keep on trying. You know, I've never really cared what anybody did so long as they tried at it. I just plain like people who try. It doesn't matter what, so long as they get out there and work their bahoolas off.*

On September 30, 1975, heavyweight boxing champ Muhammad Ali retained his World Heavyweight Title after defeating the formidable "Smokin' Joe" Frazier. He recalls that victorious moment: *The screams are so loud they sound far away. Then the crowd, pushing, shoving, reporters shouting. They want something from me. Something more. Some words or comment. But I'm too tired. Besides, I already told them. And I already told you. Didn't you hear me? I said I was The Greatest.*

Ali's boxing career was characterized by a passion to win—a passion that gave him a tactical advantage over his rivals. In the ring he didn't seem to care about ego, money or titles as much as beating his ring-mate. To him it was a mental game, a game he played with beauty and finesse, but with the zeal of a child. He fought for himself, for his home town, for his family and for the black race, battling not only his opponents, but the widespread prejudice of the time. He fought for Islam, for he is also a religious man as well as a political one. But most of all, he just loved to fight: broken jaws, torn muscles, split-open lips and cracked skulls were all a part of his mission, as he perceived it—a mission to bring power and recognition to black people everywhere.

The Making of a Champion

In 1959 the boxer was still using the name he was born with, Cassius Clay. That year he won his first major title, the Chicago Golden Gloves Championship. Then in 1964, after deciding that his name would no longer reflect his heritage as the descendent of slaves, he began calling himself "Muhammad Ali." In doing so, he wished to bring honor to the religion he had chosen: Islam. Three years later, citing both religious and political conviction, Ali refused induction into the Army and received a five-year jail sentence. Critics warned that his decision—not to mention a five-year layoff—would ruin his career. Instead, Ali's face has become the most widely recognized in the world.

Ali proved that his commitment to his religion was typical of his loyalty to his family and to his values. He is a complex man who was willing to forego his World Championship bout with Sonny Liston rather than renounce his ties with controversial Black Muslims. Despite his willingness to fight anyone, anytime, anywhere, he refused to fight the Viet Cong, saying he had nothing against them.

Ali may have displayed the most intense bravado the world has ever seen. His constant litany of self-praise and self-promotion outside the ring seemed decidedly un-American to some. He often made up poems that denigrated his opponents and proclaimed his own greatness.

Originally, the public scoffed at Ali's incessant claims to be "the greatest fighter that ever lived," but they soon fell in love with the man who could "float like a butterfly and sting like a bee!" Though the consummate showman, he came to command supreme respect from the most hard-nosed, celebrated fighters of his time.

"Invite Muhammad to fight, and your country will share in the world spotlight," was the advance campaign that attracted bids to host bouts from various national governments, including Zaire, Malaysia, the Philippines, Egypt, Saudi Arabia, Iran, Haiti, Ireland, Switzerland, Japan, Indonesia and Canada.

Two professional bouts especially stand out in the career of this champion. In 1973 Ali lost a devastatingly brutal 12-round split decision to Ken Norton in San Diego. In the other, he regained his World Heavyweight Title from George Foreman in a towering victory.

NORTON VS. ALI … Shorty Is Watching

Before the bell rings, [my manager] Bundini whispers in my ear, "Shorty is in the living room, watching. Shorty is sitting down, crossing His legs and watching you. Just remember that." Shorty is Bundini's name for God. And during the whole time I'm struggling to take Norton out before another blow crushes into my jaw, Bundini is screaming, "Shorty's watching!"

… The stadium explodes [when the decision is announced]. Wild shouts and screams come down from the bleachers. Some boo the decision, but the screams and cries of "NORTON!" "NORTON!" drown them out…. Those voices out there are not just a "hometown reaction." It's the reaction of White America …

Why did I lose? I think back to the second round when Norton got in through my guard and crashed a left up against my jaw. I know exactly when the blow came. I felt a snap and a sudden gush of blood in my throat …

"If it's broke," Bundini is saying, "we've got to stop the fight." But he knows I won't stop. There are thirteen more rounds to go, and I can win.

After the loss the former champion returned to Louisville to see if he would still be accepted. Until then, he had always returned home the conqueror: two Golden Gloves Championships, some AAU titles, an Olympic Gold Medal, the World Heavyweight Title, and, after his exile from boxing, as The Undefeated. This time he found the hometown fans loved him as much as ever.

FOREMAN VS. ALI … The Half-Dream Room

After the Norton defeat Ali was determined to regain the title. He hoped that George Foreman, then World Champion, would give him a shot and accept his challenge. A ten-million-dollar deal was signed for the Ali-Foreman matchup in Zaire on October 30, 1974.

Ali was ready to work his rope-a-dope move (a tactic in which he leans back against the ropes to rest, fends off blows with his arms and lets his foe punch himself out) and his "Ali Shuffle" (a quick, smooth shuffling of his feet followed by a thunderous hook). For Ali, the fight was more than just a chance to regain a title: it was the embodiment of his personal calling. *George is The Champion, and the world listens to The Champion. There are things I want to say, things I want the world to hear. I want to be in a position to fight for my people. Whatever I have to do tonight, George will not leave Africa The Champion.*

… CLANG! ROUND TWO … I move to the center, jab and dance and jab. But I know now that my danger is not in the corners or on the ropes, but in dancing six steps to George's three…. It won't be George who'll be exhausted by round nine. It'll be me…. I decide not to wait until I'm tired to play the ropes, but to take the corners while I'm fresh and still strong, to gamble on the ropes all the way …

A crowbar in George's right hand crashes through my guard into my head, knocks me into the room … the room I had planned to take George into, the half-dream room. My head vibrates like a tuning fork. Neon lights flash on and off.

CLANG! ROUND THREE … George's "murder" round. But if he expects me to be quiet on the day I'm supposed to die, he's mistaken…. He throws his heaviest bomb, it curls around my head and we clinch so tight I feel his heart pounding. I bite his ear. "Is that the best you can do sucker? Is that all you got Chump? You ain't got no punch! You in big trouble, boy!"

When the round ends, my head is humming. But the round of my execution is over, and all I will do now is plot the time when my turn comes

The Will to Win

The outcome of the Foreman fight ultimately turned on which man was to display the greater will to win. As the 7th round drew to a close, Ali still believed that he had the bigger heart:

The bell rings and I feel pain all over me…. How long can I stand up under this barrage? I've got to go for the kill before he gets his second wind.

CLANG! ROUND EIGHT … George looks like King Kong when he comes at you…. Only a

man who knows what it is to be defeated can reach down to the bottom of his soul and come up with the extra ounce of power it takes to win when the match is even. I know George wants to keep The Champions Crown, but is he willing to pay the price? Would he lay out his life?

It's time to go all out. Toe to toe. George pours out a long left, and I cross my right over it. Now I've got to lay it all down on the line. If the price of winning is to be a broken jaw, a smashed nose, a cracked skull, a disfigured face, you pay it if you want to be King of the Heavyweights. If you want to wear the crown, you can play it careful only until you meet a man who will die before he lets you win. Then you have to lay it all on the line or back down and be damned forever.

The crowd eggs me on: "ALI! ALI! BOMAYE!" … I shoot a straight right to his jaw with all the snap and power that's in me. I strike him almost flush on the chin, and he stands still …

I'm ready to follow through with combinations, but I see he's slowly falling, a dazed look in his eyes. I know he's entering the room of the half-dream for the first time in his life. George is down, his eyes glazed. He's listening to the tuning forks humming in his head, bats blowing saxophones, alligators whistling, neon signs blinking.

The referee begins the count. George will later protest that he was the victim of a short count, and I can understand why. In the half-dream room time seems to stretch out slow, like rubber, and unless you've been there before, you'll never know how fast it goes by.

I watch every lift of the referee's arm. I remember thinking of Frazier. He would never lose the crown lying on the floor. No referee could count over his body as long as he had blood in it.

"Six … seven … eight … " George is turning over slowly.

"Nine … ten!" George is on his feet, but it's over. The referee raises my hand in victory.

And the stadium explodes! People break past the paratroopers and climb over the press tables, climb into the ring … and the whole world is screaming, ALI! ALI! ALI! ALI!.

A reporter claws his way through the crowd and yells at me, "How did you do it…. What you think of George now?" I shake my head. I don't want to tell him what George has taught me. That too many victories weaken you. That the defeated can rise up stronger than the victor.

But I take nothing away from George. He can still beat any man in the world.

Except me.

Postscript: Muhammad Ali truly paid the price. In his case, "the price" proved to be a premature bout with Alzheimer's.

JACKIE ROBINSON: A LIFE REMEMBERED
by Maury Allen, Franklin Watts Publishers, 1987

In 1947 Jackie Robinson—talented athlete, bona fide family man, and proud black-rights advocate—made history when he broke baseball's color barrier. In his time he was also unquestionably the most exciting player in the major leagues.

In *Jackie Robinson: A Life Remembered*, Maury Allen compiles comments made by Robinson's teammates, opposing players, and family members to draw a revealing profile of this intensely competitive, courageous, and multifaceted man.

Robinson grew up in Pasadena, California, a predominantly white, middle-class community. After graduating from high school, the hyperactive young athlete attended Pasadena Junior College, then UCLA, starring at both institutions in football, baseball, basketball and track. While at UCLA he met his wife, Rachel Isum. She remembers how he immediately stood out in her mind, more for his character than for his athletic skills: "Jack was never ashamed of being black. In fact, he did something few blacks ever did. He always wore a white shirt. It showed off his dark skin."

After serving a stint in the Army, Jackie signed a contract with the Kansas City Monarchs of the Negro Leagues—the only place a black athlete could go to play professional baseball in 1945. Fatefully, that same year Branch Rickey, the operating head of the National League's Brooklyn Dodgers, told a few close associates that he'd decided to sign a black player for his team.

Rickey sent scouts out to look over the Negro Leagues and see what they had to offer. One of these Dodgers scouts, Clyde Sukeforth, recalls that they were told to look for someone with more than just playing ability: "[Rickey] wanted a player who could turn the other cheek and fight back by exceptional play ... keep his mouth shut, and [help] Brooklyn win ... "

Rickey quickly became interested in Robinson. "There was something about the fellow that impressed me as his being somebody special," Sukeforth recalls. "Determination was written all over his face. This wasn't a young man who would be pushed around. It wasn't hard to tell he was a highly intelligent man."

Robinson played out the 1946 season with the Dodgers' top farm club, the Montreal Royals, leading the league in batting and winning the Royals their pennant. Though he was a fan favorite in Montreal, Jackie had to endure the segregation laws of the American South during spring training, staying in a different hotel from his teammates.

Then, in 1947, came a pivotal point in baseball history: Robinson moved up to the majors. A few of his fellow Dodgers, mostly Southerners, strongly opposed playing alongside a black man; one even went so far as to circulate an anti-Robinson petition. In contrast, other Dodger players, especially team captain Pee Wee Reese, went out of their way to make Robinson feel welcome.

In any case, Jackie's hitting and base-stealing abilities quickly convinced the whole team of his value. "Salaries weren't all that big in those days, and I wasn't going to make a big fuss over what color a player was if he was helping me win," remarked an appreciative teammate.

In those days there were few blacks living in the middle-class Brooklyn neighborhoods of most Dodger fans; but stadium-goers flocked to Ebbets Field to see him play: *Into [our] narrow, traditional, segregated world ... came the black face of Jackie Robinson. For many of us in 1947, it was the first black person we recognized by name ...*

And the fans were not disappointed. Robinson was an electric player on the ball diamond, combining an intense will to win with tremendous natural ability. *He never stood still at third [base].... He bounced around. ... He made full runs toward home, just stopping at some perfect time so he could return without being caught.* "When he got caught in a rundown," remembers former catcher Joe Garagiola, "he'd have everybody in the park involved, including the vendors."

Still, the racial constraints of the time took their toll. "Those early days were awfully tough on Jackie," reflects one teammate. "I remember times on the train when nobody would sit with him or talk with him. Pee Wee always seemed to be the first to break the tension ... " Robinson received anonymous death threats; in Atlanta, the Ku Klux Klan picketed his hotel. "He was staying in those rat traps in the colored section while we were out in those fancy hotels, and that galled him.... You could see him seething when the guys complained how slow the room service was or how the porters lost a bag.... He would just take out that anger on the opposition."

Wherever he went loudmouths, in an effort to distract him, shouted racial insults from the stands. It wasn't easy for Robinson to ignore these slurs. As another teammate recalls, he "was a combative person by nature and that restraint went against his personality. He had to hold a lot in, and it angered him terribly. Holding that much anger can really hurt a man, and I think all that name-calling in those years killed him. I really do think that."

In 1947 the Dodgers won the National League pennant, going on to face the Yankees in the World Series—losing in seven games. Jackie didn't hit well in the series, but he did steal three bases. For his amazing rookie season, Robinson was awarded the National League Rookie-of-the-Year award.

More black players soon joined Robinson in the major-league ranks. The Dodgers signed Roy Campanella and Don Newcombe and in the American League, Larry Doby signed with the Cleveland Indians midway through the 1947 season. But Jackie was the forerunner, and he remained the symbolic civil rights "man" of the late 1950s and early 1960s.

Roy Campanella was an entirely different person from Jackie. Everybody loved "Campy," while they either worshiped Robinson or else outright hated him. As Joe Black, another pioneer black player, explains, "He didn't buddy around with everybody. The biggest thing in his life was just playing ball and being with Rachel and the children." Another teammate remembered that "Jackie demanded respect as an athlete, and everything he did on the field seemed aimed in that direction. He felt responsible, as if the whole black race rested on his shoulders."

Campanella discusses their differing styles: "In the early days we couldn't stay in the same hotels with the rest of the club, and when we did we couldn't eat in the dining rooms. Jackie was always annoyed by that. I didn't care that much. But he fought that hard, and one day he just sat down in the dining room, and that was that. He was served and nobody made a fuss over it.... He went after things his way, and I went after them my way."

When the Dodgers played their cross-town rivals the New York Giants, headed by former Dodgers manager Leo "the Lip" Durocher, Robinson and "the Lip" would often engage in vicious verbal battles, baiting each other to take the rivalry a step farther— perhaps into fisticuffs. The two teams had always hated each other, but Durocher and Robinson seemed to carry on an especially impassioned feud. One Dodger player looks fondly back at the spats: "The best times I ever had with Jackie were just listening to Jackie fight with Leo.... Jackie had a real sharp tongue. It was fun playing with him."

But their enmity was never personal, Durocher maintains: "Sure we had our feuds, because he wanted to win and I wanted to win.... I agitated him a little, and he agitated me back."

Still, in 1951, after Bobby Thomson hit the famous home run to win the pennant for the Giants, Robinson approached Durocher after the game and congratulated him. "That was one of the hardest things any man ever had to do, and I really appreciated that," remarked Durocher later. "Jackie Robinson had class. He was some man."

As he had at UCLA and everywhere else he'd played, Robinson gradually assumed a leadership role on the team. In 1949 he won the National League MVP award. That same year the Dodgers went to the World Series again—and they would go on to five more Series during Robinson's playing career. They finally won the Series in 1955, when they beat the New York Yankees.

That season Robinson, who'd entered the major leagues at the ripe-old age of 28, had begun to slow down, losing his fearsome quickness and speed. "Jack couldn't run the way he could earlier, but he was still some competitor," a young up-and-coming player reported. "[He] should have been the first black manager.... When I think of Jackie now, I think of him as a great player and a great man, but also as somebody who was so competitive, so intense. Jackie was like a great fighter getting ready for the heavy-weight championship of the world before every game."

Robinson was a hero and a role model to young black Americans. He constantly sought out ways to use his fame as a tool to influence and inspire black youth. As a boy, future home-run king Hank Aaron was living in Mobile, Alabama, when Robinson paid a visit: "He was dressed in suit and tie and talked to us on the street in front of the drugstore. The kids just gathered around him and listened.... He kept repeating, 'Stay in school, stay in school.' He stressed how important that was, and he said we all couldn't play in the big leagues, but we all could get a better education and make something of ourselves."

When he was traded to the Giants' organization in 1957, Robinson, 38, instead opted to retire from baseball. In ten seasons he had accumulated a batting average of .311 and broken Ty Cobb's base-stealing record. His final career hit had won game six of the 1956 World Series for the Dodgers and had proved to be his last performance in a baseball uniform. "Jack's knees were bothering him a great deal by then," remembers his wife Rachel. "He was also losing interest in baseball.... He wanted to move on to other pursuits. He wanted to get involved in things that were now more important to him than baseball."

Two years after retirement Robinson took a job as personnel director for a restaurant and began writing a column for the New York Post. He spoke out on politics—especially on racial issues—and was involved in the civil-rights movements of the '60s. He also lobbied baseball to start hiring blacks in executive positions. By then there were many black players—in both leagues and on every major-league team—but still no black managers or black executives.

In his first year of eligibility, 1962, Robinson was inducted into the Baseball Hall of Fame. As the '60s moved into the '70s, however, his name and fame faded from the limelight. He worked and raised his family, while still making occasional personal appearances and speaking engagements. When his son, Jackie Robinson, Jr., died in a car accident in 1971, Robinson made a rare appearance on television to express his grief. Viewers were shocked; suffering from diabetes, their old hero now looked weathered and fragile. With his health steadily deteriorating, Robinson's final year was a difficult one.

Upon her husband's death in 1972, Rachel Robinson asked a young minister named Jesse Jackson to render the eulogy. Jackson lauded Robinson as a dynamic, chivalrous man and commended his dramatic pioneering role in securing for blacks the rights they deserved as Americans and as human beings. Then he ended his sermon with these words: "When Jackie took the field, something reminded us of our birthright to be free.... He was the black knight. He was checking the king's bigotry and the queen's indifference. His body, his mind, his mission can not be held down by a grave."

BABE: THE LEGEND COMES TO LIFE
by Robert W. Creamer, Simon and Schuster, 1974

Babe Ruth was the first American superstar, baseball's greatest and most beloved player, bigger in his time than any movie heartthrob or political hero. In *Babe: The Legend Comes to Life*, Robert W. Creamer, who as a boy watched the slugger play in Yankee Stadium, draws on interviews with Ruth's friends, teammates, rival ballplayers and acquaintances to "produce a total biography, one that … would present all the facts and myths … the obvious and subtle things" that made Babe Ruth "a unique figure in the social history of the United States."

George Herman Ruth, born in Baltimore, Maryland, to George and Katherine Ruth, always celebrated February 7th, 1894 as his birthday. His original birth certificate lists a later date, but as Ruth once observed with characteristic bluntness, "What the hell difference does it make?"

With both parents working outside the home, young Ruth habitually avoided school, "roamed the streets" and stole from his parents. *"Looking back on my boyhood,"* he wrote in his autobiography, *"I honestly don't remember being aware of the difference between right and wrong."* As a grown man … that carefree attitude toward moral and social codes remained…. In the words of sportswriter John Drebinger, "He was the most uninhibited human being I have ever known. He just did things."

Ruth's father eventually sent his recalcitrant son to St. Mary's Industrial School for Boys, where he would go on to spend the better part of his developmental years. The boys at St. Mary's attended classes, performed house chores and, as part of their regular exercise regimen, played baseball. Ruth, as a catcher, soon became the school's star.

The prefect of discipline at St. Mary's was Brother Matthias, a giant of a man, six-and-a-half feet tall, whom Ruth later called "The greatest man I've ever known." Matthias started Ruth pitching, and it was as a pitcher that the young man attracted the attention of Jack Dunn, a baseball scout and owner of the minor league Baltimore Orioles, who signed him to a $600 contract for the 1914 season. "You'll make it, George," said Brother Matthias as Ruth walked away forever from St. Mary's.

At spring training in North Carolina, Ruth impressed the professionals with both his pitching and his hitting. In a practice game—his first with other professional ballplayers—he pummeled a towering homer that, as an eyewitness reported, "will live in the memory of all who saw it." It was a taste of things to come.

The youthful and exuberant Ruth amused the older Oriole players, who began calling him "Dunn's Babe," in reference to his boyish behavior. It was with the Orioles that Ruth traveled outside Baltimore for the first time. Everything was new to him—eating in restaurants, traveling by train, staying in hotels, even the hotel elevators. Dunn kept boosting Ruth's salary, eventually to $1800 a season, and for the first time in his life Ruth had spending money in his pocket.

The Orioles quickly rose to first place in their league. But attendance was low and Jack Dunn was losing money. One by one he sold off his players. Babe finally went to Joseph Lannin, owner of the major-league Boston Red Sox.

The Babe played little for the Red Sox in 1914; Sox skipper Bill Carrigan sent him down to the minors for most of the year. But life was not uneventful: it was during this time that Ruth met and married his first wife, Helen. *What a difference a year had made in his life…. Months before he had [been] dirt poor, untraveled, totally unsophisticated. Now, at twenty-one, he was a successful professional athlete…. He was rich…. He was married …*

The next year Ruth became a starting pitcher for the Red Sox. He also hit four home runs, a remarkable feat for a pitcher—although, interestingly, at the time home runs were not routinely celebrated. *But there were signs … that the Ruthian home run was going to change things.* The ease with which Ruth hit his homers—and the length that he hit them—made them unforgettable to baseball fans.

Meanwhile, Lannin had raised Ruth's salary to $3500. Now Babe really took to the nightlife in the big cities where the team played. He was often seen driving down Broadway in New York in a "low-slung convertible, wearing a coonskin coat … " Carrigan later explained, "You have to remember, he had grown up in that Catholic reformatory. When they let him out it was like turning a wild animal out of a cage."

The Red Sox won the pennant and the World Series in 1915, and Ruth was an important part of the team's success. Boston won the series again in 1916 and 1918, seasons in which Babe was rated as the best left-handed pitcher in baseball. But even at this point the controversial ballplayer had a habit of not remembering the names of even those teammates he'd known for years.

Increasingly, it was Ruth's hitting—specifically, his home runs—that fans flocked to the parks to see. He hammered out 11 home runs in 1918, while still a pitcher, and the Red Sox, one of the weakest-hitting teams in baseball, began to play Ruth in the outfield or at first base when he wasn't on the mound.

During the 1919 season the Red Sox moved Ruth permanently to the outfield. That year he set his first home-run mark, smacking 29 "dingers" to break all previous major-league records—at the time seen as the ultimate accomplishment, even for him. But he would eventually more than double that mark.

After the 1919 season, the Red Sox, strapped for cash, sold Ruth to the New York Yankees. "I figure the Red Sox is ruined," one disgusted fan hissed. But Harry Frazee, the new Red Sox owner, claimed the trade would help the team: He was tired of Ruth's all-night partying and his tendency to get into fights with umpires, managers, and coaches. "While Ruth is undoubtedly the greatest hitter the game has ever seen," commented Frazee, "he is likewise one of the most selfish and inconsiderate men ever to put on a baseball uniform."

Ruth was also one of the most eccentric men who ever donned a baseball uniform. Once before a game he offered an onion to a stranger as a cure for the man's cold; during a heat wave, he wore cabbage leaves under his ball cap to keep cool. But without Babe, Frazee's Red Sox suffered through almost a decade in last place, while the Yankees, flaunting the Home-Run King, were on the threshold of arguably the greatest dynasty in baseball history.

In his first two seasons as a Yankee, the swaggering Babe had the two best seasons in batting history. In the process, he launched—besides baseballs—a revolution. *The game changed more between 1917 and 1921 than it did in the next forty years.*

Up until Ruth's time, homers were rare, scores were low, and pitching dominated the game. A batter was expected to protect the plate and "punch out singles." But free-swinging Ruth, unafraid of striking out, broke the game wide open, slamming 54 homers in 1920 and putting 59 balls over the fences in 1921. "I swing big, with everything I've got," he expounded. "I hit big or I miss big. I like to live as big as I can."

Other players soon copied Babe's big swing, and home runs, along with scores, shot up throughout the majors. As fans flocked to the ballparks, the Yankees became the first club to draw more than a million in one season.

New Yorkers especially loved this larger-than-life character; the city's Italian immigrant population even christened him "Bambino." *And Ruth was made for New York.* Teammate Lee Allen remembered him as "a large man in a camel's hair coat and camel's hair cap, standing in front of a hotel, his broad nostrils sniffing at. the promise of the night." On the road Babe's roommate, Ping Bodie, only saw him on the field, and ended up carrying Ruth's luggage on and off the train. "I don't room with him," Bodie once told a reporter, "I room with his suitcase."

Ruth's play was sub-par in 1922, brilliant in '23 and '24, and again turned sour—at least for his standards—in 1925. That season, after going to three straight World Series, the Yankees fell to 7th place. Babe's attitude was no help. His open contempt for Yankee manager Miller Huggins, whom he called "The Flea," infected other players, and Huggins lost control of the team.

At one point in the season the overweight Bambino had to be transported to the hospital with an intestinal abscess—dubbed by reporters as "the bellyache heard round the world." By then most writers prophesied that he would not return to his previous dominance. But the Babe had some of his greatest seasons ahead of him. *From the ashes of 1925, Babe Ruth rose like a rocket. [In the next five years] he put on the finest display of hitting that baseball has ever seen ... 50 home runs a year [and] more than 400 yet to come ...*

Ruth's team mirrored its slugger's success, winning three straight pennants. The '27 Yankees, considered by many to be the greatest baseball squad of all time, won 110 games. Ruth hit 60 homers that year, breaking his old record, and Lou Gehrig, his teammate, hit a whopping 47. Hitting three homers in the '28 series was the apex of Ruth's career, *the happiest moment of three years of great accomplishment and relative serenity. His life would never be as uncomplicated again ...*

In 1929 Babe's wife Helen perished in a fire. Although they had been separated for three years, her death saddened him. But then Ruth met the love of his life: a widow named Claire Hodgson, whom he soon married. In 1931 Babe signed a two-year contract with the Yankees for an annual salary of $80,000. When someone mentioned that he was by far the highest-paid player in baseball, raking in even more earnings than President Herbert Hoover, the story has it that he replied, "Why not? I had a better year than he did."

In 1932 the "Sultan of Swat" began slowing down. *More and more he left the game in the late innings and let young Sammy Byrd or Myril Hoag finish up for him. Still, the Yankees went on to another World Series— Babe's tenth.*

It was in the third game of the 1932 series that Ruth hit the famous "Called-Shot" homer. Jeered by the opposing team and their fans, Babe, according to legend, pointed to the spot deep in the center-field bleachers where he would send the ball. He challenged the Cubs before 50,000 people—and went out and hit the home run.

In spite of his diminishing skills, Ruth continued to play, partly because he had it in the back of his mind to manage the Yankees, or perhaps another club. But none of the major league owners would hire him. They saw him as a selfish, undisciplined player who lacked the smarts to manage a team. "Could he have managed?" Creamer asks. *Of course.... He was baseball smart, he was sure of himself, he was held in awe by his fellow players and he was undeniably good copy. He may not have been a success ... but he should have been given the chance.*

Babe finally retired. During his last years he played a fierce game of golf and traveled all over the world. Then in 1948 he returned to Yankee Stadium for the park's 25th anniversary. Thin, frail and wasted from the cancer that would soon kill him, he donned his uniform and cap for the last time. One by one, his '23 Yankees teammates were introduced and walked out to applause from the stands. Then came Ruth's name: *He got to his feet ... and took a bat to use as a cane.... His name rang out over the public address system, the roar of the crowd began and, as W.C. Heinz wrote, "He walked out into the cauldron of sound he must have known better than any other man."*

Eight weeks later, on August 16, 1948, he died.

JIM THORPE: THE WORLD'S GREATEST ATHLETE
by Robert W. Wheeler, University of Oklahoma Press, 1978

(published in 1975 under the title Pathway to Glory)

At the 1912 Olympic Games in Stockholm, the King of Sweden proclaimed Native American Jim Thorpe as "the greatest athlete in the world." One year later Thorpe was forced to give up his Olympic gold medals in a scandal that changed the course of his life. With this warmly appreciative biography, Robert Wheeler convincingly pleads for Thorpe's exoneration, and for his reinstatement, so many years later, as "a man of unbounded good nature combined with unlimited courage and determination ..."

Born in 1888 on the Oklahoma prairie into the Sac and Fox tribes, the future athlete was named *Wa-tho-huck*, or "Bright Path" by his mother, Charlotte View. But he soon became known simply as Jim. He and his twin brother Charlie enjoyed an active childhood. Said Jim: "Our lives were lived in the open, winter and summer. We were never in the house when we could be out of it.... I was always of a restless disposition and never was content unless I was trying my skill in some game against my fellow playmates ..."

Jim's father Hiram P. Thorpe was in his own right a revered wrestler and track star. Not only did he teach his sons how to strengthen their bodies, he also counseled them to compete fairly. As one of Jim's childhood friends notes: "He made our Indian people known by his good sportsmanship ..."

Jim's childhood, however, was marred by tragedy. First his brother Charlie died of pneumonia when the boys were eight; then several years later, while attending a military school for Indian youth, Jim learned that his father had been injured in a hunting accident and was near death. Immediately the boy set out for home on foot—covering a total of 270 miles in only two weeks. His father eventually recovered, but a few months later Jim's mother died unexpectedly.

After a brief stint on a Texas ranch, Jim returned home to help his father with the farm and attended a nearby public school. In 1904, when Jim was 16, he was invited to attend the Carlisle Indian College on an athletic scholarship. Mr. Thorpe urged his son to accept. "Son, you are an Indian," he said. "I want you to show other races what an Indian can do."

At Carlisle Jim was coached by Glenn S. "Pop" Warner, the most innovative football genius of his time. Even as Jim's recruiter, Warner was amazed when he finally saw the full range of Jim's athletic prowess. One day while watching Jim practice the high jump, Warner exclaimed, "You've just broken the school record! That bar was set at five feet nine inches!"

Coach Warner was initially reticent to let Jim play varsity football because of his slender frame. But player pestered him until he agreed to play the fledgling in a few games during the 1907 season. By 1908, a seasoned Thorpe had made his presence spectacularly known—running for five touchdowns in one of the first games. In another game Jim was sidelined until the last few minutes. When Warner finally put him in, the young fullback immediately scored a touchdown in what one observer called "the single most dramatic play I have ever seen in sports": *Jim took the very first hand-off and blasted into the line with [a thunderous] crash.... When he was able to continue into their backfield, I couldn't believe my eyes! He didn't use one block on his way to the goal line seventy yards away, while all the time he kept hollering, "Out of my way! Get out of my way!"*

Later in the season the Carlisle "Indians" played against national champion Pennsylvania in what Thorpe later said was "the toughest game in my twenty-two years of college and professional football." After scoring Carlisle's only touchdown and kicking the extra point to preserve a 6-6 tie, Thorpe was named a third-team All-American. He was also a standout on the Carlisle track team, where he took first place in six out of seven events in one meet, generating the legend that he "singlehandedly" defeated Lafayette College.

After the track season, Thorpe was leaving for a summer farm job when he ran into some friends at the train station. "A couple of Carlisle ballplayers ... were going to North Carolina ... to play baseball," Thorpe reported. "I didn't enjoy farming, so I tagged along.... The manager [at Rocky Mount] offered me fifteen dollars a week to play third base; I took it ..."

Jim played for two seasons (1909–10) before the baseball league folded. Afterward, he drifted aimlessly around Oklahoma. Both his parents were now dead, and in his melancholy he jumped at the chance to return to the Carlisle football team for the 1911 season. He came back greater than ever, leading Carlisle to an 11–1 record. At season's end, Walter Camp named him a first-team All-American. Coach Warner was even more impressed: "[Jim] knew everything a football player could be taught and ... could execute the play better than the coach ever dreamed of.... He is the same way in all sports, always watching for a new motion which will benefit him. Then Thorpe has the marvelous concentrative power which he puts into every move he makes. It is a splendid sight to see him hurl a football thirty yards ... with merely an abrupt snap of the wrist, direct to the hands of the receiver ..."

Thorpe's long touchdown runs and accurate field-goal kicking soon brought him nationwide attention. Huge crowds began to come out to see him play, and sportswriters praised him heartily as "the most versatile athlete ever."

Probably Thorpe's greatest moment came in 1912, when he traveled to Sweden to represent his country in the fifth Olympiad. To everyone's surprise, he won gold medals in both the decathlon and the pentathlon, taking first place in four of the five pentathlon events. One American team official said: "It answers the allegation that most of our runners are of foreign parentage, for Thorpe is a real American, if there ever was one."

Thorpe's performance in the 110-meter hurdles for the decathlon—15.6 seconds—is truly amazing when compared with the 15.7-second time that won the individual event thirty-six years later. *Improved diets, training procedures, hurdling techniques, and equipment had not been able to break track's longest-standing record.*

Following the Olympics, Thorpe played a final winning season at Carlisle and was again selected as a first team All-American. Pete Calac, one of Thorpe's teammates, recalled: " … He was the best. He was good at everything he attempted…. [But he] never acted like he was better than any of us…. He always tried to be just one of the guys."

In 1913 reports came out that Thorpe had played minor league professional baseball three years earlier. The Amateur Athletic Union demanded an explanation. Hiding nothing, Thorpe wrote a letter to AAU president James E. Sullivan, readily admitting that he had been paid to play baseball, and adding: *I did not play for the money … but because I liked to play ball…. I received offers amounting to thousands of dollars since my victories last summer, but I have turned them all down …*

The AAU, however, stripped Thorpe of his medals and divested him of his amateur status. The press was sympathetic. Sportswriter Damon Runyon mourned that "none of his marvelous records will stand. They will be wiped out completely … although it is rather doubtful if this … will remove them from the memory of the people who follow athletic events." Editorials across the country attacked the AAU: *AAU officials think nothing of taking money for their services as managers of athletic meets … still these men … are so "pure" that they cannot be approached.* Nonetheless, Thorpe only issued a single statement: "I must have time to consider my future plans."

Despite a bevy of lucrative offers from Vaudeville promoters who wanted to cash in on his fame, Thorpe finally signed to play professional baseball with the New York Giants in 1913. He earned much less than the promoters had offered him.

From the beginning the Giants' domineering manager John McGraw clashed with the quiet Thorpe. Finally, in 1919, Thorpe was released by McGraw on the pretext that he couldn't hit a curve ball. In response, Thorpe said: "I hit .327 my last year in the National League; I must have hit a few curves." He went on to play nine more years in the minor leagues, then, in 1928, at the age of 40, he quit professional baseball.

Throughout the years Thorpe played for the Giants, he also played for football's semi-professional Canton Bulldogs, joining the team every fall at the end of baseball season. And in 1920 he had been named as president of the newly formed American Professional Football Association—the precursor of today's NFL—which he had helped to organize.

Thorpe's stamina continued to amaze his contemporaries. Walter Lingo, owner of the Oorang Indians, yet another team for which Thorpe played, revealed: "One of the secrets of his great lasting powers is the fact that he never quits training. Playing baseball in the summer, football in the fall, and [spending] the intervening months hunting, his body is in the peak of physical condition at all times…. He is the real fighting type of man when occasion demands, but at all other times is both gentle and kind…. His greatest virtue is his love of honesty and his hatred of untruthfulness or deception."

After retiring from football in 1929, the 44-year-old Thorpe supported himself by working at odd jobs through the Great Depression, sometimes for only fifty cents an hour.

Then in 1938 a group of football greats published their picks for an "All-Time" All-American Team—and every one of them selected Jim Thorpe for his own team. As the only player so honored, Thorpe was hired to go on a cross-country lecture tour. In all his lectures he pled the cause of his fellow Native Americans: "Indians, you know, are misnamed. We aren't Indians. We are Red Men and we settled this country long before the white people ever came to these shores…. There were 30,000 Indian volunteers in the last war. They fought for this country. Many gave their lives for its people and its resources. In return, the Indians should be granted full citizenship with all the rights and privileges that go with it … "

The great Native American athlete believed that his fame could be used to help expose the "Red Man's" plight. He kept a copy of a newspaper article which, he felt, "placed the final, and most misunderstood, years of his life into proper perspective." *Pity the poor Indian?* it began. *Not Jim Thorpe!… One glance is enough to convince me that Thorpe is not a descendant of the Red Men who were rooked out of Manhattan Island …*

In 1950 two Associated Press polls voted Thorpe the greatest football player and greatest male athlete of the half-century. Meanwhile, he kept himself busy promoting a young pro-wrestler, advising Warner Brothers on the film *Jim Thorpe—All-American*, and "heading an all-Indian song and dance troupe," the Jim Thorpe Show.

In 1953, at the age of 65, Thorpe died suddenly of a heart attack. Remembering the influence his own father had had on his life, Jim would have been especially proud of the eulogy offered by his daughter Grace: "[My father] had an enormous amount of personal integrity and never uttered a bad word about anyone…. His posture was always erect and his manner mild. He exuded manliness and warmth."

Jim Thorpe's life had thus left an unparalleled legacy not only in the world of sport, but in the hearts of his friends and family, where, for him, it counted even more.

Fatima's Meer's biography documents the remarkable life of South Africa's Nelson Mandela. Accused with Mandela in the 1956 treason trial, Meer was active in the organized resistance campaign of the African National Congress.

Although she was banned from her native South Africa in 1954, in 1976, and in 1981—when she and Winnie Mandela were imprisoned for five months awaiting trial—Meer subsequently returned. A professor of sociology in Durban, Meer wrote *Higher than Hope* at the Mandelas' urging. According to Winnie Mandela, "There was no better person to write such a narrative than Fatima Meer," who, through years of conversations and correspondence with Mandela, knows the man well.

Nelson Mandela was born in 1918 in Qunu, South Africa. As his younger sister Nomabandla recalls: "Our father [Hendry Mphakanyoswa Gadla] was a chief but was subsequently deposed for insubordination. He rode a horse and he had enough cattle to marry four wives. Our mother, Nosenki Fanny, was of the Right-hand House and was his third wife ... "

A "devout Christian," Nelson's mother worried about the future of her son, "Buti," as he was then called, and after consulting with her husband, the boy was sent to the village of Mqekezweni, where he would get an education. Nelson lived with the village chief, his father's uncle, who adopted the ten-year-old after the death of his father.

Of the many chiefs who visited Mqekezweni, Chief Zwelibhangile Joyi was the oldest, "shriveled and bent and so black that he was blue." Nelson delighted in Tatu Joyi's knowledge of African history: *Tatu Joyi said that the white people divided brother from brother, and split the people of Ngangelizwe into pieces and destroyed them.... A chief puts land beneath the feet of his people. Queen Victoria took away the land of the Thembu and put them into locations and put strange tribes between them, so that they would kill each other and remain forever weak against the white people.*

Nelson later researched Tatu Joyi's detailed accounts of the white man's arrival in South Africa when he studied at Fort Hare University. Indeed, Nelson confirmed that the whites had used gunfire and other forms of intimidation to suppress the African kings' *ubuntu* (humanity) and to establish their tyranny. ... *Nelson, tutored at Tatu Joyi's feet, was fired to regain that ubuntu for all South Africans.*

Expelled from Fort Hare in 1941 for persisting in his "fanatical" studies, Nelson and his brother Justice moved to the sprawling city of Johannesburg. "They had come to South Africa's industrial heart," Meer writes, " ... so they could begin to understand their own place and destiny in their motherland." But within days Justice returned to live with Jongintaba, leaving Nelson, alone, to pursue an education.

Nelson became acquainted with Walter Sisulu, a young estate agent who would become Secretary General of the African National Congress (ANC). Walter gradually drew Nelson into the world of Johannesburg politics. While completing his B.A., attending law school and

marrying Walter's cousin Evelyn, Nelson became a leader in the ANC Youth League, an organization established to awaken popular political consciousness and fight oppression.

When ANC Youth League President Anton Lembede died in 1949, Nelson, as League Secretary, was catapulted into a more prominent role in the group. Subsequently, the African National Congress adopted the Youth League's plan to protest against the Nationalist Government, and together they joined South Africa's oppressed Indian population to launch a national work-stoppage. However, the day ended tragically; 19 blacks and Indians were killed by police and 30 others were injured.

At Nelson's direction, the ANC called for a massive National Day of Protest in response to the killings. Rallies were held throughout the country; organized groups of Africans and Indians defied ordinances they deemed unjust. But when Walter Sisulu and others were jailed and Nelson was "jerked out of bed" in a first of many pre-dawn raids on ANC leaders, the demonstration was quashed.

Taking charge as president of the Youth League in 1951, Nelson thereafter replaced the exiled J.B. Marks as president of the Transvaal ANC. Now as he worked consistently to liberate his people, Nelson was often separated from his family.

The ANC's Defiance Campaign grew quickly and the South African government became desperate. *Realizing that the power of the Campaign and its international support lay in its non-violence, [the government] acted to slander [the campaign] with violence.* Although the government permitted the ANC to hold a mass prayer meeting in East London in October of 1952, within minutes the military moved in and "turned the peaceful gathering into a bloodbath." The ANC, committed to nonviolence and not knowing how to cope with such attacks, soon weakened. The government, meanwhile, outlawed any form of passive resistance and, by 1957, the campaign was all but lost.

Now forbidden to speak in public, Mandela was forced to change his tactics: he organized a "grassroots" effort relying on trade unions and covert operations. With more time on his hands, Mandela also studied for and passed his law exams, after which he opened an office at Chancellor House.

By now the Nationalists were at their strongest: ... *Their tyranny appeared invincible. They passed laws ... that deprived African, Indian and Coloured people of their homes and land*; the European-based African Education Movement went so far as to decree that there was "no place [for the] 'native'" in the South African literati. In response, Nelson Mandela called for the ANC to develop its own school system, announced a boycott of all public schools, and enlisted 1,000 volunteer teachers for the ANC system. The government countered by declaring all "unregistered" schools illegal, before forcibly closing down the classes. Ultimately, Mandela conceded to government pressure, reasoning that some form of education was preferable to none at all.

Mandela's life was now so hectic that he was rarely at home. Consequently, he and Evelyn began divorce proceedings—and although he worried about the effect it would have on his children, he was able to console them. Just weeks later Mandela was arrested along with 155 other participants of the Congress of the People, an inter-racial alliance of South Africans who sought political freedom for all fellow countrymen. While much of the resistance movement became embroiled in the trial, the Ovamboland People's Congress—which would later become the South West African People's Organization (SWAPO), an ANC ally—was formed in Capetown in 1957. That year also marked the split within the ANC along racial lines, as black members accused certain white factions of emphasizing class conflict without regard to race.

Soon after Mandela was released on bail from the Fort Prison, he met Winnie Madikizela, and "wooed her in his own way within the confines of his banning order and in between his daily attendance at the Treason Trial." When his divorce from Evelyn was finalized in June of 1958, Nelson married Winnie.

Five years after the treason trial had begun the court finally dismissed all charges, and "Nelson was released from a stranglehold that had cost him his practice and seriously jeopardized his freedom to work for his people. Although there were wild demonstrations of joy outside the courtroom, Nelson Mandela knew that his people were not winning the larger battle: *The Nationalists were ... converting the traditional chiefs from patrons and guardians of the people into lackeys of the oppressor.... African tenant farmers were expelled from white farms ... pushed into already overcrowded reserves ... forced to sell whatever livestock they possessed ...*

Subsequently on March 26, 1960 in Sharpeville, South Africa, the police gunned down 69 protestors and injured 180. As a result, 95 percent of the workforce went on strike; 30,000 marched on Caledon Square; a state of emergency was declared, both the ANC and PAC were banned, and thousands were temporarily detained by police. In response to the government's use of violence, Mandela and other ANC members set up *Umkhonto we Sizwe*, a clandestine organization that would force change through acts of sabotage against South African military installations.

In 1962 Mandela met with Ethiopia's Emperor Haile Selassie and the Commander-in-Chief of Algeria's Army of National Liberation, in order to undergo military training in those countries. On his return to South Africa, he was arrested and subsequently sentenced to five years in prison for incitement to strike and for traveling without a passport. Thus Mandela was again brought to trial, along with Walter Sisulu and others of the High Command, charged with sabotage and attempting to overthrow the state. Winnie was permitted to attend what came to be known as the "Rivonia Trial"—"providing she did not dress or behave in a manner to cause 'incidents.'" Mandela and all except two of his fellow ANC members were summarily found guilty of sabotage and sentenced to life imprisonment.

With Mandela out of the picture, "the ANC almost disappeared from the articulated consciousness of the country; a new generation of blacks grew into the Black Consciousness and confronted white tyranny with surly anger." Winnie joined this movement, a choice that brought her frequent imprisonment and torture—as well as a citation from the British as "Woman of the Year."

In 1976 the country experienced unprecedented violence. That previous year the government had introduced Afrikaans (a derivative dialect of the early Dutch settlers) into the secondary schools as its state language—a tongue that African teachers could barely teach and pupils could barely understand. And in response to a simple Soweto student protest rally, police opened fire on children. *Overnight the children became defenders of their people against the government.* Clearly, the year 1976 paved the way for a sharpening of the military confrontation between apartheid and its opposition.

The South African government meted out a brutal revenge, swooping down on Black Consciousness groups and outlawing all such organizations. Winnie was not only again publicly scorned, but was banished from Soweto, where her circle of influence had been growing. *The one name that resounded above all others was that of Mandela.... Mandela came ... to be celebrated internationally as the human symbol of freedom and human resistance against tyranny.*

The early- and mid-1980s were marked by international pressure for South African reform. In January 1985 the Rivonia men were offered their release by the Nationalist State President P.W. Botha. Nelson's response was read at the Jabulani Stadium in Soweto on 10 February, 1985, where over 10,000 people had gathered. Mandela gave an unequivocal answer to Botha's offer: "Let him renounce violence. Let him say that he will dismantle apartheid. Let him unban the people's organization, the African National Congress ... free all who have been imprisoned, banished or exiled.... I cannot sell my birthright, nor am I prepared to sell the birthright of the people to be free."

In December of 1988 the state announced that Mr. Mandela had been removed to a house at the Victor Verster prison, and that his family would be allowed to live with him there. But he declined to share his imprisonment with his family and refused any privileges denied his comrades in prison.

Then in July, 1989 *a government communiqué suddenly informed the world that Mr. Mandela had made a "courtesy call" on President Botha ... and that the two leaders had talked for forty-five minutes.... The government had openly referred to him as a "leader" ... the most significant sign yet that the stronghold of Afrikaner domination was crumbling ...*

Summary Footnote

In October, 1989, Walter Sisulu and others were freed unconditionally by new South African President F.W. deKlerk, who soon legalized the ANC. On February 11, 1990, Nelson Mandela was released from prison. He and deKlerk were awarded the Nobel Peace Prize later that year. Mandela is now serving as President of South Africa.

ALBERT SCHWEITZER, THE ENIGMA
by James Bentley, HarperCollins Publishers, 1992

In James Bentley's biography, Albert Schweitzer emerges as one of the 20th century's most widely revered men. Schweitzer was also a man of enormous contradictions, "a man who cherished his family but spent months away from them, who despised racism but supervised a missionary hospital in which only whites held positions of power, who rejected Western civilization, but returned to it … " Moreover, although he worked tirelessly to promote peace and human dignity throughout the world, Schweitzer was given to periods of abject despair. On one such occasion he even revealed: "We believed once in the victory of truth … in our fellow men … in goodness, but we do not now. We trusted in the power of kindness and peaceableness; we do not now. We were capable of enthusiasm; but we are not so now."

These bleak thoughts, however, ultimately gave way to optimism. After receiving the Nobel Peace Prize in 1953, Schweitzer told an audience, "It is my belief that one day we shall reach the point where we shall refrain from wars for moral reasons, because we feel that war is a crime against humanity."

Schweitzer was born on January 14, 1875, in the little town of Kaysersberg in Alsace, a German-speaking region of France. When Albert was one year old, the family moved to Gunsbach, where his father served as a Protestant pastor. Young Albert soon became interested in religion himself and, when he was only eight, asked for his own Bible, which proved to greatly influence Schweitzer's humanistic vision. As he later recalled: "Out of the depths of my feelings of happiness there gradually arose inside me an understanding … that we must not regard our lives as belonging to ourselves alone."

Albert clearly was not a typical child. Precociously, he had begun music instruction at the age of five, for example, and played the organ for Sunday Mass by the age of nine. But despite his accomplishments, his childhood was not particularly happy. Because his family was wealthier than others in the village, he was rejected and occasionally beaten up by his schoolmates.

Surprisingly, Albert was a poor scholar, but during this period he "found his voice." As he later recalled: "I emerged from the shell of reserve in which up till now I had hidden myself and became one who disrupted every amiable discussion."

Albert's passion for discussion, of course, proved quite advantageous when he entered the University of Strasbourg in 1893. Initially torn between his love for music and for theology, Albert ultimately decided to become a theologian. Years later he would tell a congregation: "People say that those who do theology are confronted with hard battles, because of the doubts which arise when they plunge themselves into the deep study and research of Christian doctrine and history. Such doubts and temptations have never assailed me … because I have been so certain of His spiritual presence."

Indeed, Schweitzer proved to be gifted at working out intricate theological explanations, influenced by the "inspired teachings of the brilliant theologians … at the University of Strasbourg." Publishing articles which were later translated into many languages, Schweitzer's religious studies soon made him famous throughout Europe.

After obtaining his degree in 1900, Schweitzer became a regular curate of the church of Saint-Nicolas in Strasbourg, where he was profoundly touched by a bust portraying a black man, sculpted at the hands of Frederic Auguste Bartholdi. The sculpture's "melancholy expression" so moved Schweitzer that he began to reflect on the fate of contemporary black men and women. Consequently, he decided that when he reached the age of 30 "he would devote himself to relieving the lot of the natives of Africa."

By 1910 Schweitzer had published his widely acclaimed *The Quest of the Historical Jesus* and had begun to establish himself as an internationally renowned scholar. But he decided it was now time to be "a simple human being, to do something small in the spirit of Jesus." Thus, he determined to fulfill his vow to provide "service to his fellow human beings" in Africa.

First he moved to Paris to study tropical medicine. Schweitzer planned to become a "jungle doctor" and build his own hospital in Africa. As he explained to his congregation: "For me missionary work is essentially not a religious matter. First and foremost it is a human duty that our states and nations have never undertaken…. This noble culture of ours speaks so piously of human dignity and the rights of man and then disregards the dignity and rights of countless millions, treading them underfoot simply because they live overseas or because their skins are of a different colour … "

When in February 1913 Doctor Schweitzer had completed his medical studies, he set about raising funds by giving recitals, and was soon able to afford a nurse and the equipment necessary for his first medical mission to Africa. *He also decided that his nurse [Helene Bresslau] ought to become his wife, or perhaps he felt obliged to marry her simply because few people, and particularly not her father, were pleased at the thought of an unmarried young woman leaving with her powerful male friend for the African jungle.* After marrying, Dr. and Mrs. Schweitzer, loaded down with books and supplies, took the train to Bordeaux and set out to sea on the steamer *Europe*. After a stormy journey, the couple reached the capital city of French Equatorial Africa. The afternoon of their arrival they went to work in a "filthy, leaking hut, till recently, used as a chicken coop."

While he slowly gained the trust of the Africans, Albert speedily charmed his fellow missionaries. Judging that his operating theatre in a former hen coop was inadequate, he designed and built a new hospital that "was oriented along the equator, so that the stifling sun never penetrated its wards." Mosquito netting and wooden shutters shielded the patients against insects.

By the end of their first nine months the Schweitzers had treated nearly 2,000 patients, whose chief complaints were "skin diseases, malaria, sleeping sickness, elephantiasis, heart problems, leprosy, osteomyelitis, tropical dysentery and hernias … " Schweitzer wrote: *From my own experience and that of other colonial doctors I can say that a single doctor … with the most modest equipment means very much for very many … who would otherwise have had to succumb to their fate in despair.*

In the summer of 1914 the World War created an "absurdly difficult" situation for the Schweitzers: "As Alsatians my wife and I were German nationals [and] since we were at war, my wife and I were regarded as enemy aliens—and treated as such."

In September 1917, when the new French Colonial Government restricted even further the rights of German-speaking aliens, Schweitzer and his wife were sent to a prison in Bordeaux. Later they were moved to a small camp at Saint-Remy-de-Provence, a former mental hospital where, a few years earlier, Vincent van Gogh had died. By petitioning the camp director, Schweitzer was soon given permission to practice medicine in the camp.

Thus, though they grew more and more depressed, their internment became bearable. It was at this time that Helene conceived their only child, daughter Rhena. The pregnancy, however, did nothing to improve her already poor health. Finally in July of 1918 the French government was persuaded to send them home to Strasbourg.

With Helene now suffering also from the terrible effects of tuberculosis, Schweitzer accepted an offer to return to his former positions as lecturer and preacher.

Salvation finally came from an unexpected source: Nathan Soderblom, archbishop of Uppsala, Sweden, who had read Albert's works, extended him an invitation to lecture. *His spirits were so low that he almost refused.* But, exhausted and despondent, he went to Uppsala, and there he partially recovered his failing health. Soderblom also brought about the Schweitzers' financial relief by arranging for a lecture tour and the publication of Albert's life story, *On the Edge of the Primeval Forest.* Schweitzer "did not pull any punches" in the text: *We should perceive the task that needs to be done for the coloured people not as "good works" but as duty … not as benevolence … but atonement.*

In February 1924 Schweitzer wrote his *Memoirs of Childhood and Youth.* That same month he left for Africa, leaving "the crippled Helene to care for their child." Permanently disabled as a consequence of her frequent illnesses and a skiing accident, his wife would have to experience the glory of Albert's mission vicariously, through his letters.

From this point on he would only return to Europe for his extended fund-raising tours—and to accept numerous awards and honorary doctorates. Though he always remained a rather shy person and did not revel in publicity, he did what he had to do for the benefit of his hospital.

When he returned to West Africa in 1924, Dr. Schweitzer found his hospital in a shambles; the ravages of storms and looting had taken their toll. After designing and erecting a new structure, which he called *Lambarene,* he added another 40 buildings, opening up space for several hundred more patients. Doctors and nurses who wanted to join him in providing round-the-clock medical care poured in from all over Europe. In fact, Schweitzer's problem lay not in a lack of willing and able workers but in being able to pay their scant wages.

Often exhausted, Schweitzer considered his patients both a joy and a constant irritation: *[He] had endless problems persuading patients not to take their medicines all at once. Some of his recuperating patients would bathe, unwisely, in the filthy Ogowe River. Others inserted grubby fingers under their dressings to feel their wounds. Sometimes relatives crept inside his hospital and climbed into the patients' beds, forcing the sick to sleep on the floor.* In despair at such behaviors, he once exclaimed, "What an imbecile I am to have come to stay with these savages and devoted myself to them!" At hearing this, his black assistant Joseph replied, "Yes, doctor, on earth you are a fool, but not in heaven."

His work at the hospital had caused Schweitzer to completely neglect his marriage. The Second World War, however, proved to bring Albert and Helene back together. With the clouds of hostility looming over the world, the doctor traveled to Europe in 1939 to purchase a stockpile of food and drugs. While Helene subsequently accompanied him back to Africa, her poor health finally forced her to return to Europe. She visited her husband once more in 1957, but she died in Zurich only ten days later. Three months after her death the 82-year-old Schweitzer brought Helene's ashes to Lambarene and buried them outside his study window.

Schweitzer would not abandon his work. Now aided by his daughter Rhena, he remained dedicated to humanity. But now he was an old man, unable to do as much as before. Then on August 23, 1965 he startled his fellow workers by announcing arrangements for his death. The following Friday he walked through his orchard, saying good-bye to each individual tree. A few days later, on September 4, 1965, Schweitzer died at the age of 90.

Nearly a half century earlier he had delivered one of his most moving sermons: "If you study life deeply, looking perceptively into the vast and animated chaos that is creation, the profundity of it all will stun you. You will recognize yourself in everything. That tiny beetle which lies dead in your path was a living creature, struggling like you for existence, rejoicing like you in the warmth of the sun, like you knowing fear and pain. Now it is no more than decaying matter, as you too sooner or later will be.

Later, one morning some days after Dr. Schweitzer's death, the natives sang for him, expressing their love and gratitude. One nurse remembered: "Once a native said to him, 'When you die we will have a tom-tom of a week to mourn you.' The doctor replied, 'fortunately I won't hear it.'"

THE STORY OF MY LIFE
by Helen Keller, Doubleday & Company, 1902

*H*ave you ever been at sea in a dense fog, when it seemed as if a tangible white darkness shut you in, and the great ship, tense and anxious, groped her way toward the shore ... and you waited with beating heart for something to happen? I was like that ship before my education began ...

Helen Keller was born on June 27, 1880, in Tuscumbia, Alabama. For 19 months she lived a normal childhood, speaking her first words at six months and walking for the first time when she was one. *I am told that while I was still in long dresses I showed many signs of an eager, self-asserting disposition. Everything that I saw other people do I insisted upon imitating.*

All too soon, the happy signs of infancy ended. *One brief spring, one summer rich in fruit and roses, one autumn of gold and crimson sped by.... Then, in the dreary month of February came the illness which closed my eyes and ears ...* A high fever left Helen blind and deaf. Although her memories of her early life were vague, she later recalled "the agony and bewilderment with which I awoke after a tossing half sleep, and turned my eyes ... away from the once-loved light, which came to me dim and yet more dim each day.... Gradually I got used to the silence and darkness that surrounded me and forgot that it had ever been different ... "

For five years Helen lived in darkness, her communication limited to "crude signs" or pantomimes. She realized that those around her didn't use signs to ask for bread or ice cream or water, but communicated by moving their mouths. *I stood between two persons who were conversing and touched their lips. I could not understand, and was vexed. I moved my lips and gesticulated frantically without result.*

As she grew older Helen's frustration also grew. *My failures to make myself understood were invariably followed by outbursts of passion. I felt as if invisible hands were holding me, and I made frantic efforts to free myself.*

Helen's parents were willing to do anything to augment their daughter's limited life experience. When she was six they wrote to the Perkins Institution in Boston, an organization devoted to the education of the blind. In response, in March of 1887 the Institution sent a woman named Anne Mansfield Sullivan to the Keller's home to teach Helen.

The day after she arrived Miss Sullivan gave Helen a doll. Then, using an alphabet system in which different finger positions represented letters, she spelled "d-o-l-l" into the girl's hand. "I was at once interested in this finger play," Helen recalled, "and tried to imitate it." Although she learned to spell several words by using her hand, she did not realize that there was a connection between the "finger plays" and the actual objects they represented.

Then one day Miss Sullivan took Helen to the water pump, and while cool water splashed on the girl's outstretched palm, her teacher spelled "w-a-t-e-r" into her other hand. *[In that moment], somehow the mystery of language was revealed to me, a misty consciousness as of something forgotten—a thrill of returning thought.... I knew then that "w-a-t-e-r" meant the wonderful cool something that was flowing over my hand.... I left the well-house eager to learn. Everything had a name, and each name gave birth to a new thought ...*

Once Helen learned the riddle behind language, her appetite was insatiable. *The more I handled things and learned their names and uses, the more joyous and confident grew my sense of kinship with the rest of the world.* Miss Sullivan encouraged her "to find beauty in the fragrant woods, in every blade of grass, and in the curves and dimples of my baby sister's hand ... "

Miss Sullivan next employed a collection of words printed in raised letters to teach Helen how to read. The girl "quickly learned that each printed word stood for an object, an act, or a quality." The two of them made a game of learning about sentence structure by arranging a series of objects together with word cards to fill in the blank parts of the sentence. "Until then," Helen mused, "I had been like a foreigner speaking through an interpreter."

Throughout her life Helen gave much of the credit for her amazing ability to process information and experience to Anne Sullivan: *It was my teacher's genius, her quick sympathy, her loving tact, which made the first years of my education so beautiful. It was because she seized the right moment to impart knowledge that made it so pleasant and acceptable to me.... I feel that her being is inseparable from my own.... All the best of me belongs to her—there is not a talent, or an aspiration or a joy in me that has not been awakened by her loving touch.*

On Christmas Day 1887 Helen, who had previously understood little about the holiday, woke her family with her first signed "Merry Christmas!" In May of the following year she took her first trip to Boston, to visit the Perkins Institution for the Blind. There she befriended many other blind children, with whom she conversed using Miss Sullivan's "manual alphabet." She walked on Bunker Hill and received her first history lesson. She even rode on an ocean-going steamboat and touched Plymouth Rock: *As I recall that visit North I am filled with wonder.... The treasures of a new, beautiful world were laid at my feet.... I met many people who talked with me by spelling into my hand ... the barren places between my mind and the minds of others blossomed like the rose.*

In 1890 Helen learned about Ragnhild Kaata, a deaf and blind girl in Norway who had learned to speak. No longer was Helen content to limit her conversations to hand-signing; she was "on fire with eagerness" to learn to speak. Another teacher, Miss Sarah Fuller, arrived to give Helen voice lessons. By feeling the position of Miss Fuller's mouth and tongue as she pronounced a word, Helen eventually managed to utter her first sentence: "It is warm." *It is an unspeakable boon to me to be able to speak in winged words that need no interpretation. As I talked, happy thoughts fluttered up out of my words that might perhaps have struggled in vain to escape my fingers.* She forced herself through the tremendous difficulties involved in learning to talk by constantly reminding herself, "My little sister will understand me now."

In Autumn of 1891, 11-year-old Helen penned a little story which she titled "The Frost King." Although she didn't realize it, the story she wrote was mostly paraphrased from a tale called "The Frost Fairies," which had been read to her in 1888. Her mind had retained the story's imagery, style and plot, and she later came to believe that they were her own. *I thought then that I was "making up a story," as children say, and I eagerly sat down to write it before the ideas should slip from me.... Now, if words and images come to me without effort, it is a pretty sure sign that they are not the offspring of my own mind ... It is certain that I cannot always distinguish my own thoughts from those I read, because what I read becomes the very substance and texture of my mind.* Eventually she even forgot that the story had been read to her. Nevertheless, some people persisted in spreading rumors that she had knowingly plagiarized the story. The accusations troubled Helen for many years: *Books lost their charm for me, and even now the thought of those dreadful days chills my heart.... No child ever drank deeper of the cup of bitterness than I did. I had disgraced myself.... I wept as I hope few children have wept [and] have never played with words again for the mere pleasure of the game. Indeed, I have ever since been tortured by the fear that what I write is not my own.*

In 1892, again encouraged by Miss Sullivan, Helen shook off the humiliation that had followed her first creative attempt and wrote a brief account of her life. The next year, now more confident, she traveled to Washington to attend the presidential inauguration of Grover Cleveland, and visited Niagara Falls. As she wrote in her journal: *I stood on the point which overhangs the American Falls, and felt the air vibrate and the earth tremble.* The following summer she visited the World's Fair, accompanied by Dr. Alexander Graham Bell, the educator and inventor who had first advised Helen's parents to write the Perkins Institute. The exhibits—everything from industrial machines to Egyptian mummies—fascinated Helen, who was given free rein to touch anything she wished. *In the three weeks I spent at the Fair I took a long leap from the little child's interest in fairy tales and toys to the appreciation of the real and the earnest in the workaday world.*

In the Fall of 1894, after a year of attending "regular" school, Helen enrolled at Wright-Humason School for the Deaf in New York. There she studied "vocal culture" and "lip-reading," not to mention "arithmetic, physical geography, French and German." Two years later she began classes at the Cambridge School for Young Ladies and prepared to take the admittance exams at Radcliffe College, the women's college at Harvard. Attending the school was a lifelong dream: *When I was a little girl, I visited Wellesley and surprised my friends by the announcement, "Some day I shall go to college—but I shall go to Harvard!"*

With Anne Sullivan by her side interpreting the professors' words, Helen sat through lectures at the Cambridge School. She lived in a dormitory along with several seeing and hearing girls her own age, and for the first time enjoyed the full companionship of her peers.

Between 1897 and 1899, Helen took Radcliffe's admittance exams, passing the language and history subjects without difficulty. She also passed the mathematical exams, despite complications with the braille notation. Some of the exam supervisors did not seem to appreciate the extra work it took to administer the tests to a handicapped girl. "But if they unintentionally placed obstacles in my way," Keller acknowledged, "I have the consolation of knowing that I overcame them all." She began classes at Radcliffe in 1900, determined to compete—and to succeed.

In 1902, while attending Radcliffe, Miss Keller completed *The Story of My Life*, a more complete account of her early years. It was published and became a bestseller, as well as an inspiration to millions of readers worldwide.

The darkness that enshrouded Helen Keller's life at the age of two was lifted by her learning to speak and read. From the time she read her first story at age seven to the educational experiences of her adult years, Keller "devoured everything that [came] within the reach of my hungry finger tips." Reading became, of necessity, her primary pastime, her "utopia," and one of the few arenas in which she was not "disenfranchised." She went on to devote her life to improving conditions for the handicapped and fulfilling her desire that all children should enjoy the benefits of an education. She also received great joy from meeting people and feeling the love of family and friends, among whom she counted writers Oliver Wendell Holmes and Samuel Clemens, poet John Greenleaf Whittier, and Alexander Graham Bell— some of the greatest minds of the age.

Sometimes, it is true, a sense of isolation enfolds me ... as I sit alone.... Beyond there is light, and music, and sweet companionship.... So I try to make the light in others' eyes my sun, the music in others' ears my symphony, the smile on others' lips my happiness.

PATTON, THE MAN BEHIND THE LEGEND
by Martin Blumenson, William Morrow and Company, 1985

A *throwback to the Teutonic knight, the Saracen, the Crusader, George Patton was one of America's greatest soldiers, one of the world's great captains,* writes Martin Blumenson in his biography of Patton. Blumenson, who once served in Patton's Third Army, reveals the man behind the uniform in an attempt to make the decorated general appear mortal.

George Smith Patton, Jr. was born on November 11, 1885 into a family of gentlemen and soldiers. Early on, young George decided to become a great military leader, following the tradition set by his ancestors, "who had displayed bravery, the highest manly quality.... They became beacons for the future general. His kinsmen, he believed literally, watched from above, and ... judged the actions of their descendants."

George attended Virginia Military Institute as a teen and was later appointed to West Point. He resolved to be West Point's very best cadet, even though his dyslexia made schoolwork difficult. "I am either very lazy or very stupid or both, for it is beastly hard for me to learn and as a natural result I hate to study," he wrote, expressing an "overpowering sense of [his] own worthlessness." Even though his military zeal impressed his instructors, Patton had to repeat his first year at West Point.

Doubting his courage and wanting to test his mettle under fire, he soon began to perform feats of bravery that won the attention of his instructors and classmates. Patton succeeded, and the legend began— though the general would later remark, "Naturally I am not over bold and am inclined to show emotion— a most unmilitary trait."

Perfecting "military traits" became extremely important to Patton: *All his life he honed his image, developing what he felt were the appropriate mannerisms—profanity ... aristocratic bearing, the fierce scowl, ruthlessness. And in the process he killed much of his sensitivity and warmth and thereby turned a sweet-tempered and affectionate child into a seemingly hard-eyed and choleric adult.*

Joining the cavalry after his graduation from West Point in 1909, Patton drew both respect and scorn for publicly apologizing to an enlisted man, to whom he had said "damn you" instead of "damn it." And when his face was cut by a bucking horse, a bloodied Patton impressed his men by continuing to drill them, even as blood streamed down onto his chest.

A year later, in 1910, Patton married Beatrice Ayer, a young woman from a wealthy family. Shortly thereafter, he and his wife relocated to Washington D.C., where he could be "close to those who mattered." However, it was not until 1915, when he was stationed on the Mexican border, that Patton found the chance to win the admiration of his superiors. After hostilities had broken out between Pancho Villa and American border forces, Patton, joining General John J. Pershing on an expedition into Mexico, led ten men in motorcars to the hideout of one of Villa's captains. This daring raid marked the first time that American troops had used motor vehicles in battle.

"I have at last succeeded in getting into a fight," Patton wrote to his family, which now included two daughters. Exhilarated by his own fearlessness, the officer boasted that when he first killed a man he "felt the same way he did when he hooked and landed his first swordfish, surprised by his luck."

Later, during World War I, Patton again joined Pershing, who led the American Expeditionary Force in France. Now promoted to Captain and longing for battle and personal glory, Patton quickly became an expert in the use of tanks in warfare and organized the First Light Tank Brigade. Demonstrating extreme vitality and singlemindedness, he was soon promoted to the rank of Lieutenant Colonel and, as always, his men worshiped him.

Patton espoused a philosophy of "Attack ... push forward, attack again." With this dogged mindset, he once led his men to victory even after he had sustained a gunshot wound. Promoted to Colonel, he received the Distinguished Service Medal and the Distinguished Service Cross, and was lauded as the "Hero of the Tanks" in American newspapers.

The conflict's end came as a disappointment to the aggressive warrior, who would return to his peacetime rank of Captain in the Cavalry. "Peace looks possible," he wrote his wife, "but I rather hope not, for I would like to have a few more fights." Dismayed that Americans did not want to maintain a large peacetime Army, he was not altogether satisfied with his new life: *Although the glow of Patton's wartime achievements remained to cheer him, the interwar years for him were a time of frustration.... Despite his external ebullience, he despaired. Was he growing too old to participate in another war adventure?*

When the United States entered World War II, Patton, who was first appointed to the rank of Colonel, then to Brigadier General, commanded an armored brigade. Conducting highly publicized war games in the Southwest to test deployment of large armored forces, he impressed George Marshall, Army Chief of Staff. Patton was soon promoted to Major General and awarded his second star.

In 1942, leading a difficult amphibious landing in French Morocco, Patton quickly crushed Vichy French resistance and captured Casablanca. Now his hope was to confront Rommel's German troops in North Africa. But General Dwight Eisenhower, commander of the American forces, allowed the British to play the primary role in the operation against Rommel. Consequently, Patton lost respect for Eisenhower. The commander "lacked decision and a sense of reality," railed the younger Patton. What was worse, according to him, was that Eisenhower had gone "pro-British."

When a corps of Americans suffered a humiliating defeat at the hands of Rommel and the Germans, Patton assumed command of the corps. Its men fought so effectively in Africa under his leadership that Patton received a third star.

The rising general resumed command of his armored brigade—now called the U.S. Seventh Army—and successfully invaded Italy. Patton, of course, was elated: *In a tribute to his men, he wrote, "Soldiers of the Seventh Army: Born at sea, baptized in blood, and crowned in victory in the course of 38 days of incessant battle and unceasing labor, you have added a glorious chapter to the history of war…. Your fame shall never die."*

But before long Patton's jubilation turned to despair when he was reviled and publicly censured for two occasions on which he had slapped shell-shocked men. Convinced that the soldiers had simply succumbed to cowardice, Patton believed that the blows would reawaken their manhood and their sense of duty. *… Cowardice in the face of the enemy … was the ultimate dishonor. Saving an individual from that humiliation was, in Patton's view, justified and humane.*

After spending several months in disgrace, Patton was called back into service: *Eisenhower could ill afford to lose him. Yet because of his character flaws, Eisenhower would retain him as an army commander and permit him to go no higher.*

During the invasion of France Patton was summoned to command the Third Army. Because most of his men were inexperienced in combat, however, they would not, much to Patton's chagrin, be allowed to invade the beaches. Instead the Third Army would become active only after a beachhead had been established. Though disappointed, the General prepared his soldiers to overrun the German positions.

The Third Army performed brilliantly at Normandy in 1944, and Patton once again became a national hero. Still, Patton had grown disillusioned with both Eisenhower—whom he deemed incompetent—and the British commanders. *Neither Ike or Brad has the stuff,* he wrote in his diary. *Bradley and Hodges are such nothings.* Indeed, Patton thought that if he had been placed in charge, the war would have ended much more quickly.

In 1944 and '45, Patton found himself fighting the Battle of the Bulge. The Germans had launched one last offensive, catching the allies off guard and threatening to invade Antwerp. Patton, however, brilliantly crushed the German troops and reserved for himself a place in history. Yet he credited his troops for the victory: "To me it is a never-ending marvel what our soldiers can do…. The people who actually did it were the younger officers and soldiers…. Marching all night in the cold, over roads they had never seen, and nobody getting lost, and everybody getting to the place in time—it is a marvelous feat: I know of no equal to it in military history…. I take off my hat to them."

After the Battle of the Bulge, Germany collapsed and the Allies advanced. Before the German surrender, Patton received his fourth star, becoming a full general: *Patton had … raised his Third Army to the level of the greatest fighting armies in history, comparable to Hannibal's, Cromwell's, Napoleon's, and Lee's.*

After the war's end in Europe, Patton, no longer in a command role, grew depressed, and asked to be transferred to the Pacific where the fighting continued. Instead, he was put in charge of a sector of Germany. It was then he realized that he was tired and old; he had lost his overriding confidence and zest. Sensing that he had finally fallen out of touch with the times, Patton mused: "Well the war is over…. Now the horrors of peace, pacifism, and unions will have unlimited sway…. It is hell to be old and passé and know it…. Now all is left to do is to sit around and … await the undertaker and posthumous immortality."

Now in a fight against despondency, Patton left Europe to tour the United States. He had been away for so long that he actually felt alienated from his own country. Not long after his 60th birthday, he had a premonition of his imminent death. And shortly thereafter he broke his neck in an automobile accident. He lingered, incapacitated, for a week, and then, accepting his fate with fortitude, died.

Hearing of his passing, the men he had commanded went into a state of mourning. One soldier still serving in Germany called him "one of the greatest men that ever lived," adding, "The men who served under him know him as a soldier's leader. I am proud to say that I have served under him in the Third Army…. We are making every Heinie that passes stop and take off his hat. They can't understand our feelings for him. I don't know whether or not you can understand them either."

His body was laid to rest in an American military cemetery in Luxembourg, alongside many of his fellow soldiers. After his death, Patton's popularity soared. *He died at just the right time, while his triumphs in the war remained fresh…. Had he lived, he would no doubt have felt himself to be outside the mainstream of American life. He would have turned into an anachronism.*

In a letter written during the war, one Third Army veteran described Patton's dynamic aura: *General Patton walked out on the little terrace … and when the drum, ruffles, and bugles sounded the General's march, we stood transfixed upon his appearance. Not one square inch of flesh [was] not covered with goose pimples. … That towering figure impeccably attired froze you in place and electrified the air…. He said … "I can assure you that the Third United States Army will be the greatest army in American history…. I shall drive you until hell won't have it …" He talked on to us for half an hour, literally hypnotizing us with his incomparable, if profane eloquence. When he had finished, you felt as if you had been given a supercharge from some divine source. Here was the man for whom you would go to hell and back.*

GERONIMO: HIS OWN STORY
by Fredrick W. Turner III, E.P. Dutton and Co.,1970

The Autobiography of a Great Patriot Warrior edited by S.M. Barrett, 1906; newly edited with an introduction and notes

" ... **W**hat separates the enlightened man from the savage?" Herman Melville once asked. "Is civilization a thing distinct, or is it an advanced stage of barbarism?" Such questions are more than relevant to the bleak late-19th-century Apache-Anglo conflict. The distinction between "savage" and "civilized" disappeared as white settlers often showed more ingenuity in killing than the Apaches.

In the clash that ensued, Native Americans not only lost their land but—having also been spiritually displaced—lost their cultural heritage as well. Anglo-Americans also lost, among other things, the chance to understand and appreciate the Apache longing to live in peace with their environment. Fortunately, Geronimo—the Chiricahua warrior whose feet were "planted in the roots of the soil of his Mother Earth, his hands open to receive the seasonal blessings of wind, sun, and rain, his heart reverent in the presence of wildness"—left his story as a testament to the lost legacy of his people.

Geronimo's story—supplemented by oral legends and excerpts from other memoirs and diaries—is tempered by his bitter burden as a prisoner of war. Consequently, his perspective, given in the great warrior's own voice, casts a new light on a history too often told only from the victor's point of view.

A boy-child was born in No-doyohn Canyon, Arizona, in 1829 to a noble and proudly aggressive bloodline of Chiricahua Apaches. As an infant Geronimo, whose tribal name was "Goyahkla," was "warmed by the sun, rocked by the winds, and sheltered by the trees as other Indian babes." The boy's early childhood was relatively peaceful. His mother taught him to pray to the god Usen; his father educated him in the "pleasure of the chase, and the glories of the warpath." Thus, Goyahkla integrated the skills he would find necessary to lead his people: hunting, fierce resistance, and guerrilla warfare.

While still a boy Goyahkla's father died, and he assumed the care of his mother. At age 17 he was admitted to the council of warriors and given the honor of going to war—something he had long desired. Before long, he had married and fathered three children of his own.

Then came the fateful summer of 1858, a period destined to earn him his now-famous warrior name *Geronimo*—a Spanish term connoting "Indian Resistance"—and to turn him into a vengeful, unapologetic fighter.

The entire Chiricahua tribe, which customarily ranged into Mexico each year to trade, returned to camp one evening to find that a large band of Mexicans had raided their camp and killed many of their women and children, among them Geronimo's mother and his wife and children. The loss was devastating. He describes the numbness he felt when he encountered the scene: *I stood until all had passed, hardly knowing what I would do. I had no weapon, nor did I hardly wish to fight.... I did not pray, nor did I resolve to do anything in particular, for I had no purpose left.*

The survivors returned to Arizona, where Geronimo, according to Apache custom, burned his family's tepee and all other traces of his dead. Afterwards, he pledged ruthless vengeance on those who had murdered his family, and embarked on a campaign to persuade the other tribes to join in his raids. "I could not call back my loved ones," he remembered, " ... but I could rejoice in this revenge."

The proud Chiricahua persisted with his forays into Mexico for the next 15 years. Although he was wounded at least eight separate times—and lost another wife and child to counterattacks—most of the raids were successful. Some, however, led to bitter censure for Geronimo's sometimes reckless nature, a temperament molded by his unyielding hatred. (In fact, Geronimo chose not to tell his Anglo editor that he often resorted to tricks, lies, and kidnappings in his attempts to coerce his people to continue fighting when they otherwise were ready to surrender.)

While carrying out the Mexican raids, the Apaches and the "Yankees" presented no threat to one another. Then in October of 1860, when the half-breed son of a man named Ward ran away after a brutal beating by his father, Ward accused Cochise, the Chiricahua chieftain, of stealing him. Cochise appeared at the American soldiers' tent to pronounce his innocence, but the soldiers arrested him and his men. They were told they would be held prisoner until the boy was returned.

Cochise quickly escaped, but the incident ended formal relations with the whites and launched a bloody game of strike and retreat: if a man from either group was captured, it cost him his life.

In 1863 the chief of Geronimo's band, Mangus-Colorado (roughly translated "Red Sleeves"), negotiated a peace treaty with the whites. He was promised that if he brought his tribe to live near a specified white settlement, they would be protected and provided with ample supplies.

Mangus-Colorado moved part of his tribe, intending to send for the others after sincerity of the terms of the agreement had been tested. Notwithstanding his display of trust, the chief was immediately imprisoned and his guards were ordered to shoot him if he tried to escape. Then, during his first night in prison, the guards brutally tortured and then murdered Mangus-Colorado, an act Geronimo later called "the greatest wrong ever done to the Indians."

In the spring of 1876 Geronimo was officially branded an American outlaw. He had been residing with his Chiricahua band on the Fort Bowie reservation, where they had agreed to live under terms of a peace treaty made with General Oliver O. Howard. At first Howard had seen to it that the tribe was given every provision stipulated by the treaty. The federal government, however, soon began "reinterpreting" the agreement. When Geronimo uncovered a scheme to relocate his tribe, he led a band of Chiricahuas off the Fort Bowie reservation to join his friend Victoria, chief of the Cheyenne Apaches. But after a year of constant chasing and hiding, Geronimo and Victoria surrendered themselves to agent John P. Clum.

For the next two years the Apaches lived peacefully on the San Carlos Reservation. Then, hearing a rumor that federal officers at San Carlos were planning to incarcerate the "savages," Geronimo again fled the reservation. "We thought it more manly to die on the warpath," he said, "than to be killed in prison."

A year later a cavalry regiment led by General George Crook, one of the most impressive Apache trackers of all time, caught up with Geronimo's band and convinced them to return to the reservation. Geronimo showed up some days later steering a herd of stolen cattle and horses: if the whites placed such importance on riches, the warrior explained, he was going to join the white world well-supplied. The army, of course, had no intention of permitting Geronimo to raid livestock as he saw fit, and his property was confiscated.

It wasn't long before Geronimo, suffering the sting of this latest insult to his Apache sense of decorum, again abandoned the reservation. He had coaxed two other Indian chiefs to join his band by claiming that they were about to be arrested for the murder of a third chief—a murder which had not actually occurred. When the chiefs discovered the deception, they tried to kill him, and Geronimo once more set out on the run. But after an exhausting and hopeless dash, in which he managed to elude both federal troops and Mexican bandits, he again gave himself up to Crook. "Two or three words are enough," he told the General. "... Do with me what you please. I surrender. Once I moved about like the wind. Now I surrender to you and that is all."

Geronimo nevertheless yearned to be free. Eventually, when his distrust of the white man had once again been piqued, he slipped away from the reservation for the final time. After agreeing to scout for an Army tracking expedition, the warrior turned aside when the company was about a half mile from camp, said "Adios, Senores," with a salute—and began to scale a nearby mountain. Crook, his troops unable to follow Geronimo's trail, resigned his post; he had lost his biggest catch. Years later, when he heard that Crook had died, Geronimo said, "I think that General Crook's death was sent by the Almighty as a punishment for the many evil deeds he committed."

General Nelson A. Miles replaced Crook and immediately sent a large pursuit force after the rebels with orders to kill or capture Geronimo—preferably the former. Geronimo remembered the desperation he and his band felt at the time: *We had become reckless of our lives because we felt every man's hand was against us.... [So] we gave no quarter to anyone and asked no favors.*

After five months of battling both Mexicans and federal troops, the warriors' spirits were finally broken. On September 4, 1886 Geronimo surrendered for the last time, marching to Skeleton Canyon to place himself in the custody of General Miles. A few days later he found himself aboard a train headed for Florida, where for two years he was kept at hard labor. [The terms of the surrender have since been hotly disputed. It appears, however, to have been largely unconditional, except for the guarantee that Geronimo and his band would be reunited unharmed with their families. Geronimo himself, until the day he died, swore that the accord had been directly violated more than once.]

In the spring of 1887 the Apache rebels and their families were sent to Alabama. With no property on which to build houses or raise livestock, they suffered horribly. Finally they were transported West—not to the ancestral lands promised them but to Fort Sill, Oklahoma, where Geronimo remained a prisoner.

Geronimo ends his narrative with an impassioned plea to President Roosevelt to return him and his people to their Arizona homeland: *It is my land, my home, my father's land, to which I now ask to return. I want to spend my last days there, and be buried among those mountains. If this could be I might die in peace, feeling that my people, placed in their native homes, would increase in numbers, rather than diminish as at present, and that our name would not become extinct."*

Commentary

Before Geronimo was eventually subdued, he fought one of the greatest wars of liberation in the histories of dispossessed peoples. His love of freedom, his skillful leadership and his fierce attachment to his homeland enabled him to avoid final defeat for over a decade. But these years were filled with violence, treachery and broken promises on both sides.

The Apaches' circumstances became desperate. Here was a group of people whose attachment to their land was so enduring that they were willing to pay for it with their lifeblood; running the wheels of "progress" over them was another group whose only tie to the land was, from Geronimo's perspective, "what they could rape out of it."

Encouragingly, Americans today have adopted a more balanced, judicious alliance with the earth. For Geronimo, however, change was too late in coming. He died in a military hospital in Fort Sill on February 17, 1909—a tragically ironic and uncelebrated death: After getting drunk, he died of exposure when he fell from his buggy and lay all night in the freezing rain. His behest that his body be returned to his homeland was sadly forgotten; he died a prisoner of war and was ignominiously buried in foreign soil.

FREDERICK DOUGLASS
by William S. McFeely, W.W. Norton & Company, 1991

As a man who was born a slave and who would later advise presidents, Frederick Douglass was a true American hero. He was one of the greatest orators of the 19th century and probably did more than any other individual to abolish slavery, an amazing feat considering his humble beginnings.

William McFeely's biography is an excellent study both of the early struggle for racial equality and of the troubled times in which Douglass lived. Despite fierce opposition, he worked tirelessly to achieve his goals. *Except to run free, Frederick Douglass never ran away from anything.*

McFeely relies heavily on Douglass's three autobiographies, but also consults a vast number of other sources. The resulting Frederick Douglass is thus often portrayed as human (vain, impatient and stubborn)—but no less brilliant or powerful.

In February of 1818, near the eastern shore of the Chesapeake Bay, Frederick Augustus Washington Bailey was born to a Maryland slave mother and an unknown white father. The child was raised by his grandmother, Betsey Bailey, in her small and overcrowded cabin. With the resilience and wonder of a bright child, Frederick explored the world he had entered. When the boy was six he was taken into the homes of other relatives, one of whom was Aaron Anthony, the "absentee master" who managed the grand estate at Wye House for the wealthy Lloyd family.

Frederick soon caught the attention of Lucretia and Thomas Auld, Anthony's daughter and son-in-law. When their father lost his position, the two arranged to send Frederick to Baltimore to live with Thomas's brother, Hugh Auld, his wife Sofia, and their two-year-old son. He would stay with the Aulds for nearly six years.

Sophia initiated Frederick's formal education. Just as the boy was beginning to learn to read, however, Hugh put a stop to the lessons, warning that "learning would spoil [him].... It would forever unfit him for the duties of a slave." But Frederick had by then mastered enough skills to continue teaching himself, and in his studies he developed an intense interest in the subject of slavery: "I was eager to hear any one speak of slavery. Every little while, I could hear something about the abolitionists." At age 12 he began attending Sabbath school, and at 14 he was made a teacher in the school. Then in March of 1833 Frederick was sent back to live with Thomas Auld.

After less than a year Frederick was hired out to Edward Covey, well known for "breaking" the spirit of slaves. For the next six months there were regular beatings and hard labor, plowing and tending the fields. A few days after receiving a savage whipping, Frederick fought back. After nearly two hours of grappling with Covey, neither man was able to gain the upper hand and the fight ended. Now Frederick was more determined than ever to escape slavery.

The next year, 1835, Frederick was transferred to William Freeland's farm—a much more congenial workplace, at least when compared to Covey's estate—where he worked the fields alongside four other slaves. There he spent his Sundays teaching his fellow slaves to read. Word got around, and he soon held school for 20 or 30 slaves from nearby farms. The talk at the meetings would often turn to slavery—and escaping. Before long a small group of them had hatched a plan to make their break. But before it could be carried out, they were betrayed from within. Fortunately, due to a lack of evidence, all of the slaves involved were returned to their masters.

Frederick was sent back to Baltimore to live in the home of Hugh and Sophia, there to apprentice out in the ship-caulking trade. Baltimore accommodated a large free black community, and Frederick eagerly involved himself in its churches and intellectual organizations. It was while engaged in these interests that he met and courted Anna Murray, a free woman working as a domestic servant.

Though a slave, the industrious young man soon enjoyed considerable independence. He was allowed to live apart from the Aulds, upon the stipulation that he report to Hugh each week and pay the man three dollars of his earnings. But when Frederick once was late in making a payment, he was ordered to move back in with the family and give up all of his earnings. He obeyed, but "the Auld brothers had lifted the lid of their slave's hopes too widely ever to get it shut again. Now he—with Anna—would run away."

Dressed as a sailor and carrying a packet of seaman's papers acquired from a free man, Frederick Bailey left Baltimore on September 3, 1838. Traveling by road, river and rail through Delaware and Philadelphia, after being recognized but not betrayed and having his papers demanded but not scrutinized, Frederick reached his destination: New York City. Once Anna had made her way there, too, the couple was married and set off for New England, settling down in New Bedford, Massachusetts.

To avoid capture, Frederick dropped his two middle names and changed his last name to "Douglass." He found good work caulking ships at the New Bedford shipyard, but the other men refused to work with him because of his color. He found solace as an active member of the local African Methodist Episcopal Zion congregation. *The days I spent in little Zion, New Bedford, in the several capacities of sexton steward, class leader, clerk, and local preacher ...* he wrote, *[were] among the happiest days of my life.*

At a meeting on March 12, 1839, the runaway slave spoke out against colonization (the proposal to return slaves to Africa) and told of his experiences. A notice of his speech subsequently appeared in the Liberator, published by William Lloyd Garrison, who had been instrumental in founding both the Massachusetts and the New England Anti-Slavery Societies. In the spring of 1841 the wealthy abolitionist William C. Coffin heard Douglass speak and "thought that a good many people ought to hear what the beautifully spoken, earnest young black man had to say."

At a prominent anti-slavery conference later that year, Douglass was invited to take the stage. The sermon, based on his own life story, inspired his listeners. *He paid no attention to Parker Pillsbury's advice that it was "better [to] have a little of the plantation" in his speech and [ignored] Garrison's [warning] that he should not sound too "learned" lest people not "believe you were ever a slave." At the convention's close, he was invited to become an agent of the Massachusetts Anti-Slavery Society and go out on the lecture circuit to tell the world of his experiences as a slave.*

In 1843 Douglass took to the road, leaving his wife and children sometimes for months at a time to speak out against slavery's evils. Nearly 100 audiences—some dominated by pro-slavery advocates or, worse yet, angry mobsters—heard the soaring voice of the orator.

Indeed, the antislavery movement included many different factions whose leaders often disagreed on which course to follow. Accused by some of being an agitator, Douglass had by this time distanced himself from the Anti-Slavery Society, and, as early as 1844, he was becoming a leader in his own right.

In 1845 when he published his first autobiography, *Narrative of the Life of Frederick Douglass*, he crossed the Atlantic for a tour of the United Kingdom. His visits in Scotland and England went so well that he considered settling in Edinburgh. A British friend, Ellen Richardson, began a campaign to collect donations to buy their friend's freedom from Auld and, early in 1847, Frederick Douglass returned to the United States as a free man.

While in England, Douglass had also accepted contributions to embark on publishing his newspaper, a project opposed by the Anti-Slavery Society's leaders, who felt Douglass could be more productive as a lecturer than as an editor. Nevertheless, the first issue of his *North Star* was published on December 3, 1847.

Following Douglass's formal break with the American Anti-Slavery Society in 1851—a split precipitated by his persistence in citing the U.S. Constitution to achieve emancipation—the *North Star*'s name was changed to *Frederick Douglass' Paper*, a politically charged weekly.

Shortly after Douglass had completed his second book, *My Bondage and My Freedom* (an expanded version of his autobiography, of which a third volume, *Life and Times of Frederick Douglass*, would appear in 1881), bloody skirmishes erupted in Kansas after the 1855 passage of the Kansas-Nebraska Act. *[This time those] antislavery leaders who had been pacific, in action if not always in rhetoric—Henry Ward Beecher, Gerrit Smith, and Douglass himself ... —now called on their followers to send guns to the Kansas abolitionists.* On October 16, 1859, John Brown, along with 22 fellow abolitionists, attacked and seized the Harpers Ferry arsenal; their victory was short-lived, as all were soon captured or killed.

By 1860 more and more militancy was in the air. Black Americans were as despondent as they had ever been. Efforts to end slavery seemed to have been frustrated on every side.

When Abraham Lincoln assumed the Presidency in 1861, Douglass did all he could to convince the President that emancipation of the slaves should be the main objective of the Civil War that was just underway. Finally the President had heard enough. Lincoln did announce that on January 1, 1863, he would issue a proclamation freeing the slaves in the rebellious states. Sensing that history was in the making, Douglass urged young black males to support the Union cause. As thousands of black volunteers swelled Union ranks, Douglass believed it would not only bring ultimate victory but also bring about the respect of their white neighbors. Despite his assertions that Lincoln moved too slowly on black issues, the two developed a good working relationship—which was cut short by the President's assassination on April 14, 1865, just five days after Lee surrendered to Grant at Appomattox.

The end of slavery meant anything but the end of Douglass's public life. He protested President Andrew Johnson's retrograde policies and fought even more vigorously against racism and segregation practices. The freedom fighter's new crusade was aimed at winning for blacks the right to vote. Upon ratification of the 15th Amendment in 1870, however, the power behind the movement was immediately weakened, as longtime allies were forced to choose between black causes or those of American women—who would be denied voting and other basic human rights for another half century.

Douglass spent his later years waiting for a presidential appointment. He also continued to lend his strong voice to black rights. Paul Laurence Dunbar, a poet and aspiring journalist, described a speech Douglass read, consisting of his essay "The Race Problem in America," on "Colored People's Day," August 25, 1893: *As he read his paper ... Douglass was interrupted by jeers and catcalls from white men in the rear of the crowd.... The old man tried to go on, but the mocking persisted. His hand shook ... the great orator's voice faltered. [Then to his fellow abolitionists' delight and to his enemies' dismay, his voice came again], drowning out the catcalls as an organ would a penny whistle. "Men talk of the Negro problem," Douglass roared. "There is no Negro problem. The problem is whether the American people have loyalty enough, honor enough, patriotism enough, to live up to their Constitution." On he went for an hour: " ... We Negroes love our country. We fought for it. We ask only that we be treated as well as those who fought against it." Thunderous applause followed. He had won the day and the hearts of many.*

The legacy of Frederick Douglass's fight for black rights lives on long after his death, which came on February 20, 1895.

Gerd Ruge's highly acclaimed biography *Gorbachev* recounts how a man of humble origins ultimately rose to lead the Soviet Party, dominating and altering Soviet policy so radically that his name will forever be remembered in the annals of world history.

Birth of a Reformer

On March 2, 1931, in the small Russian farming village of Privolnoye, Mikhail Sergeyevich Gorbachev was born. Perhaps his village's name, which translates to "Freedom," in some way influenced the extraordinary changes Gorbachev would someday effect. Indeed, he would make more freedom available to Soviet citizens than anyone could ever imagine.

Gorbachev's independent turn of mind may actually have been inherited from his Cossack ancestors: *A love of freedom and independence was central to [Cossacks'] lives and nowhere in Russia was there a stronger feeling for equality before the law and democracy.* Gorbachev's maternal grandfather Panteli Gopalko exemplified Cossack independence. Gopalko was one of the first post-Revolutionary Russians to organize peasants into a cooperative where they could both farm their own land and work together to improve farming methods. Gopalko was highly respected, and his approach to cooperative farming was widely copied before collectivism replaced it.

In addition to caring for her young son Mikhail, Gopalko's daughter Maria also worked on the farm. Her husband, Sergei Gorbachev, drove tractors and maintained and repaired agricultural implements. The parents worked hard and lived quietly during Mikhail's childhood—until the advent of Stalin's enforced collectivism and political purges, which resulted in the arrest of three-fourths of the regional Stravropol Party cadres Persecution of the peasants soon followed. The purges, of course, had a profound influence on Mikhail: *Although he was still a young child, he saw what was happening to the people around him. To the simple, honest people who had made the Revolution, who had fought in the Civil War, who had founded the collective farms. They had all suffered, though they were innocent. Naturally he didn't accept this.*

When Mikhail was ten, the terror finally subsided. However, shortly thereafter his country was invaded by the Germans. Throughout most of World War II the Germans occupied Privolnoye. Mikhail's father served in the Soviet army for four years, while his mother worked long hours loading trains in a neighboring region.

When the town was finally liberated, normal life resumed and school classes opened up once more. Still, for quite a long time Mikhail was unable to attend because he had no clothes to wear. When at length the boy was able to return to class, his father promised him that he would never again be forced to interrupt his studies.

In 1950, when Mikhail was accepted to the Moscow University of Law, he quickly perceived the extent to which he was considered an outsider. But in spite of his ill-fitting clothes, he gradually established some close friendships. He soon moved into a room with five other young intellectuals. They dubbed it the "open room," because it was here that they freely exchanged their ideas.

Despite his outspokenness—which at the time certainly was not a valued trait—Gorbachev joined and rose quickly through the ranks of the Young Communist League. "What I liked about him was that he achieved what he did on his own," a friend remembers. "He had no influential relatives or friends, he wasn't even from Moscow. He got there on his own merits."

Gorbachev became a full member of the Communist Party in 1952. The following year Stalin died, inaugurating a period of open debate known as "The Thaw." Muscovite students and intellectuals cautiously addressed the problems and controversies facing the Soviet Union. In the ensuing months, the citizens of Moscow demanded elections and a genuine political party, not the bureaucratic chaos they had recently endured. The pressure for political restructuring taking place in Moscow during the 1950s aroused Gorbachev's mind and heart; 30 years later, similar ideas would resurface in his politics.

It was also during this period that Gorbachev met the slim, haughty, and seemingly unattainable Raisa Titarenko, also a young intellectual. The couple later married and, after their graduation, moved to Stravopol, the capital of Gorbachev's home region. While her husband worked for the Young Communists, Raisa became a university lecturer. In 1957 she gave birth to their daughter, Irina.

The Rise of a Political Leader

Although he disagreed with many policies of new Soviet leader Nikita Khrushchev, Gorbachev continued to advance within the Party. By October 1964 he had been promoted to a department leader in the Regional Party Committee. In this capacity, he was constantly forced to grapple with the shortcomings of worker productivity and agricultural technology. To better equip himself to confront these problems, Gorbachev enrolled as a student of economics at Stravopol Agricultural College.

In 1978 Gorbachev was elevated to the position of Agricultural Secretary of the Central Committee. One of his fellow Committee members later remarked, "This was one of the rare moments in Soviet history when a man's personal qualities brought about his rise. Gorbachev was young and energetic, he had made a name for himself in the Central Committee with his speeches on agriculture, but he belonged to no clan and no one was afraid of him or jealous of him."

Gorbachev worked hard to build and maintain his reputation as a *diligent* Party member rather than a *well-connected* Party member. *[He] did not simply follow instructions from party headquarters. He made changes on his own initiative, which entailed a certain amount of risk.* Moreover, he abhorred fellow Party members' corruption and nepotism, and took every measure to avoid their hunting parties and drinking binges. He also took pains to ensure that Irina was not treated as a typical Party brat, who usually spent summers abroad. Instead, the girl stayed in Privolnoye for the holidays, working in the garden with her grandmother. She wore no fur coats or diamonds, and was treated like any other young Soviet student.

Gorbachev soon was promoted to Secretary of the Central Committee and the following year was made a member of the Politburo: Mikhail Gorbachev was now one of the 14 most powerful men in the Soviet Union.

At the death of Soviet leader Leonid Brezhnev in 1982, Gorbachev's succession to the highest ranks of Soviet power seemed all but assured when his close friend Yuri Andropov was named as Party chief. However, neither Andropov nor his aged successor, Konstantin Chernenko, were to lead the country for very long; both died shortly after taking power. Thus in 1985 the Party deputies elected Gorbachev as the new Communist Party Leader—*the* most powerful man in the Soviet Union.

On the Road to Freedom

Gorbachev, subtly at first, began piloting the Soviet Union in a new direction. Being careful only to make changes within the established bureaucracy, his first two goals were *uskorehiye*, the acceleration of modernization based on technical development, and *povorot*, a change of focus. To facilitate his new goals, Gorbachev began slowly to replace the old faces of the Party with new, liberal thinkers—reformers in his own mold.

He quickly gained allies, especially from outside the Soviet Union. Though initially hesitant, Western leaders soon gained confidence in Gorbachev and were thrilled to see a new Soviet order beginning to emerge. *The aston-ished Western world had discovered a Soviet leader with a new style—a dynamic man, quite unlike his senile predeces-sors, who already seemed to stand for a new Soviet Union.* After Gorbachev visited Great Britain, Margaret Thatcher referred to him as a man "with whom one could do busi-ness."

Back home in the Soviet Union, meanwhile, Gorbachev grappled with severe problems; increased shortages of food and supplies had beget millions of impatient, angry workers. Realizing that in order to bring reform to the country he would have to allow citizens the right to speak freely against the Party, he called for an open dialogue. He asked questions, seeking answers from the villager, the factory worker, the businessman engaged in foreign trade. His people were astonished that he expected truthful answers—that he encouraged freedom of expression. *Glasnost* had taken hold.

For the first time since "The Thaw," Soviet citizens now began to speak and write openly about the problems faced by their country. They accused the parliament of being falsely elected, and called for election by the people. The average Soviet citizen began to demand rights accorded him under the constitution—a situation unheard of before Gorbachev assumed power.

For most Soviets *perestroika*—Gorbachev's plan for economic and political reform—seemed a beneficent philosophy that promised a better life. To be sure, Soviet workers merely wanted a better standard of living, not a Westernized government. Few, however, were prepared to accept the time it would take to exact reforms and to

establish a market-driven economy. Both democracy and a better standard of living would not come all at once.

Gorbachev moved slowly, patiently, cautiously, working and making compromises within the system. Other officials—like Boris Yeltsin, whom Gorbachev had brought to Moscow as Party Secretary—preferred a more accelerated pace. Speaking on behalf of reform and against corruption, Yeltsin endorsed many of the same principles as Gorbachev, but completely disagreed with his strategies.

Once many of the older and more conservative members had retired from Congress, announcing that they were simply too old to wage the new battles that would have to be fought, the people elected in 1989 young radicals such as Yeltsin to serve in Congress—and to begin the democratic debate.

After the elections Congress appointed Gorbachev as both General Secretary of the Party and the State President, making him more powerful than even Stalin had been. Second in power was Boris Yeltsin, the newly elected President of the Russian Federation.

Now that Moscow was moving toward a multi-party system, political and special interest groups were formed. Clearly policy had to change and develop as quickly as the people generated new, reform-minded ideas. Unfortunately, Gorbachev could not keep pace.

On November 9, 1989 the Berlin Wall came down and the tangible barrier between East and West was removed. The world now recognized Gorbachev's role in the sudden liberation of millions of people. In recognition of and appreciation for his efforts, he was awarded the Nobel Peace Prize.

Gorbachev was a hero—everywhere but in the Soviet Union. As fall turned to winter, food lines began to lengthen. Nevertheless, the Supreme Soviet retained its confidence in Gorbachev and elected him in May 1990 to the new office of Soviet President.

Within six months of the election, five of the Soviet Republics declared themselves independent, and another six announced their sovereignty within a disintegrating Union. Gorbachev's presidency was in unmistakable crisis. Yeltsin, in fact, soon led movements to help win independence for the Russian Republic. Because an inde-pendent Russia would end the Communist Party, Gorbachev was forced to exercise his executive powers to repeal Russia's independence.

In an effort to retain power, Gorbachev turned to supporters on the far right, allying himself with those opposed to reform and attempting to stifle glasnost by controlling the media. On January 13, 1991 Soviet tanks and troops surged into Lithuania to crush a provincial uprising. It was evident that Gorbachev was losing the battle. Finally on Christmas Day 1991, Gorbachev resigned his presidency of the collapsed Soviet empire. The next day Boris Yeltsin assumed the Kremlin office. The once-powerful union now was reduced to an indis-tinct group of independent states struggling for economic, political and social stability.

Gorbachev had managed, nevertheless, to create a new future for his country and for the world, and to guarantee himself a prominent pedestal in the annals of history.

THE IRON LADY – *A BIOGRAPHY OF MARGARET THATCHER*
by Hugo Young, Farrar Straus Giroux, 1989

The Iron Lady not only mirrors past political events but delves into the meaning behind those events. Considered an outstanding example of British political journalism, Hugo Young's moving biography of a woman who "has intrigued the world more than any of her predecessors since Churchill" is, in the words of Kirkus Reviews, "as definitive as a biography can be of a life still in progress."

Margaret Thatcher was born on October 13, 1925 in Grantham, Lincolnshire, England, the youngest daughter of Alderman Alfred Roberts. Raised under strict Victorian values of "hard work, self-help, rigorous budgeting and a firm belief in the immorality of extravagance," she applied the teachings of her father: "He taught me that you first sort out what you believe in ... then apply it. You don't compromise on things that matter." And as Prime Minister, she held to her beliefs: "Some say I preach merely the homilies of housekeeping or the parables of the parlour ... but, I do not repent. Those parables would have saved many a financier from failure and many a country from crisis."

Margaret's entrance into Oxford University in 1943 marked the "beginning of a lifetime's dedication to Conservative politics." She earned her degree in chemistry, a discipline she plied throughout her political career. In December 1984, for example, while discussing "Star Wars" (defensive space technology) with U.S. President Ronald Reagan, she reputedly told the president in a moment of exasperation: "But, I'm a chemist. I know it won't work."

Being a natural-born leader and a strong woman with a mind of her own, she impressed many in the Conservative Party. Her political future was "crucially facilitated" by her marriage to the wealthy Denis Thatcher in 1945. Their marriage produced twins, Mark and Carol, and provided her with the financial freedom to pursue her political career with "undistracted single-mindedness."

At age 32 Thatcher won the parliamentary seat at Finchley, with a Conservative majority of 12,000. The *Finchley Press* summarized her achievement in a single ecstatic sentence: *Speaking without notes, stabbing home points with impressive hands, Mrs. Thatcher launched fluently into a clear-cut appraisal of the Middle East situation, weighed up Russia's propagandist moves with the skill of a housewife measuring the ingredients in a familiar recipe ... switched swiftly to Britain's domestic problems (showing a keen grasp of wage and trade union issues), then swept her breathless audience into a confident preview of Conservatism's dazzling future.* With the cementing of "valuable" political friendships and her own political ideologies, Thatcher rose to parliamentary prominence.

Later, the 1964 election in which Harold Macmillan was deposed and Edward Heath came into power heralded the beginning of a "new era." Heath did as he had promised, freeing up international trade, modernizing antiquated factories, and slaughtering other of government's "sacred cows." During this time Thatcher moved through junior positions that provided her little political glory but immeasurable experience for the years to come.

Heath was reelected in 1970. Viewing Margaret as a "diligent, reliable ... fit colleague," he appointed her to the Department of Education and Science. This formative experience taught her "both the limits ... and huge potential of a minister's power."

After sailing through the 1974 election, Heath appointed Thatcher to a housing policy committee. It was during this time that she began a "cautious break with Heathism" and emerged "a singularly 'political' politician ... well able to depart, where necessary, from what she personally believed to be right."

Under the tutelage of Airey Neave, who viewed her as a political genius, Thatcher won the nomination for Prime Minister of the newly formed National Coalition Government, taking control at a time when the party was ready for a return to fundamentalist Conservatism. Cautiously, she established "a philosophy most people could understand," while economist and political ally Joseph Keith drove home the message of the new "Thatcherism." She reiterated these philosophies whenever she spoke: Britain and socialism were not the same. The British inheritance—the right of every man to enjoy the rewards of his own labor—was the very essence of a free country.

To fulfill the British inheritance, she empowered a number of men and women—some highly controversial choices—to iron out, among other things, the regulations on the economy, inflation, public spending, trade union law reform, public sector pay, and public sector fights.

During her first six months in office as Prime Minister, Thatcher established her dominance and educated herself in the intricacies of foreign affairs. Expounding on her deep-rooted abhorrence of Communism, she called for European unity and common defense. In doing so, she introduced her new "international personality" during a speech in January 1976. "The Russians ... put guns before butter," she declared. "[They are] a super power only ... in the military sense ... a failure in human and economic terms." Her voice reverberating, she then urged Britain to meet the challenge of unity or "end up on the scrap heap of history."

"The Iron Lady" forcefully established her iron-willed reputation. Recognizing her own shortcomings, she commissioned leaders who would compensate for her lack of skill in certain areas, and who would accept her authoritarian style of leadership. One of these leaders was Lord Carrington, a foreign advisor chosen as her first Foreign Secretary. Of utmost importance on Carrington's agenda was the issue of Rhodesia, which had been torn by civil war for the previous seven years. After many months of seeking Rhodesian control through the ballot box, Thatcher finally saw no other option but to seize control of the former colony, a decision that led to the formal transfer of power to an independent Zimbabwe on April 17, 1980. The *Zambia Times* applauded the action, expressing that Thatcher had "left a ray of hope on a dark horizon" and that "inside the iron casing is a soft heart." She won the praise of Britons and Rhodesians alike as a champion of human rights.

Initially, positive popular opinion followed Thatcher into the war to reclaim the Falkland Islands from Argentinean occupation. *However, as soon as the war was over, the obvious question had to be addressed; that is, why had it occurred?* The report of the Franks Committee found her not guilty of negligence or of failing to provide protection for the islands before seizure had occurred. Consequently, Thatcher won a second term.

Now for the first time the Prime Minister succeeded in filling the three most senior positions in the cabinet with partisan ministers. Despite inside support, Thatcher's second term was torn with problems. The nation remained in dire straits in terms of employment, health care and defense spending. Personal scandals involving key cabinet members, the American invasion of Grenada—about which she had not been forewarned—and the imminent arrival of Cruise missiles in Britain further distressed Prime Minister Thatcher. As a result she "began to experience what most other British leaders had learned to suffer much sooner in their time." Friends, disillusioned, turned away; the press, which had compared her performance during her first term "to that of the gigantic and leonine spirit of Winston Churchill," now censured her. Her failure to accompany the Americans into Grenada was touted as a "huge failure of judgment." Still, "the quality which distinguishes politicians from most other people, is resilience," and, unlike some of her predecessors, Thatcher wasn't prone to despair. She declared: "I am in politics because of the conflict between good and evil, and I believe that in the end, good will triumph."

Thatcher set to work stripping the powerful monopoly unions of their power and bringing the budget under control. She also increased defense spending and modernized the British nuclear deterrent. The Soviets were "not to be trusted," Mrs. Thatcher explained, but negotiations would continue.

About this time she visited Hungary, a trip that eventually led her to a meeting with Mikhail Gorbachev. In December 1984, the Soviet leader brought a large delegation to London: *It proved to be a most providential occasion. Within three months, Chernenko was dead and Gorbachev had succeeded him.*

Gorbachev made a powerful impression on Thatcher, who, she said, shared two great goals: first, to stimulate effective disarmament talks and, second, to further trade and cultural exchange. Gorbachev also acknowledged a personal warmth for "his new found friend," a relationship which later enabled Thatcher to act as an interlocutor between the super powers of Russia and the United States.

While Gorbachev was still in London, Thatcher set off on a six-day world tour. On a stopover in Beijing, she undertook one of the "most momentous pieces of bilateral treaty-making [of] her time"—the surrender of the lease on Hong Kong. The last leg of her tour took her to Washington, where, "only a week after her brilliant conversations with the greatest enemy of Star Wars (Gorbachev), she would be sitting … with its most determined friend...." *Camp David might not have stopped the Star Warriors in their tracks, but it provided a frame of reference for a later address to Congress where she supported the President's continued research in nuclear deterrence—the Strategic Defense Initiative.*

Thatcher finally managed to sway public opinion back to her side: *For want of an organized, politically credible alternative, the intellectual argument in favour of Thatcherite economics had carried the day …* Further determining her success was the perception among Conservative Britons of a vibrant economy, in which even the unemployed "felt better off"; privatization had made positive inroads, and monopolies no longer held sway. The burgeoning economy became a headline story and, by the time of the election, British optimism was at an all-time high.

Consequently, Thatcher's third term cleared the way "for the pursuit of a brand of Conservatism which no longer had quite the same need to answer to the customary hazards of democratic existence." *It was in place, as it seemed unchallengeable. And so without question, was its leader: confirmed in her luxuriant conviction that she had carried Britain, by the only honest policies available, towards the destiny her people desired and the world would strive to emulate.... However, this populism … was marked by a disabling paradox:* her strong, sometimes abrasive personality soon began to wear thin on Britons; many disliked her, few loved her. What was worse, she did not seem to like them. Over-anxious to have Britain succeed and run on sound economic principles, she would not tolerate less than precision among her staff. Here she was, a populist who had lost her popularity: *She was one of us … arguably our supreme representative, the complete personification of what we were. And yet, after ten years, she remained different. In an important sense, she wasn't "one of us" at all. She was altogether too superior.*

To the end, Thatcher remained the ultimate, irrepressible fighter; as she often described herself, she "was made of sterner stuff." And in the final outcome, though loved and hated at once, Thatcher was always respected. "I hang on," she once told an interviewer after nine years as Prime Minister, "until I believe there are people who can take the banner forward with the same commitment, belief, vision, strength and singleness of purpose."

TRUMAN
by David McCullough, Simon and Schuster, 1992

"I am just a common everyday man whose instincts are to be ornery, who's anxious to be right ... " Thus did Harry Truman describe himself, and for good or ill, this is how most Americans perceive their 33rd President—as a "common man," a man of the people. But David McCullough, in his exhaustive, Pulitzer Prize-winning biography *Truman*, leaves us with a vivid, three-dimensional portrait of a most *uncommon* man—and of the dramatic times he lived through and helped shape.

Harry S Truman (the middle S, in true Truman style, is an independent entity, not an initial) was born in Lamar, Missouri, on May 8th, 1884 to John and Martha Truman, and grew up on his grandfather Solomon Young's Blue Ridge farm in Jackson County, Missouri. Young Harry's eyesight was notably bad; he was, in his own words, "blind as a mole." As a consequence, he avoided most sports, preferring to stay home and read, play the piano or spend time with his mother, whom he adored. "I was kind of a sissy," he later admitted; but boyhood friends claimed they respected his seriousness and intelligence.

After graduating high school with honors, Truman went to work first for a newspaper, then a railroad, and then a bank, until his father asked him to stay home and help with the family farm. *The family came first. If Harry harbored any regrets or resentment, he never let on.... Everything now revolved around the farm.... Everyone worked, "and woe to the loafer," as Harry remembered.*

Truman stayed on the farm for more than a decade, and took it over entirely after his father died in 1914. Then, in 1917, when America entered World War I, the 33-year-old farmer joined the National Guard and was sent to France, where he attained the rank of captain and commanded a battery of 194 men and four artillery guns. He was soon recognized for displaying "fierce courage under fire," and won the lifelong loyalty of his men.

When he returned to Missouri in 1918, Truman was a changed man; he had discovered he could lead. And just as important, in the Army Truman had made the acquaintance of Jim Pendergast, whose father Michael headed a powerful political organization in Kansas City.

In 1919 Truman married Bess Wallace, whom he had loved since childhood, and opened a Kansas City haberdashery. Times were tough in Missouri and the store eventually failed. But as fate would have it, that same year the Pendergasts asked him to run for Jackson County judge. "Mike Pendergast picked me up and put me into politics and I've been lucky," he later wrote.

The neophyte campaigner won the judgeship, and 12 years later, in 1934, the Pendergast political machine endorsed him for the United States Senate. Again Truman won the race, but it was said that he had obtained his new post "under a cloud" because of his Pendergast connections. Nevertheless, Truman remained loyal to his benefactors.

In 1940 Lloyd C. Stark, a former governor of Missouri, challenged Truman for his Senate seat. Few people, including President Roosevelt—who favored Truman because of his support for the New Deal—thought the incumbent had much of a chance to win without Pendergast backing. But Truman refused to give up. He campaigned all across the state, and pulled off a stunning political upset.

Not long afterwards, with World War II raging in Europe, Senator Truman chaired what became known as the Truman Committee, established to investigate waste and inefficiency in the awarding of defense contracts. The committee did such capable work that "often a threat to 'take everything to the Truman Committee' [was] sufficient to force a cure of abuses."

Because President Roosevelt's health was deteriorating and Democratic Party bosses cringed at the thought of "liberal pacifist" Vice President Henry Wallace assuming the Presidency, Roosevelt was pressured to pick the reluctant Truman as his 4th-term running mate. The choice was not without detractors: Truman's selection was labeled "the Missouri Compromise"; *Time* magazine, which only the summer before had lauded the Senator's committee work, now portrayed him as a "drab mediocrity [and] 'the mousy little man from Missouri.'"

Roosevelt and Truman narrowly defeated Dewey. But although the victory seemed to have rejuvenated the President, he died only 82 days after taking office. Truman felt totally overwhelmed by the weight placed upon his shoulders. "Boys," he pleaded with a group of reporters, "if you ever pray, pray for me now. I don't know whether you fellows ever had a load of hay fall on you, but when they told me yesterday what had happened, I felt like the moon, the stars, and all the planets had fallen on me." Truman's critics, meanwhile, were aghast; they saw him as shallow and naive, an unsophisticated farmer with a good heart. "If Harry Truman can be President," jeered one, "so could my next-door neighbor."

On May 7th, 1945, only three weeks after Truman had taken the Presidential oath, Germany surrendered to the Allied forces. As Russian troops scurried to occupy most of Eastern Europe, Secretary of War Henry Stimson kept Truman abreast of advances in the Manhattan Project, the top-secret development of the atomic bomb.

In July of 1945, Truman, Churchill and Stalin, the leaders of the "Big Three" Allied nations, held meetings in Potsdam, Germany. It was there that Truman received momentous news: the first atomic bomb had been successfully detonated in New Mexico. The President gave much consideration to the precedent that would be set if he introduced atomic weapons to the world. Nevertheless, continuing heavy American losses in the Pacific eventually convinced him to give the go-ahead to use the weapon against Japan.

On August 6th, 1945 an atomic bomb was dropped on Hiroshima, annihilating much of the city; four days later a second bomb devastated the city of Nagasaki. Then, with Japan reeling in shock, Truman mercifully ordered a ceasefire. "The thought of wiping out another city was too horrible," he said. Japan surrendered on August 14, eventually bringing World War II to an end.

As Truman struggled to help the nation convert to a peacetime economy, he was beset by problems: his liberal domestic programs drew immediate Congressional opposition; a series of labor strikes crippled the nation; a succession of cabinet resignations and firings became fodder for the press; and he was criticized for bringing his inexperienced Missouri "cronies" into the White House. Even his now-famous relationship with his mother became a target of ridicule. He was depicted by the media as "indecisive," "vacillating" and "disorganized," and one newsman cited Truman's "curious reluctance or even inability to think of himself as President ... "

The Republicans swept the 1946 elections in both houses of Congress—losses which some interpreted as a referendum on Truman's lackluster administration. Now he was viewed by most as not only an "ordinary" man but as one "sadly miscast" in his role.

Others, however, took a wider view. Winston Churchill, who had coined the term "Iron Curtain" just one year earlier, admired Truman's firm stand against the Russians. Undersecretary of State Dean Acheson labeled Truman "the captain with the mighty heart." Clark Clifford remained staunchly loyal; he had worked in the Truman White House during the era that produced both the Truman Doctrine—a policy which provided economic and military aid to countries threatened by interference from other states, most notably the Soviet Union—and the Marshall Plan, a program of massive economic aid to rebuild European nations. "Harry Truman and the United States saved the free world," Clifford declared categorically.

Republicans often accused the Truman administration of being "soft on Communism." This was one of the charges which led Truman in exasperation to declare that "no man in his right mind would ever wish to be President if he knew what it entailed." Nevertheless, in 1948 he decided to run for election in his own right, saying that he relished the "prospect of taking on the Republicans in an all-out, full-scale championship fight."

As usual, most observers didn't give Truman much of a chance. In addition to his other political problems, he had adopted a civil-rights stance, thereby alienating Southern Democrats and dividing his party. Many of the New Dealers in Truman's own party wanted to dump the President and nominate Dwight Eisenhower, the most popular man in the country, as the Democratic candidate. The press became openly contemptuous, branding Truman "inept and pathetic." His approval rating dipped to an all-time low.

Even before the Democratic Convention, Truman was rated so far behind Republican nominee Thomas E. Dewey that some pollsters predicted he could not possibly win. But when Truman named the much respected Alben Barkley as his running mate and promised a Democratic victory, he brought the convention to its feet.

Then the never-say-die Missourian traveled the country by train, covering 21,928 miles in his now famous "Whistle-stop Campaign." Grinning, he promised, "I'm going to give 'em hell." At each stop huge crowds gathered to hear Truman speak. Detractors claimed that people came only out of curiosity, but if so, Truman confounded their expectations. His potent message struck a responsive chord nationwide. He tore into the Republican Congress, calling its leaders "gluttons of privilege," and "cold ... cunning men [who] had stuck a pitchfork in the farmer's back." One correspondent later characterized the energetic though grueling Truman campaign as "sharp speeches fairly criticizing Republican policy and defending New Deal liberalism mixed with sophistry, bunkum piled higher than haystacks, and demagoguery tooting merrily down the track."

Meanwhile, Truman's aides were growing more and more despondent—and with good reason: newspapers were already loudly proclaiming Dewey as the next President. But to the media's mammoth chagrin, on November 2, 1948, Truman defeated Dewey in the biggest upset in the history of presidential elections. "Not one polling organization had been correct in its forecast," notes McCullough. "Every expert had been proven wrong, [and] 'a great roar of laughter arose from the land.'"

Although the late '40s and the '50s were a time of unequaled wealth and prosperity for Americans, controversy surrounded Truman's second term. The most debated issue was the President's decision to commit American troops to armed conflict in Korea. Some argued that the military intervention was nothing less than an undeclared war—in which many American lives were lost and no real objectives were achieved. Others insisted that Truman's firmness and resolve had saved South Korea from a Communist takeover.

In one of the most questionable decisions of the war, Truman revoked the command of much-decorated General Douglas MacArthur. A nationwide storm of almost hysterical protest ensued. Many in Congress called for the President's impeachment. But to Truman, the decision boiled down to a Constitutional issue: the President, acting as civilian Commander-in-Chief, should have authority over all military leaders.

Truman declined to run for reelection in 1952, despite the fact that he knew no other Democrat had a chance of defeating Dwight Eisenhower—who had changed affiliations to run on the Republican ticket. The President's reason for stepping down, writes McCullough, was simple: *For as far back nearly as he could remember, Truman had held to the ideal of the mythical Roman hero Cincinnatus, the patriot farmer who assumes command in his country's hour of peril, then returns to the plow.*

In 1953 Truman and his wife Bess, who never was comfortable living in Washington, moved back to Independence, Missouri. For the next 20 years the retired President devoted his time to working on his memoirs and organizing the Harry Truman Library, where his papers would be preserved. "I tried never to forget who I was," Truman said, "and where I'd come from and where I was going back to."

Harry S Truman died on December 26, 1972. In summing up the meaning of his Presidency to American history, McCullough quotes correspondent Eric Severeid: "I am not sure he was right about the atomic bomb, or even Korea. But remembering him reminds people what a man in office ought to be like. It's character, just character. He stands like a rock in memory now."

MY LIFE
by Golda Meir, G.P. Putnam's Sons, 1975

Golda Meir's childhood in Russia passed with few happy memories. Her most vivid impressions, she said, were marked by fear. "I didn't know then … " she wrote, "what a pogrom was, but I knew it had something to do with being Jewish and with the rabble that used to surge through town, brandishing knives and huge sticks, screaming 'Christ killers' as they looked for the Jews, and who were now going to do terrible things to me and to my family." To escape persecution, Golda's father immigrated with his family to "the golden country of America," where he—and thousands of other Jews—hoped to find safety and prosperity.

The Meirs settled in Milwaukee, and Golda's father quickly set out to fashion his family into "Americans." This transformation included wearing American clothes, speaking English instead of Yiddish, and attending school. For Golda, her family's new freedom was best characterized by a Labor Day parade in which her father marched alongside mounted police, who, instead of shooting the marchers, as the Cossacks had so often done, escorted them down the route.

But not all the Meirs were happy living in America. Golda's older sister Sheyna found only loneliness in their new home. She argued constantly with her parents and several times attempted to move out on her own. Sheyna broke with her parents finally when she contracted TB and had to be sent to a Jewish sanatorium in Denver. There, against the will of her parents, she married a Russian socialist who had escaped prison and made his way to America.

Afterwards, family pressures mounted on Golda as well. First, her mother tried to arrange a marriage for her. Golda, however, who was only 14, rejected her mother's plans. Then, thinking Golda had all the education a girl needed, her parents refused to send her to high school. Unable to bear such treatment, Golda escaped to Denver to live with her sister and continue her education there—a move which proved to be a turning point in her life.

In Russia, Golda had often listened to Sheyna and her friends discuss liberal politics; now in Denver, the independent young woman again found herself in company of her sister's circle of intellectuals—many of whom were Labor Zionists. Not only did these discussions prove to form the political ideals Golda would practice for the rest of her life, but while taking part in them she also met her future husband Morris Meyerson.

Shortly after Golda's 17th birthday, an urgent letter from her father drew her back to Milwaukee. This time her parents were less strict with her; they could see that she had matured and would no doubt move on to college in preparation to become a teacher. Her parents, especially her father, had also become involved in the local Labor Zionist movement, the same movement through which Golda had met many of the great pioneers of Zionism, who had already begun their struggle for a Jewish homeland in Palestine.

Morris, who later joined her in Milwaukee, was less enthusiastic about Golda's increasing political involvement. After organizing a successful march protesting an outbreak of anti-Semitic pogroms in Eastern Europe, Golda, dissatisfied with the breadth of her efforts, decided once and for all to unite with her fellow Zionists in Palestine. Morris understood her decision, but it took several long months of deliberation before he decided that he, too, would accompany her. In 1909 the two of them were married; Golda became Mrs. Meyerson—which later, while serving as a minister in the Israeli cabinet, she changed to its Hebrew equivalent "Meir."

Golda and her husband were joined by Sheyna, and together they sailed to Egypt. When they reached Tel Aviv, however, the newest Jewish community outside of Jaffa, they were unimpressed. After lodging there temporarily, Golda and Morris joined a kibbutz at Mehavia. It was there that Golda found a way of life "more likely than any other to offer us a channel for expressing ourselves as Zionists, as Jews and as human beings."

Golda adapted quite quickly to the stark, demanding lifestyle—and soon took up a position of leadership. Morris, though, could not adjust to the lack of privacy and artistic opportunities. When he became ill, Golda was forced to leave the kibbutz. After he recovered Golda briefly returned to the kibbutz, but because Morris refused to join her, she resigned herself to living in Jerusalem.

The ensuing four years were the most miserable of Golda's life. More than the struggle against deprivation, she felt trapped by the anxiety of providing for a family that now included two children, Sarah and Menachem. She also longed for the sense of purpose she had felt in the kibbutz. Thus, when she was asked to join the leadership of the Histadrut, a major Jewish labor union, she jumped at the chance. Morris understood—as Golda would also come to understand—that her political interests had driven an ever-widening wedge between them. Eventually she moved with the children to Tel Aviv, where Morris visited them on weekends.

During her first years with the Histadrut, Golda served on the Executive Committee, and there met the people who would later bring about Israel's statehood: David Ben-Gurion, the father of modern Israel; Levi Eshkol, Israel's third prime minister; and Berl Katznelson, the unofficial "father figure" of the Labor Zionists. Her political work on the committee also taught her the value of "pragmatic socialism"—which would form the root of her public service for the rest of her life.

While relations between Arabs and Jews had often been tenuous, in 1936 Arab "disturbances" exacerbated existing tensions. The colonial British government quickly established the Peel Commission, which was to suggest partitioning Palestine into Jewish and Arab sectors. The Arabs rejected the proposal, and, with little international sponsorship for Zionism, the British closed Jewish immigration.

The British upheld their exclusive policies throughout the long, bitter years of the holocaust. To Golda it was inexplicable that a government which fought so valiantly against Hitler could, at the same time, actively oppose Jewish immigration to Palestine. Ironically, when the British Labor Party—which had vocally supported Zionism—came to power, they pursued a policy that blocked or turned back from Palestine "illegal" ships filled with Holocaust survivors. It seemed that the gateway to the Jewish promised land would forever be closed.

Then, finally, the British government, caught in an escalating conflict between Jews and Arabs, appealed to the United Nations, which proposed a partition plan much like that of the Peel Commission. This time, despite Arab opposition, the U.N.'s affirmative vote sanctioned Israeli autonomy.

Golda cried like a child when she and other Zionist leaders signed the official Israeli Scroll of Independence. She was soon dispatched to the U.S. to lobby American Jews to arm the infant state against the Arab militias massed at its borders.

As the War of Independence unfolded, Golda witnessed little of the early action. Shortly after returning to Israel, she was sent to Moscow as first Israeli minister to Russia. Back in the country of her birth, she saw again firsthand the anti-Semitism which had so shattered her childhood.

Her stay in Moscow lasted only seven months. Ben-Gurion, Israel's first Prime Minister, called Golda home to serve as Minister of Labor in his cabinet. For seven years Golda dealt with wave after wave of Jewish immigrants. She oversaw the construction of immigrant camps, the development of language and work skills programs, and the construction of houses and communities to permanently settle the expanding populace.

During this busy period, Morris died. Though the couple had long been separated, they had always loved each other, and she privately grieved over his death.

In 1956 other sorrows took center stage in Golda's life. The Arab states continued to arm themselves against the Jewish nation. Serving as Foreign Minister, Golda was well aware of the dangers and was one of few who knew beforehand about the Sinai Offensive, an attack in which Israeli troops, in a few short days, swept across the Sinai Peninsula and Gaza Strip. Though the offensive freed the Israelis from exposure to the terrorist bases, the U.N. demanded that the Israelis withdraw and cede the territory to a peacekeeping force. As Golda attempted to negotiate a peace settlement, she realized that the international community had never understood the Israeli people or the complex nature of the Middle East conflict.

"We were the firstborn of the United Nations," she admitted, "but we were being treated like unwanted stepchildren, and I must admit that it hurt."

In her duties as Foreign Minister, Golda headed numerous outreach programs to developing African and Asian countries. Israel's enormous pool of trained specialists, however, soon gave way to Arab pressure. The ensuing Yom Kippur War forced most of these partner countries to break ties with Israel, and, once again, the Jewish state learned that "One can count on no one but oneself." This bitter lesson was only reinforced by the international indifference to Egyptian and Syrian rhetoric—and further Arab readiness to launch another attack on Israel. In the end, the world did not resist when Egypt's Nasser ordered U.N. forces out of the Sinai Peninsula. Once again Israel stood on its own—and once again, with American support, it swiftly routed its foes.

Golda, after decades of government service, observed this war from retirement. Within a short few months, however, the Labor Party called on her to head a delegation with the mission of unifying its three factions.

When her work was done, Golda hoped to return to private life. Then one night she received a phone call: Eshkol, the Prime Minister, had died of a heart attack. As "manager" of the unified Labor Party, she was asked to supervise the interim government until formal elections could be held. In the fall of 1969, at the age of 70, she was elected Prime Minister of Israel.

Her five years in office began and ended with war. Israel was determined to hold the territories gained during the Six-Day War until a permanent peace agreement could be signed. The Arabs, on the other hand, were just as adamant that Israel return the occupied lands. The result was a War of Attrition, in which Egypt, with Soviet backing, made consistent attacks on Israeli holdings. Golda, knowing that another full-scale assault would soon commence, did all she could both to initiate peace talks with Arab leaders and secure arms for her country. After several visits to Washington, she finally won U.S. assurances of continued support.

In 1973, on Yom Kippur—or sacred "Day of Atonement"—Egypt and Syria suddenly launched a two-front attack. Caught off guard, the Israelis initially gave up ground. For Golda Meir, every decision became a harrowing dilemma in which Israeli lives were at stake. Not until a few weeks into the war, with U.S. military aid on its way, did the tide turn.

In November of the same year a ceasefire agreement was signed. But the "Yom Kippur War" had taken its toll, both on the nation and its aged Prime Minister. Exhausted, Golda resigned in June of the following year.

Golda Meir's vision of Israel, a homeland for her people, has endured. Until her death at age 80 in 1978, she continued to dream of a strong and peaceful nation where her grandchildren would "grow up as free Jews in a country that is their own."

PROFILES IN COURAGE
by John F. Kennedy, Harper & Brothers, 1955

*T*his is a book about that most admirable of human virtues—courage.... These are the stories of the pressures experienced by eight United States Senators and the grace with which they endured them—the risks to their careers, the unpopularity of their courses, the defamation of their characters, and sometimes, but sadly only sometimes, the vindication of their reputations and their principles.

The eight political heroes spotlighted in John F. Kennedy's Pulitzer Prize-winning *Profiles in Courage* truly exemplify the philosophy made famous by its author: "Ask not what your country can do for you—ask what you can do for your country."

All eight men—John Quincy Adams, Daniel Webster, Thomas Hart Benton, Sam Houston, Edmund G. Ross, Congressman Lucius Quintus Cincinnatus Lamar, George Norris, and Robert A. Taft—refused to sacrifice their principles despite the most crushing opposition. Each also bucked the will of his political party, an important matter to Kennedy, who believed that politicians must sometimes rise above partisan considerations.

Four of Kennedy's heroic profiles are featured here. The idea they embody—that individuals can be a force for liberty and justice by following their convictions in the face of popular opposition—still appeals to Americans' noblest qualities.

•

John Quincy Adams was the son of the second U.S. President, John Adams, and was eventually to assume the mantle of the Presidency himself. *Harsh and intractable ... he had a tenacity of purpose, a lofty and inflexible courage, an unbending will, which never qualified or flinched before human antagonist, or before exile, torture, or death.* Unfortunately, these qualities did not serve him well in the political arena. "A politician in this country must be the man of a party," he explained. "I would fain be the man of my whole country."

Elected to the Massachusetts State Senate in 1803, Adams immediately infuriated his own Federalist party by sanctioning the views of Republican President Thomas Jefferson, who argued for individual rights over government intervention. Although ostracized by the Federalists and ignored by colleagues and constituents, he stuck to his ideals: *His guiding star was the principle ... his father had laid down many years before: "The magistrate is the servant not of his own desires, not even of the people, but of his God."*

In 1807 Adams supported an embargo bill designed to retaliate against "British aggressions upon American ships." The embargo hit New England, including his home state, harder than any other section of the country. Newspapers attacked him as "a party scavenger ... one of those ambitious politicians who lives on both land and water, and occasionally resorts to each, but who finally settles down in mud." The criticism didn't surprise Adams; early on he confided to a fellow supporter of the embargo that "This measure will cost you and me our seats ... "

As Adams predicted, the Massachusetts legislature voted to replace him at the end of his term, and instructed the state's Senators to vote for repeal of the embargo. Out of deference to his constituents' wishes, Adams straightway resigned rather than serve out his term. Eventually, his political fortunes rose again. He went on to serve a "politically independent term" as United States President, then closed out his political career in the House of Representatives.

"Far from regretting any one of those acts for which I have suffered," he said looking back, "I would do them over again ... at the hazard of ten times as much slander, unpopularity, and displacement."

•

On March 7th, 1850, a Massachusetts Senator delivered a speech that postponed the outbreak of civil war in the United States for eleven more years. That "7th of March" speech, however, ruined him politically, bringing on vicious criticism which continued even after his death.

Daniel Webster was, in the words of contemporaries, "a compound of strength and weakness, dust and divinity ... a great man with a small ambition." He was also probably the greatest orator the Congress has ever seen.

In 1850 many Southern leaders were threatening secession over the Northern states' refusal to allow the expansion of slavery into the Western territories. Virginia Senator Henry Clay asked the gifted Webster for his support on a compromise bill that would allow slave states to remain as such. A fervent abolitionist, Webster regarded slavery "as a great moral and political evil," but he was also a Union man, long famous for his impassioned cry, "Liberty and Union, now and forever, one and inseparable!" He believed that secession would lead to bloodshed and was convinced that Clay's compromise was the country's only salvation.

On the appointed day, Webster stood before a packed Senate chamber and proclaimed: "I wish to speak today, not as a Massachusetts man, nor as a Northern man, but as an American and a Member of the Senate ... " The three-hour speech that followed literally "disarmed and quieted the South." One newspaper later reported: *Webster did more than any other man in the whole country, and at a greater hazard of personal popularity, to stem and roll back the torrent of sectionalism which ... threatened to overthrow the pillars of the Constitution and the Union.*

But at the time Northern abolitionists were outraged at what they regarded as Webster's betrayal. He was labeled a "traitor to the cause of freedom." Educator Horace Mann called him "a fallen star! Lucifer descending from Heaven!"—and he lost any chance for the Presidential nomination that he had long coveted.

Webster died in 1852, "disappointed and discouraged" but true to the Union to the end. " ... No man can suffer too much, and no man can fall too soon," he proclaimed some weeks before his death, "if he suffer or if he fall in defense of the liberties and Constitution of his country."

•

Thomas Hart Benton, who served the people of Missouri in the Senate for 30 consecutive years, loved a good fight. Once he warned an opponent, "I never quarrel, sir. But sometimes I fight, sir; and whenever I fight, sir, a funeral follows, sir." But his last great fight—waged against secessionists in the South, including voters from his own state—resulted in the Democratic Senator's own political funeral.

As a longtime champion of Westward expansion, Benton was enormously popular among his fellow Missourians throughout his first four Senate terms; but by the early 1840s, Missouri, as a slave state, had begun to identify strongly with its Southern neighbors. Benton, holding to his Union ideals, suffered a steep decline in popularity and was barely elected to his fifth term in 1844. Despite the close election, he insisted on going against his party and his constituents in opposing the annexation of Texas—which would have upset the ration of slave to free states. South Carolina Senator John C. Calhoun, a pro-slavery advocate, denounced Benton as "false to the South," and the Missouri legislature agreed, pushing through resolutions that instructed all its national representatives to vote for annexation. Benton refused, calling the resolutions "the speckled progeny of a vile conjunction, redolent with lurking treason to the Union." This intransigent refusal cost him his Senate seat.

But in the end, Benton triumphed—even in death. At the outbreak of the Civil War, four years after he had surrendered to his ultimate adversary, throat cancer, Missouri declined to secede with the other Southern states, in part inspired by Benton's memory. The faith he had displayed in his last Senate report to his constituency was finally borne out: "I sometimes had to act against the preconceived opinions and first impressions of my constituents; but always with full reliance upon their intelligence to understand me and their equity to do me justice—and I have never been disappointed."

●

Edmund G. Ross, "the man who saved a President," may actually have saved the institution of the Presidency itself by casting a courageous vote that completely destroyed his own political career. One historian called this vote "the most heroic act in American history, incomparably more difficult than any deed of valor upon the field of battle."

In 1868 the "Radical Republicans," who dominated the Congress by a count of 42 to 12, sought to remove their one-time Senatorial colleague the stubborn Tennessee-born Andrew Johnson from the Presidency, all because he resisted the vengeful Reconstruction policies imposed on the South during the post-Civil War period. According to the Articles of Impeachment, they needed only a two-thirds majority (36 votes) to convict Johnson of official misconduct.

It soon became clear that the Prosecution could produce little, if any, evidence of presidential wrongdoing. Six Republicans stood up to say that, without proper evidence, they would vote for acquittal. The Radicals knew that they could not afford to lose even one of the 36 remaining Republican votes, or they would lose their necessary two-thirds majority. But at the caucus

Senator Ross, a solid Republican from Kansas who disliked the President, said his vote was still "undecided."

The Radicals were offended. Sputtered one Republican leader, "I did not think that a Kansas man could quibble against his country." As the one undecided Republican senator, Ross now received "the full brunt" of his party's pressure tactics.

" ... So far as I am concerned, though a Republican and opposed to Mr. Johnson and his policy," Ross told an associate as the trial for impeachment got under way, "he shall have as fair a trial as an accused man ever had on this earth." Mail poured in from the Senator's home state, demanding Johnson's conviction. He received scores of dire warnings, even threats of assassination if he did not vote for impeachment. *Ten minutes before the vote ... [Ross's] Kansas colleague warned him ... that a vote for acquittal would mean trumped up charges and his political death.*

"I almost literally looked down into my open grave," Ross later recalled. "Friendships, position, fortune, everything that makes life desirable to an ambitious man were about to be swept away by the breath of my mouth, perhaps forever." Still, Ross voted not guilty.

The President and the Presidency were saved; but newspapers across the country assailed the man who had "sold himself and betrayed his constituents ... basely lied to his friends, shamefully violated his solemn pledge [and] signed the death warrant of his country's liberty ... "

Ross served out the whole of his six-year term, all the while referred to as "Traitor Ross." His fellow senators shunned him as if he were a leper. Finally, upon leaving the Senate in 1871, he moved with his family back to Kansas, there to suffer "social ostracism, physical attack, and near poverty." Only late in his life did national opinion vindicate his courageous actions. It was finally recognized that, in supporting the President, the Senator from Kansas had "saved the country from ... a strain that would have wrecked any other form of government [and a] calamity greater than war ... "

●

Reflecting on the lives of these great patriots, Kennedy writes: ... *Without belittling the courage with which men have died, we should not forget those acts of courage with which men ... have lived ...*

Endnote: A Profile of the Author

Born in 1917, John F. Kennedy served his country heroically during World War II, receiving the Navy and Marine Corps Medal and a purple heart. He also served three times as a U.S. Representative from Massachusetts, and in 1952 successfully ran for the U.S. Senate. It was while recuperating from back surgery during his term as a Senator that he wrote *Profiles in Courage.*

In 1960 Kennedy was elected President of the United States. In 1963, while riding in a Dallas motorcade, he fell victim to an assassin's bullet—an incident that devastated a nation and shattered the "American Camelot" that characterized Kennedy's brief term in office.

POETS AND POETRY

epic verses and versemakers

Shakespeare's first 126 sonnets are dedicated to a young friend of his, while the rest appear to be written to a "dark lady" …

All are architects of Fate,
    Working in these walls of Time;
Some with massive deeds and great,
    Some with ornaments of rhyme.

Nothing useless is, or low;
    Each thing in its place is best;
And what seems but idle show
    Strengthens and supports the rest.

Henry Wadsworth Longfellow

If you have to dry the dishes
(Such an awful, boring chore)
If you have to dry the dishes
('Stead of going to the store)
If you have to dry the dishes
And you drop one on the floor,
Maybe they won't let you
Dry the dishes anymore.

Shel Silverstein

In these brief overviews you will become acquainted—or reacquainted—with some of the essential voices in English-language poetry over the past four and a half centuries. You will be invited into the life, times and foremost works of diverse poets such as Shakespeare, Rudyard Kipling, Dorothy Parker and Jack Prelutsky, "thought musicians" who serve both as representatives of their eras and genres and as the individual creators of individual poems. And surely you will find no form of discourse within the realm of expression that is quite so individual as a poem.

Good poetry distills and clarifies a writer's deepest engagements with life, offering up to the reader a rare "elixir" of words and emotions. Let the verses in this library sink into you one by one: the sensual rhythms of Lord Byron, the bleak and powerful imagery of Eliot, the bright, pungent darts of Dickinson, and the sharp but subtle barbs of Ogden Nash. Accept, and savor, these "music-of-the-soul" offerings.

CONTENTS

These "rough and tender" poems touch upon both human connection and separation, often referring to people's "souvenirs" …

Larry Levis

Twentieth-century Verse

Popular Poetry Today

"I want to go everywhere,
look at and listen to everything.
You can go crazy with some of the
wonderful stuff there is in life."

Shel Silverstein

There was an old man from Calcutta,
Who coated his tonsils with butta,
    Thus converting his snore
    From a thunderous roar
To a soft, oleaginous mutta.

Ogden Nash

Oh, East is East, and West is West and never the
    twain shall meet,
Till Earth and Sky stand presently at God's great
    Judgement Seat;

Rudyard Kipling

Once upon a midnight dreary, while I pondered,
  weak and weary,
Over many a quaint and curious volume of
  forgotten lore,
While I nodded, nearly napping, suddenly there
  came a tapping,
As of some one gently rapping, rapping at my
  chamber door.
'Tis some visitor,' I muttered, 'tapping at my
  chamber door—
Only this and nothing more.'

Edgar Allan Poe

No man is an island,
entire of itself;
every man is a piece of the continent,
a part of the main.
If a clod be washed away by the sea,
Europe is the less,
as well as if a promontory were,
as well as if a manor of thy friend's
or of thine own were:
any man's death diminishes me,
because I am involved in mankind,
and therefore never send to know
for whom the bell tolls;
it tolls for thee.

John Donne

I

PARADIGM POETRY

WILLIAM SHAKESPEARE
(1564–1616)

It wasn't until the age of 27—middle-aged by that era's standard—that Shakespeare began to write poetry. His often much younger contemporaries, however, agreed that he was the epitome of the master wordsmith. Time has validated that opinion—and even enhanced it.

Very little is known of Shakespeare's early life; in fact, even his later years—aside from a bit here and a piece there—are riddled with uncertainties about his personal and professional life. (For a more complete sketch of his life and legacy, please consult the "Biographies—They Made a Difference" library in Volume I of this series.)

Shakespeare is best-known for his highly dramatic and poetic plays. Herein, however, we will focus on his superb sonnets. Many themes are apparent in the Bard's poetic body of work; some are lighthearted pieces, some consist of sincere communications, and others brim with serious commentary. In all of the works, however, there breathes a surplus of power.

The following light verse was apparently written to mock a love sonnet written by an associate to his fair lady love.

SONNET CXX

My mistress' eyes are nothing like the sun;
Coral is far more red than her lips' red:
If snow be white, why then her breasts are dun;
If hairs be wires, black wires grow on her head.

I have seen roses demask'd, red and white,
But no such roses see I in her cheeks;
And in some perfumes is there more delight
Than in the breath that from my mistress reeks.

I love to hear her speak, yet well I know
That music hath a far more pleasing sound:
I grant I never saw a goddess go,
My mistress, when she walks, treads on the ground:

> *And yet, by heaven, I think my love as rare*
> *As any she belied with false compare.*

A warning against such deceivers is sounded in Shakespeare's earliest-known poem, "A Lover's Complaint."

For further I could say "This man's untrue,"
And knew the patterns of his foul beguiling;
Heard where his plants in others' orchards grew
Saw how deceits were gilded in his smiling;
Knew vows were ever brokers to defiling …

Over time, some critics have come to the conclusion that Shakespeare's sonnets are autobiographical in nature, writings through which he could relay his perceptions and experiences. Conversely, others assert that the sonnets are mere figments of Shakespeare's fertile imagination.

Shakespeare's first 126 sonnets are dedicated to a young friend of his, while the rest appear to be written to a "dark lady" who steals both his own heart and that of this friend. The poet imagines that the Dark Lady holds some sort of strange power over him, but he feels helpless to do anything about it.

SONNET CLII

In loving thee thou know'st I am forsworn,
But thou art twice forsworn, to love me swearing;
In act thy bed-vow broke, and new faith torn
In vowing new hate after new love bearing.

But why of two oaths' breach do I accuse thee,
When I break twenty I am perjur'd most;
For all my vows are oaths but to misuse thee,
And all my honest faith in thee is lost;

For I have sworn deep oaths of thy deep kindness,
Oaths of thy love, thy truth, thy constancy;
And, to enlighten thee, gave eyes to blindness,
Or made them swear against the thing they see;

> *For I have sworn thee fair - more perjur'd I,*
> *To swear against the truth so foul a lie!*

The great poet understood the power of time in the world and in the lives of people. The words, meter and rhyme all work together in this sonnet to accomplish his purpose.

SONNET LXIV

When I have seen by Time's fell hand defaced
The rich-proud cost of outworn buried age;
When sometime lofty towers I see down-razed,
And brass eternal slave to mortal rage;

When I have seen the hungry ocean gain
Advantage on the kingdom of the shore,
And the firm soil win of the watery main,
Increasing store with loss and loss with store;

When I have seen such interchange of state,
Or state itself confounded to decay;
Ruin hath taught me thus to ruminate,
That Time will come and take my love away.

> *This thought is as a death which cannot choose*
> *But weep to have that which it fears to lose.*

As powerful as time is, Shakespeare obviously believed that love could persist through time.

SONNET XXX

When to the sessions of sweet silent thought
I summon up remembrance of things past,
I sigh the lack of many a thing I sought,
And with old woes new wail my dear time's waste:

Then can I drown an eye, unused to flow,
For precious friends hid in death's dateless night,
And weep afresh love's long since cancell'd woe,
And moan the expense of many a vanish'd sight;

Then can I grieve at grievances foregone,
And heavily from woe to woe tell o'er
The sad account of fore-bemoaned moan,
Which I new pay as if not paid before,

But if the while I think on thee, dear friend,
All losses are restored and sorrows end.

Other sonnets speak of the power of love to outlast time. This one is among the most popular.

SONNET CXVI

Let me not to the marriage of true minds
Admit impediments, Love is not love
Which alters when it alteration finds
Or bends with the remover to remove:

O, no! it is an ever-fixed mark,
That looks on tempests and is never shaken;
It is the star to every wandering bark,
Whose worth's unknown, although his height be taken.

Love's not Time's fool, though rosy lips and cheeks
Within his bending sickle's compass come;
Love alters not with his brief hours and weeks,
But bears it out even to the edge of doom.

If this be error and upon me proved,
I never writ, nor no man ever loved.

Occasional despair flows through the sonnets. Shakespeare mourns disappointments, dissatisfactions, losses, the death of friends. Yet in each case, before the piece ends, his beloved Dark Lady reassures him and rejuvenates him. For a time, a new theme emerged: not only does love conquer time, it conquers all.

SONNET XXIX

When in disgrace with Fortune and men's eyes,
I all alone beweep my outcast state,
And trouble deaf heaven with my bootless cries,
And look upon myself and curse my fate,

Wishing me like to one more rich in hope,
Featured like him, like him with friends possessed,
Desiring this man's art, and that man's scope,
With what I most enjoy contented least;

Yet in these thoughts myself almost despising,
Haply I think on thee, and then my state,

Like to the lark at break of day arising
From sullen earth, sings hymns at heaven's gate;

For thy sweet love rememb'red such wealth brings,
That then I scorn to change my state with kings.

Shakespeare's "The Rape of Lucrece" is based on a historical tale of a Roman emperor's son who is entranced by the great virtue of a married noblewoman. Unable to assail that virtue, the son finally rapes his paradigm. Afterward, as she mourns the act, we hear another description of the power of time.

… Time's glory is to calm contending kings,
To unmask falsehood, and bring truth to light,
To stamp the seal of time in aged things,
To wake the morn, and sentinel the night,
To wrong the wronger till he render right;
To ruinate proud buildings with thy hours
And smear with dust their glitt'ring golden tow'rs …

Why work'st thou mischief in thy pilgrimage,
Unless thou could return to make amends?
One poor retiring minute in an age
Would purchase thee a thousand thousand friends,
Lending him wit that to bad debtors lends:
O, this dread night, wouldst thou one hour come back
I could prevent this storm, and shun thy wrack!

Shakespeare's plays frequently portrayed how mankind's appetites and lust for power or position lead to fatal mistakes that destroy lives. Further along in "The Rape of Lucrece" these same deadly motivations are in force.

So that in venturing ill we leave to be
The things we are for that which we expect;
And this ambitious foul infirmity,
In having much, torments us with defect
Of that we have; so then we do neglect
The things we have; and, all for want of wit,
Make something nothing by augmenting it.

The reader can feel Lucrece's terror as she struggles in vain to save herself by reasoning with an unreasonable man.

…. She conjures him by high almighty Jove,
By knighthood, gentry, and sweet friendship's oath,
By her untimely tears, her husband's love,
By holy human law, and common troth,
By heaven and earth, and all the power of both,
That to his borrow'd bed he make retire,
And stoop to honour, not to foul desire …

'My husband is thy friend, for his sake spare me;
Thyself art mighty, for thine own sake leave me;
Myself a weakling, do not then ensnare me;
Thou look'st not like deceit, do not deceive me;
My sights, like whirlwinds, labour hence to heave thee.
If ever man were moved with woman's moans,
Be moved with my tears, my sighs, my groans….

JOHN DONNE
(1572–1631)

"No man is an island; every man is … part of the main." John Donne penned these lines during a life spent wrestling to be part of a society which spurned him.

Born in 1572 to a middle-class English family, Donne first studied at Oxford, then at a philosophy workshop called Lincoln's Inn, and finally enlisted in the military and took part in naval raids on Spain. Electing to elope with the daughter of one of his wealthy sponsors landed him in prison for a short time. A fanatic concerning social status, his greatest desire was to be recognized as a "man of breeding." Accomplishing this feat, however, was difficult in Elizabethan England, as Catholics were unmercifully persecuted by members of the Anglican Church—including the Queen herself. Despite the fact he was sponsored by many wealthy and influential patrons, Donne failed to acquire the entitled rank of a well-bred individual.

Sometime in his early twenties, Donne renounced the Catholic Church. His reasons are unclear, but his desire to gain social favor played a major part in his decision. Otherwise knowing he would always be a second-class citizen, he simply refused to be a part of any religious rites. His poetry from this point on takes on a ferocious, raging tone in which he rails against God, Satan, death, life … virtually anything that held religious overtones. Remaining a deeply spiritual person in spite of his public outcries of rebellion, he privately felt he had damned his soul by renouncing his church.

In 1615, perhaps out of guilt—but more likely due to his continuing quest for social acceptance—Donne joined the Anglican ministry, enticed by Elizabeth's successor, King James I. The king promised a good salary; thus the poet lived out his life in relative comfort.

Virtually all of Donne's known poetry was written before 1615. His recorded sermons, however, resound with the same vigor—and anger—as his poetry. His works are characterized by robust, direct language. In spite of archaic spellings, the images created are instantly accessible to the modern reader. Many of the poems begin with a strong directive phrase; others open with an unflinching question that demands an immediate answer. Donne's inner turmoil—and perhaps his ego—gave him an urgency to write about subjects such as God and death, topics his contemporaries often either ignored or treated very lightly. In Holy Sonnet #10 he not only addresses these themes, he attacks them with relish.

Death, be not proud, though some have
   called thee
Mighty and dreadful, for thou art not so;
For those whom thou thinkest thou dost
   overthrow
Die not, poor Death, nor yet canst thou kill me.
From rest and sleep, which but thy pictures be
Much pleasure; then from thee much more
   must flow,
And soonest our best men with thee do go
Rest of their bones and souls delivery.
Thou are slave to Fate, Chance, kings, and
   desperate men,
And dost with poison, war, and sickness dwell,
And poppies or charms can make us sleep as well
And better then thy stroke. Why swell'st thou
   then?
One short sleep past, we wake eternally,
And death shall be no more; Death, thou
   shalt die!

Donne's work can be a kind of cathartic experience for those who are reluctant to confront God on His own terms. The following lines from Holy Sonnet #14 well-illustrate his near-blasphemous rantings.

… Batter my heart, three person'd God; for, you
As yet but knock, breathe, shine, and seek
   to mend;
That I may rise, and stand, o'erthrow me,
   'and bend
Your force, to break, blow, burn and make
   me new.
I, like an usurpt town, to'another due,
Labour to'admit you, but Oh, to no end,
Reason your viceroy in me, me should defend,
But is captiv'd, and proves weak or untrue.
Yet dearly' I love you, and would be loved faine,
But am betroth'd unto your enemy:
Divorce me, 'untie, or break that knot again;
Take me to you, imprison me, for I
Except you'enthrall me, never shall be free,
Nor ever chaste, except you ravish me.

Holy Sonnets reflect a tortured mind that operates somewhere between self-loathing, anger, and humble supplication. Holy Sonnets #163 and #164 most graphically depict this juxtaposition.

HOLY SONNET #163

Oh my black soul! now thou art summoned
By sickness, death's herald, and champion;
Thou art like a pilgrim, which abroad hath done
Treason, and durst not turn to whence he is fled;
Or like a thief, which till death's doom be read,
Wisheth himself delivered from prison,
But damn'd and haled to execution,
Wisheth that still he might be imprisoned.
Yet grace, if thou repent, thou canst not lack;

But who shall give thee that grace to begin?
Oh make thy self with holy mourning black,
And red with blushing, as thou art with sin;
Or wash thee in Christ's blood, which hath
   this might
That being red, it dyes red souls to white.

HOLY SONNET #164

As due by many titles I resign
My self to Thee, o God; first I was made
By Thee, and for Thee, and when I was decay'd
Thy blood bought that, the which before was
Thine,
I am Thy son, made with Thy Self to shine,
Thy servant, whose pains Thou hast still repaid,
Thy sheep, Thine image, and, till I betray'd
My self, a temple of Thy Spirit divine;
Why doth the devil then usurp on me?
Why doth he steal, nay ravish that's thy right?
Except thou rise and for thine own work fight,
Oh I shall soon despair, when I do see
That thou lov'st mankind well, yet wilt not
   choose me,
And Satan hates me, yet is loath to lose me.

Though his poetry was greatly influenced by the turbulent religious temperament of the time, Donne did not limit himself to strictly religious themes. Indeed, he explored several wide genres, including satire and romance. His romantic poetry is fraught with changing voices, sometimes opening with bold statements and closing with pitiful, meaningless maxims. "Woman's Constancy" echoes with a sense of hopelessness, perhaps born out of the feeling that if he could not love himself, no one else possibly could either.

Now thou hast loved me one whole day,
Tomorrow when thou leavest, what wilt thou say?
Wilt thou then antedate some new-made vow?
        Or say that now
We are not just those persons which we were?
Or that oaths made in reverential fear
Of Love, and his wrath, any may forswear?
Or, as true deaths true marriages untie,
So lovers' contracts, images of those,
Bind but till sleep, death's image, them unloose?
        Or, your own end to justify,
For having purposed change and falsehood, you
Can have no way but falsehood to be true?
Vain lunatic, against these 'scapes I could
        Dispute, and conquer, if I would;
        Which I abstain to do,
For by tomorrow I may think so too.

In this same poem another theme common to Donne's work is addressed: a fascination with changeability and transmutability, a fixation conceivably rising from his own betrayal of the religion of his youth.

In counterpoint, his body of work also seems to reflect a need to belong, to be an integral part of the proverbial "big picture." This idea is poignantly illustrated by Donne's most famous work, "No Man Is An Island," which appears in his *Devotions Upon Emergent Occasions, Meditation XVII*, and begins with the words: *All mankind is of one author, and is one volume; when one man dies, one chapter is not torn out of the book, but translated into a better language; and every chapter must be so translated... As therefore the bell that rings to a sermon, calls not upon the preacher only, but upon the congregation to come: so this bell calls us all: but how much more me, who am brought so near the door by this sickness....*

It then closes with:

No man is an island,
entire of itself;
every man is a piece of the continent,
a part of the main.
If a clod be washed away by the sea,
Europe is the less,
as well as if a promontory were,
as well as if a manor of thy friend's
or of thine own were:
any man's death diminishes me,
because I am involved in mankind,
and therefore never send to know
for whom the bell tolls;
it tolls for thee.

WILLIAM BLAKE
(1757–1827)

William Blake was born in London in 1757 to a middle-class family. Educated at home by his mother, who shielded her sensitive child against the severe schools of the day, Blake demonstrated an early and active imagination—as well as a talent for seeing visions, which he first expressed in drawings. His father, recognizing his artistic talent, sent him away to drawing school at the age of ten.

The youngster later was apprenticed to an engraver. When, at age 21, his apprenticeship ended, he began accepting commissions, all the while studying painting at the Royal Academy. In 1782 Blake married Catherine Battersea; a year later he printed his first poems, *Poetical Sketches*. Then in 1787 he published *Songs of Innocence*, a highly innovative creation not only in its language but also in its presentation. The poems were engraved in an ornate calligraphic style which became Blake's trademark.

Inspired by the storming of the Bastille in 1789, Blake next compiled *The Marriage of Heaven and Hell*. Then, as if to forecast the success of the French Revolution, he wrote and engraved the poem "America." To give voice to his disillusionment with the "French Reign of Terror," Blake also penned *Songs of Innocence* and *Songs of Experience*. On the 12th of August, 1827, Blake died, still poor, yet hard at work on his last project, an illustration of Dante's *Divine Comedy*.

In *Songs of Innocence* Blake first expresses some of his deepest thoughts about mankind and God. He vigorously celebrates the spirit of innocence—not only the natural state of childhood, but also the condition of simplicity and unrestrained love to which the mature soul aspires. The verses are simple, appealing to both children and adults. But the clarity and innocence are often deceiving. Beneath the rhythms—often borrowed from nursery rhymes—is a deeper significance hidden in certain symbols. In "The Lamb," for instance, the themes of shepherds and their flocks represent serenity, while the peaceful pastures symbolize a state of innocence or eternity.

THE LAMB

Little lamb, who made thee?
Dost thou know who made thee,
Gave thee life, and bade thee feed
By the stream and o'er the mead;
Gave thee clothing of delight,
Softest clothing, wooly, bright;
Gave thee such a tender voice,
Making all the vales rejoice?
Little lamb, who made thee?
Dost thou know who made thee?

Little lamb, I'll tell thee;
Little lamb, I'll tell thee:
He is called by thy name,
For He calls Himself a lamb,
He is meek, and He is mild,
He became a little child;
I a child, and Thee a Lamb,
We are called by His Name.
Little lamb, God bless thee!
Little lamb, God bless thee!

"Holy Thursday" describes an annual service at St. Paul's Cathedral on Ascension Day. The boys from the "charity schools" (orphanages) of London march to the church to give thanks for their blessings. The "beadles" spoken of are the parish officers who supervise them.

HOLY THURSDAY

'Twas on a Holy Thursday, their innocent
    faces clean,
The children walking two and two, in red and
    blue and green,
Grey headed beadles walking before with wands
    as white as snow;
Till into the high dome of Paul's they like
    Thames' waters flow.

Oh what a multitude they seemed, those flowers
    of London town!
Seated in companies they sit, with radiance all
    their own.
The hum of multitudes was there, but
    multitudes of lambs:
Thousands of little boys and girls raising their
    innocent hands.

Now like a mighty wind they raise to Heaven the
    voice of song,
Or like harmonious thunderings the seats of
    Heaven among.
Beneath them sit the agéd men, wise guardians
    of the poor.
Then cherish pity, lest you drive an angel from
    your door.

Five years later, Blake's verse had kept its simplicity, yet had taken on an entirely different mood. In *Songs of Experience*, "experience" denotes a world of disillusionment in which innocence is dashed by harsh reality. In order to emphasize this contrast, he composes many of the "songs" as ironic counterparts or parodies of the earlier poems. "The Tyger" is, for example, an ironic counterpart to "The Lamb," the "tyger" representing God's righteous anger.

THE TYGER

Tyger! Tyger! burning bright
In the forests of the night,
What immortal hand or eye
Could frame thy fearful symmetry?

In what distant deeps or skies
Burnt the fire of thine eyes?
On what wings dare he aspire?
What the hand dare seize the fire?

And what shoulder, and what art,
Could twist the sinews of thy heart?
And when thy heart began to beat,
What dread hand? and what dread feet?

What the hammer? what the chain?
In what furnace was thy brain?
What the anvil? what dread grasp
Dare its deadly terrors clasp?

When the stars threw down their spears
And watered heaven with their tears,
Did he smile his work to see?
Did he who made the Lamb make thee?

Tyger! Tyger! burning bright
In the forests of the night,
What immortal hand or eye
Dare frame thy fearful symmetry?

Between his *Songs of Innocence* and *Songs of Experience*, Blake wrote and engraved *The Marriage of Heaven and Hell*, a collection of verse, proverbs and prose allegory inspired by the new age of political freedom which Blake felt was dawning on Europe. The book consists of four parts: "The Argument," "The Voice of the Devil," "A Memorable Fancy" and the "Proverbs of Hell." "The Argument" is a free-verse piece touching upon the perversion of paradise by ecclesiastical and political tyranny. In its commentary, Blake sets forth his philosophy on good and evil. "Good" is associated with passivity and conventional wisdom; "evil," with creativity and genius. In Blake's scheme, Devils are poets and Hell is the realm of truth. Angels, on the other hand, are the souls of those pious individuals who blindly and hypocritically follow the laws of conventional morality.

THE ARGUMENT

Rintah roars & shakes his fires in the
   burden'd air;
Hungry clouds swag on the deep.

Once meek, and in a perilous path,
The just man kept his course along
The vale of death.
Roses are planted where thorns grow,
And on the barren heath
Sing the honey bees.

Then the perilous path was planted,
And a river and a spring
On every cliff and tomb;
And on the bleached bones
Red clay brought forth.

Till the villain left the paths of ease,
To walk in perilous paths, and drive
The just man into barren climes.

Now the sneaking serpent walks
In mild humility,
And the just man rages in the wilds
Where lions roar.

Rintah roars & shakes his fires in the
   burden'd air;
Hungry clouds swag on the deep.

"America" was also inspired by Europe's new-found liberty. The United States had won its revolutionary war, and France, recently having gained its own emancipation from monarchism, was embarking on what appeared to be a majestic project of renewal. Blake saw the current events unfolding around him as all part of a spiritual awakening—a struggle towards spiritual freedom. To prophesy the struggle's success, the poem was set against the backdrop of the American Revolution. Here, "Albion" refers to England, against which Washington and other American patriots had fought.

PASSAGE FROM AMERICA: A PROPHECY

The Guardian Prince of Albion burns in his
   nightly tent,
Sullen fires across the Atlantic glow to America's
   shore:
Piercing the souls of warlike men, who rise in
   silent night,
Washington, Franklin, Paine & Warren, Gates,
   Hancock & Green;
Meet on the coast glowing with blood from
   Albion's fiery Prince.

Washington spoke: "Friends of America look over
   the Atlantic sea;

A bended bow is lifted in heaven, & a heavy
iron chain
Descends, link by link, from Albion's cliffs across
the sea, to bind
Brothers & sons of America, till our faces pale
and yellow;
Heads deprest, voices weak, eyes downcast, hands
work-bruis'd,
Feet bleeding on the sultry sands, and the furrows
of the whip
Descend to generations that in future times
forget."
The strong voice ceas'd, for a terrible blast swept
over the heaving sea;
The eastern cloud rent; on his cliffs stood Albion's
wrathful Prince,
A dragon form, clashing his scales; at midnight
he arose,
And flam'd red meteors round the land of Albion
beneath;
His voice, his locks, his awful shoulders, and his
glowing eyes
Appear to the Americans upon the cloudy night.

Solemn heave the Atlantic waves beneath the
gloomy nations,
Swelling, belching from its deeps red clouds &
raging fires.
Albion is sick, America faints! enrag'd the Zenith
grew.
As human blood shooting its veins all round the
orbed heaven,
Red rose the clouds from the Atlantic in vast
wheels of blood,
And in the red clouds rose a Wonder o'er the
Atlantic sea;
Intense! naked! a Human fire, fierce glowing, as
the wedge
Of iron heated in the furnace; his terrible limbs
were fire
With myriads of cloudy terrors; banners dark
& towers
Surrounded; heat but not light went thro' the
murky atmosphere

The King of England looking westward trembles
at the vision ...

GEORGE GORDON "LORD" BYRON
(1788–1827)

When George was born in 1788, he was given
the last name of "Gordon," taken from his
mother's side of the family. At age ten, however,
he inherited the title of "Lord" Byron from a
great uncle on his father's side. After his father
deserted the family, Byron moved to Scotland
with his mother. He was first educated at
Aberdeen, then Harrow, then Trinity College,
Cambridge. Though he never earned a degree,
he did earn a reputation for wild and reckless
living.

Shortly after forsaking college, Byron and a
friend toured Europe for two years, spending
time in Portugal, Spain and Greece. His first
two cantos, "Childe Harold's Pilgrimage" and
"Oriental Tales," were inspired by his feelings
during his travels. These drawn out, meandering poems became immediately successful.

Back home in England, Byron married and
had a child. But after only one year together, the
couple separated. As one historian observed,
"Byron was wild and his wife was a prude, and
nothing else needs to be said."

After the divorce, rumors spread that Byron
had entered into an incestuous relationship
with his half-sister Augusta. When she did in
fact give girth, Byron, though he never
admitted the child was his, was forced to move
to Switzerland to escape the stinging criticism.

Apparently, these personal trials aroused
Byron's poetic muse, for during this time he
penned "Parisina," "Hebrew Melodies," "The
Prisoner of Chillon," Canto III of "Childe
Harold's Pilgrimage" and "Manfred." He later
toured Italy, where he completed Canto IV of
"Childe Harold," "Beppo" and "Don Juan."

In 1823 Byron returned to Greece, which by
then was embroiled in revolution. He quickly
took up the cause, spent vast amounts of
money supporting it, and was even made an
officer in the rebellion. But bad weather and
over-exposure caused him to become critically
ill, a sickness that led to his death in 1824. The
Greeks, who considered him a national hero,
gave him every honor accorded one of their
own fallen comrades in arms.

Critics have never been kind to Byron's
artistry. He has been accused of everything
ranging from fostering moral corruption to
perpetrating crimes against the English
language—and as a poet in search of a style.
Most likely, Byron found his voice with
"Beppo" and "Don Juan." Had he lived longer,
his work may have become more stable.

Byron often writes of loss: loss of love, of
home, of honor, of everything humanity holds
dear. This began with "Childe Harold."
Although he insisted that he did not symbolize

Harold, that Harold was a fictitious character created to link all the pieces of the "Pilgrimage," still it is easy to feel Byron's sense of loss in Harold's reveries. The image of even his dog forgetting him is strangely poignant.

CHILDE HAROLD'S PILGRIMAGE— CANTO THE FIRST
… For who would trust the seeming sighs
Of wife or paramour?
Fresh feeres will dry the bright blue eyes
We late saw streaming o'er.
For pleasures past I do not grieve,
Nor perils gathering near;
My greatest grief is that I leave
No thing that claims a tear.

And now I'm in the world alone,
Upon the wide, wide sea;
But why should I for others groan,
When none will sigh for me?
Perchance my dog will whine in vain,
Till fed by stranger hands;
But long ere I come back again
He'd tear me where he stands….

Critics have termed the "Childe Harold" cantos as an exploration in "the agony of humanity." That agony, and Byron's lifelong search for love and honor, are a significant part of "Don Juan."

CANTO THE SEVENTH
… O Love! O Glory! what are ye who fly
Around us ever, rarely to alight?
There's not a meteor in the polar sky
Of such transcendent and more fleeting flight.
Chill, and chain'd to cold earth, we lift on high
Our eyes in search of either lovely light;
A thousand and a thousand colours they
Assume, then leave us on our freezing way….

In spite of his own personal depravity, Byron clearly espoused a broadened, universal morality, and mourned its frequent absence in mankind. In Canto I of "Childe Harold," he criticizes war by way of his description of a battlefield.

… Three hosts combine to offer sacrifice;
Three tongues prefer strange orisons on high;
Three gaudy standards flout the pale blue skies;
The shouts are France, Spain, Albion, Victory!
The foe, the victim, and the fond ally
That fights for all, but ever fights in vain,
Are met—as if at home they could not die—
To feed the crow on Talavera's plain
And fertilize the field that each pretends
   to gain….

For whatever virtues he lacked, honesty was one of his redeeming characteristics. Byron never lied to himself about his morality. His feelings about his unfeigned nature are well apparent in "Childe Harold."

… If my fame should be, as my fortunes are,
Of hasty growth and blight, and dull
   Oblivion bar

My name from out the temple where the dead
Are honour'd by the nations—let it be—
And light the laurels on a loftier head!
And be the Spartan's epitaph on me,
"Sparta hath many a worthier son than he."
Meantime I seek no sympathies, nor need;
The thorns which I have reap'd are of the tree
I planted: they have torn me, and I bleed:
I should have known what fruit would spring
from such a seed….

Clearly Byron recognized that he was the root source of his own problems. "Epistle to Augusta" emphasizes this even more.

I have been cunning in mine overthrow,
The careful pilot of my proper woe.

Mine were my faults, and mine be their reward,
My whole life was a contest, since the day
That gave me being, gave me that which marred
The gift,—a fate, or will, that walked astray.

Critics mostly consider Byron's many dalliances with satire to be among his best work. They certainly were among the most popular, though some attributed this popularity to the public's appetite for gossip about the literary coterie. When one of his works was criticized, Byron struck back with the following.

TO A KNOT OF UNGENEROUS CRITICS
Rail on, Rail on, ye heartless crew!
My strains were never meant for you;
Remorseless Rancour still reveal,
And damn the verse you cannot feel.
Invoke those kindred passions' aid,
Whose baleful stings your breasts pervade;
Crush, if you can, the hopes of youth,
Trampling regardless on the Truth.
Truth's Records you consult in vain,
She will not blast her native strain;
She will assist her votary's cause,
His will at least be her applause …

English Bards And Scotch Reviewers is a collection of satire inaugurated early in Byron's career and completed after some criticism of his poetry. Unlike his attacks on critics in general, here he skewered his contemporaries on an individual basis. The following was directed toward a now-obscure acquaintance, Viscount Strangford.

For thee, translator of the tinsel song,
To whom such glittering ornaments belong,
Hibernian Strangford! with thine eyes of blue,
And boasted locks of red or auburn hue,
Whose plaintive strain each love-sick miss
  admires,
And o'er harmonious fustian half expires,
Learn, if thou canst, to yield thine author's sense,
Nor vend thy sonnets on a false pretence.
Think'st thou to gain thy verse a higher place,
By dressing Camoens in a suit of lace?
Mend, Strangford! mend thy morals and
  thy taste;
Be warm, but pure; be amorous, but be chaste:
Cease to deceive; thy pilfer'd harp restore,
Nor teach the Lusian bard to copy Moore.

Byron's satire was not limited to specific poetry. He was not above taking what we now call a "cheap shot" on almost any occasion. For example, many of Coleridge's readers share Byron's plea:

And Coleridge, too, has lately taken wing,
But like a hawk encumbered with his hood,—
Explaining metaphysics to the nation—
I wish he would explain his Explanation.

"Childe Harold's Pilgrimage," a fine example of Byron's descriptive verse, was not all written or published simultaneously. The first two Cantos were published together early in Byron's career; the third and fourth appeared separately late in his short life.

CANTO THE SECOND
… He that has sailed upon the dark blue sea
Has viewed at times … a full fair sight,
When the fresh breeze is fair as breeze may be,
The white sail set, the gallant frigate tight;
Masts, spires, and strand retiring to the right,
The glorious main expanding o'er the bow,
The convoy spread like wild swans in their flight,
The dullest sailor wearing bravely now,
So gaily curl the waves before each dashing
  prow….

Byron's love affair with Greece and its revolution provided the force behind "The Giaour."

Clime of the unforgotten brave!
Whose land from plain to mountain-cave
Was Freedom's home or Glory's grave!
Shrine of the mighty! can it be,
That this is all remains of thee?
Approach, thou craven crouching slave;
Say, is not this Thermopylae?

These waters blue that round you lave,
Oh, servile offspring of the free—
Pronounce what sea, what shore is this?
The gulf, the rock of Salamis!
These scenes, their story not unknown,
Arise, and make again your own;
Snatch from the ashes of your Sires
The embers of their former fires;
And he who in the strife expires
Will add to theirs a name of fear
That Tyranny shall quake to hear,
And leave his sons a hope, a fame,
They too will rather die than shame;
For Freedom's battle once begun,
Bequeathed by bleeding Sire to Son,
Though baffled oft is ever won
Bear witness, Greece, thy living page!
Attest it many a deathless age!

Perhaps Byron's greatest expressive piece was written about himself and his feelings. Reverting to "Childe Harold" (Canto III), we see the feeling of the creator as he views his own, enigmatic nature.

He, who grown aged in this world of woe,
In deeds, not years, piercing the depth of life,
So that no wonder waits him; nor below
Can love, or sorrow, fame, ambition, strife,
Cut to his heart again with the keen knife
Of silent, sharp endurance: he can tell
Why thought seeks refuge in lone caves, yet rife
With airy images, and shapes which dwell
Still unimpaired, though old, in the soul's
  haunted cell.

'Tis to create, and in creating live
A being more intense, that we endow
With form our fancy, gaining as we give
The life we image, even as I do now.
What am I? Nothing: but not so are thou,
Invisible but gazing, as I glow
Mixed with thy spirit, blended with thy birth,
And feeling still with thee in my crushed
  feelings' dearth.

PERCY BYSSHE SHELLEY
(1792–1822)

O wild West Wind, thou breath of Autumn's being,
Thou from whose unseen presence the leaves of
*   the dead*
Are driven, like ghosts from an enchanter fleeing …

… Be thou, Spirit fierce,
My spirit! Be thou me, impetuous one!

Drive my dead thoughts over the universe
Like withered leaves to quicken a new birth!
And, by the incantations of this verse,

Scatter, as from an unextinguished hearth
Ashes and sparks, my words among mankind!
Be through my lips to unawakened Earth

The trumpet of a prophecy! O Wind,
If Winter comes, can Spring be far behind?

"Ode to the West Wind," the best known of Shelley's "shorter" poems, conveys the visionary, prophetic role the poet saw himself playing. His political ideas were tinged with a poetic quality, and his poetry was infused with politics.

Percy Bysshe Shelley fueled his work with philosophy and politics, a radical departure from the poetry of his day. Born in Sussex, England, he was schooled at Eton and Oxford. He was expelled from Oxford, however, for publishing an inflammatory pamphlet, "The Necessity of Atheism." After leaving school, he involved himself in several political causes in Ireland and England.

In an effort to elude his creditors and escape the antagonism of his critics, Shelley set off for Italy with his second wife, wandering the countryside with a colorful group of English expatriates. It was during these bohemian wanderings that most of his best poetic work was done, including "Prometheus Unbound," "Ode to the West Wind," the "Cenci, Adonais," the more gentle "To a Skylark," and, what proved to be his last, unfinished work, "The Triumph of Life." At age 29, Shelley drowned at sea while sailing to Lerici from Leghorn.

Critic T.S. Eliot—who openly derided Shelley's subversive views—admitted that, void of those idealistic, revolutionary shades, his poetry still would have been nothing more than a "wax effigy," a metaphor taken directly from one of Shelley's own works, "In Defense of Poetry."

"Queen Mab: A Philosophical Poem," Shelley's earliest serious effort, marked the first time the poet had in any degree succeeded in fusing his artistic and political concerns. Savaged by critics who thought the poem to be simply a vehicle for his views, its chief value is its interesting handling of themes and motifs that received fuller treatment in later, more mature works.

… Now stands adorning
This lovely earth with taintless body and mind;
Blest form his birth with all bland impulses,
Which gently in his noble being wake
All kindly passions and all pure desires
All things are recreated and the flame
Of consentaneous love inspires all life.

After "Queen Mab," Shelley took to composing poems commemorating political injustices and furthering the cause of reform both in England and on the continent: "The Masque of Anarchy"—inspired by the St. Peter's Field Massacre; "Ode Written in October 1819" and "Ode to Liberty"—whose stimulus was the Spanish revolution; "Ode to Naples"—written on the occasion of the war of the kingdom of Naples against Austrian domination; "Hellas"—concerning the Greek struggle for liberation from the Turkish empire; and the two major poems "The Revolt of Islam" and "Prometheus Unbound"—both springing from signs of revolution that Shelley felt were manifesting themselves throughout the world.

More than any poet before him, Shelley defined poetry in a social sense. His notions of the role of poetry as an instrument for social and moral reform are superbly set forth in his "Defense of Poetry," written in 1820 in response to an essay challenging poets to leave civic matters to reasoners and merchants. Easily Shelley's most famous and frequently quoted prose work, in it he explained that, of all the factors giving rise to the birth of civilization, art and drama played the biggest part.

Shelley applied this innovative theory to his own verse-making. He deemed it his poetic vocation to awaken the whole of Europe, a continent spellbound by superstition and tyranny. This idea of change—of the inescapable certainty of the nature of change, not only in the seasons, but also in governments and laws—Shelley also treats in his brilliant "Ozymandias of Egypt." In all worldly rulers he sees the interceding hand of certain fate and crumbling empire.

I met a traveller from an antique land
Who said: Two vast and trunkless legs of stone
Stand in the desert. Near them, on the sand,
Half sunk, a shattered visage lies, whose frown,
And wrinkled lip and sneer of cold command
Tell that its sculptor well those passions read
Which yet survive, stamped on these lifeless things,
The hand that mocked them and the heart that fed.
And on the pedestal these words appear:
"My name is Ozymandias, king of kings:
Look on my works, ye mighty, and despair!"
Nothing beside remains. Round the decay
Of that colossal wreck, boundless and bare,
The lone and level sands stretch far away.

Of all the Romantic poets, it was Shelley who most consistently maintained a devotion to political activism. As a result, he incurred the fear and loathing of the conservative establishment. On his death, one review declared, "Shelley, the writer of some infidel poetry has drowned ... now he knows whether there be a God or no."

While it is true that in many of Shelley's works politics overshadows the poetry, the most successful of his poems are less explicitly political. Instead, bipartisan issues are stripped bare and treated separately from other contemporary affairs. Thus they become integrated as part of his overall poetical vision.

Such is the case with "Prometheus Unbound," Shelley's best long poem, in which he translates his revolutionary ideas into a universal and mythological language. Composed in 1818 in the ruins of the Baths of Caracalla in Rome, "Prometheus Unbound" is an unstageable drama based on Aeschylus's Greek tragedy *Prometheus Bound*. Where the Greek playwright used strong images of mythical beings to propel his story, Shelley takes those same images and converts the play into a socio-political allegory.

He gave man speech and speech created thought,
Which is the measure of the universe;
And science struck the thrones of Earth and heaven
Which shook but did not fall; and the harmonious
    mind
Poured forth in all-prophetic song,
And music lifted up the listening spirit
Until it walked, exempt from mortal care
Godlike o'er the clear billows of sweet sound.

And speaking of sound, it was the beautiful melody of the skylark that inspired "To the Skylark," just two years before his untimely death, one of the poet's most magnificent works, expressive metaphor insisting that human happiness and sadness are inextricably entwined. Mortals "pine for what is not"; their glee is "fraught" with "some pain"; their "sweetest songs are those that tell of saddest thought." Even so, what joy all could learn from that expressed by the heavenly skylark.

Hail to thee, blithe spirit!
    Bird thou never wert—
    That from heaven or near it
    Pourest thy full heart
In profuse strains of unpremeditated art ...

Like a poet hidden
    In the light of thought,
    Singing hymns unbidden,
    Till the world is wrought
To sympathy with hopes and fears it heeded not:

Like a high-born maiden
    In a place tower,

Soothing her love-laden
    Soul in secret hour
With music sweet as love, which overflows her
bower ...

Teach us, sprite or bird,
    What sweet thoughts are thine:
I have never heard
    Praise of love or wine
That painted forth a flood of rapture so divine ...

What objects are the fountains
    Of thy happy strain?
What fields, or waves, or mountains?
    What shapes of sky or plain?
What love of thine own kind? What ignorance of
pain?

With thy clear keen joyance
    Languor cannot be:
    Shadow of annoyance
    Never came near thee:
Thou lovest, but ne'er knew love's sad satiety.

Waking or asleep,
    Thou of death must deem
    Things more true and deep
    Than we mortals dream,
Or how could thy notes flow in such a crystal
stream?

We look before and after,
    And pine for what is not:
    Our sincerest laughter
    With some pain is fraught;
Our sweetest songs are those that tell of saddest
thought.

Yet, if we could scorn
    Hate and pride and fear,
    If we were things born
    Not to shed a tear,
I know not how thy joy we ever should come near.

Better than all measures
    Of delightful sound,
    Better than all treasures
    That in books are found,
Thy skill to poet were, thou scorner of the ground!

Teach me half the gladness
    That thy brain must know:
    Such harmonious madness
    From my lips would flow,
The world should listen then, as I am listening now.

JOHN KEATS
(1795–1821)

"If poetry can't come as naturally as leaves to a tree, it shouldn't come at all."

Naturally, the words came easily to John Keats, who wrote some of the finest lyrics in the English language. Although raised in an orphanage, by age 16 he had completed a prose translation of Virgil's *Aeneid*. A year later he turned to verse. He studied for a career in medicine, but by his twenty-first year he had determined to devote his full talents to literature.

Though his early poems were popular with the masses, they were not critically acclaimed. In a letter to his friend, James A. Hessey, he wrote: "Praise or blame has but a momentary effect on the man whose love of beauty in the abstract makes him a severe critic on his own Works. My own domestic criticism has given me pain without comparison …"

Keats founded his poetry on myths and fables, structuring verse around ideas such as beauty and truth. He once wrote in a letter that imagination, in its purity, finds sublime beauty and sublime truth. "I am certain of nothing but the holiness of the Heart's affections," he said, "and the truth of Imagination—What the imagination seizes as Beauty must be truth."

Most famous for his Odes, Keats's prime subject matter was nature, in keeping with the Romantic temperament of the time. The Ode is a form in which each stanza plays a particular role. The first stanza presents an idea, the second contradicts it, and the third reconciles the two opposing notions.

On a walking tour in the Scottish Highlands, Keats came down with the chills and a sore throat. The illness turned out to be tuberculosis, which claimed his life at the age of 25. Even during his short years, "death"—especially premature death—weighed heavily on the poet's mind. In *When I Have Fears*, Keats presages his early demise, a loss that would come, he speculated, before his pen had "gleaned my teeming brain …"

ODE TO A NIGHTINGALE
I.

My heart aches, and a drowsy numbness pains
  My sense, as though of hemlock I had drunk,
Or emptied some dull opiate to the drains
  One minute past, and Lethe-wards had sunk:
'Tis not through envy of thy happy lot,
  But being too happy in thine happiness,
    That thou, light-winged Dryad of the trees,
In some melodious plot
  Of beechen green, and shadows numberless,
    Singest of summer in full-throated ease.

II.

O, for a draught of vintage that hath been
  Cooled a long age in the deep-delved earth,
Tasting of Flora and the country green,
  Dance, and Provencal song, and sunburnt mirth!
O for a beaker full of the warm South,
  Full of the true, the blushful Hippocrene,
    With beaded bubbles winking at the brim,
And purple-stained mouth;
  That I might drink, and leave the world unseen,
    And with thee fade away into the forest dim:

III.

Fade far away, dissolve, and quite forget
  What thou among the leaves hast never known,
The weariness, the fever, and the fret
  Here, where men sit and hear each other groan;
Where palsy shakes a few, sad, last gray hairs,
  Where youth grows pale, and specter-thin, and dies;
    Where but to think is to be full of sorrow
And leaden-eyed despairs,
  Where Beauty cannot keep her lustrous eyes,
    Or new Love pine at them beyond tomorrow.

Keats was famous for his device of mixing the senses, often dizzying the reader in the process. Reveling in wine, a bird's song and, finally, forgetfulness as the pleasure of youth fades away, the poem's speaker finds that escape is impossible—and his thoughts turn inward, back into a world where suffering, death and fleeting youth still haunt the recesses of his mind.

"Ode on Melancholy" was written in the same pattern. Here, Keats admonishes the reader to embrace sadness and avoid escape, to take joy in the emotions of the present, whether good or bad.

ODE ON MELANCHOLY
I.

No, no go not to Lethe, neither twist
  Wolfs-bane, tight-rooted, for its poisonous wine;
Nor suffer thy pale forehead to be kissed
  By nightshade, ruby grape of Proserpine;
Make not your rosary of yew-berries,
  Nor let the beetle, nor the death-moth be
    Your mournful Psyche, nor the downy owl
A partner in your sorrow's mysteries;
  For shade to shade will come too drowsily,
    And drown the wakeful anguish of the soul.

II.

But when the melancholy fit shall fall
  Sudden from heaven like a weeping cloud
That fosters the droop-headed flowers all,
  And hides the green hill in April shroud;
Then glut thy sorrow on a morning rose,
  Or on the rainbow of the salt sand-wave,
    Or on the wealth of the globed peonies;
Or if thy mistress some rich anger shows,
  Emprison her soft hand, and let her rave,
    And feed deep, deep upon her peerless eyes.

III.

She dwells with Beauty — Beauty that must die;
  And Joy, whose hand is ever at his lips
Bidding adieu; and aching Pleasure nigh,
  Turning to poison while the bee-mouth sips:
Ay, in the very temple of Delight
  Veiled Melancholy has her sov'reign shrine,
    Though seen of none save him whose strenuous
tongue
Can burst Joy's grape against his palate fine;
  His soul shall taste the sadness of her might,
And be among her cloudy trophies hung.

The following two odes are perhaps Keats's finest and best known. He died within a year of completing these poems, having created living works that assured his own immortality.

TO AUTUMN

Season of mists and mellow fruitfulness!
  Close bosom-friend of the maturing sun;
Conspiring with him how to load and bless
  With fruit the vines that round the thatch-eaves run;
To bend with apples the moss'd cottage-trees,
  And fill all fruit with ripeness to the core;
    To swell the gourd, and plump the hazel shells
With a sweet kernel; to set budding more,
  And still more, later flowers for the bees,
    Until they think warm days will never cease
      For Summer has o'er-brimm'd their clammy cells.

Who hath not seen the oft amid thy store?
  Sometimes whoever seeks abroad may find
Thee sitting careless on a granary floor,
  Thy hair soft-lifted by the winnowing wind;
Or on a half-reap'd furrow sound asleep,
  Drowsed with fume of poppies, while thy hook
    Spares the next swath and all its twined flowers;
And sometimes like a gleaner thou dost keep
Steady thy laden head across a brook;
  Or by a cider-press, with patient look,
    Thou watchest the last oozings hours by hours.

Where are the songs of Spring? Ay, where are they?
  Think not of them, Thou hast thy music too,
While barred clouds bloom the soft-dying day,
  And touch the stubble-plains with rosy hue;
Then is a wailful choir the small gnats mourn
  Among the river shallows, borne aloft
    Or sinking as the light wind lives or dies;
And full-grown lambs loud bleat from hilly bourn;
Hedge-crickets sing; and now with treble soft
  The redbreast whistles from a garden-croft;
    And gathering swallows twitter in the skies.

"Ode on a Grecian Urn" explores the concept that, through art, a singular fleeting moment can be preserved for eternity.

ODE ON A GRECIAN URN

I.

Thou still unravish'd bride of quietness,
  Thou foster-child of Silence and slow Time,
Sylvan historian, who canst thus express
  A flowery tale more sweetly than our rhyme:
What leaf-fringed legend haunts about thy shape
  Of deities or mortals, or of both,
    In Tempe or the dales of Arcady?
What men or gods are these? What maidens loath?
  What mad pursuit? What struggle to escape?
    What pipes and timbrels? What wild ecstasy?

II.

Heard melodies are sweet, but those unheard
  Are sweeter; therefore, ye soft pipes, play on;
Not to the sensual ear, but, more endeared,
  Pipe to the spirit ditties of no tone:
Fair youth, beneath the trees, thou canst not leave
  Thy song, nor ever can those trees be bare;
    Bold Lover, never, never canst thou kiss,
Though winning near the goal—yet, do not grieve;
  She cannot fade, though thou hast not thy bliss,
    For ever wilt thou love, and she be fair!

III.

Ah, happy, happy boughs! that cannot shed
  Your leaves, nor ever bid the Spring adieu;
And, happy melodist, unwearied,
  For ever piping songs for ever new;
More happy love! more happy, happy love!
  For ever warm and still to be enjoyed,
    For ever panting, and for ever young;
All breathing human passion far above,
  That leaves a heart high-sorrowful and cloyed,
    A burning forehead, and a parching tongue.

IV.

Who are these coming to the sacrifice?
  To what green altar, O mysterious priest,
Leadest thou that heifer lowing at the skies,
  And all her silken flanks with garlands dressed?
What little town by river or sea shore,
  Or mountain-built with peaceful citadel,
    Is emptied of its folk, this pious morn?
And, little town, thy streets for evermore
  Will silent be; and not a soul to tell
    Why thou art desolate, can e'er return.

V.

O Attic shape! fair attitude! with breed
  Of marble man and maidens overwrought,
With forest branches and the trodden weed;
  Thou, silent form, dost tease us out of thought
As doth eternity: Cold Pastoral!
  When old age shall this generation waste,
    Thou shalt remain, in midst of other woe
Than ours, a friend to man, to whom thou say'st,
  'Beauty is truth, truth beauty—that is all
    Ye know on earth, and all ye need to know.'

MID- AND LATE-19TH CENTURY LYRICISTS

ELIZABETH BARRETT BROWNING
(1806–1861)

"All the life and strength which are in me," wrote Elizabeth Barrett Browning in 1840, "seem to have passed into my poetry." To her, life was poetry. She wrote her first poem, a birthday ode to her mother, when she was only eight years old. She received such praise for this piece that it became a common practice for her to write birthday odes for the members of her family. When she was 14, her father, Edward Barrett, published 50 copies of her epic poem "The Battle of Marathon." Following its release, poetry was to be her life's work.

Elizabeth spent considerable time reading, writing and studying, often being tutored alongside her brother Edward, whom she lovingly called "Bro." During her childhood she was exceptionally close to her ten younger brothers and sisters. The girl found as much joy in boisterous outdoor activities with her siblings as she did in writing. Her childhood was both active and happy; she excelled physically as well as mentally. However, at age 15 Elizabeth's young life took a drastic turn: she contracted measles. Shortly thereafter, she began suffering from another, undiagnosed disease. As was common in her day, she was sent away from home, spending nearly a year at the Gloucester Spa receiving treatment for a spine complaint.

After months of being isolated and in bed, upon returning home Elizabeth was weak and depressed. The melancholy was deepened by the fact that Bro had been sent to a boarding school while she was away. She missed the companionship of her brother, but also despaired the fact that, while his education would continue, hers would not. More and more troubled about being denied further training simply on the basis of gender—her whole world thus altered—poetry took on a greater significance; it became her source of being.

In 1828 Elizabeth's mother died unexpectedly, causing her to retreat even more deeply into herself and her poetry. She separated herself from her family and friends and clung desperately to her religious faith.

Four years after his wife's death, Mr. Barrett moved his family to London. Unfortunately, the climate there had an ill effect on his daughter's health. Elizabeth nearly died of a lung hemorrhage in 1838. Bro accompanied her to Torquay, Australia to recover, and it was there that she suffered the most devastating tragedy in her life: at the drowning accident of her beloved Bro, Elizabeth subsequently spent the following three months grieving in a darkened room, unable to speak or write.

Finally she returned to London, where she again picked up pen and paper, soon publishing vast amounts of poetry. In 1845, correspondence with the young poet Robert Browning commenced. After five months of exchanging letters, the two poets met. Sixteen months later, they married secretly and moved to Italy. While there, her career as a poet flourished as she expanded her poetic repertoire and took up writing about political and social issues.

At the beginning of her marriage, Browning enjoyed a reprieve from her physical ailments. For the first time in a very long time, she was healthy and happy. In 1849 she gave birth to a son. Then, in 1850, she suffered a miscarriage—her

fourth in all—and her ailments returned. For 11 years her health deteriorated, until, in 1861, Elizabeth Barrett Browning died, cradled in the arms of her husband.

HOW DO I LOVE THEE?
LET ME COUNT THE WAYS

How do I love thee? Let me count the ways.
I love thee to the depth and breadth and height
My soul can reach, when feeling out of sight
For the ends of Being and ideal Grace.
I love thee to the level of every day's
Most quiet need, by sun and candlelight.
I love thee freely, as men strive for Right;
I love thee purely, as they turn from Praise.
I love thee with the passion put to use
In my old griefs, and with my childhood's faith.
I love thee with a love I seemed to lose
With my lost saints,—I love thee with the breath,
Smiles, tears, of all my life!—and, if God choose,
I shall but love thee better after death..

Perhaps the most recognized of Elizabeth Barrett Browning's poems, "How Do I Love Thee? Let Me Count the Ways" is part of a large collection of love poems titled *Sonnets from the Portuguese*, written for Robert Browning. In this collection she explores the emotional depths and complexities of this, her most intimate bond. She was quoted as saying that a poet's primary responsibility is "to tell the truth." In *Sonnets from the Portuguese* the truth is openly declared, revealing her many-faceted relationship with her husband. The result is a wide range of poems, each possessing a profound beauty and truth.

SONNETS FROM THE PORTUGUESE X

Yet, love, mere love, is beautiful indeed
And worthy of acceptation. Fire is bright,
Let temple burn, or flax. An equal light
Leaps in the flame from cedar-plank or weed.
And love is fire. And when I say at need
I love thee ... mark! ... I love thee—in thy sight
I stand transfigured, glorified aright,
With conscience of the new rays that proceed
Out of my face toward thine. There's nothing low
In love, when love the lowest: meanest creatures
Who love God, God accepts while loving so.
And what I feel, across the inferior features
Of what I am, doth flash itself, and show
How that great work of Love enhances Nature's.

SONNETS FROM THE PORTUGUESE XIV

If thou must love me, let it be for naught
Except for love's sake only. Do not say
'I love her for her smile ... her look ... her way
Of speaking gently ... for a trick of thought
That falls in well with mine, and ... brought
A sense of pleasant ease on such a day—
For these things in themselves, Beloved, may
Be changed, or change for thee,—and love, so wrought
May be unwrought so. Neither love me for
Thine own dear pity's wiping my cheeks dry,—
A creature might forget to weep, who bore

Thy comfort long, and lose thy love thereby!
But love me for love's sake, that evermore
Thou may'st love on, through love's eternity.

SONNETS FROM THE PORTUGUESE XXXVIII

First time he kissed me, he but only kissed
The fingers of this hand wherewith I write;
And ever since, it grew more clean and white ...
Slow to world-greetings, quick with its 'Oh, list,'
When the angels speak. A ring of amethyst
I could not wear here, plainer to my sight,
Than that first kiss. The second passed in height
The first, and sought the forehead, and half missed,
Half falling on the hair. O beyond meed!
That was the chrism of love, which love's own crown,
With sanctifying sweetness, did precede.
The third upon my lips was folded down
In perfect, purple state; since when, indeed,
I have been proud and said, 'My love, my own.'

Browning also shared a deep relationship with God.
Much of her poetry, especially her early work, is profoundly
religious.

From A SABBATH MORNING AT SEA

... And though this sabbath comes to me
Without the stolid minister
And chanting congregation,
God's Spirit shall give comfort.
He who brooded soft on waters drear,
Creator on creation.

He shall assist me to look higher,
He shall assist me to look higher,
Where keep the saints, with harp and song,
An endless endless Sabbath morning,
An endless Sabbath morning,
And that sea commixed with fire,
And that sea commixed with fire,
Oft drop their eyelids raised too long
To the full Godhead's burning
To the full Godhead's burning ...

From DE PROFUNDIS

... I praise Thee while my days go on;
I love Thee while my days go on:
Through dark and dearth, through fire and frost,
With emptied arms and treasure lost,
I thank Thee while my days go on.

And having in Thy life-depth thrown
Being and suffering (which are one),
As a child drops his pebble small
Down some deep well, and hears it fall
Smiling—so I. THY DAYS GO ON ...

As Browning matured in her verse-creation, she experimented with different themes. She began to view her poetry as
a weapon with which to combat social and political wrongs. In
one of her most poignant poems "The Cry of the Children,"
the exploitation of children in the labor force is lamented.

From THE CRY OF THE CHILDREN

... Do you question the young children in the sorrow
    Why their tears are falling so?
The old man may weep for his tomorrow
    Which is lost in Long Ago;
The old tree is leafless in the forest,
    The old year is ending in the frost,
The old wound, if stricken, is the sorest,
    The old hope is hardest to be lost.
But the young, young children, O my brothers,
    Do you ask them why they stand
Weeping sore before the bosoms of their mothers,
    In our happy Fatherland?...

'For oh,' say the children, 'we are weary,
    And we cannot run or leap;
If we cared for any meadows, it were merely
    To drop down in them and sleep.
Our knees tremble sorely in the stooping,
    We fall upon our faces, trying to go;
And, underneath our heavy eyelids drooping,
    The reddest flower would look as pale as snow;
For, all day, we drag our burden tiring
    Through the coal-dark, underground;
Or, all day, we drive the wheels of iron
    In the factories, round and round ...

Personal and political, passionate and objective, lyrical
and declamatory, Browning's epic poem "Aurora Leigh,"
published in 1856, was the pinnacle of her poetic achievements. The lengthy poem's lines are perhaps autobiographical, in nature if not entirely in fact.

From AURORA LEIGH

Of writing many books there is no end;
And I who have written much in prose and verse
For others' uses, will write now for mine,—
Will write my story for my better self,
As when you paint your portrait for a friend,
Who keeps it in a drawer and looks at it
Long after he has ceased to love you ...
I, writing thus, am still what men call young;
I have not so far left the coasts of life
To travel inland, that I cannot hear
That murmur of the outer Infinite
Which unweaned babies smile at in their sleep
When wondered at for smiling; not so far,
But still I catch my mother at her post
Beside the nursery-door, with finger up,
'Hush, hush–here's too much noise!' while her sweet eyes
Leap forward, taking part against her word
In the child's riot. Still I sit and feel
My father's slow hand, when she had left us both,
Stroke out my childish curls across his knee ...
... O my father's hand,
Stroke the poor hair down, stroke it heavily,–
Draw, press the child's head closer to thy knee!
I'm still too young, too young to sit alone ...

HENRY WADSWORTH LONGFELLOW
(1807–1882)

All are architects of Fate,
    Working in these walls of Time;
Some with massive deeds and great,
    Some with ornaments of rhyme.

Nothing useless is, or low;
    Each thing in its place is best;
And what seems but idle show
    Strengthens and supports the rest.

Thus begins Longfellow's poem "The Builders," a work which reflects both his personal moral philosophy and that of the time in which he lived.

The only American honored in the Poet's Corner of London's Westminster Abbey, this professor published 12 books, in addition to writing several textbooks and much poetry. During his lifetime, his verse was translated into many languages, making him one of the most celebrated voices of the Western world.

In the seacoast town of Portland, Maine, Henry Wadsworth was born in 1807 to the eminent Longfellow family. He showed a zest for learning and, unlike many of his fellow poets, enjoyed a happy childhood. Attending Bowdoin College, he was offered a professorship of modern languages, subsequently traveling in Europe for a time to prepare himself to teach and to write grammar textbooks.

Longfellow soon married and began a career at Harvard University. Thereafter, his young wife died. His second marriage brought him six children and 18 years of relatively blissful family life. At the height of his success and fame, personal tragedy struck once more, with the death of his wife. Amid rewarding literary praise, he spent the remainder of his life alone.

In 1839, shortly after becoming a Harvard professor, Longfellow published *Voices of the Night*. One poem in this collection, "Psalm of Life," became particularly popular and served as a springboard for his career in poetry.

The Victorian age was known for its sentimentality. Longfellow also expounded on the prevalent philosophies of the day; literally thousands were writing poetry on similar themes. What set him apart, though, were his superior writing skills and the pathos that he managed to infuse in his verse.

The poem which first brought Longfellow fame has remained popular to this day. "A Psalm of Life" is a clear example of the author's moral philosophy: the individual can make a difference; therefore, each should each do all that he or she can do.

A PSALM OF LIFE
What the Heart of the Young Man Said to the Psalmist

Tell me not, in mournful numbers,
    Life is but an empty dream!—
For the soul is dead that slumbers,
    And things are not what they seem.

Life is real! Life is earnest!
    And the grave is not its goal;
Dust thou art, to dust returnest,
    Was not spoken of the soul.

Not enjoyment, and not sorrow,
    Is our destined end or way;
But to act, that each to-morrow
    Find us farther than to-day.

Art is long, and Time is fleeting
    And our hearts, though stout and brave,
Still, like muffled drums, are beating
    Funeral marches to the grave.

In the world's broad field of battle,
    In the bivouac of Life,
Be not like dumb, driven cattle!
    Be a hero in the strife!

Trust no Future, howe'er pleasant!
    Let the dead Past bury its dead!
Act, —act in the living Present!
    Heart within, and God o'erhead!

Lives of great men all remind us
    We can make our lives sublime,
And, departing, leave behind us
    Footprints on the sands of time;

Footprints, that perhaps another,
    Sailing o'er life's solemn main,
A forlorn and shipwrecked brother,
    Seeing, shall take heart again.
Let us, then, be up and doing,
With a heart for any fate;
Still achieving, still pursuing,
Learn to labor and to wait.

Longfellow's storytelling talents and his interest in history came to the fore much later with the publication of "Evangeline," "The Song of Hiawatha" and "The Courtship of Miles Standish." This latter piece differs from his others in that it is a story rather than a poem, drawing heavily from an old pilgrim's tale.

The following selection from "The Courtship of Miles Standish" accentuates Longfellow's sensitivity toward women, a unique characteristic during his time.

" … That is the way with you men; you don't
   understand us, you cannot.
When you have made up your minds, after
   thinking of this one and that one,
Choosing, selecting, rejecting, comparing one
   with another,
Then you make known your desire, with abrupt
   and sudden avowal,
And are offended and hurt, and indignant
   perhaps, that a woman
Does not respond at once to a love that she never
   suspected … "
"No!" interrupted the maiden, with answer
   prompt and decisive;
"No; you were angry with me, for speaking so
   frankly and freely.
It was wrong, I acknowledge; for it is the fate of
   a woman
Long to be patient and silent, to wait like a ghost
   that is speechless,
Till some questioning voice dissolves the spell
   of its silence.
Hence is the inner life of so many suffering
   women
Sunless and silent and deep, like subterranean
   rivers
Running through caverns of darkness, unheard,
   unseen, and unfruitful,
Chafing their channels of stone, with endless and
   profitless murmurs … "
"When from the depths of my heart, in pain and
   with secret misgiving,
Frankly I speak to you, asking for sympathy only
   and kindness,
Straightway you take up my words, that are plain
   and direct and in earnest,
Turn them away from their meaning, and answer
   with flattering phrases.
This is not right, is not just, is not true to the best
   that is in you;
For I know and esteem you, and feel that your
   nature is noble,
Lifting mine up to a higher, a more ethereal level.
Therefore I value your friendship, and feel it
   perhaps the more keenly
If you say aught that implies I am only as one
   among many,
If you make use of those common and
   complimentary phrases
Most men think so fine, in dealing and speaking
   with women,
But which women reject as insipid, if not as
   insulting."…

"Hiawatha" resulted from Longfellow's
surrendering his professorship to write full-
time. He completed this poem, along with
several lesser ones, within a year after leaving
the university. In spite of some criticism, this
poem was well received by the general population, much more so than the poet had expected.
Public readings of it began almost immediately.

Here, rhyme yields to rhythm and purpose.
Even read silently, the poem pulses with the
cadence of a chant.

From THE SONG OF HIAWATHA—
INTRODUCTION

Should you ask me, whence these stories?
Whence these legends and traditions,
With the odors of the forest,
With the dew and damp of meadows,
With the curling smoke of wigwams,
With the rushing of great rivers,
With their frequent repetitions,
And their wild reverberations,
As of thunder in the mountains? …

I repeat them as I heard them
From the lips of Nawadaha,
The musician, the sweet singer.

O my children! my poor children!
Listen to the words of wisdom,
Listen to the words of warning,
From the lips of the Great Spirit,
From the Master of Life, who made you!
"I have given you lands to hunt in,
I have given you streams to fish in,
I have given you bear and bison,
I have given you roe and reindeer,
I have given you brant and beaver,
Filled the marshes full of wild-foul,
Filled the rivers full of fishes;
Why then are you not contented?
Why then will you hunt each other?
I am weary of your quarrels,
Weary of your wars and bloodshed,
Weary of your prayers for vengeance,
Of your wranglings and dissensions;
All your strength is in your union,
All your danger is in discord;
Therefore be at peace henceforward,
And as brothers live together."

In 1861 Longfellow's second wife died in a
tragic fire. Trying to save her, the poet was
severely burned. His way of dealing with grief
was to retreat; not much of his feelings about
that death or about the ongoing Civil War were
reflected in his ensuing writings. "With me," he
once said, "all deep feelings are silent ones."
Only a quote from Tennyson that begins "Sleep
sweetly, tender heart, in peace," grace the blank
pages of his journal during this time, belying

his inner grief. Finally, 18 years later, he came to grips with the death, writing "The Cross of Snow."

THE CROSS OF SNOW

In the long, sleepless watches of the night,
A gentle face—the face of one long dead—
Looks at me from the wall, where round its head
The night-lamp casts a halo of pale light.
Here in this room she died, and soul more white
Never through martyrdom of fire was led
To its repose; nor can in books be read
The legend of a life more benedight.
There is a mountain in the distant West
That, sun-defying, in its deep ravines
Displays a cross of snow upon its side.
Such is the cross I wear upon my breast
These eighteen years, through all the
*   changing scenes*
And seasons, changeless since the day she died.

The success of Longfellow's works hinges on his moral impulse, his storytelling skill, and his understanding of a human interest in history. Their charm also rests in the poet's ability to convey a sense of serenity and peace, even in disquieting times. In final stanzas of "The Day is Done" the healing power of poetry is especially invoked to salve the troubled heart.

… Then read from the treasure volume
*   The poem of thy choice,*
And lend to the rhyme of the poet
*   The beauty of thy voice.*

And the night shall be filled with music,
*   And the cares, that infest the day,*
Shall fold their tents, like the Arabs,
*   And as silently steal away.*

EDGAR ALLAN POE
(1809–1849)

ALONE

From childhood's hour I have not been
As others were—I have not seen
As others saw—I could not bring
My passions from a common spring—
From the same source I have not taken
My sorrow—I could not awaken
My heart to joy at the same tone—
And all I lov'd—I lov'd alone—
Then—in my childhood—in the dawn
Of a most stormy life—was drawn
From ev'ry depth of good and ill
The mystery which binds me still—
From the torrent, or the fountain—
From the red cliff of the mountain—
From the sun that 'round me roll'd
In its autumn tint of gold—
From the lightning in the sky
As it pass'd me flying by—
From the thunder, and the storm—
And the cloud that took the form
(When the rest of Heaven was blue)
Of a demon in my view.

One of America's greatest poets, short-story writers and literary critics, Edgar Allan Poe's writing—regardless of genre—possessed a haunting quality. At first he was lauded only for his romantic lyric poems, horror fiction and clever detective stories. Only since World War I have his symbolic verses and tales also been appreciated.

Edgar Poe was born in Boston, Massachusetts. Deserted by his father, and his mother taken in death, the two-year-old was put in the foster home of Mr. and Mrs. John Allan, from whom he took his middle name.

Although the Allans never formally adopted Edgar, they gave him some monetary support and encouraged him to study law, which he did, attending school in London and at the University of Virginia. He proved to be an excellent student. However, in an effort to win money for books and clothing, he turned to gambling, soon became consumed in debt, and eventually withdrew from school. To appease his foster father, Poe enlisted in the army and later entered the U.S. Military Academy. But, determined to follow a literary career, the young man finally broke regulations, forcing his dismissal from the Academy. He thereafter lived with his aunt, marrying her daughter, and supported them all on the receipts from his written publications.

While editing and writing articles for several literary magazines, Poe wrote and published his first volume, *Tamerlane and Other Poems*, then *Al Aaraaf, Tamerlane and Minor Poems*. Even as one of the most successful and respected writers around, still he was underpaid, and his family often went without food.

His works are often shrouded in mystery. And, like his poetry, much of his later life as well as his death remain a mystery. Although some details about his later years are recorded, they seem to have been marked by tragedy.

Poe's love verse was written in a form called *acrostic poetry*, in which the left edge of the poem spells out a name or a word.

AN ACROSTIC

Elizabeth it is in vain you say
"Love not"—thou sayest it in so sweet a way:
In vain those words from thee or L.E.L.
Zantippe's talents had enforced so well;
Ah! if that language from thy heart arise,
Breathe it less gently forth—and veil thine eyes.
Endymion, recollect, when Luna tried
To cure his love—was cured of all beside—
His folly—pride—and passion—for he died.

In "Annabel Lee," simple rhymes and charming images heighten the work's underlying eeriness.

ANNABEL LEE

It was many and many a year ago,
* In a kingdom by the sea,*
That a maiden there lived whom you may know
* By the name of Annabel Lee;*
And this maiden she lived with no other thought
* Than to love and be loved by me …*

… And this was the reason that, long ago,
* In this kingdom by the sea,*
A wind blew out of a cloud, chilling
* My beautiful Annabel Lee;*
So that her high-born kinsmen came
* And bore her away from me,*
To shut her up in a sepulchre,
* In this kingdom by the sea.*

The angels, not half so happy in heaven,
* Went envying her and me—*
Yes!—that was the reason (as all men know,
* In this kingdom by the sea)*
That the wind came out of the cloud by night,
* Chilling and killing my Annabel Lee.*

But our love it was stronger by far than the love
* Of those who were older than we—*
* Of many far wiser than we—*
And neither the angels in Heaven above,
* Nor the demons down under the sea,*
Can ever dissever my soul from the soul
* Of the beautiful Annabel Lee.*

For the moon never beams, without bringing
* me dreams*

Of the beautiful Annabel Lee;
And the stars never rise but I feel the bright eyes
* Of the beautiful Annabel Lee;*
And so, all the night-tide, I lie down by the side
Of my darling—my darling—my life and my
bride,
* In the sepulchre there by the sea,*
* In her tomb by the sounding sea.*

Poe's most famous work, "The Raven," is an obsessively haunting piece. The visiting bird's only word is "Nevermore," a simple lament that finally emerges as a disturbing answer to each of the questions the narrator poses—questions directed both to the raven, and to himself.

THE RAVEN

Once upon a midnight dreary, while I pondered,
* weak and weary,*
Over many a quaint and curious volume of
* forgotten lore,*
While I nodded, nearly napping, suddenly there
* came a tapping,*
As of some one gently rapping, rapping at my
* chamber door.*
'Tis some visitor,' I muttered, 'tapping at my
* chamber door—*
Only this and nothing more.'

Ah, distinctly I remember it was in the bleak
* December,*
And each separate dying ember wrought its ghost
* upon the floor.*
Eagerly I wished the morrow;—vainly I had
* sought to borrow*
From my books surcease of sorrow—sorrow for
* the lost Lenore—*
For the rare and radiant maiden whom the
* angels name Lenore—*
Nameless here for evermore.

And the silken sad uncertain rustling of each
* purple curtain*
Thrilled me—filled me with fantastic terrors
* never felt before;*
So that now, to still the beating of my heart, I
* stood repeating:*
'Tis some visitor entreating entrance at my
* chamber door—*
Some late visitor entreating entrance at my
* chamber door;*
This it is and nothing more.'

… Open here I flung the shutter, when, with
* many a flirt and flutter,*
In there stepped a stately raven of the saintly days
* of yore.*
Not the least obeisance made he; not a minute
* stopped or stayed he;*
But, with mien of lord or lady, perched above my
* chamber door—*

Perched upon a bust of Pallas just above my
    chamber door—
Perched, and sat, and nothing more.

Then this ebony bird beguiling my sad fancy into
    smiling,
By the grave and stern decorum of the
    countenance it wore,
'Though thy crest be shorn and shaven, thou,'
    I said, 'art sure no craven,
Ghastly grim and ancient raven wandering from
    the nightly shore—
Tell me what thy lordly name is on the Night's
    Plutonian shore!'
Quoth the raven, 'Nevermore.'

Much I marvelled this ungainly fowl to hear
    discourse so plainly,
Though its answer little meaning—little
    relevancy bore …
… Bird or beast upon the sculptured bust above
    his chamber door,
With such name as 'Nevermore.'

But the raven, sitting lonely on that placid bust,
    spoke only
That one word, as if his soul in that one word he
    did outpour.
Nothing further then he uttered—not a feather
    then he fluttered—
Till I scarcely more than muttered: 'Other friends
    have flown before—
On the morrow will he leave me as my hopes have
    flown before.'
Then the bird said, 'Nevermore.'

Startled at the stillness broken by reply so
    aptly spoken,
'Doubtless,' said I, 'what it utters is its only stock
    and store,
Caught from some unhappy master whom
    unmerciful disaster
Followed fast and followed faster till his songs one
    burden bore—
Till the dirges of his hope that melancholy
    burden bore
Of "Never—nevermore."'

But the Raven still beguiling all my sad soul
    into smiling,
Straight I wheeled a cushioned seat in front of
    bird and bust and door;
Then, upon the velvet sinking, I betook myself
    to linking
Fancy unto fancy, thinking what this ominous
    bird of yore—
What this grim, ungainly, ghastly, gaunt, and
    ominous bird of yore
Meant in croaking 'Nevermore.'

… Then, methought, the air grew denser,
    perfumed from an unseen censer,
Swung by Seraphim whose foot-falls tinkled on
    the tufted floor.
'Wretch,' I cried, 'thy God hath lent thee—by
    these angels he hath sent thee
Respite—respite and nepenthe from thy
    memories of Lenore!
Quaff, oh quaff this kind nepenthe, and forget
    this lost Lenore!'
Quoth the raven, 'Nevermore.'

… 'Prophet!' said I, 'thing of evil!—prophet still,
    if bird or devil!
By that heaven that bends above us—by that God
    we both adore—
Tell this soul with sorrow laden if, within the
    distant Aidenn,
It shall clasp a sainted maiden whom the angels
    named Lenore—
Clasp a rare and radiant maiden, whom the
    angels named Lenore?'
Quoth the raven, 'Nevermore.'

'Be that word our sign of parting, bird or fiend!'
    I shrieked, upstarting—
'Get thee back into the tempest and the Night's
    Plutonian shore!
Leave no black plume as a token of that lie thy
    soul hath spoken!
Leave my loneliness unbroken!—quit the bust
    above my door!
Take thy beak from out my heart, and take thy
    form from off my door!'
Quoth the raven, 'Nevermore.'

And the raven, never flitting, still is sitting, still
    is sitting
On the pallid bust of Pallas just above my
    chamber door;
And his eyes have all the seeming of a demon's
    that is dreaming,
And the lamp-light o'er him streaming throws his
    shadow on the floor;
And my soul from out that shadow that lies
    floating on the floor
Shall be lifted—nevermore!

Alfred "Lord" Tennyson
(1809–1892)

Ring Out Wild Bells

Ring out, wild bells, to the wild sky,
  The flying cloud, the frosty light;
  The year is dying in the night;
Ring out, wild bells, and let him die.

Ring out the old, ring in the new;
  Ring, happy bells, across the snow;
  The year is going, let him go;
Ring out the false, ring in the true …

Ring out false pride in place and blood,
  The civic slander and the spite;
  Ring in the love of truth and right,
Ring in the common love of good.

Alfred Tennyson's poetry truly did ring out a new message of truth and human love. As one of the supreme craftsmen of the English language and chosen as Britain's national poet, he was blessed with a remarkable range of literary talent. What's more, he was highly dedicated to refining his art.

Tennyson was born in Somersby, Lincolnshire. After just a few years in school, his father became dissatisfied with the quality of his children's education and brought them home to be taught.

In 1827 Alfred and his brother Charles published *Poems by Two Brothers*, which also included pieces by another brother, Frederick. That same year Alfred went to Cambridge University, where he met Arthur Hallam. The two men became devoted friends, Hallam becoming Tennyson's biggest fan, enthusiastically encouraging his writing. In 1830, after Tennyson published *Poems, Chiefly Lyrical*, Hallam penned and published a critical essay praising the book. Tennyson, though reluctant to continue writing, nevertheless yielded to Hallam's persuasiveness, publishing another book of *Poems* in 1832.

In the fall of 1833, Hallam died unexpectedly; Tennyson was overcome with grief. For the next year and a half he struggled with depression, *In Memoriam*, a lengthy, philosophic masterpiece made up of 133 individual poems, being one of his few creations during this period. As time went on, the poet's friends urged him to publish again. Among this cadre of supporters were John Stuart Mills, Ralph Waldo Emerson and Henry Longfellow. Tennyson refused to publish his work, but he did pick up his pen and resume his career.

Finally, in 1842, economic pressures forced his hand. Another edition of *Poems* was published, then came his *The Princess*. Tennyson married in 1850 and thereafter avoided public life. In that same year, he finally published *In Memoriam*, though anonymously. The critics liked this book—and the public loved it. By the end of the year it had sold 60,000 copies, and Queen Victoria offered the 41-year-old Tennyson the position of poet laureate of England, vacant since the death of Wordsworth.

Residing in his quiet country homes, Tennyson turned out inspiring and creative works. Having long considered an Arthurian epic, in 1859 he published the first version of *Idylls of the King*, continuing to add pieces to it throughout his long life.

As the years passed, Tennyson produced six more volumes of verse and became the first poet presented with a peerage, becoming Lord Tennyson nine years before his death in 1892. His body was buried in the Poets' Corner of Westminster Abbey.

In a long struggle to deal with the death of his devoted friend Hallam, Tennyson's *In Memoriam* alternates between utter despair and hopeful abandon.

But I remained, whose hopes were dim,
Whose life, whose thoughts were little worth
To wander on a darkened earth,
Where all things round me breathed of him …

Whatever way my days decline,
I felt and feel, though left alone,
His being working in mine own,
The footsteps of his life in mine …

In words, like weeds, I'll wrap me o'er,
Like coarsest clothes against the cold;
But that large grief which these enfold
Is given in outline and no more …

The following lines from *The Princess* ring with tenderness, and are believed to have been written several years after Tennyson's first son was delivered stillborn.

As through the land at eve we went,
  And plucked the ripened ears,
We fell out, my wife and I,
O, we fell out, I know not why,
  And kissed again with tears.
And blessings on the falling out
  That all the more endears,
When we fall out with those we love
And kiss again with tears!
For when we came where lies the child
  We lost in other years,
There above the little grave,
O, there above the little grave,
  We kissed again with tears.

Though all of Tennyson's poems are lyrical in nature, some are more musical than others, such as this beautiful lullaby, also from *The Princess* collection

Sweet and low, sweet and low,
  Wind of the western sea,
Low, low, breathe and blow,
  Wind of the western sea!
Over the rolling water go,
Come from the dying moon, and blow,
  Blow him again to me;
While my little one, while my pretty one, sleeps.

Sleep and rest, sleep and rest,
  Father will come to thee soon;
Rest, rest, on mother's breast,
  Father will come to thee soon;
Silver sails all out of the west
  Under the silver moon:
Sleep, my little one, sleep, my pretty one, sleep.

While these lines have their own rhythm and melody, the loneliness of the mother waiting for her husband to come home is still readily apparent.

Tennyson's most exquisite images came from nature. "The Brook" was first published in *Maud and Other Poems*.

I come from haunts of coot and hern;
  I make a sudden sally
And sparkle out among the fern,
  To bicker down a valley.

By thirty hills I hurry down,
  Or slip between the ridges,
By twenty thorps, a little town,
  And half a hundred bridges.

I murmur under moon and stars
  In brambly wildernesses;
I linger by my shingly bars;
  I loiter round my cresses;

And out again I curve and flow
  To join the brimming river,
For men may come and men may go,
  But I go on forever.

The following images are also from *The Princess*:

The splendor falls on castle walls
  And snowy summits old in story:
The long light shakes across the lakes,
  And the wild cataract leaps in glory.
Blow, bugle, blow, set the wild echoes flying,
Blow, bugle; answer, echoes, dying, dying, dying.
  O hark! O hear! how thin and clear,
    And thinner, clearer, farther going!
  O sweet and far, from cliff and scar,
    The horns of Elfland faintly blowing!
Blow, let us hear the purple glens replying:
Blow, bugle; answer, echoes, dying, dying, dying.

One of the earliest examples of the poet's remarkable storytelling skill is "The Lady of Shalott," concerning a lady, a weaver by trade, afflicted with the curse of loneliness. Finally arrives Sir Lancelot. The lady, seeing him, leaves her loom, gets in a boat and floats toward him— but in breaking the curse forfeits her life.

… Lying, robed in snowy white
That loosely fell to left and right—
The leaves upon her falling light—
Thro' the noises of the night
She floated down to Camelot:
And as the boat-head wound along
The willowy hills and fields among,
They heard her singing her last song,
The Lady of Shalott.

"The Charge of the Light Brigade," the poetic account of a suicidal charge of British forces over open terrain during the Crimean War, is a Tennyson classic.

Half a league, half a league,
    Half a league onward,
All in the valley of Death
    Rode the six hundred.
'Forward the Light Brigade!
Charge the guns!' he said:
Into the valley of Death
    Rode the six hundred.

'Forward the Light Brigade!'
Was there a man dismay'd?
Not tho' the soldier knew
    Someone had blunder'd:
Their's not to make reply,
Their's not to reason why,
Their's but to do or die:
Into the valley of Death
    Rode the six hundred.

Cannon to the right of them,
Cannon to the left of them,
Cannon in front of them
    Volley'd and thunder'd;
Storm'd at with shot and shell,
Boldly they rode and well,
Into the jaws of Death
Into the mouth of Hell
    Rode the six hundred.

Flash'd all their sabres bare,
Flash'd as they turn'd in air,
Sabring the gunners there,
Charging an army, while
    All the world wonder'd:
Plunged in the battery-smoke
Right thro' the line they broke;
Cossack and Russian
Reel'd from the sabre stroke
    Shattered and sunder'd.
Then they rode back, but not,
    Not the six hundred.

Cannon to the right of them,
Cannon to the left of them,
Cannon behind them
    Volley'd and thunder'd;
Storm'd at with shot and shell,
While horse and hero fell,
They that had fought so well
Came thro' the jaws of Death
Back from the mouth of Hell,
All that was left of them,
    Left of six hundred.

When can their glory fade?
O the wild charge they made!

All the world wonder'd.
Honor the charge they made!
Honor the Light Brigade,
    Noble six hundred!

At age 81, just three years before his death, Tennyson picked up an old envelope and wrote "Crossing the Bar" across the back of it.

Sunset and evening star,
    And one clear call for me!
And may there be no moaning of the bar,
    When I put out to sea.

But such a tide as moving seems asleep,
    Too full for sound and foam,
When that which drew from out the boundless deep
    Turns again home!

Twilight and evening bell,
    And after that the dark!
And may there be no sadness of farewell,
    When I embark;

For though from out our bourn of Time and Place
    The flood may bear me far,
I hope to see my Pilot face to face
    When I have crossed the bar.

WALT WHITMAN
(1819–1892)

"I hear America singing, the varied carols I hear …
… Singing with open mouths their strong
melodious songs."

The poetic tradition in America was strongly influenced by Walt Whitman. Many succeeding poets (Carl Sandburg, Hart Crane, Henry Miller, Allen Ginsberg, among others) sensed the great contribution and influence this literary giant had on their work.

Whitman's poetry broke with tradition of stanzaic patterns and measured lines, which brought a certain sense of freedom and naturalness to his lines.

The second son of a carpenter/contractor, Whitman was reared by semiliterate parents in a rural village on Long Island, New York. The political and intellectual atmosphere in the home was liberal, shaped by the teachings of Quakerism. But the youth read with captivated diligence the few 19th-century novels he could procure, the "classics" of European literature, and *The Bible.*

After probing into several different professions, Whitman finally settled down to teach in the village schoolhouse. Finding he had many talents in journalism, at the age of 22 he ventured to Manhattan, eventually becoming a journeyman printer.

He soon mastered the newspaper trade and contributed short stories and essays to a local paper. Later, as editor of *The Brooklyn Daily Eagle*, he penned many lyrical poems, most of them political in orientation. However, after two years he was dismissed for his radical views. After work as editor of a New Orleans newspaper, Whitman opened up his own printing and stationery store and began writing his greatest poetry.

Leaves of Grass was published in 1855, the title springing from a biblical allusion to the nature of humanity. Few copies of the first edition sold, yet, over time, it became a classic. "One's-Self I Sing" is the first inscription and entry in the volume. In it, Whitman reveals a spiritual connection he felt between the human soul and the world at large.

One's-Self I sing, a simple separate person,
Yet utter the word Democratic, the word En-Masse.

Of physiology from top to toe I sing,
Not physiognomy alone nor brain alone is worthy
*　for the Muse,*
I say the Form complete is worthier far,
The Female equally with the Male I sing.

Of life immense in passion, pulse, and power,
Cheerful, for freest action form'd under the
*　laws divine,*
The Modern Man I sing.

In *I Hear America Singing*, Whitman celebrated the common, everyday laborer: the man or woman, mother or father who is often overlooked and taken for granted. The songs these strong Americans sing are hopeful manifestations of free enterprise and the "American Dream."

I hear America singing, the varied carols I hear;
Those of mechanics—each one singing his, as it
*　should be, blithe and strong;*
The carpenter measures his, as he measures his
*　plank or beam,*
The mason singing his, as he makes ready for work,
*　or leaves off work;*
The boatman singing what belongs to him in his
*　boat, the deckhand singing on the steamboat deck;*
The shoemaker singing as he sits on his bench, the
*　hatter singing as he stands;*
The wood-cutter's song, the ploughboy's, on his way
*　in the morning, or at noon intermission or at*
*　sundown;*
The delicious singing of the mother, or of the young
*　wife at work, or of the girl sewing or washing,*
Each singing what belongs to her, and to none else;
The day what belongs to the day—at night the party
*　of young fellows, robust, friendly,*
Singing, with open mouths, their strong melodious
*　songs.*

Combining romantic love and animal instinct with very real life-bearing situations, "O Me! O Life!" contemplates the struggle and spiritual emptiness of modern times. But the optimistic conclusions that are finally drawn are characteristic redeeming features of much of Whitman's lyrical poetry.

O me! O life! of the questions of these recurring,
Of the endless trains of the faithless, of cities fill'd
*　with the foolish,*
Of myself forever reproaching myself, (for who more
*　foolish than I, and who more faithless?)*
Of eyes that vainly crave the light—of the objects
*　mean—of the struggle ever renew'd,*
Of the poor results of all, of the plodding and sordid
*　crowds I see around me,*
Of the empty and useless years of the rest, with the
*　rest me intertwined,*
The question, O me! so sad, recurring—What good
*　amid these, O me, O life?*

Answer
That you are here—that life exists, and identity,
That the powerful play goes on, and you may
*　contribute a verse.*

Along with the other sides of life, Whitman celebrated romantic passion, and sought to expose societal repression.

THE DALLIANCE OF THE EAGLES

Skirting the river road, (my forenoon walk, my rest,)
Skyward in air a sudden muffled sound, the
dalliance of the eagles,
The rushing amorous contact high in space together,
The clinching interlocking claws, a living, fierce,
gyrating wheel,
Four beating wings, two beaks, a swirling mass
tight grappling,
In tumbling turning clustering loops, straight
downward falling,
Till o'er the river pois'd, the twain yet one, a
moment's lull,
A motionless still balance in the air, then parting,
talons loosing,
Upward again on slow-firm pinions slanting, their
separate diverse flight,
She hers, he his, pursuing.

TO A STRANGER

Passing stranger! you do not know how longingly
I look upon you,
You must be he I was seeking, or she I was seeking,
(it comes to me as of a dream,)
I have somewhere surely lived a life of joy with you,
All is recall'd as we flit by each other, fluid,
affectionate, chaste, matured,
You grew up with me, were a boy with me or a girl
with me,
I ate with you and slept with you, your body has
become not yours only nor left my body mine only,
You give me the pleasure of your eyes, face, flesh, as
we pass, you take of my beard, breast, hands, in
return,
I am not to speak to you, I am to think of you when
I sit alone or wake at night alone,
I am to wait, I do not doubt I am to meet you again,
I am to see to it that I do not lose you.

Whitman was a great admirer of Abraham Lincoln, the man and his mission. Furthermore, Lincoln was a recognizable figure who reflected the poet's own democratic ideas. "O Captain! My Captain!" is a dedication to the Union-saving president, a captain guiding his ship through troubled waters.

O CAPTAIN! MY CAPTAIN!

O Captain! my Captain! our fearful trip is done,
The ship has weather'd every rack, the prize we
sought is won;
The port is near, the bells I hear, the people all
exulting,
While follow eyes the steady keel, the vessel grim
and daring:
> *But O heart! heart! heart!*
> *O the bleeding drops of red,*

> *Where on the deck my Captain lies,*
> *Fallen cold and dead.*

O Captain! my Captain! rise up and hear the bells,
Rise up—for you the flag is flung—for you the
bugle trills;
For you bouquets and ribbon'd wreaths—for you the
shores a-crowding;
For you they call, the swaying mass, their eager
faces turning;
> *Hear Captain! dear father!*
> *This arm beneath your head;*
> *It is some dream that on the deck,*
> *You've fallen cold and dead.*

My Captain does not answer, his lips are pale
and still,
My father does not feel my arm, he has no pulse
nor will;
The ship is anchor'd safe and sound, its voyage
closed and done;
From fearful trip, the victor ship, comes in with
object won;
> *Exult, O shores, and ring, O bells!*
> *But I, with mournful tread,*
> *Walk the deck my Captain lies,*
> *Fallen cold and dead.*

THIS DUST WAS ONCE THE MAN

This dust was once the Man,
Gentle, plain, just and resolute—under whose
cautious hand,
Against the foulest crime in history known in any
land or age,
Was saved the Union of These States.

Just as he was aware of the historical significance that Lincoln played in the rescuing and restoration of a nation, Whitman, as a poet, was conscious of his own labors toward discovery and innovation. Looking back at Whitman's life as a whole, "Full of Life Now" renders a fitting self-portrait.

FULL OF LIFE NOW

Full of life now, compact, visible,
I, forty years old the eighty-third year of the States,
To one a century hence or any number of centuries
hence,
To you yet unborn these, seeking you.

When you read these I that was visible am become
invisible,
Now it is you, compact, visible, realizing my poems,
seeking me,
Fancying how happy you were if I could be with you
and become your comrade;
Be it as if I were with you. (Be not too certain but I
am now with you.)

EMILY DICKINSON
(1830–1886)

This is my letter to the world,
That never wrote to me,—
The simple news that Nature told,
With tender majesty.

Her message is committed
To hands I cannot see;
For love of her, sweet countrymen,
Judge tenderly of me!

These lines from "My Letter to the World" are but a few from one of the 1,700 poems written, while in seclusion, by Emily Dickinson. Only ten of her poems were published during her lifetime—and those without her consent—while her first volume of poetry became public four years after her death.

Dickinson was born in 1830 in Amherst, Massachusetts, and spent her life there. Her father, although an austere man, once was said to have rang the bells of the Baptist Church just so everyone in the village would come outdoors to see the sunset.

The future poetess studied at Amherst Academy—a Puritan stronghold. At age 17, her year at Mount Holyoke seminary was the only time she spent away from her parents' home. Upon her return, little by little she withdrew from the affairs of the community. Her sometime brooding verses indicate that, at this point, she could only write while observing the world from a distance.

Dickinson's writing career began at school sometime before 1858. Her work was not meant for publication, but written as additions to letters—they almost comprising poems in their own right, filled with rhyme, rhythm and riddle-like phrases. Friends and editors pleaded with her to publish her works, but these well-meaning associates succeeded in getting only a fraction into print.

In 1874 Dickinson's father died, and, eight years later, so did her mother. From then on, her only real contact with the world was with and through her sister, Lavinia, who was later responsible for bringing a few of Dickinson's works into publication.

Manifesting a New England point of view—one of tradition, self-discipline and austerity—Dickinson wrote sparse verse. Symbols of nature—such as sunlight, birds, mushrooms and such—were worthy of poetry, as well as were the classic topics of life, love and death.

Dickinson recognized what to her was an obvious overlap between religion and nature, writing in an 1856 letter: " … all have gone to church … and I have come out in the new grass to listen to the anthems."

The following poem about nature also carries religious overtones—as well as references to death.

There's a certain slant of light,
On winter afternoons,
That oppresses, like the weight
Of cathedral tunes.

Heavenly hurt it gives us;
We can find no scar,
But internal difference
Where the meanings are.

None may teach it anything,
'Tis the seal, despair,—
An imperial affliction
Sent us of the air.

When it comes, the landscape listens,
Shadows hold their breath;
When it goes, 'tis like the distance
On the look of death.

Dickinson detected the beauty in nature even when it was gloomy and depressing outside.

The sky is low, the clouds are mean,
A travelling flake of snow
Across a barn or through a rut
Debates if it will go.

A narrow wind complains all day
How someone treated him;
Nature, like us, is sometimes caught
Without her diadem.

Contrast this more mellow, somber tone with the exultation in the following verses, where the first stanza's deliberate break in rhyming pattern is then reinstated in the subsequent stanzas. After Dickinson's death, publishers often had to choose from among several renditions of a line or stanza she had tried—none of which were crossed out. In this case two versions of the first stanza exist, neither of which are rhymed.

I taste a liquor never brewed
From tankards scooped in pearl;
Not all the vats upon the Rhine
Yield such an alcohol!

Inebriate of air am I,
And debauchee of dew,
Reeling, through endless summer days,
From inns of molten blue.

When landlords turn the drunken bee
Out of the foxglove's door,

When butterflies renounce their drams,
I shall but drink the more!

Till seraphs swing their snowy hats,
And saints to windows run,
To see the little tippler
Leaning against the sun!

If Dickinson's religion was personal, it was also certain and unwavering, as in perhaps her most beloved verse.

I never saw a moor,
I never saw the sea;
Yet know I how the heather looks,
And what a wave must be.

I never spoke with God,
Nor visited in Heaven;
Yet certain am I of the spot
As if the chart were given.

The Puritan outlook—embracing a belief that true worship requires a special kind of behavior—was also evident in Dickinson's work.

Triumph may be of several kinds.
There's triumph in the room
When that old imperator, Death,
By faith is overcome.

There's triumph of the finer mind
When truth, affronted long,
Advances calm to her supreme,
Her God her only throng.

A triumph when temptation's bribe
Is slowly handed back,
One eye upon the heaven renounced
And one upon the rack.

Severer triumph, by himself
Experienced, who can pass
Acquitted from that naked bar,
Jehovah's countenance!

Emily Dickinson wrote many poems about death, but did not approach it with the preoccupation other poets often reserved for the subject.

Afraid! Of whom am I afraid?
Not Death—for who is He?
The Porter of my Father's Lodge
As much abasheth me …

Although her verse is brief, the imagery is strong and vivid. The words, rhymes and rhythms combine to generate deep impact.

I felt a funeral in my brain,
*   And mourners, to and fro,*
Kept treading, treading, till it seemed
*   That sense was breaking through.*

And when they all were seated,
*   A service like a drum*
Kept beating, beating, till I thought
*   My mind was going numb.*

And then I heard them lift a box,
*   And creak across my soul*
With those same boots of lead, again,
*   Then space began to toll*

As all the heavens were a bell,
*   And Being but an ear,*
And I and silence some strange race,
*   Wrecked, solitary, here.*

A collection of Dickinson's poems makes it clear that at one time she was deeply in love with someone. Apparently, that love not returned or fulfilled, prompted some powerful poems. Alas, in the following verse, words and phrases like "entrenched," "none suspect" and "secret" suggest that Dickinson's sweetheart was never even aware of her feelings.

Rearrange a wife's affection?
When they dislocate my brain,
Amputate my freckled bosom,
Make me bearded like a man!

Blush, my spirit, in thy fastness,
Blush, my unacknowledged clay,
Seven years of troth have taught thee
More than wifehood ever may!

Love that never leaped its socket—
Trust entrenched in narrow pain—
Constancy through fire awarded,
Anguish bare of anodyne!

Burden—borne so far triumphant—
None suspect me of the crown,
For I wear the thorns till sunset,
Then my diadem put on.

Big my secret, but it's bandaged,
It will never get away
Till the day its Weary Keeper
Leads it through the Grave to thee.

Modern advocates of the women's movement have come to view Emily Dickinson as one of the earliest examples of feminism. Even in her isolation, she was a sharp observer of life and the human race.

Success is counted sweetest
By those who ne'er succeed.
To comprehend a nectar
Requires sorest need.

Not one of all the purple host
Who too the flag today
Can tell the definition,
So clear, of victory!

As he, defeated, dying,
On whose forbidden ear
The distant strains of triumph
Burst agonized and clear!

Indeed, her seclusion may have intensified her understanding of human emotions.

What fortitude the soul contains
That it can so endure
The accent of a coming foot,
The opening of a door!

Dickinson recognized both the joys and the terrors of the quiet, introspective life.

One need not be a chamber to be haunted,
One need not be a house;
The brain has corridors surpassing
Material place.

Far safer, of a midnight meeting
External ghost,
Than an interior confronting
That whiter host.

Far safer through an Abbey gallop,
The stones achase,
Than, moonless, one's own self encounter
In lonesome place ...

By her own standard, Dickinson's life and poetry were great successes. Her epitaph might well have read:

If I can stop one heart from breaking,
I shall not live in vain;
If I can ease one life the aching,
Or cool one pain,
Or help one fainting robin
Unto his nest again,
I shall not live in vain.

CHRISTINA ROSSETTI
(1830–1894)

Rigidity, structure, conformity, propriety … these defined the Victorian world into which Christina Rossetti was born. Strict moral values and social etiquette—especially for women—were the rule. Just as the close-fitting and suffocating corset restricted a woman's body in the name of fashion, so the social rules and mores inhibited a woman's spirit in the name of propriety. Despite such constraint, Rossetti found her voice, and became one of the outstanding female poets of the 19th century.

Born into a literary family, Rossetti and her siblings were versed in the classics. The children lived in an austere home; aside from reading and writing, they had little else to occupy their time. As they matured, all of the family's children developed into notable writers.

Only 17, Christina was first in her family to publish poetry. Titled *Verses*, this work was intensely religious, reflecting the influence the Bible played in her life. Rossetti was also profoundly affected by St. Augustine's and a Kempis's religious works. Much of her work resonates with spiritual themes.

A Victorian woman was faced with three choices: marriage, sisterhood or spinsterhood. Rossetti, having declined two marriage proposals and refusing to join the All Saints' Sisterhood, was consigned the latter of the three choices, and her poetry reflects the pain of an isolated existence. Writing about the anguish born of unfulfilled love, to Rossetti, death loomed the most palatable escape. The poetess died from cancer in 1894.

The most famous of Rossetti's poems is "Goblin Market," first published in 1862. On the surface, the poem appears to be a simple nursery rhyme-like story about two sisters. On a deeper level, it is a poetic essay on repressed female sexuality.

GOBLIN MARKET

Morning and evening
Maids heard the goblins cry:
"Come buy our orchard fruits,
Come buy, come buy:
Apples and quinces,
Lemons and oranges … "

… Evening by evening
Among the brookside rushes,
Laura bowed her head to hear,
Lizzie veiled her blushes:
Crouching close together
In the cooling weather,
With clasping arms and cautioning lips,
With tingling cheeks and fingertips.
"Lie close," Laura said,

Pricking up her golden head:
"We must not look at goblin men,
We must not buy their fruits:
Who knows upon what soil they fed
Their hungry thirsty roots?"
"Come buy," call the goblins
Hobbling down the glen.
"Oh" cried Lizzie, "Laura, Laura,
You should not peep at goblin men."
Lizzie covered up her eyes,
Covered close lest they should look;
Laura reared her glossy head,
And whispered like the restless brook:
"Look, Lizzie, look, Lizzie,
Down the glen tramp little men…. "

As the poem proceeds, both girls know that they should avoid the goblin men, yet hearing them is inevitable, and, eventually, Laura succumbs to their call, exchanging a lock of her hair—a symbol of her virginity—for the sweet fruit they offer. Upon partaking of the goblins' fruit, Laura is no longer able to hear their customary cry of "Come buy, come buy." Longing for the sweet fruit, she goes out in a vain search for the goblin market. Pining for the forbidden fruit, Laura becomes sick to the point of death. Lizzie, however, having resisted the goblins' call, bravely ventures to the goblin market to purchase fruit for her sister. But the goblin men will not allow her to take fruit for someone else. They try to force her to eat of the fruit, but she fiercely resists, returning home with her clothes tattered, her body bruised, and her face covered with the juice of the enslaving fruit. When Laura sees what Lizzie has done, she rushes to her and kisses away the juice—which is no longer sweet, but bitter. But, finally, the fruit's bitterness, combined with the love of her sister, redeems Laura from her ruin.

Although "Goblin Market" cheerfully concludes with a "love conquers all" message, the vast majority of Rossetti's poetry is not nearly so optimistic. Throughout her life she struggled between striving for sacred love or secular love, believing that she could only have one or the other. She found neither; her desire for an intimate union through marriage remained unfulfilled, as did her desire to join herself with God. As a result, a preoccupation with death began to pervade the work.

Her early poetry voices a need to have a deep and meaningful relationship with God, as the final stanza of "A Christmas Carol" reveals.

… What can I give Him,
Poor as I am?
If I were a shepherd
I would bring a lamb,

If I were a Wise Man
I would do my part,—
Yet what I can I give Him,
Give my heart.

Mary Magdalene is also an expression of religious longings:

She came in deep repentance,
  And knelt down at His feet
Who can change the sorrow into joy,
  The bitter into sweet.

She had cast away her jewels
  And her rich attire,
And her breast was filled with a holy shame,
  And her heart with a holy fire.

Her tears were more precious
  Than her precious pearls—
Her tears that fell upon His feet
  As she wiped them with her curls.

Her youth and her beauty
  Were budding to their prime;
But she wept for the great transgression,
  The sin of other time.

Trembling betwixt hope and fear,
  She sought the King of Heaven,
Forsook the evil of her ways,
  Loved much, and was forgiven.

Disappointed by her religion, Rossetti hungered for an intimate earthly relationship. "L.E.L." sums up her empty, romantic yearnings of spinsterhood.

L.E.L.
"Whose heart was breaking for a little love."

Downstairs I laugh, I sport and jest with all:
  But in my solitary room above
I turn my face in silence to the wall;
  My heart is breaking for a little love.
    Though winter frosts are done,
    And birds pair every one,
And leaves peep out, for springtide is begun.

I feel no spring, while spring is well-nigh blown,
  I find no nest, while nests are in the grove:
Woe's me for mine own heart that dwells alone,
  My heart that breaketh for a little love.
    While golden in the sun
    Rivulets rise and run,
While lilies bud, for springtide is begun.

All love, are loved, save only I; their hearts
  Beat warm with love and joy, beat full thereof:
They cannot guess, who play the pleasant parts,
  My heart is breaking for a little love.

While beehives wake and whir,
  And rabbit thins his fur,
In living spring that sets the world astir.

I deck myself with silks and jewelry,
  I plume myself like any mated dove:
The praise my rustling show, and never see
  My heart is breaking for a little love.
    While sprouts green lavender
    With rosemary and myrrh,
For in quick spring the sap is all astir.

Perhaps some saints in glory guess the truth,
  Perhaps some angels read it as they move,
And cry one to another full of ruth,
  "Her heart is breaking for a little love."
    Though other things have birth,
    And leap and sing for mirth,
When springtime wakes and clothes and feeds the earth.

Yet saith a saint: "Take patience for the scythe";
  Yet saith an angel: "Wait, for thou shalt prove
True best is last, true life is born of death,
  O thou, heart-broken for a little love!
    Then love shall fill thy girth,
    And love make fat thy dearth,
When new spring builds new heaven and clean new earth."

Lonely and insecure, Rossetti longed for the solace of death. Lines from "Looking Forward" reveal a last hope for happiness.

Sleep, let me sleep, for I am sick of care;
Sleep, let me sleep, for my pain wearies me.
Shut out the light; thicken the heavy air
With drowsy incense; let a distant stream
Of music lull me, languid as a dream,
  Soft as the whisper of a summer sea …

Considered by many her finest poem, "Three Stages" lends a vivid impression of the heartache Rossetti suffered.

… The fruitless thought of what I might have been,
  Haunting me ever, will not let me rest.
A cold North wind has withered all my green,
  My sun is in the West.

But, where my palace stood, with the same stone
  I will uprear a shady hermitage:
And there my spirit shall keep house alone,
  Accomplishing its age.

There other garden-beds shall lie around,
  Full of sweet-briar and incense-bearing thyme:
There will I sit, and listen for the sound
  Of the last lingering chime.

III

TWENTIETH CENTURY VERSE

RUDYARD KIPLING
(1865–1936)

Oh, East is East, and West is West and never the
twain shall meet,
Till Earth and Sky stand presently at God's great
Judgement Seat;

These first two lines of "The Ballad of East and West" advre often quoted out of context, evidencing how Rudyard Kipling's extraordinary skill sometimes over shadowed his message. The final lines of the stanza, however, reverse the meaning of this poem.

But there is neither East nor West, Border, nor
Breed, nor Birth,
When two strong men stand face to face, though
they come from the ends of the earth!

Born in Bombay, India, to ordinary English middle-class parents, Kipling's life was far from ordinary. He spent the first years of his life in relative comfort, attended to by Indian servants. When Rudyard was six, his parents returned to England to see to the boy's education, and he and his sister were placed in the care of a couple who ran a boarding house. Kipling became a voracious reader, but the master of the house disapproved of the activity, and soon the boy's book were seized; the budding poet, it is believed, was subsequently tormented—and possibly tortured—while in this home. When his mother learned of these conditions, she immediately returned to England and placed her son in a reputable boarding school.

At age 17 Kipling was hired to write for a newspaper in India. There was unable to spend time with his family, yet the experiences of his childhood held strong sway on his work.

Kipling spent seven years writing poetry and articles for various Indian papers. He published poetry (*Departmental Ditties*) and short stories (*Plain Tales from the Hills*), both of which became popular books both in India and Europe.

In time, Kipling returned to England to live. Soon, he married—and, for him, life had finally blessed him with bliss. While honeymooning in America, however, Kipling's bank failed, stranding the couple. With the help of relatives, they found a place to live, and Kipling resumed his writing. During this time, he published two books of verse, *Barrack Room Ballads* and *Seven Seas*. He also completed *The Jungle Book* and its sequel.

After four years in America, the Kiplings returned to England. There they lived quietly and happily, a good life interrupted only by the tragic death of their oldest daughter.

Captains Courageous and *Kim* were soon published, followed by the *Just So Stories*. In 1907 Kipling became the first Englishman to win the Nobel Prize for literature. As he grew into middle-age, he became an activist, involving himself in such events as the Boer War and World War I. His son, John, entered World War I and was soon reported as missing in action, presumed dead. This new tribulation devastated the family. After the war, Kipling withdrew from public view, and his writing took a more placid, less strident tone.

Critics of the day generally rated him highly as a writer, and not so highly as a poet. In addition to his anti-imperialist views, he tended to rely heavily on rhyme and meter—all during a time when imperialism was in vogue and Romantic poets were turning to free-verse and other experimental forms. Finally, his poetry became popular with the masses. Still, most critics continued to think of good poetry as unpopular—thus Kipling's "popular" poems couldn't be "good" poems.

Kipling is regarded a true "poet of the people." *Barrack Room Ballads* includes some of the best examples of "people poetry," such as "Danny Deever," "Mandalay," and "Gunga Din." The later lines of "Danny Deever" describes the execution of a soldier from the viewpoint of other soldiers.

… "What's that so black against the sun?" said
Files-on-Parade.
"It's Danny fightin' hard for life," the Colour
Sergeant said.
"What's that that whimpers overhead?" said
Files-on-Parade.
"It's Danny's soul that's passing now," the
Colour-Sergeant said …

"Mandalay," on the other hand, is a love story, a rhythmic masterpiece that embraces the classic line, "I've a neater, sweeter maiden in a cleaner, greener land."

… By the old Moulmein Pagoda,
Lookin' eastward to the sea,
There's a Burma girl a-settin',
And I know she thinks o' me;
For the wind is in the palm-trees,
And the temple-bells they say:
"Come you back, you British soldier;
Come you back to Mandalay!"
Come you back to Mandalay,
Where the old Flotilla lay:
Can't you 'ear their paddles chunkin'
From Rangoon to Mandalay?
On the road to Mandalay,
Where the flyin'-fishes play,
An' the dawn comes up like thunder
Outer China 'crost the Bay! …

"Gunga Din" was sometimes criticized among elitist reviewers not only for its rhyme scheme but for its explicit moral message.

... I shan't forgit the night
When I dropped be'ind the fight
With a bullet where my belt-plate should 'a' been.
I was chokin' mad with thirst,
An' the man that spied me first
Was our good old grinnin', gruntin' Gunga Din.
'E lifted up my 'ead,
An' he plugged me where I bled,
An' 'e guv me 'arf-a-pint o' water green:
It was crawlin' and it stunk,
But of all the drinks I've drunk,
I'm gratefullest to one from Gunga Din ...
　　You Lazarushian-leather Gunga Din!
　　Though I've belted you and flayed you,
　　By the livin' Gawd that made you,
　　You're a better man than I am, Gunga Din!

With the death of his son, who was missing in action, Kipling's dramatic poetry takes a totally different turn. In "A Nativity" his words clearly and consistently return to his son's well-being.

The Babe was laid in the Manger
　　Between the gentle kine—
All safe from cold and danger—
　　"But it was not so with mine,
　　(With mine! With mine!)"
"Is it well with the child, is it well?"
　　The waiting mother prayed.
"For I know not how he fell,
　　And I know not where he is laid."

... "My child died in the dark.
　　Is it well with the child, is it well?
There was none to tend him or mark,
　　And I know not how he fell."

... "But I know for Whom he fell"—
　　The steadfast mother smiled,
"Is it well with the child—is it well?
It is well—it is well with the child!"

Examples abound of Kipling's light verse in *Barracks Room Ballads* and *Seven Seas*. Unique in its lack of military overtones is the piece "When Earth's Last Picture Is Painted."

When Earth's last picture is painted
　　and the tubes are twisted and dried,
When the oldest colours have faded,
　　and the youngest critic has died,
We shall rest, and, faith, we shall need it—
　　lie down for an aeon or two,
Till the Master of All Good Workmen
　　shall put us to work anew.
And those that were good shall be happy:
　　they shall sit in a golden chair;
They shall splash at a ten-league canvas
　　with brushes of comets' hair.
They shall find real saints to draw from—
　　Magdalene, Peter, and Paul;
They shall work for an age at a sitting
　　and never be tired at all!

And only The Master shall praise us,
　　and only The Master shall blame;
And no one shall work for money,
　　and no one shall work for fame,
But each for the joy of the working,
　　and each, in his separate star,
Shall draw the Thing as he sees It
　　for the God of Things as They are!

Even Kipling's light verse could carry a sting, as this first stanza from "Old Men."

This is our lot if we live so long and labour unto
　　the end—
That we outlive the impatient years and the
　　much too patient friend:
And because we know we have breath in our
　　mouth and think we have thoughts in our head,
We shall assume that we are alive, whereas we are
　　really dead ...

Perhaps another reason the critics so disparaged Kipling's poems was they carried such moralistic messages. Indeed, his moralizing could penetrate to the heart of the blameworthy. The final lines of "The Mary Gloster" are a prime example.

... The things I knew was proper
　　you wouldn't thank me to give,
And the things I knew was rotten
　　you said was the way to live.

Because Kipling wrote about men of action, he was much loved by the common English soldiers and sailors. Often he wrote about them for a reason, as seen in "The Last of the Light Brigade."

THE LAST OF THE LIGHT BRIGADE

There were thirty million English
  who talked of England's might,
There were twenty broken troopers
  who lacked a bed for the night.
They had neither food nor money,
  they had neither service nor trade;
They were only shiftless soldiers,
  the last of the Light Brigade.

They felt that life was fleeting;
  they knew not that art was long,
That though they were dying of famine,
  they lived in deathless song.
They asked for a little money
  to keep the wolf from the door;
And the thirty million English
  sent twenty pounds and four!

… O thirty million English
  that babble of England's might,
Behold there are twenty heroes
  who lack their food to-night;
Our children's children are lisping
  to "honour the charge they made—"
And we leave to the streets and the workhouse
  the charge of the Light Brigade!

"If" was another popular poem—though rejected by the critics, perhaps for being "too neatly tied up."

If you can keep your head when all about you
Are losing theirs and blaming it on you,
If you can trust yourself when all men doubt you,
But make allowance for their doubting too; …
If you can dream—and not make dreams your
  master;
If you can think—and not make thoughts your
  aim;
If you can meet with Triumph and Disaster
And treat those two impostors just the same;
If you can bear to hear the truth you've spoken
Twisted by knaves to make a trap for fools,
Or watch the things you gave your life to broken,
And stoop and build 'em up with wornout tools:
… Yours is the Earth and everything that's in it,
And—which is more—you'll be a Man, my son!

"The Children's Song" spotlights both Kipling's own attitude toward the critics and his own personal moral code.

… Teach us to look in all our ends,
On Thee for judge, and not our friends;
That we, with Thee, may walk uncowed
By fear or favour of the crowd.

Teach us the Strength that cannot seek,
By deed or thought, to hurt the weak;
That, under Thee, we may possess
Man's strength to comfort man's distress.

Teach us Delight in simple things,
And Mirth that has no bitter springs;
Forgiveness free of evil done,
And Love to all men 'neath the sun! …

WILLIAM BUTLER YEATS
(1865–1939)

One of the greatest poets of the 20th century, W.B. (William Butler) Yeats directed the themes of his works on art, Irish nationalism, and the supernatural. Also a dramatist, he authored 26 plays. Among his many accomplishments, Yeats won the Noble Prize for Literature in 1923.

Born in Dublin, Ireland, Yeats spent his childhood in London and western Ireland, and grew up promoting the cause of the Irish. He co-founded the Irish Literary Theatre to support nationalism and encourage the writing and producing of plays about the Irish way of life.

The elements which set Yeats's verses apart were his supreme sense of diction, rhythm and metrics. His lines almost sing with a music-like cadence. *Collected Poems*, published in 1950, contains most of his verse. He later wrote *A Vision*, a guide to his theories—which serves quite useful in interpreting and understanding some of his more difficult poems.

Yeats's politics are most pronounced in the work "Easter, 1916." Here, he recounts the events of the Irish rebellion, provides the reader with a list of the central figures in that revolt, and extols the rebels' courage in the face of insurmountable odds. He loved these revolutionaries, the heroic founders of the Irish Republic.

EASTER, 1916

I have met them at close of day
Coming with vivid faces
From counter or desk among grey
Eighteenth-century houses.
I have passed with a nod of the head
Or polite meaningless words,
Or have lingered awhile and said
Polite meaningless words,
And thought before I had done
Of a mocking tale or a gibe
To please a companion
Around the fire at the club,
Being certain that they and I
But lived where motley is worn:
All changed, changed utterly:
A terrible beauty is born.

That woman's days were spent
In ignorant good-will,
Her nights in argument
Until her voice grew shrill.
What voice more sweet than hers
When, young and beautiful,
She rode to harriers?
This man had kept a school
And rode our winged horse;
This other his helper and friend
Was coming into his force;
He might have won fame in the end,
So sensitive his nature seemed,
So daring and sweet his thought.
This other man I had dreamed
A drunken, vainglorious lout.
He had done most bitter wrong
To some who are near to my heart,
Yet I number him in the song;
He, too, has resigned his part
In the casual comedy;
He, too, has been changed in his turn,
Transformed utterly:
A terrible beauty is born.

… Too long a sacrifice
Can make a stone of the heart.
O when may it suffice?
That is Heaven's part, our part
To murmur name upon name,
As a mother names her child
When sleep at last has come
On limbs that had run wild.
What is it but nightfall?
No, no, not night, but death;
What is needless death after all?
For England may keep faith
For all that is done and said.
We know their dream; enough
To know they dreamed and are dead;
And what if excess of love
Bewildered them till they died?
I write it out in a verse—
MacDonagh and MacBride
And Connolly and Pearse
Now and in time to be,
Wherever green is worn,
Are changed, changed utterly:
A terrible beauty is born.

Formulating his own theories about the nature of time and history, Yeats's ideas are in part derived from his notions of spirituality. He viewed history as a being "gyre," a symbolic whirlpool or eddy in which time is tossed and spun around, finally to disappear in the bottomless void. The complicated scheme of his poetry separates time into a series of "gyres" marking the various eras through which civilization has passed.

To Yeats, the "gyre" is an important element signaling the end of the Christian epoch and the coming of Armageddon. The "rough beast" is a sphinx-like image of the coming catastrophe which is let loose by a world where the "centre cannot hold" and extreme anarchy reigns. He also uses a spiritual symbol—the "soul of the world"—to express the concept of apocalypse.

Turning and turning in the widening gyre
The falcon cannot hear the falconer;
Things fall apart; the centre cannot hold;
Mere anarchy is loosed upon the world,
The blood-dimmed tide is loosed, and everywhere
The ceremony of innocence is drowned;
The best lack all conviction, while the worst
Are full of passionate intensity.
Surely some revelation is at hand;
Surely the Second Coming is at hand.
The Second Coming! Hardly are those words out
When a vast image out of Spiritus Mundi
Troubles my sight: somewhere in the sands of
 the desert
A shape with lion body and the head of a man,
A gaze blank and pitiless as the sun,
Is moving its slow thighs, while all about it
Reel shadows of the indignant desert birds.
The darkness drops again; but now I know
That twenty centuries of stony sleep
Were vexed to nightmare by a rocking cradle,
And what rough beast, its hour come round
 at last,

Slouches toward Bethlehem to be born?

Unlike most poets, Yeats's works improved
as he grew older. In the last ten years of his life
he turned out his best, most innovative poetry.
Throughout *Last Poems* Yeats faces head-on the
gradual weakening of his own body—and that
of civilization. In "The Swans at Coole" he finds
that after 19 autumns of counting and being
cheered by the swans in a nearby woods, now
his fading heart is "sore"; the seemingly
undying, youthful birds have awakened in him
the terrible realization of how much his life has
changed. Still, for the most part, Yeats managed
to find abundant cause to rejoice in his poetic
pursuits and celebrate his continued love of the
arts, of nature, and of sensual pleasure.

The trees are in their autumn beauty,
The woodland paths are dry,
Under the October twilight the water
Mirrors a still sky;
Upon the brimming water among the stones
Are nine-and-fifty Swans.
The nineteenth autumn has come upon me
Since I first made my count;
I saw, before I had well finished,
All suddenly mount
And scatter wheeling in great broken rings
Upon their clamorous wings.
I have looked upon those brilliant creatures,
And now my heart is sore.
All's changed since I, hearing at twilight,
The first time on this shore,
The bell-beat of their wings above my head,
Trod with a lighter tread.
Unwearied still, lover by lover,

They paddle in the cold
Companionable streams or climb the air;
Their hearts have not grown old;
Passion or conquest, wander where they will,
Attend upon them still.
But now they drift on the still water,
Mysterious, beautiful;
Among what rushes will they build,
By what lake's edge or pool
Delight men's eyes when I awake some day
To find they have flown away?

In "Sailing to Byzantium" the narrator
leaves the natural world to sail over the seas,
coming to rest at a far-off region of the mind.
As the mind's journey over territory and time
ends, the poet becomes a prophet, all-knowing,
all-wise, timeless—much in the same way Yeats
himself tried to span history with his literary
efforts.

SAILING TO BYZANTIUM
I
That is no country for old men. The young
In one another's arms, birds in the trees,
—Those dying generations—at their song,
The salmon-falls, the mackerel-crowded seas,
Fish, flesh, or fowl, commend all summer long
Whatever is begotten, born, and dies.
Caught in that sensual music all neglect
Monuments of unageing intellect.

II
An aged man is but a paltry thing,
A tattered coat upon a stick, unless
Soul clap its hands and sing, and louder sing
For every tatter in its mortal dress,
Nor is there singing school but studying
Monuments of its own magnificence;
And therefore I have sailed the seas and come
To the holy city of Byzantium.

III
O sages standing in God's holy fire
As in the gold mosaic of a wall,
Come from the holy fire, perne in a gyre,
And be the singing-masters of my soul.
Consume my heart away; sick with desire
And fastened to a dying animal
It knows not what it is; and gathers me
Into the artifice of eternity.

IV
Once out of nature I shall never take
My bodily form from any natural thing,
But such a form as Grecian goldsmiths make
Of hammered gold and gold enamelling
To keep a drowsy Emperor awake;
Or set upon a golden bough to sing
To lords and ladies of Byzantium
Of what is past, or passing, or to come.

ROBERT FROST
(1874–1963)

THE ROAD NOT TAKEN

Two roads diverged in a yellow wood,
And sorry I could not travel both
And be one traveler, long I stood
And looked down one as far as I could
To where it bent in the undergrowth;

Then took the other, as just as fair,
And having perhaps the better claim,
Because it was grassy and wanted wear;
Though as for that the passing there
Had worn them really about the same,

And both that morning equally lay
In leaves no step had trodden black.
Oh, I kept the first for another day!
Yet knowing how way leads on to way,
I doubted if I should ever come back.

I shall be telling this with a sigh
Somewhere ages and ages hence:
Two roads diverged in a wood , and I—
I took the one less traveled by,
And that has made all the difference.

Like his poem, Robert Lee Frost has made all the difference in American poetry. A four-time Pulitzer Prize winner, Frost's earliest poems are as splendidly composed as his later ones. Finding inspiration in the landscapes, folkways and simple speech mannerisms of New England, his works have been much lauded and loved for their incisive simplicity.

"The Road Not Taken" exemplifies Frost's straightforward style and depth. Though not always understood simply, his effects are dependent on a certain slyness for which the reader needs to be prepared. During a lecture, Frost explained that this poem was not meant to be an allegory or metaphor of some sort, but simply an account of a time he and a friend took a walk in the woods. Coming to a fork in the road, each decided to take a different route—and eventually they ended up in the same place. The difference between the roads was a matter of opinion, the poet pointed out, not a matter of greatness.

The work of Frost is direct and graceful; its language is unadorned. Of course—as is the case with most great poetry—a measure of ambiguity leaves room for interpretation. He employed traditional meters and rhyme schemes in his writing as well as a definite narrative which gave his verse subtly and power. One supposed the last line of "Stopping By Woods on a Snowy Evening" (" … miles to go before I sleep") was a rather overt reference to approaching death, or some sort of disguised death-wish. To these interpretations, Frost replied, "No, it means to get the hell out of there."

Frost's father passed away soon after Frost's birth in California, whereupon his mother moved the family to New England. There the would-be poet briefly attended Dartmouth College, worked on a country paper, and then turned to teaching school. He also studied at Harvard for two years, but concluded that formal study was not his style. While later in life he accepted invitations to lecture at several universities, he spent most of his time farming a few acres of ground in New England.

However, it was in England that Frost's brilliant career was truly born. His first two volumes of verse were published there and, after receiving critical acclaim, were also published in the United States.

While Frost often turned his attentions to serious themes and ideas, he did not hesitate to apply humor to the most horrible condition. In the following two works—both touching on the theme of the final apocalypse—his wit is readily apparent.

FIRE AND ICE

Some say the world will end in fire,
Some say in ice.
From what I've tasted of desire
I hold with those who favor fire.
But if it had to perish twice,
I think I know enough of hate
To say that for destruction ice
Is also great
And would suffice.

U.S. 1946 KING'S X

Having invented a new Holocaust,
And been the first with it to win a war,
How they make haste to cry with fingers crossed,
King's X—no fairs to use it any more!

In the "Mending Wall" Frost again turns to humor to undermine the solemn question of how it is that any of us can get along, save for the walls which keep us apart. In this verse, the narrator and his neighbor perform the simple chore of repairing a stone wall. The narrator cannot see the sense in it, but his neighbor is firm in his belief that "good fences make good neighbors."

THE MENDING WALL

Something there is that doesn't love a wall,
That sends the frozen-ground-swell under it,
And spills the upper boulders in the sun,
And makes gaps even two can pass abreast.
The work of hunters is another thing:
I have come after them and made repair

Where they have left not one stone on a stone,
But they would have the rabbit out of hiding,
To please the yelping dogs. The gaps I mean,
No one has seen them made or heard them made,
But at spring mending-time we find them there.
I let my neighbor know beyond the hill;
And on a day we meet to walk the line
And set the wall between us once again.
We keep the wall between us as we go.
To each the boulders that have fallen to each.
And some are loaves and some so nearly balls
We have to use a spell to make the balance:
'Stay where you are until our backs are turned!'
We wear our fingers rough with handling them.
Oh, just another kind of out-door game,
One on a side. It comes to little more:
There where it is we do not need the wall:
He is all pine and I am apple orchard.
My apple trees will never get across
And eat the cones under his pines, I tell him.
He only says, 'Good fences make good neighbors.'
Spring is the mischief in me, and I wonder
If I could put a notion in his head:
'Why do they make good neighbors? Isn't it
Where there are cows?
But here there are no cows.
Before I built a wall I'd ask to know
What I was walling in or walling out,
And to whom I was like to give offence.
Something there is that doesn't love a wall,
That wants it down.' I could say 'Elves' to him,
But it's not elves exactly, and I'd rather
He said it for himself. I see him there
Bringing a stone grasped firmly by the top
In each hand, like an old-stone savage armed.
He moves in darkness as it seems to me—
Not of woods only and the shade of trees.
He will not go behind his father's saying,
And he likes having thought of it so well
He says again, 'Good fences make good
    neighbors.'

Frost regarded neighbors—and the concept of neighborliness—with warmth and tenderness. In "A Time to Talk" he endorses taking time to nurture such kinship.

A TIME TO TALK

When a friend calls to me from the road
And slows his horse to a meaning walk,
I don't stand still and look around
On all the hills I haven't hoed,
And shout from where I am, What is it?
No, not as there is time to talk.
I thrust my hoe in the mellow ground,
Blade-end up and five feet tall,
And plod: I go up to the stone wall
For a friendly visit.

"Stopping by Woods on a Snowy Evening" is among Frost's most puzzling works. Though speculation abounds as to its interpretation, the author maintained a stubborn silence about the poem's possibilities.

STOPPING BY WOODS ON A SNOWY EVENING

Whose woods these are I think I know.
His house is in the village though;
He will not see me stopping here
To watch his woods fill up with snow.
My little horse must think it queer
To stop without a farmhouse near
Between the woods and frozen lake
The darkest evening of the year.
He gives his harness bells a shake
To ask if there is some mistake.
The only other sound's the sweep
Of easy wind and downy flake.
The woods are lovely, dark and deep,
But I have promises to keep,
And miles to go before I sleep,
And miles to go before I sleep.

Frost, especially at the height of his career, held public readings where his magnificent voice kept listeners spellbound. His oratory powers were showcased at John F. Kennedy's Inauguration, where the poet delivered the Inaugural Poem "The Gift Outright" to a nationwide audience. Here he speaks sensitively yet with perspective of an American historical dilemma.

THE GIFT OUTRIGHT

The land was ours before we were the land's.
She was our land more than a hundred years
Before we were her people. She was ours
In Massachusetts, in Virginia.
But we were England's, still colonials,
Possessing what we still were unpossessed by,
Possessed by what we now no more possessed.
Something we were withholding made us weak
Until we found out that it was ourselves
We were withholding from our land of living,
And forthwith found salvation in surrender.
Such as we were we gave ourselves outright
(The deed of gift was many deeds of war)
To the land vaguely realizing westward,
But still unstoried, artless, unenhanced,
Such as she was, such as she would become.

JAMES JOYCE
(1882–1941)

First and foremost known as a writer of prose (his fiction and short story collections are masterpieces), the poetry of James Joyce is no less skillfully executed. In fact, his poetic offerings best reveal the true identity of the writer. Simple and direct, the work mirrors the inner reflections of a genius.

James Joyce, born in Dublin, Ireland, was educated at Jesuit schools and earned a degree in modern languages at University College Dublin. His ambitions were to be a writer and to study medicine. He gave up the second dream to teach English in Yugoslavia, during which time he published his poems in a small volume titled *Chamber Music*. Joyce lived most of his married life in Paris, France and Zurich, Switzerland. Through the years, he published a number of prose works and another collection of verse called *Pomes Penyeach*.

The success of Joyce's poetry rests in its clear, "musical" language. Almost totally lacking in complexity, many critics have been led to regard them instead as lyrics. In part, they *are* lyrics. Joyce was an excellent singer and loved music, and his *Chamber Music* collection was regarded as, apart from poetry, a suite of songs arranged "approximately allegretto, andante, cantabile, mosso." Indeed, it was his hope that the poems would eventually be set to music, as suggested by the collected works' first poem.

I

Strings in the earth and air
  Make music sweet;
Strings by the river where
  The willows meet.

There's music along the river
  For Love wanders there,
Pale flowers on his mantle,
  Dark leaves on his hair.

All softly playing,
  With head to the music bent,
And fingers straying
  Upon an instrument.

Poem XII from *Chamber Music* was brought to life one night when a lady friend remarked that the moon "looked tearful." Joyce, never one to perpetuate a cliché, d.isagreed. To him the moon looked like "the chubby hooded face of some jolly fat [monk]."

XII

What counsel has the hooded moon
  Put in thy heart, my shyly sweet,
Of Love in ancient plenilune,

Glory and stars beneath his feet—
A sage that is but kith and kin
  With the comedian Capuchin?

Believe me rather that am wise
  In disregard of the divine,
A glory kindles in those eyes,
  Trembles to starlight. Mine, O Mine!
No more be tears in moon or mist
  For thee, sweet sentimentalist.

Though his poems were simple and direct, Joyce wielded a varied form, capable of exploring the entire spectrum of human events, from love to war.

XXII

Of that so sweet imprisonment
  My soul, dearest, is fain—
Soft arms that woo me to relent
  And woo me to detain.
Ah, could they ever hold me there

Gladly were I a prisoner!

Dearest, through interwoven arms
  By love made tremulous,
That night allures me where alarms
  Nowise may trouble us;
But sleep to dreamier sleep be wed
Where soul with soul lies prisoned

XXXII

Rain has fallen all the day.
  O come among the laden trees:
The leaves lie thick upon the way
  Of memories.
Staying a little by the way
  Of memories shall we depart.
Come, my beloved, where I may
  Speak to your heart.

XXXVI

I hear an army charging upon the land,
And the thunder of horses plunging, foam about
  their knees:
Arrogant, in black armour, behind them stand,
Disdaining the reins, with fluttering whips, the
  charioteers.
They cry unto the night their battle-name:
I moan in sleep when I fear their whirling
  laughter.
They cleave the gloom of dreams, a blinding flame,
Clanging, clanging upon the heart as upon an
  anvil.
They come shaking in triumph their long,
  green hair:
They come out of the sea and run shouting by
  the shore.
My heart, have you no wisdom thus to despair?
My love, my love, my love, why have you left
  me alone?

In order to perfect his writing skills, Joyce took to using devices such as abstraction and imagery to develop new themes. One outstanding thematic poem is "Ecce Puer," written as a dual piece, both to commemorate the near-concurrent saddening death of the poet's father and joyous birth of his grandson.

ECCE PUER

Of the dark past
A child is born
With joy and grief
My heart is torn.

Calm in his cradle
The living lies.
May love and mercy
Unclose his eyes!

Young life is breathed
On the glass;
The world that was not
Comes to pass.

A child is sleeping:
An old man gone.
O, father forsaken,
Forgive your son!

Poems from *Chamber Music* clearly demonstrate Joyce's haunting love affair with romantic imagery and simple emotion.

XIV

My dove, my beautiful one,
   Arise, arise!
   The night-dew lies
Upon my lips and eyes.

The odorous winds are weaving
   A music of sighs:
   Arise, arise,
My dove, my beautiful one!

I wait by the cedar tree,
   My sister, my love,
   White breast of the dove,
My breast shall be your bed.

The pale dew lies
   Like a veil on my head.
   My fair one, my fair dove,
Arise, arise!

As if not content to allow the thought to finish, he picks up where he left off in the very next stanzas.

XV

From dewy dreams, my soul, arise,
   From love's deep slumber and from death,
   For lo! the trees are full of sighs
      Whose leaves the morn admonisheth,

Eastward the gradual dawn prevails
   Where softly-burning fires appear,
Making to tremble all those veils
   Of grey and golden gossamer.

While sweetly, gently, secretly,
   The flowery bells of morn are stirred
And the wide choirs of faery
   Begin (innumerous!) to be heard.

Perhaps Joyce's most lyrical—and romantic—sense is illustrated best in the following.

XVI

O cool is the valley now,
   And there, love, will we go
For many a choir is singing now
   Where Love did sometime go.
And hear you not the thrushes calling,
   Calling us away?
O cool and pleasant is the valley
   And there, love, will we stay.

WILLIAM CARLOS WILLIAMS
(1883–1963)

THIS IS JUST TO SAY

I have eaten
the plums
that were in
the icebox

and which
you were probably
saving
for breakfast

Forgive me
they were delicious
so sweet
and so cold

In his poetry, William Carlos Williams created an American voice. Rather than staying within the formal conventions of most previous traditions, he chose to express American English in the rhythm of American speech, on "a measure of the ear." His style was new—and, at times, was criticized as insubstantial.

On one occasion, during a television interview with Williams, it was pointed out that one of his poems, containing lines such as "2 partridges/2 mallard ducks/a Dungeness crab" was nothing more than "a fashionable grocery list." Williams readily admitted that it was in fact a grocery list. "But is it poetry?" he was then asked. Williams' response was classic—and classically stated his overall philosophy toward writing. Said he: " … In prose, an English word means what it says. In poetry, you're listening to two things … you're listening to the sense, the common sense of what it says. But it says more. That is the difficulty." The lines of his verse, he went on to explain, when studied for their rhythmic qualities, form a "jagged pattern." He considered this pattern as the soul of his poetry; the words and the meaning—if there was one—was secondary.

Williams was born to immigrant parents in Rutherford, New Jersey, where he remained virtually the entire 80 years of his life. Unlike many writers of his day who traveled to Europe, he chose to live in American society and focus upon American themes. Known widely in his time as the "doctor-poet," as a practicing medical doctor he produced the bulk of his work at the busy height of his career.

A clear example of his approach to poetry is "Le Medecin Malgre Lui," published in 1915, in which, through self-examination, Williams mocked those physicians who were more style than substance. He saw hypocrisy in many doctors whose offices were meticulously and glamorously outfitted, yet gave substandard—or worse—medical care.

Oh I suppose
I should wash
the walls of my office
polish the rust
from my instruments and keep them
definitely in order
build shelves in the laboratory
empty out the old stains
clean the bottles
and refill them,
buy another lens,
put my journals on edge instead of
 letting them lie flat
in heaps—then begin
ten years back and
gradually
read them to date
cataloguing important
articles for ready reference.
I suppose I should
read the new books.
If to this I added
a bill at the tailor's
and at the cleaner's
grew a decent beard
and cultivated a look
of importance—
Who can tell? I might be
a credit to my Lady of Happiness
and never think anything
but a white thought!

Williams advocated using speech unencumbered by special significance or meaning. A man "makes a poem," he once said, and the reader should be able to read it. He felt that a poet's first duty was "to lift by use of his imagination and the language he hears, the material conditions and appearances of his environment to the sphere of the intelligence where they will have new currency …"

Experimenting with natural speech, Williams adapted his work to a variety of speakers whose voices reflected different emotions. "The Widow's Lament in Springtime" takes this route.

Sorrow is my own yard where the new grass
 flames as it has flamed often before but not
 with the cold fire that closes round me this year.
Thirty-five years I lived with my husband.
The plumtree is white today with masses of flowers.
Masses of flowers load the cherry branches
 and color some bushes yellow and some red
 but the grief in my heart is stronger than they
for though they were my joy formerly, today I
 notice them
 and turned away forgetting.
Today my son told me that in the meadows,
at the edge of the heavy woods in the distance,
 he saw
 trees of white flowers.

I feel that I would like to go there
  and fall into those flowers
  and sink into the marsh near them.

New directions in poetry were opened through Williams' use of unadorned images. "The Red Wheelbarrow" uses very simple language to portray its message.

THE RED WHEELBARROW

so much depends
upon

a red wheel
barrow

glazed with rain
water

beside the white
chickens.

In this poem, the wheelbarrow, the rain and the chickens are not presented as symbols representing larger ideas. They are, according to Williams, intended to express their own importance within the context of the poem—"no ideas but in things."

This simple use of "things" also appears in "Poem (As the Cat)."

As the cat
climbed over
the top of

the jamcloset
first the right forefoot

carefully
then the hind
stepped down
into the pit of
the empty
flowerpot

Symbolism, however, did become a part of Williams' later works. In his lengthy epic poem "Paterson," he relies on abstraction as well as concrete images to support his notions.

… a bud forever green,
tight-curled upon the pavement, perfect
in juice and substance but divorced, divorced
from its fellow, fallen low—

Divorce is
the sign of knowledge in our time,
divorce! divorce! …

In "Asphodel, That Greeny Flower," the concept of image is put in perspective.

Are facts not flowers
and flowers facts

or poems flowers
or all words of the imagination
interchangeable?

To Williams, everything can be conceived in the imagination; thus, objects, ideas, facts, images, etc. are all interchangeable.

As a physician, Williams maintained a close and continuous contact with humanity. He saw patients daily, a practice which found voice in his poetry.

A COLD FRONT

This woman with a dead face
has seven foster children
and a new baby of her own in
spite of that. She wants pills

for an abortion and says
um hum, in reply to me …

… She looks at me with her mouth
open and blinks her expressionless
carved eyes, like a cat
on a limb too tired to go higher

from its tormentors …

"The Old Men" is another piece which reflects doctor-poet's acute, clinical ability to observe.

Old men who have studied
every leg show
in the city …

Old men cut from touch
by the perfumed music—
polished or fleeced skulls
that stand before
the whole theater

in silent attitudes
of attention—

… Solitary old men for whom
we find no excuses—
I bow my head in shame
for those who malign you.

Old men
the peaceful beer of impotence
be yours!

In "The Poor," the idea of scrutinizing people themselves is combined with detailed descriptions of their surroundings.

It's the anarchy of poverty
delights me, the old
yellow wooden house indented
among the new brick tenements

Of a cast iron balcony
with panels showing oak branches
in full leaf. It fits
the dress of the children

reflecting every stage and
custom of necessity—
Chimneys, roofs, fences of
wood and metal in an unfenced

age and enclosing next to
nothing at all: the old man
in a sweater and soft black
hat who sweeps the sidewalk—

his own ten feet of it
in a wind that fitfully
turning his corner has
overwhelmed the entire city

For Williams, the theory of a poem did not spring from the ethereal, abstract heights, but from the factual, down-to-earth depths. "To a Dog Injured in the Street" demonstrates Williams's ability to develop generalizations from isolated events.

It is myself
not the poor beast lying there
yelping with pain
that brings me to myself with a start—
as at the explosion
of a bomb, a bomb that has laid
all the world to waste.
I can do nothing
but sing about it …
I remember Norma
our English setter of my childhood
her silky ears and expressive eyes …
The cries of a dying dog
are to be blotted out
as best I can …

William Carlos Williams was known as a "poet's poet" for much of his career; he was hardly recognized outside of literary circles. In 1946, after publishing well over a dozen books of poetry, the American public could no longer ignore him. Williams enjoyed increasing respect from then until his death in 1963, when, posthumously, he was awarded the Pulitzer Prize and the Gold Medal for Poetry.

SALUTATION

O generation of the thoroughly smug
    and thoroughly uncomfortable,
I have seen fishermen picnicking in the sun,
I have seen them with untidy families,
I have seen their smiles full of teeth
    and heard ungainly laughter.
And I am happier than you are,
And they were happier than I am;
And the fish swim in the lake
    and do not even own clothing.

For Ezra Pound, happiness could be found in the simple life a fisherman, not among the "exquisite and excessive" people who stroll through their lives afraid to be spoken to, yet wanting to speak. He held a vigorous affinity for the working class—and an equally vigorous distrust of the middle and upper classes.

Leaving his home town of Haley, Idaho, Pound attended Hamilton College and the University of Pennsylvania, where, in 1906, he received his M.A. in romance languages. Traveling to Europe, he became a willing and restless American expatriate living in London, Paris and Rome. A member of the Lost Generation, a group of American writers living abroad that also included Gertrude Stein and Ernest Hemingway, Pound exerted a strong influence over modern literature through his associations with other great writers.

After a time, Pound, fully enamored with the Fascist politics of Mussolini, finally settled in Rapallo, Italy, doing radio broadcasts from the 1930s through the Second World War. After the Allied forces captured Italy, Pound was imprisoned and tried for treason. Eventually he was found insane and locked up for 13 years in St. Elizabeth's Hospital. It was only through the tireless efforts of such friends as T.S. Eliot and Archibald MacLeish that Pound gained release from the asylum and permitted to return to Italy.

As a poet, Pound often employed what he called "masks" in his work, even titling one of his collections *Personae*, a reference to his technique of assuming a personality that was not his own. Likewise, in the *Odyssey* Pound assumes the voice of an ancient Greek to hide the source of his political denunciations.

In *Hugh Selwyn Mauberley*, the poet reveals via the life of the title character a living symbol of his age. Pound's own frustration with society was evident. He repeatedly denounces war and poverty. What's more, he denounces modern society's lack of appreciation for artistic merit, specifically lamenting his own, futile attempt to "resuscitate the dead art of poetry." His jour-

nalist, near-autobiographic voice tends to weave a realistic fabric of the world during the 20th Century's early decades.

HUGH SELWYN MAUBERLEY

I

For three years, out of key with his time,
He strove to resuscitate the dead art
Of poetry; to maintain "the sublime"
In the old sense. Wrong from the start—

No, hardly, but, seeing he had been born
In a half-savage country, out of date;
Bent resolutely on wringing lilies from the acorn
...

His true Penelope was Flaubert,
He fished by obstinate isles;
Observed the elegance of Circe's hair
Rather than mottoes on sun-dials.

Unaffected by "the march of events,"
He passed from men's memory in l'an trentiesme
De son eage; the case presents
No adjunct to the Muse's diadem.

II

The age demanded an image
Of its accelerated grimace,
Something for the modern stage,
Not, at any rate, an Attic grace;

Not, not certainly, the obscure reveries
Of the inward gaze;
Better mendacities
Than the classics in paraphrase!

The "age demanded" chiefly a mould in plaster,
Made with no loss of time,
A prose kinema, not, assuredly, alabaster
Or the "sculpture " of rhyme ...

V

There died a myriad,
And of the best, among them,
For an old bitch gone in the teeth,
For a botched civilization,

Charm, smiling at the good mouth,
Quick eyes gone under earth's lid,
For two gross of broken statues,
For a few thousand battered books.

As observed, Pound frequently wrestles with forces and attitudes antithetical to art and the artist. Phrases such as "I never mentioned a man but with the view / Of selling my own works," and "Don't kick against the pricks, / Accept opinion" can be found in his poetry, satirical attacks against those who write for money rather than love.

In the following work he speaks as a young Chinese woman, many miles distant and many years away.

THE RIVER-MERCHANT'S WIFE: A LETTER

While my hair was still cut straight across
my forehead
I played about the front gate, pulling flowers.
You came by on bamboo stilts, playing horse,
You walked about my seat, playing with blue
plums.
And we went on living in the village of Chokan:
Two small people, without dislike or suspicion.

At fourteen I married My Lord you.
I never laughed, being bashful.
Lowering my head, I looked at the wall.
Called to, a thousand times, I never looked back.

At fifteen I stopped scowling,
I desired my dust to be mingled with yours
Forever and forever and forever.
Why should I climb the look out?

At sixteen you departed,
You went into far Ku-to-yen,
by the river of swirling eddies,
And you have been gone five months.
The monkeys make sorrowful noise overhead.

You dragged your feet when you went out.
By the gate now, the moss is grown, the different
mosses,
Too deep to clear them away!
The leaves fall early this autumn, in wind.
The paired butterflies are already yellow with
August
Over the grass in the West garden;
They hurt me. I grow older.
If you are coming down through the
narrows of the river Kiang,
Please let me know beforehand,
And I will come out to meet you
As far as Cho-fu-Sa.

Borrowing and translating from literature, Pound never hesitated to use a line from another piece of writing or mix an allusion with another one to create a new idea or image. He was well versed in diverse poetic styles and genres, from ancient Chinese poetry to the medieval French.

Pound simplified his work with haiku-like brevity. The first draft of "In a Station of the Metro," for instance, was almost 30 lines long. Paring it down until he reached the perfect metaphor, the perfect feeling, Pound creates juxtaposition of emotion to image.

IN A STATION OF THE METRO

The apparition
Of these faces in the crowd;
Petals on a wet, black bough.

So read many of his stylized pieces.

ALBA

As cool as the pale wet leaves
of lily-of-the-valley
She lay beside me in the dawn.

This final sonnet was one of Pound's earlier works, reflecting a strict adherence to rhyme and meter. Pound later forsook this style as his confidence in his own abilities and his lust for experimentation grew. Still, the marvelous and vibrant imagery and word-choice so evident in this piece leave no doubt as to how far he would go with his poetry.

In "A Virginal" (the name taken from a small keyboard instrument popular among ladies of the Renaissance period) the poet speaks in the guise of a lover rejecting a lady, thus shrouding in imagery his bitter commentary on classical poetry. The arms that "have bound me straitly" likely constitute a pun suggesting a straightjacket. Twice Pound cries, "No, no," a clear rebuff of his castoff love, then gives the reasons behind his denunciation of the allure of traditional verse. Captivated by a freer verse, he favors the green, pure shoots of Spring.

A VIRGINAL

No, no! Go from me. I have left her lately.
I will not spoil my sheath with lesser brightness,
For my surrounding air has a new lightness;
Slight are her arms, yet they have bound me
straitly
And left me cloaked as with a gauze of ether;
As with sweet leaves; as with a subtle clearness.
Oh, I have picked up magic in her nearness
To sheathe me half in half the things that
sheathe her.
No, no! Go from me. I have still the flavor,
Soft as spring wind that's come with birchen
bowers.
Green come the shoots, aye April in the branches,
As winter's wound with her sleight hand she
staunches,
Hath of the trees a likeness of the savor:
As white their bark, so white this lady's hours.

MARIANNE MOORE
(1887–1972)

"Observer" is an appropriate title for a book of Marianne Moore's poetry. She wrote about plants, animals, birds and nature, as well as human nature—verbally freezing them for the reader to study, then finishing up near the end of a "typical" work with a moral.

Moore was born in Kirkwood, Missouri, and educated in the Metzger schools, where she studied art and drawing. She maintained an interest in art throughout her life. It was during her academic training that Moore began writing poetry. Her first works were printed in the Bryn Mawr literary and alumni magazines.

After graduation, Moore taught at the U.S. Industrial Indian School in Carlisle, Pennsylvania, where one of her students was Jim Thorpe, the Olympic gold medalist. Continuing to write poetry, she remained unrecognized until, during a stint in England, her first book, *Poems*, was published. *Observations* was published in America three years later, receiving the Dial Award.

Her poems struggled to "find" themselves, as she herself was known to revise and re-revise them meticulously—some would say compulsively. By 1935, *Selected Poems* brought Moore a wider audience range, and her later *Collected Poems* won the Bollingen Prize. For her work she received the National Book Award and the Pulitzer Prize. Other achievements included the National Institute of Arts and Letters Gold Medal for Poetry, the Poetry Society of America's Gold Medal for Distinguished Achievement, and the National Medal for Literature.

Despite her poetic prowess, her works are often difficult to identify with. In a letter to a friend, she once stated that she would not publish a book until she had penned some poems "that are easy to understand and that are beyond doubt, alluring." Yet perhaps such so-called "alluring" verse would have caused her to sacrifice her inherent rhythmic, image-producing strengths.

WHAT ARE YEARS?

What is our innocence,
what is our guilt? All are
naked, none is safe. And whence
is courage: the unanswered question,
the resolute doubt,—
dumbly calling, deafly listening—that
in misfortune, even death,
   encourages other
   and in its defeat, stirs

the soul to be strong? He
sees deep and is glad, who
accedes to mortality
and in his imprisonment rises
upon himself as
the sea in a chasm, struggling to be
free and unable to be,
   in its surrendering
   finds its continuing.

So he who strongly feels,
behaves. The very bird,
grown taller as he sings, steels
his form straight up. Though he is captive,
his mighty singing
says, satisfaction is a lowly
thing, how pure a thing is joy.
   This is mortality,
   this is eternity.

From the music of Brahms to the music of birds, Moore's language carries a musical sense. She had a knack for putting down onto paper the things that she saw.

PROPRIETY

in some such word
 as the chord
   Brahms had heard
   from a bird,
sung down near the root of the throat;
 it's the little downy woodpecker
   spiraling a tree—
   up up up like mercury;

 a not long
 sparrow-song
 of hayseed
 magnitude—
a tuned reticence with rigor
from strength at the source. Propriety is
   Bach's Solfegietto—
   harmonica and basso.

 The fish-spine
 on firs, on
 somber trees
 by the sea's
walls of wave-worn rock—have it; and
a moonbow and Bach's cheerful firmness

in a minor key.
It's an owl-and-a-pussy-

both-content
agreement.
            Come, come. It's
            mixed with wits'
it's not a graceful sadness. It's
resistance with bent head, like foxtail
            millet's. Brahms and Bach,
            no; Bach and Brahms. To thank Bach

for his
first, is wrong.
            Pardon me;
            both are the
unintentional pansy-face
uncursed by self-inspection; blackened
            because born that way.

As previously expressed, Moore's works impart not so much direct description as the pleasure of reflection, poems that make more sense the more you read them. So it is with the beginnings of "Radical," which is left for the reader to decipher its exact meaning—if, indeed, there is one. (Presumably, it's about a carrot and a left-wing movement.)

RADICAL

Tapering
to a point, conserving everything,
this carrot is predestined to be thick.
The world is
but a circumstance,
a miserable corn patch for its feet.
With ambition, imagination, outgrowth,
nutriment,
with everything crammed belligerently
inside itself, its fibres breed monopoly—
a tail-like, wedge-shaped engine with the
secret of expansion, fused with intensive heat to
the color of the set-
ting sun and
stiff ...

NEVERTHELESS

you've seen a strawberry
    that's had a struggle; yet
    was, where the fragments met,

a hedgehog or a star-
    fish for the multitude
    of seeds. What better food

than apple-seeds—the fruit
    within the fruit—locked in
    like counter-curved twin

hazel-nuts? Frost that kills
    the little rubber-plant-
    leaves of kok-saghyz-stalks, can't

harm the roots; they still grow
    in frozen ground. Once where
    there was a prickly-pear-

leaf clinging to barbed wire,
    a root shot down to grow
    in earth two feet below;

as carrots form mandrakes
    or a ram's-horn root some-
    times. Victory won't come

to me unless I go
    to it; a grape-tendril
    ties a knot in knots till

knotted thirty times,—so
    the bound twig that's under-
    gone and over-gone, can't stir.

The weak overcomes its
    menace, the strong over-
    comes itself. What is there

like fortitude! What sap
    went through that little thread
    to make the cherry red!

The process of creative expression—in particular, that of master musicians, artists and, of course, writers—intrigued the poet.

THE PAPER NAUTILUS

For authorities whose hopes
are shaped by mercenaries?
    Writers entrapped by
    teatime fame and by
commuters' comforts? Not for these
    the paper nautilus
    constructs her thin glass shell.

Giving her perishable
souvenir of hope, a dull
    white outside and smooth-
    edged inner surface
glossy as the sea, the watchful
    maker of it guards it
    day and night; she scarcely

eats until the eggs are hatched.
Buried eight-fold in her eight
    arms, for she is in
    a sense a devil-
fish, her glass ram's-horn-cradled freight
    is hid but is not crushed;
    as Hercules, bitten

by a crab loyal to the hydra,
was hindered to succeed,
    the intensively
    watched eggs coming from
the shell free it when they are freed,—
    leaving its wasp-nest flaws
    of white on white, and close-

laid Ionic chiton-folds
like the lines in the mane of
    a Parthenon horse,
    round which the arms had
wound themselves as if they knew love
    is the only fortress
    strong enough to trust to.

Moore attempted to give permanence to temporal things, using language and a sharp eye to capture a "verbal photograph" for the reader to contemplate.

SILENCE

My father used to say,
"Superior people never make long visits,
have to be shown Longfellow's grave
or the glass flower at Harvard.
Self-reliant like the cat—
that takes its prey to privacy,
the mouse's limp tail hanging
    like a shoelace from its mouth—
they sometimes enjoy solitude,
and can be robbed of speech
by speech which has delighted them.
The deepest feeling always shows itself in silence;
not in silence, but restraint."
Nor was he insincere in saying,
    "Make my house your inn."
Inns are not residences.

T.S. ELIOT
(1888–1965)

BURNT NORTON

Time present and time past
Are both perhaps present in time future,
And time future contained in time past.
If all time is eternally present
All time is unredeemable.
What might have been is an abstraction
Remaining a perpetual possibility
Only in a world of speculation.
What might have been and what has been
Point to one end, which is always present.
Footfalls echo in the memory
Down the passage which we did not take
Towards the door we never opened ...

Though Thomas Stearns Eliot published only a few of his poems, his influence on 20th-century verse is vast and profound. He struggled against the artistic temperament of Victorian England in an effort to find a new way of illustrating the world. Most of his work is a curious mix of opposites: dark and light, hope and despair, hate and love.

Eliot was the grandson of a Unitarian minister. In St. Louis, Missouri, Eliot studied in private schools, then left for Harvard where he received his M.A. degree. Traveling to Europe, England became his adopted homeland, where he converted to the Anglican Church. He found work with Faber and Faber Publishing, eventually becoming its director.

That poetry required "hard labour" for both writer and reader was Eliot's thinking, and poetry should not be limited to common language—like an advertising jingle. On occasion, he would speak with a different voice, simply for effect, as in the following poem, where the speaker addresses the listener like a Biblical prophet, evoking a near-Isaiah voice.

GERONTION

Thou hast nor youth nor age
But as it were an after dinner sleep
Dreaming of both.

Here I am, an old man in a dry month,
Being read to by a boy, waiting for rain.
I was neither at the hot gates
Nor fought in the warm rain
Nor knee-deep in the salt marsh, heaving a
cutlass,
Bitten by flies, fought.
My house is a decayed house ...

Signs are taken for wonders. "We would see a
sign!"
The word within a word, unable to speak a word,

Swaddled with darkness. In the juvescence of the
year
Came Christ the tiger

In depraved May, dogwood and chestnut,
flowering Judas,
To be eaten, to be divided, to be drunk
Among whispers ...

After such knowledge, what forgiveness?
Think now
History has much cunning passages, contrived
corridors
And issues, deceives with whispering ambitions,
Guides us by vanities. Think now
She gives when our attention is distracted
And what she gives, gives with such supple
confusions
That the giving famishes the craving. Gives
too late
What's not believed in, or if still believed,
In memory only, reconsidered passion ...

Unnatural vices
Are fathered by our heroism. Virtues
Are forced upon us by our impudent crimes ...

And an old man driven by the Trades
To a sleepy corner.

Tenants of the house,
Thoughts of a dry brain in a dry season.

In "The Love Song of J. Alfred Prufrock," Eliot assumes the utterances of an old man. The narrator, however, is actually a young man imagining himself in old age, lamenting a past lived without risk or passion. After inviting the reader through "certain half-deserted streets, / The muttering retreats / Of restless nights in one-night cheap hotels, " the poem turns to a central concern:

... And indeed there will be time
For the yellow smoke that slides along the street,
Rubbing its back upon the window-panes;
There will be time, there will be time
To prepare a face to meet the faces that you meet;
There will be time to murder and create,
And time for all the works and days of hands
That lift and drop a question on your plate;
Time for you and time for me,
And time for a hundred indecisions,
And for a hundred visions and revisions,
Before the taking of a toast and tea.

In the room the women come and go
Talking of Michelangelo.

And indeed there will be time
To wonder, "Do I dare?" and, "Do I dare?"

Time to turn back and descend the stair,
With a bald spot in the middle of my hair—
[They will say: "How his hair is growing thin!"]
My morning coat, my collar mounting firmly to
the chin,
My necktie rich and modest, but asserted by a
simple pin—
[They will say: "But how his arms and legs are
thin!"]
Do I dare
Disturb the universe?
In a minute there is time
For decisions and revisions which a minute will
reverse.

The narrator continues, sorrowing, "I have measured out my life with coffee spoons," and "No! I am not Prince Hamlet, nor was meant to be."

I grow old … I grow old …
I shall wear the bottoms of my trousers rolled.

Shall I part my hair behind? Do I dare to eat
a peach?
I shall white flannel trousers and walk upon
the beach.
I have heard the mermaids singing, each to each.

I do not think that they will sing to me.

I have seen them riding seaward on the waves
Combing the white hair of the waves blown back
When the wind blows the water white and black.

We have lingered in the chambers of the sea
By sea-girls wreathed with seaweed red and
brown
Til human voices wake us, and we drown.

Distressed by the apparent shallowness of life and the lack of God and meaning in modern times, the poet turned his pen to this disheartening theme again and again. In "The Waste Land" Eliot focused his poetic powers, enormous knowledge and great imagination to create what some consider his supreme work.

THE WASTE LAND
I. The Burial of the Dead

April is the cruellest month, breeding
Lilacs out of the dead land, mixing
Memory and desire, stirring
Dull roots with spring rain.
Winter kept us warm, covering
Earth in forgetful snow, feeding
A little life with dried tubers …

What are the roots that clutch, what branches
grow

Out of this stony rubbish? Son of man,
You cannot say, or guess, for you know only
A heap of broken images, where the sun beats,
And the dead tree gives no shelter, the cricket no
relief,
And the dry stone no sound of water. Only
There is shadow under this red rock,
(Come in under the shadow of this red rock),
And I will show you something different from
either
Your shadow at morning striding behind you
Or your shadow at evening rising to meet you;
I will show you fear in a handful of dust …

Further into the poem, Eliot's thoughts turn to the "unreal city," the bleak streets of London and his mixture of fleeting memories.

… Unreal City,
Under the brown fog of a winter dawn,
A crowd flowed over London Bridge, so many,
I had not thought death had undone so many.
Sighs, short and infrequent, were exhaled,
And each man fixed his eyes before his feet …

There in the crowded byways, overheard conversations show sordidness, sadness, loss of communication; families and friends elicit a sense of isolated separateness; humanity is wrenched apart, to exist in wretched, lonely hovels. Rats dot the landscape.

Then enters Tiresias—a seer who is both male and female—who proceeds to foretell the future stark lives of Londoners, destined to naught amid "oil and tar" riding the surface of a river's water and the merchandising of everything and everyone.

… After the torchlight red on sweaty faces
After the frosty silence in the gardens
After the agony in stony places
The shouting and the crying
Prison and place and reverberation
Of thunder of spring over distant mountains
He who was living is now dead
We who were living are now dying
With a little patience …

My friend, blood shaking my heart
The awful daring of a moment's surrender
Which an age of prudence can never retract
By this, and this only, we have existed
Which is not to be found in our obituaries
Or in memories draped by the beneficent spider
Or under seals broken by the lean solicitor
In our empty rooms …

I have heard the key
Turn in the door once and turn once only
We think of the key, each in his prison
Thinking of the key, each confirms a prison … ●

POPULAR POETRY TODAY

IV

DOROTHY PARKER
(1893–1967)

"It was quite a childhood: a terrifying father hammering her wrists; a rather lunatic stepmother hammering at her mind; a sister and a brother too remote in age for any communion…. The servants put out of reach by social convention…. She hated being a Jew and began to think that her mother had deserted her by dying. She began to hate herself." So a childhood friend describes the adolescent life of Dorothy Parker. From the time she was born until the day she died, hers was an anguished and lonely existence.

Her mother, Eliza Marston Rothschild, died shortly after her daughter's birth. Subsequently, Dorothy was raised by her Jewish father, whom she feared, and her devoutly Catholic stepmother, whom she hated.

Complicated by the fact that she, a Jewish girl, was sent to the Catholic school at the Blessed Sacrament Convent, Dorothy was troubled and unable to assimilate. Eventually she was expelled for insisting that the Immaculate Conception was really spontaneous combustion. Sent to Miss Dana's private boarding school, the girl received an intensely traditional education. Though the social rules were excessively strict, the academic atmosphere was exceptionally fertile, and the poet within her began to unfold.

Following her graduation, Parker held a series of writing jobs for various magazines. While employed by *Vogue* and *Vanity Fair*, her caustic and impeccable wit became well-known, and eventually her literary trademark. Monthly morticians' journals were frequent sources of inspiration for the titles of her poems, stories and books.

Despite the severe bitterness that dominates her writing, there was a more caring side. Compassion found expression through social activism. Being no stranger to pain and suffering, Parker was quick to take up the causes of others. In 1927 she marched against the execution of Sacco and Vanzetti; later, she helped to found the Anti-Nazi League. During the McCarthy era, Parker was blacklisted by the California State Senate Committee on Un-American Activities because of her financial contributions to learning centers in communist countries. She appeared before the New York State joint legislative committee in 1955 and pled the Fifth Amendment.

When Parker died of a heart attack at age 73, she left the bulk of her estate to the Reverend Martin Luther King Jr. She had never met him, yet admired him greatly and wanted to aid his civil rights cause.

It is not surprising that Parker left her estate to a stranger rather than to a loved one; her personal life was turbulent and sad. Commenting on Parker's final years, one of her friends wrote: "Her captains and kings had long departed. I saw her … before she died … and she said, in effect, that all those she loved were dead, and that she, herself, had been dead for a long time." The combination of a painful life mixed with a droll, sardonic wit, resulted in a truly unique poetic voice.

Drawing on her own traumatic relationships with men, Parker's chosen poetic theme was often love—or rather, failed love.

UNFORTUNATE COINCIDENCE

By the time you swear you're his,
  Shivering and sighing,
And he vows his passion is
  Infinite, undying—
Lady, make a note of this:
  One of you is lying.

As in "Unfortunate Coincidence," Parker's poems tend to follow the conventional rules of rhyme and rhythm. The fact that she adheres to such conventional rules makes her piercing wit all the more effective. The musical quality of her language lulls the reader along, then strikes with startling speed, spewing a venomous barrage of sarcasm and cynicism.

INDIAN SUMMER

In youth, it was a way I had
To do my best to please,
And change, with every passing lad,
To suit his theories.

But now I know the things I know,
And do the things I do;
And if you do not like me so,
To hell, my love, with you!

NEWS ITEM

Men seldom make passes
At girls who wear glasses.

GODSPEED

Oh, seek, my love, your newer way;
I'll not be left in sorrow.
So long as I have yesterday,
Go take your damned tomorrow!

EXPERIENCE

Some men break your heart in two,
Some men fawn and flatter,
Some men never look at you;
And that cleans up the matter.

GENERAL REVIEW OF THE SEX SITUATION

Woman wants monogamy;
Man delights in novelty.
Love is woman's moon and sun;
Man has other forms of fun.
Woman lives but in her lord;
Count to ten, and man is bored.
With this the gist and sum of it,
What earthly good can come of it?

LOVE SONG

… My love runs by like a day in June,
And he makes no friends of sorrows.
He'll tread his galloping rigadoon
In the pathway of the morrows.
He'll live his days where the sunbeams start,
Nor could storm or wind uproot him.
My own dear love, he is all my heart—
And I wish somebody'd shoot him.

MEN

They hail you as their morning star
Because you are the way you are.
If you return the sentiment,
They'll try to make you different;
And once they have you, safe and sound,
They want to change you all around.
Your moods and ways they put a curse on;
They'd make of you another person.
They cannot let you go your gait;
They influence and educate.
They'd alter all that they admired.
They make me sick, they make me tired.

SYMPTOM RECITAL

I do not like my state of mind;
I'm bitter, querulous, unkind.
I hate my legs, I hate my hands,
I do not yearn for lovelier lands.
I dread the dawn's recurrent light;
I hate to go to bed at night.
I snoot at simple, earnest folk.
I cannot take the gentlest joke.
I find no peace in paint or type.
My world is but a lot of tripe.
I'm disillusioned, empty-breasted.
For what I think, I'd be arrested.
I am sick, I am not well.
My quondam dreams are shot to hell.
My soul is crushed, my spirit sore;
I do not like me any more.
I cavil, quarrel, grumble, grouse.
I ponder on the narrow house.
I shudder at the thought of men …
I'm due to fall in love again.

The topic of life itself is treated skeptically by Parker. Aside from failed love, the single most prominent theme in her poetry is death.

THE FLAW IN PAGANISM

Drink and dance and laugh and lie,
Love, the reeling midnight through,
For tomorrow we shall die!
(But, alas, we never do.)

CHERRY WHITE

I never see that prettiest thing—
A cherry bough gone white with Spring—
But what I think, "How gay 'twould be
To hang me from a flowering tree."

CODA

There's little in taking or giving,
There's little in water or wine;
This living, this living, this living
Was never a project of mine.
Oh, hard is the struggle, and sparse is
The gain of the one at the top,
For art is a form of catharsis,
And love is a permanent flop,
And work is the province of cattle,
And rest's for a clam in a shell,
So I'm thinking of throwing the battle—
Would you kindly direct me to hell?

THE SMALL HOURS

No more my little song comes back;
And now of nights I lay
My head on down, to watch the black
And wait the unfailing gray.

Oh, sad are winter nights, and slow;
And sad's a song that's dumb;
And sad it is to lie and know
Another dawn will come.

EPITAPH

The first time I died, I walked my ways;
I followed the file of limping days.

I held me tall, with my head flung up,
But dared not look on the new moon's cup

I dared not look on the sweet young rain,
And between my ribs was a gleaming pain.

The next time I died, they laid me deep.
They spoke worn words to hallow my sleep.

They tossed me petals, they wreathed me fern,
They weighted me down with a marble urn.

And I lie here warm, and I lie here dry,
And watch the worms slip by, slip by.

RÉSUMÉ

Razors pain you;
Rivers are damp;
Acids stain you;
And drugs cause cramp.
Guns aren't lawful;
Nooses give;
Gas smells awful;
You might as well live.

Using her wit as a defense against her stinging existence, Parker's naked honesty redefined poetic expression. It was life from a different angle, a contrary and bitter viewpoint. As she often said, in more than sarcastic tones: "You might as well live."

OGDEN NASH
(1902–1971)

ARTHUR

There was an old man from Calcutta,
Who coated his tonsils with butta,
    Thus converting his snore
    From a thunderous roar
To a soft, oleaginous mutta.

Widely known as a writer of light, humorous and satirical poetry, Ogden Nash was appreciated and imitated by both his peers and rivals. And even since his death, his reputation has continued to grow.

Nash is famous for combining wit and imagination with memorable rhyme. He began his career, however, writing serious verse—sonnets and other works relating to "beauty, truth, and pain." But this early phase did not last long. "I had better laugh at myself before anyone laughs at me," he once said. Not long after, he started writing his characteristic brand of poetry honing in on the minor idiocies of humanity.

After first publishing his poems in *The New Yorker* magazine, Nash's first book, *Hard Lines*, met with immediate success. It introduced a variety of themes that he would continue to explore. Other books followed: *Many Long Years Ago* (1945), *You Can't Get There From Here* (1957), *The Old Dog Barks Backwards* (published after his death, 1972), and *I Wouldn't Have Missed It* (1975).

Nash's biting commentaries on society marked the beginning of his satirical verse and announced his two major themes: the countless problems of the contemporary city and the futility of the human quest for meaning. In fact, though whimsical in nature, his poetry cuts to the heart of deep human issues; it ridicules what he considered foolish behavior—including his own.

The poem "More About People," for example, reflects on the inexplicable correlation between work and survival.

When people aren't asking questions
They're making suggestions
And when they're not doing one of those
They're either looking over your shoulder or stepping
    on your toes
And then as if that weren't enough to annoy you
They employ you.
Anybody at leisure
Incurs everybody's displeasure.
It seems to be very irking
To people at work to see other people not working,
So they tell you that work is wonderful medicine,
Just look at Firestone and Ford and Edison,
And they lecture you till they're out of breath or
    something
And then if you don't succumb they starve you to death
    or something.
All of which results in a nasty quirk:

That if you don't want to work you have to work
to earn enough money so that you won't have to
work.

Nash was unconcerned about meter in his poetry; nor did he worry that the lines of his poems were unequal in length. He often stretched sentences over several lines to produce eye-opening and comical rhymes, as can be seen in the beginnings of "The Terrible People."

People who have what they want are very
fond of telling people who haven't what
they want that they really don't want it,
And I wish I could afford to gather all
such people into a gloomy castle on
the Danube and hire half a dozen
capable Draculas to haunt it …

The complications of modern American life and the idiosyncrasies of city living were, to Nash, food for thought, as is evident in the poem, "I Will Arise and Go Now," written in 1949.

In far Tibet
There live a lama,
He got no poppa,
He got no momma …

He got no soap,
He got no opera,
He don't know Geritol

From copra …

He got no teeth,
He got no gums,
Don't eat no Spam,
Don't need no Tums.

He love to nick him
When he shave;
He also got
No hair to save …

He use no lotions
For allurance,
He got no car
And no insurance.

No Alsop warnings,
No Pearson rumor
For this self-centered
Nonconsumer.
Indeed, the
Ignorant Have-Not
Don't even know
What he don't got.

If you will mind
The box-tops, comma,

I think I'll go
And join that lama.

This same urban theme can also be seen in "City Greenery."

If you should happen after dark
To find yourself in Central Park,
Ignore the paths that beckon you
And hurry, hurry to the zoo,
And creep into the tiger's lair.
Frankly, you'll be safer there.

Nash drew much inspiration from the animal world. His writing often showed great esteem for these souls, God's creatures.

A BAS BEN ADHEM
My fellow man I do not care for.
I often ask me, What's he there for?
The only answer I can find
Is, Reproduction of his kind.

… The finest of the human race
Are bad in figure, worse in face.
Yet just because they have two legs
And come from storks instead of eggs …

He hails himself with drum and fife
And bullies lower forms of life.

Not that I think that much depends
On how we treat our feathered friends,
Or hold the wrinkled elephant
A nobler creature than my aunt.
It's simply that I'm sure I can
Get on without my fellow man.

THE TURTLE
The turtle lives 'twixt plated decks
Which practically conceal its sex.
I think it clever of the turtle
In such a fix to be so fertile.

THE MULES
In a world of mules
There are no rules.

The poet loved to play with language, pushing puns, often grouping combinations of strange words, cleverly comparing seemingly unrelated objects, inventing words, or misspelling real words to maintain his rhyme and create a carefully planned effect.

REFLECTION OF THE FALLIBILITY OF NEMESIS
He who is ridden by a conscience
Worries about a lot of nonscience;
He without benefit of scruples
His fun and income soon quadruples.

After the birth of his first child, Nash dealt in verse with the subject of parenthood.

DON'T CRY DARLING, IT'S BLOOD ALRIGHT
Whenever poets want to give you the idea
that something is particularly meek and mild,
They compare it to a child.
Thereby proving that though poets with poetry
*   may be rife*
They don't know the facts of life.
If of compassion you desire either a tittle or a jot,
Don't try to get it from a tot …

MY DADDY
I have a funny daddy
Who goes in and out with me,
And everything that baby does
My daddy's sure to see,
And everything that baby says,
My daddy's sure to tell
You must have read my daddy's verse.
I hope he fries in hell.

In the following pieces Nash focuses on age and death. Still, he manages to maintain a certain element of humor to prevent the works from crossing into the morbid.

THE MIDDLE
When I remember bygone days
I think how evening follows morn;
So many I loved were not yet dead,
So many I love were not yet born.

CROSSING THE BORDER
Senescence begins
And middle age ends
The day your descendants
Outnumber your friends.

OLD MEN
People expect old men to die,
They do not really mourn old men.
Old men are different. People look
At them with eyes that wonder when.
… People watch with unshocked eyes;
But the old men know when an old man dies.

Nash, the master humorist, in the poem "Pastoral" explores a rural scene, getting right to the heart of the situation.

Two cows
In a marsh
Mildly munching
Fodder harsh.
Cow's mother,
Cow's daughter
Mildly edging
Brackish water.

Mildly munching
While heron,
Brackish minded,
Waits like Charon.
Two cows,
Mildly mooing;
No bull;
Nothing doing.

Although he kept a very loose sense of rhythm and meter, Nash was extremely adept at limerick-style ditties.

SAMSON AGONISTES
I test my bath before I sit,
And I'm always moved to wonderment
That what chills the finger not a bit
Is so frigid upon the fundament.

THREE SAMPLE LIMERICKS ...
An elderly bride of Port Jervis
Was quite understandably nervis,
  Since her apple-cheeked groom,
  With three wives in the tomb,
Kept insuring her during the service.

There was a young belle of old Natchez
Whose garments were always in patchez.
  When comment arose
  On the state of her clothes,
She drawled, When Ah itchez, Ah scratchez!

There was a brave girl of Connecticut
Who flagged the express with her pecticut
  Which critics defined
  As presence of mind,
But deplorable absence of ecticut.

THE TERMITE
Some primal termite knocked on wood
And tasted it, and found it good,
And that is why your Cousin May
Fell through the parlor floor today.

THE PARSNIP
The parsnip, children, I repeat,
Is simply an anemic beet.
Some people call the parsnip edible;
Myself, I find this claim incredible.

THE OCTOPUS
Tell me, O Octopus, I begs,
Is those things arms, or is they legs?
I marvel at thee, Octopus;
If I were thou, I'd call me Us.

DYLAN THOMAS
(1914–1953)

... He's a stranger, outside the season's humours,
Moves, among men caught by the sun,
With heart unlocked upon the gigantic earth.
He alone is free, and, free, moans to the sky.
... Even among his own kind he is lost,
Is love a shadow on the wall,
Among all living men is a sad ghost.
He is not a man's or woman's man,
Leper among a clean people
Walks with the hills for company,
And has the mad trees' talk by heart ...

So begins a semi-biographical collection of poems by Dylan Thomas, *Poet: 1935*. Obscure, cryptic, difficult to follow, nevertheless the potency emanating from his works radiates with energy. Although his poetry was veiled in riddle, Thomas himself was open, easy going and well-liked.

Thomas was born in Wales, son of an English teacher who had poetic aspirations himself. Though the youth's academic career was unremarkable, he did excel in English. He began entering poetry contests—which he often won—in *The Sunday Referee*, a local newspaper. From 1934 to 1936, Thomas published two books: *Eighteen Poems* and *Twenty-Five Poems*.

A third book, *The Map of Love*, containing prose pieces as well as verse, was published in 1939. His last English volume of new verse was *Death and Entrances*, published in 1946, and yet another anthology, *Collected Poems 1934-1952*, was in print before his exhausting American tour, during which he became critically ill. On November 9, 1953, he succumbed to a high fever.

Thomas's death was greatly mourned; the critics felt he was just hitting his stride both as a poet and writer. Over the years hence, his work has traveled the spectrum between critical acclaim and derision. In recent years, his poetry has enjoyed renewed interest, with Thomas himself becoming a sort of university English department "icon."

Most of Thomas's poetry is traditional in nature, focusing on birth, death, love, sex, and religion. Intermingling of these disparate themes, however, is his true hallmark. "Written for a Personal Epitaph," published at age 16, shows the poet's intuitive skill in blending themes—as well as an early preoccupation with death.

Feeding the worm
Who do I blame
Because laid down
At last by time,

Here under the earth with girl and thief,
  Who do I blame?
  Mother I blame
  Whose loving crime
  Moulded my form
  Within her womb,
Who gave me life and then the grave,
  Mother I blame.
  Here is her labour's end,
  Dead limb and mind,
  All love and sweat
  Gone now to rot.
I am man's reply to every question,
His aim and destination.

Not easily deciphered by the casual reader, Thomas's works are often compared to "puzzles" and "forbidding cliffs." His images are vivid, but not always easy to categorize. "Epitaph" demonstrates this early tendency toward abstraction, but his work just a few years later had become more complex, more imaginative, as represented by the following piece. Apparently, Thomas considered both his own life and that of the world as linked in fate and controlled by the same forces.

THE FORCE THAT THROUGH THE GREEN FUSE DRIVES THE FLOWER

The force that through the green fuse drives
  the flower
Drives my green age; that blasts the roots of trees
Is my destroyer.
And I am dumb to tell the crooked rose
My youth is bent by the same wintry fever ...

By his early 20s, with the publication of *Twenty-Five Poems*, Thomas's verses had become extremely difficult to interpret. The density of his works was deliberate, as he compacted as many images as he could into a small space. Critic Edith Sitwell, trying to analyze his writing, claimed that his density was "largely the result of the intense concentration of each phrase, packed with meaning, of the fusion (not confusion) of two profound thoughts."

Typical of that fused density are the ten sonnets included in *Altarwise By Owl-light.*

VIII

This was the crucifixion on the mountain,
Time's nerve in vinegar, the gallow grave
As tarred with blood as the bright thorns I wept;
The world's my wound, God's Mary in her grief,
Bent like three trees and bird-papped through
  her shift,
With pins for teardrops is the long wound's
  woman.
This was the sky, Jack Christ, each minstrel angel
Drove in the heaven-driven of the nails

Till the three-colored rainbow from my nipples
From pole to pole leapt round the snail-waked
  world.
I by the tree of thieves, all glory's sawbones,
Unsex the skeleton this mountain minute,
And by this blowcock witness of the sun
Suffer the heaven's children through my
  heartbeat.

Some of this sonnet's symbology is clear (the mountain, vinegar, thorns, Mary...), while much is left to the reader's interpretation. For his part, Thomas never supplied interpretations, insisting that the images were the all-important element. His feelings about those who attempt to make sense of each and every reference are clear in these lines.

TO OTHERS THAN YOU
Friend by enemy I call you out.

You with a bad coin in your socket,
You my friend there with a winning air
Who palmed the lie on me when you looked
Brassily at my shyest secret ...

I never thought to utter or think
While you displaced a truth in the air,
That thought I love them for their faults
As much as for their good,
My friends were enemies on stilts
With their heads in a cunning cloud.

Twenty-Five Poems marked a transition in Thomas's style and subject matter. Rather than follow the literary trends of his day, he decided to return to more simplistic themes and language. This poem reflects his decision.

I HAVE LONGED TO MOVE AWAY
I have longed to move away
From the hissing of the spent lie
And the old terrors' continual cry
Growing more terrible as the day
Goes over the hill into the deep sea ...

I have longed to move away but am afraid;
Some life, yet unspent, might explode
Out of the old lie burning on the ground,
And, crackling into the air, leave me half-blind ...

"After the Funeral" is also less complex, typical of the new direction Thomas had taken.

AFTER THE FUNERAL
(In memory of Ann Jones)
... I know her scrubbed and humble sour hands
Lies with religion in their cramp, her threadbare
Whisper in a damp word, her wits drilled hollow,
Her fist of a face clenched on a round pain;
And sculptured Ann is seventy years of stone ...

In his best-known poem, written in homage to his dying father, Thomas disciplined himself in both form and word, demonstrating that, far from stemming from a lack of skill, his customary free-flowing style was deliberate.

DO NOT GO GENTLE INTO THAT GOOD NIGHT

Do not go gentle into that good night,
Old age should burn and rave at close of day;
Rage, rage against the dying of the light.

Though wise men at their end know dark is right,
Because their words had forked no lightning they
Do not go gentle into that good night.

Good men, the last wave by, crying how bright
Their frail deeds might have danced in a green
bay,
Rage, rage against the dying of the light.

Wild men who caught and sang the sun in flight,
And learn, too late, they grieved it on its way,
Do not go gentle into that good night.

Grave men, near death, who see with blinding
sight
Blind eyes could blaze like meteors and be gay,
Rage, rage against the dying of the light.

And you, my father, there on the sad height,
Curse, bless, me now with your fierce tears, I pray.
Do not go gentle into that good night.
Rage, rage against the dying of the light.

Finally, Thomas's talent is displayed in rare form in "The Conversation of Prayer." (Here the hidden rhymes have been highlighted to show that they indeed exist.) As the images— that of a boy going downstairs to pray and an old man going upstairs to comfort his dying wife—cross, so do the rhymes.

THE CONVERSATION OF PRAYER

*The conversation of **prayers** about to be **said***
*By the child going to **bed** and the man on the*
* **stairs***
*Who climbs to his dying **love** in her high **room**,*
*The one not caring to **whom** in his sleep he will*
* **move***
And the other full of tears that she will be dead …

*In the fire of his **care** his love in the high **room**.*
*And the child not caring to **whom** he climbs his*
* **prayer***
*Shall drown in a grief as **deep** as his true **grave**,*
*And mark the dark eyed **wave**, through the eyes*
* of **sleep**,*
Dragging him up the stairs to one who lies dead.

SYLVIA PLATH
(1932–1963)

POPPIES IN OCTOBER

Even the sun-clouds this morning cannot manage
* such skirts.*
Nor the woman in the ambulance
Whose red heart blooms through her coat so
* astoundingly—*

A gift, a love gift
Utterly unasked for
By a sky

Palely and flamily
Igniting its carbon monoxides, by eyes
Dulled to a halt under bowlers.

O my God, what am I
That these late mouths should cry open
In a forest of frost, in a dawn of cornflowers.

Sylvia Plath was born in Boston, Massachusetts. When she was eight, her English professor-father died—a loss from which she would never recover.

Just a few months after the death, Plath published her first poem in the *Boston Traveller*. She attended Smith College and Newnham College on scholarship, and entered several writing contests, all of which she won. While at Newnham, she met another poet named Ted Hughes, whom she married. After receiving her Masters degree, she returned to Smith, where she taught English until moving to England some years later.

Plath's first poems, it seemed, were churned out tediously, nursed by thesaurus and dictionary. She became known for her ruthless perceptions of her own work; if she didn't like a single word or a line in a poem, she scrapped the entire piece. She studied different styles in an effort to find one that would fully express the anguish she felt. In fact, critics say Plath didn't truly find her own voice until after her second child was born in 1962.

Some critics have suggested that Plath's creativity stemmed from her self-destructiveness. Even as an infant she possessed this tendency. On one occasion when the little one-year-old was sitting on the beach, she immediately crawled toward the ocean, unafraid, not stopping at the water's edge. Plath's mother had to rush into the crashing waves to drag her petulant child out of the water.

At 19, Plath attempted suicide. Not unexpectedly, her poetry in the preceding months had become rife with symbols of death. Her husband, writing later, confessed that by then Plath's "poetry and death became inseparable." Still, her suffering proved to be a powerful creative impetus.

Plath explored other voices in addition to poetry. She published a radio play, a children's book, a collection of short stories, and a novel titled *The Bell Jar*, written under the pseudonym Victoria Lucas. Soon after separating from her husband and giving birth to her second child, the breadth and depth of her poetry both accelerated and expanded; gone were the plodding forays into the word books.

The Bell Jar was finally published just one month before Plath's death. After its release, she turned to writing poetry even more frantically than before, sometimes drafting three or four complete works a day.

Sylvia Plath once claimed: "Dying is an art…. I do it exceptionally well." On February 11, 1963, she took her own life.

Ironically, Plath felt an almost pathological aversion to desecration of plants and animals, or to ruin of any type, for that matter. In particular, she considered the Holocaust one of humanity's greatest insults. Using the disturbing metaphors of a Nazi death camp, she lashed out in bitterness and anger at her father's death. "Daddy" is thought to be a thinly-veiled, allegoric look into Plath's own life and death (though, of course, many of the lines are figurative).

DADDY

You do not do, you do not do
Any more, black shoe
In which I have lived like a foot
For thirty years, poor and white,
Barely daring to breathe or Achoo.

Daddy, I have had to kill you.
You died before I had time—
Marble-heavy, a bag full of God,
Ghastly statue with one gray toe
Big as a Frisco seal

And a head in the freakish Atlantic
Where it pours bean green over blue
In the waters off beautiful Nauset.
I used to pray to recover you.
Ach, du.

In the German tongue, in the Polish town
Scraped flat by the roller
Of wars, wars, wars.
But the name of the town is common.
My Polack friend

Says there are a dozen or two.
So I never could tell where you
Put your foot, your root,
I never could talk to you.
The tongue stuck in my jaw.

It stuck in a barb wire snare.
Ich, ich, ich, ich,

I could hardly speak.
I thought every German was you.
And the language obscene

An engine, an engine
Chuffing me off like a Jew.
A Jew to Dachau, Auschwitz, Belsen.
I began to talk like a Jew.
I think I may well be a Jew.

The snows of the Tyrol, the clear beer of Vienna
Are not very pure or true.
With my gypsy ancestress and my weird luck
And my Taroc pack and my Taroc pack
I may be a bit of a Jew.

I have always been scared of you,
With your Luftwaffe, your gobbledygoo.
And your neat moustache
And your Aryan eye, bright blue.
Panzer-man, panzer-man, O You—

Not God but a swastika
So black no sky could squeak through.
Every woman adores a Fascist,
The boot in the face, the brute
Brute heart of a brute like you …

If I've killed one man, I've killed two—
The vampire who said he was you
And drank my blood for a year,
Seven years, if you want to know.
Daddy, you can lie back now.

There's a stake in your fat black heart
And the villagers never liked you.
They are dancing and stamping on you.
They always knew it was you.
Daddy, daddy, you bastard, I'm through.

In "Lady Lazarus" Plath exclaims, "I have done it again. One year in every ten I manage it." Apparently referring to her previous suicide attempt, these lines became ironically prophetic.

LADY LAZARUS

I have done it again.
One year in every ten
I manage it—

A sort of walking miracle, my skin
Bright as a Nazi lampshade,
My right foot

A paperweight,
My face a featureless, fine
Jew linen.

Peel off the napkin
O my enemy.
Do I terrify?—

The nose, the eye pits, the full set of teeth?
The sour breath
Will vanish in a day.

Soon, soon the flesh
The grave cave ate will be
At home on me

And I a smiling woman.
I am only thirty.
And like the cat I have nine times to die.

This is Number Three.
What a trash
To annihilate each decade.

What a million filaments.
The peanut-crunching crowd
Shoves in to see

Them unwrap me hand and foot
The big strip tease.
Gentleman, ladies,

These are my hands,
My knees.
I may be skin and bone,

Nevertheless, I am the same, identical woman.
The first time it happened I was ten.
It was an accident.

The second time I meant
To last it out and not come back at all.
I rocked shut

As a seashell.
They had to call and call
And pick the worms off me like sticky pearls.

Dying
Is an art, like everything else.
I do it exceptionally well …

In the poet's most hopeful moments, Plath shows a strong and sensitive attention to beauty—rather like an anesthesia for the pain that haunted her. In "Black Rook in Rainy Weather" she hopes for a piecing together of lovely, inspiring moments to defend and shield herself against despair. Painful as her story is, her moments of celebration are rare—but momentous.

BLACK ROOK IN RAINY WEATHER

On the stiff twig up there
Hunches a wet black rook
Arranging and rearranging its feathers in the
    rain.
I do not expect miracle
Or an accident

To set the sight on fire
In my eye, nor seek
Any more in the desultory weather some design,
But let spotted leaves fall as they fall
Without ceremony, or portent

Although, I admit, I desire,
Occasionally, some backtalk
From the mute sky, I can't honestly complain:
A certain minor light may still
Lean incandescent

Out of kitchen table or chair
As if a celestial burning took
Possession of the most obtuse objects now and
    then—
Thus hallowing an interval
Otherwise inconsequent

By bestowing largesse, honor,
One might say love. At any rate, I now walk
Wary (for it could happen
Even in this dull, ruinous landscape); skeptical,
Yet politic; ignorant

Of whatever angel may choose to flare
Suddenly at my elbow. I only know that a rook
Ordering its black feathers can so shine
As to seize my senses, haul
My eyelids up, and grant

A brief respite from fear
Of total neutrality. With luck,
Trekking stubborn through this season
Of fatigue, I shall
Patch together a content

Of sorts. Miracles occur,
If you care to call those spasmodic
Tricks of radiance
Miracles. The wait's begun again,
The long wait for the angel,

For that rare, random descent.

SHEL SILVERSTEIN
(1932–)

"I want to go everywhere, look at and listen to everything. You can go crazy with some of the wonderful stuff there is in life."

Shel Silverstein collects his "stuff of life" in the form of highly imaginative poetry and distorted line drawings. Born in Chicago, Illinois, in 1932, he began drawing and writing at around age 14. He admits: " … I couldn't play ball, I couldn't dance. Luckily, the girls didn't want me."

Since those early years, he has established himself as a journalist, a composer, a playwright, a cartoonist, a lyricist, and a folksinger—and appeared in a 1971 movie. Even in the 1950s as a U.S. Army private in Korea and Japan, Silverstein served as a cartoonist for the Pacific edition of the *Stars and Stripes*, the American military newspaper.

Silverstein, a former ad-copy writer, never set out to be a writer specializing in children's verse until a friend urged him to visit Ursula Nordstrom, a children's book editor. Nordstrom, after much persuasion, finally convinced Silverstein that he could write for children. Ever since, he has produced books and poems that resonate with energy, attracting large followings of both juvenile and adult readers.

Silverstein's brief tale *The Giving Tree* was published in 1964, becoming his best-known work. Most of his poetry is found in two larger works titled *The Light in the Attic* and *Where the Sidewalk Ends*.

Astute observation of children and adults interacting with other children and adults, mixed with advice—both good and bad—are Silverstein's trademarks.

LISTEN TO THE MUSTN'TS
Listen to the MUSTNTS, child,
Listen to the DON'TS.
Listen to the SHOULDN'TS,
The IMPOSSIBLES, the WON'TS.
Listen to the NEVER HAVES,
Then listen close to me—
Anything can happen, child
ANYTHING can be.

Silverstein's "Hector the Collector" parodies the things people value most. Hector, the poem's protagonist, is very much surprised that what to him is a treasure is not as appreciated by others.

HECTOR THE COLLECTOR
Hector the collector
Collected bits of string,
Collected dolls with broken heads
And rusty bells that would not ring.
Pieces out of picture puzzles,
Bent-up nails and ice-cream sticks,
Twists of wires, worn-out tires,
Paper bags and broken bricks.
Old chipped vases, half shoelaces,
Gatlin' guns that wouldn't shoot,
Leaky boats that wouldn't float
And stopped-up horns that wouldn't toot.
Butter knives that had no handles,
Copper keys that fit no locks,
Rings that were too small for fingers,
Dried-up leaves and patched-up socks.
Worn-out belts that had no buckles,
'Lectric trains that had no tracks,
Airplane models, broken bottles,
Three-legged chairs and cups with cracks.
Hector the Collector
Loved these things with all his soul—
Loved them more than shining diamonds,
Loved them more than glistenin' gold.
Hector called to all the people,
"Come and share my treasure trunk!"
And all the silly sightless people
Came and looked … and called it junk.

Another poem that raises doubts about the value of things is "Ol' Man Simon."

Ol' man Simon, planted a diamond,
Grew hisself a garden the likes of none.
Sprouts all growin', comin' up glowin',
Fruit of jewels all shinin' in the sun.
Colors of the rainbow,
See the sun and rain grow
Sapphires and rubies of ivory vines …
Pure gold corn there,
Blowin' in the warm air,
Ol' crow nibblin' on the amnythyst seeds.
In between the diamonds, ol' man Simon
Crawl about pullin' out platinum weeds.
Pink pearl berries,
All you can carry,
Put 'em in a bushel and
Haul 'em into town.
Up in the trees there's
Opal nuts and gold pears—
Hurry quick, grab a stick
And shake some down.
Take a silver tater,
Emerald tomater,
Fresh plump coral melons
Hangin' in reach.
Ol' man Simon,
Diggin' in his diamonds,
Stops and rests and dreams about
One … real … peach.

The theme of frugality bordering on stinginess appears in a sad-silly poem called "Lester," in which the character is given a magic wish by the goblin in the banyan tree. But Lester, a clever lad, wishes for two more wishes, turning his one into three. The wishing for more wishes goes on and on, until Lester has "Five billion, seven million, eighteen thousand thirty-four" wishes. He then spreads them on the ground and dances around them, all the while wishing for more, and more, and more. Silverstein then concludes with the moral of his story:

… While other people smiled and cried
And loved and reached and touched and felt
Lester sat amid his wealth
Stacked mountain-high like stacks of gold,
sat and counted—and grew old.

Lester soon died, and when he was found with his zillions of wishes it was discovered that not one was missing. The poem concludes: *In a world of apples and kisses and shoes / He wasted his wishes on wishing……*

Silverstein's commentary on what is of true worth carries over into a sly little poem that parody's children's fears. In it, he paints the imagined fears as absurd, and therefore, manageable.

THE GOOGIES ARE COMING

The googies are coming, the old people say,
To buy little children and take them away.
Fifty cents for fat ones,
Twenty cents for lean ones,
Fifteen cents for dirty ones,
Thirty cents for clean ones,
A nickel each for mean ones.

The googies are coming, and maybe tonight,
To buy little children and lock them up tight.
Eighty cents for husky ones,
Quarter for the weak ones,
Penny each for noisy ones,
A dollar for the meek ones.

Forty cents for happy ones,
Eleven cents for sad ones.
And, kiddies, when they come to buy,
It won't do any good to cry.
But—just between yourself and I—
They never buy the bad ones!

The poem "Ma and God" sets up an amusing conflict between the two supreme beings in any child's life, and then speculates on who is really the higher authority.

God gave us fingers—Ma says, "Use your fork."
God gave us voices—Ma says, "Don't scream."
Ma says eat broccoli, cereal and carrots.
But God have us tasteys for maple ice cream.

God gave us fingers—Ma says, "Use your hanky."
God gave us puddles—Ma says, "Don't splash."
Ma says, "Be quiet, your father is sleeping."
But God gave us garbage can covers to crash.

God gave us fingers—Ma says, "Put your gloves on."
God gave us raindrops—Ma says, "Don't get wet."
Ma says be careful, and don't get too near to

Those strange lovely dogs that God gave us to pet.

God gave us fingers—Ma says, "Go wash 'em."
But God gave us coal bins and nice dirty bodies.
And I ain't too smart, but there's one thing for
*   certain—*
Either Ma's wrong or else God is.

In "How Not To Have To Dry the Dishes" Silverstein offers practical advice to any child wishing to escape the duty and drudgery of dish-washing.

If you have to dry the dishes
(Such an awful, boring chore)
If you have to dry the dishes
('Stead of going to the store)
If you have to dry the dishes
And you drop one on the floor,
Maybe they won't let you
Dry the dishes anymore.

But Silverstein's poetry is not all naughtiness and dubious advice. Much of his work takes on a more whimsical, funny style. "Me-Stew" and "Moon-Catchin' Net" are two of many pieces that capture his knack for fanciful whimsy—a knack that character-izes the true genius of Shel Silverstein.

ME-STEW

I have nothing to put in my stew, you see,
Not a bone or a bean or a black-eyed pea,
So I'll just climb in the pot to see
It I can make a stew out of me.
I'll put in some pepper and salt and I'll sit
In the bubbling water—I won't scream a bit.
I'll sing while I simmer, I'll smile while I'm stewing,
I'll taste myself often to see how I'm doing.
I'll stir me around with this big wooden spoon
And serve myself up at a quarter to noon.
So bring out your stew bowls,
You gobblers and snackers.
Farewell—and I hope you enjoy me with crackers!

MOON-CATCHIN' NET

I've made me a moon-catchin' net,
And I'm goin' huntin' tonight,
I'll run along swingin' it over my head,
and grab for that big ball of light.

So tomorrow just look at the sky,
And if there's no moon you can bet
I've found what I sought and I finally caught
The moon in my moon-catchin' net.

But if the moon's still shinin' there
Look close underneath and you'll get
A clear look at me in the sky swingin' free
With a star in my moon-catchin' net.

JACK PRELUTSKY
(1940–)

THE WAYS OF LIVING THINGS

There is wonder past all wonder
in the ways of living things,
in a worm's intrepid wriggling,
in the song a blackbird sings,
In the grandeur of an eagle
and the fury of a shark,
in the calmness of a tortoise
on a meadow in the dark,
… In a fish's joyful splashing,
in a snake that makes no sound,
in the smallest salamander
there is wonder to be found.

One of Jack Prelutsky's most serious poems, "The Ways of Living Things" is long on humor and vivid imagery that bring to life the real and imaginary animals that stride across the landscape of his work.

Born in Brooklyn, New York, to an electrician father and a housewife mother, Prelutsky was a brilliant and precocious child, yet restless and nonconforming in school. In spite of his undisciplined behavior, he did exhibit one glorious talent: an exceptional singing voice. By age ten he sang regularly at weddings and other occasions. Later, he attended a music-oriented high school in New York.

Prelutsky's path to fame as an opera singer came to an end after he heard the great Italian tenor Luciano Pavarotti. Knowing he could never sing like that, he moved on to other endeavors. From one occupation to the next, he spent much of his time traveling and playing the guitar.

Feeling that his life was meant to be spent in the arts but not content being a folk singer, Prelutsky ventured into drawing—spending an entire six months creating imaginary animals and writing short poems for each. At the urging of a friend, he submitted his work for publication and was informed that there was potential in the poetry, but not in his drawings. Thus encouraged, Prelutsky set out to create poems that would peak children's interest. Foregoing the trend to write "deep" and "meaningful" verse, he focused on nonsense lines laced with colorful imagery.

Prelutsky's work resonates within a child's imagination. Designed to be read out loud, some of the verses contain tongue twisters. Thus, as a child moves through a poem, here and there he learns something new about words, nature, dinosaurs—or himself.

Prelutsky's amusing works often play to the natural curiosity children have about animals.

ALLIGATORS ARE UNFRIENDLY

Alligators are unfriendly,
they are easily upset,
I suspect that I would never
care to have one for a pet.

Oh, I know they do not bellow,
and I think they do not shed,
but I'd probably be nervous
if I had one in my bed.

Alligators are not clever,
they are something of a bore,
they can't heel or catch a Frisbee,
they don't greet you at the door,
for their courtesy is lacking,
and their tempers are not sweet,
they won't even fetch your slippers
… though they just might eat your feet.

Animals—both real and imaginary—that might be unfamiliar to children are described in ways that create vivid mental pictures.

THE YAK

Yickity-yackity, yickity-yak,
the yak has a scriffily, scraffily back;
some yaks are brown yaks and some yaks are black,
yickity-yackity, yickity-yak.

Sniggildy-snaggildy, sniggildy-snag,
the yak is all covered with shiggildy-shag;
he walks with a ziggildy-zaggildy-zag,
sniggildy-snaggildy, sniggildy-snag.

HELP

Can anybody tell me, please,
a bit about the thing
with seven legs and furry knees,
four noses and a wing?

Oh what has prickles on its chin,
what's yellow, green and blue,
and what has soft and slimy skin?
Oh tell me, tell me, do.

And tell me, what has polka dots
on every other ear,
what ties its tail in twenty knots,
what weeps a purple tear?

Oh what is growling long and low
and please, has it been fed?
I think I'd really better know …
it's sitting on my head.

Prelutsky sometimes ends his poems with a punch line or otherwise unexpected surprise.

THE SHERIFF OF ROTTENSHOT

The sheriff of Rottenshot, Jogalong Jim,
wore a one-gallon hat with a ten-gallon brim.
He was short in the saddle and slow on the draw,
but he was the sheriff, his word was the law.

Jogalong Jim didn't know how to fight,
his boots were too big and his britches too tight,

he wasn't too bright and he wasn't too brave,
and he needed a haircut, a bath and a shave.

His rifle was rusty and couldn't shoot straight,
his bony old pony groaned under his weight.
The sheriff of Rottenshot, Jogalong Jim,
was lucky that nobody lived there but him.

The thought of eating strange things can be extremely funny to children.

TWICKHAM TWEER

Shed a tear for Twickham Tweer
who ate uncommon meals,
who often peeled bananas
and then only ate the peels,
who emptied jars of marmalade
and only ate the jars,
and only ate the wrappers
off of chocolate candy bars.

When Twickham cooked a chicken,
He would only eat the bones,
he discarded scoops of ice cream
though he always ate the cones,
he'd boil a small potato
but he'd only eat the skin,
and pass up canned asparagus
to gobble down the tin.

He sometimes dined on apple cores
and bags of peanut shells,
on cottage cheese containers,
cellophane from caramels,
but Twickham Tweer passed on last year,
that odd and novel man,
when he fried an egg one morning
and then ate the frying pan.

NIGEL GLINE

When Nigel Gline sat down to dine,
he yawned, "This meal's a bore!
It's nothing more than what I've had
a thousand times before.
I'm through with cheese and chocolate,
I'm done with beans and beef,
I'd like a tasty tree instead."
So Nigel ate a leaf.

He liked that leaf, and swallowed more,
then nibbled on a twig,
that hardly seemed to be enough,
his appetite was big,
the twigs were so delicious
that he started on a limb,
soon every branch upon that tree
had vanished into him.

"It's time to try the trunk!" he said,
and ate it on the spot,
the bark was easy to digest,

the knots, of course, were not.
Now Nigel Gline declines to dine,
deep roots grow from his toes,
and birds nest in the leafy boughs
that stem from Nigel's nose.

Prelutsky overstates problems that most children face such as the stress of homework and the trauma of moving, coloring them with humor. Through exaggeration and fantasy, he helps children deal sensibly with their very real concerns.

A REMARKABLE ADVENTURE

I was at my bedroom table
with a notebook open wide,
when a giant anaconda
started winding up my side,
I was filled with apprehension
and retreated down the stairs,
to be greeted at the bottom
by a dozen grizzly bears.
We tumultuously tussled
till I managed to get free,
then I saw, with trepidation,
there were tigers after me,
I could feel them growing closer,
I was quivering with fear,
then I blundered into quicksand
and began to disappear.
I was rescued by an eagle
that descended from the skies
to embrace me with its talons,
to my terror and surprise,
but that raptor lost its purchase
when a blizzard made me sneeze,
and it dropped me in a thicket
where I battered both my knees.
I was suddenly surrounded
by a troop of savage trolls,
who maliciously informed me
they would toast me over coals,
I was lucky to elude them
when they briefly looked away—
that's the reason why my homework
isn't here with me today.

WE MOVED ABOUT A WEEK AGO

We moved about a week ago,
it's nice here, I suppose,
the trouble is, I miss my friends,
like Beth, who bopped my nose,
and Jess, who liked to wrestle
and dump me in the dirt,
and Liz, who found a garter snake
and put it down my shirt.

... the more I think about them,
the more it makes me sad,
I hope I make some friends here
as great as those I had.

LARRY LEVIS
(1946–)

The voice in the poetry of Larry Levis is often alone, watching, contemplating both the rough and the tender edges between people. His work addresses the music, cities and personalities that inhabit realms. These "rough and tender" poems touch upon both human connection and separation, often referring to people's "souvenirs"—personal symbols, objects and places by which people interact with other people during the course of their lives.

Born in Fresno, California, Levis's academic career centered on English and writing, culminating with a PhD in Modern Letters from the University of Iowa. Having authored five books of poetry and one collection of short stories, his first publication, *The Wrecking Crew*, won many honors, including the United States Award of the International Poetry Forum. *The Afterlife* won the Lamont Award of the American Academy of Poets in 1976; *The Dollmaker's Ghost* won the Open Competition of the National Poetry Series; and the fourth collection, *Winter Stars*, was published in the Pitt Poetry Series in 1985. Other awards include three fellowships in poetry from the National Endowment for the Arts, a Fulbright and a Guggenheim Fellowship.

From a single scene and a nondescript group of characters, Levis reaches out and grabs his reader's entire being. A poem—such as "Decrescendo"—may begin with the story of a nameless group of musicians in an undisclosed bar on an ordinary night, but then it suddenly becomes larger, pulling the whole world, bit by bit, it seems, into the emotional landscape.

DECRESCENDO

If there is only one world, it is this one.

In my neighborhood, the ruby-helmeted
*   woodpecker's line*
Is all spondees, & totally formal as it tattoos
Its instinct & solitude into a high sycamore
*   which keeps*
Revising autumn until I look out, &
Something final will be there: a branch in
*   winter—not*
Even a self-portrait. Just a thing.

Still, it is strange to live alone, to feel something
Rise up, out of the body, against all that is,
By law, falling & turning into the pointless
*   beauty*
Of calendars ...
It is all like the doomed singers, Cooke &
Redding,
Who raised their voices against the horns;

Implacable decrescendos, & knew exactly
*   what they*
Were doing, & what they were doing was
dangerous.

The man on sax & the other on piano never had
to argue
Their point, for their point was time itself; & all
*   That one wished to say, even to close friends,*
*   One said beside that window: The trees turn; a*
*   woman*
Passing on the street below turns up her collar
*   against*
The cold; & if the music ends, the needle on the
phonograph
*   Scrapes like someone raking leaves, briefly,*
*   across*
A sidewalk, & no one alone is, particularly,
special.

That is what musicians are for, to remind us of
this, unless
Those singers die, one shot in a motel room
By a woman who made a mistake; & one dead
In a plane crash, an accident.

Which left a man on sax & another on piano
With no one to back up, &, hearing the news,
One sat with his horn in a basement in Palo Alto,
Letting its violence go all the way up, &
Annoying the neighbors until the police came,
And arresting him—who had, in fact, tears
In his eyes. And the other, a white studio
Musician from L. A., who went home & tried
To cleave the keyboard with his hands until
They bled, & his friends came, & called his wife,
And someone went out for bandages & more
*   bourbon—*

Hoping to fix up, a little, this world.

One of Levis's strengths is his ability to perceive—and define—the spaces between people. He might use the distance between lovers, for example, to define the characters' relationship; the love—or lack of love—between father and son can also be given a spatial correlation. " ... We do not choose, & do not fall apart. But we are apart," reads a line in the poem "Oklahoma."

"Distance" and "detachment," implies Levis, are not synonyms. Neither is *aloneness* synonymous with *loneliness*: sometimes, being alone makes us lonely, but sometimes the bliss of solitude—especially after a day of confronting a collective mass of humanity—is the most potent elixir of the soul.

OKLAHOMA

Often, I used to say: I am this dust; or, I am
    this wind.
And young, I would accept that.
The truth is, it was never the case.
I have seen enough dust & wind by now to know
I am a little breath that always goes the distance,
Longing requires, & to know even this will fail.
The truth is, dear friends, we fall apart;
And for mysterious reasons, not entirely clear
    to us,
We choose to live alone. The truth is,
We do not choose, & do not fall apart. But we
    are apart …

I rise, & put on my precisely faded jeans,
a black Hawaiian shirt
With ridiculous light yellow roses;
& sharp-toed cowboy boots.
    Style, after all, is a kind of humor,
Something truly beneath contempt.
Even here, on the Southern Plains, in Oklahoma
    City.

Though something, beneath the armor we put on,
Is always missing, the trouble with this wind
Is that it drives the land away: These raw cuts
In the red dirt of the roadside almost speak for
    themselves.
Are they painful? They look as if they once were.
Someday, see for yourself, & take care when you
Do so. Look closely, but take care.
And put your arms around each other's waists so
    you don't
Slip through to anything truer
Than you meant to be.

The earth, for example, has often been a lie,
And the wind its rumor.

Together, once, they drove all
The better people away.

There emerges an urban flavor in some of
the poems, bleak yet beautiful images of gritty
people bustling about—and accomplishing
little.

MY STORY IN A LATE STYLE OF FIRE

Whenever I listen to Billie Holiday, I am
    reminded
That I, too, was once banished from New York
    City.
Not because of drugs or because I was interesting
    enough
For any wan, overworked patrolman to worry
    about—
His expression usually a great, gauzy spiderweb of
    bewilderment
Over his face—I was banished from New York
City by a woman.
Sometimes, after we had stopped laughing, I
    would look
At her & see a cold note of sorrow or puzzlement
    go
Over her face as if someone else were there,
    behind it,
Not laughing at all. We were, I think, "in love."
No, I'm sure.
If my house burned down tomorrow morning, &
if I & my wife
And son stood looking on at the flames, & if, then,
Someone stepped out of the crowd of bystanders
And said to me: "Didn't you once know … ?" No.
But if
One of the flames, rising up in the scherzo of fire,
    turned
All the windows blank with light, & if that flame
    could speak,
And if it said to me: "You loved her, didn't you?"
I'd answer,
Hands in my pockets, "Yes." And then I'd let fire
& misfortune
Overwhelm my life …
That morning, when she asked me to leave,
    wearing only
The apricot tinted, fraying chemise, I wanted
    to stay.
But I also wanted to go, to lose her suddenly,
    almost
For no reason, & certainly without any
    explanation.
I remember looking down at a pair of singular
    tracks
Made in a light snow the night before, at how
    they were
Gradually effacing themselves beneath the tires
Of the morning traffic, & thinking that my only
    other choice
Was fire, ashes, abandonment, solitude. All of
    which happened
Anyway, & soon after, & by divorce. I know this
    isn't much.
But I wanted to explain this life to you, even if
I had to become, over the years, someone else to
    do it.
You have to think of me what you think of me.
    I had
To live my life, even its late, florid style. Before

You judge this, think of her. Then think of fire,
Its laughter, the music of splintering beams
& glass,
The flames reaching through the second story of
a house
Almost as if to—mistakenly—rescue someone
who
Left you years ago. It is so American, fire. So like
us.
Its desolation. And its eventual, brief triumph.

Memories are held as much in places and objects as they are in people's hearts and minds. In the previous poem, the flame spoke to the writer, drawing out of his inner self an honest answer, a guileless response that a mere person could not elicit.

In the following poem, the waves, too, hold memories and questions, but they will not release their historical recollections nor seek answers to their doubts concerning the whys and hows of human existence.

LATE SEPTEMBER IN ULCINJ
—for Colleen McElroy
Birth & Death own the little walled cottages;
Since one's illiterate, the other always speechless,
There's no real way of meeting either.
And what did you come here for if not to hear
Finality in the soft click of a latch,
Or in the long thud of the empty wavebreak?
The rocks glistening for a second after it
Would find it strange that they meant anything.
And the gull's cry, & the sore screech of a winch
On a fishing boat a hundred yards offshore,
Are the poor speech of everything there is,
An unregretting blossoming & humming …
The sea wall overlooked the rocks, the choppy
water,
Four teenagers playing solemnly with a knife
Whose falling shadow told each one of a fortune,
And a woman reading something on the beach
Who yawned, stretched, & seemed to fall asleep.
It was the custom to wear nothing there,
Where the wave sprawl on the rock cannot
remember.

This final work—a love poem still emitting Levis's constant messages of time and human bonds—exhibits the quiet style of which Levis is capable.

AS I MOVE ON WITH YOU
Different days,
Different hours,
Many faces,
bouquets of flowers,

Fantasies,
And mists,
Of dreams,

Lost away,
Onto the ways,
Of yesterday,

See the future,
Past untold,
In his arms,
Is her hold,

Watch the moments,
See me through,
As my love,
Moves on with you.

THOUGHTS WORTH PONDERING

musings for the moment

In this world there are only two tragedies. One is not getting what one wants, and the other is getting it.

Oscar Wilde

Love and work are the cornerstones of our humanness.

Sigmund Freud

Hate your job? There's a support group for that. It's called everybody and they meet at a bar.

Drew Carey

"*Thoughts Worth Pondering*" is organized, not by topic, but by mood and voice—the various moods and voices of human nature. Each separate gourmet selection of quotes is designed to be tasted, savored and re-savored, and can be accessed for escape, amusement, entertainment or insight, according to your wants and needs of the moment.

If you feel your funny bone needs a good strike, head for the pages filled with "*Classic Comedy Collections*," "*Wisecracks and Witticisms*" or "*Comic Kids' Stuff*;" if the wells of your inspiration and motivation need recharging, perhaps some thoughts under "*Lights to Live By*," "*Tutorial Tales*" or "*The Religious Voice*" will help; or if you want to infuse a little spice or controversy into you conversation, check out some entries in "*The Human Condition*" or "*Point/Counterpoint*" sections. Uplifting, informative, refining, faith-promoting, confidence-building ... the fruits we reap from others' pungent perceptions can leave fertile new furrows within our own hearts and minds to nurture the seeds of our own individual wisdom.

CONTENTS

My foul-weather friend …

Winston Churchill

I wasn't always black . . .
there was this freckle, and
it got bigger and bigger.

Bill Cosby

No one can harm you
except yourself.

Gandhi

This life is a test; it is only a test.
If it were a real life, you would
receive instructions on where to
go and what to do.

Anonymous

Her hat is a creation
that will never go out
of style; it will just
look ridiculous year
after year.

Fred Allen

Boy, those French:
They have a different
word for everything!

Steve Martin

I don't feel old.
I don't feel anything
until noon. Then it's
time for my nap.

Bob Hope

Dogs are the leaders of the planet.
If you see two life forms, one of them's
making a poop, the other one's carrying
it for him, who would you assume is in
charge.

Jerry Seinfeld

A DOSE OF STEVEN WRIGHT

A friend of mine once sent me a post card with a picture of the entire planet Earth taken from space. On the back it said, "Wish you were here."

What's another word for *Thesaurus*?

I saw a subliminal advertising executive, but only for a second.

It doesn't make any difference what temperature a room is, it's always room temperature.

I knew these Siamese twins. They moved to England, so the other one could drive.

I just installed a skylight in my apartment. The people who live above me are furious!

Babies don't need a vacation but I see them at the beach. I'll go over to them and say, "What are you doing here? You've never worked a day in your life!"

I had a friend who was a clown. When he died, all his friends went to the funeral in one car.

If you shoot at mimes, should you use a silencer?

I intend to live forever. So far, so good.

I have a large seashell collection, which I keep scattered on beaches all over the world.

I busted a mirror and got seven years bad luck, but my lawyer thinks he can get me five.

I bought my brother some gift-wrap for Christmas. I took it to the Gift Wrap department and told them to wrap it, but in different print so he would know when to stop unwrapping.

A lot of people are afraid of heights. Not me, I'm afraid of widths.

Sponges grow in the ocean. That just kills me. I wonder how much deeper the ocean would be if that didn't happen.

There is a fine line between fishing and just standing on the shore like an idiot.

Do you think that when they asked George Washington for ID that he just whipped out a quarter?

I went to a general store but they wouldn't let me buy anything specific.

You can't have everything. Where would you put it?

ELLEN DEGENERES

What's with this sudden choice of disorders we get right now? When I was a kid, we just had crazy people, that's it, just crazy people.

Our attention span is shot. We've all got Attention Deficit Disorder or ADD or OCD or one of these disorders with three letters because we don't have the time or patience to pronounce the entire disorder. That should be a disorder right there, TBD—too busy disorder.

I ask people why they have deer heads on their walls. They always say because it's such a beautiful animal. There you go. I think my mother is attractive, but I have photographs of her.

Stuffed deer heads on walls are bad enough, but it's worse when they are wearing dark glasses and have streamers in their antlers because then you know they were enjoying themselves at a party when they were shot.

In the beginning there was nothing. God said, Let there be light! And there was light. There was still nothing, but you could see it a whole lot better.

Normal is getting dressed in clothes that you buy for work and driving through traffic in a car that you are still paying for - in order to get to the job you need to pay for the clothes and the car, and the house you leave vacant all day so you can afford to live in it.

Procrastination is not the problem. It is the solution. It is the universe's way of saying stop, slow down, you move too fast…. What I'm trying to say is, if you leave tonight and you don't remember anything else that I've said, leave here and remember this: Procrastinate now, don't put it off.

We stock up on popcorn and candy like we're crossing the Sierras, don't we? "I'll have a couple of soft pretzels, a hot dog, milk duds, snocaps. Is that the largest popcorn you've got there—that bucket? You don't have a barrel or anything like that? Do you have a donkey or a pack mule or anything? Oh, and a diet coke."

I gotta work out. I keep saying it all the time. I keep saying I gotta start working out. It's been about two months since I've worked out. And I just don't have the time. Which uh..is odd. Because I have the time to go out to dinner. And uh..and watch tv. And get a bone density test. And uh.. try to figure out what my phone number spells in words.

Speaking of call-waiting: It's turned into a mini people's choice awards. Hasn't it? And you find out right away who wins or loses: You're having a pleasant conversation with what you think is a good friend. You hear the click. They tell you to hold on. You're confident they're going to come back to you. And then they come back and they say, "I've got to take this other call." And you know what that means what they just said to the other person? "Let me get rid of this other call."

Speaking of the local news: They do these teases to get you to watch late on. They're so incredibly cruel: "It could be the most deadly thing in the world and you may be having it for dinner. We'll tell you what it is tonight at 11:00."

If we don't want to define ourselves by things as superficial as our appearances, we're stuck with the revolting alternative of being judged by our actions.

So, I bought a new CD and I was trying to get it open but couldn't with all the layers. I mean plastic and then tape and the tape is like government tape. It says "open here." Is that sarcasm? And buy batteries and they are in there with layers and layers of cardboard and then scissors … you need scissors to get into scissors, what if you were buying them for the first time? You wouldn't be able to get them open. Then you try and buy a light bulb and it's this thin, thin cardboard…. What are they thinking? "Oh, they'll be fine."

The 1960s were when hallucinogenic drugs were really, really big. And I don't think it's a coincidence that we had the shows then like The Flying Nun.

Just go up to somebody on the street and say "You're it!" and just run away.

My grandmother started walking five miles a day when she was sixty. She's ninety-seven now, and we don't know where the hell she is.

15 CLASSIC, ANONYMOUS, ALL-PURPOSE RULES FOR LIVING

1. The journey of a thousand miles begins with a broken fan belt and leaky tire.

2. It's always darkest before dawn. So if you're going to steal your neighbor's newspaper, that's the time to do it.

3. Don't be irreplaceable. If you can't be replaced, you can't be promoted.

4. Always remember that you're unique. Just like everyone else.

5. Never test the depth of the water with both feet.

6. If you think nobody cares if you're alive, try missing a couple of car payments.

7. Before you criticize someone, you should walk a mile in their shoes. That way, when you criticize them, you're a mile away and you have their shoes.

8. If at first you don't succeed, skydiving is not for you.

9. Give a man a fish and he will eat for a day. Teach him how to fish, and he will sit in a boat and drink beer all day.

10. If you lend someone $20 and never see that person again, it was probably worth it.

11. The quickest way to double your money is to fold it in half and put it back in your pocket.

12. Generally speaking, you aren't learning much when your lips are moving.

13. Experience is something you don't get until just after you need it.

14. Never miss a good chance to shut up.

15. Never, under any circumstances, take a sleeping pill and a laxative on the same night.

BILL COSBY

I wasn't always black … there was this freckle, and it got bigger and bigger.

If the new … father feels bewildered and even defeated, let him take comfort from the fact that whatever he does in any fathering situation has a fifty percent chance of being right.

A new father quickly learns that his child invariably comes to the bathroom at precisely the times when he's in there, as if he needed company. The only way for this father to be certain of bathroom privacy is to shave at the gas station.

Having a child is surely the most beautifully irrational act that two people in love can commit.

Human beings are the only creatures on earth that allow their children to come back home.

Poets have said that the reason to have children is to give yourself immortality. Immortality? Now that I have five children, my only hope is that they are all out of the house before I die.

A word to the wise ain't necessary—it's the stupid ones who need the advice.

Sex education may be a good idea in the schools, but I don't believe the kids should be given homework.

Let us now set forth one of the fundamental truths about marriage: the wife is in charge.

As I have discovered by examining my past, I started out as a child. Coincidentally, so did my brother. My mother did not put all her eggs in one basket, so to speak: she gave me a younger brother named Russell, who taught me what was meant by "survival of the fittest."

Gray hair is God's graffiti.

Immortality is a long shot, I admit. But somebody has to be first.

Women don't want to hear what you think. Women want to hear what they think - in a deeper voice.

When you become senile, you won't know it.

WOODY ALLEN

Basically my wife was immature. I'd be at home in the bath and she'd come in and sink my boats.

Some guy hit my fender the other day, and I said unto him, "Be fruitful and multiply." But not in those words.

I am thankful for laughter, except when milk comes out of my nose.

A man goes to a psychiatrist and says, "Doc, my brother's crazy, he thinks he's a chicken." The doctor says, "Why don't you turn him in?" The guy says, "We would. But we need the eggs."

When I was kidnapped, my parents snapped into action. They rented out my room.

As the poet said, 'Only God can make a tree' — probably because it's so hard to figure out how to get the bark on.

On the plus side, death is one of the few things that can be done just as easily lying down.

Life is full of misery, loneliness, and suffering - and it's all over much too soon.

When we played softball, I'd steal second base, feel guilty and go back.

How is it possible to find meaning in a finite world, given my waist and shirt size?

It is impossible to travel faster than the speed of light, and certainly not desirable, as one's hat keeps blowing off.

If only God would give me some clear sign! Like making a large deposit in my name in a Swiss bank.

The food here is terrible, and the portions are too small.

There are worse things than death. Have you ever spent the evening with an insurance salesman?

More than any other time in history, mankind faces a crossroads. One path leads to despair and utter hopelessness. The other, to total extinction. Let us pray we have the wisdom to choose correctly.

My one regret in life is that I am not someone else.

It's not that I'm afraid to die, I just don't want to be there when it happens.

ACTUAL NEWS HEADLINES ...

Red Tape Holds Up New Bridges

Man Struck By Lightning Faces Battery Charge

Child's Stool Great for Use in Garden

Something Went Wrong in Jet Crash, Experts Say

Safety Experts Say School Bus Passengers Should be Belted

Milk Drinkers are Turning to Powder

If Strike isn't Settled Quickly it May Last a While

Is There a Ring of Debris around Uranus?

Miners Refuse to Work after Death

Hospitals are Sued by Seven Foot Doctors

Police Begin Campaign to Run Down Jaywalkers

Queen Mary Having Bottom Scraped

Grandmother of Eight Makes Hole in One

Blind Woman Gets New Kidney from Dad she Hasn't Seen in Years

Deaf Mute Gets New Hearing in Killing

Robber Holds Up Albert's Hosiery

Two Sisters Reunite after Eighteen Years at Checkout Counter

War Dims Hope for Peace

New Study of Obesity Looks for Larger Test Group

Eye Drops Off Shelf

Kicking Baby Considered To Be Healthy

Kids Make Nutritious Snacks

Reagan Wins on Budget, but More Lies Ahead

Farmer Bill Dies in House

Local High School Dropouts Cut in Half

Cold Wave Linked to Temperatures

Lung Cancer in Women Mushrooms

Ray Romano

Everyone should have kids. They are the greatest joy in the world. But they are also terrorists. You'll realize this as soon as they are born, and they start using sleep deprivation to break you.

… I want to be a pro golfer. It's a love/hate relationship with golf. I can come away feeling so serene, and yet, it's the thing that I can let get to me to throw a club and say curses that don't even exist. I'm obsessed with something that won't let me master it. I don't know … I need therapy.

If my father had hugged me even once, I'd be an accountant right now.

Will Rogers

I guess there is nothing that will get your mind off everything like golf. I have never been depressed enough to take up the game, but they say you get so sore at yourself you forget to hate your enemies.

Things ain't what they used to be and never were.

Be thankful we're not getting all the government we're paying for.

This country has come to feel the same when Congress is in session as when the baby gets hold of a hammer.

I never expected to see the day when girls would get sunburned in the places they do now.

Diplomacy is the art of saying "Nice doggie" until you can find a rock.

All I know is just what I read in the papers, and that's an alibi for my ignorance.

There is nothing so stupid as the educated man if you get him off the thing he was educated in.

An economist's guess is liable to be as good as anybody else's.

What the country needs is dirtier fingernails and cleaner minds.

The man with the best job in the country is the vice-president. All he has to do is get up every morning and say, "How is the president?"

I bet after seeing us, George Washington would sue us for calling him "father."

He who dies with the most toys—still dies.

When I die, my epitaph—or whatever you call those signs on gravestones—is going to read: "I joked about every prominent man of my time, but I never met a man I didn't like." I am so proud of that I can hardly wait to die so it can be carved.

Everything is changing. People are taking their comedians seriously and the politicians as a joke.

We are all here for a spell, get all the good laughs you can.

Jerry Seinfeld

It's amazing that the amount of news that happens in the world every day always just exactly fits the newspaper.

Let me ask you something–if someone's lying, are their pants really on fire?

Somebody just gave me a shower radio. Thanks a lot. Do you really want music in the shower? I guess there's no better place to dance than a slick surface next to a glass door.

Dogs are the leaders of the planet. If you see two life forms, one of them's making a poop, the other one's carrying it for him, who would you assume is in charge.

There is no such thing as fun for the whole family.

I will never understand why they cook on TV. I can't smell it. Can't eat it. Can't taste it. The end of the show they hold it up to the camera, "Well, here it is. You can't have any. Thanks for watching. Goodbye."

The big advantage of a book is it's very easy to rewind. Close it and you're right back at the beginning.

The Swiss have an interesting army. Five hundred years without a war. Pretty impressive. Also pretty lucky for them. Ever see that little Swiss Army knife they have to fight with? Not much of a weapon there. Corkscrews. Bottle openers. "Come on, buddy, let's go. You get past me, the guy in back of me, he's got a spoon. Back off. I've got the toe clippers right here."

You know you're getting old when you get that one candle on the cake. It's like, "See if you can blow this out."

According to most studies, people's number one fear is public speaking. Number two is death. Death is number two. Does that sound right? This means to the average person, if you go to a funeral, you're better off in the casket than doing the eulogy.

Men want the same thing from women that they want from their underwear …a little support, comfort, and freedom.

People who read the tabloids deserve to be lied to.

Now they show you how detergents take out bloodstains, a pretty violent image there. I think if you've got a T-shirt with a bloodstain all over it, maybe laundry isn't your biggest problem. Maybe you should get rid of the body before you do the wash.

Men don't care what's on TV. They only care what else is on TV.

I was the best man at the wedding. If I'm the best man, why is she marrying him?

Sometimes the road less traveled is less traveled for a reason.

GROUCHO MARX-ISMS

I don't care to belong to any social organization which would accept me as a member.

One morning I shot an elephant in my pajamas. How he got into my pajamas I'll never know.

Outside of a dog, a book is man's best friend. Inside of a dog it's too dark to read.

I suggest we give him ten years in Leavenworth or eleven years in Twelveworth. I tell you what I'll do. I'll take five and ten in Woolworth.

I was married by a judge. I should have asked for a jury.

I find television very educating. Every time somebody turns on the set, I go into the other room and read a book.

I never forget a face, but in your case I'll be glad to make an exception.

FIT-TO-PRINT BUMPERSTICKERS

Cover me! I'm changing lanes!

WORK HARDER: Millions on welfare depend on you!

This is not an Abandoned Vehicle

If you can read this, I've lost my trailer

If everything is coming your way, you're in the wrong lane!

If this car is being driven courteously, it's been stolen

What if the Hokey Pokey IS what it's all about?

I brake SUDDENLY for tailgaters

I is a college student

Yes, this is my truck. No, I won't help you move.

My other car is also a piece of junk

I used to have a handle on life, but it broke

As a matter of fact, I DO own the road

I respect your opinion. I just don't want to hear it.

LILLY TOMLIN

I've always wanted to be somebody but I see now I should have been more specific.

Why isn't there a special name for the tops of your feet?

I always wondered why somebody doesn't do something about that. Then I realized I was somebody.

Reality is the leading cause of stress among those in touch with it.

If love is the answer, could you please rephrase the question?

Don't be afraid of missing opportunities. Behind every failure is an opportunity somebody wishes they had missed.

Remember we're all in this alone.

We are all in this together, by ourselves.

For fast-acting relief try slowing down.

I personally think we developed language because of our deep need to complain.

If I had known what it would be like to have it all—I might have been willing to settle for less.

The trouble with the rat race is that even if you win, you're still a rat.

If you read a lot of books you are considered well read. But if you watch a lot of TV, you're not considered well viewed.

Ninety eight percent of the adults in this country are decent, hardworking, honest Americans. It's the other lousy two percent that get all the publicity. But then, we elected them.

No matter how cynical you become, it's never enough to keep up.

The road to success is always under construction.

Why is it that when we talk to God we're said to be praying, but when God talks to us we're schizophrenic?

WACKY T-SHIRT SLOGANS

Equal Opportunity Annoyer

I'm in shape … Round is a shape

Hoarse Whisperer

I don't need no Educashun

Boldly Going Nowhere

Which Is Bigger, A Bazillion Or A Gazillion?

Volunteering ... it doesn't pay

Impatience is not to be tolerated!

Save the trees. Eat a beaver.

I'm on Debt Row

Lawyers Have Feelings Too! (allegedly)

If I throw a stick, will you leave?

Behind every great man is a woman rolling her eyes.

Gene Pool Full. Get Out!

I'm Brainstorming Here (And Quite a Storm It Is)

I was trying to daydream, but my mind kept wandering

DAVE BERRY

Several readers sent in an article from the *Richmond Times-Dispatch* concerning a dump-truck driver who "dropped more than 59,000 pounds of processed human excrement on Interstate 295" and was charged with "failure to contain his load."

What I look forward to is continued immaturity followed by death.

Walking like a dork is popular among people who used to jog for their health but can no longer afford orthopedic surgery.

Not all chemicals are bad. Without hydrogen or oxygen, for example, there would be no way to make water, a vital ingredient in beer.

If a woman has to choose between catching a fly ball and saving an infant's life, she will choose to save the infant's life without even considering if there are men on base.

The leading cause of death among fashion models is falling through street grates.

You can say any foolish thing to do to a dog, and the dog will give you a look that says, "My God, you're right! I never would've thought of that!"

Dogs feel very strongly that they should always go with you in the car, in case the need should arise for them to bark violently at nothing right in your ear.

ERMA BOMBECK

When I watch Captain Picard on "Star Trek: The Next Generation," I get really depressed. Hundreds of years have passed and they still don't have a cure for baldness.

Anybody who watches three games of football in a row should be declared brain dead.

Thanksgiving dinners take eighteen hours to prepare. They are consumed in twelve minutes. Half-times take twelve minutes. This is not coincidence.

On vacations: We hit the sunny beaches where we occupy ourselves keeping the sun off our skin, the saltwater off our bodies, and the sand out of our belongings.

People shop for a bathing suit with more care than they do a husband or wife. The rules are the same. Look for something you'll feel comfortable wearing. Allow for room to grow.

What's with you men? Would hair stop growing on your chest if you asked directions somewhere?

Never accept a drink from a urologist.

Never go to a doctor whose office plants have died.

Did you ever notice that the first piece of luggage on the carousel never belongs to anyone?

A friend never defends a husband who gets his wife an electric skillet for her birthday.

I come from a family where gravy is considered a beverage.

Seize the moment. Remember all those women on the *Titanic* who waved off the dessert cart. And for what!

Marriage has no guarantees. If that's what you're looking for, go live with a car battery.

I haven't trusted polls since I read that 62% of women had affairs during their lunch hour. I've never met a woman in my life who would give up lunch for sex.

God created man, but I could do better.

Once you get a spice in your home, you have it forever. Women never throw out spices. The Egyptians were buried with their spices. I know which one I'm taking with me when I go.

There's something wrong with a mother who washes out a measuring cup with soap and water after she's only measured water in it.

Guilt: the gift that keeps on giving.

Do you know what you call those who use towels and never wash them, eat meals and never do the dishes, sit in rooms they never clean, and are entertained till they drop? If you have just answered, "A house guest," you're wrong because I have just described my kids.

When a child is locked in the bathroom with water running and he says he's doing nothing but the dog is barking, call 911.

Sometimes I can't figure designers out. It's as if they flunked human anatomy.

I've exercised with women so thin that buzzards followed them to their cars.

PAULA POUNDSTONE

Adults are always asking little kids what they want to be when they grow up because they're looking for ideas.

The problem with cats is that they get the same exact look whether they see a moth or an ax-murderer.

My mom said she learned how to swim when someone took her out in the lake and threw her off the boat. I said, "Mom, they weren't trying to teach you how to swim."

I don't have a bank account, because I don't know my mother's maiden name.

I like to work on New Year's Eve. It has a nice spirit; a nice feel about it. If you are all about the 'year-end' thing at all, then laughing with fellow human beings is a great way to start the new year.

I was court-ordered to Alcoholics Anonymous on television. Pretty much blows the hell out of the second A, wouldn't you say?

We need a twelve-step group for compulsive talkers. They would call it On Anon Anon.

MILTON BERLE

My niece just got married. I was worried at first, but this afternoon she proved that she had the homemaker's instinct. She asked my wife to give her the recipe for cold cereal!

Unlike most newlyweds, she could boil water, but the groom got tired of having it seven days a week!

While hunting, a woman said to her husband, "Of course I heard it moo. Why shouldn't a moose moo?"

A young Marine recruit was called into the office and told that he'd failed to show up for camouflage class. The young Marine asked, "How did you know?"

I wouldn't believe him if he swore he was lying!

My son was about seven when he looked into our wedding album and said, "Pop, are these pictures of the day Mom came to work for us?"

I'd admit my biggest mistakes, but between my wife, her mother and my kids, it's too close to call!

My wife and I share household chores. I dry the dishes, my wife sweeps them up.

I married her for her looks, but not the ones she's been giving me lately!

A man bought his wife a burial plot. The following year he didn't buy her nything and she complained. He answered, "You didn't use the present I bought you last year!"

A man approached his neighbor. "Joe," he asked, "will you need your golf clubs Saturday?" Joe said, "I'm playing golf all day." "Good," answered the neighbor. "Then you won't need your lawnmower!"

AGELESS "DEEP THOUGHTS" BY JACK HANDEY

(taken from the old Saturday Night Live TV program)

To me, boxing is like a ballet, except there's no music, no choreography, and the dancers hit each other.

I hope if dogs ever take over the world, and they chose a king, they don't just go by size, because I bet there are some chihuahuas with some good ideas.

Maybe in order to understand mankind, we have to look at the word itself: "Mankind." Basically, it's made up of two separate words—"mank" and "ind". What do these words mean? It's a mystery, and that's why so is mankind.

If you work on a lobster boat, sneaking up behind someone and pinching him is probably a joke that gets old real fast.

Probably the earliest flyswatters were nothing more than some sort of striking surface attached to the end of a long stick.

I wish I had a dollar for every time I spent a dollar, because then, yahoo!, I'd have all my money back.

Whenever I see an old lady slip and fall on a wet sidewalk, my first instinct is to laugh. But then I think, what if I was an ant, and she fell on me? Then it wouldn't seem quite so funny.

Why do people in ship mutinies always ask for "better treatment"? I'd ask for a pinball machine, because with all that rocking back and forth you'd probably be able to get a lot of free games.

If you ever fall off the Sears Tower, just go real limp, because maybe you'll look like a dummy and people will try to catch you because, hey, free dummy.

Children need encouragement. If a kid gets an answer right, tell him it was a lucky guess. That way he develops a good, lucky feeling.

I don't think I'm alone when I say I'd like to see more and more planets fall under the ruthless domination of our solar system.

If a kid asks where rain comes from, I think a cute thing to tell him is "God is crying." And if he asks why God is crying, another cute thing to tell him is "Probably because of something you did."

Contrary to what most people say, the most dangerous animal in the world is not the lion or the tiger or even the elephant. It's a shark riding on an elephant's back, just trampling and eating everything they see.

If I was the head of a country that lost a war, and I had to sign a peace treaty, just as I was signing I'd glance over the treaty and then suddenly act surprised. "Wait a minute! I thought WE won!"

I bet the main reason the police keep people away from a plane crash is they don't want anybody walking in and lying down in the crash stuff, then, when somebody comes up, act like they just woke up and go, "What was THAT?!"

When you die, if you get a choice between going to regular heaven or pie heaven, choose pie heaven. It might be a trick, but if it's not, mmmmmmm, boy.

Too bad you can't buy a voodoo globe so that you could make the earth spin real fast and freak everybody out.

A Taste of Mark Twain

Names are not always what they seem. The common Welsh name Bzjxxllwcp is pronounced Jackson.

Never learn to do anything. If you don't learn, you will always find someone else to do it for you.

The reports of my death have been greatly exaggerated.

I have just got a new theory of eternity. (*a remark to a table-mate while listening to a longwinded speech honoring the scientist*)

Golf is a good walk spoiled

Sometimes too much to drink is barely enough.

Denial ain't just a river in Egypt.

I am opposed to millionaires, but it would be dangerous to offer me the position.

When I was younger I could remember anything, whether it happened or not.

Under certain circumstances, profanity provides a relief denied even to prayer.

Suppose you were an idiot, and suppose you were a member of Congress; but I repeat myself ...

Such is the human race. Often it does seem such a pity that Noah ... didn't miss the boat.

Familiarity breeds contempt—and children.

Never run after your hat—others will be delighted to do it; why spoil their fun?

Be careful about reading health books. You may die of a misprint.

There are two times in a man's life when he shouldn't speculate: when he can't afford it, and when he can.

Always acknowledge a fault frankly. This will throw those in authority off guard and allow you opportunity to commit more.

Get your facts first, and then you can distort them as much as you please.

Carol Burnett

Comedy is tragedy plus time.

Giving birth is like taking your lower lip and forcing it over your head.

I don't have false teeth. Do you think I'd buy teeth like these?

Henny Youngman

When I read about the evils of drinking, I gave up reading.

A girl phoned me the other day and said, "Come on over, nobody's home." I went over. Nobody was home.

A doctor gave a man six months to live. The man couldn't pay his bill, so he gave him another six months.

A car hits a Jewish man. The paramedic says, "Are you comfortable?" The man says, "I make a good living ... "

A bum asked me, "Give me $10 till payday." I asked, "When's payday?" He said, "I don't know. You're the one working!"

I'll tell you how to beat the gambling in Las Vegas. When you get off the airplane, walk right into the propeller.

My wife's an earth sign. I'm a water sign. Together we make mud.

Those two are a fastidious couple. She's fast and he's hideous.

I was such an ugly kid…. When I played in the sandbox, the cat kept covering me up.

My wife was at the beauty shop for two hours—and that was just for the estimate.

Getting on a plane, I told the ticket lady, "Send one of my bags to New York, send one to Lod Angeles, and send one to Miami." She said, "We can't do that." I told her, "You did it last week … "

Look, I'm not going to engage in a battle of wits with you. I never attack anyone who is unarmed.

RODNEY DANGERFIELD

I met the surgeon general; he offered me a cigarette.

What a dog I got. Last night he went on the paper 4 times—3 while I was reading it.

My wife and I were happy for twenty years. Then we met.

When I was a kid my parents moved a lot—but I always found them.

My wife has to be the worst cook. I my house, we pray after we eat.

Boy is my wife stupid. It takes her an hour and a half to watch 60 Minutes.

BOB HOPE

You know you're getting old when the candles cost more than the cake.

I don't feel old. I don't feel anything until noon. Then it's time for my nap.

I was called "Rembrandt" Hope in my boxing days, because I spent so much time on the canvas.

Isn't it fun to go out on the course and lie in the sun?

I've already started receiving Christmas cards. It's wonderful to get cards early. I was up all last night—erasing.

My brother worked at the post office during the Christmas rush last year, but they had to let him go. Every time they'd hand him a load of packages he'd say, "For me?"

I'll shoot my age if I have to live to be 105.

It was so crowded the pickpockets wouldn't take your watch unless it was gift-wrapped. One of 'em had his hand in my pocket and I said, "What's the idea?" He said, "Don't get excited. I'm just making change."

People really are flocking out here, though. You should see the way our freeways are jammed day and night with people trying to get to Los Angeles from Los Angeles.

SAM LEVENSON

If your wife wants to learn to drive, don't stand in her way.

Lead us not into temptation. Just tell us where it is; we'll find it.

If you die in an elevator, be sure to push the Up button.

The simplest toy, one which even the youngest child can operate, is called a grandparent.

Insanity is hereditary—you get it from your children.

We should not permit prayer to be taken out of the schools; that's the only way most of us got through.

It's so simple to be wise. Just think of something stupid to say and then don't say it.

DAVID LETTERMAN

New York City was hosting a four-day Global Warming Summit. But today was such a nice day, they canceled it.

It's graduation time. A lot of honor students here in New York City. "Yes, Your Honor … No, Your Honor."

They have dog food for constipated dogs. If your dog is constipated, why screw up a good thing? Stay indoors and let 'em bloat.

Donald Trump doesn't have much money invested in the stock market per se. Most of his money goes into junk blondes.

… Mother's Day: The day we salute the woman we blame for all of our personal problems.

I was going to have Mom come out for Mother's Day. I thought it would be great fun. But she doesn't have enough Greyhound miles.

Jay Leno

There's a new telephone service that lets you test your IQ over the phone. It costs $3.95 a minute. If you make the call at all, you're a moron. If you're on the line for three minutes, you're a complete idiot.

I went into a McDonald's yesterday and said, "I'd like some fries." The girl at the counter said, "Would you like some fries with that?"

Today marks the 47th anniversary of the invention of the birth control pill. And for all you women out there that forgot to take yours, Happy Mother's Day!

It looks like Exxon is going to buy Mobil Oil. They say their goal is to create the largest chain of filthy restrooms in the world.

Today Jerry Springer testified before Chicago's City Council. The big issue is whether the fights on his show are real or fake. I hope they're real! Wouldn't it be horrible if those morons on his show weren't actually getting punched in the mouth?

The reason there are two senators for each state is so that one can be the designated driver.

Here's something to think about: How come you never see a headline like "Psychic Wins Lottery"?

The price of gasoline passed four dollars a gallon in California. Gas is so expensive now a lot of people are only planning summer trips within walking distance from their homes.

If God doesn't destroy Hollywood Boulevard, he owes Sodom and Gomorrah an apology.

As of July 1, Allstate Insurance Company will stop selling new policies to homeowners in California because we have too many disasters. They shouldn't have the right to call themselves "Allstate." Maybe they should change their name to "Some-states."

A Pennsylvania man is suing God. He blamed God for losing his job. The case was thrown out because God does not have access to legal counsel. There are no lawyers in heaven.

The University of Nebraska says that elderly people that drink beer or wine at least four times a week have the highest bone density. They need it—they're the ones falling down the most.

Conan O'Brien

Early on, they were timing my contract with an egg timer.

In Cleveland there is legislation moving forward to ban people from wearing pants that fit too low. However, there is lots of opposition from the plumber' union.

A study in the Washington Post says that women have better verbal skills than men. I just want to say to the authors of that study: 'Duh.'

Joan Rivers

I have flabby thighs, but fortunately my stomach covers them.

I don't exercise. If God had wanted me to bend over he would have put diamonds on the floor.

The first time I see a jogger smiling, I'll consider it.

I told my mother-in-law that my house was her house, and she said, "Get the hell off my property."

People say that money is not the key to happiness, but I always figured if you have enough money, you can have a key made.

I succeeded by saying what everyone else is thinking.

I wish I had a twin, so I could know what I'd look like without plastic surgery.

I hate housework. You make the beds, you wash the dishes and six months later you have to start all over again.

I knew I was an unwanted baby when I saw that my bath toys were a toaster and a radio.

My mother could make anybody feel guilty - she used to get letters of apology from people she didn't even know.

There is not one female comic who was beautiful as a little girl.

Martin Mull

I don't jog. It makes the ice jump right out of my glass.

Having a family is like having a bowling alley installed in your head.

A cult following is a nice way of saying very few people like you.

Never underestimate a child's ability to get into more trouble.

George Burns

The most important thing in acting is honesty. If you can fake that, you've got it made.

Too bad that all the people who know how to run the country are busy driving taxi cabs and cutting hair.

It takes only one drink to get me drunk. The trouble is, I can't remember if it's the thirteenth or the fourteenth.

If it's a good script I'll do it. And if it's a bad script, and they pay me enough, I'll do it.

At my age flowers scare me.

If you live to be one hundred, you've got it made. Very few people die past that age.

You know you're getting old when you stoop to tie your shoelaces and wonder what else you could do while you're down there.

I don't believe in dying. It's been done. I'm working on a new exit. Besides, I can't die now—I'm booked.

Retirement at sixty-five is ridiculous. When I was sixty-five I still had pimples.

This is the sixth book I've written, which isn't bad for a guy who's only read two.

When I was young I was called a rugged individualist. When I was in my fifties I was considered eccentric. Here I am doing and saying the same things I did then and I'm labeled senile.

First you forget names, then you forget faces. Next you forget to pull your zipper up and finally, you forget to pull it down.

Steve Martin

First the doctor told me the good news: I was going to have a disease named after me.

I like a woman with a head on her shoulders. I hate necks.

Comedy may be big business, but it isn't pretty.

Boy, those French: They have a different word for everything!

A day without sunshine is like, you know, night.

All I've ever wanted was an honest week's pay for an honest day's work.

I believe in equality. Equality for everybody. No matter how stupid they are or how superior I am to them.

Phillis Diller

Never go to bed mad. Stay up and fight.

Best way to get rid of kitchen odors: Eat out.

Housework can't kill you, but why take a chance?

Tranquilizers work only if you follow the advice on the bottle—keep away from children.

If it weren't for baseball, many kids wouldn't know what a millionaire looks like.

Most children threaten at times to run away from home. This is the only thing that keeps some parents going.

I want my children to have all the things I couldn't afford. Then I want to move in with them.

We spend the first twelve months of our children's lives teaching them to walk and talk and the next twelve telling them to sit down and shut up.

Always be nice to your children because they are the ones who will choose your rest home.

There's so little money in my bank account, my scenic checks show a ghetto.

A bachelor is a guy who never made the same mistake once.

Aim high, and you won't shoot your foot off.

I asked the waiter, "Is this milk fresh?" He said, "Lady, three hours ago it was grass."

The real reason your pro tells you to keep your head down is so you can't see him laughing at you.

You know you're old if your walker has an airbag.

Johnny Carson

Married men live longer than single men. But married men are a lot more willing to die.

If variety is the spice of life, marriage is the big can of leftover Spam.

New York is an exciting town where something is happening all the time, most of it unsolved.

Never use a big word when a little filthy one will do.

I was so naive as a kid I used to sneak behind the barn and do nothing.

A Carson "Carnac the Magnificent" Cavalcade

"Supervisor" … What does Clark Kent use to keep the sun out of his eyes?

"Follow the yellow brick road" … What are good directions to a urologist's office?

"The Orient Express" … What is a drink made with soy sauce and prune juice?

"The ZIP Code" … What do CIA agents have to remember to go to the bathroom?

"Igloo" … What do you use to keep your ig from falling off?

"Henry r. Block" … Name one guy who's rich after April 15th.

"Grape Nuts" … What are Ernest and Julio Gallo?

"Debate" … What do you use to catch de fish?

"Until he gets caught" … How long does a United States Congressman serve?

"A, B, C, D, E, F, G" … What were some of the earlier forms of Preparation H?

"Frathouse" … What do you call a Japanese home struck by a meteor?

"Rose Bowl" … What do you say when it's Rose's turn at the bowling alley.

"Sis boom bah" … Describe the sound made by an exploding sheep.

STEVE ALLEN

Asthma doesn't seem to bother me any more unless I'm around cigars or dogs. The thing that would bother me most would be a dog smoking a cigar.

I used to be a heavy gambler. But now I just make mental bets. That's how I lost my mind.

The purpose of having an open mind is the same as having an open mouth, the object being eventually to close it on something solid. But one should never close either mind or mouth until the general circumstances of the moment make it reasonable to do so.

WITTY AND WISE WORD DEFINITIONS

Baseball: A game which consists of tapping a ball with a piece of wood, then running like a lunatic. - *H.J. Dubiel*

Abstract Art: A product of the untalented, sold by the unprincipled to the utterly confused. - *Al Capp*

The fishing rod: A stick with a hook at one end and a fool at the other. - *Samuel Johnson*

Red light: The place where you catch up with the motorist who passed you at 60 m.p.h. a mile back. - *Robert M. Lewis*

Desk: A wastebasket with drawers. - *The Wall Street Journal*

Congress: Bingo with billions. – *Red Skelton*

Justice: A decision in your favor. - *Harry Kaufman*

Parenthood: That state of being better chaperoned than you were before marriage. - *Anonymous*

Middle age: When you begin to exchange your emotions for symptoms. - *Irvin S. Cobb*

War: A passion play performed by idiots. - *Bill Corum*

Wretched: How you pronounce "Richard" in the South. - *Anonymous*

A SAMPLING OF AMBROSE BIERCE'S OWN TELLTALE WORD DEFINITIONS

Absurdity, n.: A statement or belief manifestly inconsistent with one's own opinion.

Acquaintance, n.: A person whom we know well enough to borrow from, but not well enough to lend to.

Admiration, n.: Our polite recognition of another's resemblance to ourselves.

Anoint, v.: To grease a king or other great functionary already sufficiently slippery.

Bigot, n.: One who is obstinately and zealously attached to an opinion that you do not entertain.

Bore, n.: A person who talks when you wish him to listen.

Cabbage, n.: A familiar kitchen-garden vegetable about as large and wise as a man's head.

Confidante, n.: One entrusted by A with the secrets of B confided to herself by C.

Consult, v.: To seek approval for a course of action already decided upon.

Corporation, n.: An ingenious device for obtaining profit without individual responsibility.

Coward, n.: One who, in a perilous emergency, thinks with his legs.

Day, n.: A period of twenty-four hours, mostly misspent.

Debt, n.: An ingenious substitute for the chain and whip of the slavedriver.

Deliberation, n.: The act of examining one's bread to determine which side it is buttered on.

Destiny, n.: A tyrant's authority for crime and a fool's excuse for failure.

Edible, adj.: Good to eat, and wholesome to digest, as a worm to a toad, a toad to a snake, a snake to a pig, a pig to a man, and a man to a worm.

Egotist, n.: A person of low taste, more interested in himself than in me.

Famous, adj.: Conspicuously miserable.

Fork, n.: An instrument used chiefly for the purpose of putting dead animals into the mouth.

Happiness, n.: An agreeable sensation arising from contemplating the misery of another.

History, n.: An account, mostly false, of events, mostly unimportant, which are brought about by rulers, mostly knaves, and soldiers, mostly fools.

Land, n.: A part of the earth's surface, considered as property. The theory that land is property subject to private ownership and control is the foundation of modern society, and is eminently worthy of the superstructure.

Love, n.: A temporary insanity curable by marriage.

Marriage, n.: The state or condition of a community consisting of a master, a mistress, and two slaves, making in all, two.

Meekness, n.: Uncommon patience in planning a revenge that is worthwhile.

Optimism, n.: The doctrine that everything is beautiful, including what is ugly, everything good, especially the bad, and everything right that is wrong … It is hereditary, but fortunately not contagious.

Painting, n.: The art of protecting flat surfaces from the weather, and exposing them to the critic.

Patience, n. A minor form of despair, disguised as a virtue.

Photograph, n.: A picture painted by the sun without instruction in art.

Politeness, n.: The most acceptable hypocrisy.

Positive, adj.: Mistaken at the top of one's voice.

Pray, v.: To ask that the laws of the universe be annulled in behalf of a single petitioner confessedly unworthy.

Quotation, n.: The act of repeating erroneously the words of another.

Revolution, n.: In politics, an abrupt change in the form of misgovernment.

Success, n.: The one unpardonable sin against our fellows.

Sweater, n.: Garment worn by child when its mother is feeling chilly.

Telephone, n.: An invention of the devil which abrogates some of the advantages of making a disagreeable person keep his distance.

Vote, n.: The instrument and symbol of a freeman's power to make a fool of himself and a wreck of his country.

RED SKELTON

People in hell … where do they tell someone to go?

A fellow told me he was going to hang-glider school. He said, "I've been going for three months." I said, "How many successful jumps do you need to make before you graduate?" He said, "All of them."

All men make mistakes, but married men find out about them sooner.

Any kid will run any errand for you, if you ask at bedtime.

I'm nuts and I know it. But so long as I make 'em laugh, they ain't going to lock me up.

GEORGE CARLIN

Honesty may be the best policy, but it's important to remember that apparently, by elimination, dishonesty is the second-best policy.

Dogs lead a nice life. You never see a dog with a wristwatch.

Ever wonder about those people who spend $2 apiece on those little bottles of Evian water? Try spelling Evian backward.

If someone with multiple personalities threatens to kill himself, is it considered a hostage situation?

"I am" is reportedly the shortest sentence in the English language. Could it be that "I do" is the longest sentence?

Most people work just hard enough not to get fired and get paid just enough money not to quit.

Why do they bother saying "raw" sewage? Do some people cook that stuff?

I was thinking about how people seem to read the Bible a whole lot more as they get older; then it dawned on me … they're cramming for their final exam.

I enjoy comparing baseball and football: Baseball is a nineteenth-century pastoral game. football is a twentieth-century technological struggle. Baseball is played on a diamond, in a park. The baseball park!

Football is played on a gridiron, in a stadium, sometimes called Soldier Field or War Memorial Stadium…. In football you wear a helmet. In baseball you wear a cap. Football is concerned with downs—what down is it? Baseball is concerned with ups—who's up? In football you receive a penalty. In baseball you make an error…. Football has hitting, clipping, spearing, piling on, personal fouls, late hitting and unnecessary roughness. Baseball has the sacrifice. Football is played in any kind of weather: rain, snow, sleet, hail, fog … In baseball, if it rains, we don't go out to play. Baseball has the seventh inning stretch. Football has the two minute warning…. In baseball, during the game, in the stands, there's kind of a picnic feeling; emotions may run high or low, but there's not too much unpleasantness. In football, during the game in the stands, you can be sure that at least 27 times you're capable of taking the life of a fellow human being. And finally, the objectives of the two games are completely different: In football the object is for the quarterback, also known as the field general, to be on target with his aerial assault, riddling the defense by hitting his receivers with deadly accuracy in spite of the blitz, even if he has to use shotgun. With short bullet passes and long bombs, he marches his troops into enemy territory, balancing this aerial assault with a sustained ground attack that punches holes in the forward wall of the enemy's defensive line. In baseball the object is to go home! And to be safe!—I hope I'll be safe at home!

W.C. FIELDS

On the whole, I'd rather be in Philadelphia. (*Fields's own epitaph*)

After two days in hospital I took a turn for the nurse.

I am free of all prejudices. I hate everyone equally.

The laziest man I ever met put popcorn in his pancakes so they would turn over by themselves.

I cook with wine, sometimes I even add it to the food.

Once, during prohibition, I was forced to live for days on nothing but food and water.

A man's got to believe in something. I believe I'll have another drink.

A woman drove me to drink … and I hadn't even the courtesy to thank her.

I never drink water because of the disgusting things that fish do in it.

Always carry a flagon of whiskey in case of snakebite and furthermore always carry a small snake.

I once spent a year in Philadelphia, I think it was on a Sunday.

Start every day with a smile and get it over with.

FRED ALLEN

I like long walks, especially when they are taken by people who annoy me.

I'd rather have a full bottle in front of me than a full frontal lobotomy.

I learned law so well, the day I graduated I sued the college, won the case, and got my tuition back.

A celebrity is a person who works hard all his life to become well-known, then wears dark glasses to avoid being recognized.

An actor's popularity is fleeting. His success has the life expectancy of a small boy who is about to look into a gas tank with a lighted match.

Some movie stars wear their sunglasses even in church. They're afraid God might recognize them and ask for autographs.

Television is a medium because anything well done is rare.

I can't understand why a person will take a year to write a novel when he can easily buy one for a few dollars.

I don't have to look up my family tree, because I know that I'm the sap.

Her hat is a creation that will never go out of style; it will just look ridiculous year after year.

The first time I sang in the church choir, two hundred people changed their religion.

I always have trouble remembering three things: faces, names, and—I can't remember what the third thing is.

An advertising agency is 85 percent confusion and 15 percent commission.

He dreamed he was eating shredded wheat and woke up to find the mattress half gone.

Hanging is too good for a man who makes puns; he should be drawn and quoted.

WISECRACKS AND WITTICISMS
(One-liners, Pithy Observations)

A little nonsense now and then is relished by the wisest men.

– *Anonymous*

When buying a used car, punch the buttons on the radio. If all the stations are rock and roll, there's a good chance that the transmission is shot.

– *Larry Lujack*

A woman, on a very hot day, greeted Mr. Berra and remarked, "My, you look mighty cool today," whereupon Berra replied, "Thank you, ma'am. You don't look so hot yourself."

– *Yogi Berra*

When I coached at Niagara, we gave recruits a piece of caramel candy. If they took the wrapper off before eating it, they got a basketball scholarship; otherwise, they got a football scholarship.

– *Frank Layden*

I don't like country music, but I don't mean to denigrate those who do. And for the people who like country music, denigrate means "put down."

– *Bob Newhart*

The goodness of a pun is proportional to its intolerableness.

– *Edgar Allan Poe*

Science has not yet found a cure for the pun.

– *Robert Byrne*

The best way to convince a fool that he is wrong is to let him have his own way.

– *Josh Billings*

A person who buries his head in the sand offers an engaging target.

– *Mabel A. Keenan*

I'm pleased that television is now showing murder stories, because it brings murder back into its rightful setting—the home.

– *Alfred Hitchcock*

The same time that women came up with PMS, men came up with ESPN.

– *Blake Clark*

A pat on the back is only a few vertebrae away from a kick in the pants.

– *Dennis Crocket*

At my age, every doctor says the same thing: It's either something I have to live with—or something I have to live without.

– *Anonymous*

The best substitute for experience is being sixteen.

– *Raymond Duncan*

Parenthood: That state of being better chaperoned than you were before marriage.

– *Marcelene Cox*

Plant and your spouse plants with you, weed and you weed alone.

– *Dennis Breeze*

The imaginary friends I had as a kid dropped me because their friends thought I didn't exist.

– *Aaron Machado*

Ever have one of those nights when you didn't want to go out but your hair looked too good to stay home?

– *Jack Simmons*

As we grow older everything seems to wear out, fall out or spread out.

– *Anonymous*

My wife has never suffered from stress, but she's a carrier.

– *Blake Clark*

Television is an invention that permits you to be entertained in your living room by people you would not have in your home.

– *David Frost*

Everyone seems normal—until you get to know them.

– *Anonymous*

It's like saying she's a beautiful girl except for her face.

– *J.D. Salinger*

If Casey Stengel were alive today, he'd be turning over in his grave.

– *Yogi Berra*

When you're wearing a short skirt and walking past a crew of construction workers, always pick your nose. It acts as a deterrent to catcalls.

– *Amy Wallace*

When you are waiting for the bus and someone asks, "Has the bus come yet?" If the bus came would I be standing here?

– *Billy Connoly*

Whenever you want to marry someone, go have lunch with his ex-wife.

– *Shelley Winters*

Here lies my wife: here let her lie!
Now she's at rest, and so am I.
— *John Dryden, 17th century*

Doctor to patient: "I have good news and bad news. The good news is that you are not a hypochondriac."
— *Anonymous*

The closest to perfection a person ever comes is when he fills out a job application.
— *Stanley J. Randall*

Everyone has the ability of making someone happy, some by entering the room, others by leaving it.
— *Anonymous*

If my doctor told me that I had only six minutes to live ... I'd type a little faster.
— *Isaac Asimov*

Please, if you ever see me getting beaten up by the police, please put your video camera down and help me.
— *Bobcat Goldthwait*

Anyone who thinks the way to a man's heart is through his stomach must have flunked anatomy.
— *Anonymous*

I don't know anything about music. In my line you don't have to.
— *Elvis Presley*

How many more bathroom-window curtains must die needlessly to clothe golfers?
— *Mike Lough*

When your husband comes home with cockleburs in the cuffs of his pants, don't ask him what his score was.
— *Sam Sneed, advice to golf widows*

By the time a man's wise enough to watch his step, he's too old to go anywhere.
— *Anonymous*

I feel safer on a racetrack ... than I do on Houston expressways.
— *A.J. Foyt*

I didn't invent the hypothetical situation, but let's just suppose for a second that I did.
— *Auggie Cook*

I've got a tooth that's driving me to extraction.
— *Edgar Bergen as Charlie McCarthy*

In spite of the cost of living, it's still popular.
— *Kathleen Norris*

If you're yearning for the good old days, just turn off the air conditioning.
— *Griff Niblack*

My luck is so bad that if I bought a cemetery, people would stop dying.
— *Ed Furgol*

Three things in life are hard to do: climb a forward-leaning fence, kiss a backward-leaning woman, and say something clever when accepting a trophy.
— *Josh Pons*

It took me 17 years to get 3,000 hits in baseball. I did it in one afternoon on the golf course.
— *Hank Aaron*

Touring pro: "I'm having trouble with my long putts."
Ben Hogan: "Why don't you try hitting your irons closer to the pin?"
— *Ben Hogan*

Do not walk behind me, for I may not lead. Do not walk ahead of me,
for I may not follow. Do not walk beside me either.
Just pretty much
leave me the hell alone.
— *Anonymous*

When a husband brings his wife flowers for no reason, there's a reason."
— *Molly McGee*

I adore life, but I don't fear death. I just prefer to die as late as possible.
— *Georges Simenon*

One loss is good for the soul. Too many losses are not good for the coach.
— *Knute Rockne*

All pro athletes are bilingual. They speak English and profanity.
— *Gordie Howe*

I went to the 30th reunion of my preschool. I didn't want to go, because I've put on like a hundred pounds.
— *Wendy Liebman*

Money talks—but credit has an echo.
— *Bob Thaves*

Some days you're the bug; some days you're the windshield.
— *Anonymous*

If I'd known how much packing I'd have to do, I'd have run again.
— *Harry S Truman, on leaving office*

Learn the lines and don't bump into the furniture.
— *Noel Coward's advice to actors*

If you want to stand in the shortest line in the world, fall in behind those who think they're overpaid.
— *Bill Vaughan*

I won't say ours was a tough school, but we had our own coroner. We used to write essays like "What I'm Going to Be If I Grow Up."
— *Lenny Bruce*

There were some judgment mistakes made [at the White House].... [But] if being dumb was a criminal offense, half these senators would be in prison.
— *Sen. Ben Nighthore Campbell*

Pro and con are opposites, that fact is clearly seen. If *progress* means to move forward, then what does *congress* mean?
— *Nipsey Russell*

My problem lies in reconciling my gross habits with my net income.
— *Errol Flynn*

I became an actor because I did poorly on law school exams.
— *Fred Grandy, Actor and U.S. Congressman*

He would not blow his nose without moralizing on conditions in the handkerchief industry.
— *Cyril Connolly, on George Orwell*

I never graduated from Iowa. I was only there for two terms—Truman's and Eisenhower's.
— *Alex Karras*

A verbal contract isn't worth the paper it's written on.
— *Samuel Goldwyn*

Why do grandparents and grandchildren get along so well? They have the same enemy—the mother.
— *Claudette Colbert*

In this world of sin and sorrow there is always something to be thankful for; as for me, I rejoice that I am not a Republican.
— *H.L. Mencken*

It is a sad fact that fifty percent of marriages in this country end in divorce. But, hey, the other half end in death. You could be one of the lucky ones.
— *Richard Jeni*

My mother says I didn't open my eyes for eight days after I was born, but when I did, the first thing I saw was an engagement ring. I was hooked.
— *Elizabeth Taylor*

The only mystery in life is why the kamikaze pilots wore helmets.
— *Al McGuire*

Getting married, like getting hanged, is a great deal less dreadful than it has been made out.
— *H.L. Mencken*

To keep your marriage brimming
with love in a loving cup,
Whenever you're wrong admit it,
Whenever you're right shut up.
— *Ogden Nash*

A converted cannibal is one who, on Friday, eats only fishermen.
— *Emily Lotney*

Nothing in the world is friendlier than a wet dog.
— *Anonymous*

My greatest strength as a consultant is to be ignorant and ask a few questions.
— *Peter Drucker*

In the country of the blind the one-eyed king can still goof up.
— *Laurence J. Peter*

Old people love to give good advice. It compensates them for their inability to set a bad example.
— *Duc de La Rochefoucauld, c. 1650*

Remember that as a teenager you are in the last stage of your life when you will be happy to hear the phone is for you.
— *Fran Lebowitz*

An atheist is a guy who watches a Notre Dame-SMU football game and doesn't care who wins.
— *Dwight D. Eisenhower*

America is the country where you buy a lifetime supply of aspirin for one dollar, and use it up in two weeks.
— *John Barrymore*

How prophetic L'Enfent was when he laid out Washington as a city that goes around in circles.
— *John Mason Brown*

We pay for the mistakes of our ancestors, and it seems only fair that they should leave us the money to pay with.
— *Don Marquis*

Adam and Eve had an ideal marriage. He didn't have to hear about all the men she could have married, and she didn't have to hear about the way his mother cooked.
— *Kimberly Broyles*

Hate your job? There's a support group for that. It's called everybody and they meet at a bar.

– Drew Carey

Some people are alive only because it is illegal to kill them.

– Anonymous

The guy who marries the boss's daughter just winds up with two bosses.

– Ethel Merman

"Like vinegar to the teeth, and smoke to the eyes, so are the lazy to their employers."

– Interpretation, Proverbs 10:26

Most people would rather die than think. In fact, some do.

– Bertrand Russell

There are three kinds of lies: lies, damned lies, and statistics.

– Benjamin Disraeli

Duct tape is like "The Force." It has a light side and a dark side, and it holds the universe together.

– Anonymous

The more you speak of yourself, the more you are likely to lie.

– Johann Zimmermann

Husbands are awkward things to deal with; even keeping them in hot water will not make them tender.

– Mary Buckle

Man who stumble over the same rock twice deserve to break neck.

– Chinese proverb

A fanatic is one who can't change his mind and won't change the subject.

– Winston Churchill

Men will confess to treason, murder, arson, false teeth, or a wig. How many of them will own up to a lack of humor?

– Frank Colby

Few people blame themselves until they have exhausted all other possibilities.

– Francis Duffy

Man once subscribed to the theory of male superiority—then woman cancelled his subscription.

– Shannon Fife

There are two theories to arguing with women. Neither one works.

– Anonymous

A woman approached President Calvin Coolidge—who was well known for his introverted nature—and remarked: "You must talk to me, Mr. Coolidge. I made a bet today that I could get more than two words out of you." Coolidge coolly replied, "You lose."

– Calvin Coolidge

The fellow that owns his own home is always just coming out of a hardware store.

– Kin Hubbard

Success, I shall tell you out of the wisdom of my years, is a toy balloon among children armed with sharp pins.

– Gene Fowler

Heredity is what sets the parents of a teenager wondering about each other.

– Laurence J. Peter

Adolescence is perhaps nature's way of preparing parents to welcome the empty nest.

– Karen Savage and Patricia Adams

The best reply to an atheist is to give him a good dinner and ask him if he believes there is a cook.

– Louis Nizer

When a man is wrapped up in himself, he makes a pretty small package.

– John Ruskin

If the Republicans will stop telling lies about the Democrats, we will stop telling the truth about them.

– Adlai Stevenson

When you have no basis for an argument, abuse the plaintiff.

– Marcus Tullius Cicero, c. 100 B.C.E.

My foul-weather friend …

– Winston Churchill

You loan a hard-covered book to a friend and when he doesn't return it you get mad at him. It makes you mean and petty. But twenty-five cent books are different.

– John Steinbeck

A statesman is a politician who's been dead for ten or fifteen years.

– Harry S Truman

Actually, I'm an overnight success. But it took me twenty years.

– Monty Hall

The handwriting on the wall may be a forgery.

– Ralph Hodgson

I know only two tunes: one of them is "Yankee Doodle," and the other isn't.

– *Ulysses S. Grant*

Opera in English is, in the main, just about as sensible as baseball in Italian.

– *H.L. Mencken*

There's a difference between a philosophy and a bumper sticker.

– *Charles M. Schultz*

Maybe death and taxes are inevitable, but death doesn't get worse every time Congress meets.

– *Joan I. Welsh*

Advice to speakers: If you don't strike oil in twenty minutes stop boring.

– *Adam S. Bennion*

The recipe for a good speech includes some shortening.

– *Gene Yasenak*

The most useful of all social graces is the ability to yawn with your mouth closed.

– *Laurence J. Peter*

Please, dear God, make my words today sweet and tender, for tomorrow I may have to eat them.

– *Anonymous*

Procrastination is the art of keeping up with yesterday.

– *Don Marquis*

Some folks never exaggerate—they just remember big.

– *Audrey Snead*

How often are we offended by not being offered something we do not really want.

– *Eric Hoffer*

Television has raised writing to a new low.

– *Sam Goldwyn*

Don't be humble. You're not that great.

– *Golda Meir*

Egotism is that special something which enables a man who's in a rut to think he's in a groove.

– *Anonymous*

If you love something, set it free. If it comes back, you treasure it. If it doesn't, hunt the sucker down and kill it.

– *Anonymous*

School is like a lollipop. It sucks until it is gone.

– *Ashley Salvati*

The taxpayer—that's someone who works for the federal government but doesn't have to take a civil service exam.

– *Ronald Reagan*

There may be luck in getting a job, but there's no luck in keeping it.

– *J. Ogden Armour*

Advertising is the art of making whole lies out of half truths.

– *Edgar A. Shoaff*

If your parents didn't have any children, there's a good chance that you won't have any.

– *Clarence Day*

You've heard of the three ages of man: youth, middle age, and "you're looking wonderful!"

– *Francis Cardinal Spellman*

Henry James was one of the nicest old ladies I ever met.

– *William Faulkner*

Drive carefully. It's not only cars that can be recalled by their maker.

– *Anonymous*

Being a child isn't what it used to be. Huck Finn is a delinquent, Tom Sawyer isn't working up to capacity, and Heidi is in foster care. Jim Hawkins is too young to be a cabin boy, and whoever would let Alice just sit there doing nothing at all but dream through a summer afternoon?

– *Anonymous*

It took a genius to develop an aspirin bottle that couldn't be opened by a child capable of operating a VCR.

– *Doug Larson*

A loser is a window washer on the 44th floor who steps back to admire his work.

– *Anonymous*

Sir: My secretary, being a lady, cannot take down, in short hand, what I would like to say to you; I, being a gentleman, cannot think it; but you, being neither, can easily guess my thoughts.

– *Anonymous*

If the English language made any sense, *lackadaisical* would have something to do with a shortage of flowers.

– *Doug Larson*

If you are going to wear a hat at all, be decisive and go the whole hat. In making a courageous choice of millinery, you have nothing to lose but your head.

– *The Bedside Guardian*

Fish and visitors stink after three days.
– Anonymous

If you're going to do something wrong, at least enjoy it.
– Leo Rosten

An expert is someone called in at the last minute to share the blame.
– Sam Ewing

Always forgive your enemies—nothing annoys them so much.
– Oscar Wilde

[When] high school seniors graduate … some will seek further expansion of knowledge through a higher education. Others will go to college.
– Anonymous

What bothers me about TV is that it tends to take our minds off our minds.
– Anonymous

Stay in college, get the knowledge.
And stay there until you're through.
If they can make penicillin out of moldy bread,
they can sure make something out of you!
– Muhammad Ali

One of the hardest things to imagine is that you are not smarter than average.
– Jonathan Fuerbringer

Reality is a temporary illusion brought on by an absence of beer.
– Anonymous

I think, therefore I'm single.
– Liz Winston

In certain situations, it pays to be open, honest, and direct, and to express your true feelings. But dating is not one of those situations.
– Gibson Greetings, Inc.

Tallulah Bankhead, on meeting a former lover for the first time in years, deadpanned, "I thought I told you to wait in the car."
Do you have any problems other than that you're unemployed, a moron, and a dork?
– John McEnroe to a fan

My wife wanted to call our daughter Sue, but I felt that in our family that was usually a verb.
– Dennis Wolfberg

Remember the good old days when a juvenile delinquent was a boy who played the saxophone too loud?
– Anonymous

If you're feeling really good about life … don't worry, it will pass.
– Anonymous

… Hell, I even thought I was dead, 'till I found out it was just that I was in Nebraska.
– Gene Hackman as Lil' Bill in The Unforgiven

Everybody lies, but it doesn't matter because nobody listens.
– Nick Diamos

Blame someone else and get on with your life.
– Alan Woods

I tend to live in the past because most of my life is there.
– Herb Caen

Don't worry about people stealing your ideas. If your ideas are any good, you'll have to ram them down people's throats.
– Howard Aiken

Successful people are very lucky. Just ask any failure.
– Michael Levine

After looking at the bill for my operation, I understand why the doctors wear masks in the operating room.
– Anonymous

We live in an age when pizza gets to your home before the police.
– Jeff Marder

The world would not be in such a snarl
Had Marx been Groucho instead of Karl.
– Irving Berlin

Somebody has to do something, and it's just incredibly pathetic that it has to be us.
– Jerry Garcia of the Grateful Dead

Why does the Air Force need expensive new bombers? Have the people we've been bombing over the years been complaining?
– George Wallace

I was born with a priceless gift, the ability to laugh at the misfortunes of others.
– Dame Edna Everage

It's time to open your parachute when cars look as big as ants. If ants look as big as cars, you've waited too long.
– Ernst Luposchainsky III

Never miss a chance to keep your mouth shut.
– Robert Newton Peck

When are you going to realize that if it doesn't apply to me it doesn't matter?

— *Murphy Brown (Candice Bergen)*

A weed is a plant that has mastered every survival skill except learning how to grow in rows.

— *Doug Larson*

The object of most prayers is to wangle an advance on good intentions.

— *Robert Brault*

God in His wisdom made the fly
And then forgot to tell us why.

— *Ogden Nash*

Your worst humiliation is only someone else's momentary entertainment.

— *Karen Crockett*

If Moses had been a committee the Israelites would still be in Egypt.

— *J.B. Hughes*

Mother, food, love, and career are the four major guilt groups.

— *Cathy Guisewite*

We all basically go back to being children in the dentist's chair.

— *Arthur Benjamin*

Don't cross this field unless you can do it in 9.9 seconds. The bull can do it in 10.

— *Sign on a bison range*

It is not that the U.S. Government is an entirely comic matter; but to deal in power, ambition, and the people driven by both, a fine madness and sense of humor are handy things to have.

— *Barbara Howard, Laughing All the Way*

A new study suggests TV may contribute to clinical depression. It's what's known in scientific language as going down the tube.

— *Bill Tammeus*

Most rock journalism is people who can't write interviewing people who can't talk for people who can't read.

— *Frank Zappa*

Dear Sir, Your profession has, as usual, destroyed your brain.

— *George Bernard Shaw, letter to a journalist*

I had never had a piece of toast
Particularly long and wide,
But fell upon the sanded floor,
And always on the buttered side.

— *James Payne*

To be rich is no longer a sin; it's a miracle.

— *Anonymous*

When women are depressed they either eat or go shopping. Men invade another country. It's a whole different way of thinking.

— *Elayne Boosler*

I have long thought that the aging process could be slowed down if it had to work its way through Congress.

— *George Bush's gag writers*

I would never die for my beliefs because I might be wrong.

— *Bertrand Russell*

Adorable children are considered to be the general property of the human race. Rude children belong to their mothers.

— *Judith Martin*

We hope that, when the insects take over the world, they will remember with gratitude how we took them along on all our picnics.

— *Bill Vaughan*

If there's one major cause for the spread of mass illiteracy, it's the fact that everybody can read and write.

— *Peter De Vries*

If you're hanging around with nothing to do and the zoo is closed, come over to the Senate. You'll get the same kind of feeling and you won't have to pay.

— *Robert Dole*

The people I'm furious with are the women's liberationists. They keep getting up on soapboxes and proclaiming women are brighter than men. That's true, but it should be kept quiet or it ruins the whole racket.

— *Anita Loos*

Too often, the opportunity knocks, but by the time you push back the chain, push back the bolt, unhook the two locks and shut off the burglar alarm, it's too late.

— *Rita Coolidge*

Well, I certainly don't believe God's a woman, because if He were, men would be the ones walking around wearing high heels, taking Midol, and having their upper lips waxed.

— *Dixie Carter*

When primitive man screamed and beat the ground with sticks, they called it "witchcraft." hen modern man does the same thing, they call it "golf."

— *Ann Landers*

I would venture to guess that Anon, who wrote so many poems without signing them, was a woman.
– Virginia Woolf

Boys will be boys, and so will a lot of middle-aged men.
– Kin Hubbard

A flirtatious letter addressed to George Bernard Shaw included the line: *You have the greatest brain in the world, and I have the most beautiful body; so we ought to produce the most perfect child.* Shaw replied with: *What if the child inherits my body and your brains?*
– George Bernard Shaw

If at first you don't succeed, try looking in the wastebasket for the instructions.
– Ann Landers

A neighborhood is where, when you get out of it, you get beat up.
– Murray Kempton

Somebody's boring me. I think it's me.
– Dylan Thomas

If you couldn't read, you couldn't look up what was on television.
– From the "Leave It to Beaver" show

A lawyer with a briefcase can steal more than a thousand men with guns.
– Mario Puzo

The reason there is so little crime in Germany is that it's against the law.
– Alex Levin

A decision is what a man makes when he can't find anybody to serve on a committee.
– Fletcher Knebel

I want my data back, scumbag, and I want it back now!
– Secretary overheard conversing with her computer

Communism doesn't work because people like to own stuff.
– Frank Zappa

Don't bother discussing sex with small children. They rarely have anything to add.
– Fran Lebowitz

The surest sign that intelligent life exists elsewhere in the universe is that it has never tried to contact us.
– Calvin and Hobbes comic by Bill Watterson

I hate being a bureaucrat and will resign as soon as I know the proper procedure.
– Hector Breeze

In response to one critic's scornful accusation, "Mr. Churchill, you are drunk," Churchill replied, "And you madam, are ugly, but I shall be sober tomorrow."

Until you've lost your reputation, you never realize what a burden it was.
– Margaret Mitchell

Never accept an invitation from a stranger unless he offers you candy.
– Linda Festa

This life is a test; it is only a test. If it were a real life, you would receive instructions on where to go and what to do.
– Anonymous

A nursery school teacher was delivering a station wagon full of kids home one day when a fire truck zoomed past. Sitting in the front seat of the fire truck was a Dalmatian dog. The children fell to discussing the dog's duties. "They use him to keep crowds back," said one youngster. "No," said another, "he's just for good luck." A third child brought the argument to a close. "They use the dogs," she said firmly, "to find the fire hydrant."

As an instructor in driver education at Unionville-Sebewaing Area High School in Michigan, I've learned that even the brightest students can become flustered behind the wheel. One day I had three beginners in the car, each scheduled to drive for 30 minutes. When the first student had completed his time, I asked him to change places with one of the others. Gripping the wheel tightly and staring straight ahead, he asked in a shaky voice, "Should I stop the car?"

A little boy opened the big, old family Bible with fascination, he looked at the old pages as he turned them. Then something fell out of the Bible and he picked it up and looked at it closely. It was an old leaf from a tree that had been pressed in between pages. "Momma, look what I found," the boy called out. "What have you got there, dear?" his mother asked. With astonishment in the young boy's voice he answered, "It's Adam's suit!!!"

One summer evening during a violent thunderstorm a mother was tucking her small boy into bed. She was about to turn off the light when he asked with a tremor in his voice, "Mommy, will you sleep with me tonight?" The mother smiled and gave him a reassuring hug. "I can't dear," she said. "I have to sleep in Daddy's room." A long silence was broken at last by his shaking little voice: "The big sissy."

Nine-year-old Joey was asked by his mother what he had learned in Sunday School. Joey said, "Well, Mom, our teacher told us how God sent Moses behind enemy lines on a rescue mission to lead the Israelites out of Egypt. When he got to the Red Sea, he had his engineers build a pontoon bridge, and all the people walked across safely. He used his walkie-talkie to radio headquarters and call in an air strike. They sent in bombers to blow up the bridge, and all the Israelites were saved." The mother gasped, "Now, Joey, is that REALLY what your teacher taught you?" The boy replied, "Well, no, but if I told it the way the teacher did, you'd never believe it!"

A mother took her 3-year-old daughter to church for the first time. The church lights were lowered, and then the choir came down the aisle, carrying lighted candles. All was quiet until the little one started to sing in a loud voice, "Happy birthday to you, Happy birthday to you... "

Ever notice how a 4-year-old's voice is louder than 200 adult voices? Several years ago I returned home from a trip just when a storm hit, with crashing thunder and severe lightning. As I came into my bedroom about 2 am, I found my two children in bed with my wife, Karey, apparently scared by the loud storm. I resigned myself to sleeping in the guest bedroom that night. The next day, I talked to the children, and explained that it was fine to sleep with Mom when the storm was bad, but when I was expected home, please don't sleep with Mom that night. They said OK. After my next trip several weeks later, Karey and the children picked me up in the terminal at the appointed time. Since the plane was late, everyone had come into the terminal to wait for my plane's arrival, along with hundreds of other folks waiting for their arriving passengers. As I entered the waiting area, my son saw me, and came running, shouting, "Hi, Dad! I've got some good news!" As I waved back, I said loudly, "What's the good news?" "Nobody slept with Mommy while you were away this time!" Alex shouted. The airport became very quiet, as everyone in the waiting area looked at Alex, hen turned to me, and then searched the rest of the area to see if they could figure out exactly who his Mom was.

An acquaintance of mine who is a physician told this story about her then four-year-old daughter. On the way to preschool, the doctor had left her stethoscope on the car seat, and her little girl picked it up and began playing with it. "Be still, my heart," thought my friend, "my daughter wants to follow in my footsteps!" Then the child spoke into the instrument: "Welcome to McDonald's. May I take your order?"

A certain little girl, when asked her name, would reply, "I'm Mr. Sugarbrown's daughter." Her mother told her this was wrong; she must say, "I'm Jane Sugarbrown." The Vicar spoke to her in Sunday School, and said, "Aren't you Mr. Sugarbrown's daughter?" She replied, "I thought I was, but mother says I'm not."

Finding one of her students making faces at others on the playground, Ms. Smith stopped to gently reprove the child. Smiling sweetly, the teacher said, "Bobby, when I was a child, I was told if that I made ugly faces, it would freeze and I would stay like that." Bobby looked up and replied, "Well, Ms Smith, you can't say you weren't warned.

A Sunday school teacher asked her little children, as they were on the way to the church service, "And why is it necessary to be quiet in church?" One bright little girl replied, "Because people are sleeping."

A salesman calls this house, and the three-year-old son answers the phone. The salesman asks, "Can I talk to your mother?" The boy whispers in a very low voice, "She's busy." The salesman asks, "Can I talk to your daddy?" The kid whispers again, in a very low voice, "He's busy too." The salesman then asks, "Is there anyone else there?" The tot replies in the same quiet voice, "A policeman." The salesman inquires, "Can I talk to the policeman?" The boy repeats again, in a low whisper, "He's busy too." The salesman again questions him and asks, "Is there anyone else there?" The kid comes back in a whisper, "A fireman." The salesman then wants to know if he can talk to the fireman. And once again the tot whispers, "He's busy too." By now the salesman is really wondering what is going on. He asks the boy, "What are they all doing?" The little rug-rat replies, still in a very low whisper... "Looking for me."

LETTERS TO GOD

A teacher of children invited her students to write God and tell Him something about themselves or ask Him a question. The results were quite insightful:

Dear God...
... In bible times did they really talk that fancy?

– Jennifer

... I went to this wedding and they kissed right in church. Is that ok?

– Neil

... If you will watch in Church on Sunday I will show you my new shoes.

– Mickey D.

... I think the stapler is one of your greatest inventions.

– Ruth M.

... We read that Thomas Edison made light. But in Sunday School they said that you did it. So I bet he stoled your idea.

– Sincerely, Donna

... Please send Dennis Clark to a different camp this year.

– Peter

... Thank you for the baby brother, but what I prayed for was a puppy.

– Joyce

... I am an Amearican. What are you?

– Robert

... I think about you sometimes even when I'm not praying.

– Elliott

... Instead of letting people die and having to make new ones why don't you just keep the ones you got now?

– Jane

PROVERBS AND FROM A YOUNGSTER'S PERSPECTIVE

A first grade teacher collected well-known proverbs. She gave each child in the class the first half of the proverb, and asked them to come up with the rest. Here are some of the results:

Better to be safe than ... punch a 5th grader. Strike while the ... bug is close.

You can lead a horse to water but ... how?

Don't bite the hand that ... looks dirty.

No news is ... impossible. A miss is as good as a ... mister.

If you lie down with dogs, you ... will stink in the morning.

An idle mind is ... the best way to relax.

A penny saved is ... not much.

Children should be seen and not ... spanked or grounded.

You get out of something what you ... see pictured on the box.

When the blind lead the blind ... get out of the way.

A day without sunshine is like ... night.

Laugh and the whole world laughs with you.

Cry and ... you have to blow your nose.

A rolling stone ... plays the guitar.

The grass is always greener ... when you remember to water it.

A bird in the hand is ... a real mess.

It's always darkest just before ... I open my eyes.

The squeaking wheel gets ... annoying.

We have nothing to fear but ... our principal.

I think, therefore I ... get a headache.

Laugh and the world laughs with you. Cry, and ... someone yells, "Shut up!"

Early to bed and early to rise ... is first in the bathroom.

A journey of a thousand miles begins with ... a blister.

WISE ADVICE FROM KIDS

You can never trust a dog to watch your food.
— *Patrick, age 10*

When your dad is mad and asks you, "Do I look stupid?" don't answer him.
— *Heather, 16*

Never tell your mom her diet's not working.
— *Michael, 14*

Stay away from prunes.
— *Randy, 9*

Never pee on an electric fence.
— *Robert, 13*

When your mom is mad at your dad, don't let her brush your hair.
— *Taylia, 11*

Never allow your three-year-old brother in the same room as your homework assignment.
— *Traci, 14*

Don't sneeze in front of anyone when you're eating crackers.
— *Mitchell, 12*

Never try to hold a dust buster and a cat at the same time.
— *Kyoyo, 9*

You can't hide a piece of broccoli in a glass of milk.
— *Armir, 9*

Don't wear polka-dot underwear under white shorts.
— *Kellie, 11*

If you want a kitten, start out by asking for a horse.
— *Naomi, 15*

Felt markers are not good to use as lipstick.
— *Lauren, 9*

Don't pick on your sister when she's holding a baseball bat.
— *Joel, 10*

When you get a bad grade in school, show it to your mom when she's on the phone.
— *Alyesha, 13*

Don't try to baptize a cat.
— *Eileen, 8*

Never spit when on a roller coaster.
— *Scott, 11*

Never do pranks at a police station.
— *Sam, 10*

Listen to your brain. It has lots of information
— *Chelsey, 7*

Never dare your little brother to paint the family car.
— *Phillip, 13*

Forget the cake. Go for the icing!
— *Cynthia, 8*

When you want something expensive, ask your grandparents.
— *Matthew, 12*

Never smart off to a teacher whose eyes and ears are twitching.
— *Andrew, 9*

Don't squat with your spurs on.
— *Noronha, 13*

Wear a hat when feeding seagulls.
— *Rocky, 9*

If you are wearing suspenders with one strap down, you need to be careful going to the bathroom.
— *Anon, 10*

Don't flush the toilet when your dad's in the shower.
— *Lamar, 10*

Don't ever be too full for dessert.
— *Kelly, 10*

Never ask for anything that costs more than five dollars when your parents are doing taxes.
— *Carrol, 9*

I've learned that my daddy can say a lot of words I can't.
— *Anon, 8*

I've learned that if you want to cheer yourself up, you should try cheering someone else up.
— *Anon, 13*

I've learned that it always makes me feel good to see my parents holding hands.
— *Anon, 13*

I've learned that you shouldn't confuse a black crayon with a Tootsie Roll.
— *Anon, 10*

I've learned that gold fish don't like jello.
— *Anon, 5*

I've learned that the teacher always calls on me the time I don't know the answer.
— *Anon, 9*

THINGS I'VE LEARNED FROM MY CHILDREN

(from an anonymous mother in Austin, Texas)

A king size waterbed holds enough water to fill a 2,000 sq. foot house 4 inches deep.

If you spray hair spray on dust bunnies and run over them with roller blades, they can ignite.

A three-year-old's voice is louder than 200 adults in a crowded restaurant.

If you hook a dog leash over a ceiling fan, the motor is not strong enough to rotate a 42-pound boy wearing Batman underwear and a superman cape. It is strong enough, however, to spread paint on all four walls of a 20x20 foot room.

You should not throw baseballs up when the ceiling fan is on. When using the ceiling fan as a bat, you have to throw the ball up a few times before you get a hit. A ceiling fan can hit a baseball a long way.

The glass in windows (even double pane) doesn't stop a baseball hit by a ceiling fan.

When you hear the toilet flush and the words "Uh-oh", it's already too late.

Brake fluid mixed with Clorox makes smoke, and lots of it.

Certain Legos will pass through the digestive tract of a four-year-old.

Play Dough and *microwave* should never be used in the same sentence.

Super glue is forever.

No matter how much Jell-O you put in a swimming pool you still can't walk on water.

Pool filters do not like Jell-O.

VCR's do not eject PB&J sandwiches even though TV commercials show they do.

Garbage bags do not make good parachutes.

Marbles in gas tanks make lots of noise when driving.

You probably do not want to know what that odor is.

Always look in the oven before you turn it on.

Plastic toys do not like ovens.

The fire department in Austin has a 5-minute response time.

The spin cycle on the washing machine does not make earthworms dizzy. It will however make cats dizzy and cats throw up twice their body weight when dizzy.

A KID'S-EYE VIEW OF LOVE

What Most People Are Thinking When They Say "I Love You"?

"The person is thinking: Yeah, I really do love him. But I hope he showers at least once a day."
– *Michelle, age 9*

"Some lovers might be real nervous, so they are glad that they finally got it out and said it and now they can go eat."
– *Dick, 7*

Concerning Why Love Happens Between Two Particular People

"One of the people has freckles and so he finds somebody else who has freckles too."
– *Andrew, 6*

"No one is sure why it happens, but I heard it has something to do with how you smell.... That's why perfume and deodorant are so popular."
– *Mae, 9*

"I think you're supposed to get shot with an arrow or something, but the rest of it isn't supposed to be so painful."
– *Manuel, 8*

On What Falling In Love Is Like

"Like an avalanche where you have to run for your life."
– *John, 9*

"If falling in love is anything like learning how to spell, I don't want to do it. It takes too long."
– *Glenn, 7*

On The Role Of Beauty And Handsomeness In Love

"If you want to be loved by somebody who isn't already in your family, it doesn't hurt to be beautiful."
– *Anita C, 8*

"It isn't always just how you look. Look at me. I'm handsome like anything and I haven't got anybody to marry me yet."
– *Brian, 7*

"Beauty is skin deep. But how rich you are can last a long time."
– *Christine, 9*

Reflections On The Nature Of Love

"Love is the most important thing in the world, but baseball is pretty good too."

– Greg, 8

How Do People In Love Typically Behave?

"Mushy … like puppy dogs … except puppy dogs don't wag their tails nearly as much."

– Arnold, 10

"All of a sudden, the people get movies fever so they can sit together in the dark."

– Sherm, 8

Concerning Why Lovers Often Hold Hands

"They want to make sure their rings don't fall off because they paid good money for them."

– Gavin, 8

"They are just practicing for when they might have to walk down the aisle someday and do the holy matchimony thing."

– John, 9

Confidential Opinions About Love

"I'm in favor of love as long as it doesn't happen when 'Dinosaurs' is on television."

– Jill, 6

"Love is foolish … but I still might try it sometime."

– Floyd, 9

"Yesterday I kissed a girl in a private place …. We were behind a tree."

– Carey, 7

"Love will find you, even if you are trying to hide from it. I been trying to hide from it since I was five, but the girls keep finding me."

– Dave, 8

"I'm not rushing into being in love. I'm finding fourth grade hard enough."

– Regina, 10

Some Surfire Ways To Make A Person Fall In Love With You

"Tell them that you own a whole bunch of candy stores."

– Del, 6

"Shake your hips and hope for the best."

– Camille, 9

"Don't do things like have smelly, green sneakers. You might get attention, but attention ain't the same thing as love."

– Alonzo, 9

"One way is to take the girl out to eat. Make sure it's something she likes to eat. French fries usually works for me."

– Bart, 9

How Can You Tell If Two Adults Eating Dinner At A Restaurant Are In Love?

"Just see if the man picks up the check … "

– Bobby, 9

"Lovers will just be staring at each other and their food will get cold…. Other people care more about the food."

– Bart, 9

"See if the man has lipstick on his face."

– Sandra, 7

"It's love if they order one of those desserts that are on fire. They like to order those because it's just like how their hearts are—on fire."

– Christine, 9

How Was Kissing Invented?

"I know one reason that kissing was created. It makes you feel warm all over, and they didn't always have electric heat or fireplaces or even stoves in their houses."

– Gina, 8

How A Person Learns To Kiss

"You can have a big rehearsal with your Barbie and Ken dolls."

– Julia, 7

"You learn it right on the spot when the gooshy feelings get the best of you."

– Brian, 7

"It might help to watch soap operas all day."

– Carin, 9

When Is It Okay To Kiss Someone?

"When they're rich."

– Pam, 7

"It's never okay to kiss a boy. They always slobber all over you . . . . That's why I stopped doing it."
— *Tammy, 7*

"If it's your mother, you can kiss her anytime. But if it's a new person, you have to ask permission."
— *Roger, 6*

"The law says you have to be eighteen, so I wouldn't want to mess with that."
— *Curt, 7*

"The rule goes like this: If you kiss someone, then you should marry them and have kids with them. It's the right thing to do."
— *Howard, 8*

How To Make Love Endure

"Spend most of your time loving instead of going to work."
— *Dick, 7*

"Don't forget your wife's name . . . . That will mess up the love."
— *Erin, 8*

"Be a good kisser. It might make your wife forget that you never take out the trash."
— *Dave, 8*

"Don't say you love somebody and then change your mind . . . . Love isn't like picking what movie you want to watch."
— *Natalie, 9*

What Do Most People Do On A Date?

"Dates are for having fun, and people should use them to get to know each other. Even boys have something to say if you listen long enough.
— *Lynnette, 8*

"On the first date, they just tell each other lies, and that usually gets them interested enough to go for a second date."
— *Martin, 10*

How Do You Decide Who To Marry?

"You got to find somebody who likes the same stuff. Like if you like sports, she should like it that you like sports, and she should keep the chips and dip coming."
— *Alan, 10*

"No person really decides before they grow up who they're going to marry. God decides it all way before, and you get to find out later who you're stuck with."
— *Kirsten, 10*

What Is The Right Age To Get Married?

"Twenty-three is the best age because you know the person FOREVER by then."
— *Camille, 10*

"No age is good to get married at. You got to be a fool to get married."
— *Freddie, 6*

How Can A Stranger Tell If Two People Are Married?

"Married people usually look happy to talk to other people."
— *Eddie, 6*

"You might have to guess, based on whether they seem to be yelling at the same kids."
— *Derrick, 8*

What Do You Think Your Mom And Dad Have In Common?

"Both don't want no more kids."
— *Lori, 8*

Is It Better To Be Single Or Married?

"It's better for girls to be single but not for boys. Boys need someone to clean up after them."
— *Anita, 9*

"Single is better, for the simple reason that I wouldn't want to change no diapers. Of course, if I did get married, I'd just phone my mother and have her come over for some coffee and diaper-changing."
— *Kirsten, 10*

How Would The World Be Different If People Didn't Get Married?

"There sure would be a lot of kids to explain, wouldn't there?"
— *Kelvin, 8*

"You can be sure of one thing—the boys would come chasing after us just the same as they do now."
— *Roberta, 7*

How Would You Make A Marriage Work?

"Tell your wife that she looks pretty even if she looks like a truck."

– Ricky, 10

QUESTIONS-AND-(MOSTLY)-ANSWER TIME!

The beguiling ideas about science quoted here were gleaned from essays, exams, and classroom discussions. Most were from 5th and 6th graders. They illustrate Mark Twain's contention that the "most interesting information comes from children, for they tell all they know and then stop."

Question: What is one horsepower? Answer: One horsepower is the amount of energy it takes to drag a horse 500 feet in one second.

You can listen to thunder after lightening and tell how close you came to getting hit. If you don't hear it you got hit, so never mind.

Talc is found on rocks and on babies.

The law of gravity says no fair jumping up without coming back down.

When they broke open molecules, they found they were only stuffed with atoms. But when they broke open atoms, they found them stuffed with explosions.

When people run around and around in circles we say they are crazy. When planets do it we say they are orbiting.

Rainbows are just to look at, not to really understand.

Someday we may discover how to make magnets that can point in any direction.

South America has cold summers and hot winters, but somehow they still manage.

Most books now say our sun is a star. But it still knows how to change back into a sun in the daytime.

Water freezes at 32 degrees and boils at 212 degrees. There are 180 degrees between freezing and boiling because there are 180 degrees between north and south.

A vibration is a motion that cannot make up its mind which way it wants to go.

There are 26 vitamins in all, but some of the letters are yet to be discovered. Finding them all means living forever.

There is a tremendous weight pushing down on the center of the Earth because of so much population stomping around up here these days.

Lime is a green-tasting rock.

Many dead animals in the past changed to fossils while others preferred to be oil.

Genetics explain why you look like your father and if you don't why you should.

Vacuums are nothings. We only mention them to let them know we know they're there.

Some people can tell what time it is by looking at the sun. But I have never been able to make out the numbers.

We say the cause of perfume disappearing is evaporation. Evaporation gets blamed for a lot of things people forget to put the top on.

To most people solutions mean finding the answers. But to chemists solutions are things that are still all mixed up.

In looking at a drop of water under a microscope, we find there are twice as many H's as O's.

Clouds are highflying fogs.

I am not sure how clouds get formed. But the clouds know how to do it, and that is the important thing.

Clouds just keep circling the earth around and around. And around. There is not much else to do.

Cyanide is so poisonous that one drop of it on a dogs tongue will kill the strongest man.

A blizzard is when it snows sideways.

A monsoon is a French gentleman.

Thunder is a rich source of loudness.

Isotherms and isobars are even more important than their names sound.

It is so hot in some places that the people there have to live in other places.

The wind is like the air, only pushier.

MAXIMS AND MOTTOS
(Piercing Insights and Uncommon-Sense Advice)

Beware of unsolicited advice.

– Akiba, The Talmud

Never give advice. Look at Socrates, a noted Greek philosopher, who went around giving good advice ... and they poisoned him.

– Anonymous

The best is yet to come.

– Anonymous

Straighten up your room first, then the world.

– Jeff Jordan

You cannot plow a field by turning it over in your mind. You have to get off your butt and do something!

– Dail C. West

Nothing great was ever achieved without enthusiasm.

– Ralph Waldo Emerson

Never give in, never give in—never—in nothing, great or small, large or petty—never give in except to convictions of honour and good sense.

– Winston Churchill

The best place to find helping hands is at the end of your own arms.

– Confucius

And now here is my secret, a very simple secret: It is only with the heart that one can see rightly; what is essential is invisible to the eye.

– Antoine de Saint-Exupery

It is sometimes necessary to step backward in order to go forward.

– French saying

The shoe that fits one person pinches another; there is no recipe for living that suits all cases.

– Carl Jung

The only ones ... who will be really happy are those who have sought and found how to serve.

– Albert Schweitzer

People are lonely because they build walls instead of bridges.

– Joseph Fort Newton

The dog barks, but the caravan moves on.

– Arabic proverb

Of course everything has been said that needs to be said—but since no one was listening it has to be said again.

– Anonymous

It is better to die on your feet than live on your knees.

– Dolores Ibarruri

My duty is to obey orders.

– Stonewall Jackson

One can acquire everything in solitude—except character.

– Stendhal

The tragedy of love is indifference.

– W. Sommerset Maugham

Draw your salary before spending it.

– George Ade

Neither a borrower nor a lender be.

– William Shakespeare, Hamlet

If we don't change direction, we will arrive at where we are going.

– Richard L. Evans

News is the first draft of history.

– Benjamin Bradlee

Ideas shape the course of history.

– John Maynard Keynes

History is bunk.

– Henry Ford

History ... is a nightmare from which I am trying to awake.

– James Joyce, Ulysses

There can be no freedom or beauty about a home life that depends on borrowing and debt.

– Henrik Ibsen, A Doll's House

Whatever you have, spend less.

– Samuel Johnson

You can't help getting older, but you don't have to get old.

– George Burns

There is no substitute for hard work.

– Thomas Edison

I'm curious about jumping off a cliff, and I won't do that either.

– Herschel Walker, on why he wasn't curious about taking a drink

A small daily task, if it be really daily, will beat the labors of a spasmodic Hercules.

– Anthony Trollope

Don't blame the mirror if your face is faulty.
— *Nikolai Gogol*

Statistics are no substitute for judgment.
— *Henry Clay*

It is easier to resist at the beginning than at the end.
— *Leonardo da Vinci*

Being entirely honest with oneself is a good exercise.
— *Sigmund Freud*

You can't get spoiled if you do your own ironing.
— *Meryl Streep*

To be able to say how much you love is to love but little.
— *Petrarch*

Honor is not the exclusive property of any political party.
— *Herbert Hoover*

Always be sure you're right, then go ahead.
— *Davey Crockett*

Chill out, folks. You can't shake hands with a clenched fist.
— *Ann Landers (from I. Gandhi)*

Work keeps us from three great evils—boredom, vice and need.
— *Voltaire*

He who has begun has half done. Dare to be wise; begin!
— *Horace*

When eating bamboo sprouts, remember the man who planted them.
— *Chinese proverb*

Nothing is worth more than this day.
— *Johann Goethe*

Those who have the most to do and are willing to work will find the most time.
— *Samuel Smiles*

Failure is an event, never a person.
— *William D. Brown*

Good manners and soft words have brought many a difficult thing to pass.
— *Aesop*

Act well at the moment and you have performed a good action to all eternity.
— *Johann Kaspar Lavater*

Because half a dozen grasshoppers under a fern make the field ring with their importunate chirps, do not imagine that they are the only inhabitants of the field.
— *John Bunyan*

A teacher affects eternity; he can never tell where his influence stops.
— *Henry Adams*

Cleverness is not wisdom.
— *Euripides*

Leadership is action, not position.
— *Donald H. McGannon*

The man who insists on seeing with perfect clearness before he decides, never decides.
— *Henri Frederic Amiel*

Ask thyself, daily, to how many ill-minded persons thou has shown a kind disposition.
— *Marcus Antoninus*

A fool may be known by six things: anger without cause; speech without profit; change without progress; inquiry without object; putting trust in a stranger; and mistaking foes for friends.
— *Arab proverb*

There are only two kinds of people who fail: Those who listen to nobody, and … those who listen to everybody.
— *Thomas M. Beshere, Jr.*

Ability without ambition is like kindling wood without the spark.
— *Anonymous*

Rest is not idleness, and to lie sometimes on the grass under the trees, listening to the murmur of the water, or watching the clouds float across the blue sky, is by no means a waste of time.
— *Lord Avebury*

A wise man will make more opportunities than he finds.
— *Francis Bacon*

The ants find kingdoms in a foot of ground.
— *William Rose Benet*

We should learn, by reflecting on the misfortunes of others, that there is nothing singular in those which befall ourselves.
— *William Melmoth*

Charity should begin at home, but it should not stay there.
— *Phillips Brooks*

He who loses wealth loses much; he who loses a friend loses more; but he who loses courage loses all.
— *Miguel de Cervantes*

A single conversation across the table with a wise man is worth a month's study of books.
— *Chinese proverb*

Strive for excellence, not perfection.

– H. Jackson Brown, Jr.

Do what you can, with what you have, where you are.

– Theodore Roosevelt

Better guide well the young than reclaim them when they are old.

– Joseph Malin

Make it a rule of life never to regret and never to look back. Regret is an appalling waste of energy.

– Katherine Mansfield

Obstacles are those frightful things you see when you take your eyes off the goal.

– Hannah Moore

Every man goes down to his death bearing in his hands only that which he has given away.

– Persian proverb

It is with our judgments as with our watches; no two go alike, yet each believes his own.

– Alexander Pope

We have no more right to consume happiness without producing it than to consume wealth without producing it.

– George Bernard Shaw

It is not enough to be industrious—so are the ants. What are you industrious about?

– Henry David Thoreau

Keep your face toward the sunshine and the shadows will fall behind you.

– Walt Whitman

The measure of success is not whether you had a tough problem to deal with, but whether it's the same problem you had last year.

– John Foster Dulles

Sometimes a person has to go a very long distance out of his way to come back a short distance correctly.

– Edward Albee, Zoo Story

To live for some future goal is shallow. It's the sides of the mountain that sustain life, not the top.

– Robert M. Pirsing

There never was a day that did not bring its own opportunity for doing good that never could have been done before, and never can be done again.

– William Burleigh

To consider oneself different from ordinary men is wrong, but it is right to hope that one will remain like ordinary men.

– Publilius Syrus

Happy is he who has been able to learn the causes of things.

– Virgil

Perhaps someday it will be pleasant to remember even this.

– Virgil

No man is justified in doing evil on the grounds of expediency.

– Theodore Roosevelt

Words are easy, like the wind; faithful friends are hard to find.

– Richard Barnfield

The ladder of life is full of splinters, but they always prick the hardest when we are sliding down.

– William L. Brownell

A Good life fears not Life nor Death.

– Thomas Fuller

One vice worn out makes us wiser than fifty tutors.

– Edward G. Bulwer-Lytton

Only your real friends will tell you when your face is dirty.

– Sicilian proverb

An idle man is like a house that hath no walls; the devils may enter on every side.

– Geoffrey Chaucer

Hope is the dream of a waking man.

– Diogenes

Say as little as possible while appearing to be awake.

– William P. Rogers, on attending meetings

To acquire self-discipline and self-control, you start with a single step: you decide that you can do it.

– Norman Vincent Peale

As land is improved by sowing it with various seeds, so is the mind by exercising it with different studies.

– Pliny the Elder

In everything consider the end.

– French proverb

It is a bad plan that admits of no modification.

– Publilius Syrus

Before we passionately desire anything which another possesses, we should examine as to the happiness of the possessor.

– Francois Rochefoucauld

The wise does at once what the fool does at last.

– Baltasar Gracian

It's not how old you are, but how you are old.
— *Marie Dressler*

Habits are at first cobwebs; at last, chains.
— *English proverb*

Every path hath a puddle.
— *John Ray*

Bad habits are as infectious by example as the plague itself is by contact.
— *Henry Fielding*

It is better to shoot for the stars and miss than aim at the gutter and hit it.
— *Anonymous*

In Life as in Football
Fall Forward when you fall.
— *Arthur Guiterman*

To face despair and not give in to it, that's courage.
— *Ted Koppel*

Sometimes you can't see yourself clearly until you see yourself through the eyes of others.
— *Ellen DeGeneres*

You won't find a solution by saying there is no problem.
— *William Rostler*

When you read a classic, you do not see more in the book than you did before; you see more in you than there was before.
— *Clifton Fadiman*

Trust because you are willing to accept the risk, not because it's safe or certain.
— *Stephen C. Paul*

If you want to earn more than you get, you need to be worth more than you are paid.
— *Anonymous*

I never did anything worth doing by accident, nor did any of my inventions come by accident. They came by work.
— *Thomas A. Edison*

Common sense is not common.
— *Will Rogers*

He who can take advice is sometimes superior to him who can give it.
— *Karl von Knebel*

Our faults irritate us most when we see them in others.
— *Pennsylvania Dutch proverb*

Even a single hair casts its shadow.
— *Publilius Syrus*

One can pay back the loan of gold, but one dies forever in debt to those who are kind.
— *Malay proverb*

You never really lose until you quit trying.
— *Mike Ditka*

Eighty percent of success is showing up.
— *Woody Allen*

A rattlesnake that doesn't bite teaches you nothing.
— *Jessamyn West, The Life I Really Lived*

If you can't stand the heat, get out of the kitchen.
— *Harry S Truman*

The best thing to do behind a person's back is pat it.
— *Franklin P. Jones*

Dig the well before you are thirsty.
— *Chinese proverb*

A mule dressed in a tuxedo is still a mule. If a man calleth thee a donkey, pay him no mind. If two men calleth thee a donkey, get thee a saddle.
— *Yiddish proverb*

You get out of life just what you put into it—minus taxes.
— *Al Lerrera*

Everybody is ignorant, only on different subjects.
— *Will Rogers*

Do not free a camel of the burden of his hump. You may be freeing him from being a camel.
— *G.K. Chesterton*

The porcupine, whom one must handle gloved, may be respected, but is never loved.
— *Arthur Guiterman*

He is educated who knows how to find out what he doesn't know.
— *George Simmel*

Everyone must row with the oars he has.
— *English proverb*

He that is everywhere is nowhere.
— *Thomas Fuller*

Don't look back. Something might be gaining on you.
— *Leroy "Satchel" Paige*

Lose an hour in the morning, and you will be all day hunting for it.
— *Richard Whately*

Stopping at third base adds nothing to the score.
— *Anonymous*

This above all: to thine own self be true,/ And it must follow, as the night the day,/ Thou canst not then be false to any man.

— *William Shakespeare, Hamlet*

The middle of the road is where the white line is—and that's the worst place to drive.

— *Robert Frost*

That lucky rabbit's foot didn't work for the rabbit.

— *Anonymous*

Watch the little things; a small leak will sink a great ship.

— *Benjamin Franklin*

Plan ahead.... It wasn't raining when Noah built the ark.

— *Anonymous*

Behold the turtle: He only makes progress when he sticks his neck out.

— *James B. Conant*

Every man is a damn fool for at least five minutes every day; wisdom consists in not exceeding the limit.

— *Elbert Hubbard*

The reverse side also has a reverse side.

— *Japanese proverb*

Chronic remorse is a most undesirable sentiment.... Rolling in the mud is not the best way of getting clean.

— *Aldous Huxley*

Here's a good rule of thumb: Too clever is dumb.

— *Ogden Nash*

We should not be like misers who never enjoy what they have but only bewail what they lose.

— *Plutarch*

Many receive advice, few profit by it.

— *Publilius Syrus*

Be excellent to each other.

— *Bill and Ted's Excellent Adventure*

Little drops of water wear down big stones.

— *Russian proverb*

Men show their characters in what they think laughable.

— *Goethe*

The best of blessings—a contented mind.

— *Latin proverb*

Remember that thou art mortal.

— *Greek proverb*

If Heaven creates a man, there must be some use for him.

— *Chinese proverb*

Misfortune does not always come to injure.

— *Italian proverb*

The more stupid, the happier.

— *Chinese proverb*

If you are afraid of being lonely, don't try to be right.

— *Jules Renard*

Let your children go if you want to keep them.

— *Malcolm Forbes*

He who seizes the right moment is the right man.

— *Goethe*

Cruelties should be committed all at once.

— *Machiavelli*

Granting our wish one of Fate's saddest jokes is!

— *James Russell Lowell*

A good intention clothes itself with power.

— *Ralph Waldo Emerson*

Beware of all enterprises that require new clothes.

— *Henry David Thoreau*

Keep thy hook always baited, for a fish lurks even in the most unlikely waters.

— *Ovid*

There's small choice in rotten apples.

— *William Shakespeare*

The blow of a whip raises a welt, but a blow of the tongue crushes bones.

— *Ecclesiasticus*

We should take care not to make the intellect our god; it has, of course, powerful muscles, but no personality.

— *Albert Einstein*

Hell is truth seen too late.

— *Anonymous*

You cannot endow even the best machine with initiative; the jolliest steamroller will not plant flowers.

— *Walter Lippmann*

We lie loudest when we lie to ourselves.

— *Eric Hoffer*

Teach thy tongue to say "I do not know."

— *Maimonides*

Beware of the man of one book.

— *St. Thomas Aquinas*

Once the toothpaste is out of the tube, it is awfully hard to get it back in.

— *H.R. Haldeman*

No man sees far, the most see no farther than their noses.

— *Thomas Carlyle*

You can usually judge the caliber of a man by the size of the things that get his goat.

— *Anonymous*

Avoid as you would a pestilence—two things: fear and anger. Scientific investigation has proven that these two excesses engender poisons in the body that destroy its health and break down its efficiency.

— *Anonymous*

Whom the gods would destroy they first make mad.

— *Dryden*

Fear not that thy life shall come to an end, but rather fear that it shall never have a beginning.

— *Cardinal Newman*

Worry is a misuse of the imagination. It is assuming responsibility that God never intended you to have. It brings sorrow and saps the day of its strength.

— *Alfred A. Montapert*

Worry is as useless as sawing sawdust.

— *Anonymous*

Action speaks louder than words, but nearly as often.

— *Mark Twain*

Life is a journey. Not a camp.

— *Anonymous*

When men speak ill of thee, live so nobody will believe them.

— *Plato*

Even on the most exalted throne in the world we are only sitting on our own bottom.

— *Michel Eyquem De Montaigne*

Never get so busy making a living that you forget to make a life.

— *Anonymous*

Forbidden fruit is responsible for many bad jams.

— *Anonymous*

Men occasionally stumble over the truth, but most of them pick themselves up and hurry off as if nothing had happened.

— *Winston Churchill*

It is a bad plan that admits of no modification.

— *Publilius Syrus*

Many a man thinks he has an open mind when it's merely vacant.

— *Anonymous*

Time is a dressmaker specializing in alterations.

— *Faith Baldwin*

I dance to the tune that is played.

— *Spanish proverb*

Great souls have wills; feeble ones have only wishes.

— *Chinese proverb*

Most of us swim in the ocean of the commonplace.

— *Pio Baroja*

You can avoid having ulcers by adapting to the situation: if you fall in the mud puddle, check your pockets for fish.

— *Anonymous*

Past experience should be a guide post, not a hitching post.

— *Anonymous*

The past is a bucket of ashes, so live not in your yesterdays, nor just for tomorrow, but in here and now. Keep moving and forget the post mortems. And remember, no one can get the jump on the future.

— *Victor Hugo*

Know the difference between success and fame. Success is Mother Teresa. Fame is Madonna.

— *Erma Bombeck*

Whenever you're sitting across from some important person, always picture him sitting there in a suit of long underwear. That's the way I always operated in business.

— *Joseph P. Kennedy*

Are these things, then, necessities? Then let us meet them like necessities.

— *William Shakespeare, King Henry IV*

We do not remember days, we remember moments.

— *Cesare Pavese*

Never bend your head. Always hold it high. Look the world straight in the eye.

— *Helen Keller*

When you betray somebody else, you also betray yourself.

— *Isaac Bashevis Singer*

The brightest things you ever say/ Are those you think about next day.

— *Arnold Glasow*

The man who says just what he thinks, should think.

— *Anonymous*

What would be the use of immortality to a person who cannot use well a half hour.

— *Ralph Waldo Emerson*

Never make a promise in haste.

— *Mahatma Gandhi*

I beseech you … think it possible that you may be mistaken.

— *Oliver Cromwell*

There is no dishonor in rethinking a problem.

— *The Royal Bank of Canada, Monthly Letter*

My mind is a chest of drawers. When I wish to deal with a subject, I shut all the drawers but the one in which the subject is to be found. When I am wearied, I shut all the drawers and go to sleep.

— *Napoleon Bonaparte*

It is a wise father who throws away his old report cards.

— *Anonymous*

One must separate from anything that forces one to repeat "No" again and again.

— *Friedrich Nietzsche*

If you draw your thread too fine it will break.

— *Petrarca*

It's pretty hard to tell what does bring happiness. Poverty an' wealth have both failed.

— *Kin Hubbard*

When a man has not a good reason for doing a thing, he has one good reason for letting it alone.

— *Thomas Scott*

You win the victory when you yield to friends.

— *Sophocles*

The most important thing in a man is not what he knows, but what he is.

— *Narciso Yepes*

There are times when if you are not feeling like yourself, it is quite an improvement.

— **Anonymous**

The perpetual obstacle to human advancement is custom.

— *John Stuart Mill*

He that jokes, confesses.

— *Italian proverb*

If you want a thing done, go—if not, send.

— *Benjamin Franklin*

The go between wears out a thousand sandals.

— *Japanese proverb*

Do not give, as many rich men do, like a hen that lays an egg, and then cackle.

— *Henry Ward Beecher*

It is fine to aim high if we have developed the ability to accomplish our aims, but there is no use aiming unless the gun is loaded.

— *William Ross*

I don't want the cheese, I just want to get out of the trap.

— *Latin American proverb*

Ambition destroys its possessor.

— *The Talmud*

He that hath a head of wax must not walk in the sun.

— *George Herbert*

If we had no faults, we should not take so much pleasure in noting those of others.

— *La Rochefoucauld*

Almost all our faults are more pardonable than the methods we think up to hide them.

— *La Rochefoucauld*

Know thyself. Don't accept your dog's admiration as conclusive.

— *Mayes*

The proverb warns that, "You should not bite the hand that feeds you." But maybe you should, if it prevents you from feeding yourself.

— *Thomas Szasz*

Be thine own palace, or the world's thy jail.

— *John Donne*

It is our responsibilities, not ourselves, that we should take seriously.

— *Peter Ustinov*

Keep out of ruts; a rut is something which, if traveled in too much, becomes a ditch.

— *Arthur Guiterman*

Go to bed. Whatever you're staying up late for isn't worth it.

— *Andrew A. Rooney*

Trust, but verify.

— *Old Russian proverb*

Be not afraid of life. Believe that life is worth living and your belief will help create the fact.

— *William James*

Let us satisfy our own consciences, and trouble not ourselves by looking for fame. If we deserve it, we shall attain it; if we deserve it not, we cannot force it.

— *Seneca*

You have to believe in happiness or happiness never comes.

— *Douglas Malloch*

Do not get excited over the noise you have made.
– Desiderius Erasmus

If it's working, keep doing it.
If it's not working, stop doing it.
If you don't know what to do, don't do anything.
– Medical school advice

Beware of fishing for compliments—you might come up with a boot.
– Carol Weston

Don't ask questions of fairy tales.
– Jewish proverb

When things go wrong—don't go with them.
– Anonymous

Don't change your plans too often. One sometimes meets destiny on the road he took to avoid it.
– Quoted by Ann Landers

Don't talk about yourself; it will be done when you leave.
– Addison Mizner

I think we consider too much the good luck of the early bird, and not enough of the bad luck of the early worm.
– Franklin D. Roosevelt

Stumbling is not falling.
– Portuguese proverb

The problem when solved will be simple.
– Sign on the wall of a General Motors research laboratory

Where there is no vision, the people perish ...
– Proverbs 29:18

Victory—a matter of staying power.
– Elbert Hubbard

Don't be afraid to take a big step if one is indicated. You can't cross a chasm in two small jumps.
– David Lloyd George

He who is above the conscience of the community is as likely to be slain as he who is below.
– Harold Cooke Phillips

What you do for yourself may start you up in the world. But from there on up, it's what you do for others.
– Burton Hillis

Expect nothing; live frugally on surprise.
– Alice Walker

Lost battles do not lose a war, if our cause is just and our spirit strong.... Defeat isn't bitter if you don't swallow it.
– Ben K. O'Dell

He that is slow to anger is better than the mighty; and he that ruleth his spirit than he that taketh a city.
– Proverbs 16:32

The bigger your head gets, son, / The easier it'll be to fill your shoes.
– James J. O'Reilly, Your Life

Patience accomplishes its objective, while hurry speeds to its ruin.
– Sa'di

A patronizing disposition always has its meaner side.
– George Eliot, Adam Bede

The noblest grace that sweetens life is charity borne with selflessness.
– Anonymous

I have a real belief that life takes care of itself. And it's usually much better than what I imagine.
– Dana Delany

Blot out vain pomp; check impulse; quench appetite; keep reason under its own control.
– Marcus Aurelius

Be aware that a halo has to fall only a few inches to be a noose.
– Dan McKinnon

Never look down on anybody unless you're helping him up.
– Jesse Jackson

If we are not our brother's keeper, let us at least not be his executioner.
– Marlon Brando

The essence of life: fight as if there were no death.
– Guy de Rothschild

People ask for criticism, but they only want praise.
– W. Somerset Maugham

Striving for excellence motivates you; striving for perfection is demoralizing.
– Harriet Braiker, The Type E Woman

Fifty-one percent of being smart is knowing what you are dumb about.
– Ann Landers

You can't have everything. Where would you put it?
– Steven Wright

We must not be innocents abroad in a world that is not innocent.
– Ronald Reagan

Every man carries the entire form of human condition.

– Michel de Montaigne

Life is a succession of lessons which must be lived to be understood.

– Ralph Waldo Emerson

The worst-tempered people I have ever met were those who knew that they were wrong.

– David Letterman

I think society has changed tremendously in the last 25 years. Today, everybody talks about their rights and privileges. Twenty-five years ago, everybody talked about their obligations and responsibilities.

– Lou Holtz

Treat your guest as a guest for two days; on the third day, give him a hoe.

– Swahili proverb

Every man is a fool for at least five minutes every day; wisdom consists of not exceeding the limit.

– Elbert Hubbard

We must not let our passion destroy our dreams.

– King Arthur, Camelot

We are all worms, but I do believe I am a glowworm.

– Winston Churchill

The great companies did not know that the line between hunger and anger is a thin line.

– John Steinbeck

The growth of a large business is merely the survival of the fittest.... The American beauty rose can be produced in the splendor and fragrance which bring cheer to its beholder only by sacrificing the early buds which grow up around it.

– John D. Rockefeller

America is an enormous frosted cupcake in the middle of millions of starving people.

– Gloria Steinem

Endeavor to be always patient of the faults and imperfections of others, for thou hast many faults and imperfections of thy own that require a reciprocation and forbearance. If thou art not able to make thyself that which thou wishest to be, how canst thou expect to mold another in conformity to thy will?

– Thomas Kempis

Service is the rent that you pay for room on this earth.

– Shirley Chisholm

If the profession you have chosen has some unexpected inconveniences, console yourself that no profession is without them ... and that all the perplexities of business are softness compared with the vacancy ... of idleness.

- Samuel Johnson

Be as smart as you can, but remember that it's always better to be wise than to be smart. And don't be upset that it takes a long, long time to find wisdom. Like a rare virus, wisdom tends to break out at unexpected times, and it's mostly people with compassion and understanding who are susceptible to it.

– Alan Alda

As a painter I shall never signify anything of importance. I feel it absolutely.

– Vincent van Gogh

If I'm such a legend, why am I so lonely?

– Judy Garland

Am I going to make mistakes as a parent? Sadly, every day. I'm looking around for the perfect parent and I haven't seen one yet.

– Paula Poundstone

The world is full of suffering; it is also full of the overcoming of it.

– Helen Keller

Music ... can name the un-nameable and communicate the unknowable.

– Leonard Bernstein

Music expresses that which cannot be put into words and that which cannot remain silent.

– Victor Hugo

The only gracious way to accept an insult is to ignore it. If you can't ignore it, top it. If you can't top it, laugh at it. If you can't laugh at it, it's probably deserved.

– Russell Lynes

Hard work spotlights the character of people: some turn up their sleeves, some turn up their noses, and some don't turn up at all.

– Sam Ewing

Wherever they burn books, they will also, in the end, burn human beings.

– Heinrich Heine

Be bold and courageous. When you look back on your life, you'll regret the things you didn't do more than the ones you did. Don't say you don't have enough time. You have exactly the same number of hours per day that were give to Pasteur, Michelangelo, Mother Teresa, Helen Keller, Leonardo da Vinci, Thomas Jefferson, and Albert Einstein.

– H. Jackson Brown, Jr.

… Even when you lack self confidence, keep in mind that if you want a woman to think you're a prince, you should treat her like a queen.

– Marilyn vos Savant

There are people who put their dreams in a little box and say, "Yes, I've got dreams, of course I've got dreams." Then they put the box away and bring it out once in awhile to look in it, and yep, they're still there.

– Erma Bombeck

Careful the things you say,
Children will listen.
Careful the things you do,
Children will see.
And learn.
Children may not obey,
But children will listen.
Children will look to you
For which way to turn,
To learn what to be.
Careful before you say,
"Listen to me."
Children will listen.

– Stephen Sondheim, Into the Woods

A friend loves you for your intelligence, a mistress for your charm, but your family's love is unreasoning; you were born into it and are of its flesh and blood. Nevertheless it can irritate you more than any group of people in the world.

– André Maurois

Politicians—especially state legislators—are disinclined to do anything constructive like spend more money on schools for fear it might become a precedent and send society down the primrose path of spending enough money on schools.

– Bill Hall

Movements born in hatred very quickly take on the characteristics of the thing they oppose.

– J.S. Habgood

The man who can't dance thinks the band is no good.

– Polish proverb

Decency is quiet, but it lasts.

– Anonymous

It's not that I want to be ungracious. I am flattered at being invited to dinner at the White House. Sort of. Maybe. Actually, I'm not at all flattered, since I know it is a political game.

– Mike Royko, syndicated columnist

Rare is the person who can weigh the faults of others without putting his thumb on the scales.

– Byron J. Langenfield

All who have meditated upon the art of governing mankind have been convinced that the fate of empires depends on the education of youth.

– Aristotle

Artists can color the sky red because they know it's blue. Those of us who aren't artists must color things the way they really are or people might think we're stupid.

– Jules Feiffer

What is destructive is impatience, haste, expecting too much too fast.

– May Sarton, Journal of a Solitude

To consider oneself different from ordinary men is wrong, but it is right to hope that one will not remain like ordinary men.

– Anonymous

The basic difference between an ordinary man and a warrior is that a warrior takes everything as a challenge, while an ordinary man takes everything either as a blessing or as a curse.

– Don Juan

There are no great people. Rather, there are great challenges that ordinary people are forced to meet.

– Anonymous

The fear of death keeps us from living, not from dying.

– Paul C. Roud, Making Miracles

Don't look … you might see.
Don't listen … you might hear.
Don't think … you might learn.
Don't walk … you might stumble.
Don't run … you might fall.
Don't make a decision … you might be wrong.
Don't live … you might die.

– Anonymous

Be sure you gurgle [laugh] three times a day for your own wellbeing. And if you can get other people to join you in your laughter, you may help keep this shaky boat afloat. When people are laughing, they're generally not killing one another.

– Alan Alda

Decide that you want it more than you are afraid of it.

– Bill Cosby

It must be the aim of education to teach the citizen that he must first of all rule himself.

– Winthrop Aldrich

I learned certain things about wasting energy. It hit me the hardest after the French [Open]. The important thing is to learn a lesson every time you lose. Life is a learning process and you have to try to learn what's best for you. Let me tell you, life is not fun when you're banging your head against a brick wall all the time.

– John McEnroe

There is a foolish corner even in the brain of a sage.

– Aristotle

The life of every man is a diary in which he means to write one story, and writes another; and his humblest hour is when he compares the volume as it is with what he hoped to make it.

– James Barrie

The heart has reasons which reason itself does not understand.

– Jacques Bossuet

More than any other time in history, mankind faces a crossroad. One path leads to despair and utter hopelessness. The other, to total extinction. Let us pray we have the wisdom to choose correctly.... Summing up, it is clear the future holds great opportunities. It also holds pitfalls. The trick will be to avoid the pitfalls, seize the opportunities and get back home by six o'clock.

– Woody Allen, "My Speech to the Graduates"

Even when we fancy that we have grown wiser, it may be only that new prejudices have displaced old ones.

– Christian Bovee

Education makes a people easy to lead, but difficult to drive; easy to govern, but impossible to enslave.

– Lord Brougham

The world is still deceiv'd with ornament.... In religion, what damned error but some sober brow will bless it, and approve it with a text, hiding the grossness with fair ornament? There is no vice so simple but assumes some mark of virtue on his outwardparts. How many cowards, whose hearts are all as false as stairs of sand, wear yet upon their chins the beards of Hercules and frowning Mars; who inward searched, have livers white as milk?

– William Shakespeare, The Merchant of Venice

I have learned silence from the talkative, tolerance from the intolerant, and kindness from the unkind; yet strangely, I am ungrateful to these teachers.

– Khalil Gibran

They say, best men are molded out of faults; and for the most become much more better for being a little bad.

– William Shakespeare, Measure for Measure

Zeal is fit only for Wise Men, but is found mostly in Fools.

– Thomas Fuller

Addiction is the number one disease in our civilization.

– Deepak Chopra

Afflictions refine some, they consume others.

– Thomas Fuller

Suffering cleanses only when it is free of resentment.

– Eric Hoffer

We can easily forgive a child who is afraid of the dark; the real tragedy of life is when men are afraid of the light.

– Plato

I think you should be a child for as long as you can. I have been successful for 74 years being able to do that. Don't rush into adulthood, it isn't all that much fun.

– Bob Newhart

The one who will be found in trial capable of great acts of love is ever the one who is always doing considerate small ones.

– Frederick William Robertson

If you were going to die soon and had only one phone call you could make, who would you call and what would you say? And why are you waiting?

– Stephen Levine

Life is like an onion; you peel it off one layer at a time, and sometimes you weep.

– Carl Sandberg

I shall never permit myself to stoop so low as to hate another man.

– Booker T. Washington

I hope that I shall always possess firmness and virtue enough to maintain what I consider the most enviable of all titles, the character of an honest man.

– George Washington

If there is light in the soul,
There will be beauty in the person.
If there is beauty in the person,
There will be harmony in the house.
If there is harmony in the house,
There will be order in the nation.
If there is order in the nation,
There will be peace in the world.
— *Chinese proverb*

Your plan for work and happiness should be big, imaginative and daring. Strike out boldly for the things you honestly want more than anything else in the world. The mistake is to put your sights too low, not to raise them too high. The definite, faraway goal will supercharge your whole body and spirit; it will awaken your mind and spirit; it will awaken your mind and creative imagination, and put meaning into otherwise lowly step-by-step tasks you must go through in order to attain your final success.
— *Henry J. Kaiser*

Whatever women do they must do twice as well as men to be thought of as half as good.
— *Ella Wheeler Wilcox*

America does not consist of groups. A man who thinks of himself as belonging to a particular national group in America has not yet become an American.
— *Woodrow Wilson*

Strength and struggle go together. The supreme reward of struggle is strength. Life is a battle and the greatest joy is to overcome. The pursuit of easy things makes men weak. Do not equip yourselves with superior power and hope to escape the responsibility and work. It cannot be done. It is following the lines of least resistance that makes rivers and men crooked.
— *Ralph Parlette*

Yesterday is history, tomorrow is a mystery, today is God's gift, that's why we call it the present.
— *Joan Rivers*

Pain nourishes courage. You can't be brave if you've only had wonderful things happen to you.
— *Mary Tyler Moore*

Now if you are going to win any battle you have to do one thing. You have to make the mind run the body. Never let the body tell the mind what to do. The body will always give up. It is always tired—morning, noon, and night. But the body is never tired if the mind is not tired. When you were younger the mind could make you dance all night, and the body was never tired…. You've always got to make the mind take over and keep going.
— *George S. Patton*

Character is what you are in the dark.
— *Dwight L. Moody*

Many hands and hearts and minds generally contribute to anyone's notable achievements.
— *Walt Disney*

Lives of great men all remind us
We can make our lives sublime,
And, departing, leave behind us
Footprints on the sands of time.
— *Henry Wadsworth Longfellow*

Great crises produce great men, and great deeds of courage.
— *John F. Kennedy*

The sign of a great man is that the closer you get, the greater he seems.
— *Chofetz Chaim, 9th century*

It is far more impressive when others discover your good qualities without your help.
— *Judith Martin*

Who is wise?
He that learns from everyone.
Who is powerful?
He that governs his Passions.
Who is rich?
He that is content.
Who is that?
Nobody.

— *Benjamin Franklin*

Valor would cease to be a virtue if there were no injustice.
— *Agesilaus*

Unfortunately large numbers of people all over the world have been specifically taught in childhood not to think, because thinking would lead to questioning the certainties of the elders, and this has not been allowed in most cultures.
— *Brock Chisholm*

Ours seems to be the only nation on earth that asks its teenagers what to do about world affairs and tells its golden-agers to go out and play.
— *Julian F. Grow*

Unblessed is the son who does not honor his parents; but if reverent and obedient to them, he will receive the same from his own children.
— *Euripides*

There are some people who have to do, in order to make their mark. They have to perform, they have to contribute. And there are some people who only have to be.
— *F. Scott Fitzgerald*

Whenever I held my newborn baby in my arms, I used to think that what I said and did to him could have an influence not only on him but on all whom he met, not only for a day or a month or a year, but for all eternity—a very, very challenging and exciting thought for a mother.

– *Rose Kennedy*

The human being who lives only for himself finally reaps nothing but unhappiness. Selfishness corrodes. Unselfishness enables, satisfies. Don't put off the joy derivable from doing helpful, kindly things for others.

– *B.C. Forbes*

Not to be able to bar poverty is a shameful thing; but not to know how to chase it away by work is a more shameful thing yet.

– *Pericles*

I've never been poor, only broke. Being poor is a frame of mind. Being broke is only a temporary situation.

– *Michael Todd*

There are only two ways of getting on in this world: by one's own industry, or by the weakness of others.

– *Jean de La Bruyere*

It's easier to love humanity as a whole than to love one's neighbor…. A low capacity for getting along with those near us often goes hand in hand with a high receptivity to the idea of the brotherhood of man.

– *Eric Hoffer*

There is only one kind of love, but there are a thousand imitations.

– *Francois Rochefoucauld*

Everybody can be great … because anybody can serve. You don't have to have a collage degree to serve. You don't have to make your subject and verb agree to serve. You only need a heart full of grace. A soul generated by love.

– *Martin Luther King, Jr.*

The bitterest tears shed over graves are for words left unsaid and deeds left undone.

– *Harriet Beecher Stowe*

If we see cruelty or wrong that we have the power to stop, and do nothing, we make ourselves sharers in the guilt.

– *Anna Sewell*

Everybody wants sympathy, but nobody wants people feeling sorry for them.

– *Beryl Pitzer*

One of the most striking differences between a cat and a lie, is that a cat has only nine lives.

– *Mark Twain*

Aging is not "lost youth" but a new stage of opportunity and strength…. The way you define yourself makes such a difference.

– *Betty Friedan*

One can savor sights and sounds more deeply when one gets really old. It may be the last time you see a sunset, a tree, the snow, or know winter. The sea, a lake, all become as in childhood, magical and a great wonder: then seen for the first time, now perhaps for the last. Music, bird songs, the wind, the waves: One listens to tones with deeper delight and appreciation—"loving well," to borrow from Shakespeare's 73rd sonnet, "that which I must leave ere long."

– *Helen Nearing*

Cocaine is God's way of telling you you've got too much money.

– *Sting, British rock star*

Fools and wise folk are alike harmless. It is the half-wise and the half-foolish who are the most dangerous.

– *Goethe*

A generation ago, most people finished a day's work and needed a rest. Now they need exercise.

– *Anonymous*

One fifth of the people are against everything all the time.

– *Robert F. Kennedy*

People can be more forgiving than you can imagine. But you have to forgive yourself. Let go of what's bitter and move on.

– *Bill Cosby*

If people were more concerned with being reconciled than with being right, the world would be a better place.

– *Judith Martin*

The proper function of Man is to live, not to exist. I shall not waste my days in trying to prolong them. I shall use my time.

– *Jack London*

How beautifully leaves grow old. How full of light and color are their last days.

– *George Burns*

Worry, self-doubt, fear, and anxiety—these are some of the culprits that bow the head and break the spirit.

– *Anonymous*

Life is either a daring adventure or nothing.
— *Helen Keller*

There must be more to life than having everything!
— *Maurice Sendak*

It's the hardest thing in the world to accept a pinch of success and leave it that way.
— *Marlon Brando*

No one can harm you except yourself.
— *Gandhi*

Character is the sum total of all our everyday choices.
— *Margaret Jensen*

Only I can change my life. No one can do it for me.
— *Carol Burnett*

Bad habits are easier to abandon today than tomorrow.
— *English proverb*

I find, by experience, that the mind and the body are more than married, / For they are most intimately united; / And when the one suffers, the other sympathizes.
— *Lord Chesterfield, Philip D. Stanhope*

Human nature is eternally hungry for recognition. The perfect food for this hunger is credit, written or spoken, acknowledgement of service rendered. Give the credit—all the credit—to the other person. When giving credit is second nature, you will take your place among the world's bigger people, for that is the way of bigness the world over.
— *James T. Mangan*

It's a complex world. I hope you'll learn to make distinctions. A peach is not its fuzz, a toad is not its warts, a person is not his or her crankiness. If we can make distinctions, we can be tolerant, and we can get to the heart of our problems instead of wrestling endlessly with the gross exteriors.... Your assumptions are your windows on the world. Scrub them off every once in a while, or the light won't come in.
— *Alan Alda, at his daughter's commencement address*

It's a strange world of language in which skating on thin ice can get you into hot water.
— *Franklin P. Jones*

Man is the animal that intends to shoot himself out into interplanetary space, after having given up on the problem of an efficient way to get himself five miles or so to work and back each day.
— *Bill Vaughan*

A strange thing about life. I am always looking for something to do.
— *Robert E. Lee*

It is hard to fight against impulsive desire; whatever it wants it will buy at the cost of the soul.
— *Heraclitus*

Education is an admirable thing, but it is well to remember from time to time that nothing that is worth knowing can be taught.
— *Oscar Wilde*

What sets the world in motion is the interplay of differences, their attractions and repulsions.
— *Octavio Paz*

We must not think our world is the only one. There are worlds outside our experience. "Call that a sunset?" said the lady to Turner as she stood before the artist's picture. "I never saw a sunset like that." "No, madam," said Turner. "Don't you wish you had?" Perhaps your world and mine is only mean because we are near-sighted. Perhaps we missed the vision not because the vision is not there, but because we darken the window.
— *"Alpha of the Plough"*

No one is so eager to gain new experience as he who doesn't know how to make use of the old ones.
— *Marie Von Ebner-Eschenbach*

There is more adventure alive in the world today than there ever was, plenty of unexplored places. Adventure is there waiting for any man with the courage to go and find it. But you'll never discover it by looking at the calendar—and counting yourself to death.
— *Louis L'Amour*

Nobody grows old by living a given number of years. Years wrinkle the skin, but to give up enthusiasm wrinkles the soul.
— *Anonymous*

It does no harm just once in a while to acknowledge that the whole country isn't in flames, that there are people in the country besides politicians, entertainers and criminals.
— *Charles Kuralt*

Nothing so needs reforming as other people's habits.
— *Mark Twain*

Youth is not a time of life—it is a state of mind, a product of the imagination, a vigor of the emotions a predominance of courage over timidity, an appetite for adventure.
— *Anonymous*

Who hears music feels his solitude peopled at once.
— *Robert Browning*

Tiny children want to learn to the degree that they are unable to distinguish learning from fun. They keep this attitude until we adults convince them that learning is *not* fun.
— *Glenn Doman*

One cannot be too extreme in dealing with social ills: besides, the extreme thing is generally the true thing.
— *Emma Goldman, Anarchism*

Dreaming permits each and every one of us to be safely insane every night of the week.
— *William Charles Dement*

Life is what happens when you are making other plans.
— *John Lennon*

In this world there are only two tragedies. One is not getting what one wants, and the other is getting it.
— *Oscar Wilde*

If a problem causes many meetings, the meetings eventually become more important than the problem.
— *Anonymous*

I see no hope for the future of our people if they are dependent on the frivolous youth of today, for certainly all youth are reckless beyond words.... When I was a boy, we were taught to be discreet and respectful of elders, but the present youth are exceedingly wise and impatient of restraint.
— *Hesiod, 8th century B.C.E.*

Love and work are the cornerstones of our humanness.
— *Sigmund Freud*

The gem cannot be polished without friction, nor man without trials.
— *Confucius*

The people who can do you the most damage are the ones who are closest to you.
— *Robert Mitchum*

I smoked pot once in my life. I thought it smelled like dirty socks and I never did it again.
— *Dick Booth*

... they praise me, and make an ass of me; now my foes tell me plainly I am an ass; so that by my foes, sir, I profit in the knowledge of myself, and by my friends I am abused.
— *William Shakespeare, Twelfth Night*

In a Nutshell: Six Ways to Make People Like You—
Principle 1: Become genuinely interested in other people.
Principle 2: Smile.
Principle 3: Remember that a person's name is to that person the sweetest and most important sound in any language.
Principle 4: Be a good listener. Encourage others to talk about themselves.
Principle 5: Talk in terms of the other person's interests.
Principle 6: Make the other person feel important —and do it sincerely.
— *Dale Carnegie*

Home is the place where, when you have to go there, they have to take you in.
— *Robert Frost*

In an age contorted by violence, I have no doubt whatever that people are born to kindness as a wind is born to movement. After all, if tenderness were rare instead of normal, wouldn't the newspapers give it headlines? MOTHER CHERISHES FAMILY—BLIND PERSON HELPED ACROSS STREET—PRISONERS VISITED—DESPERATE PEOPLE CARED FOR—BOY SHARES HIS LUNCH WITH PUPPY ... and on and on. But such events are not news; they are as common and as beautiful as dandelions.
— *Neil Millar*

Everyone is a moon, and has a dark side which he never shows to anybody.
— *Mark Twain*

I am glad every day for all the reckless things we did. If we had waited till we could afford them, now it would be too late.
— *Anonymous*

In the coldest February, as in every other month of every other year, the best thing to hold on to in this world is each other.
— *Linda Ellerbee, Move On: Adventures in the Real World*

But ah! Think what you do when you run in debt: You give to another power over your liberty.
— *Benjamin Franklin*

An honest man is one who knows that he can't consume more than he has produced.
— *Ayn Rand, Atlas Shrugged*

People of character don't allow the environment to dictate their style.
— *Lucille Kallen, The Tanglewood Murder*

Virtue is its own revenge.

– E.Y. Harburg

It was not I that sinned the sin
 The ruthless body dragged me in
Though long I strove courageously,
The body was too much for me.

– Walt Whitman

[Anger] builds nothing but can destroy everything.

– L. Douglas Wilder

It [Ku Klux Klan] gathers under its hood the mentally ill, the haters who have forgot what it is they hate or who dare not harm their real hate object, and also the bored and confused and ignorant. The Klan is made up of ghosts on the search for ghosts who have haunted the southern soul too long.

– Lillian Smith, Killers of the Dream

When I was born
I was Black
When I grew up
I was Black
When I go out in
The sun
I am Black
But you!
When you were born
You were pink
When you grow up
You are white
When you get sick
You are green
When you go out in
The sun
You are red
When you get cold
You are blue
And when you die
You are purple
And you call me
Colored!

– Anonymous African-American child

One must ask children and birds how cherries and strawberries taste.

– Johann Wolfgang Von Goethe

One moment of a man's life is a fact so stupendous as to take the lustre out of all fiction.

– Ralph Waldo Emerson

I can think of nothing less pleasurable than a life devoted to pleasure.

– John D. Rockefeller

I would rather be one mile from hell going in the opposite direction, than to be one thousand miles from hell going straight to it.

– Wilford Hinkson

We don't read and write poetry because it's cute; we read and write poetry because we are members of the human race, and the human race is filled with passion.

– Robin Williams, Dead Poets Society

The song I came to sing remains unsung. I have spent my life stringing and unstringing my instrument.

– Rabindranath Tagore

We shall cut down God knows how many trees so that we can have one edition of this book.

– R.D. Laing

Man is distinguished from all other creatures by the faculty of laughter.

– Joseph Addison

There's nothing funnier than the Human Animal.

– Walt Disney

Beware of jokes [from which] we go away hollow and ashamed.

– Ralph Waldo Emerson

Imagination is only intelligence having fun.

– George Scialabbe

The majority of us lead quiet, unheralded lives as we pass through this world. There will most likely be no ticker-tape parades for us, no monuments created in our honor. But that does not lessen our possible impact, for there are scores of people waiting for someone just like us to come along … someone who will live a happier life merely because we took the time to share what we have to give. Too often we underestimate the power of a touch, a smile, a kind word … all of which have the potential to turn a life around. It's overwhelming to consider the continuous opportunities there are to make our love felt.

– Leo Buscaglia

Insanity is doing the same thing over and over again, but expecting different results.

– Rita Mae Brown, Sudden Death

Seek always to do some good, somewhere. Every man has to seek in his own way to realize his true worth. You must give some time to your fellow man. For remember, you don't live in a world all your own. Your brothers are here too.

– Albert Schweitzer

What you think in the egotism of anger you will pay for in the humiliation of saner moments.

– Crane

Most of us will do anything to be good, except change our way of living.

– Anonymous

They sicken of the calm, who know the storm.
— *Dorothy Parker*

The notion of the "war on gangs" being successful is as realistic as the People's Republic of China telling Americans to stop being American. When gang members stop their wars and find that there is no longer a need for their sets to exist, banging will cease. But until then, all attempts by law enforcement to seriously curtail its forward motion will be in vain.
— *Kody Scott, Monster,*
An autobiography of an L.A. gang member

Nationalized health care would have: The compassion of the IRS, the efficiency of the Postal Service, the failure rate of government schools, the enforcement tactics of the Bureau of Alcohol, Tobacco and Firearms, and all at Pentagon prices!
— *Albert V. Burns*

God give us men, the time demands
strong minds, great hearts, true faith and ready hands;
Men whom the lust of office does not kill;
Men whom the spills of office cannot buy;
Men who possess opinions and a will;
Men who have honor; men who will not lie;
Men who can stand before a demagogue
and damn his treacherous flatteries without winking;
Tall men, sun crowned, who live above the fog
In public duty and in private thinking!
For while the rabble with their thumb-worn creeds,
Their large professions and their little deeds,
Mingle in selfish strife; lo! Freedom weeps!
Wrong rules the land, and waiting justice sleeps!
— *J.G. Holland*

To survive it is often necessary to fight, and to fight you have to dirty yourself.
— *George Orwell*

I am extraordinarily patient, provided I get my own way in the end.
— *Margaret Thatcher*

I wouldn't swap one wrinkle of my face for all the elixirs of youth. All of these wrinkles represent a smile, a grimace of pain and disappointment … some part of being fully alive.
— *Helen Hayes*

The tragedy of life is what dies inside a man while he lives.
— *Albert Schweitzer*

A straight line is the shortest in morals as in geometry.
— *Joseph L. Baron*

Nobody dast blame this man. You don't understand; Willy was a salesman, there is no rock bottom to the life. He don't put a bolt to a nut, he don't tell you the law or give you medicine. He's a man way out there in the blue, riding on a smile and a shoeshine. And when they start not smiling back—that's an earthquake. And then you get yourself a couple of spots on your hat, and you're finished. Nobody dast blame this man. A salesman is got to dream, boy. It comes with the territory.
— *Arthur Miller, Death of a Salesman*

Perhaps the straight and narrow path would be wider if more people used it.
— *Kay Ingram*

"Hush, don't say that—you'll lose some of your friends." My answer is simple and final: If I don't say it, I'll lose my own soul.
— *E. Stanley Jones*

Real confidence comes from knowing and accepting yourself—your strengths and your limitations—in contrast to depending on affirmation from others.
— *Judith M. Bardwick*

We all find it in ourselves to do what we have to do. People are capable of an awful lot when they have no choice…. Courage is when you have choices.
— *Terry Anderson, former hostage*

Formerly, when religion was strong and science weak, men mistook magic for medicine; now when science is strong and religion is weak, men mistake medicine for magic.
— *Thomas Szasz*

And often times excusing a fault doth make the fault worse by excuse—as patches set upon a little breach discredit more in hiding of the fault than did the fault before it was so patched.
— *William Shakespeare, King John*

We are more inclined to hate one another for points on which we differ, than to love one another for points on which we agree.
— *Charles Caleb Colton*

Half of our life is spent trying to find something to do with the time we have rushed through life trying to save.
— *Will Rogers*

How confusing the beams from memory's lamp are.
One day a bachelor, the next a grampa.
What is the secret of the trick?
How did I get old so quick?
— *Ogden Nash*

The world is quickly bored by the recital of misfortune, willingly avoids the sight of distress.
— *W. Somerset Maugham*

The happiness of others is never bearable for very long.
— *Francoise Sagan*

There is something curiously boring about somebody else's happiness.
— *Aldous Huxley*

Evil is the stone on which the good sharpens itself.
— *Dorothy Auchterlonie*

We neither get better or worse as we get older, but more like ourselves.
— *Robert Anthony*

The opportunities of man are limited only by his imagination. But so few have imagination that there are ten thousand fiddlers to one composer.
— *Charles F. Kettering*

Be not angry ...
that you cannot make others
as you wish them to be ...
since you cannot even make YOURSELF
as you wish to be.
— *Thomas a Kempis*

Per year, gangs in South Central [LA] recruit more people than the four branches of the U.S. Armed Forces do. Crack dealers employ more people in South Central than AT&T, IBM, and Xerox combined.
— *Kody Scott, Monster,*
An autobiography of an L.A. gang member

It was not the apple on the tree, but the pair on the ground, I believe, that caused the trouble in the garden.
— *M.D. O'Connor*

In any contest between power and patience bet on patience.
— *W.B. Prescott*

The man who views the world at 50 the same as he did at 20 has wasted 30 years of his life.
— *Muhammad Ali*

So much is pressing on humans today that no one has time to stand still long enough to evaluate it. They gulp life and taste nothing! They eat life and have no savor.
— *Geraldine Farrar*

Pretty much all the honest truth telling there is in the world is done by children.
— *Oliver Wendell Holmes, Sr.*

Peace can come only as a consequence of freedom.
— *Ernest L. Wilkinson*

I have never seen greater monster or miracle in the world than myself.
— *Michel De Montaigne*

Lord, what fools these mortals be!
— *William Shakespeare*

There is nobody so irritating as somebody with less intelligence and more sense than we have.
— *Don Herold*

Let Wall Street have a nightmare and the whole country has to help get them back in bed again.
— *Will Rogers*

... that is what learning is. You suddenly understand something you've understood all your life, but in a new way.
— *Doris Lessing*

It doesn't take a hero to order men into battle. It takes a hero to be one of those men who goes into battle.
— *General H. Normann Schwarzkopf*

In a consumer society there are inevitably two kinds of slaves: the prisoners of addiction and the prisoners of envy.
— *Ivan Illich*

How would I have felt standing naked in front of an armed SS officer being forced to dig a pit that I knew would be my grave? Empathy is a required element of morality.... That emotion needs to be cultivated among our children and ourselves.
— *Steven Spielberg*

Five basic reasons for the Decline and Fall of the Roman Empire from Edward Gibbon's book by the same title, published in 1788:
1) The undermining of the dignity and sanctity of the home, which is the basis for human society.
2) Higher and higher taxes: the spending of public money for free bread and circuses for the populace.
3) The mad craze for pleasure, with sports and plays becoming more exciting, more brutal, and more immoral.
4) The building of great armaments when the real enemy was within—decay of individual responsibility.
5) The decay of religion, whose leaders lost touch with life and their power to guide. And I beseech you to treasure up in your hearts these my parting words: Be ashamed to die till you have won some victory for humanity.
— *Horace Mann, his last baccalaureate*
sermon at Antioch College

A proposal that every citizen should be required to appear at reasonable intervals before a properly qualified jury to justify his existence. If he could not justify it, his existence would be swiftly and efficiently terminated.

– *George Bernard Shaw*

Age does not protect you from love but love to some extent protects you from age.

– *Jeanne Moreau*

Self-fulfillment presupposes that you have a self worth fulfilling.

– *James Q. Wilson*

Bravery is the capacity to perform properly even when scared half to death.

– *Omar Bradley*

If only there were evil people somewhere, insidiously committing evil deeds, and it were necessary only to separate them from the rest of us and destroy them. But the line dividing good and evil cuts through the heart of every human being. And who is willing to destroy a piece of his own heart?

– *Aleksandr Solzhenitsyn, Russian rights leader*

Do not lose faith in humanity: there are over a hundred million people in America who have never played you a single nasty trick.

– *Hubbard*

Hatred paralyzes life; love releases it.
Hatred confuses life; love harmonizes it.
Hatred darkens life; love illumines it.

– *Martin Luther King, Jr.*

My sense now of age is that it's a new period in life, as yet mostly unknown and untested, which has to be seen in its own terms.

– *Betty Friedan*

He worked like hell in the country so he could live in the city, where he worked like hell so he could live in the country.

– *Don Marquis*

Violence is not strength, and compassion is not weakness.

– *King Arthur, in "Camelot"*

The world is a beautiful place
to be born into
if you don't mind some people dying
all the time
or maybe only starving
some of the time
which isn't half so bad
if it isn't you.

– *Laurence Ferlinghetti*

It is not the ape, nor the tiger in man that I fear, it is the donkey.

– *William Temple*

Every human being is your counterpart. Every other human being possesses and embodies aspects of yourself: your dreams, your sorrows, your hopes.... For each of us there was a time when the world was young, a springtime of spirit that was later tested by the winters of discontent; and in the midst of each of our lives lies the haunting shadow of death. Therefore we are all quite alike; indeed at the core we are all one, all lost—and all found—in the same mysterious enterprise that is life. Hold this in your heart as you go about your day, and the world will cease to be inhabited by strangers, and the burden of life itself will no longer be a process of loneliness.

– *Daphne Rose Kingma*

Whatever you have received more than others—in health, in talents, in ability, in success—all this you must not take to yourself as a matter of course. In gratitude for your good fortune, you must render in return some sacrifice.

– *Albert Schweitzer*

I cannot believe that the purpose of life is to be "happy." I think the purpose of life is to be useful, to be responsible, to be honorable, to be compassionate. It is, above all, to matter, to count, to stand for something, to have made some difference that you lived at all.

– *Leo C. Rosten*

You can turn painful situations around through laughter. If you can find humor in anything, even poverty, you can survive it.

– *Bill Cosby*

We live very close together. So, our prime purpose in this life is to help others. And if you can't help them at least don't hurt them.

– *The Dalai Lama*

As a rule a man's a fool;
When it's hot he wants it cool;
When it's cool he wants it hot.
Always wanting what is not.

– *Anonymous*

There is scarcely any man sufficiently clever to appreciate all the evils he does.

– *La Rochefoucauld*

I reckon there's as much human nature in some folks as there is in others, if not more.

– *Edward Noyes Westcott*

God may not always come when we need Him, but He will always be on time.

– *Alex Haley*

It made me shiver, and I about made up my mind to pray and see if I couldn't try to quit bein' the kind of boy I was and be better. So I kneeled down. But the words wouldn't come. Why wouldn't they? It weren't no use to try and hide it from Him…. I knowed very well why they wouldn't come. It was because my heart wasn't right; it was because I was playin' double. I was lettin' on to give up sin, but way inside of me I was holdin' on to the biggest one of all. I was tryin' to make my mouth say I would do the right thing and the clean thing, but deep down in me I knowed it was a lie and He knowed it. You can't pray a lie. I found that out.

– *Mark Twain,*
from the words of Huckleberry Finn

When thou prayest, rather let thy heart be without words than thy words be without heart.

– *John Bunyan*

When you pray don't insult God's intelligence by asking Him to do something which would be unworthy of even you, a mortal.

– *Mme Chiang Kai-shek, I Confess My Faith*

Whenever God erects a house of prayer / The Devil always builds a chapel there. / And twill be found, upon examination, / The latter has the largest congregation.

– *Daniel Defoe*

Live in such a way that those who know you but don't know God will come to know God because they know you.

– *Anonymous*

It has been said that man is the only animal who laughs, and the only one who weeps; the only one who prays; the only one who walks fully erect; the only one who makes fires; the only one who guides his own destiny; the only one who is penitent; and the only one who needs to be.

– *David Elton Fineblood, Philosophy of Religion*

My atheism, like that of Spinoza, is true piety towards the universe and denies only gods fashioned by men in their own image to be servants of their human interests.

– *George Santayana*

Rabbi Zusya said that on that day of judgment, God would not ask him why he had not been Moses, but why he had not been Zusya.

– *Walter Kaufmann*

Seven days without prayer makes one weak.

– *Allen E. Bartlett*

He who hates a man is as if he hated God.

– *Midrash, The Talmudic Anthology*

To claim to be a Christian or Jew who loves God and neighbor and not to take an active part in the formation of social policies affecting those neighbors would seem to deny complete fulfillment of one's faith.

– *Ruben Askew*

I have always believed in God, though I have my quarrels with Him.

– *Elie Wiesel*

There can be no surer sign of decay in a country than to see the rites of religion held in contempt.

– *Niccolo Machiavelli, c. 1500*

I shall tell you a secret, my friend. Do not wait for the last judgment, it takes place every day.

– *Albert Camus*

So far as is known, no bird ever tried to build more nests than its neighbors; and no fox ever fretted because he had only one hole in the earth in which to hide; and no squirrel ever died in anxiety lest he should not lay up enough nuts for two winters instead of one; and no dog ever lost sleep over the fact that he did not have enough bones buried in the ground for his declining years.

– *Religious Telescope*

Time is so fleeting that if we do not remember God in our youth, age may find us incapable of thinking about Him.

– *Hans Christian Anderson*

In the beginning, our Creator gave all the races of mankind the same songs and the same drums to keep in touch with Him, to keep faith. But people kept forgetting. In the fullness of time, the spiritual traditions of all the peoples—they are the same—will be united again in a great gathering of their secret leaders. And they will gain power to remake the world.

– *Mohawk prophecy, told by Tom Porter*

The wise man in the storm prays to God, not for safety from danger, but for deliverance from fear.

– *Ralph Waldo Emerson*

There's not much practical [religion] in the man who lives on better terms with angels and seraphs than with his children, servants and neighbors.

– *Henry Ward Beecher*

The terrible crisis we face may be nothing less than God's call to us to reach a new level of humanity.
— *Samuel H. Miller*

At bottom every man knows well enough that he is a unique being ... and by no extraordinary chance will such a marvelously picturesque piece of diversity in unity as he is, ever be put together a second time.
— *Friedrich Nietzsche*

At any rate, I am convinced that *He* does not play dice.
— *Albert Einstein*

God is involved with humanity in a process of spiritual evolution.
— *Seth Farber*

He who merely knows right principles is not equal to him who loves them.
— *Confucius*

I think you will understand me when I say that I have never known a thinking man who did not believe in God.
— *Robert Andrews Millikan*

If we acknowledge God in all our ways, He has promised safely to direct our steps, and in our experience we shall find the promise fulfilled.
— *Edward Payson*

Practice in life what you pray for and God will give it to you more abundantly.
— *Edward R. Pusey*

If thou neglecteth thy love to thy neighbor, in vain thou professeth thy love to God.
— *Francis Quarles*

He who would be friends with God must remain alone or make the whole world his friend.
— *Mahatma Gandhi*

God has two dwellings; one in heaven, and the other in a meek and thankful heart.
— *Izaak Walton*

Grant that I may not so much seek to be consoled as to console,
To be understood as to understand;
To be loved as to love.
For it is in giving that we receive.
— *St. Francis of Assisi*

If you believe in the Lord he will do half the work, but the last half. He helps those who help themselves.
— *Cyrus K. Curtis*

An honest man is the noblest work of God.
— *Alexander Pope*

It was pride that changed angels into devils; it is humility that makes men as angels.
— *St. Augustine*

Prayer is not conquering God's reluctance but taking hold of God's willingness.
— *Phillips Brooks*

... Behold, the fear of the Lord, that is wisdom; and to depart from evil is understanding.
— *Job 28:28*

Nothing sets a person so much out of the devil's reach as humility.
— *Jonathon Edwards*

Fear knocked at the door. Faith answered. No one was there.
— *English proverb*

Show me the man who would go to heaven alone, and I will show you one who will never be admitted there.
— *Owen Feltham*

The worship most acceptable to God comes from a thankful and cheerful heart.
— *Plutarch*

What can I give Him, poor as I am? / If I were a shepherd I would give him a lamb. / If I were a wise man I would do my part, / Yet what can I give Him: Give my heart.
— *Christina Rossetti*

What shall I say when I see God?
— *Sister Madelva Wolff*

God says to me with kind of a smile,
"Hey how would you like to be God awhile
and steer the world?"
"Okay," says I, "I'll give it a try.
Where do I set?
How much do I get?
What time is lunch?
When can I quit?"
"Gimme back that wheel," says God,
"I don't think you're quite ready yet."
— *Anonymous*

Eternity is not something that begins after you are dead. It is going on all the time. We are in it now.
— *Charlotte Perkins Gillman, The Forerunner*

Sometimes a nation abolishes God, but fortunately God is more tolerant.
— *Anonymous*

When God conceived the world, that was poetry; He formed it, and that was sculpture; He varied and colored it, and that was painting; and then, crowning all, He peopled it with living beings, and that was the grand divine, eternal drama.

– *Charlotte Cushman*

A watch without a watchmaker is less incredible than a creation without a Creator.

– *Anonymous*

A synagogue or church that admitted only saints would be like a hospital that admitted only healthy people. It would be a lot easier to run, and a more pleasant place to be, but I'm not sure it would be doing the job it is here to do.

– *Harold Kushner, Who Needs God*

It may be the devil or it may be the Lord, but you're gonna have to serve somebody.

– *Bob Dylan*

We are most deeply asleep at the switch when we fancy we control any switches at all.

– *Annie Dillard, Holy the Firm*

If you're not closer to the Lord today than you were yesterday . . . guess who moved.

– *Anonymous*

The same loving hand that has created you has created me. If He is your Father He must be my Father also. We all belong to the same family. . . . Naturally I would like to give them the joy of what I believe, but that I cannot do; only God can. Faith is a gift of God but God does not force Himself.

– *Mother Teresa*

The Lord works from the inside out. The world works from the outside in. The world would take people out of the slums. [God] takes the slums out of the people, and then they take themselves out of the slums. The world would mold men by changing their environment. [God] changes men, who then change their environment. The world would shape human behavior, but [God] can change human nature.

– *Ezra Taft Benson*

Show me the way—
Not to fortune or fame,
Not how to win laurels
Or praise for my name—
But show me the way
To spread the Great Story
That "Thine is the Kingdom
and Power and Glory."

– *Anonymous*

We are born for a higher destiny than earth.

– *Bulwer*

. . . I said to the man who stood at the gate of the year:
"Give me a light, that I may tread safely into the unknown!" And he replied:
"Go out into the darkness and put your hand into the Hand of God.
That shall be to you better than light and safer than a known way."

– *M. Louis Haskins*

This must be what God sees.

– *Frank Borman, Apollo 8 astronaut, of the dwindling globe below him*

Educate men without religion and you make them but clever devils.

– *Duke of Wellington*

Morality without religion is a tree without roots; a stream without any spring to feed it; a house built on the sand; a pleasant place to live in till the heavens grow dark, and the storm begins to beat.

– *J.B. Shaw*

In the last analysis everything operates by the will of God.

– *W.R. Whitney*

The better we understand the intricacies of the atomic structure, the nature of life, or the master plan for the galaxies, the more reason we have found to marvel at the wonder of God's creation.

– *Wernher Von Braun*

Great Spirit, help me never to judge another until I have walked in my brothers moccasins two weeks.

– *Native American prayer*

Do not pray for tasks equal to your powers. Pray for powers equal to your tasks. Then the doing of your work will be no miracle, but you shall be the miracle.

– *Phillip Brooks*

I sought to hear the voice of God,
and climbed the topmost steeple
But God declared: "Go down again,
I dwell among the people."

– *Lewis Newman*

The value of persistent prayer is not that He will hear us . . . but that we will finally hear Him.

– *William McGill*

Prayer doesn't use up artificial energy, doesn't burn up any fossil fuel, doesn't pollute.

– *Margaret Mead*

The brotherhood of men would be an empty dream without the fatherhood of God.

– *Abraham Joshua Heschel*

Lord, when we are wrong, make us willing to change, and when we are right, make us easy to live with.

– Peter Marshall

I could not say I believe. I know! I have had the experience of being gripped by something that is stronger than myself, something that people call God.

– Carl Jung

How flowers become thee
And almost match thy beauty.
Oh, to be a gardener
To work the soil and plant the seed
That brings forth such beauty.

In my mind there is another garden
That grows incessantly, day and night.
In this hidden garden of the mind
I grow roses overnight
Make gingkos flourish in a trice.

What other trees do I cultivate there
In a space no larger than a melon?
How many trees
How many flowers
Are there in this wide world?

Near the center of this vast garden of the mind's eye
There grows a tree, most majestic.
It's called the tree of knowledge of good and evil.
I have tasted its fruit, both bitter and sweet.
Oh, curious is me!

I hear a whisper that there is another tree
More beautiful and the fruit thereof
More delicious than any I have ever tasted.
They say its name is the tree of life,
Or is it called the tree of paradise?

The fruit is so everlastingly sweet
That almost I forgot the other trees,
The Gingko—the Rose
And almost thee.

I, a gardener would be!
And make a paradise
Of this tangled wilderness
Betwixt me and thee.

God, be thou my gardener,
Help me make a paradise
of the wilderness of my soul.

– Dean W. Bitter

If someone comes to you entreating aid, do not say in refusal: "Trust in God; He will help," but act as if there were no God, and none to help but you.

– The Sassover, The Hasidic Anthology

Would to God that we might spend a single day really well.

– Thomas A Kempis

A little child of God ... God's last, best and, so far as we know, final expression of Himself.

– W.S. Rainsford, The Story of a Varied Life

A miracle cannot prove what is impossible; it is useful only to confirm what is possible.

– Maimonides

Oh God, help us to be master of ourselves that we may be the servants of others.

– Sir Alec Paterson

Nobody ever outgrows Scripture; the book widens and deepens with our years.

– Charles Haddon Spurgeon

Did not God
Sometimes withhold in mercy what we ask,
We should be ruined at our own request.

– Hannah More

All I have seen teaches me to trust the Creator for all I have not seen.

– Ralph Waldo Emerson

I know this world is ruled by Infinite Intelligence. It required Infinite Intelligence to create it and it requires Infinite Intelligence to keep it on its course .... It is mathematical in its precision.

– Thomas A. Edison

The more I try to unravel the mysteries of the world we live in, the more I come to the conception of a single overruling power—God.

– Henry Eyring

God is the silent partner in all great enterprises.

– Abraham Lincoln

A mighty fortress is our God,
A tower of strength ne'er failing.
A helper mighty is our God,
O'er ills of life prevailing.
He overcometh all.
He saveth from the fall.
His might and pow'r are great.
He all things did create,
And he shall reign forever more.

– Martin Luther

We act in faith, and miracles occur.

– Dag Hammerskjold

Even if you're on the right track, you'll get run over if you just sit there.

– Will Rogers

Certain thoughts are prayers. There are moments when, whatever the attitude of the body, the soul is on its knees.

– Victor Hugo

There is no brotherhood of man without the fatherhood of God.

– Henry Martyn Field

Behind everything stands God.... Do not avoid, but seek, the great, deep, simple things of faith.

– Phillips Brooks

I would not lift my little finger to defend the western world against communism if I thought that man were just a machine with no spark of divinity in him.

– Dwight D. Eisenhower

He who has ceased to pray has lost a great friendship.

– Richard L. Evans

I would rather walk with God in the dark than go alone in the light.

– Mary Gardiner Brainard

We are perishing for want of wonder, not for want of wonders.

– Gilbert Keith Chesterton

Nothing in life is more wonderful than faith—the one great moving force which we can neither weigh in the balance nor test in the crucible.

– Sir William Osler

I have lived, seen God's hand through a lifetime, and all was for the best.

– Robert Browning

If radio's slim fingers can pluck a melody
From night—and toss it over a continent or sea;
If the petaled white notes of a violin
Are blown across the mountains or the city's din;
If songs, like crimson roses, are culled from thin blue air—
Why should mortals wonder if God hears prayer?

– Ethel Romig Fuller

It is not permitted us to know everything.

– Horace

Your task, to build a better world,
God said, I answered, How?
This world is such a large, vast
place, so complicated now,
And I so small and useless am,
There's nothing I can do. But God
in all his wisdom said,
Just build a better you ...

– Anonymous

We don't know what water is. We don't know what electricity is. We don't know what heat is. We have a lot of hypotheses about these things, but that is all. But we do not let our ignorance about these things deprive us of their use.

– Thomas A. Edison

The disease with which the human mind now labors is want of faith.

– Ralph Waldo Emerson

If a door slams shut it means that God is pointing to an open door further on down.

– Anna Delaney Peale

A perfect faith would lift us absolutely above fear.

– George MacDonald

God's in his heaven—
All's right with the world!

– Robert Browning

To believe only possibilities is not faith, but mere philosophy.

– Sir Thomas Browne

God had so much love in him he had to make us to get some love out.

– Rachel, age 9

The Indian sees no need for setting apart one day in seven as holy day, since to him all days are God's.

– Charles E. Eastman, The Soul of the Indian

If mountains can be moved by faith, is there less power in love?

– Frederick W. Faber

Religion is not proficiency in the fine art of spiritual knowledge, but just the love of God and our neighbour.

– Fr. Andrew

I find the doing of the will of God leaves me no time for disputing about His plans.

– George MacDonald

If men were only a little more aware of what they are all doing together this very moment, they would feel as if they were in church, singing in a chorus. How they all love one another without knowing it, and how beautiful it would be if they knew! If only they could do consciously what they now do unawares!

– Paul Claudel

Where there is hate, let me sow love;
Where there is injury, pardon;
Where there is doubt, faith;
Where there is despair, hope;
Where there is darkness, light.

– St. Francis of Assisi

We shall match your capacity to inflict suffering with our capacity to endure suffering. Do to us what you will and we shall continue to love you.

– Martin Luther King, Jr.

All good moral philosophy is but a handmaid to religion.

– Francis Bacon

Life is an adventure in forgiveness.

– Norman Cousins

Let me not pray to be sheltered from dangers but to be fearless in facing them.
Let me not beg for the stilling of my pain but for the heart to conquer it.
Let me not look for allies in life's battlefield but to my own strength.
Let me not crave in anxious fear to be saved but hope for the patience to win my freedom.
Grant me that I may not be a coward, feeling your mercy in my success alone;
but let me find the grasp of your hand in my failure.

– Rabindranath Tagore

It is impossible for the mind which is not totally destitute of piety, to behold the sublime, the awful, the amazing works of creation and Providence, the heavens with their luminaries, the mountains, the oceans, the storm, the earthquake, the volcano, the circuit of the seasons, and the revolutions of empire—without marking in them all, the mighty hand of God, and feeling strong emotions and reverence toward the Author of these stupendous works.

– Timothy Dwight

Creation means the transformation of an otherwise chaotic world into a thing of order and beauty. It is the shaping of an indifferent matter into a world of value.

– J.E. Boodin

Experience of the spiritual world is not only possible in special moments of ecstasy but is waiting for us within every experience, however ordinary.

– A. Victor Murray

In God's economy, nothing is wasted. Through failure, we learn a lesson in humility which is probably needed, painful though it is.

– Bill Wilson, co-founder, Alcoholics Anonymous

Spread love everywhere you go: first of all in your own house. Give love to your children, to your wife or husband, to a next door neighbor.... Let no one ever come to you without leaving better and happier. Be the living expression of God's kindness; kindness in your face, kindness in your eyes, kindness in your smile, kindness in your warm greeting.

– Mother Teresa

What a piece of work is man, how noble in reason, how infinite in faculty, in form and moving how like an angel, in appearance HOW LIKE A GOD.

– William Shakespeare

We have not lost faith, but we have transferred it from God to the medical profession.

– George Bernard Shaw

All of our great political leaders believed in God. The most beautiful music, the finest art, the greatest writings and the most advanced political systems were all produced by those who believed in God.

– Wilford Hinkson

... We hold these truths to be self-evident, that all men are created equal, that they are endowed by their Creator with certain unalienable rights, that among these are Life, Liberty and the pursuit of Happiness.

– Thomas Jefferson, Declaration of Independence

Through the thick gloom of the present, I see the brightness of the future as the sun in heaven. We shall make this a glorious, an immortal day. When we are in our graves, our children will honor it. They will celebrate it with thanksgiving, with festivity, with bonfires, and illuminations. ...Before God, I believe the hour is come. My judgment approves this measure, and my whole heart is in it. All that I have, and all that I am, and all that I hope, in this life, I am now ready here to stake upon it.... It is my living sentiment, and by the blessing of God it shall be my dying sentiment. Independence now, and Independence forever.

– John Adams

There is a God! The herbs of the valley, the cedars of the mountains, bless Him. The insect sports in His beam; the bird sings Him in the foliage; the thunder proclaims Him in the heavens; the ocean declares His immensity. Man alone has said, "There is no God!"

– Anonymous

There are no facts yet wrested from the intriguing mysteries of this strange, onrushing cosmos which can in any degree disprove the existence and intelligent activities of an unconditioned, personal God.... For science is indeed "watching God work."

– Morritt Stanley Congdon

The destiny of mankind is not decided by material computation. When great causes are on the move in the world ... we learn that we are spirits, not animals ...

– Winston Churchill

Man, himself, is the crowning wonder of creation; the study of his nature the noblest study the world affords.

– William Gladstone

Ye call me Master,
And obey me not;
Ye call me light,
And seek me not;
Ye call me life,
And desire me not;
Ye call me wise,
And follow me not;
Ye call me fair,
And love me not;
Ye call me rich,
And ask me not;
Ye call me eternal,
And seek me not;
Ye call me gracious,
And trust me not;
Ye call me noble,
And serve me not;
Ye call me mighty,
And honor me not;
Ye call me just,
And fear me not;
If I condemn you,
Blame me not.

– Inscription in the cathedral at Tubeck, Germany

… We would stop in at the church very often because I wanted [our children] to know that church was something for every day in the week, it wasn't … just for a special day or special hour; that you could pray or that you could talk to God any time and He would be there, He would listen to you. He would give you advice or sympathy or whatever it was you felt you needed.

– Rose Kennedy

I like to speak of prayer as listening. We live in a culture that is terribly afraid to listen. We'd prefer to remain deaf. The Latin root word of the word *deaf* is "absurd." Prayer means moving from absurdity to obedience. Let the words descend from your head to your heart so you can begin to know God. In prayer, you become who you are meant to be.

– Henri Nouwen

People who pray for miracles usually don't get miracles…. But people who pray for courage, for strength to bear the unbearable, for the grace to remember what they have left instead of what they have lost, very often find their prayers answered…. Their prayers helped them tap hidden reserves of faith and courage which were not available to them before.

– Harold S. Kushner

… Where there is a plan, there is intelligence, and an orderly, unfolding universe testifies to the truth of the most majestic statement ever uttered—"In the beginning—God."

– Arthur H. Compton

There is no burden of the spirit but is lightened by kneeling under it. Little by little, the bitterest feelings are sweetened by the mention of them in prayer.

– William Mountford

THE TOUCH OF THE MASTER'S HAND
By Myra B. Welch

'Twas battered and scarred, and the auctioneer
Thought it scarcely worth his while
To waste much time on the old violin,
But held it up with a smile.
"What am I bidden, good folks," he cried,
"Who'll start the bidding for me?
A dollar, a dollar, then, two! Only two?
Two dollars, and who'll make it three?
Three dollars, once; three dollars, twice;
Going for three … " But no,
From the room, far back, a grey-haired man
Came forward and picked up the bow;
Then, wiping the dust from the old violin,
And tightening the loose strings,
He played a melody pure and sweet
As a caroling angel sings.

The music ceased, and the auctioneer,
With a voice that was quiet and low,
Said: "What am I bid for the old violin?"
And he held it up with the bow.
"A thousand dollars, and who'll make it two?
Two thousand! And who'll make it three?
Three thousand, once; three thousand, twice;
And going and gone," said he.

The people cheered, but some of them cried,
"We do not quite understand
What changed its worth?" Swift came the reply:
"The touch of a master's hand."

And many a man with life out of tune,
And battered and scarred with sin,
Is auctioned cheap to the thoughtless crowd,
Much like the old violin.

A "mess of potage," a glass of wine;
A game—and he travels on.
He is "going" once, and "going" twice,
He's "going" and almost "gone."

But the Master comes and the foolish crowd
Never can quite understand
The worth of a soul and the change that's wrought
By the touch of the Master's hand.

According to the theory of aerodynamics, as may be readily demonstrated through wind tunnel experiments, the bumblebee is unable to fly. This is because the size, weight and shape of his body in relation to the total wing-spread makes flying impossible. The bumblebee, being ignorant of these scientific truths, goes ahead and flies anyway and makes a little honey each day.

– Anonymous

When I do good, I feel good, when I do bad, I feel bad, and that's my religion.

– Anonymous

Hope begins in the dark, the stubborn hope that if you just show up and try to do the right thing, the dawn will come. You wait and watch and work: you don't give up.

– Anne Lamott

He has achieved success who has lived well, laughed often and loved much; who has enjoyed the trust of pure women, the respect of intelligent men and the love of little children; who has filled his niche and accomplished his task; who has left the world better than he found it, whether by an improved poppy, a perfect poem or a rescued soul; who has never lacked appreciation of earth's beauty or failed to express it; who has always looked for the best in others and given the best he had; whose life was an inspiration; whose memory a benediction.

– Bessie Anderson Stanley

Thee lift me, and I lift thee, and together we ascend.

– John Greenleaf Whittier

The friend who can be silent with us in a moment of despair or confusion, who can stay with us in an hour of grief and bereavement, who can tolerate not-knowing, not-curing, not-healing, and face with us the reality of our powerlessness—that is the friend who cares.

– Henri Nouwen, Out of Solitude

People tell me "don't"—I do. They say "can't"—I prove I can.

– Lily Havey, Japanese internment survivor

You're on the road to success when you realize that failure is merely a detour.

– William G. Milnes, Jr.

They conquer who believe they can. He has not learned the first lesson of life who does not every day surmount a fear.

– Ralph Waldo Emerson

Think of all the beauty still left around you and be happy.

– Anne Frank, Diary of a Young Girl

Only he who attempts the ridiculous can achieve the impossible.

– Will Henry

Anyone who says something is impossible is always being interrupted by someone doing it.

– Anonymous

As long as you're going to be thinking anyway, think big.

– Donald Trump

The people who get on in this world are the people who get up and look for the circumstances they want, and, if they can't find them, make them.

– George Bernard Shaw

You're a good man, Charlie Brown.

– Charles M. Schulz, Peanuts comic strip

Move out, man! Life is fleeting by.
Do something worthwhile, before you die.
Leave behind a work sublime,
that will outlive you, and time!

– Alfred A. Montapert

What do we live for, if it is not to make life less difficult for each other?

– George Eliot

Occasionally in life there are those moments of unutterable fulfillment which cannot be completely explained by those symbols called words. Their meanings can only be articulated by the inaudible language of the heart.

– Martin Luther King, Jr.

The happiness of life is made up of minute fractions—the little, soon-forgotten charities of a kiss or smile, a kind look, a heartfelt compliment—countless infinitesimals of pleasurable and genial feeling.

– Samuel Taylor Coleridge

He drew a circle that shut me out—
Heretic, rebel, a thing to flout.
But love and I had the wit to win:
We drew a circle that took him in.

– Edwin Markham

Obstacles are those frightful things you see when you take your eyes off your goal.

– Henry Ford

All the beautiful sentiments in the world weigh less than a single lovely action.

– James Russell Lowell

Discovery consists in seeing what everybody has seen and thinking what nobody has thought.

– Albert Szent-Gyorgyi

A mediocre idea that generates enthusiasm will go further than a great idea that inspires no one.

– Mary Kay Ash

For us is the life of action, of strenuous performance of duty; let us live in the harness, striving mightily; let us rather run the risk of wearing out than rusting out.

– Theodore Roosevelt

We need to be motivated by a new Spirit from within. Stir us out of our apathy and put the fire of love and goodness in us to move and motivate us to bigger and better days.

– Supreme Philosophy of Man

LIVE so enthusiastically you cannot fail.

– Dorthea Brande

You must do the thing you think you cannot do.

– Eleanor Roosevelt

Give me men with fire in their bowels.

– Oliver Cromwell

Creativity inspires more creativity. Saints are sinners who kept on trying. If you're feeling low, don't despair. The sun has a sinking spell every night, but it comes back up every morning. The way I see it, if you want the rainbow, you gotta put up with the rain.

– Dolly Parton

Our world was not designed to be fair. If you demand it, and use that unanswered demand to excuse a lack of drive, you'll be miserable and unsuccessful.... So don't ask for fairness and don't let your limitations hold you back. Take what you have and get what you want with it. Being happy is your own personal duty. Don't listen to those who say, "It's not done that way." Maybe it's not, but maybe you'll do it anyway. Don't listen to those who say, "You're taking too big a chance." Michelangelo would have painted the Sistine floor, and it would surely be rubbed out by today.... I firmly believe that if you follow a path that interests you, not to the exclusion of love, sensitivity, and cooperation with others, but with the strength of conviction that you can move others by your own efforts, and do not make success or failure the criteria by which you live, the chances are you'll be a person worthy of your own respect.

– Neil Simon

If we are intended for great purposes, we are expected to overcome great trials.

– Alfred A. Montapert

Attempt the impossible in order to improve your work.

– Bette Davis

There are defeats more triumphant than victories.

– Michel De Montaigne

Admitting Error clears the Score
And proves you Wiser than before.

– Arthur Guiterman

We must view young people not as empty bottles to be filled, but as candles to be lit.

– Robert H. Shaffer

The game was to just find something about everything to be glad about—no matter what 'twas.... You see, when you're hunting for the glad things, you sort of forget the other kind.

– Eleanor H. Porter, Pollyanna

God created memory so that we might have roses in December.

– Italo Svevo

Our business in life is not to get ahead of others, but to get ahead of ourselves—to break our own records, to outstrip our yesterday by our today.

– Stewart B. Johnson

You gotta walk that lonesome valley,
You gotta walk it by yourself,
Ain't nobody else gonna walk it for you.

– William H. Armstrong, Sounder

… Courage must come from the world within,
The man must furnish the will to win.
So figure it out for yourself, my lad,
You were born with all that the great have had,
With your equipment they all began.
Get hold of yourself, and say: "I can."

– Edgar A. Guest

… And the world will be better for this,
That one man, scorned and covered with scars,
Still strove, with his last ounce of courage,
To reach the unreachable star.

– Joe Darion, Man of La Mancha

Whoever is happy will make others happy too. He who has courage and faith will never perish in misery.

– Anne Frank

The soul would have no rainbow had the eyes no tears.

– John Vance Cheney

They never told me I couldn't.

– Tom Dempsey

Don't wait for your ship to come in; swim out to it.

– Anonymous

Do not turn away, through cowardice, from despair. Go through it.... Pass beyond. On the other side of the tunnel you will find light again.

– Andre Gide

Be bold—and mighty forces will come to your aid.

– Basil King

Little minds are tamed and subdued by misfortune, but great minds rise above it.

– Washington Irving

The tree that never had to fight
For sun and sky and air and light,
But stood out in the open plain
and always got its share of rain,
Never became a forest king
But lived and died a scrubby thing.

The man who never had to toil
to gain and farm his patch of soil,
Who never had to win his share
Of sun and sky and light and air,
never became a manly man
But lived and died as he began.

Good timber does not grow with ease,
The stronger wind, the stronger trees.
The further sky, the greater length.
The more the storm, the more the strength.
By sun and cold, by rain and snow,
In trees and men good timbers grow.

Where thickest lies the forest growth
We find the patriarchs of both.
And they hold counsel with the stars
Whose broken branches show the scars
Of many winds and much of strife.
This is the common law of life.

– Douglas Malloch

Never give way to melancholy; resist it steadily, for the habit will encroach. I once gave a lady two-and-twenty recipes against melancholy: one was a bright fire; another, to remember all the pleasant things said to and of her; another, to keep a box of sugarplums on the chimney piece, and a kettle simmering on the hob.

– Sydney Smith

Roy has a great asset—20 percent vision. He wears thick glasses with an extra strong lens. So he never sees an obstacle in his path and goes on to success.

– John Tigrett, on publisher Roy Thomson

Nothing is worth more than this day.

– Goethe

There ain't nothing from the outside can lick any of us.

– Margaret Mitchell, Gone with the Wind

Here and there, and now and then, God makes a giant among men.... It is not the critic who counts, nor the man who points out how the strong man stumbled or where the doer of deeds could have done better. The credit belongs to the man who is actually in the arena; whose face is marred by dust and sweat and blood; who strives valiantly; who errs and comes short again and again; ... who, at the best, knows in the end the triumph of high achievement; and who, at the worst, if he fails, at least fails while daring greatly, so that his place shall never be with those cold and timid souls who know neither victory nor defeat.

– Theodore Roosevelt

You cannot make yourself feel something you do not feel, but you can make yourself do right in spite of your feelings.

– Pearl S. Buck

The day will come when, after harnessing space, the winds, the tides and gravitation, we shall harness for God the energies of love. And on that day, for the second time in the history of the world, we shall have discovered fire.

– Tielhard de Chardin

You give but little when you give of your possessions. It is when you give of yourself that you truly give.

– Kahlil Gibran

The second mile of hard work is what makes the difference between the exhilaration of achievement and the acceptance of mediocrity.

– F. David Stanley

If I can stop one Heart from breaking
I shall not live in vain.
If I can ease one Life the Aching
Or cool one Pain
Or help one fainting Robin
Unto his Nest again
I shall not live in vain.

– Emily Dickinson

Nothing can stop the man with the right mental attitude from achieving his goal; nothing on earth can help the man with the wrong mental attitude.

– Thomas Jefferson

Triumph is a great word, but it is the first syllable that counts. Who ever found any meaning in "Umph"?

– Anonymous

True heroism is remarkably sober, very undramatic. It is not the urge to surpass all others at whatever cost, but the urge to serve others at whatever cost.

– Arthur Ashe

There are three rules for success. The first is: Go on. The second is: Go on. And the third is: Go on.

– Crane

"Brave Adm'r'l, say but one good word;
What shall we do when hope is gone?"
The words leapt like a leaping sword;
"Sail on! sail on! sail on! and on!"

– Joaquin Miller

It is invariably the tree that has been stressed and challenged surviving in a high, windy place that yields the wood I value most.

– Harry Nohr, World Class Wood Designer

All we are given is possibilities—to make ourselves one thing or another.

– Ortegay Gasset

Commitment is the stuff character is made of; the power to change the face of things. It is the daily triumph of integrity over skepticism.

– Shearson/Lehman Bros.

In the city, a road with no exit is marked Dead End. In the country, we call these roads lanes. I always think that it is sad to label anything a dead end. No one wants to explore it then. But walking down a lane is romantic and exciting. I hesitate to venture down a dead-end road, but I look for lanes to explore with a favorite friend. An unexpected building, a rare flower, a quiet peace all wait for me on country lanes.

– Kathleen S. Abrams

The difference between a lady and a flower girl is not how she behaves, but how she is treated. I shall always be a flower girl to Professor Higgins because he always treats me as a flower girl and always will. But I know that I shall always be a lady to Colonel Pickering because he always treats me as a lady and always will.

– Eliza Doolittle from My Fair Lady

Forgiveness is the fragrance of the violet that clings fast to the heel that crushed it.

– Anonymous

To be astonished at anything is the first movement of the mind toward discovery.

– Louis Pasteur

If I have seen farther than other men, it is by standing on the shoulders of giants.

– Sir Isaac Newton

We are not interested in the possibility of defeat.

– Victoria, Queen of Great Britain

... I live the way I wish. There are always people who will object. If you're short, tall people diminish you. If you're tall, shorter people don't like you. If you're alive, people wish you were dead. I do the best I can for the most I can ...

– Robert Mitchum

I have used all my doubt as energy, and created with it. I have used all my pain as energy, and created with it. I have used all my anxiety as energy, and created with it. I plan to use my death as energy, and create with it ...

– Stymean Karlen

Seize the day! Make your lives extraordinary.

– From the movie Dead Poets Society

Every day someone does something that couldn't be done.

– Anonymous

Not failure, but low aim, is crime.

– Anonymous

On a garden wall in Peking, China, was a brass plate about two feet long with these words:
Enjoy yourself. It is later than you think!
Well, maybe it is later than you think; why don't you do something about it?

– Charles W. Miller

Did you tackle that trouble that came your way
With a resolute heart and cheerful?
Or hide your face from the light of day
With a craven soul and fearful?

Oh, a trouble's a ton, or a trouble's an ounce,
Or a trouble is what you make it.
And it isn't the fact that you're hurt that counts,
But only how did you take it?

You are beaten to earth? Well, well, what's that?
Come up with a smiling face.
It's nothing against you to fall down flat,
But to lie there—that's disgrace.

The harder you're thrown, why the higher you bounce.
Be proud of your blackened eye!
It isn't the fact that you're licked that counts,
It's how did you fight and why?...

– Edmund Vance Cooke

For all the trials and tears of time,
For every hill I have to climb,
My heart sings but a grateful song ...
These are the things that make me strong.

– Anonymous

If I can stop one heart from breaking,
I shall not live in vain;
If I can ease one life the aching,
Or cool one pain,
Or help one fainting robin
Unto his nest again,
I shall not live in vain.

– *Emily Dickinson*

I'd look at one of my stonecutters hammering away at a rock, perhaps a hundred times without as much as a crack showing in it. Yet, at the hundred and first blow it would split in two, and I knew it was not that blow that did it, but all that had gone before.

– *Jacob A. Riis*

You cannot dream yourself into a character. You must hammer and forge yourself one.

– *Froude*

Two men bearing each a heavy load
Met one day in a narrow road.
The bully blurted loud, abusive, cruel:
"I don't back up for any fool."
Said the other in kindly spirit true:
"I feel very much the same as you—
Except I do."

– *E.L.M.*

Sir Andrew Barton said, I'm hurt,
I'm hurt, but I'm not slain.
I will lay me down and bleed awhile,
then rise and fight again.

– *Anonymous*

Unemployment and despair can lead to desperation. But most people will not commit desperate acts if they have been taught that dignity, honesty and integrity are more important than revenge or rage; if they understand that respect and kindness ultimately give one a better chance at success ...

– *Deseret News*

Happiness is excitement that has found a settling down place, but there is always a little corner that keeps flapping around.

– *E.L. Konigsburg,*
from The Mixed-Up Files of
Mrs. Basil E. Frankweiler

No star is ever lost we once have seen,
We always may be what we might have been.

– *Adalaide A. Proctor*

I was raised by two sick people who taught me insanity and fear and hatred. I was raised in hell, chaos felt like home. Result: I learned to land on my feet in any situation. I can stand face to face with the cruelest of ogres.

– *Steven J. Wolin, The Resilient Self*

THE BEATITUDES OF THE AGED
by Victor Hugo

Blessed are they who understand my faltering step and palsied hand.
Blessed are they who know that my ears today must strain to catch the things they say.
Blessed are they who seem to know that my eyes are dim and my wits are slow.
Blessed are they who looked away when coffee spilled at the table today.
Blessed are they with a cheery smile who stopped to chat for a little while.
Blessed are they who never say you've told that story twice today.
Blessed are they who know the ways to bring back memories of yesterdays.
Blessed are those who ease the days on my journey home in loving ways.
Blessed are they who make it known that I'm loved respected and not alone.
Blessed are they who know I'm at a loss to find the strength to carry the cross.
I don't want to get to the end of my life and find that I just lived the length of it. I want to have lived the width of it as well.

– *Diane Ackerman*

Life loves to be taken by the lapel and told: "I am with you kid. Let's go."

– *Maya Angelou*

Vision is the art of seeing things invisible.

– *Jonathan Swift*

... Our doubts are traitors, and make us lose the good we oft might win by fearing to attempt.

– *William Shakespeare, Measure for Measure*

We are face to face with our destiny and we must meet it with a high and resolute courage. For us is the life of action, of strenuous performance of duty; let us live in the harness, striving mightily; let us rather run the risk of wearing out than rusting out.

– *Theodore Roosevelt*

Somebody said that it couldn't be done,
But he with a chuckle replied
That "maybe it couldn't,"
but he would be one
Who wouldn't say so till he'd tried.

So he buckled right in with a trace of a grin
On his face. If he worried he hid it.
He started to sing as he tackled the thing
That couldn't be done, and he did it.

– *Edgar A. Guest*

Ah, but a man's reach should exceed his grasp,
Or what's a heaven for?

– *Robert Browning*

The most welcomed people of the world are never those who continually look back upon the trials, the sorrows, the failures, the bitter frustrations of yesterday, but those who cast their eyes forward with faith, hope … courage, happy curiosity.

– James Francis Cooke

By perseverance the snail reached the Ark.

– Charles Hadon Spurgeon

If a man is called to be a street sweeper he should sweep streets even as Michelangelo painted, or Beethoven composed music. He should sweep streets so well that all the host of heaven and earth will pause and say, here lived a great sweeper who did his job well.

– Martin Luther King, Jr.

I know of no higher fortitude than stubbornness in the face of overwhelming odds.

– Louis Nizer

A winner is someone who recognizes his God-given talents, works his tail off to develop them into skills, and uses these skills to accomplish his goals.

– Larry Bird

Every friend represents a world in us, a world possibly not born until they arrive, and it is only by this meeting that a new world is born.

– Anais Nin

Courage is not limited to the battlefield or the Indianapolis 500 or bravely catching a thief in your house. The real tests of courage are much deeper and much quieter. They are the inner tests, like remaining faithful when nobody's looking, like enduring pain when the room is empty, like standing alone when you're misunderstood.

– Charles R. Swidoll

When things go wrong as they sometimes will,
When the road you're treading seems all up hill,
When the funds are low and debts are high,
And you want to smile, but have to sigh.

When care is pressing you down a bit,
Rest—if you must—but don't you quit.
Life is queer with its twists and turns,
As every one of us sometimes learns,

And many a failure turns about
When he might have won had he stuck it out.
Don't give up, though the pace seems slow—
You might succeed with another blow.

Often the goal is nearer than
It seems to a faint and faltering man,
Often the struggler has given up
When he might have captured the victor's cup.

And he learned too late, when the night slipped down,
How close he was to the golden crown.
Success is failure turned inside out—
The silver tint of the clouds of doubt—

And you never can tell how close you are,
It may be near when it seems afar;
So stick to the fight when you're hardest hit—
It's when things seem worst that you mustn't quit.

– Anonymous

Just Do It!

– Nike advertising slogan

The ninety and nine are with dreams content;
But the hope of a world made new
Is the hundredth man who is grimly bent
On making that dream come true.

– Anonymous

Nothing in the world can take the place of persistence.
Talent will not; nothing is more common than unsuccessful men with talent. Genius will not; unrewarded genius is almost a proverb. Education will not; the world is full of educated derelicts. Persistence and determination alone are omnipotent. The slogan "Press on" has solved and always will solve the problems of the human race.

– Calvin Coolidge

Courage is not the absence of fear but the ability to carry on with dignity in spite of it.

– Scott Turow, The Burden of Proof

It is said the one machine can do the work of fifty ordinary men. No machine, however, can do the work of one extraordinary man.

– Tehyi Hsieh

From the biographies of the world's celebrities:
Thurlow Weed walked two miles through the snow with pieces of rag carpet about his feet for shoes, that he might borrow a book.
Milton wrote "Paradise Lost" in a world he could not see, and then sold it for fifteen pounds.
John Bunyan wrote "Pilgrim's Progress" in prison, at the behest of conscience and in disregard of the edict of his accusers.
Carlyle, after lending the manuscript of the "French Revolution" to a friend, whose servant carelessly used it to kindle a fire, calmly went to work and rewrote it.
Handel practiced on his harpsichord in secret, until every key was hollowed by his fingers to resemble the bowl of a spoon.

– Leaders of Men

If it is to be, it is up to me.

– E. Wilford Edmar

Tenderness toward those weaker than ourselves strengthens the heart toward life itself. The moment we understand and feel sorry for the next man and forgive him, we wash ourselves, and it is a cleaner world.

– Albert Schweitzer

He who has struggled in the dark best knows the radiance of the light.

– Anonymous

The power that makes grass grow, fruit ripen, and guides the bird in flight is in us all.

– Anizia Yezierska, Red Ribbon on a White Horse

If you want to lift yourself up, lift up someone else.

– Booker T. Washington

To the good I would be good; to the not-good I would also be good, in order to make them good.

– Lao-Tzu

The great pleasure in life is doing what people say you cannot do.

– Walter Bagehot

Eagles: When they walk, they stumble. They are not what one would call graceful. They were not designed to walk. They fly, and when they fly, oh, how they fly, so free, so graceful. They see from the sky what we never see.

– Dr. Thomas C. Lee, inscription given with a painting of an eagle to a paraplegic medical student at Georgetown University Medical School

Far away there in the sunshine are my highest aspirations. I may not reach them, but I can look up and see their beauty, believe in them and try to follow where they lead.

– Louisa May Alcott

Expect trouble as an inevitable part of life, and when it comes, hold your head high, look it squarely in the eye and say, "I will be bigger than you. You cannot defeat me." Then repeat to yourself the most comforting of all words, "This too shall pass." Maintaining self-respect in the face of a devastating experience is of prime importance.

– Ann Landers

Out of suffering have emerged the strongest souls.

– E. H. Chapin

I have found the paradox that if I love until it hurts, then there is no hurt, but only more love.

– Mother Teresa

Believe that you have it, and you have it.

– Desiderius Erasmus

In the long run men hit only what they aim at. Therefore, though they should fail immediately, they had better aim at something high.

– Henry David Thoreau

Don't be afraid to give up the good to go for the great.

– Kenny Rogers

If you would attain to what you are not yet, you must always be displeased by what you are. For where you were pleased with yourself there you have remained. But once you have said, "It is enough" you are lost. Keep adding, keep walking, keep advancing; do not stop, do not turn back, do not turn from the straight road.

– St. Augustine

Any song that moves you to joy or tears has greatness. Everything in life should be enjoyed for what it is.

– Marguerite Piazza, Metropolitan Opera

If you cannot win, you must win.

– Reb Menshim Mendl of Kotsk

If we are ever to enjoy life, now is the time—not tomorrow, nor next year, nor in some future life after we have died. The best preparation for a better life next year is a full, complete, harmonious, joyous life this year. Today should always be our most wonderful day.

– Thomas Dreier

This is the beginning of a new day. God has given me this day to use as I will. I can waste it—or use it for good, but what I do today is important, because I am exchanging a day of my life for it! When tomorrow comes, this day will be gone forever, leaving in its place something that I have traded for it. I want it to be gain, and not loss; good, and not evil; success, and not failure; in order that I shall not regret the price that I have paid for it.

– W. Heartsill Wilson

It was a little thing for the janitor to leave a lamp swinging in the cathedral at Pisa, but in that steady swaying motion the boy Galileo saw the pendulum, and conceived the idea of thus measuring time.

– Anonymous

Teach only love, for that is what you are.

– A Course In Miracles

Let miracles replace all grievances.

– Foundation for Inner Peace

The best way out of a difficulty is through it.

– Will Rogers

... You're in the trap called here. But you can get out of it. You can get there from here. The goal, the objective—the dream!—they are all attainable. The first step is to take the first step—raise one foot off dead center. You're not compelled to achieve your aspiration by one soaring flight, not even by giant steps, only one foot at a time. After the first footstep, the second is easier, the third is surer, the fourth is faster. Suddenly the miracle happens. Your mind is off the footsteps and only on the dream. Only you're not dreaming the dream anymore—you're living it. Winning. Getting the best of yourself.

– Katherine Nash

Don't bunt, aim out of the ball park. Aim for the company of the immortals.

– David Ogilvy

Some folks are natural born kickers. They can always find a way to turn disaster into butter.

– Katherine Paterson, Lyddi

Nothing ever built arose to touch the skies unless some man dreamed that it should, some man believed that it could, and some man willed that it must.

– Charles F. Kettering

You win some, you lose some, and some get rained out, but you gotta suit up for them all.

– J. Askenberg

When you come to the end of your rope, tie a knot and hang on.

– Franklin D. Roosevelt

It's not what happens *to* us, but what happens *in* us that supremely counts.

– Anonymous

Whenever we conquer our fears, whenever we do with love and courage the things we have to do, then no matter what the results may seem to be at the time, we are victorious and we are counted as those who have been a success.

– Dale E. Turner

When I was a cub in Milwaukee I had a city editor who'd stroll over and read across a guy's shoulder when he was writing a lead. Sometimes he would approve, sometimes he'd say gently, "Try again," and walk away. My best advice is, try again. And then again. If you're for this racket, and not many really are, then you've got an eternity of sweat and tears ahead. I don't just mean you. I mean anybody.

– Red Smith

.. Because I'm good enough
I'm smart enough
And doggone it, people like me.

– Al Franken as Stuart Smalley,
Saturday Night Live

All maxims have their antagonistic maxims; proverbs should be sold in pairs, a single one being but a half-truth.

— *William Mathews*

You're right from your side, I'm right from mine.
— *Bob Dylan, "One Too Many Mornings"*

You can't teach an old dog new tricks.
— *Old English saying*

You're never too old to learn.
— *Old English saying*

And if any mischief follow, then thou shalt give life for life. Eye for eye, tooth for tooth, hand for hand, foot for foot, burning for burning, wound for wound, stripe for stripe.
— *The Bible, Exodus 21:23–25*

[Capital Punishment] … tells our children that it is OK to meet violence with violence.
— *Mario Cuomo*

Son, we live in a world that has walls, and those walls have to be guarded with guns … because deep down in places you don't talk about at parties, you want me on that wall—you need me on that wall. I have neither the time nor the inclination to explain myself to a man who rises and sleeps under the blanket of freedom I provide and then questions the manner in which I provide it…. I would rather you just say thank you.
— *Jack Nicholson, A Few Good Men*

Every gun that is fired, every warship launched, every rocket fired, signifies, in the final sense, a theft from those who hunger and are not fed, those who are cold and are not clothed. The world in arms is not spending money alone. It is spending the sweat of its laborers, the genius of its scientists, the hopes of its children.
— *Dwight David Eisenhower*

Nothing could have been more obvious to the people of the early twentieth century than the rapidity with which war was becoming impossible. And as certainly they did not see it. They did not see it until the atomic bombs burst in their fumbling hands.
— *H.G. Wells*

The emotional security and political stability in this country entitles us to be a nuclear power.
— *Sir Ronald Mason*

My child is an honor student.
— *Bumper sticker*

My kid beat up your honor student.
— *Bumper sticker*

A society that views graphic violence as entertainment … should not be surprised when senseless violence shatters the dreams of its youngest and brightest …
— *Deseret News*

It's cool seeing people being blown up, shot, squished, and chopped.
— *Boy, age 8 from Misti Snow, Take Time To Play Checkers*

The highest result of education is tolerance.
— *Helen Keller*

What are schools for if not indoctrination against Communism?
— *Richard Nixon*

Absence makes the heart grow fonder.
— *Thomas Haynes Bayly*

Out of sight, out of mind.
— *Proverb*

It is conceivable that religion may be morally useful without being intellectually sustainable.
— *John Stuart Mill*

The fact that a believer is happier than a skeptic is no more to the point than the fact that a drunken man is happier than a sober one.
— *George Bernard Shaw*

Only the shallow know themselves.
— *Oscar Wilde*

There are many people who have the gift, or failing, of never understanding themselves. I have been unlucky enough, or perhaps fortunate enough to have received the opposite gift.
— *Charles de Talleyrand*

Public opinion in this country is everything.
— *Abraham Lincoln*

Know the true value of time; snatch, seize, and enjoy every moment of it. No idleness, no laziness, no procrastination; never put off till tomorrow what you can do today.
— *Lord Chesterfield*

Never do today what you can do as well tomorrow, because something may occur to make you regret your premature action.
— *Aaron Burr*

If all mankind minus one were of one opinion, and only one person were of the contrary opinion, mankind would be no more justified in silencing that one person than he, if he had the power, would be justified in silencing mankind.

— *John Stuart Mill*

I consider myself a Christian, Hindu, Moslem, Jew, Buddhist, and Confucian.

— *Mohandas Gandhi*

The equal toleration of all religions … is the same thing as atheism.

— *Pope Leo XIII*

Satan is indeed loose in the world—and he is racism.

— *Elie Wiesel*

I don't see much future for the Americans…. Everything about the behavior of American society reveals that it's half judaized and half negrefied. How can one expect a state like that to hold together?

— *Adolf Hitler*

What's right about America is that although we have a mess of problems, we have the great capacity—intellect and resources—to do something about them.

— *Henry Ford II*

Whoever kindles the flames of intolerance in America is lighting a fire underneath his own home.

— *Harold E. Stassen*

Capitalism did not arise because capitalists stole the land … but because it was more efficient than feudalism. It will perish because it is not merely less efficient than socialism, but actually self-destructive.

— *J.B.S. Haldane*

Socialism is only workable in heaven where it isn't needed and hell where they've got it.

— *Cecil Palmer*

Under capitalism man exploits man; under socialism the reverse is true.

— *Polish proverb*

Tobacco, divine, rare, superexcellent tobacco, which goes far beyond all the panaceas, potable gold and philosopher's stones, a sovereign remedy to all disease.

— *Robert Burton, c. 1600*

To measure up to all that is demanded of him, a man must overestimate his capacities.

— *Goethe*

Cigarettes dull the faculties, stunt and retard the physical development, unsettle the mind, and rob the persistent user of will power and the ability to concentrate.

— *Dick Merriwell*

… All faiths do harm. We may define faith as a firm belief in something for which there is no evidence. When there is evidence, no one speaks of faith. We do not speak of our faith that two and two are four or that the earth is round. We only speak of faith when we wish to substitute emotion for evidence.

— *Anonymous*

We are told that faith could remove mountains, but no one believed it; we are now told that the atomic bomb can remove mountains, and everyone believes it.

— *Bertrand Russell*

God must love the common man, he made so many of them.

— *Abraham Lincoln*

No woman can call herself free who does not own and control her body. No woman can call herself free until she can choose consciously whether she will or will not be a mother.

— *Margaret Sanger*

Any use whatsoever of matrimony exercised in such a way that the act is deliberately frustrated in its natural power to generate life is an offense against the law of God and of nature, and those who indulge in such are branded with the guilt of a grave sin.

— *Pope Pius XI*

This country was formed for the white, not the black man. And looking upon African slavery from the same viewpoint held by the noble framers of our constitution, I for one have ever considered it one of the greatest blessings (for both themselves and us) that God ever has bestowed upon a favored nation.

— *John Wilkes Booth*

… That peculiar disease of intellectuals, that infatuation with ideas at the expense of experience that compels experience to conform to bookish preconceptions.

— *Archibald MacLeish*

A book is the only place in which you can examine a fragile thought without breaking it, or explore an explosive idea without fear that it will go off in your face…. It is one of the few havens remaining where a man's mind can get both provocation and privacy.

— *Edward P. Morgan*

I have a dream that one day in the red hills of Georgia, the sons of former slaves and the sons of former slave owners will be able to sit together at the table of brotherhood ... that one day even the State of Mississippi, a state sweltering with the heat of injustice, sweltering with the heat of oppression, will be transformed into an oasis of freedom and justice ... that my four little children will one day live in a nation where they will not be judged by the color of their skin but by the content of their character.

– Martin Luther King, Jr.

Good swimmers are oftenest drowned.

– Thomas Fuller

God must hate the common man, he made him so common.

– Philip Wylie

I think every woman wants to look up to a man, if she has any sense.

– Katharine Hepburn

When you want anything said, ask a man. If you want anything done, ask a woman.

– Margaret Thatcher

I owe all my success in life to having been always a quarter of an hour beforehand.

– Horatio Nelson

Better early than late; better late than never.

– Anonymous

Punctuality is the virtue of the bored.

– Evelyn Waugh

I don't agree with you, but I'd fight to the death to protect your right to say it.

– Anonymous

It's a great pity the right to free speech isn't based on the obligation to say something sensible.

– Anonymous

What mother wouldn't go to jail to help her suffering child?

– Mildred Kaitz, who received a summons for growing marijuana to help her son who has multiple sclerosis

The blood lust by the DA against marijuana users is being used to justify an abuse of civil rights.

– William F. Buckley, Jr.

I will fight with all the vigor God has given me, any step that would expand the opportunities for people to self-destruct.

– U.S. Rep. Charles Rangel

Marijuana [damages] brain cells and respiratory systems, decreased hormone production in both sexes, acute memory loss, lower immune systems, miscarriages and stillbirths.

– Stephen Greene, deputy administrator, Drug Enforcement Administration

Here we are, we're alone in the universe, there's no God, it just seems that it all began by something as simple as sunlight striking on a piece of rock. And here we are. We've only got ourselves. Somehow, we've just got to make a go of it. We've only got ourselves.

– Jean, The Entertainer, by John Osborne

But if from thence thou shalt seek the Lord thy God, thou shalt find him, if thou seek him with all thy heart and with all thy soul.

– The Bible, Deuteronomy 4:29

The love of money is the mother of all evil.

– Phocylides, 6th century, B.C.E.

We are told that the love of money is the root of all evil; but money itself is one of the most useful contrivances ever invented: it is not its fault that some people are foolish or miserly enough to be fonder of it than of their own souls.

– George Bernard Shaw

It is not the creation of wealth that is wrong, but love of money for its own sake.

– Margaret Thatcher

The love of unearned money is the root of all evil.

– Anonymous

They have taken sin and made it as mediocre as non-sin. Gambling is no longer a vice, it's just play. Pretty soon they will have people convinced that gambling is doing God's work.

– Vicki Abt, sociologist

We are simply following the demographics. We did not put arcade games in for the purpose of addicting children and we have not hired Joe Camel as our spokesman.

– Larry Wolf, CEO, MGM Grand

Do as you would be done by.

– Lord Chesterfield

I'll be damned if I want most folks out there to do unto me what they do unto themselves.

– Toni Cade Bambara

Man tends to increase at a greater rate than his means of subsistence; consequently he is occasionally subjected to a severe struggle for existence.

– Charles Darwin

Do not do unto others as you would they should do unto you. Their tastes may not be the same.

— *George Bernard Shaw*

Do not do for others what they can do for themselves.

— *Anonymous*

We declare henceforth that all animals shall enjoy these inalienable rights: The right to freedom from fear, pain and suffering—whether in the name of science or sport, fashion or food, exhibition or service. The right, if they are wild, to roam free, unharried by hunters, trappers or slaughterers…. And finally the right, at the end, to a decent death—not by a club, by a trap, by harpoon, cruel poison or mass extermination chamber. We have only one creed—to speak for those who can't.

— *The Fund for Animals, Inc.*

The only people with a right to complain about what I do for a living are vegetarian nudists.

— *Ken Bates,
one of California's 700 licensed fur trappers*

If someone was unhappy being tall, would those same people call for sawing off his legs?

— *Anonymous response*

And God blessed them, saying, Be fruitful, and multiply…

— *The Bible, Genesis 1:22*

We are going to monitor every minute of your broadcast news, and if this kind of bias continues … you just might find yourself having a little trouble getting some of your licenses renewed.

— *Frank Shakespeare*

They can't censor the gleam in my eyes.

— *Charles Laughton*

It is true that liberty is precious—so precious that it must be rationed.

— *Vladimir Lenin*

Those who deny freedom to others, deserve it not for themselves.

— *Abraham Lincoln*

Never does nature say one thing and wisdom another.

— *Juvenal*

Nature is usually wrong.

— *James Whistler*

In failing circumstances no man can be relied on to keep his integrity.

— *Ralph Waldo Emerson*

This old anvil laughs at many broken hammers. There are men who can't be bought.

— *Carl Sandburg*

Our rocket has bypassed the moon. It is nearing the sun, and we have not discovered God.

— *From a 1960 Moscow radio broadcast*

There are no facts yet wrested from the intriguing mysteries of this strange, onrushing cosmos which can in any degree disprove the existence and intelligent activities of an unconditioned, personal God. For science is indeed "watching God work."

— *Morritt Stanley Congdon*

It's called jury duty, not jury inconvenience. It is an obligation, not an interruption.

— *Newsweek, public service advertisement*

Jury: A group of twelve men who, having lied to the judge about their hearing, health and business engagements, have failed to fool him.

— *H.L. Mencken*

You know what I think about violence. For me it is profoundly moral, more moral than compromises and transactions.

— *Benito Mussolini*

Social justice cannot be attained by violence. Violence kills what it intends to create.

— *Anonymous*

Guns are neat little things, aren't they? They can kill extraordinary people with very little effort.

— *John W. Hinckley, Jr.,
President Ronald Reagan's attempted assassin*

In 1988, handguns killed
7 people in Great Britain
19 in Sweden
53 in Switzerland
25 in Israel
13 in Australia
8 in Canada
and 8,915 in the United States.
God Bless America.

— *Poster by Center to Prevent Handgun Violence*

We don't have to be what you want us to be.

— *Bill Russell*

The hottest place in hell is reserved for those who in the time of great moral crisis maintain their neutrality.

— *Dante Alighieri*

I don't know, I don't care, and it doesn't make any difference.

— *Jack Kerouac*

When in Rome do as the Romans do.
— *Billy Joel, Storm Front*

Fear of losing is what makes competitors so great. Show me a gracious loser and I'll show you a permanent loser.
— *O.J. Simpson*

Every man's got to figure to get beat sometime.
— *Joe Louis*

The pessimist is the man who believes things couldn't possibly be worse, to which the optimist replies, "Oh yes they could."
— *Vladimir Bukovsky*

The optimist proclaims we live in the best of all possible worlds, and the pessimist fears this is true.
— *James Branch Cabell*

Freedom of the press is not an end in itself but a means to the end of a free society.
— *Felix Frankfurter*

A free press can, of course, be good or bad, but, most certainly, without freedom it will never be anything but bad.
— *Albert Camus*

If the 1st Amendment means anything, it means that a state has no business telling a man, sitting alone in his own house, what books he may read or what films he may watch.
— *Thurgood Marshall, unanimous opinion guaranteeing the right to possess in one's home material that might be regarded as obscene in public*

Nobody, including the Supreme Court, knows what obscenity is.
— *Norman Dorsen*

People keep writing songs about how rock 'n' roll will never die. Well, rock 'n' roll died a long time ago. It never even made it into the '60s. A certain joy went out of rock 'n' roll, and what was left was militancy—which I guess makes sense because of the times.
— *Joni Mitchell*

That is, rock 'n' roll is only rock 'n' roll if it's not safe ... the real thing is always brash. Violence and energy—that's really what rock 'n' roll is all about.
— *Mick Jagger*

What joy in that light cloud!
— *Ermanno Wolf-Ferrari, on smoking*

What's done is done.
— *Shakespeare, Macbeth*

I want all hellions to quit puffing that hell fume into God's clean air.
— *Carrie Nation*

There is nothing so aggravating as a fresh boy who is too old to ignore and too young to kick.
— *Kin Hubbard*

Children love and want to be loved and they very much prefer the joy of accomplishment to the triumph of hateful failure. Do not mistake a child for his symptom.
— *Dr. Erik Erikson*

Oh, call back yesterday, bid time return.
— *William Shakespeare, Richard II*

Women are not men's equals in anything except responsibility. We are not their inferiors, either, or even their superiors. We are quite simply different races.
— *Phyllis McGinley*

There is only one sex.... A man and a woman are so entirely the same thing that one can scarcely understand the subtle reasons for sex distinction with which our minds are filled.
— *George Sand*

To curse is to pray to the Devil.
— *German proverb*

Grant me some wild expressions, Heavens, or I shall burst.
— *George Farquhar*

Art is meant to disturb. Science reassures.
— *Georges Braque*

We especially need imagination in science. It is not all mathematics, nor all logic, but it is somewhat beauty and poetry.
— *Maria Mitchell*

The individual who commits violence in the name of peace is already on the road to becoming that which he hates.
— *Lawrence J. Peter, The Peter Program*

There's no question in my mind but that rights are never won unless people are willing to fight for them.
— *Eleanor Smeal*

The proliferation of guns must be stopped.... We must also stop glorifying the materialism that drives people to violence.
— *Marian Wright Edelman*

Better Red than dead.
— *Anonymous*

A bit of shooting takes your mind off your troubles—it makes you forget the cost of living.
– Brendan Behan

When a nation's young men are conservative, its funeral bell is already rung.
– Henry Ward Beecher

There are no more liberals…. They've all been mugged.
– James Q. Wilson

Better that we should die fighting than be outraged and dishonored…. Better to die than to live in slavery.
– Emmeline Pankhurst

When even despair ceases to serve any creative purpose, then surely we are justified in suicide.
– Cyril Connolly

Often the test of courage is not to die but to live.
– Vittorio Alfieri

The first thing we do, let's kill all the lawyers.
– William Shakespeare, King Henry VI

Thou shalt not avenge.
– The Bible, Leviticus 19:18

Open thine heart not to every man, lest he requite thee with a shrewd turn.
– The Bible, Ecclesiastics 8:19

"Come into my parlor," said the spider to the fly.
"'Tis the prettiest sight you ever did spy."
– Mary Howitt

Men can know more than their ancestors did if they start with a knowledge of what their ancestors had already learned. This is why a society can progress only if it conserves its traditions, then refines and builds.
– Distilled Wisdom

Is it progress if a cannibal uses knife and fork?
– Stanislaw J. Lec

We are a religious people whose institutions presuppose a Supreme Being.
– William O. Douglas

God is still the best medicine that we physicians can ever prescribe. But He expects us to team up with Him and utilize our wits, plus all the available drugs and other techniques that scientists have developed.
– Dr. George W. Crane

The Atomic Age is here to stay—but are we?
– Bennett Cerf

I believe in an America where the separation of church and state is absolute …
– John F. Kennedy

No country without an atom bomb could properly consider itself independent.
– Charles De Gualle

Everything according to reason.
– Cardinal Richelieu

Pure logic is the ruin of the spirit.
– Antoine De Saint-Exupery

Whatever choice Elizabeth Bouvia may ultimately make, I can only hope that her courage, persistence and example will cause our society to deal realistically with the plight of those unfortunate individuals to whom death beckons as a welcome respite from suffering.
– Lynn Compton

Euthanasia is a long, smooth-sounding word, and it conceals its danger as long as smooth words do, but the danger is there, nevertheless.
– Pearl Buck, The Child Who Never Grew

In all my years of public life I have never obstructed justice.
– Richard M. Nixon

Give the investigators an hors d'oeuvre and maybe they won't come back for the main course.
– Richard M. Nixon

Madam, we took you in order to have children, not to get advice.
– Charles XI

But if God had wanted us to think with our wombs, why did he give us a brain?
– Clare Boothe Luce

Our goal is not the conquest of Iraq—it is the liberation of Kuwait. It is my hope that somehow the Iraqi people can, even now, convince their dictator that he must lay down his arms, leave Kuwait, and let Iraq itself rejoin the family of peace-loving nations …
– George Bush, speech to nation, January 1991

… How many deaths will it take 'til he knows that too many people have died?
– Bob Dylan, "Blowin' in the Wind"

Troops are made to let themselves be killed.
– Napoleon Bonaparte

Greed is good! Greed is right! Greed works! Greed will save the U.S.A.!
– Michael Douglas, Wall Street

We're Going To War To Defend People Who Won't Let Women Drive?

– Button

When you buy a pill and buy peace with it you get conditioned to cheap solutions instead of deep ones.

– Max Lerner

Big mouthfuls often choke.

– Italian proverb

When the European settlers landed on these wonderful shores they ... could not even have lasted that first winter had it not been for the kindness of the Native American. The Native American kept us Europeans alive because he felt it was his duty.... The Native American gave us food and taught us how to use these foods because he felt he should, and now he is very sorry. He is tragically sorry.

– Jeff Smith

I don't feel we did wrong in taking this great country away from them. There were great numbers of people who needed new land, and the Indians were selfishly trying to keep it for themselves.

– John Wayne

To knock a thing down, especially if it is cocked at an arrogant angle, is a deep delight to the blood.

– George Santayana

One more such victory and we are lost.

– Plutarch, Pyrrhus

You have put me in here a cub, but I will come out roaring like a lion, and I will make all hell howl!

– Carry Nation, on her imprisonment

There's no greater gap between our good intentions and our misguided consequences than you see in the welfare system.

– Bill Clinton

This is classic Clinton: overpromise, underdeliver, and then try to fudge the difference.

– William Bennett

We look forward to the time when the power of love will replace the love of power. Then will our world know the blessings of peace.

– William Gladstone

Let him who desires peace prepare for war.

– Vegetius, 4th century

Do we fear our enemies more than we love our children?

– Bumper Sticker

I'm sick of hearing about twelve-step programs for healing and recovery. What we need are fewer twelve-step programs and more twelve-gauge shotguns.

– Name withheld by request

It is men, not women, who have promoted the cult of brutal masculinity; and because men admire muscle and physical force, they assume that we do too.

– Elizabeth Gould Davis

And who was wrong?
And who was right?
And did it matter in the thick of the fight?

– Billy Joel, The Nylon Curtain

On behalf of the people of the United States, I extend sincere condolences to the people of North Korea on the death of President Kim Il Sung. We appreciate his leadership in resuming the talks between our governments. We hope they will continue as appropriate.

– Statement issued by President Bill Clinton on the death of Kim

I'm at a loss to understand his statement extending "sincere condolences" to the people of North Korea on "behalf of the people of the United States." Perhaps President Clinton has forgotten that Kim Il Sung was responsible for the war that caused the loss of more than 54,000 American lives and 100,000 Americans wounded.

– Senator Bob Dole, July 9, 1994

I got a mama who joined the Peace Corps when she was sixty-eight, I got one sister who's a Holy Roller preacher. Another wears a helmet and rides a motorcycle. And my brother thinks he's going to be President. So that makes me the only sane one in the family.

– Billy Carter, brother of Jimmy Carter

I might say, first of all, I don't have any control over what my brother says or what he does ...

– Jimmy Carter

Are you not ashamed of heaping up the greatest amount of money and honor and reputation, and caring so little about wisdom and truth and the greatest improvement of the soul?

– Socrates

The more I read him, the less I wonder that they poisoned him.

– Thomas Macaulay, about Socrates

To have a reason to get up in the morning, it is necessary to possess a guiding principle. A belief of some kind. A bumper sticker if you will.

– Judith Guest, "Ordinary People"

There's a difference between a philosophy and a bumper sticker.

– Charles M. Schulz

Patience is necessary, and one cannot reap immediately where one has sown.

– Soren Kierkegaard

Lack o' pep is often mistaken fer patience.

– Kin Hubbard

Technology—the knack of so arranging the world that we don't have to experience it.

– Max Frisch

I'm not convinced that the world is in any worse shape than it ever was. It's just that in this stage of almost instantaneous communication, we bear the weight of problems our forefathers only read about after they were solved.

– Burton Hillis

The American reading his Sunday paper in a state of lazy collapse is perhaps the most perfect symbol of the triumph of quantity over quality…. Whole forests are being ground into pulp daily to minister to our triviality.

– Irving Babbitt

There was only one catch and that was Catch-22, which specified that a concern for one's own safety in the face of dangers that were real and immediate was the process of a rational mind. Orr was crazy and could be grounded. All he had to do was ask; and as soon as he did, he would no longer be crazy and would have to fly more [combat] missions. Orr would be crazy to fly more missions and sane if he didn't, but if he was sane he had to fly them. If he flew them he was crazy and didn't have to; but if he didn't want to he was sane and had to.

– Joseph Heller, Catch-22

Anyone who isn't confused doesn't really understand the situation.

– Edward R. Murrow

DEEP IDEAS
(Penetrating Reflections, Thought Fodder)

So few of us really think. What we do is rearrange our prejudices.

– George Vincent

Often you get the best insights by considering extremes—by thinking of the opposite of that with which you are directly concerned.

– C. Wright Mills

Life is absurd and meaningless—unless you bring meaning to it, unless you make something of it. It is up to us to create our own existence.

– Alan Alda

Each person's only hope for improving his lot rests on his recognizing the true nature of his basic personality, surrendering to it, and becoming who he is.

– Sheldon Kopp

Statistically, the probability of any one of us being here is so small that you'd think the mere fact of existing would keep us all in contented dazzlement of surprise.

– Lewis Thomas, The Lives of A Cell: Notes of A Biology Watcher

Nothing is interesting if you're not interested.

– Anonymous

Be neither a hammer nor a nail.

– Anonymous

Often men can see farther through a tear than through a telescope.

– Leo J. Muir

Complete success alienates a man from his fellows, but suffering makes kinsmen of us all.

– Elbert Hubbard

Children have never been very good at listening to their elders, but they have never failed to imitate them.

– James Baldwin

If we could be twice young and twice old, we could correct all our mistakes.

– Euripides

To be seventy years young is sometimes far more cheerful and hopeful than to be forty years old.

– Oliver Wendell Holmes

What separates the enlightened man from the savage? Is civilization a thing distinct, or is it an advanced stage of barbarism?

– Herman Melville

We cannot put off living until we are ready. The most salient characteristic of life is its coerciveness; it is always urgent, "here and now," without any possible postponement. Life is fired at us point blank.

– Ortega y Gasset

We will be better and braver if we engage and inquire than if we indulge in the idle fancy that we already know—or that it is of no use seeking to know what we do not know.

– Plato

Nothing is more desirable than to be released from affliction, but nothing is more frightening than to be deprived of a crutch.

– James Baldwin

[People] take the images outside them for reality and never allow the world within to assert itself.

– Hermann Hesse

Science without religion is lame, religion without science is blind.

– Albert Einstein

I know well what I am fleeing from, but not what I am in search of.

– Michel de Montaigne, c. 1550

Man, if you gotta ask, you'll never know.

– Louis Armstrong, when asked to define jazz

As if you could kill time without injuring eternity.

– Henry David Thoreau

The acts of this life are the destiny of the next.

– Persian proverb

To see things in the seed, that is genius.

– Lao-tzu

Why should we be in such desperate haste to succeed, and in such desperate enterprises? If a man does not keep pace with his companions, perhaps it is because he hears a different drummer.

– Henry David Thoreau

It is impossible to escape the impression that people commonly use false standards of measurement—that they seek power, success, and wealth for themselves and admire them in others, and that they underestimate what is of true value in life.

– Sigmund Freud

Everything intercepts us from ourselves.

– Ralph Waldo Emerson

Let us lament as over stomachs, minds who do not eat. If there is anything more poignant than a body agonizing for want of bread, it is a soul which is dying of hunger for light.

– Victor Hugo, Les Miserables

It's an abnormal world I live in. I don't belong anywhere. It's like I'm floating down the middle. I'm never quite sure where I am.

– Arthur Ashe

A speech is a solemn responsibility. The man who makes a bad thirty-minute speech to two hundred people wastes only a half hour of his own time. But he wastes one hundred hours of the audience's time—more than four days—which should be a hanging offense.

– Jenkins Lloyd Jones

A special ability means a heavy expenditure of energy in a particular direction, with a consequent drain from some other side of life.

– Carl Jung

A day ... is a miniature eternity.

– Ralph Waldo Emerson

As long as there are sovereign nations possessing great power, war is inevitable.

– Albert Einstein

If you would convince a man that he does wrong, do right. Men will believe what they see. Let them see.

– Henry David Thoreau

The world is a looking glass, and gives back to every man the reflection of his own face.

– William Makepeace Thackery

In the midst of winter, I finally learned that there was in me an invincible summer.

– Camus

It is very strange ... that the years teach us patience; that the shorter our time, the greater our capacity for waiting.

– Elizabeth Taylor

Being a philosopher, I have a problem for every solution.

– Robert Zend

Perhaps any of us could get along with perfect people. But our task is to get along with imperfect people.

– Richard L. Evans

He who would find a friend without faults will be without friends.

– Anonymous

On second thought, when the meek eventually inherit the earth it will probably be in such a condition that nobody would have it.

– Laurence J. Peter

Mediocrity tends to draw downward what is up but not upward what is down.

– Anonymous

Pity the meek, for they shall inherit the earth.

– Don Marquis

Those who know the truth are not equal to those who love it, and those who love it are not equal to those who live it.

– Confucius

If you are visited by pain, examine your conduct.

– The Talmud

Would there be this eternal seeking if the found existed?

– Antonio Porchia

A woman, in her sleep, dreamt Life stood before her, and held in each hand a gift—in the one Love, in the other Freedom. And she said to the woman, "Choose!" And the woman waited long; and she said, "Freedom!" and Life said, "Thou has well chosen. If thou hadst said, 'Love' I would have given thee that thou didst ask for; and I would have returned to thee no more. Now the day will come when I shall return. In that day I shall bear both gifts in one hand." The woman, in her sleep, laughed.

– Olive Schreiner

Every act alters the soul of the doer.

– Oswald Spengler

Lots of people want to ride with you in the limo, but what you want is someone who will take the bus with you when the limo breaks down.

– Oprah Winfrey

Like the greedy merchants of bazaars, if we get out of life what we ask for, we are unhappy for not having asked for more.

– Paul Eldridge

The glory of friendship is not the outstretched hand, nor the kindly smile nor the joy of companionship; it is the spirited inspiration that comes to one when he discovers that someone else believes in him and is willing to trust him.

– Ralph Waldo Emerson

The supreme happiness of life is the conviction of being loved for yourself, or, more correctly, being loved in spite of yourself.

– Victor Hugo

We are such stuff
As dreams are made on,
 and our little life
Is rounded with a sleep.

– William Shakespeare

The comfort of having a friend may be taken away, but not that of having had one.

– Seneca

Sometimes, [prejudice is] like a hair across your cheek. You can't see it, you can't find it with your fingers, but you keep brushing at it because the feel of it is irritating.

– Marian Anderson

I am content with what I have, little be it, or much.

– John Bunyan

Adversity reveals and shapes character.

– Anonymous

The face of the enemy frightens me only when I see how much it resembles mine.

– Stanislaw J. Lec

Two may talk together under the same roof for many years, yet never really meet; and two others at first speech are old friends.

– Mary Catherwood "Marianson" Mackinac

I would rather be a superb meteor, every atom of me in magnificent glow, than a sleepy and permanent planet.

– Jack London

I like trees because they seem more resigned to the way they have to live than other things do.

– Willa Cather

After the game, the king and pawn go into the same box.

– Italian proverb

If an ass goes traveling, he will not come home a horse.

– Thomas Fuller

Believe nothing, no matter where you read it, or who said it—even if I have said it—unless it agrees with your own reason and your own common sense.

– Guatama Buddha

To know what you are, you must first investigate and know what you are not.... The clearer you understand that on the level of mind you can be described in negative terms only, the quicker will you come to the end of your search ...

– Sri Nisargadatta Maharaj

What struck me most was the silence. It was a great silence, unlike any I have encountered on Earth, so vast and deep that I began to hear my own body; my heart beating, my blood vessels pulsing, even the rustle of my muscles moving over each other seemed audible.

– Aleksei Leonov, first man to walk in space

Everyone believes in something. It might be God or no God, manifest greed for money or power, a career or a friend, science, a principle—something. Remember, whatever it is we place before ourselves is what we run toward. When we commit to high ideals, we succeed before the outcome is known. Your life is worth a noble motive.

– Walter Anderson

It is man's destiny to ponder on the riddle of existence and, as a by-product of his wonderment, to create a new life on this earth.

– Charles F. Kettering

God made the world round so we would never be able to see too far down the road.

– Isak Dinesen

Why do you climb philosophical hills? Because they are worth climbing.... There are no hills to go down unless you start from the top.

– Margaret Thatcher

The unrecorded past is none other than our old friend, the tree in the primeval forest which fell without being heard.

– Barbara Tuchman

Very often it happens that a discovery is made whilst working upon quite another problem.

– Thomas Edison

The intellect has little to do on the road to discovery. There comes a leap in consciousness, call it intuition or what you will, and the solution comes to you and you don't know how or why.

– Albert Einstein

One is sorry one could not have taken both branches of the road. But we were not allotted multiple selves.

– Gore Vidal

Trying to define yourself is like trying to bite your own teeth.

– Alan Watts

Humor [is] something that thrives between man's aspirations and his limitations. There is more logic in humor than in anything else. Because, you see, humor is truth.

– Victor Borge

Dog scientists, hoping to make life better for their species, struggle to understand the principle of the doorknob.

— *Gary Larson cartoon*

As in a game of cards, so in the game of life, we must play what is dealt to us, and the glory consists, not so much in winning as in playing a poor hand well.

— *Josh Billings*

Nothing is inevitable until it happens.

— *A.J.P. Taylor*

We are all refugees of a future that never happened.

— *Lee Weiner*

What you are to be you are now becoming.

— *Cameron Beck*

We tend to think things are new because we've just discovered them.

— *Madeleine L'Engle, A Wind in the Door*

Change occurs when you become what you are, not when you try to become what you are not.... Change seems to happen when you have abandoned the chase after what you want to be (or think you should be) and have accepted—and fully experienced—what you are.

— *Janette Rainwater*

There is a period near the beginning of every man's life when he has little to cling to except his unmanageable dream, little to support him except good health, and nowhere to go but all over the place.

— *E.B. White*

The fundamental law of nature is that all force must be kept in balance. When any force goes off on a tangent, there is a smash.

— *Thomas Edison*

The one thing that can be safely predicted about life is that it is unpredictable.... There is nothing on earth that in the twinkling of an eye is not subject to change.

— *Richard L. Evans*

Don't think! Thinking is the enemy of creativity. It's self-conscious, and anything self-conscious is lousy. You can't try to do things; you simply must do them.

— *Ray Bradbury*

In a consumer society there are inevitably two kinds of slaves: the prisoners of addiction and the prisoners of envy.

— *Ivan Illich*

Man himself is a visitor who does not remain.

— *Anonymous*

Hell is yourself, [and the only redemption is] when a person puts himself aside to feel deeply for another person.

— *Tennessee Williams*

The opposite of love is not hate, it's indifference. The opposite of art is not ugliness, it's indifference. The opposite of faith is not heresy, it's indifference. And the opposite of life is not death, it's indifference.

— *Elie Wiesel*

Now, a cautious mountaineer seldom takes a step on unknown ground which seems at all dangerous that he cannot retrace in case he should be stopped by unseen obstacles ahead. This is the rule of mountaineers who live long.

— *John Muir*

The price of hating other human beings is loving oneself less.

— *Eldridge Cleaver*

Although we know that God is merciful, please, God, do not have mercy for those people who created this place.

— *Elie Wiesel, speaking at anniversary of the liberation of Auschwitz death camp*

We have confused the free with the free and easy.

— *Adlai E. Stevenson*

Cosmic upheaval is not so moving as a little child pondering the death of a sparrow in the corner of a barn.

— *Thomas Savage*

Life does not accommodate you, it shatters you. It is meant to, and it couldn't do it better. Every seed destroys its container or else there would be no fruitation.

— *Florida Scott-Maxwell*

The true joy of life [is] being used for a purpose recognized by yourself as a mighty one ... being thoroughly worn out before you are thrown to the scrap heap ... being a force of nature instead of a feverish, selfish clod of ailments and grievances.

— *George Bernard Shaw*

The analysis of character is the highest human entertainment.

— *Isaac Bashevis Singer*

Civilization is hideously fragile [and] there's not much between us and the horrors underneath, just about a coat of varnish.

— *C.R. Smith*

We are told that when Jehovah created the world he saw that it was good. What would he say now?
— *George Bernard Shaw*

People change and they forget to tell each other.
— *Lillian Hellman*

When a friend speaks to me, whatever he says is interesting.
— *Jean Renoir*

We don't believe in rheumatism and true love until after the first attack.
— *Marie Von Ebner-Eschenbach*

The thing that makes you exceptional, if you are at all, is inevitably that which must also make you lonely.
— *Lorraine Hansberry*

The significance of man is that he is that part of the universe that asks the question—what is the significance of man?
— *Cal Lotus Becker*

What difference does it make if the thing you are scared of is real or not?
— *Toni Morrison, Song of Solomon*

To be sure, the dog is loyal. But why, on that account, should we take him as an example? He is loyal to men, not to other dogs.
— *Karl Kraus*

To treat your facts with imagination is one thing, but to imagine your facts is another.
— *John Burroughs*

The least of things with a meaning is worth more in life than the greatest of things without it.
— *Carl Jung*

There is nothing so well-known as that we should not expect something for nothing—but we all do and call it Hope.
— *Edgar Watson Howe*

Every reform movement has a lunatic fringe.
— *Theodore Roosevelt*

Of course everything has been said that needs to be said—but since no one was listening it has to be said again.
— *Anonymous*

If we don't change direction, we will arrive at where we are going.
— *Richard L. Evans*

Things don't change. You change your way of looking, that's all.
— *Carlos Castaneda*

The quizzical expression of the monkey at the zoo comes from his wondering whether he is his brother's keeper, or his keeper's brother.
— *Evan Esar*

You never conquer a mountain. You stand on the summit a few moments; then the wind blows your footprints away.
— *Arlene Blum, Annapurna*

The destruction of the past is perhaps the greatest of all crimes.
— *Simone Weil, The Need for Roots*

Where does the white go when the snow melts? I would like to know because I'm very curious ... and it seems like a mystery.
— *Rachel, age 8*

Men imagine that thought can be kept secret, but it can not; it rapidly crystallizes into habit, and habit solidifies into circumstance.
— *James Allen*

To be able to say how much love, is to love but little.
— *Petrarch*

Even though your kids will consistently do the exact opposite of what you're telling them to do, you have to keep loving them just as much.
— *Bill Cosby*

The malignant disease of the "what-ifs."
— *Dr. Robert L. DuPont*

What is destructive is impatience, haste, expecting too much too fast.
— *May Sarton, Journal of a Solitude*

The price one pays for pursuing any profession, or calling, is an intimate knowledge of its ugly side.
— *James Baldwin*

There is no moral virtue in being endowed with genius rather than talent: It is a gift of the gods or the luck of the genes.
— *Dorothy Auchterlonie*

The great corrupter of public man is the ego.... Looking at the mirror distracts one's attention from the problem.
— *Dean Acheson*

The trouble with dreams is that they're just synaptic meanderings—gossamer mind fiction— so that one minute everything is perfect and this thing you've been chasing is so CLOSE you can almost inhale it, and the next, WHAM. It's gone, and you're back in reality because no matter how wonderful a dream is, it's never really real.
— *Advertisement for the Oldsmobile Aurora*

Who is not afraid of pure space—that breath-taking empty space of an open door? But despite fear, one goes through to the room beyond.

– Anne Morrow Lindbergh

Order is the shape upon which beauty depends.

– Pearl Buck

Take heed how you disguise yourself and copy others. Stick to nature if you desire to please, for whatever is fictitious and affected, is always insipid and distasteful.

– Charles Palmer

If only no one had told them I was mad. Then I wouldn't be.

– Kate Millett, The Looney-Bin Trip

People often say that this or that person has not yet found himself. But the self is not something that one finds. It is something that one creates.

– Thomas Szasz

If you would understand your own age, read the works of fiction produced in it. People in disguise speak freely.

– Arthur Helps

Almost the whole world is asleep—everybody you know, everybody you see, everybody you talk to … only a few people are awake and they live in a state of constant total amazement.

– Meg Ryan, Joe vs. the Volcano

The hardest thing to explain is the glaringly evident which everybody has decided not see.

– Ayn Rand, The Fountainhead

I know not what the world will think of my labors, but to myself it seems that I have been but as a child playing on the seashore; now finding some prettier pebble or more beautiful shell than my companions, while the unbounded ocean of truth lay undiscovered before me.

– Sir Isaac Newton

A hundred times every day I remind myself that my inner and outer life depends on the labors of other men, living and dead, and that I must exert myself in order to give in the measure as I have received and am still receiving.

– Albert Einstein

I'm very healthy. And I have an eternal curiosity. Then, I think I'm not dependent on any person. I love people, I love my family, my children…. But inside myself is a place where I live all alone and that's where you renew your springs that never dry up.

– Pearl Buck

Science, freedom, beauty, adventure. What more could you ask of life? Aviation combined all the elements I loved…. I began to feel that I lived on a higher plane than the skeptics of the ground; one that was richer because of its very association with the element of danger they dreaded, because it was freer of the earth to which they were bound. In flying I tasted the wine of the gods of which they could know nothing …

– Charles Lindbergh

In the last analysis, it is our conception of death which decides our answers to all the questions that life puts to us.

– Dag Hammarskjold

The dead of midnight is the noon of thought.

– Anna Letitia Barbauld

To go fishing is the chance to wash one's soul with pure air, with the rush of the brook or the serenity of a lake, and the shimmer of the sun on blue water. It brings meekness and inspiration from the decency of nature, charity toward tackle-makers, patience toward fish, a mockery of profits and egos, a quieting of hate, a rejoicing that you do not have to decide a darned thing until next week. And it is discipline in the equality of men—for all men are equal before fish.

– Herbert Hoover

The sense of obligation to continue is present in all of us. A duty to strive is the duty of us all. I felt a call to that duty.

– Abraham Lincoln

The barriers are not yet erected which shall say to aspiring talent, thus far and no farther.

– Ludwig van Beethoven

If you can't have faith in what is held up to you for faith, you must find things to believe in yourself, for a life without faith in something is too narrow a space to live.

– George E. Woodbury

I think we are well advised to keep on nodding terms with the people we used to be, whether we find them attractive company or not. Otherwise they turn up unannounced and surprise us, come hammering on the mind's door at 4 a.m. of a bad night and demand to know who deserted them, who betrayed them, who is going to make amends.

– Joan Didion

By his very success in inventing labor-saving devices, modern man has manufactured an abyss of boredom that only privileged classes in earlier civilizations have ever fathomed.

– Lewis Mumford

If only we'd stop trying to be happy, we could have a pretty good time.

– *Edith Wharton*

Creative minds always have been known to survive any kind of bad training.

– *Anna Freud*

You can no more win a war than you can win an earthquake.

– *Jeanette Rankin*

Talent is a question of quantity. Talent does not write one page— it writes three hundred.

– *Jules Renard*

It is often the scientist's experience that he senses the nearness of truth when … connections are envisioned. A connection is a step toward simplification, unification. Simplicity is indeed often the sign of truth and a criterion of beauty.

– *Mahlon Hoagland*

The psychic task which a person can and must set for himself is not to feel secure but to be able to tolerate insecurity.

– *Erich Fromm*

No trumpets sound when the important decisions of our life are made. Destiny is made known silently.

– *Agnes De Mille*

I'll appreciate my gift of choice today and linger in the past only as it benefits the better part of the present.

– *Anonymous*

I am a Pilgrim on the edge,
on the edge of my perception.
We are travelers at the edge,
We are always at the edge of our perception.

– *Scott Mutter*

Each honest calling, each walk of life, has its own elite, its own aristocracy based upon excellence of performance.

– *James Bryant Conant*

Children begin by loving their parents; as they grow older they judge them; sometimes they forgive them.

– *Oscar Wilde, The Picture of Dorian Gray*

In philosophy, it is not the attainment of the goal that matters; it is the things that are met with by the way.

– *Havelock Ellis*

The wrong way always seems the more reasonable.

– *George Moore*

All things are possible until they are impossible— and even the impossible may only be so as of now.

– *Pearl Buck*

Opposition may become sweet to a man when he has christened it persecution.

– *George Eliot, Janet's Repentance*

Without feeling, a work does not have soul. If you feel it before you do it, then it will be right.

– *John Prazen*

We possess nothing in the world—a mere chance can strip us of everything—except the power to say "I."

– *Simone Weil, Gravity and Grace*

The real voyage of discovery consists not in seeking new landscapes but in having new eyes.

– *Marcel Proust*

I am secretly afraid of animals—of all animals except dogs, and even of some dogs. I think it is because of the us-ness in their eyes, with the underlying not-usness which belies it.

– *Edith Wharton*

Power can be taken, but not given. The process of the taking is empowerment in itself.

– *Gloria Steinem, Outrageous Acts and Everyday Rebellions*

This great misfortune—to be incapable of solitude.

– *Jean De La Bruyere*

The key to the prison of depression is simply to become truly your own best friend.

– *Dorothy Rowe*

We told that boy when he marched away that he was fighting a war to end all wars. He fell, believing.

– *Bruce Barton*

There are things that are worth dying for—the honor of one's country, the sanctity of the home, the virtue of women, and the safety of little children. But, if they are worth dying for, they are worth living for!

– *George W. Truett*

Peace is not a passive but an active condition, not a negation but an affirmation. It is a gesture as strong as war.

– *Mary Roberts Rinehart*

The universe is a stairway leading nowhere unless man is immortal.

– *E.Y. Mullins*

Peace is more than the absence of aggression. It is the creation of a world community in which every nation can follow its own course without fear of its neighbors.

– Lyndon B. Johnson

We sleep, but the loom of life never stops and the pattern which was weaving when the sun went down is weaving when it comes up tomorrow.

– Henry Ward Beecher

History fades into fable; fact becomes clouded with doubt and controversy; the inscription molders from the tablet; the statue falls from the pedestal. Columns, arches, pyramids, what are they but heaps of sand; and their epitaphs, but characters written in the dust?

– Washington Irving

Yes, we did produce a near perfect Republic. But will they keep it? Or will they in the enjoyment of plenty lose the memory of Freedom? Material abundance without character is the surest way to destruction.

– Thomas Jefferson

The stairway of time ever echoes with the wooden shoe going up and the polished boot coming down.

– Jack London

The mind is no match with the heart in persuasion; constitutionality is no match with compassion.

– Everett M. Dirksen

Modern man worships at the temple of science, but science tells him only what is possible, not what is right.

– Milton S. Eisenhower

Perhaps the only true dignity of man is his capacity to despise himself.

– George Santayana

Society is frivolous, and shreds its day into scraps, its conversations into ceremonies and escapes.

– Ralph Waldo Emerson

Last, but by no means least, courage—moral courage, the courage of one's convictions, the courage to see things through. The world is in a constant conspiracy against the brave. It's the age-old struggle—the roar of the crowd on one side and the voice of your conscience on the other.

– Douglas MacArthur

In the final analysis, our most basic common link is that we all inhabit this small planet. We all breathe the same air. We all cherish our children's future. And we are all mortal.

– John F. Kennedy

For, on this shrunken globe, men can no longer live as strangers. Men can war against each other as hostile neighbors, as we are determined not to do; or they can coexist in frigid isolation, as we are doing. But our prayer is that men everywhere will learn, finally, to live as brothers.

– Adlai E. Stevenson

Miracles occur naturally as expressions of love. The real miracle is the love that inspires them. In this sense everything that comes from love is a miracle.

– Marianne Williamson, A Return To Love

Not to engage in the pursuit of ideas is to live like ants instead of like men.

– Mortimer Adler

James D. Newton shared the following: When Thomas Edison was working on improving his first electric light bulb, the story goes, he handed the finished bulb to a young helper, who nervously carried it upstairs, step by step. At the last possible moment, the boy dropped it—requiring the whole team to work another 24 hours to make a second bulb.

When it was finished, Edison looked around, then handed it to the same boy. The gesture probably changed the boy's life. Edison knew that more than a bulb was at stake.

Lucien Stryk, Takashi Ikemoto and Taigan Takayama, in their book *Zen Poems of China and Japan*, write: When a rebel army took over a Korean town, all fled the Zen temple except the abbot. The rebel general burst into the temple, and was incensed to find that the master refused to greet him, let alone receive him as a conqueror.

"Don't you know," shouted the general, "that you are looking at one who can run you through without batting an eye?"

"And you," said the abbot, "are looking at one who can be run through without batting an eye."

The general's scowl turned into a smile. He bowed low and left the temple.

One day a not-so-well-known painter asked Albert Einstein to sit for a portrait. The famous mathematician replied, "No, no, no, I do not have time."

But when the painter confessed that he desperately needed the money he would get for the picture, Einstein replied, "Well, that's another story. Of course I'll sit."

When eight-year-old Joey's little sister underwent a necessary operation, it turned out she had lost so much blood she was in need of an immediate transfusion. Joey's blood type was the same as his little sister's. "Will you give your sister some of your blood?" asked the doctor.

Joey paused for a long time before he agreed.

The boy tried to be brave as the blood was being drawn from his veins, but the doctor noticed that he was growing paler and paler. When the draw was complete, Joey looked up at the doctor and timidly asked, "I was just wondering how long it will be before I die?" The doctor looked down at Joey and said, "Do you think people die when they give blood?"

"Well, yes sir," replied Joey.

"And you were willing to die for your sister?"

"Yes, sir," he said quietly.

Gandhi repeated a principled story of his time: I saw a very small girl walking up a hill, carrying an infant boy on her shoulders and said to her, "This boy is too heavy for you."

"Not at all," replied the girl. "He's my brother."

As *Golf Digest*'s Jerry Tarrde explains: Rule 6 in golf is the Ten Commandments packed into one. It means you cannot lie, cheat or steal. You cannot conceal the truth or spread disinformation ...

The best example of Rule 6 at work occurred in 1968, when Roberto De Vicenzo of Argentina signed for a score that was one stroke higher than he actually deserved and thereby lost the chance to participate in a playoff for the Masters. When the mistake was brought to his attention, he didn't blame the scorekeeper or the tournament officials. And he didn't hire a lawyer.

His comment will live for as long as golf is played. In the ultimate demonstration of sportsmanship he said: "What a stupid I am."

In life, too few of us are ever willing to admit it.

On one crucial hole of a national championship golf match, the great Bobby Jones drove his ball into the woods. While searching for it, he accidentally nudged the ball with his foot. Though the act was unseen by anyone else, Jones promptly penalized himself one stroke—the margin of his defeat.

After the defeat, when Alistair Cooke commended him for his act of honesty, Jones remarked, "You might as well praise a man for not robbing a bank."

A quick-thinking Voltaire, facing an angry Francophobic London mob which was shouting for his death, called out, "Englishmen! You want to kill me because I am a Frenchman! Am I not punished enough, in not being an Englishman?" whereupon the pacified crowd then cheered his words and escorted him to safety.

A visitor was admiring a painting in the studio of Renoir, who was noted for the voluptuousness of his nudes. "How do you achieve such realistic flesh tints?" he asked.

"Who can say?" shrugged the French impressionist. "I keep adding a stroke here and a stroke there until I am satisfied that everything is right."

"But how do you know when it is exactly right?" prodded the visitor.

Confided Renoir, "When I feel like pinching."

Kim Woo-Choong, founder of the Korean-based Daewoo Group, a conglomerate with annual sales of $25 billion—more than Coca-Cola or Nabisco—forged his determination as a young refugee in wartime Korea.

When Kim was 14-years-old, his father was kidnapped by North Koreans and the young boy was thrown into the sober responsibility of feeding his family. He sold newspapers from a makeshift shack along a river, which was forced to close during inclement weather.

Following one storm he had only a few coins to give the family for the day's meals. When he arrived home, his mother said, "We've already eaten. You must be hungry, so eat." In truth, there had been only one bowl of rice, and his brothers had all been put to bed hungry.

I thought I would cry, said Kim. "I had a bowl of noodles on the way home," he lied. "You should eat."

"I had learned a valuable lesson," he recalls. "You must be generous with others, but severe with yourself."

E.E. Edgar divulged the humility of a friend: Until he reached middle age, French artist Paul Cezanne lived a hand-to-mouth existence. Then a Paris dealer held an exhibition of his paintings, and overnight he caught on.

During his first visit to the exhibition, Cezanne was touched by the warmth of the reception accorded him. But something else impressed him more. He pointed at the canvases on the walls and whispered to a friend: "Look, they're framed!"

Henri Dunant, a wealthy 30-year-old Swiss banker and financier was sent by his government to propose a business deal to Napoleon III. He found Frenchman on the plain of Solferino, seconds away from entering a battle with the Austrians. Dunant sat and watched the battle, transfixed—entranced by the horror taking place below him. After the battle had ended, Dunant entered the small town. Driven by the compassion and sympathy at the suffering he witnessed, he declared that the world should abolish the barbarous act of war.

When Dunant returned to Switzerland he became a fanatic on the subject of peace—preaching it everywhere. His business suffered and he eventually went broke. Still, he persisted.

At the first Geneva Conference he carried his one-man assault against war. As a result, the first international law against war was passed. In 1901 Dunant was awarded the first Nobel Peace prize. Despite his nearly hopeless financial state, he donated all his prize money to the worldwide movement he had founded.

Despite the fact he died almost totally forgotten by the world, he needed no monument to mark his grave—except the symbol of the organization he founded—the everlasting monument of the Red Cross.

Some time ago a 10-year-old boy entered a coffee shop and sat down. When approached by the waitress he asked, "How much is an ice cream sundae?"

"Fifty cents," she replied.

The boy studied the number of coins in his hand and then asked, "How much is a dish of plain ice cream?"

The waitress, becoming impatient, replied brusquely, "Thirty-five cents."

The boy looked at the coins again and ordered the plain ice-cream. The waitress brought his order and placed the bill on the table next to it. When the boy finished, he paid the cashier and left. When the waitress returned to pick up his empty plate, she paused and swallowed hard. There, placed neatly beside the empty dish, were two nickels and five pennies as her tip.

When Dr. Robert J. Oppenheimer, supervisor of the creation of the first atomic bomb, was asked by a congressional committee if there was any defense against the weapon, he quickly responded, "Certainly."

"And that is … " they inquired.

Dr. Oppenheimer looked over the hushed, expectant audience and subtly whispered, "Peace."

Oliver Wendell Holmes once attended a meeting in which he was the shortest man present. "Dr. Holmes," quipped a friend, "I should think you'd feel rather small among us big fellows."

"I do," retorted Holmes. "I feel like a dime among a lot of pennies."

Once, Napoleon suddenly appeared at one of

his camps at Boulogne-sur-Mer. His first words to Marshal Soult on arrival were, "How much time do you require to be able to embark?"

"Three days, sire," he was told.

"I can only give you one," replied Napoleon.

"That's impossible," said the Marshal.

"'Impossible' is not a word in my dictionary. Erase it from yours," commanded Napoleon.

•

The challenge that awaits reminds me of the ancient coat of arms of the royal family of Spain. Before Columbus set sail to cross the Atlantic, it was believed that the world ended out there somewhere past Gibraltar. To the Spanish, one of their real glories was that they were the last outpost of the world, and that their country fronted right on the great beyond. Therefore the royal coat of arms showed the Pillars of Hercules, the great columns guarding the Strait of Gibraltar, and the royal motto said plainly *Ne Plus Ultra*, meaning, roughly, "There is no more beyond here."

But then, when Columbus returned, he had actually discovered a whole new world out there. The ancient motto was now meaningless. In this crisis someone at Court made a noble and thrifty suggestion, which was immediately adopted by Queen Isabella. It was simply that the first word, *Ne*, be deleted. Now the motto on the coat of arms read—and has read ever since—just two words: *Plus Ultra*— "There is plenty more beyond."

•

Jacques Lipchitz, the sculptor, spent his youth in Paris, where he was a close friend of Soutine, Modigliani, and Chagall. One day a friend complained that he was dissatisfied with the light he painted on his canvases, and went off to Morocco, seeking a change in light. He found, however, that the light in his Moroccan canvases was no different. Lipchitz then advised him, "An artist's light comes from within, not from without."

•

The late Christopher Reeve, who lived the final 11 years of his life as a quadriplegic, shared this thought with Oprah Winfrey in 1998: Anything can happen to anybody. I remember the last movie I did I played a paraplegic in a movie called *Above Suspicion*, and I went to a rehab center and worked with the people there so I could simulate being a paraplegic. And every day I would get in my car and drive away and go, "Thank God, that's not me," and seven months later I was in this condition. And I remember in a way the smugness of that, as if I was privileged in a way.

The point is we are all one great big family and any one of us can get hurt at any moment. So that taught me a really big lesson about complacency. We should never walk by somebody who's in a wheelchair and be afraid of them or think of them as a stranger. It could be us—in fact, it is us.

•

Before Lou Little became the most successful football coach in Columbia University history, he coached for Georgetown University. There was one boy on his team who, although not a great football player, served as a great morale booster for the team. Little was fond of the boy and even let him play on occasion.

One day, about a week before the big finale game of the season, the boy's mother called coach Little with bad news—the boy's father had died that morning. The boy used to go arm-in-arm around the campus with his father. Little knew he would take the news hard. Little broke the news to the boy, who immediately left for home—only to return three days later to ask the coach if he could start in the big game. "I think it's what my father would have liked most," he said. After a brief hesitation, Little agreed, provided the boy only stay in a play or two.

True to his word, Little started the boy—but never took him out. For 60 jarring minutes the boy played inspired football, running, blocking, and tackling like an All-American, and sparking the team to victory. After the game Little threw his arms around the boy and asked him what got into him.

The boy answered, "Remember how my father and I used to go about arm-in-arm? There was something about him very few people knew. Dad was blind. And I knew today would be the first time he would ever see me play."

•

Upon being dismissed from his government job in the custom house, Nathaniel Hawthorne arrived home in deep despair. With his head hung he told his tale with all hopelessness to his wife, who didn't waste a minute before she set pen and ink on the table, lit the fireplace, and sat him down. Putting her arms around his shoulders she said, "Now you will be able to write your novel." Which of course he did, dramatically proving the statement that "out of breakdown comes possibility."

One day Count Leo Tolstoy was stopped on the street by a beggar who appeared emaciated and weak. The author searched his pockets for a coin to give the starving man and discovered that he did not carrying a single penny. Taking the worn hands of the beggar's between his own he said, "Do not be angry with me, my brother; I have nothing with me."

The sunken face of the beggar immediately became illuminated as he replied, "But you called me brother—that was a great gift."

•

After Michelangelo completed the statue of Moses, the Renaissance sculptor stared at his work, scrupulously studying it for a long time, and then suddenly struck the knee of the masterpiece in anger crying, "Why dost thou not speak?"

Michelangelo's eternal search for divine perfection was the very fuel for his compulsive artistic drive.

•

Many years ago in the city of Hamburg, the saintly philosopher Moses Mendelssohn fell in love with a charming woman named Fruntje. He approached her father, Guggenheim, to inform him of his love for her. Guggenheim, referring to Mendelssohn's hunched back, the result of a curvature of the spine, replied, "Well, you are a philosopher and a wise man, so you will not take it amiss. The girl said she became frightened when she saw you because of your appearance."

This did not surprise Mendelssohn, and he immediately asked to speak with Fruntje. Although she avoided looking at him throughout the conversation, Mendelssohn was able to lead the conversation to the subject that was on his mind. Timidly, Fruntje asked if he, too, believed in marriages that were made in heaven. Mendelssohn said that yes, he did, and then went on to relate an unusual story: "As you know, they call out in Heaven at the birth of a boy, 'This one will get that girl for a wife.' When I was born, my future wife was also thus announced, but it was added, 'She will, alas, have a terrible hump.' I shouted, 'Oh, Lord, a girl who is humpbacked will very easily become bitter and hard. A girl should be beautiful. Good Lord, give the hump to me, and let her be handsome and well formed!'"

Fruntje immediately accepted his proposal and soon became the faithful and devoted wife of Mendelssohn.

•

It was the year 1870 and the Methodists were having their annual conference in Indiana. The presiding Bishop was asking the group for an interpretation of current events, when the president of the college where the conference was being held volunteered his input: "I think we are in a very exciting age."

The Bishop asked him to expound. The president continued, "I believe we are coming into a time when we will see, for example, wonderful inventions. I believe men will fly through the air like birds."

The Bishop Wright, visibly disturbed by this scientifically-based comment proclaimed, "This is heresy, this is blasphemy; I read in my Bible that flight is reserved for the angels. We will not have such talk here in my area." And he returned home to his two young sons, Orville and Wilbur.

•

B. Charles Hostetter told of a remarkable happening: Some time ago, a young mother took her baby and embarked on a journey over the hills of South Wales during a terrible blizzard. However, overtaken by the relentless freezing snow, she was never able to arrive at her destination. A search party later located her frozen body beneath the snow.

As the would-be rescuers dug her body out, they were surprised to find that she had no outer clothes on. But as they lifted her corpse, they learned why: The selfless mother had taken them off to wrap around her baby. When they unwrapped the child, they found him still alive and in amazingly good condition.

The son was David Lloyd George, who grew up to be the prime minister of Great Britain during World War I. He was known as one of England's greatest statesmen. The vital sacrifice his mother had made was a noted contribution to all of humanity.

•

In his 42-year career as coach of the University of Chicago, Amos Alonzo Stagg was the idol of students and graduates alike. He was especially noted for his uncompromising honesty.

This honesty was illustrated on one specific occasion when Stagg's champion baseball team was defending its college title. It was the final play, the batter had singled, and one of Stagg's players was racing home with the winning run. "Get back to third base," Stagg yelled to his man. "You cut it by a yard!"

"But the umpire didn't see me!" cried the runner.

"That doesn't make any difference!" Stagg yelled, "Get back!"

The game was lost, but a character battle was won.

•

In the year 1884, a young American man died while visiting Europe. His parents were heartbroken; the boy had had his whole life ahead of him. Rather than erect an ornate grave, they began to consider some kind of living memorial to their son, one that would help other young men like him. Thus, they arranged to meet with Charles Eliot, the president of Harvard University.

When the ordinary, unpretentious couple arrived in his office and explained about their son and their intention of establishing a memorial, such as a building or the likes, Eliot crisply responded with a suggestion of aristocratic disdain, " ... What you suggest costs a great deal of money." He obviously didn't think this ordinary couple capable of such a donation.

The woman paused and rose slowly. "Mr. Eliot," she said, "what did this entire university cost?"

Eliot muttered a figure amounting to several million dollars.

"Oh, we can do better than that," she said. And the plain, unpretentious couple contributed $26 million for a memorial to their son—to be named Leland Stanford, Jr. University.

•

It was somewhere around the year 635 when St. Aidan, bishop of Northumbria, was given a fine horse by his good friend King Oswin, ruler of the former British province of Deira. Upon meeting a beggar down the road, the bishop immediately dismounted his horse and gave the fine animal, including all its costly trappings, to the poor man. When the king heard of this, he summoned Aidan. "Why did you give away the horse that we specially chose for your personal use when we knew that you had need of one for your journeys? We have many less valuable horses that would have been suitable for beggars."

Aidan replied, "Is this foal of a mare more valuable to you than a child of God?" The king thought for a minute and suddenly cast his sword aside to kneel at Aidan's feet and beg his forgiveness. Of course he was immediately forgiven. And as Aidan watched the king go, he became very sad. When his chaplain asked why, he replied, "I know that the king will not live long, for I have never seen a king so humble as he is. He will be taken from us as the country is not worthy to have such a king."

A few years later King Oswin was treacherously killed by his northern neighbor, King Oswy.

•

When Leonardo da Vinci was working on the face of Jesus in his painting "The Last Supper," he became angry with a certain man and lost his temper with him—lashing out at him with bitter words and threats. When he returned to his canvas, he attempted to continue his work but found himself unable to do so.

Thus, he lay down his tools and searched for the man to ask his forgiveness. The man accepted his apology and Leonardo returned to his workshop and finished the work.

William Allen White, the man responsible for establishing the *Emporia Gazette* as a national newspaper, generously gave 50 acres of parkland to his home town. When asked to explain his action, he replied, "This is the last kick in a fistful of dollars I am getting rid of. I have tried to teach people that there are three kicks in every dollar: one, when you make it—and how I love to make a dollar; two, when you have it—and I have the Yankee lust for saving. The third kick is when you give it away—and it is the biggest kick of all."

•

In 1825 Pope Leo XII went on a visit to the jail of the Papal States. Upon arriving, he insisted on questioning each of the prisoners as to how they had ended up there. Every man, with the exception of one, begged their innocence. The one man who did not, humbly admitted that he was both a forger and a thief. Turning to the prison warden, Pope Leo sternly commanded, "Release this rascal at once. I do not wish that his presence should corrupt all these noble gentlemen here!"

•

A few years ago a man decided to visit a fellow member of his church, since he had not seen him there for a while. When asked where he had been, the man responded "The church makes too many demands. It is always asking for money or time or something.

"You know," the visitor said, "twenty-five years ago a son was born to me. From the moment he came into this world, he took my time and energy and he cost me plenty of money—first the hospital bills, then the toys and food, then shoes, books, and lessons. I had to haul him from dances and to Boy Scouts. And then one day, just as he was about to graduate from college, my son was infected with a terrible disease and he died." Attempting to hold back the tears, he continued, "Since that time, my boy has not taken one minute of my time, nor cost me one cent—not one cent."

•

Harry Emerson Fosdick relates: When an American soldier in France won the Croix de Guerre, he refused to wear it. When asked why he did not wear it proudly as he should, the soldier explained, "I was no good back home. I let my sister and my widowed mother support me. I was a deadbeat. And now they have given me the Croix de Guerre for something I did at the front. I am not going to put it on. I am going back home first. I am going to win out there. I am going to show my mother that I can make good at home. Then I will put on the Croix de Guerre."

He is not the first to have discovered that being heroic in a crisis is sometimes even easier than being useful at home.

As the great sculptor Phidias was carving the statue of Diana to be placed in the Acropolis, he seemed to be taking an unusually long time on the back side of the head. He was meticulously bringing out every strand of hair as far as possible, when someone remarked, "That figure is to stand a hundred feet high, with its back to the marble wall. Who will ever know what details you are putting there?"

Phidias replied, "I will know." And he continued with his painstaking detail.

* * *

As told by E.E. Edgar: At the bedside of H.G. Wells, who was in his last illness, an old friend attempted to get a conversation going by recalling incidents of years gone by. Wells, though, evinced little interest.

"I have no time to dwell on where I have been," he finally said. "I am too busy thinking of where I am going."

* * *

During World War II Jimmy Durante was doing a tour of veterans' hospitals under the supervision of Ed Sullivan. At one rehabilitation center on Long Island, Ed warned Jimmy that they were on a tight schedule and there would be no time for encores or they would miss their plane. But when the time came for them to leave, there was Durante—doing an encore.

Sullivan frantically motioned from behind the curtain for Durante to come off stage. Jimmy quickly walked over to Ed and said, "Look, Ed, plane or no plane, I can't leave—look at the pair of soldiers clapping in the second row."

Ed looked over and spotted the two one-armed veterans—clapping together with their good arms. The fact that they missed their plane suddenly became inconsequential.

* * *

One evening at the White House, during the William Howard Taft presidential administration, an incident occurred that sought to inspire parents in sustaining their relentless duty of discipline.

The President and his family were at the dinner table when Taft's youngest son made a surprisingly disrespectful remark to his father. The table was suddenly quiet. Finally, the first lady addressed her husband. "Well," she said, "aren't you going to punish him?"

Taft thought for a minute and then responded, "If the remark was addressed to me as his father, he certainly will be punished. However," he added, "if it was addressed to the President of the United States, that is his constitutional privilege."

It was the celebration of the brilliant conductor Arturo Toscanini's 80th birthday. Clusters of people were standing around the room, talking, when someone asked Toscanini's son what his father ranked as his most important achievement. "For him there can be no such thing," replied the son. "Whatever he happens to be doing at the moment is the biggest thing in his life, whether it is conducting a symphony or peeling an orange."

* * *

It was the first week of October in 1843. A certain man was attending the ceremonies of the new Athenaeum at Manchester, when he felt a sudden inspiration to write a story that would arouse the people's awareness of the need to improve conditions of the poor. One week later he returned to London and started his composition.

As the story began to take form, he fell under its spell, laughing and weeping in turn with his characters. For seven weeks he labored relentlessly on the manuscript.

At last, on December 18, 1843, his masterpiece was completed, and the first edition appeared on the bookstalls of London. Unaware that he had written a classic, Charles Dickens was astonished when he learned that the entire six thousand copies of A Christmas Carol had sold out within twenty-four hours.

* * *

The harvest of 1783 was a poor one, but the bailiffs of the estates at Chavaniac owned by Marquis de Lafayette, the French general and politician who helped to found the revolutionary National Assembly, had managed to fill the barns with wheat anyway. "The bad harvest has raised the price of wheat," said the bailiff. "This is the time to sell."

Lafayette thought about the hungry peasants in the surrounding villages. "No," he replied, "this is the time to give."

* * *

Tom Mahoney of *American Legion Magazine* shares the following: When the French scientist Louis Pasteur was stricken with a cerebral thrombosis, during the construction of a laboratory that the government was building for him, his condition seemed so hopeless that the government ordered the construction to be stopped. When Pasteur heard of this news his condition began to rapidly decline.

His friends, aware of what was happening, appealed to Emperor Napoleon III, who responded to their plea and ordered construction resumed. Pasteur suddenly began an amazingly rapid recovery. And in the completed laboratory he went on to conquer rabies and several other diseases.

Several years ago an American woman journalist had been sent to China to cover a story. While there she witnessed a frail Catholic Sister cleansing the gangrenous sores of wounded soldiers. "I wouldn't do that for a million dollars!" she informed the Sister.

Without pausing from her work, the Sister humbly replied, "Neither would I."

⬤

Sunshine Magazine's Maeanna Chesterton-Mongle relates the following event: It was a sleety and slushy day in New York. Pedestrians were hurrying along 42nd Street with their coat collars pressed around their ears, scarcely looking up to glance at passers-by. A young black man, carrying a heavy valise in one hand and a huge suitcase in the other, was rushing toward Grand Central Station, slipping and skidding along the walk as he went.

Suddenly a hand reached out and took the valise, and a pleasant voice said, "Let me take one, brother! Bad weather to have to carry things."

The black man was a little reluctant, but the other man insisted that it was on his way and it was no trouble. All the way to the station the two chatted like old friends.

Years later, Booker T. Washington told his story. "That was my first introduction to Theodore Roosevelt," he said.

⬤

Alexander the Great noticed Diogenes, the great philosopher, staring attentively at a large collection of human bones and asked what he was looking for.

"I am searching for the bones of your father," said the philosopher, "but I cannot distinguish them from those of his slaves."

⬤

Famed English artist J.M.W. Turner once invited Charles Kingsley into his studio to see a painting of a storm at sea. Kingsley was full of admiration for the reality of the landscape. "How did you do it, Turner?" he asked.

The artist's answer was indeed inspiring: "I wished to paint a storm at sea, so I went to the coast of Holland and engaged a fisherman to take me out in his boat in the next storm. The storm was brewing, and I went down to his boat and asked him to bind me to its mast. Then he drove the boat out into the teeth of the storm. The storm was so furious that I longed to lie down in the bottom of the boat and allow it to blow over me. But I could not: I was bound to the mast. Not only did I see that storm and feel it, but it blew itself into me, till I became part of the storm. And then I came back and painted that picture."

⬤

Poet Vachel Lindsay told of an experience that happened to him one night when he was very tired

and hungry. He stopped at a farmhouse and asked to stay overnight. He had no money, but offered to pay for his lodging by reciting original poetry. The housewife was not interested in poetry and replied, "We cannot keep you, but those people there may," and she pointed across the field to a small house.

Lindsay went to the house, where the man welcomed him and invited him in, saying, "You may stay if you are willing to put up with what we have."

The house consisted of two very small rooms. There was no rug on the floor, no window shades, and not a piece of furniture worth more than two dollars. There was only a rickety old table, surrounded by a few broken chairs, a small bed and an old stove.

When Lindsay left the next morning, he was inspired. "That man had nothing," he told a friend, "and gave me half, and we both had abundance."

⬤

One day the Baron de Rothschild was approached by a man who needed a loan of $1,000. The Baron agreed to grant the loan, if the client would provide an endorser. The man could not think of a single person who would accept that responsibility. Finally, nearly ready to give up, he told the Baron that the only person who trusted him was God Almighty.

The Baron looked thoughtful for a moment, then replied, "He will be fine. I'll accept Him as an endorser." He asked the man to sign the note, and on the back he wrote, "Endorsed by God Almighty."

Six months later the client returned to pay back his note, but the Baron refused payment. The man looked confused and asked him to explain why. The Baron replied with a smile, "My dear friend, the Endorser has already repaid the loan."

⬤

After the death of Chaim Weizman, Ben-Zvi was called to the presidency of Israel. On the first day of his presidency he returned home at night and found a sentry marching up and down in front of his residence. When he asked the soldier what he was doing there, the young officer replied that he was sent by the Chief of Staff as an honor guard before the home of the President. Ben-Zvi was amazed. He entered his home and within a few minutes came out again into the cold, wintry, night air.

"Look here," he said to the soldier, "It's cold outside. Come in and have a cup of hot tea."

The soldier informed him that he was not allowed to leave his post. The President went inside once again and asked his wife to make some hot tea. Once again he walked out and, addressing the sentry, said, "Look, I have an idea. You go in and have a cup of tea. I will stand outside with your gun and take your post."

FANTASTIC FACTS

oddities, inquiries and curiosities

What is the most
widely sung tune in
the English-speaking
world?

Who was the former heavyweight
champion sentenced in 1992 to
six years in prison for date rape?

In what form did
God first appear
to instruct Moses?

In what part of the body does
a stroke occur?

I n the grand tradition of Volume 1's "Trivia to Learn By" sections, *"Fantastic Facts"* offers some all-new, all-fun collections of intriguing questions and eye-opening answers. But this library boasts a few new twists:

Some 47 specific, custom-tailored categories to help armchair experts delve faster and more selectively into the topics that engage them most; and a *"Did you know that …"* sampling of "fast facts" tucked handily under every heading, to be used as warm-up fodder and easy reference.

So, check out our *"Rest and Relaxation"* section before planning your next vacation. And on the road you can impress your travelmates with tidbits from *"World Travels," "Creepy Crawlers," "Music to My Ears"* or at-your-fingertip brainteasers from dozens of other categories.

It's free fun and enlightenment, anytime, anywhere. So … learn on!

CONTENTS

What British theoretical physicist wrote *A Brief History of Time*?

How many seconds are there in a day?

What notoriously confident tennis player said, "My greatest strength is that I have no weakness"?

What nation do more tourists visit than any other?

How many bottles
make up a "magnum"
of champagne?

The last execution
held in the Tower of
London took place
during what war?

What IQ score is considered
to mark the beginning of the
genius level?

...The FDA allows an average of 30 or more insect fragments and one or more rodent hairs per 100 grams of peanut butter?

...Diet product spending has actually decreased in the past two decades, while non-diet product purchases ballooned by billions of dollars?

...Women burn fat more slowly than men, by a rate of about 50 calories—about one chocolate-chip cookie's worth—per day?

...Americans annually spent an estimated $300 billion dining out?

...In ancient China and certain parts of India mice are considered a great delicacy?

...A 16-cup tub of buttered movie theater popcorn has more grams of fat in it than a bacon-and-egg breakfast, a Big Mac with fries, and a full steak dinner combined (at least before modifications were made by the theaters starting in the mid-90s)?

...The name "pretzel" was derived from the early Latin word *brachiatus*, meaning "having branch-like arms," because its shape resembles a pair of folded arms?

...The "57" in Heinz '57 sauce refers to the "nearly three-score" varieties of the product; in 1923, Heinz offered flavors that included "grape jelly," "peanut butter," "cherry preserves," and "cream of pea soup"?

...A full 12 percent of the total quantity of colas sold are consumed with—or instead—of breakfast.

Gastronomical Gourmet

• The "science of dining" or "the art of eating well" is known as _____; and one who is an expert in this field—a "connoisseur of good food"—goes by what name(s)?
–*Gastronomy; gastronome (gastronomer, gastronomist), gourmet or epicure*

• Devoured at the rate of about 1.2 billion pounds a year, what is America's favorite snack food? –*Potato chips*

• What is the pasta noodle whose name means "tongues" in Italian? –*Linguine*

• What dessert is traditionally served to fans at the Wimbledon tennis tournament each year? –*Strawberries and cream*

• Which "shade" of turkey meat contains the most fat and calories, white or dark? –*Dark*

• What sounds do Rice Krispies make in Dutch-speaking countries, comparable to our English "snap, crackle and pop"? –*"Pif, paf, pof"*

• What is the English translation for the popular Italian dish "pie"? –*Pizza*

• Taking its name from a Sanskrit term meaning "horn-shaped" and used as a staple in Chinese soups and stir-fries for thousands of years, in the west this spice is used mainly in sweets. In fact, Queen Elizabeth I is reputed to have invented a type of cookie that bears its name. What is this spice—and the name of Elizabeth's runaway popular cookie?
–*Ginger; the gingerbread man*

• Chinese cooking has a unique history. Name these Chinese/Asian-originated foods:
    A health-giving aphrodisiac.
      –*Ginseng*
    Called a "miniature orange."
      –*The kumquat*
    Beijing's most famous dish.
      –*Peking duck*
    A popular condiment with Asian origins.
      –*Ketchup (comes from 'kecap', the Malayan word for condiment)*

• With over 6 billion sold each year, what is the world's bestselling brand of cookie? –*Nabisco's 'Oreo'*

• Name, in order of preference, the three most popular ice cream flavors in America. –*Vanilla, chocolate and butter pecan*

• Who was the Baby Ruth candy bar named after? (Hint: No, it wasn't baseball player Babe Ruth.) –*Ruth Cleveland, daughter of President Grover Cleveland and the first baby girl ever born in the White House*

• Elephants love this "nut," even though it grows underground. –*The peanut, actually a légume*

• What is the name of a breakfast product made up of edible letters? –*Alphabits*

• Food names can range from the whimsical to the tantalizingly oblique. Fill in the blanks below with the correct terms:
    "Albany beef" is actually a fish known as _____. –*Sturgeon*

The "Barbary Fig," "India Fig," or "Indian Pearl" is more commonly known in North America as the _____ _____.
    –*Prickly pear*
A "tenderloin trout" is really a _____.
    –*Catfish*
The dried-fruit pastries known as "funeral pies" are usually filled with _____.
    –*Raisins*
The common cornmeal "hoecake" or "johnnycake" was originally known as _____cake because itinerant preachers could pack it away for months without fear of mold or spoilage.
    –*"Journey"*
"Indian snacks"—dried, salted and cured strips of beef—are known by the Quechua derivative _____.
    –*Jerky*
"Farmer" cheese is also known as _____ cheese. –*Cottage*
"Cherrystones" are a delicacy found near the sea; usually they are known as _____.
    –*Clams*
The deep-sea anglerfish—a popular restaurant menu item—is commonly known as the _____.
    –*Monkfish*

• In the Middle Ages, what soup was believed to be an aphrodisiac? –*Chicken soup*

• Give the city, nationality or place-name widely associated with each of these foods:
    Baked beans.
        –*Boston*
    Sourdough bread.
        –*San Francisco*
    Rye bread.
        –*New York*
    Clam chowder.
        –*New England or Manhattan*
    Fried chicken.
        –*Kentucky*
    Oven cooking. –*Dutch*
    Waffles.
        –*Belgian*

• In 1955, Quaker Oats made an unusual offer: free in each box of cereal was a folded paper. What did it award the bearer?
–*Lawful deed to one square inch of land in Canada's Yukon Territory*

• What major "Flintstone" character is missing in a bottle of children's Flintstone Chewable Vitamin tablets? –*Betty Rubble*

• What are the external buds on a potato called?
–*Eyes*

• What tropical fruit serves as the traditional garnish for ham? –*Pineapple*

• What is the world's most popular tropical fruit? –*The mango*

• What fruit is mentioned most often in the Bible? –*The fig*

• What are the blue veins in blue cheese made up of? –*Mold*

• The following products originally went by different names. Give the more current name that replaced the original.
    "Little Short-Cake Fingers"
        –*Twinkies*
    "Kandy Kake"
        –*Baby Ruth Candy*
    "Fairy Fluff"
        –*Cotton Candy*
    "Brad's Drink"
        –*Pepsi-Cola*
    "Fruit smack flavored syrup" (before being marketed in its dehydrated form)
        –*Kool-Aid*

• What percentage of fat is saved by opting for a margarine spread over butter?
–*None—both are 100 percent fat*

• According to 172-pound Larry Coker (who formerly weighed 750 pounds), of the 70 million Americans who try to lose weight annually, what is the rate of permanent success?
–*Two percent*

• A submarine sandwich is known by several different names, depending on which region of the U.S. you're in. Give the regional English word for this oblong sandwich in each of the following areas:
    Philadelphia.
        –*"Hoagie"*
    Upstate New York.
        –*"Bomber"*
    New York City.
        –*"Wedge"*
    Boston.
        –*"Grinder"*
    Miami.
        –*"Cuban sandwich"*
    Kansas City.
        –*"Italian"*

THE MEASURE OF ALL THINGS
did you know that ...

...The base of the Great Pyramid of Egypt is large enough to cover ten football fields?

...Atomic clocks are accurate to a few millionths of a second a year?

...If you piled a billion one-dollar bills one on top of another, the pile would be 70 miles high?

...Disneyland sells enough soft drinks every year to fill a five-acre lake?

...New York City has 230 miles of subway track?

...The distance required for an average-length freight train (carrying about 100 cars) to come from a speed of 60 miles per hour to a complete stop is a full mile?

...Basketball Hall-of-Famer Bob Lanier wore a size 22 shoe?

Get Out Your Gauges

• Why is a manhole round? *If it were any other shape, its cover could conceivably be turned so that it could fall through the hole*

• Both the English and metric systems of measuring temperature use the "degree" as their units. The English system is measured in degrees "fahrenheit." What is the temperature scale for the metric system called? And, for each scale, at what temperatures does water freeze and boil?
—Centigrade (or celsius); 0 and 100 degrees centigrade, 32 and 212 degrees fahrenheit

• In circular measures, if 90 degrees equals one "quadrant," what does 30 degrees equal?
—One "sign" – originally named for the 12 signs of the Zodiac (which occur at 30-degree intervals along the astrological circle)

• What are the common dimensions of a credit card?
—3 3/8 by 2 1/8 inches

• One "sidereal" (or "astral") day—the time it takes for Earth to revolve once around its axis in relation to the background stars—is short of the 24-hour solar day by about how many minutes? *—Four minutes*

• Centennial is to 100 years as _____ is to 1,000 years. *—Millennial*

• The prefix *deci* is to a tenth as the prefix *nano* is to a _____. *—Billionth*

• The states of Washington, California, Nevada, and most of Oregon lie in what time zone? *—Pacific*

• Of what significance was the date Jan. 1, 2001?
—It was technically the first day of the 21st century

• How long is the Statue of Liberty's nose? How wide is her mouth? *—4 feet long; 3 feet wide*

• On average, how many visits to the bathroom does an American make on a daily basis? How much time does this add up to throughout a lifetime?
—Six trips, for a total of 47 minutes daily, which adds up to 2 "bathroom years" in an average lifetime

• How long is the average duration of a yawn?
—Six seconds

• An earthquake that measures 8 on the Richter scale would be how many times stronger than one measuring 4? *—10,000 times stronger*

• How long did it take the estimated 400,000 men who worked on it to complete the construction of the Great Pyramid of Egypt? *—20 years*

• About how long would it take to walk once around the Pentagon? *—20 minutes*

• What unit is used to assess the weight of precious stones and gems? What is the term used to express the purity of gold? *– "Carat"; "karat"*

• If Barbie—the long-legged, big-busted, shiny-blonde-haired doll—were a real five-foot-nine-inch model, what would her actual measurements be? On the opposite end of the scale, what would be the measurements of Popeye's 29-year-old girlfriend Olive Oyl? *—Barbie would have a 36-inch bust, a 17-inch waist, and 32-inch hips; Olive, 19-19-19*

• How many seconds are there in a day? *—86,400*

• What unit is used for measuring the height of horses? *—A "hand"—which is equal to 4 inches*

• What is a "Branock device" used to measure?
—Shoe size

• A surveyor standing on a mountain peak can figure out where he is on a map by measuring the azimuth (relative angles) to two other points of reference that are known to him and the distance between them. What is this method commonly called? *–Triangulation*

• What fraction of an iceberg shows above water?
—About one-ninth

• Name the brand of stopwatch used on the TV series "60 Minutes." *—Heuver*

• In the fairy tale, how long did Sleeping Beauty sleep? *—100 years*

DRIVIN' MY CAR
did you know that ...

…Each year consumers burn enough gas in bumper-to-bumper traffic to drive to the sun and back more than 300 times?

…Driving with the air-conditioner on reduces gas mileage by approximately 2.5 miles per gallon?

…The "Father of Traffic Safety," William Phelps Engo—the man who originated modern traffic regulations—never drove a car? (He relied on a chauffeur.)

…The first electric traffic light was installed in Cleveland in 1914?

…It is an estimated 62 times safer to travel by plane than by highway, according to per-mile fatality rates?

…A combustion engine puts out more power at lower altitude than at higher altitude, due to greater air pressure and oxygen density?

…The first Grand Prix race, held in 1901, was won with an average speed of 46 mph?

…John and Horace Dodge had built an auto empire that, by 1920, was cranking out 1,000 cars a day—and that both of these extraordinary men were illiterate?

…Most American automobile horns give off the musical note F?

…Front seat belts weren't offered as standard equipment in cars until 1963—and rear seat belts two years later?

On the Road Again

• How many cow hides does it take to make the leather interior for one Lexus GS300? –*Five*

• If, on cue, every person in the United States were to climb into a car, how many, on average, would be in each car? If everyone in the country of Ecuador did the same thing, how crowded would the average car be? –*In the U.S. there would be 1.7 persons per car; in Ecuador, 132 would be in each car*

• What name did the Nissan company originally go by? –*Datsun*

• Name the vehicle used by Luke Skywalker to cover the desert terrain of his home planet of Tatooine in the 1977 film "Star Wars." –*The 'Landspeeder'*

• What company manufactures the Corvette Stingray? –*General Motors*

• Who founded the city of Detroit back in the 17th century? –*Antoine Cadillac*

• Name the consumer activist whose book *Unsafe at Any Speed* (1965) led to the passage of the 1966 National Traffic and Motor Vehicle Safety Act. –*Ralph Nader*

• What type of car was featured as the General Lee on CBS's 1979 "Dukes of Hazard" series? –*A 1967 Dodge Charger*

• What was the name of the classic car featuring a pop-up shield used by James Bond to defy bullets in the 1967 movie "Thunderball"? What was the name of the car that turned into a submarine in his 1977 movie "The Spy Who Loved Me"? –*An Austin Martin; a Lotus Esprit*

• What did Grandpa Munster of TV's "The Munsters" series call his 160-mph coffin-on-wheels? –*'Dracula'*

• Actor James Dean, baseball manager Billy Martin, actress Jayne Mansfield, General George Patton, mogul John D. Rockefeller and Princess Di all had one thing in common. What was it? –*Each died due to injuries in an auto accident*

• What does "MSRP" stand for in automobile commercials? –*"Manufacturer's Suggested Retail Price"*

• What German auto proudly advertised itself as the only car that would float on water? (Though it will definitely float, it won't float indefinitely.) –*The Volkswagen Beetle*

• Name the car that goes with each of these advertising mottos.
  "A car ahead"
  　　　–*Honda*
  "We are driving excitement"
  　　　–*Pontiac*
  "It just feels right"
  　　　–*Mazda*
  "I love what you do for me"
  　　　–*Toyota*
  "The relentless pursuit of perfection"
  　　　–*Lexus*
  "Quality is job one"
  　　　–*Ford*
  "Cars that make sense"
  　　　–*Hyundai*
  "A different Kind of Company. A Different Kind of Car."
  　　　–*Saturn*

• What do the *initials of the Fiat Automobile stand for?* – *"Fabrica Italiana Automobile Tovino"*

• What automobile company's logo consists of an emblem with a three-pointed star? –*Mercedes Benz*

• When a hot-rod brandishes "Snowballs," what feature is it showing off? – *White-wall tires*

• What is a CBer referring to when talking about a "pregnant roller skate?" –*A Volkswagen Beetle*

• What automobile model—famous as a dismal market failure—was named after Henry Ford's only child? –*The Edsel*

• How are "Vince" and "Larry" employed by the U.S. Department of Transportation?
–*As the famous pair of crash-test dummies*

• What device made its debut in Cleveland, Ohio, August 5, 1914, on the corner of Euclid Avenue and East 105th Street? – *The traffic light*

• Identify the name of the "car movie" from each description below:
  • Features a race across the United States stars Burt Reynolds, Farrah Fawcett, Sammy Davis, Jr., Dom Deluise, and a host of others. – *"Cannonball Run"*
  • Lengthy story about a 1908 race from New York to Paris. – *"The Great Race"*
  • A black TransAm, a dumb Southern cop, CB radios, and—again—Burt Reynolds –*"Smokey and the Bandit"*
  • All about the first black racing champion—Richard Pryor. – *"Greased Lightning"*
  • Matthew Broderick borrows a Ferrari for the day. – *"Ferris Bueller's Day Off"*
  • Its star is a DeLorean. – *"Back to the Future"*
  • Stars Robin Williams as a sleazy car salesman. – *"Cadillac Man"*

• What was the most popular car ever made?
–*The Volkswagen Beetle (In the U.S. sales reached five million between 1949 and 1981—when U.S. production stopped—and total worldwide sales reached 21 million by 1992)*

• What choice of color, by a wide margin, is the favorite for American vehicles?
–*White, at about 20%*

• According to odds-maker William Hill in London, what are the odds that Britain will switch to driving on the right-hand side of the street before the year 2005? –*250 to 1*

NUMEROUS NUMBERS
did you know that …

… The average number of letters used in a movie title is 17?

… There are 1575 steps from the ground floor to the top of the Empire State Building?

… According to the Library of Congress, of their 16.4 million books 300,000 of them are officially overdue?

… The parking lot at Bloomington, Minnesota's massive Mall of America has 13,000 parking spaces—a fact that led to some 2,000 shoppers requesting help to find their cars in 1993?

… Each year over three billion Christmas cards are sent throughout the world?

Let Me Count the Ways
• If you started counting (1, 2, 3 …), what is the first number you would say that contained the letter "d"? –*One hundred*

• What do the numbers 11, 69 and 88 all have in common?
–*They read the same right-side up and upside down*

• What IQ score is considered to mark the beginning of the genius level? –*140*

• If you are a U.S. citizen, what is the breakdown of the "mysterious code" represented by the numbers on your social security card? –*The first three digits show what part of the country you applied from, the next two signify the year you applied—again, conveyed in code—and the last four digits denote your "citizen's number," kept on file by the government*

• In what sort of work are you most likely to use "Mach" numbers? –*Test pilot*

• What famed fictional group of three consisted of Porthos, Aramis and Athos? And who was the fourth, perhaps better-known member of this group?
–*The Three Musketeers; d'Artagnan*

• Each of the following sets of three items forms a part of a larger group involving a number. Identify the group:
Anger, envy, pride
    –*The Seven Deadly Sins*
Frogs, locusts, hail
        –*The ten Biblical plagues of Egypt*
John, Thomas, Simon
        –*Jesus's Twelve Apostles*
Carpenter, Cooper, Shepard
        –*The seven original U.S. astronauts*
Capitoline, Esquiline, Palatine
        –*The seven hills of Rome*
Jane, Anne, Catherine
        –*Wives of Henry VIII*

• "When you're torn between two of these, the best rule is to choose the lesser." What are the items in question? –Two evils

• According to Robert Louis Stevenson's novel *Treasure Island*, how many men are there on a dead man's chest? –15

• What renowned Parisian courtier, when she died in 1971, left a legacy of perfume named by number? –Coco Chanel

• What is the rank of the Roman soldier who was in charge of a hundred-man unit? –Centurion

• Which directions do you travel on odd-numbered highways in the United States? On even-numbered highways? –North and south; east and west

• How many days constitutes a "fortnight"? –14

• If your true love gave you all of the gifts described in the song "The Twelve Days of Christmas," how many total birds would be fluttering about your home?
–23 (1 partridge, 2 turtle doves, 2 French hens, 4 "calling birds," 6 geese ('a laying), and 7 swans ('a swimming)

• Speaking of Christmas, in what Christmas song are the ages 1 and 92 mentioned?
–"Chestnuts Roasting on an Open Fire"

• How many holes (or indentations) are there on a Chinese Checker board? –121

• What numeric nickname is given the clubhouse at a golf course? –The 19th Hole

• What are the last four digits of the IRS agency's toll-free telephone number? –1040

• How many times can the digit 9 be found in the numbers between 1 and 100? –20

• How many times does the word "One" appear on the face side of a one-dollar bill? How about on the reverse side? And how about the isolated digit "1" on the face and reverse sides? – "One" appears twice on the face and six times on the back; "1" appears four times on the face and four times on the back—for a grand total of 16 "big ones."

• What is the number commonly used in journalism to signify the end of a newspaper story? –30

• How many steps lead up to a gallows? How many loops are tied in a hangman's noose? –In both cases, 13

• What is the number of herbs and spices in the mixture that coats the chicken at KFC? –11

• What fictional character lives in the Hundred Acre Wood? –Winnie the Pooh

ONE FOR THE MONEY
did you know that ...

…When your bank deducts 15, 20 or more dollars from your account as compensation for a bounced check, the bank only expends about one dollar and a quarter's worth of manpower, computer power, overhead and mailing costs to process the matter?

…Live pigs recently replaced money as a form of payment at a steel spring manufacturing plant in Belgrade, Yugoslavia?

…Inner-city Los Angeles families spend on the average 36 percent of their income on food, while their suburbanite counterparts spent only 12 percent?

…The I.R.S. allows taxpayers to take thousands of dollars in deductions for vanity surgery such as facelifts, breast enlargements and nose jobs, if business related, but health club fees and weight-reducing programs are not deductible?

…Typical hospital expenses for a child struck by gunfire total more than $14,000—the same as a full-year's tuition at an average private college?

…If people in their 30s invested the $25.00 a month usually spent on credit card interest they'd have more than $57,200 by the time they reached age 65?

…Credit-card fraud costs consumers over $7.00 per year for each card they carry?

…Americans spend approximately $25 billion each year on beer? (This amount, incidentally, could prevent the yearly deaths of over four million impoverished children around the world.)

…The lowest denomination of paper money, a one-penny banknote, was issued by Fiji in 1942?

Financial Windfalls
• About how much money is consumed on military purposes every 13 days by the world's armed nations? –About $25 billion

• What country was the first to use paper money—known as "white deerskin money"—beginning in 140 B.C.E.?
–China, the Han Dynasty

• Which is the highest U.S. denomination *ever* issued for public circulation? The highest bill *currently* in circulation? –$10,000; 100-dollar bill

• What is the estimated annual cost to U.S. taxpayers for keeping secret government documents classified? *–$20 billion a year (at least three times more than NASA's total budget)*

• Per person, how much did it cost the U.S. Census Bureau to conduct the 1990 census? *–$10 (for a total of $2.51 billion)*

• In 1969, how much did comedian Eddie Murphy pay for a flowered headband worn by rock star Jimi Hendrix? *–$19,500*

• Coins and paper money which must be accepted for payment of debts is known as legal _____. *–Tender*

• Today an average-size tube of Colgate toothpaste sells for about $3.00. How much would buying Colgate—or about any other toothpaste brand—set you back in the small West-African country of Cameroon? What about China? *–Over $6.00; about $5.50*

• What is the meaning of the words *Annuit Coeptis*, printed on the $1 bill? What do the eye and the pyramid represent? *–"He (God) has favored our undertakings"; the all-seeing deity and strength*

• From what source is the Nobel Peace Prize money derived? *–Interest earned on the $9.2 million bequeathed for that purpose by Swedish scientist Alfred Nobel at the time of his death in 1896*

• Pennies are made up of only 2.5 percent copper. Which other metal makes up bulk of the little copperheads? *–Zinc*

• What is the average life span of a $1 bill? *–18 months*

• The one-dollar bill, of course, is the most circulated denomination of U.S. currency. What is the second most used denomination? *–The $20 bill*

• What's known as a "C-note"? *–A 100-dollar bill*

• It's not legal for the portrait of someone who is ____ _____ to appear on American currency. *–Not dead*

• Whose likeness appears on currency of a whopping 34 countries? *–Queen Elizabeth II's*

… It takes about the same amount of energy to make 20 cans from recycled aluminum as it does to make one can from the raw mineral ore?

… Each person living in an industrial nation expends an average of ten tons of rock and mineral products every year?

… It takes 42 different minerals/metals to construct a telephone handset, and the most unadorned TV set contains at least 35?

… The gold coating found on the face masks worn by astronauts is what protects them from the sun's fierce radiation?

Can You Dig It?

• Roman soldiers were paid in part with a salt ration called "salarium argentum," which is where the modern term _____ comes from. *–"Salary"*

• The presence of particular metals serves what purpose in a fireworks display? *–The metals are the source of the varied brilliant colors*

• Give the name of the metal or mineral that assists in each of the following bodily functions:

Essential for manufacturing red blood cells.
    –Iron
Required for bone and cell growth and for normal functioning of the nervous system.
    –Manganese
Maintains fluid and mineral balance, assists nerves and muscles, and helps the heart function normally.
    –Potassium
Aids the body in producing healthy blood cells.
    –Zinc
Assists in maintaining healthy muscles, red blood cells and proteins in the hair and nails.
    –Selenium
Builds strong bones and teeth; helps nerve function and blood clotting.
    –Calcium

• What metal is derived from the German "kobold," meaning "goblin"?
    –Cobolt

• What is carbon-14 primarily used for?
    –To date objects

• Give the mineral/metal used for each of the following products:

Jewelry, electrical conductors, heat shields
    −*Gold*

Thermometers, mercury vapor lamps, electric switches
    −*Mercury*

Batteries, radioactive shields, bullets, fishing weights
    −*Lead*

Pottery, china, bricks
    −*Clay*

Glass, computers, lubricants, water repellents
    −*Silica*

Cement, mortar, building stone
    −*Limestone*

Mirrors, photographic film, utensils, old coins
    −*Silver*

Fertilizers and animal feed
    −*Phosphates*

Electrical cable and pennies (before 1982)
    −*Copper*

Pennies minted after 1982
    −*Zinc*

Steel girders, nails, tools, magnets
    −*Iron*

Beverage containers and airplane bodies
    −*Aluminum*

Plaster, wallboard, alabaster
    −*Gypsum*

• The French expression *puvoir hydrogen* means "hydrogen power." How is this term more commonly expressed?
−*The pH level*

• What metallic element—the least dense of any metal—is used as an antidepressant in medicines?
−*Lithium*

• Of the 118 (and growing) identified elements, only eight make up 98 percent of the Earth's crust. Name them.
−*Oxygen, silicon, aluminum, iron, calcium, sodium, potassium and magnesium*

• What color is diamond dust?
−*Black*

• A diamond will not dissolve in acid. What is the only thing that can destroy it?
−*Intense heat*

CRIME AND CORRUPTION
did you know that …

…By the time a child finishes elementary school she will have witnessed an estimated 8,000 murders and 100,000 acts of violence on television?

…Though not one "witch" was burned in the early days of Salem, Massachusetts, 19 women and young girls were hanged on the town's barren "Gallows Hill"?

…In the past decade, in the range of 50,000 children were killed by guns in the U.S.—a figure roughly equivalent to the number of Americans killed in the Vietnam War?

…Arrests for violent crimes perpetrated by American youths under the age of 18 jumped from 54,596 in 1970 to 104,137 in 1992—a 91% hike?

…Elliot Ness, a real-life FBI agent, was instrumental in locking up mobster Al Capone, cleaning up corrupt cops, instituting The Cleveland Police Academy, and founding Cleveland's Boys Town?

…An independent source estimates the cost of crime in the U.S. at over million and a half dollars per minute?

…Some 3,862 prisoners were executed in the U.S. between 1930 and 1980?

…Nationwide, a woman is beaten ever 15 seconds?

…In 1991, James Campbell, a chemist at Virginia Tech, was caught manufacturing methamphetamines in a university laboratory, yet was acquitted on the legal defense that he had only tried it after watching the TV program "48 Hours" and hearing correspondent Dan Rather explain the process for making speed?

On the Wrong Side of the Law
• Someone who pulls fraudulent or deceptive deals may be called a "con"—an expert at evoking and then abusing the trust of his target. What is the word *con* short for? −*Confidence, as in "confidence man"*

• In 1978, Dan White, a former policeman, shot and killed San Francisco's mayor George Moscone. White's attorney brought in a battery of psychiatrists to testify in his behalf. What was one especially peculiar testimony? −*It was claimed that White's addiction to Twinkies, Coca-Cola and potato chips resulted in extreme blood-sugar level variations, exacerbating his manic depression which, in turn, led to his psychopathic behavior*

• What popular soul singer was arrested for brandishing a shotgun in his office building while demanding to know who had used his private toilet? –*James Brown*

• On April 4, 1993, police in Charles City, Virginia, apprehended a runaway drug dealer without breaking into a sweat. A brief fashion fad at the time, what was the suspect wearing that made it so easy to spot him? –*L.A. Gear's Light Gears—battery-powered sneakers that flash red lights when the heels hit the ground*

• Mohammed Salemeh was arrested as a suspect in the 1993 World Trade Center bombing, which killed six people. How was Salemeh caught? –*He appeared at a rental center to reclaim his $400 deposit on the van he had used in the bombing*

• On his way to the electric chair, what did James Donald French helpfully submit as a possible headline for the next morning's newspaper? – *"French Fries"*

• Gifted con-artist Victor "The Count" Lustig devoted his entire life to carrying out various scams. However, in 1922 one con game in particular made him the most infamous cheat of all time. What was it? –*He sold the Eiffel Tower to a scrap-metal dealer for $50,000*

• What bit of religious advice did Victor Lustig give for dealing with a potential con victim? –*Wait for the mark to reveal his religious affiliation, then become a member of the same church*

• Gangster Al "Scarface" Capone claimed he had received his scar in World War I. Problem was, Capone never served in World War I. Where did his scar actually come from?
–*He was knifed in Brooklyn—in a fight over a woman—while working as a bouncer in a saloon*

• Capone's nickname was "Scarface." His brother, Ralph, was assigned the primary duty of intimidating prospective customers into buying Al's liquor. What was Ralph's nickname? – *"Bottles"*

• What was Charlie "Lucky" Luciano's real first name? What other three infamous gangsters linked up with him in 1917? –*Salvatore; Luciano was joined by Frank Costello, Benny "Bugsy" Siegel, and Meyer Lansky*

• What Mafia leader's nickname was "Teflon Don" before he was sentenced to life in prison on July 23, 1992 after being found guilty on 44 counts of racketeering and murder? Who finally ripped away the criminal cover of this mob kingpin? –*John Gotti; he was betrayed by his lieutenant, Salvatore "Sammy the Bull" Gravano*

• In 1934 police arrested a carpenter and charged him with the 1932 murder of Charles and Anne Lindbergh's 20-month-old son Charles Augustus, Jr. What is the name of this man who was convicted and executed in 1936 for the crime? Also, what law was subsequently passed by Congress making it a federal offense to transport a kidnap victim across state lines? –*Bruno Richard Hauptmann; the "Lindbergh law"*

• The doodles of a judge once triggered an appeal from a death-row inmate. What did the judge draw on the letter setting the date for this inmate's execution? –*A smiley face*

• Buying event tickets at regular prices and selling them at inflated prices is commonly known as _____. –*Scalping*

• Name "The Rock" that became known as "America's Devil's Island"—a prison characterized by maximum security, minimum privilege, and a rule of silence. Also, what was its unofficial "slogan"? –*Alcatraz (finally closed in 1963 amid protests against its "cruel methods" of punishment); it was jokingly referred to as "A Super Prison for Super Prisoners"*

• What criminal mastermind, said to have played a role in fixing the 1919 World Series, was nicknamed, among other things, "Mr. Big," the "Brain," and the "Fixer"? –*Arnold Rothstein*

• Who was the former heavyweight champion sentenced in 1992 to six years in prison for date rape? –*Mike Tyson*

• Give the correct definition for the following slang crime terms:
   "Air dance"
         –*Execution by hanging*
   "Black act"
         –*Picking a lock in the dark*
   "Meat-eater"
         –*A policeman or politician who accepts a bribe*
   "Chicago overcoat"
         –*A 1920s underworld term for a coffin*
   "State chemists"; "state electricians"
         –*Executioners who kill condemned prisoners by lethal injection or electric chair, respectively*

• Name the young Massachusetts woman who allegedly killed her father and stepmother with an ax in 1892, but was acquitted largely due to her exemplary charitable and religious activities?
–Lizzie Borden

• What was the sentence received by James Earl Ray for killing Martin Luther King, Jr. in 1968?
–He was sentenced to 99 years in prison

• What are "Saturday night specials"?
–Inexpensive handguns

• In 1925, John T. Scopes, a young biology teacher from Dayton Tennessee, was convicted for breaking a state law. What was his crime?
–Teaching the theory of evolution

• Who "takes the cake" in rate of shoplifting convictions—men or women?
–Women shoplifters outnumber men by four or five to one

• What were the real names of Butch Cassidy and the Sundance Kid?
–Cassidy was born Robert Leroy Parker on April 1, 1866 in Circleville, Utah; the Sundance Kid was born Harry Longbaugh in Phoenixville, Pennsylvania in 1870

• What are the three basic symbolic concepts in Chinese philosophy that represent the "Triads"—Chinese secret societies which function as crime syndicates?
–Heaven, Earth and Man

THE '60S AND '70S
did you know that ...

…The "pass/fail" grading system took hold in colleges and universities across the U.S. during the mid-sixties when it became clear to a sympathetic faculty that low grades could send students on a long trip to Vietnam?

…In 1963 the Zone Improvement Plan (ZIP Codes) was implemented by the U.S. Post Office, carving the nation into 43,000 parts— and dramatically improving mail sorting efficiency?

Those Were the Days?
• What colorful food additive did the Food and Drug Administration approve in 1962 that would be declared carcinogenic 16 years later?
–Red Dye #2

• What popular mid-sixties fashion trend, originated by fashion designer Mary Quant, was often worn with knee-high boots?
–The mini skirt

• Former First Lady Jackie Kennedy became a trendsetter when she "wrapped" two of her best-known features in mystery with one of these articles designed in 1961 for a Madison Avenue store called Purdy. What were they?
–Wrap-around sunglasses

• The Scott Paper Company put out a special line of easy-to-care-for dresses for $1.25 each in 1966 and advertised them as "flexible, fire-resistant and reinforced by rayon scrim." What were the dresses actually made of?
–Paper

• In 1964, a new beachwear item left Bob Hope saying, "Instead of Playboy, the guys will be buying Ladies Home Journal." He added that "It leaves nothing to the imagination, and at my age it's good to have an imagination." Phyllis Diller, however, quipped, "When I wore one, everyone thought I was Albert Schweitzer." What were Hope and Diller talking about?
–The topless bathing suit

• What was the name of the hairdo made popular by Olympic gold-medal figure skater Dorothy Hamill in 1976? –The wedge

• What was the title of the 1969 movie that became the first and only X-rated production to win the Academy Award for Best Picture?
–"Midnight Cowboy" (Its rating has since been lowered to R)

• For two years during the '70s Mattel put out a doll called "Growing Up Skipper." What happened to this doll when her arm was turned?
–*Her breasts grew*

• When this series debuted in 1964, it was immediately panned as one of the dumbest, most cliche-infested television sitcoms in history. Nevertheless, it did become a smash hit—with syndicated reruns still popular. What is the series?
–*"Gilligan's Island"*

• What highly-rated 1968-to-1973 comedy show featured the classic one-liners "You bet your bippy," "Here comes the judge" and "Sock it to me! Sock it to me!"?
–*"Rowan and Martin's Laugh-In"*

• In 1962 the Mashed Potato, the Loco-Motion, the Frug, the Monkey and the Funky Chicken were all in vogue. What were they?
–*Dances*

• What historic musical event commenced August 15, 1969 on Max Yasgur's dairy farm in Bethel, New York? How long did the event last?
–*The Woodstock Music Festival (originally scheduled for Woodstock, N.Y.); three days*

• What popular campus activity, practiced primarily by sororities and fraternities in the 1960s, was rejuvenated by the 1978 movie premier of "National Lampoon's Animal House"?
–*Toga parties*

• Name the "sport" that had college students of the 1960s trying to see how many bodies would fit into a common curbside compartment.
–*Phone booth packing*

• Name the district in San Francisco associated in the '60s with "hippies" and other segments of the "counter culture." –*Haight-Ashbury*

• In 1975 these trademarked items were cared for, nurtured, and treated like little pampered pooches. What were they? –*Pet Rocks*

• What requirement was enacted as a law by LBJ in 1965 in response to evidence linking a common consumer product to significant health hazards? –*Manufacturers must put health warnings on cigarette packs*

• What round yellow 1970s fad accessories were inscribed with thin black lines and often accompanied by the words "Have a Nice Day"?
–*Smile buttons*

• In 1975 one-time stockbroker Josh Reynolds bolstered his assets by creating a temperature-sensitive juju, which he claimed could reveal the wearer's state of mind. What was the name of this trinket? –*The trademarked "Mood Ring"*

• Name the landmark 1973 U.S. Supreme Court case that barred states from preventing abortion in the first six months of pregnancy.
–*Roe vs. Wade*

• What 1960s fad, dubbed as America's "exotic dance and party rouser," had kids bending over backwards? –*The Limbo*

• What term became famous—or infamous—as a designation for the wholesale firing that took place in the midst of the Watergate Scandal on the evening of October 20, 1973?
–*The Saturday Night Massacre*

• Name the teenage heiress who was dragged screaming from her apartment in a kidnapping by the Symbionese Liberation Army on February 4, 1974—and then after being apprehended months later by FBI agents, was accused of adopting her captors' radical beliefs and convicted of bank robbery? –*Patty Hearst*

• Name the tall, leafy, herbaceous annual plant known in the Latin as "cannabis sativa."
–*Marijuana*

• On November 22, 1963, the CBS daytime soap-opera "As World Turns" was interrupted by the somber voice of "the most trusted man in America" announcing the assassination of President John Kennedy. Who was this eminent announcer?
–*CBS newsman Walter Cronkite*

• What Monday-evening ABC television program debuted in the fall of 1970 and became an immediate fixture—since shown on ESPN? –*"Monday Night Football"*

• Name the type of light that guided the mid-70s into an era of "dark illumination," as kids decorated their rooms with glowing black velvet posters. –*Ultraviolet, or "black" light*

MYTHICAL PROPORTIONS
did you know that ...

... Roman men once used a type of sacred thong—a "februa," which became a symbol of Juno, Roman goddess of marriage and fertility—as an "instrument of purification"? (They believed that striking a woman with this thong during the month of February would ensure her fertility.)

... In Norse mythology, Asgard is not only the home of the gods but also the center of the universe?

... The three "Graces" in Greek mythology refer to the three daughters of Zeus, all goddesses of fertility and named for the pleasing appearance of fertile gardens and fields?

For the Love of Zeus!

• What 9800-foot mountain peak, straddling the border of Thessaly and Macedonia, is professed to be the home of the Greek gods? –*Mt. Olympus*

• What ore, a primary source of atomic energy, is named after the primeval Greek sky god who became the grandfather of the classic Olympian gods? –*Uranium (after the god Uranus)*

• What flower, sporting varied and striking colors, was named for the Greek goddess of the rainbow? –*The 'iris'*

• What insect-eating plant—with somewhat heart-shaped leaves—was named for the Roman goddess of love? –*The Venus flytrap*

• What month was named for the Roman god of war? (Hint: Most soldiers did not look forward to marching to war in the middle of winter.) –*March (from the Roman god Mars)*

• Name the poor nymph whose unsettling love for Narcissus caused her to pine away until nothing but her voice remained. –*Echo*

• What common English word is derived from the name of a Greek god who had a human torso combined with the horns, ears and legs of a goat—enabling him to arouse terror in lonely places? –*Panic*—from the Greek shepherd god Pan

• What English verb is derived from the name of a king in Greek mythology whom Zeus punished by hanging fine fruit just above his head—which rose out of reach when he tried to eat it? –*'Tantalize'—from the Greek king Tantalus*

• What English word for a soft, gentle breeze comes from the name of the Greek god of the West Wind? –*Zephyr*

• According to Greek mythology, who had "the face that launched a thousand ships ... "? What was the result of this beauty's abduction? –*Helen, wife of King Menalaus of Argos; her abduction by Paris, a Trojan prince, brought on the Trojan War*

• In Greek mythology, what name refers to the "primal void" that gave birth to Earth, the infernal regions, Love, Darkness, and Night? –*Chaos*

• Name the two ravens that perched on the shoulder of the Nordic god Odin to inform him of worldly secrets. –*Thought and Memory*

• What day of the week was named after the Norse god of thunder and storm who was also the protector of mankind? –*'Thursday', from the Norse god Thor*

• What was unique about the birth of Athena, the Greek goddess of war, wisdom and handicrafts? –*She was born fully armed from the head of her sky-god father Zeus, the supreme ruler of Olympus*

• What was the punishment that Sisyphus was sentenced to in Hades for having cheated death? –*He was forced to eternally roll a stone up a hill every morning, only to have it roll back down every night*

• In Greek mythology, who is the goddess of victory? –*Nike—sometimes portrayed as an "aspect" of Athena*

• In Greek mythology, who lost a footrace because she couldn't ignore the golden apples dropped in her path by Hippomenes, her suitor? –*Atlanta*

• Three Greek beings—Clotho, who spins the thread of our life, Lachesis, who determines its length, and Atropos, who cuts it off—present each mortal at birth with both good and evil gifts. By what name do these providence-providers go by? –*The three "Fates"*

• Queen Jocasta hanged herself when she found out that her husband was also her son. Who was her unfortunate consort—given a new shot at fame in the 20th century when Freud linked his name to his theory of childhood development? –*Oedipus*

• What mythological mother of 14 sons and 14 daughters was punished for her arrogance by being changed to a column of stone, whose face remained forever wet with tears over her slain children? –*Niobe*

• Who were the winged dragon-like creatures with writhing snakes for hair whose looks turned men to stone? –*The Gorgons*

THE MEDIA JUNGLE
did you know that ...

...CBS News ex-anchor Dan Rather used to invent and give play-by-play accounts of fictitious football games while walking to his elementary school in Wharton, Texas?

...Although Horace Greeley has always been given credit, it was actually John Soule who, in an 1851 article for the Terre Haute Express, coined the phrase "Go west, young man ... "?

...Playing on the rivalry of the "yellow kid" comic strip that appeared in 1895, two newspapers, The New York World and The New York Journal, coined the phrase "yellow journalism."

...The powerful media moguls that owned the above-mentioned papers were, respectively, William Randolph Hearst and Joseph Pulitzer?

The Fourth Estate

• Name the magazine that corresponds to the mottos or "mission statements" given below:

"The magazine for men"
  –Esquire
"The humor magazine"
  –National Lampoon
"The weekly news magazine"
  –Time
"The magazine of news significance"
  –Newsweek

• On February 9, 1993, "Dateline NBC" was forced to publicly apologize for a scandal which caused new NBC president Michael Gartner to resign. What was the scandal?
–"Dateline" rigged a GM truck with explosives to simulate a "scientific" crash-test demo

• What controversial political figure was named *Time* magazine's "Man of the Year" for 1979?
–Iran's Ayatollah Khomeini

• Who was the first woman to anchor a nightly television network newscast?
–Barbara Walters

• What radioactive, extremely tall Japanese movie star once made appearances on the covers of *Time* and *Newsweek* magazines? And how tall was he?
–Godzilla; 164 feet tall

• When King Kong's giant mechanical hand was pictured on *Time* magazine's cover in 1976, who was it clutching in its grasp?
–Actress Jessica Lange

• What was journalist Nellie Bly's real name? What stunt did this tough newswoman pull off in 1889 that put her name in the record books?
–Elizabeth Cochrane (Seaman); she traveled around the world in 72, not 80, days

• Name the editorial columnist and TV personality who founded *The National Review*?
–William F. Buckley, Jr.

• The cover of August 1991's Vanity Fair magazine sported a controversial photo of actress Demi Moore. What two startling factors sparked the controversy?
–Moore was both nude and in her last trimester of pregnancy

• In 1871 The New York Herald sent journalist Sir Henry Morton Stanley to Africa to find a Scottish missionary-explorer. What was this explorer's name and what was he looking for when Stanley met him?
–David Livingston; he was attempting to trace the source of the Nile River

• While serving in the U.S. Army during World War II, what future CBS-TV "60 Minutes" reporter penned a brilliant and cynical novel of young love titled *Tell Me About Women*?
–Harry Reasoner

• After establishing Christian Science and the Church of Christ Scientist, what woman, at the ripe old age of 87, founded the magazine *The Christian Science Monitor*?
–MaryBaker Eddy

... In his earlier years as a bachelor actor, Tom Selleck appeared twice on TV's "The Dating Game"—and lost out to other contestants both times?

... Mattel's billionaire Barbie doll's full name is Barbie Millicent Roberts?

... At the height of his fame Fred Astaire's feet were insured for $650,000?

... After comic actor Groucho Marx lost $240,000 in the 1929 two-day stock market crash, his insomnia became so bad that he often would call people in the middle of the night just to insult them?

... When preeminent cartoonist Charles Schulz was in high school the yearbook staff turned down his offer to include a few of his comic strips? (His work still appears in several thousand newspapers in dozens of countries.)

... Famed German composer Ludwig van Beethoven sometimes poured ice water over his head in an effort to stimulate his brain?

... When another musical genius, Wolfgang Amadeus Mozart, was just two years old he correctly picked out a pig's squeal as a "G-sharp"?

Little-Known Facts About Well-Known People

• What popular late network newscaster was a high school drop-out? *–ABC's Peter Jennings*

• Statesman Winston Churchill suffered a lifelong inability to enunciate one particular letter of the alphabet; thus, he wrote all his speeches with this terminal letter carefully eliminated. What letter was it? *– "S"*

• What naturalist, plagued by a lifetime of nervous disorders, turned to science because his stutter precluded him from becoming a minister? (Hint: In a bit of irony, ministers were later to be counted among his most ardent detractors.) *–Charles Darwin, father of the theory of evolution*

• In their early years, Sir Winston Churchill, Thomas Edison, Albert Einstein, Henry Ford and Sir Isaac Newton were all once considered what?
–Incorrigible students and failures in school

• What did Michelangelo, Leonardo da Vinci and Jack the Ripper each have in common? *–They were left-handers*

• After all his narrow escapes, what was the cause of Harry Houdini's ultimate demise? –On what U.S. holiday did he die? *Acute appendicitis overtook him on Halloween day, 1926*

• Born in Hot Springs, Iowa, her measurements—according to her late creator—are 70-30–32. Name her. *–Miss Piggy*

• Who holds the still-standing record for the most fan mail ever received? (Hint: Children have sent him hundreds of millions of letters over the years.) *–Mickey Mouse*

• What was the color of actress Jayne Mansfield's house and automobile? *–Pink, her favorite hue*

• What good-luck object does Opera singer Luciano Pavarotti carry in his pocket whenever he sings? *–A bent nail*

• This actor lost 45 lbs. in 1993 in order to play the part of Andrew Beckett, an AIDS victim fighting wrongful termination. Name him, and the award-winning film.
–Tom Hanks; "Philadelphia"

• Carol Burnett signaled her grandmother every week at the end of her show to let her know everything was all right. What was this trademark signal?
–She would tug slightly on her left earlobe

• After divorcing husband Don Johnson, who is actress Melanie Griffith's current hunky main squeeze?
–Actor Antonio Banderas

• Give the name of each of these celebrities' famed exes:
Superstar rocker Mick Jagger
 –Model Jerry Hall
Film mogul Stephen Spielberg
 –Actress Amy Irving
Singer/actress Whitney Houston
 –R&B singer/dancer Bobby Brown
Former Beatle Paul McCartney
 –Model Heather Mills
Actor Tom Arnold
 –Actress Rosanne Barr
Singer Jessica Simpson
 –Nick Lachey
Actress Nichol Kidman
 –Actor Tom Cruise
Actress Jennifer Aniston
 –Actor Brad Pitt
Actress Carmen Electra
 –Rock guitarist Dave Navarro and ex-basketballer Dennis Rodman

• Provide the names of the spouses who divorced and later *remarried* each of these celebrities:
Elizabeth Taylor (actress)
 –Richard Burton
William Saroyan (writer)
 –Carol Marcus
Milton Berle (comedian)
 –Joyce Matthews
Dorothy Parker (writer)
 –Alan Campbell
Robert Wagner (actor)
 –Natalie Wood
Jayne Wyman (actress)
 –Fred Karger
Elliot Gould (actor)
 –Jenny Bogard

• Among his many accomplishments, football star Joe Namath will forever be remembered for modeling what product for a television commercial?
–Beautymist pantyhose

• What Academy Award-winning actor often registers at hotels under the name of Lord Greystoke? –Marlon Brando

• What first name was Oprah Winfrey born with? –Orpah

• Just days after the death of film star Rudolph Valentino, an anonymous woman mysteriously placed 13 roses on his grave. By what nickname was this legendary figure later known? –"The Lady in Black"

• Who was the first big-time American celebrity whose AIDS diagnosis became public knowledge?
–Rock Hudson

• One-time movie actor Dick Wilson did not gain his fame from his film work, but rather as what grocery clerk? What product did he tout, and what famous line did he commonly recite as this character?
–Mr. Whipple; toilet tissue; "Don't squeeze the Charmin"

• What rock star was once elected homecoming queen by his alma mater, the University of Houston?
–Alice Cooper

• Upon what comedian did columnist Walter Winchell confer the nickname "Thief of Bad Gags"?
–Milton Berle

• The play/movie "Amadeus" fancifully attributes Mozart's murder to a jealous fellow composer, the intellectual Antonio Salieri, who openly questioned why God would give such a wondrous gift to a 35-year-old brat. According to some historians, how did Salieri carry out his plan? In fact, what was the probable cause of Mozart's death?
–He poisoned his rival; he likely died of overwork and typhus

• What commercial product did both rock musician Dr. John and model/actress Brooke Shields pose for as babies? –Ivory soap

• The birth name of this comedian/actor is Albert Einstein. What is his stage name? –Albert Brooks

• Singer Neil Diamond won a scholarship to New York University, where he majored in biology in hopes of becoming a doctor. In what sport did he win his scholarship? –Fencing

• This country singer, who also took the lead role in several movies, was a Rhodes Scholar in his youth. Name him.
–Kris Kristofferson

• What actress/model held the title of "Miss Pro Tennis" in 1968? –Farrah Fawcett

AT THE MOVIES
did you know that …

… Sales of undershirts plummeted 40 percent shortly after Clark Gable opened his shirt to reveal a bare chest in 1934's "It Happened One Night"?

… It took John Hughes only four days to write the script for the 1983 comedy film "National Lampoon's Vacation"?

… The little-known 1966 movie "The Persecution and Assassination of Jean-Paul Marat as Performed by the Inmates of the Asylum of Charenton Under the Direction of the Marquis de Sade" is the longest-titled film in history?

… While viewing daily film takes from the 1937 Humphrey Bogart gangster movie "Marked Woman," producer Hal Wallis objected to a puny-looking extra standing among the tough guys, and when asked why he had used this actor, the director's response was that the insignificant little extra wasn't really an actor but an actual member of the Lucky Luciano gang who had been cast to add realism?

That's a Wrap!
• What was German war-leader Adolph Hitler's favorite movie? –"King Kong"

• What film's climactic fight scene has BruceLee breaking Jackie Chan's neck?
–"Enter the Dragon"

• Actor William Pratt was once considered a hopeless cause by producers and directors because of his lisp. However, after answering an agent's advertisement in Billboard magazine, this 23-year-old became world famous for his contributions to Universal Studio's "Frankenstein." What is William Pratt's stage name? –Boris Karloff

• A hot new trend in films was launched with the 1986 release of the Academy Award-winning feature "Platoon." Similar flicks, such as "Full Metal Jacket" and "Hamburger Hill," followed one on top of the other. What was the fad behind their success? –The craze for realistic and ultra-violent Vietnam War movies

• What Pixar movie was first to receive a rating higher than G? –"The Incredibles"

• What 1981 Academy Award-winning movie, starring Mary Tyler Moore, Donald Sutherland and Timothy Hutton, marked Robert Redford's directorial debut? –"Ordinary People"

• At a total running time of 85 hours, what was the longest movie ever produced?
– *"The Cure for Insomnia" (1987)*

• Bing Crosby and Bob Hope starred in a series of movies that featured the word "road" in each title. What was their first "Road" movie called?
– *"The Road to Singapore"*

• The following actors masqueraded as opposite gender in movies. Name the movie from the actor and the year the movie came out:
Robin Williams, 1993
– *"Mrs. Doubtfire"*
Gyenyth Paltrow, 1998
– *"Shakespeare in Love"*
Barbra Streisand, 1983
– *"Yentl"*
Tony Curtis, 1959
– *"Some Like It Hot"*

• The year 1939 marked an apex in movie making. Answer these questions from that splendidly memorable year:
The name of Humphrey Bogart's one-and-only horror film? What was Bogart's role? – *"Return of Dr. X"; he played child-killer Maurice Xavier*

What famous Southern-belle role did Bette Davis turn down in 1939 because she thought her leading man would be Errol Flynn, whom she refused to work with? What actress was pushed into stardom after landing the role Davis had declined? Scarlet O'Hara of "Gone With the Wind"; – *Vivian Leigh*

Who was first offered the male lead in "Gone With the Wind" but turned it down, saying, "I'm glad it'll be Clark Gable who's falling flat on his face … "? – *Gary Cooper*

W.C. Fields was offered $75,000 to play an ultimately wise and good-hearted con-man in an epic fantasy motion picture. What was the role, and why—even though it was written with Fields in mind—did he decline it? – *"The Wizard of Oz"; he wanted $100,000*

• What 1930 German "cabaret" film kicked off the acting career of Marlene Dietrich?
– *"The Blue Angel"*

• What is the name of the famous trademark lion for Metro Goldwyn Mayer (MGM) studios? – *Leo*

• What 1987 Steve Martin movie was actually a modern-day remake of Edmond Rostand's classic "Cyrano de Bergerac"? – *"Roxanne"*

• Name the irreverent underground animator who produced the first landmark X-rated cartoon, "Fritz the Cat" (1972), and then went on to make a feature-length animated movie of J.R.R. Tolkien's G-rated classic "The Lord of the Rings" (1978). – *Ralph Bakshi*

• Brian de Palma's 1984 film "Scarface" holds the dubious distinction of using the four-letter F-word a record number of times. How many times was this word spoken during the film?
– *206 (an average of once every 29 seconds)*

• What two common "eat-it-it's-good-for-you" items were combined to create Linda Blair's realistic looking "vomit" in the 1973 film "The Exorcist"? – *Split-pea soup and oatmeal*

• What was used for the blood in the infamous black-and-white shower scene from Alfred Hitchcock's 1960 thriller-classic "Psycho"?
– *Chocolate sauce*

• Alfred Hitchcock always made a brief "cameo" appearance in each of his films; however, in the 1944 movie "Lifeboat," the entire storyline was set in a lifeboat out at sea and there was no opportunity for "Hitch" to dip in and out of the action. What was the ingenious solution that ensured his appearance in this film?
– *He placed a photo of himself on a newspaper that is read on camera by one of the characters (He is the "before" specimen on a before-and-after ad for a diet product)*

• What two iconic Hollywood actors both turned down the part of young Corleone in "The Godfather" (1972), leaving Al Pacino to play the role?
– *Robert Redford and Warren Beatty*

• The high-grossing 1989 Spielberg film "Indiana Jones and the Last Crusade" is cherished by blunder buffs for its record number of mistakes found in a single movie. What is wrong with the following scenes?
The beginning of the film shows young Indy crossing the Atlantic in 1938 by airliner and, later, embarking for the return journey by airship (blimp). – *Transatlantic passenger air service didn't begin until 1939, one year later; and transatlantic airship services had ceased in 1937, the year before Indy is shown traveling by blimp*

In the airport lounge in Berlin, two passengers are depicted reading identical German newspapers. – *The papers are dated 1918, 20 years before the year in which the film is set*

An intertitle reading "The Republic of Hatay" is immediately followed by a scene in which the ruler is addressed as "Your Royal Highness."
–*A republic, by definition, has no royal rulers*

• And before leaving the same subject, how old was Sean Connery when he played the father of 46-year-old Harrison Ford (Indiana Jones) "The Last Crusade"? –*58*

• What physical characteristic would have prevented actor Tom Cruise, who played the lead role in "Top Gun," from actually becoming a naval pilot in real life? –*The Navy requires that officers be 5 feet 10 inches tall, and Cruise is only 5'9"*

• Legendary movie mogul Samuel Goldwyn was notorious for his frequent abuse of the English language. Fill in the blanks to complete the following classic "Goldwynisms":
"Our comedies are not to be _____ at."
   –*Laughed*
"I don't think anybody should write his autobiography until after he's _____."
   –*Dead*
"We've passed a lot of _____ since then."
   –*Water*
"I would be sticking my head in a _____."
   –*Moose*
"I can't make it, but I hope you'll give me a _____."
   –*Raincoat*
To a supposedly valuable employee who was leaving the studio: "It always makes me very unhappy to say good-bye to a _____ in my machine."
   –*Clog*
After a sculptor commented on the beauty of Mrs. Goldwyn's hands: "Go ahead, make a _____ of them."
   –*Bust*

• What famous director broke his own 1982 record for the all-time top-grossing film with another blockbuster in 1993? What were the names of the two record-smashers in question? –*Steven Spielberg, with his 1993 film "Jurassic Park" and 1982 classic "E.T."*

• What star-studded 2001 flick was originally meant to feature, among others, Bruce Willis, Danny Glover, Luke Wilson and Owen Wilson? –*"Ocean's Eleven"*

TELEVISION TIDBITS
did you know that …

… Ninety-eight percent of U.S. households own at least one television set—and most own more than one?

… Some viewers of "Gilligan's Island" actually sent letters to the U.S. Coast Guard asking them to rescue the castaways?

… Jack Nicholson guest-starred in two episodes of "The Andy Griffith Show"?

… Comedian David Letterman was first to perform the sticky stunt of "velcro wall-jumping" before a national audience in the mid 1980s, which brought about an immediate increase in popularity in his late-night television show?

… Producers of "Saturday Night Live" had their doubts about hiring John Belushi? (They were afraid he was not disciplined enough for live TV.)

… The characters in the sitcom "Barney Miller"—Captain Miller, Inspector Luger, Wojo, Fish, and Lt. Scanlon—were made honorary detectives by the New York Police Department?

Tuning In To the Tube
• A cable television company serving Columbia, South Carolina, needed to occupy a vacant channel while awaiting the start-up of their new Science-Fiction channel. In the interim they chose a fairly innocuous—some might even say "monotonous"—scene to occupy the vacant channel's screen. But when the channel finally began regular broadcasting, complaints were so numerous that the company had to acquire another channel on which to resume running their temporary picture. What was this soothing scene? –*A camera aimed full time at an aquarium*

• What is the first name of Andy Griffith's character in the TV series "Matlock"? –*Benjamin*

• Name the 1960s TV spy spoof immortalized by its star, Don Adams. Also, what apologetic phrase did Adams employ in every episode after botching an assignment or committing some other blunder? –*"Get Smart"; "Sorry 'bout that, Chief"*

• Who succeeded musician Doc Severinson when Jay Leno became host of "The Tonight Show"? –*Branford Marsalis*

• Another TV star known for his bungling ways was Don Knotts. What two popular sitcoms did he appear in? – *"The Andy Griffith Show"* and *"Three's Company"*

• Match these TV/movie superheroes with their secret identities:
  Superman
    – *Clark Kent*
  The Shadow
    – *Lamont Cranston*
  Spiderman
    – *Peter Parker*
  The Incredible Hulk
    – *Dr. David Banner*
  Wonder Woman
    – *Diana Prince*

• Johnny Carson took over the reins of the "Tonight Show" from Jack Parr; to whom did he pass them to when he "dismounted" in 1992? – *Jay Leno*

• Name the mellifluous-voiced British-born American who hosted Masterpiece Theatre for the Public Broadcasting Service from 1971 until his death in 1992. – *Alistair Cooke*

• Who "did" the voice for Magnum P.I.'s heard-but-not-seen boss on the show? – *Orson Welles*

• What TV sitcom took an uncouth family from the backwoods of the Ozarks and introduced them to the glamors of California? – *"The Beverly Hillbillies"*

• What phrase appears on the UFO poster in Fox Mulder's office on "The X-Files"? *"I Want to Believe"*

• Who made his acting debut as Mickey in "The Little Rascals," then grew up to portray a tough street cop named "Baretta"? – *Robert Blake*

• Name the TV military sitcoms that go with the settings described below:
  A World War II German POW camp known as Stalag 13
    – *"Hogan's Heroes"*
  An Old West military outpost (the perfect location for this "comedy of arrows")
    – *"F Troop"*
  A basic-training boot camp for the United States Marine Corps
    – *"Gomer Pyle, USMC"*
  A WWII P.T. boat under the command of actor Ernest Borgnine
    – *"McHale's Navy"*
  An Army surgical hospital camp during the Korean War
    – *"M*A*S*H"*

• Who of the original M*A*S*H regulars previously was a U.S. Army soldier who served in Korea—though it was after the War was over)? – *Jamie Farr*

• Name the four shows that were direct spin-offs of the series "All In the Family." – *"Maude," "The Jeffersons," "Archie Bunker's Place"* and *"Gloria"*

• "Corey," "Jeff" and "Timmy" have all been owners of what famous TV and movie pet? – *Lassie*

• What famous late Chinese martial arts icon guest-starred in a two-part episode of "Batman" as the Green Hornet's right-hand-man, Kato? – *Bruce Lee*

• Name the plush, purple, PBS reptile who teaches children to love everyone. – *Barney the Dinosaur*

• What two classic horror-spoof sitcoms first ran between 1964 and 1966 on national TV? – *"The Munsters"* and *"The Addams Family"*

• Who composed the opening music for the TV game show "Jeopardy"? – *The show's creator Merv Griffin*

• Like today's Vanna White, Jay Silverheels was a TV "sidekick." Who was he sidekick to, and what was his television name? – *The Lone Ranger; Tonto*

• What was the occupation of Jack Tripper, Jack Ritter's character in "Three's Company"? – *Chef*

• What was the name of the professor on "Gilligan's Island"? – *Roy Hinkley*

• What does the T. stand for as the initial in Captain James T. Kirk's name from the Television series "Star Trek"? – *Tiberius*

• Name the leading TV character played by the indicated actor from each series below:
  "The Man from U.N.C.L.E."
  (Robert Vaughn)
    – *Napoleon Solo*
  "The Fugitive" (David Janssen)
    – *Richard Kimble*
  "Batman" (Adam West)
    – *Bruce Wayne*
  "The Six Million Dollar Man"
  (Lee Majors)
    – *Col. Steve Austin*

• Who was the voice of "Charlie" on the television series "Charlie's Angels"? – *John Forsythe*

• What were the full names of the characters Starsky and Hutch in the TV series that went by the same title?
−*Dave Starsky and Ken Hutchinson*

• Supply the name of the actor who portrayed the enigmatic character Larry "Bud" Melman on "Late Night With David Letterman"?
−*Calvert de Forrest*

• What body parts were "bionic" on the "Six Million Dollar Man" and the "Bionic Woman" characters? −*His left eye, right arm and both legs; her right ear, right arm and both legs*

• Name the three original "Charlie's Angels" of the 1970s. −*Kate Jackson, Farrah Fawcett and Jaclyn Smith*

• In April, 1970, a few days after the riot trial on the "Chicago 8" had ended, radical Abbie Hoffman appeared on the Merv Griffin Show. Censors, however, never allowed Hoffman's shirt to be seen by the public. What symbol was his shirt fashioned to represent?
−*The American Flag*

• What were the names of Tom and Joan Bradford's eight children in the 1977-1981 comedy-drama "Eight Is Enough"?
−*Mary, Joanie, Nancy, Elizabeth, Susan, David, Tommy, and Nicholas*

CARTOONS & CARICATURES
did you know that …

… Bugs Bunny, the smart-alecky "wascally wabbit" created by Warner Brothers animator Chuck Jones, first appeared as a hare in "Porky's Hare Hunt" (1938)? (He was changed into a quick-witted rabbit for later films.)

… Pat Sullivan's creation Felix the Cat, after making his debut in 1923 and having his animated short-films shown to children during afternoon matinees, was the first cartoon character to gain superstardom?

Comic Strips and Animations
• What is the name of Batman's butler? *Alfred*

• In "Blondie," what are the names of Dagwood and Blondie Bumstead's two children? Dagwood's boss and his wife's names?
−*Alexander and Cookie; Mr. Dithers and Cora*

• What is Fred and Wilma Flintstone's home telephone number? −*BC 1234*

• In the comic strip "Beetle Bailey," what is the name of the camp he and his fellow soldiers are stationed at? −*Camp Swampy*

• What is "Mr. Magoo's" first name? −*Quincy*

• Patterned after the popular Sherlock Holmes stories, what comic strip character first appeared in 1931? −*Dick Tracy*

• Give the name of these "Dennis the Menace" characters:
    Dennis's easily-riled next-door neighbor and his more easy-going wife
        −*George and Martha Wilson*
    Dennis's father and mother
        −*Henry and Alice Mitchell*
    The local librarian
        −*Miss Davis*
    Dennis's best friend
        −*Joey*
    Dennis's self-proclaimed "girlfriend"— actually, the bane of his existence
        −*Margaret Wade*

• What cartoon hero was sweet on Sweet Polly Purebred? −*Underdog*

• What satirical comic book, created in the 1950s, gave us coverman Alfred E. Neuman with his "What, me worry?" smile? −*MADD magazine*

• Name the first feature-length animated film, released by Disney Studios in 1937.
−*"Snow White and the Seven Dwarfs"*

• What was the first cartoon series ever to be broadcast during prime time? – *"The Flintstones"*

• What DC Comics hero died in 1992 during a battle with an invader named Doomsday who came from another dimension? – *Superman*

• What is Doonesbury's first name? – *Michael*

• In the Popeye comics, who was Popeye's formidable 372-pound enemy? What was his name in the Popeye films and TV shorts that followed? – *Brutus; Bluto*

• Name the cartoon character that brought to life each of these famous lines:
"Shhh, I'm hunting wabbits."
    – *Elmer Fudd*
"Hello, all you happy people!"
    – *Droopy the dog*
"Oh, my darlin', oh, my darlin', oh, my darlin' Clementine."
    – *Huckleberry Hound*
"Ah, what's up, doc?"
    – *Bugs Bunny*
"You're dethhhpicable!"
    – *Daffy Duck*
"Ablee, ablee, ablee, ablee—that's all folks!"
    – *Porky Pig*
"Thufferin' thuccotash!"
    – *Sylvester the Cat*
"Exit, stage left."
    – *Snagglepuss the Lion*
"El kabong!"
    – *Quick Draw McGraw*
"I tawt I taw a puddy tat."
    – *Tweety bird*
"Yabba-dabba-doo!"
    – *Fred Flintstone*

• Name the creative production team that brought America both "The Flintstones" and "The Jetsons." – *William Hanna and Joseph Barbera*

• Who were the original members of the "Fantastic Four" super-hero pack? – *Mr. Fantastic, Invisible Girl, The Human Torch and The Thing*

• Creator Jim Davis called his popular tubby character "A little bit of Archie Bunker and Morris the Cat tossed together." To whom was he referring? – *Garfield the Cat*

• Name the editor of Clark Kent's "The Daily Planet" newspaper in Metropolis? Who portrayed him in the celebrated Superman movies of the 1980s? – *Perry White; Jackie Cooper*

• What is the last name of Linus and Lucy in the "Peanuts" comic strip? – *Van Pelt*

FUN AND GAMES
did you know that ...

… The craze of swallowing goldfish was initiated during a 1939 bull session at Harvard University's Holworthy Hall by freshman Lothrop Withington Jr., son of a prominent Boston lawyer—and soon everyone was following suit?

… The biggest-selling toy of the year 1957 was the Hula Hoop?

… The Slinky, a loosely coiled spring toy, made its debut in November 1945—and has been crawling down America's stairways ever since?

… "Patience," "Canfield," "Klondike" and "Spider" are all variations of the card game Solitaire?

… When it was first introduced on Mississippi riverboats in the 1800s, the game of poker originally went by the name "Bluff"?

Games People Play

• In the game of Chess, what is the maximum number of squares a king can move in any given direction? A queen? – *Only one; eight*

• Which color always moves first in a Chess game? – *White*

• What aromatic World Championship contest takes place annually in Beaver, Oklahoma? – *The World Championship Cow Chip Throwing Contest*

• Gambling has been legalized in all but two U.S. states. Which two states still do not allow any form of organized gaming? – *Hawaii and Utah*

• In 1978 Bob Speca, Jr. had 100,000 of these standing at one time before they all toppled with the help of a klutzy ABC-TV cameraman. What were they? – *Dominoes*

• What are the playing tiles commonly called in the game of Dominoes? – *Bones*

• "Art & Literature," "Science & Nature" and "Sports & Leisure" are three of the six categories in the classic Trivial Pursuit board game. Name the other three categories. – *"Geography," "Entertainment" and "History"*

• What Chinese parlor game, first popularized as early as 500 B.C.E., became a fad among upper-class Americans during the 1920s? – *Mah-Jongg*

• What suspect in the game of Clue has the same name as a popular condiment?
–*Colonel Mustard*

• How many flat colored squares are there on a Rubik's Cube? –*54*

• In the game of Backgammon, how many playing pieces does each player start with? –*15*

• Exceeding 80 million sales since its invention in 1935, what is the world's all-time bestselling board game? –*Monopoly*

• Answer these other questions about the game of Monopoly:
> What household item—often associated with a sometimes tedious chore—is used as a player token?
> > –*An iron*
> What two articles of clothing are used as tokens?
> > –*A hat and a shoe*
> What property, according to Monopoly aficionados, is landed on most often?
> > –*Illinois Avenue*
> What is the rent for Boardwalk with a hotel?
> > –*$2,000*
> How many total properties are there on a Monopoly board?
> > –*28*

• In what game does the word *fudgies* mean "mistakes"? –*Marbles*

• What toy can let you "walk the dog," go all the way "around the world," then come home to "sleep?" –*The yo-yo*

• What is the stretchable, bouncing, viscous toy that is packaged and sold in plastic eggs? –*Silly Putty*

• What was the high-bouncing, hard-rubber sphere sold to Wham-O by Norman Stingley in 1965? –*The Super Ball*

• What is the common name for an alabaster marble? –*An "alley"*

• What category of adrenaline-inducing mechanical contraptions includes heavy-duty performers like the "Texas Cyclone" and "Mister Twister"? –*Roller Coasters*

• What kind of footwear, first fabricated in 1760 by Belgium's Joseph Merlin, exploded into an international craze in the late 1970s and early 1980s? –*Roller Skates*

• Another roller craze was sparked by Jan and Dean in their 1965 hit "Sidewalk Surfing." Name the still-popular mode of transportation that this duo celebrated in song. *The skate board*

• These skates, featuring wheels arranged in a straight-line configuration and used in sports like "asphalt hockey," are known as what? –*Rollerblades*

• What is the measurement used in Frisbee tournaments to determine how long a Frisbee remains airborne? –*"Maximum Time Aloft"*

• What game, from the Japanese word *Paka* (meaning "to eat"), gobbled up a generous share of the six-billion-dollar video game business during 1982? –*Pac-Man*

• Name the gravity-defying thrill that took America by storm in 1991. –*Bungee jumping*

• Take a gamble and come up with the definition of the gambling terms listed in the left-hand column:
> Another name for Blackjack
> > –*Twenty-one*
> Gambling's "ivories"
> > –*Dice*
> "Doped Cards"
> > –*A marked deck*
> A "Fruit Machine"
> > –*A slot machine*
> The three colors on a roulette wheel
> > –*Red, green and black*
> Roulette's country of origin
> > –*France*
> The "suicide king"
> > –*The king of hearts*

... According to "Harper's Magazine Index," a staggering—or "only," depending on how you see the statistic—six percent of Americans say they find life "dull"?

... Britain's Queen Elizabeth II took a course when she was 18 to acquire skills to help with the war effort, and enjoyed the class so much that she took it on as a hobby? And what did this course cover? Heavy mechanics, of course; she learned to strip and service engines.

... Today's men and women average around 40 hours of free time each week, compared to only 34 "spare" hours 40 years ago?

... More Americans visit zoos each year than go to all sporting events combined?

... Former U.S. President Ronald Reagan spent 24 percent of his time in office on vacation or at Camp David compared to the 10 percent vacation-time taken by his predecessor Jimmy Carter?

... Renowned U.S. attorney Clarence Darrow, an avid crossword puzzle fan, once tried in embarrassment to hide the crossword he was working on from H.G. Wells, who replied, "Don't be foolish. I work two of them every day of my life"?

... Over half of an "average" modern teen's spare time is filled tuning into music or digital programming on some high-tech device?

... "Food" was listed as the number-one worry for those planning and carrying out a social event?

Don't Worry, Be Happy!
• What is the preferred reading material for the 66 percent of Americans who admit to reading in the bathroom? –*Reader's Digest*

• As a husband, Austrian psychoanalyst Sigmund Freud often engaged in "collective" competitions with his family. What did the Freuds collect? –*Mushrooms*

• What did the late Palestinian political leader Yasir Arafat do to relax? –*He watched cartoons*

• Name the miniatures, distributed by Joshua L. Cowen, that hit an all-time sales high in 1941. Also, what company distributed these favorite collectables? (Hint: Gomez Addams of the "Addams Family" TV sitcom loved to crash

them to "ease his mind.") –*Electric trains; the Lionel Corporation*

• Almost any kind of leisure activity can become a hobby. Name the four general, overlapping categories that most hobbies fall under.
–*The arts, collecting, handicrafts, and games and sports*

• Identify the type of hobbyist that matches each of these scientific designations:
Deltiologist
   –*Post card collector*
Spelunker
   –*Cave explorer*
Philatelist
   –*Stamp collector*
Lepidopterist
   –*Moth and butterfly collector*
Pugilist
   –*Boxer*
Notaphile
   –*A banknote collector*
Bandophile
   –*A cigar band collector*

• What are you doing if you interlace a "warp" and "weft"? –*Weaving*

• A "kiln" and a "kick wheel" are used in what hobby? –*Pottery-making*

• The terms "yarn over," "popcorn" and "cast on" belong to what creative diversion? –*Knitting*

• What activity does a "piscatologist" participate in? –*Fishing*

• What soothing sport uses "plugs" and "leaders"? –*Also fishing*

• What is another name for a "natatorium"? –*A swimming pool*

• What are a "bucket hitch" and a "fisherman's bend"? –*Types of knots*

• What type of hobbyist might be interested in "first-day-issues"? –*A stamp or magazine collector*

OLD TESTAMENT TEST
did you know that ...

... Abraham wasn't the only Old Testament father to face the prospect of sacrificing a child? (Centuries later, a homeward-bound Gileadite general named Jephthah in the book of Judges vowed to sacrifice "whatever shall first come out ... of my house to meet me" in thanksgiving for his victorious return from Mizpah. When he was greeted by his "only child" Adah, the father, heartsick, cried out, "Alas, my daughter!" Nevertheless, with Adah's determined blessing, he eventually carried out his vow. See Judges 11:34-40)

... "Lucifer"—literally meaning "Lightbearer" or "Full of light"—our best-known name for the Devil, is mentioned only once in the Old Testament (Isaiah 14:12), and not at all in the New Testament?

... The word *Maher-shalal-hash-baz* (See Isaiah 8:1 and 3), meaning "To speed to the spoil, he hasteneth the prey," is the longest word in the Old Testament?

... According to legend, the names of the two thieves crucified at Jesus' right and left were named Disma and Gestas, and that after ordering the crucifixion Pontius Pilate supposedly went and killed himself?

... The respective traditional symbols of Matthew, Mark, Luke and John as the Four Evangelists are a man, a lion, an ox and an eagle?

It's In the Book!

• Most know that Adam and Eve's first two sons were Cain and Abel. Who was their third son? –*Seth*

• An early English Bible, published in 1560, was given a nickname for its rendition of a verse from Genesis that has Adam and Eve sewing fig leaves together to make themselves a certain type of clothing. What is the nickname that honors this Edenic garb? –*The Breeches Bible*

• Who asked, "Am I my brother's keeper?" –*Cain, speaking to the Lord after slaying his brother Abel*

• What Old Testament characters used these other well-known lines—and to whom is each speaking?

"It is not good for the man to be alone ... " (Gen. 2:18). –*The Lord God, speaking to no one in particular*

"Ye shall not surely die.... Ye shall be as gods, knowing good and evil." (Gen. 3:4-5). –*The serpent in the Garden of Eden, speaking to Eve*

"God hath made me to laugh ... " (Gen. 21:6). –*Sara, speaking to no one in particular about the birth of her and Abraham's son, Isaac*

"Get thee from me ... see my face no more; for in that day thou seest my face thou shalt die." (Exodus 10:28). –*Pharaoh, to Moses*

"Speak; for thy servant heareth." (I Sam. 3:10). –*The boy Samuel, to the Lord*

"Come to me, and I will give thy flesh unto the fowls of the air, and to the beasts of the field." (I Sam. 17:44). –*The Philistine giant Goliath, to young David*

"And though after my skin worms destroy this body, yet in my flesh shall I see God." (Job 19:26). –*Job, to Bildad the Shuhite*

"Did we not cast three men bound into the midst of the fire?... Lo, I see four men loose, walking ... and they have no hurt ..." –*King Nebuchadnezzar, to his counselors concerning the casting of Shadrach, Meshach and Abed-nego into the fiery furnace*

• What is the name of the large sea monster that represents the forces of evil in the Old Testament? –*Leviathan*

• What was—and is—the name of the city where Samson brought down the pillars, killing over 3,000 Philistines, including himself? –*Gaza*

• According to the book of Genesis, how old was Noah when he died? –*950 years old*

• What feathered black long-distance flightmasters brought meat and bread to Elijah as he hid by the brook east of Jordan? –*Ravens (see I Kings 17:6)*

• What were the only two animals on Noah's ark mentioned specifically in scripture? –*A raven and a dove*

• What name does the Bible assign to Noah's wife? –*"Noah's wife"*

• How many people were aboard Noah's ark during the time of the Great Flood? –*Eight (Noah, his wife, their three sons, and their son's wives)*

• What were the names of Noah's three sons? –*Shem, Ham and Japheth*

• What happened to Lot's wife when she disobeyed God's commandment and looked back toward the sinful cities of Sodom and Gomorrah as she and her family fled before the holocaust sent by God to consume them? –*She was turned into a pillar of salt*

• In what form did God first appear to instruct Moses? –*A burning bush*

- Name the Old Testament book that contains the famous chapter beginning, "To every thing there is a season …" –*Ecclesiastes*

- Give the dimensions of Noah's ark, according to Genesis. –*It was 300 by 50 by 30 cubits (one cubit equals about 18 inches)*

- What is the fifth of the Ten Commandments? –*"Honor thy father and thy mother … "*

- Name the Old Testament book that tells the remarkable story of the love between a Moabite woman and her Israelite mother-in-law. Also, name these two women. –*Ruth; Ruth and Naomi*

- Name the Canaanite fertility god whose worship became synonymous with evil among the Israelites—in part because, like many other Near-Eastern divinities, he required human sacrifice. –*Baal*

- Coverdale's Bible of 1535 was nicknamed the "Bug Bible" because it translated Psalm 91:5 as "Thou shalt not need to be afrayed for eny bugges by night." What is the more modern translation that replaces the word "bugges" in the King James Version? –*"Terrors" ("Bugges" related to the bogeyman and bugaboos that still "haunt" current English usage; it once did refer to all scary notions and elusive phenomena, and not just insects*

- What was the name of the wooden chest that contained the stone tablets inscribed with the Ten Commandments? –*The Ark of the Covenant*

- According to Genesis, why did Cain have a mark placed on him after he killed his brother? –*To protect him from anyone who might want to kill him in retaliation for his murder of Abel*

- Name the two women Jacob, father of the "twelve tribes," married. Which was his favorite? What was their relationship to each other? –*Leah and Rachel; Jacob "loved Rachel"; the wives were sisters*

- King Ahaziah, along with 102 of his soldiers, was executed by fire for trying to capture what great prophet of Israel? –*Elijah "the Tishbite"*

- How were Korah, Dathan, Abiram and their families punished for rejecting Moses's authority and founding their own congregation? –*They were swallowed by the earth*

- What is the last word in the Old Testament, in the book of Malachi? –*"Curse"*

A WOMAN'S WORLD
did you know that …

… In 1958 Julia Child was the first woman to be "christened" a full-fledged "Chef," a title traditionally held only by men in this profession?

… Women represent approximately 63 percent of all persons over the age of 18 living below the poverty level?

… Women make up 70 percent of all migraine headache sufferers?

… Los Angeles resident Alice Wells was sworn in as the first policewoman in the United States on September 12, 1910?

… According to a survey conducted in 1991 by a research firm and Cornell University, female executives receive a promotion an average of every 2.6 years, while their male colleagues must wait an average of 3.3 years?

… The number of woman-owned businesses increased a dramatic 57 percent in the past several decades?

… Recent statistics show that women with master's degrees, working year round and full time, earn only about the same amount as men with associate degrees?

… French dancer and notorious World War I German spy Mata Hari (born Margaretha Geertruida Zeele), after being arrested in a Paris hotel in 1917, was said to have smiled and winked at the firing squad as they raised their rifles to shoot her?

There is Nothin' Like a … Woman!

- In 1992, what nation had the highest percentage of women in their legislature? –*Finland, with 38.5%*

- Who, in 1849, became the first female medical doctor? –*Elizabeth Blackwell*

- In 1853 Antoinette Brown Blackwell became the first formally educated woman minister. What church did she belong to? –*The Congregationalist Church*

- In 1853, who founded the *Una*, the first women's rights magazine? –*Paulina Wright Davis (1813-1876*

- After allowing current title holder Nicole Dunsdon to complete her reign in October 1992, what country successfully lobbied to have its national beauty contest canceled, claiming that it was degrading to women? –*Canada*

• In 1939 an acclaimed black female contralto was barred from singing in Washington's Constitutional Hall because of her race. Who was she? –*Marian Anderson*

• In 1959, Anita Bryant—who later became the spokeswoman for Florida orange juice—represented what state in the Miss America Beauty pageant? –*Oklahoma*

• What woman was rejected by 29 medical schools before finally gaining admission, and went on to become the first licensed woman doctor in the U.S.? –*Elizabeth Blackwell*

• What well-known women's activist was arrested and convicted of attempting to vote in the 1872 U.S. national election? –*Susan B. Anthony*

• Who was the first First Lady ever to obtain a college education?
–*Lucy Hayes, wife of Rutherford B.*

• What military-leader "Maid of Orleans" was condemned for heresy and burned at the stake?
–*Joan of Arc*

• Aside from the fictional, idealistic representations of "Justice" and "Liberty," name the three females who have appeared on U.S. currency.
–*Martha Washington, Pocahontas and Susan B. Anthony*

• Who was the notorious Wild West character who was said to have had 12 husbands, who dressed, cursed and shot like a man, and was buried beside Wild Bill Hickok in Deadwood, South Dakota?
–*Martha Jane Canary, a.k.a. Calamity Jane*

• What revolutionary woman educator served as president of the National College Equal Suffrage League from 1908-1917 and as president of Bryn Mawr College, Pennsylvania, from 1894-1922?
–*Martha Carey Thomas*

• Former British Prime Minister Margaret Thatcher's nickname was what? –*"The Iron Lady"*

• Who were the first two women to head the two major political parties in the U.S. –*Jean Westwood headed the Democratic Party in 1972; Mary Louise Smith, in 1974, was first to lead the Republicans*

• Who was the first woman to run for President of the United States, and in what year?
–*Victoria Woodhull of Homer of Ohio, in 1872*

• In 1933, Frances Perkins, serving under F.D. Roosevelt, became the first female cabinet member. What "semi-ironic" position did she hold? –*Secretary of Labor*

• Of the 2200 persons quoted in the current edition of "Bartlett's Familiar Quotations," how many are women? –*Only 164*

• What little-known woman worked alongside Eli Whitney to invent the cotton gin?
–*Catherine Greene*

• What American social worker and founder of Chicago's Hull House won the 1931 Nobel Peace Prize for her work in the Women's International League for Peace and Freedom? –*Jane Addams*

• What gracious woman was founder of the Special Olympics? –*Eunice Kennedy Shriver*

• Who was the first woman to appear on a U.S. postage stamp? –*Queen Isabella of Spain in 1893*

• Also in the year 1893, what nation of the world became the first to grant women the right to vote? When—and with what Amendment to the Constitution—did the U.S. grant this right?
–*New Zealand; 1920 with the 19th Amendment*

• Martha Mitchell, wife of former Nixon Attorney General John Mitchell, earned a nickname for her often outrageous comments on liberals, protesters and reporters. What was this tongue-in-cheek nickname? –*"The Mouth That Roared"*

• Who was the only female to win the U.S. Medal of Honor? What services did she render during the Civil War to merit this award? –*Mary Walker; she served as a surgeon in the 52nd Ohio Regiment*

• The actress who played opposite John Wayne in the 1970 film "Rio Lobo" became 20th Century-Fox's president of production 10 years later. What is her name? –*Sherry Lansing*

• Noted for her studies of the cultures of the Pacific Islands, the United States and Russia, who was born Dec. 16, 1901?
–*Anthropologist Margaret Mead*

• What "loose-trousered" fashion itemdid woman's rights activist Amelia Bloomer popularize? –*Bloomer*

• What is the name of the Hollywood stunt woman and race-car driver who set 22 records in various racing sports—and, incidentally, was born deaf? –*Kitty O'Neil*

• Hired in 1973 by Frontier Airlines, who was the first female commercial airline pilot in the U.S.?
–*Emily Warner*

ROMANCE AND MARRIAGE
did you know that ...

... According to *Longevity* magazine, over 50 percent of married men and women do not consider their current spouse their best-ever lover?

... A study done by *McCall's* magazine reported that the divorce rate is 23 percent lower in cities with Major League baseball teams than in those without a team?

... August, rather than June, is, by a small margin, actually the most popular month for weddings?

... Studies indicate that a man who kisses his wife goodbye in the morning when he leaves for work averages a higher income than those who don't? Also, men who kiss their wives before leaving for work live five years longer than those who don't?

... In the old rhyme " ... something old, something new, something borrowed, something blue," blue is symbolic of the blood of royalty, since both the bride and groom were considered to be "royal" on their wedding day?

... Women who complete 16 or more years of school are less likely to divorce their first husbands?

... A majority (two-thirds, actually) of kissers turn their heads to the right when kissing?

... The science of kissing is called philematology?

... Among the Germanic Goths of the year 200, a man usually married a woman from within his own community. When there were too few women, however, the prospective groom would kidnap his bride from a neighboring village. The bridegroom was accompanied by his strongest and best friend, who helped him capture his bride. Thus comes the term "best man."

Love Makes the World Go 'Round

• Brides are traditionally placed to the left of the groom. Why might this be? –*Going back to the Goths, after the groom captured his bride he placed her at his left, thus freeing his sword hand against sudden reprisal*

• According to English folklore, what is the most *unlucky* day of the week to be wed? (Hint: Surprisingly, it's the most popular day for today's couples.) –*Saturday*

• How many years of marriage are celebrated on the Crystal Anniversary? –*15*

• Gifts made of what materials are traditionally given on these other wedding anniversaries:
  1st? –*Paper*
  5th? –*Wood*
  10th? –*Tin or aluminum*
  25th? –*Silver*
  30th? –*Pearl*
  50th? –*Gold*
  60th? –Yellow diamond

• Monogamy—being married to one spouse—is the most common form of marriage in our modern society. How many other known forms of marriage are there? Name them.
–*There are three others: Polygyny—one husband several wives; Polyandry—one wife, several husbands; and Group marriage—several husbands and wives*

• What Old Testament prophet had 700 wives and 300 concubines?
–*Solomon (I Kings 11:3)*

• Mongkut of Siam—the king represented in the famous play "The King and I"—was the most married person in history. How many wives did he have?
–*He was known to have a total of 9,000 wives and concubines*

• What would a groom traditionally do to ensure that his bride did not trip, and thus bring bad luck, while entering their new home's front door for the first time as husband and wife?
–*He would carry her over the threshold*

• Name the famous person who made each of the following rollicking statements about marriage:
  "A man may be a fool and not know it—but not if he is married."
    –*H.L. Mencken*

  "I've only slept with the men I've been married to. How many women can make that claim?"
    –*Elizabeth Taylor*

  "I don't think I'll get married again. I'll just find a woman I don't like and buy her a house."
    –*Lewis Grizzard*

  "We would have broken up except for the children. Who were the children? Well, she and I were."
    –*Mort Sahl*

"Gettin' married's a lot like getting into a tub of hot water. After you get used to it, it ain't so hot."
—*Minnie Pearl*

• Who was Xanthippe's husband? (Hint: He was a famed Greek philosopher.) —*Socrates*

• According to a recent opinion poll, British women would rather give up sexual relations than having to abstain from what gastronomical delight? —*Chocolate*

• Besides a number of friends and relatives, what two large and unusual guests were present at the second wedding of Elizabeth Taylor and Richard Burton? —*A couple of hippopotami*

• The tradition of playing pranks on the newlywed couple began with the aim of warding off evil spirits. What would be the logic of having steadfast friends do such things to the newlyweds? —*It was done in hopes that the spirits would take pity on the couple for already being picked upon enough, and would leave them alone*

• What is the significance of wearing an engagement ring on the fourth or "ring" finger of the left hand?
—*Traditional belief held that a delicate nerve ran from that finger directly to the heart*

• Name the pioneering pair of sex therapists who filed for divorce in 1992.
—*William H. Masters and Virginia E. Johnson*

A BRITISH HODGEPODGE
did you know that ...

…A Brit who is accused of harassment, vandalism or other abusive or marginally illegal behavior often first receives an ASBO ("Anti-Social Behaviour Order"), a civil order demanding that he or she stop the offensive behavior. If the order is breached, the offender may then be brought up on criminal penalties?

…The UK is made up of several thousand islands, with England, Scotland and Wales forming the largest island?

…The most northerly British land masses are the Shetland Islands, which became part of the UK in 1472 when they were taken from Norway in reparation for an unpaid wedding dowry? (In fact, even today many of the Islands' 22,000 residents feel more devoted to their Scandinavian origins than those of the British.)

…The farthest one can get inland from the sea in the UK is only about 70 miles?

…Britain, in 1840, was the first country to issue a postage stamp, the *Penny Black* featuring a portrait of Queen Victoria?

Cheerio … and All That Rot!
• "Gurning," a British tradition that supposedly dates back to 1267, has grown into a competition that today takes place in the northwest of England. What is gurning?
—*The art of pulling ugly face*

• The traditional "Bangers and Mash" is a popular menu item in many British pubs. What is Bangers and Mash?
—*Sausages and mashed potato*

• What is black pudding made from? —*Blood*

• What might one do with an OED?
—*Look up a word definition (stands for Oxford English Dictionary)*

• The geographical location of zero (0) longitude passes through the UK at a certain location, from which the term _____ Mean Time (GMT) is derived. What is this city?
—*Greenwich*

• What British theoretical physicist wrote *A Brief History of Time*? —*Stephen Hawking*

• Which king, according to legend, received an arrow to the eye and was killed in the Battle of Hastings in 1066? Who led the conquering forces? —*King Harold II; William of Normandy*

• Who is the London-born creator of the World Wide Web? –*Sir Timothy Berners-Lee*

• What are the last five words of Charles Dickens' "A Christmas Carol," and which character are they credited to?
– *"God Bless us, Every One!"; Tiny Tim*

• What is the name of the legal holiday celebrated in Britain and Canada that refers to the custom of giving gift boxes to faithful employees on the day after Christmas? –*Boxing Day*

• Only one member of the Royal Family has competed at the Olympic Games, at age 21 winning the equestrian event at the 1976 Montreal Games. Who is the Royal, who today serves as a member of the International Olympic Committee? –*Princess Anne*

• What is the full name of Queen Elizabeth II? –*Elizabeth Alexandra Mary Windsor*

• What was the name of Britain's—and the world's— first national airlines, launched in 1924? –*Imperial Airways*

• What is a "self-canceling trafficator"? – *The British term for a turn signal*

• Who was England's longest-reigning monarch, ruling 1837 through 1901? –*Victoria*

• The tune "Greensleeves" was said to have been composed by what famous Englishman? –*Henry VIII*

• Each area of the British Isles maintains its own customs, national costumes, flags and symbols. What part of Britain do you associate with tartans? –*Scotland*

• No native snakes inhabit Ireland. Who was said in legend to have banished the serpents from the isle? –*St. Patrick*

• What British rockers, before reaching stardom, once worked …
    As a grave digger?
        –*Rod Stewart*
    In a slaughterhouse?
        –*Ozzy Osboure*
    As a porter in a mental institution?
        –*Mick Jagger*

• Named "Archibald Leach" at his birth in London in 1904, what would-be comedian and actor sailed to the U.S. in 1920 to work on Broadway, then moved to Hollywood in 1931, there to become a movie icon? –*Cary Grant*

• What writer inspired the band name "The Doors"? ("… when the doors of perception open … ") –*Aldous Huxley*

• London post boxes, public telephones and iconic double-decker busses are red. But predominantly what color are the city's taxis? –*Black*

• "Caber Tossing" is one of the strength and skill events held at the annual Scottish Highland Games. What is a caber?
–*A large, 18-foot, 120-pound wooden beam*

• Famed Brits Charles Darwin, Winston Churchill and Lewis Carroll all shared what speech impediment?
–*Each stammered when talking*

• In 1620 the Pilgrim Fathers left Plymouth, England and set sail for America aboard two ships, not just the Mayflower. Suffering bad leaks, the other ship returned to port, where all boarded the Mayflower for the crossing. What was the name of this unhistorical, unseaworthy ship? –*The Speedwell*

• London's hub consists of five major roads converging at a junction featuring a statue of Eros. What is this location called?
–*Piccadilly Circus (be forewarned, however, that there is no circus there)*

CHEERS AND BOTTOMS UP!
did you know that ...

... "Huffcup," "mad dog," "Father Whoreson," "Angel's Food," "dragon's milk" and "left leg" were all common terms for beer in Elizabethan England?

... It took the Nestle Company eight years to develop the first instant coffee?

... Bordeaux wine is usually aged in casks made of oak?

... Fifty percent of Americans start their day with a cup of coffee?

Raise a Glass

• What thirst-quenching drink is sometimes referred to as "Adam's Ale"? – *Water*

• Name the rum, sugar and lime cocktail that takes its name from a town in Cuba. – *Daiquiri*

• Name the "Englishman's Drink."
– *"The Bloody Mary"*

• What drink was called "Tonsil Paint" in the Old West? – *Whiskey*

• Name the alcoholic drink that matches each of the following descriptions:
Sweet vermouth mixed with whiskey.
   – *A Manhattan*
Rum, mixed with pineapple and coconut milk.
   – *Pina Colada*
Red wine laced with fresh fruit.
   – *Sangria*
Ginger ale, a cherry and grenadine.
   – *A Shirley Temple*
Whiskey chased by beer.
   – *A Boiler Maker*
Tequila, triple sec and lime juice.
   – *A Margarita*

• The fragrance of a coffee bean is called its "aroma." Fill in the blanks of these other coffee terms:
_____ refers to the sense of heaviness, richness and thickness one tastes when drinking the warm beverage. – *Body*
Deriving its name from its foam or "cap," which resembles the hooded robes of a certain class of Italian friars, _____ is a concoction of espresso and steamed, foamed milk. – *Cappuccino*
_____ coffee is made from very strong black beans, ground extra fine and brewed by mechanically forcing hot water through the grounds. – *Espresso*

• What was Ludwig Roselius's motivation when he decided to "decaffeinate" coffee in 1900?
– *He believed that the death of his father, a coffee taster, was caused by too much caffeine*

• As first spoken in Old-English pubs, what, purportedly, did it mean to "mind one's ps and qs"? – *To keep an accounting of a customer's consumption by pints and quarts*

• How many bottles make up a "magnum" of champagne? – *Two*

• Burgundy wine comes in large bottles. What is the name of this bottle, equivalent in size to eight standard bottles? – *A Methusalah*

• In the year 800 sheep from Ethiopian flocks got a caffeine buzz from eating coffee leaves and berries; humans soon picked up the habit. Answer the following questions about this bean-made brew:
What type of coffee has the highest caffeine content?
   – *Perked (with 108 mg per five-ounce serving)*
On average, how many cups of coffee does an American coffee-drinker consume per day?
   – *A tad over three and a half cups*
"Specialty" coffees—usually pre-flavored with nuts and powders—are growing in popularity. Name the top-selling five flavors.
   – *Vanilla Nut, Irish Cream, Chocolate, Vanilla, and Macadamia Nut*

... Boca Grande, Florida, boasts a trio of streets named "Damn If I Know," "Damn If I Care" and "Damn If I Will"?

... The American people adopted "In God We Trust" as their national credo in 1956?

... Chicago comprises the largest variety of ethnic groups in the entire Great Lakes region?

... A vast majority of airline pilots rate Washington, D.C.'s National Airport the country's most challenging airport at which to land?

O See Can You Say ...

• What two states have never adopted Daylight Saving Time? *–Arizona and Hawaii*

• What is the only U.S. state that does not have a motto? *–Alaska*

• But for the flip of a coin, what Oregon city was nearly named "Boston"? *–Portland*

• What exclusive part of Boston, Massachusetts, was once called both "Mount Whoredom" and "Satan's Seat," due not only to the several hundred prostitutes that plied their trade there but also to the countless taverns that occupied the area? *–Beacon Hill*

• In what U.S. state can travelers enjoy the *Zydeco*, the accordion-based music of French-speaking Creoles? *–Louisiana*

• What is the "treasure state," which every year turns out hundreds of pounds of flawless sapphires? *–Montana*

• What Michigan city did Kellogg's Cereal adopt as its world "breakfast city?" *–Battle Cree*

• Name the U.S. city associated with the following well-known descriptions:
　　"The Rubber Capital of the World"
　　　　–Akron, Ohio
　　"Pittsburgh of the South"
　　　　–Birmingham, Alabama
　　"Celery City"
　　　　–Kalamazoo, Michigan
　　"Pretzel City"
　　　　–Reading Pennsylvania
　　"Insurance City"
　　　　–Hartford, Connecticut
　　"Cement City"
　　　　–Allentown, Pennsylvania

• A tiny, disease-transmitting tick was named after the Connecticut town in which the illness was first reported. Name the town. *–Lyme*

• The "windy city" of Chicago actually ranks 16th on the list of all-time windiest American cities. With average wind speeds of 13.1 miles per hour, what, in truth, is the windiest city in America? *–Great Falls, Montana*

• Name the U.S. state with the most national park sites. *–Alaska, with eight*

• Name these national park sites by these summaries of their most prominent features:
　　A one-mile-deep canyon.
　　　　–The Grand Canyon (Arizona)
　　Boasts the highest point on the Atlantic coast
　　of the U.S.; rugged coastlines and sandy beaches.
　　　　–Acadia (Maine)
　　The world's greatest geyser area; forests, waterfalls,
　　and a wide variety of wildlife.
　　　　–Yellowstone (Wyoming)
　　Two active volcanoes; rare plants and animals.
　　　　–Volcanoes National Park (Hawaii)
　　High mountains; large hardwood and evergreen
　　forests. *–Great Smoky Mountains (North Carolina)*
　　Giant rock arches, windows and towers formed by
　　erosion. *–Arches (Utah)*
　　Huge underground caves and strange rock
　　formations. *–Carlsbad Caverns (New Mexico)*
　　The greatest single-peak glacier system in the
　　United States. *–Mount Rainier (Washington)*
　　A subtropical wilderness with plentiful wildlife.
　　　　–The Everglades (Florida)

• Which state has the greatest number of hazardous waste sites? *–New Jersey, with nearly 100*

• Name the U.S. city (actual or created) made famous by each of the following characters:
　　Wyatt Earp
　　　　–Tombstone, AZ
　　Batman
　　　　–Gotham City
　　Dick Tracy
　　　　–Anytown America
　　Dirty Harry
　　　　–San Francisco, CA
　　Robocop
　　　　–Detroit, MI

• Who designed the American flag? (Hint: It was not Betsy Ross.) *–Francis Hopkinson, a naval flag designer*

• In what state is the Greater Cincinnati International Airport located? *–Kentucky*

• Identify the following Manhattan sites:
　　This educational institution was originally known
　　as Kings College. *–Columbia University*
　　Sports Illustrated magazine is published here.
　　–Time-Life Building
　　NBC studios are located here. *–The G.E. Building*
　　This complex included the twin towers.
　　–The World Trade Center

The world's largest Gothic cathedral.
–*Church of St. John the Divine*
New York's two major train stations.
–*Grand Central and Pennsylvania stations*
It's known as the "Showplace of the Nation."
–*Radio City Music Hall*
David Letterman's new "really big sheeew" place.
–*The Ed Sullivan Theater*
This museum is noted for its contemporary art collection and original architecture.
–*The Guggenheim Museum*
The famous structure that earned the state its nickname. –*The Empire State Building*

• The world's largest living plant is said to be a 3,500-year-old tree that stands 272 feet tall. What is the name of this giant and where is it located?
–*The General Sherman Tree is a giant sequoia in Sequoia National Park, California*

• Which state's residents, in median age, are the youngest? The oldest? –*Utah, with a median age of around 26; Florida, with a median age of 37 years*

• What are the only two states whose names include the letter "X"? –*New Mexico and Texas*

• What state name is the only one to contain the letter "Z"? –*Arizona*

• What is the only state with the letter "J" in its name? –*New Jersey*

• There is only one letter of the alphabet that is not in a state name. What is it? –*"Q"*

• With one exception, the name of every state in the Union contains two or more syllables. Which is the exception? –*Maine*

• What does the word *Nevada* mean in Spanish? –*"Snow-clad"*

• The motto of Kansas is *Ad Astra Per Aspera.* What is the English translation? –*"To the stars through difficulties"*

• Which U.S. city is home to a voodoo museum? –*New Orleans, Louisiana*

• Where can you go to longingly view a hundred $10,000 bills on display? (What's the total amount of cash on display?) –*Blinton's Horseshoe Club in Las Vegas, Nevada; a million dollars*

• Give the name of the island that lies among the southern edge of a major U.S. city and where you can take a walk down a three-mile boardwalk, watch sharks and beluga whales at the aquarium, and experience the thrill of the "Cyclone." (Hint: It was once home to countless rabbits.) –*Coney Island*

WORLD TRAVELS
did you know that …

… China's illustrious Beijing Duck Restaurant can seat 9,000 people at a time?

… Since the running of the bulls began at Pamplona, Spain in 1926, only 13 people have been killed? (Attendance at the eight-day event increased dramatically when Ernest Hemingway made famous the running of the bulls in his novel *The Sun Also Rises.*)

… The world's largest musical instrument can be found in Atlantic City, N.J.'s Municipal Auditorium? (The impressive organ has 33,112 pipes that range from one quarter of an inch to 64 feet in length.)

… The Mediterranean sea gets its name from the Latin phrase meaning "sea in the middle of land"?

… Aberdeen, Maryland, boasts the world's only tank museum?

… If you wanted to travel down the world's longest river, you would go to the Nile in Egypt, at 4,160 miles (though not all of it can be navigated)?

… The volume of water in the Amazon river is greater than that of the next 8 largest rivers in the world combined?

Jetlag in the Global Village
• What nation do more tourists visit than any other? –*France*

• What are the three official languages of Switzerland? –*French, German and Italian*

• Name the group of Pacific islands, located off the coast of Ecuador, in which unusual animals such as Giant tortoises, marine iguanas and tool-using finches can be spotted.
–*The Galapagos Islands*

• What is the name of Israel's counterpart to the U.S. dollar? –*The shekel*

• The rand, named from a prosperous gold-mining region in Africa, is the official currency of what country? –*South Africa*

• A famous bridge built in Lima, Peru, in 1610 is still used today. Its mortar, however, was mixed using a singular viscous liquid in place of water. As reflected by the bridge's name, what liquid was used? –*Egg whites from 10,000 eggs; The Bridge of Eggs*

• Name the country that was created in 1929 by an agreement between the Roman Catholic Church and the government of Italy.
–*Vatican City*

• What massive edifice is made up of 2,300,000 blocks, each weighing 2.5 tons?
–*The Great Pyramid of Giza, Egypt*

• What structure is 180 feet tall and tips over 16 feet to one side? (Scientists give it only another 100 years or so before it collapses.)
–*The Leaning Tower of Pisa (Pisa, Italy)*

• The driest desert in the world is not the Sahara in the Middle East, but what desert located where? –*The Patagonia Desert in the most southern region of South America*

• Tourists from what country spend the most per capita of any other visitors? –*Japan*

• Travelers have often said of this city that "you can die after you see it." Name this most beautiful city. –*Naples, Italy*

• What zoo boasts the largest collection of animals in the world?
–*The San Diego Zoo in California*

• Where would you find Angel Falls, the world's highest waterfall, at 3,212 feet tall? –*Venezuela*

• Copenhagen's most famous landmark is a statue that greets ships arriving in Copenhagen harbor. What does this statue depict, and what Dane inspired it? –*'The Little Mermaid', from Hans Christian Andersen's fairy tale*

• Name the country in which you can visit King Solomon's Mines. –*Israel*

• The Dead Sea, lying between Israel and Jordan, lays claim to what two distinctive traits?
–*It's the lowest place on Earth (its surface is 1,312 feet below sea level) and the world's saltiest lake*

• Central America's Lake Nicaragua, once infested by pirates, is the world's only fresh-water lake to be infested by what toothy fish?
–*Sharks*

• What is the most frequent trip-spoiling ailment travelers experience, especially when visiting less-developed countries? What is it most commonly caused by?
–*Diarrhea; water, including ice cubes*

• What is unique about the Ayres Rock located in Australia's Mount Olga National Park?
–*Its circumference measures over five miles*

• According to travel guidebooks, what can a traveler do to avoid experiencing the above-mentioned "unmentionable" ailment?
–*Use bottled water for both drinking and brushing teeth*

• The second most common travelers' affliction is frequently contracted in Africa, Central and South America, Asia and in some South Pacific islands. It can be prevented by taking medication and using an insect repellent. Name this deadly disease. –*Malaria*

• Another bit of travelers' advice includes avoiding food from street vendors, since a certain disease can be transmitted through water, food, and generally unsanitary conditions. What is this disease? –*Hepatitis A*

• Both athletes and spectators from all over the world traveled to the capital of Bosnia for the 1984 Winter Olympics. Name this city.
–*Sarajevo*

• Which country boasts the most islands, with approximately 81,000? (An "island" is defined as a land mass of at least 100 meters squared.)
–*Finland*

• Borneo is the only island shared by three different countries. Name them.
–*Indonesia, Malaysia and Brunei*

• What city in China is home to the Temple of Heaven landmark? –*Beijing*

• The world's busiest airport, with over 79 million passengers passing through in 2003, is located where? –*Atlanta, Georgia USA (Hartsfield International)*

• What two New York structures—one built in 1883 and one in 1931—were, at their respective completions, each labeled "the eighth wonder of the world"?
–*The Brooklyn Bridge and the Empire State Building*

• Name the romanticized vehicles that glide up and down the canals of Venice. And what color are they painted? –*Gondolas; black*

• If you visited Liverpool, England, what would you call its residents? –*Liverpuddlians*

… Every time you breathe in, you inhale at least one or two of the same molecules you inhaled as a baby with the first breath you took?

…The chemical compound carbon dioxide, which makes up less than one percent of dry air, can suffocate plants and animals if administered in levels that are too concentrated?

… Physicist Albert Einstein was denied security clearance from the U.S. government when he first arrived to work on the atom bomb prior to World War II?

…The colorless material called celluloid—often used in the manufacturing of toys, toilet articles and film—was the result of attempts to produce better billiard balls?

Proton and Electron Soup

• Decompression sickness—known by pilots as "altitude sickness" and by deep sea divers as "the bends"—is linked to a release of gas bubbles into body tissues, resulting in pain, shock, or even death. Name this most abundant gas. (Hint: It makes up about 70 percent of the air you breathe.) –*Nitrogen*

• What element was observed through a spectroscope for the first time in 1868? During what event was it observed?
–*Helium; during a solar eclipse*

• Name the inert gas that fills the lighted tubes of advertising signs and Las Vegas casinos.
–*Neon*

• What pungent, water-soluble gas was first produced by camel dung near Egypt's Temple of Ammon—the place from which the gas derived its name?
–*Ammonia*

• Give the name of the unstable gas that accounts for the sharp, fresh odor that is sometimes present in the air after a lightning storm. –*Ozone*

• Nitrous oxide can cause feelings of euphoria if inhaled. What is the name of this mirth-producing compound, and who developed it—a man who, incidentally, later committed suicide.
– *"Laughing gas"; Horace Wells*

• "The smallest unit of a substance that retains the properties of that substance" is the simple definition of a what? –*A molecule*

• Matter that does not enter into chemical reactions is known as what? –*Inert*

• A _____ is a substance that controls the rate of a chemical reaction. –*Catalyst*

• What essential ingredient, common to many expensive cosmetics, is, in its native form, a foul-smelling tar-like substance extracted from the fleece of sheep? –*Lanolin*

• The atoms in this chemical compound are a chain in the form H-O-O-H (two hydrogen atoms connected by two oxygen atoms), and is sometimes used for bleaching hair. What is this chemical? –*Hydrogen Peroxide*

• What type of substance turns blue litmus paper red? Conversely, what substance will turn a red piece of litmus blue? –*An acid; a base*

• The temperature at which a gas becomes a liquid is known as its _____ point. The temperature at which a liquid becomes a solid?
–*Condensation; freezing*

• Given the reputation of Italy's Lucrezia Borgia, Duchess of Ferrara during the early 16th century, which of the following would she have found most handy to have around: calcium chloride, sodium carbonate, strychnine, or pizza? –*Strychnine, a poison (calcium chloride is the compound making up common table salt, and sodium carbonate is the gas in soda pop … which can wash down your pizza!)*

• Cement, mixed with sand and water, turns to what over time? –*Concrete*

• When water is frozen to create ice, what chemical changes occur? –*The chemical composition (H_2O) of its molecules remains the same (only the structure—how the molecules themselves are "stacked"—is changed upon freezing)*

• What would you most likely do with the compound $MgSO_4$: power a car with it, use it to blow up a building, add it to water and soak one's feet, or use it to fertilize a lawn?
–*Soak one's feet—it's the formula for Epsom salt*

• A liquid is a type of matter that has a definite _____ but no definite _____.
–*Volume; shape*

… Seventy percent of all the hats sold each year in the U.S. are baseball caps?

… Until the 1870s, baseball games were played without the use of gloves?

… Lyricist Jack Northwood, who wrote "Take Me Out To the Ball Game," did not actually attend his first game until 34 years after writing the song?

… Tennis star Tracy Austin appeared on the cover of World Tennis magazine at age four and Sports Illustrated at age 13?

… In Thailand, teams of soldiers play tug-of-war against a team of elephants, who wear T-shirts to identify themselves as the opposing team?

C'mon, Be a Sport!

• What is listed as the most dangerous sport by American insurance companies? –Football

• In what high school sport are the most injuries reported? –Each year 62% of participants in girls' cross country report an injury

• What is the name marathon runners attach to the physiological phenomenon that typically affects them after 20 miles, caused by the loss of glycogen to the muscles and often resulting in severe cramps and fever? – "Hitting the Wall"

• What notoriously confident tennis player said, "My greatest strength is that I have no weakness"? –John McEnroe

• Why was American football nearly banned in 1905? Who finally stepped in to save the sport? –18 players were killed during games that year; President Theodore Roosevelt took steps to make the game safer

• What is the only country to have played in every World Cup tournament since its inception in 1930? –Brazil

• What basketball squad, organized in Chicago by Abe Saperstein in 1926, remains one of the few professional teams without a home court. –The Harlem Globetrotters

• In 1915 the Indianapolis 500 was won by Ralph DePalma. However, DePalma did not drive across the finish line; he didn't even finish the race inside his Mercedes. How did he win? –He pushed his car the last mile and a half

• What do the initials in former Buffalo Bills great running back—and infamous defendant—O.J. Simpson's name stand for? –Orenthal James

• For the following universities and colleges, give the rather feeble name chosen for their sports-team mascot:
    Whitman College (Washington)
        –Missionaries
    St. Bonaventure College (New York)
        –Bonnies
    Centenary College (Louisiana)
        –Gentlemen
    Whittier College (California)
        –Poets
    New York University
        –Violets
    University of Pennsylvania
        –Quakers
    Heidelberg College (Ohio)
        –Student Princes
    University of New England (Maine)
        –Pilgrims

• Often presumed to be ice hockey, what is actually the official national sport of Canada? –Lacrosse

• What purpose do the dimples on a golf ball serve? –They allow the ball to travel faster and farther

• Today's "rough terrain" bicycles more commonly go by what name? –Mountain bikes

• The sport of climbing mountains with as little equipment as possible is called what? –Rock climbing

• Organized in 1845, the New York Knickerbockers became the first U.S. professional team in what sport? –Baseball

• What color of attire does the home team usually wear in basketball? –A white or light-colored uniform

• In 1990, what championship event attracted a then-record TV audience of over 1 billion people? –The World Cup finals

• Name the three sporting events that are won by moving backwards. –Tug of war, the backstroke (in swimming) and sculling (rowing)

• Prior to the year 1875, when one of its lawns was set aside for a tennis game, for what sport was England's famed Wimbledon Tennis complex designed? –It was the All England Croquet Club

• What is the common term for three consecutive strikes in bowling? –*A turkey*

• What is the name of the area located immediately behind the pins in bowling? –*The pit*

• What is the most popular participant sport in the U.S.? –*Fishing*

• What are the three general classifications of skis? –*Downhill, jumping and cross country*

• In horseshoes, what is the distance between the stakes? –*40 feet*

• What is China's fast-paced national sport? –*Table Tennis (Ping-Pong)*

• What novel sports competition, held during the 1992 Labor Day weekend in Grayslake, Illinois, sparked a controversial complaint from members of the Outdoor Power Equipment Institute? –*The first national lawnmower racing championship (participants were chastised for failing to promote safe and effective use of outdoor equipment)*

• Give the name of the real-life sports figures portrayed in the following films:
"The Pride of the Yankees"
     –*Lou Gehrig*
"Raging Bull"
     –*Jake Lamotta*
"Fear Strikes Out"
     –*Jimmy Piersall*
"The Pride of St. Louis"
     –*Dizzy Dean*
"Field of Dreams"
     –*"Shoeless" Joe Jackson*

• Name the sport originally known as *sphairistike.*
     –*Tennis*

OLYMPIC GOLD
did you know that ...

... The early Olympic Games (c. 1400 B.C.E. to 394, when conquering Roman Emperor Theodosius ordered them ended) played an important part of Greek religious festivals? (The exciting athletic contests were regarded as pleasing to the spirits of the dead.)

... The ancient Games permitted competition only between male athletes?

... Norwegian-born American Anders Haugen garnered fourth place in the large hill ski jump during the 1924 Winter Olympics in France, but 50 years later, when Anders was 83, was awarded the bronze medal when a scoring error was discovered?

... Tons of snow had to be shipped in from Canada in order to hold the 1980 Winter Olympics at Lake Placid, New York?

Faster, Higher, Farther
• Fill in the following blanks in these statements about the Olympics (and identify the Olympic event to which each statement applies):
The rapid-fire pistol target holds a resemblance to a small _____ _____.
     –*Human figure (shooting)*
The first perfect "10" score to be awarded in this event went to _____ _____ at the 1976 Olympics.
     –*Nadia Comaneci (gymnastics)*
The pool is required to contain a minimum of 8 _____, each 7 to 9 feet wide.
     –*Lanes (swimming)*
The _____ is considered by many to be the ultimate test to determine the world's best all-around athlete.
     –*Decathlon (track and field)*
In this event, running at top speed the men approach the _____ from one end, while the women approach it from the side.
     –*Horse (gymnastics)*
Water temperature is required to be within a two-degree range between _____ and _____ degrees Fahrenheit.
     –*78 and 80 (swimming)*
The _____ _____ measures 16 feet 3 inches long by 4 inches wide, and stands nearly 4 feet off the floor.
     –*Balance Beam (gymnastics)*
The only track-and-field event in which a world record has never been set in the Olympics is the _____ .
     –*Discus*

- Which two countries are the only to have participated in every Olympiad since its inception in 1896? –Greece and Australia

- Name the 10 track-and-field events that make up the Decathlon. Which of these ten is generally run last? –100-meter, 400-meter, and 1500-meter runs; 110-meter hurdles; high jump; long jump; javelin throw; pole vault; shot put; and discus throw; the 1500-meter race is last

- The "iron-man" triathlon—an event requiring its entrants to swim 2.4 miles, immediately move to a 112-mile bike race, and end with a 26.2-mile marathon run—has been an Olympic event for how many years? –It is not an event sponsored by the Olympics

- After winning the women's 100-meter dash against favored Stella Walsh of Poland in the 1936 Berlin Olympics, Missouri's Helen Stephens was accused by the screaming crowd of being a man. How did Olympic officials solve the problem? –They insisted that Stephens disrobe in front of the crowd

- What were the original five events of the pentathlon in ancient Greece? –Leaping, running, wrestling, and throwing both the discus and the spear

- Name the two Olympic decathlon champions that each appeared on the front of Wheaties breakfast cereal boxes. –Bob Mathis and Bruce Jenner

- What two sites have hosted the Olympic Winter games twice? –Lake Placid, New York and St. Moritz, Switzerland

- What great athlete was an Olympic gold medalist in track and field, and later went on to win ten major golf titles? –Babe Didrikson-Zaharias

- What well-known pediatrician was an oarsman for the Yale crew that won the 1924 Olympic Gold Medal in Paris? –Br. Benjamin Spock

- What country's delegation is the only one that commonly refuses to dip its flag during the opening-day Olympic parade? –The United States

- What notorious state leader was Head of Ceremonies at these same 1936 Berlin Games? –Dictator Adolph Hitler

- What was the first non-European site to host the Winter Olympics? –Lake Placid, New York

- The athletes from what country are always first to march in the Olympic parade at the opening-day ceremonies? What country is always the last to receive the accolades of the crowd? –Greece; the host country

- Canada won the Winter Olympics gold medal in hockey every year until 1936. What country finally broke their stranglehold on Olympic hockey titles? –Great Britain

- Rudi Ball was the only one of "these" to play hockey for the German squad in the 1936 Winter Olympics. What distinguished Ball from his teammates? –He was the only Jewish member of the German team

- Give the names of the three Winter Olympic game sites that end with the letter O. –Oslo, Norway, Sarajevo, Yugoslavia and Sapporo, Japan

- Great Britain's Princess Anne, the only member of the royal family to have participated in the Olympics (winning gold in equestrian), was also the only competitor at the 1976 Montreal Olympics that did not have to undergo what kind of test? –A sex test

- Polish Olympic Gold Medal track star Stella Walsh became the first female to run 100 yards in less than 11 seconds. What startling bit of information about her was discovered upon her death several decades later? –"She" was actually a "he"

- An athlete competing from a country in the Southern Hemisphere won a rare Winter Olympics medal in the 1992 Albertville Games. Who won the Silver Medal in slalom skiing, and what "down-under" country was she from? –Annelise Coberger; New Zealand

- In 1952 Emil and Dana Zatopek became the first married couple each to win a Gold Medal at an Olympics. In which two events did they prevail? –Emil won the men's marathon and Dana the women's javelin throw

- The first American ever to participate in the modern Olympic Pentathlon in 1912 later became a famed U.S. Army general. Name him. –General George S. Patton

- What is the only Olympic sport that is timed to the one thousandth of a second? –The luge

- What twin brothers won the Gold and Silver medals in the 1984 Winter Olympics men's slalom? –Phil and Steve Mahre

WAR AND PEACE
did you know that …

…Applicants seeking routine jobs at the atomic bomb development "Manhattan Project" facilities near Los Alamos, New Mexico, between 1942 and 1945 were automatically disqualified if they were literate?

…Leo Tolstoy's famed Russian novel *War and Peace*, set during the Napoleonic War, is jammed with over 500 characters?

Wars and Weaponry

• What important front-line capacity did late movie mogul Walt Disney hold during World War I?
–He was an ambulance driver for the allies

• The building located at Prinsengracht 263—one of the most well-known addresses to emerge from World War II—is a major tourist attraction today. What is the significance of this structure, located in Amsterdam, The Netherlands? *–It's the annex above which Jewish diarist Anne Frank and her family lived for two years while hiding from the Nazis*

• What was classical Greek inventor/mathematician Archimedes' fatal "death-ray"? (Hint: Legend has it that it was used to set fire to an attacking fleet of Roman ships.) *–Sunlight reflected by high-powered mirrors*

• In the Nazi army of the 1940s, the "Brownshirts" were ordinary foot soldiers. By contrast, who were the "Blackshirts"? *–They were elite troopers chosen as bodyguards for high-ranking officials*

• The son of a famed foreign leader was captured by Germany during World War II. Instead of accepting an offer to exchange prisoners, the leader allowed his son to die in a prison camp. Who was this infamously ruthless man? *–Joseph Stalin*

• Today the initials "CD" most commonly refer to *Compact Disc*. What did these same initials represent for the average U.S. citizen during the 1940s? *–Civil Defense*

• What war has been referred to as "The War of Faulty Communications," since it might have been avoided entirely had telegraphic communications existed then? (Hint: Two days before war was declared, Britain had agreed to repeal the laws that were the chief excuse for fighting. However, the news did not reach President Madison in time to avert hostilities.) *–The War of 1812*

• What Spartan king headed a small army of 300 Spartans against a vastly superior Persian force in the 480 B.C.E. Battle of Thermopylae, all dying in the conflict?
–King Leonidas

• Which type of explosive device derived its name from the tropical pomegranate fruit?
–The grenade

• What eight countries are currently suspected or known to have nuclear weapons? *–The United States, Russia, The United Kingdom, China, India, France, Israel and South Africa (Others, notably North Korea and Iran, are at present working towards them.)*

• This American Civil War hero, known as Frank Thompson, fought at Bull Run in 1861 and Fredericksburg in 1862; he also spied behind Confederate lines disguised as a female. What was particularly unusual about Thompson? *–"He" was actually Sarah Edmonds, who had initially disguised herself as a man*

• Name the Civil War Confederate general who was accidentally shot and killed by one of his own men.
–Stonewall Jackson

• During the Persian Gulf War, the U.S. Defense Department substituted euphemisms for many common sites, situations and events. What does each of these more politically-accepted euphemisms refer to?
  "Airborne Sanitation" *–Shooting down enemy planes*
  "An Armed Situation" *–War*
  "Collateral Damage" *–Killing innocent victims*
  "Suppression of Assets" *–Bombing key buildings*
  "Effort" *–A bombing attack*
  "Security Review" *–Censorship*
  "Servicing the Target" *–Killing the enemy*
  "Weapons Systems" *–Bombs*

• What was the result of the first bomb dropped by the German Luftwaffe on the Russian city of Leningrad during World War II? *–It killed the only elephant in the city's zoo*

• Upon its development by Richard Gatling in 1862, what "death-instrument" weapon was deemed so horrible that it was said no war could ever be fought again? *–The machine gun*

• What did the Germans name the large cannon they used to bombard Paris during World War I? *–Big Bertha*

• What Italian soldier and patriot, whose conquest paved the way for his country's unification, extended the unusual recruiting statement "I offer thirst, forced marches, battles and death"—subsequently drawing thousands of 19th-century Italians to defend the banner? *–Giuseppe Garibaldi*

• What term, interpreted to mean "divine wind," was used in World War II to describe the actions of Japanese air force fliers crashing their bomb-laden planes into enemy targets? *–Kamikaze*

• The last execution held in the Tower of London took place during what war? *–World War II*

• Name the Union Army cavalry commander, labeled "Little Phil" during the Civil War, who offended many loyal Texans in his district with the words, "If I owned Texas and Hell, I would rent out Texas and live in Hell." *–Philip Sheridan*

…On one occasion the Coca-Cola Company was presented an offer to buy out the bankrupt Pepsi-Cola Company for $1,000, but—confident that they would continue to monopolize soft-drink sales—corporate executives refused the offer, missing the opportunity to strangle the very company that would soon become its arch-rival?

…New York businessman Richard Charles Drew conceived of and opened the first blood bank back in 1940? (Unfortunately, because Drew was black, he was not allowed to contribute blood to his own bank.)

…The largest industrial complex in the world—occupying a whopping 204.3 acres of floor space—is the Nizhiny Tagil Railroad Car and Tank Plant located near Moscow, Russia?

…Back in 1956 two men named Henry and Richard established a company called H&R Block to assist people with the odious task of preparing their taxes?

…The McDonald's corporation has overtaken the U.S. Army as the world's largest staff trainer?

…Ford Motor Company president Ernest Breech, when asked if his company would be interested in manufacturing the Volkswagen after the war, decided it was "not worth a damn," and instead chose to produce the Edsel, which proved a $350 million failure?

…Eli Whitney, inventor of the cotton gin, did not strike it rich with his invention, but made the majority of his money as a New England gun manufacturer, acquiring lucrative contracts from the government?

…Chain stores account for 72% of all grocery sales in the U.S.?

Buying, Selling and Industry-Making

• What successful businessman has an ice-cream-cone-shaped swimming pool in the back yard of his California home?
–*Irvin Robbins (Burton Baskin's partner)*

• What do the three M's stand for in the 3M company?
–*Minnesota Mining and Manufacturing*

• What do the M's stand for in M&M's candy?
–*Victor Mars and his associate Mr. Merrie, who developed the candy in 1941*

• My Little Pony, GI Joe, and Mr. Potato Head are all toys marketed by what company? –*Hasbro*

• What product corresponds with each of the following inauspicious foreign brand names and descriptions:
  In Japan, Green Piles can be found in many lawn and garden centers.
    –*Fertilizer*
  In China, Pansy is certainly not a fresh scented flower; in fact, it is a brand of _____ _____.
    –*Men's underwear*
  In Spain, Colon Plus is not a breakfast cereal, but rather a _____ _____.
    –*Liquid detergent*
  In Greece, this Zit could, in principle, be "popped," since it is a _____-_____ _____ _____.
    –*Lemon-lime soft drink*
  In Sweden, Krapp is a fitting name for this brand of _____ _____.
    –*Toilet tissue*
  In Japan, Mucus is something you may want to sample after all.
    –*A soft drink*
  In Sweden, a big Plopp would be a welcome energy boost after work.
    –*Chocolate bar*

• What automobile manufacturer produced the Gremlin—and, in 1976, promptly reduced its price by 7.8 percent to $2995? –*American Motors*

• In 1992, the Pro-Line Cap Company in Fort Worth, Texas, was cited by OSHA (the Occupational Safety and Health Administration) for not having adequate restroom facilities for its female employees. How did the company solve the problem?
–*They fired all 30 of their female employees*

• What was the first home appliance introduced by Sunbeam? –*The iron*

• What is the name of the chubby little man made of Michelin tires who can be seen on the covers of Michelin travel guides? –*Bibendum*

• What do the BVD initials stand for in the brand of men's underwear? (Hint: It does not stand for "Baby"s Ventilated Diapers.") –*The company's founders, Bradley, Voorhees and Day*

• The name of a popular skin cream—originally called "Dr. Bunting's Sunburn Remedy"—was changed because it soon became fashionably known as the concoction that "knocks eczema"? –*Noxzema*

• Jules Lederer, husband of former advice columnist Ann Landers, borrowed $5,000 and turned it into a $10 million business. Name the company. *–Budget Rent-A-Car*

• What distinctive marketing gimmick—a strategy with respect to dollars-and-cents merchandise pricing which is still widely used today—did Melville E. Stone introduce in 1875? *–He subtracted a penny from an item's price, making it appear to be cheaper (i.e. $1.99 instead of $2.00)*

• What is the name of the fictional company that supplies "The Road Runner" cartoon's Wile E. Coyote with explosives and other devices used in his attempt to capture his rival? *–Acme*

• In 1951 Topps became the first manufacturer of this product and continues to hold its #1 spot in the market today. Name this collectable commodity. *–Baseball (and now other sports) cards*

EVERY BODY'S HUMAN
did you know that ...

... Even if the stomach, the spleen, 75 percent of the liver, 80 percent of the intestines, one kidney, one lung, and virtually every organ from the pelvic and groin area were removed, the human body could still function quite normally?

... Tears which are incited by air-borne irritants (i.e. when cutting onions or when getting a whiff of ammonia) differ in composition from those tears shed out of emotion?

... By the time you turn 70, your heart will have beat some two-and-a-half billion times (figuring on an average of 70 beats per minute)?

... The human sense of smell is so keen that it can detect the odors of certain substances even when they are diluted to 1 part in 30 billion?

... The lens of the eye continues to grow throughout a person's life?

... Most people age 60 have lost half of their taste buds?

... Every square inch of the human body has an average of 32 million bacteria on it?

... A full one-half to three-fourths of the heat produced by the body is lost through the head?

... More than a century ago Darwin claimed that facial expressions could actually intensify emotions, thus, people could really be happier if they forced themselves to smile? (In our day scientists have noticed that an increase in the chemical hormone serotonin brings on heightened feelings of well-being, and that smiling accelerates the manufacture of this "natural narcotic.")

... On average, a human being loses 40 to 100 strands of hair a day?

... Fingernails grow about three times faster than toenails?

... We shed about 600,000 particles of skin every hour—about 1.5 pounds a year?

How's a Body To Know?
• If you climbed to an elevation of 63,000 feet above sea level, what would your blood do?
–At normal body temperature, your blood would boil

• In what part of the body does a stroke occur?
–The brain

• How many linear feet of nerve fiber are contained in one square inch of skin from the human hand?
–Approximately 72 feet

• How many muscles does it take to smile? To frown? –*17; 43*

• A baby's body has 300 bones at birth, but by adulthood, how many does it have? –*206*

• What part of the body is actually a projection of the thyroid cartilage of the larynx? (Hint: It's named after a prominent Bible character.) –*The Adam's Apple*

• When you sit in a tub of water for an hour or so, the skin on your hands and feet become wrinkled. Why is this? –*These outer, thicker layers of skin expand due to water retention*

• What explosive bodily discharge can exceed a speed of 100 mph" –*A sneeze*

• What is the location of the "20 moons" that grace the human body? –*The base of the finger nails and toe nails*

• What is the medical explanation for someone turning white from fear? –*When frightened, the blood vessels constrict, pressing blood away from the skin to the center of the body*

• What are the gluteus maximus's claim to fame— besides the fact that you can sit on them? –*They are the largest muscles in the body*

• What "piliferous" growth on the human body cannot be destroyed by cold, change in climate, water or other natural forces, is resistant to many kinds of acids and corrosive chemicals—and therefore is hated by all amateur plumbers? –*Hair (Aside from its vulnerability to fire, human hair is nearly impossible to destroy.)*

• Statistically, what growing percentage of men in the U.S. are sexually impotent? –*One out of ten men admit to the affliction*

• Where on the human body is the *philtrum* located? –*It is the indentation in the middle of the area between the nose and the upper lip*

• If hit by lightening, which of the five senses is most likely to be lost? –*Hearing*

• If you eat too much, what temporarily happens to your sense of hearing? –*It becomes duller*

• As you descend into a deep underground mine shaft, what happens to your body weight? –*It decreases ever so slightly*

• Which lung in the human body is larger, the left or the right? –*The right*

• What part of the human body receives no supply of blood, and therefore must obtain its oxygen from the air? –*The cornea of the eye*

…Comedian Dom DeLuise wrote a children's book about an ugly caterpillar who is transformed into a butterfly titled *Charlie the Caterpillar*?

…In 1985 London education officials removed the classic novel *The Adventures of Tom Sawyer* from school libraries because they deemed it both "racist" and "sexist"?

"Once Upon a Time …"

• In 2006, what twin professional football players published a children's book titled *By My Brother's Side*? –*Tiki and Ronde Barber*

• What were Cinderella's slippers originally made of before a translation error transformed them to "glass" in the 1600s? –*Fur (the word glauser was used to describe the "shine" of the slippers' fur)*

• What well-known writer of adult spy novels authored the children's story titled Chitty Chitty Bang Bang? –*Ian Fleming*

• What basic reader series of books for young children was written by Zerna A. Sharp? –*Dick and Jane*

• What was Lewis Carroll's birth name and every-day profession? –*Rev. Charles Lutwidge Dodgson was a lecturer on mathematics at Christ Church, Oxford*

• Identify the "Jacks" in the following nursery rhymes:
He tried to raise his cholesterol level.
    –*Jack Sprat*
He suffered a pretty serious head trauma.
    –*Jack, from "Jack and Jill"*
He was nice to cats.
    –*Jack Stout*
His table manners left something to be desired.
    –*Jack Horner*

• Who is the carrot-topped nine-year-old who bears the unique middle name of "Provisionia Gaberdina Dandeliona Ephraimsdaughter," and lives in the villa Villekula with her purple spotted horse? –*Pippi Longstocking*

• What were the names of Cinderella's two ugly stepsisters? –*Anastasia and Drizella*

• Panned by critics, what pop singer superstar recently put out a series of children's books? –*Madonna*

• Three animals refused to help make the bread—but later were most eager to eat it—in the tale of "The Little Red Hen." Name them. And who finally did help the exasperated mother with the bread-making?
–*Cat, Duck and Pig; her children*

• What Dr. Seuss character stole Christmas?
–*The Grinch*

• Name the title book character who was born in a flower and slept in a cradle made out of a walnut shell. –*Thumbelina*

• What nationality was Aladdin of "Aladdin and the Magic Lamp" fame? –*Chinese*

• Where did *The Wonderful Wizard of Oz* author L. Frank Baum allegedly obtain the name of his magical kingdom? –*From a tag on one of his filming cabinets labeled "O-Z"*

• Give the title of Dr. Seuss's first book, which was rejected by 28 different publishers before one finally decided to give it a chance. What was the birth name of this creator of delightfully nonsensical verse? –*And to Think That I Saw It on Mulberry Street; Theodor Seuss Geisel*

• As a young girl, an imaginative and widely-read children's author sewed flowers onto her father's sweater, named her doll after a tractor, and was in the lowest reading group in her first-grade class. Who is this author of children's works? –*Beverly Cleary*

• This tale of the Arabian Nights begins with the command "Open sesame." Name the tale. –*"Ali Baba and the Forty Thieves"*

• *Anthropomorphism* is the assigning of human attributes to things that are not human. Give the name of each of the following anthropomorphic works of fiction:
 The classical English work about Mr. Toad, Rat and Mole.
  –*The Wind in the Willows*
 The Watty Piper story about a persistent "coupled" character.
  –*"The Little Engine That Could"*
 A story about a mongoose and a cobra.
  –*"Rickki-tikki-tavi"*
 The medieval beast epic about the lion, the wolf, the bear and the fox.
  –*"Reynard the Fox"*

• In the story "Pinocchio," what is the name of:
 Geppetto's cat and goldfish?
  –*Figaro and Cleo*
 Pinocchio's friend and "conscience"?
  –*Jiminy Cricket*

The bully who coaxes Pinocchio to spend his "father's" money on candy?
  –*Lampwick*
The puppetmaster who captures Pinocchio?
  –*Stromboli*
The whale who swallows both Geppetto and Pinocchio?
  –*Monstro*

• What is the favorite food of the Hobbits, created by J.R. Tolkien? –*Mushrooms*

• What Raymond Briggs book was removed in 1979 from elementary classrooms in Holland, Michigan, due to several parental complaints about its portraying Santa Claus as having a negative attitude toward Christmas?
–*Father Christmas*

• What book, written by Claire H. Bishop and Kurt Wise, describes the exploits of a boy who could swallow the sea, of his brother with an iron neck, of a third brother who could stretch and stretch his legs, of a fourth who could not be burned, and of yet a fifth brother who could hold his breath indefinitely?
–*The Five Chinese Brothers*

• Name the animal that Lewis Carroll describes as "frumious" in his poem "Jabberwocky."
–*The Bandersnatch*

• Jacob and Wilhelm are the first names of what two storytelling siblings? –*The Brothers Grimm*

• By what pen name is the author Elizabeth Forest better known? –*Mother Goose*

• In *The Phantom Tollbooth*, a novel by Norton Juster, what is the rival city of the city Dictionopolis? –*Digitopolis*

...William Faulkner's name was originally spelled with no letter "U"? (When the error was made by the typesetter on his first novel, he decided to leave it rather than create a hassle.)

...The Encylopaedia Britannica was banned and pulped in Turkey in 1986 amid accusations that it spread "separatist propaganda"?

...The FBI has a voluminous thousand-page file on writer Dorothy Parker? (Although she never proved to be member of the Communist Party, her record does show that she was a member of the League of Women Shoppers.)

Power of the Pen

• Three writers—Lewis Carroll (best-known for his *Alice's Adventures in Wonderland*), Thomas Jefferson (drafter of the Declaration of Independence) and Ernest Hemingway (author of *For Whom the Bell Tolls*)—each shared a particular writing habit. What was it?
—*They all wrote standing up*

• Samuel Clemens (Mark Twain) once compiled a 1-through-27 list of people and things to be rescued from a burning boarding house. What was the first item on the list? The last thing to be rescued?
—*Fiancées; Mothers-in-law*

• What English Dame is the world's top-selling fiction writer, having penned a total of 78 mystery novels that have sold an estimated two billion copies worldwide? —*Agatha Christie*

• Agatha Christie, in 1926, did something rather mysterious for 11 days back in 1926—an event she expressly left unexplained.
—*She suddenly and unexplainably disappeared*

• "Excuse my dust" was the suggested epitaph of what irreverent writer/poetess? —*Dorothy Parker*

• What American poet always used lowercase letters when signing or printing his poetry? What did the initials used in his literary signature stand for? —*e.e. cummings; Edward Estlin*

• Besides great writing ability, what did authors Voltaire, Oscar Wilde and Henry David Thoreau have in common? —*Each spent time in jail or prison (Thoreau for only a night)*

• What 19th-century Russian medical doctor wrote a number of short stories and plays, which since have gained popularity in translation? —*Anton Chekhov*

• During his brief tenure as a bank teller, certain "shortages" were noted, and, convicted of embezzlement, he, too, spent a few years in prison. Who was this preeminent short story artist? —*O. Henry*

• Identify the author and arguable greatest work by these briefest of summaries of their life experiences:

Employed his adventures in Alaska in his writing.
—*Jack London; "Call of the Wild"*
Described his and his dog's travels across America.
—*John Steinbeck; "Travels With Charlie"*
His best-known play centered on a Marilyn Monroe-type character.
—*Arthur Miller (who was married to Monroe; "After the Fall"*
Dramatized the torment of his and his family's life in his plays. *Eugene O'Neill;*
—*"Long Day's Journey Into Night"*
Jungian analysis and use of symbolism define his works. *Hermann Hesse;*
—*"Steppenwolf"*
Greatest play was inspired by his sister Rose's tough life. *Tennessee Williams;*
—*"The Glass Menagerie"*

• What is the title of the Abbie Hoffman book which purportedly can only be checked out by members of Congress? —*Steal This Book*

• What eccentric author, in an attempt to be drummed out of West Point, appeared for a public military parade wearing the requisite white gloves and a belt, but nothing more? (Indeed, he was soon expelled for "gross neglect of duty.") —*Edgar Allan Poe*

• Who was the author of *The Autobiography of Alice B. Toklas*? —*Gertrude Stein*

• Who were Scarlet's twin admirers in Margaret Mitchell's *Gone With the Wind*?
—*Stuart and Brent Tarleton*

• Name the book that was author Joyce Jillson's response to *Real Men Don't Eat Quiche*.
—*Real Women Don't Pump Gas*

• What acclaimed Boston-born poetess had a habit of smoking big black cigars? —*Amy Lowell*

• What novel did Charles Dickens leave unfinished at his death? —*The Mystery of Edwin Drood*

• What is the Feb. 2, 1905 birthplace of novelist Ayn Rand, author of the acclaimed *The Fountainhead* (1943) and *Atlas Shrugged* (1957)? —*St. Petersburg (Leningrad), Russia*

• In which direction of the compass did Charles Dickens always face when writing—and aimed his head when sleeping? –*North*

• What author waged an unsuccessful campaign to become Mayor of New York City in 1969? –*Norman Mailer*

• Name the Russian writer who compared Stalin's mustaches to cockroaches and, as a result, was sent to a death camp. –*Osip Mandelstam*

• What plumed gratuity did T.S. Eliot once release under his chair at a staid London restaurant? –*A live pigeon*

• What is the subject of the do-it-yourself guides that are annual bestsellers—and whose sales in the U.S. are especially brisk in late March and early to mid-April? –*Income tax guidebooks*

• What Daniel Defoe work of fiction was based on the real-life adventures of Alexander Selkirk? –*Robinson Crusoe*

• Name the novel written by English author Anthony Burgess in which the title is based on a mechanical citrus fruit. –*A Clockwork Orange*

• Who was the real Poor Richard who authored the Almanacs? –*Benjamin Franklin*

• Identify the famous writer who, due to his tallness, was known to use the top of his refrigerator as a table to write his books. –*Thomas Wolfe*

• What did author Timothy Dexter do in response to criticism over the lack of punctuation in his book *A Pickle for the Knowing Ones*? –*In the book's second edition he published an entire page of nothing but punctuation marks*

• Which of the Apollo XI astronauts didnot write a book? –*Neil Armstrong, first man on the moon*

• Give the name of the Stephen King novel about a burial ground used for reincarnation—and, harder still, spell it correctly. –*Pet Sematary*

THE ANIMAL FAIR
did you know that ...

...Bulls are colorblind? (The traditional red cape used by bullfighters is primarily for aesthetic purposes; it is the movement that attracts the bull's attention.)

...A chameleon's tongue is more than twice the length of its body?

...All pet hamsters are descended from a single female wild golden hamster found in Syria in 1930—found already with a litter of 12 young.

...Some 1.5 billion dollars is spent on pet food each year in the U.S., four times more than is spent on baby food?

...In just one hour a single little brown bat can catch 1,200 mosquitoes-sized insects?

...Once the female lays its single egg, the male penguin takes over the job of incubating it for the next two months? (During this period the male does not eat, and will lose up to 40 percent of its body weight.)

...The tiny hummingbird egg—2,000 times smaller than that of an ostrich—is half an inch long, a third of an inch wide and weighs but half a gram?

...The quills of a newborn porcupine are soft enough to touch, but within about four hours they turn into the sharp, prickly needles for which these animals are notorious?

...The average male Alaskan brown bear weighs 250 pounds compared to the 487 pounds for the Pennsylvanian brown bear?

...A pigeon's bones weigh less than its feathers?

...A skunk will not bite and throw its scent at the same time?

...The human nose can detect a skunk's smell up to one mile away?

...The only known animal that will eat a skunk is the great horned owl?

...The average cow will give nearly 200,000 glasses of milk in her lifetime?

It's a Wild World Out There!
• What one characteristic differs in twin calves born of the opposite sex compared to those born of the same gender? –*Opposite-sexed calves are sterile*

• Appropriately enough, what is the middle name of George Grinnel, who, in 1886, founded the Audubon Society, named in honor of naturalist John James Audubon? –*Bird*

• How many times a second can a woodpecker peck? –*20/sec.*

• What is the color in the name of the largest living Rhino? –*White*

• Compared to humans, how many cervical vertebrae does a giraffe's neck contain? –*Seven—the same number as you have*

• Which is the only cat species that cannot retract its claws? –*The cheetah*

• What is the name of the female offspring of a mule? –*Mules are sterile—they have no offspring*

• What is the underside of a horse's hoof called—a semi-hard area that peels off several times a year with new growth? –*The "frog"*

• What animal undertakes the longest annual migration, traveling upwards of 21,000 miles each year? –*The Arctic Tern*

• What animals, besides humans, can suffer from sunburn?
–*Pigs, walruses and light-toned horses*

• What was likely the earliest animal domesticated by man? (Hint: The answer is not the dog.) –*The reindeer*

• The poison-arrow frog has enough poison to kill how many people? –*About 2,200*

• As far as is known, what is the only animal that never gets sick and is immune to every known disease, including cancer? –*The shark*

• About how many hours a day do each of the following animals sleep?
  The sloth
    –*20 hours*
  The elephant
    –*2 hours*
  The horse
    –*5 hours*
  The shrew
    –*It does not sleep at all*
  The squirrel
    –*14 hours*
  The koala
    –*18 hours*
  The rat
    –*13 hours*

• What rodent, long prized for its extraordinarily soft fur, is native to the Andes Mountains of South America? –*The Chinchilla*

• What two kinds of dairy cows are named after the British islands in which their breeds originated? –*Guernseys and Jerseys*

• Which arctic animal has traditionally held an important role in the lifestyle and economy of the Lapp peoples?
–Where are these herders found? *Reindeer; in the extreme northern climes of Norway*

• Provide the name of the animal that completes the following phrases:
  To keep the _____ from the door is to ward off hunger.
    –*Wolf*
  In the lap of luxury, one is said to live high on the _____.
    –*Hog*
  A carefree person is said to be happy as a _____ at high tide.
    –*Clam*
  If you're looking to escape responsibility, you're trying to _____ out of it.
    –*Weasel*

• What common trait does the hummingbird, the loon, the swift, the kingfisher and the grebe share? –*They are all birds that cannot walk*

• Why would it be said of the Great Auk, the Dodo, the Labrador duck, the Carolina parakeet and the Passenger pigeon that they have only a past but no future? –*They are extinct*

• What are the names of the two huge lions that guard the entrance to the New York Public Library's central research branch in Manhattan? –*Patience and Fortitude*

• What do camels store in their humps that, when combined with oxygen molecules from inhaled air, forms water? –*Fat*

• Camels have three _____ to protect them against blowing sand? –*Eyelids*

• Where on earth is the only place where packs of camels (dromedaries) roam wild? (Hint: It's not the Middle East, though camels are imported there from this mystery country.) –*Australia*

• The bird lives in a hole in the ground, is almost blind, lays only one egg each year, and yet has survived for more than 70 million years. What is it? –*The kiwi, New Zealand's flightless national bird*

• What is the only known *eusocial* vertebrate, a toothy, powerful-jawed mammal that lives in colonies similar to those of ants and termites, with a single fertile queen giving birth to nonreproductive workers and soldiers? –*The molerat*

• The world's smallest mammal lives in Thailand and weighs less than a penny. What is it? –*The bumblebee bat*

• What two animals describe the up-and-down action of the stock market? –*Bull and Bear*

• What animal appears on the Izod Lacoste polo shirt? (Hint: It's not an alligator.) –*It's a crocodile*

• In most species of songbirds, only the males sing. What two primary purposes does this action serve? –*To protect territory and to attract a mate*

• What is the other name for a wildebeest, a type of wild African cattle? –*The gnu*

• What kind of an animal does "hog wool" come from? –*A year-old sheep*

• What kind of archaic animals are the Diplodocus and the Pteranodon? –*They are dinosaurs*

• Give the name of the "repetitive" bird that deposits its egg in the nests of other birds. –*The cuckoo*

• Speaking of eggs, identify the following egg-laying animals by their descriptions:
    This waddling bird lays but one egg per year.
        –*The penguin*
    This queen lays 30,000 eggs daily.
        –*The termite*
    This huge soaring bird lays only one egg every two years.
        –*The California condor*
    This bi-valve mollusk produces some 500 million eggs per year.
        –*The oyster*

CREEPY CRAWLERS
did you know that …

…Birds avoid eating the colorful Monarch butterfly because its diet of leaves from the poisonous milkweed plant gives it a bad taste?

…The notorious germ-carrying housefly can transport bacteria as far away as 15 miles from the original source of contamination?

…When more than one threat is present, a fly's central nervous system will overload, causing immobilization?

…Only full-grown male crickets can chirp?

…A tarantula spider can live a full two years without food—but when it catches its food, it can devour it quickly? (A tarantula can ingest an entire mouse—including the bones—in only a day and a half.)

…If it ever escaped into the wild, a single slug of the Giant African Snail species could conceivably reproduce itself 16 quadrillion times over a five year period?

…A snail's self-produced protective "foot film" makes it able to crawl along the cutting edge of a razor without injuring itself?

…The sinister ichneumon wasp injects her eggs into a host's body, paralyzing its victim without killing it, then tortures its prey after the eggs hatch by eating its fatty deposits and digestive organs before consuming the heart?

Bugs and Things—"Creepy" and Otherwise

• What is the only state in the U.S. where houseflies cannot live and breed? –*Alaska*

• What is the world's fastest insect, capable of speeds of up to 50 mph and of traveling 85 miles a day? –*The dragonfly*

• What incestuous insect creates her own husband from scratch and then copulates with her sons within a few days of laying the eggs—after which her sons immediately die? –*The female mite*

• Name the insect that is roasted and eaten by the handful by many native South African tribes. (Hint: These same "party snacks" in turn try to eat the natives out of house and home.) –*Termites*

• What is the only species a queen bee will use her stinger on? –*Another queen bee*

• What insect kills more people worldwide than do all the poisonous snakes combined. –Honeybees

• What effect does hard rock music, played to colonies of termites, have on the insects? –With accompaniment, they chew through wood at twice the normal rate

• How much honey does a single honeybee produce over a lifetime? –Only about a 12th of a teaspoonful

• What is the origin of the killer bee that is now making its way north into regions of the United States? –It escaped from an experimental breeding colony in Brazil 35 years after it was introduced

• What are "cooties"? –A type of body lice

• What insect seriously damaged the fruit, nut and vegetable crops of California in the 1980s? –The Mediterranean fruit fly

• In proportion to its size, what insect has the largest brain of any living creature on Earth? –The ant

• What pesky insect has been found by researchers to be the perfect lab specimen, since it resists disease, can survive radical surgery and, if beheaded, dies, not from decapitation, but rather from starvation? –The roach

• What is known as the hardiest of all the world's insects—feeling equally at home at the frigid North Pole as in the steamiest equatorial jungle? –The mosquito

• The blood of mammals is red. What color is an insect's blood? A lobster's? –Yellow; blue

UNDER THE SEA
did you know that ...

... The tropical sea anemone willingly provides shelters to a colony of damselfish, but if approached by damselfish outside its colony it will sting them to death?

... The aggressively fierce walking catfish— originally imported from Asia as an aquarium oddity—escaped from Florida breeding tanks in the 1970s, is able to breath and crawl on land, and can eat other fish up to seven inches long?

... A tuna can traverse a hundred miles of ocean in a single day?

... Most fish do not sleep, though their constant motion is marked by periods of reduced activity? (A few fish have been found to "sleep" in coral reefs by leaning against rocks or standing on their tails.)

... As a result of the "stress" of swimming in small tanks, nearly 10 percent of the blue fin and yellow fin tuna in the Tokyo Sea Life Park aquarium are reported to have developed bumpy, deformed faces and/or dislodged eyes?

... The elephant seal, the largest seal known to man, can grow as long as 20 feet and weigh some 8,000 pounds?

... The four-eyed tropical anableps fish can browse underwater with one set of eyes while scanning above water with the other pair?

... The Johnsonia Eriomma is more commonly called the "bigeye fish" because its eyes are a full one-fifth as long as its body?

... A blue whale's heart weighs upwards of 1200 pounds?

... Biologists from Cornell University recently found that families of sperm whales, separated geographically from one another, develop radically different vocal repertoires?

... The Nile perch, known as the "elephant of the water," has proven to be a severely misguided ecological experiment, having devoured most of the 300 other fish species in Africa's Lake Victoria since its introduction in 1960?

Thar She Blows!

• Which fish, unable to get enough oxygen from the water, can actually drown? (They have to surface about every five minutes to breathe.) —*Electric eels*

• At 188 decibels, more shrill than a pneumatic drill, what is believed to be the loudest sound produced by any living animal? —*The whistle of the blue whale*

• What creature could look at you with 35 large blue eyes? —*The scallop*

• Imported to the United States as a food source in the 1870s, what giant cousin of the goldfish paves its muddy way by uprooting aquatic plants, often rendering its environment uninhabitable for other species? —*Carp*

• What female fish stores her eggs in the abdominal pouch of her mate? —*The sea horse*

• Depending on which of the over 200 species you are referring to, this sea animal's tentacles vary in number from just a few to more than 800; some tentacles are less than an inch long, while others trail 120 feet (about ten stories) down into the water. What kind of sea creature are we talking about? —*The jellyfish*

• Name the jellyfish that is capable of inducing a sting more lethal than an entire nest-full of wasps? —*A Portuguese Man-of-War*

• Name the four stages of growth that the salmon fish passes through. —*Fry, pan, smelt and grilse*

• Where is the most likely place to catch a sardine? —*There is no such fish as a "sardine"; canned sardines generally contain young herring or pilchard*

• What happens to goldfish when they either go without adequate illumination or are placed in a body of running water? —*They lose their color*

• What starfish, commonly associated with the Pacific Ocean, is known for the damage it has done to many of the world's coral reefs? —*The crown-of-thorns starfish*

• What flatfish is born with two eyes, one on each side of its head, but eventually ends up with both eyes moving to the top of its head? —*The turbot*

• What sea creature is made up of 98 percent water and will virtually disappear if washed up to shore and allowed to dry? —*The jellyfish*

• When threatened, what fish will engorge itself with water and display its sharp spines, often frightening away enemies as large and formidable as the tiger shark? —*The porcupine fish*

• Name the luminous fish whose male species eventually attaches itself to the female, becoming completely connected. —*The Anglerfish (all the male angler's internal organs—with the exception of the reproductive system—are fused to its female companion)*

• For what purpose were Goldfish originally bred by the Chinese? —*Strictly culinary*

• It grows from the size of pea to a 150-pound behemoth, perhaps 30 feet across, in only two years, its entire life-span. What is it? —*The Pacific Giant Octopus*

• What is the largest creature without a backbone, weighing some 2.5 tons and growing up to 55 feet long? —*The giant squid (It's eyes can be a foot or more in diameter.)*

• What eight-legged sea animals also have two kidneys and three hearts? —*Both the octopus and the squid*

• What is the strainer in a certain class of whale's mouth referred to? —*The baleen*

• Provided it's not caught and eaten, what is the lifespan of a trout? —*Four years*

• What marine mammal sleeps at night just below the surface of the water, frequently rising to the surface for air? —*Dolphins*

• What was the intimidating promotional line used to advertise the 1978 movie "Jaws II"? —*"Just when you thought it was safe to go back in the water ... "*

RAINING CATS AND DOGS
did you know that ...

...According to the American Animal Hospital Association, over 65 percent of cat owners admitted that if their pet needed emergency medical treatment, they would treat the pet before themselves?

...The only dogs that bark regularly are those that come in contact with humans or other domesticated dogs? (Dogs in the wild rarely if ever bark.)

...Chow Chows were originally bred for three reasons: as a great pet/hunter/helper, to keep people warm with their furry hides, and as food—like pigs or cows?

...There are about 100 different breeds of cats?

...The backward-facing hooks (or *papillae*) on a cat's tongue provide the necessary roughness for grooming its fur and for scraping meat off bones?

...Despite the long-time domestication factor, there is no genetic barrier between dogs and wolves?

..."Mixed breeds" and "cross breeds" are NOT the same? (Mixed breed dogs have various lineage that is most likely unknown, while a cross breed is a combination of only two different breeds.)

...Mixed breed dogs are less likely to suffer from inherited diseases and disabilities than are pure-bred dogs?

...The Bloodhound doesn't need to smell blood to find someone who is lost? (It is said that his name instead means *blooded hound,* or aristocratic.)

...A skilled tracker dog can easily distinguish between individual scents, but fails only when it comes to the scent of identical twins?

...The Canary Islands were not named after canaries, but for large dogs? (The Latin name, *Canariea insulae,* means "Islands of Dogs.")

...Often after being petted, a cat will clean himself in an attempt to get the "person" smell off?

...In 1885 the English banned as inhumane the use of dogs for hauling carts?

...Newfoundlands have webbed feet, making them great swimmers and divers, while Bassets, on the other hand, can't swim? (Their legs are too short to keep their heavy, long bodies afloat.)

...Possibly due to their higher-pitched voices, cats respond better to women than to men?

Canines vs. Felines

• Name the wild dog largely associated with the Australian continent. *The dingo*

• Albert Schweitzer once said: "There are two means of refuge from the miseries of life: _____ and ____." According to Schweitzer, what are these two soothing life requisites? *–Music and cats*

• "Beauty without vanity, strength without insolence, courage without ferocity, and all the virtues of man without his vices." What Romantic poet, devastated upon the death of his beloved Newfoundland, named Boatswain, had these words inscribed upon the dog's gravestone? *–Lord Byron*

• What is the most popular cat derivation in the United States? *–The Siamese*

• When cats walk or run, they step with both left legs, then both right legs, etc. What are the only other two animals to do this? *–The camel and the giraffe*

• All dogs have a normal body temperature of between 100 and 102 degrees Fahrenheit, with the exception of one. What dog has a body temperature that reaches upwards of 104 degrees? (Hint: It needs to conserve all the warmth it can.) *–The Mexican Hairless*

• What hunting/guard dog derived its name from a German tax collector, who, aware of the unpopularity of his job and bent on protecting his person, developed this exceptionally fierce breed? *–Doberman pinscher*

• According to TV show "Breed All About It," royalty and the rich used to keep small lap dogs for an unusual reason, specifically to sleep with. How did this practice benefit the dog's moneyed owner? *–With the dog under the covers before retiring, bedbugs, fleas, etc. would go onto the dog instead of themselves*

• What was the penalty for killing a cat in Egypt 4,000 years ago? *–Death*

• What would you calla cat-lover? A person afraid or hateful of cats? *–Ailurophile; ailurophobe*

• According to a 27-year-old New York City study, what breed of dog is known to bite the most? The least? *–German police dog; golden retriever*

• What is unique about the Basenji dog? *–It doesn't bark.*

• Compared to a human's five million scent-sensitive cells, how many smell cells does a German shepherd dog have? *–220 million*

• What are the three most commonly used names for dogs in the U.S.? *–Rover, Spot and Max*

- When a cat rubs against your leg, what two things is it accomplishing? –*Showing affection and applying its personal scent on you*

- The cat referred to in Lewis Carroll's *Alice's Adventures In Wonderland* is of what breed? –*The fabricated "Cheshire" breed*

- Give the dog terms that match each of the following definitions:
    The bulldog's drooping lip.
        –*The chops*
    The part of the body located in front of the chest.
        –*The brisket*
    A spotted nose.
        –*A butterfly nose*
    Where the tip of the ear falls over the orifice, covering it.
        –*A button ear*
    A pointed or pricked ear.
        –*A tulip ear*
    A short round foot with high, well-developed knuckles.
        –*A cat foot*
    Pendulous folds of skin under the throat.
        –*The dewlap*
    The tops of the hip joints.
        –*Hucklebones*

- Interestingly enough, what is the ancient Egyptian word for cat, which literally means "to see"? –*Mau*

- In which country did the French poodle originate? –*Germany*

- What dog breed arose in Egypt about 5,000 years ago, later coming to England sometime before the 9th century, where it was bred by aristocrats to hunt such small game as hares. –*The greyhound*

- Cats seem to talk or send messages with their tails. Interpret what a cat is saying by the following tail positions:
    Straight up in the air.
        –*He likes you*
    Slightly raised and curved outward.
        –*She's curious*
    Fluffed out and lowered.
        –*He's afraid*
    A twitching tip.
        –*She's irritated*
    Arched back, bristled tail.
        –*He's ready to fight*

- An expression originated with the Eskimos and referred to a night so cold that one had to bed down with three dogs to keep warm. What is this term? –*"Three dog night"—adopted by the band of the same name*

…Bette Midler, Barry Manilow and many other famous vocalists got their start in a club in New York City called The Continental Baths, located in the basement of the Ansonia Hotel?

…Comedian Peter Sellers had "In the Mood" played at his funeral as an inside joke?

…On Jan 1, 1960 late country singer Johnny Cash gave his first free concert at California's San Quentin Prison? (Coincidentally, Merle Haggard was in the audience during Cash's performance.)

…Rock artists Jim Morrison, Jimi Hendrix and Janis Joplin each died at the tender young age of 27?

…Australian-based rock group Men At Work got the inspiration for their name from a road sign?

The Beat Goes On
- What do the famous rock groups The Doors, The Who, The Rolling Stones, The Beach Boys and The Grateful Dead all have in common? –*None of the groups ever won a Grammy Award*

- Who sings the hit single "All I Wanna Do," adapted from the poem "Fun" by Wyn Cooper? –*Sheryl Crow*

- What comedian/singer recorded his first song in a bathroom across the hall from the radio station where he worked? What was the name of the song? –*"Weird Al" Yankovic; "My Bologna"*

- What physical feature does country-western singer Dolly Parton share with rock 'n roll singer Pat Benatar? –*They both stand only five feet tall*

- At the group's first major show, what popular rock band made its entrance by skydiving from a plane into Anaheim Stadium? –*Van Halen*

- What rock-'n'-roll song was first to hit #1 on the charts? Who sang it? –*"Rock Around the Clock," by Bill Haley and the Comets*

- What did Grace Slick, lead singer of Jefferson Airplane (or Starship), name her daughter? –*god (with a lower case g)*

- What Captain and Tenille song examines the intricacies of rodent romance? For what other song did the duo receive a Grammy in 1975? –*"Muskrat Love"; "Love Will Keep Us Together"*

• What song, crooned by Ernie of "Sesame Street," topped the charts in 1970?
−*"Rubber Duckie"*

• Given the artist and the year, identify each Grammy-winning "Best Record" title:
Norah Jones, 2003
−*"Come Away With Me"*
Eric Clapton, 1993
−*"Tears In Heaven"*
Dixie Chicks, 2007
−*"Not Ready To Make Nice"*
Celine Dion, 1999
−*"My Heart Will Go On"*
Bobby McFerrin, 1988
−*"Don't Worry, Be Happy"*
Natalie Cole, with Nat "King" Cole, 1992
−*"Unforgettable"*
Ray Charles & Norah Jones, 2005
−*"Here We Go Again"*
USA for Africa, 1985
−*"We Are the World"*
Bette Midler, 1989
−*"Wind Beneath My Wings"*
Christopher Cross, 1980
−*"Sailing"*
The Eagles, 1978
−*"Hotel California"*
Michael Jackson, 1983
−*"Beat It"*
Phil Collins, 1990
−*"Another Day In Paradise"*
The 5th Dimension, 1969
−*"Aquarius" ("Let the Sun Shine")*
Roberta Flack, 1973
−*"Killing Me Softly With His Song"*
Frank Sinatra, 1966
−*"Strangers In the Night"*
Tina Turner, 1984
−*"What's Love Got to Do With It?"*

• Elvis Presley's loyal following of friends, bodyguards and musicians were referred to by what nickname? −*The "Memphis Mafia"*

• What is the most widely sung tune in the English-speaking world?
−*"Happy Birthday to You"*

• What punk rocker died of an overdose before he could be brought to trial for the murder of his girlfriend, Nancy Spungen, who was found dead in New York City's Chelsea Hotel on October 17, 1978? −*Sid Vicious*

• Carly Simon's 1972 hit "You're So Vain" was said to have been inspired by the actions of what actor? −*Warren Beatty*

• Who wrote "Leaving on a Jet Plane," made famous by Peter, Paul and Mary? −*John Denver*

• Identify the famous pop/rock music groups that once went by these names:
The Paramours
−*The Righteous Brothers*
Caesar and Cleo
−*Sonny and Cher*
Johnny and the Moondogs
−*The Beatles*
Carl and the Passions
−*The Beach Boys*
Big Thing
−*Chicago*
The Golden Gate Rhythm Section
−*Journey*
Sparrow
−*Steppenwolf*
Earth
−*Black Sabbath*

• "Angel of Harlem" was U2's tribute to what soulful jazz singer who died in 1959, impoverished, at the age of 44? −*Billie Holiday*

• Complete the words from the following Grateful Dead songs:
"Standing on the _____."
−*Moon*
"Ramble on _____ and _____."
−*Rose and rose*
"Brown eyed _____."
−*Woman*
"Fire on the _____."
−*Mountain*

• Actor Dustin Hoffman once challenged Paul McCartney to compose a ballad based on the haunting last words of artist Pablo Picasso. McCartney took the dare, and as a result recorded what song with his group, Wings?
−*"Drink to Me …"*

• Who is considered by most musical "in-the-knows" to be the most successful family in music history? −*The Jacksons*

• What pop/rock 'n roll feature artist(s) gave us each of these "trademark" titles?
"Sad Songs"
−*Elton John*
"Born in the U.S.A."
−*Bruce Springsteen*
"Piano Man"
−*Billy Joel*
"Tapestry"
−*Carole King*
"You've Got a Friend"
−*James Taylor*
"U Can't Touch This"
−*M.C. Hammer*
"Every Breath You Take"
−*The Police*

"Monday, Monday"
 –The Mamas and the Papas
"Bridge Over Troubled Water"
 –Simon and Garfunkel
"Stayin' Alive"
 –The Bee Gees
"Stop! In the Name of Love"
 –The Supremes
"I Heard It Through the Grapevine"
 –Marvin Gaye
"Oh Pretty Woman"
 –Roy Orbison
"My Girl"
 –The Temptations
"The Dock of the Bay"
 –Otis Redding
Breaking Up is Hard to Do"
 –Neil Sedaka
"Jump"
 –Van Halen

• What animal appears on the cover of many of Pink Floyd's albums? –A pig

• Who was awarded the very first Gold Record in 1958 for his song "Catch a Falling Star"? –Crooner Perry Como

• What did the slogan on folk singer Woody Guthrie's guitar read? –This Machine Kills Facists

• Name the rock group most closely associated with each of the following performers:
 Robert Plant
  –Led Zepplin
 Jerry Garcia
  –The Grateful Dead
 Brian Jones
  –The Rolling Stones
 Roger Daltry
  –The Who
 Belinda Carlisle
  –The Go-Go's
 David Lee Roth
  –Van Halen
 Fred Mercury
  –Queen
 Jim Morrison
  –The Doors

• Coincidentally, what song were the Rolling Stones playing during their famous Altamont Speedway free concert when one of the Hell's Angels security force members knifed a member of the audience (an act that was captured on film)? –"Under My Thumb"

THE GRIM REAPER
did you know that …

…A majority of fire-related deaths are due to smoke inhalation rather than burns?

…Teenagers are 50 percent more susceptible to catching a cold than people over 50?

…Ninety percent of teenagers suffer from some form of acne?

…Men successfully commit suicide three times more frequently than women do—but women attempt suicide two to three times more often than men?

…Over 80 percent of professional boxers have suffered brain damage?

…Fewer than ten people were present at "founder of Communism" Karl Marx's funeral in 1883?

…In 1888, the worst hailstorm ever recorded hit Moradabad India, killing 246 people?

…The world's deadliest famine, which killed an estimated 30 million people in China between 1959 and 1961, was not revealed to the rest of the world until 20 years later?

…Amnesty International, the worldwide organization for the defense of human rights, estimates that there are in the neighborhoodof half a million prisoners of conscience throughout the world, and many others who have been summarily executed by governments?

…According to a recent study, nearly half of all deaths occur within three months after a person's birthday, while only eight percent die during the three-month period preceding a birthday? (Researchers hypothesize that the period following a birthday is anticlimactic, whereas the period before is viewed as a subconscious psychological goal to be achieved.)

Death, Disease and Injury
• Which of the following is currently the least likely to cause death: smoking, nuclear power, home appliances, or hand guns? –Nuclear power, by far (as far as we know)

• The symptoms of this common ailment are usually brought about as a result either of allergic reactions or exercise, which precipitate a narrowing of the bronchial tubes. What is the name of this malady? –Asthma

• Death is known as one of life's two inevitable misfortunes. Name the other, as implied by Benjamin Franklin. –*Taxes*

• In the United States, how many years does it take before a missing person can be declared legally dead? –*Seven*

• What person was burned at the stake in 1431, the same year Vlad Dracula was born? Where did the burning take place?
–*Joan of Arc; Rouen, France*

• How many young men were killed while playing in college football games during the 1905 season? During a typical season nowadays? –*18; today, with improvements in equipment, the number of annual football-related deaths can be counted on one hand*

• Name the form of cancer that involves the uncontrolled growth of white blood cells, or leukocytes. –*Leukemia*

• What is the highly transmittable disease that is often referred to as "the kissing disease?" –*Mononucleosis*

• Which of the following sources expose Americans to the *largest* amount of radiation: buildings, television sets, medical diagnoses, or nuclear reactors? –*Medical diagnoses*

• If you have *Verruca Vulgaris*, what are you suffering from? –*Warts*

• Millionaire businessman Howard Hughes suffered from a fear of public places (agoraphobia). What other phobia did he have? –*Mysophobia—the fear of germs*

• Give the common term used to describe the disruption of our circadian rhythm as the result of a lengthy airplane flight. –*Jet lag*

• What necessary substance secreted by the pancreas lowers the body's blood sugar levels, and, if not produced in sufficient quantities, can cause diabetes? –*Insulin*

• Name the condition that often afflicts the elderly, which is characterized by painful, inflamed and fragile joints. –*Arthritis*

• When 16-year-old Anissa Ayala of California was diagnosed with leukemia in 1993, what well-publicized—and, according to some, ethically questionable—action did her parents take to successfully save her life? –*They conceived a baby to serve as a bone marrow donor for their older daughter*

• What is the virus that causes AIDS? –*Human Immunodeficiency Virus (HIV)*

• What is the name of the bizarre neurological disorder in which one hand acts independently of the other and against the body's wishes—sometimes pinching, slapping or striking its owner? –*The Dr. Strangelove Syndrome*

• Throughout history, what dreaded "bad air" disease has been carried by anopheles mosquitoes? –*Malaria*

• What percentage of the U.S. population seek some form of mental health treatment each year? –*About 11 percent*

• Comedian Sid Caesar was known to have tonsurphobia—a fear of _____. –*Having his hair cut*

• Novelist John Cheever had gephyrophobia, or fear of _____ _____. –*Crossing bridges*

• On February 26, 1992, Beijing worker Xu Denghai was hospitalized with a "twisted intestine." In fact, Xu was the third such case in several weeks since this craze had swept China. What was the cause of these mysterious injuries? –*Excessive play with a Hula Hoop*

• Give the name of the psychiatric disorder that corresponds with the following definitions:
 People who suffer from this ailment mistrust everyone and cannot abandon constant suspicions that someone is "out to get them."
 –*Paranoia*
 Self-love is healthy, to a certain degree. However, this illness is manifested by excessive love of self, including delusions of grandeur and a constant need for attention.
 –*Narcissism*
 People who survive a trauma may have painful recollections or nightmares, and during an "episode" may in fact behave as if they were reliving the trauma.
 –*Post-Traumatic Stress Disorder*
 Primary symptoms of this illness include delusional thinking, usually accompanied by auditory or visual hallucinations. It seems there is an inherited vulnerability to this disease.
 –*Schizophrenia*
 This disease is characterized by the establishment of two or more separate identities that seem to be responsible for a specific feeling or act of the individual.
 –*Multiple Personality Disorder (split personalities)*

- Roman emperor Augustus Caesar suffered from this "black" phobia, known as Achluophobia. What couldn't Caesar bring himself to do? *–Sit in the dark*

- What is the only thing that can truly sober up a liquor-intoxicated person? *–Time*

- What typically minor injury is a first-time snow skier most likely to sustain? *–Sunburn*

- What animal's skin can be successfully grafted onto the human body to repair burns? *–A pig's*

- British Queen Elizabeth I suffered from anthophobia. What was she afraid of? *–Roses*

- In the 1990s, the Consumer Product Safety Commission banned for sale more than 10 brands of this type of product, considering them a health threat to children because they contained lead. What were they? *–Crayons*

- According to German researchers, on what day of the week is the risk of heart attack greatest? *–Monday (nearly 50 percent greater than on any other day)*

- In 1846 a group of 87 pioneers left Illinois on a wagon migration to California. In accordance with Lansford Warren Hastings' authoritative guidebook *Emigrant's Guide to Oregon and California*, they took a new route around the southern tip of the Great Salt Lake and became snowbound in the Sierra Nevada Mountains. Forced to camp for four months, the 47 survivors eventually resorted to cannibalism to ward off starvation. What was the name of this ill-fated company? *–The Donner Party, led by George Donner*

SUPERSTITIONS AND FOLKLORE
did you know that …

… The selling of personal horoscopes is big business around the world?

… According to Old-English folklore, if a rabbit or a hare crosses the road in front of you, you must take off your hat, spit on it, and put it back on your head?

… Standing in front of a latrine and inhaling the stench, being in the presence of pigs, and applying the entrails of a young pigeon or newborn puppy to the forehead were all anti-plague remedies prescribed throughout 14th-century Europe?

… For centuries wearing a blue shirt or dress has been believed to ward off witches, who, apparently, were thought to abhor the color?

… Of gypsies, peasants and gamblers (three groups considered by many to be of the most superstitious in the world), gamblers are regarded as the most superstitious?

Charmed, I'm Sure

- A superstition is a traditional belief that a certain action or event can cause or foretell an apparently unrelated event. Many superstitions deal with important life passages, such as birth, marriage, pregnancy, and death. A causal superstition involves taking a deliberate action to ensure good luck or avoid bad luck. Identify what the alleged result will be for each of the following actions or events:

A newborn child is carried *upstairs* before being carried *down* a flight of stairs.
–He or she will rise to success in the world

A child is born on a Sunday.
–He or she will enjoy good luck

You drop a knife or fork on the floor.
–Company is coming

A young woman pins a four-leaf clover to her door.
–She will marry the first bachelor who passes through

Knocking on wood.
–You will avoid bad luck

A bride and groom see one another on their wedding day prior to the ceremony.
–They will have bad luck

At a wedding, the guests throw rice at the newlyweds.
–The marriage will result in many children

When a person dies, the doors and windows of the room are left open.
–The spirit of the departed can leave in peace

A person always carries a silver dollar with him.

    —He will have good luck

A pregnant woman eats unhealthy foods.

    —Her child will bear an unwanted birthmark

• Some superstitions likely derived from a practical origin. For example, besides any supernatural effects, what might be the practical result of hanging a bag of garlic around a child's neck to ward off disease? *—Its smell keeps away other children—including those carrying any contagious virus*

• Similarly, many people believe that lighting cigarettes for three persons from a single match will bring bad luck. For what practical reason may this superstition have started? (Hint: It may have originated among soldiers during World War I.) *—At night, a match that stayed lit long enough to light three cigarettes provided an easy target for the enemy*

• Name the lucky object that is both "looked over" in song—and most often overlooked in our everyday travels. *—A four-leaf clover*

• In fact, finding a four-leaf clover or a horseshoe is said to be a good omen, and is an example of a *sign* superstition. Sign superstitions foretell an event without any conscious action by the person involved. Breaking a mirror or spilling salt, for instance, brings bad luck. What do each of these signs supposedly mean?

    You hear a dog howling in the night.

        —Death is near

    You meet a person with red hair.

        —He or she has a quick temper

    You see a ring around the moon.

        —Rain is on its way

• What other animal, besides black cats, brings bad fortune—since, it is said, witches often transform themselves into this animal? *—Hares*

• According to Japanese belief, a sick person should not be given cut flowers, which soon wither and die. What would be a more appropriate gift, representing hope for the patient's recovery? *—A potted plant*

• Similarly, what would one include inside a gift of a purse or wallet to ensure that the recipient will always be blessed with sufficient money? *—Money*

• What is *teratology*? *—The study of monsters*

• Upon the death of a professional magician, what does tradition stipulate that a colleague do with the deceased's magic wand? *—Break it over the casket*

• What is *tasseography*? *—Tea leaf reading*

• Millions of people place great importance in—and base critical decisions on—the position of the sun, moon, planets and stars. What is this the name of this study? *—Astrology*

• What would be a proper meal for a fairy? *—Milk, cream and butter*

• According to legend, the gift of eloquence can be obtained by kissing the Blarney Stone. However, the stone must be kissed in a specific way to obtain this gift. How must it be kissed—and where is the stone located? *—With the head hanging downward; in Blarney Castle near Cork, Ireland*

• Considered an omen of bad luck, what is the name of the legendary ghost ship—the subject of one of Wagner's operas—which is said to wander forever off the Cape of Good Hope? *—The Flying Dutchman*

• What number did musical composer Frederic Chopin fear so intensely that he refused to compose music on this day of the month, and would not live in a house with that number anywhere on it? *—Seven*

• Complete the following well-known superstitions—most often espoused by con men—by filling in the following blanks:

    If your _____ _____ itches, rub it on the seat of your pants.

        —Left hand

    Giving money to a _____ will bring you good luck.

        —Stranger

    In order to ensure that a police officer won't harass you, always _____ over your left shoulder when you see one.

        —Spit

    Never _____ on rainy days.

        —Work

    Never take advantage of anyone with a _____.

        —Harelip

• If a lycanthrope looked in the mirror, what might his reflection show? *—A werewolf*

• To a folklorist, what is "The Grateful Dead"? (Hint: It is not a rock group.) *—It is a tale in which a young man buries a corpse at great personal risk to himself and then obtains a bride with the help of the appreciative dead*

• Induced sneezing, jumping up and down, and swallowing dead bees in honey were all techniques used by both men and women throughout the centuries to prevent what? *—Conception of a child*

... A woman walking past a crew of construction workers can keep herself from being hassled by picking her nose—an act that creates an immediate deterrent?

... Since bees are infuriated by the gas that comes out of our mouths when we breathe, the best way to avoid a bee sting is to hold your breath?

... Mark Twain once made the astute observation that "It is better to keep your mouth shut and appear stupid than to open it and remove all doubt"?

... If everyone who owned a fax machine switched to half-page cover sheets rather than full-page, it would save nearly two million miles of unrecyclable fax paper a year?

Mother Knows Best

• What is the best way to escape an attack by killer bees? *–Run in a zigzag motion*

• The following are statistically documented ways to stretch life expectancy. Guess the amount of time a person can expect to add or subtract from her life by following these bits of advice:

> Install a smoke detector in your home.
> > *–Add Nine Days*
> Drink tall glasses of chlorinated swimming-pool water rather than regular tap water.
> > *–Slice off half-a-day*
> Drive a sedan rather than a compact car.
> > *–Add 70 days*
> Always wear a seat belt.
> > *–Tack on 69 days*
> Try to come in contact with snakes and bees as often as possible.
> > *–Subtract 12 hours for each bite or sting*

• "Remain still until you are floating, then slowly rotate to a horizontal position and roll yourself onto firm ground." What are you doing if you're following this advice?
–Extracting yourself from quicksand

• According to the King James Version of The Bible, which commandment advises us against "keeping up with the Joneses"?
–The 10th—"Thou shalt not covet ... "

• If a grizzly bear begins to attack you, what is the best way to respond?
–Curl up in a ball and play dead

• When Bob Hope met nightclub singer Anthony Dominick Benedetto, he advised him to change his name—which he did. What did he change it to? *–Tony Bennett*

• What was the staunch Miss Post advising against when she recommended the following restrictions: "Certainly not in church, or during recitation periods in school.... And certainly not when wearing formal clothes"?
–Against chewing gum in public

• To combat the problem of misplacing your keys or locking them in your car, Shell Oil once came up with a list of suggestions. Identify the advice that corresponds with each clue:

> It may be more cumbersome to lug around, but this item is easier to find when you are in a hurry.
> > *–Use an extra-large key ring*
> Instead of using your car's automatic door-lock system, _____.
> > *–Always lock your door from the outside using the key*
> If you follow this piece of advice, you will always be able to enter your vehicle, since most people generally carry this around with them.
> > *–Carry an extra key in your purse or billfold*

• According to Benjamin Franklin's "Poor Richard's Almanac," what else besides fish "begins to stink in three days"? *–House guests*

• From the same source ("Poor Richard's Almanac"), what is the best way to learn the value of money? *–Try to borrow some*

... A screaming baby can produce a sound level of 90 decibels, five decibels higher than the level that will cause permanent hearing loss?

... Several recent studies have proven that preschoolers whose mothers smoked 10 or more cigarettes per day during pregnancy have significantly lower IQs than children of nonsmokers?

... Prenatal and infant deaths are significantly higher among males than females?
... A fetus reacts to sound as early as the fourth month from conception, and, as a newborn, will most likely turn toward a female voice in preference to that of a male?

Heavy With Child

• What does a human embryo develop into after about eight weeks? *–A fetus*

• What part of a newborn baby accounts for one-quarter of its entire weight?
–Its head

• A gamete is a functional sex cell—either an egg or a sperm—which can unite with a gamete of the opposite sex. What results in the fusion of two gametes? *–A zygote*

• What blood type is the father sure not to have if a mother with O-type has a B-type baby?
–O-type

• How many children did the average married American woman give birth to in the 1600s?
–13

• In the year 1900, what were the most popular first names given to boy and girl American babies? *–John and Mary*

• What is the synthetic hormone that is used intravenously to either initiate contractions or speed up the progress of labor? *–Pitocin*

• This approach to childbirth, pioneered by the doctor it was named for, relies on intensive training and practice to substitute useful responses to the stimulus of labor contractions in place of counterproductive ones. What is this method called?
–Lamaze, developed by French obstetrician Fernand Lamaze

• What is the process in which eggs are fertilized in a test tube and then implanted into the uterus? *–In-vitro fertilization*

• In the U.S., what are the odds of having twins?
–1 in 90

• The fertilization of two ovum results in what type of twins? What is the result of a single egg cell that is fertilized, which then divides into two equal parts?
–Fraternal twins; identical twins

• Which parent's chromosome determines the sex of the baby? *–The father's*

• What is another name for "pregnancy-induced hypertension"?
–Toxemia, or preeclampsia

• Name the yellowish liquid which is excreted from the mammary gland as a precursor to breast milk. *–Colostrum*

• Uterine contractions occur early in pregnancy but are not usually felt until the last trimester. These mild contractions, often perceived as a moderate hardening of the uterus, are not strong enough to deliver a baby. What are they referred to? *–"Braxton Hicks"*

• After how many weeks of pregnancy is a miscarriage considered a "premature birth" rather than a "spontaneous abortion"?
–20 weeks

• Doctors once believed that a pregnant woman should limit her overall weight-gain to about 15 pounds. What is considered an acceptable weight-gain during pregnancy now?
–Between 25 and 35 pounds

• If both expectant birth parents have three brothers and no sisters, what sex is their baby likely to be?
–There remains a 50-50 chance of having either a boy or a girl; gender has not been proven to be genetically determined

• According to the National Center for Health Statistics, in what month of the year are most babies born? What is the top birth day?
–September; Tuesday

… John Quincy Adams, U.S. President from1825 through1829, frequently went out "skinny-dipping" in the Potomac River before sunrise?

… As the nation's "largest-ever" President, Grover Cleveland stood more than six feet tall and weighed over 300 pounds while in office? (A few weeks after his birth, his mother said of him, "He is very large for his age and grows fat every day.")

… Richard M. Nixon's nickname in college was "Iron Butt"—and in law-school he was dubbed "Gloomy Gus"?

… President William H. Harrison served the shortest term in office, dying of pneumonia in 1841 just 31 days after taking the presidential oath? (He probably contracted the illness after walking in the rain, having refused to ride during his inaugural parade.)

… President Franklin D. Roosevelt served a total of 12 years, 1 month and 8 days in the White House—and, in 1939, was the first President to speak on television?

… Upon the death of President William H. Harrison, John Tyler was the first Vice President to serve as unelected President?

White House Goings-on

• Which U.S. President never won election to either the office of the Vice President or President? *–Gerald Ford*

• Since President James Buchanan was not married, who acted as First Lady during his term in office? *–His niece, Harriet Lane*

• Name the President who appears on the $500 bill. What about the $1,000 and $5,000 bills (though the latter is not currently in circulation)? *–William McKinley ($500); Grover Cleveland ($1,000) and James Madison ($5,000)*

• Who were the only grandfather and grandson to have both served as President? *–William H. (1841) and Benjamin Harrison (1889-1893)*

• Who were the only father and son to serve as President? *–John Adams (1797-1801) and John Quincy Adams (1825-1829)*

• Which President seemed to enjoy showing off his gallbladder scar after his operation? *–Lyndon B. Johnson*

• What former First Lady purportedly administered a professional judo flip to a New York news photographer for taking pictures of her outside a movie house in 1969? *–Jacqueline Kennedy Onassis*

• How many of his eight years in office did George Washington live in the White House? *–Zero—the White House was completed during Washington's successor John Adams's term*

• Which President had the most children? *–John Tyler, with 15*

• Who was the U.S. Presidential retreat Camp David named after? *–David Eisenhower II, grandson of Dwight D. Eisenhower*

• Before President Eisenhower changed the name of the retreat, what name was it known by? *–Shangri-La*

• Alexander Hamilton was killed in 1804 while engaged in a duel with whom? *–Thomas Jefferson's Vice President, Aaron Burr*

• Name the first U.S. President ever to visit the former Soviet Union. *–Richard Nixon*

• What two former presidents died on the same day, and on what "select" day in 1826 did they die? *–John Adams (at age 90) and Thomas Jefferson (83) both died on July 4 (By a remarkable coincidence, Adams's last words were, "Thomas Jefferson still lives.")*

• Who was the only former Vice President to later be elected President but did not succeed the President under whom he served? *–Richard Nixon*

• When most of the White House gardeners were drafted to fight in WWI, what creative substitute did President Woodrow Wilson use to mow the lawn? *–A small flock of sheep*

• Besides Washington, Jefferson, Van Buren and Lincoln, name the other five U.S. Presidents who did not attend college. *–Taylor, Fillmore, Andrew Johnson, Cleveland and Truman*

• George Washington, Dwight D. Eisenhower, Ulysses S. Grant and Zachary Taylor all served in what post before assuming the Presidency? *–General in the U.S. Army*

• Shortly after President Ronald Reagan was shot in 1981, what cabinet member declared, "I'm in control"? *–Secretary of State Alexander Haig*

• What special orders did the press receive after Franklin Roosevelt was crippled by in 1921—eleven years before he assumed the Presidency? –*There were to be no pictures taken of him that showed his legs*

• Which President was the first to grow a beard in office? –*Abraham Lincoln*

• What celebrated poet performed a reading at President John F. Kennedy's inauguration? –*Robert Frost*

• Most people believe that JFK, at 43 years old, was the youngest President ever elected to office. Actually, he was second youngest. Who, at age 42, held this distinction among Presidents? –*Theodore Roosevelt*

• Most Americans know that Kennedy was the first and only Roman Catholic to serve as President, and that the Presidency has been filled by a number of Methodists (Polk, A. Johnson, Grant, McKinley …), Presbyterians (Jackson, Lincoln, Wilson, Eisenhower …), Unitarians (both Adamses, Jefferson, Taft …) and Episcopalians (Washington, Madison, Monroe, FDR, Ford, Bush …). Name the Presidents affiliated with the following religions:
Disciples of Christ
   –*James Garfield, LBJ and Reagan*
Baptist
   –*Warren G. Harding and Bill Clinton*
Congregationalist
   –*Calvin Coolidge*
Friend (Quaker)
   –*Herbert Hoover and Richard Nixon*

• Which President was known as a "genius for inactivity"—averaging 10 hours of sleep a day and another 10 of loafing—leaving four hours for work? –*Calvin Coolidge*

• Name the former U.S. President who admitted to shooting his sister in the rear end with a BB gun when he was 15. –*Jimmy Carter*

• Only one president served two non-consecutive terms. Who was this President, and who was elected to take over the reigns of office between his terms? –*Grover Cleveland; Benjamin Harrison (1889-1893)*

• Name the five offices, in order, that are in line of succession to the Presidency. –*The Vice-President, Speaker of the House of Representatives, President Pro Tempore of the Senate, Secretary of State and, if all else fails, the Secretary of the Treasury, in turn, succeed the President*

• Which former U.S. President earlier appeared on a 1942 cover of Cosmopolitan magazine dressed in a Navy uniform? –*Gerald Ford*

• What is the annual salary for the President of the United States? –*$400,000*

• Name the limited right that the President may invoke to withhold information from Congress. –*Executive privilege*

• Who were the only two men elected to Congress after serving as President? –*John Quincy Adams (1831-1848) and Andrew Johnson (1874-1875)*

• Who is the only U.S. President known to have reported sighting a UFO? –*Jimmy Carter*

• What six Presidents have shared the common name of "James"? –*Madison, Buchanan, Monroe, Garfield, Polk and Carter*

• What was the title of the play President Lincoln was viewing at Ford's Theater on the evening of April 14, 1865, the night of his assassination? –*"Our American Cousin," written by Tom Taylor*

• What was Gerald R. Ford's recorded birth name before he was adopted as an infant by his mother's new husband, Gerald R. Ford, Sr.? –*Leslie Lynch King, Jr.*

• Which President was sworn into office on an airplane? –*Lyndon B. Johnson, following Kennedy's assassination in 1963*

...The last time the United States could boast a national budget surplus was in 1835-36?

...There are seven obvious yet perplexing coincidences about former U.S. Presidents Abraham Lincoln and John F. Kennedy: (1) both were assassinated, (2) both were shot in the head from behind, (3) both were shot on a Friday, (4) both of their wives were present at the time, (5) Lincoln's assassin (John Wilkes Booth) was born in 1839 while Kennedy's (Lee Harvey Oswald) was born in 1939, (6) Lincoln's personal secretary was surnamed Kennedy while Kennedy's was surnamed Lincoln, and (7) Lincoln was elected in 1860, Kennedy in 1960?

...Tibet, in which 75 percent of the citizens are still illiterate and make the equivalent of only $80 per capita income a year is currently controlled and occupied by Chinese communists?

Political Platforms

• What modern-day technologically advanced nation at one time voluntarily gave up guns for more than 200 years? *–Japan (1637-1853)*

• Name the country that at one time required foreign visitors to wade through a trough of disinfectant upon entering its borders. *–Albania*

• What reformer organized the 1903 "March of the Mill Children," demanding an end to child labor—traipsing a route from Philadelphia to President Theodore Roosevelt's summer home?
–Mary Harris Jones ("Mother Jones")

• Another reformer espoused "The Great Leap Forward," designed to revitalize The People's Republic of China's economy by communizing industry. Who pushed this plan in 1958, leading to 20 million Chinese starving to death? *–Mao Zedong*

• Who was the first democratically elected President of Russia? *–Boris Yeltsin, 1991*

• Hailing a new era of freedom and cooperation, what country finally had its first all-race election in 1994? *–South Africa*

• What famous film star and director took time out of his career to serve as mayor of the small town of Carmel, California? *–Clint Eastwood*

• During the 1940 U.S. presidential election campaign, the Democratic and Republican parties were joined by a third party. What was the name of this party, and who ran for president on its ticket?
–The Surprise Party; comedienne Gracie Allen, George Burns's wife

• What political party, founded by dime novelist Ned Buntline in the 1850s, is today known as the American Party? (Hint: Since this party's adherents were opposed to U.S. immigration policies—especially of allowing Irish-Catholic immigrants—they each took an oath of secrecy.)
–The Know Nothing Party

• In its 2,500-year history, which country had never held an election until 1987? What percentage of the population voted that year?
–Ethiopia (Abyssinia); 96 percent

• What is the earliest-known system of publically displayed laws, set forth by a Babylonian ruler around 1760 B.C.E.? *–The Code of Hammurabi*

• What more common term has been replaced by these more politically correct—perhaps "politically comical"—terms?

Differently interesting; charm-free
–Boring
Uniquely coordinated
–Clumsy
Terminally inconvenienced
–Dead
Morally different; ethically disoriented
–Dishonest
Sobriety deprived
–Drunk
A previously recounted humorous narrative
–An old joke
An unaffiliated applicant for private-sector funding
–A panhandler
A nontraditional shopper
–A shoplifter
Melanin impoverished
–Caucasian
A directionally impoverished person
–A vagrant

• Who is the British version of the United States' Uncle Sam? *–John Bull*

• What international incident nearly led to a nuclear confrontation between the U.S. and Russia in 1962? *–The Cuban Missile Crisis*

• On which continent have most of the countries gained their independence only during the last 30 years? *–Africa*

• What country houses more than a dozen of the world's largest banks in terms of total assets?
–Japan

• What country held its first-ever democratic elections on Jan. 30, 2005? *–Iraq*

... Ivan IV Vasilievich, the unifier and first Czar of Russia and best known as Ivan the Terrible, was dubbed with this infamous title after ordering thousands of political executions among his subjects and, in a fit of rage, murdering his own heir—his eldest son?

... Famed physicist Albert Einstein was once offered—but turned down—the presidency of Israel?

Kings, Commanders and Czars

• Name the Mongolian sovereign whose territorial conquests (4,860,000 square miles of tribal control, including much of present-day Russia and China) between the years1206 and 1227 exceeded the total combined conquests of Alexander the Great, Attila the Hun and Napoleon Bonaparte (4,350,000 square miles). –*Genghis Kahn*

• What common bond do the terms *Ming, Shang, Tang, Sung, Han* and *Ch'ing* all share? –*They all refer to Chinese dynasties*

• French Emperor Napoleon Bonaparte exhibited a zeal for conquest and control. But what small, feeble creatures could allegedly make this great man shake, sweat, scream and cry for help? –*Kittens*

• What 1953 female graduate of Mt. St. Vincent College in New York City went on to become a world leader from 1986-1992? –*Corazon Aquino, President of the Philippines*

• During the 480-odd years between 1068 and 1547, eight King Henrys ruled over England. Which Henry was responsible for each of the following?

In connection with his famed attraction to women, he is remembered for his break with papist Rome, which resulted in the creation of the Church of England.
–*Henry VIII*

This King's argument with Thomas Becket, the Archbishop of Canterbury, eventually led to Becket's murder.
–*Henry II*

Also known as Henry of Lancaster, this ruler became king after seizing the throne from Richard II. He left the crown with a huge debt.
–*Henry IV*

Also known as Henry Tudor, he instituted the Court of the Star Chamber simply to curb the power of the nobles.
–*Henry VII*

While his brother, the rightful monarch, was abroad, he generously crowned himself king.
–*Henry I*

As a ruler during the War of the Roses, he suffered from acute periods of insanity and was eventually sent to prison—where he was murdered.
–*Henry VI*

This incompetent sovereign survived in power for an eternal and intolerable 45 years; in his old age he relinquished most of his power to his son Edward.
–*Henry III*

• Between 1239 and 1972, Great Britain also boasted eight King Edwards. Identify each Edward from the following descriptions:
He expelled the Jews from England in 1290.
–*Edward I*

The eldest son of Queen Victoria, he brought international goodwill to England and was a highly popular king.
–*Edward VIII*

According to the widely accepted story told by Sir Thomas More, this boy-king was suffocated in the Tower of London upon the order of Richard III.
–*Edward V*

The brief rule of this frail young son of King Henry VIII was dominated by relatives and advisors. Protestantism was established in England during his reign.
–*Edward VI*

He abdicated after less than one year to marry an American-born divorcee.
–*Edward VIII*

• Name the Zimbabwian president who passed a law in 1983 declaring it a crime to make fun of his name. –*President Canaan Banana*

• A decisive battle that took place on December 2, 1805 is known as the Battle of the Three Emperors. Who are the three emperors referred to? –*Napoleon I of France, Alexander I of Russia, and Francis I of Austria*

• Which English king, born June 4, 1738, is best known in the U.S. for losing the American colonies? –*King George III (Coincidentally, his visit to Eton College in England is still celebrated annually on July 4, the day Americans celebrate their independence.)*

• By a former marriage, actress Sophia Loren is sister-in-law to the son of a well-known world ruler. Who was this most loathed dictator? –*Benito Mussolini*

• Name the world leaders who went by the following nicknames:

This South American leader (1783-1830), known as "The Liberator," made his whole life a quest for his continent's independence.
–Simon Bolivar

Also known as "The Liberator," this Irish nationalist leader served in the British House of Commons from 1775 to 1847.
–Daniel O'Connell

This Frankish ruler (688-c.741), whose surname literally means "The Hammer," finally halted the Muslim invasion of Europe.
–Charles Martel

Commonly surtitled "The Upright," this direct successor of Mohammed became the first Muslim caliph.
–Abu Bakr

Known as "Mr. Republican" (1889-1953), this "party patriot" was a U.S. Senator from Ohio and son of a former U.S. President.
–Robert Alphonso Taft

• What did Emperor Menlik II of Abyssinia (now Ethiopia) do with the electric chair he ordered from the U.S.? *–He used the chair as a throne (When he made the order, electricity was not yet available in his country to power the chair.)*

• What enigmatic world leader has made cameo appearances in several Hollywood films? (Hint: He's an avowed socialist.) *–Fidel Castro*

• According to the Bible, who was the first king of Israel? *–Saul*

THOSE AMAZING PEOPLE
did you know that ...

... In 1972 a student skydiver dropped 3,300 feet without his parachute opening, landed on his face, and a few minutes later got up and walked away with only a broken nose and a few missing teeth?

... In 1985 a 14-year-old boy in perfect health heard of his girlfriend's desperate need for a heart transplant and publicly vowed that he would give his life if he could save hers? A few days later, the boy collapsed due to a blood clot in the brain and was pronounced brain-dead. His heart was donated to his girlfriend, who recovered completely.

... In September 1954, Mrs. Hewlett Holdges of Sylacuaga, Alabama, was napping in her living room when a meteorite crashed through her roof and hit her? (She was only slightly injured.)

... Two retarded brothers named George and Charles, known as the Bronx Calendar Twins and featured in a 1966 edition of *Life* magazine, can, in just seconds, calculate the day of the week for any date over a period of 80,000 years?

... Roy C. Sullivan, a retired park ranger from Virginia, survived seven direct lightning strikes during his career (struck in 1942, '69, '70, '72, '73, '76 and '77) making him the most lightning-struck—perhaps most "revolting"—person on record?

... The subject of the Emmy-winning movie "The Woman Who Willed a Miracle," the prodigious savant Leslie Lemke is blind, and yet he possesses an extraordinary memory and is able to sing and play the piano with amazing talent?

Believe It Or Not ...

• Already a double-leg amputee when shot down and captured by the Nazis, Douglas Bader, one of England's greatest fighter pilots, persistently tried to escape from his POW camp. What did the German guards finally do to stop his escape efforts?
–They confiscated one of his artificial legs

• Born in 1674 in Germany, Matthew Buchinger played 12 musical instruments, danced the hornpipe, was an expert with a pistol, and excelled in bowling, calligraphy and magic. Besides these amazing accomplishments, what physical characteristics made this man even more remarkable? *–He was only 28 inches tall and had no arms or legs*

549

• In 1901 Anna Edson Taylor was the first person to take the 186-foot plunge off Niagara Falls. After being helped from the cushioned barrel in which she was enclosed, what fact did she admit that made her feat even more audacious? *–She could not swim*

• Chang and Eng, a set of twins born in 1811 to Chinese parents living in Siam (now Thailand), worked for P.T. Barnum's circus, after which they married and fathered 22 children. On the same day in 1874, they died. What was extraordinary about these twin boys?
–They were conjoined at the hip (thus the name "Siamese Twins") and remained fused throughout their lives

• On December 13, 1982, this well-known sports figure, while out jogging, saved the life of 67-year old Jessie Dye by freeing her from a burning automobile—after which he continued his jog. Who is this heroic athlete?
–Former Heisman Trophy winner and professional running-back Herschel Walker

• After losing both hands in a dynamite explosion, what actor wrote his 1949 autobiography titled *Victory in My Hands? –Harold Russell*

• What autistic mathematical savant, currently residing in Salt Lake City, Utah, was the inspiration for the character played by actor Dustin Hoffman in the Academy Award-winning movie "Rain Man"? *–Kim Peak*

• This amazing couple has been around since the 1300s and is still going strong. They take the place of anyone whose true identity is unknown—and their names can be found on death certificates, birth certificates and legal documents. Who are they? *–John and Jane Doe*

• During the Revolutionary War, an exhausted army messenger nearly collapsed at a Connecticut home—unable to ride any farther. A 16-year-old girl finished the messenger's mission, riding the remaining 40 miles—at night, on horseback—to summon the needed reinforcements. A statue in Carmel, New York, commemorates her act. What is this American heroine's name? *–Sybil Ludington*

• In 1983, when 11-year-old Samantha Smith of Maine wrote a letter to Soviet leader Yuri Andropov pleading with him to stop the nuclear arms race, what was Andropov's response? Also, what tragedy occurred two years later? *–Samantha was invited to visit him at the Kremlin, which she did; she and her father were killed in a plane crash*

WORD SOUND-ALIKES
did you know that …

Riddled To Death!

• The answer to each of the following riddles is a pair of sound-alike—but not spelled-alike—words (heterographs). Identify the words:

I rent a home on the boundary between two countries. I'm a _____ _____.
  –Boarder and border
This happens when two female deer take naps.
  –Does doze
Seven rather feeble days.
  –A weak week
How would you tell an item of footwear to go away?
  –Shoo, shoe!
When a large, powerful African animal joins a band of fighters that hide in trees, ambush the enemy, and go on sudden raids, what do you call him?
  –A guerrilla gorilla
This is the money the government collects on the sale of tiny nails.
  –A tacks tax
When Mr. Cornseed finally achieved the status of a high-ranking army officer, what was he called?
  –Colonel Kernel
This year's fashionable country lodging is the ____ ____.
  –In Inn
What is immovable writing paper called?
  Stationary stationery
What award could you win for sticking your nose into other people's business?
  –A Meddle Medal

• Identify the sound-alike pairs or triplets for the following set of definitions:

To modify or change; an elevated table upon which religious services may be performed.
  –Alter; altar
Inactive or unemployed; one that is adored; an event of rural simplicity.
  –Idle; idol; idyll
A line formed by sewing two pieces of material together; to give the impression of being.
  –Seam; seem
Entirely; having several perforations; associated with divine power.
  –Wholly; holey; holy
To have measured a certain amount; to walk in water.
  –Weighed; wade
A portion or element; freedom from disagreement.
  –Piece; peace

Most important; a thick growth of hair down the neck.
–Main; mane

In the direction of; a cardinal number; in addition.
–To; two; too

To prefer above others; masticates.
–Choose; chews

To have rented for a specified period of time; lowest in importance or rank.
–Leased; least

Of recent origin; having apprehended with clarity; either of two large African antelopes.
–New; knew; gnu

• Homographs are words that are spelled alike but pronounced differently. Find the single word to fit each set of dual definitions below:

The *tiny sixty seconds* passed swiftly.
–Minute

He'll *give* the *gift* after dinner.
–Present

He looked *sickly* in his *pointed* hat.
–Peaked

I suggest you *get back to* typing your *summary of job qualifications.*
–Resume

The professor *exposes us* to endless lectures on boring *topics.*
–Subjects

He'll *speak closely* with the people who *live and work together.*
–Commune

It will *enrage* him to smell the pleasant *burning aroma.*
–Incense

Her opinions *differ* from his in this *struggle.*
–Conflict

NOBODY ASKED, BUT…
did you know that …

…A person walks the equivalent of twice around the world in an average lifetime?

…More than half the people in the U.S. are technophobic—afraid in one way or another to familiarize themselves with modern points of technology?

…When you put a shell next to your ear the sound you hear is not that of the ocean, but rather the sounds around you and those coming from inside your ear (amplified by the vibration of air molecules bumping into each other)?

…An average of 400 billion gallons of fresh water are used worldwide every day?

…According to *Glamour* magazine, more than 40 percent of American women are now a size 14 or larger, compared to the women's fashion-industry standard size 8?

…Before buttons became a common suit coat-cuff adornment, they were first sewn on the cuffs of midshipmen to keep them from wiping their noses with their sleeves?

…Gardiner Greene Hubbard, appointed to be the first president of the National Geographic Society in 1888, was also Alexander Graham Bell's father-in-law?

…The visible lightning bolt you see during a thunderstorm is not coming from the sky but actually traveling upward from the ground?

…During a severe hailstorm in Mississippi on May 11, 1894, an eight-inch-long gopher turtle, completely encased in ice, fell to the ground?

…At least 1,000 tons of dust from outer space enters the atmosphere every year and makes its way to Earths surface?

Since You're Still Reading …

• What is unique about the words *silver, purple, orange* and *month*? *–No other word in the English language rhymes with them*

• What letter of the alphabet is located at the top of an optometrist's eye chart? *–"E"*

• How many times a month does the average American male cry? The average female? *–1.5; over 5*

• How many words is a regular lead pencil capable of writing? *–About 50,000*

• When shipped from England to the United States, what item was classified by Customs officials as a "large antique"?
–The London Bridge

• On a standard cube, how many more corners than sides are there? –Two (eight corners, six sides)

• What letter is to the left of "V" on a computer keyboard? –"C"

• According to custom, which side of a cow would you sit on during milking time?
–The left

• Name the annual award which is presented by the National Council of Teachers of English to a specific public figure or agency who uses the most deceptive, evasive and confusing language? –The Doublespeak Award

• What Patuxet/Wampanoag Indian achieved fame for helping the Pilgrims survive their first winter in America? –Squanto

• Of the 25 highest mountains on Earth, in what single area can you find 19 of them?
–The Himalayas, in Tibet

• Earth's longest mountain chain is the Mid-Atlantic Ridge, a submarine chain which splits nearly the entire Atlantic Ocean north to south. What country's land mass was formed by one of these mountains rising above the sea surface?
–Iceland

• What do veteran sailors term a comrade who has not yet crossed the equator?
–A Polliwog

• According to the book 52 Ways to Live a Long and Healthy Life, what percentage of adults are happy with their physical appearance?
–Four percent

• What inspired Leo Gerstenzag to invent Q-Tips cotton swabs in 1923?
–He saw his wife use cotton on the end of a tooth-pick to clean their baby's ears

• What couple created the first "Barbie" doll in their basement in 1959? Who is the doll named after?
–Elliot and Ruth Handler; their only daughter

• How long would it take a lightly-clothed person to freeze to death in Antarctica—or, for that matter, anywhere else—at a temperature of -70 degrees Fahrenheit?
–Only about 60 seconds

• What appurtenance did American Reverend Jonathan Scobie invent while visiting Okinawa, Japan in 1869? –The rickshaw

• Give the kn– word that matches each of these quasi-definitions:
   One nautical mile an hour.
      –A knot
   A "treasured" fort.
      –Knox
   Casting on a needle.
      –Knitting
   A benevolent international organization of Roman Catholic men.
      –Knights of Columbus
   Probably the most useful of all the common tools used by people.
      –The knife
   A bag worn on the back during hikes.
      –A knapsack
   To strike with a hard blow.
      –Knock
   The patella
      –The kneecap
   A small rounded hill.
      –A knoll
   To ring or sound a bell (especially for a funeral).
      –Knell
   Understanding gained through experience or study (as in the phrase, "_____ is swell!").
      –Knowledge

INDEX

SCARAB